The Babylonian Talmud

The Babylonian Talmud

A Translation and Commentary

Volume 16
Tractate *Sanhedrin*

Jacob Neusner

HENDRICKSON PUBLISHERS

ISBN 1-56563-707-0

The Babylonian Talmud: A Translation and Commentary, by Jacob Neusner, reproduces the complete text of his thirty-six volume edition originally published as *The Talmud of Babylonia: An Academic Commentary* in the University of South Florida Academic Commentary Series (1994–1999). This Hendrickson edition reproduces this material with permission and provides new front matter, a new introduction to the whole work, and new introductions to each tractate.

Printed in the United States of America

First Printing — November 2005

Quotations from the Mishnah not found within the text of the Babylonian Talmud itself are taken from *The Mishnah: A New Translation*. (Translated by Jacob Neusner; New Haven, Conn.: Yale University Press, 1988). Used with permission.

Library of Congress Cataloging-in-Publication Data

Neusner, Jacob, 1932–
    [Talmud of Babylonia]
    The Babylonian Talmud : a translation and commentary /
Jacob Neusner.
       p. cm.
    Comprises the full 37 tractates with new introduction and
commentary.
    ISBN 1-56563-707-0 (alk. paper)
    1. Talmud—Commentaries. I. Title.
    BM504.N44 2005
    296.1'2507—dc22

                                   2005022399

Table of Contents

Volume 16: *Sanhedrin*

Introduction to Tractate *Sanhedrin*

Sanhedrin deals with the organization of the Israelite government and the courts and punishments administered thereby. The court system is set forth in the Mishnah's statement of matters (Mishnah tractate *Sandhedrin* 1:1–5:5), the death-penalty (Mishnah tractate *Sanhedrin* 6:1–11:6), and extra-judicial penalties (Mishnah tractate *Sanhedrin* 9:5–6, 10:1–6). The penalties other than capital punishment, that is, perjury (with variable penalties), banishment, and flogging, are set forth in the next tractate, *Makkot*.

I. The court system

    A. Various kinds of courts and their jurisdiction
    B. The heads of the Israelite nation and the court system
    C. The procedures of the court system: property cases
    D. The procedures of the court system: capital cases

II. The death penalty

    A. Stoning
    B. The four modes of execution that lie within the power of the court and how they are administered
    C. Stoning
    D. Burning or decapitation
    E. Strangulation
    F. Extra-judicial punishment
    G. Death at the hands of Heaven: denial of eternal life

While Scripture supplies many facts, the Talmud organizes matters in its own way. The details of the organization of the court system do not derive from the written Torah, nor are the specificities of the death penalty supplied there. Scripture's contribution is therefore episodic. Deuteronomy 16:18–20 specifies appointing judges and Deut 17:8–13 provides for an appellate system. The death penalty for murder is specified in Num 35:30 and that it must rely on the testimony of two or three witnesses in Deut 17:6–7. The comparison of the high priest with the king (Mishnah tractate *Sanhedrin* 2:1–5) rests on Lev 21:10–12 (for the high priest) and Deut 17:14–20 (for the king). The death penalty involving hanging the body on a tree until night (but with burial on the same day) is found in Deut 21:22–23. The death penalty for the stubborn and rebellious son is found in Deut 21:18–21. The city that is wiped out because of idolatry is treated in Deut 13:12–18. Scripture contributes facts for the law in *Sanhedrin* on specific topics, but the shape and program of the tractate as a whole cannot be predicted on the basis of the Torah.

In its overarching structure tractate *Sanhedrin* moves from property cases to capital cases. Then within capital cases *Sanhedrin* addresses the penalties for catalogued crimes (from the most severe to the lightest crimes). Lastly the law turns to the most severe penalty of all: the penalty that only the Heavenly court can impose.

The auxiliary portion of the tractate then proceeds from capital to corporal punishment. The order of the whole tractate is: (1) the earthly court and property cases; (2) the earthly court and capital punishment; (3) the Heavenly court; and, then appended, (4) corporal punishment. This order of exposition identifies for us what is at issue when the topic of punishment for criminal acts is addressed. The rabbinic sages approach the topic of criminal justice bearing in mind a profound theological issue: how God's justice is to be done on earth in such a way as to express God's mercy, even for sinners and criminals.

1

Bavli Tractate Sanhedrin
Chapter One
Folios 2A-18A

1:1-6

A. (1) Property cases [are decided] by three [judges];

B. (2) those concerning theft and damages, before three;

C. (3) [cases involving] compensation for full-damages, half-damages [Ex. 21:35], twofold restitution [Ex. 22:3], fourfold and fivefold restitution [Ex. 21:37], by three;

D. (4) "cases involving him who rapes [Deut. 32:28-29], him who seduces [Ex. 22:15-16], and him who brings forth an evil name (Deut. 22:19), by three," the words of R. Meir.

E. And sages say, "He who brings forth an evil name is [tried] before twenty-three, for there may be a capital case."

M. 1:1

A. (5) [Cases involving the penalty of] flogging [Deut. 25:2-3] are before three.

B. In the name of R. Ishmael they said, "Before twenty-three."

C. (6) [The decision to] intercalate the month is before three.

D. (7) "[The decision to] intercalate the year is before three," the words of R. Meir.

E. Rabban Simeon b. Gamaliel says, "With three do they begin, with five [more] they debate the matter, and they reach a final decision with seven [more] [judges].

F. "But if they reached a decision [to intercalate the year] with three judges, [the year is] intercalated."

M. 1:2

A. (8) "The laying of hands [on a community sacrifice] by elders and the breaking of the heifer's neck [Deut. 21:1-9] are done by three judges," the words of R. Simeon.

B. R. Judah says, "By five."

1

C.   (9) The rite of removal of the shoe [breaking the levirate bond] (Deut. 25:7-9) and the exercise of the right of refusal are done before three judges.
D.   (10) [The evaluation of] fruit of fourth-year plantings [which is to be redeemed [(Lev. 19:23-25)] and of second tithe (Deut. 14:22-26) whose value is not known is done before three judges.
E.   (11) Assessment of the value, [for purposes of redemption,] of things which have been consecrated is done before three judges.
F.   (12) [Property pledged as security for] vows of valuation, in the case of movables, is evaluated by three [judges].
G.   R. Judah says, "One of them must be a priest."
H.   And [evaluation of property pledged as security for vows for valuation] in the case of real estate is done by nine and a priest.
I.   And so for [the valuation-vow covering] men.

M. 1:3

A.   (1) Cases involving the death penalty are judged before twenty-three judges.
B.   (2) The beast who commits or is subjected to an act of sexual relations with a human being is judged by twenty-three,
C.   since it is said, "And you will kill the woman and the beast" (Lev. 20:16).
D.   and it says, "And the beast you will slay" (Lev. 20:15).
E.   (3) An ox which is to be stoned is judged by twenty-three,
F.   since it is said, "And the ox will be stoned, and also its master will be put to death" (Ex. 21:29).
G.   Just as [the case of the master], leading to the death-penalty, [is adjudged], so is the [case of] the ox, [leading to] the death-penalty.
H.   The wolf, lion, bear, panther, leopard, and snake a capital case affecting them is judged by twenty-three.
I.   R. Eliezer says, "Whoever kills them first acquires merit."
J.   R. Aqiba says, "Their capital case is judged by twenty three."

M. 1:4

A.   (1) They judge a tribe, a false prophet [Deut. 18:20], and a high priest, only on the instructions of a court of seventy-one members.
B.   (2) They bring forth [the army] to wage a war fought by choice only on the instructions of a court of seventy-one.
C.   (3) They make additions to the city [of Jerusalem] and to the courtyards [of the Temple] only on the instructions of a court of seventy-one.
D.   (4) They set up sanhedrins for the tribes only on the instructions of a court of seventy-one.
E.   (5) They declare a city to be "an apostate City" [Deut. 13:12ff.] only on the instructions of a court of seventy-one.
F.   And they do not declare a city to be "an Apostate city" on the frontier,
G.   [nor do they declare] three [in one locale] to be apostate cities,
H.   but they do so in the case of one or two.

M. 1:5

A.   The great sanhedrin was [made up] of seventy-one members,

B.   and the small one was twenty-three.

C.   And how do we know that the great sanhedrin was to have seventy-one members?

D.   Since it is said, "Gather to me seventy men of the elders of Israel" (Nm. 11:16).

E.   Since Moses was in addition to them, [lo, there were seventy one.]

F.   R. Judah says, "It is seventy."

G.   And how do we know that a small one is twenty-three?

H.   Since it is said, "The congregation shall judge, and The congregation shall deliver" (Num. 35: 24, 25) –

I.   one congregation judges, and one congregation saves – thus there are twenty.

J.   And how do we know that a congregation is ten? Since it is said, "how long shall I bear with this evil congregation [of the ten spies]" (Num. 14:27) – excluding Joshua and Caleb.

K.   And how do we know that we should add three more?

L.   From the implication of that which is said, "You shall not follow after the many to do evil" (Ex: 23:20), I derive the inference that I should be with them to do good.

M.   If so, why is it said, "After the many to do evil"?

N.   Your verdict of acquittal is not equivalent to your verdict of guilt.

O.   Your verdict of acquittal may be on the vote of a majority of one, but your vote for guilt must be by a majority of two.

P.   [2B] Since there cannot be a court of an even number of members [twenty-two], they add yet another – thus twenty-three.

Q.   And how many residents must there be in a town so that it may be suitable for a sanhedrin?

R.   One hundred-twenty.

S.   R. Nehemiah says, "Two hundred and thirty, equivalent in number to the chiefs of groups of ten [Ex. 18:21]."

M. 1:6

I.1   A.   [Property cases [are decided] by three [judges]; those concerning theft and damages, before three:] *do not cases concerning theft and damages fall within the classification of property cases [that they have to be singled out]?*

B.   *Said R. Abbahu, "The purpose of the framer of the passage is to spell out [what property cases are], thus,* 'What cases fall into the classification of property cases? They are cases such as those that concern theft and damages. But cases involving admissions that loans have been made and transactions of loans do not fall into that category.' [Schachter, p. 4, n. 3: There are claims supported by witnesses attesting the defendant's former admission of his liability, or who were actually present at the time of the transaction]."

C.   *And it was necessary to refer both in general to monetary cases, and also in particular to cases concerning theft and damages.*

D.   *For had the Tannaite authority made reference solely to property cases [without further specification], I should have concluded that even cases involving admissions that loans have been made and transactions of loans fall into the same category.*

Accordingly, the Tannaite authority made explicit reference to cases of theft and damages.

E.   *And had the formulation made reference only to cases of theft and damages and not made reference to the more general category of property cases, I should have reached the conclusion that the classification encompasses even cases of admissions of loans and transactions of loans.*

F.   *I might have further assumed that the reason the authority framed matters in particular with reference to theft and damages was that the very principle that three judges are required is written with explicit reference to cases of theft and damages.*

G.   *As to cases of theft, it is written,* "The householder shall come near to the judges" (Ex. 22:7), a verse that speaks of damages. But what difference does it make to me whether the damage is to one's body or one's property.

H.   *Accordingly, the Tannaite authority made reference to property cases and further made explicit that in the classification at hand are involved cases of theft and damages, but not cases of admissions and transactions involving loans.*

I.   *Now what, further is the reason for excluding such cases?*

J.   *If one might wish to propose that it is because trials for such cases do not require three judges,*

K.   and has not R. Abbahu said, "If two judges dealt with monetary cases, in the view of all parties, their judgement is null"?

L.   *Hence [the reason for excluding such cases] is that we do not require the judgment of experts [in the cases of conflicting claims as to loans].*

M.   *[Testing this thesis, we ask:] What is the exegetical principle in the mind of the authority at hand.* [At issue here is the interpretation of Ex. 22:9, "For every breach of trust ... of which one says, 'This is it,' the case of both parties shall come before God." Now do we maintain that "one passage is interwoven with another"? Specifically, do we hold that at hand is a transposition that applies the rule just now stated also to loans as well as to bailments, the topic to which the verse makes explicit reference? If we do take that reading, then just as we require three judges for a case involving a bailment, so we require three judges in a case involving a loan. Thus:] *If, then, the authority before us maintains that in the present instance we have a transposition of verses [in such wise that the rules governing the case of a property claim are the same as those governing the case of a loan,] then surely we should require expert judges [for the case of a loan, just as much as we do for a property case].*

N.   *And if he maintains that, at hand, we do not have a transposition of passages, then why does he insist that there be three judges to begin with? [If we do not apply to cases involving loans the procedural requirements governing property cases, then why do so in the detail at hand at all?]*

O.   *In point of fact the authority at hand does maintain that [we interpret the cited verse in such a way as to suppose] that we have an interposition of one matter [in the midst of another, with the* consequence that we hold the cited verse to speak not only of bailments but also of loans]. In point of fact, on that account, one should require expert judges for cases involving loans.

P. *The reason that, nonetheless, the authority before us does not require experts in such cases is on account of the view of R. Hanina.*

Q. For R. Hanina said, "As a matter of the law as the Torah would have it, the same rule would govern both capital and property cases in respect to diligent examination of the witnesses.

R. **[3A]** "For it is written, 'One manner of judgment shall you have' (Lev. 24:22).

S. "Why is it then that sages have maintained that property cases do not involve the diligent testing of the witnesses? So as not to shut the door before people who need to take loans. [Schachter, p. 5, n. 8: Creditors would refuse to advance loans should difficulties confront them in collecting their debts, and the same consideration has led to the suspension of the law regarding the need of expert judges.]"

T. If [cases involving property do not require experts, then if the judges make an error,] they should not have to pay compensation [the injured party who has suffered from their error. For that provision protects inexpert judges in general, and, if you have accepted such a class of judges, you should extend to the judges the normal protection.]

U. All the more so, such a provision would lock the door against those who need to take out loans. [The creditors would have no recourse in a case of judicial error.]

V. *If so, the Mishnah at hand presents two distinct laws. First, it indicates that property cases are judged by three ordinary people. Second, it indicates that cases involving theft or damages are to be judged by three experts. Furthermore, why does the framer of the passage make reference to the fact that three judges are required [in each case, if the one clause, namely M. 1:1B, simply serves to explain the other, namely, M. 1:1A]?*

W. *Rather, said Raba, ["The framer of the passage has presented two different rules. As to the matter of the trial of cases involving loans, they do not require expert judges, on account of the position laid forth by] R. Hanina."*

I.2 A. [Explaining the matter of three judges in cases involving loans], R. Aha, son of R. Iqa, said, "*On the basis of the rules of the Torah itself, a single judge also would be suitable to judge the case. For it is said, 'In justice you [singular] shall judge your neighbor' (Lev. 19:15). But on account of idle folk [who pass their opinion without knowing the law, three are required.]*"

B. *But merely because they are three, may they not turn out to be idle folk [merely passing their opinion]?*

C. *It is not possible that among the three will be no one who has learned the law.*

D. *If that is the case, then, if they make a judicial error, they should not be free of having to make restitution [on the grounds that an expert is exempt if he makes an error from having to make up the loss]?*

E. *[If that were the rule], how much the more so would idle meddlers get involved in judging cases.*

F. *[Since Raba, above, and Aha concur that ordinary folk may judge cases], on what point do Raba and R. Aha, son of R. Iqa, differ?*

G. *They differ on the statement of Samuel, "If two people judged a case [in place of the three], their decision is valid. But they are called a presumptuous court."* Raba rejects Samuel's view [because, in his view, the Torah requires three judges to deal with a case], while R. Aha, son of R. Iqa, concurs with Samuel's view.

II.1   A.   **Cases involving compensation for full-damages, half damages [twofold restitution, fourfold and fivefold restitution, are judged by three judges] [M. 1:1C]:**

B. *Cases involving compensation for full damages fall into the category of cases involving damages. [Why then make explicit the fact that these two are tried by three judges?]*

C. *It is because the framer of the passage wished to make reference to cases involving compensation for half-damages that he included, within his formula, a reference also to cases involving claims for full damages.*

D. *But cases involving claims for half-damages likewise fall into the category of claims for damages.*

E. *The Tannaite authority first made reference to cases involving property claims of an ordinary character [in which the compensation is indemnification, dictated by the nature of the claim], and then he made distinct reference to cases in which the compensation takes the form of a fine [rather than being assessed against the actual damages that have been inflicted].* [Schachter, p. 6, n. 8: A fine imposed upon the owner for not guarding his animal from causing damage, as distinct from damages in cases of mayhem, which are considered indemnity.]

F. *That explanation well serves him who maintains that a claim for half-damages falls into the category of a fine.* But in the view of him who has said that a claim for half-damages falls into the category of [indemnification for loss of] property, what is there to be said?

G. *Rather, since the framer of the passage wished to make reference, in his formulation, to cases involving two-fold, four-fold, and five-fold damages,* **[3B],** *all of which constitute payments not assessed in accord with the actual damage that has been done, he framed matters also to encompass the matter of half-damages, which likewise [by definition] are not assessed in accord with the actual damage that has been done, and, quite naturally, since he made reference to half-damages, he included in his formulation reference to whole damages as well.*

II.2   A.   How on the basis of Scripture do we know that [trials of this classification take place before] three judge courts?

B. *It is in accord with that which our rabbis have taught on Tannaite authority:*

C.   "'Then the householder shall come near to the judge' (Ex. 22:8) – lo, one; 'The case of both parties shall come before the judge' (Ex. 22:9) – lo, two; and 'He whom the judge shall condemn shall pay double to his neighbor' (Ex. 22:9) – lo, three, [thus the three verses specify that three judges must be involved in the case]," the words of R. Josiah.

D.   R. Jonathan says, "The first allusion to a judge serves to introduce the topic, and further exegetical meaning cannot be imputed to the first occurrence of a word [which serves simply to supply the facts of the matter]. Rather: 'The case of both parties shall come before the judge' (Ex. 22:9) – lo, one. 'And he whom the judge shall condemn shall pay double to his neighbor' (Ex. 22:9) – lo, two. You cannot have a court with an even number of judges, so add yet another, thus three in all."

E.   *May we say at issue is whether or not further exegetical meaning may be imputed to the first occurrence of a word? Thus? one master takes the position that further exegetical meaning may be imputed to the first occurrence of a word, and the other master maintains that further exegetical meaning may not be imputed to the first occurrence of a word.*

F.   *No, all parties concur that, indeed, one may not impute to the first occurrence of a word further exegetical meaning. What R. Josiah will say to you [in response to Jonathan's criticism of his proof] is this: "[If the purpose of the passage at hand were merely to specify the need for a judge, and if that were its sole meaning,] then the author of the passage should have said, '*And the householder shall come near to the judge [using the word for judge alone, rather than the word which serves to mean both 'judge' and 'God.'] *Why does the verse at hand make use of the word that bears the double meaning of both 'judge' and 'God'? That produces the inference that a secondary issue, the number of judges on the court, also is subject to discussion [with the result as specified above.]"*

G.   *And R. Jonathan?*

H.   *He takes the view that the framer of the passage used commonplace language [and the choice of the word in question was not to convey yet a secondary sense]. That ordinary usage is illustrated by the saying, "He who has a trial should go to a trial-judge."*

I.   *But does R. Josiah not concur that a court must be made up of an odd number of judges? And has it not been taught on Tannaite authority:* R. Eliezer, son of R. Yosé the Galilean, says "What is the meaning of the verse of Scripture, ' ... to incline after many to wrest for yourself a court made up of an uneven number of judges.'"

J.   *[Indeed, he does not concur, since] he accords with the view of R. Judah, who holds that there are to be seventy judges. For we have learned in the Mishnah:* **The great sanhedrin was made up of seventy one members. ... R. Judah says, "It is seventy"** *[M. 1:6A, F].*

K.   *But I may propose that R. Judah addresses the composition only of the great sanhedrin, concerning which there are relevant verses of Scripture, but as to other courts, does he take the view [that a court need not be made up of an odd number of judges]? And should you say there is indeed no difference, have we not learned in the Mishnah:* **"The laying of hands on a community sacrifice by elders and the breaking of the heifer's neck are done by three judges,"** **the words of R. Simeon. R. Judah says, "By five" [M. 1:3A-B].** *In this connection it has been said, "What is the scriptural basis for the position of R. Judah? '...and they shall lay hands...' (Lev. 4:5) – thus speaking of at least two persons, and further specifies, '...the elders...' (Lev. 4:5), thus speaking of at least two persons. Since there cannot be a court with an even number of judges, they add on one more, thus yielding five."* [Hence Judah will not accept a court with an even number of judges, except in the case of the great sanhedrin. Josiah cannot appeal to Judah as his precedent.]

L.   *The position of R. Josiah goes further than R. Judah's. For R. Judah speaks specifically of the great sanhedrin, in maintaining that there need not be an odd number of judges, but other courts must have an odd number of judges, while R. Josiah maintains that for all other courts too, there cannot be an even number of judges.*

M.   *Now in Josiah's view, how are we to explain the word, "to incline" (Ex. 23:2) [from which we have derived the principle that the court must have an odd number of judges]?*

N.   *One may apply that reference to courts that try capital cases but not to courts that try property courses. But lo, we have learned in the Mishnah:* **[In judging property cases], if two judges say, "He is innocent," and one says, "He is guilty," he is innocent. If two say, "He is guilty," and one says, "He is innocent," he is guilty [M. 3:6I-J].**

O.   *We may maintain that the cited passage does not accord with the view of R. Josiah [since it assumes we have an odd number of judges trying a property case].*

P.   *You may maintain that it accords even with the view of R. Josiah.* [Schachter, p. 9: He will agree that the decision of the majority is valid even in civil cases] *by virtue of an argument* a fortiori. *This argument rests on the rule covering capital cases. If in capital cases, which deal with more severe penalties, the All-Merciful has said, "Follow the majority," how much the more so [will we follow the majority, and hence require an uneven number of judges], in a property case?*

II.3   A. *Our rabbis have taught on Tannaite authority:*
        B. **Property cases [are brought before] three judges [M. 1:1A].**
        C. **Rabbi says, "Before five, so that the decision may be reached by three" [T. San. 1:1A-B].**
        D. *But if there is a court of three judges, will the decision not be reached by two? [And in both cases, there is a majority, whether it is three out of five or two out of three].*
        E. *This is the sense of Rabbi's statement: It is because the court verdict must be reached by three judges [not merely a majority of the court, without reference to the actual number of judges]. Therefore Rabbi takes the view that when the Scripture requires three judges, it is for the final verdict that the three are required.*

F.   R. Abbahu made fun of this thesis: "But if that is the principle at hand, then the great sanhedrin should have a hundred and forty one members, so that the final verdict will be reached by seventy one. The lesser sanhedrin should have to have forty-five members, so that the final decision will be with twenty-three members. But the text states, 'Gather to me seventy men of the elders of Israel' (Num. 11:16), and thus the All-Merciful speaks of the number that must be gathered at the time of their assembly, namely, seventy. So too, 'The congregation shall judge and the congregation shall deliver' (Num. 35:24), [on the basis of which the make-up of a lesser sanhedrin is determined to be twenty-three judges,] speaks of the time at which the congregation undertakes judgment [of the case]. So too, 'The householder shall come near to the judges' (Ex. 22:7) speaks of the time at which the plaintiff comes before the court. That is the moment at which three judges must be present [and not in the rendering of the verdict, which may be done by two.] Rather, this is the scriptural basis for the view of Rabbi: 'They shall condemn' (at Ex. 22:7) makes use of the plural verb with reference to the subject, 'judges.' Thus two judges are required. Now when the word 'judges' occurs below, and when it occurs earlier, we assign the same meaning to each use of the word. Just as the later occurrence indicates that two judges are required, so the earlier occurrence indicates that two judges are required. Since you cannot have a court with an even number of judges, yet another must be added to the number, yielding five in all."

G.   **[4A]** *And rabbis?*

H.   *They hold that the word is written in the singular form [lacking a consonant would demand a plural reading, and hence stands for only a singular subject, hence one judge, not two, is required.]*

II.4   A.   *Said R. Isaac bar Joseph said R. Yohanan, "Rabbi, R. Judah b. Roes, the House of Shammai, R. Simeon, and R. Aqiba, all take the view that* we read Scripture in the way in which the supplied vowels direct it to be read."

      B.   *As to Rabbi, evidence is as we have just now stated [that we interpret the word in accord with the supplied vowels, thus as a plural, rather than in accord with its consonantal form, which is in the singular].*

      C.   *R. Judah b. Roes, as it has been taught on Tannaite authority:*

      D.   *For it has been taught on Tannaite authority:*

      E.   A disciple asked R. Judah b. Roes, "I read [at Lev. 12:5, 'If she bear a female child, she shall be unclean for two weeks'] the consonants as 'two weeks.' Is it possible that a woman who bears a female child should be unclean for seventy days [reading the consonants in that way]?"

      F.   He said to them, "The Scripture has imposed uncleanness followed by a period of cleanness on the occasion of birth of a male, and, in the case of the female, it is for double the period specified for a male. So too we when the Scripture imposes a period of uncleanness in a male, for a female it should be double that same period [and hence, since it is a week of uncleanness on the occasion of the birth of a male, it should be two weeks – not seventy days – for the female]."

G.   After they had gone forth, he ran after them, brought them back, and said to them, "You do not require [the argument I just made], since we pronounce the word as 'two weeks', and the principle is that we follow the version of Scripture in the way in which the supplied vowels direct that it should be read."

H.   The House of Shammai?

I.   *It accords with that which we have learned in the Mishnah:*

J.   **The House of Shammai say, "Any offering, the drops of blood of which are to be tossed on the outer altar, if one properly tossed blood one time, produces atonement. But in the case of the sin-offering, two tossings of the blood done properly on the outer alter are required to effect atonement."**

K.   **And the House of Hillel say, "Even a sin-offering, the blood of which was properly tossed only one time, effects atonement" [M. Zeb. 4:1A-C].**

L.   *And said R. Huna, "What is the scriptural basis for the position of the House of Shammai?* Scripture makes reference to the horns of the altar three times [at Lev. 4:25, 30, and 34, with the noun read as a plural all three times, even though in two of the three occurrences the vowel specifying the female plural is not written]. Thus there are six allusions to the horns of the altar. Four cover the description of the proper carrying out of the religious duty [if done rightly], and two to indicate what is at a minimum required [so that if not properly done two times, the act is null].

M.   "The House of Hillel say, "We find that, since the word for 'horns of the altar' is written in the plural one time [yielding two], but is written twice lacking the full spelling out of the plural form,] [so yielding only two more, that is, two singletons], we have in all four allusions. The sense then is that the blood must be done properly, by way of carrying out the religious duty, three times, but it must be done properly at least one time." [So the House of Shammai read the words in accord with the supplied vowels, and the House of Hillel read them only in accord with the consonants.]

N.   *But perhaps the sense is that all of the references to "horns of the altar" pertain to the proper conduct of the religious duty [but do not indicate what, at a minimum, must be done]?*

O.   *We do not find the case of an act of atonement all by itself* [Schachter: without an accompanying rite].

P.   R. Simeon?

Q.   *It is in accord with that which we have learned on Tannaite authority:*

R.   Two sides of the sukkah must be in accord with the law pertaining to them [as solid walls], but the third wall may be even so small as a handbreadth in size.

S.   R. Simeon says, "Three of them must accord with the law applying to them, but the fourth may be only a handbreadth."

T.   *What is at issue between them?*

U.   *Rabbis take the view that we are governed by the inherited spelling out of the words at hand, and R. Simeon takes the position that it is the manner in which the received vowels dictate the pronunciation of the passage that we read the passage.*

V.   *To spell this out: rabbis take the view that we are governed by the inherited spelling out of the words at hand [the consonants, without the vowels]. Thus the word for tabernacles (sukkot) [which occurs at Lev. 23:42-3] is written twice defectively [lacking the letter that signifies the feminine plural] and once properly, so yielding four references in all [the two read as if in the singular, the one read in the plural]. You deduct one reference for simply announcing the matter, leaving three. The received legal tradition is that one of the walls may be of diminished size, namely, a handbreadth [with the result that, as rabbis maintain, two must be of standard size and one of a handbreadth].*

W.   *R. Simeon takes the position that [reading all three occurrences of the word for tabernacle as plurals] we have six such references. We remove one verse of Scripture for simply announcing the matter, leaving four. The received law that one of the walls may be of diminished size, namely, a handbreadth [with the result that three must accord with the law, the fourth being merely a handbreadth].*

X.   And R. Aqiba?

Y.   *As it has been taught on Tannaite authority:*

Z.   R. Aqiba says, "How on the basis of Scripture do we know that a quarter-log of blood that derives from two corpses [with each corpse by itself contributing less than the requisite volume] imparts uncleanness when overshadowed [because the blood from two distinct sources is held to join together to form the requisite volume]?

AA.   "As it is said, 'He shall not go into any dead body' (Lev. 21:11). [Schachter: The plural *nafshot*, translated body, indicates that] even though there are two persons [from which the blood has flowed], their blood constitutes a single volume [to form the requisite amount to impart uncleanness in the tent of a corpse]."

BB.   And rabbis? The word is written in the singular form [and so the requisite proof does not flow from it]. [Aqiba wishes to read the word as the vowels dictate, rabbis in accord with the consonants only.]

CC.   *To this proposition [at A] R. Aha bar Jacob objected, "Is there no one else [apart from those listed earlier] who does not concur that the mode of reading a word indicated by the supplied vowels dictates the meaning?*

DD.   *"And has it not been taught on Tannaite authority:*

EE.   *"'You shall not boil a kid in the milk of its mother' (Ex. 23:19).*

FF.   *"'Is it possible that we should read the word for milk as though it were the word for fat [since both use the same consonants]?*

GG.   **[4B]***"Surely you must therefore maintain that the mode of reading a word is dictated by the supplied vowels [Schachter, p. 12, n. 8: And this is disputed by no one, as otherwise there would be no foundation for the prohibition.]*

HH.   *"Therefore it must follow that all parties concur that the supplied vowels dictate how a word must be read [with the result that we ignore the consonantal meaning and follow only that provided by the vowels]." [We shall now review the several disputes and prove that all parties concur on that principle.]*

II.   *As to the dispute between Rabbi and rabbis, it concerns the following point of difference:*

JJ.   *Rabbi takes the view that the word* "whom the judges shall condemn" (Ex. 22:8) *speaks of two other judges* [Schachter, p. 12, n. 11: and that accounts for his view that five judges are required], while rabbis hold that the word speaks of the judges both in the verse in which it occurs as well as in the preceding clause [Schachter: the word in each case being taken as plural of majesty, and so no additional judges are implied].

KK.   *R. Judah b. Roes has no rabbinical opposition in any event.*

LL.   *As to the House of Hillel:*

MM.   *It is in accord with that which has been taught on Tannaite authority:*

NN.   The word, "He shall make atonement" occurs three times [at Lev. 4:26, 31, 35] in connection with the sin-offering [demonstrating that if the blood is properly tossed even one time only, that suffices to attain atonement in the case of a sin-offering].

OO.   The reason for that repeated stress is on account of a possible logical argument to the contrary [which, by formulating matters as it does, Scripture forestalls.]

PP.	The proposed argument is as follows: The word "blood" is used with reference to tossing the blood of an offering below the red line that divided the altar into two horizontals, and the word blood is used with reference to tossing the blood of offerings that has to go above that same red line.
QQ.	Just as, in the case of blood that has to be tossed below the red line, if one has tossed the blood properly one time only, he has achieved atonement, so in the case of blood that is tossed above the red line, if it is properly tossed one time only, the priest has effected atonement.
RR.	[At the same time,] one may take the following route:
SS.	The word "blood" is used in connection with offerings the blood of which is tossed onto the outer altar, and the word "blood" is used in connection with offerings the blood of which is tossed on the inner altar.
TT.	Just as blood that is tossed on the inner altar is such that, if only one of the requisite tossings of the blood should be lacking, the sacrifice is null and accomplished nothing, so with respect to blood that is tossed against the outer altar, if only one of the requisite tossings of blood is lacking, the sacrifice is nought. [This second proof, then, would vitiate the conclusion of the first.]
UU.	Now let us see which is the dominant analogy: We should construct an argument concerning blood that is sprinkled on the outer altar on the basis of a case involving blood that is sprinkled on the outer altar, and let us not construct an argument concerning blood that is sprinkled on the outer altar from the case of blood that is sprinkled on the inner altar [thus rejecting the first of the two proposed arguments].
VV.	Or let us take this route: Let us construct an argument governing the sprinkling of the blood of the sin-offering, which is done on the four corners of the altar, from the case of a sin-offering, with the blood sprinkled on the four corners of the altar. But let proof not derive from the case of an offering which is not a sin-offering and does not involve the four corners of the altar.
WW.	[Since we can, through logical argument, produce contradictory results, it is necessary for] Scripture to state three times, "He shall make atonement."
XX.	This then deals with the problem of logic [just now spelled out, in the following way:]
YY.	"He shall atone" even though he has tossed the blood only three times.
ZZ.	"He shall atone" even though he has sprinkled the blood only two times.

AAA. "He shall atone" even though he has only tossed the blood only once.

BBB. *As to R. Simeon and rabbis, at issue is this matter:*

CCC. *R. Simeon takes the view that no verse of Scripture is necessary to indicate that sukkah-roofing is required, while rabbis take the view that a verse of Scripture is necessary to indicate that sukkah-roofing is required.*

DDD. *As to R. Aqiba and rabbis, at issue is this matter:*

EEE. *R. Aqiba holds that the word for "any body" refers to two corpses, not only to one, while rabbis maintain that the word speaks of only one corpse.*

FFF. *Is it truly the case that all parties concur that the supplied vowels indicate how a word is to be read and so what it means?*

GGG. *But has it not been taught on Tannaite authority:*

HHH. "The word for frontlets [referring to phylacteries] occurs three times, two times lacking the indication of the plural, one time including that full spelling [at Deut. 6:8, 9:18, and Ex. 13:16].   that indicates there are four [sections of Scripture to be inserted into the phylacteries]," the words of R. Ishmael.

III. R. Aqiba says, "It is not necessary [to resort to such a proof], for the letters for the first half of the word, in the Katpi language, stand for two, and the letters for the second half of the word, in Afriki, stand for the word two."

JJJ. *It must, therefore, follow that there is dispute [concerning whether or not the determinant is the supplied vowels]. But where there is a dispute, it is where the pronunciation of the word in accord with its vowels differs from the pronunciation of the word as dictated solely by the consonants. [Where the vowels indicate the presence of a letter which the consonants do not present, there we shall have a dispute, but not otherwise.]*

KKK. *But in such a case as the word for "milk" which is the same in its consonantal form as the word for "fat," where the letters are the same for both pronunciations, [there really is universal agreement that] the word is read in accord with the received vowels and in that way alone.*

LLL. But lo, there is the case of the verse, "Three times in the year all your males shall appear before the Lord" (Ex. 23:17) [in which the word for "shall appear" may be read "shall see," hence, "shall see the Lord"]. In this case, the two meanings are to be imputed to exactly the same consonantal construction, and yet there is a dispute [as to whether we follow the received vowels or the consonantal form alone].

MMM. *For it has been taught on Tannaite authority:*

NNN. Yohanan b. Dahabai says in the name of R. Judah b. Tema, "He who is blind in one eye is exempt from having to bring an appearance-offering [on a pilgrim festival, such as is specified at Ex. 23:17], for it is said, 'He will appear.' 'He will appear' just as he sees, that is, just as one comes to see, so he comes to be seen. Just as seeing is with two eyes, so being seen is with two eyes. [Schachter: As the Lord comes to see with both eyes, so should he who comes to be seen by Him come with both eyes]."

OOO. Rather, said R. Aha, son of R. Iqa, "Scripture has stated, 'You shall not boil a kid in its mother's milk' (Ex. 23:19). What is forbidden is the act of boiling. [Schachter, p. 15, n. 3: Boiling is a term applicable only to a liquid, such as milk, and not to fat, which would require such a word as roasting. Therefore we must read the word at hand as milk, not as fat.]"

II.5 A. *Our rabbis have taught on Tannaite authority:*

B. Property cases are to be tried by a court of three judges. **[5A]** But if the judge was recognized by the community as an expert, he may judge even all by himself.

C. Said R. Nahman, "Someone such as myself may judge property cases alone."

D. And so said R. Hiyya, "Someone such as myself may judge property cases alone."

E. *[Interpreting the foregoing statements,] the question was raised: Is the sense, "Such as myself," that I have mastered legal traditions and learned how to reason about them, and, furthermore, have gotten authorization [to judge by myself]," with the further implication that someone who has not gotten authorization to judge by himself [and has done so] produces an invalid judgment? Or is it the sense that even if one has not gotten authorization, [if he judges by himself], his judgment is valid?*

F. *Come and take note: Mar Zutra, son of R. Nahman, judged a case by himself and made an error. He came before R. Joseph [to find out whether he had to make restitution]. He said to him, "If they accepted you as judge in their case [even though you would judge as an individual], you do not have to make restitution for the error, and, if not, you have to make restitution." What the precedent yields is that the fact that even though one has not gotten authorization, should he judge by himself, his judgment is a valid one.*

H. *That indeed is the inference.*

II.6 A. *Said Rab, "One who wants to judge cases with the proviso that, if he makes a judicial error, he is exempt from having to make restitution, had best get authorization from the house of the exilarch."*

B. *And so said Samuel, "Let such a one gain authorization from the house of the exilarch."*

II.7 A. *It is self-evident that authorization granted here for judging cases here, or that granted there for judging cases there [in the Land of Israel], or authorization granted here for judging cases there [in the Land of Israel] is valid.*

B. *The reason is that here [in the exilarch] we have "the scepter," while there they have only "the law-giver" [Gen. 49:10].*

C. *For it has been taught on Tannaite authority:*

D. "The scepter shall not depart from Judah" (Gen. 49:10) speaks of the exilarchs of Babylonia, who govern Israel with the authority of the scepter [officially, by right].

E. "And a lawgiver" (Gen. 49:10) speaks of the grandsons of Hillel in the Land of Israel, who [merely] teach Torah in public [but do not have standing as a government].

F. *The real question is this:] Is authorization granted there valid for judging cases here?*

G. *Come and take note: Rabbah bar Hana judged a case and made an error. He came before R. Hiyya, who said to him, "If they accepted you as judge in their case, you do not have to make restitution for the error, and, if not, you have to make restitution." Now, in point of fact, Rabbah bar Hana had indeed taken authorization [there]. What is the implication of the case? It is that authorization granted there for use here is invalid.*

J. *That implication indeed emerges.*

K. *Is it then the case that such authorization [granted in the Land of Israel is invalid in Babylonia?] And lo, when Rabbah bar R. Huna had a dispute with the staff of the exilarch, he said, "I do not have my authorization from you. I have my authorization from my father, my master, and my father, my master, has authorization from Rab, and Rab has authorization from R. Hiyya, and R. Hiyya has authorization from Rabbi [in the Land of Israel]." [So authorization from there to here is assumed to be valid.]*

M. *It was any old argument that he threw at them.*

N. *If that is the case, if then authorization from there to here is invalid, then why did Rabbah bar Hana seek authorization at all?*

O. *It was for the purpose of judging cases in the towns on the frontiers.*

II.8 A. What is "authorization"?

B. *[The following story answers the question by means of illustration.] When Rabbah bar Hana was going down to Babylonia, R. Hiyya said to Rabbi [Judah the Patriarch],* "My nephew, son of my brother, is going down to Babylonia. May he make decisions on matters of religious prohibition?"

C. "He may make decisions on matters of religious prohibition?"

D. "May he judge cases of civil law?"

E. "He may judge cases of civil law."

F. "May he declare firstborn beasts [to be blemished and so] permitted for ordinary use?"

G. "He may declare firstborn beasts [to be blemished and so] permitted for ordinary use."

H. *When Rab was going down to Babylonia, R. Hiyya said to Rabbi,* "My nephew, son of my sister, is going down to Babylonia. May he make decisions on matters of religious prohibition?

I. "He may make decisions on matters of religious prohibition?"

J. "May he judge cases of civil law?"

K. "He may judge cases of civil law."

L. "May he declare firstborn beasts [to be blemished and so] permitted for ordinary use?"

M. "He may not declare firstborn beasts [to be blemished and so] permitted for ordinary use."

N. *Why did [Hiyya] differentiate between his nephew, son of his brother, and his nephew, son of his sister?*

O. *And if you should wish to reply that that is how things happen to be, has not a master said, "Aibu, Hana, Shila, Mareta, and R. Hiyya all were sons of Abba bar Aha Karesela of Kafri"? [So*

Rab was son of the brother of R. Hiyya, as well as son of his sister.]

P.   *Rab was son of the brother of the sister of R. Hiyya [on his mother's side], and Rabbah was son of his brother alone.*

Q.   *And if you prefer, I shall explain that* **[5B]** it was because of his [distinguished] sagacity, for it is written, "Say to wisdom, you are my sister" (Prov. 7:4).

R.   *As to his response to the question, "May he declare firstborn beasts [blemished and so] permitted for ordinary use," which was, "He may not do so," why would he not permit him to do so?*

S.   *If one might wish to propose that it was because he was not learned, lo, we have just said that he was very learned.*

T.   *But it was because he was not expert in the character of disqualifying blemishes.*

U.   But has not Rab said, "I spent eighteen months with s shepherd of domesticated cattle in order to learn which blemish is permanent and which passes [and so would not disqualify the beast]"?

V.   Rather, it was to pay special respect to Rabbah bar Hana.

W.   *And if you wish, I shall propose that it was because of the very fact that Rab was altogether too familiar with disqualifying blemishes. He might therefore permit a beast for ordinary use on the basis of a blemish that ordinary folk might not fully recognize. The result, then, would be that people would say that in the case of such a blemish, Rab permitted the beast, and so people would come to permit secular use of a beast affected by a merely transient blemish.*

X.   "May he make decisions on matters of religious prohibition?"

Y.   "He may make decisions on matters of religious prohibition."

Z.   *But if [an authority] has learned the rules properly, what need does he have to gain permission to judge such cases?*

AA.   It was because of an actual case.

BB.   *It has been taught on Tannaite authority.*

CC.   One time Rabbi came to a certain place and saw that the people were kneading their dough in a state of susceptibility to cultic uncleanness [by wetting it down with a liquid that imparts susceptibility to the flour, which, when dry, is insusceptible in line with Lev. 11:32, 34]. He said to them, "On what account are you kneading your dough in a state of susceptibility to cultic uncleanness?"

DD.   They said to him, "A certain disciple came by and taught us, 'Swamp-water does not impart to dry flour the susceptibility to uncleanness.'"

EE.   *But what he had said was eggs, and they though he had said swamp-water [since the consonants are the same, and the vowels shift only slightly], [with the result that they erred].*

FF.   *They made a further mistake with respect to the following:* **Water of Qarmyon and water of Pugah are unfit [for use in mixing with the ashes of the red cow to make purification water], because they are swamp water [M. Par. 8:10I-J].**

GG.   *The people drew the conclusion that, since these classes of water are unfit for mixing with the ashes of the red cow to form purification-water they also will not impart susceptibility to uncleanness [to dry flour].*

HH.   *But that is not the law. The point is that, for use for mixing purification-water, we require running water [and swamp-water does not fall into that classification]. But here, with respect to imparting susceptibility to uncleanness, any sort of liquid [among the specified ones, including water] does impart susceptibility to uncleanness.*

II.   *It has been taught on Tannaite authority:*

JJ.   At that moment they made the decree that a disciple may not give a decision on a matter of religious prohibition unless he gains permission from his master.

II.9   A.   *Tanhum, son of R. Ammi, came to Hattar. He gave the following exposition to the people:* "It is permitted to soak grain before grinding it for use on Passover [despite the concern that the grain may be leavened, because, Schachter states, p. 18, n. 6: Leavening, the result of dampness, does not occur in this, as the grain is ground immediately after washing.]"

       B.   *They said to him, "Is it not R. Mani of Tyre here. And it has been taught on Tannaite authority:* 'A disciple may not give a decision on a matter of religious prohibition in the locale of his master unless he is at least three parasangs away from him, a distance equivalent to the breadth of the camp of Israel.'"

       C.   *He said to them, "That never came to my mind!"*

II.10 A.   *R. Hiyya saw a man standing in a graveyard. He said to him,* "Are you not son of Mr. So-and-so, a priest?"

       B.   *He said to him, "Yes. But the father of that man [me] was strong-headed, and he gazed upon a divorced woman and, with her, produced profaned seed [in the form of children who were unsuited to be in the priestly caste, as children of a priest and a divorced woman, in line with Lev. 21:14]."*

II.11 A.   *It is self-evident that if authorization is granted only in part [for one purpose, not for some other], that is valid [as in the case of Rab]. What is the rule on authorization granted on the basis of a condition?*

B.
Come and take note: R. Yohanan said to R. Shemen, "Lo, you act under our authorization, until you come back to us."

Judgment of Cases by Fewer than Three Judges

II.12   A.
[Reverting to the] body [of the text cited above at I.2]:

B.
Said Samuel, "Two who judged a case produce a valid judgment, but they are called 'a presumptuous court.'"

C.
In session R. Nahman stated this tradition. Raba objected to R. Nahman, **"Even if two judges declare him innocent and two declare him guilty but one of them says, "I don't know," they have to add to the number of the judges [M. 3:6L-N].** *Now if the judgment of Samuel is valid, let the case fall into the category of the judgment of a court made up of two judges [and why add a third]?"*

D.
That case is to be distinguished from the present issue, for, in that matter, to begin with the court went into session in the presumption that three judges would decide the case. In the present circumstance, it was not in the presumption that three judges would decide the case that the court went into session.

E.
A further objection was raised to Samuel's view: **Rabban Simeon b. Gamaliel says, "Judgment is by three [judges], and arbitration is by two arbitrators. The force of arbitration is greater than the force of a court decision. For if two made a judgment the litigants have the power to retract. If two who effected an arbitration, the litigants do not have the power to retract" [T. San. 1:9I-L].** [6A] *And if you wish to maintain that Rabban Simeon b. Gamaliel's colleagues differ from him, has not R. Abbahu stated, "If two persons judged a case, all parties concur that their judgment is invalid."*

F.
Do you simply throw the opinion of one authority against that of someone else? [Schachter, p. 19, n. 8: Why should Samuel, unlike R. Abbahu, hold that the rabbis differ from R. Simeon b. Gamaliel?]

II.13   A.
Reverting to the text cited above:

B.
R. Abbahu said, "If two persons judged a property case, all parties concur that their judgment is invalid."

C.
R. Abba objected to R. Abbahu, "'If one has judged a case, declaring the liable party to be exempt and the exempt party to be liable, declaring what is clean to be unclean or what is unclean to be clean, what he has done is done. But he has to make restitution out of his own property.' [This rule would surely contradict Abbahu's position, since the effect of the decision of even a single judge is valid.]"

D. *With what sort of a case do we deal here? It is a case in which the litigants accepted the authority of the individual to judge their case.*

E. *If that is the case, why does he have to make restitution out of his own property [for his judicial error]?*

F. *It is because they originally said to him, "Judge the case for us in accord with the Torah, [and he has not met that stipulation]."*

G. *Said R. Safra to R. Abba, "In what aspect did the error consist? If we say that it was in a matter of law made explicit in the Mishnah, has not R. Sheshet said R. Assi said, 'If one has made an error in a matter made explicit in the Mishnah, he simply retracts his decision.' Rather, it is an error in reasoning among contradictory views."*

H. *What would such a case –* an error in reasoning among contradictory view *– involve?*

I. *Said R. Pappa, "It would be exemplified by a matter of law in which two Tannaite authorities or two Amoraic authorities differ, and a definitive statement of the decided law is not laid down. But there is a customary view in circulation to act in accord with one of the contending parties, and the judge at hand went and made a decision in accord with another of the parties. This would constitute an error in reasoning among contradictory views.*

II.14   A. *May we propose [that the issue between Samuel's and Abbahu's views of whether two persons may judge a case] follows lines of a dispute between Tannaite authorities?* **"Arbitration is with three judges," the words of R. Meir. And sages say, "With one" [T. San. 1:1C-D].** *Now if we make the assumption that both parties concur that we treat as equivalent arbitration and trial of a case, then would it not follow that the dispute at hand concerns the following principle: One authority holds that a trial must be before three judges [as Meir says], while the other authority maintains that a case is judged by two judges [and at issue, then, is the matter on which Abbahu and Samuel differ].*

B. *No, all parties concur that a case is tried before three judges. Here what is the point at issue? One authority holds that we treat as comparable arbitration and judgment of a case at trial. The other authority maintains that we do not treat as comparable arbitration and the judgment of a case at a trial.*

C. *May we say, then, that there are three opinions among Tannaite authorities on the matter of arbitration? One authority says it is before three authorities, one before two, and one before one?*

D. *Said R. Aha, son of R. Iqa, and some say, R. Yemar, son of R. Shelemia, "He who holds that it is done with*

two would accept the arbitration even of a single
individual. *The reason that he wants to have two
arbitrators is to that there will be [two] witnesses
[namely, the arbitrators] [if needed]."*

E. *Said R. Ashi, "What follows from the facts is that*
an act of formal acquisition is not necessary
in an arbitrated case. *For if you suppose that an
act of acquisition is required, then why should the
Tannaite authority at hand require three
arbitrators? He should suffice with two, with the
parties then being bound by an act of acquisition*
[in which they pledge themselves to adhere
to the award (Schachter)]."

F. *The decided law is that arbitration must be
accompanied by an act of acquisition* [Schachter,
p. 21, n. 4: because, strictly speaking, the
decision is not one of law, and unless the
parties have bound themselves by an act of
acquisition, they can retract].

Composite on Arbitration as Alternative to a Legal Contest

II.15   A. *Our rabbis have taught on Tannaite authority:*
         B. Just as judgment is done before three judges, so an arbitration is
reached by three judges.
         C. [6B] Once the court process has been completed, one has not got the
right to arbitrate.

II.16   A. R. Eleazar, son of R. Yosé the Galilean, says, "It is forbidden to
arbitrate, and whoever arbitrates a case [after judgment has been
passed] – lo, this one sins.
         B. "And whoever praises the arbitrator – lo, this one curses [the
Omnipresent].
         C. "Concerning such a person it is said, 'He who blesses the arbitrator
blasphemes the Lord' (Ps. 10:3).
         D. "But let justice pierce the mountain, as it is written, 'For judgment is
God's' (Deut. 17).
         E. " And so Moses' motto was: Let the law pierce the mountain. But
Aaron loved peace and pursued peace and would make peace
between one person and another, as it is said, 'The Torah of Truth
was in his mouth and unrighteousness was not found in his lips, he
walked with me in peace and uprightness and did many turn away
from iniquity' (Mal. 2:6)."
         F. **R. Eliezer [T.: b. Jacob says, "Why does Scripture say, 'He who
blesses a robber blasphemes the Lord' (Ps. 10:3)?**
         G. **They made an analogy. To what is the matter to be compared?
To] someone who stole a seah of wheat, ground it into wheat,
baked it into bread, and separated dough-offering from the bread
[for the priest], and then fed the bread to his children.] How is
such a person to say a blessing? It is no blessing but a curse.**
         H. **"Concerning such a person it is said, 'When the robber blesses, he
blasphemes the Lord'"** [T. San. 1:2].

J.   R. Meir says, "The reference to one who robs speaks only of Judah. For it is written, 'And Judah said to his brothers, What profit is it if we slay our brother' (Gen. 37:26) [using the same root as the verb for arbitrate]. And whoever blesses Judah, lo, such a person blasphemes, and it is in that context that it is said, ''When the robber blesses, he blasphemes the Lord.''

II.17   A.   R. Joshua b. Qorha says, "It is a religious duty to arbitrate, as it is said, 'Execute the judgment of truth and peace in your gates' (Zech. 8:16).

B.   "Now is it not so that in any case in which there is a judgment [of truth], there is no peace, and in any case in which there is peace, there is no judgment of truth?

C.   "So what is the judgment [of truth] which also contains peace?

D.   "You have to say, This is arbitration."

E.   And so it says in the case of David, "And David acted with judgment and charity to all his people" (2 Sam. 8:15).

F.   Now is it not so that in any case in which there is judgment, there is no charity, and in any case in which there is charity , there is no judgment?

G.   So what is the judgment in which there also is charity?

H.   You have to say, This is arbitration [T. San. 1:3].

I.   [If] one has judged a case, declaring the guiltless to be guiltless, and imposing liability on the guilty party,

J.   if one then sees that he has imposed liability on a poor man,

K.   he takes [the necessary funds for restitution] out of his own pocket and gives it to him, this is a case of true justice and charity.

L.   [That is how he turns out to do] true justice with this one and charity with that one, justice to the one who gets his property back.   Charity to that one, since he has paid from his own property [T. San.1:4I].

M.   To Rabbi, this view of matters presented a problem. If matters were as stated, then rather than saying, "To all his people" (2 Sam. 8:15), it should say only, "to the poor."

N.   Rather, Rabbi says, "[Following T.'s phrasing:] "[If] one has judged a case, declaring the guiltless to be guiltless and imposing liability on the guilty party,

O.   "he turns out to do charity with the one who is liable,

P.   "for he removes the stolen goods from his possession.

Q.   "and he does justice to the innocent party, for he restores to him what belongs to him" [T. San. 1:5].

R.   R. Simeon b. Menassia says, "[Sometimes one should arbitrate, and sometimes he should not arbitrate].

S.   "Two who came before someone to judge [their case] –

T.   "before one has heard what they have to say,

U.   "or if he has heard what they have to say but does not know in which direction the case should turn,

V.   "he has the right to say to them, 'Go out and seek arbitration.'

W.   "But once he has heard what they have to say and knows in which direction the case should turn,

X.   he has no right to say to them, 'Go out and seek arbitration.'

Y.   "Just as it is written, 'The beginning of strife is as when one lets out water; therefore before the matter is laid bare, leave off contention' (Prov. 17:14) —

Z.   "Before the ruling is clear, you are free to abandon it.

AA. "Once the decision is clear, you do not have the right to abandon it" [T. San. 1:6].

BB. R. Judah b. Laqish would say, "Two who came before someone for judgment —

CC. "one strong and one weak —

DD. "before one has heard what they have to say,

EE. "or if one has heard what they have to say, but does not yet know in which direction the case should turn,

FF. "he has the right to say to them, 'I am not going to be subject to you [and to take your case],'

GG. "lest the stronger party turn out to be liable, and the stronger one go after him.

HH. "But if one he has heard what they have to say and knows in which direction the case should turn,

II.   "he has not got the right to say to them, 'I am not going to be subject to you [and to take your case].

JJ. "For it is said, 'You shall not be afraid before man, for judgment is God's' (Deut. 1:17)" [T. San. 1:7].

KK. R. Joshua b. Qorha says, "How do we know that, if a disciple was sitting before his teacher [who was acting as a judge] and knew something for the case of the poor man and something against the case of the rich man, you are not free to keep silent?

LL. "Scripture says, 'You shall not be afraid before man, for judgment is God's' (Deut. 1:17).

MM. [B. lacks:] "Do not hold back what you have to say because of man" [T. San. 1:8]

NN. R. Hanin says, "You may not hold back your view on anyone's account. The judges should know Whom they judge, and before Whom they judge, and Who it is Who judges with them.

OO. "And the witnesses should know about Whom they give testimony, and before Whom they give testimony, and with Whom they give testimony, and Who it is Who is a witness with them,

PP. "since it is said, 'Then both the men before whom the controversy is shall stand before the Lord' (Deut. 19:17).

QQ. "And it is said, 'God stands in the congregation of God and in the midst of judges he judges' (Ps. 82:1).

RR. "And concerning Jehoshaphat it is said, 'Consider what you do, for you judge not for man but for God' (II Chron. 19:6).

SS. "Now perhaps a judge might say, 'What do I need this trouble for?'

TT. "But has it not truly been said, 'He is with you in the matter of judgment' (2 Chron. 19:6).

UU. "You have to take account only of what your own eyes see."

II.18   A.   *What marks the conclusion of the trial?*

B.   Said R. Judah said Rab, "[The statement by the judges,] 'Mr. So and so, you are liable. Mr. So and so, you are innocent.'"

C.   Said Rab, "The decided law accords with the view of R. Joshua b. Qorha."

D.   *Is this the case? And lo, R. Huna was a disciple of Rab, and when litigants would come before R. Huna, he would say to them, "Do you want me to judge the case or to arbitrate it?"* [Schachter, p. 24, n. 5: Hence we see that Rab does not favor R. Joshua b. Qorha's opinion, as it is unlikely that Huna, the disciple, would deviate from the ruling of the master]."

II.19   A.   *What is the sense of "religious duty" as it was used by R. Joshua b. Qorha?* [7A] *It is a religious duty to say to them, "Do you want me to judge the case or to arbitrate it?"*

B.   *If so, then what we have is nothing other than the opinion of the first authority [who favors arbitration].*

C.   *At issue between them is whether or not it is a religious duty.*

D.   R. Joshua b. Qorha maintains that it is a religious duty.

E.   The first Tannaite authority maintains that it is merely an option.

F.   *But that is the position of R. Simeon b. Menassia .*

G.   *At issue between them is the rule prevailing* once one has heard the claims of both parties and knows to which side the judgment will incline. At that point, you are not permitted to say to them, "Go and arbitrate the matter."

II.20   A.   *There is a difference of opinion [concerning Ps. 10:3, cited above] on the part of R. Tanhum bar Hanilai. R. Tanhum bar Hanilai has said, "The cited verse of Scripture speaks only with regard to the making of the Golden Calf. For it is said, 'And when Aaron saw it, he built an altar before it' (Ex. 32:5)."*

B.   What did he see?

C.   *Said R. Benjamin bar Japheth said R. Eleazar, "He saw Hur slain before him. He reasoned, 'If I do not listen to them, they will do to me what they did to Hur, and in me will be carried out the verse of prophecy, "Shall the priest and the prophet be slain in the sanctuary of God" (Lam. 2:20), and they will never have a remedy. It is better that they make the calf, since they may find a remedy in repentance.'"*

II.21   A.   *Now as to the other Tannaite authorities [cited above, who favor arbitration even after a case has been heard], how do they interpret the verse, "The beginning of strife is as one that lets out water"* (Prov. 17:14)?

B.   *They explain it in accord with the view of R. Hamnuna.*

C.   For R. Hamnuna said, "The beginning of a person's judgment comes with the issue of study of Torah, for it is said, 'The beginning of judgment concerns the letting out of water' [and water stands for Torah]."

D.   *Said R. Huna, "Strife is compared to a rush of water, that gets broader as water pushes through."*

E.   *Abbayye the Elder said, "It is like [Schachter:] planks of a wooden bridge; the longer they lie, the firmer they grow."*

II.22   A.   *There was a man who went around saying, "Happy is the one who hears [something] and remains indifferent. A hundred evils pass him by."*

B.   Said Samuel to R. Judah, "A verse of Scripture is written along these same lines: 'He who lets out water [of strife] causes the beginning of judgment' (Prov. 17:14). [The numerical value of the Hebrew letters for the word for judgment is a hundred], thus, it is the beginning of a hundred evils."

C.   There was a man who went around saying, "For two or three acts of theft, the criminal is not put to death [but he ultimately will be caught]."

D.   Said Samuel to R. Judah, "There is a pertinent verse of Scripture: 'So says the Lord, For three transgressions of Judah but for four I will not reverse [the judgment]' (Amos 2:6)."

E.   There was a man who went around saying, "There are seven pits open for the good man, [who escapes them all], but one suffices for an evil-doer."

F.   Said Samuel to R. Judah, "There is a pertinent verse of Scripture: "The righteous man falls seven times but rises up again' (Prov. 24:16)."

G.   There was a man who went around saying, "When you go forth from a trial, take your cloak, sing a song, and go your way."

H.   Said Samuel to R. Judah, "There is a pertinent verse of Scripture: 'And all this people also [Schachter: including the losers] shall come to their place in peace' (Ex. 18:23)."

I.   There was a man who went around saying, "The woman sleeps and her basket falls."

J.   Said Samuel to R. Judah, "There is a pertinent verse of Scripture: 'By laziness the rafters sink in' (Qoh. 10:18)."

K.   There was a man who went around saying, "The man [Schachter:] on whom I relied raised his club against me."

L.   Said Samuel to R. Judah, "There is a pertinent verse of Scripture: 'Yes, mine own familiar friend, in whom I trusted and who ate my bread, has lifted up his heel against me' (Ps. 41:10)."

M.   There was a man who went around saying, "When our love was strong, we could sleep on the blade of a sword. Now that our love is not strong, a bed sixty cubits wide is not enough for us."

N.   Said R. Huna, "There are pertinent verses of Scripture. In the beginning, it is written, 'And I will meet with you and speak with you from above the ark cover' (Ex. 25:22). And it is taught on Tannaite authority: The ark was nine handbreadths high and the cover a handbreadth, so ten in all. Then it is written, 'As for the house which king Solomon built for the Lord, the length of it was three score cubits, the breadth twenty, the height thirty' (1 Kgs. 6:2).

O.   *"But in the end it is written, 'Thus says the Lord, The heaven is my throne and the earth my footstool. Where is the house that you can build for me' (Is. 66:1)."*

II.23   A.   *How do we know that the word [translated above as] "be afraid" also can stand for "gather in"?*

B.   Said R. Nahman, "Scriptures has said, 'You shall not drink of the wine, nor gather in the grapes' [using the same root] (Deut. 28:39)."

C.   *R. Aha bar Jacob said, "Proof derives from here: 'She provides her bread in the summer and gathers [using the same root] her food in he harvest' (Prov. 6:8)."*

D.   *R. Aha, son of R. Iqa, said, "Proof derives from here: 'A wise son gathers in summer' (Prov. 10:5)."*

In Praise of Justice and True Judges

II.24   A.   Said R. Samuel bar Nahmani said R. Jonathan, "Every judge who renders a true and faithful judgment brings the Presence of God to rest on Israel, as it is said, 'God stands in the congregation of God, in the midst of the judges he judges' (Ps. 82:1).

B.   "And every judge who does not render a true and faithful judgment drives the Presence of God to abandon Israel, as it is said, 'Because of the oppression of the poor, because of the sighing of the needy, now will I arise, says the Lord' (Ps. 12:6)."

C.   And R. Samuel bar Nahmani said R. Jonathan said, "From every judge who unjustly takes something from one party and assigns it to the other, the Holy One, blessed be he, takes away his life, as it is said "Do not rob from the poor because he is poor, nor oppress the afflicted in the gate, for the Lord will plead their cause and will despoil of life those who despoil them' (Prov. 22:22-23)."

D.   And R. Samuel bar Nahmani said R. Jonathan said, "A judge should always imagine that a sword is hanging between his loins [ready to cut him into two], and Gehenna is open beneath him, **[7B]** as it is said, 'Behold, it is the litter of Solomon [Schachter: standing for the presence of God], and round about it are three score of the mighty men of Israel [disciples of sages]; they all handle the sword and are expert in war, and every man has his sword upon his flank because of the dread of night' (Song 3:7-8) – the dread of Gehenna, which is like the night."

II.25   A.   *R. Josiah, and some say. R, Nahman bar Isaac, gave an exposition, "What is the meaning of the verse of Scripture, 'O house of David, thus says the Lord, Execute justice in the morning and deliver the spoiled out of the hand of the oppressor' (Jer. 21:12)?*

B.   "Now is it only in the morning that judges work, and do they not work throughout the day?

C.   "But if a matter is clear to you as the morning light, then state it, and if not, do not state it."

D.   *R. Hiyya bar Abba said R. Jonathan said, "Proof derives from here: 'Say to wisdom,. You are my sister' (Prov. 7:4). If the matter is* as clear to you as is the fact that your sister is forbidden to you, then say it, and if not, do not say it."

II.26   A.   Said R. Joshua b. Levi, "When ten judges go into session to judge a case, an iron chain is hanging on the neck of all of them [since responsibility for the decision is shared equally by them]."

    B.   *That is self-evident.*

    C.   *No, it was necessary to make it explicit, only to deal with the case of a disciple who is in session before his master.*

    D.   *When a case would come to R. Huna, he would call and bring together ten rabbis from he house of a master, saying "It is so that each should carry chips from the beam."*

    E.   *When a case involving a disqualified beast [brought by a slaughterer for evaluation] came to R. Ashi, he would call and bring together all of the slaughterers of Mata Mehassia, saying, "It is so that each would carry chips from the beam."*

II.27   A.   *When R. Dimi came, he said that R. Nahman bar Kohen gave an interpretation, "What is the meaning of that which is written, 'The king by justice established the land, but he who loves gifts overthrows it'* (Prov. 29:4)?

    B.   "If the judge is like a king, who needs nothing [from anyone else but knows the law on his own], he will establish the land. But if the judge is like a priest who goes begging at the threshing places [to collect the priestly gifts], he will destroy it."

II.28   A.   *The administration of the patriarchate appointed a judge who had not studied the law. They said to Judah bar Nahmani, the spokesman for R. Simeon b. Laqish, "Stand at his side as the spokesman [who repeats in a loud voice what the master wishes to say to the assembled throng]."*

    B.   *He arose and bent down to him [to hear what he wished to say], but the unqualified man said nothing.*

    C.   *He [Judah] commenced, saying, "'Woe to him who say to wood, 'Awake! and to the dumb stone, 'Arise!' Can this teach? Behold it is overlaid with gold and silver, and there is no breath at all in the midst of it'* (Hab. 2:19).

    D.   "The Holy One, blessed be he, is going to exact punishment from those who set [up such as this], as it is written, 'But the Lord is in his holy Temple, let all the earth keep silent before him' (Hab. 2:19)."

II.29   A.   Said R. Simeon b. Laqish, "Whoever appoints a judge who is unworthy is as if he plants an asherah in Israel.

    B.   "For it is said, 'Judges and offices shall you appoint' (Deut. 16:18), and, nearby, 'You shall not plant an Asherah of any kind of tree' (Deut. 16:19)."

    C.   Said R. Ashi, "And if one does so in a place in which there are disciples of sages, it is as if he planted it right next to the altar, for it is said, 'Beside the altar of the Lord your God' (Deut. 16:19)."

II.30   A.   It is written, "You shall not make with me gods of silver or gods of gold" (Ex. 20:23). *Gods of silver and gods of gold are what one may not make, but is it permitted to make ones of wood?*

    B.   Said R. Ashi, "The verse refers to a judge who comes on account of silver or a judge who comes on account of gold."

II.31   A.   *When Rab would come to court, he would say this, "With a bitter soul he goes forth to death. The needs of his house he has not attended to. He goes home empty-handed. Would that his coming home should be as is his going forth."*

B.   When he would see a crowd following him, he would say, "'Though his excellence mount up to the heavens and his head reach unto the clouds, yet shall he perish forever, like his own dung' (Prov. 27:24)."

II.32   A.   *When on the Sabbath that coincided with a festival people would lift up Mar Zutra the Pious onto their shoulders, he would say this, "'For riches are not for ever nor does the crown endure for all generations' (Prov. 27:24)."*

II.33   A.   *Bar Qappara gave an exposition, "Whence in Scripture do we derive the basis for the rabbis' saying,* **Be deliberate in judgment [M. Abot 1:1]?**

B.   "As it is written, 'Neither shall you go up by steps upon my altar' (Ex. 20:26). Next comes the verse, 'And these are the judgments' (Ex. 20)27). [Schachter, p. 30, n. 7: The juxtaposition shows that for judgments one should proceed slowly and avoid large paces, as one does on ascending the altar.]"

C.   Said R. Eliezer, "How on the basis of Scripture do we know that a judge should not trample over the heads of the holy people?

D.   "As it is said, 'Neither shall you go up by steps upon my altar' (Ex. 20:26), and next comes the verse, 'And these are the judgments' (Ex. 20:27)."

E.   "These are the judgments which you shall set before them" (Ex. 20:27).

F.   *What is required is, "which you shall teach them."*

G.   *Said R. Jeremiah, and some say, R. Hiyya bar Abba, "This refers to the tools of the judges' craft."*

H.   *When R. Huna would go in to take up a case, this is what he said, "Bring out the tools of my craft: the rod, the strap, the ram's horn, and the sandal [for flogging, administering the thirty-nine stripes, the rite of excommunication, and the rite of removing the shoe (Deut. 25:5-10), respectively]."*

II.34   A.   "And I shall command your judges at that time" (Deut. 1:16):

B.   Said R. Yohanan, "This concerns the rod and strap, to be used cautiously."

C.   "Hear the causes between your brothers and judge righteously" (Deut. 1:16):

D.   Said R. Hanina, "This is a warning to the court not to listen to the claim of one litigant before the other comes to court, and a warning to the litigants not to plead before the judge before the other party comes to court. *The word for 'hear' may also be read 'announce.'*"

E.   *R. Kahana said, "Proof derives from here, 'You shall not take up a false report,' (Ex. 23:1) may be read, 'Do not mislead' [Schachter, p. 31, n. 10: with reference to the litigant, that he should not attempt to win over the judge to his side by stating his case in the absence of his adversary]."*

F.   "You shall judge righteously" (Deut. 1:16):

G.   R. Simeon b. Laqish said, "First of all make sure the judgment is accurate, and then pronounce it."

H. "Between a man and his brother" (Deut. 1:16):
I. Said R. Judah, "Even in cases such as dividing a house from an upper room."
J. "And the stranger that is with him" (Deut. 1:16):
K. Said R. Judah, "Even a case involving division of an oven and a cooking stove."
L. "You shall not show recognize persons in judgment" (Deut. 1:16):
M. R. Judah says, "You shall not recognize anyone."
N. R. Eleazar says, "You shall not treat anyone as a stranger [Schachter: even if he is your enemy]."
O. *The landlord of Rab came before him with a case. he said to him, "Are you not my landlord?"*
P. *He said to him, "Yes." [The man continued,] "I have a case for trial."*
Q. *He said to him, " [8A] I am disqualified to judge a case for you."*
R. *Rab said to R. Kahana, "Go, judge his case." [Kahana] saw that the man was behaving presumptuously toward him. He said to him, "If you pay attention, well and good, but if not, I shall remove Rab from your mind."*
S. "You shall hear the small and the great alike" (Deut. 1:17):
T. Said R. Simeon b. Laqish, "It means that you should regard as equally valuable a case involving a penny and one involving a great fortune."
U. *What is the practical use of the law? If I should say that it means one should pay close attention to the case and produce a valid judgment, that is self-evident. Rather, it means to give the case priority [if its turn should come up].*
V. "You shall not be afraid before anyone, for judgment is God's" (Deut. 1:17):
W. Said R. Hama, son of R. Hanina, "Said the Holy One, blessed be he, 'It is not enough for the wicked judges unjustly to take money from this one and hand it over to that one, but they impose upon me the trouble of retrieving the money and handing it back to its rightful owner.'"
X. "And the case that is too hard for you, bring to me" (Deut. 1:17):
Y. Said R. Hanina, and some say, R. Josiah, "For saying this thing Moses was punished.
Z. "For it is said, 'And Moses brought their cause before the Lord' (Num. 27:5)."
AA. *To this point R. Nahman bar Isaac objected, "Is it written, 'And I shall announce it'? What is written is, 'I shall hear it,' meaning, if I have learned the applicable law, I have learned it, and if not, I shall go and learn it."*
BB. *Now [the case of the daughters of Zelophehad involves] that which has been taught on Tannaite authority:*
CC. **The pericope of inheritance was suitable to have been written in behalf of Moses, our Master, but the daughters of Zelophehad had the merit that it should be written in their behalf.**
DD. **The pericope of the wood-gatherer [Num. 15:32] was suitable to have been written in behalf of Moses, our master, but the**

wood-gatherer was so condemned that it was written on his account.

EE.   This serves to teach you that [Schachter] evil is brought about through the agency of sinful men, and good through that of worthy men [T. Yoma 4:12].

FF.   It is written: "And I commanded you judges at that time" (Deut. 1:16) and it is written," I commanded you at that time" (Deut. 1:18).

GG.   Said R. Eleazar said R. Simlai, "The first constitutes a warning to the community that reverence for the judge should govern them, and a warning to the judge to bear the burden of the community."

HH.   To what extent?

II.   Said R. Hanan, and some say, R. Shabbetai, "'As the nursing father carries the sucking child' (Num. 11:12)."

JJ.   It is written, "You [Joshua] must go with this people" (Deut. 31:7), and it is written, "For you shall bring the children of Israel" (Deut. 31:23). [In the first instance, Joshua is equal to the people, in the second, he is leader (Schachter)].

KK.   Said R. Yohanan, "Said Moses to Joshua, 'You and the elders of the generation with them [shall be equal].'

LL.   "Said the Holy One, blessed be he, 'Take a staff and browbeat them [to show your authority]. A generation has a single spokesman, not two."

II.35   A.   *It has been taught on Tannaite authority:*

B.   A summons is by the authority of three.

C.   *What is the meaning of "summons"?*

D.   *If you wish to propose that reference is made to the call to say Grace, has it not been taught on Tannaite authority:* "The summons and the call to say Grace are done by a quorum of three." *And if you propose that the meaning of the Tannaite teaching, is to provide a secondary expansion of the first clause, thus,* "What is a summons? it is a summons to say Grace after Meals," *has it not been taught,* "A summons is on the authority of three, and the summons to say Grace after Meals is on the authority of three"? *Therefore, what is the sense of "summons" [in the Tannaite citation with which we began]?*

E.   It is a summons to court.

F.   *It would be illustrated by what Raba said, "If a court of three judges is in session, and the bailiff goes for the court and issues his summons in the name of only one of the judges, he has said nothing. [His summons is effective] only if he speaks in the name of all of them."*

J.   *That rule applies on a day on which a court is not in session. But on a day on which a court is in session, we have no objection [to a summons in the name of one judge only]."*

III.1   A.   **Cases involving twofold restitution [M. 1:1C]:**

B.   R. Nahman bar Hisda sent word to R. Nahman bar Jacob, "May our master instruct us.

C.   "As to cases involving the imposition of penalties [fines], how many judges are required?'

D.   *What question did he raise before him? Lo, we have learned in the Mishnah:* **It is with three judges [M. 1:1C].**

E. *What he was asking him was about the power of an individual who was a certified expert. May such a person by himself judge a case involving penalties, or may he not do so?*

F. *He said to him, "You have learned to repeat the passage as follows:* **Cases involving twofold, four-fold and fivefold restitution are judged by three.**

G. *"What is the sense of three? Should I say it is done by three ordinary persons? Has not the father of your father stated in the name of Rab, 'Even ten men who are common folk are disqualified to judge cases involving penalties'? Accordingly the passage must speak of certified expert. And it has specified that they too must be three."*

IV.1 A. **"...cases involving him who rapes, him who seduces, and him who brings forth an evil name (Deut. 22:19), by three," the words of R. Meir. And sages say, "He who brings forth an evil name is tried before twenty-three, for there may be a capital case." [M. 1:1EA-F]:**

B. *And should a case involving a case involving a capital crime come forth, what difference would it make?* [Schachter, p. 34: Since there are no witnesses yet known to be available to corroborate the husband's suspicion, is it not merely a monetary case, involving only the payment of the marriage-settlement?]

C. *Said Ulla, "At issue is whether or not we take account of the effect of the husband's gossip.* [Schachter, p. 35, n. 1: As soon as the charge is made before the court, the report might be bruited, and witnesses, of whom the husband may at the moment be unaware, may come to support it, the charge thus becoming capital.] *R. Meir takes the view that* we do not take account of the possibility of gossip, [with the result that we do not suppose unknown witnesses may come forth later on.]. *Sages take the view that* we do take into account the possibility of gossip."

D. *Raba said, "All parties concur that we do not take account of the possibility of gossip [with the result that we also do not concern ourselves with the possibility that witnesses will come forth to turn it into a capital case]. At issue is whether we take account of the honor owing to the judges who were appointed at the outset [in the concern that we may have a capital case, but then dismissed later on when it turns out that we have only a property case, concerning payment of the marriage-settlement]. In what sort of case do we concern itself? In one in which a court of twenty-three judges is assembled to judge a capital case [that may be in hand], and then [when the witnesses on a capital crime do not materialize], the court breaks up. The plaintiff then claims, Let three at any rate say to judge the property claim at hand.* [Schachter: The sages, in order to protect the dignity of those judges who would have left, require them to reassemble, while R. Meir does not hold this view.]"

E. *[8B] An objection was raised:* **And sages say, "He who brings forth an evil name [M. 1:1E], in a case in which one lays claim concerning money, is judged by three; [in a case in which the issue is] capital punishment, it is before twenty-three"** [cf. M. 1:1F] [T. San. 1:ZE-G]. *Now, to the position of Raba the cited passage poses no problem.* If the case involved a claim for money to begin with, a court of three judges hears it. If the case involved a capital crime to begin with, even if in the end it deals only with a property claim, the case must be heard by twenty-three judges. *But it poses a problem to Ulla* [for in Ulla's view, rabbis' take account of the husband's suspicions alone as involving a capital charge (Schachter, p. 36, n. 9)].

F.   *Said Raba, "I and the lion of the club explained the matter – and who is that? It is R. Hiyya bar Abin – in the following way: Here with what case do we deal? It is one in which* the husband brought witnesses to testify that the wife had committed adultery, and the father [successfully] brought witnesses to prove that the husband's witnesses were perjurers. When the husband comes to collect the property claim from the husband [who now owes the value of the marriage-contract, which he had sought to gain through the perjury], the case is tried with by a court of three judges. But as to the capital charge, twenty-three judges [try the case]."

G.   *Abbayye said, "All parties concur that we do take account of the effect of the gossip of the husband, and we further take account of the honor owing to the first judges [who make up the court of twenty-three]. With what sort of case do we deal here? It is with a case in which [before the woman committed adultery, she was] warned without specification [as to the form of the death-penalty she would receive if she committed the act she planned]. [Why only three judges are required in Meir's view is now to be specified. He concurs with Yosé b. R. Judah.] The Tannaite authority at hand [opposed to Meir] concurs with that which has been taught on Tannaite authority:* **As to all others liable to the death-penalty imposed by a court as listed in the Torah, they convict them only on the testimony of witnesses, after warning, and after they inform him that [what he is going to do] subjects him to liability to the death-penalty in court. R. [Yosé b. R.] Judah says, 'Only if they will inform him specifically of the sort of death-penalty to which he will be subjected,' [T. San. 11:1A-C].** [Thus, in the case at hand, the woman will not be liable to the death-penalty, so the appropriate court is one that deals only with the property claim]."

H.   *R. Pappa said, "Here we deal with a woman who is in the status of an associate [knowledgeable in the law], and at issue is the dispute between R. Yosé b. R. Judah and rabbis. For it has been taught on Tannaite authority:* R. Yosé b. R. Judah says, 'An associate [knowledgeable in the law] does not require suitable admonition [prior to a crime, so as to render him liable to punishment], because admonition is demanded only to permit a distinction between one who does the deed unknowingly and the one who does it knowingly [and the associate surely will know the law and therefore needs not be told the specific form of the death-penalty to which he will become liable should he commit the act in prospect.]"

I.   *R. Ashi said,* **[9A],** *"We deal with a case in which people gave a warning to the woman that she would be liable to a flogging but did not warn her that she would be liable to the death-penalty. And at issue is the dispute between R. Ishmael and rabbis. For we have learned in the Mishnah:* **Cases involving the penalty of flogging are before a court of three judges. In the name of R. Ishmael they said, 'Before one of twenty-three judges.' [M. 1:2A-B].** *"*

J.   *Rabina said, "At issue is a case in which one of the witnesses against the woman turns out to be a relative or otherwise invalid. And the dispute concerns what is debates between R. Yosé and Rabbi in regard to the position of R. Aqiba. For we have learned in the Mishnah:* **R. Aqiba says, 'The mention of the third [witness] is only to impose upon him a strict rule and to treat the rule concerning him as the same as that applying to the other two. And if Scripture has imposed a punishment on someone who gets involved with those who commit a transgression precisely equivalent to that which is imposed on those who themselves commit the transgression, how much the more so will [Heaven] pay a just reward to the one who gets involved with those who do a religious duty precisely equivalent to that which is paid to those who themselves actually do the religious duty!'"** Jut as, in the case of two [witnesses], if one of them turns out to be a relative or otherwise invalid, the testimony of both of them is null, so in the case of three [if] one of them turns out to be a relative or otherwise invalid, the testimony of all three of them is null. How do we know that the same rule applies even in the case of a hundred? Scripture says, 'Witnesses.' Said R. Yosé, 'Under what circumstances? In the case of trials for capital crimes. But in the case of trials in property litigations, the testimony may be confirmed with the remaining [valid witnesses].' Rabbi says, 'All the same is the rule governing property cases and capital cases.' This is the rule when [both witnesses] warned the transgressor. But if they had not joined in warning the transgressor, what [9B] should two brothers do who saw someone commit homicide? [M. Mak. 1:7-L,1:8].**"

K.   *Or, if you prefer, I shall propose that the case at hand is one in which others [than the actual witness] admonished the woman, but the witnesses to the deed did not admonish the woman. And at issue is the dispute of R. Yosé and rabbis, as we have learned in the Mishnah:* **"R. Yosé says, 'Under no circumstances is one put to death unless both witnesses against him have admonished him, as it is said, 'At the testimony of two witnesses' (Deut. 17:6). [M. Mak. 1:9F-G].**

N.   *And if you prefer, I shall propose that the case at hand is one in which the witnesses were contradicted during the cross-examination [Schachter:] regarding accompanying circumstances but corroborated each other during cross-examination [on such matters as date, time, and place]. At issue, then is the dispute between Ben Zakkai and rabbis. For we have learned in the Mishnah:* **There was a precedent in which Ben Zakkai investigated [the witnesses] by asking about the stalks of figs [that were on the tree under which the crime had been committed] [M. San. 5:2B]."**

IV.2   A.   Said R. Joseph, "If the husband brought witnesses that the wife had committed adultery, and the father brought witnesses who proved the husband's witnesses to be perjurers, the witnesses who had testified in behalf of the husband are put to death, but they do not have to pay monetary compensation [for the loss of the marriage-contract that they had conspired to cause to the wife's family.] If the husband then went and brought witnesses who proved the father's witnesses to have been perjurers, the witnesses who had testified in behalf of the father are put to death but they also have to pay monetary compensation [to the husband, for having conspired to force him to pay off the marriage-settlement]. That is, they pay monetary compensation to this one [the husband] and are put to death on account of that one [the earlier witnesses]."

B.   And R. Joseph said, "If someone testified, 'Mr. So-and-so had sexual relations with Mr. Such-and-such against the latter's will, the victim and another party may join together to give testimony to have the criminal put to death. If he testified that it was with the assent of the victim, then the victim is wicked, and the Torah has said, 'Do not put your hand with the wicked to be an unrighteous witness' (Ex. 23:1)."

C.   Raba said, "A person is regarded as related to himself [for the purpose of giving testimony, and, consequently, someone may not so testify as to convict himself.] [Hence, the victim's testimony about himself is null, and he may testify against the perpetrator.] [Schachter, p. 39, n. 7: Consequently, his evidence is valid only with regard to the criminal but not to himself, on the principle that we consider only half of his testimony as evidence.]"

D.   Said Raba, "[If someone testified,] '[10A] 'Mr. So-and-so has had sexual relations with my wife,' he and another party may join together to form the requisite number of witnesses to impose the death-penalty on the adulterer, but not to impose the death-penalty on the wife."

E.   *Of what fact does Raba thereby propose to inform us? Is it that we recognize a division in what a person says [and so accept testimony so far as it affects one party, but not so far as it affects another]? That is what he has just said [in the case of the sodomist].*

F.   *What might you have supposed? That a person is regarded as related to himself is a principle we invoke for the person himself, but not for his wife? So we are informed [that the same principle applies to his wife].*

G.   And Raba said, "[If witnesses testified,] 'So-and-so has had sexual relations with a betrothed girl,' and the witnesses were proved to be perjurers, they are put to death, but they do not have to make monetary restitution to the accused [who, if found guilty, would have lost the value of the marriage-settlement that was coming to her]. [If they had testified,] 'Mr. So-and-so's daughter...,' and were proven to be perjurers, they are put to death but also have to pay monetary compensation. They pay monetary compensation to the one party and are subjected to the death-penalty on account of the other party."

H.   And Raba said, "[If witnesses testified,] 'Mr. So-and-so committed an act of bestiality with an ox,' and the witnesses are proven to be perjurers, they are put to death but do not have to pay monetary compensation [for the death of the ox]. 'It was with the ox belong to Mr. So-and-so,' if they are shown to be perjurers, they are put to death and have to pay monetary compensation. monetary compensation on this one's account, death on that one's account."

I. *But why is it necessary to provide yet another example? The same point is made in both instances.*

J. *[Raba framed the present case] to deal with the following question. For Raba raised the following question, "[If someone testified,] 'Mr. So-and-so committed an act of bestiality with my ox,' what is the law? Do we maintain that a man is regarded as related to himself [for purposes of testimony, in which case, as we saw above, he may not testify to his own disadvantage], but a person is not regarded as related with regard to his property [so in the latter case, he may indeed give valid testimony as to what has taken place with his ox]? Or do we maintain that a person is regarded as related to his property?"*

K. *After he had raised the question, he went and settled it: "A person is regarded as related to himself but a person is not regard a regarded as related to his property."*

V.1 A. **Cases of flogging [are tried by a court of] three judges [M. 1:2A]:**

B. *What is the scriptural source for this rule?*

C. Said R. Huna, "Scripture says, '[The judges] judge them' (Deut. 25:1), the plural refers to two judges, and since a court cannot have an even number of judges, they add an additional one to the court, making three in all."

D. *If so, then take up the following words in the same verse, "... acquitting the innocent and condemning the guilty" (Deut. 25:1). [Since the plural is used in both verbs,] shall we then say that, "acquitting" demands two more judges, and "condemning" yet two more, requiring a court of seven in all?*

E. *The cited language is needed to deal with the point of Ulla. For Ulla has said,* "Whence in the Torah do we find an allusion to the disposition of perjured witnesses?"

F. *An allusion to the disposition of perjured witnesses?! Lo, it is written,* "Then you shall do to him as he had proposed by perjury to do to his brother" (Deut. 19:19)!

G. *Rather, the question must be,* "Whence in the Torah do we find an allusion to the fact that perjured witnesses are to be flogged?

H. "As it is written, '... acquitting the innocent and condemning the guilty...' (Deut. 25:1). [The verse continues, 'then if the guilty man deserves to be beaten, the judge shall cause him to lie down and be beaten...' (Deut. 25:2). In the assumption that the reference to acquitting and condemning refers to the judges, we ask:] Merely because the judges 'justify the righteous and condemn the wicked,' does it follow that 'the guilty man deserves to be beaten'? [Schachter: The text cannot therefore refer to judges,] so the case must be as follows: *We deal with witnesses whose testimony has convicted a righteous man, and other witnesses have come along and vindicated the righteous man to begin with and so turned the other witnesses into wicked men. In this case:* 'If the guilty man deserves to be beaten, the judge shall cause him to lie down and be beaten...' (Deut. 25:2R)."

I.   But why not derive the same proposition from the commandment, "You shall not bear false witness" (Ex. 20:16)?

J.   Because [at Ex. 20:16] you have a negative commandment in which no deed is done, and in the case of any negative commandment in which no concrete deed is carried out, you do not inflict flogging. [Hence the proof is required as given, for the proposed proof-text will not serve.]

VI.1 A. **In the name of R. Ishmael they said, "By twenty-three" [M. 1:2B].**

B.   *What is the scriptural basis for the position of R. Ishmael?*

C.   *Said Abbayye, "It derives from establishing an analogy on the basis of the use of the same word, 'guilty party,' in two contexts, the present one and the one involving those who are condemned to be put to death. Here it is written, 'If the guilty man deserves to be beaten' (Deut. 25:2), and elsewhere, 'Who is guilty of death' (Num. 35:31). Just as in that latter case the court that imposes the penalty must be made up of twenty-three judges, so here a court of twenty-three judges is required."*

D.   Raba said, "Flogging comes instead of the death-penalty."

E.   *Said R. Aha, son of Raba, to R. Ashi, "If so, what need is there, in the case of a flogging, to make an estimate of the victim's health [to see whether or not he can take the flogging]? Let him be flogged, and if he dies, he dies [since the flogging is a form of the death-penalty in any event.]"*

F.   He said to him, "Scripture has said, 'Then your brother should be dishonored before your eyes' (Deut. 25:3). This means that, when the flogging is given, it is given to someone who is alive."

G.   *But lo, as to that which has been taught on Tannaite authority:* **If the physicians have estimated that he can take twenty stripes, they impose on him only a number of stripes that is divisible by three, and how many would that be? It is eighteen [T. Mak. 4:0 12]. [10B]** *But why not give him twenty-one, for, if he should perish because of the twenty-first lash, he still would be alive when it was inflicted?*

H.   He said to him, "Scripture has said, 'Then your brother will be dishonored before your eyes' (Deut. 25:3), *meaning, after he has been flogged, he must remain your brother in your sight, and that would not be the case [if he should die at the end of the twenty-first lash]."*

VII.1 A. **The decision to intercalate the month is before a court of three judges [M. 1:2C]:**

B.   *The word choice of the Mishnah-sentence at hand is not "calculation" [of the time at which the new month begins], let alone "sanctification" [of the new month, when it begins], but rather "intercalation" [of the new month]. Let the court not sanctify [the new month on the thirtieth day], and then, on its own, it will be automatically intercalated.* [Schachter, p. 42, n. 4: The commencement of the month was dated from the time when the earliest visible appearance of the new moon was reported to the sanhedrin. If this happened on the thirtieth day of the current month, that month was considered to have ended on the preceding day, the twenty-ninth, and was called deficient. But if not, announcement was made on the thirtieth day, that day was reckoned to the current month, which was then called full, and the ensuing day was considered the first of the next month.] [Why we do not speak of the calculation as to the months to be intercalated or given an additional day, since in given year, no fewer than four months nor more than eight months could be full. Again, we ask why the formal "sanctification" of the new moon by proclamation on the thirtieth day is not mentioned.]

C. *Said Abbayye, "Repeat the language of the Mishnah in the form:* **Sanctification of the new month** [rather than intercalation, to deal with the foregoing question]. *So too it has been taught on Tannaite authority:* "'**The sanctification of the new month and the intercalation of the year are done by a court of three judges,' the words of R. Meir [T. San. 2:1A].**'"

D. *Said Raba, "But lo, the language of the Mishnah is 'intercalation.'"*

E. *Rather said Raba, "The sense of the passage is that* the sanctification of the new month takes place on the day of intercalation, in a court of three judges. After the day on which intercalations takes place, there is no further rite of sanctification. *And whose opinion is before us? It is R. Eleazar b. Sadoq. For it has been taught on Tannaite authority:* **R. Eleazar b. Sadoq says, 'If the new moon did not appear at its proper time, they do not conduct a rite of sanctification for it, for we take for granted that in Heaven they already have conducted the rite of sanctification of the new moon.'" [M. R.H. 2:7].**"

F. *[Proposing a different view of the sense of the passage from that proposed by Raba,] R. Nahman said, "The rite of sanctification of the new moon takes place after the declaration of intercalation of the new month, in a court of three judges. No rite of sanctification takes place on the day on which the intercalation is pronounced. And whose view is this? It is that of Pelimo. For it has been taught on Tannaite authority:* Pelimo says, '[If the new moon has appeared] at the proper time time, they do not conduct a rite of sanctification for it. If it was not in its proper time, they do conduct a rite of sanctification for it.'"

G. *R. Ashi said, "The upshot is that the language of the Mishnah refers to the calculation of the new month, and what is the sense of 'intercalation'? It is, 'calculation [of whether or not the month is to get an extra day]' And [the reason that intercalation is the word used is that], since the framer of the passage planned to make reference to the intercalation of the year, he framed the passage to refer, also to the intercalation of the month. What follows is that the calculation of the month requires court action, but the sanctification of the month does not. And in accord with whom is this position? It is in line with the view of R. Eliezer, as it has been taught on Tannaite authority:* R. Eliezer says, 'Whether the new moon appears at the expected time or not at the expected time, it is not to be subjected to a rite of sanctification.' "'For it has been said in Scripture, "you shall sanctify the fiftieth year" (Lev. 25:10), which bears the implication that while you sanctify years, you are not to sanctify months.'"

VIII.1 A. **Rabban Simeon b. Gamaliel says, "With three [do they begin to intercalate the year, with five more they debate the matter, and** they reach a final decision with seven judges. But if they reached a decision to intercalate the year with three judges, the year is intercalated]" [M. 1:2E-F]:

B.   *It has been taught on Tannaite authority:*

C.   How is a case in which, as Rabban Simeon b. Gamaliel has said, "With three do they begin to intercalate the year, with five more they debate the matter, and they reach a final decision with seven judges"?

D.   [If] one says to go into sessions, and two say not to go into session, the opinion of the individual is null as a minority.

E.   [If] two say to go into session, and one says not to go into session – they add two more to their number and debate the matter [with five.]

F.   [If] two say that it requires intercalation, and three say that it does not require intercalation – the opinion of the two is null because it is a minority.

G.   [If] three say it requires, and two say it does not require [intercalation], then they add two more to their number.

H.   [B. lacks:] Then they reach a final decision with seven."

I.   For a quorum may not be less than seven" [T. San. 2:1C-I]

J.   *As to the numbers of three, five, and seven, what do they stand for?*

K.   *There is a dispute about that matter between R. Isaac bar Nahmani and one who was with him, and who was that? It is R. Simeon b. Pazzi. Some say it was R. Simeon b. Pazzi and one who was with him, and who was that? It was R. Isaac bar Nahmani.*

L.   One said, "They stand for the number of words in the three verses of the priestly benediction [Num. 6:24-26]."

M.   The other said, "They stand for 'the three keepers of the threshold' (2 Kings 25:18), 'the five of those who saw the king's face' (2 Kings 25:19), and the seven 'who saw the king's face' (Est. 1:14)."

N.   *R. Joseph repeated the matter on Tannaite authority,* "The three, five, and seven, stand, respectively, for 'the three keepers of the threshold,' five 'who saw the king's face,' and seven 'who saw the king's face.'"

O.   *Said Abbayye to R. Joseph, "Why did you not explain this reason to us until now?"*

P.   *He said to them, "I did not know that you were wondering about the matter. Did you ever ask me something which I refused to tell you?"*

VIII.2   A.   *Our rabbis have taught on Tannaite authority:*

B.   The year is intercalated only **[11A]** by people who are specifically appointed for that task.

C.   There was the case concerning Rabban Gamaliel. He announced, "Call up seven [qualified persons] to the upper room [to intercalate the year]. When he got up there, he found eight. He said, "Who is the one who came up without authorization? Let him go down."

D.   Samuel the younger got up and said, "I am the one who came up without authorization. I did not come up to intercalate the year, but it was only because I needed to learn how the law is actually carried out."

E. He said to him, "Remain seated, my son, every year is worthy to be intercalated by you. But sages have ruled, 'The year is intercalated only by people who are specifically appointed for that task.'"

Stories about Samuel the Younger; The Chain of Tradition of Humility

F. *In point of fact, it was not Samuel the younger, but it was someone else, and [Samuel] acted as he did to spare embarrassment to the other.*

G. *There was the parallel incident, in which Rabbi was in session and giving an exposition.* He smelled garlic. He said, "Who ate garlic? Let him go out."

H. R. Hiyya got up and left.

I. All of the others got up and left too.

J. The next day R. Simeon, son of Rabbi, found R. Hiyya. He said to him, "Are you the one who annoyed father yesterday [by eating garlic]?"

K. He said to him, "Let not such a thing happen in Israel."

L. *Where did R. Hiyya learn such conduct? He learned it from the case of R. Meir.*

M. *For it has been taught on Tannaite authority:*

N. There was the case of a woman who came to the study-house of R. Meir and said to him, "Rabbi, one of you betrothed me through an act of sexual relations [and I do not know which one it is, but I wish a divorce]."

O. R. Meir stood up and wrote out for her a writ of divorce and gave it to her.

P. All of those present got up and wrote out a writ of divorce for her and gave it to her.

Q. *And where did R. Meir learn such behavior?*

R. *He learned it from Samuel the younger.*

S. *And where did Samuel the younger learn it?*

T. *He learned it from Shecaniah, son of Jehiel.*

U. For it is written, "And Shecaniah, son of Jehiel, one of the sons of Elam, answered and said to Ezra, We [including himself] have broken faith with our God and have married foreign women of the peoples of the land; yet now there is hope in Israel concerning this thing" (Ezra 10:2).

V. *And where did Shecaniah, Son of Jehiel, learn it? He learned it from Joshua, as it is written,* "The Lord said to Joshua, Get you up, wherefore, now, are you fallen upon your face? Israel has sinned" (Josh. 7:10-11).

W. He said before him, "Lord of the world, who has sinned?"

X. He said to him, "Am I an informer? Go, cast lots."

Y. *And if you wish, I shall propose that he learned it from Moses, for it is written,* "And the Lord said to Moses, How long will you refuse to keep my commandments and my laws" (Ex. 16:28)

[Schachter, p. 46, n. 1: Though no blame was attached to Moses, he is included to spare the offenders from humiliation].

VIII.3   A.   *Our rabbis have taught on Tannaite authority:*

B.   **[In T.'s version, which has minor differences from B.'s:] When the latter prophets died, that is, Haggai, Zechariah, and Malachi, then the Holy Spirit came to an end in Israel.**

C.   **But even so, they made them hear [Heavenly messages] through an echo.**

D.   **One time [Sages] gathered together in the upper room of the house of Guria in Jericho, and a heavenly echo came forth and said to them, "There is a man among you who is worthy to receive the Holy Spirit, but his generation is unworthy of such an honor."**

E.   **Sages all set their eyes upon Hillel the elder.**

F.   **And when he died, they said about him, "Woe for the pious man, woe for the humble man, the disciple of Ezra" [T. Sot. 13:3].**

G.   **Then another time they were in session in Yabneh and heard a heavenly echo saying, "There is among you a man who is worthy to receive the Holy Spirit, but the generation is unworthy of such an honor."**

H.   **Sages set their eyes upon Samuel the younger.**

I.   **At the time of his death what did they say? "Woe for the pious man, woe for the humble man, the disciple of Hillel!"**

J.   **Also he said at the time of his death, "Simeon and Ishmael are destined to be put to death, and the rest of the associates will die by the sword, and the remainder of the people will be up for spoils.**

K.   **"After this, great disasters will fall."**

L.   **Also concerning R. Judah b. Baba they ordained that they should say about him, "Woe for the humble man, woe for the pious man, disciple of Samuel the Small." But the times did not allow it [T. Sot. 13:4].**

M.   For people may not made a public lamentation for those put to death by the government.

VIII.4   A.   *Our rabbis have taught on Tannaite authority:*

B.   The year is intercalated only if the patriarch approves.

C.   **There is this precedent: Rabban Gamaliel went to ask for authorization from the government in Syria, and he did not come back right away, so they intercalated the year on the condition that Rabban Gamaliel would concur.**

D.   **And when he came back, he said, "I concur."**

E.   **So the year turned out to be deemed to have been intercalated [M. Ed. 7:7I-K].**

VIII.5   A.   *Our rabbis have taught on Tannaite authority:*

B.   They intercalate the year only when it needs it,

C.   because of the [condition of] the roads,

D.   because of the bridges,

E.   because of the passover ovens,

F. and because of the residents of the Exile, who have left home and not been able to reach [Jerusalem].

G. But they do not [intercalate the year] because of snow, cold, or the Exiles who have not year set out [for the pilgrimage].

H. [T. adds:] But all of those factors do they treat as additional reason [for intercalating] the year. And if they intercalated they year [on these counts], lo, it is deemed intercalated [T. San. 2:12]

VIII.6 A. *Our rabbis have taught on Tannaite authority:*

B. They do not intercalate the year because [the season of the] kids, lambs, or pigeons has not yet come.

C. But in the case of all of them, they regard it as a support [for intercalating] the year.

D. But if they declared the year to be intercalated [on the basis of their condition], lo, this is deemed intercalated [T. San. 2:4].

E. How so?

F. R. Yannai says in the name of Rabban Simeon b. Gamaliel who said [In Aramaic], "We inform you that the pigeons are tender and the spring lambs thin, and the spring season has not yet come,

G. "and it is proper in my view, so I have added thirty days to this year" [T. San. 2:5].

H. *An objection was raised [to the framing of G]:* How long a span of time constitutes the intercalation of the year? Thirty days. Rabban Simeon b. Gamaliel says, "A month." [How then can the foregoing assign to Simeon b. Gamaliel the language that it chooses?]

I. Said R. Pappa, "If people wish, they say, 'A month,' and if they wish, they say, 'Thirty days.'"

J. *Come and take note of the difference between* **[11B]** *the arrogant ancients and the humble moderns. For it has been taught on Tannaite authority:*

K. Rabban Gamaliel and sages, were in session on the steps to the Temple.

L. And Yohanan, the scribe, was before them, with three scrolls prepared before him.

M. [Gamaliel] said to [Yohanan], "Take one scroll and write:

N. *"[In Aramaic]: 'To our brethren, residents of Upper Galilee and residents of Lower Galilee, May your peace increase. We inform you that the time for the removal has come, to set apart the tithes from the olive vats.'*

O. *"Take the second letter and write: 'To our brethren, residents of the [upper south and residents of the lower] south, may your peace increase.' We inform you that the time for the removal has come, to set apart tithes from the sheaves of grain.'*

P. *"Take the third letter and write: 'To our brethren, residents of the Exile of Babylonia, and residents of the Exile of Media, and of all the other Exiles of Israel, may your peace increase forever.' We inform you that the pigeons are still tender, the lambs are thin, and the spring-tide has not yet come. So as it is proper in my view and in the view of my colleagues, we have added thirty days to this year" [T. San. 2:6].*

Q.   *Perhaps [the modesty shown in this letter comes] after Gamaliel had been deposed. [Since he had lost office and regained it, he would have included reference to his associates in his letter, while Simeon b. Gamaliel need not have had to do so.]*

VIII.7   A.   *Our rabbis have taught on Tannaite authority:*

B.   **On account of three signs do they intercalate the year, because of the [premature state of] the grain, because of the condition of the produce of the tree[s], and because of the lateness of the spring equinox.**

C.   **On account of any two of these they will intercalate the year, but on account of only one of them, they will not intercalate the year.**

D.   **[T. adds: But if they declared the year to be intercalated, lo, this is deemed intercalated.]**

E.   **If the premature state of the grain was one of them, they would rejoice.**

F.   **R. Simeon b. Gamaliel says, "Also on account of the lateness of the spring equinox" [T. San. 2:2].** [Schachter, p. 49, n. 5, explains that the four seasons follow the solar calendar. Should the season that begins at the summer solstice, June 21, extend until after the Sukkot festival or the season that begins at the winter solstice, December 21, extend until the sixteenth of Nisan, a month would be added to the year, so that the festivals might fall in their natural seasons, Passover in spring, Sukkot in fall. That is the point of reference of Simeon b. Gamaliel.]

G.   *The question was raised: Did he mean, "On account of the lateness of the equinox they rejoiced, or on account of the lateness of the equinox they intercalated the year"?*

H.   *The question stands.*

VIII.8   A.   *Our rabbis have taught on Tannaite authority:*

B.   **On account of [evidence of conditions in] three regions [viewed as distinct districts] do they intercalate the year: Judea, TransJordan, and Galilee.**

C.   **On account of evidence produced in two of them they intercalate the year, but on account of evidence deriving from only one of them they do not intercalate the year.**

D.   **[T. adds:] But if they declared the year to be intercalated, lo, this is deemed intercalated.]**

E.   **And if the land of Judea was one of the two regions, they would rejoice,**

F.   **because of the first fruits of grain which come only from Judah [for the altar]. [T. San. 2:3].**

VIII.9   A.   *Our rabbis have taught on Tannaite authority:*

B.   **They intercalate the year only in Judah,**

C.   **and if they intercalated in Galilee, lo, it is deemed to have been intercalated.**

D.   **Hananiah of Ono gave testimony [before Rabban Gamaliel], "[They intercalate they year <u>only</u> in Judah,] and if they intercalated the year in Galilee, it is not deemed to have been intercalated [T. San. 2:13].**

E.   *Said R. Judah, son of R. Simeon b. Pazzi, "What is the scriptural basis for the position of Hananiah of Ono? Scripture states, 'Unto his habitation* shall you seek and thither shall you come' (Deut. 12:5). The sense is, 'Every inquiry that you undertake shall concern only the habitation of the Omnipresent [which is Judea].'"

VIII.10 A. *Our rabbis have taught on Tannaite authority:*

B. [The court] may intercalate the year only by day, and if they have conducted the rite at night, it is not deemed to have been intercalated.

C. And the court may sanctify the new month only by day, and if they have conducted the rite of sanctification by night, it is not deemed to have been sanctified.

D. *Said R. Abba, "What verse of Scripture makes that point [C]?* 'Blow the horn at the new moon, at the covering of the moon our feast day' (Ps. 81:4). What is the festival on which the moon is covered? One must say it is the New Year [which comes at the first of the month of Tishri. All other festivals occur on some day other than the first of the lunar month.]

E. "And it is written, 'For this is a statute for Israel, a judgment of the God of Jacob' (Ps. 81:4).

F. "Just as judgment takes place by day, so the sanctification of the month must take place by day."

VIII.11 A. *Our rabbis have taught on Tannaite authority:*

B. They do not intercalate the year [12A] in a time of famine.

C. **R. [B. lacks] Meir says, "Lo, Scripture says, 'And there came a man from Baal Shalisha, and he brought the man of God bread of the firstfruits, twenty loaves of barley, and fresh ears of corn in his sack' (2 Kings 4:42).**

D. **"And is it not so that there is no place in which the produce ripens earlier in the entire Land of Israel than in Baal Shalisha? And even so, he offered as first fruits only that one species [which he had brought to the man of God].**

E. **"Should you claim it was wheat? Scripture refers to barley.**

F. **"Is it possible to say that he brought it before the sheaf of first grain had been offered [on the sixteenth of Nisan, so allowing the consumption of the produce of the new year for the first time]? Scripture says, 'And he said, Give it to the people, so that they may eat' (2 Kings 4:43). So it was afterward.**

G. **"So if follows that the year was suitable for intercalation.**

H. **"Now why did Elisha not intercalate it?**

I. **"Because it was a year of famine, and the whole people was running around to the threshing floors." [T. San. 2:9]**

VIII.12 A. *Our rabbis have taught on Tannaite authority:*

B. **They do not intercalate the year before the New Year,**

C. **and if they did intercalate it, it is not deemed intercalated.**

D. **But on account of necessity they do intercalate it forthwith after the New Year.**

E. **Even so: they intercalate only Adar [T. San. 2:7].**

F. *Is this so [that the year may be intercalated only after the New Year at Tishri]?*

G. And lo, people sent [from the Land of Israel] to Raba, "A pair [of disciples] has come from Raqqat [Tiberias], who had been taken by an eagle [Roman legion], and in their possession were things made at Luz, *such as what?* Such as purple [thus, show-fringes]. And through the merit supplied by divine mercy and through their own merit they came forth whole.

H.   "The offspring of the loins of Nahshon [the patriarch of the Land of Israel, descended from Nahshon, so Ex. 6:23] wanted to set up one nesib [bearing the dual sense of 'officer' and 'month'], but that Edomite [Roman] did not give them permission. But those who belong to the gatherings got together and established a nesib in the month in which Aaron the priest died [which is the month of Ab, prior to Elul and Tishri]." [Thus we see that the year may be intercalated through the addition of a month even prior to Tishri.].

I.   *To be sure, they made the calculation at that time, but they did not actually let the decision be known.*

J.   *How do we know that the word nesib means a month?*

K.   *It is in line with that which is written,* "Now Solomon had twelve officers [nesibim] throughout Israel, who supplied the king and his staff monthly through the year" [thus the word means both officer and month] (1 Kings 4:7).

L.   *But is it not written,* "And one officer that was in the land" (1 Kings 4:19)?

M.   R. Judah and R. Nahman:

N.   One said, "One was appointed over all the rest of them."

O.   The other said, "That one served for the intercalated month [in which he was to supply provisions]."

VIII.13 A. *Our rabbis have taught on Tannaite authority:*

        B. **They do not intercalate a year in advance.**

        C. **[T. adds:] And if they did intercalate a year in advance, it is not deemed intercalated.**

        D. **And they do not [at one time] intercalate one year after another [successively] for three years.**

        E. **[T. adds:] R. Simeon says, "They do intercalate one year after another."**

        F. **Said R. Simeon, "There is this precedent. R. Aqiba was imprisoned, and [at one time] he intercalated three years [sequentially], one after the other."**

        G. **They said to him, "From there do you derive proof? But it was because the court was in session and was reckoning the need for one year after another, in its proper time"** [T. San. 2:8].

VIII.14 A. *Our rabbis have taught on Tannaite authority:*

        B. They do not intercalate the year either in the case of the Seventh Year or in the case of the year after the Seventh Year.

        C. When are they accustomed to intercalate the year? In the year before the Seventh Year.

        D. Members of the house of Rabban Gamaliel would intercalate the year in the year after the Seventh Year.

        E. *And this involves the dispute of the following Tannaite authorities:*

        F. *It has been taught on Tannaite authority:*

G. People may not import vegetables from abroad. But our rabbis permitted it [to provide for the needs of the community during the Seventh Year, when people could not farm their land].

H. *What is the point at issue?*

I. R. Jeremiah said, "At issue is whether we take account of the possibility that dirt [which, beyond the boundaries of the Land of Israel, is cultically unclean with corpse-uncleanness] is attached to the vegetables. [Gamaliel did not scruple, so he had no reason to worry about famine, since imported produce would be available.]

VIII.15 A. *Our rabbis have taught on Tannaite authority:*

B. **They do not intercalate the year when there is uncleanness.**

C. **R. Judah says, "They do so."**

D. **Said R. Judah, "There is this precedent. Hezekiah the King of Judah intercalated the year when there was uncleanness, and he prayed for mercy for himself,**

E. **"for it is said, 'For a multitude of the people, even the men of Ephraim and Manasseh, Issachar and Zebulun, had not cleaned themselves, [12B], yet they ate the Passover otherwise than it is written. For Hezekiah prayed for them, saying, 'May the Lord in his goodness pardon every one' (II Chron. 30:18)" [T. San. 2:10]**

F. **R. Simeon says, "If it was a matter of intercalating such a year when there is uncleanness, it is indeed deemed to be intercalated. But why did he pray for mercy for himself?**

G. **"But [Hezekiah] intercalated Nisan in the month of Nisan itself, and they only intercalate Adar."**

H. **R. Simeon b. Judah says in the name of R. Simeon, "Also: because he made Israel celebrate a second Passover" [T. San. 2:11]**

I. A master has said, "R. Judah says, "They do [intercalate the year when there is uncleanness]."

J. *It follows that, in Judah's view, a condition of uncleanness affecting the community is suspended [but not simply treated as null. While some hold that, when there is a condition of uncleanness affecting the community as a whole, that condition is treated as null, Judah's position is that it is held in suspense. Therefore he intercalates the year, so as to allow for a rite of purification. In his view only if it were unavoidable would the uncleanness be treated as null.] But lo, it has been taught on Tannaite authority:*

K. "Whether or not the front-plate is actually on the high priest's forehead, it propitiates," the words of R. Simeon.

L. R. Judah says, "While it is till on his forehead, it propitiates. If it is no longer on his forehead, it does not propitiate."

M. Said R. Simeon to [Judah], "The condition of the high priest on the Day of Atonement will prove the matter. For on that day the front-plate is not on his forehead, and yet it serves to propitiate [and render acceptable sacrifices offered in a state of uncleanness, in line with Ex. 28:36-38]."

N. Said R. Judah to [Simeon], "Omit reference to the Day of Atonement, on which uncleanness affecting the community is permitted [and abrogated. So the case at hand proves nothing.]" [Thus uncleanness affecting the community is treated as null, vs. J.']

O. *But in accord with your view [that we intercalate the year so as to avoid uncleanness affecting the community as a whole on the occasion of the Passover-offering], the passage at hand contains an inner contradiction.*

P. Specifically, R. Judah says, "They intercalate the year when there is uncleanness. And there is this precedent: Hezekiah the king of Judah intercalated the year when there was uncleanness, and he prayed for mercy for himself." [Why pray for mercy for himself, it what he did was correct?]

Q. *The passage is improperly formulated, and this is how it should be given:*

R. "People may not intercalate the year on account of uncleanness, but if they have done so, it is deemed intercalated. R. Judah says, 'It is not intercalated. And R. Judah said...'" [Now the point of praying for mercy is clear.]

S. *If so, the following passage poses a problem, namely,* R. Simeon says, "If it was a matter of intercalating such a year when there is uncleanness, it is deemed to be intercalated." *In line with the revised formulation of the passage, what he says is the same thing as what the first authority [Judah] has said!*

T. *Said Raba, "At issue is the rule pertaining not after the fact but to begin with. [Simeon says even to begin with one may intercalate on account of uncleanness. Judah accepts after the fact what has already been done.]"*

U. *So too it has been taught on Tannaite authority:* People, to begin with, do not intercalate the year on account of uncleanness. R. Simeon says, "They do intercalate the year."

V. In any event, why did [Hezekiah] pray for mercy on his account?

W. It is because: They only intercalate the month of Adar, but he intercalated the month of Nisan in the month of Nisan itself.

X.   A master has said, "For they only intercalate the month of Adar, but he intercalated the month of Nisan in the month of Nisan."

Y. *But did Hezekiah not concur that the verse,* "This month shall be to you the beginning of months" (Ex. 12:2) *speaks of Nisan, meaning, there is only one Nisan and not a second one?* [Schachter, p. 55, n. 6: Once Nisan has been proclaimed it cannot be re-proclaimed Adar, making the ensuing month Nisan.]

Z. *He erred in the matter enunciated by Samuel.*

AA. For Samuel said, "People may not intercalate the year [adding an extra month] on the thirtieth day of Adar, since it is appropriate to declare that day to be the first of Nisan [when Adar should have only twenty-nine days]."

BB.	[Hezekiah] took the view that we do not invoke the argument, "Since it is appropriate..." [with the result that on the thirtieth day of Nisan he intercalated a month into the year.] [He prayed because he later on realized his mistake].
CC.	[Supply:] *So too it has been taught on Tannaite authority:*
DD.	**People on the thirtieth day of Adar may not intercalate a month into the year since it is appropriate to declare that day as the first of Nisan.**
EE.	**R. Simeon b. Judah says in the name of R. Simeon, "Also: because he made Israel celebrate a second Passover" [T. San. 2:11D].**
FF.	*How so? [Why did he think it was correct and then change his mind?]*
GG.	Said R. Ashi, "It was a case in which the Israelites were half unclean and half clean, and women [who were not unclean] completed the number of those who were clean and formed the majority of them.
HH.	*"To begin with he theorized that women were subject to the obligation to offer a Passover-offering on the first Passover. Only a minority of the women were unclean, so a minority of the women were then to be put off to make the offering on the second Passover [held a month later for those unclean on the occasion of the first.].*
II.	*"Then he reached the conclusion that women offer a Passover-offering on the first Passover [not as an obligation but] only as an optional matter, so that [among those who were obligated to offer a Passover-offering on the first Passover] a majority [now, entirely males] were unclean. But if a majority of those obligated to make the offering are unclean, they are not told to postpone and bring their offering on the second Passover, [but they offer it on the first one]."*
JJ.	*Returning to the body of the text just now discussed:* Samuel said, "People may not intercalate the year [adding an extra month] on the thirtieth day of Adar, since it is appropriate to declare that day as the first of Nisan [when Adar should have only twenty-nine days]."
KK.	*If people have actually intercalated the year on that day, what is the rule?*
LL.	Said Ulla, "On that day people do not conduct a rite of sanctification of the new month."
MM.	If they did conduct a rite of sanctification, what is the law?

NN.   Said Raba, "The intercalation is nullified."

OO.   R. Nahman said, "The month is both intercalated and sanctified."

PP.   *Said Raba to R. Nahman, "Since from Purim to Passover are thirty days, and since from the advent of Purim we give public expositions of the laws of Passover, for it has been taught on Tannaite authority,* **People raise questions about the laws of Passover thirty days prior to Passover, and Rabban Simeon b. Gamaliel says, 'For two weeks' [T. Meg. 3]** –

QQ.   *"If on the thirtieth day when the new month arrives, they postpone the new month [of Nisan], people will well end up treating with disregard the prohibition of leaven [on Passover] [having in error celebrated the Passover a month earlier]!"*

RR.   *He said to him, "People will know that the intercalation of the year depends upon calculations, and will say that it was the proper calculation that had not been reached by the rabbis until this point. [On that account the consideration raised by Raba is of no weight.]"*

VIII.16   A.   Said R. Judah, said Samuel, "'People intercalate the year only if the summer season is short of completion by the larger part of the month [of Tishri so that, in the year that is a candidate for intercalation, if we do not add a month, then the bulk of Tishri will pass before the autumnal equinox has been reached. In simple terms, it means that the larger part of Tishri, must fall prior to September 21.] 'What would constitute the larger part of the month of Tishri? 'Sixteen days," the words of R. Judah, [so the new month of Tishri must fall by September 5]. **[13A]** R. Yosé says, 'Twenty-one days' [so the new month of Tishri must fall by September 13.]

             B.   "Now the two of them interpret the same verse: 'And the month of the ingathering at the season of the year' (Ex. 34:22). [The sense is that the month of ingathering must fall within the autumnal season, beginning in Tishri]. *One authority [Judah] takes the view that the entirety of the feast of ingathering* [that is, Tabernacles, from 15 to 21 Tishri] [Schachter, p. 58, n. 1: beginning with the day when the work of ingathering is permitted, the sixteenth day of the month of Tishri, the day after the Festival of Tabernacles] *must be included in the autumnal season [hence if the summer season is short of completion by sixteen days, the new autumnal season begins on the seventh and will thus not include all the days when the work or ingathering is permitted (Schachter)]. The other authority takes the view that only part of the festival of ingathering [Sukkot] must be encompassed* [Schachter, p. 58, n. 4: Hence its possible delay until the twenty-first of the month, but not later, because the twenty-second of Tishri is a full festival day again, on which no gathering of crops is permitted.]"

             C.   [We now raise a distinct, but related issue, on whether we assign the day on which the new season begins – that is, September 21 – to the summer season, now ending, or to the fall season, now beginning. What we wish to know is the position of the authorities at hand on that question.] *What is the theory [of the parties at hand on the issue of whether the day on which the season starts is held to belong to the season now ending or to the one now beginning]?*

D. *If they take the view that the day on which the season shifts belongs to the completion [of the season that is ending], then even if it were not so* [Schachter: short of completion as sixteen days for Judah or twenty-one days for Yosé, but fifteen or twenty days, respectively,] it will accord neither with him who requires that the entire Festival [of Tabernacles] falls within the autumnal season [thus beginning no later than sixteen days after September 21] *nor with him who requires that only part of the Festival [of Tabernacles] falls within the autumnal season thus beginning no later than twenty-one days after September 21].* [Schachter, p. 58, n. 8: For even if the day marking the change in season coincides with the sixteenth or twenty-first day after September 21 the new season will commence only on the following day.]

E. *It must follow that both parties assume that day that marks the change in the season is assigned to the incoming season and so is joined to the beginning of the new season.*

F. *An objection was raised:* "The day marking the change in the season marks the end of the old season," the words of R. Judah. R. Yosé says, "It marks the beginning of the new season."

G. *And furthermore, it has been taught on Tannaite authority:* **They intercalate the year only if the spring equinox is distant by the better part of a month. And how much is the better part of a month? Sixteen days.**

H. **R. Judah says, "Two thirds of a month, twenty days"** [so no part of Tabernacles will come into the fall]. [Schachter, p. 58, n. 11: **This refutes Samuel on both points (a) R. Judah holds here that part of the Feast is sufficient; and (b) in his view the Tequfah-day commences the new season, and does not end the last.**]

I. **R. Yosé says, "They make a reckoning of the year. If before Passover there still are lacking sixteen days of the equinox, they intercalate another month.** (Schachter, p. 59, n. 2: **For if not, the summer season would not end until the 21st of Tishri, the new one beginning on the 22nd. The two seasons, the spring and summer, consist of hundred and eighty-two days, and the five lunar months between Nisan and Tishri consist of hundred and forty seven days which, when added to the fourteen days of Nisan and the twenty-one days of Tishri make a total of hundred and eighty-two days. The Tishri or Fall season beginning on the 22nd of the month will thus not include any part of the Festival of Ingathering.] [If] before the Festival [there are lacking] sixteen days before the autumnal equinox, they do not intercalate it."**

J. **R. Simeon says, "Even if it was lacking sixteen days before the Festival [of Sukkot], they do intercalate it"** [T. San. 2:7].

K. Others say, "[Schachter: The year is intercalated even if the season is short of completion] by less than half of the month. And how much is that? Fourteen days."

L. *There is indeed a problem [in contradictory statements of Judah, as explained above].*

M. A master has said: "R. Judah says, 'Two thirds of a month, twenty days.'

N. **"R. Yosé says, 'They make a reckoning of the year. If before Passover there still are lacking sixteen days of the equinox, they intercalate another month [T. San. 2:70-R]."**

O. *This is the same view as R. Judah's! [Both authorities include only part of the Festival of Tabernacles in the autumnal season, but not the whole of it.]*

P. *At issue between them is the status of the day on which the seasons change.* [Schachter, p. 59, n. 9: According to R. Judah, that day completes the previous *Tequfah*, consequently, if twenty days have passed and the sun has reached its new cycle on the 21st, the new season begins on the 22nd, in which case not even part of the Feast of Ingathering is included; whilst according to R. Yosé's calculation, even if the solstice occurs on the 21st day, that day is added to the new cycle.]

Q. A master has said: **R. Yosé says, ['They make a reckoning of the year. If before Passover there still are lacking sixteen days of the equinox, they intercalate another month.] If there are lacking sixteen days before the autumnal equinox, they do not intercalate the year'** [T. San. 2:7R]."

R. *In R. Yosé's view, therefore, it is when there are sixteen days short of the day of the turning of the season do we not intercalate, but if we are seventeen or eighteen days short, we do intercalate.*

S. *But has he not said, "If before Passover there still are lacking sixteen days of the equinox, they do intercalate" and so, if it is less, they do not!*

T. *No, in neither case do people intercalate. But since in the opening clause he wished to frame matters as "sixteen days before Passover," in the latter segment the passage is repeated as, "Sixteen days before the Festival" [but we do not limit the matter to sixteen, and even if the shortage is somewhat more than that, the year still does not get a new month].*

U. **R. Simeon says, "Even if it was lacking sixteen days before the Festival of Sukkot, they do intercalate it"** [T. San. 2:7E].

V. *But is this not the view of the authority cited at the outset?*

W. [13B] *At issue is whether* we assign the day on which the seasons turn to the concluding season, or to the one now beginning. *But we do not know which party holds which view.*

X. Others say, "The year is intercalated even if the season is short of completion by less than half of the month. And how much is that? Fourteen days."

Y. *What is their view [on the matter of assigning the day of the turning of the season to the closing or the opening season]? If they maintain that the day on which the seasons change is assigned to the season now concluding, and that we insist that the entirety of the Feast of Tabernacles fall within the new [autumnal] season, then, in point of fact, it is so. [The fall season will begin on the fifteenth of Tishri, while the Festival of Tabernacles begins on the sixteenth.]*

Z. *Said R. Samuel bar R. Isaac, "The 'others' speak in point of fact of the advent of the vernal season. For it is written, 'Observe the month of Abib [that is, spring]' (Deut. 16:1). The meaning is, 'Make sure that the beginning of the vernal season takes place on a day in Nisan [Schachter: when the moon is still in the process of renewal]." [Schachter pp. 60-61, n. 10: That accounts for the limit of fourteen days, after which it is on the wane.]"*

AA. *But why not intercalate a day in Adar* [Schachter, p. 61, n. 1: Which would bring in the new season on the thirteenth day, when the moon is still waxing, rather than cause the derangement of a whole month; and though the first day of Passover must not fall on Monday, Wednesday or Friday, and the addition of a day might cause that, it would not matter, because the limitation of the days on which Passover may commence is due to the desire to avoid New Year falling on Sunday, Wednesday or Friday, and that could be avoided by adding a day to one of the normally defective months between Nisan and Tishri.]

BB. *Said R. Aha b. R. Jacob, "The Tannaite authority counts from higher to lower numbers and frames matters as follows:* One may intercalate only in the lesser part of the month [down to the fourteenth day of the month]. [Schachter, p. 61, n. 3: But if there is actually a shortage of fourteen days, only the month of Adar is intercalated.] And how much is that? It is fourteen days."

CC. *Rabina said, "In point of fact 'others' do refer to Tishri [and not to Nisan, as Samuel bar Isaac has claimed]. And 'others' take the view that we require the entirety of the Festival of Tabernacles to fall within the autumnal season, on the one side, and also that the first day of the Festival likewise.* [Schachter, p. 61, n. 5: And being of the view that the seasonal day completes the season, if there is a shortage of fourteen days, in which case the new autumnal season will begin on the fifteenth day, the first day of the Feast will not be included in it, so that intercalation is justified.]"

DD.   But it is written, "The Feast of Ingathering" (at the season of the year) [Ex. 34:22, meaning that the Feast must fall within the autumnal season, after September 21]! [Schachter: meaning the day on which ingathering is permitted.]

EE.   [They understand the sense as], "The Feast which occurs in the season of ingathering."

IX.1   A.   **"The laying of hands [on a community sacrifice by elders and the breaking of the heifer's neck are done by three judges," the words of R. Simeon. R. Judah says, "By five," [M. 1:3A-B]:**

B.   *Our rabbis have taught on Tannaite authority:*

C.   [With reference to Lev. 4:15: "And the elders of the congregation shall lay their hands upon the head of the bull before the Lord...":] Since it says, "And the elders... shall lay hands," is it possible to suppose that elders from any source whatsoever [will suffice]?

D.   Scripture says, "of the congregation."

E.   Since it says, "Of the congregation," is it possible to suppose that unimportant members of the congregation [will suffice]?

F.   Scripture says, "The congregation," meaning, "those who are distinguished in the congregation."

G.   And how many are they to be?

H.   "'...shall lay hands...' [in the plural] indicates that two are required, and 'elders of...' indicates that two are required, and since there cannot be an even number in a court, another is to be added to the lot, yielding five in all," the words of R. Judah.

I.   R. Simeon says, "'Elders of...' indicates that two are to do it, and since there cannot be an even number in a court, another is to be added, yielding three in all."

J.   *But so far as R. Simeon is concerned, is it not written, "...shall lay hands..."?*

K.   *That is required to make its own point [indicating what the elders in fact are to do].*

L.   *And R. Judah?*

M.   *No statement of the sort is required, for if it is the case that "...shall lay hands..." does not serve the purpose of providing an occasion for deriving an exegetical lesson, it would have been sufficient for the text to state, "As to the elders of the congregation, their hands shall be on the head of the bull."*

N.   *And R. Simeon?*

O.   *If that is how the matter were written, I might have reached the conclusion that the meaning of "on" was "nearby" [and not right on the head, as the verse's present formulation makes explicit].*

P.   *And R. Judah?*

Q.   *That lesson is to be derived from the use of the word "head" in the present case and the similar usage in reference to the burnt-offering [Lev. 1:4 being explicit that one lays his hand on the head of the burnt-offering].*

R.   *And R. Simeon?*

S.	*He derives no lesson from the appearance of the word "head" both here and in reference to the burnt-offering.*
IX.2	A. *It is taught on Tannaite authority:*
	B. **Laying on of hands and laying on of hands for elders are done with three [judges] [T. San. 1:1E].**
	C. *What is the meaning of "laying on of hands," and what is the meaning of "laying on of hands for elders"?*
	D. *Said R. Yohanan, "It means the laying on of hands for the designation of elders [as authorized judges]."*
	E. *Said Abbayye to R. Joseph, "Whence in Scripture do we derive proof that the laying on of hands for the designation of elders is done by a court of three judges?*
	F. *"Should one propose that the proof derives from the following text, 'And he laid his hand upon him' (Num. 27:23), then it should be sufficient for a single sage to lay hands. And should you claim that Moses [in the cited verse] stood in the stead of the seventy-one, then seventy-one should be required for the laying on of hands."*
	G. *It is an unsolved problem.*
	H. *Said R. Aha, son of Raba, to R. Ashi, "Is it necessary to lay hands in a physical sense?"*
	I. *He said to him, "One 'lays hands' by calling the candidate master [rabbi] and assigning him authorization to judge cases involving penalties."*
IX.3	A. *[Since the Mishnah-rule states that the laying on of hands is done by three, we now ask:] And can not a single individual lay hands?*
	B. And lo, said R. Judah said Rab, "Now may that man's memory be blessed, and his name is R. Judah b. Baba. For if it were not for him, the laws of penalties would be forgotten in Israel."
	C. "Be forgotten"?! *But people would have learned them afresh! Rather:* **[14A]** "The laws of penalties would have been nullified.
	D. "For once the evil government made a decree against Israel, that whoever laid hands would be killed, whoever had hands laid on would be killed, a town in which there was a rite of laying on hands would be wiped out, and the boundaries within which such a rite took place would be uprooted.
	E. "What did R. Judah b. Baba do? He went and took up a position between two high hills, between two large towns, and between the Sabbath limits of two towns [so that the penalty would not apply to either one of them, thus sparing them the effects of the decree], between Usha and Shefaram. There he laid hands on five elders. And these are they: R. Meir, R. Judah, R. Simeon, R. Yosé, and R. Eleazar b. Shammua."
	F. R. Avia adds to the list the name of R. Nehemiah.
	G. [Judah in Rab's name continues,] "When the enemies found out about them, he said to them, 'My sons, run.'
	H. "They said to him, 'Master, what will happen to you?'
	I. "He said to them, 'Lo, I am set firm before them like a stone that no one can turn over.'
	J. "People say that [the enemy] did not move from there until [Schachter:] they had driven three hundred iron spear-heads into his body, making it like a sieve."

K. *[The story does not prove that a single individual may lay on hands because] there were others with him, but the reason that they were not taken into account is on account of the honor owing to [the Martyred] R. Judah b. Baba.*

L. *And was R. Meir subject to the laying on of hands of R. Judah b. Baba? And lo, said Rabbah bar bar Hana said R. Yohanan, "Whoever says that R. Meir was not subject to laying on of hands by R. Aqiba merely errs."*

M. R. Aqiba laid hands on him but [others] did not accept [the validity of the act], while R. Judah b. Baba laid hands on him and [others] did accept the validity of the act.

IX.4   A. Said R. Joshua b. Levi, "The rite of laying on of hands does not apply outside of the Land."

B. *What is the meaning of, "The rite of laying on of hands does not apply..."? If one should propose that judges outside of the Land in no way judge cases involving penalties, lo, we have learned in the Mishnah:* **The sanhedrin applies both in the Land and outside of the Land [M. Mak. 1:10E].**

D.   *Rather, it is that, outside of the Land, there is no rite of laying on of hands.*

E.   *It is self-evident that if those who lay hands are outside of the Land, and those on whom hands are to be laid are inside the Land, lo, we have said that one does not [lay hands]. But if those who lay hands are inside the Land and those on whom hands are to be laid are outside of the Land, what is the law?*

F.   *Come and take note: R. Yohanan was distressed concerning R. Shemen bar Abba, because he was not with them so as to have hands laid on [in the Land].*

G.   *As to R. Simeon b. Zerud, and another was with him, namely, R. Jonathan b. Akmai, and some say, it was R. Jonathan b. Akmai, and one who was with him, namely, R. Simeon b. Zerud, one who was with him received the laying on of hands, and one who was not with him did not receive laying on of hands. [A disciple outside of the Land cannot receive the laying on of hands.]*

IX.5   A. *R. Hanina and R. Hoshaia did R. Yohanan aim to subject to the laying on of hands, but the opportunity did not arise. This bothered him very much. They said to him, "Let the master not be troubled about this.*

B. *"[Why not? Because] we come from the house of Eli, concerning which* R. Samuel bar Nahman said R. Jonathan said, 'How do we know that members of the house of Eli are not subject to the laying on of hands? As it is said, "And there shall be no elder in your house forever" (1 Sam. 2:32). Now what is the meaning of the word "elder"? If one should propose it literally means an old man, lo, it is said, "And all the increase of your house shall die as young men" (1 Sam. 2:32). Therefore it must speak of the laying on of hands.'"

IX.6   A. *R. Zera would hide himself so as not to have hands laid on. For R. Eleazar said, "Always be accepting [the authority of others] and so endure."*

B. *When he heard the following statement of* R. Eleazar, *"A man does not rise to a position of greatness unless all of his sins are forgiven," he made himself available.*

C. *When they laid hands on R. Zera, they sang this to him: "Not with paint, nor with rouge, nor with dyed hair, but full of charm."*

IX.7 A. *When they laid hands on R. Ammi and R. Assi, they sang this to them: "Only people of this sort, only people of this sort. Do not lay hands to rule over us [Schachter:] half-wits and third-wits."*

IX.8 A. *When R. Abbahu came from the Torah-session to the emperor's house, the ladies of the emperor's house came forth and sang in his honor, "Master of his people, spokesman of his nation, torch of light.*

B. *"Blessed be your coming in peace."*

X.1 A. **The breaking of the heifer's neck [as prescribed at Deut. 21:1-9] is done by a court of three [judges, "the words of R. Simeon. R. Judah says, "By five"] [M. 1:3A-B].**

B. Our rabbis have taught on Tannaite authority:

C. "'Then your elders and your judges shall come forth' (Deut. 21:1-2):

C. "'Your elders' indicate that two are required.

D. "'Your judges' indicates that another two are required.

E. "A court cannot be of an even number, so they add on to their number yet another, lo, there are five," the words of R. Judah.

F. R. Simeon says, "'Your elders' indicates that they are two, and a court cannot be an even number, so they add to them yet another, lo, three in all."

G. *But R. Simeon also has to deal with the fact that "Your judges" also has been written.*

H. *That he requires to prove a different point entirely, namely, to indicate that they must be the select among the judges.*

I. *And R. Judah derives that fact from the use of the word "your elders."*

J. *And R. Simeon? [He argues as follows:] "If the All-Merciful had written, 'Elders,' I might have reached the conclusion that even ordinary elders of the market place [would suffice]. So the All-Merciful wrote, 'Your elders.' And if the All-Merciful had written merely, 'Your elders,' I might have reached the conclusion that even members of a lesser sanhedrin would suffice. Accordingly, the All-Merciful wrote, 'Your judges,' to indicate that they are to be among the select of your judges."*

K. *And R. Judah derives the lesson from the use of "elders," in the verse,* "The elders of the congregation" (Lev. 4:15) [as well as in the present context]. Just as, at that passage, the reference is to select among the congregation, so here too it must be the select among the congregation.

L. *But if in such a way one can derive the besought lesson for the entire rule from the cited passage, then what need is there to say, "Your* elders and your judges"? [That is, if Judah can derive from Lev. 4:15 the rule that five elders are necessary, why introduce the exegesis of "and your judges" for proof that five judges are necessary? He has made that point quite admirably on the basis of a different verse.]

M.   *But the use of the word "and" in the word "and your judges" is what serves to indicate the number [of judges that are required].*

N.   *And R. Simeon? In his view the use of the word "and" bears no supererogatory implications whatsoever.*

O.   *But then how do you deal with the possibility of the following: "And they shall come forth" (Deut. 21:2) means that two must do so, "and they shall measure" (ibid.) means that two must do so In the view of R. Judah, then, there should be nine, and in the view of R. Simeon, lo, there are seven. [That is, the verbs appearing in the same verse appear to add another four judges to the requisite number. The problem confronts both authorities.]*

P.   *[No, in the view of neither party should that conclusion be drawn. For] the cited language is required for the following purpose. As it has been taught on Tannaite authority: "And they shall go forth" (Deut. 21:2) means,* they *and not their agents.*

Q.   *"And they shall measure" indicates that even if the corpse is found* **[14B]** *within the limits of a particular town [in which case there is no reason to measure between one town and another], they still should take the measurement.*

R.   *For it is a religious duty to take up the task of measuring.*

X.2 A.   *[The formulation of] the Mishnah-paragraph at hand [when it specifies that we deal with members of the sanhedrin] does not accord with the view of R. Eliezer b. Jacob.*

B.   *For it has been taught on Tannaite authority:* R. Eliezer b. Jacob says, "'Your elders' refers to the sanhedrin.

C.   "'Your judges' refers to the king and the high priest."

D.   "'The king,' as it is written, 'Your king by judgment establishes the land' (Prov. 29:4).

E.   "'And the high priest,' as it is written, 'And you shall come to the Levitical priests and to the judge who will be...' (Deut. 17:9)." [Cohen, *Sotah*, p. 227, n. 9: "And" is understood as "even," therefore the priests acted as judges, and since one in particular is specified in "the judge" it must be the high priest.]

F.   *The following question was raised: Is it solely with reference to the king and high priest that R. Eliezer b. Jacob differs, but, so far as the sanhedrin is concerned, he concurs with either R. Judah or R. Simeon? Or perhaps he differs also with respect to the sanhedrin [insisting that] all those who are present must be members of the sanhedrin?*

G.   *Said R. Joseph, "Come and take note [of the following relevant case]."* [If] the whole of the great sanhedrin was found in Bethpage by a rebellious elder and he rebelled against them [in their entirety], is it possible to suppose that his rebellion is taken into account? [That is, if a local judge rejected the decision of the great sanhedrin and went and ruled contrary to their decision, what is the rule?] Scripture states, "And you will arise and go up to the place..." (Dec. 17:8) [at which the great sanhedrin is located]. This teaches that it is the location which indicates [where the rebellion is to be punished. If the ruling of the great sanhedrin did not come from Jerusalem, rebellion against that ruling is null. Now what has happened is that a rebellious elder has come across the great sanhedrin. He can be declared rebellious only by the court of seventy-one. He asked the court at hand – which just happens to be the same membership as the high court in Jerusalem – and then he rejected their ruling. What did he do? He went home and instructed the people to act as he had originally done, without taking account of the ruling of the high court. But if the court did not issue its decision <u>in Jerusalem</u>, the matter is null, as shown in the proof-text.] *Now exactly how many [members of the great sanhedrin] had gone forth from Jerusalem? If we say that only part of the court had gone forth, [in such a case can there be a ruling that the man is a rebellious elder? Surely not, for] some of those who had remained behind may be of the same view as the accused. [In the case he can claim minority support. Accordingly, we can invoke the possibility of the man's being condemned as a rebellious elder] only if, as is self-evident, the whole of the court [great sanhedrin] had gone forth. [So that is the supposition at hand.] Now for what purpose will the court have gone forth? If it is for a merely optional matter [and not an obligatory one] can the entire court leave its chambers in such a way? And is it not written,* "Your navel is like a round goblet, wherein no mingled wine is wanting" (Song 7:3). [This is regarded as referring to the sanhedrin and is understood as requiring that at least a third of the sanhedrin must be present at any session.] This indicates, then, that if one of the members has to go forth [e.g., to the toilet], if there are remaining twenty-three members, equivalent to an ordinary, small sanhedrin, he may do so. But if not, he may not do so. *Accordingly, it is self-evident that the entire court could have gone forth only to carry out a religious obligation. And for what purpose? Is it not for the purpose of taking the measurements in connection with a heifer whose neck was to be broken because of the discovery of a neglected corpse? And this would then represent the theory of R. Eliezer b. Jacob [who thus would require the presence of the entire sanhedrin]. [The question raised above thus has been answered.]*

H. Said Abbayye to [Joseph, who has supplied the proof], "Perhaps it was an exodus from the city in order to add to the territorial limits of the city and the courtyards. *For we have learned in the Mishnah:* **Only a court of seventy-one may add ground to the city and to the courtyards [M. Shebu. 2:2]."**

I. *But it has been taught on Tannaite authority in accord with the view of R. Joseph:* If [a rebellious elder] found the court at Bethpage and rebelled against them, for instance, if the court had gone forth to measure the distance in connection with the breaking of the neck of a heifer or in order to add to the territory of the city and the courtyards, is it possible that his act of rebellion should take effect? Scripture says, "And you will arise and you will go up to the place" (Deut. 17:8), which teaches that it is the location that causes [the law at hand to take effect. If the act of rebellion does not involve a decision reached by the high court in its proper meeting place, which then is rejected by the elder at hand, the act of rebellion is null.]

XI.1   A.   **The evaluation of fruit of fourth-year plantings [which is to be redeemed (Lev. 19:23-250] and of second tithe [Deut. 14:22-26], the value of which is not known, is done before three judged [M. 1:3D]:**

      B.   *Our rabbis have taught on Tannaite authority:*

      C.   **What is the definition of second tithe, the value of which is not known? It is, for example, wine which has formed a film, produce which has begun to rot, or coins which are rusty [M. M.S. 4:26].**

      D.   *Our rabbis have taught on Tannaite authority:*

      E.   **Produce in the status of second tithe, the value of which is not known is redeemed according to the valuation of three bidders and not according to the valuation of three who are not bidders even if one of the bidders is a non-Israelite, even if one of the bidders is the owner of the produce [T. M.S. 3:5A-D].**

      F.   *R. Jeremiah raised the question, "What is the law applying to three bidders who are in partnership?"*

      G.   *Come and take note:* A man and his two wives may bid for the redemption of produce in the status of second tithe, the value of which is not known. [So partners may do so.]

      H.   *But perhaps it involved a case such a R. Pappa and [his wife, who was] daughter of Abba of Sura, [who was an independent business woman].*

XII.1   A.   **Assessment of the value for purposes of redemption of things which have been consecrated is done before three judges [M. 1:3E]:**

      B.   *Our version of the Mishnah-law does not accord with the version of the following Tannaite authority. For it has been taught on Tannaite authority:* R. Eliezer b. Jacob says, "Even the assessment for purposes of redemption of a hook that belongs to the sanctuary must be a court of ten men."

      C.   *Said R. Pappa to Abbayye, "Now there is no problem in explaining the position of R. Eliezer b. Jacob, for he has ruled in accord with the view of Samuel. For Samuel said, 'The word "priest" occurs ten times in the chapter [on redeeming various things in that have been sanctified to the Temple, Lev. 27:8, 11-13, 14, 18, 23. Hence ten must be on the court that assesses the value of the property and determines the monetary equivalent to be paid to the Temple.]' But how do the rabbis find evidence that three will suffice for that task? And should you say that it is because the word 'priest' appears three times in relationship to [one of the components of the cited chapter], the word 'priest' occurs four times with respect to the redemption of real estate, on which account, by that reasoning, it should be necessary to have only four on the court to evaluate real estate. And if you should claim that that is indeed the case, have we not learned in the Mishnah:* **Evaluation of property pledged as security for vows for valuation in the case of real estate is done by nine and a priest [M. 1:3H].** *So what is there to say? That with the item at hand the number of ten allusions to the priest is complete? Then in the case of the other consecrated objects [which have to be assessed,] if* *there are six references to priests,* then six judges should be on the court for the purpose of assessing those objects!"

F. *The question stands over.*

XIII.1 A. **Property pledged as security for vows of valuation, in the case of movables, is evaluated by three judges [M. 1:3F]:**

B. *What is the meaning of evaluating property pledged as security for vows in the case of movables?*

C. Said R. Giddal said Rab, "We deal with a case in which someone says, 'The valuation of this object is incumbent on me.'"

D. For said R. Giddal said Rab, "**[15A]** He who says, 'The valuation of this utensil [which is not subject to valuation at all] is incumbent on me' must pay the value of the utensil."

E. *What is the reason?* A person knows that a Valuation does not pertain to a utensil. The donor therefore deliberately made the declaration [using the language of Valuations but] intending to pay the actual market worth of the object.

F. *Then the language at hand, ...vows of valuation, in the case of movables..., should rather be,* "the assessment of the Valuation-vow covering movables."

G. *Then repeat the version as,* The assessment of the Valuation-vow covering movables.

H. R. Hisda said Abimi [said], "It speaks of one who has paid over movables in payment of a vow of Valuation."

I. *If so, ... valuation in the case of movables... should be* "movables in the status of Valuation."

J. *Then repeat the version, as, ... movables in the status of Valuation.*

K. R. Abbahu said, "We deal with a case of one who has said, 'My valuation is incumbent on me.' When the priest comes to collect, then movables are assessed by a court of three judges and real estate by one of ten judges."

L. *Said R. Aha of Difti to Rabina, "Now to be sure, to remove property from the category of what has been sanctified, we require a court of three judges. But why do we need a court of three judges to bring into the possession of the sanctuary this same property?"*

M. *He said to him, "It is a matter of logic. What difference is there between bringing property into the possession of the sanctuary and taking it out of the possession of the sanctuary? What is the reason for having such a court to withdraw property [by redeeming it for cash] from the possession of the sanctuary? It is because one might make an error. The same consideration applies to bringing property into the domain of the Temple.!"*

XIV.1 A. **R. Judah says, "[One of them must be a priest" [M. 1:3G]:**

B. *Said R. Pappa to Abbayye, "Now there is no problem to the position of R. Judah in Scripture's referring to a priest in this connection. But as to rabbis [who do not require a priest on the board of assessors], why should Scripture have referred to a priest?"*

C. *It is a question.*

XV.1 A. **And evaluation of property pledged as security for vows for valuation in the case of real estate is done by nine ordinary men and a priest [M. 1:3H]:**

B. *Whence in Scripture do we derive this rule?*

C.   Said Samuel, "The chapter at hand [Lev. 27] makes reference to priest ten times. One serves for supplying the law [that a priest must be included]. The others serve to exclude non-priests, in sequence. But since one exclusion in sequence with another serves not to limit but to encompass, the result is that a valuation may be made by nine non-priests and one priest."

D.   *R. Huna, son of R. Nathan, objected, "But then might I say that five must be priests and five Israelites [treating each set of references as a distinct entity, so the first reference to a priest excludes an Israelite, the second, which is redundant, encompasses an Israelite, and so on down]."*

E.   *That is a question.*

XVI.1   A.   **And so for the evaluation-vow covering men [M. 1:31]:**

B.   But can a man be declared sanctified [for purposes of evaluation for dedication of his value to the Temple]?

C.   "[Indeed so,]" said R. Abbahu, "In a case in which one says, 'My worth is incumbent upon me [to pay to the Temple].'"

D.   *So it has been taught on Tannaite authority:*

E.   He who says, "My worth is incumbent on me" – they make an estimate of his value in accord with that of a slave sold in the market.

F.   And a slave is in the classification of real estate.

XVI.2   A.   *R. Abin raised the question, "As to hair that is ready for shearing, how is it assessed? Is it assessed as if it were already sheared, and therefore by a court of three assessors? Or is it regarded as fully attached [as immovable property] and therefore assessed by a court of ten?"*

B.   Come and take note of the following: He who declares his slave to be sanctified – the laws of sacrilege do not apply [to the slave].

C.   Rabban Simeon b. Gamaliel says, "The laws of sacrilege do apply to his hair."

D.   *And the passage reaches us with the* obiter dicta *that at issue in the dispute is hair that is ready to be shorn.*

E.   *That proves the point.*

F.   *May we say, further, that the Tannaite authorities to be cited below debate about the same point as the Tannaite authorities just now cited:*

G.   *For we have learned in the Mishnah:*

H.   **R. Meir says, "There are things which are tantamount to being in the ground but still are not deemed to be immovable property like the ground."**

I.   **And sages do not concur with his view.**

J.   **How so?**

K.   **"Ten fruit-laden vines I handed over to you" –**

L.   **and the other says, "They were only five" –**

M.   **R. Meir imposes an oath.**

N.   **And sages say, "Whatever is attached to the ground is like the ground" [M. Shebu. 6:5A-G].**

O.   *In this connection, said R. Yosé bar Hanina, "We deal in the dispute at hands with grapes that are ready to be harvested. One party takes the view that they are in the status of already having been cut. The other party maintains they they are not regarded as if they have already been cut."*

P. *[No, the two cases are not comparable], for you may say that even R. Meir [would not see them as parallel]. R. Meir maintains his position in the cited case because, so long as people leave the grapes, if they are not gathered they deteriorate. But in the case of one's hair, so long as one leaves it, it continues to improve in value, [so the cases are not comparable, since one man may not cut the hair].*

XVII.1 A. **Cases involving the death-penalty [are judged before twenty-three judges. The beast who commits or is subjected to an act of sexual relations with a human being is judged by twenty-three...] [M. 1:4A-B]:**

B. *The framer of the passage states as a final judgment that there is no distinction between the case of a beast having sexual relations as with a man and one having sexual relations a with a woman.*

C. *Now in regard to the case of a beast's having sexual relations as with a woman, there is no difficulty, for it is written, "*And you shall slay the woman and the beast.*" (Lev. 20:16) [so the mode of trial for the beast is the same as the mode of trial for the woman].* But how do we know that [the mode of judging the case of] a beast who had sexual relations as with a man [is the same as the mode of judging when the man is on top]?*

D. It is written, "Whoever lies with a beast shall surely be put to death" (Ex. 22:18). Now [since we know that fact from Lev. 20:16], if the passage cannot serve for the case in which a man has sexual relations with the beast [as the activity party, for that is covered by Lev. 20:15], apply it to one in which he is the passive party.

F. *The All-Merciful has framed matters using the language of man as the active party to establish an analogy between the passive and the active participant. Just as, in the case of a man who has sexual relations with a beast as the active party, the man and the cow are judged by a court of twenty-three judges, so in the case of a man as a passive party with whom a beast has sexual relations, he and the ox are judged by a court of twenty-three judges.*

XVIII.1 A. **An ox that is to be stoned is judged by a court of twenty-three, since it is said, "And the ox will be stoned and also its master will be put to death" (Ex. 21:29). Just as the case of the master, leading to the death-penalty, is judged so is the case of the ox, leading to the death-penalty [judged by a court of twenty-three judges] [M. 1:4E-G].**

B. Said Abbayye to Raba, "How do we know that the verse, 'And the ox will be stoned and also its master will be put to death' (Ex. 21:29) serves to make the point that **just as the case of the master, leading to the death-penalty, is judged, so is the case of the ox, leading to the death-penalty is judged by a court of twenty-three judges?** **[15B]** *Might I rather say that it indicates only that the owner of the ox is to be put to death?"*

C. *If so, Scripture should have written, "*And also its owner*" and then said nothing more [so indicating that the owner is to be executed].*

D. *But had the All-Merciful phrased matters in this way, I might have supposed that the owner should be put to death through stoning.*

E. *How could anyone make such a supposition! If the owner had killed someone, he is put to death by the sword. If his property is stoned, [should he then be stoned also]? [Stoning is regarded as a more severe mode of inflicting the death penalty, and will not be assigned to the owner in the present circumstance.]*

F.   *Then might one suppose that the reason that the All-Merciful has written, "He will be put to death" is to assign to him an easier mode of execution, removing from him the penalty of death by the sword and applying to him instead death by strangulation [regarded as less painful]?*

G.   *Well, that possibility would pose no problems to one who maintains that strangulation is the more severe mode of execution [for the owner will not suffer more than his beast], but in the view of him who has said that strangulation is the less severe mode of execution, what is there to say?*

H.   *Do not let the matter come to mind!* For it is written, "If there be laid on him a ransom" (Ex. 21:30), and, if you should imagine that he is liable to the death-penalty, it is not written, "You shall not take a ransom for the life of a murderer" (Num. 35:31)? [Schachter, p. 74, n. 13: And surely if he is to be executed he is considered as such].

I.   *To the contrary, that is the very point of the text. If the man commits murder, it is not enough for him to pay a ransom, but he is put to death. If his ox has killed someone, however, he then shall redeem his soul with a mere money-payment.* [Schachter, p. 74, n. 14: And where there is no offer of a ransom, he is to be put to death. And the question, "Perhaps the verse means to indicate capital punishment for the owner" remains.]

J.   *Rather, said Hezekiah, and so did a Tannaite authority of the house of Hezekiah say, "Scripture has said, 'He who smote [a human being] shall surely be put to death, he is a murderer' (Num. 35:31). For a murder he has carried out you put him to death, but you do not put him to death for a murder committed by his ox."*

XVIII.2 A.   *The question was raised,* "An ox [that sinned by coming near] Mount Sinai [cf. (Ex. 19:13)] – by what sort of court was it judged?

B.   "Do we derive the rule applicable to that specific circumstance from the rule applicable for the oncoming generations, or do we not do so?"

C.   *Come and take note:* Rami b. R. Ezekiel taught on Tannaite authority, "'Whether it be beast or man, it shall not live' (Ex. 19:13). Just as a man is judged by a court of twenty-three judges, so a beast is judged by a court of twenty-three judges."

XIX.1 A.   **The wolf, lion [bear, a panther, leopard, and snake – a capital case affecting them is judged by a court of twenty-three] [M. 1:4H]:**

B.   Said R. Simeon b. Laqish, "[Eliezer's view applies to] a case in which they have killed someone, but otherwise that is not [the rule]." *Therefore he takes the view that these beasts are capable of being trained and also are subject to ownership.*

C.   R. Yohanan said, "[Eliezer holds the position he states] even if they did not kill anymore." *Therefore he takes the position that they are not capable of being trained and also are not subject to ownership."*

D.   *We have learned in the Mishnah:* **R. Eliezer says, "Whoever kills them first acquires merit" [M. 1:4I]:** *Now from the viewpoint of R. Yohanan, what is the meaning of "acquires merit"? It means that he acquires the merit of owning their hides. But as to R. Simeon b. Laqish, of what does one acquire merit? Since they have killed someone [as is Simeon b.*

Laqish's postulate], the rabbis treat them as equivalent to one who has been found guilty [of the death penalty], and no benefit may be derived from such a one.

E.   What merit is then acquired? It is merit vis a vis Heaven.

F.   A Tannaite teaching has been repeated in accord with the view of R. Simeon b. Laqish:

G.   **An ox which caused death – all the same [is the law for] an ox which caused death and any other sort of domestic or wild beast [T.: or fowl] which caused death – their [trial for the penalty of] death is [before] twenty-three [judges].**

H.   **R. Eliezer says, "An ox which caused death – its death is before twenty-three judges.**

I.   **"But as to any other sort of domestic or wild beast or fowl which has caused death – whoever comes along and kills them first has acquired merit in Heaven,**

J.   **[T. adds:] "as it is said, 'And you will kill the woman and the beast,' and it is said, 'And the beast you will kill (Lev. 20:16, 20:15)" [cf. M.1:41I] [T. San. 3:1A-D].**

XX.1   A.   **R. Aqiba says, "Their capital case is judged by twenty-three" [M. 1:4J]:**

B.   R. Aqiba says the same thing as the first authority [at at M. 1:4H]?

C.   At issue between them is the case of the snake.

XXI.1   A.   **They judge a tribe, a false prophet, and a high priest only on the instructions of a court of seventy-one members [M. 1:5A]:**

B.   As to the tribe at hand, what was the sin that it committed? If I should propose that it is a tribe that violated the laws of the Sabbath, while one can concede that the All-Merciful has made a distinction between trials for individuals and those for whole communities, that distinction applies to cases involving idolatry. But in cases involving the violation of other religious duties, did the law make such a distinction? Rather the trial [of M. 1:5A] concerns a tribe that was misled [to commit idolatry].

C.   This then implies that the community at large is tried under the procedures applying to a very large group of people [but not a whole community]. But that accords with the views of neither R. Josiah nor R. Jonathan. For it has been taught on Tannaite authority:

D.   How large a town is subject to the law applying to a town that is to be wiped out [on grounds of communal guilt for idolatry]?

E.   "From ten to a hundred [male inhabitants]," the words of R. Josiah. [The town of Deut. 13:14 may not be a village, involving fewer than ten adult males, nor more than a hundred, which would be too large a metropolis for the present context.]

F.   R. Jonathan says, "From a hundred up to the greater part of a tribe."

G.   Now even R. Jonathan takes the view that it is the greater part of the tribe, but he does not apply the law [of Deut. 13:14] to the entirety of a tribe!

H.   Said R. Mattenah, "We deal here [at M. 1:5A] **[16A]** with a case in which the head of a tribe has sinned. Has not R. Ada bar Ahbah said, 'Every great matter they shall bring to you' (Ex. 18:22), means every matter concerning a great man'?" Here too, [the head of the tribe] falls into the category of a great man, [and if such a one has committed idolatry, he is tried before a sanhedrin of seventy-one members]."

I.   [Proposing a different point of reference for M. 1:5A:], Ulla said R. Eleazar [said], "It is a case in which people come to court concerning the division of the tribal inheritances. This must be as at the first division of the Land of Israel. Just as, in the original division of the Land, disputes came to a court of seventy-one, so for generations afterward the rule is the same."

J.   Then may one say that just as the original division took place through the use of the urn, the Urim and the Thummim, with all Israel present, so nowadays such disputes are settled by appeal to the urn, with the Urim and Thummin, and with all Israel present?

K.   *Rather, the answer given in accord with R. Mattenah is superior.*

L.   *Rabina said, "In point of fact the Mishnah-rule speaks of the case of a tribe that was misled into idolatry. And as to your question that we should judge such a case in accord with the law applying to a large community, that indeed is so. Even though we put them to death as individuals, we do judge them in a court that serves for a large community. Has not R. Hama, son of R. Yosé, said R. Oshaia said, '"You shall bring forth that man and that woman" (Deut. 17:5) – a man or a woman do you bring out to your gates, but you do not bring out the entirety of a town to your gates'? Here too a man or a woman you bring forth to your gates, but you do not bring the entirety of a tribe to your gates."*

XXII.1   A.   **A false prophet [M. 1:5A]:**

B.   *What is the scriptural source for this rule?*

C.   Said R. Yosé b. R. Hanina, "We draw an analogy based upon the occurrence of the word 'presumption' both in the present context and in that of the rebellious elder.

D.   "Just as, in the latter case, the trial is before a court of seventy-one, so here too the trial is before a court of seventy-one."

E.   *But lo, when the word "presumption" occurs, it refers to a capital case, and a capital case is tried before a court of twenty-three judges.*

F.   Rather, said R. Simeon b. Laqish, "We establish an analogy based on the use in common of the word 'word' both in the present context [Deut. 18:20: 'The prophet that shall speak a word'], and in that of the rebellious elder [Deut. 17:10: 'And you shall do according to the word']. [Schachter, p. 77, n. 10: The need of seventy-one for the false prophet, therefore, is derived from the passage relating to the rebelliousness of the elder, which must be directed against the major sanhedrin.]"

G.   *But why not reverse the argument and derive the rule governing the rebellious elder by analogy through the common use of the word "presumption" from the case of the false prophet?*

H.   *One may establish an analogy based on the common use of the word "word," and one may not derive the rule by establishing an analogy based on the common use of the word "presumption."*

XXIII.1   A.   **The high priest [M. 1:5A]:**

B.   *What is the scriptural source of this rule?*

C.   Said R. Ada bar Ahbah, "It is as Scripture says, 'Every great matter they shall bring to you' (Ex. 18:22). [The meaning is] matters involving a great [man] [in high office]."

D. *An objection was raised on the basis of the following:* "A great matter" (Ex. 18:22) speaks of a difficult one.

E. You say it refers to a difficult matter. But perhaps it refers only to matters pertaining to a great man.

F. When Scripture says, "Hard cases they brought to Moses" (Ex. 18:26), a clear reference to a difficult case is at hand. [So the proof-text just now adduced cannot serve, as we have claimed, for another verse has made that point so the proof-text at hand makes a different point, as specified.]

G. *[Ada b. Ahbah's proof] accords with the view of the following Tannaite authority. For it has been taught on Tannaite authority:*

H. "A great matter" (Ex. 18:22) refers to matters pertaining to a great man [e.g., a high priest].

I. You say that reference is to matters affecting a great man, but perhaps it means only a difficult matter.

J. When Scripture refers to "a difficult matter" [at Ex. 18:26], lo, there is clear reference to a difficult matter. How, then am I to interpret "great matter" [at Ex. 18:22]? It can speak only matters affecting a great man.

K. *And according to [the first of the two] Tannaite authorities [who has "great matter" speak of difficult cases,] what need is there for Scripture to refer to the same matter [difficult cases] twice?*

L. *One provides the commandment, the other addresses the carrying out of the commandment.*

M. *And the other [Tannaite authority]?*

N. *If that were the case, Scripture should have written the word "great" two times or the word "difficult" two times. Why does it refer on one occasion to "great" [matter] and the other to "difficult" matter?*

O. *Two lessons derive from [the variation in word-choice].*

XXIII.2 A. *R. Eleazar raised the question, "What sort of court would be required to judge the case involving the ox of a high priest [that had gored and killed a man]? Do we place it into the classification of the court involving the trial for the death-penalty of its master? Or do we place it into the category of the court involving the trial for the death penalty of any sort of master [without reference to the status of the high priest]?"*

B. *Said Abbayye, "Since [Eleazar] raises the question with reference to the high priest's ox, it would follow that the question involving the property of the high priest is self-evident to him. [Such a matter would come before a court of three judges.]"*

C. *But surely that is self-evident!*

D. *[Nay it had to be made explicit.] What might you have said? Since Scripture states, "Every matter pertaining to the great man" (Ex. 18:22), it would mean, "all matters pertaining to a great man." Lo, we are informed [otherwise, namely, that too is an issue].*

XXIV.1 A. **They bring forth the army to a war fought by choice only on the instructions of a court of seventy-one [M. 1:5B]:**

B. *What is the scriptural source for this rule?*

C. Said R. Abbahu, "Scripture says, 'And he shall stand before Eleazar the priest, [who shall inquire for him by the judgment of the Urim before the Lord. At his word shall they go out and at his word they

shall come in, both he and all the children of Israel with him, even
all the congregation]' (Num. 27:21-22).

D.   "'He' speaks of the king.

E.   "'And all the children of Israel with him' refers to the priest
anointed for war.

F.   "'And even all the congregation' refers to the sanhedrin."

G.   *But perhaps it is the sanhedrin that is instructed by the All-Merciful to
inquire of the Urim and Thummim?*

H.   *Rather, the proof derives from what R. Aha bar Bizna said R. Simeon the
Pious said,* "There was a harp suspended over David's bed. At
midnight a north wind would blow through it, and it would play
on its own. David would get up right away and take up Torah-
study until dawn. At dawn the sages of Israel would come in to
him. They said to him, 'Our lord, king, your people Israel need
sustenance.'

I.   "He said to them, 'Make a living off one another.'

J.   "They said to him, 'A handful of meal is not enough for a lion, and
a pit cannot be filled up by its own dirt.'

K.   "He said to them, 'Go and organize marauders.'

L.   "Forthwith they took counsel with Ahitophel and ask advice of the
sanhedrin and address questions to the Urim and Thummim."

M.   *Said R. Joseph, "What verse of Scripture shows this?*

N.   "'[16B] 'And after Ahitophel was Benaiah, son of Jehoiada, and
Abiathar, and the captain of the king's host was Joab' (1 Chr.
27:34).

O.   "'Ahitophel' is the adviser, and so it is written, 'And the
counsel of Ahitophel which he counselled in those days was as
if a man inquired from the word of God' (2 Sam. 16:23).

P.   "'Benaiah son of Jehoiada' speaks of the Sanhedrin.

Q.   "'Abiathar' refers to the Urim and Thummim.

R.   "And so it is written, 'And Benaiah, son of Jehoiada,
supervised the Kerethites and Pelethites' (1 Chr. 18:17).

S.   "Why were they called 'Kerethites' and 'Pelethites'?

T.   "Because they gave definite instructions [a play on the
word KRT, which is the root for cut, hence, 'speak
decisively,' and also for the name of the group], and
because they did wonderful deeds [a play on the root PL',
wonder], respectively.

U.   "After this: 'And the captain of the king's host was Joab"'
(1 Chr. 27:34). [Schachter, p. 80, n. 13: Only after the
Sanhedrin had authorized a war was there any need for
Joab, the chief general.]"

V.   *Said R. Isaac, son of R. Ada, and some say R. Isaac bar Abodimi,
"What verse of Scripture, [supports the view that there was a
harp over David's bed]? 'Awake my glory, awake psaltery
and harp, I will wake the dawn' (Ps. 57:9)."*

XXV.1 A. **They make additions to the city of Jerusalem [and to the
courtyards of the Temple only on the instructions of a court of
seventy-one] [M. 1:5C]:**

B.   *What is the scriptural basis for this rule?*

C. Said R. Shimi bar Hiyya, "Scripture has stated, 'According to all that I show you, the pattern of the tabernacle [and the pattern of all the furniture thereof] even so shall you make it' (Ex. 25:9) – in the coming generations. [Schachter, p. 81, n. 2: Just as the position and bounds of the tabernacle were regulated by Moses, representing the Great Sanhedrin, so must the boundaries of the city and Temple Courts be decided upon by the Great Sanhedrin."]

D. *Raba objected,* "As to all the utensil that Moses made, the act of anointing them served to sanctify them, while, in the future, the act of making use of them served to dedicate them. *Now why should that be the case? Why not invoke the principle, ' – in the coming generations'* [the same procedures must be followed as in the time of Moses]?"

E. *That case is different, for Scripture has said [explicitly in their regard],* "And he had anointed them and sanctified them [in particular]" (Num. 7:1), meaning, them in particular did he consecrate through anointing, and not the ones that would be used in coming generations [which did not require] anointing.

F. *May I propose,* "... them by means of anointing, and also for coming generations, it may be done either by anointing or by actual use in the liturgy."?

G. Said R. Pappa, "Said Scripture, '... wherewith they shall minister in the sanctuary' (Num. 4:12). Scripture has assigned their [sanctification] to the actual ministry to the Temple."

H. *Why then lay special emphasis upon "them" [at Num. 7:1]* [which appears to serve as an exclusion, which in face of the said verse is unnecessary (Schachter, p. 81, n. 9)]?

I. *If Scripture had not referred to them, in particular, I might have concluded that, for the generations to come, [these utensils would be consecrated] both by anointing and also by actual use in the sacred service, for so it is written, "So shall you make it" (Ex. 25:9) [even in coming generations]. Accordingly, the All-Merciful wrote, them meaning,* "those objects in particular are consecrated through anointing, and those used in coming generations will not be consecrated through anointing."

XXVI.1 A. **They set up sanhedrins for the tribes [only on the instructions of a court of seventy-one] [M. 1:5D]:**

B. *What is the basis for this rule?*

C. *It is in accord with the fact that we find that Moses founded sanhedrins, and [as before] Moses acted in the place of a court of seventy-one.*

D. Our rabbis have taught on Tannaite authority:

E. How on the basis of Scripture do we know that judges are to be appointed for Israel?

F. It is on the basis of the verse, "Judges you shall make for yourself" (Deut. 16:18).

G. As to officers [to carry out the court's decrees]?

H. Scripture says, "Officers you shall appoint..." (Deut. 16:18).

I. Judges for each tribe?

J. 'From the statement, "Judges... for your tribes' (Deut. 16:18).

K. "Officers for each tribe?

L. "Officers... for your tribes." (Deut. 16:18).

M.	Judges for each town?
N.	"Judges in all your gates."
O.	'Officers for each town?
P.	Officers in all your gates" (Deut. 16:18).
Q.	R. Judah says, "One person is appointed above all the rest of them, as it is said, 'You will make for yourself' (Deut. 16:18)."
R.	Rabban Simeon b. Gamaliel says, "'For your tribes' and 'they shall judge' means that it is a religious duty for a tribe to judge cases involving its own tribe." [T. San. 3:10E].

XXVII.1 A. **They declare a city to be "an apostate city" only on the instructions of a court of seventy-one [M. 1:5E]:**

B. *What is the scriptural basis for this rule?*

C. Said R. Hiyya bar Joseph said R. Oshaia, "It is because Scripture has said, 'Then you shall bring forth that man or that woman' (Deut. 17:5), meaning an individual man or woman you bring forth to your gates [where there is an ordinary court to try capital cases, namely a court of twenty-three judges], but you do not bring an entire town to your gates [to such an ordinary court. An entire town has to be tried before seventy-one judges]."

XXVIII.1A. **And they do not declare a city to be an apostate city if it is on he frontier [M. 1:5F]:**

B. *What is the Scriptural basis for this rule?*

C. *Because the All-Merciful has said, "In your midst" (Deut. 13:14) – and not on the frontier.*

XXIX.1 A. **Nor do they declare three apostate cities in one locale [M. 1:50]:**

B. For it is written, "Concerning one of the cities" (Deut. 13:13 – but they do declare one or two, as it is written, "of your cities" (Deut. 13:13).

C. *Our rabbis have taught on Tannaite authority.*

D. "[Concerning] one [of the cities]" (Deut. 13:13) – one, but not three.

E. You say the sense is one but not three. But perhaps it means only one but not two?

F. When Scripture says, "Your cities," lo, it has made reference to two. How, then, am I to interpret, "One"? It is one, and not three.

G. *On some occasions Rab said, "It is in one court that one does not declare three cities to be apostate, but two or three courts do so [to three]."*

H. *And sometimes Rab said, "Even in the case of two or three courts they may not do so. Under no circumstances may they do so."*

I. *What is the reason behind Rab's view?*

J. *It is because [one does not make the Israelite settlements of the Land] bald [by wiping out too many towns].*

K. Said R. Simeon b. Laqish, "That rule pertains to a single locale, but in the case of two or three distinct locales, courts may declare [several] towns to be apostate cities [and subject to destruction]."

L.   R. Yohanan said, "They do not declare [two or three towns, even in diverse areas, to be apostate] so as not to make the Land bald."

M.   *It has been taught on Tannaite authority in accord with the view of R. Yohanan:*

N.   **They do not declare three towns to be apostate towns in the Land of Israel, so as not to wipe out [Israelite] settlement in the Land of Israel.**

O.   **But they declare one or two (to be apostate cities].**

P.   **[T. adds:] R. Simeon says, "Even two they may not declare, but they may declare one town in Judah and one town in Galilee [to be apostate towns]."**

Q.   **And near the frontier they may not declare even one town to be an apostate town.**

R.   **so that gentiles will not break through and wipe out settlement in the Land of Israel. [T. San. 14:1D-H].**

S.   *What is the reason?*

T.   So that gentiles will not hear of the matter and destroy the Land of Israel.

U.   *But can we not adduce the rule [that one should not declare a border town to be apostate] from the statement of the All-Merciful,* "From your midst" (Deut. 13:14) – *and not from the border?*

V.   *It is the view of R. Simeon, who explains the reason behind the ruling of Scripture.*

XXX.1 A. **The great sanhedrin was made up of seventy-one members [M. 1:6A]:**

B. *What is the reason for the position of rabbis [who hold that it was seventy-one, as against Judah, who says that it was only seventy], for they say that* **Moses was in addition to them [M. 1:6E]?**

C. Scripture has said, "That they may stand there **[17A]** with you" (Num. 11:16), *meaning, "And you with them" [and in addition to them].*

D. And R. Judah?

E. "With you" is on account of the Presence of God [Schachter, p. 83, n. 9: In order to deserve that the Presence should rest on them.... But it does not teach that Moses was to be counted in addition to them].

F. And rabbis?

G. Scripture has said, "And they shall bear the burden of the people with you" (Num. 11:17) – *and you with them.*

H. And R. Judah?

I. "With you" means people who are equivalent to you.

J. And rabbis?

K. *They derive that same point from the verse.* "So shall they make it easier for you and bear the burden with you? (Ex. 18:22) [speaking of the lesser sanhedrin, of twenty-three], and the large sanhedrin [of seventy-one] is derived from the rule governing the lesser one.

XXX.2   A.   *Our rabbis have taught on Tannaite authority.*

B.   "But there remained two men in the camp" (Num. 11:26).

C.   But there are those who say, "Their names, [Eldad's and Medad's] remained in the urn."

D.   For when the Holy One, blessed be he, said to Moses, "Gather to me seventy of the elders of Israel" (Num. 11:16), Moses thought to himself, "How shall I do it? If I choose six from each [of the twelve] tribes, there will be two extra. If I choose five from each tribe, there will be ten too few. If I choose six from one tribe and five from another, I shall cause jealousy among the tribes."

E.   What did he do? He chose six from each tribe and took seventy-two slips. On seventy of them he wrote, "Elder," and two he left blank. He mixed them up and put them in an urn. He said to them, "Come and take your slip." To each in whose hand the slip marked "Elder" came up, he said, "Heaven has already sanctified you for the task."

F.   To each whose slip came up blank, he said, "The Omnipresent has not chosen you, and what for my part can I do?"

G.   Along these same lines, you find in Scripture, "You shall take five shekels apiece by the poll" (Num. 3:47).

H.   Said Moses, "Now what shall I do with the Israelites? If I say to someone, 'Pay off the price of your redemption and go forth,' he will say to me, 'The son of Levi has already redeemed me.'"

I.   What did he do? He took twenty-two thousand slips and wrote on each of them, "Son of Levi," and on two hundred seventy-three he wrote, "Five shekels." He mixed them together and put them into an urn.

J.   He said to them, "Take your slips." To him in whose hand a slip marked, "Son of Levi" came up, he said, "The son of Levi has already redeemed you."

K.   To whom in whose hand "Five shekels]" came up, he said, "Pay your redemption-price and go."

XXX.3   A.   R. Simeon says, "They remained in the camp. When the Holy One blessed be he said to Moses, 'Gather for me seventy men' (Num. 11:16), Eldad and Medad said, 'We are not worthy of that high position.'

B.   "Said the Holy One, blessed be he, 'Since you diminished yourselves, lo, I shall add greatness to your greatness.'

C.   "What is the greatness that he added to them?

D.   "It was that all the others prophesied and then ceased to prophesy, but they prophesied and did not cease to prophesy."

E.   And what was the prophesy that they delivered?

F.   They said, "Moses is going to die and Joshua will bring Israel into the Land."

G.   Abba Hanin says in the name of R. Eliezer, "They prophesied concerning the matter of the quail: 'Arise, quail, arise, quail.'"

H.   R. Nahman says, "They prophesied concerning Gog and Magog, as it is said, 'So says the Lord God, Are you he of whom I spoke in olden time by my servants, the prophets of Israel, that prophesied in those days for many years that I would bring you against them? (Ez. 38:17). Instead of 'years' read 'two' [using the same consonants but different vowels].

I. "And who are the two prophets who prophesied the same message in the same prophesy? You have to say it was Eldad and Medad."

J. A master said, "All of the other prophets prophesied and then ceased to prophesy, but they prophesied and did not stop.

K. *"How do we know that the others stopped? If you might wish to propose that it is on account of the verse of Scripture, 'They prophesied but did so no more' (Deut. 5:19), then take note of the verse, 'A great voice that did not cease' (Deut. 5:19). Does this too bear the meaning that it went on no more? Rather, it must have the sense of 'it did not cease,' and so too in the proof-text.*

L. *"Rather the proof derives from here. It is written, 'And they prophesied' (Num. 11:25), but in the case of Eldad and Medad it says, 'They were going on prophesying (Num. 11:27), that is, continuing to prophesy."*

M. *Now from the viewpoint of him who said that they prophesied, "Moses will die," that is in line with [Joshua's request], "My lord, Moses, forbid them."*

N. *But from the viewpoint of him who said that they prophesied about the other two matters, [either the quail or about Gog and Magog], why did Joshua say, "My lord, Moses, forbid them"?*

O. *It was because it was improper conduct, because it was as if a disciple were making a decision of law in the presence of his master [which is not to be done].*

P. *Now from the viewpoint of those who hold the other two positions [that the prophesy had to do with the quail or with the coming of Gog and Magog], that is why it is written, "Would that all the Lord's people were prophets" (Num. 11:29).*

Q. *But from the viewpoint of him who said that the prophesy was, "Moses will die," did this please him? [Why did he praise such a prophecy?]*

R. *In his presence they did not complete their prophesy [so he did not hear that part of it].*

S. *What is the sense of "forbid them" [as Joshua said]?*

T. [Joshua] said to them, "Lay on them public responsibilities, and they will stop [their prophesying] on their own."

XXXI.1 A. **And how do we know that we should add three more [to the two 'congregations of ten judges each]? [M. 1:6J]:**

B. *But in the end [in a sanhedrin of twenty-three judges] you will never come up with a majority of two for a verdict of guilt. If eleven vote for acquittal and twelve for guilt, still it is a majority of one one [and that is null, since two are needed for a verdict of guilty]. If ten vote for innocence and thirteen for guilt, there is a majority of three for guilt.*

E. Said R. Abbahu, "You find [a majority of two] only where they add to the court, and this represents the opinion of all parties.

F. *"In the case of a large sanhedrin [of seventy] it would be possible to produce such a majority in accord with the opinion of R. Judah, who has said that such a court has seventy [not seventy-one] members.* [Schachter, p. 86, n. 7: It might happen that thirty-six condemn and thirty-four acquit.]"

G. And R. Abbahu said, "When they add to the court, a court with an even number of judges may emerge to begin with."

H. *That is self-evident. [If one judge is in doubt, then there are only twenty-two judges to participate. If you add two, there will be twenty-four judges.]*

I. *What might you have said? The one who has said, "I do not know" is in the status of one who is present, so that, if [later on] he makes a statement, we pay attention to him.*

J. *So we are informed that the one who has said, "I do not know, is as if he is not present at all, and if he were to state an opinion, we do not pay any attention to him.*

XXXI.2 A. Said R. Kahana, "A sanhedrin every member of which reached the conclusion that the accused is guilty must dismiss the accused [right away].

B. *"What is the reason? We have learned that one has to keep the case over night, so as to discover grounds for acquitting the accused. But in this case the participants will not see any grounds to acquit the accused."*

XXXI.3 A. Said R. Yohanan, "They seat on a sanhedrin only people of stature, wisdom, good appearance, mature age, who can recognize sorcery, and speak seventy languages, so that there should be no need of a sanhedrin to listen to testimony through an interpreter."

B. Said R. Judah said Rab, "They seat in a sanhedrin only people who can find arguments to declare a dead creeping thing clean on the basis of the law of the Torah."

C. Said Rab, "I shall provide an argument that it is clean. [17B] Now if a snake, which by killing a human being may increase uncleanness, is not unclean, a dead creeping thing, which cannot kill a person and so increase uncleanness, surely should be clean as well."

D. *But that is not a sound argument, as we see from the case of an ordinary thorn [about which the same argument can be constructed, but no one can imagine that it is unclean].*

XXXI.4 A. Said R. Judah said Rab, "In any town in which there are not two who can speak and one who can understand [seventy languages] people may not set up a sanhedrin."

F. In Betar there were three [such linguists]. In Yavneh, there were four: R. Eliezer, R. Joshua, and R. Aqiba, and Simeon of Teman gave arguments before [the court] [while sitting on] the ground [Schachter, p. 88. n. 1: because he was as yet unqualified owing to his immaturity, yet he was allowed to take part in the discussion].

G. *An objection was raised:* [A sanhedrin] with three [linguists is characterized by] wisdom, and if there is yet a fourth [linguist], there is no more exalted court.

H. *[Rab, who requires two linguists] accords with this Tannaite authority. For it has been taught on Tannaite authority:* [A sanhedrin with] two [linguists is character by] wisdom and if there is a third, there is no more exalted court.

XXXI.5 A. "Those who derive arguments before sages" refers to Levi before Rabbi.

B. "Those who argue before sages" refers to Simeon b. Azzai and Simeon b. Zoma, Hanan the Egyptian and Hananiah b. Hakhinai.

C. *R.Nahman bar Isaac repeated the matter in terms of five names:* Simeon, Simeon, Simeon, Hanan, and Hananiah.

D. "Our rabbis in Babylonia" refers to Rab and Samuel.

E. "Our rabbis in the Land of Israel" refers to R. Abba.

F. "The judges of the Exile" refers to Qarna.

G. *"The judges of the Land of Israel"* refers to R. Ammi and R. Assi.

H. *"The judges of Pumbedita"* refers to R. Pappa bar Samuel.

I. *"The judges of Nehardea"* refers to R. Adda bar Minyomi.

J. *"The elders of Sura"* refers to R. Huna and R. Hisda.

K. *"The elders of Pumbedita"* refers to R. Judah and R. Ina.

L. *"The sharp wits of Pumbedita"* refers to Ipah and Abimi, sons of Rahbah.

M. *"The Amoraim of Pumbedita"* refers to Rabbah and R. Joseph.

N. *"The Amoraim of Nehardea"* refers to R. Hama.

O. *"Those of Neharbela taught"* refers to Rammi bar Berabi.

P. *"They say in the master's house"* refers to R. Huna.

Q. But did not R. Huna himself say, "They say in the house of the master"?

R. Rather, it is R. Hamnuna.

S. *"They say in the West"* refers to R. Jeremiah.

T. *"They sent from there"* refers to R. Yosé bar Hanina.

U. *"They ridiculed that statement in the West"* refers to R. Eleazar.

V. And lo, "They sent from the West in accord with the opinion of R. Yosé bar Hanina" [is an available formulation]?

W. *Rather, reverse matters:*

X. *"They sent from there"* refers to R. Eleazar.

Y. *"They ridiculed that statement in the West"* refers to R. Yosé bar Hanina.

XXXII.1 A. **And how many residents must there be in a town so that it may be suitable for a sanhedrin? One hundred twenty [M. 1:6Q-R]:**

B. *What do these one hundred twenty do?*

C. **Twenty-three are there for a lesser sanhedrin, and there have to be three rows of twenty-three [behind the court], lo, ninety-two.**

D. **There have to be ten men employed full time in the synagogue and otherwise unemployed, lo, a hundred and two.**

E. **[B. lacks: R. Judah says,] "There have to be two scribes, two court officers, two litigants, two witnesses, two prepared to prove the witnesses are perjurers, two further witnesses to testify as to the perjury of the ones who are to testify against the original witnesses" [T. San. 3:9D] – lo, a hundred and fourteen.**

F. *And it has been taught on Tannaite authority:*

G. In any town in which there are not the following ten officials a disciple of a sage is not permitted to live: a court inflicting the penalty of flogging and [other sorts of] penalties, a charity fund collected by two officials and divided up by three, a synagogue, a bath house, a privy, a physician, an expert [at circumcision], a notary, and a teacher of children.

H.   In the name of R. Aqiba they have said, "Also various kinds of produce, because various kinds of produce keep the eyes bright."

XXXIII.1A.   **R. Nehemiah says, "Two hundred thirty [residents]" [M. 1:6S]. [T. adds:] and the law is in accord with his opinion.**

B.   **Rabbi says, "Two hundred and seventy-seven" [T. San. 3:9F-G].**

C.   But has it not been taught on Tannaite authority:

D.   Rabbi says, "Two hundred seventy-<u>eight</u>"?

E.   There is no contradiction, the one represents the view of R. Judah, the other of rabbis. [Judah wants seventy on the sanhedrin, rabbis, seventy-one.]

XXXIII.2A.   *Our rabbis have taught on Tannaite authority:*

B.   "And place such over them to be rulers of thousands, rulers of hundreds, rulers of fifties, and rulers of tens" (Ex. 18:21):

C.   "The rulers of thousands" were six hundred.

D.   "The rulers of hundreds" were six thousand.

E.   "The rulers of fifties" were twelve thousand.

F.   "The rulers of tens" were sixty-thousand.

G.   The total number of judges is Israel was seventy-eight thousand six hundred.

The Mishnah-chapter consists of three catalogues of the sorts of courts competent to try various kinds of cases, specifically, courts of three judges (M. 1:1-3), of twenty-three (M. 1:4), and of seventy-one (M. 1:5, 6). Cases involving civil law fall into the first list, a catalogue of twelve entries; those involving capital punishment into the second, a list of three entries; and matters of public policy, five in all, constitute the third list. M. 1:6 complements M. 1:4, 5, by explaining the numbers of judges required to make up courts of seventy-one and twenty-three, respectively. The relationship between the Talmud and the Mishnah is spelled out in Chapter Twelve.

2

Bavli Tractate Sanhedrin
Chapter Two
Folios 18A-22B

2:1-2

A. A high priest judges, and [others] judge him;

B. gives testimony, and [others] give testimony about him;

C. performs the rite of removing the shoe [Deut. 25:7-9], and [others] perform the rite of removing the shoe with his wife.

D. [Others] enter levirate marriage with his wife, but he does not enter into levirate marriage,

E. because he is prohibited to marry a widow.

F. [If] he suffers a death [in his family], he does not follow the bier.

G. "But when [the bearers of the bier] are not visible, he is visible; when they are visible, he is not.

H. "And he goes with them to the city gate," the words of R. Meir.

I. R. Judah says, "He never leaves the sanctuary,

J. "since it says, 'Nor shall he go out of the sanctuary' (Lev. 21:12)."

K. And when he gives comfort to others

L. the accepted practice is for all the people to pass one after another, and the appointed [prefect of the priests] stands between him and the people.

M. And when he receives consolation from others,

N. all the people say to him, "Let us be your atonement."

O. And he says to them, "May you be blessed by Heaven."

P. And when they provide him with the funeral meal,

Q. all the people sit on the ground, while he sits on a stool.

M. 2:1

A. The king does not judge, and [others] do not judge him;

B. does not give testimony, and [others] do not give testimony about him;

C. does not perform the rite of removing the shoe, and others do not perform the rite of removing the shoe with his wife;

75

D.   does not enter into levirate marriage, nor [do his brother] enter levirate marriage with his wife.

E.   R. Judah says, "If he wanted to perform the rite of removing the shoe or to enter into levirate marriage, his memory is a blessing."

F.   They said to him, "They pay no attention to him [if he expressed the wish to do so]."

G.   [Others] do not marry his widow.

H.   R. Judah says, "A king may marry the widow of a king.

I.   "For so we find in the case of David, that he married the widow of Saul,

J.   "For it is said, 'And I gave you your master's house and your master's wives into your embrace' (II Sam. 12:8)."

                                        M. 2:2

I.1   A.   A high priest judges [M. 2:1A]:

        B.   *That is self-evident.*

        C.   *It was necessary to make that point in the context of the statement that* **others judge him.**

        D.   *That too is self-evident.* If others do not judge him, how can he serve as a judge? *For has it not been written,* "Gather yourselves together, yes, gather together" (Zeph. 2:1), *on which R. Simeon b. Laqish said,* "[The word for gather together bears the meaning of adorn, in consequence of which:] Adorn yourself and afterward adorn others."

        E.   *Rather, since the framer of the passage wished to make reference to* **the king, who does not judge others and is not judged by others,** *he made reference in his clause on the high priest to the fact that* **he does judge and is judged by others.**

        F.   *And if you wish, I shall propose that what the framer of the passage teaches is in line with that which has been taught on Tannaite authority:* **A high priest who committed homicide [if he did so] deliberately, he is executed; [if he did so] inadvertently, he goes into exile to the cities of refuge [Num. 35:9ff.]. [If] he transgressed a positive or negative commandment, [T: or, indeed, and of the commandments,] lo, he is treated like an ordinary person in every respect. [T. San. 4:1A-C].**

        G.   [Proceeding to the exegesis of the passage of Tosefta just now cited;] **If he did so deliberately, he is executed:**

        H.   *That is self-evident.*

        I.   *It was included because of the other part of the statement,* **If he did so inadvertently, he goes into exile to the cities of refuge.**

        J.   *But that fact also is self-evident.*

        K.   *It was necessary to make it explicit. It might have entered your mind to claim that since it is written,* "And he shall dwell therein until the death of the high priest" (Num. 35:25), *only one who is subject to the remedy of return [at the death of the high priest] is subject to the rule [of taking refuge in the city to begin with]. But someone who is not subject to the remedy of return [at the death of the high priest] should not go into exile at all. For we have learned in the Mishnah:* **[18B] He who kills a high priest and a high priest** who committed involuntary manslaughter never leaves [the city of refuge] [M. 2:7B-D].

L. *I might then have concluded that such a one should not go into exile at all.*

M. *[The framer of the passage] tells us that that is not the case.*

N. *But might I say that it is indeed the case?*

O. Scripture has said, "Every man slayer may flee there" (Deut. 19:3) – *including even a high priest.*

P. **If he transgressed a positive or negative commandment, or indeed any of the commandments, lo, he is treated like an ordinary person in every respect [T. San. 4:1C].**

Q. *Is it not possible that he will not transgress?*

R. *This is the sense of the passage: If he transgressed a positive or negative commandment, lo, he is treated like an ordinary person in every respect.*

S. *That is self-evident.*

T. *It might have entered our mind to say that, since we have learned in the Mishnah,* **A tribe, a false prophet, and a high priest, are judged only by a court of seventy-one judges [M. 1:6],** *in which connection R. Ada bar Ahbah said, "'Every great matter they shall bring to you' (Ex. 18:22), meaning matters involving a great [important] man, [such as the high priest], one should reach the conclusion that any and every matter affecting a great man [must come to such a court].*

U. *So we are informed [that that is not the case].*

V. *But perhaps that indeed is the case?*

W. *Is it written, "Matters affecting a great man"? What is written is, "A great matter," meaning, something that is quite literally a matter of importance.*

II.1 A. **Gives testimony and others give testimony about him [M. 2:1B]:]**

B. *And has it not been taught on Tannaite authority:*

C. "And hide yourself from them" (Deut. 22:4) – There are times in which you do hide yourself, and there are times that you do not hide yourself. How so? In the case of a priest, if [the man who needs help] is in a grave yard [where a priest may not go, for fear of contracting corpse uncleanness], or if it is an elder and the work involved is not in accord with the honor owing to him, or if it is a case in which his own work is greater in value than that of his fellow, for such a case it is written, "And you shall hide yourself. [Schachter, p. 94, n. 7: In the same way the duty of bearing testimony should be abrogated in favor of a high priest, since it is not in keeping with his exalted office.]

D. Said R. Joseph, "He gives testimony for the king."

E. *But have we not learned in the Mishnah:* **The king does not judge and others do not judge him [M. 2:2A], he does not give testimony and others do not give testimony about him [M. 2A:2B]?**

F. Rather, said R. Zera, "He gives testimony for the son of the king."

G. But the son of a king falls into the category of an ordinary person!

H. Rather: He gives testimony before the king.

I. **And lo, the king does not join in the session of a sanhedrin [T. San. 2:15A]!**

J. *On account of the honor owing to the high priest, the king will come and join in the session of the sanhedrin. The court then will take the testimony of the high priest. Then the king will go his way, and the rest of us [the rabbis] will then look into the case [on which the high priest has testified].*

II.2 A. *Reverting to the body of the text just now cited:*

B. **The king does not join in the session of a sanhedrin,**

C. **and neither the king nor the high priest joins in the session called for intercalating the year. [T. San. 2:15A-B].**

D. As to a king in the sanhedrin, *it is written,* "You shall not speak in a case" (Ex. 23:2), [reading the consonants differently, it is] "You shall not speak against the head [of the judges]." [Schachter, p. 94, n. 13: If the king were a member of the sanhedrin, other members would be inclined to suppress their opinions in deference to him.]

E. **And neither the king nor the high priest joins in the session called for intercalating the year:**

F. **The king,** on account of the army's wages [for he would have a special interest in whether or not the year gets an extra month, if he is paying the army by the year],

G. **and the high priest,** because of the cold in the fall [he would oppose adding an extra month, which places the Day of Atonement late in autumn].

H. *Said R. Pappa, "The latter statement bears the implication that the year's seasons fall [Schachter:] with the normal lunar months. [Schachter, p. 95, n. 4: When the year is intercalated, the weather in Tishri (ordinarily: September) is the equivalent of that of Marheshvan (ordinarily: October) in an ordinary year].*"

I. *Is this the case? And lo, there were three cowboys, who were standing [and talking], and rabbis overheard them speaking.*

J. *One of them said, "If the early and late sowing [wheat, barley] sprout together, it is Adar, and if not, it is not Adar."*

K. *The second said, "If the morning frost is harsh enough to kill an ox, but at mid-day the ox lies in the shade of a fig-tree and scratches its hide [because of heat], it is a Adar, and if not, it is not Adar."*

L. *The third said, "When your breath can blow against a strong east wind, it is Adar, and if it is not, it is not Adar."*

M. *The rabbis forthwith intercalated the year* [Schachter, p. 95, n. 9: Thus we see that the purpose of intercalation is to readjust the seasons, and the second Adar then has the climate of the first Adar in normal years, therefore Tishri will have its usual degree of heat in an intercalated year.]

N. *But do you thing that rabbis would intercalate the year depending on cowboys?*

O. *They depended on their own calculations and the views of the cowboys supported their decision.* [Schachter, p. 95, n. 10: In case, therefore, intercalation has been prompted by a reason other than the readjusting of the seasons, the weather will vary according to the months.]

III.1 A. **He performs the rite of removing the shoe, and others perform the rite of removing the show with his wife [M. 2:1C]:**

B. *Does the Tannaite authority at hand take the view that there is no difference whether the widow was merely betrothed or was partner to a fully consummated marriage?*

C. *Now there is no difficulty understanding the rule in the case of* a widow of a fully consummated marriage, you have a case of an affirmative religious duty and a prohibition ["A virgin of his people he shall take to wife" (Lev. 21:14) as against "A widow he shall not take" (Lev. 21:14)]. [So the high priest does not marry the widow at hand.] **[19A]** And a positive religious duty cannot set aside a negative one and a positive one. *But as to doing so when the relationship is merely one of betrothal why should he not [marry her, rather than going through the rite of removing the shoe]?* Let a positive religious duty come and set aside a negative religious duty. [The positive religious duty is to take the deceased childless brother's widow as his wife, so Deut. 25:5ff. The negative religious duty is not to marry a non-virgin, as indicated].

D. *It is a decree against his having sexual relations [to effect the levirate marriage] on account of later acts of sexual relations [which are not subject to a religious duty. He will have carried out his duty only by the first act of sexual relations.]*

E. It has been taught on Tannaite authority along these same lines; If [the high priest] went ahead and had sexual relations with the widow of his deceased childless brother, the first act of sexual relations has effected acquisition. But he is forbidden to go ahead and have further sexual relations with her, [but has to divorce her].

IV.1 A. **If he suffers a death in his family, he does not follow the bier [M. 2:1F]:**

B. *Our rabbis have taught on Tannaite authority:*

C. *"Neither shall he go out of the sanctuary" (Lev. 21:12):*

D. He should not go out with them, but he may go out after them. How so?

E. **When the bearers of the bier are not visible, he is visible, and when they are visible, he is not [M. 2:1G].**

V.1 A. **"And he goes with them to the city gate," the words of R. Meir. R. Judah says, "He never leaves the sanctuary, since it says ..." [M. 2:1H-J]:**

B. *Has R. Judah given [Meir] a good argument?*

C. *R. Meir may say to you, "If that is the sense of the verse at hand [as Judah explains] it, then he should also not go to his own home. But this is the sense of the matter: 'From the sanctuary he shall not go forth' means he should not go forth from his status as sanctified. But since in the*

*present matter there is provision for giving full recognition to that status,
he will not come to have contact [with corpse-matter]."*

D.   And R. Judah?

E.   *On account of his bitter mourning, it might happen that [unknowingly] he
will come into contact with corpse-matter.*

VI.1   A.   **When he gives comfort to others [M. 2:1K]:**

B.   *Our rabbis have taught on Tannaite authority:*

C.   **[And when] he stands in the line to give comfort to others, the
prefect of the priests and the anointed [high] priests who has now
passed out [of his position of grandeur] are at his right hand, and
the head of his father's house, the mourners, and all the people
are at his left.**

D.   **[When] he stands in the line to receive comfort from others [as a
mourner], the prefect of the priests is at his right hand, and the
head of the father's houses [the priestly courses] and all the
people are at his left hand [T. San. 4:1 I, F].**

E.   *But [in the latter case] the anointed high priest who has left office does not
come to him. Why not? [The present high priest] might be upset at his
presence, thinking, "[My predecessor] is happy at my misfortune."*

VI.2   A.   *Said R. Pappa, "The present teaching on Tannaite authority yields
three points: First, the prefect is the same as the one called in the
Mishnah's version 'the one who is appointed.' Second, the mourners
stand and the people pass by them. Third, the mourners are to the left
of those who come to give comfort."*

VI.3   A.   *Our rabbis have taught on Tannaite authority:*

H.   The original practice was for the mourners to stand still and all the
people to pass by them. There were two families in Jerusalem who
competed with one another. This one said, "I shall pass first," and
that one said, "I shall pass first." Sages ordained that the people
should stand still and the mourners should pass by.

B.   Said Rammi bar Abba, "In Sepphoris R. Yosé restored the
original practice, so that the mourners would stand still and all
the people would pass by."

C.   And said Rammi bar Abba, "In Sepphoris R. Yosé ordained
that a woman should not walk through the market place with
her children behind her, on account of an incident that took
place."

D.   And said Rammi bar Abba, "In Sepphoris R. Yosé
ordained that women should talk aloud in the privy, so as
to preserve privacy [since men would know not to come
in]."

E.   Said R. Menassia bar Avat, "I asked R. Josiah, the elder, in the
cemetery of Husal, and he said to me, 'There can be no line of
comforters less than ten people, not counting the
mourners,'and that is the case whether the mourners are
standing and all the people passing by them, or whether the
mourners pass by and all the people are standing still.'"

VII.1   A.   **And when he receives consolation from others [M. 2:1M]:**

B.   *The question was raised: When he comforts others, what does he say to
them?*

C.   *Come and take note:* And he says, "May you be comforted."

D.   *Now to what circumstances would such a statement pertain? If one should propose that it is when others comfort him, could he say to them, "Be comforted"? That would represent some sort of enchantment that he set against them! Rather it is that, when he comforts others, he says to them, "Be comforted."*

E.   *That indeed is definitive proof.*

VIII.1 A.   **The king does not judge, and others do not judge him [M. 2:2A]:**

B.   Said R. Joseph, "That law applies only to Israelite kings. But as to the kings of the house of David, such a king judges and others judge them. For it is written, 'House of David, thus says the Lord, execute justice in the morning' (Jer. 21:12)."

C.   *Now if others do not judge him, how can they judge others?* And has it not been written, 'Ornament yourselves and be ornamented' (Zeph. 2:1), interpreted by R. Simeon b. Laqish to mean, 'Adorn yourself and then adorn others'?"

D.   *What then is the reason that Israelite* **kings are not judged and do not judge**?

E.   It is because of a case that actually took place.

F.   *King Yannai's agent killed someone. Simeon b. Shetah said to sages, "Set your eyes against him and let us judge him." They sent a message to him, "Your agent has killed someone."*

G.   *He sent back to them, "Send him to me."*

H.   *They replied to him, "You come too. 'If a warning has been given to its owners' (Ex. 21:29) is what the Torah has said, so let the owner of the ox come and take responsibility for his ox."*

I.   *The king came and took his seat.*

J.   Simeon b. Shetah said to him, "King Yannai, stand on your feet, so that people can give evidence against you. And it is not before us that you stand, but before Him who spoke and brought the world into being that you stand, as it is said, 'Then both the men between whom the controversy is shall stand' (Deut. 19:17)."

K.   He said to him, "It is not as you say, but as your fellows will say."

L.   **[19B]** [Simeon] looked to his right, and the sages looked to the ground. He looked to the left, and they looked to the ground.

M.   Said Simeon b. Shetah to them, "You are lost in thought? Let the Master of thought come and exact a penalty from you."

N.   Forthwith Gabriel came and knocked them to the ground, and they all died.

O.   At that moment they ruled: **The king does not judge and others do not judge him, he does not give testimony and others do not give testimony about him [M. 2:2A-B].**

IX.1 A.   **He does not perform the rite of removing the shoe, and others do not perform the rite of removing the shoe with his wife... [R. Judah says, "If he wanted to perform the rite of removing the shoe or to enter into levirate marriage, his memory is a blessing"] [M. 2:2C-E]:**

B.   *Is what R. Judah says] true? And has not R. Ashi said, "Even in the opinion of him who maintains that,* as to a patriarch who was willing to forego the honor owing to him, the honor is foregone, but as to a king who was willing to forego the honor owing to him, the honor owing to him is not foregone, for it is said, 'You shall in any way set him as a king over you' (Deut. 17:15), meaning that fear of him should remain over you"?

C.   *A matter involving a religious duty is different [in Judah's view].*

X.1   A.   **Others do not marry his widow [M. 2:2G]:**

B.   *It has been taught on Tannaite authority:*

C.   They said to R. Judah, "[David] married women of the royal family who were permitted to him, Merab and Michal, [but these were not his widows]."

D.   **His disciples asked R. Yosé, "How did David marry two sisters while both were yet alive?"**

E.   **He said to them, "He married Michal after the death of Merab."**

F.   **R. Joshua b. Qorha says, "His act of betrothal of Merab was made in error, as it is said, 'Give me my wife, Michal, whom I betrothed at a price of a hundred foreskins of the Philistines' (2 Sam. 3:14). [T. adds: Just as his act of betrothal was not a completely valid one, so his marriage was not a completely valid one]" [T. Sot. 11:18-19].**

G.   *From what sort of scriptural proof is this conclusion to be derived?*

H.   Said R. Pappa, "Michal is my wife, and Merab is not my wife."

I.   *And what sort of error in the betrothal was there?*

J.   It is as it is written, "And it shall be that the man who kills him the king will enrich him with great riches and will give him his daughter" (1 Sam. 17:25).

K.   *David went and killed him. [Saul] said to him, "You have a debt with me [which I owe to you], and* **one who betroths a woman by forgiving a debt does not accomplish the woman's betrothal."** *[Saul] went and gave her instead to Adriel, as it is written, "But it came to pass at the time when Merab, Saul's daughter, should have been given to David, that she was given to Adriel the Meholathite to wife" (1 Sam. 18:19).*

L.   *[Saul] said to [David], "If you want me to give you Michal, go and bring me a hundred foreskins of Philistines."*

M.   *He went and brought him a hundred foreskins of Philistines.*

N.   *He said to him, "Now you have with me an unpaid debt [which I owe you], and also a perutah [coin]."*

O.   *Saul had the notion that, where there is a loan and a small coin, [the creditor] is thinking about the loan [in any transaction or exchange with the debtor, hence David will be thinking about the loan and his act of betrothal once more would be null]. But David was thinking that where there is a loan and a coin, one's thought is about the coin.*

P.   *And if you wish, I shall propose that all parties concurred that where there is a loan and a coin owing, one's thought is on the coin. But Saul took the view that [the foreskins] were worthless anyhow, while David took the view that they were fit for dog- or cat-food.*

Q.   *And how does R. Yosé interpret the language, "Give me my wife, Michal" (2 Sam. 3:14)?*

R.   *R. Yosé interprets it in a way consistent with his reasoning in general. For it has been taught on Tannaite authority:* **R. Yosé would interpret confused verses of Scripture: "It is written,**

'But the king took the two sons of Rizpah the daughter of Ayah whom she bore to Saul, Armoni and Mephibosheth, and the five sons of Michal, the daughter of Saul, whom she bore to Adriel the son of Barzillai the Meholathite (2 Sam. 21:8).

S. "Now where do we find that Michal was given to Adriel the son of Barzillai the Meholathite? Was she not given only to Palti the son of Laish who was of Gallim, as it is said, 'And Saul had given Michal, his daughter, David's wife, to Palti, the son of Laish, who was of Gallim' (1 Sam. 25:44).

T. But Scripture thereby links the marriage of Merab to the marriage of Michal. Just as the marriage of Michal to Palti the son of Laish was in transgression, so the marriage of Merab to Adriel was in transgression" [T. Sot. 11:17A-C].

U. *And as to R. Joshua b. Qorhah, is it not written,* "And the five sons of Michal, the daughter of Saul, whom she bore to Adriel" (2 Sam. 21:8)?

V. R. Joshua can say to you: **But did Michal produce them? And is it not so that Merab produced them? But Merab gave birth to them and Michal raised them, so they were called by Michal's name, [T. adds: as it is said, 'And the women of the neighborhood gave him a name, saying, A son has been born to Naomi' (Ruth 4:17)] [T. Sot. 11:20].**

W. [T. lacks:] "This serves to teach you that whoever raises an orphan in his house is regarded by Scripture as if he had given birth to him.

X.2 A. *R. Hanina says, "Proof [of the proposition just now cited] derives from the following verse of Scripture:* 'And the women of the neighborhood gave him a name, saying, A son has been born to Naomi' (Ruth 4:17)."

B. "Now did Naomi give birth to the child? Was it not Ruth? But Ruth gave birth to the child, and Naomi raised him, so he bore Naomi's name."

C. R. Yohanan said, "Proof [of the same proposition] derives from here: 'And his wife, the Judahite [Bithia, the daughter of Pharaoh] bore Yered, father of Gedor [and Heber, father of Soco,the child, and Naomi raised him, so he bore Naomi's name."

C. *R. Yohanan said, "Proof [of the same proposition] derives from here:* 'And his wife, the Judahite [Bithia, the daughter of Pharaoh] bore Yered, father of Gedor [and Heber, father of Soco, and Jekuthiel, father of Zanoah], and these are the sons of Bithia, daughter of Pharaoh, whom Mered took' (1 Chr. 4:18).

D. ("Mered was Caleb, and why was he called Mered? Because he rebelled (MRD) against the counsel of the spies.)

E. "And did Bithia give birth [to Moses], and did not Jochebed do so?

F. "But while Jochebed gave birth to him, Bithia raised him, therefore he bore her name."

G.   R. Eleazar said, "Proof derives from here: 'You have with your arm redeemed your people, the sons of Jacob and Joseph, Selah' (Ps. 77:16). Did Joseph beget [the people]? Was it not Jacob? But Jacob begot them and Joseph kept them alive, therefore they bore his name."

H.   Said R. Samuel bar Nahmani said R. Jonathan, "Whoever teaches Torah to his fellow's son is credited by Scripture as if he begat him,

I.   "as it is said, 'Now these are the generations of Aaron and Moses' (Num. 3:1), and later, 'These are the names of the sons of Aaron' (Num. 3:1), so teaching the lesson that Aaron begat them and Moses taught them [Torah], and therefore they bore his [Moses'] name."

J.   "Therefore thus says the Lord to the house of Jacob, who redeemed Abraham' (Is. 29:22):

K.   Now where in Scripture do we find that Jacob redeemed Abraham?

L.   Said R. Judah, "He redeemed him from the trouble of raising children [because Abraham had few children, while Jacob had many]. That is in line with what is written, 'Jacob shall not now be ashamed, neither shall his face now wax pale' (Is. 29:22).

M.   "'He shall not now be ashamed' – of his father.

N.   "'Neither shall his face now become pale' – because of his grandfather."

X.3   A.   It is written "Palti" (at I Sam. 25:44), and it is written "Paltiel" (2 Sam. 3:15) [so the second husband of David's undivorced wife had two names].

B.   Said R. Yohanan, "He was really called Palti, and why was he later called Paltiel? Because God (el) saved him from transgression [namely, marrying an already-married woman].

C.   "What did [God] do? He put a sword between him and her [so they did not have sexual relations], saying, 'Whoever gets involved in this matter will be pierced by this sword.'"

D.   But is it not written, "And her husband Palti went with her" (2 Sam. 3:16)?

E.   That he became like her husband [but he was not in fact ever he husband].

F.   But is it not written, "He went weeping" (2 Sam. 3:16)?

G.   It was on account of the loss of the religious duty [Schachter: of self-restraint]."

H.   "He followed her to Bahurim" (2 Sam. 3:16): Both of them [Palti and his wife] were like youths [bahurim], who had not tasted the flavor of sexual relations [having remained celibate for their marriage].

I.   Said R. Yohanan, "The strong desire affecting Joseph [Gen. 39:7-13] was modest for Boaz, and the strong desire affecting Boaz [Ruth 3:8-15] was modest for Palti ben Laish.

J. "The strong desire affecting Joseph was modest for Boaz, in line with that which is written, 'And it came to pass at midnight, and the man was startled' (Ruth 3:8)."

K. What is the meaning of "was startled"?

L. Said Rab, "His penis became as hard as a turnip top. [A play on the consonants for 'was startled' which are shared with the word for turnip.]"

M. [20A] [Yohanan continues], "And the strong desire affecting Boaz was modest for Palti ben Laish" – as we have said.

N. Said R. Yohanan, "What is the meaning of the verse of Scripture, 'Many daughters have done valiantly, but you excel them all' (Prov. 31:29)?

O. "'Many daughters have done valiantly' refers to Joseph and Boaz.

P. "'And you excel them all' speaks of Palti, son of Laish."

Q. Said R. Samuel bar Nahman said R. Jonathan, "What is the meaning of the verse of Scripture: 'Grace is deceitful and beauty is vain, but a woman who fears the Lord shall be praised' (Prov. 31:30)?

R. "'Grace is deceitful' speaks of Joseph.

S. "'Beauty is vain' speaks of Boaz.

T. "'A woman who fears the Lord shall be praised' speaks of Palti ben Laish.

U. "Another interpretation: 'Grace is deceitful' speaks of the generation of Moses.

V. "'Beauty if vain' speaks of the generation of Joshua.

W. "'A woman who fears the Lord shall be praised' speaks of the generation of Hezekiah.

X. "Another interpretation: 'Grace is deceitful' speaks of the generation of Moses and Joshua.

Y. "'Beauty is vain' speaks of the generation of Hezekiah.

Z. "'A woman who fears the Lord shall be praised' speaks of the generation of R. Judah b. R. Ilai.

AA. "They said concerning R. Judah b. R. Ilai that six disciples [in his time] would cover themselves with a single cloak but [nonetheless] would spend their time studying Torah [despite gross want]."

The Talmud systematically takes up the sentences of the Mishnah-paragraph and explains them. The secondary expansions do not change the picture of a carefully-crafted document, for we do know the rules of forming composites.

2:3

A. [If] [the king] suffers a death in his family, he does not leave the gate of his palace.

B. R. Judah says, "If he wants to go out after the bier, he goes out,

C. "for thus we find in the case of David, that he went out after the bier of Abner,

D. "since it is said, 'And King David followed the bier' (2 Sam. 3:31)."

E. They said to him, "This action was only to appease the people."

F. And when they provide him with the funeral meal, all the people sit on the ground, while he sits on a couch.

I.1   A.   *Our rabbis have taught on Tannaite authority:*

B.   In a place in which women are accustomed to go forth after the bier, they go forth in that way. If they are accustomed to go forth before the bier, they go forth in that manner.

C.   R. Judah says, "Women always go forth in front of the bier.

D.   "For so we find in the case of David that he went forth after the bier of Abner.

E.   "For it is said, 'And King David followed the bier' (2 Sam. 3:31)."

F.   They said to him, "That was only to appease the people [M. 2:3D-E].

G.   "They were appeased, for David would go forth among the men and come in among the women, go forth among the women and come in among the men,

H.   "as it is said, 'So all the people and all Israel understood that it was not of the king to slay Abner' (2 Sam. 3:37)."

I.2   A.   *Raba expounded, "What is the meaning of that which is written, 'And all the people came to cause David to eat bread' (2 Sam. 3:35)?*

B.   "It was written, 'to pierce David' [with a K], but we read, 'to cause him to eat bread' [with a B].

C.   "To begin with they came to pierce him but in the end to cause him to eat bread."

I.3   A.   Said R. Judah said Rab, "On what account was Abner punished? Because he could have prevented Saul but did not prevent him [from killing the priest of Nob, 1 Sam. 22:18]."

B.   R. Isaac said, "He did try to prevent him, but he got no response."

C.   And both of them interpret the same verse of Scripture: "And the king lamented for Abner and said, Should Abner die as a churl dies, your hands were not bound or your feet put into fetters" (2 Sam. 2:33).

D.   *He who maintains that he did not try to stop Saul interprets the verse in this way:* "Your hands were not bound nor were your feet put into fetters" — *so why did you not try to stop him?* "As a man falls before the children of iniquity so did you fall" (2 Sam. 3:33).

E.   *He who maintains that he did try to stop Saul but got no response interprets the verse as an expression of amazement:* "Should he have died as a churl dies? Your hands were not bound and your feet were not put into fetters."

F.   *Since he did protest, why "As a man falls before the children of iniquity, so did you fall"?*

G.   *In the view of him who has said that he did protest, why was he punished?*

H.   Said R. Nahman bar Isaac, "Because he held up the coming of the house of David by two and a half years."

II.1   **A.**   **And when they provide him with the funeral meal, [all the people sit on the ground, while he sits on a couch] [M. 2:3F]:**

B.   *What is the couch?*

C.   *Said Ulla, "It is a small couch* [Schachter, p. 106, n. 3: not used for rest but placed in the home merely as an omen of good fortune]. *"*

D.   *Said rabbis to Ulla, "Now is there something on which, up to that time, he had never sat, and now we seat him on that object?"*

E.   *Raba objected to this argument, "What sort of problem is this? Perhaps it may be compared to the matter of eating and drinking, for up to this point we gave him nothing to eat or drink, while now we bring him food and drink. But if there is a question, this is the question:* As to a couch [of the present sort], it is not necessary to lower it but it is stood up. *Now if you think that the couch under discussion is a small couch [such as was described above], why is it not necessary to lower it? Has it not been taught on Tannaite authority:* He who lowers beds [in the house of mourning] does not lower the mourner's bed alone but all of the beds in the house.' *[So why not lower the one under discussion?]"*

F.   *But what is the problem? Perhaps it falls into the category of a bed set aside for the storage of utensils, concerning which it has been taught on Tannaite authority:* If it was a bed set aside for storing utensils, it is not necessary to lower it. *Rather, if there is a problem, this is the problem:* R. Simeon b. Gamaliel says, "As to a small couch, one loosens the loops, and it will fall on its own." *Now if you maintain that it is a small couch [such as was described above], are there any loops?*

G.   *Rather, when Rabin came, he said, "One of the rabbis told me, and it was R. Tahalipa by name, that he would frequent the leather-workers market, and he asked one of them, 'What is a couch?' And he was told, 'It is the name of a bed of skins.'* [Schachter, p. 107, n. 2: Its strapping consisted of leather instead of ropes. Not being supported by long legs, it stood very low, and therefore on practical grounds, the first Tannaite authority maintains that is must not be undone and lowered, as the leather will be spoiled through the damp earth, while Rabban Simeon b. Gamaliel holds that there is no fear of this.]"

H.   Said R. Jeremiah said R. Yohanan, "A couch **[20B]** has its webbing affixed on the inside, while a bed has its webbing affixed on the outside."

I.   *An objection was raised:* **At what point in the process of manufacture do wooden objects become susceptible to uncleanness [as useful objects]? As to a bed and a cradle, it is when they have been sanded with a fish-skin [M. Kel. 16:1]** **[which polishes the surface].** *Now if a bed has its webbing on the outside of the frame, what need is there to smooth the wood with a fish-*

*skin? [The webbing covers the wood anyhow]. But both sorts have the
webbing on the inside, and the webbing of a bed is inserted through slits,
while the webbing of a couch is inserted through loops.*

J.   Said R. Jacob said R. Joshua b. Levi, "The decided law accords
            with the opinion of Rabban Simeon b. Gamaliel."

K.   Said R. Jacob bar Ammi, "In the case of a bed the poles of
            which protrude, it is enough to set it up [on one side]
            [Schachter, p. 107, n. 8: because if actually lowered, it may
            appear to be standing in its usual position, since then the poles
            protrude upwards]."

The entire Talmud is devoted to the amplification of the Mishnah's
materials.

2:4A-D

A.   [The king] calls out [the army to wage] a war fought by choice on
            the instructions of a court of seventy-one.

B.   He [may exercise the right to] open a road for himself, and
            [others] may not stop him.

C.   The royal road has no required measure.

D.   All the people plunder and lay before him [what they have
            grabbed], and he takes the first portion.

I.1   A.   *But has not the point [of M. 2:4A] already been made on Tannaite
            authority:* **They bring forth the army to wage a war fought by
            choice only on the instructions of a court of seventy-one [M.
            1:5B]**?

       B.   *Since the Tannaite framer of the passage dealt with all sorts of matters
            pertaining to the king, he included also a reference to his* **bringing forth
            the army to wage war by choice.**

I.2   A.   Said R. Judah said Samuel, "Everything included in the chapter [1
            Sam. 8] on the king the king is permitted to do."

       B.   "But Rab said, 'What is stated in that chapter is included only to
            make the people fear [having a king], as it is said, "You shall in any
            manner set him as king over you" (Deut. 17:15) meaning that fear of
            him should be upon you.'

       C.   *The foregoing dispute follows along the lines of a dispute among
            Tannaite authorities, as follows:*

       D.   **R. Yosé says, "Everything that is spelled out in the pericope
            of the king the king is permitted to do."**

       E.   **R. Judah says, "That pericope is written only to make the
            people revere him [cf. M. San. 2:5C],**

       F.   **"for it is written, 'You will surely set a king over you' (Deut.
            17:14), so that fear of him will be upon you."**

       G.   **And so did R. Judah say, "Three commandments were
            imposed upon the Israelites when they came into the land.**

       H.   **"[They were commanded] to appoint a king, to cut off the
            descendents of Amalek and to build the chosen House.**

       I.   **[T. adds:] "If so, why were they punished in the days of
            Samuel [for wanting a king]? Because they acted too soon."**

J.   R. Nehorai says, "This pericope was written only because of [future] complaints [with the king],

K.   "For it is said, 'And you will say, I will set a king over me' (Deut. 17:14)."

L.   *It has been taught on Tannaite authority:* R. Eleazar [b. R. Yosé] says, "The elders asked in the proper way, as it is said, 'Give us a king to judge us' (1 Sam. 8:6).

M.   "But the ordinary folk went and spoiled matters, as it is said, 'That we also may be like all the nations, and our king will judge us and go before us to fight our battles' (1 Sam. 8:20)" [T. San. 4:5H-Q].

I.3   A.   *It has been taught on Tannaite authority:*

      B.   R. Yosé says, "Three commandments were imposed upon the Israelites when they came into the land. They were commanded to appoint a king, to cut off the descendents of Amalek, and to build the chosen House" [T. San. 4:5K-L].

      C.   Now I do not know which of them comes first.

      D.   When Scripture says, "The hand upon the throne of the Lord, the Lord will have war with Amalek from generation to generation" (Ex. 17:16), one must conclude that first of all they are set up a king.

      E.   For "throne" refers only to the king, as it is said, "The Solomon sat on the throne of the Lord as king" (1 Chr. 29:23).

      F.   Still, I do not know whether they are to build the chosen House first, or to cut off the seed of Amalek first.

      G.   When Scripture says, "And when he gives you rest from all your enemies round about," then it goes on, "Then it shall come to pass that the place which the Lord your God shall choose" (Deut. 12:10), we reach the conclusion that first of all comes cutting off the seed of Amalek.

      H.   So too in the case of David it says, "And it came to pass when the king dwelt in his house, and the Lord had given him rest from his enemies round about," and then it goes on, "that the king said to Nathan the prophet, See, now, I dwell in a house of cedars" (2 Sam. 7:1-2).

I.4   A.   Said R. Simeon b. Laqish, "At first Solomon ruled over the creatures of the upper world, as it is said, 'Then Solomon sat on the throne of the Lord as king' (1 Chr. 29:23). Then he reigned over the creatures of the lower world, as it is written, 'For he had dominion over all the region on this side of the river, From Tifsah even to Gaza' (1 Kgs. 5:4)."

      B.   Rab and Samuel:

      C.   One said, "Tifsah is at one end of the world, Gaza at the other."

      D.   *The other said, "Tifsah and Gaza were next to one another.*

      E.   And just as he ruled over Tifsah and Gaza, so he ruled over the entire world."

F.	But in the end he ruled only over Israel, as it is said, "I, Qohelet, have been king over Israel" (Qoh. 1:12).
G.	Then he ruled over Jerusalem alone, as it is written, "The words of Qohelet, son of David, king of Jerusalem" (Qoh. 1:12).
H.	In the end, he ruled only over his own bed, as it is written, "Behold it is the bed of Solomon, three score mighty men are about it" (Song 3:7).
I.	In the end he ruled only over his staff, as it is written, "This was my portion from all my labor" (Qoh. 2:10).
J.	Rab and Samuel:
K.	One said, "[All he had at the end] was his staff." The other said, "He had his pitcher."
L.	*Did he or did he not recover [his glory]?*
M.	Rab and Samuel:
N.	One said, "He did." The other said, "He did not."
O.	*The one who said that he did not return to his high position says that he first was king and then an ordinary person, and the one who said that he reverted to his glory holds that first he was king, then an ordinary person and finally king again.*

II.1	A.	**He may open a road for himself, [and others may not stop him]** [M. 2:4B]:
	B.	[With reference to M. 2:4D: **All the people plunder... and he takes the first portion**], *our rabbis have taught on Tannaite authority:*
	C.	The royal treasuries [of a defeated foe] belong to the king, and as to the rest of the spoil that the army takes, half is for the king and the other half is for the people.
	D.	*Said Abbayye to R. Dimi, and some say to R. Aha, "Now there is no difficulty in understanding that the royal treasuries should go to the king. That is as things should be. But how on the basis of Scripture do we learn that as to the rest of the spoil, half goes to the king and half to the people?"*
	E.	*[The reply:]* "As it is written, **[21A]**, 'And anointed [Solomon] unto the Lord to be prince and Sadok to be priest' (1 Chr. 29:22). An analogy is drawn between the prince and Sadok. Just as, in the case of Sadok, half belonged to him and half to his brothers [the other priests], so in the case of the prince, half belongs to him and half to his brothers."
	F.	*And how do we know that that was the fact with Sadok himself?*
	G.	*As it has been taught on Tannaite authority:*
	H.	Rabbi says, "'And [the showbread] shall be for Aaron and his sons' (Lev. 24:9) – half to Aaron, half to the sons."

The program of glossing predominates, even though a few rather substantial composites are inserted as supplements of one sort or another.

2:4E-I

E. "He should not multiply wives to himself" (Deut. 17:17) – only eighteen.

F. R Judah says, "He may have as many as he wants, so long as they do not entice him [to abandon the Lord (Deut. 7:4)]."

G. R. Simeon says, "Even if there is only one who entices him [to abandon the Lord] – lo, this one should not marry her."

H. If so, why is it said, "He should not multiply wives to himself"?

I. Even though they should be like Abigail [1 Sam. 25:3].

I.1 A. *Does the dispute [at M. 2:4F, G] bear the implication that R. Judah seeks out the reasoning behind a verse of Scripture, and R. Simeon does not seek out the reasoning behind a verse of Scripture? But do we not find just the opposite? For it has been taught on Tannaite authority:*

B. "As to a widow, whether she is poor or rich, people do not exact a pledge from her, for it is said, 'You shall not take the widow's raiment as a pledge' (Deut. 24:17)," the words of R. Judah. R. Simeon says, "If she is rich, they do exact a pledge from her. If she is poor they do not exact a pledge from her, because one is liable to return it to her, and so may give her a bad name among her neighbors [by constant visitations]." *In that connection we raised the question, What is the sense of that statement? This is the sense of that statement:* Because you take a pledge from her, you are liable to return the object to her, and so you give her a bad name among neighbors [so Simeon]. *What follows is that R. Judah does not take account of the reasoning behind a verse of Scripture, and R. Simeon does take account of the reasoning behind a verse of Scripture.*

C. *In general R. Judah does not take account of the reasoning behind a verse of Scripture, but the present case is different, for he spells out the reason given in the Scripture itself.* What is the reason that "he shall not multiply wives to himself"? It is because "his heart should not be turned aside."

D. And R. Simeon?

E. *He may reply to you that in general, we do interpret the reason behind a verse of Scripture. In the present case, therefore, the Scripture should have stated, "He should not multiply wives to himself" and then fallen silent. I should then have stated on my own then,* "What is the reason that he should not multiply them? So that his heart should not turn away." Why make "not turning away" explicit therefore? To indicate, **Even if there is only one who entices him to abandon the Lord, lo, this one should not marry her [M. 3:4H].**

F. Then how shall I explain the sense of "He should not multiply"?

G. **Even one like Abigail [M. 2:4I].**

I.2 A. *As to the number of eighteen [specified at M. 2:4E], what is the source for that number?*

B. *It is from the following verse of Scripture:* "And unto David were sons born in Hebron, and his first-born son was Amnon, of Ahinoam the Jezreelites, the second, Chileab, of Abigail, the wife of Nabal the Carmelite, the third Absalom, son of Maacah; the fourth, Adonijah, son of Haggith; and the fifth, Shefatiah, son of Abital, and the sixth,

Ithream, of Eglah, David's wife. These were born to David in Hebron" (2 Sam. 3:2-5). *And the prophet said to him,* "And if that were too little, then would I add to you the like of these and the like of these" (2 Sam. 12:8). *Each "like of these" means six more [since the referent is the original six], so eighteen in all.*

C.   *Rabina objected, "Might I say that 'Like of these' stands for twelve, and the second such reference means twenty-four* [Schachter, p. 113, n. 3: He increased the number in geometrical progression, 6, 12, 24]?"

D.   *So it has been taught on Tannaite authority:* "He should not multiply wives to himself" (Deut. 17:17) – more than twenty-four.

E.   *In the view of him who interprets the "and," the number is forty-eight.*

F.   *It has been taught on Tannaite authority along these very lines:* "He should not multiply wives to himself" (Deut. 17:17) – more than forty-eight.

G.   *And what is the reason for the view of the Tannaite authority who framed the Mishnah-passage at hand?*

H.   *Said R. Kahana, "He draws an analogy between the first 'and the like' and the second 'and the like.' Just as the former refers to six, so the latter refers to the six."*

I.   *But there was Michal [beyond the six wives who are listed]?*

J.   Rab said, "Eglah is Michal, and why was she called Eglah? Because she was as beloved of him as a calf [eglah] is of its mother.

K.   "And so it is said, 'If you had not ploughed with my heifer' (Jud. 14:18)."

L.   *But did Michal have children? And is it not written,* "And Michal, daughter of Saul, had no child to the day of her death" (2 Sam. 6:23)?

M.   Said R. Hisda, "To the day of her death she had none, but on the day of her death she had one."

N.   *Now where, in point of fact, is the number of sons reckoned? It is in Hebron. But the case involving Michal took place in Jerusalem, for it is written,* "Michal, daughter of Saul, looked out at the window and saw King David leaping and dancing before the Lord, and she despised him in her heart" (2 Sam. 6:16).

O.   And R. Judah, and some say R. Joseph, said, "Michal took her due punishment, which was childlessness."

P.   *Rather, one might propose,* prior to that event she had children, but afterward she had none.

Q.   [Referring to the issue of the number of eighteen specified in the Mishnah-paragraph], is it not stated, "And David took concubines and wives out of Jerusalem" (2 Sam. 5:13)?

R.   It was to reach the number of eighteen [wives].

S.   *What is the difference between wives and concubines?*

T.   Said R. Judah said Rab, "Wives are with a marriage contract and a rite of betrothal, concubines are without a marriage contract and without a rite of betrothal."

I.3   A.   Said R. Judah said Rab, "David had four hundred sons, all of them born of beautiful captive women. All grew long locks plaited down the back. All of them seated in golden chariots.

And they went forth at the head of troops, and they were the powerful figures in the house of David."

B. And R. Judah said Rab said, "Tamar was the daughter of a beautiful captive woman. For it is said, 'Now, therefore, I pray you, speak to the king, for he will not withhold me from you' (2 Sam. 13:13). Now if you hold that she was the daughter of a valid marriage, would the king ever have permitted [Amnon] to marry his sister? But, it follows, she was the daughter of a beautiful captive woman."

C. "And Amnon had a friend, whose name was Jonadab, son of Shimeah, David's brother, and Jonadab was a very subtle man" (2 Sam. 13:3): Said R. Judah said Rab, "He was subtle about doing evil."

D. "And he said to him, Why, son of the king, are you thus becoming leaner... And Jonadab said to him, Lay down on your bed and pretend to be sick... and she will prepare the food in my sight... and she took the pan and poured [the cakes] out before him" (2 Sam. 13:4ff.): Said R. Judah said Rab, "They were some sort of pancakes."

E. "Then Amnon hated her with a very great hatred" (2 Sam. 13:15): *What was the reason?*

F. Said R. Isaac, "One of his hairs got caught [around his penis and cut it off] making him one whose penis had been cut off."

G. *But was she the one who had tied the hair around his penis? What had she done?*

H. *Rather, say, she had tied a hair around his penis and made him into one whose penis had been cut off.*

I. *Is this true? And did not Raba explain, "What is the sense of the verse, 'And your renown went forth among the nations for your beauty' (Ez. 16:14)? It is that Israelite women do not have armpit or pubic hair."*

J. *Tamar was different, because she was the daughter of a beautiful captive woman.*

K. "And Tamar put ashes on her head and tore her garment of many colors" (2 Sam. 13:19):

L. *It was taught on Tannaite authority in the name of R. Joshua b. Qorhah, "Tamar established a high wall at that time [protecting chastity]. People said, 'If such could happen to princesses, all the more so can it happen to ordinary women.' If such could happen to virtuous women, all the more so can it happen to wanton ones!"*

M. Said R. Judah said Rab, "At that time they made a decree **[21B]** against a man's being alone with any woman [married or] unmarried."

N. *But the rule against a man's being along with [a married woman] derives from the authority of the Torah [and not from the authority of rabbis later on]. For R. Yohanan said in the name of R. Simeon b. Yehosedeq, "Whence in the Torah do we find an indication against a man's being alone [with a married woman]? As it is said, 'If your brother, of your mother, entice you' (Deut. 13:7). And is it the fact that the* son of one's mother can entice, but the son of the father cannot entice? Rather, it is to tell you that a son may be alone with his mother, and no one else may be alone with any of the consanguineous female relations listed in the Torah."

O.   Rather, they made a decree against a man's being alone with an unmarried woman.

P.   "And Adonijah, son of Haggith, exalts himself, saying, I will be king" (1 Kgs. 1:5):

Q.   Said R. Judah said Rab, "This teaches that he tried to fit [the crown on his head], but it would not fit."

R.   "And he prepares chariots and horses and fifty men to run before him" (1 Kgs. 1:5):

S.   So what was new [about princes' having retinues]?

T.   *Said R. Judah said Rab, "All of them had had their spleen removed [believed to make them faster runners] and the flesh of the soles of their feet cut off [Schachter, p. 115, n. 12: so that they might be fleet of foot and impervious to briars and thorns]."*

Unit I clarifies the deeper methodological issue at M. 2:4F-G, and unit II deals with M. 2:4E.

2:4J-N

J.   **"He should not multiply horses to himself" (Deut. 17:16) – only enough for his chariot.**

K.   **"Neither shall he greatly multiply to himself silver and gold" (Deut. 17:16) – only enough to pay his army.**

L.   **"And he writes out a scroll of the Torah for himself" (Deut. 17:17)**

M.   **When he goes to war, he takes it out with him; when he comes back, he brings it back with him; when he is in session in court, it is with him; when he is reclining, it is before him,**

N.   **as it is said, "And it shall be with him, and he shall read in it all the days of his life" (Deut. 17:19).**

I.1   A.   *Our rabbis have taught on Tannaite authority:*

B.   "He shall not multiply horses to himself" (Deut. 17:16).

C.   Is it possible to suppose that [he may not possess] even sufficient animals for his chariots and horsemen?

D.   Scripture says, "To himself," meaning, for his own use he does not multiply them, but he does have a multitude for his chariots and horsemen.

E.   How shall I explain the use of the words "horses" [rather than his horses]?

F.   This refers to horses that remain idle.

G.   How do we know that even a single horse that remains idle violates the commandment not to multiply horses?

H.   Scripture states, "That he should multiply a horse" (Deut. 17:16).

I.   But if the rule is that even a single horse that is idle falls under the prohibition against not multiplying horses, why does Scripture speak of horses in the plural as well?

J. It is to indicate that should one violate the rule, he is liable for violating a negative commandment on account of each horse.

K. *[To review:] The basic consideration, then, is the fact that the All-Merciful has written the word "for himself." Had it not done so, might we have supposed that even the number sufficient for his chariots and horsemen he may not possess? [Surely not, since the king has to have an army.]*

L. *No, it was necessary to make that specification ["to himself"] to allow the king to have a large number [of horses in his army].*

II.1 A. **Neither shall he greatly multiply to himself silver and gold" (Deut. 17:16) – only enough to pay his army [M. 2:4K]:**

B. *Our rabbis have taught on Tannaite authority:*

C. "Neither shall he greatly multiply to himself silver and gold" (Deut. 17:16):

D. Might one suppose that the prohibition covers even enough to pay his army?

E. Scripture says, "To himself" – to himself he may not multiply silver and gold, but he may multiply silver and gold sufficient to pay his army.

F. *[To review:] The reason therefore appears to be that the All-Merciful has written "to himself." Had it not written "to himself," should I have supposed that even sufficient funds to pay his army he may not collect?*

G. *No, it was necessary to include the exclusionary reference, to allow for a large budget.*

H. *Now if you maintain that the word "to himself" serves an exegetical purpose, how will you explain the equivalent usage in "He shall not multiply wives to himself" (Deut. 17:16)?* It serves to exclude from the rule ordinary people, [who may have any number of wives].

II.2 A. *R. Judah contrasted verses as follows:* "It is written, 'And Solomon had forty thousand stalls of horses for his chariots' (1 Kgs. 5:6), and elsewhere, 'And Solomon had four thousand stalls for horses and chariots' (2 Chr. 9:25). How so? If he had forty thousand stables, each one of them had four thousand horse stalls, and if he had four thousand stables, each one of them had forty thousand horse stalls."

B. *R. Isaac contrasted verses as follows:* "It is written, 'Silver was nothing accounted for in the days of Solomon' (1 Kgs. 10:21), and it is written, 'And the king made silver to be in Jerusalem as plentiful as stones' (1 Kgs. 27:3), [so silver did have some value]. *There is no contradiction.* The former verse refers to the time before Solomon married the daughter of Pharoah, the latter verse refers to the time after he married the daughter of Pharoah."

C. Said R. Isaac, "When Solomon married the daughter of Pharoah, Gabriel came down and stuck a reed in the sea, and a sandbank gathered around it, on which the great city of Rome was built."

D. And said R. Isaac, "On what account were the reasons behind rules of the Torah not revealed? Because two verses of Scripture contain an account of the reasons [behind them], and the greatest one in the world [Solomon] stumbled in them.

E.   "It is written, 'He shall not multiply wives to himself' (Deut. 17:17: 'That his heart not turn away'), and Solomon said, 'I shall have many wives, but my heart will not turn away.'

F.   "And it is written, 'When Solomon was old, his wives turned away his heart' (1 Kgs. 11:4).

G.   "And it is written, 'He shall not multiply to himself horses' (Deut. 17:17: 'so as not to bring the people back to Egypt') and Solomon said, 'I will have many horses, but I will not bring the Israelites back to Egypt.'

H.   "And it is written, 'And a chariot came up and went out of Egypt for six hundred shekels of silver' (1 Kgs. 10:29)."

III.1   A.   **And he writes out a scroll of the Torah for himself (Deut. 17:17) [M. 2:4L]:**

B.   *It has been taught on Tannaite authority:*

C.   But that is one the condition that he not take credit for one made by his ancestors.

D.   Said Rabbah, "Even though one's fathers have left him a scroll of the Torah, it is his religious duty to write one for himself, as it is said, 'Now therefore write you this song for yourself' (Deut. 31:19)."

E.   *Abbayye objected [citing a Tannaite teaching],* "And the king writes a scroll of the Torah for himself, so that he should not take credit for one made by his ancestors. That applies to a king, not to an ordinary person."

F.   *No, it was necessary to indicate that he should have two scrolls of the Torah.*

G.   *So it has been taught on Tannaite authority:* **"And he shall write for himself the repetition of this Torah" (Deut. 17:18):**

H.   **He writes for himself two scrolls of the Torah, one that goes out and comes in with him, and one that remains in his treasury.**

I.   **The one that goes out and comes in with him does not, in point of fact, go in with him to the bath house or to the privy, for it is said, "And it shall be with him and he shall read in it" (Deut. 17:19) – thus referring to places in which it is proper to read in it [T. San. 4:8F, cf. 4:7I].**

Composite on the Writing and Revelation of the Torah

III.2   A.   Said Mar Zutra, and some say Mar Uqba, "In the beginning the Torah was given to Israel in Hebrew writing and in the Holy Language [of Hebrew]. Then it was given to them in the time of Ezra in Assyrian writing and in the Aramaic language. The Israelites chose for themselves Assyrian letters and the Holy Language and they left for common folk Hebrew letters and the Aramaic language."

B.   *Who are the common folk?*

C.   Said R. Hisda, "The Samaritans."

D.   *What is "the Hebrew writing"?*

E.   Said R. Hisda, "The <u>Libunaah</u>-script."

III.3   A.   *It has been taught on Tannaite authority:*

B. R. Yosé says, "Ezra was worthy for the Torah to have been given by him, had not Moses come before him. Concerning Moses 'going up' is stated, and concerning Ezra 'going up' is stated. Concerning Moses 'going up' is stated, as it is said, 'And Moses went up to God' (Ex. 19:3). And concerning Ezra, 'going up' is stated, as it is written, 'And he, Ezra, went up from Babylonia' (Ezra 7:6). Just as in the case of 'going up' mentioned in connection with Moses, he taught Torah to Israel, as it is said, 'And the Lord commanded me at that time to teach you statutes and judgments' (Deut. 4:14), [so in the case of 'going up' mentioned in connection with Ezra, he taught Torah to Israel,] as it is said, 'For Ezra had prepared his heart to expound the law of the Lord and to do it and to teach in Israel statutes and judgments' (Ezra 7:10)"

C. And even though the Torah was not given through [Ezra], the script was changed through him.

D. For it is said, [22A] "And the writing of the letter was written in the Aramaic character and interpreted in the Aramaic tongue" (Ezra 4:7).

E. [T. adds:] Just as its interpretation was in Aramaic, so its writing was in Aramaic.

F. And it says, "But they could not read the writing, nor make known to the king the interpretation thereof" (Dan. 5:8) –

G. [T. adds:] this teaches that on that day it was given [and not before].

H. And it says, "And he shall write a copy of this law" (Deut. 17:18) – A Torah which is destined to be changed.

I. And why was [the language] called Assyrian? Because it came up with them from Assyria.

J. It has been taught on Tannaite authority: Rabbi says, "In Assyrian writing the Torah was first given to Israel, and when they sinned, it was changed to Ro as.

K. "But when they repented [T: attained merit in the time of Ezra], Assyrian returned to them, as it is said, 'Turn you to the stronghold, you prisoners of hope, even today do I declare that I will bring back the change unto you' (Zech. 9:12)" [T. San. 4:7L-Y].

L. Why is it called "Assyrian"? Because its script is upright [a play on the consonants shared by the words 'Assyrian' and 'upright'].

M. R. Simeon b. Eleazar says in the name of R. Eleazar b. Parta, who spoke in the name of R. Eleazar of Modi'in, "In the present kind of writing [the Torah] never changed in any way, it says, 'The hooks (vavs) of the pillars' (Ex. 27:10) – 'vavs' that are written like pillars. Just as pillars do not change, so 'vavs' do not change.

N. "And it says, 'And unto the Jews according to their writing and language' (Est. 8:9) – Just as their language has not changed, so their writing has not changed.

O. [T. inserts here:] "And why is it called Assyrian (ashur)? Because they are upright (me'usharim) in their manner of shaping letters."]

P. If so, how shall I interpret, "And he shall write for himself a copy of this law" (Deut. 17:17)?

Q. [This teaches that he writes for himself] two Torahs, one which comes in with him and goes out with him, and one which he leaves in his treasury [T. San. 4:8A-E].

R. As to the one that is to go out and come in with him, he makes it in the form of an amulet and ties it on to his arm, as it is said, "I have set God always before me" (Ps. 16:8).

S. *As to the other [who does not think the writing was changed by deducing that fact from the use of the word "a copy of this Torah"], how does he treat the verse, "I have set God always before me"?*

T. *He interprets that verse in accord with what R. Hannah bar Bizna said.*

U. For R. Hannah bar Bizna said R. Simeon the Pious said, "He who prays has to see himself as if the Presence of God is before him, as it is said, 'I have set God always before me' (Ps. 16:8)."

V. *Now, from the viewpoint of R. Simeon, who takes the view that the script did not change, what is the meaning of the statement, "They could not read the writing nor make known to the king the interpretation thereof" (Dan. 5:8)?*

W. *Said Rab, "The passage was written in Gematria [Schachter, p. 121, n. 4: either a cryptograph which gives, instead of the intended words, its numerical value, or a cipher produced by the permutation of letters, as in this case]: YTT YTT ADK PWGHMT. How did he interpret it to them? [Schachter, p. 121, n. 6: By interchanging the letters of the alphabet, the first with the last, the second with the one before the last, the Hebrew then reads:] Mene, Mene, Tekel, Upharsin: 'Mene, God has numbered your kingdom and brought it to an end. Tekel, you are weighed in the balances and are found wanting. Peres, your kingdom is divided and given to the Medes and the Persians' (Dan. 5:8ff.)."*

X. *Samuel said, [Schachter, p. 121, n. 7: The original words were written vertically, not horizontally, thus:] MMTWS, NNKPY, AALRN."*

Y. *R. Yohanan said, "[From left to right, thus] ANM ANM LKT NYSRPW."*

Z. *R. Ashi says, "It was written in such a way that [Schachter, p. 122, n. 2: Daniel shifted the second letter of each word to the beginning:] NMA NMA KTL PWRSYN."*

What is interesting is that the materials derive from Tosefta's complement to the present Mishnah-chapter, which seems to me to mean that a plan for how a given chapter of the Mishnah moved from document to document, from the Mishnah itself to the Tosefta, from the Tosefta to the framer of the Talmud is at hand. For nothing in the Mishnah's language demands the discussion before us, and the program of topics in the Mishnah hardly prepares us for what we find, first in the Tosefta, only then in the Bavli.

2:5

A. [Others may] not ride on his horse, sit on his throne, handle his scepter.

B. And [others may] not watch him while he is getting a haircut, or while he is nude, or in the bath-house,

C. since it is said, "You shall surely set him as king over you" (Deut. 17:15) – that reverence for him will be upon you.

I.1 A. Said R. Jacob said R. Yohanan, "Abishag would have been permitted to be married to Solomon, but was forbidden to be married to Adonijah.

  B. "She would have been permitted to Solomon, because he was king, and the king is permitted to make use of the scepter of [a former] king.

  C. "But she was forbidden to Adonijah, for he was an ordinary person."

I.2 A. *And what is the story of Abishag [and Bath Sheba]?*

  B. It is written, "King David was old, stricken in years... His servants said to him, Let there be sought..." And it is written, "They sought for him a pretty girl..." and it is written, "And the girl was very fair, and she became a companion to the king and ministered to him" (1 Kgs. 1:1-5).

  C. *She said to him, "Let's get married."*

  D. *He said to her, "You are forbidden to me."*

  E. *She said to him, "When the thief fears for his life, he seizes virtue."*

  F. He said to them, "Call Bath Sheba to me."

  G. And it is written, "And Bath Sheba went into the king to the chamber" (1 Kgs. 1:15).

  H. Said R. Judah said Rab, "At that time [having had sexual relations with David] Bath Sheba wiped herself with thirteen cloths [to show that he was hardly impotent, contrary to Abishag's accusation]."

  I. Said R. Shemen bar Abba, "Come and take note of how difficult is an act of divorce. For lo, they permitted King David to be alone [with the woman], but they did not permit him to divorce [one of his other wives]."

The Evils of Divorce, Particularly of an Aging Wife

I.3 A. Said R. Eliezer, "Whoever divorces his first wife – even the altar weeps tears on that account, for it is said, 'And this further did you do, you cover the altar of the Lord with tears, with weeping and with sighing, in so much that he regards not the offering any more, nor receives it with good will at your hand' (Mal. 2:13). And it is written, 'Yet you say, Why? Because the Lord has been witness between you and the wife of your youth, against whom you have dealt treacherously, though she is your companion and the wife of your covenant' (Mal. 2:14)."

I.4 A. Said R. Yohanan, and some say, R. Eleazar, "A man's wife dies only if people ask for money from him and he does not have it, as it is said, 'If you have not wherewith to pay, why should he take away the bed from under you' (Prov. 22:27)."

B.   And R. Yohanan said, "Any man whose first wife dies is as if the Temple was destroyed in his day. For it is said, 'Son of man, behold I take away from you the desire of your eyes with a stroke, yet you shall not make lamentation nor weep, neither shall your tears run down.' And it is written, 'And I spoke to the people in the morning, and at evening my wife died.' And it is written, 'Behold I will profane my sanctuary, the pride of your power, the desire of your eyes' (Ez. 24:16-18)."

C.   Said R. Alexandri, "For every man whose wife dies in his lifetime the world grows dark, as it is said, 'The light shall be dark because of his tent and his lamp over him shall be put out' (Job 18:6)."

D.   R. Yosé bar Hanina said, "His steps grew short, as it is said, 'The steps of his strength shall be straightened' (Job 18:7)."

E.   R. Abbahu said, "His good sense fails, as it is said, 'And his own counsel shall cast him down' (Job 18:7)."

I.5   A.   Said Rabbah bar bar Hannah said R. Yohanan, "It is as difficult to match people up as it is to split the Red Sea, as it is said, 'God sets the solitary in families, he brings prisoners into prosperity' (Ps. 68:7)."

      B.   Is that really the accepted view? And did not Rab Judah say Rab said, "Forty days prior to the formation of the foetus, an echo goes forth and proclaims, 'The daughter of Mr. So-and-so is assigned to Mr. Such-and-such, [the house of Mr. So-and-so is assigned to Mr. Such-and-such, the field of Mr. So-and-so is assigned to Mr. Such-and-such.'"]

      C.   *There is no contradiction between the implications of the cited views. The former refers to the first marriage, the latter to the second.*

I.6   A.   Said R. Samuel bar Nahman, "Everything can be replaced except for the wife of one's youth,

      B.   "as it is said, 'And a wife of one's youth, can she be rejected?' (Is. 54:6)."

I.7   A.   *R. Judah repeated on Tannaite authority to his son, R. Isaac, "A man finds true serenity only with his first wife, as it is said, 'Let your fountain be blessed and have joy of the wife of* **[22B]** *your youth'* (Prov. 5:18)."

      B.   *He said to him, "Such as whom?"*

      C.   *He said to him, "Such as your mother."*

      D.   *Is this so? And did not R. Judah recite for R. Isaac, his son, the verse of Scripture, "And I find more bitter than death the woman whose heart is snares and nets" (Qoh. 7:26)?*

      E.   *And he said to him, "Such as whom?"*

      F.   *He said to him, "Such as your mother."*

      G.   *She was easy to anger but easy to appease with a good word.*

I.8   A.   Said R. Samuel bar Onia in the name of Rab, "A woman is unformed, and she makes a covenant only with him who turns her into a utensil, as it is said, 'For your maker is your husband, the Lord of hosts is his name' (Is. 54:5)."

B. *It has been taught on Tannaite authority:*

C. A man dies only for his wife, and a woman dies only for her husband.

D. A man dies only for his wife, as it is said, "And Elimelech, Naomi's husband, died" (Ruth 1:3).

E. And a woman dies only for her husband, as it is said, "And as for me, when I came from Padan, Rachel died for me" (Gen. 48:7).

II.1 A. **And others may not watch him [while he is getting a haircut] [M. 2:5B]:**

B. *Our rabbis have taught on Tannaite authority:*

C. A king gets a haircut every day, a high priest on Fridays, an ordinary priest once in thirty days.

D. "A king gets a haircut every day," as it is said, "Your eyes shall see the king in his beauty" (Is. 33:17).

E. "A high priest on Fridays:" Said R. Samuel bar Nahman said R. Yohanan, "Since the priestly watches change [each Friday]."

F. "An ordinary priest once in thirty days:" because it is written, "Neither shall they shave their heads nor allow their locks to grow, they shall only poll their heads' (Ez. 44:20).

G. *We establish an analogy on the basis of the use of the word "allow their locks to grow" both here and in regard to the Nazirite. Here it is written,* "They shall not let their locks grow" (Ez. 44:20) *and there it is said,* "He shall let the locks of the hair of his head grow long" (Num. 6:5). *Just as in the latter context, it is a matter of thirty days, so here it is a matter of thirty days.*

H. *So too we have learned:* **A pledge of Naziriteship not bearing a specified number of days lasts for thirty days [M. Naz. 1:3A].**

I. *And how do we know it in that case?*

J. *Said R. Mattenah, "It is because Scripture has said, 'He will be holy' (Num. 6:5), and the numerical value of the letters for the word 'will be' is thirty."*

K. *Said R. Pappa to Abbayye, "May I propose that it means they should not let their hair grow long [for a full month] [so Schachter]?"*

L. *He said to him, "If it were written, 'They shall not let their hair grow long,' it would have been as you say. But now that it is written, 'They may not let their locks grow long,' the sense is, they may let it become long, but not too long."*

M. *If that is the case, then the rule should apply now, just as does the rule governing excessive use of wine [by priests]. Just as in the case of wine, it was at the time that one came to the Temple that it was forbidden, but when one did not come to the Temple, it was permitted, so in the case of those who let the hair grow long, when one can come to the Temple it is forbidden, but when one cannot come to the Temple, it should be permitted.*

N.   *But is it the case that wine is permitted [even now] when it is not possible to come to the Temple? And has it not been taught on Tannaite authority:*

O.   Rabbi says, "I maintain that priests may not drink wine at any time, but what can I do? For the calamity that has overcome them [in the destruction of the Temple] also is their remedy [since they can drink wine until the Temple is rebuilt]." *And Abbayye said, "In accord with whose view do priests drink wine these days? It is in accord with the view of Rabbi."*

Q.   *That leaves the inferences that, from the viewpoint of rabbis, they are forbidden to drink wine.*

R.   *What is the reason in that special case? It is because of the hope that the Temple will be rebuilt quickly, so that we shall require a priest who is in shape to participate in the Temple cult, and [if priests are drinking wine routinely] such a one will not be available.*

S.   *But can not the same consideration apply here too, namely, we should require a priest who is in shape to participate in the Temple cult [and if the priests let their hair grow long, such a one will not be available]?*

T.   *In this case it is possible that the priest can quickly get a haircut and go into the Temple.*

U.   *But in the other case it is possible that the priest will take a snooze and be ready to go into the Temple.*

V.   *That is in line with R. Aha's statement, "A short walk or a little sleep take away the effects of wine."*

W.   *But in that regard has it not been stated,* Said R. Nahman said Rabbah bar Abbuha, "That statement applies to one who has drunk no more than a quarter-log of wine, but if someone has drunk more than a quarter-log, a walk makes him all the more tired, and sleep will cause all the more drunkenness."

X.   *R. Ashi said, "Those priests who are drunk defile the sacred service, so the rabbis made a decree against priests' drinking wine. Those whose hair is too long do not defile the service, so the rabbis made no decree against that condition."*

Y.   *An objection was raised:* **The following priests are subject to the death-penalty [if they participate in the cult]: those** who have excessively long hair and those who are drunk [T. Ker. 1:5C]. *Now as to the drunk ones, that is in line with the verse of Scripture,* "Drink no wine or strong drink, you or your sons with you, so that you do not die" (Lev. 10:9). *But what is the proof text for those with excessively long hair?*

Z. *The ones who are drunk are comparable to the ones with long hair. It is written,* "Neither shall they shave their heads nor let their locks grow long," followed by, "Neither shall they drink wine" (Lev. 10:9). Just as drunkenness [during the sacred service] is subject to the death-penalty, so participating in the rite with excessively long hair likewise is subject to the death-penalty. *And on the same basis:* Just as priests who are drunk desecrate the sacred service, so priests with excessively long hair desecrate the sacred service.

AA. *That is indeed a question.*

II.2 A. *Said Rabina to R. Ashi, "As to this teaching [that priests whose hair is too long should not officiate and are subject to the death-penalty if they do], before Ezekiel came along, who stated it?"*

B. *[The reply of Ashi:]* "And in accord with your reasoning *[that there should have been a source prior to Ezekiel], what do you make of what R. Hisda said? [R. Hisda said] 'This matter we did not learn from the Torah of Moses, until Ezekiel came along and taught it to us:* '"No alien, uncircumcised in heart and uncircumcised in flesh shall enter my sanctuary to serve me" (Ez. 44:9). Now, before Ezekiel came along, who taught it?' But it was learned as a tradition, and Ezekiel came along and supplied scriptural support for the tradition, and here too, it was a tradition, and Ezekiel came along and supplied a scriptural basis for it."

C. *What is the sense of the statement,* "They shall only poll their heads" (Ez. 44:20)?

H. *It was taught by a Tannaite authority:* "Hair cut in the Julian style."

I. *And what is that style?*

J. *Said R. Judah said Samuel, "An unusual hair cut."*

K. *What is it like?*

L. *Said R. Ashi, "[Schachter, p. 128:] The ends of one row of hair lie alongside the roots of the next."*

M.	They asked Rabbi, "What sort of haircut did the high priest get?"
N.	He said to them, "Go and look at the haircut of [my son-in-law,] the son of Eleasa."
O.	*It has been taught along these lines on Tannaite authority:*
P.	Rabbi says, "It is not for nothing that the son of Eleasa spent so much money for a haircut, but so that he may show what sort of haircut a high priest got."

Unit I is introduced because of the reference at M. 2:5A to using the king's scepter; the further units then continue the foregoing, that is, the theme of the difficulty of divorce and the same general topic, long-term marriage. The focus of interest – priests' haircuts, priests' abstention from wine – indicates that the relevant units have been assembled for a purpose quite other than the amplification of the Mishnah-paragraph at hand. Choosing the entire, completed construction for the present setting came only after the entire composition was complete.

3

Bavli Tractate Sanhedrin
Chapter Three
Folios 23A-31B

3:1

A. Property-cases are [decided by] three [judges] [M. 1:1A].

B. This litigant chooses one [judge], and that litigant chooses one judge, and then the two of the [litigants] choose one more," the words of R. Meir.

C. And sages say, "The two judges choose one more."

D. "This party has the right to invalidate the judge chosen by that one, and that party has the right to invalidate the judge chosen by this one," the words of R. Meir.

E. And sages say, "Under what circumstances?

F. "When he brings evidence about them, that they are relatives or otherwise invalid.

G. "But if they are valid [judges] or court-certified experts, he has not got the power to invalidate them."

H. "This party invalidates the witnesses brought by that one, and that party invalidates the witnesses brought by this one," the words of R. Meir.

I. And sages say, "Under what circumstances?

J. "What he brings evidence about them, that they are relatives or otherwise invalid.

K. "But if they are valid [to serve as witnesses], he has not got the power to invalidate them."

I.1 A. *What is the meaning of the statement,* **This litigant chooses one and that litigant chooses one**? *Surely three [judges] should be enough?* [The sense of the question (Schachter, p. 129, n. 3) is that it is assumed each litigant selects a court, and the two courts choose a third court, which tries the case. Schachter: Hence the questions, why such a clumsy proceeding? Cannot the two litigants jointly select one court which shall try the action?]

105

B.   *This is the sense of the passage:* If this litigant chooses one court for himself, and that one chooses another, then they must together choose a third. [But that is the case only if they differ on the selection of the court. If they do not, then the procedure at hand is not followed.]

I.2   A.   *May even a debtor hold up matters [in the way just described]? [Or must he go to the court chosen by the creditor?]* And has not R. Eleazar said, "That rule applies only to the creditor. But as to a debtor, they force him to go to court in the town of [the creditor]"?

B.   *This accords with what* R. Yohanan said, "This rule applies to law courts set up in Syria." *Here too the rule applies to law courts set up in Syria.*

I.3   A.   *But does [the stated procedure] not apply to court-certified experts?* [Can these too not be disqualified by the debtor (Schachter)?]

B.   *R. Pappa said, "You may even maintain that the rule applies to court-recognized experts, for instance, the court of R. Huna and of R. Hisda.*

C.   *"The debtor has the right to say, 'Am I causing you any inconvenience?'* [Schachter, p. 130, n. 5: For while it is just that the debtor shall not have the power of putting the creditor to great trouble in choice of locale, seeing that the debtor is under an obligation to the creditor, this objection does not hold good when the two courts are so close to one another.]"

I.4   A.   *We have learned in the Mishnah:* **And sages say, The two judges choose a third" [M. 3:1C]:** *Now if it should enter your mind that matters are as we have proposed, that is, that we speak of each litigant's choosing a court, after the litigants have invalidated a court, will that court go and select yet another court! [Surely this is absurd.]*

B.   *And, furthermore, what is the sense of* **This litigant chooses one, and that litigant chooses one [M. 3:1B]?**

C.   *But this is the sense of the passage:* When this litigant chooses for himself one judge, and that litigant chooses for himself another judge, then the two of them choose for themselves one more.

D.   *What is the point in doing it this way?*

E.   *They said in the West in the name of R. Zera,* "Since this party chooses one judge for himself, and that party chooses another judge for himself, and the two of them then choose a third judge, the judgment of the case will be true, [and all parties will trust the decision]."

II.1   A.   **And sages say...[M. 3:1C]:**

B.   *May we say that at issue is the view stated by R. Judah in the name of Rab? For* R. Judah said Rab said, "Witnesses are not to sign a bond unless they know who is going to sign with them." *R. Meir does not concur with the statement made by R. Judah in the name of Rab, and rabbis concur with the statement made by R. Judah in the name of Rab.* [Schachter, p. 130, n. 13: Meir does not require the witnesses to know beforehand who will join them; and in the same way, it is unnecessary for the two judges to know beforehand whether the third will be a fit and proper person, therefore the third is selected by the litigants.]

C.   *No, that is not the case. All parties concur in the view of R. Judah in the name or Rab, and all concur that [the third judge] must be appointed only*

> *with the knowledge and consent of the already appointed judges. Where there is a dispute, it is in the matter of whether or not the litigants must concur in the appointment of the third judge. R. Meir takes the view that [for the third judge] we also require the knowledge and consent of the litigants. Rabbis maintain that while we require the knowledge and consent of the other judges, we do not require the knowledge and consent of the litigants.*

D.   *Reverting to the body of the foregoing statement:*

E.   R. Judah said Rab said, "Witnesses are not to sign a bond unless they know who is going to sign with them."

F.   *So too it has been taught on Tannaite authority:*

G.   Scrupulous people in Jerusalem would not sign a bond unless they knew who was going to sign with them, and they would not take a seat on a court unless they knew who was going into session with them, and they would not join a banquet unless they knew who was going to recline with them.

III.1   A.   **This party has the right to invalidate the judge chosen by that one ... [M. 3:1D]:**

B.   *Does a litigant have the power to invalidate a judge?*

C.   Said R. Yohanan, "The rule pertains to Syrian courts, but not to court-authorized expert judges."

D.   *On that basis of the concluding statement:* **And sages say, "Under what circumstances? When he brings evidence about them, that they are relatives or otherwise invalid. But if they are valid judges or court-certified experts, he has not got the power to invalidate them" [M. 3:1E-G],** *it would follow that R. Meir makes reference also to court-authorized expert judges!*

E.   *This is the sense of the matter:* But if they were valid [judges] they enter the status of court-authorized experts and a litigant cannot declare them to be invalid.

G.   *Come and take note:* **They said to R. Meir, "He does not have the power to invalidate a judge publicly acknowledged as expert" [T. San. 5:2b].**

H.   *State matters in this way:* He does not have the power to invalidate a judge that the public have accepted upon themselves as an expert.

I.   *So too it has been taught on Tannaite authority:* "A litigant may continue rejecting a judge until he undertakes [Schachter: that the action shall be tried] before a court of publicly acknowledged experts," the words of R. Meir. [Schachter, p. 132, n. 2: Hence it is evident that even Meir agrees that experts cannot be rejected.]

J.   *But lo, witnesses fall into the category of experts [since they know what they have seen], and yet R. Meir has said,* **"This party invalidates the witnesses brought by that one, and that party invalidates the witnesses brought by this one" [M. 3:1H].** [So J's premise is contradicted.]

K.   *But lo, in this regard we have the following statement:* Said R. Simeon b. Laqish, "Could a holy mouth have made such a statement?" [How can we permit a litigant to reject the witnesses brought by opposing side?]:

L. *It has been repeated as,* "the witness" [singular]. [Schachter, p. 132, n. 5: Each can reject only a single witness produced by the other; a single witness, of course, is not on a par with an expert recognized by the court or an expert court.] [The argument of K is countered.]

M. *But a single witness for what purpose? If one should say that it is in a monetary case, the All-Merciful has invalidated such testimony, [requiring, after all, two witnesses]. If it is as to the existence of an oath, then a single witness is believed as if he were two, [and so in what sort of case can we be confronting a valid, single witness]?*

N. *It is indeed in a monetary case, and it is necessary to make such a statement, to deal with a case in which the litigant has accepted the evidence of a single witness as though it were two.*

O. *What then does the statement tell us? Is it that one can retract? We have learned this already:* "**If one litigant said to the other, 'I accept my father as reliable,' 'I accept your father as reliable,' 'I accept as reliable three herdsmen to serve as judges,'" R. Meir says, "He has the power to retract." And sages say, "He has not got the power to retract"** [M. 3:2A-C]. [23B] *And in this regard, R. Dimi, son of R. Nahman, son of R. Joseph, said, "For example, if [the litigant] had accepted him as one [of the three judges]."* [Thus we see that the revised statement goes over familiar ground.] [Schachter, p. 132, n. 11: And since one of the three judges is ineligible by biblical law, he may retract; so here, since one witness cannot impose payment by biblical law, although he was accepted as trustworthy, he may retract. Consequently we were already informed of this.]

P. *No, it was necessary to provide two versions of the same principle, [each to deal with a different angle of the matter.] For had the Tannaite authority spoken only of "My father" or "Your father," I might have supposed that it is specifically in such a case that rabbis take the view that he cannot retract [once he has accepted him], because his father or the other party's father is suitable to serve in general, [and not suitable only in the case at hand]. But as to treating one witness as equivalent to two, in general such testimony is not suitable, so I should have said that in such a case, sages concur with R. Meir. [We learn that that is not so.] And had we heard that latter instance, it is in that latter instance that R. Meir takes the position that he does, but in the other, I might have supposed that he concurs with the view of rabbis. [That too is not the case.] Accordingly, it is necessary to express the matter twice.*

Q. *But since the Tannaite framer of the passage in the first clause speaks of "judge," and in the second, "witness" [of the order], it must follow that he has chosen his words very carefully [and so Simeon b. Laqish's thesis cannot stand, since it involves a less than literal reading of the evidence]!*

R. *Said R. Eleazar, "We deal with a case in which a litigant and a third party came forward to invalidate them. [Schachter, p. 133, n. 5: and two have authority to reject, but actually the reference is to two witnesses.]"*

S.   *But does a litigant have such power? He is an interested party in the testimony of the other. [What kind of a witness is he?]*

T.   *Said R. Aha, son of R. Iqa, "We deal with case, for instance, in which [the litigant] has made a public allegation of the invalidity of the other party."*

U.   *What sort of allegation? If I should say it is an allegation that the other party is a robber, does [the litigant] have the power to make such an allegation, since he is an interested party?*

V.   *Rather, it is an allegation as to a disqualification based on a family matter [Schachter: for example, the descendant of an unliberated slave cannot testify]. R. Meir takes the view that the two [the litigant and the other] may give testimony as to the invalidity in the witness's family history, and the man is automatically invalidated. But rabbis hold that, in the end, the litigant is an interested party [and so may not give that sort of testimony either].*

W.   *When R. Dimi came, he said R. Yohanan [said], "The dispute applies to the case of two groups of witnesses. R. Meir maintains that* a litigant has to validate [what he says in respect to his second set of witnesses]. [Schachter, p. 134, n. 1: Therefore, the defendant is not regarded as an interested party when he testifies to the family unfitness of one of the first pair, since the plaintiff is bound to adduce the second set in any case, who are themselves sufficient. Should the plaintiff be unable to adduce a second set, he is the cause of his own loss.] Rabbis take the view that a litigant does not have to validate [what he says in respect to his second set of witnesses], [Schachter, p. 134, n. 2: Consequently, not withstanding his first assertion, he can insist on basing his claims on the first pair of witnesses only, and so the defendant becomes an interested party in seeking to disqualify one of these witnesses]. *But in the case of a single set of witness, all parties concur that* [a litigant] has not got the power to invalidate [the witnesses brought by the other party]."

X.   R. Ammi and R. Assi said before R. Dimi: "What if there is available only a single set of witnesses?"

Y.   "If there is available only a single set of witnesses"! But have you not just stated, "But in the case of a single set of witnesses, all parties concur that a litigant has not got the power to invalidate the witnesses brought by the other party,"?

Z.   Rather, "If the second set of witnesses turns out to be relatives or otherwise invalid, what is the rule?'

AA.   He said to them, "The first set of witnesses has already given its testimony [and that has been accepted and cannot now be rejected]."

BB.   *There are those who say:* Said R. Ashi, "The first set of witnesses has already given testimony."

III.2   A.   · *May we say that at issue is the same principle debated between Rabbi and Rabban Simeon b. Gamaliel. For it has been taught on Tannaite authority:*

B.   He who comes to court on the strength of evidence based both on a deed and on proof of usufruct [to establish a now-contested claim to a field] has his case judged on the strength of the deed," the words of Rabbi.

C.   Rabban Simeon b. Gamaliel, says, "His case is judged on the strength of the evidence of usufruct."

D.   *In that regard we reflected as follows: Could it mean it is with the testimony as to usufruct and* not *as to the testimony provided by the deed? [Surely not, thus] I should say, "Also with the testimony as to usufruct. And the fact of the case is that at issue is whether it is necessary for the defendant to validate [his claim].* [Schachter, p. 135, n. 2: Rabbi maintains that the whole statement must be verified and therefore the deed is necessary, while Simeon b. Gamaliel holds that it need not be verified, just as though he had never made it, and therefore the evidence as to usufruct suffices. Rabbi then agrees with Meir, and Simeon b. Gamaliel with rabbis.]

E.   *No, that is not the case. As to the view of Rabban Simeon b. Gamaliel all parties are unanimous. [Meir and rabbis reject Simeon's view.] Where there is a dispute, it is in regard to the position of Rabbi. For R. Meir concurs with the view of Rabbi. Rabbis, by contrast, will say to you, "The position taken by Rabbi there applies only to the matter of the evidence as to ownership established through usufruct. For this serves if there is evidence that there was a deed. But here, in which the standing of one set of witnesses does not depend upon the standing of another set of witnesses, even Rabbi will concur that it is not necessary for one litigant to validate [his statements in full (Schachter)]."*

III.3   A.   *When Rabin came, he said R. Yohanan [said], "The first clause [of the Mishnah, M. 3:1D]* **[24A]** *speaks of a case in which the witnesses are invalid but the judges are valid. [The litigant proposes to reject both the witnesses and the judges,] and since he proves his case against the witnesses, we accept his claim also against the judges. The latter clause of the Mishnah [M. 3:1H] speaks of a case in which the judges are invalid and the witnesses valid. [The litigant here proves his case against the judges and not the witnesses], so that, since the judges are invalid, the witnesses also are treated as invalid. [That is why, from Meir's position, in both instances we allow one litigant to dismiss the evidence or the judges produced by the other.]"*

B.   *To this thesis Raba objected, "With regard to the view that, since the judges are invalid, the witnesses are provided invalid, the judges also are treated as invalid, in such a case there can always be resort to another court. But since the litigant has proven the judges of the other party invalid, should we say that the witnesses also are invalid? Lo, where will the opposed litigant find other witnesses? He has no more."*

C.   *It is necessary to postulate, therefore, that the opposed litigant* does *have another set of witnesses.*

D.   *But if he does not have another set of witnesses, what will be the result? Will you claim that, here too, [in Rabin's view] the litigant cannot invalidate the witnesses? That is what R. Dimi has already said!*

E.   *At issue between them is the argument of whether or not we invoke the claim that "since... " [since the one thing is so, we concede the other as well]. [Rabin] affirms that reasoning, [Dim] does not.*

III.4   A.   *Returning to the body of the text above:*

B.   Said R. Simeon b. Laqish, "Could a holy mouth have already made such a statement? [How can we permit a litigant to reject the witnesses brought by the opposing side?]"

C.   *It has been repeated as,* "The witness" [in the singular].

D.   Can this [obviously stupid mistake] be true? And did not Ulla say, "He who sees R. Simeon b. Laqish in the school house [sees him] as if he rips up mountains and grinds them against one another"?

E.   Said Rabina, "And is it not the case that whoever sees R. Meir in the school house [sees him] as if he rips up mountains still greater and grinds them against one another? *This is the sense of what he said:* Come and take note of how much [the sages of the Land of Israel] prize one another.

III.5   A.   *It is like the case of when Rabbi was in session and stated,* "It is forbidden to store up cold water [to preserve its cool quality for the Sabbath]."

B.   Said before him R. Ishmael b. R. Yosé, "Father would permit people to store up cold water [to keep it cool]."

C.   He said to him, "The elder has already given a decision, [so I retract my ruling]."

D.   Said R. Pappa, "Come and take note of how much they prize one another. For if R. Yosé were alive, he would sit humble before Rabbi. For lo, R. Ishmael b. R. Yosé filled his father's place and he sat humbly before Rabbi. Yet [Rabbi] has said, 'The elder has already given a decision, [so I retract my ruling].'"

III.6   A.   *Said R. Oshaia, "What verse of Scripture indicates it?* 'And I took unto me the two staves, the one I called 'Graciousness' and the other I called 'injurers,'" (Zech. 11:7).

B.   "'Graciousness' refers to the disciples of sages who are in the Land of Israel, who give pleasure to one another in legal studies.

C.   "'Injurers' refers to the disciples of sages who are in Babylonia, who do injury to one another in their study of the law."

D.   "Then he said, 'These are the two anointed ones' (Zech. 4:14). 'And two olive trees by it'" (Zech. 4:3).

E.   Said R. Isaac, "Yishar refers to the disciples of sages who are in the Land of Israel, who are smooth [and easy going] with one another in study of the law, like olive oil.

F.   "'And two olive trees by it' refers to disciples of sages who are in Babylonia, who are bitter toward one another in legal discussions as olive trees' [wood]."

G.   "Then I lifted up my eyes and saw, and behold there came forth two women, and the wind was

	in their wings, for they had wings like the wings of a stork. And they lifted up the measure between the earth and the heaven. Then I said to the angel who spoke with me, Whither do these bear the measure? And he said to me, To build her a house in the land of Shinar" (Zech. 5:9-11):
H.	Said R. Yohanan in the name of R. Simeon b. Yohai, "This refers to the hypocrisy and arrogance which descended upon Babylonia."
I.	*But did arrogance descend upon Babylonia?*
J.	And did not a master state, "Ten measures of arrogance descended upon the world. Elam took nine of them, and the rest of the world, one."
K.	*Yes, that is indeed the case, for it came down to Babylonia and then went on to Elam.*
L.	Note that it is written, "To build her a house in the land of Shinar."
M.	*So indeed it is proved.*
N.	And has not a master stated, "A symptom of arrogance is poverty," *and did not poverty descend upon Babylonia?*
O.	*What is the meaning of poverty? It is poverty of Torah,*
P.	for it is written, "We have a little sister and she has no breasts" (Song 8:8), on which R. Yohanan remarked, "This refers to Elam, which has had the merit of studying but not of teaching [the Torah]."
Q.	*What is the meaning of the word "Babylonia"?*
R.	Said R. Yohanan, "A rich admixture of Scripture, Mishnah, Talmud."
S.	"He has made me dwell in dark places like those that have long been dead" (Lam. 3:6):
T.	Said R. Jeremiah, "This refers to the mode of Talmud-learning carried on in a Babylonia."

The framer of the Talmud clearly had difficulty in working out the sense of the Mishnah-paragraph and assembled diverse theses on the matter. I have followed Schachter as indicated, but major text-problems require solution.

3:2

A.	"If one litigant said to the other, 'I accept my father as reliable,' 'I accept your father as reliable,' 'I accept as reliable three herdsmen [to serve as judges],'"
B.	R. Meir says, "He has the power to retract."
C.	And sages say, "He has not got the power to retract."

D. [If] one owed an oath to his fellow, and his fellow said, "[Instead of an oath], take a vow to me by the life of your head,"

E. R. Meir says, "He has the power to retract."

F. And sages say, "He has not got the power to retract."

I.1 A. *Said R. Dimi, son of R. Nahman, son of R. Joseph, "[We deal with] a case [at M. 3:2A-C] in which one of the parties accepted such a person as one of the judges."*

B. Said R. Judah said Samuel, "The dispute concerns a case in which [the creditor has agreed to say, should the judges favor the debtor,] 'The debt is forgiven to you.' But in a case in which [the debtor said to the creditor, should the judges favor the creditor,] 'I shall pay you,' all parties concur that [the debtor] has the power to retract [his agreement]." [Schachter, p. 139, n. 5: Less authority is required to rule that one retains what is already in his possession, since possession itself affords a presumption of ownership, than to transfer money from one to another. Hence, only in the former case do the rabbis rule that an undertaking to abide by the decision of an unqualified judge is binding, but not in the latter.]

C. R. Yohanan said, "The dispute pertains to a case in which [the debtor said to the creditor, if the judges rule in favor of the creditor,] 'I shall pay.'"

D. *The question was raised [in interpreting what Yohanan has said], Does he hold that there is a dispute in the case in which the debtor has said, "I shall pay you" [should the court as now constituted so rule], but in a case in which the creditor has said, "The debt will be forgiven to you," all parties concur that one cannot retract? Or is it possible that whether in the one circumstances or in the other circumstance, the same dispute pertains?*

E. *Come and take note:* For Raba has said, "The dispute pertains to a case in which the debtor said to the creditor, 'I shall pay you,' but in a case in which the creditor said to the debtor, 'The debt will be forgiven to you,' all parties concur that he cannot retract." *Now if you maintain the view that [Yohanan] holds that there is a dispute* when the debtor has said to the creditor, "I shall pay you [if the court as presently constituted so orders me]," while in a case in which the creditor says to the debtor, "The debt will be forgiven to you," all parties concur that he cannot retract, *then Raba says exactly what R. Yohanan says, [so Yohanan's position is clear]. If you say that one way or the other, there is a dispute then in accord with whose opinion does Raba make his statement?*

F. *[Within the present thesis,] Raba gives his own opinion. [What Yohanan holds has no bearing.]*

G. *R. Aha bar Tahalipa objected to what Raba said,* "'**If one owed an oath to his fellow and his fellow said, 'Instead of an oath, take a vow to me by the life of your head,' R. Meir says, 'He has the power to retract.' And sages say, 'He has not got the power to retract'** [M. 3:2D-F]. [24B] *Would this not deal with a case of someone who has taken an oath and not paid, in which case it* *is analogous to case in which* the creditor says to the debtor, 'The money will be forgiven to you'? [Schachter, p. 140, n. 4: The plaintiff agrees to abandon his claim as the result of an irregular procedure, whether in the choice of judges or in the form of the oath. This shows that they differ also in respect of 'It be remitted to thee.']"

H. No, the case involves someone who takes an oath in order to collect [*what is owing, rather than someone who takes an oath in order to avoid paying off*]. *In such a case, then, it is equivalent to claiming,* "... I shall pay you...."

I. *The Tannaite authority has presented the case* where the matter depends upon the judgment of others [in which the defendant accepts the judgment of people who cannot serve as judges], *and the Tannaite authority also presents the case* where the matter depends upon the judgment of the [plaintiff].

J. *It was, moreover, necessary to present the same principle in the two distinct cases [of M. 3:2A and D]. For had the Tannaite authority presented only the case in which the defendant makes the matter depend upon the judgment of others, in such a case R. Meir takes the view that the defendant may retract, for he has not decisively agreed to hand over the right of assigning ownership [to the court]. For [in making a mental reservation] he has said, "who can say that the court will give the right of ownership to the other party?" [The reservation is such that his original agreement is null.] But in a case in which the plaintiff has the matter depend upon his own judgment, I might say that [Meir] concurs with rabbis that he cannot retract later on. And had we learned the other case, in such a case rabbis might have taken the view that they did, but in the former, I might have said that rabbis concur with R. Meir. Accordingly, it was necessary to state both cases.*

I.2 A. Said R. Simeon b. Laqish, "There is a dispute about the rule pertaining before the completion of the court decision, but after the completion of the court decision, all agree he cannot retract."

B. And R. Yohanan said, "About retraction after the completion of the court decision there is a dispute."

C. *The following question was raised:* Is the sense of the foregoing statement that the dispute applies after the decision has been handed down, but before the decision has been handed down all parties concur that the litigant can retract? *Or perhaps is it his view that one way or the other, there is a dispute?*

D. *Come and take note of the following statement made by Raba,* "If a litigant has accepted as his judge a relative or an invalid person [proposed by the other party], if this is prior to the completion of the trial, he can retract. If this is after the completion of the trial, he cannot retract."

E. *Now if you take the view that there is a dispute after the completion of the trial, but before the completion of the trial, all parties concur that a litigant can retract, then Raba accords with R. Yohanan vis a vis the position of rabbis. But if you maintain that whether it is before or after the trial is complete, there is a dispute, then in accord with*

		whose view is Raba's statement made? Does it not then indicate that there is a dispute [about retraction] after the completion of the trial?
	F.	*It does indeed show that that is the case.*
I.3	A.	R. Nahman bar Rab sent a message to R. Nahman bar Jacob, "May our master teach us: Is the dispute applicable only to the period prior to the completion of the trial, or does it apply as well to the period after the completion of the trial [so that the litigants may retract even then?] And in accord with which authority is the decided law?"
	B.	He sent word to him, "The dispute pertains to the period after the completion of the trial, and the decided law accords with the view of sages."
	C.	*R. Ashi said, "This is what he sent to him: 'Does the dispute pertain to a case in which [the debtor said], "I shall pay you back" [should the court order me to do so], or does it pertain to a case in which [the creditor said], "I shall forgive the debt to you," and in accord with which authority is the decided law?'*
	D.	*"He sent word to him, 'The dispute pertains to a case in which the debtor said, "I shall pay you," and the decided law accords with the view of sages.'"*
	E.	*That is how the matter was repeated on Tannaite authority in Sura.*
	F.	*In Pumbedita this is how it was repeated on Tannaite authority:* Said R. Hanina bar Shelemiah, "They sent word from the house of Rab to Samuel, 'May our master teach us: What is the law as to the [issue of retraction] prior to the completion of the trial, and in a case in which [a litigant has agreed not to retract through the making of] an act of acquisition?'
	H.	"He sent them word, 'No valid action can take place after an act of acquisition, [and therefore can be no retraction],:

The entire Talmud is a sustained inquiry, beginning to end. My divisions mark off subunits of the whole. I cannot imagine a more successful inquiry into the issues and arguments of a Mishnah-paragraph.

3:3

A.	And these are those who are invalid [to serve as witnesses or judges]:
B.	he who plays dice; he who loans money on interest; those who race pigeons; and those who do business in the produce of the Seventh Year.
C.	Said R. Simeon, "In the beginning they called them, 'Those who gather Seventh Year produce.' When oppressors became many [who collected taxes in the Seventh Year], they reverted to call them, 'Those who do business in the produce of the Seventh Year.'"
D.	Said R. Judah, "Under what circumstances? When [the afore-named (B)] have only that as their profession. But if they have a

profession other than that, they are valid [to serve as witnesses or judges]."

I.1   A.   **[he who plays dice:]** *What does a dice-player do wrong [that he should be invalid as a witness or judge]?*

      B.   *Said Rami bar Hama, "It is because [gambling] is based on an agreement to pay that one hopes will not come to pass, and such an agreement does not effect acquisition."*

      C.   *R. Sheshet said, "Something of that sort does not fall into the category of an agreement to pay that one hopes will not come to pass. Rather, [the reason a gambler is not acceptable is that]* people of that sort do nothing productive."

      D.   *What is at issue [between Rami and Sheshet]?*

      E.   *There is the difference in the case of one who has learned another trade [besides gambling]. [Sheshet would accept an amateur gambler as a judge, Rami would not.]*

      F.   *But have we not learned in the Mishnah:* **Said R. Judah, "Under what circumstances? When the afore-named have only that as their profession. But if they have a profession other than that, they are valid [to serve as witnesses or judges]," [M. 3:3D]?**

      H.   *Does that not indicate that the prevailing thesis of our Mishnah-paragraph is that it is because such as these are not engaged in a productive occupation? That presents a problem, therefore, to Rami bar Hama.*

      I.   *And should you say that rabbis differ from R. Judah,* has not R. Joshua b. Levi said, "In any setting in which R. Judah has said, **[25A]** 'Under what circumstances?' or 'In what case?" that statement serves only to explain the position of sages [with whom Judah concurs]."

      J.   R. Yohanan said, "The expression, 'Under what circumstances?' serves to explain, but 'In what case?' serves to establish a point of difference.'

      K.   *In any event, all parties concur that [when Judah says,]* "Under what circumstances?" *the purpose is to explain what sages have said.*

      L.   *Now will you argue by simply quoting one authority in contradiction to another authority? One authority holds that [the cited language indicates] a point of difference, and the other authority holds that the cited language does not indicate a point of difference.*

      M.   *And do they not differ? And has it not been taught on Tannaite authority:*

      N.   Whether [one of those listed] has only that as his profession and whether he does not have only that as his profession, lo, such a one is invalid. [So there is a direct point of conflict here.]

      O.   *That statement represents R. Judah speaking in the name of R. Tarfon. For it has been taught on Tannaite authority.* R. Judah says in the name of R. Tarfon, "In point of fact, none of them is a Nazirite, because vows of Naziriteship apply only when they are accurately spelled out. [Schachter, p. 144, n. 8, citing Rashi: this proves that in Tarfon's opinion an undertaking dependent on an unknown circumstance is not binding, and therefore the same applies to gambling, each gambler undertaking to pay his opponents without knowing the latter's strength, and therefore the gambler is akin to a robber, whether gambling is his sole occupation or not.]"

II.1 A.   **He who loans money on interest [M. 3:3B]:**

	B.	Said Raba, "One who borrows money on interest is invalid to serve as a witness."
	C.	*But have we not learned in the Mishnah:* **One who loans money on interest... [M. 3:3B]**?
	D.	The point is that any loan on interest [disqualifies all parties to the transaction (Schachter)].
II.2	A.	*Two witnesses gave testimony against Bar Binithos. One said, "In my presence he lent money on interest." The other party said, "To me he lent money on interest." Raba [accepting the evidence of both] declared Bar Binithos to be invalid.*
	B.	*And lo, it is Raba who has said that* one who borrows money on interest is invalid to testify, for such a one is wicked, and the Torah has said not to accept the testimony of a wicked person [cf. Ex. 23:1]!
	C.	*Raba is consistent with another position of his, for* Raba said, "A man is regarded as relation of his own, so a man may not incriminate himself." [So Raba accepted what the man said about the third party and ignored what he said about himself.]
II.3	A.	*There was a butcher who was found to be selling* terefah-*meat under his own authority. R. Nahman declared the man invalid [as a butcher] and sent him out.*
	B.	*The man let his hair and nails grow [as a sign of repentance. R. Nahman considered declaring him valid once again.*
	C.	*Said Raba to him, "Perhaps he is practicing deception."*
	D.	*What is his remedy?*
	E.	*It accords with what R. Idi bar Abin said.*
	F.	For R. Idi bar Abin said, "He who is suspect of selling terefah-meat has only the remedy of going to a place in which people do not know him and returning a lost object of great value, or declaring as terefah-meat a piece of meat of great value that belongs to himself."
III.1	A.	**Those who race pigeons [M. 3:3B]:**
	B.	*What are pigeon-racers?*
	C.	*Here it is explained [as one who says to another], "If your pigeon beats mine...."*
	D.	R. Hama b. Oshaia said, "It is a fowler [Schachter, p. 145, no. 11: one who puts up decoy birds to attract other birds from another's dove cote.]"
	E.	*Why does the one who holds that it is one who says to another, "If your pigeon beats mine....," not concur that it is a fowler?*
	F.	He will say to you, "A fowler is forbidden merely for the sake of public peace, [but is not a thief].
	G.	*And why does the one who holds that it is a fowler not maintain that it is one who says to another, "If you your pigeon beats mine...."?*
	H.	*He will say to you, "This is nothing other than a gambler. [The Mishnah, would not say, "This is nothing other than a gambler.] [The Mishnah would not say the same thing twice.]"*
	I.	*And the other party?*
	J.	*In the case [gambling], the Tannaite law speaks of* one who depends upon his own intelligence, while in the other, he speaks of

depending on the skill of one's pigeon [so the law has to speak of two separate cases].

K.   *And it is necessary to address both cases. For had the Tannaite authority spoken of depending on one's own abilities, it is in such a case in which the participant has not decided to effect acquisition [to the other party, should he lose,] for he maintains,* **[25B]** *"I am confident that I know more than he does."*

L.   *But in the case of one who relies upon the skill of his pigeon, I might say [that the rule] does not [apply, since such a mental reservation cannot apply]. And had the Tannaite authority spoken only of one who depends upon the skill of his pigeon, [then the profit of the bet would be illegal], because the gambler would have thought, "Things depend on the rattle, and I know how to make the rattle work better than he does," but as to one who depends upon his own skills, I might say that the law is not the same. Accordingly it was necessary to specify both cases.*

M.   *An objection was raised:* **He who plays dice [M. 3:31] – this refers to one who plays with blocks of wood.**

N.   **And not only does the law apply to one who plays with blocks of wood, but even to one who plays with nut-shells or pomegranate shells.**

O.   **When does such a person reform himself? When he undertakes to break his blocks of wood and to carry out a complete reformation. [T San. 5:2A-D],**

P.   **So that he will not gamble even at no stakes.**

Q.   **One who lends on interest [M. 3:3B]: All the same are one who lends and one who borrows.**

R.   **When do we recognize their repentance?**

S.   **When they tear up bonds of indebtedness owing to them and [undertake] to carry out a complete reformation [T. San. 5:2E].**

T.   *And they do not lend an interest even to a gentile.*

U.   **Those who race pigeons [M. 3:3B3] – this refers to one who trains pigeons.**

V.   **And not only one who trains pigeons, but even one who trains any other sort of domesticated beast, wild beast, or bird,**

W.   **When are they held to have repented? When he undertakes to break those things which disqualify him and to carry out a complete repentance – –**

X.   *So that they will not practice this vice even in the wilderness.*

Y.   **Sabbatical traders? They are those who [B.:] do business in produce of the seventh year. [T.: who sit idle during the other six years of the septennate. Once the Seventh Year comes, they stretch out their hands and legs and do business in produce of transgression.]**

Z.   **When is their repentance accomplished?**

AA.   **When another year of release arrives, and he will refrain [so one may test him and find that he has reformed himself completely].**

BB.   **R. Nehemiah says, "It must be a reform through property, not merely a reform through what he has said.**

CC.   **"How so?**

DD. "[He must say,] 'These two hundred denars I collected from the sale of Seventh Year [of transgression].' Then [he must] hand them out to the poor" [T. San. 5:25 J-O].

EE. *Now we see that included in the Tannaite statement are cattle* [Schachter, p. 147, n. 5: parallel with pigeons as being trained for racing]! *Now from the viewpoint of him who has said that [under discussion is one who says,] "If your pigeon beats my pigeon," that is how we find included in the list a reference to domesticated beasts. But in the view of him who has said that under discussion is a fowler, does a domesticated beast fall into this category?*

FF. *Indeed so, in the case of a wild ox. For we have learned in the Mishnah:* **A wild ox falls into the category of domesticated cattle. R. Yosé says, "It falls into the category of a wild beast"** [M. Kil. 8:6].

III.2 A. *A Tannaite authority [stated]:* They added to the list robbers and those who impose a sale by force [even though they pay a fair market value].

B. *But a robber is prohibited on the basis of the law of the Torah.*

C. *It was necessary to include in the list [a robber] who grabs something found by a deaf-mute, idiot, and minor. To begin with people thought that that was not commonplace, or because of keeping the peace in general [it was deemed robbery], [but the Torah itself did not prohibit such action so such a robber could testify]. But when they recognized that, in the final analysis, it is a theft of property, rabbis declared such people to be invalid. As to those who impose a sale by force, to begin with it was supposed that such a person in any event pays money [for what he takes], and the imposition [through pressure] was incidental. But when [sages] saw that such people in fact just grab [what they want], rabbis made a decree against them.*

III.3 A. *A Tannaite authority [taught]:* They further added to the list cowboys, tax-collectors, and tax-farmers.

B. *As to cowboys, at first it was thought that it is an incidental act of theft [that they just happen to graze their herds on other people's land]. Once they saw that it was done intentionally, and they drove the herd there to begin with, they made a decree against them.*

C. *As to tax-collectors and tax farmers, at first it was thought that they take only what is specified as the tax. Once they saw that they took more [that the defined tax], they declared them invalid.*

D. Said Raba, "As to the cowboys of whom rabbis have spoken, all the same are one who herds large cattle and one who herds small cattle."

E. *And did Raba make such a statement? And did Raba not say, "One who herds small cattle in the Land of Israel is invalid [as a witness or judge], but one who does so outside of the Land is valid. In the case of one who herds a large cattle, even in the Land of Israel such a one is valid"?*

F. *That statement applies to breeders.*

G. *That moreover is a logical view, for lo, it has been taught on Tannaite authority:* "**I accept as reliable three herdsmen**" [M. 3:2A] [**and they are acceptable**]. [**But otherwise they are not qualified**]. *Now does this not indicate that they are not qualified as witnesses?*

H. *No, they are not qualified as judges. That would be shown, also, by the explicit reference to three herdsmen. Had it been a reference to their serving as witnesses, why make reference to three [when it is usually two witnesses, not three]?*

I. *Then would it not mean that at issue is their serving as judges?*

J. *But why make reference to three herdsmen? Any group of three men who had not learned the law also should be unacceptable [unless a litigant made explicit that he accepts them as judges]?*

K. *This is the sense of what he has said:* "Even such as these, who are not ordinarily found in a settled area."

III.4 A. Said R. Judah, "A shepherd under ordinary circumstances is invalid.

B. "A tax-collector under ordinary circumstances is valid."

C. *The father of R. Zera served as a tax-collector for thirteen years. When the canal-supervisor [who collected money for maintaining the canals] would come to town, when he would see rabbis, he would say to them,* "'Come, my people, go into your chambers' (Is. 26:20)."

D. *When he saw other people who lived in the town, he would say, "The canal-supervisor is coming to down. Now he will kill the father before the son and the son before the father." [The effect was to depopulate the town.]*

E. **[26A]** *Everybody went and hid. When the man came, he said to him, "From whom shall I collect taxes?"*

F. *When he died, he said, "Take the thirteen small coins that I have bound up in my sheet and give them back to Mr. So-and-so. For I took them from him and I did not need them [to pay the tax after all]."*

IV.1 A. **Said R. Simeon, "In the beginning they called them, 'Those who gather Seventh Year produce.' [When oppressors became many, they reverted to call them, 'Those who do business in the produce of the Seventh Year'"] [M. 3:3C]:**

B. *What is the sense of this statement?*

C. *Said R. Judah, "This is the sense of this statement,* "'In the beginning, they ruled that those who gather Seventh Year produce are valid [as witness or judges]. Those who trade in it are invalid. *When those who offered money to the poor became many, so the poor went and gathered Seventh Year produce for themselves and brought it to those [who offered the money],* [sages] retracted and ruled, "Both this one [who gathers Seventh Year produce] and that one [who trades in it] are invalid.'"

E. *The sons of Rahbah objected, "But the language,* **When oppressors became many,** *then should rather be,* **When traders became many!** *Rather: 'In the beginning they ruled that both this one [who gathered the produce] and that one [who traded in it] are invalid. When oppressors became many – (and who are they? they are the collectors of taxes paid in kind, in accord with what R. Yannai announced, 'Go and sow your fields in the Seventh Year, on account of the taxes to be paid in kind'",) they retracted and ruled that those who collect such produce are valid, while those who trade in it are invalid."*

IV.2 A.   *R. Hiyya bar Zaranoqi and R. Simeon b. Yehosedeq were going to intercalate the year in Assya. R. Simeon b. Laqish met them and joined them. He said, "I shall go along and see how they do it."*

     B.   *He saw a man ploughing. He said to them,* "He is a priest, and he is ploughing."

     C.   They said to him, "He can claim, I am an imperial employee in [the property]."

     D.   *Later on they saw another man, who was pruning his vineyard.*

     E.   He said to them, "He is a priest, and he is pruning the vineyard."

     F.   They said to him, "He can claim that he needs [the twigs] to make a bale for the wine-press."

     G.   He said to them, "The heart knows whether it is woven or crooked [a play on the root shared by both words]."

     H.   *Which did he say first? If one should say that it was the first remark, then the other could have given the same excuse, namely, "I am an imperial employee in it." Rather, the latter must have come in the beginning, and only later did he make the other remark.*

     I.   *What difference did it make that he noted that the men [violating the law] were priests?*

     J.   *It is because they are suspect of not observing the taboos of the Seventh Year. For it has been taught on Tannaite authority:* **A seah of heave-offering which fell into a hundred seahs of produce which was grown in the Seventh Year – lo, this is neutralized. If it falls into less than this amount of prohibited produce, let all of the produce rot [T. Ter. 6:3, trans. Avery-Peck, p. 183].** *And we have the following reflection on the rule:* Why should the produce be left to rot? Why not let it be sold to a priest at the price of heave-offering, deducting only the value of that one seah? *To this question R. Hiyya said in the name of Ulla,* "That indicates that priests are suspect of not scrupling in the matter of produce of the Seventh Year."

     K.   *They said [of Joshua b. Levi], "He is a pain in the neck."*

     L.   *When they got there, they went up to the roof and drew the ladder up from below.*

     M.   *[Simeon b. Laqish] went to R. Yohanan and said to him,* "Are men who are suspect about violating the Seventh Year valid to intercalate the year?"

     N.   *Then he said,* "There is no problem to me, since it is parallel to the case of the three cowboys, and rabbis made their calculations depending upon their view."

     O.   *Then he went and said,* "The cases really are not parallel. In that case the rabbis were the ones who made their calculations and intercalated that year. But here it is a conspiracy of wicked men, and a conspiracy of wicked men does not come under consideration [to constitute a board to intercalate the year]."

     P.   *Said R. Yohanan, "That is sad."*

     Q.   *When the men came before R. Yohanan, they said to him,* "He called us cowboys, and the master did not say a thing to him!"

     R.   *R. Yohanan said to them,* "Had he even called you shepherds, what could I have said to him?"

IV.3 A.   *What is a conspiracy of wicked men?*

B.   *Shebna gave expositions before thirteen myriads, while Hezekiah gave expositions before eleven myriads. When Sennacherib came and besieged Jerusalem, Shebna wrote a message and shot it on an arrow: "Shebna and his associates are prepared to make peace, Hezekiah and his followers are not prepared to make peace."*

C.   For it is said, "For lo, the wicked bend the bow, they make ready their arrow upon the string" (Ps. 11:2).

D.   *Hezekiah was afraid. He said, "Is it possible – God forbid – that the opinion of the Holy One, blessed be he, follows the majority. Since the majority are ready to give up, should we too give up?"*

E.   The prophet came and said to him, "Do not say a conspiracy, concerning all of whom this people do say, A conspiracy" (Is. 8:12).

F.   "It is a conspiracy of the wicked, and a conspiracy of the wicked does not come under consideration [to make a decision]."

G.   [When Shebna] went to carve out a sepulchre for himself among the graves of the house of David, the prophet came and said to him, "What have you here and whom have you here, that you have hewn here a sepulchre? Behold, the Lord will hurl you down as a man is hurled" (Is. 22:16). ["You will go away into exile."]

A.   *Said Rab, "Exile for a man is more difficult than for a woman."*

H.   "Yes, he will surely cover you" (Is. 22:16): Said R. Yosé b. R. Hanina, "This teaches that the skin disease broke out on him. Here is it is written, 'Surely cover ...,' and with reference to the skin disease it is written, 'He shall cover his upper lip' (Lev. 13:45)."

I.   "He will violently roll and toss you like a ball into a large country" (Is. 22:18):

J.   *A Tannaite authority [stated],* "He went after the shame of his master's household. Therefore his glory was turned to shame. *When he was going out [to surrender to Sennacherib], Gabriel came along and shut the gate in front of his retinue.*

K.   **[26B]** *"[When the Assyrians] asked, 'Where is your retinue,' he said to them, 'They have gone back on me.'"*

L.   *"They said to him, '"If so, you are ridiculing us."'* They pierced his heels, hung him on the tails of their horses, and dragged him on brambles and thorns."

M.   *Said R. Eleazar, "Shebna indulged himself. Here it is written, 'Go to a companion-steward' (Is. 22:15) and elsewhere it is written, 'And she became a companion-steward to him' (1 Kgs. 1:4). [The same word serves as a companion or a steward.]"*

N.   "When the foundations are destroyed, what has the righteous wrought?" (Ps. 11:3).

O.   R. Judah and R. Ina: One said, "If Hezekiah and his companions had been wiped out [by Shebna], 'what would the Righteous [God] have wrought?'"

P. The other said, "If the house of the sanctuary had been destroyed, 'what would the Righteous [God] have wrought?'"

Q. And Ulla said, "If the intentions of that wicked man had not been upset, 'what would the righteous [Hezekiah] have wrought?'"

R. *Now from the viewpoint of the one who has said,* "If the intentions of that wicked man had not been upset, what would the righteous have wrought?" *that is in line with the verse of Scripture,* "When the foundations are destroyed" (Ex. 7:23). *And from the viewpoint of the one who has said,* "If the house of the sanctuary had been destroyed, what would the Righteous have wrought?" *that is in line with what we have learned in the Mishnah:* **Once the ark was taken away, there remained a stone from the days of the earlier prophets, called Shetiyyah [M. Yoma 5:2A].** [The word used in the verse at hand, translated "foundations" therefore may speak of the "foundations of the house of the sanctuary."] *But as to the view of him who has said,* "If Hezekiah and his companions had been wiped out, what would the Righteous have wrought?" *where do we find that the righteous are called "foundations"?*

S. As it is written, "For the pillars of the earth are the Lord's and he has founded the world upon them" (1 Sam. 2:8) [and the righteous are the foundations].

T. *Or if you prefer, it derives from this verse:* "Wonderful is his counsel and great his wisdom" (Is. 28:29).

U. Said R. Hanan, "Why is [Torah] called wisdom [using the word appearing in the verse cited above]? Because it weakens one's power [the verb for weaken using the same root]."

V. Another answer to the question: It is called such because it was given in secret on account of Satan.

W. Another answer: It is founded on words, which are not material, yet the world rests on them.

X. Said Ulla, "Worries affect one's Torah-study, for it is written, 'He abolishes the thought of the skilled, lest their hands perform nothing substantial' (Job 5:12)."

Y. Said Rabbah, "If they do it for its own sake [rather than for a reward], [worries] have no affect.

Z. "For it is written, 'There are many thoughts in man's heart, but the counsel of the Lord is what shall stand' (Prov. 19:21).

AA. "Counsel in which the word of the Lord is found will stand forever."

V.1 A. Said R. Judah, "[**Under what circumstances? When the afore-named have only that as their profession. But if they have a profession other than that, they are valid to serve as witnesses or judges"] [M. 3:3D]:**

B.   Said R. Abbahu said R. Eleazar, "The decided law accords with the view of R. Judah."

C.   And said R. Abbahu said R. Eleazar, "In the case of all of those [listed in the Mishnah-paragraph] it is necessary to make an announcement in court [as to their invalid status]."

D.   *R. Aha and Rabina dispute about the case of a shepherd.*

E.   *One said, "It is necessary to make an announcement as to his status."*

F.   *The other said, "It is not necessary to do so."*

G.   *Now from the viewpoint of the one who has said that it is not necessary to make such an announcement, that is in line with the statement of* R. Judah in Rab's name, "Any shepherd is invalid" [so it is hardly necessary to say so in a specific instance]. *But from the viewpoint of the one who has said it is necessary to make such an announcement, what is the sense of the statement,* "Any shepherd is invalid"? [Schachter, p. 156, n. 4: Once a proclamation is made, he ceases to be a shepherd in general and becomes an individualized person.]   [So an announcement in one case is counterproductive.]

H.   *It is that, in general, we make such a proclamation [that he is invalid as a witness, even though we have no evidence that he has driven his flock into other peoples' property].*

V.2   A.   *There was the case of a deed of gift that bore the signature of two thieves.*

B.   *R. Pappa bar Samuel considered declaring it valid, for lo, no announcement had been made concerning their [status as known thieves].*

C.   *Said R. Raba to him, "While we require an announcement as to the character of a robber as defined by rabbis, do we require the same sort of public announcement on the status of a robber as defined by the law of the Torah? [Currently we do not, and the deed is invalid on its own, without reference to the failure of the court to reject the testimony of the two robbers]."*

V.3   A.   Said R. Nahman, "Those who 'eat something else' [accept charity from gentiles] are invalid for testimony.

B.   *"That applies when they do so in public, but if it is in private, the rule does not apply.*

C.   *"And as to doing so in public, we have stated that rule only in a case in which it is possible for the recipient to derive support in secret but he disgraces himself in public.*

D.   *"But if it is not possible for him to do so, then it is his way of sustaining life [and not reprehensible]."*

E.   Said R. Nahman, "One suspected of having sexual relations with a consanguineous women is valid to give testimony."

F.   *Said R. Sheshet, "Answer, my lord! This man will have forty stripes on his shoulders [for violating the sexual taboo] and yet is he valid to give testimony?"*

G. Said Raba, "And R. Nahman concedes that, in the matter of testimony given concerning the status of a woman, such testimony is invalid [if given by that man]."

H. *Said Rabina, and some say, R. Pappa, "That rule applies only to free a woman from marital bonds, but as to subjecting her to marital vows, we have no objection [to his testimony]."*

I. *That is self-evident. [Why not accept his testimony when he has no interest in the matter?] What might you have said? Such a situation [her getting married] would be his preference [for the woman, since she would not make demands and be available to him when he wanted her]. For it is written, "Stolen waters are sweet" (Prov. 9:17). So we are informed that, [so far as this man is concerned,] the longer she remains in her present status, the more available she will be to him.*

L. *And R. Nahman said, "One who steals [produce from the fields] in Nisan or in Tishri does not fall into the category of a thief.* That rule applies to a sharecropper, and to some small volume of produce, and for some sort of produce on which labor is now complete."

M. *The sharecropper of R. Zebid stole a qab of barley, and another stole a cluster of unripe dates, and he declared them invalid [as witnesses].*

V.4 A. *Some grave-diggers buried a corpse on the first festival day of Pentecost.*

B. *R. Pappa excommunicated them and declared them invalid to give testimony.*

C. *But R. Huna, son of R. Joshua, declared them valid to give testimony.*

D. *Said R. Pappa to him, "But lo, they are wicked."*

E. *[The other had the theory that] they thought they were doing a religious duty.*

F. *"But lo, I excommunicated them."*

G. *"They thought that the rabbis in that way carried out an act of expiation for their [sin]."*

V.5 A. *It has been stated:*

B. [27A] As to a witness who is proved to have conspired to commit perjury,

C. Abbayye said, "[When between the time he gave his testimony and the time he was proved a perjurer, some days have elapsed], his status as a witness is treated as invalid retrospectively [Schachter, p. 158, n. 6: from the time he began to give his evidence in court, and all the evidence he has given in the intervening period becomes invalidated]."

D. And Raba said, "It is only from that point onward that he becomes an invalid witness."

E. Abbayye said, "Retrospectively he is treated as an invalid witness, *for from the moment at which he gave his [perjured] testimony, he entered the status of the wicked, and the Torah has said,* 'Do not put your hand with the wicked' (Ex. 23:1), meaning, 'Do not make a wicked man a witness."

F. Raba said, "It is only from that point onward that he becomes an invalid witness, for the law governing the demonstration of conspiratorial perjury [involving two false witnesses who have agreed to testify against a man] constitutes an anomaly [Schachter]. *[How so?] Why do you rely upon these two witnesses [who testify against the original witnesses and claim they are perjurers]? Rely on the others [the original pair]!*

G.   *"Accordingly, you have agains t [this witness] only a [claim that applies] from the time of the application to him of the anomalous [law] and onward."*

H.   *There are those who say that Raba concurs in Abbayye's reasoning. But on what grounds has he ruled that the disqualification [is not retroactive] but only from that point onward?*

I.   *It is on account of causing loss to the purchasers.* [Schachter, p. 158, n. 9: If purchasers have transacted business through documents signed by the perjured witnesses, having been unaware of their disqualification, they would become involved in considerable loss, should their evidence be declared invalid.]

J.   *What would be at issue [between the two theories of Raba's position]?*

K.   *A case in which two witnesses gave evidence against one witness [as a perjurer, but not against the other witness in the case].*

L.   *Or there would also be the case in which the grounds for disqualifying the witness was that he was a robber.* [Schachter, p. 159, n. 2.: Here again the argument that it is an anomalous procedure no longer holds good.]

M.   *And R. Jeremiah of Difti said, "R. Pappa made a concrete decision in a case in accord with the position of Raba."*

N.   *Mar, son of R. Ashi said, "The decided law accords with the view of Abbayye."*

O.   *And the decided law accords with the view of Abbayye in six matters.*

V.6   A.   As to an apostate who eats carrion because he is hungry, all parties concur that he is invalid [as a witness].

B.   If he did so out of spite [to defy the law],

C.   Abbayye said, "He is invalid."

D.   Raba said, "He is valid."

E.   Abbayye said, "He is invalid, *because he falls into the category of the wicked, and the All-Merciful has said, 'Do not put your hand with the wicked' (Ex. 21:1)."*

F.   Raba said, "He is valid. *We require that [the wicked act be done] for a gainful purpose [and not merely as a provocation, in which case we ignore the act]."*

G.   *An objection was raised:* "Do not accept the wicked as a witness" means, "do not accept as a witness someone who is a despoiler [Schachter, p. 160, n. 3: who violates another's rights to satisfy his own greed]," referring to robbers and people who violate oaths.

H.   *Does this not mean that all the same are vain oaths and oaths dealing with property? [In that case, like a vain oath, which is merely provocative, so eating carrion, simply as act of spite, disqualifies a person as a witness].*

I. *No, both references deal with oaths involving property, and why is the word used in the plural? [It is not to encompass two types of oaths, but simply to speak of] oaths in general.*

J. *An objection was raised:* "Do not make a wicked man a witness. Do not make a despoiler a witness. This refers to robbers and those who lend on interest." *[This wicked act involves concrete gain, not merely spite, and that constitutes] a refutation of the view of Abbayye, does it not?*

K. *It indeed constitutes a refutation of his view.*

L. *May we say that the following Tannaite dispute runs parallel [to that of Abbayye and Raba]?*

M. **"One who has been proved a perjurer is invalid for giving testimony in regard to any matter of the Torah," the words of R. Meir.**

N. **Said to him R. Yosé, "Under what circumstances? In the case of one who has been proved a perjurer in a capital-case [M. 1:8E]. But if he has been proved a perjurer only in a property-case, he is valid in a capital-case [T: he is invalid only in regard to that specific matter of testimony along]" [T. Mak. 1:11A-B].**

O. *May we then say that Abbayye accords with the view of R. Meir and Raba with the view of R. Yosé?*

P. *[That is to say,] Abbayye accords with the view of R. Meir, who has said that we declare [the witness disqualified] in major cases on account of [his disqualification in] minor ones.*

Q. *And Raba concurs with R. Yosé, who holds the view that we impose disqualification on witnesses' right to testify in minor cases on the basis of disqualification in major ones, but we do not impose disqualification in a major case on account of disqualification in a minor one.*

R. *No, as to the view of R. Yosé, the authorities at hand do not dispute.* [Schachter, p. 161, n. 3: Abbayye can certainly <u>not</u> agree with Yosé, for he can in no wise hold that a perjured witness in civil cases is eligible in capital cases].

S. *Where there is a dispute, it concerns the view of R. Meir.*

T. *Abbayye concurs with the position of R. Meir.*

U. *And Raba maintains that R. Meir holds his position in the case at hand only in the instance of one who has been proven a perjurer in a monetary case, because such a one who has behaved badly toward heaven [by taking an oath that has now been proved to be false in a monetary claim] and also has behaved badly toward human beings [in that same monetary case].*

V. *But in the present case, in which the man has behaved badly toward heaven [by eating carrion], but has not behaved badly toward human beings, that is not the rule.*

W. *And the decided law accords with the view of Abbayye.*

X. *But has Abbayye not been refuted?*

Y.   *That [received law that served to refute Abbayye's ruling]
        accords with the position of R. Yosé.*

Z.   *Even though it does derive from R. Yosé, where there is a
        dispute between R. Meir and R. Yosé, the decided law
        accords with the view of R. Yosé.*

AA.   *That case is different, because the Tannaite authority who
        framed the passage gave the view of R. Meir anonymously
        [and so as the decided law, rather than as the opinion of a
        single individual].*

BB.   *And where does this anonymous version of the law [in
              accord with Meir's] view occur?*

CC.   *It is in the case of Bar Hama, who killed someone. The
              exilarch said to R. Abba bar Jacob, "Go, look into the
              matter. If beyond doubt he has committed murder, put
              out his eyes."*

DD.   *Two witnesses came to court and testified that had
              beyond doubt he committed murder.*

EE.   *[Bar Hama] went and brought two witnesses who
              testified against one of the two witnesses against him,
              [in the following way]:*

FF.   *One [of the two witnesses brought by Bar Hama]
              testified, "In my presence he stole a qab of barley."*

GG.   *The other testified, "In my presence he stole **[27B]** the
              handle of a spear."*

HH.   *[Abba] said to [Bar Hama], "What were you thinking?
              That the law accords with R. Meir [that one who is
              proved a perjurer in a monetary matter also is
              dismissed as a witness in a capital case]?*

II.   *"Where there is a dispute between R. Meir and R.
              Yosé, the divided law accords with R. Yosé. And
              as to R. Yosé, has he not said:* **One who has been
              proved a perjurer only in a property-case is
              valid to testify in a capital-case [T. Mak. 1:11B]?"**

JJ.   *Said R. Pappi to him, "That rule applies only in a case
              in which a Tannaite authority has not given R. Meir's
              version of the rule anonymously. But here the
              Tannaite authority has given R. Meir's version of the
              rule anonymously."*

KK.   *And where do we find out that that is the fact?*

LL.   *May we say that it is from the following rule,
                    which we have learned in the Mishnah:*

MM.   **Whoever is worthy to judge capital-cases is
                    worthy to judge property-cases, and there is
                    one who is worthy to judge property-cases
                    and is not worthy to judge capital-cases [M.
                    Nid. 6:4F].**

NN.   *Now whose opinion [is given anonymously,
                    therefore as the decided law, in the present rule]?*

OO.   *Should we propose that it is R. Yosé's opinion, lo,
                    we have the fact that, in his view, one who has
                    been proven a perjurer in a monetary-case*

	remains valid to testify in a capital-case even though he is invalid to testify in a property-case.
PP.	*Is it not, then, R. Meir's view?*
QQ.	*Why [are we required to turn to Meir]? Perhaps the passage speaks of people who are invalid because of [defective] genealogy.*
RR.	*For if you do not conclude that that is the reference, take note of the concluding part of the same passage:*
SS.	**Whoever is suitable to judge is suitable to give testimony, but there is one who is suitable to give testimony but is not suitable to judge [M. Nid. 6:4G].**
TT.	*Why would he be unsuitable? Because he has been proved to be a perjurer in a capital-case? But could such a one be suitable to judge a property-case? Lo, in the opinion of all parties, such a one is invalid [to judge or testify in a property-case].*
UU.	*Accordingly, it must speak of one who is invalid in one account of impaired genealogy.*
VV.	*Here too [M. Nid. 6:4F] we speak of one who is invalid on account of impaired genealogy.*
WW.	*But what follows is where the rule has been given anonymously [in the version that Meir would approve].*
XX.	*As we have learned in the Mishnah:* **And these are those who are invalid to serve as witnesses or judges: he who plays dice, he who loans money on interest, those who race pigeons, and those who do business in the produce of the seventh year [M. 3:3A-B],** and slaves. **This is the governing criterion: For any sort of testimony for which a woman is not valid, they too are not valid [cf. T. San. 5:2V].**
YY.	*Whose opinion is before us? Should we propose that it is R. Yosé, lo, there is the matter of testimony in capital-cases, which a woman is not valid to give, but which they are valid to give. Is it not then the position of R. Meir [stated anonymously and therefore as the decided law]?*
ZZ.	*Bar Hama got up and kissed him on his feet and pledged to pay the poll-tax for him for the rest of his life* [for it is now proved that evidence of people declared invalid because of monetary perjury in a monetary case is invalid in a capital case. One of the witnesses against Bar Hama was thus disqualified (Schachter)].

In all matters we remain well within the framework of discourse on the Mishnah-passage at hand, so the entire composition serves to explain or amplify the Mishnah-paragraph.

3:4-5

A.	And these are relatives [prohibited from serving as one's witnesses or judges]: (1) one's father, (2) brother, (3) father's brother, (4) mother's brother, (5) sister's husband, (6) father's sister's husband, (7) mother's sister's husband, (8) mother's husband, (9) father-in-law, and (10) wife's sister's husband –
B.	they, their sons, and their sons-in-law;
C.	but the step-son only [but not the step-son's offspring].
D.	Said R. Yosé, "This is the version of R. Aqiba. But the earlier version [is as follows]:
E.	"His uncle, the son of his uncle [Lev. 25:49] and anyone who stands to inherit him [M. B.B. 8:1]."
F.	And anyone who is related to him at that time,
G.	[If] one was a relative but ceased to be related, lo, that person is valid.
H.	R. Judah says, "Even if his daughter died, if he has sons from her, lo, [the son-in-law] is deemed a relative.

3:4

A.	"One known to be a friend and one known to be an enemy –
B.	"one known to be a friend – this is the one who served as his groomsman;
C.	"One known to be an enemy – this is one who has not spoken with him for three days by reason of outrage."
D.	They said to [Judah], "Israelites are not suspect for such a factor."

3:5

I.1	A.	[And these are relatives prohibited from serving as one's witnesses or judges: one's father:] *What is the scriptural basis for the rule at hand?*
	B.	*It accords with what our rabbis have taught on Tannaite authority:*
	C.	"Fathers shall not be put to death for the children" (Deut. 24:16).
	D.	What is the sense of the passage?
	E.	If it is to teach that fathers should not be put to death on account of the transgression of children, or children on account of the transgression of the fathers, lo, it already has been stated, "Every man shall be put to death for his own sin" (Deut. 24:16).
	F.	Rather, "Fathers shall not be put to death for the children" must mean, "through the testimony given by children" and "Children will not be put to death for the fathers" must mean, "through the testimony given by fathers."
	G.	And is it not the case that children will not be punished for the transgression of the fathers?
	H.	*And has it not been written, "Visiting the iniquities of the fathers upon the children" (Ex. 34:7)?*

I.   That passage speaks of those who adhere to the pattern of deeds of their fathers.

J.   *That is in accord with what has been taught on Tannaite authority:*

K.   "And also in the iniquities of their parents shall they pine away with them" (Lev. 26:39). That passage speaks of those who adhere to the pattern of deeds of their fathers.

L.   You maintain that it is when they adhere to that pattern of deeds. But perhaps it refers even to a case in which they do not adhere?

M.   When it says, "Every man shall be put to death for his own sin" (Lev. 26:39), lo, [we speak of those who do not adhere to their fathers' deeds, so the passage at hand must speak of] those who do adhere to their fathers' deeds.

N.   And is that not the case? And lo, it is written, "and they shall stumble upon another" (Lev. 26:37).

O.   This means that one person will stumble on account of the transgression of his brother.

P.   It teaches that all of them are held responsible for one another [so one may bear the sin of another].

Q.   That passage speaks of a case in which someone could have prevented [evil from being done] and did not do so.

I.2   A.   [28A] *We have found proof, therefore, that fathers may not testify against children and children against fathers, all the more so fathers [that is, brothers] cannot testify against one another.*

B.   *How do we know that sons cannot testify against sons [that is, cousins, sons of fathers who are brothers]?*

C.   If matters were otherwise, Scripture should have written, "Fathers shall not die on account of the testimony of a son."

D.   *What is the meaning of the use of the plural, "sons"? It serves to indicate that even sons [may not testify] against one another.*

E.   *We have found proof, therefore, that sons may not testify against one another. How do we know that sons [brothers may not testify together in a case involving a third party]?*

F.   *Said Rami b. Hama, "It is based on reasoning, as it has been taught on Tannaite authority:* 'Witnesses are declared to be perjurers [and have to suffer the penalty they conspired to inflict] only if the two of them are so proved [by corroborating one another's perjured testimony].' *Now if you take the view that brothers together may testify against a third party, it may turn out that a perjured witness may be put to death on the basis of testimony given by his brother* [supporting what he had said in testimony at the trial]. [Schachter, p. 166, n. 5: For had no one else supported him, he could not have been declared a perjured witness. Consequently, he would incur the death penalty through his kinsman's testimony.]"

G.   *Said Raba to him, "And according to your reasoning, let us take up that which we have learned in the Mishnah:* **[If there are] three brothers, and another party joins together with each of them [to give evidence of three years of usufruct of a given property, which will prove that the claimant has established right of ownership] – lo, these constitute three distinct acts of testimony. And they count as a single act of witness should the evidence be proved false [M.**

B.B. 3:4F-H]. It thus turns out that a perjured witness will have to pay monetary compensation on the basis of the testimony given by his brother. *But the penalty for false testimony derives from evidence brought by others. Here too, the penalty of false testimony will derive from evidence brought by others [so the consideration raised by Rami B. Hama is not decisive].* But if it were so [that brothers may testify together in a case involving a third party,] then Scripture should read, 'And a son on account of fathers,' or, 'and they on account of the fathers.' *Why the stress on 'and sons'? It is to show that sons [related persons] may not testify together in regard to outsiders.*"

I.3   A.   *We now have proven that people related through the father [may not give evidence together]. How do we know that people related through the mother may not do so?*

        C.   Scripture makes reference to "fathers" two times. If [the second, instance] is not needed to deal with the category of the father's relatives, apply it to the category of the mother's relatives [so excluding them from the list of those who may judge or testify].

        D.   *We have now proven that [these parties] may not participate in a decision of guilt. How do we know that they also may not participate in a decision leading to acquittal?*

        E.   Scripture makes reference to "they shall be put to death" two times. If [the second, repeated instance is not needed to deal with the category of cases involving a decision of guilt,] apply it to the category of cases involving a decision of innocence.

        F.   *We have now proven that the rule is such in capital-cases. How do we know that it is the same for property-cases?*

        G.   Scripture has said, "You shall have one law" (Lev. 24:22), a law that is equal for you [in all sorts of cases].

II.1   A.   **[and their sons-in-law:]**
               [Schachter, p. 167, n. 5: To understand Rab's statement and the others that follow it is necessary to give some explanation of affinity and consanguinity in Talmudic law. Relationships between persons are divided into two categories: (a) relationships between persons governed by the ties of consanguinity, i.e., persons of the same blood either lineally or collaterally; (b) relationships through marriage, i.e., affinity. And on the principle that man and wife are considered as one, the relatives of the one are related to those of the other by affinity. Again, the rules by which kinsfolk are excluded from bearing testimony for or against each other affect only certain degrees of relationship, e.g., relatives in the first degree, such as father and son, or brothers may not testify for or against those of the first degree, e.g., a nephew for his uncle; relatives in the second degree may not testify for or against each other, e.g., first cousins. On the other hand, relatives in the third degree may testify for or against relatives in the first, e.g., a grand-nephew in respect of an uncle, and relatives in the third degree may testify for or against relatives in the second degree, e.g., first cousins for second cousins. It should be noted that the ineligibility is mutual.]
               Said Rab, "My father's brother [my paternal uncle] may not give testimony for me, nor may his son or son-in-law, and so too, I may not testify for him, nor my son or son-in-law. But why should this

be the case? Would this not involve relationships of the third and first removes? [Schachter, p. 167, n. 7: Rab's son is a grand-nephew of Rab's uncle, hence Rab's son is a relative of the third degree (or remove) to Rab's uncle, who is of the first degree in relation to Rab's father]. *But we have learned [in the Mishnah at hand] that relatives of the second remove [are forbidden to testify for] relatives of the second remove [e.g., first cousins], and relatives of the second remove cannot testify for those of the first remove [uncles], but not that relatives of the third remove may not testify for relatives of the first remove."*

B. *What is the sense of "one's son-in-law" which has been listed in our Mishnah paragraph [at M. 3:4B]? It is the son-in-law of one's son.* [Schachter, p. 168, n. 3: The Mishnah is therefore to be explained thus: All these – including the uncle – with their sons and their sons' sons-in-law, hence this teaches the inadmissibility of relatives of the third degree].

C. *But should the Tannaite authority not include the [uncle's] son's son* [which is a more direct way of stating a third degree of relationship (Schachter)]?

D. *In framing matters as he has, the Tannaite authority has informed us of a peripheral fact, namely, the husband is equivalent [in the counting of relationships] to his wife.* [Schachter, p. 168, n. 5: Just as the daughter of his uncle's son is a relation of the third degree, so is her husband.]

E. *Then let us consider that which R. Hiyya has taught on Tannaite authority:*

F. [The Mishnah lists] eight generative relationships which add up to twenty-four [each counted along with the son and the son-in-law]. *[But if the son-in-law of the uncle's son counts as a relative of the third degree] they are, in point of fact, thirty-two [eight fathers, sons, grandsons, and sons-in-law of sons].*

G. Accordingly, [M. 3:4B] refers to one's son-in-law [and not to the son's son-in-law]. *And why does [Rab] call him the son-in-law of [the uncle's] son [Schachter]?*

H. *Since the relationship derives from [affinity, that is, marriage], he is counted as yet another generation [a third degree relation (Schachter, p. 168, n. 12)].*

I. *If that is the case, then we deal with one in the third degree vis a vis one in the second degree.* [Schachter, p. 168, n. 13: A man and his uncle's son-in-law are in the relationship of the second to the third degree. Thus if A and B are brothers, then C, A's son, and B are second and first degrees; C and D, B's sons, are two seconds; therefore C and E, B's sons-in-law, rank as second and third, since a son-in-law according to the last answer is one degree further removed than a son.] *[And testimony involving a third and second degree relation is forbidden], while Rab permits it* [Schachter, p. 169, n. 1: in that he said, "I, my son and my son-in-law (a relative of the third degree) may not bear testimony against my uncle," from which it may be inferred that Rab's son (third degree) may bear testimony against the uncle's son (second degree)].

J. *Rab accords with the view of R. Eleazar.*

K.   *For it has been taught on Tannaite authority:*

L.   R. Eleazar says, "Just as father's brother [my uncle], as well as his son and his son-in-law, may not testify against me, so the son of father's brother as well as his son and his son-in-law, may not testify against me."

M.   *Still we deal with relatives of the third and second degrees [Schachter, p. 169, n. 3: C and F, B's grandson, are second and third degrees], and Rab validates testimony of people who stand in that relationship.*

N.   *Rab concurs with him on one point and differs from him on another.*

O.   *What is the scriptural basis for the view of Rab?*

P.   It is because Scripture has said, "Fathers shall not be put to death for sons and sons... (Deut. 24:16). Now the use of the word "and" serves to encompass yet another generation [within the list of those disqualified for testimony concerning one another].

Q.   And R. Eleazar? [Schachter, p. 169, n. 8: Why does he rule that even second and third degrees are inadmissible?]

R.   *The All-Merciful has said, "Upon sons" with the sense that the invalidity of fathers' testimony is thrown onto the sons [Schachter, p. 169, n. 10: that is, who are disqualified in respect of the fathers are likewise disqualified in respect of the sons.]*

II.2 A.   Said R. Nahman, "The brother of my mother-in-law may not testify for me; the son of the sister of my mother-in-law may not testify for me.

      B.   *"So does the Tannaite authority repeat the matter:* **Sister's husband, father's sister's husband, mother's sister's husband... they, their sons, and their sons-in-law [M. 3:4A-B]."**

II.3 A.   *Said R. Ashi, "When we were at Ulla's house, the question troubled us: As to the brother of one's father-in-law, what is his status? As to the son of the brother of one's father-in-law, what is his status? As to the son of the sister of one's father-in-law, what is his status?*

      B.   *"He said to us, 'You have learned in the Mishnah:* **Brother, father's brother, mother's brother... they, their sons, and their sons-in-law [M. 3:4A-B]**.*"*

II.4 A.   *Rab went to buy* **[28B]** *parchment. People asked him,* "What is the law on a man's testifying concerning the wife of his step-son?"

      B.   *[He answered,] "In Sura they rule that the husband is equivalent to his wife. In Pumbedita they rule that a wife is equivalent to her husband [so the evidence is inadmissible.]"*

      C.   For R. Huna said Rab said, "How do we know that a woman is equivalent [as to testimony] to her husband?

      D.   "As it is written, 'The nakedness of your father's brother you shall not uncover, you shall not approach his wife, she is your aunt' (Lev. 18:14). But is she not the wife of one's uncle [not the father's sister]? So we see that a woman is equivalent to her husband."

III.1 A.   **The mother's husband [step-father], sons and sons-in-law [M. 3:4A-B]:**

      B.   *[The mother's husband's] son is one's brother [so this is not a new item, and why should the Mishnah repeat itself]?*

C. *Said R. Jeremiah, "It was necessary to include the item only to exclude a brother's brother [son of the step-father by another wife]* [Schachter, p. 169, n. 14: though he is not related to him, but only through his brother]."

D. *R. Hisda declared valid the testimony of the [step-] brother's brother.*

E. *They said to him, "Have you not heard what R. Jeremiah said?"*

F. *He said to them, "I have not heard it," meaning, "it makes no sense to me."*

G. *If so, then [the step-father's son] is his brother!*

H. *[The Tannaite authority] lists his brother on his father's side and his brother on his mother's side.*

III.2 A. Said R. Hisda, "The father of the groom and the father of the bride may give testimony concerning one another.

B. *"They relate to one another only as does the lid to the barrel [not fastened on top at all]."*

III.3 A. Said Rabbah bar bar Hannah, "A man may testify concerning his betrothed wife [prior to the consummation of the marriage]."

B. *Said Rabina, "That rule applies only if it is to take property away from her, but as to assigning property to her, he is not believed. [It will ultimately accrue to his advantage.]"*

C. *But that is not the case. There is no difference between removing property from her and assigning property to her: he is not believed.*

D. *Why should you think otherwise? Is it because of what R. Hiyya bar Ammi said in the name of Ulla, "As to a priest's betrothed wife, he does not enter the status of a relative responsible for burying the deceased [who cannot eat holy things, so Deut. 26:14], nor does he contract corpse uncleanness on her account, and the same rule applies to her. If she dies, he does not inherit her estate. If he dies, she does collect her marriage-settlement"? But that rule is because the All-Merciful has made the matter depend upon her being his wife in a consummated marriage, and a betrothed wife does not fall into that category [not being related in the flesh]. Here, by contrast, [we do not admit the evidence of a relative]* [Schachter:] *because of mental affinity, and such mental affinity does exist her [in the case of a betrothed woman and her groom].*

IV.1 A. **But the step-son only [and not the stepson's offspring] [M. 3:4C]:**

B. *Our rabbis have taught on Tannaite authority:*

C. The step-son only.

D. R. Yosé says, "A brother-in-law [the wife's sister's husband]."

E. *And another Tannaite statement has it this way:*

F. A brother-in-law only.

G. R. Judah says, "A step-son."

H. *What is the sense of the passage?*

I. *Should we propose that the sense is, "The step-son alone, and the same rule applies to the brother-in-law," and R. Yosé comes along to say, "The brother-in-law alone, and the same rule applies to the step-son"? Then the Mishnah-passage as it stands, which states,* **One's sister's husband, his son and son-in-law [M. 3:4A-B]** *accords with whom? It can be neither R. Judah nor R. Yosé [since both concur that the brother-in-law alone is excluded].*

J.   *If, again, we propose that the sense is otherwise, [as will be spelled out], there is still a problem. Namely, is this what the passage means: "His step-son alone, but his brother-in-law, his son and father-in-law [are excluded]," and R. Yosé comes along to say, "His brother-in-law alone, but his step-son, his son and his son-in-law [are excluded]? Then what R. Hiyya has taught, namely, "There are eight generative relationships, which produce twenty-four [categories that cannot testify for one another], accords with neither R. Yosé nor R. Judah.*
      [In their view, there will be nine generative relationships.] [Schachter, p. 172, n. 7: According to Judah, the brother-in-law is included in the list; according to R. Yosé there is to be added the step-son.]

K.   *This is the sense of the passage:* One's step-son alone, but as to his brother-in-law, his son and son-in-law [also are prohibited to testify]. *R. Yosé comes along to say, "His brother-in-law alone, and all the more so his step-son."*

L.   *Then the Mishnah at hand accords with R. Judah's view, and the Tannaite teaching, R. Yosé's.*

M.   R. Judah said Samuel said, "The decided law accords with R. Yosé.

IV.2   A.   *There was a deed of gift which bore as signatories two brothers-in-law. R. Joseph considered validating it, for R. Judah said Samuel said, "The law accords with R. Yosé."*

B.   *But Abbayye said to him, "How do you know that it is the R. Yosé of the Mishnah's version, validating the testimony of brothers-in-law? Perhaps it is R. Yosé of the Tannaite teaching, who invalidates it?"*

C.   *Do not let such a possibility enter your mind. For Samuel said, "Such as Phineas and I, who are brothers and brother-in-law [cannot testify for one another], but brothers-in-law under ordinary circumstances pose no problem."*

D.   *But perhaps the sense of his statement was, "For example, Phineas and I" with the sense that he was his brother-in-law [and that was why Samuel and Phineas could not testify for one another, not — in Samuel's formulation — merely because they were brothers]?*

E.   *[Joseph then] said to him, "Go and establish ownership through the testimony of the witnesses to the delivery of the writ, in accord with the rule of R. Eleazar [who regards those witnesses as the decisive one]."*

F.   But did not R. Abba say, "R. Eleazar concurs in the case of a writ disqualified on the base of its own character that it is invalid [and here we have invalid witnesses]"?

G.   *[Joseph] said to him, "Go along. I am not permitted to grant you the right of possession."*

V.1   A.   **R. Judah says, "[Even if his daughter died, if he has sons from her, lo, the son-in-law is deemed a relative" [M. 3:4H]:**

B.   Said R. Tanhum said R. Tabela said R. Barona said Rab, "The decided law accords with the view of R. Judah."

C.   Raba said R. Nahman [said], "The decided law does not accord with R. Judah."

D.   So did R. Rabbah bar bar Hannah say R. Yohanan said, "The decided law does not accord with R. Judah."

E.   *There are those who repeat the statement of Rabbah bar bar Hannah in the following connection:*

F.   R. Yosé the Galilean gave the interpretation, "And you shall come to the priests, Levites, and judge who will be in those days' (Deut. 17:9). And will anyone imagine that someone can go to a judge who will not be in his time?

G.   "But this refers to someone who had been a relative but ceased to be related [and later on such a judge may try one's case, as against M. 3:4H]."

H.   Said Rabbah bar bar Hannah said R. Yohanan, "The decided law accords with the view of R. Yosé the Galilean."

V.2   A.   *The sons of the father-in-law of Mar Uqba* **[29A]**, *who were no longer related to him [since their sister, Mar Uqba's wife, had died] came to him for a trial. He said to them, "I am not valid to try your case."*

B.   *They said to him, "What is your view? Does it accord with R. Judah [at M. 3:4H]? We shall bring a letter from the West which indicates that the decided law does not accord with the view of R. Judah."*

C.   *He said to them, "Is it with a* qab *of wax that I cleave to you? I told you that I am invalid to judge your case only because you will not pay attention to court rulings anyhow!"*

VI.   A.   **One known to be a friend – this is the one who served as his groomsman [M. 3:5B]:**

B.   For how long [does the relationship last]?

C.   Said R. Abba said R. Jeremiah said Rab, "For all seven days of the wedding banquet."

D.   *And rabbis in the name of Raba say, "Even beyond the very first day [the relationship is null]."*

VII.1 A.   **One known to be an enemy – this is one who has not spoken [with him for three days by reason of outrage] [M. 4:5C]:**

B.   *Our rabbis have taught on Tannaite authority:*

C.   "And he was not an enemy" (Num. 35:23) – then he may give testimony for him.

D.   "Neither sought his harm" (Num. 35:23) – then he may judge his case.

E.   *We have shown that an enemy [may not testify or serve as judge]. How do we prove that a friend may not do so?*

F.   *This is how to read the same verses:*

G.   "And he was not an enemy" (Num. 35:23) – not a friend, then he may give testimony for him.

H.   "Neither sought his harm" (Num. 35:23) – nor his advantage, then he may judge his case.

I.   *But is the word "friend" actually written?*

J.   *Rather it is based on reasoning. Why is the "enemy" listed? It is because of his [Schachter:] disaffection. Then a friend also [is excluded], because of his [Schachter:] friendly inclination.*

K.   *And as to rabbis [who do not disqualify known enemies or friends], how do they interpret the language, "And he was not his enemy neither sought his harm" (Num. 35:23)?*

L.	*One indicates that [such a one] may not serve as a judge in that case.*
M.	*And as to the other clause, this accords with that which has been taught on Tannaite authority:*
N.	Said R. Yosé, son of R. Judah, "'And he was not his enemy, neither sought his harm' (Num. 35:23): on the basis of this verse we learn that two disciples of sages who hate one another do not sit on the same case [as judges]."

The secondary exposition of M. 1:1A-3:1A now turns to exclusions by reason of family ties. The basic entry, M. 3:4A-C, is clear as given. The earlier version, E, simply excludes all male relatives who stand to inherit. The second clarification, after Yosé's, is at M. 3:4F-H. F-G take account of the possibility of one's ceasing to be related, e.g., if one's wife died. Judah does not differ, but merely qualifies the matter. M. 3:5 continues Judah's saying. He now adds two items to the original list, and his additions are rejected for the stated reason, but only after B-C, a rather fulsome exposition of their own. While the Talmudic discussion seems protracted, it is carefully focused upon the materials of the Mishnah. The Talmud focuses upon its usual program of exegesis and amplification.

3:6-7

A.	How do they test the witnesses?
B.	They bring them into the room and admonish them.
C.	Then they take everyone out and keep back the most important of the group.
D.	And they say to him, "Explain: How do you know that this one owes money to that one."
E.	If he said, "He told me, 'I owe him,' 'So-and-so told me that he owes him,'" he has said nothing whatsoever,
F.	unless he says, "In our presence he admitted to him that he owes him two hundred zuz."
G.	And afterward they bring in the second and test him in the same way.
H.	If their testimony checks out, they discuss the matter.
I.	[If] two [judges] say, "He is innocent," and one says, "He is guilty," he is innocent.
J.	[If] two say, "He is guilty," and one says, "He is innocent," he is guilty.
K.	[If] one says, "He is innocent," and one says, "He is guilty," –
L.	or even if two declare him innocent and two declare him guilty –
M.	but one of them says, "I don't know,"
N.	they have to add judges.

M. 3:6

A.	[When] they have completed the matter, they bring them back in.
B.	The chief judge says, "Mr. So-and-so, you are innocent," "Mr. So-and-so, you are guilty."

	C.	Now how do we know that when one of the judges leave [the court], he may not say, "I think he is innocent, but my colleagues think he is guilty, so what can I do? For my colleagues have the votes!"
	D.	Concerning such a person, it is said, "You shall not go up and down as a talebearer among your people" (Lev. 19:16).
	E.	And it is said, "He who goes about as a talebearer and reveals secrets, [but he that is faithful conceals the matter]" (Prov. 11:13).

M. 3:7

I.1	A.	*How do they speak to [the witnesses, when they admonish them, M. 3:6B]?*
	B.	*Said R. Judah, "This is what they say to them, 'As vapors and wind without rain, so is he who boasts himself of a false gift' (Prov. 25:14)."*
	C.	*Said Raba, "They can [dismiss the curse and] say, 'Seven years may a famine last, but by the gate of a skilled artisan it does not pass.'"*
	D.	*Rather, said Raba, "They say to them, 'As a maul and a sword and a sharp arrow, so is a man who bears false witness against his neighbor' (Prov. 25:18)."*
	E.	*Said R. Ashi, "They can say, 'Seven years may a famine last, but a man does not die before his years [have run out].'"*
	F.	*Rather, said R. Ashi, "Nathan bar Mar Zutra told me, 'We say to them,* "False witnesses are despised by the ones who have paid them, as it is written, 'And set two men, base fellows, before him, and let them bear witness against him, saying, You cursed God and the king' (1 Kgs. 21:10)." [Jezebel, who had hired them, called them base fellows.]'"
II.1	A.	**If he said, "He told me, 'I owe him,' ...unless he says,, "In our presence he admitted to him that he owes him two hundred zuz"** [M. 3:6E-F]:
	B.	*This supports the position of R. Judah, for* R. Judah said Rab said, "One has to say [to the witnesses to a transaction], 'You are my witnesses' [at which point the testimony is valid]."
	C.	*It has also been stated:*
	D.	Said R. Hiyya bar Abba said R. Yohanan, "'You owe me a maneh,' and the other party said to him, 'Yes,' and the next day, the first party said to him, 'Give it to me,' and the other one said, 'I was joking with you' – the latter is exempt [from having to pay unless he has instructed the bystanders to be his witnesses]."
	E.	So too it has been taught on Tannaite authority:
	F.	"You have a maneh of mine."
	G.	The other party said to him, "Yes."
	H.	The next day he said to him, "Give it to me."
	I.	The other party said to him, "I was joking with you" – the latter is exempt.
	J.	And not only so, but even if he had hidden witnesses behind a fence and said to him, "You have a maneh of mine," and the later said to him, "Yes."
	K.	"Do you want to admit it before Mr. X and Mr. Y?"
	L.	He said to him, "I'm afraid that you may drag me to court."

M.	On the next day, he said to him, "Give it to me."
N.	He said to him, "I was joking with you."
O.	He is exempt.
P.	But that rule does not apply to someone who incites people to commit idolatry.
Q.	*Whoever mentioned that classification of criminal?!*
R.	*The text has a part missing, and this is how it should read:*
S.	If [the debtor] made no such claim [that he was only joking], the court does not enter such a plea in his behalf. But in capital cases, even though the accused did not enter such a plea, the court enters that plea for him. But such a plea is not entered for one who incites [Israelites] to idolatry.
T.	*Why is an inciter different?*
U.	*Said R. Hama bar Hanina, "In the address of R. Hiyya bar Abba I heard that the inciter is in a separate category, for the All-Merciful has said, 'Neither shall your eyes pity him, neither shall you conceal him' (Deut. 13:9)."*

II.2

A.	Said R. Samuel bar Nahman said R. Jonathan, "How do we know that a plea is not entered in behalf of an inciter?
B.	"We learn that fact from the original snake [in the Garden of Eden]."
C.	For R. Simlai said, "The snake could have entered many pleas but he entered none.
D.	"And why did the Holy One, blessed be he, not enter a plea for him?
E.	"Because he himself did not plead.
F.	*"And what plea could the snake have made?*
G.	"He could have said, 'When there is a teaching of the master and a teaching of the disciple, to whom do people listen? It is to the teaching of the master.' [Schachter, p. 178, n. 6: So Eve, even though seduced by me, should have obeyed the command of God.]"
H.	[Eve revised God's commandment to her. At Gen. 3:3 she indicated that she could not touch the tree, while in fact God had said only not to eat the fruit. Accordingly,] said Hezekiah, "How do we know from Scripture that one who adds to what God has said detracts from it?
I.	"It is from the following verse: 'God has said, You shall not eat of it nor touch it' (Gen. 3:3)."
J.	*R. Mesharshayya said, "The proof is from here:* Two cubits and a half shall be his length' (Ex. 25:17. [If one removes the first letter of the word for two cubits, it will be two hundred. By adding the first letter the number at hand is reduced from two hundred to two.]"
K.	R. Ashi said, "From, 'Eleven curtains' (Ex. 26:7) [the same sort of proof]."

II.3

A.	Said Abbayye, "The ruling [that one can plead he was joking unless he explicitly recognized the witnesses and validated their testimony of what he was about to do] is the case only if the man says, 'I was

only joking with you.' But if he had said, **[29B]** 'The incident never happened at all,' he is assumed to be a confirmed liar."

B. *R. Pappa, son of R Aha bar Ada, said to him, "This we say in the name of Raba 'People do not remember pointless remarks.'* [Schachter, p. 179, n. 3: What one says in jest is not remembered. His total denial therefore does not weaken his case.]"

II.4 A. *Someone hid witnesses against his neighbor behind bed-curtains. He said to him, "You have a maneh of mine."*

B. *He said to him, "Yes."*

C. *He said to him, "May those who are here, awake or asleep, testify against you?"*

D. *He said to him, "No."*

E. *R. Kahana ruled, "Lo, he said to him, 'No.'"*

II.5 A. *Someone hid witnesses against his neighbor in a grave. He said to him, "You have a maneh of mine."*

B. *He said to him, "Yes."*

C. *"May the living and dead testify against you?"*

D. *He said to him, "No."*

E. *R. Simeon b. Laqish ruled, "Lo, he said to him, 'No.'"*

II.6 A. *Said Rabina, and some say R. Pappa, "From what R. Judah said Rab said, 'One has to say to the witnesses, "You will be my witnesses,"' it follows that there is no difference whether the debtor said it, or the creditor said it and the debtor is silent. For [when the debtor goes free in the cited cases], it is only because the debtor said, 'No.' Had he remained silent, things would have been different."*

II.7 A. *Someone had the name "A basket of debts." He said, "Who has a claim against me except for Mr. A and Mr. B?"*

B. *The two named brought him and laid claim on him in court before R. Nahman.*

C. Said R. Nahman, "Someone would ordinarily avoid presenting himself as wealthy."

II.8 A. *There was a man who was called, "A mouse lying on money" [that is, a miser].*

B. *When he lay dying, he said, "Mr. A and Mr. B have a claim of money against me." After he died, they came and laid claim against the estate.*

C. *They came before R. Ishmael, son of R. Yosé.*

D. *He said to them, "When we invoke the principle, 'Someone ordinarily avoids presenting himself as wealthy,' that applies while he is in good health. But it does not apply after death."*

E. *[The estate] paid half and were brought to court for the other half. The heirs came before R. Hiyya. He said to them, "Just as some one ordinarily avoids presenting himself as wealthy while he is alive, so a man ordinarily avoids presenting his children as wealthy [and that is why the man said he owed a lot of money, when in fact he did not]."*

F. *They said to him, "May we go and retrieve the funds we have already paid?"*

G. *He said to them, "The elder has already made his decision."*

II.9 A. If someone admitted the claim before two witnesses, and this was confirmed by an act of acquisition, they may then prepare a bond [covering the debt, even though the debtor did not instruct the scribe to do so]. But if not, they do not do so.

B. If he admitted the debt before three witnesses and no act of acquisition confirmed the matter,

C. Rab said, "Nonetheless, they prepare the bond."

D. R. Assi said, "They do not prepare the bond."

E. *There was a case, and Rab took into account the opinion of R. Assi.*

II.10 A. *Said R. Ada bar Ahbah, "Sometimes a deed of acknowledgement of a debt [before three witnesses, without an act of acquisition] may be written up, sometimes not.*

B. *"If [the witnesses] happened to be together, we do not write such a writ. If [the claimant deliberately] gathered them together [to serve as his witnesses], then we do write it."*

C. *Raba said, "Even if he gathered the witnesses together, we do not write such a writ, unless he says to them, 'You serve as judges for me.'"*

D. *Mar, son of R. Ashi, said, "Even if he gathered the witnesses together and said to them, 'You serve as judges for me,' we do not write such a write unless he designated a meeting place and called [the debtor] to come to court."*

II.11 A. *[If the debtor] conceded a claim for movables and [the witnesses] effected a formal title [given over by the debtor], they write a writ [of record], and if not, they do not write one.*

B. *If the claim has to do with real estate, and there was no formal title, what is the rule?*

C. Amemar said, "They do not write a writ."

D. Mar Zutra said, "They write it."

E. *And the decided law is that they write it.*

II.12 A. *Rabina came to Damharia. Said to him R. Dimi, son of R. Huna of Dimharia, to Rabina, "What is the law concerning movables that are as his [in the domain of the debtor]?"*

B. *He said to him, "It falls into the category of real estate."*

C. *R. Ashi said, "Since [the debt] has still to be collected, that is not the case."*

II.13 A. *There was a deed of acknowledgement of debt that lacked the phrase, "He said to us, 'Write and sign and deliver to him...'"*

B. *Both Abbayye and Raba ruled, "That accords with the position of R. Simeon b. Laqish.*

C. "For R. Simeon b. Laqish said, 'It is an assumption that witnesses sign a document only if [the vendor] is an adult.' [Schachter, p. 181, n. 6: The sale of a legacy before that age is invalid and it is taken for granted that witnesses are aware of this law. So also in this case, where the admission was made before two witnesses, and without an act of the transfer of ownership, the latter would know that they could not write a deed without the debtor's instructions; hence they must have been so instructed.]"

D. *To this position R. Pappa, and some say, R. Huna, son of R. Joshua, objected, "And is there something that we do not know but the scribes of the court do know? [The law is not known to all judges, so why assume the witnesses knew it?]"*

	E.	*They addressed the question to the scribes of Abbayye's court, who knew the rule. They turned to the scribes of Raba's court, who also knew the law.*

II.14 A. *A deed of acknowledgement had written it, "An aide memoire of the statements of so-and-so," [rather than the requisite, "an aide memoire of testimony by witnesses"], [30A] and was worded wholly as a court document [though signed by two, not three men], but omitted the phrase, "We were in session as three judges, and one of them then withdrew."* [Schachter, p. 182, n. 4: If one of the three judges necessary for the authentication of a document died before signing it, the document should be so worded.]

B. *Rabina considered ruling, "This accords with the rule of R. Simeon b. Laqish."*

C. *Said to him R. Nathan bar Ammi, "This is what we rule in the name of Raba: 'In any such case we take account of the possibility of a court that ruled in error [thinking that two judges, not three, would be sufficient to validate the writ].'"*

D. *Said R. Nahman bar Isaac, "If the language contains the words, 'A court,' it is not necessary [to scruple about a court in error]."*

E. *But perhaps it is a presumptuous court?*

F. *For Samuel said, "If two men judged a case, their judgment stands, but they are called a presumptuous court."*

G. *But the document at hand contained the inscription, "The court of Rabbana Ashi"* [Schachter, p. 182, n. 10: The signatories belonged to his school and they, no doubt, were aware that two cannot compose a court.]

H. *But perhaps the rabbis of the court of R. Ashi took the position of Samuel.*

I. *But written in the document were the words, "Rabbana Ashi instructed us to write [the deed]."* [Schachter, p. 183, n. 1: The court must therefore have been legally constituted, since he would not have asked two to form a court.]

II.15 A. *Our rabbis have taught on Tannaite authority:*

B. **If someone said [to the heirs], "I saw your father hiding money in a box, chest, or cupboard," and he said, "They belong to so-and-so," or "they are in the status of second title [to be brought to Jerusalem and there spent on the purchase of food]," if the money was in the house, the statement is null.**

C. **If the money was in the field, his statement is valid.**

D. **The governing principle is this: In any case in which he has the power to take the money [but did not do so], his statement is confirmed. If he does not have the power to take the money, he has said nothing.**

E. **If [heirs] saw their father hiding money in a box, chest, or cupboard, and he said, "They belong to So-and-so," "They are in the status of second tithe," if it was so as to give instructions, his statement stands. But if it was so as to practice deception, he has said nothing.**

F.   If one was upset about money his father had left him, and the master of dreams came and said to him, "They are such and so, in a given place, for a given purpose, e.g., for second tithe" – –

G.   there was such a case, and [sages] ruled, "Words that are spoken in dreams make no difference one way or the other" [T. M.S. 5:9-11, with different wording].

III.1   A.   If two judges say, "He is innocent," [and one says, "He is guilty," he is innocent] [M. 3:7I]:

B.   *[Where the judges differ,] how do they word the court order?*

C.   R. Yohanan said, "'He is innocent.'"

D.   R. Simeon b. Laqish said, "'Judge X and Judge Y declare him innocent, Judge Z declares him liable.'"

E.   R. Eleazar said, "'On the basis of the [judges'] discussion, Mr. So-and-so was declared innocent.'"

F.   *What is the point of disagreement?*

G.   *The point of disagreement is whether [the dissenting judge] has to take a share in paying reparations [to the guilty party, should the court turn out to have erred].*

H.   *For the one who says, "[The document states,] 'He is innocent,'" will hold that the dissenting judge nonetheless has to pay a share in restitution for judicial error.*

I.   *And the one who has said, "'Judge X and Judge Y declare him innocent, and Judge Z declares him guilty,'" he does not have to pay.*

J.   *But from the viewpoint of him who says, "[The document simply says,] 'He is innocent,'" in which case the dissenting judge does have to pay, why cannot that judge say to them, "Had you listened to me, you too would not have had to pay"? [Why does he share in the liability?]*

K.   *Rather, this is what is at issue between them: It is whether the others have to pay the share of the dissenting judge [who surely does not have to pay anything].*

L.   *In the opinion of the one who says, "[the document reads,] 'He is innocent,'" the majority-judges do have to pay the share of the dissenting judge*

M.   *In the view of him who says, "[The document reads,] 'Judge X and Judge Y declare him innocent, and Judge Z declares him liable,'" they do not have to pay the share of the dissenting judge.*

N.   *And in the view of him who has said [that the language of the document is], "He is innocent," so they have to pay the share of the dissenting judge, why should they not say to him, "Had you not been with us, no judgment could have come from the court at all" [so your presence is partly at fault for our having to make restitution]?*

O.   *Rather, this is what is at issue between them: It is on the count of "You shall not go up and down as a talebearer among your people" (Lev. 19:16).*

P.   R. Yohanan said, "[The document says merely], 'He is innocent,' on the grounds that one should not go about as a talebearer [and the names of the dissenting judges are not to be revealed on that count]."

Q.		R. Simeon b. Laqish said, "'Judge X and Judge Y declare innocent, and Judge Z declares liable,' *for otherwise the verdict would produce a misleading impression."*
R.		*R. Eleazar holds that this party is correct and that party is correct, and on that account he has the scribes write as follows: "After their discussion [so signifying disagreement] Mr. X was declared to be exempt [of any obligation to pay].'"*
IV.1	A.	**When they have completed the matter,, they bring them back in [M. 3:7A]:**
	B.	*Whom do they bring back?*
	C.	*Should we say that it is the litigants? But they are standing right there.*
	D.	*Rather, it is the witnesses [whom they bring back].*
	E.	*In accord with whose view is the Mishnah framed?*
	F.	*It cannot be in accord with R. Nathan, for it has been taught on Tannaite authority:*
	G.	**The testimony of witnesses is confirmed only if they had been in sight of one another.**
	H.	**R. Joshua b. Qorha says, "Even though this one was not opposite that one."**
	I.	**Under no circumstances is their testimony confirmed unless both of them are [heard] at the same time.**
	J.	**R. Nathan [T.: Simeon] says, "They hear out the testimony of this one on one day, and when his fellow comes on the next day, they give a hearing to what he has to say as well"** [T. San. 5:5F-I]. [Schachter, p. 185, n. 6: Hence if it is the witnesses who are admitted after a decision has been arrived at, which implies the necessity of their joint appearance, this interpretation of the law is not in accord with the view of Nathan as given.]
	K.	*In point of fact, it is the litigants, and the view at hand is that of R. Nehemiah.*
	L.	*For it has been taught on Tannaite authority:*
	M.	R. Nehemiah says, "This was the practice of the more scrupulous judges of Jerusalem. They bring on the litigants and listen to their claims, then bring in the witnesses and listen to their testimony, then take them all outside and debate the matter."
	N.	*But has it not been taught on Tannaite authority:*
	O.	"When they have completed dealing with the matter, they bring the witnesses back in?"
	P.	*That rule has been formulated not in accord with the view of R. Nathan.*
IV.2	A.	*Reverting to the body of the text just now cited:*
	B.	**The testimony of witnesses is confirmed only if they had been in sight of one another.**
	C.	**R. Joshua b. Qorha says, "Even though this one was not opposite that one"** [T. San. 5:5F-G].
	D.	*What is at issue here?*
	E.	*If you wish, I shall propose that it has to do with a biblical verse, and if you wish, I shall propose that it has to do with a matter of reasoning.*
	F.	*[As to the latter possibility, we ask about the exact fact as to which testimony is given, thus, at issue is the particular maneh to which each witness testifies. For] the maneh concerning*

which this witness testifies will not be the one concerning which that witness testifies, and the maneh, concerning which that witness testifies is not the same as the maneh concerning which this witness testifies [unless both see the transaction simultaneously].

G.   *The other party takes the view that both witnesses testify about the transfer of manehs in general, [and not about the particular coin at hand]. [So the witnesses prove the fact that a loan has been made.]*

H.   *And if you wish, I shall explain that at issue is the interpretation of a verse of Scripture.*

I.   For it is written, "And he is a witness, whether he has seen or known of it" (Lev. 5:1).

J.   *And it has been taught on Tannaite authority:*

K.   Now it is said, "One witness shall not rise up against a man" (Deut. 19:15). Since it is said, "A witness," do I not know that it is only one witness? Why then does Scripture specify that only one witness is involved when that is obvious?

L.   It serves to indicate the generative principle that in any case in which "witness" is stated, lo, two witnesses are under discussion, unless Scripture makes it explicit for you that only a single witness is at hand.

M.   *Now the All-Merciful [at Lev. 5:1] has used the singular, to indicate that [testimony is valid] only if both witnesses see the event simultaneously.*

N.   *And the other party?*

O.   "He is witness, whether he has seen or known of it" (Lev. 5:1) shows that, in any event, [disjoined testimony is acceptable].

IV.3 A.   **Under no circumstances is their testimony confirmed unless both of them are heard at the same time.**

B.   **R. Nathan says, "They hear out the testimony of this one on one day, and when his fellow comes on the next day, they give a hearing to what he has to say as well" [T. San. 5:5H-I].**

C.   *What is at issue here?*

D.   *If you wish, I shall propose that it has to do with a biblical verse, and if you wish, I shall propose that it has to do with a matter of reasoning.*

E.   *If you wish, I shall propose that it has to do with a matter of reasoning.*

F.   *One party takes the view that when a single witness comes to court, it is to prove the necessity that the accused take an oath, but not to prove that he actually owes the money.* [Schachter, p. 186, n. 11: Hence when witnesses testify separately, the evidence of neither proves liability, and therefore the two testimonies cannot be combined].

G.   *The other authority takes the view that even though they appear simultaneously, do they in any event testify with a single voice? [Obviously not. Nonetheless, the testimony of the two is joined together to validate the court action. So when they come* separately], *the evidence that they bring also may be joined together.*

H. *And if you wish, I shall propose that at issue is the interpretation of a verse of Scripture:*

I. "[And he is a witness, whether he has seen or known it], if he does not utter it, then he shall bear his iniquity" (Lev. 5:1).

J. **[30B]** *All parties concur with the view of rabbis who differ from R. Joshua b. Qorha [and maintain that both witnesses must simultaneously see the deed]. At issue here is whether or not we establish an analogy between reporting what they have seen and the actual seeing of the incident.*

K. *One authority holds that we establish an analogy between reporting the incident and seeing it, and the other party does not maintain that we establish an analogy between reporting the incident and seeing it [in which case, in the latter's view, it may be testimony spread out over several days].*

IV.4 A. *R. Simeon b. Eliaqim was watching for an occasion on which to ordain R. Yosé, son of R. Hanina, but nothing came up. One day he was in session before R. Yohanan. He said to them, "Does anybody know whether or not the law follows the view of R. Joshua b. Qorha?"*

B. *Said to him R. Simeon b. Eliaqim, "This one knows."*

C. *He said to him, "Let him say so."*

D. *He said to him, "First let the master ordain him."*

E. *He ordained him. He said to him,* "My son, tell me how you have heard matters?"

F. He said to him, "This is what I have heard, that R. Joshua b. Qorha concurs with R. Nathan [that the evidence may be disjoined and need not be simultaneous]."

G. *He said to him, "Did I ask for this information? Now if in the case of what is primary, which is the actual seeing of the event together, R. Joshua b. Qorha has said that we do not require simultaneous witness to what has happened [on the part of both at once], is there any issue of his view on requiring a simultaneous narrative later on?"*

H. He said to him, "Since you have come up [to high rank], you do not have to go down again."

I. *Said R. Zera, "We may then infer that once a person has been ordained as a major authority, the ordination is indelible."*

IV.5 A. Said R. Hiyya bar Abin said Rab, "The law is in accord with R. Joshua b. Qorha's view, both in respect to real estate and in respect to movables."

B. Ulla said, "The law accords with R. Joshua b. Qorha in real estate but not in respect to movables."

C. *Said Abbayye to him, "Since you declare the decided law, you would imply that rabbis differ. But did Raba not say in the name of R. Huna in the name of Rab, 'Sages concur with R. Joshua b. Qorha in the matter of testimony concerning real estate'? And R. Idi bar Abin repeated the formulation of Qorha's version of the laws of damages, 'Sages concur with R. Joshua b. Qorha in testimony concerning firstlings, in testimony concerning real estate, in testimony concerning a claim of ownership established through usufruct,* and in testimony concerning puberty signs for males and females.'"

D.   *Do you argue merely by citing conflicting authorities? One authority holds that they differ, and the other authority reasons that they do not differ.*

E.   *What is the point about the statement concerning testimony involving puberty signs for males and females? If we say that the evidence under discussion concerns the appearance of one hair [below] at the genitals and another hair [above] at the belly, that is, in point of fact, half of the requisite facts of the case and half of the requisite testimony. Rather,* one witness says, "There are two down below," and one witness says, "There are two up above."

IV.6   A.   *Said R. Joseph, "I say in the name of Ulla, 'The law accords with R. Joshua b. Qorha both as to real estate and as to movables."*

B.   *The rabbis who come from Mahoza say, "R. Zera said in the name of Rab, "That is the case of trials concerning evidence concerning real estate but not movables."*

C.   *Rab is consistent with his reasoning, for* Rab said, "[One witness's testimony that A has] admitted [he owes money to B, when that testimony is given on one day] followed by similar testimony of admission of a loan given later on, or [testimony concerning] admission [that the loan is owing], following [testimony concerning] the making of the loan join together [to establish the fact of liability. Both may refer to the same transaction]. But testimony as to the transaction of a loan given after other such testimony, or testimony concerning the transaction of a loan after testimony concerning the admission of a loan, do not join together."

E.   *R. Nahman bar Isaac found R. Huna, son of R. Joshua. He said to him, "What is the difference in testimony concerning the transaction of a loan given after other such testimony, so that such testimony is not joined together [to form valid evidence that the loan was made? Is it because the maneh which this one saw is not the same as the maneh which that one saw? But the same argument applies to the testimony concerning admission of a loan. For the admission of a loan concerning the maneh that this one alleges he has witnessed is not the same as the admission of a loan concerning the maneh that that party alleges he has witnessed!"*

F.   *We deal with a case in which [the debtor] said to the latter witness, "Concerning this maneh about which I confessed before you, I confess also before Mr So-and-so."*

G.   *But if that is the case, the latter of the two witnesses will know it, but the former of the two will not know it.*

H.   *We deal with a case in which [the debtor] went and said to the former of the two witnesses, "Concerning the <u>maneh</u> about which I confessed before you, I have also confessed before Mr. So-and-so."*

I.   *[Nahman] said to him, "May your mind be at rest, as you have given my mind rest."*

J. *He said to him, "Why be at rest? Did not Raba, and some say, R. Sheshet say, 'Throw a hatchet [at this answer]! All we have at hand is the case of testimony concerning admitting the loan taken after testimony concerning the loan.* [Schachter, p. 190, n. 5: For since it is necessary, according to this answer, that each witness shall know what the other has seen, it follows that an admission after a loan must be explained likewise, viz., he must have said to the latter witness: The <u>maneh</u> I have admitted receiving in your presence, I borrowed in the presence of so-and-so; and then he must have gone and said to the former witness: The <u>maneh</u> which I borrowed in your presence, I have admitted receiving before so-and-so. Why then did Rab need to state both laws?]

K. *He said to him, "This is what I have heard about you people. 'You tear down palm trees and put up palm trees.'"*

L. The Nehardeans say, "Whether we have a case of testimony concerning admission of a loan after another such testimony, or testimony concerning admission of a loan after testimony concerning the transaction of the loan, whether it is testimony concerning transaction of a loan after other such testimony, whether it is testimony of transaction of a loan after admission of a loan, in all such cases the two acts of testimony join together [to establish the fact that the loan is owing]."

M. *This is in accord with whom? It accords with R. Joshua b. Qorhah.*

IV.7 A. Said R. Judah, "Testimony of two witnesses who contradict one another under examination [in respect to peripheral issues, e.g., details of the weather that day] is valid in property-cases."

B. *Said Raba, "It is reasonable to suppose that the statement of R. Judah pertains to a case in which one says, 'The money was paid] out of a black bag,' and the other says, 'It is out of a white bag.' But if one witness says, 'It was a black [old] maneh,' and the other one says, 'It was a white [new] maneh,' the testimony does not join together."*

C. And would testimony about a black bag [or a white one] in capital-cases not join together? And has not R. Hisda said, "All the same is the evidence of one who says, 'He killed him with a sword,' and the other says, 'It was with a dagger that he killed him.' This would not be valid testimony. But if one says, 'He was wearing black clothes,' and the other says, 'He was wearing white clothes,' lo, this is valid testimony?"

D. [31A] *Are you arguing simply by quoting conflicting authorities? The Nehardeans say, "Even if one witness says, 'It was a black maneh,' and the other says, 'It was a white maneh,' their testimony joins together." In accord with whom do they rule? It is in accord with R. Joshua b. Qorha."*

E. *Now you may well say that that is the view of R. Joshua b. Qorha in a case in which the witnesses do not contradict one another [and then the disjoined testimony is acceptable]. But in a case in which the*

*witnesses contradict one another, has he made that same statement?
But the Nehardeans rule in accord with the following Tannaite
authority, for it has been taught on Tannaite authority:*

F.   Said R. Simeon b. Eleazar, "The House of Shammai and the
House of Hillel do not differ concerning two groups of
witnesses, one of which says that the loan is for two hundred
zuz, the other of which says that it is for a hundred. For within
the frame of two hundred zuz a hundred zuz is encompassed.

G.   "Concerning what do they differ?

H.   "It is concerning a single group of witnesses.

I.   "For the House of Shammai say, 'The testimony is divided
[since one witness cannot be right, so there is only a single
witness at hand, and the claim is null].'

J.   "And the House of Hillel say, 'Encompassed in the claim that
two hundred zuz are owing is the claim that one hundred zuz
[a maneh] are owing [and so there is valid testimony as to the
smaller of the two sums]."

IV.8   A.   If one witness says, "It was a jug of wine,"

B.   and the other witness says, "It was a jug of oil" –

C.   *there was a case of this kind, which came before R. Ammi.*

D.   *R. Ammi imposed upon the defendant the requirement to pay the
value of the jug of wine out of the value of a jug of oil [since oil is
more expensive, the smaller of the two claims was proved].*

E.   *In accord with whose position did he make this ruling? It is in
accord with the position of R. Simeon b. Eleazar.*

F.   *Now I might concede that R. Simeon b. Eleazar made such a
ruling in a case in which, within the sum of two hundred zuz a
maneh [a hundred zuz] is encompassed.*

G.   *But did he make his ruling in a case of this sort [in which the
character of what had been lent was at issue]?*

H.   *The ruling applies only in a case [in which the witnesses attested
not the actual wine or oil but] the value thereof.*

IV.9   A.   One says, "It was in the upper room," and the other says, "It
was in the lower room."

B.   Said R. Hanina, "A case of this kind came before Rabbi, who
joined the testimony of the two witnesses."

V.1   A.   **Now how do we know [that when one of the judges leaves the
court, he may not say... [M. 3:7C]:**

B.   *Our rabbis have taught on Tannaite authority:*

C.   **How do we know that when one of the judges leaves the court, he
may not say, "Lo, I think he is innocent, but my colleagues think
he is guilty, so what can I do? For my colleagues have the votes!"?**

D.   **Scripture says, "You shall not go up and down as a talebearer
among your people" (Lev. 19:16).**

E.   **And it is said, "He who goes about as a talebearer and reveals
secrets" (Prov. 11:13).**

F.   *There was a disciple about whom there was a rumor that he had
reports something that had been said in the school house twenty-two
years earlier. R. Ammi expelled him from the school house, saying
"This man tells secrets."*

The Talmud's discussion of the Mishnah at hand, while wide-ranging, remains cogent. For the Mishnah introduces the issue of testimony and evidence. While the Talmud completes its treatment of the Mishnah's reading of the issue, it moves on to closely related but essentially fresh issues, especially the matter of disjoined testimony, subjected to particularly thorough analysis. While the Talmud seems somewhat prolix, in fact it is entirely cogent and pursues a carefully defined program.

3:8

A. So long as [a litigant] brings proof, he may reverse the ruling.

B. [If] they had said to him, "All the evidence which you have, bring between this date and thirty days from now,"

C. [if] he found evidence during the thirty-day-period, he may reverse the ruling.

D. [If he found evidence] after the thirty-day-period, he may not reverse the ruling.

E. Said Rabban Simeon b. Gamaliel, "What should this party do, who could not find the evidence during the thirty-day-period, but found it after thirty days?"

F. [If] they had said to him, "Bring witnesses,"

G. and he said, "I don't have witnesses,"

H. [if] they had said, "Bring proof,"

I. and he said, "I don't have proof"

J. and after a time he brought proof, or he found witnesses –

K. this is of no weight whatsoever.

L. Said Rabban Simeon b. Gamaliel, "What should this party do, who did not even know that he had witnesses on his side but found witnesses? Or who did not even know that he had proof, but who found proof?"

M. [If] they had said to him, "Bring witnesses,"

N. and he said, "I have no witnesses,"

O. "Bring proof," and he said, "I have no proof,"

P. [If] he saw that he would be declared liable in court and said, "Let Mr. So-and-so and Mr. Such-and-such [now] come along and give evidence in my behalf,"

Q. or if [on the spot] he brought proof out of his pocket –

R. lo, this is of no weight whatsoever

I.1 A. Said Rabbah bar R. Huna, "The decided law accords with the view of Rabban Simeon b. Gamaliel."

B. And said Rabbah bar R. Huna, "The law does not accord with the opinion of sages."

C. *That is self-evident! Since he has said, "The law accords with the view of Rabban Simeon b. Gamaliel," it goes without saying that we know the law does not accord with sages.*

D. *What might you have said? That rule applies to begin with, but after the fact not. So we are informed that [if the court had in fact rejected his evidence and ruled against him], we bring the case back to court and retry it.*

II.1   A.   **If they had said to him, "Bring witnesses," ...Said Rabban Simeon b. Gamaliel... [M. 3:8F-L]:**

B.   Said Rabbah bar R. Huna said R. Yohanan, "The decided law accords with the opinion of sages."

C.   And said Rabbah bar R. Huna said R. Yohanan, "The decided law does not accord with the view of Rabban Simeon b. Gamaliel."

D.   *That is self-evident! Since he has said, "The law accords with the view of sages," it goes without saying that we know the law does not accord with Rabban Simeon b. Gamaliel.*

E.   *In so stating matters he informs us that in that particular aspect the law does not accord with Rabban Simeon b. Gamaliel, but in all the rest of the items the law does accord with Rabban Simeon b. Gamaliel.*

F.   *This then sets aside the statement of Rabbah bar bar Hannah that R. Yohanan said, "In any case in which Rabban Simeon b. Gamaliel teaches the law in our Mishnah, the law is in accord with him, except for the matter of surety, the rule of Sidon, and the 'latter proof' [that is, M. 3:8F-L]."*

II.2   A.   *A minor boy was called to court before R. Nahman. He said to him, "Do you have witnesses?"*

B.   *He said to him, "No."*

C.   *"Do you have proof?"*

D.   *He said to him, "No."*

E.   *R. Nahman declared him liable. The boy left weeping. Some people heard him. They said to him, "We know about your father's business activities, [and we can testify in your behalf]."*

F.   *R. Nahman ruled, "In such a case even sages will concur, for a child might well not know about his father's business activities."*

II.3   A.   *There was a woman [trustee appointed by creditor and debtor of a bond] who produced a bond [against a given debtor] but said to him, "I know that this bond has been paid off."*

B.   *R. Nahman accepted her testimony.*

C.   *Said Raba to R. Nahman, "In accord with whom? Is it in accord with Rabbi, who said, 'Right of ownership of "letters" is attained only through handing over the note'? [Schachter, p. 195, n. 6: If a creditor wishes to make over a debt, he can do so merely by handing the note to the assignee. Hence in our case the woman could have claimed ownership of the note, on the plea that it has been handed to her not as trustee but in transference of the debt. Consequently her statement that the bill was paid may be regarded as true."]*

D.   *He said to him, "This case is different, because if the woman had wanted, she could have burned the note."*

E.   *There are those who say that R. Nahman did not accept her testimony. Raba said to R. Nahman, "And lo, if she had wanted, [31B] she could have burned the note."*

F.   *[He replied,] "Since the bond had been established in court as valid, we do not accept the claim that if she had wanted, she could have burned the note."*

G.   *Since it was established in court, we cannot say she could have burned it.*

H.   *Raba objected to R. Nahman, "A receipt that bears witnesses must be authenticated by its signatories. If there are not any witnesses on the document, but it was produced by a trustee, or of it is written on the bond under the signatures of witnesses, it is valid. [Schachter, p. 195, n. 10: For the note is in the creditor's possession, and he would certainly not have permitted a false receipt to be written thereon.] Therefore a trustee is believed."*

I.   *That constitutes a refutation of the ruling of R. Nahman.*

II.4 A.   When R. Dimi came, he said R. Yohanan [said], "One may go on producing proof to contradict the decision, until he runs out of arguments and then says, 'Let Mr. X and Mr. Y come near and testify in my behalf.' [This implies that, having stated he has no more evidence, he asks that witnesses be heard (Schachter)]."

B.   *There is an internal contradiction in this statement.*

C.   *First you say, "...until he runs out of arguments" – thus conforming to the view of rabbis [who maintain that when the man says he has no more evidence, his case is closed].*

D.   *Then you say, "Let Mr. X and Mr. Y come near and testify in my behalf," which accords with the position of Rabban Simeon b. Gamaliel.*

E.   *Now should you propose to maintain that the entire formulation accords with the view of Rabban Simeon b. Gamaliel, and the passage is formulated as to spell out the meaning at hand, that is, what is the sense of, "...until he runs out of arguments"? It is, "Let Mr. X and Mr. Y come near and testify in my behalf," lo, said Rabbah bar bar Hannah said R. Yohanan, "In every passage in which the opinion of Rabban Simeon b. Gamaliel is taught in our Mishnah, the decided law accords with his view except for the matters of the pledge, Sidon, and the bringing of 'final proof.' [So Yohanan takes the view that once the litigant says that he has no more proof, he cannot introduce any more, contrary to the proposed interpretation of his statement]."*

F.   [Here is now a better version:] When R. Samuel bar Judah came, he said R. Yohanan [said], "A litigant may continue bringing proof to upset a decision, until he completes his arguments, and they say to him, **"Bring witnesses," and he said, "I don't have witnesses," and they said to him, "Bring proof," and he said, "I don't have proof"** [M. 3:8F-I].

I.   But if witnesses arrived from overseas, or if his father's pouch had been left with an outsider, lo, he may [still later] produce that proof and upset the decision.

II.5 A.   When R. Dimi came, he said R. Yohanan [said], "He who drags his fellow to court – one says, 'Let us have the trial here,' and the other says, 'Let us go to the place of the assembly,' they force him to go to the place of the assembly."

B.   Said R. Eleazar before him, "My lord, he who claims a maneh against his fellow – must he spend a maneh to collect a maneh? Rather, they force him to have the trial in his own town."

C.   *It has been stated along these same lines on Amoraic authority:*

D.   Said R. Safra, "In the case of two litigants who contested the venue of a trial – one says, 'Let us have the trial here,' and the other says, 'Let us go to the place of the assembly' – they force him to have the trial in his town. And if a question comes up for inquiry, they write it and send it. And if one litigant says, 'Write down for me the basis for your decision in trying me, they write it down and give it to him."

E.   The deceased childless man's widow has to go after the surviving brother [to where he lives] so that he may release her [of the levirate relationship].

F.   How far?

G.   Said R. Ammi, "Even from Tiberias to Sepphoris."

H.   *Said R. Kahana, "What verse of Scripture indicates it? 'Then the elders of his town shall call him' (Deut. 25:28) – but not the elders of her town."*

I.   *Said Amemar, "The decided law is that they force him to go to the place of the assembly."*

J.   *Said R. Ashi to Amemar, "And lo, R. Eleazar said, 'They force him to have the trial in his own town.'"*

K.   "That is the case when the debtor made such a claim on the creditor. But if the creditor made such a claim, 'The borrower is slave to the lender' (Prov. 22:7)."

II.6   A.   *They sent a message [from the court in the Land of Israel] to Mar Uqba, "To him whose splendor is like that of the son of Bithia [Moses], Peace to you. Uqban, the Babylonian, complained before us, 'Jeremiah, my brother, has placed obstacles in my path.' Speak [judge, order] to him and get him moving so that he will appear before us in Tiberias."*

B.   *Now the text contains a contradiction.* You say, "Speak to him," *therefore "you are to judge him." Then:* "And get him moving so that he will appear before us in Tiberias," *therefore "send him here."*

C.   *Rather, this is what they said:* "Speak to him: you try the case. If he pays attention, well and good. And if not, get him moving and let him appear before us in Tiberias."

F.   *R. Ashi said, "It was a case involving judicial penalties, and in Babylonia they do not judge such cases. And the reason that they sent a message to him in this way was to pay respect to Mar Uqba."*

The triplet sets the anonymous view, that the court has the right to lay down a time-limit on the bringing of relevant evidence, against the opinion of Simeon b. Gamaliel, that such a limitation is unfair. Since the first two cases clearly spell out what is at issue, it is only the third which is interesting, and that is from Simeon's viewpoint. Here even he concedes that evidence supposedly not available when called for, but produced at the last minute, it apt to be trumped-up.

4

Bavli Tractate Sanhedrin
Chapter Four
Folios 32A-39B

4:1-2

A. The same [laws] apply to property cases and capital cases with respect to examination and interrogation [of witnesses],

B. as it is said, "You will have one law" (Lev. 24:22).

C. What is the difference between property cases and capital cases?

D. Property cases [are tried] by three [judges], and capital cases by twenty-three.

E. In property cases they begin [argument] with the case either for acquittal or for conviction, while in capital cases they begin only with the case for acquittal, and not with the case for conviction.

F. In property cases they decide by a majority of one, whether for acquittal or for conviction, while in capital cases they decide by a majority of one for acquittal, but only with a majority of two [judges] for conviction.

G. In property cases they reverse the decision whether in favor of acquittal or in favor of conviction, while in capital cases they reverse the decision so as to favor acquittal, but they do not reverse the decision so as to favor conviction.

H. In property cases all [judges and even disciples] argue either for acquittal or conviction. In capital cases all argue for acquittal, but all do not argue for conviction.

I. In property cases one who argues for conviction may argue for acquittal, and one who argues for acquittal may also argue for conviction. In capital cases the one who argues for conviction may argue for acquittal, but the one who argues for acquittal has not got the power to retract and to argue for conviction.

J. In property cases they try the case by day and complete it by night. In capital cases they try the case by day and complete it [the following] day.

K.   In property cases they come to a final decision on the same day
      [as the trial itself], whether it is for acquittal or conviction. In
      capital cases they come to a final decision for acquittal on the
      same day, but on the following day for conviction.

L.   (Therefore they do not judge [capital cases] either on the eve of
      the Sabbath or on the eve of a festival.)

                              M. 4:1

A.   In cases involving questions of [B. adds: property[uncleanness
      and cleanness they begin [voting] from the eldest. In capital cases
      they begin from the side [with the youngest].

B.   All are valid to engage in the judgment of property cases, but all
      are not valid to engage in the judgment of capital cases,

C.   except for priests, Levites, and Israelites who are suitable to marry
      into the priesthood.

                              M. 4:2

I.1   A.   [The same laws apply to property cases and *capital cases with
            respect to examination and interrogation of witnesses:] Do property
            cases require examination and interrogation of witnesses? An objection
            was raised [to that proposition]:* If the date was inscribed on the writ,
            "On the first of Nisan, in the year of release," and others came
            along and said to them [the witnesses to the writ], "How in the
            world can you have signed that writ, for lo, you were with us on
            that day in such and such a place," their testimony remains valid,
            and the writ remains valid, for we take into account the
            possibility that they postdated the writ [wrote the writ earlier but]
            when they wrote it out" [T. Mak. 1:2G-I]. *Now if you maintain that
            we require examination and interrogation of the witnesses, how can we
            take account of the possibility that they postdated the writ when they wrote
            it out? [That would have come out in the interrogation, and in any event
            if we accept such a claim, why interrogate the witnesses at all?]*

      B.   *And by your reasoning you should find a problem in the following passage
            of the Mishnah:* Antedated bonds are invalid. [By antedating the
            document, the creditor gains rights, to which he is not entitled,
            against the property of the debtor. But postdated bonds are valid.
            [By postdating the document, the creditor voluntarily restricts his
            own legal rights against his debtor's property] [M. Sheb. 10:5C-D,
            trans. Newman, p. 206]. *Now if you maintain that we require
            examination and interrogation of witnesses to the bond, why should
            postdated bonds be regarded as valid?* [These too could be forgeries.
            Schachter p. 201, n. *: Hence even if the loan itself is attested as
            having taken place, it should rank as only a verbal loan, which
            cannot be collected from property sold even after it was incurred.]

      C.   *[The fact that we raise the issue on the basis of the passage of the Tosefta, of
            secondary authority, rather than of the Mishnah, of primary authority]
            poses no problem, since we raise our objection on the basis of a stronger
            issue. Specifically, even in the case of a date of the first of Nisan in the
            Sabbatical Year, on account of which it would not be common for people to
            make loans [which would be nullified in the Seventh Year] and so would
            not likely claim, "Perhaps they postdated it when they wrote it," for one*

      would not want to weaken the force of his bond, even in such a case, since the Seventh Year only at the end nullifies existing debts, we declare the bond valid [Schachter, p. 202, n. 3: by assuming its writing has been postponed to the Sabbatical Year. Thus, this assumption, since it is possible, is made in spite of its improbability, a loan in the Sabbatical Year still being rare. How much more so is the assumption to be made in normal cases. Why then should the witnesses be examined on the date, since even if it is disproved, their testimony holds good?]

D.   *In any event the cited passage presents a problem [to the rule of the Mishnah before us].*

I.2   A.   Said R. Hanina, "As a matter of Torah-law, **the same [rules] apply to property cases and capital cases with respect to the examination and interrogation of witnesses as it is said, 'You will have one law.' (Lev. 24:22) [M. 4:1A-B].**

      B.   "Then on what account did they rule that property cases do not require examination and interrogation of witnesses?

      C.   "It is so that you will not shut the door before those who wish to take out loans [by making it difficult for the lender to collect."

      D.   *But deal with the following:* [32B] If the judges made an error in their verdict, they should not have to make restitution. [Why not make this rule too?]

      E.   All the more so will you turn out to shut the door before those who wish to take out loans.

I.3   A.   *Raba said, "The rule at hand [which requires examination and interrogation of witnesses in property cases] deals with cases involving judicial penalties, while the other passages [which do not require examination of witnesses] deal with cases of admission that a debt exists and cases of transactions in loans. [In such cases the procedure would discourage creditors from lending money.]"*

      B.   *Said R. Pappa, "Both rules [that of the Mishnah, requiring interrogation, and the others cited, not requiring it] deal with matters of admissions of existing debts and transactions of loans. The former speak of a case involving suspicious circumstances, the latter does not."*

      C.   *That accords with the statement of R. Simeon b. Laqish. For R. Simeon b. Laqish contrasted [apparently conflicting verses of Scripture].* "It is written, 'In justice you shall judge your neighbor' (Lev. 19:15). And elsewhere it is written, 'Justice, justice shall you follow' (Deut. 16:20. [The repetition of 'justice' indicates that strict justice must be followed, hence rules such as interrogation of witnesses]. Why [does the word justice appear twice in one verse but only once in the other]? The verse [that repeats the word justice] refers to a case involving suspicious circumstances [therefore interrogation of witnesses is necessary]. The other verse refers to a case in which there are no suspicious circumstances [hence no interrogation is required].

      D.   *R. Ashi said, "The Mishnah-passage may be reconciled with the contradictions pointed out above as we have now explained. As to the verses of Scripture, one refers to strict justice, the other to arbitration."*

      E.   *So has it been taught on Tannaite authority:*

F.   "Justice, justice shall you follow" (Deut. 16:20): One reference to "justice' speaks of the strict justice of a trial, the other of arbitration.

G.   How so? Two boats going on a river which meet – if both of them pass together, they will both sink. If they go one after another, they will both pass safely.

H.   So too two camels going up the ascent at Bet Horon which meet – if they both try to go onward together, they will both fall. If they go up one after the other, they both will make it safely.

I.   How [do they proceed]?

J.   If one of the asses was loaded and one of them was not loaded, the one that was not loaded gives way to the one that was loaded.

K.   If one of the asses was nearer [its destination] and the other not near, the one that was nearer gives way before the one that was not near.

L.   If both of them were near or both far, they should make a compromise among them and the one will pay compensation to the next [for the loss]. [T. B.Q. 2:10B-I].

I.4

A.   *Our rabbis have taught on Tannaite authority:*

B.   "Justice, justice shall you follow" (Deut. 16:20):

C.   [This means] seek out a well-qualified court,

D.   [such as] R. Eliezer in Lydda, [or] Rabban Yohanan b. Zakkai in Beror Hayyil.

E.   *It was taught on Tannaite authority:*

F.   If you hear the sound of the grinding of the wheel in Boreni, it is a sign that the week following the birth of a son has been fulfilled [and the circumcision is at hand].

G.   [If you see] the light of a lamp in Beror Hayyil, it is the sign that there is a banquet there.

H.   *Our rabbis have taught on Tannaite authority:*

I.   "Justice, justice shall you follow" (Deut. 16:20):

J.   [This means] seek out sages in session,

K.   [such as] R. Eliezer in Lydda, Rabban Yohanan ben Zakkai in Beror Hayyil, R. Joshua in Peqiin, Rabban Gamaliel in Yabneh, R. Aqiba in Bene Beraq, R. Mattia in Romi, R. Hanania b. Teradion in Sikhni, R. Yosé in Sepphoris, R. Judah b. Beterah in Nisibis, R. Joshua in the Exile, Rabbi in Bet Shearim, sages in the hewn-stone chamber.

II.1

A.   **In property cases they begin [argument with the case either for acquittal or for conviction, while in capital cases they begin only with the case for acquittal and not with the case for conviction] [M. 4:1E]:**

B.   *What do they say [for the defense]?*

C.   *Said R. Judah, "This is what we say [to the witnesses for the prosecution], 'Who will say that matters are as you claim?'"*

D.   *Said Ulla to him, "And lo, we should shut them up!"*

E.   *And let them be shut up! Has it not been taught on Tannaite authority:*

F.   **R. Simeon b. Eleazar says, "They move the witnesses from place to place to confuse them so that they will retract" [T. San. 9:1A]?**

G.   *Are the cases parallel? In that case the witnesses are put off in the natural course of events, while here, by our own act we put them off.*

H.   *Rather, said Ulla, "This is what we say to them, 'Do you [the defendant] have witnesses to prove that they form a conspiracy for perjury?'"*

I.   Said Rabbah to him, "But do we open the trial with an argument for the acquittal for this party which also constitutes an argument for the conviction of the other party?"

J.   *But does this encompass an argument for conviction? Have we not learned in the Mishnah:* **Witnesses who have conspired to commit perjury are not put to death [for their perjury] unless the court process has been completed [M. Mak. 1:6A]**? [Here, by contrast, the trial is just beginning, and the perjured witnesses can go off free if the accused is not convicted.]

K.   *This is the sense of my statement: If this one remains silent until the end of the court process and then brings witnesses and demonstrates that the witnesses against him form a conspiracy to commit perjury, it turns out to be the conviction of the other party!*

L.   *Rather, said Rabbah, "We say to him, 'Do you have witnesses to contradict [the witnesses against you]?'"*

M.   *R. Kahana said, "[We say], 'From what you have said, it would appear that the accused is innocent.'* [Schachter, p. 206, n. 2: The judges start by pointing out the weak features of the prosecution, e.g., even if certain statements of the prosecution are proved true, they do not show the guilt of the accused.]"

N.   *Both Abbayye and Raba say, "We say to him, 'If you did not kill anyone, do not be afraid'"*

O.   *R. Ashi said, "Let anyone who has any information for the acquittal of this party come and present it in his behalf.'"*

P.   *It has been taught on Tannaite authority along the lines of the position of Abbayye and Raba:*

Q.   Rabbi says, "'If no man have lain with you and if you have not gone aside...' (Num. 5:19).

R.   "[33A] On the basis of this verse we learn that in capital trials the court begins first with arguments for acquittal."

III.1 A.   **In property cases they reverse the decision [whether in favor of acquittal or in favor of conviction, while in capital cases they reverse the decision so as to favor acquittal but they do not reverse the decision so as to favor conviction] [M. 4:1G]:**

B.   *An objection was raised on the basis of the following:* **If one judged a case, declaring a liable person to be free of liability, declaring the person free of liability to be liable, declaring what is clean to be unclean, declaring what is unclean to be clean, what he has done is done. But he pays compensation from his own funds [M. Bekh. 4:4D-F].** [Why not retract the decision, in line with M. 4:1G?]

C.   *Said R. Joseph, "There is no contradiction. Here [where the decision may be changed] we deal with the decision of an expert, and there [where the decision cannot be changed but the judge has to pay compensation for his error], it is the decision of one who was not an expert."*

D.   *But in the case of the decision of a judge who was an expert, do we retract the decision? And lo, it has been taught on Tannaite authority:* **But if he** was an expert recognized by a court, he is free from the liability of paying [M. Bekh. 4:4G] [but the decision holds good. So the expert-judges' decision also cannot be reversed].

E.   Said R. Nahman, "In the one case [where the decision may be retracted] it is where there is a court superior in learning and in numbers, and where [the decision may not be retracted] it is where there is no superior court in wisdom and in numbers [to reverse the decision]."

F.   R. Sheshet said, "Here we speak of a case in which the error was in a teaching in the Mishnah [and the decision may be revoked], while there we deal with an error in critical reasoning [in which case the decision may not be revoked]."

G.   For R. Sheshet said R. Assi said, "If one has erred in a matter that is taught in the Mishnah, the decision is to be retracted. If the error lay in critical reasoning, the decision is not to be retracted."

H.   *Said Rabina to R. Ashi, "Even if one has erred in a matter attributed to R. Hiyya and R. Oshaia [e.g., in materials assembled in collections of Tosefta imputed to their authorship]?"*

I.   *He said to him, "Yes".*

J.   *[He asked] "And even in a matter attributed to Rab and Samuel?"*

K.   *He said to him, "Yes."*

L.   *"And even in matters attributed to me and to you?"*

M.   *He said to him, "Are we hackers of swamp-reeds? [Of course!]"*

III.2   A.   What is an example of "a matter of critical reasoning"?

B.   *Said R. Pappa, "It would involve, for example, a case in which there is a dispute on an issue between two Tannaite authorities or two Amoraic authorities, in which a statement of the decided law in accord with one or the other of the authorities has not been laid down. The judge at hand happened to make a decision in accord with one of them, but the trend of discussion in point of fact follows the other. This would be the case of an error involving critical analysis."*

C.   *An objection was raised by R. Hamnuna to R. Sheshet:*

D.   "There was the precedent of the case of a cow which had had its womb removed. R. Tarfon had the cow fed to the dogs [as invalid for Israelite consumption]."

E.   "The case came before sages, and they declared it permitted. Said Todos, the physician, 'Neither a cow nor a pig leaves Alexandria without their ripping out its womb, so that it will not bear offspring."

F.   "Said R. Tarfon, 'There goes your ass, Tarfon' [since he assumed he would have to pay restitution]."

G.   "Said to him R. Aqiba, 'R. Tarfon, you are exempt, for you are an expert recognized by a court, and any expert recognized by a court is free from the liability of paying' [M. Bekh. 4:4H-M]."

H.   *"Now is you were right [that an error in a Mishnah-law warrants retracting a decision], then he should have said to him,* 'You have erred concerning a rule of the Mishnah, and one who errs in a rule of the Mishnah may simply retract his decision.'"

I.   *The sense of [Aqiba's statement] is to give two reasons [that Tarfon is exempt]: first,* "You have erred in a law of the Mishnah and may retract;" *and furthermore, moreover,* "You have erred in a matter of critical reasoning, and you are an expert publicly acknowledged by the court, and whoever is an expert recognized by a court is free from the liability of paying."

J.   *Said R. Nahman bar Isaac to Raba, "How could R. Hamnuna raise an objection to R. Sheshet from the case of the cow? As to the cow, lo, he fed it to the dogs, and there is no possibility of giving it back!"*

K.   *This is what he meant to say to him: "If you claim that if one has erred in the matter of a Mishnah-law, he may not retract, therefore the decision stands, that is why R. Tarfon was concerned. So [Aqiba] said to him,* **"You are exempt, for you are an expert recognized by a court, and any expert recognized by a court is free from the liability of paying [compensation]."**

L.   *But if you maintained that if one errs in a matter of Mishnah-law, he may indeed retract the decision, he should have said to him, "If the cow were still available, your decision would not have stood, and you would have done nothing [demanding reparations], now too you have done nothing whatsoever.* [Schachter, p. 208, n. 9: Seeing that Aqiba did not argue in that manner, it can be inferred that if one errs regarding a law cited in the Mishnah, the decision may not be reversed.]

M.   [Dealing with the contradiction], said R. Hisda, "At that passage [M. Bekh. 4:4] we deal with the case in which a judge personally took the beast from one party and disposed of it [in which case the decision cannot be reversed], and in the present matter [the rule of M. San. 4:1G, in which, in a property case, we may retract the decision], we deal with a case in which the judge did not personally remove [property] from one party and hand it over to the other."

N.   *Now [that thesis poses no problem in the case in which] a judge declared one liable who in fact was exempt. For example, it would be a case in which he removed property from one party and personally handed it over to the other party. But if one is supposed to have declared the liable party to be exempt, how can we find an equivalent case? [All the judge has done is to leave the property in the hands of the person who now has it.]*

O.   *It would be a case in which the judge said to him, "You are exempt [from having to make a payment]."*

P.   *But in this case he has not personally taken from the one party and handed it over to the other party!*

Q.   *Since he has said, "You are exempt," it is as if he took property from one party and handed it over to the other party.*

R.   *But what about our Mishnah-paragraph, in which it is taught:* **In property cases they reverse the decision whether in favor of acquittal or in favor of conviction [M. 4:1G]?**

S.   *Now in the matter of reversing the decision in a case of acquittal we could find such a case, for example, when the judge said to him, to begin with, 'You are liable," but he did not personally take property from the one and hand it over to the other.*

T.   *But if it was on the side of the world, how would you find such a case?*

U.   *It would be where the judge said to him, "You are exempt."*

V.   *But you have just said that once the judge has said to him, "You are exempt," it is as if he had taken property from one party and personally handed it over to the other party.*

W.   *The Mishnah-passage makes a single statement [not two]:* In property cases they reverse the decision in exemption of the one party, which is a decision of liability to the other party.

X.   *Along these same lines, in respect to capital cases:*

Y.   **In capital cases they reverse the decision so as to favor acquittal [33B], but they do not reverse the decision so as to favor conviction [M. 4:1G].**

Z.   **They retract the decision so as to favor acquittal –** *acquittal alone.*

AA.   **And they do not retract the decision to favor conviction –** acquittal for one which is conviction for another.

BB.   *Conviction for whom?*

CC.   *That is no problem, it would be conviction [to the detriment of] the one who is to redeem the blood.*

DD.   *On account of avoiding a decision detrimental to the one who redeems the blood, should we put this one to death?*

EE.   *And moreover, what is the sense of the language, whether...whether... [which indicates that we deal with two statements, not one]?*

FF.   *That is a problem.*

GG.   Rabina said, "[As to R. Hisda's statement that where the guilty party is found innocent, the decision cannot be reversed, since that would involve taking from one and giving to the other], it would be illustrated by a case in which the plaintiff held a pledge in his hand, and the judge took it from him.

HH.   "'If he declared the clean to be unclean' would be illustrated by a case in which a judge [personally made the object unclean himself] by bringing it in contact with a reptile.

II.		"'If he declared the unclean to be clean' would be illustrated by a case in which the judge personally mixed [the fruit he had declared clean] with the fruit [of the one who had brought the question, in fact thereby rendering the entire lot unclean]."
IV.1	A.	**In capital cases they reverse the decision [so as to favor of acquittal but not so as to favor conviction] [M. 4:1G]:**
	B.	How on the basis of Scripture do we know that, if someone goes forth from court having been declared guilty, and one [of the judges] said, "I have arguments to offer in behalf of a verdict of innocence," that we bring the convicted man back?
	C.	Scripture says, "You shall not kill the guiltless" (Ex. 23:7).
	D.	And how do we know on the basis of Scripture that one who goes forth from court having been declared innocent, and one of the judges said, "I have arguments to offer in behalf of a verdict of guilty," that we do not bring the man back?
	E.	Scripture says, "And the one who has been declared righteous you shall not slay" (Ex. 23:7).
	F.	*Said R. Shimi bar Ashi, "And it is the opposite with one who incites [Israelites to commit idolatry]. For it is written, 'You shall not spare nor shall you conceal him" (Deut. 13:9)."*
	H.	*R. Kahana derived the same lesson from the verse, "But you shall surely kill him" (Deut. 13:10).*
	I.	*R. Zera asked R. Sheshet, "What is the law [about bringing back to court someone who has been held] and sent into exile [for unintentional homicide]? [Can he be brought back to court if one of the judges said 'I have arguments to offer in behalf of a verdict of innocence'? Yes.]"*
	J.	*"For we establish an analogy between that case and the present one through the common use, in both instances, of the word 'murderer.'"* *[Just as a murderer can be brought back, so too can a person who committed unintentional homicide.]*
	K.	*"What is the law concerning those who are liable to be flogged?"*
	L.	*"It comes through establishing an analogy between the one and the other area of law through the use, in common, of the word 'wicked.'"*
	M.	*So too has it been taught on Tannaite authority:*
	N.	How do we know that the same rule applies in cases of those liable to exile?
	O.	We establish an analogy through the common use of the word "murderer."
	P.	And how do we know that that is the law in the case of those liable to a flogging?
	Q.	From the use of the word "wicked" in both contexts.
V.1	A.	**But they do not reverse the decision so as to favor conviction [M. 4:1G]:**
	B.	Said R. Hiyya bar Abba said R. Yohanan, "And that applies if one has made a mistake about a matter about which the Sadducees do not concur [something not in Scripture], but if one has erred in a matter about which the Sadducees concur [which is to say, something actually written out in Scripture], *then it is something you learn in school [and there is no reason to reverse the conviction]."*

C.   *R. Hiyya bar Abba asked R. Yohanan, "If one made an error in a law about an adulterer or an adulteress, what is the law? [Schachter, p. 211, n. 12: Whereas other criminal cases lend themselves to mistakes in judgment, owing to the investigation of the manifold details accompanying the act, in cases of illicit intercourse, once the act is done, there is no room for error.]"*

D.   *He said to him, "While the fire is lit, go harvest your pumpkin and roast it."*

E.   *So too it has been stated on Amoraic authority:*

F.   *Said R. Ammi said R. Yohanan, "If one made an error in a case involving an adulterer, the decision is retracted."*

G.   *In what sort of cases do they not retract a decision?*

H.   Said R. Abbahu said R. Yohanan, "In a case, for instance, in which one made an error about sodomy [for this would be something on which the Sadducees do not concur, Scripture not being explicit about it]."

VI.1   A.   **In property cases all [argue either for acquittal or conviction, in capital cases all argue for acquittal, but all do not argue for conviction] [M. 4:1H]:**

B.   All encompasses even the witnesses.

C.   *May we say that the Mishnah-paragraph represents the view of R. Yosé b. R. Judah and not rabbis?*

D.   *For it has been taught on Tannaite authority:*

E.   *"'But one witness shall not testify against any person'" (Num. 35:30) – whether to testify for a verdict of innocence or for guilt.*

F.   R. Yosé b. R. Judah says, "One may testify for innocence, but may not testify for a verdict of guilt." [So Yosé would concur with the statement of the Mishnah, as interpreted at B, and rabbis would not.]

G.   Said R. Pappa, "The Mishnah-paragraph refers to one of the disciples [not one of the witnesses], and it represents the view of all parties."

H.   [34A] *What is the Scriptural basis for the view of R. Yosé b. R. Judah?*

I.   *It is because Scripture has said, "But one witness shall not testify against any person that he die" (Num. 35:30).*

J.   *"So that he die" he may not testify, but so as to acquit the accused he may testify.*

K.   And rabbis?

L.   *Said R. Simeon b. Laqish, "It is because the witness would appear to have a personal interest in his testimony [for acquittal, to avoid being convicted as a part of a conspiracy for perjury, and that is why he changes his testimony]."*

M.   *And how do rabbis interpret the language, "...that he die"?*

N.   *They apply that verse to the case of testimony from one of the disciples.*

O.   *For it has been taught on Tannaite authority:*

P.   If one of the witnesses said, "I have an argument to offer in favor of the defendant," how do we know that we pay no attention to him?

R.   And how do we know that if one of the disciples said, "I have an argument against the defendant," we do not pay attention to him?

S.   Scripture says, "One shall not testify against any person that he die" (Num. 35:30) [but he may do so for acquittal (Schachter)].

VII.1 **A.**   **In capital cases one who argues [for conviction may argue for acquittal, but the one who argues for acquittal has not got the power to retract and to argue for conviction] [M. 4:1I]:**

      B.   Said Rab, "The rule applies only to the time of the give and take of argument in the case. But when the verdict has been reached, one who has argued in favor of innocence may retract and argue in favor of guilt."

      C.   *An objection was raised on the basis of the following:* **And the next day they would get up and come to court. The one who favors acquittal says, "I declared him innocent yesterday, and I stand my ground and declare him innocent today." And the one who declares him guilty says, "I declared him guilty yesterday, and I stand my ground and declare him guilty today." The one who argues in favor of guilt may now argue in favor of acquittal, but the one who argues in favor of innocence may not now go and argue in favor of guilt [M. 5:5C-F].** *Now "the next day" is the time at which the verdict has been reached [and the one who voted for innocence cannot then change his vote, contrary to Rab's statement].*

      D.   *But according to your reasoning [and the position you have taken], on the next day is there no more give and take? In point of fact the rule before us speaks of a time of give and take.*

      E.   *Come and take note:* **[If thirty-six vote for conviction and thirty-five vote for acquittal,] they debate the matter, until one of those who voted for conviction accepts the arguments of those who vote for acquittal [M. 5:5S].** *Now if it is the case [that even at the point of a verdict, one who favors innocence may change his mind], the passage should also repeat matters in the reverse [so that one of those who voted for innocence may then accept the arguments of those who vote for guilt].*

      F.   *The Tannaite framer of the passage will go back and refer to a verdict of innocence while not doing so for a verdict of guilt.*

      G.   *Come and take note of the following that was said by R. Yosé bar Hanina,* "If one of the disciples voted in favor of innocence and then died, they regard him as though he were still alive and standing in his place [taking the same position, and so they count his vote]." *And why should this be the case? May we not claim that, if he were alive, he might have reversed himself?*

      H.   *But now, at any rate, he has not reversed himself [so we could count his original vote].*

      I.   *And lo, they have sent from there,* "In accord with the view of R. Yosé bar Hanina, the opinion of our master [Rab] is excluded. [Schachter, p. 214, n. 1: Therefore his ruling not to consider an eventual change of opinion is due to the fact that he holds that at the promulgation of the decision one cannot retract]."

J.   *What was said was,* "Do not exclude [the opinion of our master, Rab]."

K.   *Come and take note:* **And two judges' clerks stand before them, one at the right and one at the left. And they write down the arguments of those who vote to acquit and of those who vote to convict [M. 4:3C].** *Now there is good reason to write down the premises of those who vote to convict, since the next day they may perceive a fresh argument and it may be necessary to postpone judgment over night* [to give the judges a chance to change their minds. Hence the necessity of recording their statements to show that they have changed their grounds for conviction, so necessitating a further postponement (Schachter, p. 214, n. 4). *But why write down the premises of those who vote to acquit? Is it not because, if they should perceive a fresh argument, we pay no attention to them at all?*

L.   *No, it is so that two judges should not give a single reason based on two different verses of Scripture.*

M.   *That accords with what R. Assi asked R. Yohanan,* "If two judges gave a single argument on the basis of two different verses of Scripture, what is the law?"

N.   He said to him, "They count them only as one [vote]."

O.   *How do we know on the basis of Scripture that that is the fact?*

P.   *Said Abbayye,* "It is because Scripture has said, 'God has spoken once, but I have heard two [different things] because strength belongs to God' (Ps. 62:12).

Q.   "One verse of Scripture may yield a number of arguments, but one argument cannot derive from a number of verses of Scripture."

R.   *The house of R. Ishmael's Tannaite authority [taught as follows:]* "'And like a hammer that breaks the rock in pieces' (Jer. 23:29). Just as a hammer splits a rock into many pieces, so a verse of Scripture may yield a number of arguments."

VII.2   A.   *What would be an example of how a single argument may emerge from two different verses of Scripture?*

B.   *Said R. Zebid,* "It would be exemplified by that which we have learned in the Mishnah: **The altar sanctifies that which is appropriate to it. R. Joshua says, 'Whatever is appropriate to the altar-fires, if it has gone up on to the fires, should not go down, since it is said, "This is the burnt-offering, that which goes up on the hearth on the altar" (Lev. 6:9). Just as the burnt-offering, which is appropriate to the altar-fires, if it has gone up, should not go down, so whatever is appropriate to the altar-fires, if it has gone up, should not go down.' Rabban Gamaliel says, 'Whatever is appropriate to the altar, if it has gone up, should not go down, as it is said, "This is the burnt-offering on the hearth on the altar" (Lev. 6:2). Just as the burnt-offering, which is appropriate to the altar, if it has gone up, should not go down, so whatever is appropriate to the altar, if it has gone up, should not go down.'** [M. Zeb. 9:1A-C].** *Now what is it that both authorities include [among things not to be removed from the* *altar]? It is invalid objects. One authority [Joshua] brings proof of that fact from the word 'firewood' and the other [Gamaliel] proves it from the word 'altar.'* [Schachter, p. 215, n. 10: Now at thís stage it is assumed that since both deduce the same general principle from two different verses, there is not real disagreement between them. This affords an illustration of 'one law drawn from two different verses.']"

C. *But in the case at hand, do the two authorities differ at all? Note the concluding part of the same Mishnah-paragraph:* **Rabban Gamaliel and R. Joshua differ only on the matter of the blood and the drink offerings. For Rabban Gamaliel says, "They should not [having been placed on the altar] be taken down," and R. Joshua says, "They should be taken down" [M. Zeb. 9:1D-F].**

D. *Rather, said R. Pappa, "[The example derives from a Tannaite teaching." For it has been taught on Tannaite authority:* R. Yosé the Galilean says, "Since it is said, [34B] 'Whatever touches the altar shall be holy' (Ex. 29:37), I might draw the inference that that is the case whether the substance is suitable for the altar or not suitable for the altar. Scripture then says, '[Now this is what you shall offer on the altar: two] lambs' (Ex. 29:37). This implies that just as lambs are suitable for the altar, so everything suitable [for the altar goes up and is not removed." R. Aqiba says, "'...burnt-offering...' (Ex. 29:38). Just as a burnt-offering is suitable, so anything that is suitable [goes up and does not come down]." *What is it that both then exclude? It is invalid substances. One authority derives proof from the reference to "lambs," and the other authority derives proof from the reference to "burnt-offering."*

E. *But has not R. Adda bar Ahba stated, "At issue between the authorities is a bird in the status of a burnt-offering that is in fact invalid. The one who derives proof from the reference to 'lambs' then rules that the law applies to lambs but not to birds in the status of a burnt-offering. And the one who derives his proof from the reference to 'burnt-offering' will conclude that even a bird offering as a burnt-offering is covered by the law at hand."*

F. *Rather, said R. Ashi, "It is in accord with that which has been taught on Tannaite authority:* "Blood shall be imputed to that man he has shed blood" (Lev. 17:4). This serves to include the one who sprinkles [blood of a sacrifice outside of the Temple courts within the liability of extirpation," the words of R. Ishmael. R. Aqiba says, "'...Or a sacrifice' (Lev. 17:4), serving to encompass the case of one who sprinkles [the blood, as above]." *And what is it that both encompass with these distinct proof-texts? It is the matter of sprinkling. One authority derives proof from the words, "Blood shall be imputed," and the other from, "Or a sacrifice."*

G. *But has not R. Abbahu stated, "At issue between them is the one who both slaughtered and sprinkled the blood of the sacrifice*

outside of the Temple. [The person who did so acted
unwittingly. He must bring a sin-offering in atonement. Does
he bring one offering, covering both deeds, or two offering, one
for each?] In the view of R. Ishmael, he is liable for only one sin-
offering [since the same verse that covers the prohibition for
sprinkling outside the court also prohibits slaughtering outside
the court], R. Aqiba maintains that he is liable for two sin-
offerings [on both counts, since the penalty for sprinkling and
the penalty for slaughtering outside the Temple court come from
different verses]."

H.   But lo, it has been stated in this regard, Said Abbayye, "Even in
the view of R. Aqiba, he is liable for only a single sin-offering, for
Scripture has said, 'There you shall offer your burnt
offerings and there you shall do all that I command you'
(Deut. 12:14). In this way the All-merciful has treated all acts
[of the sacrificial rite in the same classification]. [Schachter, p.
217, n. 10: Hence there is only this one verse which
commands that all acts of sacrifice, which includes
slaughtering and sprinkling, shall be done in the
prescribed fashion. Therefore transgression of both
involved only one sacrifice.]"

VIII.1 A. **In property cases they try the case by day [and complete it by
night. In capital cases they try the case by day and complete it the
following day] [M. 4:1J]:**

B.   What is the scriptural basis for this rule?

C.   Said R. Hiyya bar Pappa, "It is because Scripture has said, 'And let
them judge the people at all times' (Ex. 18:22) [even by night]."

D.   If that is the case, then why not begin the trial by night too?

E.   The answer accords with the statement of Raba. For Raba contrasted
verses: "It is written, 'And let them judge the people at all
times' (Ex. 18:22). And it is written, 'And in the day that he
causes his sons to inherit' (Deut. 21:16). [In the latter verse, we
are told that a civil suit is taken up by day. How do [we
resolve the apparent discrepancy between the two verses]? The
day is the time for the beginning of the trial, and the night may
well serve for the end of the trial and the delivery of the
verdict."

VIII.2 A. The Mishnah-passage before us does not accord with the view of R. Meir.
For it has been taught on Tannaite authority:

B.   R. Meir would say, "What is the meaning of the verse of Scripture,
'According to their words shall every controversy and every
leprosy be' (Deut. 21:5)? What have controversies [about civil
matters] to do with [considerations of] leprosy? Scripture links civil
suits to decisions on leprosy [to make the following points]. Just as
decisions on the status of lepers are made by day, as it is written,
'And in the day on which the raw flesh appears in him' (Lev. 13:14),
so decisions in civil suits are taken by day.

D.   "And just as decisions on leprosy cannot be made by blind men, as
it is written, 'Wherever the priest looks' (Lev. 13:12), so civil suits
may not be decided by blind men.

E. "The text further links decisions on leprosy to decisions on civil suits [imposing on the former rules governing the latter], thus, just as civil suits may not be tried by relatives, so decisions on leprosy may not be made by relatives.

F. "Should you further propose that, just as civil suits must be decided by three judges, so decisions on matters of leprosy must be settled by three priests,

G. "and it is a matter of logic: if a person's property is disposed of by three, should not the status of his own body all the more so be settled by three?

H. "to forestall this conclusion, Scripture states, 'When he shall be brought to Aaron, the priest, to one of his sons, the priests' (Lev. 13:2), in which you learn that even a single priest may inspect leprosy-signs."

VIII.3 A. *There was a blind man in the vicinity of R. Yohanan, who would judge cases, and R. Yohanan did not object in any way.*

B. *How could he have done so, for has not R. Yohanan stated, "The decided law is in accord with the Mishnah when it is stated anonymously [not in the name of a specific authority]"? And we have learned in [an anonymous passage] of the Mishnah:* **Whoever is suitable to judge is suitable to give testimony, but there is one who is suitable to give testimony but is not suitable to judge [M. Nid. 6:4G].** *And R. Yohanan stated, "That statement serves to encompass one who is blind in one eye [who can give testimony but not judge a case]."*

E. *R. Yohanan took note of a different passage of the Mishnah, one that is given anonymously, namely:* **In property cases they try the case by day and complete it by night [M. 4:1J].**

F. *What makes one anonymous Mishnaic rule more reliable than some other?*

G. *If you like, I shall say that an anonymous statement of the law that conforms to collective opinion is preferable [to one which, we know from other evidence, speaks only for an individual. Meir's view and the anonymous version of Meir's view therefore must take second place.]*

H. *And if you like, I shall propose that the framer of the Mishnah has cited the [anonymous version of the law in accord with the opposition to Meir] in the context of laws on the conduct of trials [and not merely incidentally].*

I. *And how does R. Meir deal with the verse,* "And let them judge the people at all times" (Ex. 18:22)?

J. *Said Raba, "It serves to include a cloudy day [in the proper time for holding civil cases or for examining leprosy-signs]." For we have learned in the Mishnah:* **They do not examine leprosy-signs at dawn or at sunset, or inside the house; or on a cloudy day, because the dim appears bright; or at noon, because the bright appears dim [M. Neg. 2:2A-D].** [But, in Meir's view, they would try a <u>civil</u> case on a cloudy day, and in that aspect he would distinguish the one sort of procedure from the other.]

M.   *And how does R. Meir interpret the verse of,* "And in the day that he causes his sons to inherit" (Deut. 21:16)? [Since Meir proves his point from the analogy of trials of civil cases to examination of leprosy-signs, how does he deal with the alternative proof for day-time trials, supplied here?]

N.   *He requires that to serve as a proof-text for the following teaching on Tannaite authority given by Rabbah b. Hanina before R. Nahman:*

O.   "'And in the day that he causes his sons to inherit' (Deut. 21:16):

P.   "By day you divide up an estate, and you do not divide up an estate by night."

Q.   *He said to him,* "But would you then say that one who dies in daytime may leave his estate to his children, while one who dies in the nighttime may not leave his estate to his children? Perhaps you refer to lawsuits concerning legacies [that these like any other civil suits must take place by day [Schachter, p. 219, n. 15)]?" For so it has been taught on Tannaite authority: "And it shall be for the children of Israel a statute of judgment" (Num. 27:11). [This sentence refers to inheritance-laws.] That statement imposes upon all of the laws of the chapter at hand the rules governing civil cases in general.

T.   *That accords with what R. Judah said Rab said. For R. Judah said Rab said,* "If three people came into visit the sick, [who wished to direct the disposition of his estate for them, if they wish, they write out [his instructions as a will], and if they wish, they serve as a court [and carry out the instruction directly]. But if two were there [not three], they write out [and witness] the will, but they can not serve as a court."

V.   And R. Hisda said, "That has been taught only if they came by day. But if they came by night, they write out a will and do not serve as a court, because they constitute witnesses, and a witness cannot serve as a judge."

W.   *He said to him,* "Yes indeed, that is just what I meant."

IX.1   A.   **In capital cases, they try the case by day [and complete it the following day] [M. 4:1J]:**

B.   *What is the scriptural basis for this rule?*

C.   *Said R. Shimi bar Hiyya,* "Scripture has said, 'And hang them up unto the Lord in the face of the sun' (Num 25:4) [thus, by day, not by night]."

D.   *Said R. Hisda,* "How do we know that the word at hand means 'hanging'? As it is written, 'And we will hang them up to the Lord in Gibeah of Saul, the chosen of the Lord' (2 Sam. 21:6), and it is written **[35A]**, 'And Rizpah, the daughter of Aiah, took sack-cloth and spread it for her upon the rock, from the beginning of harvest' (2 Sam. 21:6). [Schachter: So they must have been hanged on trees]."

IX.2	A.	It is written, "And the Lord said to Moses, take all the chiefs of the people" (Num. 25:4).
	B.	While the people had sinned, how had the chiefs of the people sinned?
	C.	Said R. Judah said Rab, "Said the Holy One, blessed be he, to Moses, 'Divide them up into courts' [to try sinners." [Schachter, p. 221, n. 3: The verse is accordingly translated: Take the chief chiefs of the people and appoint them as judges and hang up them whom they shall condemn].
	D.	*What is the reason [for this instruction]? If we say that it is because* **two are not to be judged on a single day [and condemned to death] [M. San. 6:4M],** has not R. Hisda stated, "The rule applies only to two different forms of inflicting the death penalty, but if it is a single form of the death penalty, they do judge any number of cases in one day"? Rather it is so that "God's wrath may turn away from Israel" (Num. 25:4).
X.1	A.	**In property cases they come to a final decision on the same day as the trial itself, [whether it is for acquittal or conviction. In capital cases they come to a final decision for acquittal on the same day but on the following day for conviction] [M. 4:1K]:**
	B.	*What is the scriptural basis for this rule?*
	C.	*Said R. Hanina, "It is in line with this verse of Scripture: 'She that was full of justice, righteousness lodged in her, but now murderers' (Is. 1:21) [Schachter, p. 221, nos. 8-9: Judgment was held over ['lodged over night'] lest points for acquittal might be found. But now they do not postpone the verdict until the next day and so are murderers.]"*
	D.	*And Raba said, "Proof is from here: 'Relieve the oppressed' (Is. 1:17). [We have a play on words, that yields] [Schachter:] 'Bless the judge who reserves his verdict.'"*
	E.	*And the other? "Relieve the oppressed [by attending to the plaintiff] and not the oppressor [the defendant]."*
	F.	*And as to [Raba], how does he interpret the verse, "And she that was full of justice" (Is. 1:21)?*
	G.	*He interprets that verse as does R. Eleazar in the name of R. Isaac. For R. Eleazar said R. Isaac said, "In the case of any fast day on which gifts to the poor are kept overnight, it is as if one sheds blood, as it is said, 'She that was full of justice, but now that charity [is made to lodge therein (and postponed overnight), they are as murderers]' [Schachter] (Is. 1:21)."*
	I.	*And that rule pertains specifically to postponing distribution of bread and dates, but as to money, wheat, or barley, there is no objection [to postponing distribution by a day].*
XI.1	A.	**Therefore they do not judge [capital cases either on the eve of the Sabbath or on the eve of a festival] [M. 4:1L]:**
	B.	*What is the reason? Because it is impossible. How could someone do it? If someone were to try a case on Friday and complete the verdict on that day, perhaps they might find reason to convict the accused, in which case they would have to postpone the judgment overnight.*

C.   *But have the trial on Friday and complete the decision on the Sabbath, and if he is guilty put him to death on the Sabbath.*

D.   Capital punishment does not override the restrictions of the Sabbath.

E.   *Then why not put him to death in the evening?*

F.   *We require that the execution take place "in the face of the sun" (Num. 25:4) [in daytime].*

G.   *Then complete the trial on the Sabbath and put the convicted felon to death on Sunday.*

H.   You will turn out to delay the course of justice [Schachter] [by postponing the execution].

I.   *Then why not conduct the trial on Friday and complete the verdict on Sunday?*

J.   *The judges might forget their reasons [for taking the positions that they did].*

K.   Even though **two judges' clerks stand before them, one at the right and one at the left, and they write down the arguments of those who vote to acquit and of those who vote to convict [M. M. 4:3C-D]?**

L.   *Granted that they write down what they say, still, once the heart forgets, it is forgotten. Therefore it is not possible.*

XI.2   A.   Said R. Simeon b. Laqish to R. Yohanan, "The burial of a neglected corpse should override the restrictions of the Sabbath, on the basis of the following argument <u>a fortiori</u>:

B.   "Now if the performance of the Temple cult, which overrides the Sabbath is set aside on account of the burial of a neglected corpse, [the Sabbath, restrictions of which are abrogated for the Temple service, all the more so should be overridden for the burial of a neglected corpse].

C.   *"[And how do we know that observance of the Sabbath is set aside on account of the requirement to bury a neglected corpse?]*

D.   *"It is learned from the teaching concerning* "And on account of his sister" (Num. 6:7). [A Nazirite may not render himself unclean even should his father, mother, brother, or sister die.]"

E.   *So it has been taught on Tannaite authority:* "On account of his father, his mother, brother, and sister" [a Nazirite should not contract corpse-uncleanness, in connection with the necessity of burying them], (Num. 6:7).

F.   What is the purpose of this statement?

G.   Lo, if on a Nazirite was going to slaughter his Passover-sacrifice or to circumcise his son, **[35B]** and he heard that a relative had died, is it possible that to bury that person, the Nazirite should contract corpse-uncleanness?

H.   You say, "He shall not become unclean."

I.   Is it possible that, just as he may not contract corpse-uncleanness to bury his sister, so he may not contract corpse-uncleanness to bury a neglected corpse?

J.   Scripture states, "And on account of his sister" (Num. 6:7). For his sister he may not contract corpse uncleanness, but he <u>must</u> contract corpse-uncleanness on account of a neglected corpse.

K.   [Simeon b. Laqish reverts to the original argument,] if the restrictions of the Sabbath are set aside on account of the conduct of the sacrificial cult, is it not logical that the burial of a neglected corpse should override the restrictions of the Sabbath [which overrides the cult]?"

L.   He said to him, "Executing a condemned criminal should prove the contrary, for it will override the requirements of the sacrificial cult but it will not override the restrictions of the Sabbath."

M.   [He replied,] But executing a convicted criminal <u>should</u> override the restrictions of the Sabbath, on the basis of an argument <u>a fortiori</u>:

N.   "Now if the conduct of the Temple cult, which overrides the restrictions of the Sabbath, is itself overridden by the requirement to execute a murderer, as it is said, 'You shall take him from my altar that he may die' (Ex. 21:14), the Sabbath restrictions which are overridden by the Temple cult, surely should give way to the execution of the condemned criminal.

O.   *Said Raba, "The matter has already been settled by a Tannaite authority of the house of R. Ishmael."*

P.   *For a Tannaite authority of the house of R. Ishmael [said], "You shall not kindle a fire [on the Sabbath]' (Ex. 35:3). What is the purpose of this statement?"*

Q.   What is the purpose of this statement?! [We all know the answer]. If we speak from the viewpoint of R. Yosé, [that one should not kindle a flame] is singled out so as to indicate that [kindling a flame] is simply a negative commandment [violation of which is punished by flogging. Other violations of the Sabbath are punished by execution through stoning.]

R.   If we speak from the viewpoint of R. Nathan, it is singled out in order to indicate that we treat a singular and punishable act each distinct violation of Sabbath-law [not grouping all of them and penalizing the whole].

S.   *For it has been taught on Tannaite authority:*

T.   "Specification of kindling a flame [as a prohibited act] serves to place such an act in the category of a negative commandment," the words of R. Yosé.

U.   R. Nathan says, "It serves to treat as a distinct act [punished by itself] that deed [or any other deed in violation of the Sabbath]."

V.   Rather, said Raba, "What posed a problem to the Tannaite authority was the word 'habitations' [at Ex. 35:3, not to kindle a flame 'in all of Israel's habitations']. Why is that word included?

W.   "[Here is what troubled the Tannaite authority at hand:] Since the Sabbath is an obligation that pertains to the person, and since an obligation pertaining to the person applies both in the Land and outside of the Land, why did the All-Merciful include the word 'habitations' [which speaks of the Land of Israel in particular]?"

X.   In the name of R. Ishmael a disciple said, "It is because it is written, 'And if a man has committed a sin worthy of death and he be put to death' (Deut. 21:22). I might then take the view that that may be done whether on a weekday or on the Sabbath. In that case how shall I carry out the verse, 'Those who profane [the Sabbath] shall certainly be put to death' (Ex. 31:14)? It would refer to other forms of labor prohibited on the Sabbath, but not carrying out the death penalty imposed by a court.

Y.   "Or perhaps that statement encompasses also the execution of criminals convicted by a court.

Z.   "In that case how shall I interpret 'And he shall be put to death' (Deut. 21:22)?

AA.   "It would speak of weekdays, and not the Sabbath.

BB.   "Or perhaps it means that the execution is carried out even on the Sabbath?

CC.   "Scripture states, 'You shall not kindle a fire throughout your habitations' (Ex. 35:3), and elsewhere it is written, "And these things shall be for a statute of judgment for you throughout your generations in all your habitations' (Num. 35:29).

DD.   "Just as 'habitations' in that context speaks of matters pertaining to courts, so 'habitations' here speaks of matters pertaining to courts.

EE.   "Now when the All-Merciful has said, 'You shall not kindle a fire in all your habitations' (Ex. 35:3) [that must encompass not imposing the death penalty for the Sabbath, since one form of the death penalty is through 'burning.' So one cannot inflict the death penalty on the Sabbath, despite the argument a fortiori given above. And it further follows that one may not bury a neglected corpse on the Sabbath either.]"

FF.   *Said Abbayye, "Now that you have shown that* the death penalty does not override the restrictions of the Sabbath, it should follow that the death penalty does not override the requirements of the Temple cult. This would be based on an argument a fortiori.

GG.   "Now, if the Sabbath, which is set aside in favor of the requirements of the Temple cult, does not give way to the need to inflict the death penalty, the Temple cult, itself, which does override the restrictions of the Sabbath, surely should not give way before the requirement to inflict the death penalty.

HH.   "And as to the verse of Scripture, 'You shall take him from my altar that he may die' (Ex. 21:14) [which contradicts the foregoing proposition], that speaks of an offering made in behalf of an individual, which also would not override the restrictions of the Sabbath. [On the Sabbath offerings in

		behalf of individuals, as distinct from the community as a whole, are not prepared.]"
	II.	Said Raba, "Inflicting the death penalty should not override the offering of a sacrifice in behalf of an individual, on the basis of an argument a fortiori:
	JJ.	"[36A] Now if a festival, prohibitions of which are set aside on account of the requirement of an individual to bring an offering [e.g., the Passover, the appearance-offering, and the like], does not give way before the requirement to inflict the death penalty on a convicted felon, the offering of an individual, which does override the restrictions of the festival day, surely should not give way before the requirement to inflict the death penalty."
	KK.	*[The contrary view, that inflicting the death penalty does override the offering of a sacrifice in behalf of an individual] poses no problems to the position of him who has said,* "Offerings brought in fulfillment of vows and freewill offerings are not offered on a festival day."
	LL.	*But from the viewpoint of him who has said,* "Offerings brought in fulfillment of vows and freewill offerings are offered on the festival day," *what is there to say [to the argument just now presented?]* [Schachter, p. 226, n. 6: The premise being correct, the deduction is likewise correct, viz., that an execution cannot supersede a private offering. How then can the verse, "You shall take from my altar," be reconciled with this conclusion?]
	MM.	*Rather, said Raba, "[The position of Abbayye is not acceptable] from the viewpoint of him who has said that offerings brought in fulfillment of vows and freewill offerings are offered on the festival day, for in such a case, the cited verse, 'From my altar' simply does not apply* [Schachter, p. 226, n. 7: for as shown above, if Abbayye's reasoning is accepted, execution does not suspend even private offerings. To what then can 'From my altar' refer?]
	NN.	*"But even from the viewpoint of him who has said, 'Offerings brought in fulfillment of vows and freewill offerings are not offered on the festival day, [in which case the cited verse may refer to private offerings, nonetheless, Abbayye's view is not acceptable].*
	OO.	"For is it not written, 'From my altar' with the sense of 'my altar in particular. What is that altar? It is the altar on which the daily whole offering is made.
	PP.	*"And in that connection, the All-Merciful has stated, 'You shall take him from my altar that he may die' (Ex. 21:14).* [Schachter, p. 226, n. 11: Thus Scripture expressly stands in the way of the argument a fortiori proposed by Abbayye (Schachter, p. 226, n. 11)]."
XII.1	A.	**In cases involving questions of property, uncleanness and cleanness, [they begin voting from the eldest, In capital cases they begin from the side (with the youngest)] [M. 4:2A]:**

B.   *Said Rab, "I was among those who voted in the house of Rabbi, and it was from me that they began to count."*

C.   *But have we not learned in the Mishnah:* **They begin voting from the eldest [Rabbi should count first]?**

D.   *Said Rabbah, son of Raba, and some say, R. Hillel, son of R. Vallas, "The voting in the house of Rabbi was different, For there all votes began from the side [as an act of humility on the part of Rabbi]."*

XII.2   A.   And said Rabbah, son of Raba, and some say, R. Hillel, son of R. Vallas, "From the time of Moses to Rabbi, we do not find the combination of foremost status in learning in Torah and preeminence in worldly greatness joined in a single person."

B.   *And is that not so? And there was the case of Joshua?*

C.   *With him was Eleazar [equal in learning].*

D.   *There was Phineas? With him were the elders.*

E.   *There was Saul? With him was Samuel.*

F.   *But lo, [Samuel] died before him? We refer to the entire lifetime [of such a unique figure].*

G.   *There was David? With him was Ira the Jairite [2 Sam. 20:26].*

H.   *But lo, [Ira] died before him? We refer to the entire lifetime [of such a unique figure].*

I.   *There was Solomon? With him was Shimei, son of Gera [2 Sam. 19:18].*

J.   *But lo, [Solomon] killed [Shimei]? We refer to the entire lifetime.*

K.   *There was Hezekiah? With him was Shebnah.*

L.   *But he was killed [during Hezekiah's lifetime]? We refer to the entire lifetime.*

M.   *There was Ezra? No, with him was Nehemiah, son of Hachaliah.*

N.   Said R. Ada bar Ahbah, "I too say, 'From the time of Rabbi to R. Ashi, we do not find the combination of learning in Torah and worldly greatness joined in a single person."

O.   *Do we not? And lo, there was Huna bar Nathan.*

P.   *Huna bar Nathan was subordinate to R. Ashi.*

XIII.1   A.   **In capital cases they begin from the side [M. 4:2A]:**

B.   *What is the scriptural basis for this rule?*

C.   Said R. Aha bar Pappa, "Said Scripture, 'You shall not speak in a case (ryb)' (Ex. 23:2), meaning "do not speak against the chief judge (rb)' [a shift in meaning attained by supplying the consonants of "in a case' with different vowels]."

D.   *Rabbah b. b. Hannah said R. Yohanan [said], "Proof derives from here, 'And David said to his men, gird you on every man his sword, and they girded on every man his sword; then David also girded on his sword' (1 Sam. 25:13). [Schachter, p. 228, n. 3: The question whether Nabal the Carmelite's act was to be treated as rebelliousness against the king was here discussed and a vote taken in the form of girding on the sword. David was the last to express his opinion.]"*

XIII.2 A. Said Rab, "A person may teach his disciple [the rule on capital offenses] and then vote right along side of him in capital cases [with master and disciple each having a separate vote]."

B. *An objection was raised on the basis of the following passage:*

C. **And in matters pertaining to questions of uncleanness or of cleanness, as to the father and his son, the master and his disciple, both of them are counted as two votes.**

D. **In property and capital cases and cases involving flogging, the sanctification of the new month, or the intercalation of the year, they count as only one [T. San. 7:2 O-R].**

E. **[36B]** *When Rab made that statement, he referred to such disciples as R. Kahana and R. Assi, who required Rab's mastery of traditions but did not need help in reasoning about them."*

XIII.3 A. Said R. Abbahu [speaking of M. 4:1-2], "There are ten points of difference in the rules governing trials for property cases from those for capital cases.

B. "And none of those differences pertains to the trial of an ox that is to be stoned, except for the requirement of a court of twenty-three judges, that alone."

C. *What is the scriptural source for that rule [B]?*

D. *Said R. Aha bar Pappa, "It is because Scripture has said, 'You shall not bend the judgment of your poor in his cause' (Ex. 23:6) [Schachter, p. 228, n. 13: This is interpreted to mean that judgment must not be inclined in favor of conviction by a majority of only one].*

E. *"The judgment of your poor you may not bend, but you may bend the judgment in the case of an ox that is to be stoned. [Schachter, p. 229, n. 2: From this it may be inferred that the procedure in the trial of an ox to be stoned is other than that of capital cases, except in the number of judges, and that difference is extended to all the other peculiarities of capital procedure, since the object of particularly applying that procedure in capital cases was to achieve the acquittal of the accused – not so with an ox]."*

F. *Do you say there are ten? But they are only nine. But ten are listed.*

G. *It is [nine] because the rule that not everyone is valid to serve and the requirement that there be twenty-three judges constitute a single rule.*

H. *And lo, there is another. For it has been taught on Tannaite authority:*

I. **The eunuch and one who has never had children are [T.: suitable for judging property cases but are not suitable for judging capital cases] not to be seated on a Sanhedrin.**

J. **R. Judah adds [to the list] also the one who is too harsh or too forgiving [M. 4:2B-C] [T. San. 7:5A-B].**

K. And the opposite to these rules apply in the case of one who incites [Israel to commit idolatry], for the All-Merciful has said, "Neither shall you spare, nor shall you conceal him" (Deut. 13:9).

XIV.1 A. **All are valid to engage in the judgment of property cases, [but all are not valid to engage in the judgment of capital cases] [M. 4:2B].**

B. *What classification of persons does the specification of "all" serve to include?*

C. *Said R. Judah, "It includes children of prohibited marriages."*

D. *Lo, we have learned that in the Mishnah in a different context:* **Whoever is worthy to judge capital cases is worthy to judge property cases,** and there is one who is worthy to judge property cases and is not worthy to judge capital cases [M. Nid. 6:4F]. *And in reflection on that passage, it was asked, "...to include what classification of persons?" And [in that connection], said R. Judah, "It includes children of prohibited marriages."*

E. *In point of fact, one such reference includes a proselyte, the other, the child of a forbidden union.*

F. *And it was necessary to make both points explicit. For had we the rule concerning the proselyte, I might have supposed that [he may judge property because] he can enter the congregation [marrying Israelite], but the child of an illegal union [who may not enter the congregation and marry an Israelite] may not judge [property cases]. And had we learned the rule governing the child of an illegal union, I might have supposed that that is because he derives from valid seed, but a proselyte, who does not derive from a valid seed, would not be suitable [for judging property cases]. So it was necessary to specify both facts.*

XV.1 A. **But all are not valid to engage in the judgment of capital cases [M. 4:2B]:**

B. *What is the reason for this rule?*

C. *It accords with what R. Joseph repeated on Tannaite authority, "Just as a court must be clear in righteousness, so it must be clear of all blemishes."*

D. *Said Amemar, "What is the verse of Scripture that says so? 'You are fair, my love, and there is no blemish in you/ (Song 4:7)."*

E. *But perhaps this refers to the absence of physical blemishes [on the persons of the judges]?*

F. *Said R. Aha bar Jacob, "Scripture has said, 'That they may stand there with you' (Num. 11:16). 'With you' means those who are equivalent to you."*

G. *But then perhaps the rule in that case is [in particular] on account of the Presence of God [with Moses] [and the rule would not apply now]?*

H. *Rather, said R. Nahman bar Isaac, "Scripture has said, 'And they shall bear with you' (Ex. 18:22), meaning, they must be like you."*

In the aggregate we must conclude that the organizer of the Talmud has simply arranged his materials to serve as line by line expansions of the Mishnah's rules. The outline in Chapter Twelve shows how this works.

4:3-4

A. **The sanhedrin was [arranged in the shape of a half of a round threshing-floor [that is, as an amphitheatre],**

B. **so that [the judges] should see one another,**

C. **And two judges' clerks stand before them, one at the right and one at the left.**

D. **And they write down the arguments of those who vote to acquit and of those who vote to convict.**

E. **R. Judah says, "Three: One writes the opinion of those who vote to acquit, one writes the opinion of those who vote to convict, and**

the third writes the opinions both of those who vote to acquit and
of those who vote to convict."

M. 4:3

A. [37A] And three rows of disciples of sages sit before them.
B. Each and every one knows his place.
C. [If] they found need to ordain [a disciple to serve on the court],
D. they ordained one who was sitting in the first row.
E. [Then] one who was sitting in the second row joins the first row,
and one who was sitting in the third row moves up to the second
row.
F. And they select for themselves someone else from the crowd and
set him in the third row.
G. [The new disciple] did not take a seat in the place of the first
party [who had now joined in the court] but in the place that was
appropriate for him [at the end of the third row].

M. 4:4

I.1   A.   *What is the scriptural source for the rule [at M. 4:3A]?*
      B.   Said R. Aha bar Hanina, "It is because Scripture has said, 'Your
           navel is like a round goblet, wherein no mingled wine is wanting'
           (Song 7:3).
      C.   "'Thy navel' refers to the sanhedrin.
      D.   "Why is it called 'navel'?
      E.   "Because it is in session [on the Temple mount] at the navel of the
           world.
      F.   "Why is it called 'round'?
      G.   "Because [like a round shield] it protects the entire world.
      H.   "Why is it called 'goblet'? Because it is shaped like the moon [as is
           the goblet]. [Schachter, p. 231, n. 11: They were seated in circular
           form like a moon.]
I.2   A.   "Wherein no mingled wine is wanting:"
      B.   [If] one of them had to go out, he looks around to see whether
           there would be twenty-three left [after he departs]. If there
           would be twenty-three left, enough for a small Sanhedrin, he
           goes out, and if not, he does not go out.
      C.   [T.: unless there would be twenty-three left] [T. San. 7:1J-K].
I.3   A.   "Your belly is like a heap of wheat" (Song 7:3): just as in the
           case of a heap of wheat, everyone derives benefit,
      B.   so with the sanhedrin everyone benefits from their
           deliberations.
I.4   A.   "Set about with lilies" (Song 7:3): For even through a fence
           made up only of lilies [the members of the sanhedrin] will
           make no breaches.
      B.   *That is in line with what a min said to R. Kahana, "You say that
           a menstruating woman may be alone with her husband. Is it
           possible that there can be fire near two without singeing
           it?"*
      C.   He said to him, "The Torah has given testimony in our
           regard:

D.	"'Set about with lilies:' For even through a fence made up only of lilies [Israelites] will make no breaches."
E.	*R. Simeon b. Laqish said, "Proof derives from here:* 'Your temples are like a pomegranate split open' (Song 6:7): Even the empty-heads among you [play on the consonants that serve for both 'temple' and 'empty'] are as full of the accomplishment of religious duties as a pomegranate."
F.	*R. Zira said, "Proof derives from here:* 'And he smelled the scent of his raiment' (Gen. 27:27). Do not read it as 'remain' but as 'his traitors.' [Schachter, p. 232, n. 10: Even those who are traitors to Judaism diffuse the fragrance of good deeds]."

I.5

| A. | *There were some transgressors who lived in the neighborhood of R. Zira, who tried to draw them near so that they would return in penitence. Rabbis criticized him [for this relationship]. When R. Zira died, [the wicked men] said, "Up to now, the burned man with dwarfed legs would pray for mercy for us. Now who will pray for mercy for us?"* |
| B. | *They reflected on the matter in their hearts, and they carried out an act of repentance.* |

I.6

A.	*Said Abbayye, "We may infer from this rule that, when they move, all of them move."*
B.	*But cannot [the one who moves up a row] now say to them, "Up to now I was sitting at the head [of my row], and now you have seated me at the tail]"?*
C.	*Said Abbayye, "They may say this to him:* 'Be a tail to lions and not a head to foxes'" [M. Abot 4:15]."

Once the proof-text, Song 7:3, is introduced in unit I, the remainder of the passage at hand carries forward the exegesis of that verse, mostly in the context of the present theme.

4:5

A.	How do they admonish witnesses in capital cases?
B.	They would bring them in and admonish them [as follows]: "Perhaps it is your intention to give testimony on the basis of supposition, hearsay, or of what one witness has told another;
C.	"[or you may be thinking], 'We heard it from a reliable person'"
D.	"Or, you may not know that in the end we are going to interrogate you with appropriate tests of interrogation and examination.
E.	"You should know that the laws governing a trial for property cases are different from the laws governing a trial for capital cases.
F.	"In the case of a trial for property-cases, a person pays money and achieves atonement for himself. In capital cases [the accused's] blood and the blood of all those who were destined to be born from him [who was wrongfully convicted] are held against him [who testifies falsely] to the end of time.
G.	"For so we find in the case of Cain who slew his brother, as it is said, 'The bloods of your brother cry' (Gen. 4:10).

H.　"It does not say, 'The blood of your brother,' but, 'The bloods of your brother' – his blood and the blood of all those who were destined to be born from him."

I.　Another matter: 'The bloods of your brother' – for his blood was spattered on trees and stones.

J.　Therefore man was created alone, to teach you that whoever destroys a single Israelite soul is deemed by Scripture as if he had destroyed a whole world.

K.　And whoever saves a single Israelite soul is deemed by Scripture as if he had saved a whole world.

L.　And it was also for the sake of peace among people, so that someone should not say to his fellow, "My father is greater than your father."

M.　And it was also on account of the minim, so that the minim should not say, "There are many domains in Heaven."

N.　And to portray the grandeur of the Holy One, blessed be He. For a person mints many coins with a single seal, and they are all alike one another, But the King of kings of kings, the Holy One, blessed be He, minted all human beings with that seal of his with which he made the first person, yet not one of them is like anyone else. Therefore everyone is obligated to maintain, "On my account the world was created."

O.　Now perhaps you [witnesses] would like now to say, [37B] "What business have we got with this trouble?"

P.　But it already has been written, "He being a witness, whether he has seen or known, if he does not speak it, then he shall bear his iniquity" (Lev. 5:1).

Q.　And perhaps you might want to claim, "What business is it of ours to convict this man of a capital crime?"

R.　But has it not already been said, "When the wicked perish there is rejoicing" (Prov. 11:10).

M. 4:5

I.1　A.　*Our rabbis have taught on Tannaite authority:* What is the sense of "conjecture'?

　　B.　He says to them, "Perhaps this is what you saw: he was running after his fellow into a ruin [with a sword in his hand]. [The victim ran in front of him into a ruin, and then the other went after him into the ruin]. You went in after them and found [the victim slain on the floor], with a knife in the hand of the murderer, dripping blood."

　　C.　"If this is what you have seen, you have seen nothing [you must be admonished that this is not valid evidence]."

　　D.　*It has been taught on Tannaite authority:* **Said Simeon b. Shatah,** "May I [not] see consolation, if I did not see someone run after his fellow into a ruin, [with a sword in his hand, and the pursued man went before him into a ruin, and the pursuer ran in after him,] and then I came in right after him, and saw [the victim] slain, with a knife in the hand of the murderer, dripping blood, and I said to him, 'You evil person! Who killed this one? [May I [not] see consolation if I did not see him [run in here].] **Either you killed him or I did! But what can I do to you? For your blood is not handed over to me, For lo, the Torah has said, 'At the testimony of two witnesses or at the testimony of three witnesses shall he who is on trial for his life be put to death' (Deut. 17:6).**

E. **"'But He who knows the thoughts of man will exact punishment from that man.'**

F. **He did not move from the spot before a snake bit him, and he died" [T. San. 8:3].**

G. *But is this one subject to death by snake bite?* For has not R. Joseph said, and so too did the house of Hezekiah teach: "From the day on which the house of the sanctuary was destroyed, even though the sanhedrin ceased to be, the four forms of inflicting the death penalty did not cease to be."

H. Lo, they surely have ceased!

I. Rather, "the law governing the four forms of the death penalty has not ceased to be.

J. "He who became liable to the death penalty through stoning either falls from the roof or is trampled by a wild beast.

K. "He who became liable to the death penalty through burning either falls into a fire or is bitten by a snake.

L. "He who became liable to the death penalty through decapitation either is handed over for execution by the government, or thugs attack him [and cut off his head].

M. "He who becomes liable to the death penalty through strangulation either drowns in a river or dies by a quinsy."

N. One may reply that that man was already guilty on account of a different sin as well.

O. For a master has said, "Someone who is liable to the death penalty on two different counts is subjected to the more severe of the two."

II.1 A. **On the basis of supposition [M. 4:5B]:**

B. *It is in capital cases that we do not accept testimony based on supposition [or conjecture]. Lo, in the case of property cases, we do so.*

C. *In accord with whose view is that statement made?*

D. *It accords with R. Aha, for it has been taught on Tannaite authority:*

E. **R. Aha says, "A camel which was covering females among the camels, and one of the camels was found dead –**

F. **"[the owner of the one in heat] is liable, in the certainty that this one killed it" [T. B.Q. 3:6Q-R].**

G. *And in accord with the reasoning just now proposed [B], it is in particular in capital cases that we reject hearsay evidence. Lo, in property cases we accept it. And yet, have we not learned in the Mishnah.*

H. **If he said, "He told me, 'I owe him,' 'So-and-so told me that he owed him,'" he has said nothing whatsoever, unless he says, "In our presence he admitted to him that he owes him two hundred zuz? [M. 3:6E-F].** *Therefore, even though that form of evidence is also invalid in property cases, we state the rule in particular for capital cases.*

Here too even though that form of evidence is also invalid in property cases, we state the rule in particular for capital cases.

III.1   A.   **Know that ... [M. 4:5]:**

B.   Said R. Judah, son of R. Hiyya, "[Gen. 4:10, 'The bloods of your brother cry...'] teaches that Cain made on Abel, his brother, wound after wound, blow after blow, for he did not know from which one the soul would go forth, until he came to his neck."

C.   And said R. Judah, son of R. Hiyya, "From the day on which the earth opened its mouth to receive the blood of Abel, it has never again opened up, for it is said, 'From the edge of the earth have we heard songs, glory to the righteous' (Is. 24:16).

D.   "'From the edge of the earth' and not from the mouth of the earth.'"

E.   Hezekiah, his brother, objected, "'And the earth opened her mouth' (Num. 16:32)."

F.   He said to him, "For evil the earth opened, but not for good [and it was only to swallow Korah]. [Schachter, p. 237, n. 5: The opening to receive Abel's blood is accounted for good, to hide Cain's guilt.]"

G.   And said R. Judah, son of R. Hiyya, "Exile atones for half of one's transgressions. To begin with, it is written [about Cain], 'And I shall be a fugitive and a wanderer' (Gen. 4:14).

H.   "And afterward: 'And he dwelt in the land of wandering' (Gen. 4:14). [Schachter, p. 237, n. 7: The other half of the course, 'to be a fugitive' was remitted because of his exile.]"

III.2   A.   [Since Cain went into exile, the subject is pursued:] Said R. Judah [said Rab,] "Exile atones for three things.

B.   "For it is said, 'Thus says the Lord, He who abides in this city shall die by the sword, famine, and pestilence, but he who goes out and falls away to the Chaldeans who besiege you shall live, and his life shall be unto him for a prey' (Jer. 21:8-9). [Schachter, p. 237, n. 8: He who remained at home was subject to these three evils, but wandering and its consequent hardships outweighed them all.]"

C.   Said R. Yohanan, "Exile atones for everything, for it is said, 'Thus says the Lord, Write this man childless, a man that shall not prosper in his days, for no man of his seed shall prosper sitting upon the throne of David and ruling any more in Judah' (Jer. 22:30).

D.   *"After [the king] was exiled, it is written,* 'And the sons of Jechoniah, the same is Assir, Shealtiel, his son ... ' (1 Chr. 3:17). [So he was not childless, and through exile he had atoned for his sins.]"

E.   "Assir" because his mother conceived in prison [a word using the same consonants].

F.   "Shealtiel" because God planted him in a way different from the way in which people usually are planted. We know that a woman cannot become pregnant through intercourse done standing up, **[38A]** but she became pregnant through intercourse done standing up.

G.   Another explanation: "Shealtiel" because God consulted [using the same root] [sages] concerning his oath. [So as to have it remitted].

	H.	"Zerubbabel" because he was conceived in Babylonia.
	I.	And what was his name? It was Nehemiah, son of Hachaliah.
III.3	A.	*Judah and Hezekiah, sons of R. Hiyya, were seated at a meal before Rabbi and they were not saying anything. He said to the [waiter], "Give more strong wine to the young men so that they will say something."*
	B.	*When the wine had [Schachter] taken effect, they commenced by saying*, "David will not come until the two houses of patriarchal authority come to an end, specifically, the head of the exile in Babylonia and the patriarch in the Land of Israel.
	C.	"For it is said, 'And he shall be for a sanctuary, for a stumbling block and for a rock of offense to both houses of Israel' (Is. 8:14)."
	D.	He said to them, "You toss thorns into my eyes, my sons."
	E.	Said R. Hiyya to Rabbi, "Do not take offense. The numerical value of the letters composing the word, 'wine,' is seventy, and the same is so for the word, 'secret.' When wine goes in, secrets come out."
III.4	A.	*Said R. Hisda said Mar Uqba, and some say, said R. Hisda, Mari bar Mar expounded, "What is the meaning of the verse of Scripture,* 'And so the Lord has hastened the evil and brought it upon us, for the Lord our God is righteous' (Dan. 9:14)?
	B.	"Because 'the Lord is righteous' 'does he hasten the evil and bring it upon us'"
	C.	"Indeed so. The Holy One, blessed be he, acted in a righteous way with Israel by bringing the exile of Zedekiah while the exile of Jechoniah was still alive.
	D.	"It is written with reference to the exile of Jechoniah, 'And the craftsmen and smiths, a thousand' (2 Kgs. 24:16).
	E.	"[Since the word for craftsman may be read as 'deaf,' we may say,] as soon as they opened discourse, everyone became as deaf.
	F.	"[Since the word for smith may be read to mean, 'close,'] as soon as they completed the discussion of a law, it was not again taken up.
	G.	"How many were they? A thousand."
	H.	Ulla said, "He put the exile up by two years [Schachter:] as compared with the period indicated by venoshantem. [Schachter, p. 239, n. 6: And ye shall have been long (lit., 'grown old'), Deut. IV, 25. The numerical value of \ (6+50+6+300+50+400+40) is eight hundred and fifty-two. Subtracting two years according to this Haggadah, there are eight hundred and fifty-two. Subtracting two years according to this Haggadah, there are eight hundred and fifty years left, which is the length of time between Israel's entry into Palestine and the destruction of the Temple. The Temple was erected in the four hundred and eightieth year from the Exodus out of Egypt, and it stood for four hundred and ten year. Subtracting forty years for the period of their wanderings in he desert, we

reach a total of eight hundred and fifty years. That acceleration by two years is here regarded as a 'righteous' (i.e., charitable) act, since it averted the complete destruction threatened in Deut. IV, 26.]

I. *Said R. Aha bar Jacob, "That calculation indicates that 'promptness' for the Lord of the world means eight hundred and fifty two years* [Schachter, p. 239, n. 7: (7) For the following verse states, Ye shall speedily perish completely from off the land. Thus by 'speedily' God meant 852 years, alluded to by we-noshantem]."

IV.1   A. Therefore [man was created alone] [M. 4:5J]:

B. *Our rabbis have taught on Tannaite authority:*

C. On what account was man created alone?

D. So that the minim should not say, "There are many domains in heaven" [M. 4:5].

E. Another matter:

F. [T.:] Man was created one and alone.

G. And why was he created one and alone in the world? Because of the righteous and the wicked

H. So that the righteous should not say, "We are the sons of the righteous one," and so that the evil ones should not say, "We are the sons of the evil one."

I. Another matter: Why was he created one and alone? So that families should not quarrel with one another. For if now, that man was created one and alone, they quarrel with one another, had there been two created at the outset, how much the more so! [cf. M. 4:5L].

J. Another matter: Why was he created one and alone? Because of the thieves and robbers. And if now, that he was created one and alone, people steal and rob, had there been two, how much the more so! [T. San. 8:4A-E].

V.1   A. To portray the grandeur ... [M. 4:5N]:

B. *Our rabbis have taught on Tannaite authority:*

C. [T:] Another matter: Why was he created one and alone?

D. To show the grandeur of the king of the kings of kings, blessed be he.

E. For if a man mints many coins with one mold, all are alike.

F. But the Holy One, blessed be he, mints every man with the mold of the first man [T: for with a single seal, he created the entire world], and not one of them is like another [T. from a single seal all those many diverse seals have come forth],

G. as it is said, "It is changed as clay under the seal, and all this things stand forth as in a garment" (Job 38:14) [M. 4:5N] [T. San. 8:5A-D].

H. And on what accounts are faces not like one another?

I. On account of imposters,

J. so no one should see a lovely house or woman and say "It is mine" [T.S: jump into his neighbor's field or jump in bed with his neighbor's wife],

K. as it is said, "And from the wicked their light is withheld and the strong arm is broken" (Job. 38:15).

L.   *It has been taught on Tannaite authority:* **R. Meir says, "The omnipresent has varied a man in three ways: appearance, intelligence, and voice**

M.   **intelligence, because of robbers and thieves, and appearance and voice, because of the possibilities of licentiousness" [T. San. 8:6A-F].**

N.   *Our rabbis have taught on Tannaite authority:*

O.   **Man was created on Friday [T.: last in order of creation.**

P.   **And why was man created last?**

Q.   **So that the** <u>minim</u> **should not be able to say, "There was a partner with him in his work [of creation]" [cf. M. 4:5M; [T. San. 8:7].**

R.   **Another matter: [Why was he created last]?**

S.   **So that he should not grow proud.**

T.   **For they can say to him, "The mosquito came before you in the [order of the] works of creation."**

U.   **Another matter: So that he might immediately take up the doing of a religious duty. [T. San. 8:8].**

V.   **Another matter: So that he might enter the banquet at once [with everything ready for him].**

W.   **They have made a parable: To what is the matter is comparable?**

X.   **To a king who built a palace and dedicated it and prepared a meal and [only] afterward invited the guests.**

Y.   **And so Scripture says, "The wisest of women has built her house" (Prov. 9:1).**

Z.   **This refers to the King of the kings of kings, blessed be He, who built his world in seven [days] by wisdom.**

AA.   **"She has hewn out her seven pillars" (Prov. 9:1) – these are the seven days of creation.**

BB.   **"She has killed her beasts and mixed her wine" (Prov. 9:2) – these are the oceans, rivers, wastes, and all the other things which the world needs.**

CC.   **And afterwards: She has sent forth her maidens, she cries on the high places of the city, Who is simple – let him turn in hither, and he who is void of understanding (Prov. 3:4) – these refer to Adam and Even [T.: mankind and the wild beasts [T. San. 8:9A-H].**

DD.   **"Upon the highest places of the city" (Prov. 9:14):**

EE.   *Rabbah b. b. Hanna contrasted these verses:* "It is written, 'Upon he top of the highest places' (prov. 9:3) and it is written, 'On a seat on the high places' (Prov. 9:14).

FF.   **"At first 'on top,' and then, 'upon a seat.'"**

GG.   **"Who is thoughtless, let him turn in hither, as for him who lacks understanding, she says to him" (Prov. 9:4):**

HH.   **Said the Holy One, blessed be he, "Who enticed this one?**

II.   **"It is a woman who spoke to him, for it is written, 'He who commits adultery with a woman lacks understanding' (Prov. 6:32)."**

The Creation of Man. The Minim.
Debates with Unbelievers.
The Emperor and the Patriarch.

V.2   A.   *It has been taught on Tannaite authority:*

B. R. Meir would say, "The first man was [formed out] of dust gathered from every part of the world,

C. "for it is said, 'Your eyes saw my unformed substance' (Ps. 139:16), and it is written, 'The eyes of the Lord run to and fro through every part of the earth' (Zech. 4:10)."

D. Said R. Oshaiah in the name of Rab, "As to the first man, [38B], his body came from Babylonia, his head from the Land of Israel, and his limbs from other lands."

E. *As to his private parts? Said R. Aha, "They come from Aqra deAgma."*

V.3 A. Said R. Yohanan bar Hanina, "The day [on which Adam was made] was twelve hours.

B. "At the first hour the dust for making him was gathered together. At the second hour he was made kneaded into an unformed mass. At the third hour his limbs were shaped. At the fourth hour breath was poured into him. At the fifth hour he stood on his feet. At the sixth hour he named [the beasts]. At the seventh hour Eve as mated with him. At the eighth hour they went to bed two and came away from bed four. At the ninth hour he was commanded not to eat from the tree. At the tenth hour he went rotten. At the eleventh hour he was judged. At the twelfth hour he was sent off and went his way.

C. "For it is written, 'Adam tarries not in honor' (Ps. 49:13)."

D. Said Rami bar Hama, "A vicious wild beast can rule over man only if [man] appears to him as a domesticated beast.

E. "For it is said, 'Men are overruled when they appear as beasts' [So Schachter] (Ps. 49:13)."

V.4 A. Said R. Judah said Rab, "When the Holy One, blessed be he, proposed to create man, he created a group of ministering angels. He said to them, 'Shall we make man in our image?'

B. "They said to him, 'Lord of the ages, what sort of things will he do?'

C. "He said to them, 'These are the sorts of the things he will do."

D. "They said before him, 'Lord of the ages, 'What is man that you are mindful of him, and the son of man that you think of him' (Ps. 8:5)?

E. "He poked his little finger among them and burned them up, and so too did he do with the second group of ministering angels.

F. "The third group said to him, 'Lord of the ages, As to the first two groups that spoke to you, what good did they do? The whole world is yours. Whatever you want to do in your world, go and do it.'

G. "When he reached the time of the men of the generation of the flood and the men of the generation of the division of languages, whose deeds were corrupt, they said to him, 'Lord of the worlds, did not the first groups of ministering angles speak well to you?'

H. "He said to them, 'Even to old age, I am the same, and even to hoary hairs will I carry' (Is. 46:4)."

V.5 A. Said R. Judah said Rab, "The first man stretched from one end of the world to the other, as it is said, 'Since the day that God created man upon the earth, even the one end of heaven to the other' (Deut. 4:32).

B.   "When he turned rotten, the Holy One, blessed be he, put his hand on him and cut him down to size,

C.   "for it is said, 'You have hemmed me in behind and before and laid your hands upon me' (Ps. 139:5)."

D.   Said R. Eleazar, "The first man stretch from the earth to the firmament, as it is said, 'Since the day that God created man upon the earth, and from one end of the heaven to the other' (Deut. 4:32).

E.   "When he turned rotten, the Holy One, blessed be he, put his hand on him and cut him down to size,

F.   "for it is said, 'You have hemmed me in behind and before' (Ps. 139:5)."

G.   *But the two verses are contradictory.*

H.   *This refers to its measure, and that to its.*

V.6   A.   And said R. Judah said Rab, "The first man spoke Aramaic.

B.   "For it is written, 'How weighty are your thoughts to me O God' (Ps. 139:17). [Schachter: 'Weighty' and 'thoughts' are Aramaisms.]"

C.   That is in line with what R. Simeon b. Laqish said, "What is the meaning of that which is written, 'This is the book of the generations of Adam' (Gen. 5:1)?

D.   "This teaches that the Holy One, blessed be he, showed [Adam] each generation and those who expounded for it, each generation and those who served as its sages.

E.   "When he came to the generation of R. Aqiba, he took pleasure in his mastery of Torah and was saddened by the form of his death.

F.   "He said, 'How much a source of grief are your friends to me, O God' (Ps. 139:17). ['Weighty' may take on the meaning of a source of heaviness and grief, and the word for 'thoughts' in Aramaic bears the meaning in Hebrew of 'friends' (Schachter)]."

V.7   A.   And R. Judah said Rab said, "The first Man was a min.

B.   "For it is said, 'And the Lord God called to Adam and said to him, where are you' (Gen. 3:9), meaning, 'Where has your heart gone?'"

C.   Said R. Isaac, "He drew out his foreskin [to obliterate the mark of circumcision].

D.   "Here it is written, 'But like Adam, they have transgressed the covenant' (Hos. 6:7), and it is written further, 'He has broken my covenant' (Gen. 17:14)."

E.   R. Nahman said, 'He denied the very principle [that God ruled]. Here it is written, 'They have transgressed the covenant' (Hos. 6:7), and elsewhere it is written, 'Because they forsook the covenant of the Lord their God' (Jer. 22:9) [speaking of belief in God's rule]."

V.8   A.   *There we have learned in the Mishnah:* **R. Eliezer says, "Be diligent to study the Torah and know what to say to an unbeliever" [M. Abot 2:14].**

B.   Said R. Yohanan, "That rule applies to a gentile unbeliever. But as to an Israelite unbeliever, *all the more is he beyond the rule.*"

V.9   A.   Said R. Yohanan, "In every passage in which the minim have found evidence for their heresy, [in which God is spoken of in the plural], a refutation for their position is provided right at hand.

B.   "'Let us make man in our image' (Gen. 1:26) – And God created [in the singular] man in his own image' (Gen. 1:27).

C. "'Come, let us go down and there confound their language' (Gen. 11:7) – 'And the Lord came down [in the singular] to see the city and the tower' (gen. 11:5).

D. "'Because there were revealed to him God' (Gen. 35:7) – 'Unto God who answers me in the day of my distress' (Gen. 35:3).

E. "'And what great nation is there that has Gad so night [in the plural] into it, as the Lord our God is unto us whenever we call upon him [singular]' (Deut. 4:7).

F. "'And what one nation in the earth is like your people, Israel, whom God have gone [plural] to redeem for a people unto himself [singular]' (2 Sam. 7:23).

G. "'Till thrones were placed and one that was ancient did sit' (Dan. 7:9)."

H. *And what need was there for all of these passages?*

I. *The answer accords with what R. Yohanan said.*

J. *For* R. Yohanan said, "The Holy One, blessed be he, does nothing unless he consults with the heavenly family.

K. "For it is said, 'The matter is by the decree of the watchers and the sentence by the word of the Holy Ones' (Dan. 4:14)."

L. *Now all of the others are suitably [explained], but how shall we explain* "Till thrones were placed" (Dan. 7:9)?

M. One is for him, the other for David.

N. *As it has been taught on Tannaite authority:*

O. "One is for him, the other for David," the words of R. Aqiba.

P. Said to him R. Yosé, "Aqiba, how long are you going to treat in a profane way the Presence of God?

Q. "Rather, one is for bestowing judgment, the other for bestowing righteousness."

R. *Did he accept this answer or not?*

S. *Come and take note, for it has been taught on Tannaite authority:*

T. "One is for bestowing judgment and the other for bestowing righteousness," the words of R. Aqiba.

U. Said to him R. Eleazar b. Azariah, "Aqiba, what business have you in matters of lore? Go over to rules governing the skin disease [of Lev. 13] and uncleanness imparted through overshadowing of the corpse [in Ohalot=Num. 19:1ff.].

V. "Rather, one is a throne for a seat, the other for a footstool for his feet."

V.10 A. *Said R. Nahman, "If someone knows how to refute the position of the minim as well as does R. Idit, let him undertake to refute them, and if not, he should not reply to them."*

B. *Said a min to R. Idit, "It is written, 'And to Moses he said, Come up to the Lord' (Ex. 24:1). Ought it not have said, 'Come up to me'?*

C. He said to him, "This refers to Metatron, who is called by the name of his master, for it is written, 'For my name is in him' (Ex. 23:21)."

D. *"If so, let us worship him."*

E. *"It is written, 'Be not rebellious against him' (Ex. 23:21). 'Do not exchange me for him.'"*

F.   *"If so, what need do I have for the statement, 'He will not pardon your transgression' [since Metatron has no right to do so anyhow]?"*

G.   *He said to him, "By the faith that we hold ! We should not accept him even as a messenger, for it is written, 'And he said to him, if you personally do not go out with us' (Ex. 33:15)."*

V.11   A.   *A min said to R. Ishmael b. R. Yosé, "It is written, 'Then the Lord caused to rain upon Sodom and Gomorrah brimstone and fire from the Lord' (Gen. 19:24). It should have said, 'From him.'"*

B.   *A certain laundryman said to him, "Let me answer him. It is written, 'And Lamech said to his wives, Ada and Zillah, Hear my voice, you wives of Lamech' (gen. 4:23). It should have said, 'my wives.'*

C.   *"But that just is how Scripture says things, and here too, that just is how Scripture says things."*

D.   *[Ishmael] said to him, "How do you know that?"*

E.   *"I heard it from the public lesson of R. Meir."*

F.   *For said R. Yohanan, "When R. Meir would give a public lecture, he would speak one third of the time on traditions [of law], a third on lore, and a third on parables."*

G.   And said R. Yohanan, "R. Meir had three hundred parables of foxes, and of them all we have only three. **[39A]** 'The fathers have eaten sour grapes and the children's teeth are set on edge' (Ex. 18:2).

H.   "'Just balances, just weights' (Lev. 19:36). 'The righteous is delivered out of trouble and the wicked comes in in his stead' (Prov. 11:8)." [Schachter, p. 246-7, n. 14: dawn started here. Rashi gives the parables in question, as follows, combined in a single story. [Cf., however, Ms. M.: 'We have only one.'] A fox once craftily induced a wolf to go and join the Jews in their Sabbath preparations and share in their festivities. On his appearing in their midst the Jews fell upon him with sticks and beat him. He therefore came back determined to kill the fox. But the latter pleaded: 'It is no fault of mine that you were beaten, but they have a grudge against your father who once helped them in preparing their banquet and then consumed all the choice bits.' 'And was I beaten for the wrong done by my father?' cried the indignant wolf. 'Yes,' replied the fox, 'the fathers have eaten sour grapes and the children's teeth are set on edge. However,' he continued, 'come with me and I will supply you with abundant food.' He led him to a well which had a beam across it from either end of which hung a rope with a bucket attached. The fox entered the upper bucket and descended into the well whilst the lower one was drawn up. 'Where are you going?' asked the wolf. The fox, pointing to the cheese-like reflection of the moon, replied: 'Here is plenty of meat and cheese; get into the other bucket and come down at once.' The wolf did so, and as he descended, the fox was drawn up. 'And how am I to get out?' demanded the wolf. 'Ah' said the fox, 'the righteous is delivered out of trouble and the wicked comes in in his stead. Is it not written, Just balances, just weights'?]

V.12   A.   Said the emperor [printed ed.: infidel] to Rabban Gamaliel, "Your God is a thief, for it is written, 'And the Lord God caused a deep sleep to fall upon Adam, and he slept, and he took one of his ribs' (Gen. 2:21)."

B.　*[The emperor's] daughter said to him, "Let me answer him." She said to [the emperor], "Give me a commander [and troops]."*

C.　He said to her, "What do you need him for?"

D.　He said to him, "A thief invaded us last night and stole a silver goblet and left a gold one."

E.　He said to her, "Would that they should come invade us every day!"

F.　"And was it not good for the first Man, that one rib should be taken for him, and a serving maid should be given to him to serve him?"

G.　*He said to her, "What I meant to say only was that he should have taken [the rib] from him in public."*

H.　*She said to him, "Bring me a piece of meat." They brought it to her. She put it in her armpit and then took it out and said to him, "Eat a piece of this."*

I.　*He said to her, "It disgusts me."*

J.　*She said to him, "And with the first man too, if she had been taken from him in full light of day, she would have been disgusting to him."*

V.13　A.　*The emperor said to Rabban Gamaliel, "I know what your God is doing."*

B.　*[Gamaliel] was overcome and sighed.*

C.　*He said to him, "Why so?"*

D.　*He said to him, "I have a son overseas, and I miss him and I ask you to tell me about him."*

E.　*He said, "Do I know where he is?"*

F.　*He said to him, "What is going on on earth you do not know, what is going on in heaven are you going to know?"*

V.14　A.　The emperor said to Rabban Gamaliel, "It is written, 'He counts the number of the stars' (Ps. 147:4). *What's the big deal? I can count the stars."*

B.　*[Gamaliel] took some quinces and put them into a sieve. He twisted them about. He said to him, "Count them."*

C.　*He said to him, "Keep them still."*

D.　*He said to him, "The firmament goes around this way too."*

E.　*There are those who say that this is what he said to him, "I can count the stars."*

F.　*He said to him, "Tell me how many are your molars and other teeth."*

G.　*He put his hand into his mouth and counted them.*

H.　*He said to him, [What is in your mouth you don't know, what is in the firmament are you going to know?"*

V.15　A.　The emperor said to Rabban Gamaliel, "He who created the mountains did not create the wind, as it is said, 'For lo, there is one who forms mountains and one who creates wind' (Amos 4:13)."

B.　"But how about this verse having to do with Adam: 'And he created...' (Gen. 1:27) 'and he formed...' (Gen. 2:7)? Here too, will you claim that the one who created this did not create that one?

C.　"There is an area of a handbreadth square in man, with two apertures [the eye and the ear], and since it is written, 'He who plants the ear, shall he not hear, he who forms the eye, shall he not see' (Ps. 94:9), here too, will you say that the one who created this did not create that?"

D.　He said to him, "Yes."

E.   He said to him, "When someone dies, the two [creators] have to be brought to a common opinion."

V.16 A.   *Said a magus to Amemar, "The part of you from the middle and above belongs to Hormiz, and the part of you from the middle and downward belongs to Ahormiz."*

B.   *He said to him, "If so, how can Ahormiz let Hormiz piss on the ground."*

V.17 A.   *Caesar said to R. Tanhum, "Come, we shall all be one people."*

B.   *He said, "Well and good. But we who are circumcised cannot become like you, so you circumcise and become like us."*

C.   *He said to him, "You have said a good word. But whoever wins an argument with the king has to be thrown to the beasts."*

D.   *They threw him to the beasts, who did not eat him.*

E.   *A min said to him, "The reason that they did not eat him is that they were not hungry."*

F.   *They threw him in, and the animals ate him.*

V.18 A.   *An emperor said to Rabban Gamaliel, "You say that wherever there are ten, the Presence of God comes to rest. How many Presences of God are there?"*

B.   *He called [Caesar's] servant and struck him with his ladle, saying to him, "Why is there sun in Caesar's house [and you let it in]?"*

C.   *He said to him, "The sun fills the whole world."*

D.   *"Now if the sun, which is only one of the thousand thousands of myriads of servants of the Holy One, blessed be he, fills the whole world, the Presence of the Holy One, blessed be he, himself, how much the more so!"*

V.19 A.   Said a min to R. Abbahu, "Your God is a joker [ridiculing the prophets].

B.   "For he said to Ezekiel, 'Lie down on your left side' (Ez. 4:4) and it is written, 'Lie on your right side' (Ez. 4:6)."

C.   *A disciple came along and said to him, "What is the reason for the Sabbatical Year?"*

D.   *He said to him, "Now I shall say something to you both which will be appropriate to the question of each of you. Said the Holy One, blessed be he, to Israel, 'sow seed for six years, and let the land rest in the Seventh Year, so that you shall know that the land belongs to me.'*

E.   "Now they did not do so, and they sinned and went into exile.

F.   "The custom of the world is that when a province rebels against a mortal king, if he is cruel, he kills all of them, if he is merciful, he kills half of them, if he is unusually forgiving, he punishes the greatest ones among them with torture.

G.   "For the Holy One, blessed be he, inflicted pain on Ezekiel so as to wipe away the sins of Israel."

V.20 A.   Said a min to R. Abbahu, "Your God is a priest. For it is written, 'That they take heave-offering for me' (Ex. 25:2) [and that sort of offering is assigned to priests, so God is a priest].

B.   *"Now when he buried Moses, in what did he immerse [to remove the corpse-uncleanness he contracted through the burial]?*

C.   *"Should you say it was in water, is it not written, 'Who has measured the waters in the hollow of his hand' (Is. 40:12)? [The water would not suffice]"*

D.   *He said to him, "He immersed in fire, for it is written, 'For lo, the Lord will come in fire' (Is. 66:15)."*

E. *"And is immersion in fire effective?"*

F. *He said to him, "Quite to the contrary, the main point of immersion [for purification] is in fire, for it is written, '*And all that cannot stand fire you shall pass through water' (Num. 31:23)."

V.21 A. *Said a min to R. Abina, "*It is written, 'Who is like your people, Israel, a unique people on earth' (2 Sam. 7:23)?

B. *"What is so good about you? You are joined [in the same category] with us, for it is written, '*All the nations are as nothing before him' (Is. 40:17)."

C. *He said to him, "*One of you [Balaam] has testified in our behalf. For it is written, **[39B]** 'And [Israel] shall not be counted among the nations' (Num. 23:9)."

V.22 A. R. Eleazar contrasted verses, "It is written, 'The Lord is good to all' (Ps. 145:9), and it is written, 'The Lord is good to those who wait for him' (Lam. 3:25).

B. "The matter may be compared to the case of a man who has an orchard. When he waters it, he waters the whole thing.

C. "When he prunes it, he prunes only the good trees."

VI.1 A. **Therefore man was created alone [4:5J]:**
"And there went out a song throughout the host" (1 Kgs. 22:36) Exegesis of the Story of Ahab's death at Ramoth in Gilead]

B. "And there went out a song throughout the host" (1 Kgs. 22:36) [at Ahab's death at Ramoth in Gilead].

C. Said R. Aha b. Hanina, "'When the wicked perish, there is song' (Prov. 11:10).

D. "When Ahab, b. Omri, perished, there was song."

E. *But does the Holy One, blessed be he, rejoice at the downfall of the wicked?*

F. *Is it not written, "*That they should praise as they went out before the army and say, 'Give thanks to the Lord, for his mercy endures forever' (2 Chr. 20:21),

G. and said R. Jonathan, "On what account are the words in this psalm of praise omitted, 'Because he is good'? Because the Holy One, blessed be he, does not rejoice at the downfall of the wicked."

H. For R. Samuel bar Nahman said R. Jonathan said, "What is the meaning of the verse of Scripture, 'And one did not come near the other all night' (Ex. 14:20)?

I. "At that time, the ministering angels want to recite a song [of rejoicing] before the Holy One, blessed be he.

J. "Said to them the Holy One, blessed be he, 'The works of my hands are perishing in the sea, and do you want to sing a song before me?'"

K. Said R. Yosé bar Hanina, "He does not rejoice, but others do rejoice. *Note that it is written, '*[And it shall come to pass, as the Lord rejoiced over you to do good, so the Lord] will cause rejoicing over you by destroying you' (Deut. 28:63) – and not 'so will the Lord [himself] rejoice'"

L. *That proves the case.*

VI.2 A. "And dogs licked his blood] and harlots washed themselves, [according to the word of the Lord which he spoke]" (1 Kgs. 22:38):

B.   Said R. Eleazar, "This was to carry out two visions, one of Micaiah, the other of Elijah.

C.   "In regard to Micaiah it is written, 'If you indeed return whole, the Lord has not spoken by me' (1 Kgs. 22:28).

D.   "As to Elijah, it is written, 'In the place where dogs licked blood of Naboth' (1 Kgs. 21:19)."

E.   Raba said, "The reference is to actual harlots. Ahab was a cold man, and Jezebel made two pictures of harlots on his chariot, so that he would see them and heat up."

F.   "And a certain man drew his bow innocently and smote the king of Israel' (1 Kgs. 22:34):

G.   R. Eleazar said, "It was in all innocence."

H.   Raba said, "It was to perfect two visions, the one of Micaiah, the other of Elijah. ['Perfect' uses the same root as 'innocence.']"

VI.3   A.   It is written, "And Ahab called Obadiah, who was in charge of the household. Now Obadiah fear the Lord very much" (1 Kgs. 18:3):

B.   *What did he say?*

C.   Said R. Isaac, "He said to him, 'In the case of Jacob it is written, 'I have observed the signs, and the Lord has blessed me [Laban] on your account' (Gen. 30:27). In the case of Joseph, it is written, 'The Lord blessed the Egyptian's house for Joseph's sake' (Gen. 39:5). The house of 'that man' [me] has not been blessed. Is it possible that you do not fear God?'

D.   "An echo came forth and said, 'Now Obadiah feared the Lord very much' (1 Kgs. 18:3). But the house of Obadiah is not designated to receive a blessing."

E.   Said R. Abba, "What is said with regard to Obadiah is greater than what is said with regard to Abraham.

F.   "For with respect to Abraham, the word 'very much' is not written, while with regard to Obadiah, the word 'very much' is written."

VI.4   A.   Said R. Isaac, "On what account did Obadiah have the merit of receiving prophecy? Because he hid a hundred prophets in a cave.

B.   "For it is said, 'For it was so when Jezebel cut off the prophets of the Lord that Obadiah took a hundred prophets and hid them, fifty to a cave' (1 Kgs. 18:4)."

C.   *Why fifty?*

D.   Said R. Eleazar, "He took to heart the lesson of Jacob, for it is said, 'Then the camp that is left shall escape' (Gen. 32:9)."

E.   R. Abbahu said, "Because a cave cannot hold more than fifty."

VI.5   A.   "The vision of Obadiah. Thus said the Lord God concerning Edom" (Obad. 1:1):

B.   *What made Obadiah in particular [the appropriate choice of a prophet to] speak against Edom?*

C.   Said R. Isaac, "Said the Holy One, blessed be he, 'Let Obadiah come, who dwelled among two wicked people [Ahab and Jezebel] but did not learn from their deeds, and prophesy against the wicked Esau, who dwelled among two righteous people [Isaac and Rebecca] and did not learn from their deeds."

D.   Ephraim the Contentious, disciple of R. Meir, in the name of R. Meir, said, "Obadiah was an Edomite proselyte. *That is in line with*

		what people say, '[Schachter:] *From the very forest itself comes the handle of the axe that fells it.'"*
	E.	"And [David] smote Moab and measured them with a line, casting them down to the ground" (2 Sam. 8:2):
	F.	*Said R. Yohanan in the name of R. Simeon b. Yohai, "That is in line with what people say, 'From the very forest itself comes the handle of the axe that fells it.'"*
	G.	When R. Dimi came, he said, "'[Schachter:] The joint putrefies from within.'"
VI.6	A.	"Then he took his first-born son, who should have reigned in his place, and offered him for a burnt offering upon the wall" (2 Kgs. 3:27):
	B.	Rab and Samuel:
	C.	One said, "It was an offering for the sake of heaven."
	D.	The other said, "It was an offering to idolatry."
	E.	*Now in line with the view of the one who said, "It was an offering for the sake of Heaven," that is in line with the following verse of Scripture:* "And there came great wrath on Israel" (2 Kgs. 3:27) [Schachter, p. 254, n. 2: because of their failure to show loyalty to God in comparison with the devotion shown by the Moabite king].
	F.	*But in line with the view of the one who said, "It was an offering for idolatry," why did "great wrath come on Israel"?*
	G.	*It is in accord with what R. Joshua b. Levi said.*
	H.	*For R. Joshua b. Levi contrasted verses of Scripture:* "It is written, 'Neither have you done according to the ordinances of the nations that were round about you' (Ez. 5:7), but is also is written, 'But you have done according to the ordinances of the nations that were round about you' (Ez. 11:12).
	I.	"You did not do as did the upright among them, but you did in accord with the deeds of the disreputable ones among them."
VI.7	A.	"And they departed from him and returned to the earth" (2 Kgs. 3:27):
	B.	Said R. Hanina bar Pappa, "At that moment the wicked ones of Israel descended to the lowest rung [of depravity]."
	C.	"And the damsel was fair, up to being exceedingly so" (1 Kgs. 1:4):
	D.	Said R. Hanina b. Pappa, "She did not yet reach even half of the beauty of Sarah, for it is written, 'up to being... exceedingly so,' but not attaining 'exceedingly.'"

The Talmud follows the program of the Mishnah-paragraph, augmenting the theological themes with mostly-relevant illustrative materials, including a large portion of Tosefta's topical complement. While the units on biblical lore appear to be prolix, in fact they serve the themes of the Mishnah – and in a rather disciplined way at that. I must admit I cannot account for the concluding unit, on Ahab.

5

Bavli Tractate Sanhedrin
Chapter Five
Folios 40A-42A

5:1-5

A. They interrogated [the witness] with seven points of interrogation:

B. (1) In what septennate? (2) In what year? (3) In what month? (4) On what day of the month? (5) On what day [of the week]? (6) At what time? (7) In what place?

C. R. Yosé says, "(1) On what day? (2) At what time? (3) In what place? (4) Do you know him? (5) Did you warn him [of the consequences of his deed]?"

D. [In case of] one who worships an idol: Whom did he worship, and with what did he worship [the idol]?

M. 5:1

A. The more they expand the interrogation, the more is one to be praised.

B. The precedent is as follows: Ben Zakkai examined a witness as to the character of the stalks of figs [under which the incident took place].

C. What is the difference between interrogation [about the date, time, and place] and examination [about the circumstances]?

D. In the case of interrogation, [if] one witness says, "I don't know the answer," the testimony of the witness is null.

E. [In the case of] examination, [if] one of the witnesses says, "I don't know," or even if both of them say, "We don't know," their testimony nonetheless stands.

F. All the same are interrogation and examination: When [the witnesses] contradict one another, their testimony is null.

M. 5:2

199

A. [If] one [of the witnesses] says, "It was on the second of the month," and one of the witnesses says, "It was on the third of the month," their testimony stands,

B. for one of them may know about the intercalation of the month, and the other one may not know about the intercalation of the month.

C. [if] one of them says, "On the third," and one of them says, "On the fifth," their testimony is null.

D. [If] one of them says, "At two," and one of them says, "At three," their testimony stands.

E. [If] one of them says, "At three," and one of them says, "At five," their testimony is null.

F. R. Judah says, "It stands."

G. [If] one of them says, "At five," and one of them says, "At seven," their testimony is null.

H. For at five the sun is at the east, and at seven the sun is at the west.

M. 5:3

A. And afterward they bring in the second witness and examine him.

B. If their statements check out, they begin the argument in favor of acquittal.

C. [If] one of the witnesses said, "I have something to say in favor of acquittal,"

D. or [if] one of the disciples said, "I have something to say in favor of conviction,"

E. they shut him up.

F. [If] one of the disciples said, "I have something to say in favor of acquittal," they promote him and seat him among the [judges], and he did not go down from that position that entire day.

G. If there is substance in what he says, they pay attention to him.

H. And even if [the accused] said, "I have something to say in my own behalf," they pay attention to him,

I. so long as there is substance in what he has to say.

M. 5:4

A. If they found him innocent, they sent him away. If not, they postpone judging him till the next day.

B. They would go off in pairs and would not eat very much or drink wine that entire day, and they would discuss the matter all that night.

C. And the next day they would get up and come to court.

D. The one who favors acquittal says, "I declared him innocent [yesterday], and I stand my ground and declare him innocent today."

E. And the one who declares him guilty says, "I declared him guilty [yesterday] and I stand my ground and declare him guilty today."

F. The one who argues in favor of guilt may [now] argue in favor of acquittal, but the one who argues in favor of innocence may not now go and argue in favor of guilt.

G. [If] they made an error in some matter, the two judges' clerks remind them [of what had been said].

H. If they now found him innocent, they sent him off.

I. And if not, they arise for a vote.

J. [If] twelve vote for acquittal and eleven vote for conviction, he is acquitted.

K. [If] twelve vote for conviction and eleven vote for acquittal,

L. and even if eleven vote for acquittal and eleven vote for conviction,

M. but one says, "I have no opinion,"

N. and even if twenty-two vote for acquittal or vote for conviction,

O. but one says, "I have no opinion,

P. they add to the number of the judges.

Q. How many do they add? Two by two, until there are seventy-one.

R. [If] thirty-six vote for acquittal and thirty-five vote for conviction, he is acquitted.

S. [If] thirty six vote for conviction and thirty-five vote for acquittal, they debate the matter, until one of those who votes for conviction accepts the arguments of those who vote for acquittal.

M. 5:5

I.1 A. *What is the source of this rule [concerning seven points of interrogation]?*

B. Said R. Judah, "It is because Scripture has said, 'Then you shall inquire and search and ask diligently' (Deut. 13:15), and it is said, 'And if it be told you and you shall hear it, then you shall inquire diligently' (Deut. 17:4), and it says, 'And the judges shall inquire diligently' (Deut. 19:18). [Thus seven questions are specified.]"

C. **[40B]** *But might I say that the rule for each is as specified [and since the three cited verses refer, respectively, to trials concerning the apostate city, the trial of an idolator, and witnesses proved conspiring to commit perjury], then there should be three questions for the case of the apostate city, two for idolatry, and two for the trial for perjury? For if it were the case [that on any charge, we have to pose seven questions to the witnesses,] the All-Merciful should have written all entries in a single setting [e.g., seven references to searching and asking diligently in the matter of the apostate city].*

D. [Schachter:] *Since all seven are severally prescribed, the requirements of each are inferred from the other* [Schachter, p. 258, n. 11: since close examination is stated in the case of each, the three charges are assimilated to each other, and therefore the questions that are to be put in one case are to be put in the others too], *and since that is the case, it is as if the seven items were stated with reference to each type of trial.*

E. *But the three types of trials really are not equivalent to one another.*

F. *[Why not?] The apostate city does not fall into the category of the others [idolators' and perjurers' trials], because the property [of the others] is spared [while the property of an apostate city is condemned too].*

G. *A trial for idolatry is not parallel to the other two, for the idolator is put to death by the sword.*

H. *The trial of the conspiratorial witnesses does not fall into the category of the other two, because others [but not the conspiratorial witnesses] are subject to admonition in advance. [So the proposed argument does not work.]*

I. *[We shall now propose an exegetical argument:] Let us derive the commonality of the cases from the use of the word "diligently" [in all three verses cited above], and the use of that word constitutes the establishment of an analogy among the three passages serving no other purpose. Were it to serve some other purpose, one could refute the proposed analogy.*

J. *But in point of fact it serves no other purpose, for Scripture could as well have written, "And they shall inquire and they shall search" without using the word "diligently." But Scripture in using that word made a variation in its formulation by stating, "diligently," so that the use of the word is with no other purpose [but to establish an analogy as proposed just now].*

L. *Now as to the two uses, it indeed serves no other purpose, for the Scripture could have stated matters in some other way. But as to the apostate city, how should matters have been said in some way other than they are phrased? All usages in that instant are required.*

M. *No, there too the reference serves no other purpose and is available for establishing the analogy. For Scripture could have stated, "Asking, you shall ask," or "Searching, you shall search" [which would have conveyed the same meaning].*

N. *But the framer of Scripture has made use of a variant mode of expression when he used the word "diligently," which indicates that it was to leave the phrase available for the purpose proposed here.*

I.2   A.   [Since trials covering idolatry, punished by stoning, and perjury, punished by decapitation in the case of perjury in a murder trial, now have been shown to require cross-examination through seven questions, we proceed to deal with other cases, in which the two further modes of inflicting the death penalty are invoked]. *We may infer the requirement to cross-examine witnesses in cases in which the death penalty is through strangulation, on the basis of an argument a fortiori from the requirement of the same in cases ending in the death penalty through stoning or decapitation. [The former are regarded as milder modes of execution than strangulation.]*

      B.   *And we infer by an argument a fortiori that the same mode of careful cross examination is required for cases involving the death penalty of burning, on the basis of the fact the same is required in cases ending in stoning. [Here, stoning is regarded as more severe mode of execution than burning; decapitation is less severe.] [If we require cross examination for the one, we surely should do so in the other.]*

      C.   *That poses no problems to the view of rabbis, who maintain that stoning is a more severe mode of execution.*

      D.   *But in the view of R Simeon, who holds that burning is the more severe mode of execution, what is there to be said?*

      E.   Rather, said R. Judah, "'Behold, if it be truth and the thing certain' (Deut. 13:15) [concerning the apostate city], and 'Behold, if it be truth and the thing certain' (Deut. 17:4) [concerning the idolator] provides eleven [instances of inquiry]. [Schachter, p. 260, n. 16: 'If it be truth' implies that a question is put to ascertain it, likewise, 'And if the thing be certain' implies another question, hence the two sentences imply another four questions in addition to the seven]. *Seven cover the seven questions, and taking away three required for the argument from analogy [diligently in inquiries for idolatry, conspiratorial perjury, and the apostate city], leaves one.*

F. *"That [extra entry], from R. Simeon's viewpoint, is to encompass trials in which the death penalty is burning, and, from the viewpoint of rabbis, [who prove that fact from an argument a fortiori from stoning], it may be explained that, as to a matter that can be proved from an argument a fortiori, Scripture may at times take the bother to write it out on the basis of a specific allegation of a verse of Scripture.*

G. *R. Abbahu made fun of this explanation, "Might I say that the usage serves to add an eighth question for interrogation?"*

H. *But is it possible that there are to be eight questions for interrogation?*

I. *Why not? For lo, there is the possibility of adding the question concerning what time within the hour [the event took place].*

J. *And so too it has been taught on Tannaite authority:*

K. They interrogated him with eight questions.

L. *Now that view [that there are eight inquiries] poses no problems to the position of Abbayye vis a vis R. Meir, who has said, "Someone will error in no way at all." In the formulation that says, "Someone may make a minor error," there is no problem either. [As to Abbayye on Meir, we assume that witnesses will not err by half an hour, and if they say that the murder they witnessed took place at 4:30, and they are proved to have been elsewhere at that hour, we do not assume the murder they saw took place at 4 or 5 (Schachter). So too, one may ask at what part of the hour the event took place.]*

M. *But as to the position of Abbayye vis a <u>via</u> R. Judah, who said, "Someone may make an error by as much as half an hour,"*

N. *and from the viewpoint of Raba, who has said, "People may make an error of still greater a magnitude than that," what is there to say? [How shall we reach eight points of interrogation], that is to say, to utilize the eleventh proof-text]?*

O. *One may encompass questions on which year in the Jubilee.*

P. *But that is covered by the question, **In what septennate** [M. 5:1B]?*

Q. *Rather, the question will be, In which Jubilee.*

R. *And the other party?*

S. *Since the witness has stated in which year of the septennate, it is not necessary to ask in which Jubilee.*

II.1 A. **R. Yosé says, ["On what day? At what time? In what place? Do you know him? Did you warn him of the consequences of his deed?"] [M. 5:1C]:**

B. *It has been taught on Tannaite authority:*

C. Said R. Yosé to sages, "In accord with your view, if someone came and said, 'Last night he killed him,' one says to him, 'In what septennate? In what year? In what month? On what day of the month?'"

D. They said to him, "But in accord with your position, if someone came and said, 'He killed him just now,' one still has to say to him, 'On what day? At what time? In what place?'

E.   "But even though it is not necessary [in this particular case to ask such questions], we pose those questions.'

F.   *That accords with the view of R. Simeon b. Eleazar [that they move the witness from place to place to confuse him (T. San. 9:1A)]. Here too, even though it is not necessary, we impose these tests upon the witness, in accord with the view of R. Simeon b. Eleazar."*

G.   *And R. Yosé? The case of testimony, "Last night he killed him," is commonplace in most matters of testimony. But, "Just now he killed him" is not common in most cases of testimony.*

III.1   A.   **Do you know him [M. 5:1C]:**

B.   *Our rabbis have taught on Tannaite authority:*

C.   "Do you know him? Did he kill a gentile? Did he kill an Israelite? Did you admonish him? Did he accept the admonishment? Did he [Schachter:] admit his liability to the death penalty? Did he commit murder within the span of the utterance [that he made, admitting his liability]?

D.   In the case of idolatry: "What idol did he worship? Did he worship Peor? Did he worship Merqolis? With what did he conduct the rite? Was it by a sacrifice? Incense? Libation? Prostration?"

III.2   A.   Said Ulla, "How on the basis of the Torah do we know that it is necessary to admonish [the felon prior to his act, so that we may know that what he did was with full knowledge of the consequences]?

B.   "As it is said, 'And if a man shall take his sister, his father's daughter, or his mother's daughter, and see her nakedness' (Lev. 20:17).

C.   "Now does the matter depend upon what he sees? [Surely it depends upon what it is done.]

D.   "But unless he is shown the reason for the prohibition [of what he proposes to do, he is not culpable.]

E.   "Since this matter does not pertain the extirpation [41A], apply it to the penalty of flogging."

F.   *Answering the same question a Tannaite authority of the house of Hezekiah [taught], "'And if a man come presumptuously upon his neighbor to slay him with guile' (Ex. 21:14) – for witnesses admonished him, and he still acted intentionally."*

G.   *A Tannaite authority of the house of R. Ishmael [taught], "'And they who found him gathering wood' (Num. 15:33) – for they had warned him and he continued to collect the wood."*

H.   *A Tannaite authority of the house of Rabbi [taught], "'On account of the word that he humbled his neighbor's wife' (Deut. 22:34) – it was on account of matters pertaining to words."*

I.   *And it is necessary [that we have all three proofs]. For had the All-Merciful written the rule only in respect to the prohibition of sexual relations with one's sister, I might have supposed that those who are liable to flogging must be admonished, but those who are liable to the death penalty may be punished even though they were not warned in advance. So Scripture stated, "If a man come presumptuously [in a case in which the death penalty pertains]. And if the All-Merciful had stated that the rule requiring admonition applies in the case, "If a man come presumptuously," I might have concluded*

		that that rule pertains to a crime punishable by the sword, which is a lighter form of execution, but as to a case in which the penalty is stoning, which is a more severe form of execution, I might have had that that is not the rule. So it was necessary to make that point.
	J.	*And why was it necessary to make the same point twice with respect to crimes punishable by stoning [both for the one who gathered wood on the Sabbath, the other in respect to the betrothed maiden]?*
	K.	*In the perspective of R. Simeon, it serves to encompass crimes punishable by burning. In the view of rabbis, even though one may prove a matter through an argument a fortiori, Scripture will take the trouble and write the matter out [expressly].*
	L.	*And why should Scripture not have stated the rule [requiring admonition] in the case of those who are stoned on account of their crimes, and the other classifications of crimes would have been derived from that fact [by an argument a fortiori]?*
	M.	*Here too, a matter which can be shown to be the case by an argument a fortiori Scripture may well take the trouble to write out explicitly.*
III.3	A.	"Did he admit his liability to the death penalty"?
	B.	*How do we know that this is a requirement?*
	C.	Said Raba, and some say Hezekiah, "Scripture has stated, 'He who is to die shall be put to death' (Deut. 17:6).
	D.	"[He is put to death only] if he admits his liability to the death penalty."
III.4	A.	Said R. Hanan, "Witnesses who have testified against a betrothed maiden [that she has been unfaithful], who then were proved to have been formed conspiracy for perjury, are not to put to death. [Though had the woman been found guilty, she would have been put to death, in this case the perjurers do not suffer retaliation].
	B.	"[Why not?] Because they can plead, "Our intent was to prohibit her from consummating the marriage to her betrothed husband [but not to have her put to death]."
	C.	*But lo, they had admonished her [if their evidence had been valid. What sort of a defense is this?]*
	D.	*It was a case in which they had not admonished her [or claimed to have done so].*
	E.	*If they had not admonished her, on what basis could she have been subject to the death penalty?*
	F.	*We deal with a wife in the status of an associate [who is presumed to know the law], and that accords with the position of R. Yosé b. R. Judah.*
	G.	*For it has been taught on Tannaite authority:*
	H.	R. Yosé b. R. Judah says, "It is not necessary to admonish an associate [who is presumed to know the law and the consequences of violating it], for the purpose of admonition is only to allow for the distinction between inadvertent and deliberate action [but the associate knows the law and therefore could not act out of ignorance of the consequences]."
	I.	*Then if [the witnesses] cannot be put to death, how could the woman be subject to the death penalty? For you have at hand* testimony which is not subject to a test as to conspiratorial perjurers, and any testimony that is not subject to the test for conspiratorial perjury does not fall into the category of testimony at all.

J. *That is exactly the sense [of R. Hanan],* "Since the perjurers cannot be executed, because they can claim, 'We intended to prohibit her from marrying her betrothed husband,' she too is not subject to the death penalty. The reason is that this is testimony which is not subject to a test [as to conspiratorial perjury, and any testimony that is not subject to the test for conspiratorial perjury does not fall into the category of testimony at all]."

K. *And as to a woman in the status of an associate, who, we have determined, is subject to the death penalty in accord with the theory of R. Yosé b. R. Judah, how do you find an appropriate case [in which she would be subject to execution, since for their part the witnesses would not be subject to the death penalty if they are proved perjurers]?*

L. It would be a case in which the woman committed adultery and went and did so a second time.

M. The witnesses can claim, "We came to prohibit her from marrying her second lover." [So that would not exemplify matters.]

N. We deal with a case in which she committed adultery against her first husband [Schachter, p. 265, n. 7: to whom she is already prohibited in consequence of their earlier relations] or with a relative [Schachter, p. 265, n. 8: whom she is absolutely forbidden to marry at all].

O. *Why single out a betrothed woman for the present case? The same would apply even to a married one.*

P. *That is indeed so, but the distinctive point is that even in the case of this woman, who has not yet lived with the man, the witnesses may make the claim,* "We came to prohibit her from marrying her betrothed husband."

III.5 A. Said R. Hisda, "If one said, 'He killed him with a sword,' and the other said, 'He killed him with a dagger,' this is 'not certain' testimony [in line with Deut. 13:15, 17:4: 'Behold, if it be truth and the thing certain' (Schachter, p. 265, n. 9)].

B. "If one says, 'His clothing was black,' and the other says, 'His clothing was white,' lo, this is 'certain.' [These statements do not refer to the act, but only to the circumstances]."

C. *An objection was raised from the following:*

D. "Certain" means that [all elements of the testimony must stand] firm. If one says, "He killed him with a sword," and the other says, "It was with a dagger that he killed him,"

E. if one says, "His clothing was black," and the other says, "His clothing was white," this is not certain.

F. *R. Hisda explained the passage [vis a vis clothing] to refer to a scarf with which the murderer had strangled the other [so we speak not of clothing but of the murder weapon in particular, in which case the clothing] falls into the category of a sword or dagger.*

G. *Come and take note:* If one says, "His sandals were black," and the other says, "His sandals were white," this is not certain [testimony, and is null, contrary to Hisda's claim as to what constitutes valid evidence].

H. *Here too, it would be a case in which* the murderer kicked the victim with his sandal and so killed him.

I.   *Come and take note of the following:* **The precedent is as follows: Ben Zakkai examined a witness as to the character of the stems of figs [M. 5:2B].**

J.   Said Rami b. Hama, "It would be a case in which [the witnesses testified that] he had cut off a fig on the Sabbath, *on account of which he would be subject to the death penalty. [In this case what sort of fig is at hand matters as to the actual crime]."*

K.   *But has it not been taught on Tannaite authority:*

L.   They said to him, "He killed him under a fig tree" [and that is the context for the testimony at hand, contrary to Rami's thesis at J].

M.   Rather, said Rami bar Hama, "It would be a case in which the murderer was accused of piercing the deceased with the sharp end of a fig branch."

N.   *Come and take note:* He said to them, "As to this fig tree, were its stalks thin or thick? Were the <u>figs</u> black or white?" [!] [Schachter, p. 266, n. 7: Now surely he could not have killed anyone with the <u>figs</u>. This proves that the meaning is that the witnesses deposed that the accused had killed his victim under or near a fig-tree, and thus this again refutes Hisda.]

O.   *Rather, said R. Joseph, "Can anyone object on the basis of the position of Ben Zakkai? Surely he is in his own category, for he treats as equivalent to one another both interrogation and examination* [and maintains (Schachter, p. 266, n. 8:) just as contradictions on the latter invalidated the evidence, so on the former. The general view disagrees with this, and Hisda's dictum was likewise in accordance with the general view.]

IV.1 A.   **[Ben Zakkai examined a witness as to the character of the stalks of figs under which the incident took place.:]** Who is this "Ben Zakkai"?

B.   *If we should proposed that it is R. Yohanan ben Zakkai, did he ever sit in a sanhedrin [that tried a murder case]? And has it not been taught on Tannaite authority:* The lifetime of R. Yohanan ben Zakkai was a hundred and twenty years. For forty years he engaged in trade, for forty years he studied [Torah], and for forty years he taught. *And it has been taught on Tannaite authority:* Forty years before the destruction of the Temple the sanhedrin went into exile and conducted its sessions in Hanut. And said R. Isaac bar Abodimi, "That is to say that the sanhedrin did not judge cases involving penalties."

C.   *Do you think it was cases involving penalties? [Such cases were not limited to the sanhedrin but could be tried anywhere in the Land of Israel!] Rather, the sanhedrin did not try capital cases. And we have learned in the Mishnah:* **After the destruction of the house of the sanctuary, Rabban Yohanan b. Zakkai ordained ... [M. R.H. 4:1].** [So the final forty years encompassed the period after the destruction of the Temple, and Yohanan could not, therefore, have served on a sanhedrin that tried capital cases.]

D.   *Accordingly, at hand is some other Ben Zakkai [than Yohanan b. Zakkai]. That conclusion, moreover, is reasonable, for if you think that it is Rabban Yohanan ben Zakkai, would Rabbi [in the Mishnah-passage] have called him merely, "Ben Zakkai"? [Not very likely.] And lo, it has been taught on Tannaite authority:* There is the precedent that Rabban Yohanan ben Zakkai conducted an interrogation about the stalks on the figs [so surely this is the same figure as at M. 5:2B].

E.   *But [at the time at which the incident took place, capital cases were tried by the sanhedrin and] he was a disciple in session before his master. He said something, and the others found his reasoning persuasive,* **[41B]** *so they adopted [the ruling] in his name. When he was studying Torah, therefore, he was called Ben Zakkai, as a disciple in session before his master, but when he [later on] taught, he was called Rabban Yohanan ben Zakkai. When, therefore, he is referred to as Ben Zakkai, it is on account of his being a beginning [student] and when he is called Rabban Yohanan b. Zakkai, it is on account of his status later on.*

V.1 A.   **The precedent is ... What is the difference between interrogation [about the date, time and place] and examination [about the circumstances]? [M. 5:2B-C]. [In the case of examination, if one of the witnesses says, "I don't know," or even if both of them say, "We don't know," their testimony nonetheless stands (M. 5:2E)].** What is the meaning of, **"even if both of them say ..."**?

B.   *Surely it is obvious that, if one of them says,* "I don't know," *the testimony is validated, so if both of them say so, the testimony obviously will be valid?* [Schachter, p. 268, n. 5: For if one is ignorant on a certain point, the other's knowledge therefore is valueless. Hence whatever evidence is valid when one is ignorant is also valid when both are ignorant.]

C.   *Said R. Sheshet,* "The reference is to the opening clause, [dealing with interrogation]. And this is the sense of the passage: 'In the interrogation, even if both of them say, "We know," but one of them [the third of three witnesses to the same crime] says, "I don't know," the testimony is null.' In accord with whose view is this interpretation? It accords with the position of R. Aqiba, who treats as analogous [the testimony of] three witnesses and [the testimony of] two [imposing upon both the same rules of evidence]."

D.   *Said Raba,* "But lo, [the language of the passage at hand] explicitly says, **Their testimony nonetheless stands [M. 5:2E]!**"

E.   *Rather, said Raba,* "This is the sense of the passage: Even in the case of interrogation, if two witnesses say, "We know," but one of the witnesses [of a group of three] says, "I don't know," their testimony nonetheless stands.' In accord with which authority is the passage framed? It is not in accord with the view of R. Aqiba."

VI.1 A.   **[What is the difference between interrogation about the date, time, and place and examination about the circumstances? In the case of interrogation, if one witness says, "I don't know the answer," the testimony of the witness is null. In the case of examination, if one of the witnesses says, "I don't know," or even if both of them say, "We don't know," their testimony nonetheless stands. All the same are interrogation and examination: When the witnesses contradict one another, their testimony is null:]** *R. Kahana and R. Safra were repeating [rules of] the sanhedrin in the house of Rabbah. Rami bar Hama met them. He said to them, "What is it that you people say about [the laws of] the sanhedrin at the house of Rabbah?"*

B.   *They said to him, "And what should we say about the rules of sanhedrin by themselves [without respect to what Rabbah has to teach us]? What's your problem?"*

C.   *He said to them, "On the basis of this passage:* **What is the difference between interrogation [about the date, time and place] and examination [about the circumstances], in the case of interrogation, if one witness says, 'I don't know the answer,' the testimony of the witness is null. In the case of examination, if one of the witnesses says, 'I don't know,' or even if both of them say, 'We don't know,' their testimony nonetheless stands [M. 5:2C-E],** [I have the following problem:]

D.   *"since the requirement to conduct both procedures rests on the authority of the Torah, what validates the distinction between interrogation and examination?"*

E.   *They said to him, "Now wait a minute. In the case of interrogation, if one of them said, 'I don't know,' their testimony is null, because in this case you have testimony which is not subject to the test of conspiratorial perjury. In the case of examination, if one of them said, 'I don't know,' their testimony nonetheless stands, because you do have testimony which you can subject to the test of conspiratorial perjury."*

F.   *He said to them, "If this is what you have to say about the rules, then you have a great deal to say about them."*

G.   *They said to him, "It was because of the patience of the master that we spoke about the matter a great deal. If it had been on account of his contentiousness, we should have said not a thing about it."*

VII.1 A.   If one of the witnesses says, ["It was on the second of the month," and one of the witnesses says, "It was one the third of the month, their testimony stands, for one of them may know about the intercalation of the money and the other one may not know about the intercalation of the month] [M. 5:3A-B]:

B.   Until what day [of the month do we assume that people may not know whether it is a full month of thirty days or a defective one of twenty-nine days]?

C.   Said R. Aha bar Hanina said R. Assi said R. Yohanan, "Until the greater part of the month [has gone by]."

D.   *Said Raba, "Also we have learned that view in the Mishnah itself:* **If one of them says, 'On the third,' and one of them says, "on the fifth,' their testimony is null [M. 5:3C].** *Now why should that be the case? Might I not say that one party knows about the intercalation of two months and the other party does not know about the intercalation of two months? Rather, is it not because once the greater part of a month has passed people know [the calendar]?"*

E.   *To the contrary, I may say to you, indeed people do not know when the greater part of the month has gone by [that a month has been intercalated], [so the Mishnah-passage proves nothing]. But people do know about the sounding of the ram's horn [to signal the advent of the new month]. Our basic claim, then, is that someone may err in the case of the sounding of the ram's horn one time, but he is not likely to err about the sounding of the ram's horn two times.* [Schachter, p. 270, n. 3, 4: Though knowing that the ram's horn had been sounded, he may have erred once as to the day on which it was sounded] [but one would not make two mistakes in that connection].

Topical Appendix on Reciting the Blessing over the New Moon

VII.2 A.   And said R. Aha bar Hanina said R. Assi said R. Yohanan, "Up to what point in the month do people say the blessing over the new month?

   B.   "Until its [Schachter:] concavity is filled up."

   C.   And how long does that take?

   D.   Said R. Jacob Idi said R. Judah, "Up to seven [days]."

   E.   *The Nehardeans say, "Up to sixteen [days]."*

   F.   [42A] *And both parties concur with the view of R. Yohanan, but one holds that it is [Schachter] until it is like a strung bow, and the other, until it is like a sieve.*

   G.   Said R. Aha of Difti to Rabina, "[After a week has passed, in line with Judah's view at D, one may nonetheless] say the blessing, ' ... who is good and does good.' [Even though it is no longer a new moon, still the moon continues to grow, so the cited blessing is called for.]"

   H.   *He said to him, "But when the moon is waning [in the given lunar month], should we then say the blessing, '... true judge' [which is said on the occasion of bad news], that [in the earlier part of the lunar month] we should say the blessing, 'Who is good and does good'?"*

   I.   *Then why not say both [one for the earlier part, the other for the later part, of the lunar month]?*

   J.   *Since this is the usual course of events, it is not necessary for us to say any blessing at all.*

VII.3 A.   And said R. Aha bar Hanina said R. Assi said R. Yohanan, "Whoever says a blessing for the new moon at the proper time is as if he receives the Presence of God.

   B.   *"here it is written, 'This month ...' (Ex. 12:1), and elsewhere, 'This is my God, and I shall glorify him' (Ex. 15:2)."*

VII.4 A.   *A Tannaite authority of the house of R. Ishmael [stated], "If Israel had had the sole merit of receiving the presence of their father in heaven month by month, it would have been enough for them."*

   B.   *Said Abbayye, "Therefore we should say the blessing standing."*

   C.   *Maremar and Mar Zutra would be helped up on the shoulders [of others] so as to say the blessing.*

VII.5 A.   *Said R. Aha to R. Ashi, "In the West, they say the blessing, 'Blessed ... is he who renews the months.'"*

   B.   *He said to him, "A blessing such as that our women recite. Rather, it accords with the view of R. Judah. For R. Judah said, '[We say,] "Blessed ... who with his word created the heavens, and with the breath of his mouth all of their hosts. He assigned to them a rule and a time, so that they should not vary from their assignment. They rejoice and take pleasure in doing the will of their creator, working in truth, for their task is truth. And he instructed the moon to come anew as a crown of beauty for those who are sustained for from the womb. For they are destined to be renewed as is she, so as* to glorify their creator on account of the glory of his dominion. Blessed are you, Lord, who renews each month."'"

VII.6 A. "For with wise advice you shall make your war" (Prov. 24:6):

B. Said R. Aha bar Hanina said R. Assi said R. Yohanan, "In whom do you find [ability to conduct] the 'war of the Torah' [of rigorous reasoning]? He who possesses 'the wise advice' of Mishnah-learning."

C. *R. Joseph recited in his own regard,* "Much increase of grain is by the strength of the ox" (Prov. 14:4).

VIII.1 A. **If one of them says, "At two," [and one of them says, "At three," their testimony stands] [M. 5:3D]:**

B. Said R. Shimi bar Ashi, "The rule applies only to differences in hours [of the day for there is a margin of error]. But if one of them says, 'It was before dawn,' and the other says, 'It was after dawn,' their testimony is null."

C. *That is self-evident.*

D. Rather: If one of them says, "It was before dawn,' and the other says, "It was just during sunrise, ..."

E. *That too is self-evident.*

F. *[No, it requires explicit statement, for] what might you have thought? The witness was referring to the glow [before sunrise] and he saw only a gleam [but thought it was sunrise]. So we are informed that we do not [treat that as a routine margin of error].*

IX.1 A. **And afterward they bring in [the second witness and examine him ... and he did not go down from that position that entire day] [M. 5:4A-F]:**

B. *That day and no more?*

C. *And has it not been taught on Tannaite authority:*

D. **If there is substance in what he says [the disciple] did not go down from that position ever.**

E. **And if not, he did not go down from that position that entire day [M. 5:4D],**

F. **so that people should not say, "His going up was his downfall [T. San. 9:3D-F].**

G. *Said Abbayye, "Refer [the allusion to that entire day] to a case in which there was no substance in what he says."*

X.1 A. **If they found him innocent, they sent him away. If not, they postpone judging him till the next day. They would go off in pairs and would not eat very much or drink wine that entire day [M. 5:5A-B]:**

B. *What is the reason for not [drinking] wine?*

C. Said R. Aha bar Hanina, "Scripture has said, "[It is not] for princes [RWZN] [to say], Where is strong drink' (Prov. 31:4).

D. "Those who are dealing with the secrets [RZW, letters appearing in the word for princes] of the world should not get drunk."

XI.1 A. **They debate the matter [until one of those who votes for conviction accepts the arguments of those who vote for acquittal] [M. 5:5S]:**

B. *And if they do not accept [the arguments]?*

C. Said R. Aha, "They dismiss [the accused]."

D. And so said R. Yohanan, "They dismiss [the accused]."

E.   *Said R. Pappa to Abbayye, "Then let him go free to begin with [if the court of seventy-one produces no clear majority? Why debate, when the entire court is not likely to convict?]"*

F.   *He said to him, "This is what R. Yohanan said, 'It is so that they should not leave the court while in a state of confusion.'"*

G.   *There are those who say, Said R. Pappa to Abbayye, "And why add to the court?* Why not just dismiss him from the original court [of twenty-three judges]? [Schachter, p. 273, n. 7: If there was then no clear majority, both sides should have endeavored to win one more vote over to their opinion, and in the case of failure, he should have been set free there and then.]"

H.   *He said to him, "R. Yosé takes your view."*

I.   *For it has been taught on Tannaite authority:*

J.   R. Yosé says, "Just as they do not add to a court of seventy-one judges, so they do not add to a court of twenty-three judges."

XI.2 A.   *Our rabbis have taught on Tannaite authority:*

B.   **In property cases [the court may] rule, "The case is stale."**

C.   **In capital cases [the court may] not rule, "The case is stale [T. San. 7:7A-B].**

D.   *What is the sense of, "The case is stale"?*

E.   *Should I say, "The case is a difficult one [requiring protracted debate]? Then one should reverse the formulation of this rule just now cited [and dismiss a case capital case on the grounds that the debate is too prolonged. One should in point of fact dismiss the accused under such circumstances.]*

F.   *Said R. Huna bar Manoah in the name of R. Aha son of R. Iqa, "Reverse matters."*

G.   *R. Ashi said, "Under no circumstances should you reverse matters. What is the sense of 'The case is stale'? The case has been subjected to most learned [debate]."*

H.   *An objection was raised on the basis of the following:* **The chief judge alone has the right to say, "The case is stale" [T. San. 7:7C].** *Now if you maintain that the sense of the statement is, "The case has been subjected to most learned [debate]," then there is no problem in having the chief judge make such a pronouncement. But if you hold that the sense of the phrase is, "The case is a difficult one," it surely would not be appropriate for the chief judge to make such a statement, since he thereby disgraces himself.*

L.   Indeed so, for the one who pronounces his own disgrace himself is not the same as one who is pronounced a disgrace by others [so it is better for the chief judge, than for a lesser one, to make the statement].

M.   *There are those who state this as follows:*

N.   *Now if you maintain that the sense of the statement is, "The case is a difficult one," then that is in line with the principle: The one who pronounces his own disgrace is not the same as the one who is pronounced a disgrace by others. But if you hold that the sense of the statement is, "The case has been subjected to most learned [debate], "should the chief judge praise himself in such a manner? And has it not been written, "Let*

O.   another praise you, and not your own mouth" (Prov. 27:2)?

O.   *A rule governing court procedure is in its own category, for it is the duty of the head of the court to pronounce [the verdict]. For so we have learned in the Mishnah:* **When they have completed the matter, they bring him back in. The chief judge says, "Mr. So-and-so, you are innocent," "Mr. So-and-so, you are guilty" [M. 3:7A-B].**

Most of the Talmud focuses upon the exposition of the Mishnah-chapter at hand. Only an extended collection of materials forming a tradental aggregate (Aha-Assi-Yohanan) carries us far from the topic at hand.

6

Bavli Tractate Sanhedrin
Chapter Six
Folios 42B-49A

6:1A-G

A. [When] the trial is over, [and the felon is convicted], they take him out to stone him.

B. The place of stoning was well outside the court, as it is said, "Bring forth him who cursed [to a place outside the camp]" (Lev. 24:14).

C. One person stands at the door of the courthouse, with flags in his hand, and a horseman is some distance from him, so that he is able to see him.

D. [If] one [of the judges] said, "I have something to say in favor of acquittal," the one [at the door] waves the flags, and the horseman races off and stops [the execution].

E. And even if [the convicted party] says, "I have something to say in favor of my own acquittal," they bring him back,

F. even four or five times,

G. so long as there is substance in what he has to say.

I.1
A. *Now was the place of stoning merely outside the court and no farther?*

B. *And has it not been taught on Tannaite authority,*

C. The place of stoning was outside the three camps?

D. *Yes, it is as you say. But the reason that the author of the passage has stated matters this way is to indicate that if the court should go into session outside of the three camps, they establish a place of stoning outside the court, so that it will not appear as if the court is committing murder, or so that there may be the possibility of saving the man [by establishing some distance between the place at which the verdict is handed down and the place of stoning].*

I.2
A. *What is the scriptural basis [for the rule that the place of stoning must be outside the three camps]?*

B. *It is as our rabbis have taught on Tannaite authority:*

C. "Bring forth him who cursed [to a place] outside the camp" (Lev. 24:14).

D. That is, outside the three camps.

E. You say that it is outside the three camps. But perhaps it means only outside a single camp?

F. Here the phrase, "outside the camp" is used (Lev. 24:14) and elsewhere, with regard to bulls that were burned up [as whole offerings], it is said, "Outside the camp" (Lev. 12:21).

G. Just as in that context, it means outside the three Israelite camps, so the same rule applies here.

H. *And how do we know that is the case in that context?*

I. *It is as our rabbis have taught on Tannaite authority:*

J. "The whole bullock he shall carry away outside the camp" (Lev. 12:12).

K. That means, outside the three camps.

L. You say that it is outside the three camps.

M. But may it not mean outside one camp?

N. When, with respect to the bull offered for the community [in case of an unwitting public transgression], Scripture says, "Outside the camp," there is no need for Scripture to say so explicitly, for lo, it already has been stated, "And he shall burn it as he has burned the first bullock" (Lev. 12:12). Accordingly, the statement requires carrying it beyond the second camp.

O. And when it says, with respect to the ashes [Schachter, p. 276, n. 12: beyond which the burning is to take place], "Outside the camp," which Scripture also need not make explicit, since it already has been stated, "Where the ashes are poured out shall it be burned" (Lev. 4:12), the statement further requires carrying it beyond the third camp.

P. But why not interpret [the phrase, "without the camp" (Lev. 24:14), in the sense imputed to that phrase] in the context of sacrifices slaughtered outside [of the proper location, the Temple]? Just as, in that context, the meaning is "outside the one camp," so there the meaning would be, "outside the one camp"? [Hence the requirement is outside one camp, not all three].

Q. It is more logical [to derive the meaning of the phrase] from [its sense in the context of] the bullocks that are to be burned, for [Schachter:] they have the following points in common: [1] "Bring forth ... without the camp" (Lev. 12:12), [2] the bringing forth is a prerequisite to the act, and [3] atonement. [Schachter, p. 277, n. 3: In both cases there is a positive command, "Bring forth." Further, bringing forth without the camp is a prerequisite for the fitting performance of the act, whereas in the case of sacrifices slaughtered outside the Temple court it is a transgression. Moreover, the burning of the bullock is an atonement for the high priest and the whole congregation, and stoning likewise is an atonement for the malefactor; but that feature is absent in the case of sacrifices slaughtered without.]

R. Quite to the contrary, [he should have derived the meaning of the phrase] from [its sense in the context of] sacrifices slaughtered outside the Temple, [Schachter:] since they have the following in common: [1] human being, [2] sinners, [3] life is taken and [4] the application of the rule that the sacrifice is rendered refuse by an improper attitude of the officiating priest. [Schachter, p. 277, n. 4: "Without the camp" in both places refers to a human being, the blasphemer was to be taken without the camp, and a human being slaughtered without the camp, while in connection with the bullocks that are burned, the phrase speaks of animals. The blasphemer and the one who slaughters outside the camp both commit sins, while the bullock is not a sinner. In both cases the leading "outside the camp" occurs in order to take life, that of the blasphemer and the sacrifice yet to be slaughtered, while the bullocks already have been slaughtered, while "without the camp" with respect to the bullocks speaks only of the case after they have been slaughtered. Finally, the law of unfitness caused by the improper intention of the officiating priest has no application to the two items at hand, neither to stoning – by definition – nor to sacrifices slaughtered outside of the Temple.]

	S.	*It is better [to derive the meaning of the word as it occurs in one context relating to a prerequisite to proper performance from its meaning in another such setting* [as above Schachter, p. 277, n. 3].
I.3	A.	*[Dealing with the same issue], R. Pappa said, "Where did Moses dwell? It was in the camp of the Levites. And the All-Merciful said to him, 'Bring forth him that has cursed outside the camp' (Lev. 24:14), meaning outside the camp of the Levites.*
	B.	*"'And they brought him who had cursed outside the camp' (Lev. 24:14), means outside the camp of the Israelites [since specifying, once more, 'outside the camp' must have been intended to supply another meaning.]"*
	C.	*[No,] it was necessary to indicate the carrying out [of what God had commanded].*
	D.	*[No,] the carrying out is stated explicitly:* "**[43A]** "And the Children of Israel did as the Lord had commanded Moses" (Lev. 24:23).
	E.	*Then how do you deal with the following verse:* "And they stoned him with a stone" (Lev. 24:23). [Schachter, p. 278, n. 7: It was not needed to show how the execution was carried out, as that was already stated in the words quoted above; hence by analogy this too needs a distinctive interpretation.]
	F.	*It was required to serve the purpose of the following teaching on Tannaite authority:*
	G.	"And they stoned him with a stone" (Lev. 24:23) –
	H.	"Him," – and not his clothing, [so the man is naked].
	I.	"A stone," for if he died after being struck by a single stone, [the rite] has been properly carried out.
	J.	*And it was necessary to write both "stone" and "stones" [at Num. 15:36, the gatherer of woods is stoned with <u>stones</u>]. For had the All-Merciful written only, "stone," I might*

have supposed that when the guilty party did not die from a blow by a single stone, we should not bring other stones with which to kill him. The All-Merciful had to write, "stones." And if the All-Merciful had written only, "stones," I might have supposed that in the first place, one has to bring two stones. So the All-Merciful wrote, "stone."

K.   Now [why does] the Tannaite authority at hand invoke the notion that "it is written" [that is, referring to the argument from analogy worked out in unit II] [while Pappa deduces the matter in a different way]?

O.   This is what he meant to say, "If it had not been written, that is, even if the verse [cited by Pappa] were not available, I should have been able to derive the rule by analogy. Now that we are able to derive the rule from a verse of Scripture, of course there is no need to invoke an argument by analogy,"

I.4   A.   R. Ashi said, "Where did Moses dwell? It was in the camp of the Levites. And the All-Merciful said to him, 'Bring forth him that has cursed outside the camp' (Lev. 24:14), meaning outside the camp of the Levites.

B.   "'Outside the camp' – outside the camp of the Israelites.

C.   "'And they brought him who had cursed outside the camp' (Lev. 24:14) this serves to indicate the carrying out [of what God had commanded]."

D.   But the carrying out is stated explicitly: "And the children of Israel did as the Lord had commanded Moses" (Lev. 24:23).

E.   That was necessary for two purposes, first to indicate [that the participants in the rite] lay hands [on the guilty party], and second to indicate [that the execution is carried out by pushing the man [off a high place].

F.   The rabbis said to R. Ashi, "In your view, then, concerning all these references to 'he shall take out,' that are noted in the context of the bullocks that are to be burned, how do you interpret them?"

G.   This is a problem.

II.1   A.   **One person stands ... [M. 6:1C]:**

B.   Said R. Huna, "It is obvious to me that the same rule applies to the stone which is used for the stoning, the tree on which the corpse is hung, the sword with which the criminal is put to death, and the scarf with which he is strangled. All of them are [paid for by the funds] of the community. What is the reason? Because we cannot say to a man to go and supply his own property so that he may be put to death."

C.   But, R. Huna asked, "As to the flag with which they wave and the horse that runs and holds up the execution [M. 6:1C], to whom to they belong? Since they serve to save the man himself, should they come from his own property? Or perhaps since the court is obligated to provide for saving the man, should these things come from public funds?"

D. *And further, with regard to what R. Hiyya bar R. Ashi said R. Hisda said,* "As to him who goes forth to be put to death, they give him a glass of wine containing a grain of frankincense, so as to distract him, as it is said, 'Give strong drink to him who is ready to perish and wine to the bitter in soul' (Prov. 31:6).'

E. *And it has also been taught on Tannaite authority,*

F. The aristocratic women in Jerusalem would voluntarily provide it.

G. *But if the aristocratic women had not voluntarily provided it, who would have done so?*

H. *Surely it comes from public funds, since it is written, "Give" – of what is theirs.*

III.1 A. **[If one of the judges said, "I have something to say in favor of acquittal:]** R. Aha bar Huna asked R. Sheshet," If one of the disciples said, 'I have an argument to make in behalf of a verdict of innocence,' and then the disciple was struck dumb, what is the law?"

B. *R. Sheshet blew into his hands, "If someone was struck dumb? Even on the other side of the world [there may be someone who has an argument to give]! [Obviously, we deal with realities.]"*

C. *But in that case, no such statement has been made, while here, such a statement has been made.*

D. *What is the rule?*

E. *Come and take note of what R. Yosé bar Hanina said, "If one of the disciples who voted for acquittal died, they regard him as if he were living and taking a position on the case."*

F. *If he voted to acquit, that is so, but if he did not vote to acquit, that is not so.*

G. *That is obvious to me. Where there is a question for you is if he had said [that he would do so]. [Schachter, p. 280, n. 7: When R. Yosé states, "argued for acquittal," did he mean that he must have given reasons for his statement, or that he merely said he could do so, even if he was subsequently prevented from giving his reasons?]*

IV.1 A. **And even if the convicted party says [M. 6:1E]:**

B. **[Must there be substance in what he has to say] even the first and the second time?** *Has it not been taught on Tannaite authority:*

C. **[And even if the convicted party says, "I have something to say in favor of my own acquittal," they bring him back (M. 6:1E)], one time, two times, [T: Even three times],**

D. **whether or not there is substance in what he has to say, they bring him back [T: pay attention to him]. From that point on, if there is substance in what he has to say, they bring him back [pay attention to him], and if not, they do not [pay attention to him] [T. San. 9:4H-J].**

E. *Said R. Pappa, "Explain the passage, From the second time onwards, [that is, the third time and beyond]."*

IV.2 A. *How do [the judges] know [whether or not there is substance]?*

B. *Said Abbayye, "They send along a pair of rabbis. If there is substance in what he says, they affirm it, if not, they do not."*

C. *And let them send [a pair of rabbis] along with him to begin with?*

D.   *Because he is frightened, he may not be able to say everything that he*
        wants [so twice he is allowed to speak in his own behalf without
        preliminaries].

The Talmud fairly systematically works its way through the
Mishnah's rulings.

6:1H-J

H.   [If] they then found him innocent, they dismiss him,
I.   And if not, he goes out to be stoned.
J.   And a herald goes before him, crying out, "Mr. So-and-so, son of
        Mr. So-and-so, is going out to be stoned because he committed
        such-and-such a transgression, and Mr. So-and-so and Mr. So-
        and-so are the witnesses against him. Now anyone who knows
        grounds for acquittal – let him come and speak in his behalf!"

I.1   A.   *Said Abbayye, "And it is necessary to say [at M. 6:1J], 'On such and such*
                a day, at such and such an hour, in such and such a place.' Perhaps there
                are people who have knowledge of the matter and they will come and prove
                the witnesses against the man to be perjurers."

II.1   A.   A herald goes before him [M. 6:1J]:
        B.   *Just before [the execution], but not prior to that time.*
                [Schachter, p. 281-2, supplies a full translation of the following,
                which is omitted in censored editions of the Talmud and is not
                found in the standard printed text, translated here. What follows is
                verbatim Schachter's translation.]
        C.   This implies, only immediately before [the execution], but not
                previous thereto. [In contradiction to this] it was taught: On
                the eve of the Passover Yeshu was hanged. For forty days
                before the execution took place, a herald went forth and cried,
                'He is going forth to be stoned because he has practiced sorcery
                and enticed Israel to apostasy. Any one who can say anything
                in his favor, let him come forward and plead on his behalf.'
                But since nothing was brought forward in his favor he was
                hanged on the eve of the Passover!
        D.   Ulla retorted: Do you suppose that he was one for whom a
                defense could be made? Was he not a Mesith [enticer],
                concerning whom Scripture says, Neither shalt thou spare,
                neither shalt thou conceal him (Deut. 13:9)? With Yeshu
                however it was different, for he was connected with the
                government [or royalty, i.e., influential].
        E.   Our Rabbis taught: Yeshu had five disciples, Matthai, Nakai,
                Nezer, Buni and Todah. When Matthai was brought [before
                the court] he said to them [the judges], Shall Matthai be
                executed? Is it not written, Matthai [when] shall I come and
                appear before God? (Ps. 42:3). Thereupon they retorted: Yes,
                Matthai shall be executed, since it is written, Matthai [when]
                shall [he] die and his name perish (Ps. 41:6). When Nakai was
                brought in he said to them: Shall Nakai be executed? It is not
                written, Naki [the innocent] and the righteous slay thou not
                (Ex. 23:7)? Yes, was the answer, Nakai shall be executed, since

it is written. In secret places does Naki [the innocent] slay (Ps. 10:8). When Nezer was brought in, he said: Shall Nezer be executed? Is it not written, And Nezer [a twig] shall grow forth out of his roots (Is. 11:1). Yes, they said, Nezer shall be executed, since it is written, But thou art cast forth away from the grave like Nezer [an abhorred offshoot] (Is. 14:19). When Buni was brought in, he said: Shall Buni be executed? Is it not written, Beni [my son], my first born (Ex. 4:220. Yes, they said, Buni shall be executed, since it is written, Behold I will slay Bine-ka [thy son] thy first born (Ex. 4:23). And when Todah was brought in, he said to them: Shall Todah be executed? Is it not written, A psalm for Todah [thanksgiving] (Ps. 100:1)? Yes, they answered, Todah shall be executed, since it is written, Whoso offereth the sacrifice of Todah [thanksgiving] honoreth me. (Ps. 50:23)

II.2   A.   [43B] Said R. Joshua b. Levi, "Whoever sacrifices his impulse to do evil and confesses on that account is regarded by Scripture as though he had honored the Holy One, blessed be he, in the two worlds, this world and the world to come, for it is written, 'Who offers the sacrifice of confession honors me' (Ps. 50:23)."

     B.   R. Joshua b. Levi said, "When the Temple stood, a person would offer a burnt offering, and the reward of a burnt offering would go to his credit, or he would do the same with a meal offering, and the reward of a meal-offering would go to his credit.

     C.   "But he who is humble is regarded by Scripture as though he had offered up all sacrifices.

     D.   "For it is said, 'The sacrifices of God are a broken spirit' (Ps. 51:19).

     E.   "And his prayers are not rejected, for it is written, 'A broken and contrite heart, O God, you will not despise' (Ps. 51:19)."

Unit I complements M. 6:2J, and unit II.1 (in Schachter's translation of the Munich manuscript) illustrates the law. Unit II.2 is attached because of the exegesis of Ps. 50:23.

6:2

A.   [When] he was ten cubits from the place of stoning, they say to him, "Confess," for it is usual for those about to be put to death to confess.

B.   For whoever confesses has a share in the world to come.

C.   For so we find concerning Achan, to whom Joshua said, "My son, I pray you, give glory to the Lord, the God of Israel, and confess to him, [and tell me now what you have done; hide it not from me.] And Achan answered Joshua and said, Truly have I sinned against the Lord, the God of Israel, and thus and thus I have done" (Josh. 7:19). And how do we know that his confession achieved atonement for him? For it is said, "And Joshua said, Why have you troubled us? The Lord will trouble you this day"

(Josh. 7:25) – This day you will be troubled, but you will not be troubled in the world to come.

D.   And if he does not know how to confess, they say to him, "Say as follows: 'Let my death be atonement for all of my transgressions.'"

E.   R. Judah says, "If he knew that he had been subjected to perjury, he says, 'Let my death by atonement for all my sins, except for this particular sin [of which I have been convicted by false testimony]!'"

F.   They said to him, "If so, then everyone is going to say that, so as to clear himself."

I.1   A.   *Our rabbis have taught on Tannaite authority:*

B.   The word, "I pray you," [at Josh. 7:19] means only supplication.

C.   When the Holy One, blessed be he, said to Joshua, "Israel has sinned" (Josh. 7:11), he said to him, "Lord of the world, Who sinned?"

D.   He said to him, "Am I a squealer? Go and cast lots."

E.   He went and cast lots, and the lot fell on Achan. He said to him, "Joshua, by lot are you going to accuse me? You and Eleazar the priest are the two great figures of the generation. If I were to cast lots concerning you, the lot would come up on one of you."

F.   He said to him, "I ask you not to cast doubt on the lots, for the Land of Israel is destined to be divided up by lot, as it is said, 'The land shall be divided by lot' (Num. 26:55). So make confession."

G.   *Said Rabina, "He enticed him in words: 'We are not we going to ask anything more from you than a mere confession. Confess to him and be exempt [from further penalty].'"*

H.   Forthwith: "Achan answered Joshua and said, Of a truth, I have sinned against the Lord, the God of Israel, and thus have I done" (Josh. 7:20).

I.   Said R. Assi said R. Hanina, "This teaches that Achan committed sacrilege on the occasion of three *herems*, twice in the time of Moses, and once in the time of Joshua, for it is written, 'I have sinned, and thus and thus have I done' (Josh. 7:20)."

J.   R. Yohanan said in the name of R. Eleazar b. R. Simeon, "It was five times, four in the days of Moses, and once in the days of Joshua, as it is said, 'I have sinned and thus and thus have I done' (Josh. 7:20) [a sentence containing five words in Hebrew (Schachter)]."

K.   What is the reason that he was not punished until that time?

L.   Said R. Yohanan in the name of R. Eleazar b. R. Simeon, "Because concealed transgressions were not punished until the Israelites had crossed the Jordan."

I.2   A.   This matter is subject to dispute among Tannaite authorities:

B.   "The hidden things belong to the Lord our God, but the things that are revealed belong to us and our children for ever" (Deut. 29:28):

C.   Why [in the Hebrew version] are the words "to us and to our children" as well as the first letter of the word "for ever" dotted on the top?

D. "This teaches that punishment was not inflicted on account of hidden sins until Israel had crossed the Jordan," the words of R. Judah.

E. Said to him R. Nehemiah, "And is punishment ever [even afterward] inflicted on account of hidden sins? And has it not been stated, 'Until eternity' [but not before]?

F. "But just as punishment was not inflicted for hidden sins, so punishment was not inflicted for infractions committed in public, until the Israelites had crossed the Jordan."

G. *Then* **[44A]** *why was Achan punished [prior to that time]?*

H. *It was because his wife and children knew about it.*

I. "Israel has sinned" (Josh. 7:11):

J. Said R. Abba bar Zabeda, "Even though it has sinned, it remains Israel."

K. *Said R. Abba, "This is in line with what people say: 'A myrtle standing among reeds is still a myrtle and still called a myrtle.'"*

I.3 A. "Yes, they have even transgressed my covenant which I have commanded them, yes, they have even taken of the devoted thing and have also stolen it, and dissembled also, and they have even put it among their own property" (Josh. 7:11):

B. Said R. Ilaa in the name of R. Judah bar Misparta, "This teaches that Achan violated all five books of the Torah, for the word 'yes' ['even'] is used five times."

C. And said R. Ilaa in the name of R. Judah bar Misparta, "Achan had covered up the sign of his circumcision. Here it is written, 'They have even transgressed my covenant' (Josh. 7:11), and elsewhere it is stated, 'He has broken my covenant' (Gen. 17:14). [So 'covenant' refers to the mark of circumcision.]"

D. *That is perfectly obvious.*

E. *What might have you maintained? [Achan] would not have violated a religious duty that fell upon his own body. So we are informed [that that was not the case and he violated even that requirement].*

I.4 A. "And because he has wrought a wanton deed in Israel" (Josh. 7:19):

B. Said R. Abba bar Zabeda, "This teaches that Achan had sexual relations with a betrothed girl. *It is written here,* 'Because he has wrought a wanton deed," *and it is written elsewhere,* 'For she has wrought a wanton deed in Israel' (Deut. 22:21)."

C. *That is perfectly obvious.*

D. *What might you have maintained? [Achan] would not have permitted himself to violate the law to such an extent. So we are informed [that that was not the case, and he did violate that rule as well].*

E. *Rabina said, "His punishment is like that of a betrothed girl [who had committed adultery], that is, execution by stoning."* [Schachter, p. 287, n. 1: He should legally have been burned for taking of the things under the ban, cf. Josh. 7:15.]

I.5 A. *Said the exilarch to R. Huna, "It is written, 'And Joshua took Achan the son of Zerah and the silver and the mantle and the wedge of gold and his sons and his daughters and his oxen and his asses and his sheep and his tent and all that he had' (Josh. 7:24). While he had sinned, how had his sons and daughters sinned?"*

B.   *He said to him, "And by the same reasoning, we must ask,* If he had sinned, how had all Israel sinned?

C.   "It is written, 'And all Israel with him' (Josh. 7:24).

D.   "But [Joshua took all Israel to the execution] in order to impose his rule on them, and here too it was for the same purpose. [But they were not in fact executed.]"

I.6   A.   "And they burned them with fire and stoned them with stones" (Josh. 7:25):

B.   By two modes [of inflicting the death penalty]?

C.   Said Rabina, "What was suitable for burning was burned, what was suitable for stoning was stoned."

I.7   A.   "And I saw among the spoil a goodly mantle of Shinar and two hundred shekels of silver" (Josh. 7:21):

B.   *Rab said, "It was [Schachter:] a silk mantle."*

C.   *Samuel said, "It was a cloak dyed with alum."*

I.8   A.   "And they laid them down before the Lord" (Josh. 7:23):

B.   Said R. Nahman, "He came and threw them down before the Lord. He said, 'Lord of the world, on account of these will [as many people as constitute] a majority of the great sanhedrin [thirty-six of seventy-one] be put to death?

C.   "For it is written, 'And the men of Ai smote of them about thirty six' (Josh. 7:5)."

D.   *And it has been taught on Tannaite authority,* "It was actually thirty-six," the words of R. Judah.

E.   Said to him R. Nehemiah, "Were they thirty six? And is it not stated, '<u>about</u> thirty six'? But this refers to Jair, son of Manasseh, who was reckoned as equivalent in value to the majority of a sanhedrin."

I.9   A.   Said R. Nahman said Rab, "What is the sense of the verse of Scripture, 'The poor uses entreaties, but the rich answers insolently' (Prov. 18:23)?

B.   "'The poor uses entreaties' refers to Moses.

C.   "'The rich answers insolently' refers to Joshua."

D.   *What is the scriptural basis for that view? Should we say that it is because it is written,* "And they laid them down before the Lord" (Josh. 7:23), R. Nahman said "He came and threw them down before the Lord"?

F.   Phineas did it that way, for it is written, "Then Phineas stood up and laid out prayer, and so the plague was stayed" (Ps. 106:30), and R. Eleazar said, "It is not said, 'And he prayed,' but 'And he laid out prayer,' teaching that he behaved contentiously with his creator.

G.   "He came and cast [Zimri and Cozbi, Num. 25:7ff.] before the omnipresent, and said before him, 'Lord of the world, on account of these should twenty-four thousand Israelites fall?'

H.   "For it is written, 'And those that died by the plague were twenty-four thousand' (Num. 25:9)."

I.   *But [it derives] from the following [that Joshua spoke in an insolent way,]* "[And Joshua said, Alas, O Lord,] why have you brought this people over the Jordan" (Josh. 7:7).

J.   Moses also spoke in that way, "Why have you dealt ill with this people?" (Ex. 5:22).

> K.   *Rather, [proof derives] from here:* "Would that we had been content to dwell beyond the Jordan" (Josh. 7:7)!

I.10   A.   "And the Lord said to Joshua, Get you up" (Josh. 7:10):

> B.   R. Shila expounded this verse, "Said the Holy one blessed be he to him, 'Your [sin] is more weighty than theirs. For I commanded, "And it shall be when you have passed over the Jordan you shall set up [these stones]" (Deut. 27:4), but you went a distance of sixty miles [to Gerizim and Ebal after crossing the Jordan before setting them up].'"

> C.   *After he had gone out, Rab appointed an Amora [to deliver his message to those assembled], and interpreted [matters in this way]:* "'As the Lord commanded Moses his servant, so did Moses command Joshua, and so did Joshua; he left nothing undone of all that the Lord had commanded Moses' (Josh. 11:15).

> D.   "What then do the words, 'Get you up' (Josh. 7:10) mean?

> E.   "He said to him, 'You were the one who caused them [to sin]' [Schachter: p. 289, n. 3: by forbidding them the spoil of Jericho].

> F.   "So [God] said to him in regard to Ai, 'And you shall do to Ai and her king as you did to Jericho and her king, [only the spoil thereof and the cattle thereof shall you take as a prey].' (Josh. 8:2) [But Joshua was not to proclaim a ban of herem on Ai, as he had done on Jericho]."

I.11   A.   "And it came to pass when Joshua was by Jericho that he lifted up his eyes and looked ... And he said, No, but I am captain of the host of the Lord, I am now come. And Joshua fell on his face to the earth and bowed down" (Josh. 5:13-14):

> B.   *How did he do this? And has not R. Yohanan said,* "It is forbidden for someone to greet his fellow by night, *for we take account of the possibility that it might be a shade"? [So how did Joshua greet the man and talk with him?]*

> C.   *That case is different, for [the man] had said to him,* "I am captain of the host of the Lord, I am now come ..." [thus identifying himself].

> D.   *But maybe he was lying?*

> E.   *We have a tradition that [a being such as this] will not express the Name of heaven in vain.*

> F.   [44B] [The stranger] said to him, "Last night you neglected the daily whole offering of the evening and now you have neglected the study of Torah. [Schachter, p. 289, n. 10: The conversation took place during the night when fighting was at a standstill, and they should have been studying the law.]

> G.   "On which account have you come?" [said Joshua.]

> H.   He said to him, "I have now come [on account of your failure to study Torah]."

> I.   Forthwith: "And Joshua lodged that night in the midst of the vale" (Josh. 5:13).

> J.   And R. Yohanan said "This teaches that he spent the night in the depths of the law."

> K.   Said Samuel bar Onia in the name of Rab, "Study of the Torah is more important than offering the daily whole-offerings. For it is said, 'I have now come ...' (Josh. 5:13)."

I.12   A.   *Said Abbayye to R. Dimi, "How in the West do you apply this verse: 'Go not forth hastily to strife, for what will you do in the end of it, when your neighbor has put you to shame. Debate your cause with your neighbor, but do not reveal the secrets of another' (Prov. 25:8-9)?"*

B.   [He said to him,] "When the Holy One, blessed be he, said to him, 'Go and tell Israel, An Amorite was your father, and a Hittite was your mother' (Ez. 16:3), the [Schachter:] intercessory spirit [Gabriel] said before the Holy One, blessed be he, 'Lord of the world, if Abraham and Sarah come and stand before them, will you speak this way to them and humiliate them?

C.   "'"Debate your cause with your neighbor, but do not reveal the secret of another!"'"

D.   *And does [Gabriel] have so much freedom [to speak to God in this way]?*

E.   Indeed so, for said R. Yosé b. R. Hanina, "He bears three names: intercessor, sealer, and locker – intercessor, because he intercedes and argues against the Most High, sealer, because he seals off the sins of Israel, locker, because once he has closed [discourse on those sins], no one again can reopen discourse about them."

F.   "Had you prepared your prayer before your trouble came" (Job 36:19):

G.   Said R. Eleazar, "A person should always get his prayer ready for trouble, for had Abraham not gotten his prayer for trouble ready between Beth El and Ai [Gen. 12:8] not a single one of (the wicked of) Israel should have been left as a remnant and survivor [in the time of Joshua, when the battle of Ai was fought]."

H.   R. Simeon b. Laqish said, "Whoever puts forth great effort in prayer down below will have none to oppose him up above."

I.   R. Yohanan said, "A person should always seek mercy that all [the heavenly beings] may strengthen his power, so that he will not have opposition up above."

II.1   A.   **And how do we know that his confession achieved atonement for him [M. 6:2C]?**

B.   *Our rabbis have taught on Tannaite authority:*

C.   And how do we know that his confession achieved atonement for him?

D.   For it is said, "And Joshua said, Why have you troubled us? The Lord will trouble you this day"] (Josh. 7:25).

III.1   A.   **"This day you are troubled, but you will not be troubled in the world to come" [M. 6:2C].**

B.   And it is written, "And the sons of Zerah are Zimri, Ethan, Heman, Calcol, Darda, five in all" (1 Chr. 2:6).

C.   *What is the sense of "five in all"?*

D.   **They are five in all destined for the world to come [cf. T. San. 9:5D-F].**

E.   *Here it is Zimri, but elsewhere Achan [Josh. 7:24].*

F.   Rab and Samuel:

G.   One said, "His name was Achan, and why was he called Zimri? Because he acted like Zimri."

H.   The other said, 'His name was Zimri, and why was he called Achan? Because he [Schachter:] wound the sins of Israel about them like a serpent [Achan = snake in Greek, echidna]."

IV.1 **A.** **And if he does not know how to confess ... R. Judah says ... so as to clear themselves [M. 6:2D-F]:**

B. And why not let them clear themselves?

C. It is so as not to discredit the court and the witnesses.

IV.2 **A.** *Our rabbis have taught on Tannaite authority:*

B. **There was the case of a man who went out to be executed. He said, "If I have committed this sin, then let my death not be atonement for all my sins. But if I did not commit this sin, let my death be atonement for all my sins, and the court and all Israel are guiltless, but let the witnesses against me not enjoy forgiveness forever."**

C. **Now when sages heard this statement, they said, "It is not possible to bring him back, because the verdict had already been decreed. But let him be put to death, and let [Schachter] the chain [of responsibility] ever hang on the neck of the witnesses" [T. San. 9:5C].**

D. *It is self-evident [that he cannot by his confession retract the court's decree], for he surely has not got the power to do so.*

E. *It is indeed necessary to indicate that fact, to deal with a case in which the witnesses retract.*

F. *But if the witnesses retract, what difference does it make?*

G. *Once a witness has made his statement, he cannot then go and retract and make some other statement.*

H. *It is necessary to deal with a case in which [the witnesses give a reason for what they have said, as in the case of Baya the tax collector].*

[Schachter, pp. 292-3, n. 6: In the case in question he had denounced the tax defaulters to the Government, an act which, of course, aroused the enmity of the people. According to Rashi, the subject matter of the text is connected with this name as follows: The funeral of the said collector coincided with that of a very pious man, but accidentally the coffins were exchanged, so that the honor intended for the Rabbi was paid to the other, and vice versa. An explanation of the happening was given by the Rabbi in a dream to one of his pupils who was disturbed at the occurrence, and he also informed him that severe punishment lay in store for Simeon b. Shetah in the world to come for the neglect of his duty in tolerating eighty women in Ashkelon guilty of sorcery. Simeon, on being informed about it, took a serious view of the matter and had them executed. The relatives of these women, however, inflamed with a passion for revenge, plotted against his son, charging him with a capital crime, as a result of which he was sentenced to death. On his way to the place of execution the condemned man protested his innocence so vehemently that even the witnesses were moved to admit the falsity of their evidence, giving as ground for their former act their feelings of enmity against Simeon b. Shetah. Yet their latter statement was not accepted, according to the law expounded in the text, that a witness is not to be believed when he withdraws a former statement.]

The Mishnah's reference to Achan explains why the former of the Talmud has developed a sizable conglomerate of materials on that subject.

6:3

	A.	[When] he was four cubits from the place of stoning, they remove his clothes.
	B.	"In the case of a man, they cover him up in front, and in the case of a woman, they cover her up in front and behind," the words of R. Judah.
	C.	And sages say, "A man is stoned naked, but a woman is not stoned naked."
I.1	A.	[45A] *Our rabbis have taught on Tannaite authority:*
	B.	["When he was four cubits from the place of stoning, they remove his clothes.]
	C.	"In the case of a man, they cover him up in front [M. 7:3A-B] in part, and in the case of a woman, in front and in back in part.
	D.	"For a woman is wholly subject to licentious thoughts," the words of R. Judah [T. adds: which he said in the name of R. Eliezer].
	E.	And sages say, "A man is stoned naked, but a woman is not stoned naked" [M. 7:3C] [T. San. 9:6B-D].
	F.	*What is the scriptural basis for the view of rabbis?*
	G.	Scripture says, "And stone him" (Lev. 24:14).
	H.	*What is the sense of "him"?*
	I.	*If I maintain, "him" but not "her," is it not written, "You shall bring forth that man or that woman" (Deut. 17:5)? But the sense must be <u>him</u> without clothing, but her <u>with</u> clothing.*
	J.	R. Judah says, "'... him' – without his clothing, *and there is no difference between a man and a woman [in this regard].* [Schachter, p. 294, n. 1: Since the emphatic word, 'him,' serves for one exclusion, that of clothes, it cannot serve as excluding women from that requirement.]"
I.2	A.	*Does this then imply that rabbis take account of licentious thoughts, while R. Judah does not? Lo, we have heard the traditions in exact reverse, for so we have learned in the Mishnah:* **And a priest grabs her clothes. If they tear, they tear, and if they are ripped up, they are ripped up. He does so until he bares her breast. And he tears her hair apart** [Num. 5:18]. **R. Judah says, "If she had pretty breasts, he did not let them show, and if she had pretty hair, he did not pull it apart"** [M. Sot. 1:4E-G].
	B.	*Said Rabbah, "The reason for the other rule is this: the woman may go forth vindicated in court, and [if beforehand they saw her nude] the junior*

priests will lust after her. In the present case, lo, the woman is stoned.
[No one takes account of necrophilia.]"

C. *And should you maintain that by looking at her nude, the men will think lustful thoughts about some other woman [which we should want to forestall], has not Rabbah stated, "We have learned that the sexual desire is aroused only by what the eyes actually see."*

D. *Said Raba, "[Shall we then say that] the statement by R. Judah contradicts another statement of R. Judah, while the statement of rabbis at hand does not contradict another statement of rabbis? [Surely not!]"*

E. *Rather, said Raba, "The statement of R. Judah does not contradict another statement of R. Judah, as we have just explained, and the statement of rabbis likewise does not contradict another statement of rabbis. Here what is the scriptural basis [for rabbis' view that one must humiliate the woman, even if she is not unclean]?* 'So that all women may be taught not to do after your lewdness' (Ez. 23:48). [Accordingly, there is no consideration shown to the accused woman.] But in that other instance, [namely, stoning the woman to death], you have no greater warning than that."

F. *Now should you wish to propose that both be done to her [namely, humiliation as well as stoning],* said R. Nahman said Rabbah bar Abbuha, "Said Scripture, 'You shall love your neighbor as yourself' (Lev. 19:18). Select for him a praiseworthy form of death [and do not needlessly humiliate him in the process]."

G. *May I propose that Tannaite authorities differ with regard to the view of R. Nahman?*

H. *No, all parties concur with the view of R. Nahman. But here the dispute at hand is that one authority [rabbis] holds the position that humiliation is worse than the pain of death, and the other party [Judah] holds that the pain of death is worse than humiliation.*

Unit I.1 provides a scriptural basis for the Mishnah-paragraph's rule, and unit I.2 then compares the present rulings of the named authorities with positions taken by them in a parallel case.

6:4A-G

A. **The place of stoning was twice the height of a man.**
B. **One of the witnesses would push him over from the hips, so [hard] that he turned upward [in his fall].**
C. **He turned him over on his hips again [to see whether he had died].**
D. **[If] he had died thereby, that sufficed.**
E. **If not, the second [witness] would take a stone and put it on his heart.**
F. **[If] he died thereby, it sufficed.**
G. **And if not, stoning him is [the duty] of all Israelites, as it is said, "The hand of the witnesses shall be first upon him to put him to death, and afterward the hand of all the people" (Deut. 17:7).**

I.1 A. *It has been taught on Tannaite authority:*
     B. **And with his own height, lo, the place of stoning was three heights of a man [T. San. 9:6F].**

C.   *Do we require such a height? And an objection was raised on the basis of the following:* [It is all the same whether one digs a pit, a trench, cavern, ditches, or channels: he is liable. Why then is it written, A pit (Ex. 21:33)]? Just as a pit [under discussion] is one which is [sufficiently deep] to cause death, namely, ten handbreadths in depth, so anything which is [sufficiently deep] to cause death will be at least ten handbreadths in depth [M. B.Q. 5:5F-H].

D.   [The reason that three times a human being's height is required here], said R. Nahman said Rabbah bar Abbuha, "is that Scripture has said, 'You will love your neighbor as yourself' (Lev. 19:18), [meaning,] select for him a pleasant form of death [and do not inflict needless suffering]."

G.   *If so, let it be even higher?*

H.   *That would cause disfigurement [of the corpse].*

II.1 A.   **One of the witnesses would push him over [from the hips] [M. 6:4B]:**

B.   *Our rabbis have taught:*

C.   How do we know that [the death penalty is executed] by throwing someone down?

D.   Scripture says, "And he shall be cast down" (Ex. 19:13).

E.   And how do we know [that the death penalty is executed] by stoning?

F.   Scripture says, "He shall be stoned" (Ex. 19:13) [Cf. Deut. 22:24].

G.   And how do we know that [it is executed] both by stoning and by throwing down?

H.   Scripture says, "Stoning, he shall be stoned or thrown down" (Ex. 19:13).

I.   And how do we know that if he died after being thrown down, the matter is accomplished?

J.   Scripture says, "...or cast down" (Ex. 19:13).

K.   And how do we know that that is to be done in the generations to come?

L.   [45B] Scripture says, "And stoning, he shall be stoned" (Ex. 19:13).

III.1 A.   **And if not, the second witness would take a stone [and puts it on his heart] [M. 6:4E]:**

B.   *Takes it?* [All by himself?!] *And has it not been taught on Tannaite authority:*

C.   **R. Simeon b. Eleazar says, "There was a stone there, [a load so heavy that] it was a burden for two to carry. One would take it and put it on his heart. If he died thereby, it sufficed" [T. San. 9:6G-H].**

D.   *But from your viewpoint, the cited passage poses a problem, for it states that while [it was a load so heavy that] it was a burden for two to carry, nonetheless, one takes it and puts it on his heart.*

E.   *But the point is that he lifts it up with his friend's help and he himself throws it, so that it may drop with force.*

IV.1 A.   **And if not, stoning him is the duty of all Israelites [M. 6:4G]:**

B.   *But has it not been taught on Tannaite authority: It was never necessary for someone to do it a second time?*

C.   *Did I say that anyone did it? I said that if necessary, [that is how it would be done].*

E. Said a master, "A stone was there...! *But has it not been taught on Tannaite authority:*

F. **All the same are the stone with which [a person] is stoned, the tree on which he is hung, the sword with which he is killed, and the scarf with which he is strangled – all of them are buried with him [T. San. 9:8A II].** [So how can we say that a particular stone was used regularly for this purpose?]

G. *The sense is that they make ready and bring others to take their place.*

H. They are buried with him?

I. *But has it not been taught on Tannaite authority:*

J. **They are not buried with him [cf. T. San. 9:8A]?**

K. *Said R. Pappa, "What is the sense of 'with him?' In the area affected by his [corpse]."*

IV.2 A. Said Samuel, "If [after they have testified], the hand of the witnesses should be cut off, the condemned is exempt from the penalty of stoning.

B. *"What is the scriptural basis for this rule? We require that 'the hand of the witness shall be first upon him to put him to death' (Deut. 17:7), and [that condition] would not be [fulfilled in the present case]."*

C. *In that case, how would you deal with the testimony of witnesses who are without hands to begin with? In such a case would they be ineligible to testify?*

D. *That case is different, for Scripture has said, "The hand of the witnesses" (Deut. 17:7), with the sense of the "hand that they had already possess."* [Schachter, p. 1 297, n. 12: But if they lack hands at the outset they are eligible to testify.]

E. *An objection was raised [based on the following passage]:*

F. **[He whose trial ended and who fled and was brought back before the same court – they do not reverse the judgment concerning him and retry him].**

G. **In any situation in which two get up and say, "We testify concerning Mr. So-and-so that his trial ended in the court of such-and-such, with Mr. So-and-so and Mr. So-and-so as the witnesses against him,"**

H. **lo, this one is put to death [M. Mak. 1:10A-D].** [Schachter, p. 297, n. 14: He is executed even in the absence of the original witnesses. This proves that the injunction in Deut. 17:7 is not indispensable but only desirable when possible.]

I. *Samuel interpreted the case to speak of a situation in which the witnesses were the ones who had originally testified.*

J. *But do we require that every verse be carried out just as it is written?*

K. *And has it not been taught on Tannaite authority:*

L. "He who killed him shall surely be put to death, he is a murderer" (Num. 35:21).

M. I know only that he is to be put to death with the mode of execution that is stated in Scripture in that regard.

N. How do we know that, if you cannot put him to death in the mode of execution prescribed by Scripture, you may put him to death in any other means by which you can do so?

O. Scripture says, "He who killed him shall surely be put to death" – by any means.

P.   *But that case is different because Scripture has made it explicit, "He shall surely be put to death...."*

Q.   *Then let us construct an argument from that case [Schachter, p. 298, n. 6: that just as there, where he should be decapitated, he is nevertheless executed by any means possible, so here too, where he should be hurled down by the hands of the witnesses, he is still to be executed even if their hands have been cut off].*

R.   It is because you have references to "murderer" and "avenger of blood," that is, two verses of Scripture that serve to make the same point, and in any case where two verses of Scripture serve to make the same point, one cannot derive [any further arguments from them].

S.   *As to the murderer, it is just as we said now.*

T.   *As to the avenger of the blood, what is [the source of the same lesson]?*

U.   *It is as it has been taught on Tannaite authority:*

V.   "The avenger of blood shall himself put the murderer to death" (Num. 35:19).

W.   It is the religious duty that the avenger of the blood do it.

X.   But how do we know that if there is no avenger of the blood, the court appoints an avenger of the blood for [the deceased]?

Y.   As it is said, "When he meets him" (Num. 35:19) – under all circumstances. [Schachter, p. 298, n. 12: This shows that the provisions of an avenging kinsman are not limited to the precise statement of the Bible.]

Z.   *Said Mar Kashisha, son of R. Hisda, to R. Ashi, "And do we not require that the verse of Scripture be carried out in exactly the manner in which it is written?*

AA.   *"And have we not learned in the Mishnah:*

BB.   **[If] one of them was maimed in the hand, lame, dumb, blind, or deaf,**

CC.   **he is not declared a rebellious and incorrigible son,**

DD.   **since it is said, "Then his father and his mother will lay hold of him" (Deut. 21:20) – so they are not maimed in their hands;**

EE.   **"and bring him out" – so they are not lame;**

FF.   **"and they shall say" – so they are not dumb;**

GG.   **"This is our son" – so they are not blind;**

HH.   **"He will not obey our voice" – so they are not deaf [M. San. 8:4 F-L].**

II.   *"What is the reason for this rule?*

JJ.   *"Is it not because we have to carry out the verse exactly as it is written?"*

KK.   *No, that case is different, because the entire verse of Scripture is superfluous [and so has to be carried out literally, but in other cases that would not be the rule].*

LL.   *Come and take note:*

MM.	If the apostate city does not have a street [to which to carry out the goods of the people], it cannot be condemned as an apostate city," the words of R. Ishmael.
NN.	R. Aqiba says, "If it has no street, they make a street for it [for that purpose]."
OO.	*The dispute up to this point is only that one authority maintains that we require the street to be there to begin with, and the other authority takes the view that a street made just now falls into the category of one that has been there from the beginning. But all parties surely concur that we require that the verse be carried out just as it is written.*
PP.	*It is a [principle subject to] Tannaite dispute.*
QQ.	*For we have learned in the Mishnah:*
RR.	[With respect to Lev. 14:14, which has the priest daub blood on the thumb, big toe, or right ear of the leper as part of the rite of purification,] **if the leper did not have a thumb, big toe, or right ear, he can never have purification.**
SS.	**R. Eliezer says, "One puts the blood on their place, and has carried out his obligation."**
TT.	**R. Simeon says, "If he put it on the left side [instead of on the right], he has carried out his obligation" [M. Neg. 14:9E-G].**

The Talmud works its way through the Mishnah-paragraph's statements, unit I.1 takes up M. 6:4A, unit II.1, M. 6:4B, unit III.1, M. 6:4E. unit IV.1, M. 6:4G. Then unit IV.2 introduces a speculative question, invited by the topic of the Mishnah-paragraph but hardly demanded by it.

6:4H-M

H.	**"All those who are stoned are hung on a tree [afterward]," the words of R. Eliezer.**
I.	**And sages say, "Only the blasphemer and the one who worships an idol are hung."**
J.	**"As to a man, they hang him facing the people, and as to a woman, her face is toward the tree," the words of R. Eliezer.**
K.	**And sages say, "The man is hung, but the woman is not hung."**
L.	**Said to them R. Eliezer, "And did not Simeon b. Shetah hang women in Ashkelon?"**
M.	**They said to him, "He hung eighty women, and they do not judge even two on a single day."**

I.1	A.	*Our rabbis have taught on Tannaite authority:*
	B.	"And if he be put to death, then you shall hang him on a tree" (Deut. 21:22).
	C.	Might one not think that all those who are put to death are hung?
	D.	Scripture states, "For he is hanged because of a curse against God" (Deut. 21:23).

E. "Just as the one who blasphemes [is executed] by stoning, so all who are subject to execution by stoning [are hung]," the words of R. Eliezer [=M.6:4H].

F. Sages say, "Just as the blasphemer is one who has denied God's rule, so all who have denied God's rule [are hung]," [=M.6:4I].

G. *What is at issue?*

H. *Rabbis interpret scripture in accord with the rule of the general and the particular, and R. Eliezer interprets it in accord with the rule of extension and limitation.*

I. *Rabbis interpret scripture in accord with the rule of the general and the particular, thus:*

J. "And if he be put to death, then you shall hang him" (Deut. 21:22) *constitutes a general rule.*

K. "Because of a curse against God" (Deut. 21:23) *constitutes a particularization [of that general rule].*

L. *Now if the two clauses had been stated side by side, we should have reached the conclusion that the general rule is limited to what is made explicit in the particularization [of the rule].*

M. *So only this one [who has cursed God] but no one else [would have been encompassed].* **[46A]** *But seeing that they are given separately from one another, the formulation serves to encompass one who commits idolatry, for such a one is parallel to [the blasphemer] in every aspect.*

N. *And R. Eliezer interprets the passage in accord with the rule of extension and limitation, thus:*

O. "And if he be put to death, then you shall hang him" (Deut. 21:22) *constitutes an extension.*

P. "Because of a curse against God" (Deut. 21:23) *then constitutes a limitation on the foregoing extension.*

Q. *If the two phrases had been stated side by side, they would together have served to encompass only the one who is guilty of idolatry, who falls into the same category in every aspect.*

R. *But seeing that the two are given separately from one another, the construction serves to encompass all others who are put to death by stoning.*

II.1 A. **As to a man, they hang him ... [M. 6:4J].**

B. *What is the scriptural basis for the position of rabbis?*

C. Scripture states, "And you shall hang him" (Deut. 21:22) – him but not her.

D. And R. Eliezer? "Him" – without his clothing.

E. *And rabbis? That is indeed the case. But Scripture has said, "And if a man has committed a sin" (Deut. 21:22 – a man but not a woman.*

F. *And how does R. Eliezer interpret the phrase "And if a man has committed a sin"?*

G. *Said R. Simeon b. Laqish, "In his view that serves to exclude the stubborn and rebellious son [meaning that a man may be dealt with in this way, but not a son who has not reached manhood. Furthermore, a son cannot be declared rebellious once he has reached manhood at thirteen].*

H. *But has it not been taught on Tannaite authority:*

I.   "A stubborn and rebellious son first is stoned and then hanged," the words of R. Eliezer. [This excludes Simeon's thesis on Eliezer's reading of the cited verse.]

J.   Rather, said R. Nahman bar Isaac, "It serves [in Eliezer's view] to encompass a stubborn and rebellious son.

K.   "What is the scriptural basis for this view? Scripture has said, 'And if a man has committed a sin' – a man and not a son.

L.   "Sin – referring to one who is put to death on account of his [already committed] sin – excluding a stubborn and rebellious son, who is put to death on account of what he will become [not what he now has done].

M.   "Accordingly, you have one exclusionary phrase after another such phrase, and when there is one exclusionary phrase after another such phrase, it serves only to encompass [what the two phrases on their face would exclude. Hence the stubborn and rebellious son is subject to the stated law, just as Eliezer maintains in the Tannaite teaching.]"

III.1   A.   **Said to them R. Eliezer, "And did not Simeon b. Shetah hang women in Ashkelon?" [M. 6:4L]**

B.   Said R. Hisda, "That teaching applies only when there are two different modes of inflicting the death penalty, but if it is a single mode of inflicting the death penalty, they do judge [any number of capital cases in a single day].

C.   *But lo, the case of Simeon b. Shetah involved a single mode of inflicting the death penalty, and lo, they have said to him, that they judge only [one capital case a day].*

D.   *Rather, if the matter was stated, this is how it was stated:*

E.   [Said R. Hisda.] "That teaching applies only in the case of a single form of the death penalty that looks like two different forms of the death penalty.

F.   *"What would such a case be? For example, if there were two transgressions [punishable by death].*

G.   "But if it is a single form of the death penalty and a single transgression, they do judge [any number of capital cases on one day]."

H.   *R. Adda b. Ahbah objected,* **"They do not judge two [capital] cases in one day, even an adulterer and an adulteress [T. San. 7:2A]."**

I.   *R. Hisda interpreted this passage [H] to speak of t*he daughter of a priest and her lover [executed by different means], or of the daughter of a priest and the witnesses who come to prove that the witnesses against her are conspiratorial perjurers [in which, again the witnesses and the girl are punished in different ways].

III.2   A.   *It has been taught on Tannaite authority:*

B.   R. Eliezer b. Jacob says, "I heard that a court may inflict floggings and penalties not in accord with the law of the Torah.

C.   "But this is not so as to violate the teachings of the Torah, but so as to establish a fence around the Torah.

D.   "And there is the precedent concerning one who rode a horse on the Sabbath in the time of the Greeks, and they brought him to court and stoned him, not because it was appropriate, but because the times required it.

E.   "And there was another precedent concerning a man who had sexual relations with his wife under a date tree, and they brought him to court and flogged him, not because it was appropriate, but because the times required it.

Unit I takes M. up M. 5:3H-I, providing the expected scriptural basis for the Mishnah's rulings. Unit II moves on to M. 6:4J and does the same. Units III.1, 2 deal with the extra-legal penalties imposed by Simeon b. Shetah, M. 6:4M. So the entire composition is constructed around the Mishnah's statements.

6:4N-S, 6:5-6

N.   How do they hang him?
O.   They drive a post into the ground, and a beam juts out from it, and they tie together his two hands, and thus do they hang him.
P.   R. Yosé says, "The post leans against a wall, and then one suspends him the way butchers do it."
Q.   And they untie him forthwith.
R.   And if he is left overnight, one transgresses a negative commandment on his account, as it is said, "His body shall not remain all night on the tree, but you will surely bury him on the same day, for he who is hanged is a curse against God" (Deut. 21:23).
S.   that is to say, On what account has this one been hung? Because he cursed the Name, so the Name of Heaven turned out to be profaned.

M.6:4N-S

A.   Said R. Meir, "When a person is distressed, what words does the Presence of God say? As it were: 'My head is in pain, my arm is in pain'.
B.   "If thus is the Omnipresent distressed on account of the blood of the wicked when it is shed, how much the more so on account of the blood of the righteous!"
C.   And not this only, have [sages] said, but whoever allows his deceased to stay unburied overnight transgresses a negative commandment.
D.   But [if] one kept [a corpse] overnight for its own honor, [e.g.,] to bring a bier for it and shrouds, he does not transgress on its account.
E.   And they did not bury [the felon] in the burial grounds of his ancestors.
F.   But there were two graveyards made ready for the use of the court, one for those who were beheaded or strangled, and one for those who were stoned or burned.

M. 6:5

A.   When the flesh had rotted, they [they do] collect the bones and bury them in their appropriate place.

B.	And the relatives [of the felon] come and inquire after the welfare of the judges and of the witness.
C.	As if to say, "We have nothing against you, for you judged honestly."
D.	[46B] And they did not go into mourning.
E.	But they observe a private grief, for grief is only in the heart.

M. 6:6

I.1	A.	*Our rabbis have taught on Tannaite authority:*
	B.	Had Scripture stated, "If he has sinned, then you shall hang him," I might have maintained that first the felon is hung, and then he is put to death, just as the government does it.
	C.	Scripture accordingly says, "And he be put to death, then you shall hang him" (Deut. 21:22).
	D.	The felon is put to death and afterward hung.
	E.	How so?
	F.	They delay matters until close to sunset, then they complete the court process and put him to death, then they hang his body.
	G.	One person ties him up and then another unties him, so as to carry out the religious duty of hanging [the body].
I.2	A.	*Our rabbis have taught on Tannaite authority:*
	B.	"[Then you shall hang him on] a tree" (Deut. 21:22).
	C.	May I suppose that that would apply whether the tree is cut down [from the ground] or whether it is attached to the ground?
	D.	Scripture says, "You shall surely bury him" (Deut. 21:22).
	E.	That applies to [a tree] that now lacks only burial, excluding use of one that lacks both felling and burial. [So the tree has to have been cut down before it is used.]
	F.	R. Yosé says, "It refers to one that lacks only burial, excluding this one, which lacks both uprooting and burial. [Thus the post should not be driven into the ground.]"
	G.	*And rabbis? They treat uprooting as of no consequence.*
II.1	A.	That is to say, On what account has this one been hung? Because he cursed the Name [M. 6:4S]:
	B.	*It has been taught on Tannaite authority:*
	C.	R. Meir says, ["T.: Why does Scripture say, 'For one who is hanged is cursed by God' (Deut. 21:23)?]
	D.	"The matter is comparable to two brothers, who were identical twins in one town. One was made king [over the whole world], and the other joined a gang of thieves.
	E.	"[T.: After a while this one who had gone out to join the thieves was caught, and] the king commanded to crucify him on a cross.
	F.	"And everyone who saw him said, 'It looks as though the king is being crucified.' The king commanded them to cut him down.
	G.	"[T.: Therefore it is said, 'For one who is hanged is a curse of God]." [T. San. 9:7A-E].
III.1	A.	R. Meir said, "[When a person is distressed...]" [M. 6:5A]:
	B.	*What is the basis [of Meir's interpretation of the word 'a curse of ...'* (QLLT)]?
	C.	*Said Abbayye, "It is as if he said, 'It is not light' (QL LYT)."*

D.   *Said Raba to him, "If so, what he should have said, is, 'My head is* <u>heavy</u>
      for me, my arm is <u>heavy</u> *for me.'"*

E.   *Rather, said Raba, "It is like one who said, 'Everything is light for me
      (QYL LY).'"* [Schachter, p. 306, n. 11: Euphemistically for 'heavy,'
      as no one is inclined to speak evil in connection with his own
      person.]"

F.   *But the word under discussion [a curse of ...] is needed to make its
          own point [and is not available for exegetical purposes].*

G.   *If so, Scriptural should have said, "One who curses." Why state
          matters as "a curse of ..."?*

H.   *And might I say that the whole verse serves for that one purpose?*

I.   *If so, [in line with Raba's view] the passage should have said
          "lightness of" (QLT). Why [write the word with two L's] (QLLT)?
          It is to indicate that two [meanings are to be derived from the word].*

IV.1 A. **And not this only have sages said, [but whoever allows his
          deceased to stay unburied overnight transgresses a negative
          commandment] [M. 6:5C]:**

B.   Said R. Yohanan in the name of R. Simeon b. Yohai, "How on the
      basis of Scripture do we know that one who keeps his deceased
      overnight violates a negative commandment? Because Scripture
      says, 'You shall surely bury him' (Deut. 21:23).

C.   "On the basis of the cited verse [we learn that] one who keeps his
      deceased overnight violates a negative commandment."

D.   *There are those who say:*

E.   Said R. Yohanan in the name of R. Simeon b. Yohai, "Where in
      the Torah do we find an allusion to burial [as the required way
      of dealing with the deceased]?

F.   "Scripture says, 'You shall surely bury him' (Deut. 21:23).

G.   "On the basis of the cited verse we derive an indication in the
      Torah concerning the requirement of burial."

Burial as the Preferred Mode of Disposition of the Deceased

IV.2 A. *Said King Shapur to R. Hama, "When in the Torah is there proof that
          one has to bury the deceased?"*

B.   *He remained silent and said nothing.*

C.   *Said R. Aha bar Jacob, "The world is handed over to idiots. He should
          have said to him, 'For you shall surely bury' (Deut. 21:23) [which
          surely indicates burial is required]!"*

D.   *[But that passage may merely indicate] that one should make a casket [for
          the deceased].*

E.   *[But it is stated] "You shall surely bury him" (Deut. 21:23).*

F.   *[To King Shapur] that would not have carried [a general] meaning.*

G.   *Then he should have said to him that [Scripture reports that] the righteous
          are buried.*

H.   *[Shapur] could have said that that was the custom in general.*

I.   Since the Holy One blessed be he buried Moses [it should have
      indicated to Shapur that Scripture requires burial].

J.   *That too was so as not to diverge from accepted practice.*

K.   *Come and take note: "And all Israel shall make lamentation for him
      and bury him" (1 Kgs. 14:33).*

L.   *That too was so as not to diverge from accepted practice.*

M.   "They shall not be lamented, nor shall they be buried; they shall be as dung upon the face of the ground" (Jer. 16:4).

N.   *That too was so as to diverge from accepted practice.*

IV.3   A.   *The question was raised: Is burial [performed] for [the purpose of avoiding] disgrace or for [the sake of] atonement?*

B.   *What difference does it make?*

C.   *It would matter in a case in which one said, "I do not wish to be buried." If you say it is to avoid disgrace, he would not have the power [to inflict such a disgrace on his relatives]. But if you say it is for the sake of atonement, then he means that he does not want atonement [so even if he is buried, he does not attain forgiveness* (Schachter, p. 308, n. 9)].

D.   *What [then is the purpose]?*

E.   *Come and take note [of the fact] that the righteous are buried [so the biblical narrative indicates]. Now if you say [that the reason is] to afford atonement, do the righteous need atonement?*

F.   *Indeed they do, for it is written, "For there is not a righteous man upon earth who does good and sins not" (Qoh. 7:20).*

G.   *Come and take note: "And all Israel shall make lamentation for him, and they shall bury him, [for only he of Jeroboam shall come to the grave]" (1 Kgs. 14:13).*

H.   *Now if you should maintain that it was so that he should have atonement, this proves that the others also should be buried so that they should have atonement.*

I.   *This one, who was a righteous man, is the one who should have atonement. But this proves that those should not have atonement.*

J.   *Come and take note: "They shall not be lamented, neither shall they be buried" (Jer. 16:4). [Schachter, p. 309, n. 1: If burial is a means of expiation, why should they too not attain it?]*

K.   *It is so that they should not have atonement [for their sins].*

IV.4   A.   *The question was raised: Is the eulogy for the sake of the living or for the sake of the dead?*

B.   *What difference does it make?*

C.   *It helps us to deal with a case in which someone said before dying, "Do not pronounce a eulogy for me." Or it may serve to require the fee for the eulogy to be paid by the heirs, [for they will have to do so if it is for the deceased, but they may dispense with it if it is for their sake].*

D.   *Come and take note: "And Abraham came [from afar] to mourn for Sarah and to weep for her" (Gen. 23:2).*

E.   *If you say it is for the honor of the living, then for the honor of Abraham did they hold up Sarah's burial?*

F.   *Sarah herself wanted it that way so as to honor Abraham on her account.*

G.   *Come and take note: "And all Israel shall make lamentation for him and they shall bury him" (1 Kgs. 14:13).*

H.   *If you say it is for the sake of the living, is his family worthy for such honor to be paid on their account?*

I.   *The righteous want people to be honored on their account.*

J.   *Come and take note: "They shall not be lamented, nor shall they be buried" (Jer. 16:14).*

K.   *The righteous do not want evil-doers to be honored on their account.*

L.   *Come and take note:* "You [Zedekiah] shall die in peace and with the burnings of your fathers, the former kings who were before you, so shall they make a burning for you, and they shall lament you, saying, Ah! Lord" (Jer. 34:5).

M.   *Now if you say that it is for the honor of the living, what difference did they make to him [since Zedekiah would be the last king of Judah]?*

N.   *This is the sense of what he said to him:* "Through you will Israel be honored, as they were honored through your fathers."

O.   [47A] *Come and take note:* "In whose eyes a vile person is despised" (Ps. 15:4). This speaks of Hezekiah, King of Judah, who dragged the bones of his father on a bier of ropes. *Now if it is for the sake of the living, why [did he do it]? [Schachter, p. 310, n. 4: Surely he had no right to deprive the living of their due.]*

P.   *It was so that his father might be have atonement.*

Q.   *And on account of atonement for his father, did he deprive Israel of honor?*

R.   *The Israelites themselves were pleased to give up honor for the sake of [his atonement].*

S.   *Come and take note:* [Judah the Patriarch] said to [his testators], "Do not hold eulogies for me in the various towns [but only before large audiences in cities]." *Now if you say that is for the sake of the living, what difference did it make [to Judah the Patriarch]?*

T.   *It was so as to give greater honor to the Israelites [by having large audiences gathered for his sake."]*

U.   *Come and take note of the following:* **But if one kept the corpse overnight for its own honor, for example, to bring a bier for it and shrouds, he does not transgress on its account [M. 6:5D].**

V.   *Is not the sense of "for its honor," "for the honor of the deceased]?*

W.   *No, it is for the honor of the living.*

X.   *And for the honor of the living do people keep the deceased overnight?*

Y.   *Indeed so.* When the All-Merciful said, "His body shall not remain all night upon the tree" (Deut. 21:22), that rule applies to a case in which it would be humiliating. *But here, where there is no intent to humiliate the corpse, it is not objectionable.*

Z.   *Come and take note:* If [a mourner] kept the body overnight for the deceased's honor, to let word get out to the small towns, to bring professional mourners, to bring a casket and shrouds, then he does not violate the rule, for whatever he does is only for the honor of the deceased. [Hence the oration is for the sake of the deceased.]

AA.   *This is the sense of the passage:* Whatever one does for the honor of the living does not constitute a disgrace for the ceased.

BB.   *Come and take note:* R. Meir says, "This is a good sign for the deceased, indicating that penalty is exacted from him in this world when he dies [and not afterward]: that he is not given a eulogy; that he is not buried; that a wild beast drags his carcass; or that it rains on his bier. This would be a good omen for the deceased." *This proves that it is for the sake of the deceased [that the eulogy is spoken].*

CC.   *It does indeed prove it.*

V.1 A.   **They did not bury [the felon in the burial grounds of his ancestors] [M. 6:5E-F]:**

B.   Why such arrangements [as having two burial grounds, M. 6:5F]/

C. It is because people do not bury a wicked person next to a righteous person.

D. For R. Aha bar Hanina said, "How [on the basis of Scripture] do we know that people do not bury a wicked person next to a righteous person? As it is said, 'And it came to pass as they were burying a man that behold, they spied a band and they cast the man into the sepulchre of Elisha, and as soon as the man touched the bones of Elisha he revived and stood up on his feet' (2 Kgs. 13:21). [This was the old prophet of Beth El, so the wicked man was not to be buried with a righteous one (Schachter, p. 311, n. 9)]."

E. *Said R. Pappa to him, "But perhaps it was to carry out [the request of Elisha to Elijah], 'Let a double portion of your spirit be upon me' (2 Kgs. 2:9)? [Since Elijah had raised one person from the dead, Elisha wanted to raise two, but he had only raised the son of the Shunamite. Then the desired proof is not at hand.]"*

F. *He said to him, "If that is the case, what is the sense of the following, that is taught on Tannaite authority: 'He rose on his feet but he did not go home'?"*

G. "Then how do you deal with, 'Let a double portion of your spirit be upon me'? Where did he resurrect [two people]?"

H. He said to him, "Said R. Yohanan, 'It is that he healed the leprosy of Naaman, which is accounted as equivalent to death. 'For it is said, "Let her not, I pray you, be as one who is dead"' (Num. 12:12).'"

K. And just as they do not bury a wicked person next to a righteous person, so they do not bury a grossly wicked person next to a mildly wicked person.

V.2 A. *And why not set up four burial grounds [to cover the four modes of execution]?*

B. **Two burial grounds** *is what has been learned as the tradition in this case.*

V.3 A. Said Ulla said R. Yohanan, "If one [inadvertently] ate forbidden fat, and, [in penance,] set aside an animal for an offering, but [before actually sacrificing the beast] apostatized, and then repented, once the sacrifice has been put off, it has been put off [it is invalidated since apostates cannot offer sacrifices], and remains so. [It cannot now be used for the original, inadvertent sin.]"

B. *It has been stated on Amoraic authority along these same lines:*

C. Said R. Jeremiah said R. Abbahu said R. Yohanan, "If one [inadvertently] ate forbidden fat and in penance set aside an animal for an offering, but then lost his sanity, and then regained his sanity, once the sacrifice that has been put off, it has been put off [it is invalidated, since the man, when not in command of his senses, cannot bring the offering], and remains so [and cannot now be used for the original, inadvertent sin]."

D. *And it is necessary [to have both teachings]. For had we learned only the former, we might have concluded that, because the man himself is responsible, through his own actions, for the sacrifice's being put off, [the animal cannot again be used], but here, where the animal has* been set aside in the natural course of events, I might say that it is as if the man who had set it aside was merely sleeping [and in no way bears responsibility for the postponement of the use of the animal in expiation for his sin]. [So the beast may be used.] And if we had learned only the present case, it is because the man has not the power to recover, but in the first case, where the man has the power to revert, one might hold [that the animal has] not [been permanently invalidated]. Accordingly, it is necessary to have both rulings.

E.   Said R. Joseph, "We too have learned on Tannaite authority [the same point as has just now been made, namely]: **If in [the apostate city] there were offerings intended for use on the altar, they are left to die. Things which are consecrated for the upkeep of the house are to be redeemed [T. San. 14:5A-B].** And in that connection we reflected as follows: Why should they be left to die? If [the inhabitants of the apostate town] are put to death, do they not have atonement? So let the animals [afterward] be offered to the Most High! Then [the reason that they are not offered up] surely is that, once they have been put off [and not offered up, the animals at the moment belonging to the apostate town], they are permanently put off [and may not be offered at all, just as Yohanan has said in the foregoing]."

F.   Said Abbayye to him, "And do you think that if a wicked person dies in his wicked state, he gains atonement through his death? If he dies in his wicked state, he does not gain atonement through his death. For R. Shemaiah taught, 'Is it possible [to suppose] that, if a priest's parents left the ways of the community, he should contract corpse uncleanness [in order to bury them, although he otherwise may not contract corpse-uncleanness]? Scripture states, 'Among his people,' Lev. 21:2). The rule [that the priest may contract corpse-uncleanness in connection with the burial of his parents] applies to [a parent] who had performed deeds appropriate to his people.' [This would indicate that merely because a person has died, he does not gain expiation for is sins. The parent after death remains a sinner. There has to be penitence.]"

G.   Said Raba to [Abbayye], "And you will compare the case of one who is put to death in his wicked state to that of one who died in his wicked state? In the case of the one who dies in his wicked state, since he dies in a natural way, he does not have atonement on that account. By contrast, if he is put to death in his wicked state, he does have atonement on that account. You may know that that is the case, for it is written, 'A psalm of Asaph. O God, the heathen are come into your inheritance, they have defiled your holy temple, they have given the dead bodies of your servants to be food for the fowl of the heaven, the flesh of your saints to the beasts of the earth' (PS. 79:1-2). Who are these servants and saints? Is the meaning of 'saints' not those who actually are your saints? Those who are referred to as 'your servants' are those who to begin with were liable to be put to death, and, once they have been put to death, are now called 'servants'?"

H.   Said Abbayye to [Raba], "Do you propose to compare **[47B]** those who have been put to death by the government to those who have been put to death by an [Israelite] court? As to those who have been put to death by the government, since they have been put to death without a proper trial, *[their death] serves as atonement for them. But those who have been put to death by an Israelite court, since they have received a proper trial, when they are put to death, [their death] does not serve as atonement for them. You may know that that is the case, for we have learned in the Mishnah:* **They did not bury the felon in the burial grounds of his ancestors [M. 6:5E].** *Now if you maintain that once such a one has been put to death, it serves as atonement, then let him be buried [in the family burial plot]!"*

I. *[He replied] "We require both execution and [shameful] burial [to attain atonement]."*

J. *R. Ada bar Ahbah objected,* **"And they did not go into mourning. But they observe a private grief, for grief is only in the heart [M. 6:6D-E].** *Now if you maintain that once [the felon] has been buried [in a shameful manner], that serves as suitable atonement, then let the relatives mourn!"*

K. *[He replied] "We require that the flesh rot [before we concede that there has been expiation of sins], for note that the passage goes on:* **When the flesh had rotted, they then collect the bones and bury them in their appropriate place [M. 6:6A]."**

L. *That is decisive proof of the proposition.*

V.4 A. R. Ashi said, "At what point do the rites of mourning commence? It is from when the grave is closed with the grave-stone.

B. *"When is atonement achieved? When the body has seen a bit of the pain of the grave.*

C. *"Therefore, if [the rites] have been suspended [as in the case of the convicted felon], they are suspended [and not required].*

D. *"If so, why must the flesh be consumed [before secondary burial]? [as stated at M. 6:6A]?*

E. *"Because to do otherwise is not possible. [One cannot get at the bones before the flesh is destroyed.]"*

V.5 A. *As to the grave of Rab, people would take dirt from it for an attack of fever on the first day.*

B. *They came and informed Samuel. He said to them,* "They do quite properly. It is ordinary dirt, and ordinary dirt does not become forbidden [as something belonging to the dead,] for it is written, 'And he cast the dust thereof on the graves of common people' (2 Kgs. 23:6).

C. *"The dirt of the grave of ordinary people is compared to idolatry. Just as, when an idol is attached to the ground, it is not forbidden, for it is written,* 'You shall utterly destroy all the places where the nations that you are to dispossess served their gods, upon the high mountains' (Deut. 12:2), meaning, gods upon the high mountains, but not mountains which themselves serve as their gods,

D. *"so here too what is attached [to the ground] is not forbidden."*

E. *An objection was raised [based on the following]:* He who digs a grave for his father and who then went and buried him elsewhere – lo, this one [who dug the grave] may never be buried in [that grave]. [The grave was prepared for a particular corpse and cannot be used for someone else. It is then assumed that the dirt of the grave is subject to the same prohibition and may not be used for any other purpose. That would represent an objection to Samuel, C-D].

F.   *Here, with what sort of case do we deal?* With a grave that is built up [and is not part of the ground at all. The reason the grave is prohibited at E is simply that it was prepared by the man for his father. It would be disrespectful to use it for some other purpose.]

G.   *Come and take note:* A new grave [not assigned to any particular corpse] is permitted [to be used] for benefit. But if an abortion has been placed there, it is forbidden [to be used] for benefit. [And the parallel is that even natural soil is forbidden in this context (Schachter, p. 316, n. 1)].

H.   *Here too we deal with a grave that is built up [and not part of the ground at all].*

I.   *Come and take note.* **It comes out that one may say, there are three kinds of graves: a grave that is discovered, a grave that is known, and a grave that inconveniences the public. A grave that is discovered – one may empty it out. [Once] one has emptied it out, its place is clean, and it is permitted for benefit. A grave that is known – one may not empty it out. [If] one has emptied it out, it is unclean, and it is forbidden [to be used] for benefit [T. Oh. 15:9].** A grave that inconveniences the public – one may empty it out. Once one has emptied it out, its place is clean, but it is forbidden for benefit.
[This proves that natural soil can also be forbidden (Schachter, p. 316, n. 11)].

N.   *Here too we deal with a grave that is built up.*

O.   But is it permitted to empty out a grave that is discovered? *It may be that a neglected corpse is buried there, and a neglected corpse takes possession of the place in which it is buried.*

P.   *The case of a neglected corpse is different, because it is subject to public knowledge [once it is found and buried].*

V.6   A.   *It has been stated on Amoraic authority:*

B.   He who weaves a shroud for a corpse –

C.   Abbayye said, "It is forbidden [to use for some other purpose]."

D.   Raba said, "It is permitted."

E.   Abbayye said, "It is forbidden *[to use for some other purpose, because] designating [an object for a given purpose] matters.* [Schachter, p. 316, n. 15: Mere designation for the dead subjects it to the same law as though it has actually been employed for the purpose]."

F.   Raba said, "It is permitted, *[because] designating [an object for a given purpose] does not matter."*

G.   *What is the scriptural basis for the view of Abbayye?*

H.   *He establishes an analogy based on the use of the word* "there" *both here [in connection with the deceased,* "And Miriam died there and was buried there" (Num. 20:1)] *and there, in the case of the heifer whose neck was broken [on account of the discovery of a neglected corpse, Deut. 21:4,* "And he shall break the heifer's neck there"]. *Just as in the case of the rite of the heifer whose neck is to be broken, once the act of designation [for the present purpose] has taken place, a prohibition [affects whatever has been designated, e.g., the heifer], so in the case of what is designated [for the dead, the mere act of designation] imposes a prohibition*

[so that what is designated for the dead cannot be used for some other purpose.]

I. *And Raba derives the meaning of the word,* "there," [used with reference to Miriam, Num. 20:1], from the meaning of the use of the word "there" in connection with idolatry. [In the latter case it is as follows: "You shall surely destroy all the places there where the nations which you are to dispossess serve their gods" (Deut. 12:2).] *Just as, in the case of what is used for idolatry, mere designation for that purpose does not impose a prohibition on what is designated, so here the mere act of designation does not impose a prohibition.*

J. *And what is the reason that Raba does not derive the sense of the word from the case of the heifer whose neck is to be broken?*

K. *He will say to you,* "**[48A]** *We derive the rule governing objects that are actually used, and not merely designated, from the rule covering equivalent objects [and objects designated for idolatry are not affected by the designation, but are affected only by actual use], so we must exclude the case of the heifer whose neck is to be broken, which itself [by mere designation] falls into the category of what is sanctified.*"

L. *And what is the reason that Abbayye does not derive the sense of the word from the case of idolatry?*

M. *He will say to you,* "*We derive the rule for ordinary usage from a matter of ordinary usage, and we do not derive the rule for ordinary usage from idolatry, which is uncommon. [Ordinary usage involves what is permitted by law, and that would include both the preparation of shrouds for the dead and also the rite of breaking the heifer's neck, but it would not include idolatry.]*" [Schachter, p. 317, n. 7: Mere designation in connection with idolatry does not impose a prohibition, because, since it is abnormal (forbidden), one may repent and never use it for the purpose. But in the case of the other two, if permitted (and certainly if obligatory), once they are designated for that purpose they will certainly be used, unless unforeseen circumstances intervene. Therefore the mere designation suffices to give them the same status as though they had actually been used.]

N. *An objection was raised on the basis of the following:* **A head-wrap, which is susceptible to become unclean with midras-uncleanness [imparted through pressure of standing, lying, or sitting upon an object by a person afflicted with the modes of uncleanness specified at Lev. 15], and which [a woman] put on a scroll [and so will not be used for sitting, lying, or standing, by such a person and therefore serves a different purpose entirely] is then rendered insusceptible of midras-uncleanness [by the shift in the use to which the object is put] but falls into the category of susceptibility to uncleanness [on account of corpse-uncleanness or other uncleanness]. [The head-wrap will no longer serve for sitting, so it loses its former susceptibility. But it remains susceptible to other forms of uncleanness.] [M. Kel. 28:5A].** [What this proves is that designation of an object for a given purpose does matter, and that supports Abbayye's view and contradicts Raba's.]

O. *[Raba] may reply, [That is the case if she actually assigned it and also put it on [tied it around] the scroll.*

P.   *Why both assigning it and tying it around the scroll? [Why not merely the former of the two actions?]*

Q.   *The answer is in accord with what R. Hisda said. For R. Hisda said, "As to a scarf which one designated for use in tying up phylacteries, if one tied up phylacteries in it, it is forbidden to tie up coins in it. If one designated it for that purpose but did not tie anything up in it, or tied something up in it but did not designate it for that purpose, [it is permitted for to use it for coins].*

R.   *As to the position of Abbayye, who holds that an act of designation matters, if one designated it for use for phylacteries, even though he did not tie something up in it, or if he tied something up in it, [and] if he also designated it for that purpose, it is indeed forbidden. But if he did not designate it for that purpose, it is not forbidden.*

S.   Come and take note: As to a sepulchre which one built for a person still alive – it is permitted to derive benefit from it. If one added to it a single row of stones for a deceased person, it is forbidden to derive benefit from it. [The row of stones is not of consequence, hence the original designation mattered.]

T.   *Here with what case do we deal? With a case in which the corpse was actually buried.*

U.   *If so, what does it matter that one added a row of stones? Even if he had not added a row of stones, one could not make use of the sepulchre.*

V.   *It is necessary to indicate that item, to show that even if the body was removed, [the prohibition remains valid].*

W.   Rafram b. Papa said R. Hisda said, "If one can pick out that particular row of stones, he takes away the stones and it is permitted to use the tomb again."

X.   Come and take note: He who digs a grave for his father and went and buried him in another grave – lo, this person may not be buried there ever. [This shows that mere designation matters.]

Y.   *The reason is [not designation but] the honor owing to the father. That is surely reasonable, for are not the concluding lines of the same passage:* Rabban Simeon b. Gamaliel says, "Even in the case of one who hews stones for the burial of his father and then goes and buries him somewhere else – lo, this one may not be buried in a grave using those stones ever." *Now if you say that the operative consideration is the honor owing to the father, there are no problems. But if you say that it is because of the principle that designation matters [and so affects the stones at hand], would someone take the view that yarn spun for weaving a shroud [is forbidden? Surely not!]* [Schachter, p. 319, n. 10: For Abbayye only maintains that if a shroud is actually woven and so fit for its purpose, it is forbidden through mere designation. But what yarn is spun, although its ultimate destiny is to be woven into a shroud, is not forbidden, since, as yarn, it is useless for its purpose. Similarly, when stones are prepared for building a tomb, they should not become forbidden. Hence the prohibition must be on account of filial respect, not designation.]

Z.   *Come and take note:* As to a newly-dug grave, it is for permitted [to be used] for benefit [in some other context]. If one placed an abortion in it, it is forbidden [to be used] for benefit. If one placed an abortion there, it is indeed [forbidden], but if one did not <u>do</u> so, it is not forbidden. [Hence mere designation for use as a grave does not make any difference.]

AA. *[No, that is not the correct conclusion]. The same law applies if one has not placed an abortion in the grave. But matters are so formulated to exclude the view of Rabban Simeon b. Gamaliel, who has said,* "Abortions do not take possession of the grave into which they are placed." *Thus, matters are so formulated as to make clear that they do.*

BB. *Come and take note:* **The surplus of money collected for burying the dead is used for the dead. The surplus of money collected for a particular deceased person is used for his heirs [M. Sheq. 2:5/O-P].** [The surplus funds collected for burying a poor man must be used for other poor deceased. What is collected for a specific person may be used by the heirs for any other purpose, once the costs of the funeral are met. Hence designation does not matter.]

CC. *Here with what case do we deal? With a case in which the funds were collected while the man was yet alive.*

DD. *But the Mishnah-passage at hand does not say so, [for it says:* **The surplus of money collected for burying the dead is used for the dead. The surplus of money collected for a particular deceased person is used for his heirs [M. Sheq. 2:5/O-P].**

EE. *But it was taught on Tannaite authority in that connection:* If they collected for the dead without further specification, this would constitute the surplus of funds collected for the dead, which is assigned to other deceased in need. If they collected for a particular deceased person, this is money the surplus of which goes to the heirs.

FF. *But in accord with your reasoning, let me cite the concluding passage [which shows that designation does make a difference]:* **R. Meir says, "The surplus of money collected for a particular deceased person is left over until Elijah comes." R. Nathan says, "With surplus of money collected for a particular deceased person, they build a sepulchre on his grave. [M. Sheq. 2:5Q-R]. Or they sprinkle perfume before his bier" [T. Sheq. 1:120].**

GG. *But Abbayye explains [this passage] in accord with his view, and Raba explains [this passage] in accordance with his view.*

HH. *Abbayye explains this passage in accord with his view, maintaining that all parties concur that designation makes a difference. The first of the three authorities holds that what is needed by the deceased falls into the domain of the deceased, and what is not needed by the deceased does not fall into the domain of the deceased.* [And, Abbayye continues,] *R. Meir is in doubt whether or not that latter money falls into the domain of the deceased, on which account no one should touch that money until Elijah comes. And R. Nathan finds it self-evident that the excess does fall into the domain of the deceased, on which account one builds a sepulchre on his grave.*

II. *Raba explains matters in accord with his basic principle. All parties concur that designation makes no difference. The first of the three authorities maintains that while [the people who collect the funds] have humiliated [the deceased] [by making a public collection for burying him], he forgives the embarrassment for the sake of his heirs [so they may benefit from the surplus]. R. Meir is in doubt about*

> whether or not the deceased forgives the humiliation [of a public collection for his burial], on which account no one should touch the money until Elijah comes. R. Nathan finds it self-evident that the deceased does not forgive the humiliation, on which account one should purchase a sepulchre for his grave or perfume to scatter before his bier.

JJ.   *Come and take note:* If the deceased's father and mother were putting clothing on the corpse [as an expression of grief] it is a religious duty for others to save them [so that they not go to waste]. [But here we have designation of the objects for the corpse, and as we see, it does not make a difference].

KK.   **[48B]** *[But that is not really designation at all,] because what they did in that case they did out of grief.*

LL.   *If so, take account of that which is taught in this regard on Tannaite authority:*   Rabban Simeon b. Gamaliel said, "Under what circumstances?   In a case in which the clothing has not actually touched the bier. But if the clothing has actually touched the bier, it is forbidden [to remove it]." [If the act occurred only because of grief, there has been no formality of designation at all. Why should they be forbidden?   This challenges the explanation just now offered.]

MM.   *Ulla explained the passage, "This statement speaks of a bier that is buried with the corpse, [and the clothing is forbidden] because it might be confused with the shrouds of the deceased."*

NN.   *Come and take note:*   In the case of a bag which one made for phylacteries, it is forbidden to put money into it.   If one put phylacteries into [a bag not made for that purpose], it is permitted to put money into it. [Designation makes a difference in the former case.]

OO.   *Read the passage to mean,* If he made it and put phylacteries in it, then it is forbidden to put money into it, and this accords with the position of R. Hisda [requiring both designation and actual use].

PP.   *Come and take note:* If one says to a craftsman, "make me coverings for a [holy] scroll or a bag for phylacteries, before one has made use of them for the Most High, one is permitted to make secular use of them.   Once one has made use of them for the Most High, one is no longer permitted to make secular use of them. [Mere designation makes no difference, contrary to Abbayye's view.]

QQ.   *In point of fact, there is a dispute among Tannaite authorities, for it has been taught on Tannaite authority:* If one covered phylacteries with gold or attached to them the hide of an unclean beast, the phylacteries are invalid.   If one attached to them the hide of a clean beast, they are valid.   That is the case, even though one did not tan the hide for that purpose.   Rabban Simeon b. Gamaliel says, "Even in the case of the hide of a clean beast, the phylacteries are invalid unless one tanned the hide for the purpose of the use of phylacteries.   [In the mind of the anonymous authority, designation makes no difference, so there is no reason to require it. That would be Raba's position. Simeon b. Gamaliel takes the view that designation does make a difference, and that is Abbayye's view.]

RR.	*Said Rabina to Raba, "Is there any locale in which people set the corpse aside while weaving shrouds for it?"*
SS.	*He said to him, "Indeed so, in the case, for example, of the deceased of Harpania."*
TT.	*Maremar gave an exposition, "The decided law accords with the view of Abbayye."*
UU.	*And rabbis say, "The decided law accords with the view of Raba."*
VV.	*And the decided law accords with the view of Raba.*

V.7

A. *Our rabbis have taught on Tannaite authority:*

B. Those put to death by the court – their property goes to their heirs.

C. But those put to death by the king – their property goes to the king.

D. And R. Judah says, "Those put to death by the king – their property goes to their heirs."

E. They said to R. Judah, "It says, 'Behold he [Ahab] is in the vineyard of Naboth, where he has gone down to take possession' (I Kgs. 21:18)."

F. He said to them, "It was because he was the son of his father's brother, [and] it was appropriate [to come] to him as an inheritance."

G. "And did [Naboth] not have many children?"

H. He said to them, "And did he not kill both him and his children, as it is said, 'Surely I have seen yesterday the blood of Naboth and the blood of his sons, says the Lord; and I will requite you in this plat, says the Lord' (II Kgs. 9:26)."

I. *And as to rabbis [how do they deal with the statement that they were killed]?*

J. *That refers to the sons who would have come forth from him.*

K. *Now from the viewpoint of him who has said that their property goes to the king, that is in line with the following verse of Scripture:* "Naboth cursed God and the king" (1 Kgs. 21:13). [Schachter, p. 324, n. 1: This points to his culpability for treason to the king in addition to blasphemy, which is punished by the court; hence his estate would fall to the crown]. *But from the viewpoint of him who has said that their property goes to the heirs, why specify that he cursed the king too?*

L. *And in accord with your reasoning, why mention that he had cursed God? But it was to outrage [the judges], and here too, it was to outrage [the judges]* [Schachter, p. 324, n. 8: to make the crime appear more heinous].

M. *From the viewpoint of him who has said that the estate goes to the king, that is in line with the following verse of Scripture:* "And Joab fled to the tent of the Lord and caught hold of the horns of the altar" (1 Kgs. 2:28), and it is said, "And he said, No, but I will die here" (1 Kgs. 2:30). [Schachter, p. 324, n. 10: He declined to be tried by the king so that his estate might not be confiscated]. *But from the position of him who says that the estate goes to the heirs, what difference did it make to him?*

N. *It would be to gain time.* [Schachter, p. 324, n. 11: He wished to gain the time which it would require to take his message to the king and bring back an answer.]

O.   "And Benaiah brought back word to the king saying,
            Thus said Joab and thus he answered me" (1 Kgs.
            2:30):

P.   He said to him, "Go tell him, 'You will not do two
            things to this man [me]. If you kill me, you have to
            accept the curses with which your father cursed me
            [for the murder of Abner, 2 Sam. 3:29. That curse then
            was to be Joab's punishment (Schachter, p. 324, n. 14)].

Q.   "But if you [Schachter:] are unwilling to submit
            thereto, you must let me live and suffer from your
            father's curses against me."

R.   "And the king said to him, Do as he has said, and fall
            upon him and bury him" (1 Kgs. 2:21). [Solomon thus
            accepted the curses (Schachter)].

V.8   A.   Said R. Judah said Rab, "All of the curses that David
            issued against Joab were carried out on David's own
            descendants.

      B.   "'Let there not fail from the house of Joab one who has an
            issue or is a leper or leans on a staff or falls by the sword or
            lacks bread' (2 Sam. 3:29).

      C.   "'One who has an issue' pertains to Rehoboam, for it is
            written, 'And king Rehoboam made the effort to get up on
            his chariot to flee to Jerusalem' (1 Kgs. 12:18), and it is
            written, 'And what chariot one who has an issue rides on
            shall be unclean' (Lev. 15:9).

      D.   "'A leper' pertains to Uzziah, for it is written, 'But when he
            was strong, his heart was lifted up so that he did corruptly
            and he trespassed against the Lord his God, for he went
            into the Temple of the Lord to burn the incense upon the
            altar of incense' (2 Chr. 26:6) and it is written, 'And the
            leprosy broke forth on his forehead' (2 Chr. 26:19).

      E.   "'He who leans on his staff' refers to Asa [2 Kgs. 15:8], for
            it is written, 'Only in the time of his age he suffered from
            his feet' (1 Kgs. 15:23)."

      F.   In this regard R. Judah said R. Said, "He had gout."

      G.   *Mar Zutra, son of R. Nahman, asked R. Nahman, "What is
            it?"*

      H.   He said to him, "It is like a needle in raw flesh."

      I.   *How did he know it?*

      J.   *If you wish, I may propose that he had personally felt
            it; and if you wish I shall say that he had learned it
            from his master; and if you wish, I shall say, because*
            "The secret of the Lord is with those who fear
            him, and his covenant to make them know it" (Ps.
            25:14).

      K.   [Resuming Judah's statement in Rab's name,] "'Josiah, as it
            is written, 'And the archers shot at king Josiah' (2 Chr.
            35:23)."

      L.   In this regard said R. Judah said Rab, "They turned his
            entire body into a sieve."

M.   [Resuming Judah's statement in Rab's name,] "'Who lacks bread' refers to Jechoniah. For it is written, 'And for his allowance, there was a continual allowance given him by the king' (2 Kgs. 25:30)."

N.   *Said R. Judah said Rab, "This is in line with what people say:* '**[49A]** *Be cursed but do not curse [someone else].'"*

V.9 A.   [Reverting to V.7R:] *They brought Joab to court. [Solomon] said to him, "Why did you kill Abner?"*

B.   *He said to him, "I was redeemer of the blood [shed by him] of Asahel [his brother].* [Schachter, p. 326, n. 5: Joab's brother, who pursued Abner when he fled for his life, after having been defeated by Joab at Gibeon while fighting for Ishbosheth, Saul's surviving son, 2 Sam. 2:23]."

C.   He said to him, "Asahel was in pursuit, [since Abner killed him in self-defense, 2 Sam. 2:8-32 (Schachter)]."

D.   He said to him, "He should have saved himself by cutting off one of his limbs, [but he did not have to kill him.]"

E.   He said to him, "He could not do it."

F.   *He said to him, "Now if at exactly the fifth rib he had the capacity [to take aim], as it is written,* 'Abner with the hinder end of the spear smote him at the waist' (2 Sam. 2:23),

G.   (on which R. Yohanan said, "It was at the fifth rib, where the gall bladder and liver are suspended" [Schachter]),

H.   *"should he not have been able to aim at one of his limbs [instead of killing him]?"*

I.   *[Solomon] said, "Let us move on from the case of Abner. Why did you kill Amasa [2 Sam. 17:25, 19:14]?"*

J.   *He said to him, "Amasa had rebelled against the throne, for it is written,* 'Then said the king to Amasa, Call me the men of Judah together within three days ... So Amasa went to call the men of Judah together, but he tarried' (2 Sam. 20:)."

K.   *[Solomon] said to him, "Amasa made an exegetical basis out of the particles 'but' and 'only.' [How so?] He came upon them as they commenced their study of a tractate. He said, 'It is written,* "Whoever he be that shall rebel against your commandments and shall not hearken to your words in all that you command him shall be put to death' (Josh. 1:18). 'Is it possible that that is the case even with respect to study of the Torah [so that the violation of the king's commandment incurs death even if it is ignored so as to continue Torah-study]? 'Scripture says, "Only be strong and of good courage" (Josh. 1:18). [Schachter, p. 327, n. 2: Hence the duty to fulfill the king's command does not apply where one is engaged in the study of the Torah. According to the view held by Amasa, God's law seemed more important to him than the will of the king, and no transgression was involved in waiting until they had finished their study.]"

L.   *"But you yourself are the one who rebels against the king, for it is written, '*And the tidings came to Joab, for Joab had turned after Adonijah, though he had turned not after Absalom' (1 Kgs. 2:28)."

M.   *What is the sense of* "though he had turned not ..."?

N.   Said R. Judah, "He proposed to turn after him but did not do so."

O.   *What is the reason that he did not turn after him?*

P.   Said R. Eleazar, "David was still vigorous."

Q.   R. Yosé b. R. Hanina said, "The star of David still was ascendant."

R.   For R. Judah said Rab said, "David had four hundred sons, all children of beautiful captive women. They all had long locks and would march at the head of retinues. They were the influential men in David's regime."

S.   *[What has been said about Joab] contradicts what was said by R. Abba bar Kahana. For R. Abba bar Kahana said, "Were it not for David, Joab could not have made war, and were it not for Joab, David could not have engaged in the study of Torah. For it is written, 'And David executed justice and righteousness for all his people, and Joab, the son of Zeruiah, was in charge of the host' (2 Sam. 8:15-16). What is the reason that 'David executed justice and righteousness for all his people'? It was because 'Joab, son of Zeruiah, was in charge of the host.' And what is the reason that 'Joab was in charge of the host'? It was because 'David executed justice and righteousness for all his people.' 'When Joab was come out from David, he sent messengers after Abner and they brought him back from Bor-Sira' (2 Sam. 3:26)."*

T.   *What is "Bor Sira"?*

U.   Said R. Abba bar Kahana, "Bor [a well, hence, a pitcher of water] and a 'thorn bush' caused Abner to be killed." [Schachter, p. 328, n. 4: The explanation of this statement is found in J. Sotah I, where one of the reasons given for Abner's death was his indifference to the effecting of a reconciliation between Saul and David, instead of seeking which, he rather endeavored to increase their hatred. He did not take advantage of the following two occasions when he might have brought about the reconciliation: One, when Saul entered the cave of En-Gedi where David and his band were hidden, and the latter, though he could have destroyed his pursuer, contented himself with merely cutting of the skirt of his robe (I Sam. 24:4). The second time, in the wilderness of Ziph, when David found Saul sleeping and took the spear and jug of water from beside his head (ibid. 24:12ff.) subsequently reproaching Abner for not watching better over the King. Abner, however, made nought of this generous treatment of Saul by David, contending that the jug of water might have been given to David by one of the servants, whilst the skirt of the robe might have been torn away by a thorn-bush, and left hanging. These two incidents are hinted at in the words <u>Bor</u> (well, i.e., a jug of water), and <u>Sira</u> (a thorn-bush)].

V. "And Joab took him aside into the midst of the gate to speak with him quietly" (2 Sam. 3:27):

W. Said R. Yohanan, "He judged him in accord with the rule of the sanhedrin.

X. *"He said to him, 'Why did you kill Asahel?'*

Y. *"'Asahel was in pursuit.'*

Z. "'You should have saved yourself from him through one of his limbs.'

AA. *"'I could not do it to him that way.'*

BB. *"'Now you were able to aim directly at the fifth rib, yet could you not aim at one of his limbs?'"*

CC. "To speak with him quietly" (2 Sam. 3:27):

DD. Said R. Judah said Rab, "It concerned the pulling off of the shoe."

EE. [Schachter, p. 328, n. 8: The word is here derived from NSL, to draw or pull off. Joab is supposed to have inquired from Abner in what way a one-armed woman would loosen the shoe in the ceremony of halisah (v. Deut. 25:9). On his replying that she would do it with her teeth (cf. Yeb. 105a), he asked him to demonstrate it, and as he stooped low to do so, he smote him. This incident is hinted at in David's words of farewell to Solomon: "He (sc. Joab) shed the blood of war in peace, – and put the blood of war in the shoes that were on his feet" (1 Kgs. 2:3)].

FF. "And he smote him there at the waist" (2 Sam. 3:27):

GG. Said R. Yohanan, "At the fifth rib, where the gall-bladder and liver are suspended."

HH. "And the Lord will return [Joab's] blood upon his own head, because he fell upon two men more righteous and better than he" (1 Kgs. 2:32):

II. "Better" because they interpreted the particles that indicate "but" and "only" while he did not interpret those particles.

JJ. "Righteous" because they were commanded by word of mouth [to kill the priests of Nob], and they did not do it, while he was commanded only in a letter, and he did it.

KK. "But Amasa did not beware of the sword that was in Joab's hand" (2 Sam. 20:10):

LL. Said Rab, "Because he was not suspicious of him."

MM. "'And he was buried in his own house in the wilderness" (1 Kgs. 2:23):

NN. *Was his house a wilderness?*

OO. Said R. Judah said Rab, "It was like a wilderness. Just as the wilderness is free for everyone, so Joab's house was free for everyone [who wanted hospitality].

PP. "Another interpretation: 'Like a wilderness'. 'Just as the wilderness is free of robbery and fornication, so the house of Joab was clean of robbery and fornication."

QQ. "And Joab kept alive the rest of the city" (1 Kgs. 11:8):

RR. *Said R. Judah, "Even fish soup and fish hash he would taste and then divide up [to the poor]."*

There are two sizable, autonomous discussions, imparting to the Talmud at hand special interest. The first is on the principle of whether merely designating something for a given purpose produces concrete consequences. The second is the rather lengthy discourse on Joab. While both constructions certainly came into being independent of any interest in Mishnah-exegesis, the latter, at least, hardly gives the appearance of being merely tacked on. The exegesis of the Mishnah-paragraphs at hand is carried out systematically. But as to the discussion on whether or not designation makes a difference, I see no obvious point of intersection with the Mishnah-paragraphs before us. The composition itself is sustained and completely persuasive, but I am puzzled on why it was found appropriate here. My best guess is that the theme of burial rites satisfied the redactor who chose it for the present Talmud. The basic issue of the disposition of the estates of those put to death by the court accounts for the inclusion of the massive unit at the end.

7

Bavli Tractate Sanhedrin
Chapter Seven
Folios 49B-68A

7:1

A. **Four modes of execution were assigned to the court, [listed in order of severity]:**

B. **(1) stoning, (2) burning, (3) decapitation, and (4) strangulation.**

C. **R. Simeon says, "(2) Burning, (1) stoning, (4) strangulation, and (3) decapitation" [M. 9:3].**

D. **This [procedure considered in Chapter Six,] is [how] the religious requirement of stoning [is carried out].**

I.1 A. Said Raba said R. Sehora said R. Huna, "Any passage stated by sages in numerical order in fact does not list matters in order of priority or posteriority except for the matter of the seven substances. *As we have learned in the Mishnah:* **Seven substances do they pass over a bloodstain [to see whether it is blood or dye]: tasteless spit, water from boiled grits, urine, nitre, soap, Cimolian earth, and lion's leaf [M. Nid. 9:6A-B].** *And it is taught at the end of the same passage:* **If one rubbed them on out of order, or if one rubbed on all seven substances at once, he has done nothing whatsoever [M. Nid. 9:7K]."**

B. *R. Papa, the elder, in the name of Rab stated, "The same principle pertains also to the catalogue of* **four modes of execution.** *Since R. Simeon disputes the sequence, it indicates that the framer of the passage for his part has listed them in precise order."*

C. *And the contrary position [Raba's view, that omits reference to M. San. 7:1]?*

D. *[When he made his statement,] it did not include passages subject to dispute [but only those in which the list is stated anonymously and hence in the name of the collegium of sages].*

E. *R. Papa said, "Also the order of rites on the Day of Atonement [is meant to be exact]. For we have learned in the Mishnah:* **The entire** rite of the Day of Atonement is stated in accord with its proper order. If one did one part of the rite before its fellow, he has done nothing whatsoever [M. Yoma 5:7A-B]."

F. *And the contrary position?*

G. *That statement merely imposes an additional stringency.*

H. R. Huna, son of R. Joshua, said, "Also the order of the daily whole offering, about which it is taught on Tannaite authority: **This is the correct order of the daily whole offering [M. Tamid 7:3].**

I. *And the contrary position?*

J. *That statement is meant merely to describe the proper way of doing things [but not an indispensable sequence of actions].*

K. *[Raba's statement that a listing by number bears no significance] serves to exclude the conduct of the rite of removing the shoe [Deut. 25:5-10]. [which does no have to follow a given sequence of steps]. For we have learned in the Mishnah:* **The proper conduct of the rite of removing the shoe [is as follows]: He and his deceased childless brother's widow come to court. And they offer him such advice as is appropriate for him, since it says, "Then the elders of the city shall call him and speak to him" (Deut. 25:8). And she shall say, "My husband's brother refuses [to raise up for his brother a name in Israel. He will not perform the duty of a husband's brother to me]" (Deut. 25:7). And he says, "I do not want to take her" (Deut. 25:7). And [all of this] they say in the Holy Language. "Then his brother's wife come to him in the presence of the elders and removes his shoe from his foot and spits in his face" (Deut. 25:9) – spit which is visible to the judges. And she answers and says, "So shall it be done to the man [who does not build up his brother's house]" (Deut. 25:10) [M. Yeb. 12:6A-I].** And R. Judah said, "The proper conduct of the rite of removing the shoe is that the woman makes her statement, then the man makes his statement, then the woman removes the shoe and spits and makes her statement." *And we reflected on that statement: What exactly does he wish to tell us? The order is made explicit by our Mishnah-paragraph itself! This is what he wishes to tell us:* this is precisely how the religious duty should be carried out, but if one reverses the order, we have no objection on that account.

L. *So too it has been taught on Tannaite authority:*

M. Whether the removing of the shoe came before the spitting or the spitting before the removing of the shoe, what is done is valid.

N. *[Raba's statement] further excludes that which we have learned in the Mishnah:* **The high priest serves in eight garments and an ordinary priest in four: tunic, breeches, head-covering, and girdle. The high priest in addition wears the breastplate, apron, upper garment and frontlet [M. Yoma 7:5A-C].** *And it has been taught on Tannaite authority:* How do we know that nothing should come before the breeches? As it is said, "He shall put on the holy linen tunic, and the linen breeches shall be upon his flesh" (Lev. 16:4).

O. *And what is the reason that the Tannaite authority of the passage lists the tunic first?*

P. *Because Scripture lists it first.*

Q.   *And why does Scripture list it first?*

R.   *Because it covers the whole of the body, which is better for him. [But that is not the order in which the priest puts on the garments, as is now clear.]*

II.1 A.   **Stoning, burning [M. 7:1B]:**

B.   Stoning is a more severe [mode of execution] than burning [as listed in sequence at M. 7:1B, against Simeon's order at M. 7:1C]. because it is assigned to the blasphemer and idolator.

D.   *Why is this a more severe offense?* Because [the guilty party] has laid hands on the principle [i.e., the basis of the faith].

E.   To the contrary, burning is the more severe [mode of execution], because it is assigned to the daughter of a priest who fornicated.

F.   *And why is that a more severe offense?* Because she thus profanes her father['s genealogical sanctity].

G.   *[50A] Rabbis [behind the passage as it stands before us] take the view that [a priest's daughter who is] a married woman is taken out to be burned [and not strangled, as are others] but not a betrothed maiden. [An Israelite's daughter who commits adultery while in the status of a betrothed maiden is stoned, and the same penalty should apply to the priest's daughter. She is not an exception.] Since the All-Merciful, however, has singled out the priest's daughter who is in the status of a betrothed maiden, to declare that she shall be executed by stoning, this indicates that stoning is the more severe mode [of execution].*

H.   *Stoning is a more severe [mode of execution] than decapitation,* for it is assigned to the blasphemer and the idolator.

I.   *And why is this a more severe offense?*

J.   *It is as we have already stated.*

K.   To the contrary, decapitation is the more severe [mode of execution], for it is assigned to the men of an apostate town. *And what more severe penalty applies to them [in addition]?* That their property is destroyed [along with them].

L.   But now say, what power is greater, that of the one who entices another to sin, or that of the one who is enticed? You have to agree that it is the power of the one who entices. *And it has been taught on Tannaite authority:* Those who entice the apostate town [to apostasy are put to death] through stoning [which then proves that] stoning is the more severe [mode of execution, as compared to decapitation].

M.   Stoning is a more severe mode of execution than strangulation, for it is assigned to a blasphemer and idolator.

N.   *And why is this a more severe offense?*

O.   *It is as we have already stated.*

P.   To the contrary, strangulation is the more severe [mode of execution], for it is assigned to one who strikes his father or mother. *And why is that a more severe offense?* Because the honor owing to them is deemed analogous to the honor owing to the Omnipresent.

Q.   *But since the All-Merciful singled out the betrothed girl of the Israelite caste, separating her from the category of the married woman of Israelite caste [who has fornicated], assigning the penalty of strangulation rather than stoning, that proves that stoning is the more severe mode of execution.*

R.   Burning is a more severe [mode of execution] than decapitation, for it is assigned to a priest's daughter who fornicated.

S.   *And why is this a more severe offense?* Because she profanes her father'[s genealogical sanctity].

T.   To the contrary, decapitation should be deemed the more severe, for it is assigned to the men of the apostate town.

U.   *And what more severe penalty applies to them [in addition]?* That their property is destroyed [along with them].

V.   "Her father" is stated in connection with stoning [Deut. 22:2], the betrothed girl who fornicated is stoned because she has played the whore in her father's house], and "her father" is stated in connection with burning [a priest's daughter who fornicated is burned with fire, so Lev. 21:9, for having "profaned her father"]. Just as, when "her father" is stated with reference to stoning, stoning is deemed more severe than decapitation, so when "her father" is stated with reference to burning, burning is deemed more severe than decapitation.

W.   Burning is a more severe mode [of execution] than strangling, because it is assigned to the daughter of a priest who fornicated.

X.   *And why is this a more severe offense?*

Y.   *It is as we have already stated.*

Z.   To the contrary, strangulation is the more severe [mode of execution], for it is assigned to one who hits his father or his mother.

AA.   *And why is this a more severe crime?*

BB.   *Because the honor owing to them is deemed analogous to the honor owing to the Omnipresent. Since the All-Merciful singled out the case of a married woman, daughter of a priest, from the case of married women of Israelite caste, who had committed adultery, assigning the penalty of burning rather than strangulation, that indicates that burning is the more severe [mode of execution].* [Freedman, p. 335, n. 5: since the priest's daughter profanes her father in addition to disgracing herself].

CC.   Decapitation is a more severe [mode of execution] than strangulation, for it is assigned to the men of the apostate town.

DD.   *And what more severe penalty applies to them [in addition]?* That their property is destroyed [along with them].

EE.   To the contrary, strangulation is the more severe [mode of execution], for it is assigned to one who strikes his father or his mother.

FF.   *And why is this a more severe offense?* Because the honor owing to them is deemed analogous to the honor owing to the Omnipresent.

GG.   *Nonetheless, one who lays hands on the principle [i.e., the basis of the faith] is guilty of a more severe offense [as is the case with the execution of the inhabitants of an apostate town.*

III.1 A.   **R. Simeon says [M. 7:1C]:**

B.   Burning is a more severe [mode of execution] than stoning, for it is assigned to a priest's daughter who fornicated. *And why is this a more severe offense?* Because she has profaned her father's [genealogical sanctity].

C.   To the contrary, stoning is the more severe [mode of execution], for it is assigned to the blasphemer and the idolator. *And why is this a*

	more severe offense? Because such a one has laid hands on the principle [i.e., the basis of the faith].
D.	*R. Simeon is consistent with his views expressed elsewhere, for he has said, "All the same are the betrothed girl and the married woman [who have committed adultery]. They are taken out and burned. But since the All-Merciful has singled out the priest's daughter who was betrothed and assigned her a different penalty, namely, burning, rather than the stoning [that applies to an Israelite's daughter in the same status], this proves that burning is the more severe [mode of execution].*
E.	Burning is a more severe [mode of execution] than strangulation, for it is assigned to a priest's daughter who fornicated. And why is this a more severe offense?
F.	*It is as we have stated.*
G.	To the contrary, strangulation is the more severe [mode of execution], for it is assigned to one who strikes his father or his mother.
H.	*And why is this a more severe offense?* Because the honor owing to the parents is deemed analogous to the honor owing to the Omnipresent.
I.	*Since the All-Merciful singled out the married woman who is the daughter of a priest from the married women who is of Israelite caste and assigned her a different penalty, namely, burning rather than strangulation, thus proves that burning is the more severe [mode of execution].*
J.	Burning is a more severe [mode of execution] than decapitation, for it is assigned to the daughter of a priest who has fornicated.
K.	*And why is this a more severe offense?*
L.	*It is as we have already stated.*
M.	To the contrary, decapitation is the more severe [mode of execution], for it is assigned to the men of an apostate down.
N.	*And what more severe penalty applies to them [in addition]?*
O.	That their property is destroyed [along with them].
P.	*So now say:* Which is the greater power, the power of the one who entices [others to commit idolatry] or the power of the one who is enticed? **[50B]** You must say it is the power of the one who entices.
Q.	And this yields an argument a fortiori: If burning is more severe than strangulation, which is more severe than decapitation, which is a less severe mode of execution, is it not an argument a fortiori [that burning is a more severe mode of execution than decapitation]?
R.	Stoning is a more severe [mode of execution] than strangulation, for it is assigned to a blasphemer and an idolator.
S.	*And why is this a more severe offense?*
T.	*It is as we have already said.*
U.	To the contrary, strangulation is the more severe [mode of execution], for it is assigned to the one who strikes his father or his mother.
V.	*And why is this a more severe offense?*
W.	*Because the honor owing to them is deemed analogous to the honor owing to the Omnipresent.*

X.   *Since the All-Merciful has singled out a betrothed girl of Israelite caste who fornicated, from a married women of Israelite caste, assigning the penalty of stoning rather than strangulation, thus proves that stoning is a more severe [mode of execution].*

Y.   Stoning is a more severe [mode of execution] than decapitation, for it is assigned to the blasphemer, etc.

Z.   To the contrary, decapitation is the more severe, since it is assigned to the men of an apostate town.

AA.   And what more severe more severe penalty applies to them [in addition]? That their property is destroyed [along with them].

BB.   So now say: which is more powerful, the one who entices or the one who is enticed? You must say it is the power of the one who entices.

CC.   And this yields an argument a fortiori:

DD.   If stoning is more severe than strangulation, which is more severe than decapitation, which is a less severe mode of execution,

EE.   is it not an argument a fortiori [that stoning is a more severe mode of execution than decapitation]?

FF.   Strangulation is a more severe [mode of execution] than decapitation, for it is assigned to the one who strikes his father or his mother.

GG.   *And why is this a more severe offense?*

HH.   *It is as we have said.*

II.   To the contrary, decapitation is the more severe [mode of execution], for it is assigned to the men of an apostate town.

JJ.   *And what more severe penalty applies to them [in addition]?*

KK.   It is that their property is destroyed [along with them].

LL.   So now say: Which power is greater, the power of the one who entices [another to commit idolatry], or the power of the one who is enticed? One must say it is the power of the one who entices.

MM.   *And it has been taught on Tannaite authority:*

NN.   Those who entice the apostate town [to idolatry are executed] by stoning.

OO.   R. Simeon says, "By strangulation."

III.2 A.   *A pearl in the mouth of R. Yohanan:*

       B.   **A betrothed girl, a priest's daughter, who committed adultery [is executed] by stoning.**

       C.   **R. Simeon says, "By burning."**

       D.   **If she committed adultery with her father, she is [executed] by stoning.**

       E.   **R. Simeon says, "By burning" [T. San. 12:2].**

       F.   *What does this passage teach us?*

       G.   In the view of the rabbis, it is that a married woman [who is daughter of a priest and commits adultery] goes forth to be burned, but not a betrothed girl.

       H.   *From the viewpoint of R. Simeon, all the same are a betrothed girl and a married woman [daughters of priests, who commit adultery]. In both cases they go forth to be burned.*

       I.   *And what is the reason?*

J.   *It is that, in the view of rabbis, stoning is the more severe [mode of execution], and, in the view of R. Simeon, burning is the more severe [mode of execution].*

K.   *The practical difference [of all this] is that if someone is declared liable to the death penalty on two different counts, each with its [mode of execution], he is condemned in accord with the more severe of the two penalties.*

III.3 A.   *What [evidence is there concerning the view of] R. Simeon [that the daughter of a priest, whether betrothed or married, is executed for the crime of adultery by burning]?*

B.   *It is accord with that which has been taught on Tannaite authority:*

C.   R. Simeon says, "Two encompassing principles have been stated with reference to the priest's daughter." [Freedman, p. 338, n. 3: One encompassing principle refers to a betrothed girl, the other to a married woman. When the Torah states, "And the man who commits adultery with another man's wife, even he who commits adultery with his neighbor's wife, the adulterer and the adulteress shall surely be put to death" (Lev. 20:10). This is a general law regarding a married woman, in which a priest's daughter should be included. Likewise the law in Deut. 22:23f.: "If a damsel that is a virgin be betrothed to a husband, and a man find her in the city and lie with her, then you shall bring them both out to the gate of the city and stone them." This is a general principle for an adulterous betrothed girl, which should embrace the priest's daughter too.]

D.   *[Do you mean to say that these rules speak] of a priest's daughter and not an Israelite's daughter?*

E.   *I should say, "Also to a priest's daughter."*

F.   Now Scripture has singled out the married [priest's daughter] from the [category of the] married [Israelite's daughter], and the betrothed [priest's daughter] from the [category of the] betrothed [Israelite's daughter].

G.   Now if the reason for singling out the married [priest's daughter] from the [category of the] married [Israelite's daughter] was [Scripture's wish] to impose a stricter penalty upon the priest's daughter, so too when Scripture singled out the betrothed [priest's daughter] from the [category of the] betrothed Israelite's daughter], it was to impose a stricter penalty on her.

H.   But false witnesses [who testify] against a married woman who is a priest's daughter [and claim she has committed adultery when she has not, and so are subjected to the same penalty that they proposed to inflict on her], fall into [exactly the same] category as false witnesses against a married woman who is an Israelite's daughter.

I.   And false witnesses who testify against the betrothed daughter of a priest fall into the same category as false witnesses against the betrothed daughter of an Israelite.

III.4 A.   *Our rabbis have taught on Tannaite authority:*

B.   "And the daughter of any priest, if she profane [herself]" (Lev. 21:9):

C.   Might one think [that that is the case] even if she had profaned the Sabbath?

D.   Scripture states, "by playing the whore" (Lev. 21:9):

E.   It is concerning the profanation that involves whoredom that Scripture speaks.

F.   Might one think [that that is the case] even if she were unmarried?

G.   [No, that cannot be the case, for] "her father" is stated in the present context (Lev. 21:9), and "her father" is stated elsewhere (at Deut. 22:21).

H.   Just as in the latter passage [at issue] is an act of prostitution by a woman tied to a husband, so too here [at issue] is an act of prostitution by a woman tied to a husband.

I.   But perhaps the [analogous] usage of "her father" is intended to exclude everyone else? [Freedman, p. 340, n. 1: Only if she committed incest with her father is she punished by burning, but not for playing the harlot with others.]

J.   When Scripture states, "She profanes [herself]" (Lev. 21:9), it must mean that that act may take place with any man.

K.   How then am I to interpret [the use of] "her father"?

L.   "Her father" is stated here [at Lev. 21:9] and "her father" is stated elsewhere [at Deut. 22:21].

M.   Just as in the latter passage [at issue] is an act of prostitution by a woman tied to a husband, so here too [at issue] is an act of prostitution by a woman tied to a husband.

N.   If in the latter case (Deut. 22:21) [Scripture states] "a maiden," and she is merely betrothed, so here (Lev. 21:9) [does not Scripture imply] "a betrothed maiden" [who is a priest's daughter]?

O.   How do I know [from Scripture, that the death penalty for prostitution applies equally to a priest's daughter who is] a married maiden [i.e., a married girl under the age of twelve-and-a-half], or [a priest's daughter who is] an adult betrothed woman, or [a priest's daughter who is] an adult married woman, or even [a priest's daughter who is] an old woman [beyond her child-bearing years, hence cannot produce an illegitimate child]?

P.   Scripture states, "And the daughter of any priest (Lev. 21:9) – under all circumstances.

III.5 A.   "The daughter of a priest" (Lev. 21:9):

B.   [51A] I know only that that rule applies if she is married to a priest [as will be explained].

C.   If she is married to a Levite, an Israelite, an idolator, one of impaired priestly stock, one born of a union of a couple not legally permitted to wed at all, or to a Temple slave, how do we know [that the same rule applies]?

D.   "And the daughter of a man who is a priest" (Lev. 21:9) – even if she is not herself married to a priest.

III.6 A.   "And the daughter of a priest, if she profanes herself by playing the harlot, she profanes her father; she shall be burned in fire" (Lev. 21:9).

B.   [Interpret the latter phrase to mean as follows:] She shall be burned but the man who had intercourse with her shall not be burned.

C.   She shall be burned, but the witnesses who testify falsely against her shall not be burned.

D.   R. Eliezer says, "[Since the verse says she profanes her father one may derive the following in conclusion:] If [she had intercourse]

with her father, she shall be burned. But if [she had intercourse]
with her father-in-law, she is stoned."

E.   A master said, "Is it possible [the above Scriptural verse] also
refers to her [profaning herself by] profaning the Sabbath?

F.   "[No, that is impossible, for] profaning the Sabbath invokes
stoning [whereas the above verse specifies only burning]."

G.   *Said Raba, "Who holds the view [that she shall be burned for
violating the Sabbath]? It is R. Simeon, [for he] said that burning is a
more severe [punishment than stoning]. [Simeon] might reason that
since the Merciful One treated priests more strictly than Israelites by
giving [the former] more commandments [than the latter], then God
would invoke a more severe penalty if a priest violated the Sabbath
than if an Israelite had violated the Sabbath. Thus, one might
conclude that if a priest violates the Sabbath, he or she incurs
burning, whereas if an Israelite violates the Sabbath, he or she incurs
the less severe penalty of stoning.] [Scripture indicates this line of
reasoning is incorrect; for it states,] "if she play the harlot" [that is
only for harlotry does a priest's daughter invoke burning, not
for the profanation of the Sabbath."*

H.   *But what difference is there between a woman priest and a male priest
[so that Scripture specifically indicates that a woman priest does not
invoke burning?]*

I.   *[Had Scripture not mentioned a woman of priestly descent] I might
have arrived at the following incorrect conclusion. I might think a
priest is punished by the less severe punishment of stoning because he
is permitted to work on the Sabbath in the Temple service; but since a
woman of priestly origins is not permitted to do so, her punishment
should be stoning. [The Scriptural verse thus] teaches us [that that is
not the case]."*

J.   "Might one think that that is the case even if she was
unmarried?"

K.   Lo, it is written, "By playing the harlot"? [So why should that
have been an issue, since an unmarried woman does not
commit whoredom if she has sexual relations.]

L.   *The passage is framed in accord with the view of R. Eliezer, who has
said,* "If an unmarried man had sexual relations with an
unmarried woman, not intending thereby to effect a marital
bond, he has turned her into a whore."

M.   But perhaps the force of the analogous usage is to indicate that
only 'her father' is meant, so excluding everyone else?

N.   *What would be the sense of the passage? Is it that she had an
incestuous sexual relationship with her father? Then why specify
that this is the daughter of a priest? Even if it were the daughter of
an Israelite, the rule would be the same.*

O.   It would accord with what Raba said, "R. Isaac bar Abodimi
said to me, 'The word "they" occurs in two related passage, so
too the word "wickedness." [Freedman, p. 342, n. 1: In Lev.
18:10 it is stated: The nakedness of thy son's daughter, or of
they daughter's daughter, even their nakedness thou shalt not
uncover: for they (hennah) are thine own nakedness. Further
it is written (ibid. XVIII, 17): Thou shalt not uncover the

nakedness of a woman and her daughter, neither shalt thou take her son's daughter, or her daughter's daughter, to uncover her nakedness; for they (hennah) are her near kinswomen: it is wickedness (zimmah). Just as in the latter verse, intercourse with one's wife's daughter is treated as with her granddaughter, so in the former case, incest with one's daughter is the same offense as with one's granddaughter. Though this is not explicitly stated, it is deduced from the fact that hennah occurs in both cases. Further, in Lev. 18:17 it is stated: And if a man take a wife and her mother, it is wickedness (zimmah); they shall be burnt with fire. The use of zimmah in Lev. 18:17 and Lev. 18:10 show that burning by fire is the penalty in both cases; and the use of hennah in Lev. 18:17 and Lev. 18:10 shews that in Lev. 18:10 too the penalty is burning (cf. the Euclidean axiom: the equals of equals are equal. Thus we see that incest between a man, even an Israelite, and his daughter is punished by burning. How then could we assume that the verse under discussion, which decrees burning as a penalty for whoredom by a priest's daughter (implying the exclusion of an Israelite's daughter), refers to incest with one's father, and consequently what need is there for the deduction from she profaneth?]

P.　　*It was necessary to state the verse as is,* [Freedman, p. 342:] *For I would think that this whole passage treats of incest with one's father and the penalty of burning is prescribed here intentionally to obviate Raba's deduction.* [Freedman, p. 342, n.2: show that only a priest's daughter, who is differently punished. In that case, the identical phrasing of the verses cited by Raba would have to be otherwise interpreted]. So we are informed that that is not the case."

III.7　A.　"The daughter of a priest" (Lev. 21:9):

B.　I know only that the rule applies if she was married to a priest. If she was married to a Levite, an Israelite, an idolator, one of impaired priestly stock, one who was born of a union of a couple not legally permitted to wed at all, or to a Temple slave, how do we know that the same rule applies?

C.　Scripture says, "And the daughter of a man who is a priest' (Lev. 21:9) – even though she is herself not of the priestly caste."

D.　*Merely because the girl is married to one of these, does she cease to be the daughter of a priest? And furthermore, does it say, "A priest's daughter married to a priest [in particular]"?*

E.　*It might have entered your mind to suppose that, when the All-Merciful said, "If she profane herself by playing the whore," at issue was solely a girl who to begin with does so. But in this case, since she is already in the situation of one who has profaned her status [the rule should not pertain].*

F.　For a master has said, "'If the priest's daughter is married to a non-priest [she may not eat of an offering of holy things] (Lev. 22:12) [this verse teaches that] if she has sexual relations with one who is unfit for her, he disqualifies her [from eating food in the present status]. If she marries a Levite or an Israelite that is also the case, for it is said, '[But if a priest's daughter be a widow or divorced and have no child] and returns to her father's house, as in her youth, [she shall eat of her father's meat]' (Lev. 22:13)." *That bears the implication that when she is with him [the Levite or Israelite], she was not eating such food. I might then have supposed that, under those same circumstances, she should not suffer the penalty of burning. Accordingly, the cited verse indicates that that is not the case.*

III.8   A.   *The ruling [that a priest's daughter married to the offspring of a union of parents who cannot legally married is put to death through burning] does not accord with the view of R. Meir [who says the penalty is by strangling]. For we have learned in the Mishnah:*

B.   **"The daughter of a priest who married an Israelite and afterwards [unintentionally] ate heave-offering pays the principal, but does not pay the [added] fifth.**

C.   **"And [if she commits adultery] her death is by burning.**

D.   **"[If] she married any person who is ineligible [for marriage to priestly stock, e.g., a bastard (M. Yeb. 6:2), and then unintentionally ate heave-offering],**

E.   **she pays the principal and the [added] fifth.**

F.   **"And [if she commits adultery] her death is by strangling," – the words of R. Meir.**

G.   **But sages say, "Both of these [women] pay the principal, but do not pay the [added] fifth,**

H.   **"and [if they commit adultery] their death is by burning," [M. Ter. 7:2, trans. Alan J. Avery-Peck].** [Avery-Peck explains: The daughter of a priest who marries an Israelite. While such a woman is of priestly lineage, because of the marriage she becomes an outcast and loses the right she had while living in her father's house to eat holy things. The problem is whether such a woman still is treated as a person of priestly status, or whether she is treated as an ordinary Israelite. The issue is disputed by Meir, C-G, and sages, H-I. The key to the exegesis of the pericope is in what on the surface appears to be a secondary dispute at D+G vs. I. Meir distinguishes between a priest's daughter who marries an Israelite of unimpaired stock, and one who marries an Israelite who is not fit for marriage to priests. His point is made through the contrast. Upon divorce or widowhood the woman at D returns to her father's house and regains her previously held priestly rights. It follows for Meir that she is treated like a person of priestly status. If she commits adultery, she is executed by burning, as are all women of priestly caste who commit adultery (Lev. 21:9, M. San. 9:1). This is not the case at G. where the woman has married an Israelite of impaired lineage. Such a woman never may return to her father's house. Meir holds, therefore, that she is treated under the law as an Israelite. If she is unfaithful, her death is by strangulation, as it is for all Israelite women who are unfaithful (M. San. 11:1). On this basis we readily can interpret Meir's view regarding the restitution these women pay if they unintentionally eat heave-offering. The priest's daughter who marries an Israelite of unimpaired stock is treated like a person of priestly status. If she eats heave-offering she does not pay the added fifth, which is paid only by non-priests. Since she had no right to eat the heave-offering, however, she must replace it, as would any priest who ate heave-offering belonging to some other priest. For this reason she pays the principal. This is not the case at F. Since here the woman is treated like an Israelite, if she eats heave-offering, she must pay both the principal and the added fifth. Sages reject Meir's distinction. By birth the woman is of priestly stock. This is not changed by her marriage to a non-priest, even one of impaired lineage. After her marriage she does not have the right to eat heave-offering. If she does so anyway, since she is of priestly stock, she need not pay the added fifth required of non-priests. If she commits adultery, her death is by burning, as it is in the case of all unfaithful priestly women.]

III.9   A.   R. Eliezer says, "If she committed adultery with her father, she is put to death through burning, and is if she did so with her father in law, it is through stoning."

B.   *What is the meaning of the foregoing statement?*

C.   *Should one propose that "her father" means that she committed adultery with her father, and "with her father in law" means that she committed adultery with her father in law, then why address in particular the case of the daughter of a priest?*

D.   *Even if it were the daughter of an Israelite, the penalty of committing adultery with the father is punishable by burning, and with the father-in-law, by stoning.*

E.   But the phrase, "with her father" means "in the domain of her father," and "with her father in law" means in the domain of her father in law. [The former, then, is betrothed, the latter fully wed.]

F.   *In accord with whose view is the statement of Eliezer made, then? It cannot be in accord with the view of rabbis, for have they not said that* a married woman [who committed adultery] goes forth to execution through burning?

G.   And that penalty could not apply, then, to the betrothed girl [as Eliezer claims].

H.   *It furthermore cannot accord with the view of R. Simeon, for has he not said that* the same penalty, namely, burning, applies to both the betrothed girl and the married woman?

I.   *And it could also not accord with R. Ishmael, for has he not said [in a passage given below] that* the betrothed girl [who commits adultery] goes forth to execution through being burned, but not a married woman, so that, when in the domain of her father in law [as a married woman, should she commit adultery,] she is put to death by being strangled [and not through stoning]?

J.   *Rabin sent word in the name of R. Yosé b. R. Hanina, "This is the sense of the teaching [of Eliezer].* In point of fact it accords with rabbis. And this is the sense of what he has said: In any case in which the penalty of a woman who has committed adultery is more lenient than that inflicted on her father for incest [with his daughter] *and what would such a case be?* It is the case of an Israelite's daughter, for, if the Israelite's daughter is married [and commits adultery], she would be put to death through strangling [while her father is put to death through burning] *then in the present case, namely,* that of the priest's daughter, she would be put to death in the same way as the father, namely through burning. But in any case in which the mode of execution of the woman who has committed adultery is more stringent than that inflicted of her father [for incest with his daughter] *and what would such a case be?* It is the case of an Israelite's daughter who is betrothed [and commits adultery], for an Israelite's daughter who is betrothed would be put to death through stoning then in the present case, namely that of the priest's daughter, she would be put to death in the mode of execution that would apply to her father-in-law should he commit incest, and that is, through stoning."

K. *To this interpretation R. Jeremiah objected, "But does the passage at hand speak of penalties that are more or less stringent than one another? [Obviously not. The explanation is a complete fabrication.]"*

L. Rather, said R. Jeremiah, "[51B] The statement of Eliezer] accords with the position of R. Ishmael. This is the sense of his statement: 'With her father' means that when she is in the domain of her father [as an engaged girl, and commits adultery], she is put to death through burning, while 'with her father-in-law' means that if she commits adultery [literally] with her father-in-law, she is put to death through stoning. If, on the other hand, she committed adultery with anyone else, she is put to death through strangling."

M. *Said Raba, "How can there be a distinction in the reading of the two halves of his statement? Either both clauses refer to literal [incest], or both refer to the domain in which she is located [that is to say, as an engaged or married woman, respectively]."*

N. *Rather, said Raba, "The passage accords with the position of R. Simeon [in line with his view that burning is the most severe mode of execution].* R. Eliezer takes the view that the married woman is in the same category as the betrothed woman. Just as, with an engaged girl [who commits adultery], [the penalty imposed upon a priest's daughter who commits adultery] is raised one step [over that applicable to an Israelite's daughter who commits adultery], that is to say, from death by stoning to death by burning, so in he case of a married woman [who commits adultery], we raise the severity of the mode of execution [should such a woman commit adultery] by one step, that is to say, from strangulation to stoning."

O. *To this explanation R. Hanina objected, "But R. Simeon takes the view that both categories of woman [should they commit adultery] are put to death through burning."*

P. *Rather, said Rabina, "In point of fact [Eliezer] accords with rabbis. The assigned views, however, have to be exchanged, so that if she commits adultery while in her father's house [as a betrothed girl], she is put to death through stoning, and if it is in her father-in-law's domain [as a married woman], it is through burning. And as to [Eliezer's] use of the phrase, 'with her father,' it is simply a common usage."*

Q. *Said R. Nahman said Rabbah bar Abbuha said Rab, "The decided law accords with the message that was sent by Rabin in the name of R. Yosé b. R. Hanina."*

R.   Said R. Joseph, "That is a legal decision that will only apply to the times of the Messiah [since the law is not carried out at this time in he modes of execution specified by the Mishnah]!"

S.   Said Abbayye to him, "If that is the case, then people should not repeat the laws governing the cultic slaughter of animals designated as Holy Things, since these two are laws that will be applicable only after the Messiah comes [and rebuilds the Temple]. But the principle is to expound these laws and receive a reward for doing so, and here too, we expound the laws and receive a reward for doing so."

T.   [He replied], "This is the sense of what I said: What do I need a decision on the practical law? As the discussion went on, for what purpose would anyone have stated a concrete legal decision?"

III:10 A.   What is the source for R. Ishmael's statement?

B.   It has been taught on Tannaite authority:

C.   "'And the daughter of any priest, if she profanes herself by playing the whore' (Lev. 21:9):

D.   "Scripture speaks of a girl who is betrothed.

E.   "You say that Scripture speaks of a girl who is betrothed, but perhaps it refers even to one who is married.

F.   "Scripture says, 'And the man who commits adultery with another man's wife, even he who commits adultery with his neighbor's wife, both the adulterer and the adulteress shall be put to death' (Lev. 20:10).

G.   "All categories of persons are encompassed within the terms 'adulterer' and 'adulteress.' Now Scripture has singled out the daughter of an Israelite [who commits adultery,] who is to be put to death through stoning, and the daughter of a priest [who commits adultery], who is to be put to death through burning.

H.   "Now, when Scripture made explicit references to the daughter of an Israelite, who, if she committed adultery, was to be put to death through stoning, it then specified that it was a betrothed girl and not a married woman.

I.   "So too when Scripture singled out the daughter of a priest [who committed adultery], it indicated that she was to be put to death through burning. Scripture thus referred to a betrothed girl and not a woman.

J.   "Perjured witnesses and the lover [of a married woman, who committed adultery] also were encompassed within the verse, 'If a false witness rise up against any man to testify against him that which is wrong ...] then you shall do to him as he had conspired to do to his brother' (Deut. 19:16-19).

K.   "Now what aspect of a conspiracy to commit perjury can apply to the lover?

L.   "Rather: The penalty to be inflicted on a conspiracy of perjury against the woman had fallen into the category of the death penalty to be inflicted on the lover [of the married woman], in line with the simple statement of Scripture, 'And you shall do to him as he had conspired to do to his brother' (Deut. 19:19) – to his brother and not to his sister," the words of R. Ishmael. [Freedman, p. 347, n. 2: When a priest's daughter commits adultery, she is burned, but her lover is stoned; hence if witnesses testified falsely on such a charge, they are to be stoned, not burned.]

M. R. Aqiba says, "The same rule applies both to the betrothed girl and to the married woman [who have committed adultery]. They go forth to be put to death through burning.

N. "Is it possible that that is the case even if the woman is unmarried?

O. "Here it is stated, 'Her father,' and elsewhere the same word is used. Just as in the latter case an act of whoredom applies only if the woman is subject to a husband, so here too the act of whoredom is punishable only if she is subject to a husband."

P. Said R. Ishmael to him, "Just as, in that latter passage, she is a girl who is betrothed, so here, she is a girl, and she is betrothed, [but if she is a married woman, the punishment she should be different]."

Q. Said R. Aqiba to him, "Ishmael, by brother, I explain the language, 'and the daughter' where it would have sufficed to say merely 'the daughter.' [This additional word, and, serves to encompass the married woman]."

R. He said to him, "And because you interpret the additional use of the word 'and' in connection with the daughter, should we take out this woman and [impose a more stringent mode of execution and so burn her [as a penalty]?

S. "If the use of the word 'and' serves to encompass the married woman, then why not encompass within the law also the unmarried woman [instead of freeing her from all penalty]?

T. "And if the use of the superfluous 'and' serves to exclude the unmarried woman [from all penalty], then let it serve also to omit all reference even to the married woman."

U. *And R. Aqiba's view? The argument by analogy serves to exclude reference to the unmarried woman, and the use of the additional word, "and," with reference to the daughter, serves to encompass the married woman.*

V. *And R. Ishmael? He takes the view that since [Aqiba] has said to him that the exegesis was based on the superfluous use of the word, "and," it bore the further implication that he had retracted the argument by analogy.*

W. *And how does R. Ishmael interpret the superfluous "and" with reference to the daughter?*

X. *He requires it to serve the purposes of the teaching on Tannaite authority of the father of Samuel bar Abin:* "Is it possible to suppose that just as the Scripture has made distinctions among male priests between those who are unblemished and those who bear blemishes [who cannot participate in the Temple cult], so we should distinguish among the daughters of priests [along the same lines, e.g., with regard to an act of adultery, punishing blemished daughters of the priestly caste who commit adultery as if they were of the Israelite caste and not burning them as their mode of execution]? Scripture uses the word" 'and' where it is not needed [to serve the purpose of proving that all daughters of the priestly caste, whatever their physical condition, are put to death by burning should they commit adultery]."

Y.   And R. Aqiba? [How does he prove the same proposition]?

Z.   He derives it from the verse, "[For the offerings of the Lord made
            by fire and the bread of their God] they do offer; therefore they
            shall be holy" (Lev. 21:6). [Freedman, p. 348, n. 6: "Therefore
            they shall be holy" is an emphatic assertion of their holiness,
            implying that they do not lose it even if blemished.]

AA.   And R. Ishmael?

BB.   *If I had to derive proof from that passage, I should have reached the
            conclusion that the statement applies to* them, *but not to their
            daughters. So we are informed [by the use of the extra "and" that the
            daughters are included as well].*

CC.   *And as to R. Ishmael,* **[52A]** *how does he deal with the verse, "She
            profanes her father" (Lev. 21:9)?*

DD.   *He interprets it along the lines of that which has been taught on
            Tannaite authority:*

EE.   R. Meir would say, "What is the meaning of the statement, 'She
            profanes her father' (Lev. 21:9)?

FF.   "If [her father] had been treated as holy, now he is treated as
            ordinary.

GG.   "If he had been paid honor, now he is treated with disgrace.

HH.   "They say, 'Cursed is he who produced such a child, cursed is
            he who raised her, cursed is he who brought her forth from his
            loins.'"

II.   *Said R. Ashi, "In accord with whom do people call a wicked man,
                'Son of a wicked man,' even if it is a wicked man who is son of a
                righteous man? It is in accord with the Tannaite authority just
                now cited."*

IV.1 A.   **This procedure is how the religious requirement of stoning is
            carried out [M. 7:1D]:**

      B.   *What is the sense of the Tannaite authority in saying,* **This procedure is
            how the religious requirement of stoning is carried out?**

      C.   *It is because, just prior, it has been taught:* **When the trial is over, they
            take him out to stone him. The place of stoning was well outside
            the court ... [M. 6:1A-B].** *Now since the framer of the passage planned to
            make reference to the religious duty of inflicting the death penalty through
            burning, he made reference, also, to the religious duty of inflicting the
            death penalty through stoning.*

While the Talmud at hand is somewhat protracted, it is remarkably
cogent, taking up only a few problems and treating them at some length.
So once more the impression that the document is somewhat prolix turns
out, upon closer analysis, to be inaccurate.

7:2

A.   **The religious requirement of burning [is carried out as follows]:**

B.   **They would bury him up to his armpits in manure, and put a
      towel of hard material inside one of soft material, and wrap it
      around his neck.**

C.   **This [witness] pulls it to him from one side, and that witness
      pulls it to him at the other side, until he opens up his mouth.**

D.   And one kindles a wick and throws it into his mouth, and it goes down into his bowels and burns his intestines.

E.   R. Judah says, "Also this one: if he died at their hands [through strangulation], they will not have carried out the religious requirement of burning [in the proper manner].

F.   "But: They open his mouth with tongs, against his will, kindle a wick, and throw it into his mouth, and it goes down into his bowels and burns his intestines."

G.   Said R. Eleazar b. Sadoq, "There was the case of a priest who committed adultery.

H.   "And they put bundles of twigs around her and burned her."

I.   They said to him, "It was because the court of that time was not expert [in the law]."

I.1   A.   *What is a wick [M. 7:2D]?*
      B.   Said R. Mattenah, "It is a strip of lead."

I.2   A.   *How do we know [that death through burning is carried on in this way, rather than in that posited at M. 7:2H]?*

      B.   We establish an analogy between the meaning of the word "burning" used in the context of the death penalty [Lev. 21:9], and the meaning of the word "burning" used in connection with the congregation of Korach [Num. 17:4].

      C.   Just as, in that latter case, it involved burning the soul, with the body intact, so in the present case, it involves burning the soul, with the body intact.

      D.   R. Eleazar said, "We establish an analogy governing the word 'burning' in the present context from the meaning of the word 'burning' in the case of Aaron's sons.

      E.   "Just as in that case [Lev. 10:6] it involved burning the soul, with the body intact, so here there must be burning of the soul with the body intact."

      F.   *What is the scriptural basis for the position of the one who derives evidence from the congregation of Korach?*

      G.   It is because it is written, "[Speak to Eleazar ... that he take up the censers out of the burning ...], the censers of these sinners against their own souls" (Lev. 17:2), indicating that their souls were burned while the body was intact.

      H.   *And the other party?*

      I.   *He maintains that that passage refers, literally, to burning. And what is the sense of* "against their own souls"? *That they incurred liability to the burning of the souls on account of matters having to do with their souls.*

      J.   *This accords with the view of R. Simeon b. Laqish.*
      K.   *For R. Simeon b. Laqish said, "What is the meaning of the verse, 'With hypocritical mockers in feasts, they gnashed upon me with their teeth' (Ps. 35:16)?*

      L.   "On account of the hypocrisy that they showed to Korach on account of the banquet [that he laid out for them], the prince of Gehenna sharpened his teeth against them."

M.   *Now as to the view of him who derives the meaning of the passage from the case of the sons of Aaron, on what scriptural basis does he reach his view?*

N.   It is because it is written, "And they died before the Lord" (Lev. 10:12), that is, death of an ordinary character.

O.   *And the other party?*

P.   *That passage alludes to burning, literally.*

Q.   *And what is the sense of the statement, "They died before the Lord"? It began within, as is the case with an ordinary death.*

R.   *That accords with what has been taught on Tannaite authority:*

S.   Abba Yosé b. Dosetai says, "Two streams of fire spurted forth from the house of the holy of holies and divided into four and entered the two nostrils of this one and the two nostrils of that one and burned them up [internally]."

T.   But lo, it is written, "And the fire devoured them" (Lev. 10:12) – [them, and not another thing, so what is excluded]?

U.   "Them" – and not their garments.

V.   *And why not derive [the mode of inflicting the death penalty through burning] by analogy to the disposition of the bulls that are to be burned up [Lev. 4:12ff.]? Just as in that case, burning is meant literally, so here, burning should be meant literally.*

W.   *It is more reasonable to derive the analogy to a case involving a human being, for in the case of a human being [there are the following shared traits]: it is a human being, the act involves a sin, the human being has a soul, and in a human being there is no issue of an improper motive's rendering the death invalid [while for a sacrificial beast, if a priest forms the intention of eating the meat after the prescribed limits, the sacrifice is invalidated].*

X.   *To the contrary, it would be better to derive the matter from the analogy supplied by the bulls that are to burned, for [while the cases of Aaron's sons and the congregation of Korach were one-time events only], the mode of killing in the case of the bulls that are to be burned serves for generations to come* [Freedman: permanency. Freedman, p. 351, n. 6: The law of execution by fire, as that of sacrifices, was of permanent validity, whereas in the other two cases their deaths were unique, the result of miracles confined to particular times.]

Y.   *The former consideration are more numerous.*

Z.   *As to the one who derives the analogy from the case of the congregation of Korach, what is the reason that he did not derive the analogy from the death of the sons of Aaron?*

AA.   *That case involved burning in a literal sense.*

BB.   *And why not derive the analogy from that case anyhow?*

CC.   Said R. Nahman said Rabbah bar Abbuha, "Scripture has said, 'But you shall love your neighbor as yourself' (Lev. 19:18), meaning, choose for him a form of execution that is easy [and the burning of the body is painful]."

DD.   *But if there is the exegesis provided by R. Nahman, what need do I have for the argument by analogy at all?*

	EE.	*Were it not for the argument by analogy, I might have concluded that the burning of the soul with the body left intact is not a mode of burning at all.*
	FF.	*And if the principle derived solely from the exegesis,* "You shall love your neighbor as yourself" (Lev. 19:18), then one should collect many bundles of twigs, so that the victim will burn up quickly.
	GG.	*So we are informed [of the appropriate mode of burning].*
I.3	A.	Now Moses and Aaron were walking on the way, and Nadab and Abihu were walking behind them, with all Israel after them. Said Nadab to Abihu, "When will these two elders die, so that you and I may become leaders of the generation?"
	B.	Said the Holy One, blessed be he, to them, "Now let us see who will bury whom."
	C.	*Said R. Pappa, "That is in line with what people say: 'There are many old camels bearing the hides of young camels.'"*
I.4	A.	Said R. Eleazar, **[52B]** "What is a disciple of a sage like in the view of an ordinary person?
	B.	"At the outset he is like a gold ladle.
	C.	"If he talks with him, he is like a silver ladle.
	D.	"If he accepts some sort of benefit from him, he is like an earthenware ladle.
	E.	"Once it is broken, it cannot ever be repaired." [Freedman, p. 352, n. 4: This passage is inserted here because the assembly of Korach has just been mentioned, who were scholars (Num. 16:2). These, becoming overfamiliar with Korach and accepting gifts from him, lost his esteem, until ultimately he incited them to support him in his revolt against Moses.]
I.5	A.	Imrata, daughter of Teli, was the daughter of a priest who committed an act of adultery.
	B.	R. Hama bar Tubiah had her surrounded by twigs and burned.
	C.	*Said R. Joseph, "You erred in two matters. You erred in the matter of R. Mattenah [on how the execution through burning was to be done]. And you erred in that which has been taught on Tannaite authority: 'And you shall come to the priests, Levites, and judge that shall be in those days"* (Deut. 17:9). This verse teaches that when there is a priest [at the altar], there is judgment [of capital cases in the Jewish courts, including inflicting capital punishment], but when there is no priest, there is no such judgment.'"
II.1	A.	**Said R. Eleazar b. Sadoq, "There was the case of the daughter of a priest who committed adultery ..." [M. 7:2G]:**
	B.	Said R. Joseph, "It was a court made up of Sadduccees."
	C.	*Did [Eleazar] say this to them, and did they answer him in this way? And has it not been taught on Tannaite authority:* **Said R. Eleazar bar Sadoq, "I was a child, and I was riding on my father's shoulders, and I saw the daughter of a priest who had committed adultery, and they put bundles of twigs around her and burned her" [M. 7:2G-H]. They said to him, "You were a child, and a child has no evidence [to contribute to our discussion]" [T. San. 9:11A-B].**

D.	*[Since the argument in the cited passage is different from the one at M. 7:2I, one must explain that] there were two separate cases [about which he reported].*

E.	*Which one did he report first of all? If one should propose that it was this first one [cited at M. 7:2I] that he reported to them first, the one that took place when he was an adult, and they paid no attention to him, would he then have told them a story of what happened when he was a minor and expect to have them pay attention to him?*

F.	*Rather, it was this one [at T. San. 9:11A-B] that he told them first, and when they said to him, "You were a child" then he told them the story of what happened when he was an adult, and* **they said to him, "It was because the court of that time was not expert in the law" [M. 7:2I].**

The Talmud closely follows its usual program of Mishnah-interpretation. It begins, unit I, with a comment on a word-choice, and then proceeds, as usual, to an extensive account of the basis, in Scripture – here, scriptural analogies – for the rule in the Mishnah.

7:3A-F

A.	**The religious requirement of decapitation [is carried out as follows]:**

B.	**They would cut off his head with a sword,**

C.	**just as the government does.**

D.	**R. Judah says, "This is disgusting.**

E.	**"But they put his head on a block and chop it off with an ax."**

F.	**They said to him, "There is no form of death more disgusting than this one."**

I.1	A.	*It has been taught on Tannaite authority:*

B.	**Said R. Judah to sages, "I too recognize that it is a disgusting form of death, but what shall I do?**

C.	**"For lo, the Torah has said, 'You will not follow their ordinances' (Lev. 18:3)" [T. San. 9:11C-H].**

D.	*And rabbis? [They reply], "Since execution through the sword is written in the Torah, it is not a matter of learning [our rules] from what [gentiles] do.*

E.	*And if you do not concede that point, as to that which we have learned on Tannaite authority,* **They make burnings in honor of deceased kings, and this is not forbidden on the count of being one of the ways of the Amorites [T. Shab. 7:18],** *how can we make such a pyre? And lo, it is written, 'You will not follow their ordinances' (Lev. 18:3)! But since the matter of a funeral pyre is written in the Torah, as it is written, 'But you shall die in peace and with the burning of your fathers ... so shall they burn for you' (Jer. 34:5), it is not from [the gentiles] that we learn the practice. Here too, since it is in the Torah that execution by the sword is written, it is not from the gentiles that we learn the practice."*

I.2	A.	*And as to what we have learned in the Mishnah:* **And these are those who are put to death through decapitation: the murderer and the**

townsfolk of an apostate town [M. San. 9:1D-E], [What is the scriptural basis for decapitation in these crimes]?

B. *Now with respect to the apostate town, it is written,* "You shall surely smite the inhabitants of that town with the edge of the sword" (Deut. 13:18). *But how do we know that that is the case for the murderer?*

C. *As it has been taught on Tannaite authority:* "He shall surely be avenged" (Ex. 21:20). I do not now the form of this vengeance. When Scripture says, "I will bring a sword upon you, that shall execute the vengeance of the covenant" (Lev. 26:25), one has to say that this form of vengeance is through the sword.

D. And might I say that one has to pierce the man through?

E. It is written, "With the edge of the sword."

F. *Then might I say that one cuts the felon in half [lengthwise]?*

G. Said R. Nahman said Rabbah bar Abbuha, "Scripture has said, 'You shall love your neighbor as yourself' (Lev. 19:18), meaning that you should choose for him a form of death that is easy."

H. *[Since the context of Ex. 21:20 is vengeance for the death of a slave], we have found that when one has killed a slave [he is put to death through decapitation]. How do we know that if one killed a free man, the same rule applies?*

I. Is it not an argument <u>a fortiori</u>?

J. If one kills a slave, he is put to death through decapitation. If he killed a free man, should it be merely through strangulation [that he is put to death]?

K. *That argument poses no problem to the view of him who has said that strangulation is the lighter form of execution. But in the view of him who has said that strangulation is the more severe form, what sort of argument can you supply?*

L. *It derives from that which has been taught on Tannaite authority:* "So you shall put away the built of the innocent blood among you" (Deut. 21:9)

M. The case of all those who shed blood is compared to the case of the heifer whose neck is to be broken.

N. Just as in that case, the execution takes places with a sword at the neck, so here the execution takes place with a sword at the neck.

O. If one should propose that, just as in that case, it is done with an ax at the nape of the neck, so here too it should be done with an at at the nape of the neck, [the answer derives from the argument already given].

P. Namely, said R. Nahman said Rabbah bar Abbuha, "Scripture has said, 'You will love your neighbor as yourself' (Lev. 19:18), meaning to choose for him a form of death that is easy."

Unit I.1 expands upon the Mishnah's argument. Unit I.2 then supplies the proof, on the basis of Scripture, to which unit I refers.

7:3G-J

G. **The religious requirement of strangulation [is carried out as follows:]**

H.   They would bury him in manure up to his armpits, and put a towel of hard material inside one of soft material, and wrap it around his neck.

I.   This [witness] pulls it to him from one side, and that witness pulls it to him at the other side,

J.   until he perishes.

I.1   A.   *Our rabbis have taught on Tannaite authority:*

B.   ["And the man who commits adultery with another man's wife, even he who commits adultery with his neighbor's wife, the adulterer and the adulteress shall surely be put to death" (Lev. 20:10)]. "A man" – excluding a minor.

C.   "... who commits adultery with another man's wife" – excluding the wife of a minor.

D.   "His neighbor's wife – excluding the wife of others [idolators].

E.   "' ... shall surely be put to death' – through strangulation.

F.   "You say that it is through strangulation.

G.   "But perhaps it is only through one of any of the other modes of inflicting the death penalty that are stated in the Torah?

H.   "Now do you say so? In any passage in which there is reference in the Torah to 'death-penalty' without further specification, you do not have the right to impose the death penalty in a stringent manner but only in a lenient manner," the words of R. Josiah.

I.   R. Jonathan says, "It is not because this is the mot lenient of the modes of execution, but because in any passage in the Torah in which there is reference to the death-penalty without further specification, it is to be inflicted only through strangulation."

J.   [In support of this same proposition] Rabbi says, "There is reference to death inflicted at the hand of heaven and there is reference to death inflicted at the hand of man.

K.   "Just as death inflicted at the hand of heaven is such that there is no physical mark [on the body], so death inflicted at the hand of man [in the same sort of passage] is death in which there is no physical mark [on the body], [and that is strangulation]."

L.   *And might I say that that is burning [in the manner described just now]?*

M.   *Since the All-Merciful has specified that the daughter of a priest]who commits adultery] is put to death through burning, it must follow that adultery under discussion here is* not *punished by the death penalty inflicted through burning [but in some other way than that specified at the counterpart]."*

N.   [53A] *Now there are no problems from the viewpoint of R. Jonathan, since Rabbi has already provided an explanation of his reasoning. But as to R. Josiah, on what basis do we know that the death penalty is inflicted through strangulation in any event? Might I say it is through decapitation?*

P.   *Said Raba, "We have a tradition that there are four modes of inflicting the death penalty [M. 7:1A]."*

Q.   *What is the sense of the statement, "It is not because it is the most lenient form of the death penalty" [at I, above]?*

R.   *The dispute follows the lines of that between R. Simeon and rabbis [at M. 7:1].*

I.2   A.   *Said R. Zira to Abbayye, "As to the rest of those who are put to death through stoning, in connection with those cases Scripture does not explicitly specify that stoning is the mode of inflicting the death penalty, so that stoning is the choice mode of execution is a proposition we derive by analogy to the case of the necromancer or wizard [put to death through stoning], on the basis of which relevant phrase [of those specified at B] do we derive that fact? Do we derive that fact from the phrase, 'They shall surely be put to death'? Or do we derive it from the phrase, 'Their blood shall be upon them' (Lev. 20:27)?" [The relevant verse is as follows: 'A man or a woman who has a familiar spirit or who is a wizard they shall surely be put to death; they shall stone them with stones; their blood shall be upon them.'] [Freedman, p. 357, n. 7: In the case of all other malefactors who are stoned, though stoning is not explicitly stated, the two phrases, 'They shall surely be put to death' and 'their blood shall be upon their head' occur.]*

       B.   *He said to him,* "We derive the fact that they are put to death through stoning from the phrase, common to those other cases as well as to the case of the wizard or necromancer, 'Their blood shall be upon them.' For if we should derive the matter from the phrase, 'They shall surely die,' what need do I have for the phrase concerning 'their blood'? *But what is the purpose of the repeated use of the statement about 'their blood'? It is to supply the needed analogy to tell us that stoning applies in both cases. What need do I have, then, for the phrase, 'They shall surely die'"*

       C.   *It accords with that which has been taught on Tannaite authority:*

       D.   "'He who smote him shall surely die. He is a murderer' (Num. 35:21).

       E.   "'I know only that that applies to a mode of execution that is specified in Scripture in his regard.

       F.   "'How do I know that, if you cannot put him to death through the mode of execution that is specified in his connection in Scripture, you may put him to death through any means of inflicting death that you can use?

       G.   "'Scripture says, "He who smote him shall surely die" (Num. 35:21), meaning, by any means at all.'"

       H.   *Said R. Aha of Difti to Rabina, "As to deriving the proof from the phrase, 'He shall surely die,' what was the difficulty that troubled him [leading him to raise the question at all]? Should I propose that the difficulty lay in the case of the penalty to be inflicted on the married woman who committed adultery [who, we know, suffers the death penalty through strangulation]? That is to say, one should derive the mode of execution in her case from the analogy of the words, 'He shall surely die' used in connection with the necromancer and wizard, so that, just in that case, the penalty is inflicted through stoning, so here it is inflicted by stoning.* [Freedman, p. 358, n. 5: Instead of regarding it as an unspecified death penalty, why not treat it as explicit, in virtue of the phrase, 'They shall surely be put to death,' written also in the case of adultery with a married woman?] *But since the All-Merciful made it explicit that the betrothed girl who committed adultery is put to death through stoning, it must follow that the married woman who committed adultery would not be put to death through stoning, [so that problem really is null]. Rather, it was the fact that he who his father or mother [is put to death through strangulation] that troubled him.* [This is the difficulty:] one should derive proof from the case of the necromancer or wizard [that he is stoned. Why? Because the phrase at hand, 'He shall surely be put to death' is used of the one who hits his mother or father as well, at Ex. 21:15]. *But rather than deriving the mode of execution in the case of the necromancer or wizard, why not derive it from the case of a married woman [who is put to death through strangulation], for you do not have the right to derive a stringent mode of execution for him when you can derive a lenient mode of execution from him. [So what was the problem that led to his question?]* [Freedman, p. 358, n. lo: For the same phrase occurs in the three places, namely, the necromancer, put to death through stoning, the married woman, put to death through strangulation, and he hits his father or mother, which has to be deduced from the one or the other. It follows that one must incline to leniency. So even if the dedication were made from the phrase, 'They shall surely be put to death,' it would be still correct to say that one who hits his father or mother is strangled.]"

I.   *He said to him, "What troubled him was the case of all of the others who are put to death through stoning. For if it is from the phrase, 'They shall surely be put to death,' that we derive the fact that the mode of executing them is through stoning, why derive that fact from the case of the necromancer or wizard? Derive it from the case of the married woman who committed adultery [on the principle that we impose the more lenient form of the death penalty]."*

Unit I.1 contributes the information of who is put to death through the mode of execution at hand, with the not-incidental information of why death is inflicted in just this way, namely, there is no mark on the body. Unit I.2 then presents a much more complex problem of the scriptural basis for imposing the death penalty in this way, linked, as is clear, to unit I's proof on the basis of the adultery of the woman. So the composition is quite cogent, even though the two units are entirely distinct from one another – a fine piece of construction.

7:4 A-R

A.   These are [the felons] who are put to death by stoning:

B.   He who has sexual relations with his mother, with the wife of his father, with his daughter-in-law, with a male, and with a cow;

C.   and the women who brings an ox on top of herself;

D.   and he who blasphemes, he who performs an act of worship for an idol, he who gives of his seed to Molech, he who is a familiar spirit, and he who is a soothsayer;

E.   he who profanes the Sabbath,

F.   he who curses his father or his mother.

G.   he who has sexual relations with a betrothed maiden,

H.   he who beguiles [entices a whole town to idolatry],

I.   a sorcerer,

J.   and a stubborn and incorrigible son.

K.   He who has sexual relations with his mother is liable on her account because of her being his mother and because of her being his father's wife [Lev. 18:6-7, 20:11].

L.   R. Judah says, "He is liable only on account of her being his mother alone."

M.   He who has sexual relations with his father's wife is liable on her account because of her being his father's wife and because of her being a married woman,

N.   whether this is in the lifetime of his father or after the death of his father,

O.   whether she is only betrothed or already married [to the father].

P.   He who has sexual relations with his daughter-in-law is liable on her account because of her being his daughter-in-law and because of her being another man's wife,

Q.   whether this is in the lifetime of his son or after the death of his son [Lev. 20:12,

R.   whether she is only betrothed or already married [to the son].

I.1   A.   *It has been taught on Tannaite authority:*

         B.   R. Judah says, "If his mother was not fit to be married to his father, he is liable only on the count of her being his mother [but not on the count of her being a married woman] [T. San. 10:1A].

         C.   *What is the meaning of his statement* if she was not fit to be married to his father? *Should we say that it is* a marriage forbidden on pain of liability to extirpation and liability to the death penalty at the hands of a court? [That is, the father is subject to the death penalty either at the hands of heaven or at human hands on account of his marriage to this woman]. *Then it would follow that the rabbis take the view that even though the woman is not fit for the father, [there is a twofold penalty]. But [given the penalties of death] the father in point of fact has no sacramental bond to his woman at all! [So how can the son incur the penalty of having sexual relations with a married woman, when in point of fact she is not a married woman?] It must follow that [Judah's sense is that she is not fit for the father because the couple falls into the category of those who, if they marry], are subject to the penalty for violating a negative commandment [but not to the penalty of extirpation or execution by a court]. Then it follows that R. Judah concurs with R. Aqiba, who held that there is no sacramental bond between a couple who, [if they wed,] are subject to liability for violating a negative commandment.*

         D.   *To this proposition, R. Oshaia raised the objection,* "[A general rule did they lay down in regard to the levirate woman, widow of a deceased childless brother: any sister-in-law who is prohibited as one of the forbidden degrees of Leviticus Chapter Eighteen neither executes the rite of removing the shoe, specified at Deut. 25:5-10, nor is taken into levirate marriage.] [If she is prohibited to her brother-in-law by reason of a prohibition on account of a commandment or a prohibition on account of sanctity, she executes the rite of removing the shoe but is not taken in levirate marriage. [53B] **A prohibition on account of a commandment is a secondary grade of forbidden degrees on account of the rulings of scribes [M. Yeb. 2:3, 2:4A].**

E. *"Now why do they call such [marriages]* 'prohibited on account of a commandment as a secondary grade of forbidden degrees on account of rulings of scribes'? *Because it is a commandment to obey the teaching of sages.*

F. **"A prohibition on account of the sanctity of the levir is a widow married to a high priest, or a divorcee or a woman who has executed the rite of removing the shoe married to an ordinary priest [M. Yeb. 2:4B].**

G. *"And why do they call such marriages* 'prohibited on account of the sanctity of the levir' *Because it is written,* 'The priests shall be holy unto their God' (Lev 21:6).

H. *"And in this connection it has been taught on Tannaite authority: R. Judah reverses these definitions.* **[T. Yeb. 2:4J: R. Judah says, 'A widow wed to a high priest, or a divorcee or a woman who has undergone the rite of removing the shoe wed to an ordinary priest, fall into the category of those prohibited on account of a commandment. A secondary grade of forbidden degrees (listed at Leviticus Chapter Eighteen) on account of rulings of scribes constitutes a prohibition on account of sanctity.']** *Now while he reverses the definition, for both categories he nonetheless requires the rite of removing the shoe, [hence recognizing that a marital bond of some sort existed between the priest and the woman improperly wed to him, that is, in violation of the negative commandment that such a woman not be wed to a priest.] If, then, you maintain the view that R. Judah accords with R. Aqiba, then, since in R. Aqiba's view, couples who, if they wed, are liable for violating a negative commandment are in the status of couples who, if they wed, are subject to extirpation, and couples who, if they wed, become liable to the penalty of extirpation do not fall into the category of a marriage sufficiently strong to impose the obligation to undergo the rite of removing the shoe, let alone the obligation of levirate marriage should the husband die childless [there being no valid and legal connection between this man and this woman at all], [how could Judah concur that there is any obligation, in the present context, to undergo the rite of removing the shoe? Aqiba would never impose such an obligation, as we see.]"*

I. *[The reply:] [Judah] made his statement in accord with the position of the anonymous authority of the Mishnah-paragraph at hand but, in point of fact, he does not concur with the premises of that authority. [Judah maintains that there is no requirement of either removing the shoe or levirate marriage.]*

II.1 A. *When R. Isaac came, he repeated the Mishnah passage as we have learned it:* **'R. Judah says, "He is liable only on account of her being his mother" [M. 7:4L].'**

B. *[He then said,] "And what is the scriptural basis for his view [that the rule applies not only when she is forbidden to the father, but under* all *circumstances?]"*

C. *Said Abbayye, "It is because Scripture has said,* '[The nakedness of your father or the nakedness of your mother you shall not uncover;] she is your mother' (Lev. 18:7).

D.   "It is **because she is his mother** that you impose liability, and you do not impose liability because she is a married woman."

E.   *How then do you deal with the following:* "The nakedness of your father's wife you shall not uncover; it is your father's nakedness," (Lev. 18:8)? [Surely it means] you impose liability because she is his father's wife, and you do not impose liability [in this case] because she is his mother [his step-mother]?

F.   *Rather, in the present case, we deal with his mother who is his father's wife, then [Freedman:] one verse implies the exclusion of maternal incest [as the offense], and the other excludes incest with his father's wife [as the offense].* [Freedman, p. 362, n.1]: thus leaving no grounds for punishment at all.]

G.   *Now if she is his mother but not his father's wife, he is liable, and, if she is his father's wife but not his mother, he is liable. But if she is his mother and also his father's wife, will he not be liable at all? [That is absurd!] And furthermore, from the viewpoint of rabbis too, is it not written, "She is your mother" (Lev. 18:7)?*

H.   *Rather, they require that verse to make the point of R. Shisha, son of R. Idi [given presently].*

I.   *R. Judah also requires the same verse to make the point of R. Shisha, son of R. Idi.*

J.   [We shall now prove the sought point from the viewpoint of rabbis, that a double-liability is incurred, in line with M. 7:4K and against Judah's view at M. 7:4L:] The matter is in line with what R. Aha, son of R. Iqa, said, "Scripture has stated, '[...you shall not uncover] her nakedness' (Lev. Lev. 18:8). On one count of nakedness you impose liability, and you do not impose liability on two counts of nakedness."

K.   *How then do you deal with the following verse:* "You shall not uncover the nakedness of your daughter-in-law; she is your son's wife; you shall not uncover her nakedness" (Lev. 18:15). In this case, too, do we maintain that only on one count of nakedness you impose liability, but you do not impose liability on two counts of nakedness? *But have we not learned in the Mishnah:* **He who has sexual relations with his daughter-in-law is liable on her account because of her being his daughter-in-law and because of her being another man's wife, whether this is in the lifetime of his son or after the death of his son [M.7:4P].** *And here R. Judah does not differ! [So what has K contributed?]*

L.   *But since she is one person, even though there are prohibitions on two counts, it is written, "...her nakedness...," and here too, since she is one person, even though there are prohibitions on two counts, it is written, "...her nakedness...."*

M.   *Rather, [since the proposed proof does not work,] Raba said, "R. Judah takes the view that 'The nakedness of your father' refers to [the prohibition of sexual relations with] one's father's wife. Then, through the argument by analogy, he deduces that that is the case whether she is his father's wife who is also his mother, or his father's wife who is not also his mother.*

N.   "How, further, do we know that the penalty applies if he has sexual relations with his mother who is not his father's wife? Scripture

says, '... the nakedness of your mother you will not uncover, she is
your mother' (Lev. 18:8). [Then Judah concludes], 'On the count of
her being his mother you impose liability upon him, and you do not
impose liability upon him on the count of her being his father's
wife." [Freedman, p. 362, n. 1, states: Thus, Raba agrees with
Abbayye that R. Judah's reason is the limitation implied in the
phrase 'she is thy mother'. But he disposes of the consequent
difficulty, viz., that of the verse, it is thy father's nakedness, in the
following way: The dictum, The nakedness of thy father shalt thou
not uncover, refers to his father's wife, whether his mother or not;
and so far, (without an additional limiting phrase) it is implied that
in both cases the interdict is on account of paternal, not maternal
consanguinity. Hence, when the following verse states, (The
nakedness of thy father's wife thou shalt not uncover:) it is thy
father's nakedness, it cannot mean that guilt is incurred only on
account of paternal, but not maternal relationship, since that has
already been implied in the preceding verse, the nakedness of thy
father ... shalt thou not uncover. Therefore the limitation
undoubtedly intended by the latter verse must be otherwise
interpreted. (This is done further on.) Now, since the nakedness of
thy father would imply that whether she is his mother or not he is
penalized on account of paternal consanguinity, it follows that
when the same verse inserts a limiting clause, 'she is thy mother',
the limitation must apply to that which has already been expressed,
viz., that the father's wife, if also one's mother, is forbidden on
account of maternal, not paternal, consanguinity.]

O.   **[54A]:** *In support of Raba's view it has been taught on Tannaite
       authority to the same effect:*

P.   "[And the man who lies with his father's wife has uncovered
      his father's nakedness; both of them shall surely be put to
      death; their blood shall be upon them" (Lev. 20:11)]; "A man"
      excludes a minor.

Q.   "...who lies with his father's wife ..." bears the implication that
      that is whether it is his father's wife who is his mother, or his
      father's wife who is not his mother.

R.   How then do I know that the rule applies to his mother who is
      not his father's wife?

S.   Scripture states, "He who has uncovered his father's
      nakedness." And that phrase bears no meaning on its own
      [since its point is self-evident], and so it is available to establish
      an analogy, from which the law may be derived on the basis of
      [Freedman]: identity of meaning [which will be spelled out in
      a moment]

T.   "They shall surely be put to death" – through execution by
      stoning.

U.   You maintain that it is execution by stoning, but perhaps it
      means only execution by any one of the modes of execution
      that are prescribed in the Torah?

V.   Here it is stated, "Their blood shall be upon them" and in the
      case of the necromancer or wizard, it is stated, "Their blood
      shall be upon them" (Lev. 20:27).

W.   Just as in that passage, the mode of execution is stoning, so here the mode of execution is stoning.

X.   Now we have deduced the penalty [to be inflicted]. Whence do we derive an admonition [indicating that the act is forbidden to begin with? The verse at hand serves to impose a penalty, but not to prohibit the deed.]

Y.   Scripture states, "The nakedness of your father you shall not uncover" (Lev. 18:7).

Z.   "The nakedness of your father" refers to the wife of your father.

AA. You say that it refers to the wife of your father. But perhaps it refers literally to the nakedness of your father? [The prohibition then is against having sexual relations with one's father.]

BB. Here is it stated, "The nakedness of your father you shall not uncover" (Lev. 18:8) and elsewhere it is stated, "The nakedness of his father he has uncovered" (Lev. 20:1).

CC. Just as in that passage Scripture speaks of sexual relations between man and woman, so here too it is of sexual relations between man and woman that Scripture speaks.

DD. And the implication is that that is the case whether it is his father's wife who also is his mother, or his father's wife who is not his mother.

EE. Then how do I know that the prohibition applies also to his mother who is not his father's wife?

FF. Scripture says, "The nakedness of your mother you shall not uncover" (Lev. 18:7).

GG. I thus deduce only that one is admonished not to do so, for Scripture has treated his mother who is not his father's wife as equivalent to his mother who is also his father's wife.

HH. How then do I know from in Scripture the penalty [to be inflicted for such a deed]?

II. Here it is stated, "You shall not uncover the nakedness of your father" (Lev. 18:8) and elsewhere it is written, "The nakedness of his father he has uncovered" (Lev. 20:11).

JJ. Just as, in the [matter of the] admonition, the Scripture has treated his mother who is not his father's wife as equivalent to his mother who is his father's wife, so with respect to the penalty [to be inflicted], the Scripture treats his mother who is not his father's wife as equivalent to his mother who is his father's wife.

KK. "She is his mother" teaches that it is on account of her being his mother that you impose liability upon him, and you do not impose liability upon him because she is his father's wife [as Judah would have it].

LL. *And rabbis? this refers literally to his father's nakedness.*

MM. *But that prohibition surely derives from the statement, "You shall not lie with mankind as with womankind" (Lev. 18:22).*

NN. On the basis of that verse, a penalty on two counts is incurred [in the case of relationship between father and son].

OO. *And that accords with the view of R. Judah.*

PP. For R. Judah has said, "A 'gentile' who has sexual relations with his father is liable on two counts."

QQ. "One who has sexual relations with his uncle is liable on two counts."

RR. *Said Raba, "It stands to reason that this statement of R. Judah speaks of an Israelite, [who has committed] an unwitting act, and [refers to the issue of] an offering. The reference to a gentile serves merely as a euphemism. For if you maintain that he referred literally to a gentile, then the penalty for the act is death, and you surely are not going to execute him twice! [So the point that there are two counts of liability is senseless, unless it refers, as Raba says, to an Israelite, an unwitting act, and the issue of the number of sin-offerings he must bring.]"*

SS. *So too it has been taught on Tannaite authority:* He who has sexual relations with his father is liable on two counts. He who has sexual relations with his uncle is liable on two counts.

TT. *There are those who maintain that that statement does not accord with the position of R. Judah [of our Mishnah] [for obvious reasons] and there are those who maintain that that statement accords even with R. Judah.*

UU. [As to the view of the latter:] He derives evidence [of a twofold penalty in this case] on the basis of an argument a fortiori derived from the case of the father's brother.

VV. Now if in the case of the father's brother, who is [merely] a relative of the father, he is liable on two counts, in the case of the father will he not all the more so be liable on two counts? [Freedman, p. 35, n. 3: The liability of the son on account of sexual relations with the father's brother is deduced from the verse, "You shall not uncover the nakedness of your father's brother, you shall not approach his wife" (Lev. 18:14). Since his wife is specifically prohibited, the first half of the verse must be understood literally. Consequently, it is twice prohibited, for it is also included in the prohibition of Lev. 17:22, and hence a double penalty is incurred.

WW. *And at issue is the dispute of Abbayye and Raba [on the issue of whether we impose penalties merely on the basis of logical argument]. One authority holds that* we do impose penalty for a crime merely on the basis of a logical argument [such as just now has been given]. *And the other party maintains the view that* we do not impose a penalty on the basis of a logical argument.

XX. [Reverting to the issue at hand:] in the view of rabbis, how do we derive an admonition not to commit adultery with the wife of one's father [since they interpret "the nakedness of your father" literally (Freedman, p. 365, n. 6)]?

YY. *They derive it from the statement,* "The nakedness of your father's wife you shall not uncover" (Lev. 18:8).

ZZ. *And R. Judah? He takes the view that that verse serves to admonish* one not to have sexual relations with the father's wife after the father has died.

AAA. *And the rabbis? They derive that point from the end of the verse at hand:* "It is your father's nakedness [even after death]."

BBB. *And R. Judah? He derives from that statement the fact that* one is penalized on the count of her being his father's wife, but he is not penalized on the count that she is a married woman.

CCC. *But lo, we have learned in the Mishnah:* **He who has sexual relations with his father's wife is liable on her account because she is his father's wife and also, because she is a married woman, whether this is in the lifetime of his father or after the death of his father [M. 7:4M-N].** *And R. Judah does not express disagreement with that statement. [So how can be take the position just now imputed to him?]*

DDD. *Said Abbayye, "He does not dispute it in the external teaching on Tannaite authority [but not in the Mishnah's version of the same matter].*

EEE. *And how do rabbis derive from Scripture that one who has sexual relations with his father's wife after his father's death is punished? Now from the viewpoint of R. Judah, there is no problem, for he finds evidence in an argument by analogy. But how do the rabbis prove the same point?*

FFF. *They will say to you, "'He has uncovered his father's nakedness'* (Lev. 20:11), *on the basis of which R. Judah establishes his argument by analogy, from our viewpoint serves to prove that one is punished if he has sexual relations with his father's wife after his father's death."*

GGG. *And how do rabbis prove that* he is punished if he has sexual relations with his mother who is not his father's wife?

HHH. Said R. Shisha, son of R. Idi, "Scripture has said, 'She is your mother' (Lev. 18:7). This shows that Scripture has treated his mother who is not his father's wife as equivalent to his mother who is his father's wife [on the basis of the analogy of the word mother.]"

III.1 A. He who has sexual relations with his daughter-in-law (M. 7:4P).

B. *[While the Mishnah imposes liability on the count of her being his daughter-in-law and on the count of her being another man's wife,] why not in addition impose a penalty on the count of her being his son's wife?*

C. Said Abbayye, "Scripture began its statement by referring to his daughter-in-law [at Lev. 28:15:'You shall not uncover the nakedness of your daughter-in-law...she is your son's wife, you shall not uncover her nakedness'] and then concluded with a reference 'to his son's wife,' to tell you that his daughter-in-law falls into the same category as his son's wife, [and so a single count is involved]."

Unit I.1 presents a different version of Judah's position, M. 7:4L, since the Mishnah does not introduce the issue of her not being "fit to be married" to the father, while the external Tannaite version does add that consideration. That issue then carries in its wake the question of the grounds on which the woman is not fit to be married to her husband. So the exegetical interest lies in the explanation of the Tosefta's version. Unit II.1 introduces the more complicated question of the number of counts on which a person is going to be punished, the scriptural basis for the several views, and the diverse issues emerging on the basis of those facts. The discussion is substantial, but continuous and cogent. Unit III.1 then briefly raises the same question for M. 7:4P. So the Talmud ignores the bulk of the Mishnah's materials and deals principally with one clause only.

7:4 S-V

S.   He who has sexual relations with a male [Lev. 20:13, 15-16], or a cow, and the woman who brings an ox on top of herself.

T.   if the human being has committed a sin, what sin has the beast committed?

U.   But because a human being has offended through it, therefore the Scripture has said, "Let it be stoned."

V.   Another matter: So that the beast should not amble through the market place, with people saying, "This is the one on account of which Mr. So-and-so got himself stoned."

I.1   A.   *How do we know [on the basis of Scripture] that the penalty of pederasty is stoning?*

B.   *It is in line with what our rabbis have taught on Tannaite authority:*

C.   ["If a man lies with a man, as the lyings of a woman, both of them have committed an abomination; they shall surely be put to death; their blood shall be upon them" (Lev. 20:13)]: "A man" – excluding a minor.

D.   "...lies also with a man..." – whether adult or minor.

E.   "...as the lyings of a woman..." – Scripture thus informs you that there are two modes of sexual relations with a woman.

F.   Said R. Ishmael, "Lo, this comes to teach a lesson but is itself subject to a lesson. [Freedman, p. 367, n. 5: For the phrase "the lyings of a woman" is redundant insofar as it teaches that even unnatural pederasty is punishable, since all pederasty is such. Hence its teaching is thrown back upon itself, viz., that unnatural cohabitation is punishable when committed incestuously.]"

G.   "They shall surely be put to death" – by stoning.

H.   You say that it is by stoning. But perhaps it is by one of the other modes of inflicting the death penalty prescribed in the Torah.

I.   Here it is stated, "Their blood shall be upon them," and in the case of the necromancer and the wizard, it is stated, "Their blood shall be upon them" is. Just as in that passage, the mode of execution is stoning, so here the mode of execution is stoning.

J.   [54B] Accordingly, we have deduced the mode of execution. Whence do we derive an admonition [that the act is forbidden to begin with]?

K.   Scripture states, "You shall not lie with mankind as with womankind; it is an abomination" (Lev. 18:22).

L.   From this passage we derive the admonition that applies to the one who lies [with the male].

M.   Where in Scripture do we find an admonition that applies to the passive partner?

N. "Scripture states, 'There shall be no sodomite among the sons of Israel' (Deut. 23:18), and it is said, 'And there were also sodomites in the land, and they did according to the abominations of the nations which the Lord has cast out before the children of Israel,' (1 Kgs. 14:24). [Freedman, p. 368, n. 1: Just as abomination applies to sodomy in the latter verse, so it applies to it in the former too; thus it is as though the former verse read, 'There shall be no sodomite among the sons of Israel, it is an abomination.' And just as the 'abomination' implicit here applies to both parties, so the 'abomination' explicitly stated in Lev. 18:22 refers to both]," the words of R. Ishmael.

O. R. Aqiba says, "It is not necessary [to derive proof in that way]. Lo, Scripture says, 'You shall not lie with mankind as with womankind' (Lev. 20:13). Read it as, 'You shall not be lain with....'"

II.1 A. [**He who has sexual relations...a cow:**] How on the basis of Scripture do we know that the rule applies to a beast?

B. *It is in accord with that which our rabbis have taught on Tannaite authority:*

C. ["And if a man lie with a beast, he shall surely be put to death, and you shall slay the beast" (Lev. 20:15)]: "A man" – excludes a minor.

D. "...lie with a beast" – whether young or mature.

E. "He shall surely be put to death" – by stoning.

F. You say that it is by stoning. But perhaps it is by one of the other modes of inflicting the death penalty that are prescribed in the Torah.

G. Here it is stated, "And you shall kill the beast," and elsewhere it is stated, "You shall surely kill him [and you shall stone him with stones]" (Deut. 13:10).

H. Just as, in that passage, the mode of execution is stoning, so here, too, the mode of execution is stoning.

I. In this way we have learned how the penalty is inflicted on one who has sexual relations [with a beast].

J. Whence do we learn that the same penalty applies to [the beast] who is so treated?

K. Scripture says, "Whosoever lies with a beast shall surely be put to death" (Ex. 22:18).

L. Now since this passage is not required to deal with the one who has sexual relations with the beast [who is dealt with in the passage just now cited], then apply it to the beast with which a man has sexual relations.

M. So we have derived the penalty applying both to the active and to the passive party.

N. Whence do we derive an admonition [that one not to do so]?

O. Scripture states, "Neither shall you lie with any beast to defile yourself with it" (Lev 18:23).

P. "In this passage we derive an admonition for the one who as sexual relations with a beast.

Q. "Whence do we derive an admonition against permitting a beast to have sexual relations with a human being?

R.   "Scripture says, 'There shall be no sodomite of the sons of Israel, (Deut. 23:18), and elsewhere it is stated, 'And there were also sodomites in the land...' (1 Kgs. 14:24)," the words of R. Ishmael.

S.   R. Aqiba says, "This proof is not necessary. Lo, Scripture says, 'You shall not lie with any beast', meaning, you shall not permit any sort of lying."

II.2 A.   He who has sexual relations with a male or serves as a passive partner of a male –

B.   Said R. Abbahu, "In the view of R. Ishmael, he is liable on two counts, one on the count of, 'You shall not lie with mankind,' and the other on the count, 'There shall not be a sodomite of the sons of Israel.

C.   "But on the view of R. Aqiba, he is liable on only one count, 'You shall not lie' and 'you shall not be lain with' constitute a single statement [each one based on revocalization of a single passage]."

D.   He who has sexual relations with a beast and he who serves as a passive partner of a beast –

E.   "Said R. Abbahu, "In the view of R. Ishmael, he is liable on two counts, one based on, 'You shall not lie with any beast,' and the other based on, 'There shall be no sodomite of the sons of Israel.'

F.   "But in the view of R. Aqiba, he is liable only on one count, since, 'your lying' and 'your being lain with', constitute a single admonition."

G.   Abbayye said, "Even in the view of R. Ishmael, one is liable on only one count. For 'There shall be no sodomite' speaks of sexual relations among men [not beasts]."

H.   *Then what is the scriptural basis, in R. Ishmael's view, for an admonition against playing the passive partner [with a beast]?*

I.   *One may derive it from the following verse:* "Whosoever lies with a beast shall surely be put do death" (Ex: 23:18). Now if this does not refer to one who takes the active part [since that matter is covered by Lev. 18:23], apply it to the one who takes the passive role. *The All-Merciful thus refers to the passive partner in the language applying to the active partner, so indicating that, just as the active partner is subject to a penalty and an admonition, so the passive partner is subject to a penalty and an admonition.*

II.3 A.   He who is a passive partner for a male and for a beast –

B.   Said R. Abbahu, "In the view of R. Aqiba, he is liable on two counts, one on the count of, 'You shall not lie [with mankind]' (Lev. 18:2), and the other on the count, 'You shall not lie [with any beast]' (Lev. 18:23).

C.   "But in the view of R. Ishmael, he is liable on only one count, both items deriving from the verse, 'There shall be no sodomite' (Deut. 23:18)."

D.   *Abbayye said, "Even in the view of R. Ishmael, he is liable on two counts, for it is written, 'Whosoever lies with a beast shall surely be put to death' (Ex. 22:18). If this does not refer to the active partner*

		[since that is dealt with elsewhere], apply the verse to the passive partner.
	E.	*"And the All-Merciful has singled out the passive partner with a phrase referring to the active partner to indicate that, just as the active partner is subject to a penalty and an admonition, so the passive partner is subject to a penalty and an admonition."*
	F.	But one who has sexual relations with a male or serves as a passive partner for him, and one who has sexual relations with a beast or serves as a passive partner for him, whether in the view of R. Abbahu and whether in the view of Abbayye,
	G.	so far as R. Ishmael is concerned is liable on three counts,
	H.	and so far as R. Aqiba is concerned, is liable on two counts.
II.4	A.	*Our rabbis have taught on Tannaite authority:*
	B.	As to sexual relations with a male, sages have not treated a minor boy as equivalent to an adult, but as to sexual relations with a beast, sages have treated a minor girl as equivalent to an adult.
	C.	*What is the meaning of* "sages have not treated a minor boy as equivalent to an adult?"
	D.	Said Rab, "They have not treated sexual relations of a male less than nine years old as equivalent to sexual relations of a male of nine years [or older]."
	E.	And Samuel said, "They have not treated sexual relations with a minor girl less than three years as equivalent to sexual relations with a minor girl of three years [or older]."
	F.	*What principle is under dispute?*
	G.	*Rab takes the view that whoever is subject to laws governing sexual relations with another is subject to the laws governing a passive partner, and whoever is not subject to the laws governing sexual relations with another is not subject to the laws governing a passive partner. [The nine-year-old is able to have sexual relations so is subject to the prohibition of serving as a passive partner].*
	H.	*And Samuel takes the view that what is written is "...as with the lyings of a woman" (Lev. 18:22, [which take effect from the age of three years].*
	I.	*It has been taught in accord with the view of Rab on Tannaite authority:*
	J.	A male nine years and one day old **[55A]** who has sexual relations with a beast, whether vaginally or anally, and a woman who serves as passive partner to a beast, whether in vaginally or anally, is liable.
III.1	A.	**[and the woman who brings an ox on top of herself:]** R. Nahman son of R. Hisda expounded, "In the case of a woman there are two ways in which sexual relations may take place, but in the case of a beast, only one." [Freedman, p. 372, n.1: The reference is to bestiality. If a woman allows herself to be made the subject thereof, whether naturally or not, she is guilty. But if a man commits bestiality, he is liable only for a connection in a natural manner, but not otherwise. – Thus Rashi. Tosafot, more plausibly, explains it thus: If one commits incest or adultery with a woman, whether naturally or not, guilt is incurred; but bestiality is punishable only for a connection in a natural manner, but not otherwise.]

B.   R. Pappa objected, "To the contrary, in the case of a woman, since it is the natural thing, one is liable only on account of normal sexual relations, but as to 'some other thing' one should not be liable. In the case of a beast, in which the entire procedure is not natural, one should be liable on account of having sexual relations with any orifice at all." [Freedman, p. 372, n.2: The meaning according to the interpretation of Tosafot is clear. Yet R. Pappa's objection is not made in order to prove that unnatural incest is not culpable (which, in fact, it is), but that if a distinction is to be drawn, unnatural bestiality is far more likely to be liable than unnatural incest. On Rashi's interpretation, R. Pappa's objection is explained thus: Since a woman is naturally the passive object of sexual intercourse, it follows that she should be punished for bestiality only when the connection is carried out in a natural way. But as man is the active offender in an unnatural crime he should be punished even for unnatural connection. It must be confessed that this is not without difficulty, and hence Tosafot rejects Rashi's explanation, which is based on a slightly different reading.]

III.2   A.   *It has been taught on Tannaite authority:*
         B.   A male nine years and one day old who has sexual relations with a beast, whether via the vagina or the anus,
         C.   And a woman who has sexual relations with a beast, whether via the vagina or the anus, is liable.

III.3   A.   Said Rabina to Raba, "As to him who commits the first stage of sexual relations with a male, what is the law?"
         B.   What is the law? He who commits the first stage of sexual relations with a male falls into the category of the verse of Scripture, "...with mankind as with womankind" (Lev. 18:20)[1]
         C.   But as to one who commits the first stage of sexual relations with a beast, what is the law?
         D.   *He said to him, "Since [Freeman:] the culpability of the first stage of incest, which is explicitly stated with reference to one's paternal or maternal aunt, is redundant there, for it is likened to the first state of intercourse with a menstruating woman, apply its teaching to the first stage of bestiality [as being punishable].* [Freedman, p. 372-3, n.6: In respect of one's paternal or maternal aunt, Scripture states, 'And you shall not uncover the nakedness of your mother's sister or of your father's sister, for he uncovers his near kin' (Lev. 20:19). The word for 'he uncovers' is understood as meaning the first stage of sexual intercourse, and this verse teaches that this is a culpable offense. But this teaching is superfluous, for in the preceding verse the same is taught of a menstruating woman, which serves as a model for all forbidden human sexual intercourse. Hence the teaching, being redundant, here is applied to the first stage of bestiality.]"
         E.   *Now since sexual relations with a beast constitute a crime punishable by death at the hands of a court, why should Scripture treat the commission of the first stage of such an act as subject to liability to extirpation? [That is the punishment for sexual relations with an aunt.] It should rather have been stated with respect to crimes punishable by death at the hand of a*

         court, so that one might derive liability to the death penalty in a court from a crime which is likewise subject to the death liability.

F.   *Since the entire verse at hand [Lev. 20:19, on sexual relations with an aunt] is stated for the purpose of deriving new rulings, another such derivation is included in the verse.*

III.4 A.   R. Ahadboi bar Ammi asked R. Sheshet, "He who reaches the first stage of sexual activity through masturbation – what is the law?"

        B.   *He said to him, "You disgust us."*

        C.   *Said R. Ashi, "What is the issue that troubles you? In the case at hand it is not possible. Where it is possible is where one has sexual relations with a flaccid penis. In the view of him who ruled that* he who has sexual relations, with a flaccid penis, with consanguineous relations is exempt from all penalty, here too such a one is exempt. *And in the view of him who ruled that* such a one is liable, here too he is liable, on two counts, since he is [Freedman:] simultaneously the active and passive partner of the deed."

III.5 A.   *The question was asked of R. Sheshet, "As to an idolator who had sexual relations with a beast – what is the law? [For the stoning of the beast], we require both a stumbling stock and disgrace, and while the beast indeed is a stumbling block, there is no consideration of disgrace [since gentiles do this sort of thing routinely]. Or perhaps if there is a stumbling block even though there is no consideration of disgrace,* [the beast is put to death]."

        B.   *Said R. Sheshet, "You have learned on Tannaite authority:* 'If trees, which neither eat nor drink nor breathe, are subject to the decree of the Torah to be destroyed and burned up [at Deut. 12:3, "And you shall burn their groves with fire"], because they have served man as a stumbling block, he who diverts his fellow from the paths of life to the paths of death how much the more so!' [The beast, then, should be destroyed.]"

        C.   *In that case, what about the case of an idolator who worships his beast? Should it not be forbidden and put to death?*

        D.   *But is there anything which is not forbidden for an Israelite but is forbidden for a gentile? [If an Israelite worships his cow, it is not forbidden. So there surely can be no prohibition if a gentile worships it.]*

        E.   *But if an Israelite worshipped it, it should be forbidden, along the lines of a beast that is subjected to sexual relations by a man.*

        F.   Said Abbayye, "In that case [that of an act of bestiality], the disgrace is great, while in this case [animal worship] the disgrace is little."

        G.   But take the case of trees [as above, Deut. 12:3], in which the disgrace is slight, and the Torah has said that they are to be burned and destroyed.

        H.   *We speak of the case of animate creatures, on which the All-Merciful has had pity.* [Freeman, p. 275, n.2: Hence, only where there is much degradation, as in bestiality, is an animal destroyed; but trees are destroyed even when the disgrace is not great.]

        I.   Raba said, "The Torah has said that it is because the animal derived benefit from the sin that it is to be put to death."

        J.   But lo, the trees did not derive benefit from the sin, and the Torah has said that they are to be burned and destroyed.

K.   *We speak of the case of animate creatures, for the All-Merciful has had pity on them.*

L.   [Answering the question with which we began,] *come and take note:* **Another matter: So that the beast should not amble through the market place, with people saying, "This is the one on account of which Mr. So-and-so got himself stoned: [M. 7:4V].** *Now since this second reason* **[55B]** *involves both a stumbling block and disgrace, does the first reason [at M. 7:4U, "Because a human being has offended through it"] involve a stumbling block with disgrace, for instance, when a gentile has sexual relations with a beast?*

M.   *No, the considerations in the second of the two reasons involve both a stumbling block and disgrace. And as to the first of the two reasons, what is proposes to tell us is that, even in a case where there is disgrace without a stumbling block, there also would be liability.*

N.   *What would that involve? It would be the case of* an Israelite who by inadvertence had sexual relations with a beast, in accord with the inquiry of R. Hamnuna. [Freedman, p. 375, n.7: When bestiality is committed in ignorance, one has not sinned, yet he has greatly degraded himself.]

O.   *For R. Hamnuna raised the question, "In the case of an Israelite who inadvertently had sexual relations with a beast, what is the law? We require both a stumbling block and disgrace, and here, while we do have a matter of disgrace, we do not have a stumbling block. Or perhaps it suffices that there be disgrace even though there is no consideration of a stumbling block."*

P.   [Answering the question with which we began,] *said R. Joseph, "Come and take note:* **A girl three years and one day old is betrothed by intercourse. And if a Levir has had intercourse with her, he has acquired her. And one can be held liable on her account because of the law prohibiting intercourse with a married woman. And she imparts uncleanness to him who has intercourse with her when she is menstruating, to convey uncleanness to the lower as to the upper layer [of what lies beneath]. If she was married to a priest, she may eat food in the status of priestly rations. If one of those who are unfit for marriage with her had intercourse with her, he has rendered her unfit to marry into the priesthood. If any of those who are forbidden in the Torah to have intercourse with her had intercourse with her, he is put to death on her account, but she is free of responsibility [M. Nid. 5:4]. Any of those who are forbidden** – even a beast! *And lo, in this case there is disgrace, but there is no consideration of a stumbling block, and yet it is taught that such a one is put to death on her account."*

Q.   *In that case, since the girl does it intentionally, there also is the consideration of a stumbling block, but it is the All-Merciful who has had pity on her – on her, not on the beast.*

R.   [Answering the question with which we began,] *said Raba, "Come and take note:* **A boy nine years and one day old who had intercourse with his childless brother's widow has acquired her. But he cannot give her a writ of divorce until he comes of age. And he is made unclean by a menstruating woman, to convey** uncleanness to the lower as to the upper layer. And he disqualifies, but does not render a woman qualified to eat heave-offering. And through bestiality he spoils a beast for use on the altar, and it is stoned on his account. And if he had intercourse with any of all the prohibited relationships stated in the Torah, they are put to death on his account. But he is free of responsibility [M. Nid. 5:5]. *Now here is a case where there is disgrace but no stumbling block, and it is taught that it is stoned on his account!"*

S.   *Since it was a deliberate act, it also was a stumbling block, and it is the All-Merciful that had pity on him – on him the All-Merciful had pity, but not on the beast.*

T.   [Answering the question with which we began,] *Come and take note:* **Another matter: So that the beast should not amble through the market place, with people saying, "This is the one on account of which Mr. So-and-so got himself stoned" [M. 7:4V].** *Now is it not the case that, since the second of the two reasons deals with a case in which there was a stumbling block and also disgrace, in the first of the two reasons we have a disgrace without a stumbling block? And what would such a case involve?* An Israelite who inadvertently had sexual relations with a beast.

U.   *No, the second of the two reasons involves a stumbling block and a disgrace, and the first involves a stumbling block without disgrace. And what would such a case involve? An idolator who had sexual relations, along the lines of the question addressed to R. Sheshet.*

Unit I.1 provides a scriptural basis for the law of M. 7:4S, that stoning applies to the sin at hand. Unit II.1 goes on to the execution of the cow of M. 7:4S. Unit III.1 then raises a secondary question, flowing from unit II, and unit III.2 is continuous with unit III.1. The further units ten develop themes pertinent to the rule at hand but in no way constructed to serve as exegesis or amplification for that rule.

7:5

A.   He who blasphemes [M. 7:4D1] [Lev. 24:10] is liable only when he has fully pronounced the divine Name.

B.   Said R. Joshua b. Qorha, [56A] "On every day of a trial they examine the witnesses with a substituted name, [such as], 'May Yosé smite Yosé.'

C.   "[Once] the trial is over, they would not put him to death [on the basis of evidence given] with the substituted euphemism, but they clear the court and ask the most important of the witnesses, saying to him, 'Say, what exactly did you hear [in detail]?'

D.   "And he says what he heard.

E.   "And the judges stand on their feet and tear their clothing, and never sew them back up.

F.   "And the second witness says, 'Also I [heard] what he heard.'

G.   "And the third witness says, 'Also I [heard] what he heard.'"

I.1   A.   *A Tannaite authority [states], "... When he has cursed the divine Name by Name."*

B.   *What is the source of this rule?*

C.   Said Samuel, "It is because Scripture has stated, 'And he who blasphemes the name of the Lord...when he blasphemes the name of the Lord shall be put to death' (Lev. 24:16). [Freeman: The repetition shows that the Divine Name must be cursed by the Divine Name.]."

D.   *How do we know that the word, "blaspheme" means curse?*

E.   Because it is written, "How shall I curse [using the same root] whom God has not cursed" (Num. 23:8).

F.   *The admonition not to do so derives from here:* "You shall not curse God" (Ex. 22:27).

G.   *And might I suggest that the same word means "to pierce," [so that one may not rip up a piece of paper on which the divine Name is written]?*

H.   For it is written, "[So Jehoiada the priest took a chest] and [using the same root] pierced a hole in the lid of it" (2 Kgs. 12:10).

I.   *And the admonition would derive from here:* "You shall destroy the names of the [idols] out of that place. You shall not do so to the Lord your God" (Deut. 12:3-4).

J.   *We require that the Name be cursed by use of the divine Name, and that is not present [in the cited passage].*

K.   *But perhaps what is involved is placing two slips with the divine Name together, and piercing both of them?*

L.   *Then that would be a case in which one pierced the one and only then pierced the other [not piercing one with the other simultaneously].*

M.   *And might I suggest that what is involved is engraving the divine Name on the point of a knife and with that knife piercing [a slip on which the divine Name is written]?*

N.   *But then it is the point of the knife that does the piercing.*

O.   *And might I suggest that what is involved is the pronunciation of the Name. For it is written,* "And Moses and Aaron took these men who were identified [using the same root] by their names" (Num. 1:17), with the admonition against doing so in the following: "You shall fear the Lord your God" (Deut. 6:13)?

P.   *First , we require cursing of the Name by the use of the Name, and that is absent. Furthermore, you have here the case of an admonition in the form of an affirmative commandment, and an admonition in the form of an affirmative commandment does not fall into the category of an admonition at all.*

Q.   *If you like, I shall suggest that* Scripture has said, "And the Israelite woman's son blasphemed and cursed" (Lev. 24:11), indicating that blasphemy takes the form of a curse.

R.   *Than perhaps the prohibited deed involves doing both [blaspheming and cursing]?*

S.   *Do not let it enter your mind, for it is written,* "Bring forth him who has cursed" (Lev. 24:14), and it is not written, "Bring forth him who blasphemed and cursed." [That proves that only a single action is involved.]

The Religious Obligations of the Children of Noah:
Idolators and Slaves

I.2 A. *Our rabbis have taught on Tannaite authority:*

B. ["Any man who curses his God shall bear his sin" (Lev. 24:15)]": [It would have been clear had the text simply said,]"A man." Why does it specify, "Any"?

C. It serves to encompass idolators, who are admonished not to curse the Name, just as Israelites are so admonished.

D. And they are put to death only by decapitation, for the sole form of inflicting the death penalty in the case of the sons of Noah is by decapitation.

E. *How do we deduce from the cited verse [that idolators are not to blaspheme]?*

F. *It derives from the following verse:* "The Lord" (Gen. 2:16) [each word of the verse at hand being subjected to an exegetical exercise, as we shall see below] signifies that cursing the divine Name [is forbidden for gentiles as much as for Israelites].

G. *Said R. Isaac the Smith, "The phrase cited earlier ['any man'] serves to encompass even the use of euphemisms, and it is framed in accord with the principle of R. Meir."*

H. *For it has been taught on Tannaite authority:*

I. "'Any man who curses his God shall bear his sin' (Lev. 24:15).

J. "Why is this passage stated? Is it not already said, 'And he who blasphemes the name of the Lord shall surely be put to death' (Lev. 24:16)?

K. "Since that passage specifies, '...blasphemes the Name....,' one might think that a person is liable only on account of cursing the ineffable Name. How do I know that encompassed within the prohibition are euphemisms?

L. "Scripture states, 'Any man who curses his God' – in any manner whatsoever," the word of R. Meir.

M. And sages say, "On account of using the ineffable Name, one is subject to the death penalty, but as for euphemisms, one is subject to the admonition [not to do so, but not to the death penalty if he does so]."

N. *[Isaac's view] differs from that of R. Miasha.*

O. For R. Miasha said, "A son of Noah who cursed the Name by using euphemisms in the opinion of rabbis is liable [to the death penalty].

P. *"What is the scriptural basis for that claim? Scripture has said,* 'As well the stranger as he that is born in the land [when he blasphemes the name of the Lord shall be put to death]' (Lev. 24:16). So in the case of the proselyte or the homeborn [before we inflict the death penalty] we require cursing by the use of the divine Name in particular, but in the case of the idolator, even if he uses only a euphemism [he is subject to the death penalty]."

Q. *Then how [within this theory] does R. Meir interpret the words, "as well the stranger as he that is born in the land"?*

R. The proselyte and the homeborn [who are guilty of blasphemy] are put to death by stoning, but the idolator [who is guilty of blasphemy] is put to death by decapitation.

S.   *One might have supposed that, since the law was extended to encompass them, it encompassed them for all purposes. So we are informed that that is not the case.*

T.   *And as to the theory of R. Isaac the Smith vis a vis rabbis, how are we to interpret the phrase,* "as well the stranger as he that is born in the land"?

U.   *We require that phrase to indicate that [in the case of an Israelite, guilt is incurred only if he curses] the divine Name by using the divine Name, while in the case of the idolator, we do not require the use of the divine Name in cursing the divine Name [before we impose a penalty].*

V.   Why then has Scripture used the phrase, "When any man..."? The Torah speaks in the language used by ordinary men.

I.3   A.   *Our rabbis have taught on Tannaite authority:*

B.   **Concerning seven religious requirements were the children of Noah commanded: setting up courts of justice, idolatry, blasphemy, [cursing the Name of God], fornication, bloodshed, thievery, and cutting a limb from a living beast [T. A.Z. 8:4].**

C.   [56B] **R. Hananiah b. Gamaliel says, "Also on account of blood deriving from a living beast."**

D.   **R. Hidqa says, "Also on account of castration."**

E.   **R. Simeon says, "Also on account of witchcraft."**

F.   **R. Yosé says, "On account of whatever is stated in the pericope regarding the children of Noah are they subject to warning, as it is said, 'There shall not be found among you any one who burns his son or his daughter as an offering, any one who practices divination, a soothsayer or an augur or a sorcerer or a charmer or a medium or a wizard or a necromancer' (Deut. 18:10-11).**

G.   **"Is it possible then that Scripture has imposed a punishment without imparting a prior warning.?**

H.   **"But it provides a warning and afterward imposes the punishment.**

I.   **"This teaches that he warned them first and then punished them."**

J.   **R. Eleazar says, "Also as to mixed seeds, it is permitted for a child of Noah to sow seeds which are mixed species and to wear garments of mixed species of wool and linen. But it is prohibited to breed a hybrid beast or to graft trees" (T. A.Z. 8:6K-O, 8:7, 8:8].**

K.   *What is the scriptural basis for this rule?*

L.   *Said R. Yohanan, "It is in the following verse of Scripture: '*And the Lord God commanded Adam saying, Of every tree of the garden you may freely eat' (Gen. 2:16).

M.   "'And he commanded' – this refers to setting up courts of justice, for Scripture says, 'For I know him, that he will command his children and his household after him, and they shall keep the way of the Lord, to do justice and judgment'(Gen. 18:19).

N.   "'The Lord' – this refers to blasphemy, and so it is written, 'And he who blasphemes the name of the Lord shall surely be put to death' (Lev. 24:16).

O.   "'God' – this refers to idolatry, as it is written, 'You shall have no other gods before me' (Ex. 20:3).

P.	"'Adam' – this refers to murder, as it is written, 'Whoever sheds the blood of a man, by man shall his blood be shed' (Gen. 9:6).
Q.	"'Saying' – this refers to adultery, as it is written, 'They say, If a man put away his wife and she go from him and became another man's (Jer. 3:1). [Freedman, p. 383, n.5: Thus 'saying' is used in connection with adultery.]
R.	"'Of every tree of the garden' – but not of robbery. [A person may not eat what does not belong to that person. Freedman, p. 383, n. 6: Since it was necessary to authorize Adam to eat of the trees of the garden, it follows that without such authorization– when something belongs to another–it is forbidden.]
S.	"'You may freely eat' – but not a limb cut from a living animal."
T.	*When R. Dimi came, he repeated matters in reverse:*
U.	"'God' – this refers to courts of justice."
W.	*Surely "God" refers to courts of justice, for it is written, "And the householder will come near to God" (Ex. 22:7).*
X.	*But on what basis do we conclude that, "And he commanded" refers to idolatry?*
Y.	*R. Hisda and R. Isaac bar Abedimi: One said, "'They have turned aside quickly out of the way which I commanded them; they have made them a molten calf' (Ex. 32:8)."*
Z.	*The other said, "'Ephraim is oppressed and broken in judgment, because he willingly walked after the commandment' (Hos. 5:11) [in which context, 'commandment' speaks of idolatry]."*
AA.	*What is at issue between them?*
BB.	*At issue is the case of* an idolator who made an idol but did not bow down to it.
CC.	*In the view of him who has said that [the prohibition of gentiles' idol-worship is in the verse,]* "They have made them a golden calf,"] one is liable from the time of the making of the idol [even without worshipping it].
DD.	*In the view of him who has said that the source of the prohibition is in the verse,* "Because he willingly walked after the commandment," one is liable only after he has followed the idol and worshipped it.
EE.	Said Raba, "And is there anyone who maintains that if an idolator merely makes an idol but does not worship it, he is liable? *Has it not been taught on Tannaite authority:* **On account of things for which an Israelite court inflicts the death penalty, the children of Noah are subject to warning. If the Israelite court does not inflict a death penalty, the children of Noah are not admonished concerning such actions [cf. T. A.Z. 8:4G].** *What then is excluded by that statement? Is it not to exclude the case of an idolator who made an idol but did not bow down to it [an act for which a court will not inflict the death penalty on an Israelite]?"*
FF.	*Said R. Pappa, "No, it serves to exclude the acts of embracing and kissing idols [which actions are not punishable]."*

GG.   *Embracing and kissing what sort of idols? If I should say that it refers to doing so with an idol that is usually worshipped in this way, then such a one is subject to the death penalty anyhow. Rather, it serves to exclude [punishment for doing so with idols that are] not usually worshipped in this way.*

HH.   **Setting up courts of justice:** *Are the children of Noah subject to a commandment in this regard? And has it not been taught on Tannaite authority:* The Israelites were given ten commandments at Marah, seven of which the children of Noah had already accepted, to which were added [for Israel] the laws of setting up courts of justice, observing the Sabbath, and honoring father and mother. **Courts of justice,** as it is written, "There [at Marah] he made for them a statute and an ordinance" (Ex. 15:25). **Sabbath observance, and honoring of father and mother,** as it is written, "as the Lord thy God commanded thee" (Deut. 5:15 and 5:16). [The term "commanded thee," used in both the fourth and fifth commandments, suggests that both of these had been given before the giving of the Decalogue at Sinai. These must therefore constitute the statute and ordinance of Marah.]

II.   Said R. Judah, "'As he commanded thee' refers to the events at Marah."

JJ.   Said R. Nahman in the name of Rabbah bar Abbuha, "[The commandment at Marah] served to institute trial by an assembly of judges, with witnesses and formal admonition."

KK.   *If so, why say "to which courts of justice were added" [since that addition involved only legal procedure and not actual laws]?*

LL.   Rather, said Raba, "[The commandment at Marah] served to institute penal fines."

MM.   *But even so, should it not have been said, "and courts of justice were added"?*

NN.   *Rather, said R. Aha b. Jacob, "[The commandment at Marah] served to indicate that they must establish courts in every district and town."*

OO.   *But were not the children of Noah already commanded to do this? And has it not been taught on Tannaite authority:* **Just as Israelites are commanded to call into session in every district and town courts of justice, so the sons of Noah were commanded to call into session in every district and town courts of justice (T. A.Z. 8:4D].**

PP.   *Rather, said Raba, "The Tannaite authority at hand [who claims that the requirement to establish courts of justice in gentile communities was added at Marah, and not earlier] is a Tannaite authority of the house of Manasseh, who omits references, in the list of the commandments to the sons of Noah, to courts of law and to blasphemy, and instead adds to the list the prohibitions of emasculation and mixing seeds. For a Tannaite authority of the house of Manasseh [said],* 'Seven commandments were assigned to the children of Noah: the prohibition of idolatry, adultery, murder, robbery, cutting a limb from a living creature, emasculation, and mixing seeds.'

QQ. "R. Judah says, 'The first man was commanded only concerning idolatry, for it is said, "And the Lord God commanded Adam" (Gen. 2:16).'

RR. "R. Judah b. Baterah says, '"Also concerning cursing the divine Name."'

SS. "And there are those who say, '"Also concerning setting up courts of justice."'

TT. *In accord with which authority is the following statement that R. Judah said Rab said,* "[God said to Adam,] 'I am God. Do not curse me. I am God. Do not exchange me for another. I am God. Let my fear of me be upon you [and so establish justice].*

UU. *In accord with whom? It is in accord with "there are those who say."*

VV. *Now if the Tannaite authority of the house of Manasseh interprets the verse, "And God commanded..." (Gen. 2:16), then even these other [commandments, listed earlier, also should be on his list, and not only the ones he includes]. If he does not interpret the verse, "And God commanded..." (Gen. 2:16), then what is the scriptural basis for the items he does include?*

WW. *Indeed he does not interpret the cited verse, and he derives each item from a verse of its own.*

XX. As to idolatry and adultery, **[57A]** it is written, "The earth also was corrupt before God" (Gen. 6:11), *and a Tannaite authority of the house of R. Ishmael [taught],* "In every passage in which it is stated, 'was corrupt,' the reference is always to adultery and idolatry.

YY. Adultery, as it is said, 'For all flesh had corrupted its way upon the earth' (Gen. 5:11).

ZZ. Idolatry, for it is written, 'Lest you corrupt yourselves and make you a graven image...' (Deut. 4:16).

AAA. *And the other party [who interprets the verse, "And the Lord commanded..." (Gen. 6:11)]?*

BBB. *The cited verse simply reveals the way they did things.*

CCC. Murder, as it is written, "Whoever sheds a man's blood..." (Gen. 9:6).

DDD. *And the other party?*

EEE. *The verse at hand simply indicates that [murderers] are to be executed.*

FFF. Robbery, as it is written, "As the wild herbs, have I given you all things" (Lev. 9:3), and R. Levi said, "As the wild herbs and not as garden herbs [which belong to private individuals]."

GGG. *And the other party? The cited verse serves the purpose of permitting people to eat meat.*

HHH. Cutting a limb from a living animal, as it is written, "But flesh with the life thereof, which is the blood thereof, shall you not eat" (Gen. 9:4).

III. *And the other party? That verse serves to permit people to eat creeping things.*

JJJ.		Emasculation, as it is written, "Bring forth abundantly in the earth and multiply therein" (Gen. 9:4).
KKK.		*That verse serves merely to speak of a blessing in general.*
LLL.		Mixing seeds, as it is written, "Of fowl after their kind" (Gen. 6:20).
MMM.		*And the other party? That refers to mating [indicating merely that the species mate more readily with one another than with outsiders.*

I.4   A.   Said R. Joseph, "[Disciples] of the house of one master said, 'On account of [violating] three religious duties are children of Noah put to death: on account of adultery, murder, and blasphemy.'"

B.   *To this statement, R. Sheshet objected, "There is no problem with regard to murder, for it is written, 'Whoever sheds the blood of man by man shall his blood be shed' (Gen. 9:6). But what is the source for the other two? If one derives them from the matter of murder, then all of them should also be subject to the death penalty, and not only those listed. If it is because they are included through the reference to 'any man' (Lev. 24:15, Lev. 18:6, thus covering blasphemy and adultery], then they should also encompass idolatry [from the use of the phrase, 'any man [at Lev. 20:2]."*

C.   *Rather, said R. Sheshet, "[Disciples] of the house of one master have said, 'On account of four commandments a son of Noah may be put to death [on account of idolatry, plus those listed at A]."*

D.   *And is a son of Noah put to death on account of idolatry?*

E.   *And has it not been taught with reference to idolatry:* **Because of matters on account of which an Israelite court inflicts the death penalty, the children of Noah are subject to warning [T. A.Z. 8:4G].** They are subject to warning, but they are <u>not</u> put to death.

F.   Said R. Nahman bar Isaac, "A warning that pertains to them constitutes also a sentence of death."

I.5   A.   R. Huna, R. Judah, and all the disciples of Rab say, "On account of seven commandments a son of Noah is put to death. *The All-Merciful revealed that fact of one of them, and the same rule applies to all of them."*

B.   *Is a son of Noah put to death on account of robbery? And has it not been taught on Tannaite authority:* **Concerning robbery: if one has stolen or robbed and so too in the case of stealing a beautiful captive woman and in similar cases, a gentile doing so to a gentile, or a gentile doing so to an Israelite – it [what is stolen] is prohibited. And an Israelite doing so to a gentile – it [what is stolen] is permitted [T. A.Z. 8:5C-E].** *Now if matters were [as you say], should it not teach, "One is liable," [not "permitted", treating only the stolen object]!*

C.   *It is because the framer of the passage wished to repeat at the end, "***An Israelite doing so to a gentile – it [the stolen object] is permitted,"** *that he used the language in the opening clause,* **It is prohibited.'**

D.   *But in every passage in which there is liability to a penalty, it is made explicit, for the opening clause states:* **Concerning bloodshed, a gentile who kills a gentile, and a gentile who kills an Israelite are liable, but an Israelite who kills a gentile is exempt [T. A.Z. 8:5A-B].**

E. *In that passage how else might the framer of the passage expressed matters? Could he have said, "It is forbidden..it is permitted..."? [Surely not.]*

F. *And has it not been stated on Tannaite authority:* **Gentiles and shepherds of small cattle and those who raise them make no difference one way or the other [in figuring out whose lost object to seek first] [T. B.M. 2:33A].**

G. **And similar acts, in the case of robbery:** *what would be an example? Said R. Aha bar Jacob, "It is necessary only* to cover the case of a worker in a vineyard [who munches as he eats]." *But when would this be culpable? If it is at the time that the work is complete, then it is permitted. If it is not at the time that the work is complete, it is a perfectly standard form of robbery.*

H. Rather, said R. Pappa, "It is necessary to take account of robbery of something of value of less than a perutah."

I. *If that is the case, why should it be stated that if* **a Samaritan does so to an Israelite, it is forbidden [to keep the object]?** *Does [the Israelite] not write off the object?*

J. *Granted that afterward he indeed does write off the object, at the time that [the theft] takes place, it does give distress to the owner.*

K. *[Now you say that] the commission of such an act by one Samaritan against another falls into the same category of similar acts. But since [we assume that] the Samaritan will not write off the object, it again is a perfectly standard form of robbery.*

L. But R. Aha the son of R. Iqa says, "It covers the case of one who withholds the wages of a hired man. A gentile who does so to a gentile, or a gentile who does so to an Israelite, are liable. But an Israelite who does so to a gentile is exempt.'

M. **And similar acts in the case of a beautiful captive woman:** *what would be an example?*

N. When R. Dimi came, he said R. Eleazar said R. Hanina said, "A son of Noah who designated a slave-girl for his slave-boy and [thereafter] had sexual relations with her is put to death on that account."

O. *And similar acts in the case of murder is not listed at all in the Tannaite teaching.*

P. Said Abbayye, "If it were found to have been taught on Tannaite authority, then it would represent the view of R. Jonathan b. Saul."

Q. *For it has been taught on Tannaite authority:* R. Jonathan b. Saul says, "[If a man] pursues his fellow to kill him, and [the pursued] could save himself by lopping off one of the [pursuer's] limbs and did not do so [but rather killed him], **[57B]** he is put to death on his account."

I.6 A. *R. Jacob bar Aha found that it was written in the book of the lore of the house of Rab,* "A son of Noah is put to death by a court consisting of a single judge,

B. "on the testimony of a single witness,

C. "not after appropriate admonition,

D. "on the testimony of a man but not on the testimony of a woman,

E. "but even if the witness is a relative."

F.   In the name of R. Ishmael it is said, "He is put to death even for the murder of an embryo."

G.   *What is the source of this statement?*

H.   Said R. Judah, "Scripture says, '"And surely the blood of your lives will I require". (Gen. 9:5)

I.   "[The fact that it is I who shall require" indicates that] it may be a court made of of even one judge alone.

J.   "'At the hand of every thing will I require it' (Gen. 9:5) – even without admonition.

K.   "'And at the hand of man' (Gen. 9:5) – even a single witness.

L.   "'At the hand of man' (Gen. 9:5) – not at the hand of a woman.

M.   "'His brother' – even a relative."

N.   In the name of R. Ishmael it is said, "He is put to death even for the murder of an embryo."

O.   *What is the scriptural basis of the view of R. Ishmael?*

P.   Since it is written, "Whoever sheds the blood of a man within a man [B'DM], his blood shall be shed" (Gen. 9:6).

Q.   What sort of "man" is located "within a "man"?

R.   One must say it is the embryo in the mother's womb.

S.   *And the former of the two authorities [who reject as Ishmael's view]?*

T.   *He is a Tannaite authority of the house of Menasseh, who has said,* "As to all death penalties that pertain to sons children of Noah, they are carried out in all cases only by strangulation." *He then assigns the phrase,* "within a man" *to the concluding part of the verse at hand, and he interprets it in this way:* "By man [B'DM] his blood will be shed."

U.   *What then is the form of bloodshed of a human being which takes place in such a way that [the blood remains] within the man's body? One must say it is strangulation.*

V.   *R. Hamnuna objected [to the proposition that gentile women do not have to impose justice and so may not testify, as stated at D,L],* "And is a woman not subject to the same commandment? Lo, it is written, 'For I know him that he will command his sons and household after him, and they shall keep the way of the Lord to exercise charity and judgment' (Gen. 18:19) [and the household includes women]."

W.   *[Hamnuna] raised the question and he settled it:* "'His sons' – to impose justice, and 'his household' – to do righteousness [that is, acts of charity]."

I.7   A.   Said R. Abia the elder to R. Pappa, "Might I propose that a daughter of Noah who committed murder should not be put to death?

B.   "'At the hand of man [who committed murder]'– and not the hand of woman' is what is written [at Gen. 9:6]."

C.   *He said to him, "This is what R. Judah said,* '"He who sheds the blood of man" – under any circumstances.'"

D.   *"May I propose that* a daughter of Noah who committed adultery should not be put to death, for it is written, 'Therefore shall a man forsake his father and mother and cleave to his wife' (Gen. 2:24), meaning, a man and not a woman?"

E. *He said to him, "This is what R. Judah said, '"And they shall be as one flesh" (Gen. 2:24), so that Scripture went and treated the two as one [applying the statement to both parties].'"*

I.8 A. *Our rabbis have taught on Tannaite authority:*

B. "[A man, a man shall not approach any who is near of kin to him, to uncover their nakedness" (Lev. 18:6):] As to the word, "A man," why does Scripture say it twice? It serves to encompass Samaritans [gentiles], indicating that they are admonished, just like Israelites, against sexual relations with close relatives.

C. *Does that proposition derive from the present passage? Surely it derives from the following: "'[And the Lord commanded...,] saying...'(Gen. 2:16) [as interpreted above, 56B] – this refers to adultery."*

D. *That passage refers to adultery within their own group, the present passage refers to adultery with our group. For it has been taught on Tannaite authority at the end of the passage at hand:*

E. If [a Samaritan (gentile)] had sexual relations with an Israelite, he is tried in accord with the laws governing Israelites.

F. *What practical difference does this law make [since the penalty in both cases is death]?*

G. Said R. Nahman said Rabbah bar Abbuha, "It is necessary only [to indicate] that there must be a 'congregation' of judges [twenty-three], appropriate testimony, and admonition."

H. *Is this act [of adultery] with a Jewish woman a lesser offense [that the protection of Jewish law should be accorded to him]? [Had the act been committed with a Samaritan woman, he would not enjoy the protection of the provisions in the foregoing list.]*

I. *Said R. Yohanan, "The law is necessary only to cover the case of [his committing adultery with] a betrothed girl, for in their law, there is no such category. In that case we try by him by our law."*

J. *But as to [his adultery with] a married woman, do we try him in accord with their law? Has it not been taught on Tannaite authority:*

K. If he had sexual relations with a betrothed girl, he is put to death by stoning. If with a married woman, he is put to death by strangulation.

L. *Now if he is judged in accord with their law, he should be put to death by decapitation.*

M. *Said R. Nahman bar Isaac, "What is the sense of 'a married woman' in the passage at hand? It would be a case in which* the woman had entered the marriage canopy but the marriage had not been consummated. *In their law, there is no such category [as a capital crime], so he is judged in accord with our law [as though she were fully married]."*

N. *For R. Hanina taught on Tannaite authority:* "The category of a married woman who has had sexual relations exists to their legal system, but the category of a married woman who has entered the marriage canopy but not yet had sexual relations does not exist in their legal system."

I.9 A. *It has been taught on Tannaite authority in accord with the view of R. Yohanan:* **In the case of any form of prohibited sexual relationship for which an Israelite court inflicts the death** penalty, the children of Noah are subject to warning. If an Israelite court does not inflict the death penalty in the case at hand, a son of Noah is not subject to warning with respect to it," the words of R. Meir. And sages say, "There are many prohibited relationships with respect to which an Israelite court does not inflict the death-penalty, and the children of Noah are warned with respect to them. If one has had sexual relations with a woman prohibited by Israelite law, he is tried in accord with Israelite law. If he had sexual relations in violation of Noahide law, he is judged in accord with Noahide law. But only the prohibition of sexual relations with a betrothed maiden falls into the category at hand, in which Israelite law prohibits such a relationship and Noahide law does not]" [T. A.Z. 8:G-I]. *But [included in that last category, in which Israelite law prohibits a type of relationship gentile law permits] is the case, also, of the woman who has entered the marriage canopy but not had sexual relations [and who, by Jewish law, is regarded as a married woman]?*

B.   *This Tannaite authority is the one of the house of Manasseh, who has said that in the case of every death penalty imposed on Noahides, the mode of execution is strangulation, and both for Israelite and for foreign law, in the present case, the mode of execution is the same, namely strangulation.*

C.   *And does R. Meir maintain that* in the case of any form of prohibited sexual relationship for which an Israelite court inflicts the death penalty, the children of Noah are subject to warning? *And lo, it has been taught on Tannaite authority:* A proselyte [58A] whose mother, when she conceived him, was not in a state of sanctification but who [because, while pregnant, the mother had converted to Judaism] was [then] born in a state of sanctification, is subject to the laws of consanguinity on his mother's side, but he is not subject to the laws of consanguinity on his father's side. How so? If he married his sister on his mother's side [a half-sister, born of his mother and a different father], he must divorce her. [If it was] a [half-] sister on his father's side [born of a different mother], he may keep her [as his wife]. If it was his father's sister by his father's mother, he must put her away. If it was his father's sister by his father's father, he may remain wed to her. If it was his mother's sister by her mother, he must put her away. If it was his mother's sister by her father, R. Meir says, "He must put her away." But sages say, "He may keep her."

D.   For R. Meir held, "In the case of any consanguineous relationship on the mother's side, he must put away [such a woman]. If it is on his father's side, he may keep her. [Freedman, p. 394, n. 1: The guiding principle in all this is: 'a proselyte is as a new born babe', who stands in absolutely no relationship to any pre-conversion relation. Consequently, his brothers and sisters, father, mother, etc. from before his conversion lose his relationship on his conversion. Should they too subsequently become converted, they are regarded as strangers to him, and he might marry, e.g., his mother or sister. This is the Biblical law. But since heathens themselves recognized the law of incest in respect of maternal relations, the Rabbis decreed that this should hold good for a proselyte too, i.e., that he is forbidden to marry his maternal relations who were forbidden to him before his conversion, so that it should not be said that he abandoned a faith with a higher degree of sanctity than the one he has embraced (since he cannot be expected to understand the principle of complete annulment of relationships). In this case, since he was born in sanctity, he is really not a proselyte at all, He is so styled because he too is legally a stranger to all his father's and mother's pre-conversion relations. As for his mother's paternal sister, R. Meir held that since she is partly maternally related, she is forbidden, as otherwise it would be thought that a proselyte is permitted to marry his maternal relations. But the Rabbis held that there was no fear of this, and since the relationship is in its source paternal, it is not forbidden]. And he is permitted to marry his brother's wife [Freedman, p. 394, n.3: even his brother by his mother], his father's brother's wife, and all other relations deemed consanguineous by affinity of marital ties are permitted to him, *including the wife of his father.* If he has [already] married a woman and her daughter, he may consummate the marriage with one of them and put away the other. But to begin with, he should not do so at all. If his wife died, he may marry his mother-in-law." Others say [in his view], "He may not marry her." [Freedman, p. 384, n. 5: Now in this Baraita a number of relations forbidden to Jews on pain of death, e.g., his father's wife and his mother-in-law, are permitted to the proselyte, and hence to heathens in general; whilst a number of relations not forbidden on pain of death, e.g., his sister, his paternal and maternal aunts, are prohibited to him. This, taught in R. Meir's name, contradicts his other ruling that all forbidden degrees of consanguinity punishable by death are forbidden to heathens.]

E.   *Said R. Judah, "There is no contradiction between the one passage and the other. The one has R. Meir presenting the matter in accord with the view of R. Eliezer, the other has R. Meir presenting the matter in accord with the view of R. Aqiba." For it has been taught on Tannaite authority.'*

F.   "Therefore shall a man leave his father and his mother" (Gen. 2:24):

G.   R. Eliezer says, "'His father' means the sister of his father, 'his mother' means the sister of his mother,' [whom he may not marry]."

H.   R. Aqiba says, "'His father' means his father's wife [by another marriage, for example], and 'his mother' refers literally to his mother.'"

I.   "And he shall cleave" – and not to a male.

J.   "To his wife" – and not to his fellow's wife.

K.   "And they shall become one flesh" – one with whom one can become one flesh [in an offspring], excluding domesticated beasts and wild beasts, who cannot produce an offspring with man. [Freedman, p. 395, n. 5: Hence (since this rule applies to Noahides) Meir's dictum that heathens are forbidden those relations which are prohibited to Jews on pain of death, e.g., the father's wife, reflects Aqiba's teaching, while his ruling in the Baraita that a proselyte may marry his father's wife is the view of Eliezer, who does not interpret 'his father' as his father's wife.]

L.   A master has said [in expanding upon the foregoing], "R. Eliezer says, '"His father" means his father's sister.'"

M.   *But might I say it means literally, his father?*

N.   *That is covered by the statement, "'And he will cleave' –* and not to a male."

O.   *Might I say it means, "His father's wife?" That is covered by "'his wife' and not the wife of his fellow.'"*

P.   *Might I say that this would apply after death?*

Q.   *It is similar to the prohibition of his mother. Just as his mother [Freedman] is not a relation by marriage, so "his father" must refer to a non-marriage relationship.*

R.   "His mother" refers to his mother's sister. *But might I say that it refers literally to his mother?*

S.   *That is covered by the reference to "'His wife' and not to the wife of his fellow."*

T.   *And might I say that it would apply even after death?*

U.   *It is similar to the prohibition of "his father." Just as "his father" is not literally so, so "his mother" is not literally so.*

V.   "R. Aqiba says, "'His father' means his father's wife.'"

W.   *But might I say that it refers literally to his father?*

X.   *This is covered by the statement "And he shall cleave' –* and not to a male."

Y.   *If that is the mode of argument, then may we invoke the proof already given, namely, "'His wife' – and not the wife of his fellow?"*

Z.   *The passage at hand teaches that even after death [the father's wife] is forbidden to him."*

AA. "His mother is literally his mother."

BB. *But is this not covered by, "'To his wife' and not to his fellow's wife"?*

CC. *At issue is his mother [who is related to his father because] his father had raped her [but not married her].*

DD. *At what point is there a dispute?*

EE. R. *Eliezer maintains the view that* **[58B]** [Freedman:] *only by referring to collateral relations can "his father" and "his mother" bear similar interpretations.* [Freedman, p. 396, n. 2: For they cannot both be literal, since his father is prohibited by "and he shall cleave," nor can they both refer to relationship by marriage, since his mother is a blood-relation.]

FF.   *R. Aqiba takes the position that it is better to refer the phrase of "his father" to his father's wife, who is covered by the reference [at Lev. 18:8] to "the nakedness of his father," and not to his father's sister, who falls merely in the category [at Lev. 18:12] of "his father's kin" and not his father's nakedness.*

GG.   *Come and take note:* "And Amram took Jochebed, his aunt, as his wife" (Ex. 6:20): *Was this not his aunt on his mother's side [as against Eliezer's view]?*

HH.   No, it was his aunt on his father's side. [His father's maternal sister would have been forbidden (Freedman)].

II.   *Come and take note:* "And yet indeed she is my sister, she is the daughter of my father but not of my mother" (Gen. 20:12). *Would this not contain the implication that the daughter of the mother is forbidden [as against Aqiba's view?]* [Freedman, p. 396, n. 8: For since he interprets the verse as referring to his father's wife and his mother, who are forbidden on pain of death, he evidently regards those who are forbidden under penalty of excision as permissible, and his mother's daughter is only thus forbidden, but not on pain of death.]

JJ.   *But do you think so? Was she his sister? She was the daughter of his brother, and since that was the case, there is no difference whether this was his brother by the same father or by the same mother, being permitted in either case.*

KK.   *But this is the sense of what [Abraham] said to [Abimelech], "I have a relationship with her as a sister on my father's side [she is the daughter of my half-brother by my father], but not on my mother's side. [Freedman, p. 396, n. 10: Not that she would have been forbidden in that case, but this was stated merely for the sake of exactness.]"*

LL.   *Come and take note:* On what account did Adam not marry his daughter? It was so that Cain would be able to marry his sister, as it is said, "For I said the world shall be built up by grace" (Ps. 89:2). *But were it not the case [that it was an act of grace,] she would have been forbidden [to Cain, because one cannot marry a paternal sister].*

MM.   *[To the contrary,] once that relationship was permitted, it remained so.*

NN.   Said R. Huna, "A Samaritan is permitted to marry his daughter.

OO.   "And if you say, 'On what account did Adam not marry his daughter?' It was so that Cain would be able to marry his sister, so that 'the world shall be built up by grace' (Ps. 89:2)."

PP.   *There are those who say,* Said R. Huna, "A Samaritan may not marry his daughter.

QQ.   "You may know that that is the fact, for Adam did not marry his daughter."

RR.   *But that is not the correct implication to draw. The reason in that case was so that Cain could marry his sister, so that "the world shall be built up by grace" (Ps. 89:2).*

I.10   A.   Said R. Hisda, "A slave is permitted to marry his mother and permitted to marry his daughter,

        B.   "for he has ceased to fall into the category of the Samaritan [gentile] and has not yet entered the category of Israelite."

I.11   A.   When R. Dimi came, he said R. Eliezer said R. Hanina said, "A Noahide who set aside a slave-girl for his slave-boy and then had sexual relations with her is put to death on her account."

        B.   *From what point [is she so designated]?*

        C.   *Said R. Nahman, "From the time that he referred to her as the girl friend of so-and-so."*

        D.   When is she no longer bound to him?

        E.   Said R. Huna, "From the time that she walks about in the market with her head uncovered."

I.12   A.   Said R. Eleazar said R. Hanina, "A son of Noah who had anal intercourse with his wife is liable, for it is said, 'And he shall cleave' (Gen. 2:24) – [by vaginal] and not by anal intercourse."

        B.   Said Raba, "Is there anything on account of which an Israelite is not liable and a Samaritan is liable?"

        C.   Rather, said Raba, "A son of Noah who had anal intercourse with the wife of his fellow is exempt."

        D.   *What is the scriptural basis for that view?*

        E.   "' ... to his wife' and not to the wife of his fellow, 'And he shall cleave ...' [by vaginal] and not by anal intercourse."

I.13   A.   Said R. Hanina, "An idolator who hit an Israelite is liable to the death penalty.

        B.   "For it is said, 'And he looked this way and that way, and when he saw that there was no man, he slew the Egyptian' (Ex. 2:12). [Freedman, p. 398, n. 6: Thus Moses slew the Egyptian for striking an Israelite, proving that he had merited it.]"

        C.   And R. Hanina said, "He who hits an Israelite's jaw is as if he hits the jaw of the Presence of God.

        D.   "For it is said, 'One who smites man [an Israelite] attacks the Holy One' (Prov. 20:25)."

I.14   A.   Said R. Simeon b. Laqish, "He who raises his hand against his fellow, even though he did not actually hit him, is called a wicked man.

        B.   "For it is said, 'And he said to the wicked man, Why would you smite your fellow' (Ex. 2:13).

        C.   "It does not say, 'Why <u>did</u> you smite,' but rather, 'Why would you smite.' Thus, even though he had not actually hit him, he is called a wicked man."

        D.   Said Zeiri said R. Hanina, "He is called a sinner, as it is said, 'But if not, I will take it by force' (1 Sam. 2:16), and it is written, 'Wherefore the sin of the young men was very great before the Lord' (1 Sam. 2:16)."

        E.   R. Huna said, "His hand should be cut off, for it is said, 'The uplifted arm should be broken' (Job 38:15)."

        F.   *R. Huna ordered a hand to be cut off.*

        G.   R. Eleazar says, "His only remedy is burial, for it is written, 'And as for a man of uplifted arm, for him is the earth' (Job 22:8) [Freedman]."

H. And R. Eleazar said, "The ground has been given over only for strong-armed men, as it is said, 'But as for the strong-armed man, for him is the earth' (Job 22:8)."

I.15 A. And R. Simeon b. Laqish said, "*What is the meaning of the verse of Scripture,* 'He who serves his land [meaning: tills his plot] shall be satisfied with bread' (Prov. 12:11)?

B. "If a man turns himself into a slave for his property, he shall have enough bread, and if not, he shall not have enough bread."

I.16 A. And R. Simeon b. Laqish said, "An idolator who keeps the Sabbath incurs the death penalty,

B. "for it is said, 'And a day and a night they shall not rest' (Gen. 8:22).

C. "And a master has said, 'The very admonition concerning them carries with it the death penalty.'"

D. *Said Rabina, "Even if he observed Monday as the Sabbath [he is liable]."*

E. *And why is this not included in the seven Noahide commandments?*

F. *Included there are laws which one observes by abstention, not by positive action.*

G. [59A] *And lo, establishing courts of justice is a matter of taking positive action, and that item is included in the list!*

H. *That is both a positive commandment and commandment involving abstention [from injustice].*

I.17 A. And R. Yohanan said, "An idolator who takes up study of the Torah incurs the death penalty.

B. "For it is said, 'Moses commanded the Torah for us, an inheritance' (Deut. 33:4) – for us an inheritance, and not for them."

C. *And why is this not included in the seven Noahide commandments?*

D. *If we read the word as "inheritance," then he is subject to prohibition against stealing it, and if we read it as "a betrothed girl" [by changing the pronunciation of the Hebrew word], then [Torah] falls into the category of a betrothed girl, and one who violates her is punished by stoning.*

E. *An objection was raised:*

F. R. Meir says, "Whence do we know that even an idolator, should he take up study of the Torah, is equivalent to a high priest?

G. "For it is said, '[You shall therefore keep my statutes and my judgments,] which, if a man do them, he shall live by them' (Lev. 18:5); priests, Levites, and Israelites are not specified, but only a man.

H. "From that formulation you learn that even an idolator, should he engage in study of the Torah, is equivalent to a high priest."

I. *The reference [to a gentile's study of Torah] is among the seven commandments that apply to them.*

I.18 A. R. Hanina says, "Also [children of Noah must not eat] blood drawn from a living beast."

B. *Our rabbis have taught on Tannaite authority:*

C. "But flesh with the life thereof, which is the blood thereof, you shall not eat" (Gen. 9:4).

D. This refers to not eating a limb cut from a living beast.

E.   R. Hanina b. Gamaliel says, "It refers also to blood drawn from a living beast."

F.   *What is the scriptural basis for the view of R. Hanina b. Gamaliel?*

G.   *He reads the cited verse in this way:* "Flesh with its life you shall not eat, blood with its life you shall not eat."

H.   *And rabbis? That verse serves to permit the eating of creeping things.*

I.   Along these same lines, you may say: "Only be sure that you do not eat the blood, for the blood is the life, and you may not eat the life with the flesh" (Deut. 12:23) [Freedman, p. 401, n. 2: Thus the blood being equated with the life, it may not be eaten while "the life is with the flesh," that is, while the animal remains alive.]

J.   *And rabbis? They interpret the verse to refer to the blood of the arteries, with which the soul flows out. [That blood is forbidden too.]*

I.19   A.   *Why was it necessary to state [the commandments just cited] to the sons of Noah and then to repeat them at Sinai?*

B.   *The answer accords with what R. Yosé b. R. Hanina said.*

C.   For R. Yosé b. R. Hanina said, "Every religious duty that was stated to the children of Noah and then repeated at Sinai applies both to this group [the gentiles] and to that group [the Israelites].

D.   "If it was stated to the children of Noah and not repeated at Sinai it is intended for the Israelites, not for the children of Noah.

E.   "And [in that category] was have only the prohibition of [meat containing] the sciatic nerve, *speaking in accord with the view of R. Judah, [who holds that it was forbidden to the children of Jacob]."*

F.   Said a Master, "Every religious duty that was stated to the children of Noah and then repeated at Sinai applies both to this group and to that group."

G.   *To the contrary, since the law was repeated at Sinai, surely it was stated to Israel and not to the children of Noah!*

H.   *Since the practice of idolatry was stated at Sinai and we find that idolators are penalized on its account, it follows that that prohibition [and hence others in its category] was stated both to this group and to that group.*

I.   "If it was stated to the children of Noah and not repeated at Sinai, it is for the Israelites, not for the children of Noah."

J.   *To the contrary, since it was not stated at Sinai, it was addressed to the children of Noah and not to Israel.*

K.   *There is nothing that is permitted to Israelites and forbidden to idolators.*

L.   *There is nothing? Lo, there is the case of the beautiful captive woman.*

M.   *The reason in that case is that the gentiles are not permitted to make conquests anyhow.*

N.   And there is the theft of something worth less than a penny [which gentiles treated as a crime but Israelites do not].

O. *The idolators are not forgiving [and so regard such a paltry sum as of value, so if someone steals such a sum, he is punished. Israelite courts would not punish a theft of such a sum.]*

P. "Every religious duty that was stated to the children of Noah and then repeated at Sinai applies both to this group and to that group."

Q. [59B] Lo, there is the case of circumcision, which was stated to the children of Noah, for it is written, "You shall keep my covenant" (Gen. 17:9), and it was repeated at Sinai: "And in the eighth day the flesh of his foreskin shall be circumcised" (Lev. 12:3). Now that commandment was addressed to Israel and <u>not</u> to the sons of Noah.

R. *That [repetition of the rule] served the purpose of permitting [the observance of the rite on the Sabbath. [How so?]*

S. "By day" – even [if the eighth day falls] on the Sabbath.

T. And lo, there is the commandment to be fruitful and multiply, which was stated to the children of Noah, for it is written, "And you, be fruitful and multiply (Gen. 9:7), and was repeated at Sinai, as it is written, "Go say to them, get you into your tents again" (Deut. 5:27).

U. Yet the religious duty to be fruitful and multiply applies to Israel and not to the children of Noah.

V. *The latter statement serves to indicate that in any matter adopted by a vote [of sages], another vote is necessary for repeal.* [Deut. 5:27 is taken to allow people to resume sexual relations that had been suspended, as described at Ex. 19:15, three days before the giving of the Torah.]

W. *If so, then each of the Noahide laws may be explained away as serving another purpose.*

X. *This is the sense of the statement at hand: "As to the admonition, what need was there to go and repeat it?"*

Y. "And in that category we have only the instance of the prohibition of [meat containing] the sciatic nerve, *stated in accord with the view of R. Judah."*

Z. *But [circumcision and procreation] also were not repeated [at Sinai].* [Freedman, p. 403, n. 5: For ... their repetition being for a definite purpose is not a repetition at all.]

AA. [Freedman:] *These two were repeated, though for a purpose, but this [other item] was not repeated at all.*

BB. *[As to the question about stating the rule of circumcision to the Noahides and repeating it at Sinai], if you wish, I shall explain as follows:*

CC. *As to circumcision, to begin with it was addressed to Abraham by the All Merciful [and not to the children of Noah]:* "You shall keep my covenant therefore, you and your seed after you in their generations" (gen. 17:9) – you and your seed will do so, but others need not do so.

DD. *Then how about the sons of Ishmael? They too should be liable.*

EE. [Not so, for the verse states,] "For in Isaac shall your seed be called" (Gen. 21:22).

FF. *Then the children of Esau should be liable?*

	GG.	"In Isaac," but not all [descendants of] Isaac.

GG.   "In Isaac," but not all [descendants of] Isaac.

HH.   *R. Oshaia objected, "But how about the children of Keturah. They then should not be liable [to circumcise but they are liable to do so]."*

II.   *Has not R. Yosé bar Abin, and some say, R. Yosé bar Hanina, said, "'[And the uncircumcised child, the flesh of whose foreskin is not circumcised, that soul shall be cut off from his people;] he has broken my covenant' (Gen. 17:14) – serving to encompass the children of Keturah"?*

I.20   A.   Said R. Judah said Rab, "As to the first man, he was not permitted to eat meat.

B.   "For it is written, 'Therefore I have given you all the herbs], to you it shall be for food and to all the beasts of the earth' (Gen. 1:29-30) – [herbs], and the beasts of the earth shall not be for you [to eat].

C.   "And when the children of Noah came, [God] permitted [meat] to them.

D.   "For it is said, '[Every moving thing that lives shall be meat for you;] even as the green herb [now] have I given you all things' (Gen. 9:3).

E.   "Is it possible to suppose that the prohibition of cutting a limb from a living beast should not apply to [the children of Noah]?

F.   "Scripture says, 'But flesh with the life thereof, which is the blood thereof, you shall not eat' (Gen. 9:4).

G.   "Is it possible that the rule applies even to creeping things?

H.   "Scripture says, 'But' [implying a limitation on the applicability of the rule at hand]."

I.   *What is the basis of that conclusion?*

J.   Said R. Huna, "' ... the blood thereof ...' refers to a creature whose blood is distinct from the flesh. That then excludes creeping things, whose blood is not distinct from the flesh."

K.   *It was objected [to Rab's proposition about Adam as a vegetarian]:* "And rule over the fish of the sea" (Gen. 1:28): *Is this not for purposes of eating?*

L.   *No, it is for purposes of work.*

M.   *And do fish work?*

N.   *Indeed so, in accord with the inquiry of Rahbah. For Rahbah raised the question, "If one drove a wagon with a goat and a* <u>shibbuta</u>-*fish [would this involve a violation of the rule not to plow with an ox and an ass together, Deut. 22:10]?"*

O.   *Come and take note:* " ... and over the fowl of the heaven" (Gen. 1:28): *Is this not for the purposes of eating?*

P.   *No, it is for purposes of work.*

Q.   *And do fowl work?*

R.   *Indeed so, in accord with the inquiry of Rabbah b. R. Huna, "If one has threshed [grain] using geese or cocks, in the view of R. Yosé b. R. Judah [who rules on Deut. 25:4, not muzzling the ox while it treads out grain], what is the rule?"*

S.   *Come and take note:* "... and over every wild beast that crawls on the earth" (Gen. 1:28): *That statement serves to encompass even the snake.*

T.   *It is in line with that which has been taught on Tannaite authority:*

U. R. Simeon b. Menassia says, "Woe for the valuable servant that has perished from the earth. For had the snake not been cursed, every Israelite would have assigned to him two valuable snakes. One would he send to the north and one he would send to the south, to bring back to him gemstones, precious stones, and pearls. And not only so, but they should tie a strap under its tail, with which it would produce earth for the gardens and untilled ground [of the Israelites]."

V. *An objection was raised [to the foregoing claim that Adam was not permitted to eat meat]:* R. Judah b. Tema would say, "The first man reclined in the Garden of Eden, and the ministering angels roasted meat for him and strained wine for him. The snake looked in and saw all of this glory [that was coming to Adam] and envied him."

W. That refers to meat that came down from heaven.

Y. *And is there such a thing as meat that comes down from heaven?*

Z. *Indeed so, in line with the following:* R. Simeon b. Halafta was *walking along the way. Lions met him and growled at him. He cited the verse,* "The young lions roar for prey" *(Ps. 104:21). Two pieces of meat came down [from him]. One they ate, the other they left. He took it along and came to the school house. He asked about it, "Is this an unclean thing or is it a clean [and edible] one?"*

AA. They said to him, "Nothing unclean comes down from heaven."

DD. R. Zira asked R. Abbahu, *"If something came down from heaven in the form of an ass, what is the law?"*

EE. *He said to him, "You screeching jackal! Lo, they have said to him, 'Nothing unclean comes* down from heaven.'"

I.21 A. **R. Simeon says, "Also witchcraft [is forbidden to the children of Noah]" [T. A.Z. 8:6M]:**

B. *What is the scriptural basis for the view of R. Simeon?*

C. *It accords with what is written in Scripture:* **[60A]** "You shall not permit a witch to live" (Ex. 22:17), and thereafter: "Whoever lies with a beast shall surely be put to death" (Ex. 22:18). Whoever falls into the category of "whoever lies with a beast" [thus including the children of Noah] falls into the category of "You shall not permit a witch to live."

I.22 A. **R. Eleazar says, "Also as to mixed seeds" [T. A.Z. 8:8A]:**

B. *What is the scriptural basis for this position?*

C. Said Samuel, "Scripture states, 'You shall keep my statutes ... ' (Lev. 19:19), meaning the statutes that I have already ordained for you, hence: 'You shall not let your cattle gender with a diverse kind; you shall not sow your field with mixed seed' (Lev. 19:19).

D. "Just as for your beast, the prohibition is against hybridization, so in respect to your field, the prohibition is against hybridization.

E. "Just as the prohibition applies to your beast whether in the Land or outside of the Land, so with respect to your field, the prohibition applies whether it is in the Land or outside of the Land."

F. Then how do you deal with the following:

G. "You shall therefore keep my statutes" (Lev. 18:26)? *Does this too refer to statutes that I have already ordained? [In that case the children of Noah have to keep all the commandments.]*

H.   *There it means,* "You shall keep my statutes [which I already have given]". *Here,* "You shall keep my statutes" – *meaning, statutes which to begin with [I now give] you shall keep.* [The version of Lev. 19:19 places "statutes" first in the verse, that is, those already in hand, but in Lev. 18:26, "You shall keep" comes first, so "the statutes that follow" are beginning at that point (Freedman, p. 407, n. 1)].

II.1   A.   **Said R. Joshua b. Qorha ... [M. 7:5B]:**

B.   Said R. Aha bar Jacob, "One is liable only if he curses the name made up of four letters, *thus excluding a name made up of two letters, which is not subject to a curse [and use of which is not punishable]."*

C.   *That is self-evident, since we have learned in the Mishnah:* **May Yosé smite Yosé [M. 7:5B]** [in which "Yosé" stands for the four-lettered name of God].

D.   *What might you have supposed? That the framer of the passage chose a phrase at random? So we are informed that that is not the case [and Yosé stands for the four-lettered name of God].*

E.   *There are those who report as follows:*

F.   Said R. Aha bar Jacob, "That implies that the four-lettered name of God also falls into the category of a name of God."

G.   *That is self-evident. Have we not learned in the Mishnah,* **May Yosé smite Yosé [M. 7:5B]?**

H.   *What might you have supposed? That the penalty for cursing God applies only if one makes use of the great name of God [containing forty-two letters], and the framer of the passage has chosen a phrase at random?*

I.   *So we are informed that that is not the case.*

III.1   A.   **Once the trial is over [M. 7:5C]:**

B.   *How do we know that* **[the judges] rise to their feet [M. 7:5E]?**

C.   Said R. Isaac bar Ammi, "Scripture has said, 'And Ehud came to him, and he was sitting in a summer room, which he had for himself alone, and Ehud said, I have a message from God to you. And he rose out of his seat' (Judges 3:20).

D.   "Now is it not an argument a fortiori? If Eglon, king of Moab, who was a gentile and knew God only by a nickname, rose up, in the case of an Israelite, involving the Ineffable Name, now much the more so!?

E.   And how do we know that **they tear their clothing [M. 7:5E]?**

F.   From the following: "Then came Eliakim, the son of Hiliah, who was superintendent of the household, and Shebna the scribe, and Joah the son of Asaph the recorder, to Hezekiah, with their clothes torn, and told them the words of Rab-Shakeh" (2 Kgs. 18:37).

IV.1   A.   **And never sew them back up [M. 7:5E]:**

B.   *How do we know this?*

C.   *Said R. Abbahu, "We derive an analogy on the basis of the use of the word 'tear.' Here it says,* 'With their clothes torn' (2 Kgs. 18:37). *And elsewhere it is said,* 'And Elisha saw [Elijah's ascension] and he cried, My father, my father, the chariot of Israel and the horsemen thereof.' And he saw him no more; and he took hold of his own clothes and tore in them two shreds' (2 Kgs. 2:12). *Since it says,* 'tore them in two,' *would I not know that they were shreds? Why* then does Scripture specify, 'tears'? It teaches that they were to remain torn forever."

IV.2 A. *Our rabbis have taught on Tannaite authority:*

B. All the same are the one who actually hears [the blasphemy] and the one who hears it from the one who heard it. Both are liable to tear their garments.

C. But the witnesses are not liable to tear their garments, for they already did so at the moment when they heard the original blasphemy.

D. But if they did so at the moment when they heard the original blasphemy, *what difference does that make? Lo, they are now hearing it again!*

E. *Do not let that argument enter your mind, for it is written,* "And it came to pass, when King Hezekiah heard it, that <u>he</u> tore his clothes? (2 Kgs. 18:37).

F. King Hezekiah tore his clothes, but they did not tear their clothes.

IV.3 A. Said R. Judah said Samuel, "He who hears the name of God [blasphemed] by an idolator does not have to tear his clothes, whose blasphemy the king and court tore their clothes], in point of fact, he was an Israelite apostate.

B. And R. Judah said Samuel said, "People tear their clothes only on account of the four-lettered name of God [used as a curse]."

C. *That then would exclude hearing a euphemism, on account of which one does not [tear clothes].*

D. *And this differs from the view of R. Hiyya in two matters.*

E. For R. Hiyya said, "He who hears the name of God blasphemed these days is not liable to tear his clothes, for if you do not take that position, it will result that peoples' entire garments will be full of rents [Freedman: one's garments would be reduced to tatters]."

F. *Now from whom [would one hear these curses]? Should you say that it is from Israelites, are the Israelites so wanton?*

G. *Rather, it is clear that he assumes the curses come from idolators.*

H. *And if you should propose that what they are saying is that four-lettered name of God, do they know it?*

I. *Does it not, rather mean, that they curse by using a euphemism?*

J. *And it further follows that he speaks of the present age, in which one is not liable, but in olden times, one was liable.*

K. *That proves it.*

V.1 A. **And the second witness says, "Also I heard what he heard" [M. 7:5F]:**

B. Said R. Simeon b. Laqish, "It follows from this rule that the language, 'Also I heard what he heard,' is valid in property cases as well as in capital cases.

C. *"But rabbis imposed a stricter rule [in requiring each witness to speak for himself]. But here, because it is not possible [to allow the second to repeat what the first has said], rabbis established the practice as permitted by the law of the Torah. For if it should enter your mind that this is an invalid mode of testimony, then merely on account of the notion that it is not possible [to do things otherwise], are we going to put a man to death? [Surely not.]"*

VI.1   A.   **And the third witness says, "Also I heard what he heard" [M. 7:5G]:**

        B.   *The unattributed statement at hand accords with the principle of R. Aqiba, who treats three witnesses as equivalent to two.*

I.1, II.1ff., serve as Mishnah-exegesis. A large composite on the Noahide commandments is then inserted on account of the issue of whether gentiles who curse God are punished on that account. One of the seven Noahide commandments was to refrain from blasphemy. The cited passage of Tosefta then is subjected to a systematic analysis in what follows. I can think of no more persuasive evidence that the entire construction represents a compositor's theory of how matters should be compiled and arranged. Once we deal with the Tosefta-passage, we proceed to follow up each of its elements. The topic of the Noahide commandments draws in its wake interest in the rights and obligations of gentiles in general, as well as in the status of the first man. So, in all, we have what elsewhere might fill up half a chapter of Talmud, all composed in a rather orderly way and inserted whole on a rather trivial pretext. As a subdivision, however, we can readily explain the flow of argument and therefore the rather solid logic of composition.

7:6

    A.   **[60B] He who performs an act of worship for an idol [M. 7:4D] –**

    B.   **all the same are the one who performs an act of service, who [actually] sacrifices, who offers up incense, who pours out a libation offering, who bows down,**

    C.   **and the one who accepts it upon himself as a god, saying to it, "You are my god."**

    D.   **But the one who hugs, it, kisses it, polishes it, sweeps it, and washes it,**

    E.   **anoints it, puts clothing on it, and puts shows on it, [merely] transgresses a negative commandment [Ex. 20:5].**

    F.   **He who takes a vow in its name, and he who carries out a vow made in its name transgress a negative commandment [Ex. 23:13].**

    G.   **He who uncovers himself to Baal Peor [is stoned, for] this is how one performs an act of service to it.**

    H.   **He who tosses a pebble at Merkolis [Hermes] [is stoned, for] this is how one performs an act of service to it.**

I.1   A.   *What is the meaning of* **all the same are the one who performs an act of service** [M. 7:5B]?

    B.   *Said R. Jeremiah, "This is the sense of the passage:* All the same are the one who performs an act of service in the proper manner, [and] the one who sacrifices, the one who offers incense, the one who pours out a libation, and the one who bows down, even if [these other actions] are not the usual way [in which this particular statue is worshipped]."

C.   *And why not take account, also, of tossing blood [of an animal to the god]?*

D.   *Said Abbayye, "'Tossing blood' falls into the category of a libation. For it is written,* 'Their drink libations of blood will I not offer' (Ps. 16:4). [So it is covered.]"

I.2   A.   *What is the biblical source [for the fact that these acts of worship impose guilt]?*

B.   *It is in accord with what our rabbis have taught on Tannaite authority:*

C.   If Scripture had stated, "He who sacrifices shall be utterly destroyed" (Ex. 22:19) [without adding the words, "to any god,"] I might have reached the concussion that Scripture speaks of one who sacrifices Holy Things outsides of the Temple.

D.   Accordingly, Scripture states, " ... to any gods," indicating that Scripture speaks of any sort of idolatry.

E.   I know only that penalty applies to one who sacrifices. How do I know that there is a penalty for offering incense, making a libation offering [and the like]?

F.   Scripture says, " ... except to the Lord alone" (Ex. 22:19), by which Scripture limited these forms of worship [regarding them as legitimate only when performed] for the divine name.

G.   Now since there is specific reference to "sacrificing," supplying an analogy to all other acts of service that are performed within the Temple, how do I know that subject to the same prohibition of worship of other gods is an act of prostration? [That is, Deut. 17:2-5 refers to various acts of service in general. Ex. 22:19 speaks of sacrifice in particular. So one particular act of service is specified among the many covered by Deut. 17:3, thus defining what falls into that latter category by means of analogy to what is specified in the former. Whatever bears the traits of the specific items then falls into its category (Freedman, p. 411, n. 9).]

H.   [To encompass prostration, not performed in the Temple as part of an act of service], Scripture says, "And he went and served other gods and prostrated himself before them" (Deut. 17:3), followed by, "You shall bring forth that man or that woman and you shall stone them with stones" (Deut. 17:4).

I.   We have thereby derived evidence of the penalty for that action. How do we know to begin with that there is an admonition against doing it?

J.   Scripture states, "For you shall not prostrate yourself to any other god" (Ex. 34:14).

K.   Might I think that subject to the same rule are such actions as embracing the idol, kissing it, or putting on its shows [so that these acts too should be subject to the death penalty]?

L.   Scripture says, "He who sacrifices ... " (Ex. 22:19).

M.   The act of sacrifice was included in the general rule [specified at Deut. 17:2ff.], and why was it singled out? It was to draw an analogy on the basis of that action and to indicate that, just as the act of sacrifice is distinctive in that it is an act of service performed within the Temple, and it is an act of service on account of which people are liable to the death penalty [should they violate its taboos], so any act of service [performed for an idol] which is analogous to one that is carried on within the Temple and produces the death-penalty, is encompassed, thus excluding such actions as prostrating oneself to the idol.

N. Prostration, accordingly, was singled out to testify to itself, while the act of sacrifice was singled out to impart its traits on all those actions that would fall into its category.

I.3 A. A master has said, "I might have reached the conclusion that Scripture speaks of one who sacrifices Holy Things outside of the Temple [rather than of idolatry]."

B. But one who sacrifices Holy Things outside of the Temple is subject to the penalty of extirpation [while in the passage at hand, the penalty is death, so how could someone have reached such a conclusions?]

C. *It might have entered your mind to maintain that if people gave him a warning, he is subject to a death penalty [as Scripture states], while if they did not give him a warning, he is subject to extirpation [in which case the passage could well speak of sacrificing Holy Things outside of the cult, not sacrificing to an idol].*

D. *So we are informed that that is not the case.*

I.4 A. *Said Raba bar R. Hanan to Abbayye, "Might I say that* prostration is subjected to explicit discussion to impose its traits on the general rule at hand [as against the view that claims prostration was singled out to testify to its own traits, not to impose its traits on the definition of other culpable actions]?

B. *"And should you propose to reply that, in that case, why was the act of sacrifice singled out, my answer is that it was to make a point about itself.*

C. *"Specifically we take account of the intention that a priest forms while performing one act of sacrifice, namely, one for God, to carry out that act of sacrifice with the intention of serving an idol.* [That is, by referring at the passage at hand to an act of sacrifice, Scripture makes this point: If one is offering a beast to God and forms the intention of sprinkling its blood for the sake of an idol, that improper intention is taken into account and the priest is subject to punishment, even though the one sacrifice is to God and the other is to an idol.]

D. *"For it has been taught on Amoraic authority:*

E. "He who slaughters a beast, forming the intention of tossing its blood in honor of an idol and burning its fat in honor of an idol [even if he then properly slaughtered the beast with appropriate intent and did not sprinkle the blood or burn the fat in honor of an idol, so that the original, improper intent, is not actually effected in a concrete deed at all],

F. "R. Yohanan said, **[61A]** 'The carcass of the beast [thereafter] is forbidden [because of the original, improper intent. He thus invokes the rule that applies to an offering made with improper intent for the sake of God and applies it equally to an offering made with improper intent for the sake of an idol.]'

G.   "And R. Simeon b. Laqish said, 'The carcass of the beast is permitted.'

H.   *"[Now, to continue Raba bar R. Hanan's question,] there is no problem from the viewpoint of R. Yohanan.* [Freedman, p. 413, n. 2: Since Yohanan draws an analogy in respect to the animal itself, he can apply the same analogy to the offender. That is, an idolatrous intention in respect of one service is punishable, even though made in another act. Consequently, if prostration was singled out in order to illumine the entire law, the special statement of sacrificing is superfluous. Hence we are forced to the conclusion that prostration was singled out only for itself].

I.   *"But from the viewpoint of R. Simeon b. Laqish, the verse of Scripture is required [to prove the point at hand, that prostration was singled out in order to throw light upon the general law].* [Freedman, p. 413, n. 3: Since Simeon b. Laqish does not accept the analogy, we can argue thus: prostration was singled out to illumine the whole. Sacrificing was singled out to teach that though an unlawful intention in respect of one act of service made in the course of another does not affect the animal's fitness for use, it is nevertheless punishable.]"

J.   *R. Pappa raised an objection, "And from the viewpoint of R. Yohanan, is there no need for a verse of Scripture? One might argue that R. Yohanan to be sure imposes a prohibition on use of the carcass of the beast, but the man who forms the improper intention is not liable to be put to death. Then the verse comes along [and is needed] to impose upon him the liability to the death penalty."*

K.   *R. Aha, son of R. Iqa, objected, "And from the viewpoint of R. Simeon b. Laqish, is a verse of necessary actually required for the stated purpose at all?*

L.   *"So far as R. Simeon b. Laqish rules that it is permitted, that ruling applies only to the use of the carcass of the beast. But as to the status of the man who has formed the improper intention, he assuredly is subject to the death penalty.*

M.   *"In this ruling, then, there would be a parallel to the case of one who prostrates himself to a mountain. The mountain remains permitted [for ordinary use and enjoyment] but the one who worships it nonetheless is put to death through decapitation."*

N.   *Said R. Aha of Difti to Rabina, "Now let us take up the question of Raba, bar R. Hanan, to Abbayye, 'Might I say that prostration is subjected to explicit discussion to impose its traits on the general rule at hand?'*

O.   *"[If so,] then as to the verse, '[Take heed to yourself ... that you do not seek after their gods, saying,] How did these nations serve their gods? [Even so I will do the same]' (Deut. 12:30) [A verse that implies that only the normal way of serving these gods is forbidden],* what acts of service are excluded by the cited verse? [For if we claim that prostration serves to indicate that even acts of service outside of the Temple are punished, then what further acts are forbidden by the verse at hand? We already know the point that it evidently wishes to make (Freedman, pp. 413-4, n. 5)].

P.   *"And should you say that it serves to exclude the act of showing one's behind to those idols that are ordinarily served by having sacrifices made to them, that point derives, in fact, from the reference to prostration.*

Q.   *"Just as prostration is an act of honoring the idol, so every act that is interpreted as an honor [would be punished, thus excluding showing one's behind to the idol]."*

R.   [The reply:] Rather, it serves to exclude one who shows his behind to a statue of Mercury.

S.   *You might have thought that one should rule, since its appropriate act of worship is an act of disgrace, so some other act of disgrace falls into the same category]and is punishable]. So we are informed that that is not the case.*

T.   Then what about the statement of R. Eliezer: "How do we know that one who sacrifices a beast to Mercury is liable? For it is said, 'They shall not more offer their sacrifices to demons' (Lev. 17:7)"?

U.   Now if it cannot speak of a mode of worship that is the ordinary and accepted one, since it is already stated, 'How did these nations serve their gods …' (Deut. 12:30) [proving that routine modes of worship are penalized if done for idols], apply it to an unusual mode of worship of those gods. [In that case, such an abnormal mode of worship is subject to punishment.]"

V.   [Reverting to Raba's thesis that the reference to prostration imposes the traits of that action on all others, with the result that abnormal modes of worship are punishable], surely an act of worship not in accord with the usual procedure would derive from the reference to prostration [and we know from that reference that such an act is punishable. We do not need to provide the proof that Eliezer gives. Would then Eliezer's proof not show therefore that Raba's thesis is wrong?'

W.   The verse at hand proves that one who makes a sacrifice [to Mercury] merely for spite [to God] [without regarding Mercury as a god] [nonetheless is subject to penalty.] [So Raba's question is not obviated by the proof at hand and valid.]

I.5   A.   *R. Hamnuna's oxen got lost on him. [While searching for them] he met Rabbah and laid out for him two passages of the Mishnah which he deemed to contradict one another: "We have learned in the Mishnah:* **he who performs an act of worship for an idol [M. 7:6A],** *meaning that if he actually performed such an act, he is [liable] but if he merely said, 'I shall do it,' he is not liable. But we have also learned in the Mishnah:* **He who says, 'I am going to worship,' 'I shall go and worship,' 'Let's go and worship' [M. 7:10N].** *[This bears the implication that merely saying, not doing, also is penalized.]"*

      B.   He said to him, "The former passage speaks of one who says, 'I shall not accept it upon me as a god until I perform an act of worship' [so that passage, too, speaks of incurring liability only by making a statement]."

C. *Said R. Joseph, "You have simply taken views at random of two Tannaite authorities [and not all Tannaite authorities are in agreement]. It is, in point of fact, a dispute among Tannaite authorities. For it has been taught on Tannaite authority:'*

D. He who says, "Come and worship me" –

E. R. Meir declares him liable [for enticing people to commit idolatry].

F. And R. Judah declares him exempt.

G. *But in a case of their actually bowing down [to that man], all parties concur, for it is said, "You shall not make for yourself any idol" (Ex. 20:4). [Freedman, p. 415, n. 1: Hence, since they worshipped him, he is guilty as a seducer to idolatry]. Where there is a dispute, it concerns a case in which what is involved is merely a statement. R. Meir takes the view that a mere statement is consequential [and hence one is liable on that account, as a M. 7:10N], and R. Judah maintains that a mere statement is null [in lines with M. 7:6A].*

H. *[Having made reference to the present dispute], R. Joseph retracted and said, "What I said is of no consequence, for even R. Judah concurs that a mere statement may well impose liability [without its being accompanied by a concrete action]. For it has been taught on Tannaite authority:*

I. "R. Judah says, 'Under no circumstances is one liable until he says, **"I am going to worship," "I shall go and worship," "Let's go and worship" [M. 7:10N].]** [This would then concur with Meir's position, that a statement without action in the matter of incitement to idolatry is penalized.]

J. *"At issue in the dispute [between Meir and Judah] is a case in which* he incited others to worship him himself, and the people replied that they would do so.

K. *"One party maintains that if one incites people to worship himself, the others do pay attention to him, and when they said 'Yes,' they were telling the truth [and so, Meir holds, he is liable]. The other party takes the view that when one incites people to worship himself, they do not pay attention to him, for people say,* '**[61B]** *what difference is there between him and us?' So when they say 'Yes,' they [are not telling the truth but] making fun of him. Now [to reconcile the two versions of the law], the Mishnah-rule refers [at M. 7:10N] to an individual who is reenticed to commit idolatry, while the one at hand refers to a community that was enticed to commit idolatry. Since an individual will not change his mind, he will certainly go in error after [the seducer to idolatry] [and hence the mere statement matters, as at M. 7:10N], but the community as a whole will surely change their minds and not go in error after him [hence the mere statement does not matter at M. 7:6A]."*

L. *Said R. Joseph, "How do I know that [a mere statement attempting to incite an individual, not accompanied by a concrete deed, brings a penalty in the case of an individual]? As it is written, "[If your brother ... entice you ...], you shall not consent to him nor hearken to him' (Deut. 13:9). Lo, if one had consented and hearkened to him, he would be liable."*

M. *To this proof, Abbayye objected, "And is there any difference between a case in which an individual is enticed and a case in which the community is enticed [to idolatry]? Has it not been taught on Tannaite authority:*

N.   "'If your brother, son of your mother, entice you' (Deut. 13:7) – all the same is the case in which an individual is enticed and the case in which the community is enticed.

O.   "But the Scripture has made particular reference to an individual, as distinct from the community, and to the community, as distinct from the individual.

P.   "The reason that the individual is singled out from the community is so as to impose a strict penalty on the man's body and a lenient penalty on his property [which, in the case of an entire community, is destroyed along with the individual].

Q.   *"The reason that the community is distinguished from the individual is to impose a lenient rule on the penalty applicable to their bodies] since they are decapitated, not stoned] but a more strict penalty on their property [which is destroyed].*

R.   *"Now [Abbayye continues], it is in that particular aspect that the case of the individual and that of the community are distinguished from one another. In all other aspects they are identical to one another, [and hence the proposed distinction of Joseph is null]."*

S.   Rather, said Abbayye, "The one passage speaks of one who is enticed to commit idolatry by what he himself says, the other passage speaks of one who is enticed to commit idolatry by what someone else says. *In the case of one who is enticed by what he himself says, he may change his mind [so that he actually does something, he is not subject to a penalty], but if he is enticed by what some else says, he will follow the other [and so is not likely to change his mind, so he is penalized for what he says, without actually doing a thing]."*

T.   *Said Abbayye, "How do I know it? Because it is written, '*You shall not consent to him nor hearken to him' (Deut. 13:9). Lo, if one consented and hearkened [by agreeing with what a third party had to say], he is liable."

U.   *Raba said, "Both this passage and that passage refer to a case of one who is enticed by what someone else says. The one speaks of a case in which one has said to him, 'This is what it it eats, this is what it drinks, this is the good it does, this is the bad it does.' The other passage speaks of a case in which one has not said to him, 'This is what it eats, this is what it drinks, and so on.'* [If one does not make the second set of statements, the hearer may reconsider, so we impose punishment only when he actually does an act of worship (Freedman, p. 416, n. 5).]"

V.   *Said Raba, "How do I know it? As it is written, '*[If your brother entice you ... saying, let us go and serve other gods ...,] namely, of the gods of the people who are round about you, near to you or far from you' (Deut. 13:8). *What difference does it make to me whether they are near or far? But this is what he said to him, 'From the quality of the ones that are near, you may learn the quality of those that are far.' Does this then not refer to a case in which one said to him, '*This is what it eats, this is what it drinks, this is the good that it does, this is the bad that it does'?"

W.   *That indeed proves the case.*

Y.   *R. Ashi said, "The latter of the two passages of the Mishnah refers to an Israelite apostate [who is punished merely for what he says, not for what he does, since we assume he will do what he says. A loyal Israelite may change his mind.]"*

Z.   *Rabina said, The two passages mean to indicate 'not only this but even that.'* [Freedman, p. 417, n. 4: The first Mishnah-Passage states that the death penalty is imposed for engaging in idol worship; the second adds that this is so not only for actually worshipping idols but also for the mere statement of intention.]"

I.6 A.   *It has been stated on Amoraic authority:*

B.   He who does an act of worship for an idol, whether from love or from fear,

C.   Abbayye said, "He is liable."

D.   Raba said, "He is exempt."

E.   *Abbayye said, "He is liable, for lo, he has worshipped it."*

F.   *Raba said, "He is exempt. If he had accepted it upon himself as a god, he would be liable, but if not, he would not be liable."*

G.   *Said Abbayye, "And on what basis do I take this position? It is in accord with what we have learned in the Mishnah:* **He who performs an act of worship for an idol – all the same are the one who performs an act of service, etc. [M. 7:6A-B].** *Does this not mean, "All the same are he who worships out of love and he who worships out of fear'?"*

H.   *And Raba will tell you, "No, it is as R. Jeremiah has explained matters [at I A-C]."*

I.   *Said Abbayye, "And on what basis do I take this position? For it has been taught on Tannaite authority:*

J.   "'You shall not prostrate yourself to them" (Ex. 20:5) –

K.   "'To them you may not prostrate yourself, but you may prostrate yourself to a man such as yourself.

L.   "'Is it possible that one may do so even to one who is worshipped like Haman?

M.   "'Scripture says, "You will not worship them" (Ex. 20:5).'

N.   "Now Haman was worshipped on account of fear. [So, it follows, one may not worship an idol whether from love or fear, and even though one has not accepted it upon himself as a god.]"

O.   *And [what is] Raba's [view]? [He maintains that one may not bow down to one] like Haman or not like Haman: One may not bow down to one like Haman, because he himself was an idol. And not like Haman, because Haman was worshipped on account of fear, while the verse at hand speaks of worship not on account of fear.*

P.   *Said Abbayye, "And on what basis do I take this position? For it has been taught on Tannaite authority:*

Q.   "'As to the case of an anointed high priest who has unwittingly worshipped an idol,

R.   "'Rabbi says, "[He is liable] if the action was done inadvertently."

S.   "'And sages say, "He is liable only if the very principle [that one may not worship an idol] was forgotten by him." [The high priest is liable for entire ignorance that the prohibition against idolatry exists, not merely for inadvertently doing the action while knowing it should not be done.]

T.   "'And they concur that so far as his sacrifice in atonement is concerned, it is a she-goat, just as is brought by an individual.

U.   "'And they further concur that he does not have to bring a suspensive guilt-offering.'

V.   *"Now as to inadvertently carrying out an act of idolatry, what sort of action can have been contemplated?* If [the high priest] inadvertently imagined that [a temple] was a synagogue and he prostrated himself to the [idol's temple] on that account, then his heart was directed to heaven [and there is no sin here at all]. *Rather, we deal with a case in which he saw a statue of a man and prostrated himself to it. Now is he had accepted the idol as his god, then what he did was deliberate [and does not fall into the present category at all].* **[62A]** *If he did not accept the idol as his god, then what he did was null.* Rather, is it not a case in which it was done out of love and dear [Freedman, p. 419, n. 4: without knowing that this is idol worship. This constitutes inadvertency in respect of the action, but not forgetfulness or ignorance of the law, since he knows that idolatry per se is forbidden. Hence the passage supports Abbayye's ruling.]"

W.   And Raba? He will say to you, "Is it not a case in which the man says that it is permitted [to carry out such an act]?"

X.   But if it is a case in which the man says that it is permitted to carry out such an act, what we have is nothing other than a situation in which the very principle that idolatry per se is forbidden has been forgotten.

Y.   The present passage speaks of a case in which the person holds that it is entirely permitted to carry out such an action, while a case in which the principle that the act is prohibited is forgotten deals with a matter in which part of the action is to be carried out and part not carried out. [Freedman, p. 419, n. 5: If the priest declares that sacrificing and offering incense to idols are forbidden but prostration is permitted, that is called ignorance of the law; if he declares that idolatry is not prohibited at all, in Raba's opinion it is regarded as inadvertency of action.]

I.7   A.   *R. Zakkai repeated on Tannaite authority before R. Yohanan,* "If a person sacrificed, burned incense, poured out a libation, and prostrated himself [to an idol] in one spell of inadvertence [not knowing that any form of service to an idol is forbidden], he is liable on only one count."

B.   *He said to him, "Go and repeat this in public."*

C.   *Said R. Abba, "That which R. Zakkai has stated in point of fact represents a dispute between R. Yosé and R. Nathan.*

D.   *"For it has been taught on Tannaite authority:*

E.   "'The prohibition of lighting a fire [on the Sabbath, which is covered under the general prohibition not to work on the Sabbath, Ex. 20:10, and did not require specification], was singled out so as to indicate that it is [merely] a negative [commandment],' the words of R. Yosé.

F.   "R. Nathan says, 'It was singled out to signify that it is treated as distinct [from other actions, so showing that, overall, if on the Sabbath in a single spell of inadvertence one carried out a number of prohibited actions, he is liable on each count, and not solely on the single count covering all of them.]' [This would place Zakkai in Yosé's position, with Nathan rejecting the basic principle.]

G. *"From the viewpoint of him who has said that the specific reference to kindling a flame was to indicate that that commandment was simply a negative one, the specific reference to prostration before an idol serves the same purpose, namely to place that act into the category of a negative commandment.*

H. *"In the viewpoint of him who has said that the explicit prohibition of kindling a flame served to show that one is liable on each count of a number of actions in violation of the Sabbath done in a single spell of inadvertence, the same principle applies to the act of prostration, also singled out, so that if one does a number of distinct actions of service to an idol in a single spell of inadvertence, he is liable on each count."*

I. *To this proposition R. Joseph objected, "But it may well be that R. Yosé maintains that the specific reference to kindling a fire was made so as to place that act in the category of a negative commandment only because he is able to prove the other principle on the strength of a different proof-text altogether. Specifically, the fact that one should make distinctions among other acts of labor on the Sabbath [and impose liability for each one when many of them are done in a single spell of inadvertence] derives, in his view, from the verse, ' ... of one of them ...' (Lev. 4:2).*

J. *"For it has been taught on Tannaite authority:*

K. *"R. Yosé says, '"[If a soul shall sin through ignorance against any of the commandments of the Lord, concerning things which ought not to be done,] and shall do one of them (Lev. 4:2) indicates that there are occasions on which is liable on one count for all actions, and there are occasions on which one is liable for each act individually.'"*

L. *"And R. Jonathan said, 'What is the scriptural basis for R. Yosé's view? It is because it is written, "and shall do of one of them" (Lev. 4:2).'"* [Freedman, p. 421, n. 3: This is a peculiar construction. The Scripture should have written, 'and shall do one (not of) of them,' or, 'and do of them' (one being understood), or, 'and shall do one' (of them being understood). Instead of which, a partitive preposition is used before each. Hence each part of the pronoun is t o be interpreted separately, teaching that he is liable for the transgression of 'one' precept; and for part of one (i.e., for 'of one'): for 'them' (explained as referring to the principal acts); and for the derivatives 'of them' (acts forbidden because they partake of the same nature as the fundamentally prohibited acts); also, each pronoun reacts upon the other, as explained in the discussion.]

M. [What follows, to the end of this paragraph, is Freedman's translation, pp. 423-425, reproduced with only minor changes:] This teaches that liability is incurred for one complete act of violation [i.e., 'one']; and for one which is but a part of one [i.e., 'of one']; and for transgressing actions forbidden in themselves [i.e., 'them'], and for actions [the prohibited nature of which is derived] from others [i.e., 'of them']; further, that open transgression may involve liability for a number of sacrifices [i.e., 'one' = 'them'], whilst many offenses may involve but one sacrifice [i.e., 'them' = 'one']. Thus: 'one complete act of violation,' – the writing [on the Sabbath] of Simeon; 'one which is but a part of one,' – the writing of Shem as part of Simeon, 'actions forbidden in themselves' [i.e., 'them'] – the principal acts of labor forbidden on the Sabbath; 'actions [the prohibited nature of which is derived] from others [i.e., "of them"]' – the derivatives; 'one transgression may involve liability for a number of sacrifices [i.e., "one" = "them"] – e.g., if one knew that it was the Sabbath [and that some work is forbidden on the Sabbath], but was unaware that these particular acts are forbidden; 'many offenses may involve but one sacrifice [i.e., "them" = "one"]' – e.g., if he was unaware that it was the Sabbath, but knew that his actions are forbidden on the Sabbath. But here [in idol worship], since separation of actions is not derived from elsewhere, may we not say that all agree [even R. Yosé] that prostration was singled out to indicate 'separation'? [But this is so?] May not 'separation' of acts in the case of idolatry too be deduced from 'of one of them'? Thus, 'one complete act of idolatry' – sacrificing [to idols]; a part of one [i.e., 'of one'] – the cutting of one organ. 'Actions forbidden in themselves' [i.e., 'them'] – principal acts, i.e., sacrificing, burning, incense, making libations, and prostration; 'actions derived from others' [i.e., 'of them'] the derivatives of these – e.g., if he broke a stick before it; 'one transgression may involve liability for a number of sacrifices,' [i.e., 'one' = 'them'], e.g., when one knows that it is an idol [and that idolatry is forbidden], but is unaware that the particular acts in question constitute idol-worship; many offenses may involve but one sacrifice, [i.e., 'them' = 'one']; if he is unaware that it is an idol, but knows that these acts are forbidden in idol worship.

N.   *As to an act of idolatry done in inadvertence, how would it be defined?*

O.   *If one should suppose that he was worshipping a synagogue when he bowed down to [a temple of an idol], lo, his heart was directed to heaven.*

P.   *Rather, he saw a statue of a man and bowed down to it.*

Q.   *But if he had accepted it as a god, then what he did was a deliberate violation of the law.*

R.   *And if he had not accepted it as a god, then what he did was null.*

S.   *Hence what he did was out of love and fear.*

T.   *That poses no problems to Abbayye, who has held that one is liable on that account.*

U.   *But from the viewpoint of Raba, who has said that one is exempt, what is there to be said?*

V.   It is that the man maintained that it is permitted [to worship an idol]. [Freedman, p. 423, n. 6: Though this does not constitute unawareness that a particular thing is an idol worship, yet it is a case where many transgressions involve but one sacrifice.]

W.   *On that basis you may work out the problem posed by Raba to R. Nahman:* "If one is responsible for forgetting the principle of both [the Sabbath as a day on which labor is prohibited, and also that the given act of labor is prohibited on the Sabbath], what is the law?"

X.   *One may reach the conclusion that one is liable on only one count.* [Freedman, p. 424, n. 2: For if one declared that idolatry is permissible, it is as though he were unaware that a particular things was an idol. Hence if we deduce from the verse that in idolatry only one sacrifice is needed for such inadvertence, the same must apply to the Sabbath. At this stage of the discussion it is assumed, however, hat this deduction is impossible, as otherwise Raba would not have propounded his problem. Consequently the verse cannot be applied to idolatry, and Abba is justified in regarding kindling and prostration as interdependent both in interpretation and in the resultant laws and Zakkai's statement is admissible as correct – according to R. Yosé.]

Y. *That is no objection. If you can solve the problem, solve it. [What difference does it make?]*

Z. *But can you interpret the verse at hand to speak of idolatry? The cited verses speak of idolatry, while the verses under discussion concern sacrifices brought on account of the anointed priest, that is, a bullock; for the chief, a he-goat; and for an individual, a she-goat or lamb.*

AA. *In regard to idolatry, we have learned:* they concur that his sacrifice is a she-goat, as in the case of a private individual.

BB. *There is nothing further [to be said.* Freedman, p. 424, n. 8: Consequently this verse cannot teach separation of idolatrous actions.]

CC. *When R. Samuel bar Judah came, he said,* **[62B]** *"This is what [Zakkai] taught on Tannaite authority before [Yohanan]:* 'There is a more strict rule that applies to the Sabbath than applies to other religious duties, and there is a more strict rule that applies to other religious duties that does not apply to the Sabbath.

DD. "'For in the case of the Sabbath, if one has done two forbidden actions in a single spell of inadvertence, he is liable for each one separately, a rule that does not apply to other religious duties.

EE. "'The more strict rule applying to other religious duties is that if one has performed a forbidden action inadvertently, without prior intention, he is liable, which is not the rule for the Sabbath.'"

FF. A master has said, "In the case of the Sabbath, if one has done two forbidden actions ...":

GG. *How shall we illustrate that statement? If one should propose that a person did an act of reaping and one of grinding, then, in respect to other religious duties, it would be similar to eating both forbidden fat and blood. In such a case, one is liable on two counts, just as here he is liable on two counts.*

HH. *Then with respect to other religious duties, what sort of case would yield the result* that one is liable on only a single count?

II. *If one ate forbidden fat and then more forbidden fat.*

JJ. *In a parallel case involving the Sabbath it would be if one performed an act of reaping and then another act of reaping.*

KK. *In that case, however, in the one context [eating forbidden fat] he is liable on only one count, and in the other context, he also is liable on only one count.*

LL. *That is why [R. Yohanan] said to him, "Go and repeat your tradition outside."*

MM. *But what is the real problem at hand? Perhaps one may say to you that, as to the acts of reaping and grinding, subject to a rule distinct from other religious duties, the reference [to "other religious duties"] is specifically to idolatry, and it accords with what R. Ammi said.*

NN. For R. Ammi said, "If one has sacrificed, offered incense, and poured out a libation, all in a single spell of inadvertence, he is liable on only a single count," [while in the case of the Sabbath, as we see, one is liable on more than a single count].

OO.   *You cannot assign the statement only to idolatry, for the end of the same sentence reads:* "The more strict rule applying to other religious duties is that, if one has performed a forbidden action inadvertently, without prior intention, he is liable, which is not the rule for the Sabbath."

PP.   *Now what, in reference to idolatry, can possibly fall into the category of an action that has been performed inadvertently, without intention?*

QQ.   If one supposed that a temple of an idol was a synagogue and prostrated himself to it, lo, his heart was directed to heaven.

RR.   *Rather, he saw a statue of a man and bowed to it.*

SS.   *If, then, he accepted it as a god, what he did was done deliberately.*

TT.   *If he did not accept it as a god, then what he did was null.*

UU.   *Rather, what he did was out of love and awe.*

VV.   *That poses no problems to Abbayye, who has said that, in such a case, he is liable.*

WW.   *But as to the view of Raba, who has said that he is exempt, what is there to be said?*

XX.   Rather, it is one who has the view that such an action is permitted. [Freedman, p. 425, n. 3: And since he has never known of any prohibition, it is not regarded as unwitting, but as unintentional too.]

YY.   *Then this is what is not the case for the Sabbath, for, in a similar circumstance, one would not be liable at all.*

ZZ.   *[But surely that conclusion is not possible], for when Raba poses his question to R. Nahman as to the rule governing a single spell of inadvertence in each of the two contexts, it is only whether one is liable on one count or on two counts. But it never entered his mind that one would be entirely exempt from all liability.*

AAA.   *What difficulty is at hand? Perhaps one may say to you indeed that the first clause speaks of idolatry and the remainder of other religious duties.*

BBB.   *The case of inadvertence, without intention, would be one in which one had the view that [when he found there was forbidden fat in his mouth], he thought that it was spit and swallowed it [rather than spitting it out], a rule which, in a parallel case on the Sabbath, would produce the ruling of non-liability. [How so?] If one had the intention of lifting up something that was already harvested but turned out to cut something yet attached to the ground, he is exempt. [Freedman, p. 426, n. 2: Cutting or tearing out anything growing in the earth is a forbidden labor on the Sabbath. His offense was both unwitting and unintentional for (i) he had no intention of tearing out anything and (ii) he did not know that this was growing in the soil. Now, had he known that it was growing in he soil and deliberately uprooted it in ignorance of the forbidden nature of that action, his offense would have been unwitting but intentional. By analogy, had he intended to eat the melted fat, thinking that it was permitted, his offense would be regarded as unwitting but intentional. Since, however, he did not intend eating it at all, but accidently swallowed it, thinking at the same time that it was spittle, his offense was both unwitting and unintentional.]*

CCC.

This is in line with what R. Nahman said Samuel said, "He who gets involved with forbidden fat or consanguineous sexual relationships is liable, for he derived benefit from the act. [That is, if one planned to eat permitted fat but inadvertently ate forbidden fat, or planned to have sexual relations with his wife but inadvertently had them with his sister, he is liable.] If by contrast one was involved in a forbidden action on the Sabbath [and thereby did what he did not intend to do], he is exempt, for it is a deed involving full deliberation that the Torah has prohibited."

DDD.

R. Yohanan is consistent with his views expressed elsewhere, for he does not wish to apply one paragraph of a Mishnah-teaching to one circumstance, and a later paragraph to a difference circumstance." [We now have an example of that same approach of consistency.]

EEE.

For R. Yohanan said, "For whoever explains for me the Mishnah-paragraph of 'a barrel' in such a way that it accords with the position of a single Tannaite authority, I shall carry his clothes to the baths." [Freedman, p. 427, n. 2: This reference is to a Mishnah on B.M. 40b: If a barrel was entrusted to a man's keeping, a particular place being assigned to it, and this man moved it from the place where it was first set down, and it was broken – Now, where it was broken whilst he was handling it, then if he was moving it for his own purposes (e.g., to stand on it), he must pay for it; if for its sake (e.g, if it was exposed to harm in the first place), he is not liable. But if it was broken after he had set it down, then in both cases he is not liable. If the owner, however, had assigned a place to it, and this man moved it, and it was broken, whether whilst in his hand or after he had set it down: if he moved it for his sake, he is liable; if for its own, he is not. The Talmud then proceeds to explain that the first clause is in accordance with R. Ishmael, who maintained that if one stole an article and returned it without informing its owner, he is free from all further liability in respect of it. Consequently, if he moved the barrel for his own purpose (which is like stealing), and set it down elsewhere, no particular place being assigned to it, his liability have ceased. But the second clause agrees with R. Aqiba's ruling that if an article is stole and returned, the liability remains until the owner is informed of its return. Consequently, if he moved it for his own purpose, he remains liable even after it is set down. But R. Johanan was dissatisfied with this explanation, holding that both clauses should agree with one Tanna. Now, the Talmud does actually explain that it can agree with one Tanna, viz., by assuming that in the first clause the barrel was subsequently returned to its original place, but that in the second clause it was not. Consequently, it concurs entirely with R. Ishmael, but his liability continues in the second instance because he did not return it to its first place. But R. Johanan rejects this explanation, not deeming it plausible to conceive of such different circumstances in the two clauses of the Mishnah. For the same reason, when R. Zakkai taught that sometimes the Sabbath is more stringent than other precepts, and sometimes it is the reverse, R. Johanan would not accept an interpretation whereby 'other precepts' in the first clause means idolatry, whilst in the second it referred to forbidden fat.]

FFF.   *Returning to the body of the text just now cited:*

GGG.   **[63A]** Said R. Ammi, "If one sacrificed to an idol, burned incense, and poured out a libation to it, in a single spell of inadvertence, he is liable on only a single count."

HHH.   *Said Abbayye, "What is the scriptural basis for the view of R. Ammi? '[You shall not bow down to them] nor serve them' (Ex. 20:5), by which formulation Scripture has treated all of them as a single act of service."*

III.   *But did Abbayye make such a statement?*

JJJ.   And has not Abbayye said, "Why is reference in three settings made to the prohibition of bowing down for an idol [at Ex. 20:5]?

KKK.   "One covers doing so in the proper way, one covers doing so not in the proper way, and the third serves to impose a distinct liability for each act of doing so [so that if one does so three times in a single spell of inadvertence, he is liable on three counts]"?

LLL.   *[Abbayye's statement] was in fact a report of R. Ammi's viewpoint, but [Abbayye] does not concur with that viewpoint.*

MMM.   *Returning to the text just now cited:*

NNN.   Said Abbayye, "Why is reference made to the prohibition of bowing down for an idol in three settings [at Ex. 20:5]? One covers doing so in the proper way, one covers doing so not in the proper way, and the third serves to impose a distinct liability for each act of doing so."

OOO.   *But as to doing so in the proper way, is this not derived from the verse, "[How did these nations serve their gods? Even so will I do likewise]" (Deut. 12:30)?*

PPP.   Rather: "one of the references to prostration deals with a case in which one worships the idol in a normal but somewhat unusual way, one deals with the case in which one worships it not in its normal way at all, and the third serves to impose a distinct liability for each act of doing so."

II.1   A.   **The one who accepts it upon himself as a god, saying to it, "You are my god" [M. 7:6C]:**

B. Said R. Nahman said Rabbah bar Abbuha said Rab, "Once one has said to it, 'You are my god,' he is liable."

C. *For what? If it is for the death penalty, that is the explicit statement of the Mishnah-passage.*

D. Rather, it is for an offering.

E. *But is that even from the viewpoint of rabbis? For has it not been taught on Tannaite authority:* **One is liable only on account of something which is of practical consequence, such as sacrificing, burning incense, pouring out a libation, or prostrating oneself [T. 10:3B].** *And in this connection R. Simeon b. Laqish said, "Who is the Tannaite authority who includes the matter of prostration [which is hardly a concrete action in the category of a sacrifice]? It is R. Aqiba, who maintains the view that we do not require that there be a concrete deed at all [to impose liability for idolatry].*

F. *It surely must follow that rabbis take the view that we do require a concrete deed [and Rab's statement would then not represent the position of rabbis but only of an individual authority].*

G. *When Rab made that statement, it was from the viewpoint of R. Aqiba.*

H. *But if it was from the viewpoint of R. Aqiba, that is a self-evident fact. The person at hand falls into the category of a blasphemer.*

I. *What might you have said? R. Aqiba imposes the requirement of bringing an offering only in the case of a blasphemer, in which case Scripture makes explicit reference to extirpation. But here, in which case there is no explicit reference in Scripture to extirpation, I might have said that that was not the case. So we are informed that there is an analogy to be drawn* [between saying "You are my god" and blasphemy,] for it is written, "They have made a molten calf and have worshipped it and have sacrificed to it and have said, '[These are your gods, O Israel who brought you up out of the land of Egypt]" (Ex. 32:8). [So sacrificing and declaring that this is one's god are regarded as analogous actions, as Aqiba maintains].

J. Said R. Yohanan, "Were it not for the indication of the plural in the verb, 'who have brought you up,' the Israelites would have become liable to destruction. [The calf then is not the sole god, the Israelites' language indicating that God also was a divinity.]"

K. *This is subject to a dispute on Tannaite authority:*

L. Others say, "Were it not for the indication of the plural in the verb, 'who have brought you up,' the Israelites would have become liable to destruction."

M. Said to him R. Simeon b. Yohai, "Is it not the case that whoever joins together the Name of heaven and the name of 'something else' [an idol] is uprooted from the world, as it is said, 'He who sacrifices to any god, save to the Lord alone, shall be utterly destroyed' (Ex. 22:19)?

N. "What is the meaning of the plural verb?

O. "It indicates that they desired many gods."

III.1 A. **But the one who hugs it, kisses it, polishes it, sweeps it... [M. 7:6D]:**

B. When R. Dimi came [from Palestine], he said R. Eleazar [said], "On account of all [of the actions listed at M. 7:6Dff.] one is given a flogging, except for the **one who takes a vow in its name or who carries out a vow made in its name [M. 7:6R].**"

C.   *What distinguishes one who takes a vow in its name or who carries out a vow made in its name that such a one is not flogged?*

D.   It is because that constitutes a violation of a negative commandment that does not involve a concrete action.

E.   *The other items also constitute* prohibitions based on a negative commandment phrased in general terms, and people do not administer a flogging for the violation of a prohibition based on a negative commandment phrased in general terms.

F.   *For it has been taught on Tannaite authority:*

G.   How do we know that if someone eats meat from a beast before it has died, he violates a negative commandment?

H.   Scripture says, "You shall not eat anything with the blood" (Lev. 19:26).

I.   Another matter: "You shall not eat anything with the blood" means you shall not eat meat while the blood is still in the bowl [and not sprinkled].

J.   R. Dosa says, "How do we know that people do not provide a mourners' meal on account of those who are executed by a court? Scripture says, 'You shall not eat anything for one whose blood has been shed.'"

K.   R. Aqiba says, "How do we know that a sanhedrin who put someone to death should not taste any food all that day?

L.   "Scripture says, 'You shall not eat anything with bloodshed.'"

M.   R. Yohanan says, "How do we know that there is an admonition against the wayward and rebellious son? Scripture says, 'You shall not do anything to cause bloodshed' (Lev. 19:26) [Freedman's translation]."

N.   *And said R. Abin bar Hiyya, and some say, R. Abin bar Kahana, "In the case of all of these, one is not flogged, for each of these constitutes a prohibition based on a general principle."*

O.   But when Rabin came [from Palestine], he said R. Eleazar [said], "In the case of all of them, one is not flogged, except for **the case of one who takes an oath by [the idol's] name or carries out an oath made in its name.**

P.   *"What is the reason that these are differentiated so that one is not flogged?*

Q.   *"It is because these items constitute prohibitions based on a negative commandment phrased in general terms."*

R.   *But these other items constitute violations of a negative commandments that do not involve concrete actions.*

S.   *The rule follows the view of R. Judah, who has said, "*As to a negative commandment that does not involve a concrete action, the court nonetheless administers a flogging on account of a violation of such a commandment."

T.   *For it has been taught on Tannaite authority:*

U.   "'You shall let nothing of it remain until the morning, and that which remains of it until the morning you shall burn with fire' (Ex. 12:10).

V.   "In framing matters this way, the Scripture has stated a positive commandment following a negative commandment, **[63B]** so as to indicate to you that the court does not inflict a flogging on that account," the words of R. Judah.

W. R. Jacob says, "That is not the principle at hand. Rather it is because what we deal with is a negative commandment that does not contain a concrete deed, and on account of the violation of a negative commandment that does not involve a concrete deed, the court does not inflict a flogging."

X. *It must follow that R. Judah takes the view that, on such an account, the court does inflict a flogging.*

IV.1 A. **He who takes a vow in its name and he who carries out a vow made in its name transgress a negative commandment [M. 7:6F]:**

B. *How do we know that this is the case for* him who vows in its name or who carries out a vow made in its name?

C. *As it has been taught on Tannaite authority:*

D. "And you shall make no mention of the name of other gods" (Ex. 23:13):

E. **This means that one should not say to his fellow, "Wait for me by the idol of so and so,"**

F. **or, "I'll wait for you by the idol of such-and-such" [T. A.Z. 6:11A-C].**

G. "And neither let it be heard of your mouth" – that one should not take a vow or carry out a vow made by its name, nor should he cause others [gentiles] to take a vow by its name or to carry out a vow by its name.

H. Another matter: "Let it not be heard out of your mouth" – this is an admonition against one who incites or entices Israelites to practice idolatry.

I. *But the matter of inciting is stated explicitly, for it is written in that connection, "And all Israel shall hear and fear and shall do no more any such wickedness as this is among you" (Deut. 13:12).*

J. This is an admonition against one who causes Israelites to practice idolatry.

K. "Nor should he cause others [gentiles] to take a vow by its name:"

L. *This supports the viewpoint of Samuel's father.*

M. For Samuel's father said, "It is forbidden for a person to form a partnership with an idolator, lest he become liable to take an oath to him and have to take the oath by his idol."

N. "For the Torah has said, 'Neither let it be heard out of your mouth' (Ex. 23:13)."

IV.2 A. *When Ulla came, he stayed at the City of Nebo. Said Raba to him, "And where did the master lodge?"*

B. *He said to him, "In the City of Nebo."*

C. *He said to him, "Is it not written, 'And do not mention the name of other gods' (Ex. 23:13)?"*

D. He said to him, "This is what R. Yohanan has said, 'It is permitted to mention the name of any idol that is written in the Torah."

E. *"And where is this one written?"*

F. *"As it is written, 'Bel bows down, Nebo stoops' (Is. 46:1)."*

G. *And if it is not written in the Torah, may one not mention it?*

H. *To that proposition R. Mesharshia objected,* "**If one saw a flux as profuse as three, which is sufficient for one to go from Gad**

> Yon to Shiloah, which is time enough for two immersions
> and two dryings, lo, this one is entirely a zab [M. Zab. 1:5A-
> D]. [Clearly, the framer of the Mishnah was willing to refer to
> a town named for an idol.]"

I.   *Said Rabina, "Gad too is mentioned in the Torah: 'That prepare a
       table for Gad' (Is. 65:2)."*

IV.3   A.   *Said R. Nahman, "Any form of mockery is forbidden except for mockery of
            idolatry, which is permitted. For it is written, 'Bel bows down. Nebo
            stoops... they stoop, they bow down together, they could not deliver
            the burden' (Is. 46:1). And it is written, 'They have spoken: the
            inhabitants of Samaria shall fear because of the calves of Beth Aven;
            for the people therefore shall mourn over it, and the priests thereof
            that rejoiced on it for the glory thereof, which is departed from it'
            (Hos. 10:5). Do not read 'its glory' but 'his weight.'"*

IV.4   A.   *Said R. Isaac, "What is the meaning of the following verse of Scripture:
            'And now they sin more and more and have made for themselves
            molten images of their silver and idols in their image' (Hos. 13:2)?*

       B.   *"What is the meaning of* 'idols in their image'? This teaches that each
            one of them made an image of his god and put it in his pocket.
            When he called it to mind, he took it out of his pocket and
            embraced it and kissed it."

       C.   *What is the meaning of,* "Let the men that sacrifice kiss the
            calves" (Hos. 13:2)?

       D.   Said R. Isaac of the house of R. Ammi, "The servants of the
            idols would look enviously at wealthy men. They would
            starve the calves and make images of [the rich men] and set
            them up at the side of the cribs and then bring the calves out.
            When the calves would see the men, they would run after them
            and nuzzle them. [The servants] would say to the men, 'The
            idol wants you. Let him come and sacrifice himself to him.'
            [Freedman, p. 433, n. 7: Thus the verse is translated: They
            sacrifice themselves in their homage to the calves.]"

       E.   *Said Raba, "Then the verse, 'Let the men that sacrifice kiss the
            calves' should read, 'Let the calves kiss the men that sacrifice.'"*

       F.   Rather said Raba, "'Whoever sacrifices his son to an idol would
            have the priest say to him, "You have offered a great gift to it.
            Come and kiss it."'"

IV.5   A.   Said R. Judah said Rab, "'And the men of Babylonia made Succoth-
            benoth' (2 Kgs. 17:30) [among idols brought by gentiles who
            resettled Samaria after the deportation].

       B.   *"What was it?* It was a chicken.

       C.   "'And the men of Cuth made Negral (NRGL)' (2 Kgs. 17:30).

       D.   *"What was it?* It was a cock (TRNGL).

       E.   "'And the men of Hamath made Ashima' (2 Kgs. 17:30).

       F.   *"What was it?* It was a bald buck.

       G.   "'And the Avites made Nibhaz an Tarak' (2 Kgs. 17:30).

       H.   *"What are these?* A dog and an ass.

       I.   "'And the Sepharvites burned their children in fire to Adrammelech
            and Anamm*elech, the gods of Sepharvaim' (2 Kgs. 17:30).*

       J.   *"What were they?* A mule and a horse.

K.   "'Adrammelech' *means that [the mule] honors its master in carrying its load.*

L.   "'Anammelech' *means that the horse answers its master in battle.*

M.   "Also the father of Hezekiah, king of Judah, wanted to do the same to him [namely, to burn him in fire], but his mother covered him with salamander [blood and so made him fire-proof]."

IV.6 A.   Said R. Judah said Rab, "The Israelites know that idolatry was of no substance and did not perform acts of idolatry except with the intent of allowing themselves publicly to engage in consanguineous sexual relations."

B.   *R. Mesharsheyya objected, "'As those who remember their children, so they longed for their altars, and their graves by the green trees'* (Jer. 17:2).

C.   "And R. Eleazar said, 'It was like a man who yearned for his son.' [So their belief in idols was sincere.]"

D.   This was after they had cleaved to idolatry [and gotten used to it].

E.   *Come and take note:*

F.   "And I will cast your carcasses upon the carcasses of your idols" (Lev. 26:30):

G.   They say: Elijah, the righteous man, was searching among those who are starving in Jerusalem. One time he found a child who was starving and who was thrown into a dung heap. He said to him, "From what family do you come?"

H.   He said to him, "From such and such a family do I come."

I.   He said to him, "Has anyone survived from that family?"

J.   He said to him, "No one but me."

K.   He said to him, "If I teach you something by which you will live, will you learn it?"

L.   He said to him, "Yes."

M.   He said to him, "Say every day, 'Hear O Israel, the Lord our God, the Lord is one.'"

N.   He said to him, "[64A] Be silent, so as not to make mention of the name of the Lord.'

O.   It was because his father and mother had not taught him [the worship of the Lord]. He forthwith took out his little idol from his bosom and began to hug it and kiss it, until his stomach burst and his idol fell to the ground, and he fell on it.

P.   This was to carry out that which is said, "And I shall cast your carcasses upon the carcasses of your idols" (Lev. 26:30). [Thus we see that the Israelites were sincere in their idolatry.]

Q.   *This came after they had cleaved to idolatry [and gotten used to it.]*

R.   *Come and take note:*

S.   "And they cried with a loud voice to the Lord their God" (Neh. 9:4) [when the Israelites came back to Zion in the time of Ezra].

T.   *What did they say?*

U.   *Said R. Judah, and some say, R. Jonathan, "'Woe, woe, this is what destroyed the house and wiped out the temple, killed the righteous and caused Israel to go into exile from its land, and it still is dancing among us. Is it not so that you put it among us only so that we could gain a reward [for resisting it]. We don't want it, we don't want the reward for resisting it!'" [So they were deeply attracted to the idolatry.]*

V.   *This came after they had cleaved to idolatry.*

W.   *[Judah continues,] "They sat in a fast for three days and prayed for mercy. A message came down from the firmament, with the word 'truth' written on it."*

X.   Said R. Hanina, "This proves that the seal of the Holy One, blessed be he, is truth."

Y.   *[Judah goes on,] "Something in the shape of a lion's whelp made of fire came forth from the house of the Holy of Holies and said to the prophet to Israel, 'This is the tempter of idolatry.' While they held it, its hairs fell out of it, and its roar could be heard for four hundred parasangs. They said, 'What shall we do? Perhaps from heaven there will be mercy for it.'*

Z.   *"The prophet said to them, 'Throw it into a lead pot and cover it with lead to stifle its voice.'*

AA. *"For it is written, 'And he said, This is wickedness, and he cast it into the midst of the ephah and he cast the weight of lead upon the mouth of it' (Zech. 5:8).*

BB. *"They said, 'Since it is a propitious time, let us pray for mercy about the tempter of sin [so we may be saved from it].'*

CC. *"They prayed for mercy, and it was given into their hands, and they imprisoned it for three days.*

DD. *"People went looking for a fresh egg for a sick person and could not find it. [All sexual activity had ceased.]*

EE. *"They said, 'What should we do? If we ask for half-and-half [so that the power of temptation be limited by half], it will not be granted to us.'*

FF. *"They blinded its eye with rouge, so that a man will not lust for his close female relations."*

IV.7 A. Said R. Judah said Rab, "There was the case of a gentile woman who was very sick. She said, 'If that woman [I] survive this illness, she will go and worship every idol in the world.'

B.   "She recovered from the illness and went and worshipped every idol in the world.

C.   "When she came to Peor, she asked its keepers how people worship this idol.

D.   "They said to her, 'People eat beets and drink beer and then show their behinds [and fart] before it.'

E.   "She said, 'It would be better for that woman [me] to fall sick again but not to worship that idol in such a way.'

F.   [Rab continues], "But you, house of Israel, were not this way, 'who were joined to Baal Peor' (Num. 25:5) – joined like a tightly fitting seal.

G.   "'But you who cleave to the Lord your God' (Deut. 4:4) – like two dates that are stuck together."

H.   *In a Tannaite passage it is taught:*

I.   "That were joined to Baal Peor" (Num. 25:5) – like a woman's bracelet.

J.   "And you who cleave to the Lord your God" (Deut. 4:4) – literally cleaving.

IV.8 A. *Our rabbis have taught on Tannaite authority:*

B.   There is the case of Sabta of Eles, who hired his ass to a gentile woman. When she came to Peor, she said to him, "Wait for me while I go in and come out."

C. After she came out, he said to her, "Now you wait for me while I go in and come out."

D. She said to him, "Aren't you a Jew?"

E. *He said to her, "And what difference does it make to you?"*

F. He went in, showed his behind to the idol and wiped his ass on its nose, and the servants of the idol praised him, saying, "There never has been a person who served it in such a way."

G. [That is line with M. 7:6G, thus] **He who shows his behind to Baal Peor – lo, this is the way it is served,** *even though the person who does so has the intent of committing a disgrace against it.*

H. **He who throws a pebble at Mercury [M. 7:6H] – lo, this is the way it is served,** *even though the person who does so has the intent of stoning it.*

IV.9 A. *R. Menassia was going along to Be Torta. They pointed out to him, "There is an idol standing here."*

B. *He took a stone and threw it at it.*

C. *They said to him, "It is Mercury."*

D. *He said to them, "What we have learned in the Mishnah is:* **He who tosses a pebble at Merkolis [M. 7:6H]."**

E. *He came to the school house and asked [whether he had committed a sin, having intended to express contempt].*

F. *They said to him, "We have learned in the Mishnah:* **He who tosses a pebble at Merkolis [M. 7:6H]** *– even though one's intent is to stone it."*

G. *He said to them, "Then I shall go and take it away [the heap of stones that constitutes the idol]."*

H. *They said to him, "All the same are the one who takes a stone away and the one who places a stone on it – both are liable, for each one [removed] leaves room for another stone."*

Unit I.1 clarifies the sense of the Mishnah's language. Unit I.2 then seeks the biblical source for the Mishnah's rule. The inquiry proceeds through unitsI.3,4 Unit I.5 then takes up the contradiction in the implications of M. 7:6A and M. 7:10N. Units I.6, 7 are inserted because of the clarification of M. 7:6A-B. I cannot claim to have done justice to unit I.7, and, as indicated, rely upon Freedman's exposition of the passage as well as on his translation. Unit II.1 brings us to M. 7:6C, unit III.1 to M. 7:6D, unit IV.1 to M. 7:6F. Despite the diffuse appearance of sizable components of the composition at hand, the bulk of the materials are put together systematically to clarify the Mishnah's statements.

7:7A-E

A. **He who gives of his seed [child] to Molech [M. 7:4D] [Lev. 20:2] is liable only when he will both have given him to Molech and have passed him through fire.**

B. **[If] he gave him to Molech but did not pass him through fire.**

C. **passed him through fire but did not give him to Molech,**

D. **he is not liable –**

E.   until he will both have given him to Molech and have passed him through fire.

I.1   A.   *The Mishnah [at M. 7:4] refers to both idolatry in general and giving to Molech in particular [treating them as separate. This would imply that giving a child to Molech is not an act of idolatry.]*

B.   *Said R. Abin, "Our Mishnah-passage is framed in accord with him who has said that Molech is not an idol."*

C.   *For it has been taught on Tannaite authority:*

D.   One is liable for [worshipping] Molech or any other idol.

E.   R. Eleazar b. R. Simeon says, "One is liable for doing so for Molech, and exempt for doing so not for Molech" [T. San. 10:5D-E].

F.   Said Abbayye, "R. Eleazar b. R. Simeon and R. Hanina b. Antigonos have said the same thing.

G.   *"R. Eleazar b. R. Simeon has said that which we have just now cited.*

H.   *"R. Hanina b. Antigonos, as it has been taught on Tannaite authority:*

I.   "R. Hanina b. Antigonos says, 'On what account did the Torah use the word Molech [with the same root as the word for king]? It is to indicate that the prohibition pertains to any sort of thing which people have made a king over themselves, even a pebble or a splinter. [Freedman, p. 438, n. 1: This shows that he too regards any fetish as a Molech.]'"

J.   *Said Raba, "At issue between [Eleazar and Hanina] is the case of a Molech of a temporary character. [Freedman, p. 438, n. 3: Anything which was only temporarily worshipped as Molech, such as a pebble, which would obviously not be a permanent idol. According to Hanina, one is liable, and Eleazar applies the law only to a permanent idol worshipped as Molech.]"*

I.2   A.   [64B] Said R. Yannai, "One is liable only if he hands his son over to the worshippers of an idol.

B.   "For it is said, 'And you shall not give of your seed to pass through the fire to Molech' (Lev. 18:21). [Freedman, p. 438, n. 5: This proves that the offense consists of two parts, formal delivery to the priests and causing the seed to pass through the fire.]"

C.   *So too it has been taught on Tannaite authority:*

D.   Is it possible to suppose that if one passed his son through fire but did not give him to Molech [M. 7:7C], he might be liable?

E.   Scripture states, "You shall not give" (Lev. 18:21).

F.   Is it possible to suppose that if he handed his son over but did not pass him through fire [M. 7:7B], he might be liable?

G.   Scripture states, "To pass through...."

H.   If he handed over his son [to the priests] and passed him through fire, but not to Molech, is it possible that he might be liable?

I.   Scripture says, "...to Molech."

J.   If one handed his son over and passed him to Molech, but not through fire, is it possible that he might be liable?

K.   Here it is said, "to pass through...," and elsewhere it is said, "There shall not be found among you any one who makes his son or daughter pass through fire" (Deut. 18:10).

	L.	Just as in that passage it must be through fire, so in the present case it must be through fire.
	M.	Just as in the present case it must involve Molech, so in that case it must involve Molech.
I.3	A.	Said R. Aha, son of Raba, "If one passed all of his children through fire, he is exempt.
	B.	"For it is said, 'Of your seed,' but not all your seed."
I.4	A.	*R. Ashi raised the question,* "If one passed a blind son through fire, what is the law?
	B.	"If he passed through a son who was asleep, what is the law?
	C.	"If he passed through the son of his son or the son of his daughter, what is the law?"
	D.	*In any event one may solve one of these questions.*
	E.	*For it has been taught on Tannaite authority:*
	F.	"Because he has given of his seed to Molech" (Lev. 20:2).
	G.	*What is the sense of Scripture here?*
	H.	Since it is said, "There shall not be found among you any one who makes his son or his daughter pass through the fire" (Deut. 18:10), I know only that the law applies to one's own son or daughter. How do we know that it encompasses the son of his son or the son of his daughter?
	I.	Scripture says, "When he gives of his seed to Molech" (Lev. 20:4).
	J.	*The Tannaite authority opens with the verse,* "Because he has given of his seed" (Lev. 20:2) *and concludes with the verse,* "When he gives of his seed" (Lev. 20:4). *This serves to provide the occasion for yet another interpretation.* [Freedman, p. 439, n. 8: From the first verse we learn that the law applies to one's grandsons too; "When he gives" is stated in order that another law may be deducted.]
	K.	So "Because he has given of his seed" (Lev. 20:2):
	L.	I know that the rule applies to giving one's legitimate children.
	M.	How do I know that the law encompasses also invalid offspring?
	N.	Scripture says, "When he gives of his seed" (Lev. 20:4) [a superfluous statement leading to the inclusion of the other sort of offspring].
I.5	A.	Said R. Judah, **"One is liable only when he will have passed him through fire in the usual way [T. 10 San. 10:4B]."**
	B.	*What would this mean?*
	C.	*Said Abbayye, "A pile of bricks was in the middle, with fire on one side and on the other side."*
	D.	*Raba said, "It was like the bouncing about on Purim."*
	E.	*There is a Tannaite teaching in accord with the view of Raba:*
	F.	**And he is liable only when he will have passed him through fire in the usual way.**
	G.	**[If] he passed him through fire by foot, he is exempt.**
	H.	**And he is liable, moreover, only on account of those who are his natural children [T. San. 10:4B-D].**
	I.	**How so? If it was his son or daughter, he is liable.**
	J.	**[He who passes] his father, mother, or sister through fire [for Molech] is exempt.**
	K.	**He who passes through himself is exempt.**
	L.	**R. Eleazar b. R. Simeon declares him liable.**

M.   **All the same is doing so for Molech and for any other idol: one is liable.**

N.   **And R. Simeon says, "He is liable only on account of Molech alone"** [T. San. 10:5A-E].

O.   *Said Ulla, "What is the scriptural basis for the view of R. Eleazar b. R. Simeon?*

P.   *"Scripture says, 'There shall not be found among you' (Deut. 18:10) – 'among you' meaning 'within you.'"*

Q.   *And rabbis? They do not interpret the clause, "Within you."*

R.   *But have we not learned in the Mishnah:* **If one has to choose between seeking what he has lost and what his father has lost, his own takes precedence** [M. B.M. 2:11A-B]. *And in this connection, we said,* "What is the Scriptural basis for that view?" *And R. Judah said,* "Scripture has said, 'Save that there shall be no poor among you' (Deut. 15:4), meaning that what is among you [personally, your own family] takes precedence over what belongs to anyone else." [So rabbis do interpret the word "among you."]

S.   *That follows the exclusionary phrase, "Save that...."*

I.6   A.   Said R. Yosé bar Hanina, "The three references to extirpation on account of idolatry serve what purpose? [These are at Lev. 20:2-5, 'Whoever gives of his seed to Molech will I cut off from among his people,' 'And if the people of the land kill him not, then I will set my face against that man... and will cut him off,' and, at Num. 15:30: 'But the soul that does something presumptuously... shall be cut off from among his people.']

      B.   "One serves to state the penalty for worship in the normal way, one serves to state the penalty for idol worship not in the normal way, and one states the penalty for worship of Molech."

      C.   *And in the view of him who has said that* Molech falls into the general category of idolatry, what need is therefore a specific reference to extirpation as the penalty for serving Molech?

      D.   It states the penalty for him who passes his son through fire but not in the normal way.

      E.   *And as to him who has said that* the blasphemer falls into the category of one who has served an idol, what need is there to specify that extirpation applies to the blasphemer [at Num. 15:30]?

      F.   *It is in accord with that which has been taught on Tannaite authority:*

      G.   "'That soul, being cut off, shall be cut off' (Num. 15:30).

      H.   "'Being cut off' in this world; 'shall be cut off,' in the world to come," the words of R. Aqiba.

      I.   Said R. Ishmael to him, "And has it not already been said, 'That soul shall be cut off' (Num. 15:30). Are there then three worlds?

      J.   "Rather: 'And that soul shall be cut off' in this world; 'he is to be cut off' in the world to come.

      K.   "The repetition is because the Torah uses ordinary human speech [and bears no further meaning at all]."

Unit I.1 takes up M. 7:4A, and the clarification of the Mishnah is worked out at units I.2, 3. Unit I.4 raises some secondary questions based on the foregoing. Unit I.5 goes over the Tosefta's complement, and unit I.6 deals with the scriptural relevant verses. So the entire construction follows the established exegetical program.

7:7F-I

F. [65A] He who has a familiar spirit [M. 7:4D4] [Lev. 20:27] – this is a ventriloquist, who speaks from his armpits;

G. and he who is a soothsayer [M. 7:4D5] – this is one whose [spirit] speaks through his mouth –

H. lo, these are put to death by stoning.

I. And the one who makes inquiry of them is subject to a warning [Lev. 19:31, Deut. 18:10-11].

I.1 A. *What is the reason that, in the present passage, the framer of the passage refers to both one who has a familiar spirit and also a soothsayer [at M. 7:7F, G], while at the list of those who are put to their death through extirpation, the one who has a familiar spirit is included in the list, but the one who is a soothsayer is omitted [at M. Ker. 1:1]?*

B. Said R. Yohanan, "It is because both of them are encompassed in a single negative commandment [at Lev. 19:31, 'Do not recognize those who have familiar spirits or soothsayers']."

C. R. Simeon b. Laqish said, "The soothsayer is omitted [at M. Ker. 1:1], because there is no concrete deed that he does."

D. *And as to R. Yohanan, why did the framer [of the passage at M. Ker. 1:1] refer to one who has a familiar spirit [and leave out the other item]?*

E. *Because it is with that one that Scripture [Lev. 19:31] began discourse.*

F. *And as to R. Simeon b. Laqish, why does he not explain matters as does R. Yohanan?*

G. Said R. Pappa, "Because the two [categories of sorcerer] are treated distinctly when it comes to the specification of the death penalty [at Lev. 20:27: 'A man who has a familiar spirit or a soothsayer will surely be put to death.' The 'or' distinguishes the two.]"

H. *And R. Yohanan? Deeds that are distinct when they are stated in a verse that prohibits them are regarded as truly distinct, while distinctions in the expression of the death penalty applying to such deeds do not impose a difference.*

I. *And why does R. Yohanan not explain matters in accord with the view of R. Simeon b. Laqish?*

J. *He will reply to you that the Mishnah-paragraph of tractate Keritot represents the position of R. Aqiba, who has taken the view that we do not require a concrete deed [to impose the penalty of having to bring a sin-offering for an unwitting act of idolatry]. [He includes the blasphemer on the list of M. Ker. 1:1, as against the view of rabbis, who would omit the blasphemer because he is one who has not performed a concrete deed.]*

K.   *And R. Simeon b. Laqish?*

L.   *Granted that R. Aqiba does not require a substantial deed [for imposition of liability], he does require some sort of slight action [before he will require the bringing of a sin-offering for an inadvertent act of blasphemy].*

M.   *But as to the blasphemer, what sort of action is involved?*

N.   *The use of the lips constitutes an action.*

O.   *And what sort of action does a one who has a familiar spirit perform?*

P.   *He flaps his arms [so that the voice of the dead appears to come from his armpits], and that constitutes an action.*

Q.   *Is this the case even from the viewpoint of rabbis? But it has been taught on Tannaite authority:*

R.   **One is liable only for something that involves a concrete deed, such as sacrificing, offering incense, pouring out a libation, or prostrating oneself [T. San. 10:3B-C].**

S.   *In this regard Simeon b. Laqish said, "What Tannaite authority stands behind the inclusion of prostration? It is R. Aqiba, who has said that we do not require a concrete deed [to impose liability, as before]."*

T.   *And R. Yohanan said, "You may even maintain that it is the viewpoint of rabbis, since bending one's body in rabbis' view constitutes a deed."*

U.   *Now in R. Simeon b. Laqish's view of rabbis' opinion, so far as rabbis are concerned, bending one's body in prostration does not constitute a deed, while flapping one's arms, as done by a person who has a familiar spirit, does constitute a concrete deed! [What difference can there be between these obviously similar acts?]*

V.   *When R. Simeon b. Laqish made his statement [that the one who has a familiar spirit carries out an action], it was within the context of the viewpoint of R. Aqiba, but so far as rabbis are concerned, that is not the case.*

W.   *If so, then [the Mishnah-passage at M. Ker. 1:1 should specify that just as a blasphemer does not have to bring a sin-offering for inadvertent blasphemy, there being no action, so too] the one who consults a familiar spirit likewise should be excluded [from those required to bring a sin-offering] [there being no concrete action involved in what he has done either].*

X.   Rather, said Ulla, "We deal with one who has a familiar spirit who burned incense to a demon [and that involves a concrete action]."

Y.   Said Raba to him, "But burning incense to a shade constitutes an act of idolatry. [That is a separate item on the list and cannot be subsumed within the reference to one who has a familiar spirit.]"

Z.   Rather, said Raba, "The passage [at M. Ker. 1:1] refers to one who has a familiar spirit who burned incense as a charm."

AA.   Said Abbayye to him, "Burning incense as a charm constitutes merely an act of charming, [and that is merely prohibited by a negative precept (Freedman)]."

BB.	Indeed so, and the Torah has said that one one who acts as a charmer is put to death through stoning. [Freedman, p. 444, n. 2: Consequently, for unwitting transgression a sin offering is due.]
CC.	*Our rabbis have taught on Tannaite authority:*
DD.	"There shall not be found among you... a charmer" (Deut. 18:11):
EE.	All the same are the one who charms large objects and the one who charms small objects, and even snakes and scorpions.
FF.	*Said Abbayye, "Therefore one who seals up wasps or scorpions [using charms to do so], even though he intends only that they not do harm to anyone, violates a prohibition."*
GG.	*And why does R. Yohanan maintain that bending over in prostration constitutes a concrete action in rabbis' view, while in their view moving the lips does not constitute a concrete action?*
HH.	Said Raba, "The case of the blasphemer is different, because there is the issue there is what is in the heart."
II.	**[65B]** *[To this explanation of what is at issue]* R. Zira objected, *"'A conspiracy of perjurers is excluded [from the list at M. Ker. 1:1, those obligation to a sin-offering for inadvertent offense] because there is no concrete deed involved in what they have done.' Now why should this be the case? Lo, is the issue there not what is in the heart?"*
JJ.	Said Raba, "That case, involving a conspiracy of perjurers, is different, since there it is a matter of speech ['the voice']."
KK.	And in R. Yohanan's view, does not an act of speech constitute an act?
LL.	*Lo, it has been stated on Tannaite authority:* If one frightened a beast by his act of speech or drove off animals by his act of speech, R. Yohanan said, "He is liable." R. Simeon b. Laqish said, "He is exempt."
MM.	R. Yohanan said liable [because in his view] the movement of the lips constitutes a concrete deed.
NN.	R. Simeon b. Laqish said, "Exempt [because in his view] the movement of the lips does not constitute a concrete action."
OO.	Rather, said Raba, "The case of the conspiracy of perjurers is different, since they are subject to having caused an offense by what they have seen [in using their eyes, and there there is no concrete action whatsoever]."
I.2 A.	*Our rabbis have taught on Tannaite authority:*
B.	**He who has a familiar spirit – this is one who has a ventriloquist which speaks [M. 7:7F] from between his joints and from between his elbows.**
C.	**A soothsayer [M. 7:7G] – this one who has the bone of a familiar spirit in his mouth, and it speaks on its own [T. San. 10:6A-B].**
D.	*The following objection was raised:* "And your voice shall be as of one who has a familiar spirit, out of the ground" (Is. 29:4).

E.   *Does this not mean that it speaks in a natural way?*

F.   *No, it comes up and takes a seat between his joints and speaks*

G.   *Come and take note:* "And the woman said to Saul, I saw a god-like form ascending out of the earth" (1 Sam. 28:13).

H.   *Does that not mean that it speaks in a natural way?*

I.   *No, it took a seat between her joints and then spoke.*

I.3   A.   *Our rabbis have taught on Tannaite authority:*

B.   **He who inquires of the dead (Deut. 18:11) – all the same are the one who raises up the dead by divining and the one who makes inquiry of a skull.**

C.   **What is the difference between one who makes inquiry of a skull and one who raises up the dead by witchcraft?**

D.   **For the one who raises up the dead by witchcraft – the ghost does not come up in his normal way and does not come up on the Sabbath.**

E.   **But the one who makes inquiry of a skull – [the spirit] comes up in the normal way and comes up on the Sabbath [T. San. 10:7A-D].**

F.   **It goes up** – *but where to? Lo, [the skull (E)] is lying before him.*

G.   *Rather say,* **It answers in the normal way and it answers on the Sabbath.**

I.4   A.   And so too did Turnus Rufus ask R. Aqiba, "What distinguishes one day [the Sabbath] from all other days?"

B.   He said to him, "What distinguishes one man from all other men?"

C.   *"Because that is what my lord [the emperor] wants."*

D.   *"As to the Sabbath, too, that is what my Lord wants."*

E.   *He said to him, "What I meant to ask you was this: Who tells you that this particular day is the Sabbath?"*

F.   He said to him, "The Sabbation river will prove the matter, the one who has a familiar spirit will prove the matter, your father's grave will prove the matter, from which no smoke goes up on the Sabbath."

G.   He said to him, "You have shamed, disgraced, and cursed him."

I.5   A.   One who asks a question of a familiar spirit – it this not the same as one who seeks after the death?

B.   *So it has been taught on Tannaite authority:*

C.   "Or who consults the dead" (Deut. 18:11):

D.   This refers to one who fasts and goes and spends the night in a cemetery, so that the unclean spirit will come to rest on him.

E.   Now when R. Aqiba would come to this verse of Scripture, he would cry, "And if one who fasts so as to have rest on him an unclean spirit succeeds so that an unclean spirit does rest on him, he who fasts in order that a clean spirit will come to rest on him – how much the more so [should he succeed]!

F.   "But what can I do? For our sins have caused us [to be unable to fast with such a result], for it is said, 'But your iniquities have separated between you and your God' (Is. 59:2)."

G.   *Said Raba, "If they wanted, the righteous could create a world for it is said, 'But your iniquities have distinguished' (Is. 59:2)."*

H.   *Rabbah created a man. He sent it to R. Zira, who talked with him, but he did not answer him.*

I.   *He said to him, "You have come by means of enchantment, go back to the dust you came from."*

J.   *R. Hanina and R. Oshaia went into session every Friday afternoon and took up the study of the Book of Creation. They made a third-grown calf and ate it.*

I.6

A.   *Our rabbis have taught on Tannaite authority:*

B.   **One who observes the times (Deut. 18:10) –**

C.   **R. Simeon says, "This is one who rubs the semen of seven sorts of men in his eyes."**

D.   **And sages say, "This is one who holds peoples' eyes [giving them hallucinations]."**

E.   **R. Aqiba says, "This is one who reckons the times and hours, saying, 'Today is a good to go out.' 'Tomorrow is a good day to make a purchase.' 'The wheat that ripens on the eve of the Seventh Year usually is sound.' 'Let beans be pulled up to save them from becoming wormy'" [T. Shab. 7:14].**

F.   *Our rabbis have taught on Tannaite authority:*

G.   **[In T's version] Who is an enchanter?**

H.   **One who says, "My staff has fallen from my hand."**

I.   **"My bread has fallen from my mouth."**

J.   **"Mr. So-and-so has called me from behind me."**

K.   **"A crow has called to me."**

L.   **"A dog has barked at me."**

M.   **"A snake has passed at my right and a fox at my left."**

N.   **[66A] "Do not begin with me, for lo, it is dawn."**

O.   **"It is a new moon."**

P.   **"It is Saturday night" [T. Shab. 7:13].**

Q.   *Our rabbis have taught on Tannaite authority:*

R.   **"You shall not use enchantments or observe times" (Lev. 19:26):**

S.   **This speaks of those who use enchantment through weasels, birds, or fish.**

Unit I.1 deals with the relationship between M. San. 7:7 and M. Ker. 1:1. Units I.2, 3-4 take up the Tosefta's complement to our Mishnah. Units I.5, 6 define various pertinent categories of law-violators in the present context.

7:8A

A.   **He who profanes the Sabbath [M. 7:4E] – in regard to a matter, on account of the deliberate doing of which they are liable to extirpation, and on account of the inadvertent doing of which they are liable to a sin-offering.**

I.1

A.   *This statement bears the implication that there is a form of profanation of the Sabbath on account of which* people are not liable to a sin-offering should they do it inadvertently, or to extirpation if they do it deliberately.

B.   *What would it be?*
C.   *It is violation of the law of boundaries, in the view of R. Aqiba,*
D.   *or of the law against kindling a fire, in the view of R. Yosé.*

The Talmud lightly clarifies the implications of the Mishnah's statement.

7:8B-E

B.   **He who curses his father and his mother [M. 7:4F] is liable only when he will have cursed them by the divine Name.**
C.   **[If] he cursed them with a euphemism,**
D.   **R. Meir declares him liable.**
E.   **And sages declare him exempt.**

I.1   A.   *Who are the sages [of M. 7:8E]?*
       B.   *They represent the view of R. Menahem, son of R. Yosé.*
       C.   *For it has been taught on Tannaite authority:*
       D.   R. Menahem, son of R. Yosé, says, "'When he blasphemes the name of the Lord, he shall be put to death' (Lev. 24:16).
       E.   "Why is 'the Name' stated here [since the verse earlier refers to it, 'And he who blasphemes the Name of the Lord shall surely be put to death']?
       F.   "The usage teaches that the one who curses his father and mother he is liable only if he curses them with the divine Name."

I.2   A.   *Our rabbis have taught on Tannaite authority:*
       B.   "[For any man that curses his father of his mother shall surely be put to death; his father and his mother he has cursed; his blood shall be upon him" (Lev. 20:9).] Why does Scripture say "any man"?
       C.   It serves to in encompass a daughter, one of undefined sexual traits, and one who exhibits the traits of both sexes.
       D.   "'Who curses his father or his mother' – I know only that the law covers his father and his mother. How do I know that it covers his father but not his mother, or his mother but not his father?
       E.   "Scripture says, 'His father and his mother he has cursed; his blood shall be upon him' (Lev. 20:9), that is, 'he has cursed his father,' 'he has cursed his mother,'" the words of R. Josiah.
       F.   R. Jonathan says, "The verse bears the implication that it speaks of the two of them simultaneously, and it bears the implication that it speaks of each by himself or herself, unless the text explicitly treats the two of them together."

I.3   A.   "He shall surely be put to death" (Lev. 20:9). That is, by execution through stoning.
       B.   You say that it is through stoning. But perhaps it is by any one of the other modes of execution that are listed in the Torah.
       C.   Here the Scripture states, "His blood shall be upon him" (Lev. 20:9), and elsewhere it states, "[A man... who has a familiar spirit or a wizard shall surely be put to death; they shall stone them with stones;] their blood shall be upon them" (Lev. 20:27).

D.   Just as in that latter passage the mode of execution is through stoning, so in the present passage the mode of execution is through stoning.

E.   We thereby have derived evidence on the character of the penalty. Whence do we find evidence of an admonition [against the act itself]?

F.   Scripture states, "You shall not curse the judges nor curse the ruler of your people" (Ex. 22:27).

G.   If [the wayward's son's] father was a judge, he is covered by the general statement, "You shall not curse the judges."

H.   If he was the chief, he is covered in the statement, "Nor curse the ruler of your people."

I.   But if he is neither a judge nor a leader, how do we know [that he is not to be cursed]?

J.   This is how to proceed: Lo, you must construct an argument based on the definitive traits of each of the two parties, for the traits of the chief are not the same as the traits for the judge, and the traits of the judge are not the traits of the chief.

K.   The definitive traits of the judge are not the same as those of the chief, for lo, in the case of a judge, you are commanded concerning his decision [that is, to obey his decision], which is not the case for the chief.

L.   The definitive trait of the chief is that you are commanded not to rebel against him, which is not the case of the judge, in which instance you are not commanded against rebelling against him.

M.   The shared definitive trait of both types is that they fall into the category of "your people," and you are admonished not to curse them.

N.   So I introduce the case of "your father" who also is "among your people," and you are thus admonished not to curse him.

O.   [Arguing against this proposition], what indeed is the shared definitive trait [of the judge and the chief] is that both of them derive the [honor owing to them] from their high position.

P.   [No, that cannot be the consideration,] for the Torah has said, "You shall not curse the deaf" (Lev. 19:14), and so [in connection with the prohibition against cursing], Scripture speaks of the most humble who are "among your people."

Q.   But the distinctive trait of the deaf person is that his deafness has caused [him to be given special status, namely, protection against being cursed].

R.   The cases of the chief and the judge will prove to the contrary.

S.   The special trait of the chief and the judge is that their high position has caused them [to enjoy immunity from cursing]. A deaf person will prove to the contrary.

T.   Then the circular argument continues on its merry way, for the definitive trait of the one is not the same as the definitive trait of the other, and the definitive trait of the other is not the same as the definitive trait of the one.

U.   The shared trait among them all is that all of them fall into the category of "among your people," and you are admonished not to curse them.

V.   And I then introduce the cases of "your father" who is "among your people," and in his case too you are admonished against cursing him.

W.   [Not at all,] for what the several categories have in common is that they are distinguished [from the common people]. [The one set is distinctive because of its high position, the other because of deafness.]

X.   If that were the case, Scripture should have said either, "The judges and the deaf..." or "the chief and the deaf."

Y.   Why was it necessary to make references to "the judges"?

Z.   If it is not necessary to make a point concerning itself [since the judges could have been covered by the reference to the chief], apply it to another matter entirely, specifically, to the case of his father.

AA.   *That argument suffices for him who maintains that* the word used for judges [which also is the word for God] is secular [and means a judge], *but what is there to be said from the viewpoint of him who maintains that* the word here means God and is used in a sacred sense [That is, "You should not curse God"]?

BB.   *That is in accord with the following Tannaite teaching:*

CC.   "The word that serves for both God and the judges is used in a secular sense, for judges," the words of R. Ishmael.

DD.   R. Aqiba says, "The word is used in a sacred sense, for God."

EE.   And it further has been taught on Tannaite authority:

FF.   R. Eliezer b. Jacob says, "Where in Scripture do we find an admonition against cursing the Name of God?

GG.   "Scripture says, 'You shall not curse God' (Ex. 22:27)."

HH.   *From the viewpoint of the one who has said that the word is used in a secular sense, we may derive the case of the sacred from the secular usage.*

II.   *In the viewpoint of him who has said that the word is used in a sacred sense, we derive the rule covering the secular setting from the rule covering the sacred one.*

JJ.   *Now from the viewpoint of him says that the word is used in a secular sense and one derives the rule covering the sacred from the secular, there are no problems [since we have a simple argument a fortiori].*

KK.   *But from the viewpoint of him says that the word is used in the sacred sense and that one may derive the rule covering the secular setting from the one covering the sacred, perhaps there is an admonition against cursing the sacred [Judge], but there is no admonition against cursing the secular [judge].*

LL.   *If so, Scripture should have written, "You shall not revile God" [spelling the word in a less emphatic way].*

MM.   [66B] *Why say, "You shall not curse..." [spelling the word in a more emphatic way]?*

NN.   *It is to imply the rule covering both circumstances.*

Unit I.1 seeks the authority behind the rule at hand, and units I.2-3 uncover the scriptural basis for that rule.

7:9

A.　He who has sexual relations with a betrothed maiden [M. 7:4G] [Deut. 22:23-4] is liable only if she is a virgin maiden, betrothed, while she is yet in her father's house.

B.　[If] two different men had sexual relations with her, the first one is put to death by stoning, and the second by strangulation. [The second party, B. has not had intercourse with a virgin (M. 11:1). The maiden is between twelve years and one day and twelve years six months and one day old.]

I.1　A.　*Our rabbis have taught on Tannaite authority:*

B.　"If a girl that is a virgin is betrothed to a husband" (Deut. 22:23): "Girl" and not [either a minor, under twelve years, or] a mature woman.

C.　"A virgin" – and not one who has had sexual relations.

D.　"Betrothed" and not one in a fully consummated marriage.

E.　"In her father's house" – excluding a case in which the father has given the girl over to the agent of the husband.

F.　Said R. Judah said Rab, "[The Mishnah-paragraph before us] represents the view of R. Meir, but sages say that subject to the law of a betrothed girl is even a minor [and not only a girl from twelve years to twelve years six months and one day, such as is ordinarily subsumed under a reference to a 'girl.']"

G.　*Said R. Aha of Difti to Rabina, "How do we know that the Mishnah passage represents the view of R. Meir, and that the reference to 'girl' serves to exclude a minor? Perhaps it represents the view of rabbis, and the reference to 'girl' serves to exclude a mature woman but no other category of woman?"*

H.　*He said to him, "[If that were the case, then the formulation],* ...is liable only if she is a virgin, a maiden, betrothed, [while she is yet in her father's house] [M. 7:9A], *should be, '...is liable only if she is a virgin-maiden and betrothed.' And nothing further is needed [to prove the case]."*

I.2　A.　*R. Jacob bar Ada asked Rab, "If one has had sexual relations with a minor who was betrothed, in R. Meir's view, what is the law?*

B.　*"Does he exclude such an act entirely from any sort of punishment or is it from the penalty of stoning that he excludes the action [by the exegesis given at unit I]?"*

C.　*He said to him, "It stands to reason that he excludes the felon from the penalty of stoning."*

D.　*"But is it not written, '[If a man be found lying with a woman married to a husband,] then both of them shall die' (Deut. 22:22), meaning that a penalty is imposed only if both of them are treated in the same way?"*

E.　*Rab remained silent [having no answer to this argument. The implication of the argument is that if both are not penalized – and the minor girl is not penalized – then neither is penalized at all. Hence the intent of Meir should be to exclude the felon from punishment of any sort whatsoever.]*

F.　*Said Samuel, "Why should Rab had remained silent? He should have said to him, 'But if a man find a betrothed damsel in the field...] then the man* only *who lay with her shall die' (Deut. 22:25). [Sometimes the* man alone is punished, even when the betrothed consented, that is, if she was a minor (Freedman, p. 453, n. 3)]."

I.3 **A.** *The foregoing follows the lines of the following dispute among Tannaite authorities:*

 B. "'Then they shall both of them die' (Deut. 22:22) means that a penalty is imposed only when the two of them are equal," the words of R. Josiah.

 C. R. Jonathan says, "'Then the man only that lay with her shall die' (Deut. 22:25)."

 D. *And as to the other party [Jonathan], how does he deal with the statement, "Then they shall both of them die" (Deut. 22:22)?*

 E. *Said Raba, "It serves to exclude a case of mere petting [in which the woman does not reach orgasm]."* [Both must enjoy sexual gratification (Freedman, p. 453, n. 5)].

 F. *And as to the other party? A case of mere petting bears no consequences whatever [and is not penalized by the court].*

 G. *And as to the other party [Josiah], how does he deal with the reference to "the man only"?*

 H. *It accords with that which has been taught on Tannaite authority:*

 I. **It ten men had intercourse with her and she remained yet a virgin, all of them are put to death by stoning.**

 J. **Rabbi says, "The first is put to death by stoning, and the others by strangulation" [T. San. 10:9C-D].**

I.4 **A.** *Our rabbis have taught on Tannaite authority:*

 B. "And the daughter of any priest, if she profane herself by playing the whore" (Lev. 21:9).

 C. Rabbi says, "[The verse refers to] the first [such action].

 D. "And so it is written, 'Then the man only who lies with her shall die' (Deut. 22:25)."

 E. *What is the sense of this statement?*

 F. *Said R. Huna, son of R. Joshua, "Rabbi accords with the view of R. Ishmael.*

 G. *"[Ishmael] has said, 'A betrothed girl [daughter of a priest] is distinguished in that her death penalty [should she commit adultery] is through burning, but that penalty does not apply to a married woman [a priest's daughter, who committed adultery].'*

 H. *"And this is the sense of his statement: 'If the first act of sexual relations [of the priest's daughter, who was betrothed] is one of adultery, then she is put to death through burning. But if it is any later sexual act [and not the first,] she is put to death through strangulation.'*

 I. *"And what is the sense of, 'And so...'?*

 J. *"'Just as, in that other passage, Scripture speaks of her first act of sexual relations, so here too the same applies.* [Freedman, p. 454, n. 2: Just as a betrothed maiden is excepted from the punishment of a married woman, that is, strangulation, being stoned instead, which exception applies to her seducer too, and that only for the first coition, so also in the case of the priest's daughter, the exception is made only for her first coition, that is, if she is a betrothed girl and not a married woman.'"

K.   *Said R. Bibi bar Abbayye to him, "But this is not what the master (and who is it? it is R. Joseph) said.*

L.   *"Rather, Rabbi accords with R. Meir, who has said,* **If the priest's daughter married one of those who is invalid for marriage into the priesthood, she would be put to death through strangulation [M. Ter. 7:2].** In this connection Rabbi says, 'If her first act of sexual relations constitutes profanation through adultery, she is put to death through burning, and thereafter it is through strangulation.

N.   *"And what is the sense of, 'And so...'?*

O.   **[67A]** *"It serves only to call to mind [that under discussion is something done for the first time. There is no further intent to draw an analogy.]"*

Unit I.1 proves that the authority at hand is Meir, and units I.2,3+4 then at greater depth explore Meir's views. So the entire composition is unitary and sustained.

7:10A-N

A.   He who beguiles others to idolatry [M. 7:4H] – this [refers to] an ordinary fellow who beguiles some other ordinary fellow.

B.   [If] he said to him, "There is a god in such a place, who eats thus, drinks thus, does good in one way, and harm in another" –

C.   against all those who are liable to the death penalty in the Torah they do not hide witnesses [for the purposes of entrapment] except for this one.

D.   [If] he spoke [in such a way] to two, and they serve as witnesses against him,

E.   they bring him to court and stone him.

F.   [If] he spoke [in such a way] to [only] one person, [the latter then] says to him, "I have some friends who will want the same thing."

G.   If he was clever and not prepared to speak in [the friends'] presence,

H.   they hide witnesses on the other side of the partition,

I.   and he says to him, "Tell me what you were saying to me now that we are by ourselves."

J.   And the other party says to him [what he had said], and then this party says, "Now how are we going to abandon our God who is in Heaven and go and worship sticks and stones?"

K.   If he repents, well and good.

L.   But if he said, "This is what we are obligated to do, and this is what is good for us to do,"

M.   those who stand on the other side of the partition bring him to court and stone him.

N. [He who beguiles others is] one who says, "I am going to worship," "I shall make an offering," "I shall offer incense," "I shall go and offer incense," "Let's go and offer incense," "I shall make a libation," "I shall go and make a libation," "Let's go and make a libation," "I shall bow down," "I shall go and bow down," "Let's go and bow down."

I.1 A. The one who beguiles others is an ordinary fellow [M. 7:10A] – *the operative consideration is that he is an ordinary fellow, [so he is put to death through stoning].*

B. *But if he were a prophet, he would be put to death through strangulation.*

II.1 A. **Who beguiles some other ordinary fellow [M. 7:10A]:**

B. *The point is that he is an individual.*

C. *But if it had been a community, he would have been put to death through strangulation.*

D. *In accord with which authority is the Mishnah-paragraph before us?*

E. *It is R. Simeon.*

F. `For it has been taught on Tannaite authority:`

G. A prophet who enticed people to commit idolatry is put to death through stoning.

H. R. Simeon says, "Through strangulation."

I. Those who entice a town to apostasy are put to death through stoning.

J. R. Simeon says, "Through strangulation."

K. *Let us turn to the concluding passage of the same Mishnah-paragraph:* **He who beguiles others is one who says, Let's go and worship..."** [M. 7:10N], on which R. Judah said Rab said, "What is subject to discussion here is those who beguile a town to apostasy."

L. *So the passage accords with rabbis [who hold that those who beguile a town to apostasy are stoned to death, not strangled].*

M. *Accordingly, does the opening part of the Mishnah-passage accord with the view of R. Simeon, and the closing part with rabbis?*

N. *Rabina said, "The entirety accords with the view of rabbis, and the point is to say, 'not only this but also that.'"* [Freedman, p. 456, n. 1: When the Mishnah states, **He who beguiles an individual,** it is not intended to exclude a multitude, but merely to commence with the universally agreed law. Then the next Mishnah adds that the same applies to the seduction of a multitude, though this is not admitted by all.]

II.2 A. *R. Pappa said, "When the Mishnah says,* **He who beguiles others refers to an ordinary fellow who beguiles some other ordinary fellow,** [M. 7:10A], *it is for the purpose of entrapment."*

B. *So it has been taught on Tannaite authority:*

C. **Against all those who are liable to the death penalty in the Torah they do not use procedures of entrapment, except for the one who beguiles others to idolatry [M. 7:10C].**

D. **How do they do it?**

E. **They hand over to him two disciples of sages, [who are put] in an inside room, and he sits in an outside room.**

F. **And they light a candle, so that they can see him.**

G. **And they listen to what he says.**

H.   But he cannot see them.

I.   And this one says to him, "Tell me what you were saying to me now that we are by ourselves."

J.   And the other party says to him what he had said, and then this party says, "Now how are we going to abandon our God who is in heaven and worship an idol?"

K.   If he repents, well and good. But if he said, "This is what we are obligated to do, and this is what is good for us to do," then the witnesses, who hear outside, bring him to court and stone him [T. San. 10:11].

Unit I.1 seeks the authority behind the Mishnah, and unit II.1 then amplifies the Mishnah with Tosefta's complement.

7:10/O-7:11

O.   He who leads [a whole town astray] [M. 10:4H] is one who says, "Let's go and perform an act of service to an idol."

M. 7:10/O

A.   The sorcerer [M. 7:4I] – he who does a deed is liable,

B.   but not the one who merely creates an illusion.

C.   R. Aqiba says in the name of R. Joshua, "Two may gather cucumbers. One gatherer may be exempt, and one gatherer may be liable.

D.   "[Likewise:] He who does a deed is liable, but he who merely creates an illusion is exempt."

M. 7:11

I.1   A.   Said R. Judah said Rab, "Subject to the present statement of the Mishnah are those who entice a whole town to apostasy."

II.1   A.   **The sorcerer – he who does a deed is liable [M. 7:11A]:**

B.   *Our rabbis have taught on Tannaite authority:*

C.   "[You shall not permit] a sorceress [to live]" (Ex. 22:17).

D.   The same rule applies to a sorcerer and to a sorceress. Why then does Scripture speak of a sorceress?

E.   It is because it is mainly women who practice sorcery.

II.2   A.   How are they put to death?

B.   R. Yosé the Galilean says, "Here it is stated, "'You shall not permit a sorceress to live' (Ex. 22:17) and elsewhere it is written, 'You shall not allow anything that breathes to live' (Deut. 20:17).

C.   "Just as in that context [the Canaanite nations], everything is put to death through decapitation, so here it is through decapitation."

D.   R. Aqiba says, "Here it is stated, 'You shall not permit a sorceress to live' (Ex. 22:17), and elsewhere it is stated, '[There shall not a hand touch it, but he shall surely be stoned or shot through], whether it be beast or man it shall not live' (Ex. 19:13).

E.   "Just as in that passage [having to do with the avoidance of Sinai before the giving of the Torah], the penalty is through stoning, so here too the penalty is through stoning."

F.   Said R. Yosé to him, "I have drawn an analogy based on the use in two passages of the language, 'You shall not permit to live...' But you have drawn an analogy between 'It shall not live' and 'You shall not permit to live...,' [so that the language is not exactly the same in the verses that you cite]."

G. Said R. Aqiba to him, "I have drawn an analogy for the penalty to be inflicted on an Israelite from the case of an Israelite, in which setting Scripture has provided several different modes of execution, while you have drawn an analogy for the death penalty to be inflicted on an Israelite from the case of idolators, in which context Scripture has not specified a number of different modes of execution, **[67B]** but only a single mode of inflicting the death penalty."

H. Ben Azzai says, "It is stated, 'You shall not suffer a sorceress to live' (Ex. 22:17), and immediately beyond, 'Whosoever lies with a beast shall surely be put to death' (Ex. 22:18).

I. "The juxtaposition of the two topics is to indicate that, just as one who lies with a beast is put to death through stoning, so a sorceress also is put to death through stoning."

J. Said to him R. Judah, "And merely because one matter is juxtaposed to the next, shall we take this person out for execution through stoning?! [There must be better proof.]

K. "Rather, those who divine by a ghost or by a familiar spirit fall into the classification of of sorcery. Why were they singled out? It was so as to drawn an analogy to them, so as to tell you, 'Just as those who divine by a ghost or by a familiar spirit are put to death through stoning, so a sorceress who is to be executed is put to death through stoning.'"

L. *But from the viewpoint of R. Judah's arguments, we have in the case of the one who divines by the ghost and the one who consults a familiar spirit two verses of Scripture that say the same thing,* and in a case of two verses of Scripture that say the same thing, one cannot derive lessons for some other matter entirely.

M. *Said R. Zechariah, "In respect to that matter, R. Judah indeed maintains that* two verses of Scripture that say the same thing do serve to teach yet another lesson entirely."

II.3 A. R. Yohanan said, "Why are they called sorcerers?

B. "Because they deny the power of the family above [a play on the word for sorcery]."

C. "There is no one else besides him" (Deut. 4:25):

D. R. Hanina said, "Even as to sorcery, [Freedman, p. 459, n. 5: Not even sorcerers have power to oppose his decree.]"

E. *There was a woman who tried to make dirt from under the feet of R. Hanina.*

F. *He said to her, "If it works out for you, go do it. [But] 'There is no one else besides him' (Deut. 4:25) is what is written."*

G. Can this be so [that Hanina made such a statement]?

H. But did not R. Yohanan say, "Why are they called sorcerers? Because they deny the power of the family above"?

I. *R. Hanina was in a special category, because he had a great deal of merit.*

J. Said R. Aibu bar Nigri said R. Hiyya bar Abba, "'With their sorcery' (Ex. 7:22) refers to magic through the agency of demons, 'with their enchantments' (Ex. 7:11) refers to sorcery without outside help."

K.   "So it is said, 'And the flame of the sword that turns of itself' (Gen. 3:24) [thus an action taking place of itself, similarly, the word at hand connotes sorcery performed without extraneous aid (Freedman, p. 459, n. 10)]."

II.4   A.   *Said Abbayye, "If [the sorcerer] uses exact methods, it is through a demon.*

     B.   *"If the sorcery does not work through exact methods, it is through enchantment."*

     C.   Said Abbayye, "The laws of sorcery are like the laws of the Sabbath.

     D.   "There are some actions that are punished by execution through stoning, some for which there is no penalty but which are forbidden, and some that are permitted to begin with.

     E.   "He who does a deed is punishable by stoning, but he who merely creates an illusion does what is forbidden but is exempt from punishment [M. 7:11D].

     F.   *"And as to what is permitted to begin with, it accords with the matter involving R. Hanina and R. Oshaia.*

     G.   *"Every Friday afternoon they would study the laws of creation and make for themselves a third-grown calf and they would eat it."*

II.5   A.   *Said R. Ashi, "I saw the father of Qarna blow his nose hard and ribbons of silk came out of his nostrils."*

II.6   A.   "Then the magicians said to Pharaoh, This is the finger of God" (Ex. 8:19).

     B.   [Since the reference is to the creation of lice, which the Egyptian sorcerers could not do,] said R. Eleazar, "On the basis of that statement we learn that a demon cannot make a creature smaller than a barley seed."

     C.   *R. Pappa said, "By God, he cannot make a creature as large as a camel.*

     D.   *"But these he can collect and those he cannot collect."*

     E.   *Said Rab to R. Hiyya, "I myself saw a Tai-Arab take a sword and chop up a camel, then he rang a bell and the camel arose."*

     F.   *He said to him, "After this was there blood or dung? [If not], it was merely an illusion."*

     G.   *Zeira went to Alexandria in Egypt. He bought an ass. When he went to give it water, it dissolved, and in place arose a landing board.*

     H.   *They said to him, "If you were not Zeiri, we should not give you back your money. Is there anyone who buys something here without testing it with water?"*

II.7   A.   *[68A] Yannai came to an inn. He said to them, "Give me some water to drink." They brought him a flour-and-water drink.*

     B.   *He saw that the woman's lips were moving. He poured out a little of the drink, and it turned into scorpions. He said to them, "I drank something of yours, now you take a drink of mine."*

	C.	*He gave her something to drink and she turned into an ass. He mounted her and went out to the market place.*
	D.	*Her girl-friend came and nullified the charm, so he was seen riding around on a woman in the market place.*
II.8	A.	"And the frog came up and covered the land of Egypt" (Ex. 8:6):
	B.	Said R. Eleazar, "It was one frog, and it multiplied into a swarm and filled the whole land of Egypt."
	C.	*That accords with a Tannaite dispute:*
	D.	R. Aqiba says, "It was one frog and filled the whole land of Egypt."
	E.	Said to him R. Eleazar b. Azariah, "Aqiba, what have you to do with matters of lore? Stop this talking of yours and go to discuss the laws of nega-spots and tents.
	F.	"It was a single frog, and it croaked for the others, and they came."
III.1	A.	**R. Aqiba says in the name of R. Joshua [M. 7:11D]:**
	B.	*Did R. Aqiba learn his knowledge of magic from R. Joshua? And have we not learned in a Tannaite teaching [that he learned his magic from R. Eleazer]?*
	C.	When R. Eleazer fell ill, R. Aqiba and his colleagues came in to visit him. He was sitting on his bed, and they sat in the antechamber. That day was a Friday, and Hyrcanus, his son, came in to remove his father's phylacteries. [Eliezer] grew angry with him and he went out in distress.
	D.	He said to them, "It appears to me that father's mind is deranged."
	E.	[Aqiba] said to them, "His [your] mind and your mother's mind are deranged. How will one ignore a matter that is prohibited on pain of stoning and take up a matter that is prohibited merely by reason of Sabbath rest [on the authority of rabbis]. [Freedman, p. 462, n. 1: The wife had not yet kindled the Sabbath lights nor put away the Sabbath meal to keep it hot. Both of these, if done on the Sabbath, are punishable by stoning, while the wearing of phylacteries indoors is forbidden only by rabbinical ordinance. Therefore he rebuked his son and wife.]"
	F.	Since sages observed that [Eliezer's] mind was at ease, they went in and sat before him at a distance of four cubits. [This was because he had been excommunicated, so they were prohibited from coming closer than that distance.]
	G.	He said to them, "Why have you come?"
	H.	They said to him, "To study Torah we have come."
	I.	He said to them, "And up to now why have you not come?"
	J.	They said to him, "We did not have free time."
	K.	He said to them, "I should be surprised if you people die natural deaths."
	L.	R. Aqiba said to him, "What will my death be?"
	M.	He said to him, "Your death will be the most difficult of all."

N.   He raised his two arms and laid them on his heart and said, "Woe for you, these two arms of mine, for they are like to scrolls of the Torah that have been rolled up [and have not been opened and read].

O.   "I learned much Torah, I taught much Torah.

P.   "I learned much Torah, but I did not take away from my masters even so much as a dog licks up from the water of the ocean.

Q.   "I taught much Torah, but my disciples did not take away from me so much as an eye-brush takes of eye-shadow.

R.   "And not only so, but I can repeat three hundred rules concerning a bright spot [Lev. 13:2], and no one ever asked me a thing about them.

S.   "And not only so, but I can repeat three hundred laws (and some say, three thousand laws), about the planting of cucumbers, and no one has ever asked me a thing about those laws, except for Aqiba, son of Joseph.

T.   "Once he and I were walking along the way, and he said to me, 'Rabbi, teach me something about planting cucumbers.'

U.   "I said something and the whole field was filled with cucumbers.

V.   "He said to me, 'Rabbi, you have taught me how to plant them. Now teach me how to pull them up.'

W.   "I said something and all of them were collected into a single place."

X.   They said to him, "As to **the ball, shoemaker's last, amulet, leather bag containing pearls, and small weight [M. Kel. 23:1]**, what is the law? [Are they susceptible as receptacles or not susceptible?]

Y.   He said to them, "They are susceptible to uncleanness." But they can regain insusceptibility to uncleanness just as they are."

Z.   "As to a shoe on the last, what is the law?"

AA.   He said to them, "It is [insusceptible to uncleanness and so] pure," and his soul went forth as he said the word, "pure."

BB.   R. Joshua stood on his feet and said, "The vow is released, the vow is released."

CC.   At the end of the Sabbath, R. Aqiba met his [bier] as it went from Caesarea to Lud. He beat his flesh until blood flowed to the ground. He began his eulogy for the line of mourners saying, "'My father, my father, the chariot of Israel and the horsemen thereof' (2 Kgs. 2:12).

DD.   "I have many coins but there is no money-changer to straighten them all out."

EE.   *Therefore it was from R. Eleazer that [Aqiba] learned [the rules cited in the Mishnah-paragraph].*

FF.   *He learned them from R. Eleazer but did not learn the reasoning about them, and then he went and learned them from R. Joshua, who taught them how to reason about them.*

GG.   *And how, to begin with, did [Eliezer] do any such thing? And lo, we have learned in the Mishnah:* **He who does a deed is liable [M. 7:11D]**!

HH.   *If it is to practice learn so as to teach about the subject, it is a different matter, for* a master has said, "'You shall not learn to do after the abominations of these nations' (Deut. 18:9).

II.   "You may not learn in order to do, but you may learn in order to understand and to teach about it."

Units I.1, II.1 deal with the formulation of the Mishnah's rule. Unit III.1ff. take up the mode of execution, which, after all, forms the topic at hand. Unit III.1 reverts to the Mishnah-passage and supplies materials on the authority behind it.

8

Bavli Tractate Sanhedrin
Chapter Eight
Folios 68B-75A

8:1

A.   A rebellious and incorrigible son [M. 7:4J] –

B.   at what point [does a child] become liable to be declared a rebellious and incorrigible son?

C.   From the point at which he will produce two pubic hairs, until the 'beard' is full –

D.   (that is the lower [pubic], not the upper [facial, beard], but the sages used euphemisms).

E.   As it is said, "If a man has a son" (Deut. 21:18) – (1) a son, not a daughter; (2) a son, not an adult man.

F.   And a minor is exempt, since he has not yet entered the scope of the commandments.

I.1   A.   *How do we know on the basis of Scripture that a minor is exempt?*

B.   *How do we know it! For it has been explicitly taught in the Mishnah-passage before us:* **since he has not yet entered the scope of the commandments [M. 8:1F].**

C.   *And furthermore, where do we find that Scripture has imposed a penalty [on a minor] so that, in the present setting in particular, one should require a verse of Scripture to declare a minor to be exempt?*

D.   *This is what we meant to say:* Is a wayward and rebellious son put to death on account of a sin that he has actually committed? He is put to death on account of what he will end up doing. Since he will be put to death on account of what he will end up doing, then even a minor [might fall within the framework of the law].

E.   *And furthermore,* **"A son" implies, a son and not a man [M. 8:1E],** *hence a minor [so the supposition of the question is quite sound].*

F.   Said R. Judah said Rab, "It is because Scripture has said, 'When a man will have a son...' (Deut. 21:18) – a son who is close to reaching the full strength of a man."

II.1   A.   **Until the lower beard is full:**

       B.   *R. Hiyya taught on Tannaite authority,* "Until it surrounds the corona."

       C.   When R. Dimi came, he said, "Surrounding the penis and not surrounding the testicles. [The former is an earlier point.]"

II.2   A.   Said R. Hisda, "If a minor male produced a child, his son is not subject [to the law] of a wayward and rebellious son, for it is said, 'If a man has a son' (Deut. 21:18), meaning, when a man has a son, and not 'when a son has a son.'"

       B.   *But that proof-text is needed for the proposition stated by R. Judah in the name of Rab [at I F].*

       C.   *If so, Scripture should have said,* "When a son will be born to a man."

       D.   *What is the sense of,* "When a man has a son"?

       E.   *What is implied is in accord with what R. Hisda has said,* [Freedman, p. 466, n. 4: By reversing the order, the manhood of the father when betting the son is emphasized. Only if a man beget a son, but not if a minor beget one, though he is already a man when his son transgresses.]

       F.   *May I then say that the entire verse serves only for the present purpose [excluding Rab's proposition entirely]?*

       G.   *If so, Scripture should have written,* "The son of a man." *What is the sense of,* "A man has a son"? *It bears the proof for two propositions.*

       H.   *The present proposition stands at variance with the view of Rabbah. For Rabbah has said,* "A minor male cannot produce a child, for it is said, 'But if the man has no kinsmen to recompense the trespass to' (Num. 5:8).

       I.   "Now [since all Israelites are related], is it possible that any Israelite would not have a redeemer?

       J.   "But the Scripture here speaks of taking what belongs to the estate of a proselyte [who has no Israelite heirs, by definition]. [69A] And the All-Merciful thereby indicates by saying, 'A man,' that is in the case of a man that you have to go in search of a redeemer, to find out whether he has kinsmen, but if it is a minor, it is not necessary to search for kinsmen, for you may be certain that he does not have kinsmen. [That is because a minor cannot produce a child.]"

       K.   *Abbayye objected,* "'[And if any man lies carnally with a woman who is a bondmaid' (Lev. 19:20)]: 'A man' indicates that it must be an adult male.

       L.   "How do we know that the law applies to a boy nine years and one day old who is capable of having sexual relations?

       M.   "Scripture says, '<u>And</u> if a man....'"

       N.   He said to him, "To be sure, he has [semen], but he cannot produce a child, such as with grain that is not yet a third grown [which has seed but, if sown, that seed cannot germinate]."

       O.   *A Tannaite authority of the house of Hezekiah [stated],* "'But if a man came presumptuously...' (Ex. 21:14).

       P.   "A man can [Freedman:] inflame his genitals and emit semen, but not a minor."

       Q.   *Said R. Mordecai to R. Ashi,* "*How do we know that the word translated presumptuously at hand means 'heating'?*

R.		*"It is from the verse, 'And Jacob sod pottage' (Gen. 25:29)* [which uses the same root]."
II.3	A.	*Now as to the Tannaite authority of the house of Ishmael,* [who taught, 'If a man has a son'] (Deut. 21:18) means, a son but not a father [so that if the son is himself a father already, the law does not apply (Freedman, p. 467, n. 10)],
	B.	*how would such a case be possible?* [We recall that the Mishnah has defined the period of liability as that interval between the appearance of two pubic hairs and the completion of the pubic corona, a relatively brief span of time.]
	C.	*Should one maintain that the wife became pregnant after the boy had produced two pubic hairs but produced the child before the lower beard had completed encircling the penis?*
	D.	*Is there a sufficient interval [to permit the pregnancy to come to term]?*
	E.	*And has not R. Keruspedai said, "The entire period of liability of a wayward and rebellious son is only three months alone."*
	F.	*Rather, is it not a case in which the wife became pregnant prior to the husband's producing two pubic hairs and then gave birth before the beard had completely grown. [That is how the son would not be subject to the law at hand].*
	G.	*That would then prove that* a minor may produce a child.
	H.	*No, in point of fact his wife became pregnant after he had produced two pubic hairs and then gave birth after the lower beard was complete.*
	I.	*And as to the problem of the saying in the name of R. Keruspedai [that there would not be done for the pregnancy to come to term while the boy was subject to the law of the wayward and rebellious son], when R. Dimi came, he said, "In the West they say, '"A son," and not one who is fit to be called a father.'* [Freedman, p. 468, n. 1: Once his wife is impregnated, he is already fit to be called a father. But it is unnecessary to exclude him when he is already a father, for by then his hair must be fully grown, and he is automatically excluded by the limitations expressed in the Mishnah.]"
II.4	A.	*Reverting to the body of the foregoing:* Said R. Keruspedai said R. Shabbetai, "The entire period of liability of a wayward and rebellious son is only three months alone."
	B.	*But lo, we have learned in the Mishnah:* **From the point at which he will produce two pubic hairs until the beard is full [M. 8:1C].** [Is that only in three months?]
	C.	*[This is the reply:] If the beard is full, even though three months have not passed, or if three months have passed, even though the beard is not full [he is no longer liable, and that is why Keruspedai's statement is valid under all circumstances.]*
	D.	*R. Jacob of Nehar Peqod sat before Rabina, and, going into session, said in the name of R. Huna, son of R. Joshua, "From the statement of R. Keruspedai in the name of R. Shabbetai it follows that* if a woman bears a child at seven months, her pregnancy will not be discernible at a third of its term.
	E.	*"For if you think that her pregnancy will be discerned at a third of term, why should the statement at hand specify three months? It would have sufficed to specify two and a half months.* [Freedman, p. 468, n. 4: For the fetus being then

discernible, the son is fit to be called a father and is no longer liable.]"

F.   *He said to him, "Under all circumstances I should say to you that the fetus will be discernible at a third of term, [after three months, for in framing the law] we follow the majority [of cases]. [Most pregnancies go on for nine months, and the fetus is discerned at three months. That is then the point at which the son may be called a father and is no longer subject to the law of the wayward and rebellious son.]"*

G.   *They made this statement before R. Huna, son of R. Joshua, He said to him, "But in capital cases [such as this one] do we follow the majority? Has the Torah not said, 'Then the congregation shall judge and the congregation shall deliver the slayer' (Num. 35:25). [Freedman, p. 468, n. 6: This is taken to mean that in doubt the accused be given the benefit.] Can you then say that we follow the majority?"*

H.   *This statement was repeated before Rabina. He said to him, "But in capital cases do we not follow the majority?*

I.   *"Have we not learned in the Mishnah:* **If one of the witnesses says, 'It was on the second of the month,' and one of the witnesses says, 'It was on the third of the month,' their testimony stands, for one of them may know about the intercalation of the month, and the other one may not know about the intercalation of the month [M. 5:3A-B].**

J.   *"And if you maintain that we do not follow the majority, then we should rule in the present case that the witnesses testify in a precise way and so contradict one another. [Freedman, p. 469, n. 3: Since there is a minority that does not err in respect of the length of the month, why not assume that each knows the length of the preceding month?]*

K.   *"Rather, is it not because we do maintain that we follow the case of the majority, and the majority is likely to err in the matter of the intercalation of the month."*

L.   *Said R. Jeremiah of Difti, "We too have learned in the Mishnah:* **A girl three years and one day old is betrothed by intercourse. And if a Levir has had intercourse with her, he has acquired her. And they are liable on her account because of the law prohibiting intercourse with a married woman. And she imparts uncleanness to him who has intercourse with her when she is menstruating, to convey uncleanness to the lower as to the upper layer. If she was married to a priest, she eats heave-offering. If one of those who are unfit for marriage has intercourse with her, he** has rendered her unfit to marry into the priesthood. If one of all those who are forbidden in the Torah to have intercourse with her has intercourse with her, they are put to death on her account, but she is free of responsibility [M. Nid. 5:4A-H]. [69B] *Now why should this be the case [that she should be regarded as legally married at all]? I might invoke the possibility that she is barren, and it was in the supposition that she was barren, the husband would not have betrothed her [so that, in point of fact, should she prove to be barren, she is not regarded as betrothed at all]. Must we therefore not maintain that we follow the status of the majority, and the majority of women are not barren [and that is why the rule is as stated in the Mishnah]."*

M.   *No, [that is not right, for] what is the sense of "liable on her account" as the Mishnah states matters? It is to an offering.*

N.   *But lo, what it says is,* **They are put to death on her account!**

O.   At issue is her father's having sexual relations with her.

P.   *But it says,* **If one of all those who are forbidden in the Torah to have intercourse with her has intercourse with her** [not just the father]!

Q.   *So the Mishnah-rule speaks of a case in which the husband accepted her [whether or not she was barren, so the case does not make the besought point anyhow].*

II.5 A.   *Our rabbis have taught on Tannaite authority:*

B.   **A woman who commits lewdness with her minor son, who entered into the first state of cohabitation with her – –**

C.   **the House of Shammai invalidate her from marriage into the priesthood.**

D.   **And the House of Hillel declare her valid [T. Sot. 5:7A-C].**

E.   *Said R. Hiyya, son of Rabbah bar Nahmani, said R. Hisda, and some say, said R. Hisda said Zeiri, "All concur in the case of a son nine years and one day old, that his act of sexual relations is entirely valid.*

F.   *"In the case of a child less than eight years of age, [all agree that] his act of sexual relations is null.*

G.   *"The dispute pertains only to the case of a child eight years of age.*

H.   *"For the House of Shammai take the view that we derive the law from the case of* the earlier generations [when a boy of eight years could impregnate a woman], *and the House of Hillel take the view that we do not derive the law from the case of* the earlier generations."

I.   *And how on the basis of Scripture do we know that the earlier generations could produce a pregnancy [at the age of eight years]?*

J.   *May we say that the proof is as follows:*

K.   It is written, "[And David sent and inquired after the woman, and one said,] 'Is not this Bath Sheba, daughter of Eliam, wife of Uriah the Hittite'" (2 Sam. 11:3).

L.   And it is written, "Eliam, the son of Ahitophel the Gilonite" (2 Sam. 23:134).

M.   And it is written, "And he sent by the hand of Nathan the prophet, and he called his name Jedidiah [Solomon later on] because of the Lord" (2 Sam. 12:25).

N.   And it is written, "And it came to pass, after two full years [after Solomon was born] that Absalom had sheep-shearers" (2 Sam. 13:23).

O.   And it is written, "So Absalom fled and went to Geshur and was there three years" (2 Sam. 13:38).

P.   And it is written, "So Absalom dwelt two full years in Jerusalem and did not see the king's face" (2 Sam. 14:28).

Q.   And it is written, "And it came to pass after forty years that Absalom said to the king, I pray you, let me go and pay my vow which I have vowed to the Lord in Hebron" (2 Sam. 25:7).

R.   And it is written, "And when Ahitophel saw that his counsel was not followed, he saddled his ass and arose and went home to his house, to his city, and he put his household in order, and hanged himself" (2 Sam. 17:23).

S.   And it is written, "Bloody and deceitful men shall not live out half their days" (Ps. 55:24). [This proves that Ahitophel did not reach the age of thirty-five].

T.   *And it has been taught on Tannaite authority:*

U.   The entire lifespan of Doeg was only thirty-four years, and of Ahitophel only thirty-three years.

V.   *So how many years were they? Thirty-three. Then deduct the seven years, the age of Solomon at that time [that Ahitophel committed suicide], leaving twenty-six. Take off two years for three pregnancies, and it comes out that each one was eight years old when he produced a child.* [Ahitophel must have been eight years at the conception of Eliam, Eliam eight years at the conception of Bath Sheba, Bath Sheba eight years at the conception of Solomon (Freedman, p. 471, n. 3)].

W.   *But perhaps the two of them [Ahitophel and Eliam] were nine years old [when they produced conceptions], and Bath Sheba was only six years old when she conceived, for a woman is more vital. You may know that that is the case, for she had had a child earlier [before Solomon].*

X.   *The proof derives from here:*

Y.   "Now these are the generations of Terah: Terah begat Abram, Nahor and Haran" (Gen. 11:27).

Z.   Abraham was a year older than Nahor, and Nahor was a year older than Haran. So Abraham was older than Haran by two years.

AA.   And it is written, "And Abraham and Nahor took wives for themselves, the name of Abram's wife was Sarai, and the name of Nahor's wife was Milcah, daughter of Haran, father of Milcah and father of Iscah" (Gen. 11:29).

BB. (And R. Isaac said, "Iscah is the same as Sarai, and why was she called Iscah? Because she foresaw through the Holy Spirit [what would happen in the future], and this is in line with that which is written, 'In all that Sarah has said to you, hearken to her voice' (Gen. 21:12).")

CC. (Another reason: Everyone looked at her beauty.)

DD. It is written, "Then Abraham fell upon his face and laughed and said in his heart, [Shall a child be born to him who is a hundred years old? And shall Sarah, who is ninety years old, bear?]" (Gen. 17:17).

EE. *Now how much older was Abraham than Sarah? Ten years.*

FF. *And he was older than her father by two years.*

GG. *It turns out that Haran begat Sarah when he was eight years old.*

HH. *But why should we reach this conclusion? Perhaps Abraham was the youngest of the three, and the brothers were ranked in wisdom.*

II. *You may know that Scripture ranked them in accord with their wisdom, for it is written,* "And Noah was five hundred years old, and Noah begat Shem, Ham and Japheth,"

JJ. [If ranked by age,] Shem would be a year older than Ham, and Ham a year older than Japheth, so Shem was two years older than Japheth.

KK. It is written, "And Noah was six hundred years old when the flood of water was upon the earth" (Gen. 7:6), and it is written, "These are the generations of Shem. Shem was a hundred years old and begat Arphaxad two years after the flood" (Gen. 11:10).

LL. *Now can he have been a hundred years old? He must have been a hundred and two years old.* [Freedman, p. 472, n. 5: Since Noah was five hundred years old when Shem was born, and six hundred when the flood commenced, Shem must have been a hundred then. Consequently, two years later he was a hundred and two years old.]

MM. *Rather, Scripture ranked them by wisdom, and here too, Scripture ranked them by wisdom.*

NN. *Said R. Kahana, "I stated this teaching before R. Zebid of Nehardea.*

OO. *"He said to me, 'You derive the fact from that passage. And this is the proof from which we derive the same proposition:*

PP. *"'To Shem, also, the father of all the children of Eber, brother of Japheth the elder, even to him were children born' (Gen. 10:21).*

QQ. *"[This indicates that] Japhath was the oldest of the brothers."*

RR. *How do we know [that in earlier generations a boy of eight years of age could produce a child]?*

SS. *It is from the following:*

TT. "And Bezaleel, son of Uri, son of Hur, of the tribe of Judah" (Ex. 38:22).

UU.	And it is written, "And when Azubah, [Caleb's wife], died, Caleb took Ephrath, who bore him Hur" (1 Chr. 2:19).
VV.	*And when Bezaleel made the tabernacle, how old was he?*
WW.	*He was thirteen, for it is written,* "And all the wise men, who wrought all the work of the sanctuary, came every man from his work which they made" (Ex. 36:4) [Freedman: he had must reached manhood].
XX.	*And it has been taught on Tannaite authority:*
YY.	In the first year [after the Exodus] Moses made the tabernacle, in the second he put up the tabernacle and sent out the spies.
ZZ.	And it is written, "And Caleb said, I was forty years old when Moses, the servant of the Lord, [sent me from Kadesh-bernea to spy out the land]" (Jos. 14:7), "and now, lo, I am today eighty-five years old" (Josh. 14:10).
AAA.	*So how old was he? He was forty years old. Take off the fourteen years of Bezaleel's age at that time [since he was thirteen when he made the tabernacle, and this was a year later], leaving twenty-six years [as Caleb's age when Bezaleel was born]. Take off two years for three pregnancies [leaving twenty-four years], so each must have produced a child at the age of eight.*

III.1 A. **A son, not a daughter [M. 8:1E]:**

B. *It has been taught on Tannaite authority:*

C. **Said R. Simeon, "By strict law a daughter also should have been appropriate to fall into the category of the wayward and rebellious child, [70A] for everyone comes around to her to commit a sin [and she may turn out to be a whore].**

D. **"But it is the decree of Scripture: 'a son,' not a daughter" [T. San. 11:6C].**

The bulk of the materials at hand is framed around the interests of the Mishnah-paragraph. Units I.1, II.1 provide proof texts or clarifications of the Mishnah's rule. Unit II.2 expands upon the proof-text at hand. Unit II.3 is continuous with unit II.2. Unit V provides an important qualification of the law at hand. III.1 then reverts to the Mishnah-paragraph and expands upon is proof-text.

8:2

A. At what point is he liable?

B. Once he has eaten a tartemar of meat and drunk a half-log of Italian wine.

C. R. Yosé says, "A mina of meat and a log of wine."

D. [If] he ate in an association formed for a religious duty.

E. [if] he ate on the occasion of the intercalation of the month,

F. [if] in Jerusalem he ate food in the status of second tithe,

G. [if] he ate carrion and terefah-meat, forbidden things or creeping things,

H.		[if] he ate untithed produce, first tithe, the heave-offering of which had not been removed, second tithe or consecrated food which had not been redeemed [by money],
I.		[if] he ate something which fulfilled a religious duty or whereby he committed a transgression,
J.		[if] he ate any sort of food except meat, drank any sort of liquid except wine –
K.		he is not declared a rebellious and incorrigible son –
L.		unless he eats meat and drinks wine,
M.		since it is said, "A glutton and a drunkard" (Deut. 21:20).
N.		And even though there is no clear proof for the proposition, there is at least a hint for it,
O.		for it is said, "Do not be among the wine-drinkers, among gluttonous meat-eaters" (Prov. 23:20).
I.1	A.	Said R. Zira, "As to this tartemar, I do not know what it is, but since R. Yosé doubles the measure applying to wine, it follows that he doubles the measure in regard to meat.
	B.	"So it turns out that a tartemar is a half mina."
I.2	A.	Said R. Hanan bar Moledah said R. Huna, "He is liable only if he buys meat cheaply [ZWL] and eats it, buys wine cheaply [ZWL] and drinks it, for it is written, 'He is a glutton [ZWLL] and a drunkard' (Deut. 21:20) [a play on words, since the root for 'glutton' yields 'cheap.']"
	B.	Said R. Hanan bar Moledah said R. Huna, "He is liable only if he eats raw meat and drinks undiluted wine."
	C.	*Is this so?. And lo, both Rabbah and R. Joseph say,* "If he ate raw meat and drank undiluted wine, he is not regarded as a wayward and rebellious son."
	E.	Said Rabina, "What is meant by undiluted wine is wine that is diluted but not diluted, and what is meant by raw meat is meat that has been cooked but not cooked.
	F.	*"It is like charred meat that thieves eat [on the run]."*
	G.	*Both Rabbah and R. Joseph say,* "If he ate salted meat and drank wine right from the vat [before it has matured], he cannot be treated as a wayward and rebellious son."
I.3	A.	*We have learned there:* **On the eve of the ninth of Ab a person should not eat two prepared dishes, nor should one eat meat or drink wine [M. Ta. 4:7D].**
	C.	*In this regard a Tannaite authority taught,* "But one may eat salted meat and drink wine fresh from the vat.
	D.	As to salted meat, how long must it be salted?
	E.	Said R. Hanina bar Kahana, "So long as one might eat the meat of a peace-offering [two days and an intervening night].
	F.	And how long is wine regarded as fresh from the vat?
	G.	So long as it is in its first stage of fermentation.
	H.	*And it has been taught on Tannaite authority:* **Wine which still is fermenting – as long as it is fermenting, it is not liable to the law of uncovered liquids. And how long is it deemed still to be fermenting? Three days [T. Ter. 7:15 (Avery-Peck)].** What is the law here [i.e. with regard to fermenting wine]?

I.   There [with respect to not eating meat on the eve of the ninth of Ab] it is so as to diminish rejoicing. [So long as the meat is like the meat of a peace-offering, it gives the pleasure of fresh meat.]

J.   *Here it is because of its attractiveness, and even after a brief period, it is no longer attractive.*

K.   *Wine for its part is attractive only after forty days have passed.* [The son is liable only for eating and drinking what is very attractive, hence excluding meat a day old and wine less than forty days old (Freedman, p. 476, n. 2)].

The Evils of Wine and Strong Drink

I.4   A.   Said R. Hanan, "Wine has created in this world only for comforting the bereaved and for requiting the wicked.

B.   "For it is written, 'Give strong drink to him who is ready to perish [=the wicked], and wine to those of heavy heart' (Prov. 31:6)."

C.   Said R. Isaac, "What is the meaning of the statement of Scripture, 'Do not look upon wine when it is red' (Prov. 23:31)?

D.   Do not look upon wine, which makes the face of the wicked red in this world and white [with embarrassment] in the world to come."

E.   Raba said, "'Do not look upon wine when it is red' (Prov. 23:31) – do not look upon wine, which ends up as blood."

F.   *R. Kahana contrasted verses of Scripture, "It is written,* Tirash, *but we read,* tirosh [for the word for wine].

G.   "If one had merit, he is made a head (rosh). If not, he becomes poor (rash)."

H.   *Raba contrasted verses of Scripture, "It is written, 'And wine makes desolate the heart of man' but it is read, 'rejoices the heart of man.' If one has merit, wine makes him glad, if not, it makes him sad."*

I.   *And this is in line with what Raba said, "Wine and spice makes one wise."*

I.5   A.   *Said R. Amram, son of R. Simeon bar Abba, said R. Hanina, "What is the meaning of the verse of Scripture, 'Who has woe? who has sorrow? who has contentions? who has babbling? who has wounds without cause? who has redness of eyes? They who tarry long at wine, they who go to seek mixed wine' (Prov. 23:29-30)?"*

B.   *When R. Dimi came, he said, "In the West they say, in respect to this verse, that one may interpret the second part in explanation of the first, or the first in explanation of the second.* [Freedman, p. 477, n. 3: The second as explanatory of the first: who have all these evils? Those who tarry long. The second being the cause, the first the effect. <u>Vice versa</u>: For whom is it fitting to tarry long over wine? For the wicked only.]"

I.6   A.   *Ubar, the Galilean, expounded as follows: "The word 'and' is stated thirteen times with respect to wine:*

B.   "'And Noah began to be a husbandman, and he planted a vineyard, and he drank of the wine and was drunken, and he was uncovered within his tent. And Ham the father of Canaan saw the nakedness of his father and told his two brothers outside. And Shem and Japheth took a garment and laid it upon their shoulders and went backward and covered the nakedness of their father, and their faces [were backward, and they did not see their father's nakedness].

And Noah awoke from his wine and knew what his younger son had done to him' (Gen. 9:20-24). [Freedman: the conversive waw occurs thirteen times. The combination of waw yod means woe, thus there were thirteen woes; so great are the sorrows caused by drunkenness]."

C. *[On the reference to what the younger son had done to him,] Rab and Samuel [discussed the matter].*

D. One said, "He castrated him."

E. And the other said, "He had sexual relations with him."

F. *The one who said that he castrated them holds that, since he cursed him by his fourth son [the sons of Ham, Cush, Mizraim, Phut, and, fourth, Canaan, and at Gen. 10:7, Noah cursed Canaan], he cursed him because of a fourth son [which Noah could not have].*

G. *And the one who maintains that he had sexual relations with him compares the use of, "And he saw." Here: "And Ham the father of Canaan saw the nakedness of his father," and elsewhere: "And when Shechem, son of Hamor, saw her, [he took her and lay with her and defiled her]" (Gen. 34:2).*

H. *Now from the viewpoint of him who says that he castrated him, that is why he cursed him as to his fourth son in particular.*

I. *But as to him who maintains that he had sexual relations with him, why did he curse the fourth son in particular? Rather, he ought to have cursed him.*

J. *In point of fact, both took place.*

I.7 A. "And Noah began to be a husbandman and he planted a vineyard" (Gen. 9:25):

B. *Said R. Hisda said R. Uqba, and some say, Mar Uqba said R. Zakkai said,* "The Holy One, blessed be he, said to Noah, 'Noah, you should have learned from the first man, for whom it was only wine that was the cause [of all his troubles]."

C. *This accords with the view of him who has said that the tree from which the first man ate was the vine.*

D. *That is in accord with what has been taught on Tannaite authority:*

E. R. Meir says, "As to the tree from which the first man ate [and was cursed],

F. "It was a vine, **[70B]** for there is nothing that causes for man so much wailing as wine, [as it says, 'And he drank of the wine and got drunk' (Gen. 9:21)]."

G. R. Judah says, "It was wheat, for a child does not know how to call his mother and father by name before he can taste wheat, [so wheat is the source of knowledge, hence the Tree of Knowledge]."

H. R. Nehemiah says, "It was a fig tree, for the source of the curse proved also to be the remedy, as it is said, 'And they sewed fig leaves together' (Gen. 3:7)."

I.8 A. "The words of King Lemuel, the burden wherewith his mother admonished him" (Prov. 31:1):

B. Said R. Yohanan in the name of R. Simeon b. Yohai, "This verse teaches that his mother had him bound on a post [to be flogged].

	C.	"She said to him, 'What, my son? and what, the son of my womb? and what, the son of my vows?' (Prov. 31:1).
	D.	"'What my son? Everybody knows that your father feared heaven, and now people will say that his mother was the cause of his [corruption].
	E.	"'And what, the son of my womb? As to all the other wives of your father's harem, once they got pregnant, they did not see the face again. But I forced my way in so that I should have a vigorous and well-formed son. [Further acts of intercourse would make the foetus better looking.]
	F.	"'And what, the son of my vows? All the other women in your father's harem would take vows, "May I have a son worthy of the throne," but I took a vow and said, "May I have a son that is vigorous and filled with Torah-learning and fit for prophecy."
	G.	"'It is not for kings, O Lemuel, it is not for kings to drink wine [nor for princes to say, Where is a strong drink]' (Prov. 31:4).
	H.	"She said to him, 'What business do you have with kings who drink wine and get drunk and say, "What do we need God for?"?
	I.	"'Nor for princes to say, Where is strong drink' (Prov. 31:4):
	J.	"'Should he to whom all the secrets of the world are self-evident drink and get drunk?'"
	K.	*There are those who say,* "Should he, to whom all the princes of the world rise early to come to his door, drink wine and get drunk?"
	L.	Said R. Isaac, "How do we know that Solomon repented and confessed that his mother [was right]?
	M.	"As it is written, 'I am more brutish than man and have not the understanding of a man' (Prov. 30:2).
	N.	"'I am more brutish than man' refers to Noah, of whom it is written, 'And Noah began to be a husbandman' (Gen. 9:20).
	O.	"'And have not the understanding of a man' – of Adam."
II.1	A.	**If he ate in an association formed for a religious duty [M. 8:2D]:**
	B.	Said R. Abbahu, "He is liable only if he eats in an association that is made up entirely of louts."
	C.	*But have we not learned in the Mishnah:* **If he ate in an association formed for a religious duty he is not declared a wayward and rebellious son [M. 8:2D]?**
	D.	*The reason is that such an association was formed for a religious duty. Lo, if it was not formed to carry out a religious duty, even if the whole of the association was not made up of louts, he may be declared liable [and that is not limited to an association made up entirely of louts, as Abbahu has claimed]. So we are informed [by the Mishnah] that even if everyone in the association was a lout, since the association is taken up with carrying out a religious duty, he is not going to be led astray [and so penalized].*
III.1	A.	**If he ate on the occasion of the intercalation of the month [M. 8:2F]:**
	B.	*Does this bear the implication that on such an occasion they eat meat and wine?*
	C.	*And has it not been taught on Tannaite authority:*
	D.	They go up for it only with a piece of wheat bread and pulse alone.

E.		*So we are informed that even though people do not come up [to testify] carrying more than a piece of wheat bread and pulse, if he brought up meat and wine and ate it, since he was involved in performing a religious duty, he is not led astray [and so is not penalized].*
F.		*Our rabbis have taught on Tannaite authority:*
G.		Not less than ten come up for the rite of intercalating the month.
H.		People come up only with a piece of wheat bread and pulse.
I.		People come up only on the evening following the intercalation.
J.		And they come up not by day but by night.
K.		And has it not been taught on Tannaite authority:
L.		They come up not by night but by day?
M.		*This accords with what R. Hiyya bar Abba said to his sons, "Get up early and come out early, so people may know of your celebration. [But the rite took place at night.]"*
IV.1	A.	**If in Jerusalem he ate food in the status of second tithe [M. 8:2F]:**
	B.	*Since he eats it in the correct way, he will not be led astray.*
V.1	A.	**If he ate carrion and terefah-meat, forbidden things or creeping things [M. 8:2G]:**
	B.	Said Raba, "If he ate chicken, he is not condemned as a wayward and rebellious son."
	C.	*Lo, we have learned in the Mishnah:* **If he devoured carrion and terefah meat, forbidden things or creeping things [M. 8:2G] ... he is not declared a wayward and rebellious son [M. 8:2K].** Thus if he ate clean [and appropriate meat], he would be condemned as a wayward and rebellious son.
	D.	*The Mishnah speaks only of what completes the requisite volume. [If the whole measure was the meat of chicken, he would be exempt, but if it was mostly cow-meat and completed with a little chicken, he is liable.]*
VI.1	A.	**If he ate something which fulfilled a religious duty or whereby he committed a transgression [M. 8:2I]:**
	B.	**Something which fulfilled a religious duty** is a meal served to comfort mourners.
	C.	**Something whereby he committed a transgression** is a meal on a public fast.
	D.	*And what is the scriptural basis for that view?*
	E.	*Scripture has said, "He will not obey our voice" (Deut. 21:20) meaning, "our voice" and not the voice of the Omnipresent. [If he disobeys God, he does not fall into the category of a wayward and rebellious son.]*
VII.1	A.	**If he ate any sort of food except meat, or drank any sort of liquid except wine [M. 8:2J]:**
	B.	**If he ate any sort of food except meat** – *["meat" here is meant] to include even Keilah-figs.*
	C.	**If he drank any sort of liquid except wine** – *["wine" here is meant] to include even honey and milk.*
	D.	*For it has been taught on Tannaite authority:*

E. If one ate Keilah-figs or drank honey or milk, and then went into the Temple, [71A] he is liable [for entering the Temple after drinking wine.]

VIII.1   A. He is not declared a rebellious and incorrigible son unless he eats meat and drinks wine [M. 8:2K-L].

B. *Our rabbis have taught on Tannaite authority:*

C. If he ate any sort of food but did not eat meat, drank any sort of liquid but did not drink wine, he is not declared a rebellious and incorrigible son, unless he eats meat and drinks wine, since it is said, "A glutton and a drunkard" (Deut. 21:20).

D. Even though there is no clear proof for the proposition, there is at least a hint for it, for it is said, "Do not be among the wine-drinkers, among gluttonous meat-eaters" (Prov. 23:20) [M. 8:2J-O].

E. And it says, "For the drunkard and glutton shall come to poverty, and drowsiness shall clothe a man with rags" (Prov. 23:21).

F. Said R. Zira, "Whoever sleeps in the school house will find that his learning of Torah is torn into rags,

G. "For it is said, 'And drowsiness shall clothe a man with rags'" (Prov. 23:21).

The Talmud is made up of two large compositions, one treating the Mishnah in particular, and a long inserted unit on the theme of wine. For the most part the theme explains the conglomeration of materials, and there is no point at which the Mishnah-paragraph plays a role.

8:3

A. [If] he stole something belonging to his father but ate it in his father's domain,

B. or something belonging to others but ate it in the domain of those others,

C. or something belonging to others but ate it in his father's domain,

D. he is not declared a rebellious and incorrigible son – –

E. until he steals something of his father's and eats it in the domain of others.

F. R. Yosé b. Judah says, "...until he steals something belonging to his father and his mother."

I.1   A. If he stole something belonging to his father but ate it in his father's domain,

B. *even though he has ready access [to what belongs to his father], he will be afraid [and not do this very often].*

C. If he stole something belonging to others but ate it in the domain of those others,

D. *even though he is not afraid, he does not have ready access [and so will not do this very often].*

E. And all the more so if he stole something belonging to others but ate it in his father's domain,

F. *in which case he does not have ready access, and, further, is afraid [so he will not do this often].*

G.   **Until he steals something of his father's and eats it in the domain of others,**

H.   *in which case he has ready access and will not be afraid [and so will make this theft a habitual practice].*

II.1 A.   **R. Yosé b. Judah says, "...until he steals something belonging to his father and his mother [M. 8:3F]:**

B.   *Whence would his mother get domain over property?* What a wife buys is as if her husband bought it.

C.   Said R. Yosé b. R. Hanina, "It would involve something prepared for a meal for his father and for his mother."

D.   And has not R. Hanan b. Moladah said R. Huna said, "He is liable only if he will buy meat at a cheap price and drink wine acquired at a cheap price"?

E.   *Rather, I may say,* [he stole] funds for a meal designated for his father and his mother [Freedman, p. 482, n. 2: in which money the mother has an exclusive share, as *alimentation is part of the husband's obligations to the wife*].

F.   *And if you wish, I shall propose that it* was from property that a third party gave over to her, saying, "I give you this on the condition that your husband enjoy no domain over it."

The Talmud at unit I.1 presents its underlying thesis on the purpose of the law and reads each clause in light of that thesis. Unit II.2 clarifies an obvious problem in the Mishnah-paragraph.

8:4

A.   **[If] his father wanted [to put him to judgement as a rebellious and incorrigible son] but his mother did not want to do so,**

B.   **[if] his father did not want and his mother did want [to put him to judgment],**

C.   **he is not declared a rebellious and incorrigible son –**

D.   **until both of them want [to put him to judgment].**

E.   **R. Judah says, "If his mother was unworthy of his father, he is not declared to be a rebellious and incorrigible son."**

I.1   A.   *What is the sense of* **unworthy of his father** *[at M. 8:4E]? May I say that it was a marriage that produced liability to extirpation or even to the death penalty at the hands of an earthly court [e.g., an incestuous union]?*

B.   *But in any case his father remains his father and his mother, his mother.*

C.   *Rather, the sense is that he was not similar [in appearance] to his father.*

D.   *So too has it been taught on Tannaite authority:*

E.   R. Judah says, "If his mother is not like his father in voice, appearance, and stature, he cannot be declared a wayward and rebellious son."

F.   *What is the scriptural basis for that view?*

G.   It is because Scripture has said, "He will not obey our voice" (Deut. 21:10).

H.   *Since we require that the voice of the two be alike, so we require that they be alike in appearance and stature.*

I.2   A.   *In accord with which authority is the following Tannaite teaching:*

B.   **There has never been, and there never will be, a wayward and rebellious son.**

C.   **So why has the passage been written? To tell you, "Expound and receive a reward" [T. San. 11:6A-B].**

D.   *In accord with whom? The foregoing surely accords with the theory of R. Judah.*

E.   *And if you wish, I shall propose that it accords with R. Simeon, for it has been taught on Tannaite authority:*

F.   Said R. Simeon, "And because this one has eaten a tartemar of meat and drunk a half-log of Italian wine, will his father and his mother bring him out to be stoned?

G.   "But such a case has never been and will never be.

H.   "And why has it been written? It is to tell you, 'Expound and receive a reward.'"

I.   Said R. Jonathan, "I saw such a case and sat on his grave."

J.   *In accord with whom is the following that has been taught on Tannaite authority:*

K.   **An apostate town never was and is not ever going to be. And why was the matter written? To say, Expound it and receive a reward [T. San. 14:1A-B, T.'s version.]**

L.   *In accord with whom? In accord with R. Eleazer.*

M.   *For it has been taught on Tannaite authority:*

N.   R. Eleazer says, "Any town in which there is even a single mezuzah cannot be declared an apostate town."

O.   *What is the scriptural basis for that view?*

P.   Scripture has said, "And you shall gather all the spoil of it in the midst of the street thereof and shall burn them" (Deut. 13:17).

Q.   *Now if there is even a single mezuzah, it is not possible to do so, for it is written,* "And you shall destroy the names of them.... You shall not do so to the Lord your God" (Deut. 12:4).

R.   Said R. Jonathan, "I saw such a town and sat on its mound."

S.   *In accord with what authority is the following that has been taught on Tannaite authority:*

T.   **A diseased house has never come into existence and is never going to come into existence. And why was the passage written? It was to tell you, Expound and receive a reward [T. Neg. 6:1A].**

U.   *In accord with what? It is in accord with R. Eleazar b. R. Simeon, for we have learned in the Mishnah:*

V.   **R. Eleazar b. R. Simeon says, "[A house is not declared unclean] until a spot the size of two split beans will appear on two stones on two walls in the corner; its length is two split beans and its width a split bean [M. Neg. 12:3G-H].**

W.   *What is the reason for the view of R. Eleazar b. R. Simeon? It is written,* "Wall" (Lev. 14:37) *and it is again written,* "Walls" (Lev. 14:37). *What is one*

	wall that appears as two walls? It has to be at the angle at which walls meet.
X.	*It has been taught on Tannaite authority:*
Y.	**Said R. Eleazar b. R. Sadot, "There was a place on the border of Gaza, and they called it, 'A quarantined ruin.'"**
Z.	**Said R. Simeon of Kefar Akkum, "Once I went in Galilee and I saw a place that is marked off by designated stones, and they said, 'They deposited diseased stones in this place'" [T. Neg. 6:1B-C].**

Once Judah's qualification is offered, at unit I.1, the question obviously arises of whether such a case can ever come to court. Unit I.2, continuous with the foregoing, then explores that question in its own terms.

8:4F-O

F.	**[If] one of them was maimed in the hand, lame, dumb, blind, or deaf,**
G.	**he is not declared a rebellious and incorrigible son,**
H.	**since it is said, "Then his father and his mother will lay hold of him" (Deut. 21:20) – so they are not maimed in their hands;**
I.	**"and bring them out" – so they are not lame;**
J.	**"and they shall say" – so they are not dumb;**
K.	**"This is our son" – so they are not blind;**
L.	**"He will not obey our voice" – so they are not deaf.**
M.	**They warn him before three judges and flog him.**
N.	**[If] he went and misbehaved again, he is judged before twenty-three judges.**
O.	**He is stoned only if there will be present the first three judges, since it is said, "This, our son" – this one who was flogged before you.**

I.1	A.	*Does this passage prove that the Scripture must be read in a literal way, just as it is written?*
	B.	*The present case is distinctive,* **[71B]** *for the entire verse of Scripture at hand is superfluous [and available for exposition such as is given here].*
II.1	A.	**They warn him before three judges [M. 8:4M]:**
	B.	*Why? Should two not suffice?*
	C.	*Said Abbayye, "This is the sense of the passage: 'They warn him before two judges and administer a flogging before three.'"*
II.2	A.	*Whence is it stated that a wayward and rebellious son [is flogged]?*
	B.	*It is in accord with what R. Abbahu has said. For R. Abbahu has said, "We have derived an analogy from 'And they shall chastise him' which occurs two times [Deut. 22:18, Deut. 21:18].*
	C.	*"And the sense of that repeated phrase derives from the use of the word 'son,' with an analogy to the use of that same word in the phrase, 'And it shall be if the wicked man be worthy ["a son"] to be flogged' (Deut. 25:2)."*
III.1	A.	**If he went and misbehaved again, he is judged before twenty-three judges [M. 8:4/0]:**

B. *Is the cited verse, "This our son..." not used to make the point [at M. 8:4K], "This is our son" – so they are not blind?*

C. *If so, the Scripture should have stated, "He is our son."*

D. *Why: "This, our son"?*

E. *It is to permit the deduction of two rules.*

The Talmud systematically explains the Mishnah's clauses, providing a scriptural basis for the rules.

8:4P-Q

P. **[If] he fled before his trial was over, and afterward [while he was a fugitive,] the lower "beard" became full, he is exempt.**

Q. **If after his trial was done he fled, and afterward the lower beard became full, he is liable.**

I.1 A. Said R. Hanina, "A son of Noah who cursed the divine Name and afterward converted to Judaism is exempt from penalty, since the mode of trying him has undergone a change, so too the mode of inflicting the death penalty."

B. *May I say that the following passage of the Mishnah supports [Hanina's view]?* **If he fled before his trial was over, and afterward the lower "beard" became full, he is exempt [M. 8:4P].** *What is the reason for this ruling? Is it not because we invoke the rule that, since he has changed [in one aspect of culpability], he has changed [in all others]?*

C. *No, the present case is different from the other, because if he had done such a deed at this time, he would not be subject to the death penalty at all.*

D. *Come and take note:* **If after his trial was done he fled, and afterward the lower beard became full, he is liable [M. 8:4Q].** *[This would refute Hanina's view.]*

E. *Now you have said,* **If after his trial was done.** *And if his trial is done, then he is already subject to the death penalty [so there is no parallel to Hanina's case].*

F. *Come and take note:* A son of Noah who hit his neighbor or had sexual relations with his neighbor's wife and then converted to Judaism is exempt. If he did so to an Israelite and then converted to Judaism, he is liable.

G. *Now why should this be the case? May we not invoke the rule that, since his status has changed, the liability affecting him also should change?*

H. *We require a shift both in the mode of trying the man and also in the mode of inflicting the death penalty, and in this one's case, while the rules of trying him have changed, the mode of inflicting the death penalty has not changed.*

I. *But in the case of this one, while the mode of trying him has changed, the mode of inflicting the death penalty has not changed.*

J. *[How so?] While, to be sure, in the case of the murderer, to begin with he was subject to death through decapitation and he is now subject to death through decapitation, as to the one who commits adultery, to begin with he was subject to the death penalty through decapitation, but now he is subject to the death penalty through strangulation.*

K.   *But a pertinent parallel is provided by the betrothed girl, for in both instances [before, after conversion], the death penalty is the same, namely through stoning.*

L.   *But lo, the passage has been framed in the language of,* "If he did so to an Israelite," parallel to the matter of "his neighbor's wife!" [Freedman, p. 487, n. 1: His neighbor's wife must refer to a married woman, since the sacredness of betrothal alone is not recognized by gentiles. Consequently, "if he did this to an Israelite" must refer to the case of a married woman.]

M.   [*While we do indeed deal with a married woman, if one had had sexual relations with her before conversion, he would be put to death through decapitation; if it is after conversion, it is by stoning. Since stoning is a more lenient mode of execution, we maintain that] the lesser mode of execution is encompassed by the more severe [so the mode of execution cannot be said to have changed, that is, changed for the worse].*

N.   *That reply is suitable for one who maintains that decapitation is the more severe mode of execution. But as to him who maintains, as does R. Simeon, that strangulation is the more severe mode of execution, what is there to say?*

O.   *R. Simeon takes the view of the Tannaite authority of the house of Manasseh, who has said,* "All penalties of execution that apply to the sons of Noah take the form only of strangulation" [so the above argument is entirely valid].

P.   *Now to be sure, in the case of a married woman [the argument remains valid, since] to begin with the mode of execution was through strangulation and it now remains strangulation. But in the case of the murderer, to begin with the mode of execution was strangulation, while now it is through decapitation. Just as before, the lesser mode of execution [decapitation] is encompassed by the greater [which is strangulation, and the rest follows].*

Q.   *May I say that the following passage supports this argument?* If a betrothed maiden went astray [committing adultery] and then reached puberty, she is subject to the death penalty through strangulation. *But why should she not be subject to execution through stoning [as she would have been, had she remained a girl prior to puberty]? Is it not because, once the penalty changes, it changes* [Freedman, p. 488, n. 1: Though here it does not exempt her entirely, since strangulation, to which the pubescent girl is liable, is included in stoning, the punishment for the prepubescent girl]. All the more so [in a case of blasphemy], where the mode of execution wholly changes.

U.   *Has not R. Yohanan said to the Tannaite authority [who stated the passage],* "Repeat it in the form: She is put to death through stoning."

The Talmud in no way was composed to related to the Mishnah-passage at hand. It is inserted only because of its reference to the present passage. In fact it is the general principle that is at issue, not the Mishnah's rule in particular.

8:5

A. A rebellious and incorrigible son is tried on account of [what he may] end up to be.

B. Let him die while yet innocent, and let him not die when he is guilty.

C. For when the evil folk die, it is a benefit to them and a benefit to the world.

D. But [when the] righteous folk [die], it is bad for them and bad for the world.

E. Wine and sleep for the wicked are a benefit for them and a benefit for the world.

F. But for the righteous, they are bad for them and bad for the world.

G. Dispersion for the evil is a benefit for them and a benefit for the world.

H. But for the righteous, it is bad for them and bad for the world.

I. Gathering together for the evil is bad for them and bad for the world.

J. But for the righteous, it is a benefit for them and a benefit for the world.

K. Tranquility for the evil is bad for them and bad for the world.

L. But for the righteous, it is a benefit for them and a benefit for the world.

I.1   A. [72A] *It has been taught on Tannaite authority:*

      B. R. Yosé the Galilean says, "And is it the case that merely because this one has eaten a <u>tartemar</u> of meat and drunk a half-<u>log</u> of Italian wine, the Torah has said that he should be taken to court and [tried for the penalty of] stoning?

      C. "Rather, it is because the Torah has plumbed the depths of the psychology of the wayward and rebellious son.

      D. "For in the end, he will use up his father's wealth and then will want to satisfy his gluttony. Not finding the means, he will go out to the crossroads and mug people.

      E. "The Torah has said, **Let him die while yet innocent, and let him not die when he is guilty [M. 8:5B].**

      F. "For when evil folk die, it is a benefit to them and a benefit to the world.

      G. "But when the righteous folk [die], it is bad for them and bad for the world.

      H. "Wine and sleep for the wicked are a benefit for them and a benefit for the world.

      I. "But for the righteous they are bad for them and bad for the world.

      J. "Tranquility for the evil is bad for them and bad for the world.

      K. "But for the righteous it is a benefit for them and a benefit for the world.

      L. "Dispersion for the evil is a benefit for them and a benefit for the world.

      M. "But for the righteous, it is bad for them and bad for the world [M. 8:5C-L, in slightly different order].

N. [B. lacks: **Gathering together for the evil is bad for them and bad for the world.**

O. **"But for the righteous, it is a benefit for them and a benefit for the world."**]

The Talmud contributes Yosé the Galilean's reason.

8:6

A. **He who breaks in [Ex. 22:1] is judged on account of what he may end up to be.**

B. **[If] he broke in and broke a jug, if blood-guilt applies to him, he is liable.**

C. **If blood-guilt does not apply, he is exempt.**

I.1 A. *Said Raba, "What is the reason [that the householder may kill] one who breaks in?*

B. "It is because we make the assumption that no one restrains himself when it comes to protecting his property.

C. *"And this one [the thief] must have taken the view, 'If I go there, the householder will resist me and not let me [take what I want], so if he resists, I shall kill him.'*

D. "And the Torah has said, 'If he comes to kill you, you kill him first' [cf. Ex. 22:1]."

E. Said Rab, "He who breaks into a house and took utensils and got away is exempt [from having to pay for them].

F. *"What is the reason? He has acquired ownership of them by the risk of his life."*

G. *Said Rabbah, "It stands to reason that the ruling of Rab applies to a case in which the utensils were broken and no longer available for restitution, but if one took them [and they remain available], that is not the case."*

H. *By God! what Rab said applies even to a case in which he took them away.*

I. *For even in a case in which if the householder had killed him, there would have been a consideration of blood guilt; if the utensils are damaged, he remains liable. Therefore the utensils fall into the robber's domain.*

J. *Here too the utensils fall into the robber's domain.* [Freedman, p. 490, n. 1: The reasoning is as follows: when something is stolen, it loses its first ownership and passes into that of the thief, who is therefore liable for having removed it from its owner's control as for an ordinary debt. Consequently, he is liable even if it is broken. For if it theoretically remained in its first ownership, the thief would not be liable for any damage done to it. Hence in this case, since the thief, by his act of breaking in, became liable to death, restoration cannot be demanded even if the pot is intact, for liability to monetary restoration is cancelled in the face of the greater liability to death.]

K. *But that is not the case. When the All-Merciful placed the utensils into the domain of the robber, it was as to damages, but as to ownership, the property remains in the domain of the original owner. This is parallel to the case of one who borrows property [which remains in the domain of the owner, though the borrower would have to pay for any damages done to the property while he holds on to it.]*

L.   *We have learned in the Mishnah:* **[He who breaks in] ...if he broke in and broke a jug, if blood-guilt applies to him, he is liable. If blood-guilt does not apply, he is exempt [M. 8:6].**

M.   *The reason then is that he broke it, so he is exempt when no blood-guilt would apply to him [should the owner kill him], but if he only took it, he is not exempt [as against Rab's view].*

N.   *The rule at hand [of exemption from having to pay for the jug] also applies if he took it. The reason the framer of the passage says, and broke a jug, is to inform us that, if the owner should be subject to blood-guilt, even if he [the robber] broke the jug, [the robber has to pay].*

O.   *That is self-evident. The robber has done damage.*

P.   *What the framer of the passage tells us is that even if it was not intentionally [broken, liability applies].*

Q.   *What then does that tell us? That a human being always is regarded as forewarned? That we have learned in following Tannaite teaching:* **A human being always is regarded as forewarned, whether he does something inadvertently or deliberately, under constraint or willingly [M. B.Q. 2:6].**

R.   *That is a problem.*

S.   *R. Bibi bar Abbayye objected,* **"He who steals the purse of his fellow and took it out of his domain on the Sabbath – lo, this person is liable for the theft, for he had already become obligated on account of the theft of the purse before it had gone forth. If he was dragging it along and so removed it from the domain of the other, he is exempt [as to the purse] since he did not make acquisition of the purse before he had also and simultaneously violated the Sabbath [T. B.Q. 9:19A-C].** [Freedman, p. 491, n. 1: Hence we see that though the purse is still in existence, he is not bound to return it. This refutes Rab's ruling.]"

T.   *Not at all. The ruling applies to a case in which the thief threw the purse in the river [and so could not return it].*

U.   *Some rams were stolen from Raba in a break-in. The robbers returned them to him, but he would not accept them back. He said, "Since such a ruling has come forth from Rab, [it must be obeyed, and the thieves have acquired ownership of the rams.]"*

I.2   A.   *Our rabbis have taught:*

B.   **"[If a thief be found breaking in, and he be smitten that he die,] there shall no blood be shed for him, if the sun be risen upon him" (Ex. 22:1-3).**

C.   **Did the sun rise on him alone?**

D.   **But if it is as clear to you as the sun that he was not at peace with you, then kill him, but if not, do not kill him [T. 11:9F-H].**

E.   *A further Tannaite teaching:*

	F.	**"If the sun be risen upon him, there shall be blood shed for him:"**
	G.	**And did the sun rise on him alone?**
	H.	**But if it is as clear to you as the sun that he is at peace with you, do not kill him, but if not, kill him [T. 11:9F-H].**
	I.	*There is a contradiction between one unattributed teaching and another unattributed teaching.*
	J.	*There is no contradiction.* **[72B]** *The one speaks of a father robbing from his son, the other of a son robbing his father.* [The former has more compassion for the son than does the son for the father. The son must not assume the father will kill him, but the father may assume the son will kill him (Freedman, p. 492, n. 2)].
I.3	A.	*Said Rab, "I would kill anyone who broke in on me, except for R. Hanina bar Shila."*
	B.	*"What is the reason? Should I say that it is because he is a righteous man [and therefore no threat to life but], lo, in the cited possibility, he is by definition a housebreaker!* Rather, it is because I am confident in his regard that he would have mercy on me the way a father has mercy on a son."
I.4	A.	*Our rabbis have taught on Tannaite authority:*
	B.	"[If the sun be risen upon him], there shall be blood shed for him" (Ex. 22:1):
	C.	That is the case whether on a weekday or on the Sabbath.
	D.	"[If the thief be found breaking in], there shall be no blood shed for him" (Ex. 22:2).
	E.	That is the case whether on a weekday or on the Sabbath.
	F.	*Now there is no problem with the statement that there is no blood shed for him whether on a weekday or on the Sabbath. Such a statement was necessary. You might have thought that one might rule that the case may be compared to the one involving those put to death by a court, in which case, on the Sabbath we do not inflict the death penalty. Then we are taught that we do inflict the death penalty.*
	G.	*But as to the statement, "There shall be no blood shed for him" whether on a weekday or on the Sabbath, now if we do not inflict the death penalty on a weekday, is there any question about not doing so on the Sabbath?*
	H.	*Said R. Sheshet, "The statement nonetheless was necessary to deal with the case of removing a pile of dirt for the sake of such a person [who has dug his way into the house and been buried by a pile of dirt in his tunnel. We learn that the dirt must be removed even on the Sabbath, so as to safe the thief's life.]"*
I.5	A.	*Our rabbis have taught on Tannaite authority:*
	B.	"[If a thief be found breaking in] and be smitten" (Ex. 22:1) – by any one.
	C.	"And he die" (Ex. 22:1) – by any mode of death by which you can kill him.
	D.	*Now it was indeed necessary to teach, "'And be smitten' – by any man." For it might have entered your mind to maintain that it is the householder alone who will take action against the man, because someone will not refrain from defending his property, but a third*

party will not do so. So we are informed that the housebreaker is a threat, and even a third party will put him to death [if he can].

E. But as to the teaching, "'And he die' – by any mode of death by which you can kill him," what need is there for that teaching? One may derive that same fact [that any way of killing the housebreaker is permissible] from the case of the murderer. For it has been taught on Tannaite authority:

F. "He who smote him shall surely be put to death, for he is a murderer" (Num. 35:21).

G. I know only that he may be put to death by the form of death that has been stated in his regard.

H. How do I know that if you cannot put him to death in the mode of inflicting the death penalty that has been stated in his regard, you have the right to put him to death in by any means by which you can kill him?

I. Scripture says, "He shall surely be put to death" – by any means whatsoever.

J. [One might say] that that case is different [from the present one], for it is written, "He shall surely be put to death" [a phrase not stated in the present context, and it follows that proof of the same proposition in the case at hand is necessary.]

K. But why not derive the present rule from that case in any event.

L. The reason is that the matter that treats the murderer and the redeemer of the blood derives from two verses that speak of the same topic, and in the case of two verses that treat the same topic, we cannot derive any further lessons [applicable to cases other than the one at hand]. [So the proof before us is required.]

I.6 A. Our rabbis have taught on Tannaite authority:

B. "If a thief be found breaking in" (Ex. 22:1):

C. I know that only that the rule applies to a break-in [through one's walls]. How do I know that the same rule applies to a break-in through one's roof, courtyard, or outer buildings?

D. Scripture says, "If the thief be found" – anywhere [he is found as a thief].

E. If so, why does Scripture say, "Breaking in"?

F. It is because most thieves are found in a break-in [through a wall].

G. A further Tannaite teaching:

H. "[If a thief be found] breaking in" (Ex. 22:1);

I. I know only that the rule applies to a break-in [through one's walls]. How do I know that the same rule applies to a break-in through one's roof, courtyard, or outer buildings?

J. Scripture says, "If the thief be found" – wherever he is found [as a thief].

K. If so, why does Scripture state, "Breaking in"?

L. It is because the act of breaking in on his part itself constitutes the admonition [not to do so].

I.7 A. Said R. Huna, "In the case of a minor who is pursuing one, it is permitted to kill him and so to save him at the cost of his own life."

B. He maintains that it is not necessary to give an admonition to a pursuer, and there is no distinction between an adult and a minor.

C. *R. Hisda objected to R. Huna,* "The woman who is in hard labor –
    they chop up the child in her womb and they remove it limb by
    limb, because her life takes precedence over his life. If its greater
    part has gone forth, they do not touch him, for they do not set
    aside one life on account of another life [M. Oh. 7:6]. *Now why
    should that be the case? He is in the status of a pursuer [thus a threat to
    life]."*

D. *That case is different, for the threat to life derives from the action of
    heaven.*

E. *May I say that the following supports him:*

F. In the case of one who was pursuer in pursuit of his fellow to
    kill him, one says to him, "See that he is an Israelite, a member
    of the covenant, and the Torah has said, 'Whoever sheds the
    blood of man, [to save that man] his own blood shall be shed,'
    which means that one must save the blood of this party at the
    cost of the blood of that party."

G. *That statement accords with the view of R. Yosé b. R. Judah.*

H. *For it has been taught on Tannaite authority:*

I. R. Yosé b. R. Judah says, "In the case of an associate [of
    sages], there is no need for admonition, for admonition
    applies only so that the court may distinguish inadvertent
    from deliberate crime [but an associate knows the law and
    whatever he does is deliberate, by definition]."

J. *Come and take note:* "In the case of one who was in pursuit
    of his fellow to kill him, one says to him, "See that he is
    an Israelite, a member of the covenant, and the Torah has
    said, 'Whoever sheds the blood of man, [to save that
    man] his own blood shall be shed' (Gen. 9:6), which
    means that one must save the blood of this party at the
    cost of the blood of that party."

K. If [the pursuer] then said, "I know that that is how
    matters are," he is exempt [from being put to death,
    having desisted].

L. But if he said, "It is on that very condition that I act,"
    then he is liable [T. San. 11:4B-E]. [This shows that one
    has to give an admonition to the pursuer, contrary to the
    view of Huna].

M. *No, the rule at hand applies to a case in which one party was on
    one side of the canal, the other on the other said, in which case
    [the one who gives the warning] cannot save the other party.*

N. *What can one do? He has to bring him to court!*

O. *But if he were to bring him to court, there would have to be
    advance admonition.*

P. *If you want, I shall propose the following:* R. Huna may say to
    you, "I rule in accord with the Tannaite authority in the
    matter of the break-in, who has said, 'The act of breaking
    in constitutes ample admonition [against doing so, and no
    further admonition is required. The same rule applies
    here.]"

Unit I.1 provides a clarification of the reasoning of the rule at hand. I.2 cites Tosefta's complement and glosses it. I.3 is continuous with the foregoing. I.4 then takes up the exposition of the verse of Scripture on which the Mishnah's rule rests, and the same exercise occupies units I.5, 6. Only unit I.7 undertakes an independent analysis, this with reference to the requirement of admonition in the case of pursuit. The whole is an orderly and cogent composition.

8:7

A.   [73A] **And these are those who are to be saved [from doing evil] even at the cost of their lives:**
B.   **he who pursues after his fellow in order to kill him –**
C.   **after a male, or after a betrothed girl;**
D.   **but he who pursues a beast, he who profanes the Sabbath, he who does an act of service to an idol – they do not save them even at the cost of their lives.**

I.1   A.   *Our rabbis have taught on Tannaite authority:*
B.   How do we know that in the case of one who pursues his fellow to kill him, it is permitted to save [such a person from sinning] at the cost of his life?
C.   Scripture says, "You shall not stand by the blood of your neighbor" (Lev. 19:16).
D.   *Does that verse serve the present purpose? It is needed, rather, in accord with that which is taught on Tannaite authority:*
E.   How do we know that, if one sees his fellow drowning in a river, or being dragged off by a wild beast, or mugged, he is liable to save him?
F.   Scripture says, "You shall not stand by the blood of your neighbor" (Lev. 19:16).
G.   *That indeed is the case [that the verse cited earlier serves the present purpose].*
H.   *How, then, do we know that it is permitted to save such a person [from sinning] even at the cost of his life?*
I.   *We establish an argument a fortiori, on the basis of the case of a betrothed girl.*
J.   Now if, in the case of a betrothed girl, in which case the attacker comes only to inflict damage, the Torah has said that it is permitted to save her at the cost of his life,
K.   if one pursues his fellow to kill him, all the more so!
L.   But do we inflict penalties merely on the basis of the outcome of a logical argument?
M.   *A member of the house of Rabbi stated on Tannaite authority:*
N.   *It is on the basis of an argument of analogy.*
O.   "For when a man rises against his neighbor and kills him, even so in this matter" (Deut. 22:26) [in the setting of the rape of a betrothed girl].
P.   But what lesson is to be derived from the case of the murderer? [Freedman, p. 496, n. 4: For the simile itself is superfluous, since the Torah explicitly states that the maiden is not

punished. Hence it implies that a certain feature of the law of a murderer holds good here too and vice versa.]

Q. "Lo, this comes to teach a lesson but turns out to be the subject of a lesson.

R. "There is then an analogy to be drawn between the murderer and the betrothed girl.

S. "Just as in the case of the betrothed girl, it is permitted to save her at the cost of the attacker's life, so the murderer may be saved [from sin] at the cost of his life."

T. *And how do we know that the rule just now stated in fact applies to the betrothed girl herself?*

U. *It is in accord with the statement of the Tannaite authority of the house of R. Ishmael.*

V. *For the Tannaite authority of the house of R. Ishmael [taught],* "'[The betrothed girl cried,] but there was none to save her' (Deut. 2:27).

W. "But if there had been someone there to save her, then, in any means by which one may save her, one does so."

I.2 A. *Returning to the body of the cited passage:*

B. How do we know that if one sees his fellow drowning in a river, or being dragged off by a wild beast, or mugged, he is liable to save him?

C. Scripture says, "You shall not stand by the blood of your neighbor" (Lev. 19:16).

D. *Does that proposition derive from the present passage? Lo, it derives from the following passage:*

E. How do I know that one must save his neighbor from the loss of himself?

F. "'Then you shall restore him to him" (Deut. 22:2). [Freedman, p. 496, n. 7: The passage refers to restoring a neighbor's lost property. This interpretation extends it to his own person, that is, if he has lost himself, he must be helped to find his way again. Hence it also applies to rescuing one from danger].

G. *If proof derives from that passage, I might have maintained that that rule applies only to saving another as one's personal obligation, but one need not take the trouble of going out and hiring [others to do so]. So we are informed that the rule applies even to engaging others to do son.*

I.3 A. *Our rabbis have taught on Tannaite authority:*

B. **All the same are the cases of one who pursues his fellow to kill him, a male, a betrothed girl, other sorts of deeds punishable by death inflicted in the court, and those punishable by death inflicted as extirpation, people save [such persons coommitting these cries] at the cost of their own lives.**

C. **But if it was a widow married to a high priest, or a divorcee or a woman who had performed the rite of removing the shoe married to an ordinary priest, they do not save him at the cost of his life.**

D.   If the [betrothed girl] had previously been the object of the commission of a transgression, they do not save such a girl at the cost of the rapist's life.

E.   If there is another way of saving her, they do not save her at the cost of his life.

F.   R. Judah says, "If she herself had said, 'Let him be,' lest he kill her [they do not save him at the cost of his life,] [T.: even though by leaving him, he gets involved with a capital crime]" [T. San. 11:11C-F].

G.   What is the source of the foregoing?

H.   Scripture has said, "But the girl [read na'arah but written na'ar, boy] you shall do nothing, there is in the girl no sin worthy of death" (Deut. 22:26).

I.   [Since the word for girl, while read as girl, is written as boy, we understand that] when the word is written as "boy" it refers to a case of sodomous rape, and when it is read as "girl" it refers to the rape of a betrothed girl.

J.   "Sin" refers to the category of crimes for which one is liable to extirpation.

K.   "Death" refers to crimes in the classification of those punishable by death at the hand of a court.

L.   Why do I require the specification of the several items [rather than deriving all of the cases from a single example]?

M.   It was necessary to make explicit reference to each one of them [in the verse just now cited].

N.   For if the All-Merciful had made reference only to the case of homosexual rape, I might have supposed that one saves the sinner at the cost of his life in that case only, because it is not the natural way of having sexual relations.

O.   But in the case of a girl, in which case it is the natural way, I might have said one does not do so.

P.   And if the All-Merciful had made explicit the case of the girl alone, it might have been argued that in that case one takes extraordinary measures, because it inflicts injury on her [by destroying her virginity], but in the case of a boy, in which there is no injury, I might have said that is not the case.

Q.   And if the All-Merciful had made explicit these two items [73B], I might have argued that in the one case it is because it is not natural, and in the other because it inflicts injury [by destroying virginity], but in the other matter of forbidden sexual relations, in which case the form of sexual relations is natural and the consideration of inflicting injury through destroying virginity is uncommon, I might have said that that is not the case.

R.   Accordingly, the All-Merciful wrote, "...sin...."

S.   And if, furthermore, the All-Merciful had written the word, "...sin...", I might have reached the conclusion that that word encompasses even cases in which one is liable only for violating a negative commandment.

T.	*So the All-Merciful wrote, "...death...."*
U.	*And if the All-Merciful had written the word, "...death...,"* *I might have concluded that the rule applies to cases in which the court inflicts the death penalty, but it does not apply to cases in which the penalty is extirpation at the hand of heaven.*
V.	*Accordingly, the All-Merciful wrote the word, "...sin..."*
W.	*But then why should the All-Merciful not have written the words, "...sin worthy of death...," and it would not then have been necessary to make explicit reference to the case of the boy or the girl?*
X.	*That indeed is the case, but the explicit reference to the boy and the girl serve, in the one case, to eliminate [from the list of those who are saved from sin at the cost of their lives] one who is about to commit an act of idolatry, and, in the other case, to eliminate the cases of one who proposes to have relations with a beast and one who is about to violate the Sabbath.*
Y.	*But in the view of R. Simeon b. Yohai, who has held that, in he case of one about to commit an act of idolatry, it is permitted to save such a one at the cost of his life, for what purpose are the references made.*
Z.	*One serves to eliminate the case of a person about to commit bestiality [one who is not saved at the cost of his life from sin], and the other to eliminate the case of one about to violate the Sabbath.*
AA.	*[How so?] It might have entered your mind that one would encompass Sabbath violation on the analogy of the matter of idolatry, since the word "profanation" applies to both.*
BB.	*And in the view of R. Eleazar b. R. Simeon, who has said that in the case of one who profanes the Sabbath, it is permitted to save him at the cost of his life, on the basis of the analogy drawn between the Sabbath and idolatry on the basis of the appearance of the word "profanation" in both cases, what is to be said?*
CC.	*One reference serves to eliminate the case of bestiality, and, as to the other, since the All-Merciful made reference to the boy, it made reference all also to the girl [but it is not a redundancy, so Freedman, p. 498, n. 6: for though "boy" is written the context demands that "girl" be read, since the entire passage refers to a girl].*

I.4	A.	**R. Judah says, "Even if she herself had said, 'Let him be,' lest he kill her [they do not save him," etc.]:**
	B.	*What is at issue?*
	C.	Said Raba, "It is in a case in which while the girl is concerned about her virginity, she nonetheless lets him do as he wishes, so that he will not kill her.
	D.	"Rabbis take the view that the All-Merciful focuses upon the matter of the girl's virginity, and lo, the girl is concerned about her virginity, [so one may kill the rapist].

E.   *"R. Judah takes the view that the reason that the All-Merciful has said that one may kill the rapist is that the girl herself is prepared to be killed [for the sake of her honor]. But since in this case she is not prepared to be killed, [one does not kill on account of her being raped]."*

F.   *Said R. Pappa to Abbayye, "As to the case of a widow married to a high priest, there too is a consideration of dishonor [since the woman can no longer marry any other priest]."*

G.   *He said to him, "The All-Merciful takes account of a major form of dishonor, but as to a minor form of dishonor, the All-Merciful does not take account."*

I.5   A.   **Sin – this refers to the violation of rules the penalty of which is extirpation:**

B.   *An objection was raised:* **These are the girls invalid for marriage to an Israelite who nonetheless receive a fine paid as a penalty by the man who seduces them: ...he who has sexual relations with his sister [M. Ket. 3:1A,D]:** [Freedman, p. 499, n. 4: Even his sister, though "And she shall be his wife" of Deut. 22:28 is inapplicable. But if she might be saved by his life, he should not be fined. In the case of the death penalty, this principle holds good even if the offender is not actually executed or, as in this case, slain by the rescuers.]

C.   *Rabbis stated before R. Hisda, "It is at the moment at which sexual relations begin that he is exempt from being slain [to save him at the cost of his life from committing a sin]. But the penalty of paying money does not apply until the completion of the act of sexual relations."*

D.   *That explanation serves the one who maintains that* the beginning of sexual relations comes with the first "kiss" [meeting of the sexual organs], *but in the view of him who says that* the beginning of the first stage of sexual relations takes place at the point of entry of the crown of the penis into the vagina, *what is there to be said?*

E.   Rather, said R. Hisda, "We deal with a case in which the man first had sexual relations through the anus, and then went and had sexual relations through the vagina. [Freedman, p. 499, n. 8: Since she has been unnaturally violated before, whether by her brother or another, she may not be saved now by his life. Therefore he is fined for destroying her virginity. Otherwise she can be saved.]

F.   Raba said, "The rule applies where the girl permits him [to rape her], so that he will not kill her, and it represents the position of R. Judah."

G.   [74A] R. Pappa said, "It represents the case in which he has seduced her and the position of all authorities."

	H.	Abbayye said, "It applies in a case in which one could save her by cutting off one of his limbs [so the objection that he is liable to the death penalty does not apply].
	I.	"It stands within the position of R. Jonathan b. Saul."
I.6	A.	*For it has been taught on the strength of Tannaite authority:*
	B.	R. Jonathan b. Saul says, "If there is one in pursuit, who was pursuing his fellow so as to kill him, and one can save him [from the sin] at the cost of one of his limbs [rather than by killing him] and one did not do so, he is put to death on his account."
	C.	*What is the scriptural basis for the position of R. Jonathan b. Saul?*
	D.	*It is because it is written,* "If men strive [and hurt a woman], he shall surely be punished ... [and pay as the judges determine. And if any mischief follow, then you shall give life for life]" (Ex. 21:22ff).
	E.	And [in this connection] R. Eleazar said, "Scripture speaks of attempted murder [of one against the other], for it is written, 'And if any mischief follow, then you shall give life for life' (Ex. 21:22) [Freedman, p. 500, n. 8: though the murder of the woman is unintentional, thus the extreme penalty is explicable only on that assumption].
	F.	*"And even so, Scripture has said, 'If no mischief follows, he shall surely be punished.'*
	G.	*"Now if you maintain that* if one can save [the pursuer from committing sin] by taking away one of his limbs, it is not permitted to save him at the cost of his life,
	H.	*"Then you can find a case in which one is going to be punished [as Scripture here says],* in a case in which one can have saved the man from sin at the cost of one of his limbs.
	I.	*"But if you maintain that,* even if one can save [the pursuer from sin] by taking away one of his limbs, one nonetheless has the right to save him at the cost of his life, *how would you find such a case in which one might ever be punished along the lines of Scripture's statement? [Accordingly, we have Jonathan b. Saul's scriptural foundations.]"*
	J.	But the present case is to be distinguished, since here, there is death to be inflicted on account of one victim, and a monetary compensation to be paid on account of the other. [Freedman, p. 500, n. 10: He is liable to be put to death because he seeks to slay his combatant, but the monetary liability arises through his injury to the woman. Where, however, these liabilities are incurred on account of two difference persons, it may be that the one does not cancel the other.]

K.   *The present case indeed is not to be distinguished, for Rabbah has said,* "If one was pursuing his fellow and broke utensils, whether they belong to the one who is being pursued or to any other man, [the pursuer] is exempt from having to pay compensation.

L.   *"What is the reason?* The pursuer is at risk of being put to death.

M.   "But if the one who was being pursued broke utensils, if they belong to the pursuer, he is exempt from having to pay compensation.

N.   "If they belong to anybody else, he is liable.

O.   "If they belong to the pursuer, he is exempt, so that the victim's property is not treated as more valuable to him than his person [since if the victim were able to kill the pursuer, he would not be liable to the death penalty].

P.   "If they belonged to anyone else, he is liable, because he is in the situation of saving his life at the cost of someone else's property.

Q.   "And as to one who was pursuing so as to save the life of his victim and broke utensils, whether they belonged to the pursuer, the pursued, or anyone else, he is exempt from having to make compensation.

R.   "That in point of fact is not logical.

S.   "But if you maintain the contrary position, it will turn out that no one will ever try to save his fellow from a pursuer [since he will undertake risks he cannot afford]. [At any rate the proposition of K is proved.]

II.1 A. **But he who pursues a beast [profanes the Sabbath or does an act of service to an idol – they do not save them even at the cost of their own lives] [M. 8:7D]:**

B.   *It has been taught on Tannaite authority:*

C.   R. Simeon b. Yohai says, "If one performs an act of service to an idol, it is permitted even at the cost of his own life to save him from sin.

D.   "This is by an argument a fortiori: Now if on account of an offense to an ordinary person [e.g., the rape of a betrothed girl], it is permitted to save the offender even at the cost of his own life, on account of an offense to the Most High, is it not all the more so [that one should kill such a person in order to save him from sin]?"

E.   But are penalties to be inflicted merely because of logical reasoning?

F.   *He indeed takes the view that* penalties are to be inflicted because of the results of logic.

G.   *It has been taught on Tannaite authority:*

H.   R. Eleazar b. R. Simeon says, "One profaning the Sabbath may be saved from sin at the cost of his own life."

	I.	*He takes the view of his father, who has said that* penalties are to be inflicted because of the results of logic.
	J.	*And the case of the Sabbath derives from the case of idolatry by an analogy resting on the common use of the word "profanation" in respect to both sorts of actions [in regard to the Sabbath at Ex. 31:14, and in regard to idolatry at Lev. 18:21].*
II.2	A.	Said R. Yohanan in the name of R. Simeon b. Yehosedeq, "They took a vote and decided in the upper room of the house of Nitzeh in Lod, as follows: 'In the case of all transgressions that are listed in the Torah, if people say to a person, "Commit a transgression and so avoid being executed," one should commit a transgression and avoid execution, except for the matters of idolatry, sexual immorality, and murder.'"
	B.	*And may one not commit an act of idolatry [to save his life]?*
	C.	*And lo, it as been taught on Tannaite authority:*
	D.	Said R. Ishmael, "How do we know on the basis of Scripture that if people should say to someone, 'Commit an act of idolatry and do not suffer death,' that he should commit an act of idolatry and not suffer death?
	E.	"Scripture says, 'You shall live by them' (Lev. 18:5) – and not die by them.
	F.	"May I suppose that one may do so even in public?
	G.	"Scripture says, 'Do not profane my holy name, for I shall be sanctified' (Lev. 22:32)."
	H.	*Those who hold to the contrary [at Nitza's house in Lydda] accord with the view of R. Eliezer.*
	I.	*For it has been taught on Tannaite authority:*
	J.	R. Eliezer says, "[Scripture states], 'And you shall love the Lord your God with all your heart, with all your soul, with all your might.' (Deut. 6:5) If it is said, 'With all your soul (Deut. 6:5),' why is it also said, 'With all your might'? And if it is said, 'With all your might,' why is it also said, 'With all your soul'?
	K.	"But if there is someone who places greater value on his body than on his possessions, for such a one it is said, 'With all your soul.'
	L.	"And if there is someone who places greater value on his possessions than on his life, for such a one it is said, 'With all your might.'"
	M.	*And as to the matter of sexual immorality and murder?*
	N.	*It is in accord with the view of Rabbi.*
	O.	*For it has been taught on Tannaite authority:*
	P.	Rabbi says, "'For as when a man rises against his neighbor and slays him, even so is this matter' (Deut. 22:26).

Q. But what lesson is to be derived from the case of the murderer [as above]? Lo, this comes to teach a lesson but turns out to be the subject of a lesson.

R. There is an analogy to be drawn between the murderer and the betrothed girl. Just as in the case of the betrothed girl, it is permitted to save her at the cost of the attacker's life, so the murderer may be saved from sin at the cost of his life.

S. "And an analogy is further to be drawn between the case of the betrothed girl and that of the murderer.

T. "Just as in the matter or of murder, one should be killed and not commit murder, so as to a betrothed girl, let her be slain but not violate the law.

U. *"How do we know that there is the case for the murderer himself?*

V. *"It is a matter of reasoning."*

W. *That is in line with the case of one who came before Raba and said to him, "The master of my town has said to me, 'Go and kill so-and-so, and if you do not do so, I shall kill you.'"*

X. *He said to him, "Let him kill you, but do not kill. Who will say that your blood is redder than his. Perhaps the blood of that man is redder [than yours]."*

II.3 A. When R. Dimi came, he said R. Yohanan said, "[The cited rule about having to give up one's life on account only of the three sins listed] applies solely in the time in which there is no royal decree [to violate the Torah]. But if there is a royal decree, then even on account of the most inconsequential religious duty, one should be put to death and not violate the law."

B. When Rabin came, he said R. Yohanan said, "Even in the time in which there is no royal decree [to violate the Torah], one may not apply the cited rule except in private. But as to an action to be done in public, then even on account of the most inconsequential religious duty, one should be put to death and not violate the law."

C. *What would be a minor religious duty?*

D. *Raba, son of R. Isaac, said Rab said, " [74B] Even to change one's shoe lace [from what Jews regularly wore to what gentiles wore]."*

E. *And how many people constitute a public?*

F. Said R. Jacob said R. Yohanan, "A public audience is not less than ten."

G. *It is self-evident that we require the "public" to be made up of Israelites, for it is written, "But will I be sanctified among the children of Israel" (Lev. 22:23).*

H. *R. Jeremiah raised the question, "If nine are Israelites and one a gentile, what is the law?"*

I. *Come and take note of the following:*

J.   *R. Yannai, brother of R. Hiyya bar Abbar, repeated on Tannaite authority, "The meaning of the word 'among' in two passages supplies the answer.*

K.   "Here it is written, 'I will be sanctified among the children of Israel (Lev. 22:23) *and elsewhere,* 'Separate yourselves from among this congregation' (Num. 16:21).

L.   *"Just as, in the latter passage, the ten are all Israelites, so, here too, the ten must all be Israelites."*

M.   *And lo, there is the case of Esther, who violated the law in public (by marrying a gentile].*

N.   Said Abbayye, "Esther was merely in the status of the soil of the earth [and was sexually passive and therefore not an active sinner]."

O.   *Raba said, "A case in which [a violation of the law] is on account of the benefit accruing to the [persecutors and not spite] is different, for if you do not hold that view,* then how can we hand over to them our braziers and coal shovels [Freedman].

P.   *"Rather, a case in which [a violation of the law] is on account of the benefit accruing to the persecutors is different, and the same principle applied there [to Esther]."*

Q.   *Raba accords with a view of his expressed elsewhere, for Raba said, "In the case of an idolator who [out of spite] said to an Israelite, 'Cut grass on the Sabbath and throw it to cattle, and if not, I shall kill you,' the Israelite should be killed and cut it. [If he said], 'Cut it and toss it into the river,' he should be killed and not cut it. What is the reason? It is the pagan's wish to make the Israelite transgress a teaching of the faith."*

II.4   A.   *The question was addressed to R. Ammi, "Is a son of Noah commanded to accept martyrdom in the sanctification of God's name, or is he not commanded to accept martyrdom in the sanctification of God's name?"*

B.   *Said Abbayye, "Come and take note:* \The sons of Noah were given seven commandments. *But if it were the case [that martyrdom was demanded of them], there should be eight, [not seven]."*

C.   *Said Raba to him, "Those seven and whatever pertains to keeping those seven [including martyrdom, if need be]."*

D.   *What is the rule?*

E.   *Said R. Adda bar Ahbah said members of the house of Rab said, "It is written, 'In this thing, the Lord pardon your servant, that when my master goes into the house of Rimmon to worship there, and he leans on my hand, and I bow myself in the house of Rimmon' (2 Kgs. 5:18).*

F.   "And it is written, 'And he said to him, Go in peace' (2 Kgs. 5:19).

	G.	[75A] *"Now if it were so [that a Noahide has to sanctify God's name], he should not have said such a thing to him."*
	H.	*The one was in private [in which it was permitted], the other in public [when one must be martyred and not commit idolatry.*
II.5	A.	Said R. Judah said Rab, "There was the case of a man who gazed upon a woman and whose heart become sick with desire for her. They came and asked physicians, who said, 'He has no remedy unless he has sexual relations with her.'
	B.	"Sages ruled, 'Let him die but not have sexual relations with her.
	C.	"[The physicians proposed,] 'Let her stand nude before him.'
	D.	"[Sages ruled,] 'Let him die, but let her not stand nude before him.'
	E.	"'Let her talk with him behind a wall.'
	F.	"'Let him die and let her not talk with him behind a wall.'"
	G.	*There is a dispute on this case between R. Jacob bar Idi and R. Samuel bar Nahmani. One said,* "The reason is that she was a married woman."
	H.	*The other said,* "She was unmarried."
	I.	*Now if she was a married woman, that is why the rulings were as they were. But in the view of him who said that she was unmarried, why so strict a set of rulings?*
	J.	R. Pappa said, "Because of the insult to her family."
	K.	R. Aha, son of R. Iqa, said, "It was so that an Israelite woman should not be licentious."
	L.	*And why not let him marry the woman?*
	M.	*Marriage would not settle his mind, in accord with what R. Isaac said.* For R. Isaac said, "From the day on which the Temple was destroyed, the pleasure of sexual relations was taken away [from Israelites] and handed over to transgressors. For it is said, 'Stolen waters are sweet, and bread eaten in secret is pleasant' (Prov. 9:17)."

As usual, we begin, at unit I.1, with scriptural proof for the proposition of the Mishnah, M. 8:7A. Unit I.2 continues the foregoing. Units I.3-4 then complement the Mishnah-paragraph with Tosefta's treatment of the same subject. Unit I.6 concludes the foregoing. Unit II.1 moves on to M. 8:7D. From unit II.2 to the end we consider the matters for which one must accept martyrdom rather than violate the Torah. So, as usual, the entire composition serves the interests of the Mishnah-paragraph, either directly or indirectly.

9

Bavli Tractate Sanhedrin
Chapter Nine
Folios 75A-84A

9:1 A-C

A. And these are those who are put to death through burning:

B. he who has sexual relations with both a woman and her daughter [Lev. 18:17, 20:14], and a priest's daughter who committed adultery [Lev. 21:9].

C. In the same category as a woman and her daughter are [the following]: his daughter, his daughter's daughter, his son's daughter, his wife's daughter, the daughter of her daughter, the daughter of her son, his mother-in-law, the mother of his mother-in-law, and the mother of his father-in-law.

I.1 A. *The framer of the passage does not say, "He who has sexual relations with a woman whose daughter he has married,"* but rather, **He who has sexual relations with both a woman and her daughter [M. 9:1B].**

B. *What follows is that both of them are prohibited.*

C. *And who are they? They are his mother-in-law and the mother of his mother-in-law.*

D. *Then it further goes on,* **In the same category as a woman and her daughter...,** *which leads to the inference that the two that are specified are stated explicitly in Scripture, with the others derived by exegesis [from them].*

E. *That poses no problem to the view of Abbayye, who has said, "[Aqiba and Ishmael, cited below], differ on the basis on which the rule at hand is derived."*

F. *In accord with whose view is the Mishnah-passage at hand?*

G. It is R. Aqiba [who maintains that the prohibition of marriage to the mother-in-law's mother is explicitly prohibited by Scripture (Freedman, p. 507, n. 4)].

H. *But in the view of Raba, who has said, "At issue [between Aqiba and Ishmael] is the status of his mother-in-law after his wife's death [at which point the woman is no longer his mother-in-law]," in accord with authority is the Mishnah-passage at hand?*

I. *Raba will tell you, "Repeat it as follows: 'He who has sexual relations with a woman whose daughter one has married' [so obviating the question with which we began, A]."*

J. **In the same category as a woman and her daughter are...his mother-in-law, the mother of his mother-in-law, and the mother of his father-in-law [M. 9:1C].**

K. *In Abbayye's view* [Freedman, p. 508, n. 2: that burning for the first two is explicitly decreed, so that they cannot be included in 'a woman, etc.,' but are identical therewith], *since the framer of the passage wished to make reference to the mother of his father-in-law, he stated also, "His mother-in-law and the mother of his mother-in-law."* [that only the mother-in-law is forbidden on pain of death by fire, but not her mother (Freedman, p. 508, n. 3)].

L. *In Raba's view since the framer of the passage wanted to make reference to the mother of his father-in-law and the mother of his mother-in-law, he made reference also to his mother-in-law.*

I.2 A. *What is the source of the rule at hand?*

B. *It is in accord with what our rabbis have taught on Tannaite authority:*

C. "And if a man takes a woman and her mother [it is wickedness, they shall be burned with fire, both he and they]" (Lev. 20:14).

D. I know only that the law applies to marriage with both a woman and her mother. How do I know that the same law applies to [marriage with] the daughter of the woman, the daughter of her daughter, or the daughter of her son?

E. In the present passage, the word "wickedness" appears, and elsewhere the same word appears [namely, at Lev. 18:17: "You shall not uncover the nakedness of a woman and her daughter, neither shall you take her son's daughter or her daughter's daughter to uncover her nakedness, for they are her near kinswomen; it is wickedness"].

F. Just as, when the word "wickedness" occurs elsewhere, it encompasses her daughter and the daughter of her daughter as well as the daughter of her son, so here it encompasses her daughter, the daughter of her daughter, and the daughter of her son.

G. How do we know that one should treat the males as equivalent to the females?

H. Here the word "wickedness" occurs, and elsewhere, that same word occurs.

I. Just as there [at Lev. 18:17] males are treated as equivalent to females [so the son's daughter is forbidden as much as the daughter's daughter], so here the males are treated as equivalent to females.

J. How do we know that those below are treated as equivalent to those above?

K. Here the word "wickedness" occurs, and elsewhere the word wickedness occurs. Just as elsewhere those below are treated as equivalent to those above, so here those below are to be treated as equivalent to those above. And just as here, those above are treated as equivalent to those below, so elsewhere, those above are treated as equivalent to those below.

I.3   A.   A master has said, "How do we know that one should treat the males as equivalent to the females?"

     B.   *What is the sense of* "the males as equivalent to the females"?

     C.   *If we should say that one should treat the daughter of her son as equivalent to the daughter of her daughter, these derive together [from the same proof-text, based on "wickedness"].*

     D.   *Rather, it means to treat his father-in-law's mother as equivalent to his mother-in-law's mother [in both cases, incest is punished by execution through burning].*

     E.   *But if at this point we have not proved that fact in the case of the mother of his mother-in-law, can we proceed to take up the case of the mother of his father-in-law?*

     F.   **[75B]** *Said Abbayye, "This is the sense of the passage:* 'How do we know that we should treat his issue as equivalent to hers? Here the word 'wickedness' is used, and elsewhere, the word 'wickedness' is used,' and so on. [Freedman, p. 509, n.5: So we prove that his daughter, his son's daughter, or his daughter's daughter by a mistress are forbidden to him on pain of burning, just as are the wife's daughter, her son's daughter, and her daughter's daughter. For Lev. 18:17 refers to the offspring of marriage, not of seduction or outrage. On this interpretation 'male' refers to his issue, 'female' to his wife's.]"

     G.   *But lo, with reference to his issue, the word "wickedness" in point of fact is not used at all.* [Freedman, p. 509, n. 6: For that his issue is at all forbidden is derived not from Lev. 18:17 but from Lev. 18:10].

     H.   *Said Raba, "R. Isaac bar Abodimi said to me, 'We derive the application of the law to both cases from the facts, first, that 'they' appears in two related passages and the fact that 'wickedness' occurs in two.* [Freedman, p. 509, n. 7: In Lev. 18:10 it is stated, "The nakedness of thy son's daughter, or of thy daughter's daughter, even their nakedness thou shalt not uncover: for they (hennah) are thine own nakedness." Further, it is written (ibid. 18:17): "Thou shalt not uncover the nakedness of a woman and her daughter, neither shall thou take her son's daughter, or her daughter's daughter, to uncover her nakedness; for they (hennah) are her near kinswomen; it is wickedness (zimmah)." Since hennah occurs in these two passages, they are identified with each other, and zimmah in the second passage, referring to her issue, is understood to be implicit in the first too, which refers to his issue. Then the first passage is further identified with Lev. 20:14. "And if a man take a wife and her mother, it is wickedness (zimmah): They shalt be burnt with fire:" thus we derive burning for incest with his issue.]

I.4   A.   The master said, "How do we know that those below are treated as equivalent to those above?"

     B.   *What is the meaning of the phrase, "those below as those above"?*

C. *If one should wish to propose that the sense [of "those below"] is that the daughter of her son and the daughter of her daughter are equivalent to her daughter ["those above"], these derive all together from the same proof-texts.*

D. Rather, it refers to the mother of his father-in-law and the mother of his mother-in-law, treating them as equivalent to his mother-in-law.

E. *But if so, then instead of saying,* "Those below are equivalent to those above," *what is required is* "Those above are equivalent to those below". [The older generation are "those above."]

F. *Repeat the passage in just this way:* "Those above are equivalent to those below" [exactly as you propose].

G. If so, then the statement, "Here, 'wickedness' is stated, and there 'wickedness' is stated" [makes no sense]. *For, at this point, the prohibition they themselves have not yet been established through proof-texts, so the use of the word "wickedness" in their connection also can prove nothing.* [Freedman, p. 509. n. 4: At this stage, nothing has been adduced to show that incest with his mother-in-law's mother us thus punished, for 'a woman' has been translated literally. Consequently, only his mother-in-law is forbidden in this verse.]

H. Said Abbayye, "This is the sense of the passage: How do we know that we should treat the third generation above as equivalent to the third generation below [that is, the daughter's daughter and the son's daughter are forbidden, so too the father-in-law's mother and the mother-in-law's mother]?

I. "With respect to the generations below, the word 'wickedness' is used, and with reference to the generations above, the word 'wickedness' is used.

J. "Just as for the generations below, the prohibition extends for three generations, so for the generations above, the prohibitions extend for three generations.

K. "And just as with respect to the penalty, the law has treated the generations below as equivalent to the generations above, so with regard to the admonition the same is the case, the law having treated the generations above as equivalent to the generations below." [Freedman, p. 510, n. 10: For in Lev. 18:10, where the third lower generation is forbidden, nothing is said about punishment, which is derived from Lev. 20:14, as stated above. On the other hand, in Lev. 20:14, which is made to include the third generation above, though only explicitly stating the second, no formal prohibition is given. This in turn is derived from Lev. 18:10. (Both are derived through the medium of Lev. 18:17, the connecting link between the other two.) One Abbayye's interpretation it is necessary to emend the Baraitha from 'and the lower is as the upper', to 'that the upper is as the lower etc.']

L. *R. Ashi said, "Indeed, matters are just as stated [and require no revision, contrary to Abbayye's view]. And what is the sense of* "those below'? *It is "those below" in the seriousness of the prohibition.* [Freedman, pp. 510-511, n. 12: 'the upper' or higher prohibition is that of his mother-in-law, his more immediate relation, whilst the prohibition of her mother, as also of his father-in-law's mother, is regarded as 'lower', i.e. weaker, as they are a generation further removed. Hence this is its meaning: Whence do we know that his mother-in-law's mother and his father-in-law's mother, whose relationships are lower (i.e., further removed, and consequently weaker) than his mother-in-law's, are treated as his mother-in-law? It is derived from his wife's daughter: just as in the latter case, the 'lower' relation is as the 'upper' (stronger), i.e., his wife's daughter's daughter is as his wife's daughter, though more distant; so here too, his mother-in-law's mother is as she herself. This deduction is in respect of equal punishment. The second clause is explained by R. Ashi as Abbayye, as referring to the prohibition.]"

I.5 **A.** [Referring back to III A, how do we know that the male's relations are regarded as the female's relations], if so, then just as the mother of her mother is forbidden, so the mother of his mother is forbidden.

B. Said Abbayye, "Scripture says, 'The nakedness of your father or the nakedness of your mother you shall not uncover; she is your mother' (Lev. 18:7) – On account of [incest with] one's mother you impose a penalty, on account of the mother of his mother you do not impose a penalty."

C. *Said Raba, "Whether matters accord with him who has said,* [Freedman:] 'Judge from it in its entirety,' or 'Judge from it and place it on its own basis,' *this could not be deduced.* [Freedman, p. 511, n. 5: A verse is unnecessary, because his maternal grandmother could not be deduced from the gezerah shawah based on zimmah, whatever view be held on the scope of a gezerah shawah. There are two views on this. One is that the identity of law taught by a gezerah shawah must hold good in all respects, so that the case deduced is equal to the premise in all points; this is called 'judge from it and from (all) of it.' An opposing view is that the analogy holds good only in respect of the main question at issue, but that thereafter, the case deduced may diverge from its premise. This is called, 'judge from it, but place it on its own basis', i.e., confine the analogy to the main question, not to the subsidiary points.]

D. "[Freedman, p. 11:] *For on the view, 'judge from it in its entirety', [the deduction would proceed thus:] Just as her [his wife's] maternal grandmother is forbidden [to him], so is his maternal grandmother forbidden. [Then carrying the analogy] to its uttermost, just as in her case [i.e., incest with the former] is punished by fire so in his case [i.e., incest with the latter] is punished by fire.*

E. *"In the view of him who says that the execution through burning is the more severe penalty, there is the possibility of raising the following question: What is the particular trait affecting his* *wife's maternal grandfather [that she should be forbidden and the penalty of burning applies]?*

F.   "It is that his wife's mother is subject to the same penalty. [Freedman, p. 512, n. 2: Hence, since the prohibition of his wife's mother is so severe, it is natural that it should extend to her maternal grandmother too.]

G.   "But will you make such a statement in his case, for [should he have incest with] his wife, the penalty is stoning?

H.   "Furthermore, the penalty for incest with his mother is through stoning. Will the penalty for incest with his mother's mother be burning?

I.   "And furthermore, just as there is no distinction made in her case between her mother and her mother's mother, so in his case, there should be no distinction between the penalty inflicted in the case of incest with his mother and with the mother of his mother.

J.   *"And in the position of him who maintains that stoning is the more severe, on account of this problem, there is in any event no analogy.*

K.   *"[Freedman, p. 512:] Whilst on the view, 'judge from it and place it on its own basis', [the deduction would proceed thus:] Just as her [his wife's] maternal grandmother is forbidden [to him], so is his maternal grandmother forbidden. But 'place it on its own basis', thus: in the former case the punishment is burning; but in the latter, stoning, the penalty which we find prescribed for incest with his mother. Now, in the view that burning is severer, this can be refuted,* **[76A]** [Thus]: Why is her case [i.e., his wife's maternal grandmother forbidden]? Because her mother is [forbidden] on pain of death by fire. But can you say the same in his case, seeing that his mother is forbidden on pain of stoning [only]? Further, his maternal grandmother is like her's: just as in the latter case no distinction is drawn between his wife's maternal grandmother and her [his wife's] daughter, so in the former, no distinction should be allowed between his own maternal grandmother and his daughter. *Whilst on the view that stoning is severer, the analogy cannot be made on account of this last difficulty."'*

L.   If [we compare his relatives to hers], then just as his daughter-in-law is forbidden, so her daughter-in-law should be forbidden [to him, that is Freedman, p. 513, n. 5: the wife of her son by a previous husband. But she is not forbidden to him.]

M.   Said Abbayye, "Scripture has said, 'You shall not uncover the nakedness of your daughter-in-law, she is your son's wife' (Lev. 18:15), meaning, on account of the wife of your son you impose liability, but you do not impose liability on account of the wife of her son."

N.   Raba said, "[Freedman, p. 513:] *Whether it be maintained, 'judge from it in its entirety,' or 'judge from it and place it on its own basis', this could not be deduced. For on the first view, [the deduction would proceed thus:] just as his daughter-in-law is forbidden him, so is her's forbidden him. [Then carrying through the analogy] 'in its entirety,' just as in his case [the penalty] is stoning, so in her case is the penalty stoning. But if we regard stoning severer, this analogy can be refuted. [Thus]: Why is his [daughter-in-law forbidden]? Because his mother is forbidden him on pain of stoning: Can you then say the same of her daughter-in-law, seeing that incest with her mother incurs only death by fire? Moreover, her daughter is forbidden on pain of burning: shall her daughter-in-law be forbidden on pain of stoning? [No.]"*

O. [In reply to Raba:] Let his own circumstance prove to the contrary, for his daughter [should he have incest with her] produces the penalty of burning, while his daughter-in-law produces that of stoning.

P. *Rather:* Just as in his case you do not draw a distinction between his own case and that of his mother and his daughter-in-law, so in her case you should draw no distinction between her mother and her daughter-in-law. [Freedman, p. 514, n .1: Hence, incest with the latter should be punished by burning. But as has already been proved, stoning is the proper punishment; therefore the entire analogy is impossible.]

Q. [Freedman, p. 514:] *And on the view that burning is considered more severe, the analogy cannot be made because of this last difficulty. Whilst on the view, 'judge from it and place it on its own basis,' [the deduction would proceed thus:] just as his daughter-in-law is forbidden him, so is her daughter-in-law forbidden; and place it on its own basis, thus: in the former case, [his daughter-in-law] the punishment is stoning; but in the latter, burning, the punishment we find for incest with her mother. But if stoning is severer, this can be refuted. [Thus]: Why is his daughter-in-law forbidden? Because his mother is forbidden him on pain of stoning. But can you say the same of her daughter-in-law, seeing that her mother is forbidden only on pain of burning! Moreover, just as in his case, you draw a distinction between his daughter [punished by burning] and his daughter-in-law [by stoning], so in her case, you should draw a distinction between her daughter and her daughter-in-law.* [Freedman, p. 514, n. 3: i.e., just as the punishment for his daughter-in-law is severer than for his daughter, viz., stoning instead of burning, so her daughter-in-law should be more stringently interdicted than her daughter, viz., by stoning, instead of burning. But if we compare her daughter-in-law to her mother, the punishment is burning. Hence the entire deduction is impossible.]

I.6 A. How do we know that one's [own] daughter born of a woman one has raped [is forbidden]?

B.   Has not Abbayye said, "It is an argument <u>a fortiori</u>. If one is punished on account of incest with the daughter of his daughter, will he not all the more so be punished on account of his daughter?"

C.   But do [courts] inflict punishment because of a logical argument?

D.   *It serves to clarify the matter in general [but Lev. 18:10 in fact prohibits relationships with any sort of daughter].*

E.   *Raba said, "R. Isaac bar Abodimi said to me, "The matter derives from the use of the word 'they' in the two passages and the word 'wickedness' in two [as above]."*

I.7   A.   *The father of R. Abin taught on Tannaite authority,* "It is because have we have not derived from Scripture that **a man's incest with his daughter produced by a rape is punishable that it was necessary for Scripture to state, 'And the daughter of a man and a priest,** [if she profane herself through her father, she profanes him, she shall be burned with fire]' (Lev. 21:9) [cf. T. San. 12:1H]. [Freedman, p. 515, n. 4: Lev. 21:9, 'A man' is superfluous, and therefore teaches that even if she is only his daughter, not his wife's, this law holds good. By translating the rest of the verse as in the text, we deduce that an illegitimate daughter is burnt for incest with her father; and by regarding 'a man' as distinct from 'priest' (the latter being attached to the former with the copula 'and'), the deduction is made to refer to any illegitimate daughter, not only a priest's]"

B.   [Might one then reason as follows:] Just as the daughter of a priest is punished by execution through burning, but her lover is not punished by execution through burning, so incest with one's daughter produced by a rape produces the penalty of death through burning for her but not for her lover [her father]?

C.   Said Abbayye, "Said Scripture, 'She profanes her father' (Lev. 21:9). The law applies to one who profanes her father, thus excluding the case at hand, in which her father has profaned her. [So her lover, that is, her father, shares the same punishment.]"

D.   *Raba said, "In the case [of the lover of a priest's daughter, guilty with her of adultery] you have removed such a one from the penalty inflicted on the daughter of a priest and imposed upon him the penalty that applies to the daughter of an Israelite [stoning, not burning].*

E.   *"But in the present case, in accord with the death penalty of what classification of woman will you have him put to death? Will it be to that of an unmarried woman?* [Freedman, p. 516, n. 2: For if an incestuous paramour be excluded from the punishment of an adulterous woman, whether the daughter of a priest or an Israelite (since the relationship is independent of these), his law can only be assimilated to that of an unmarried woman, whose unchastity is not punished at all. But surely it cannot be maintained that an illegitimate daughter is burnt for incest with her father, though her offense is a passive one, and less than the man's, whilst he goes scot free! Hence the limitation of 'she' cannot apply to this.]"

I.8   A.   Whence do we derive the admonition that a man not commit incest with his daughter produced by his act of rape?

B.   *Now with respect to Abbayye and Raba, from the very same source from which they derive the mode of execution, they also derive the admonition [since the verses they cite contain both elements]. But* what is the equivalent for the Tannaite teaching transmitted by the father of R. Abin?

C. Said R. Ilaa, "Scripture has said, 'Do not profane your daughter to cause her to be a whore' (Lev. 19:29) [including incest, and 'daughter' involves an illegitimate one too (Freedman, p. 516, n. 5)]."

D. R. Jacob, brother of R. Aha bar Jacob, objected to this statement, "Does the cited verse, 'Do not profane your daughter to cause her to be a whore' (Lev. 19:29) serve the stated purpose? To the contrary, it is required for a quite different purpose, namely, for that in the following teaching, taught on Tannaite authority:

E. "'Do not profane your daughter to cause her to be a whore" (Lev. 19:29)"

F. "'Is it possible to maintain that Scripture speaks of a priest who may marry his daughter to a Levite or an Israelite [indicating that, since the daughter is thereby profaned, because she may no longer eat priestly rations, he is not to marry her off to a Levite or an Israelite]?

G. "'Scripture says, "To cause her to be a whore" (Lev. 19:29), meaning to refer to that sort of profanation that takes place through whoredom [and not in the context of profanation resulting in her disqualification from eating priestly rations].

H. "'So at issue is one who hands over his daughter [for a sexual liaison] not involving marriage.'"

I. [Ilaa replies], "If so, Scripture should have said, 'Do not treat profanity' [spelling the verb with one L, rather than two Ls]. Why does Scripture say, 'Do not profane [spelling the verb with two Ls]? It is to teach both lessons."

J. And how do Abbayye and Raba interpret this same verse, "Do not profane your daughter to cause her to be a whore" (Lev. 19:29)?

K. Said R. Mani, "This refers to one who marries his young daughter off to an old man."

L. It accords with that which has been taught on Tannaite authority:

M. "Do not profane your daughter to cause her to be a whore" (Lev. 19:29):

N. R. Eliezer says, "This is one who marries off his young daughter to an old man."

O. R. Aqiba says, "This refers to one who postpones marrying off his daughter once she has reached puberty."

Marrying Off One's Children in the Proper Manner

I.9 A. Said R. Kahana in the name of R. Aqiba, "You have none who is poor in Israel except because of one who is clever in acting wickedly and one who delays marrying off his daughter once she has passed puberty."

B.   *But is not the one who delays marrying off his daughter once she has passed puberty also in the category of a person who is clever in acting wickedly?*

C.   *Said Abbayye, "* **[76B]** *This is the sense of the statement at hand:* Who is one who is clever in acting wickedly? It is he who delays marrying off his daughter once she has passed puberty.'"

D.   And R. Kahana said in the name of R. Aqiba, "Be careful about someone who gives you advice in accord with his own interest."

E.   Said R. Judah said Rab, "He who marries off his daughter to an old man, and he who takes a wife for his minor son, and he who returns a lost object to a Samaritan – in respect to all of these, Scripture says, '[That he bless himself in his heart, saying, I shall have peace, though I walk in the imagination of my heart] to add drunkenness to thirst. The Lord will not spare him' (Deut. 29:18-20)."

F.   *An objection was raised:* "He who loves his wife as he loves himself, he who honors her more than he honors himself, he who raises up his sons and daughters in the right path, and he who marries them off close to the time of their puberty – of such a one, Scripture says, 'And you shall know that your tabernacle shall be in peace and you shall visit your habitation and you shall not sin' (Job 5:24). [So it is good to marry off a minor.]"

G.   *If the marriage is arranged just prior to puberty, the case is different [and meritorious].*

I.10   A.   *Our rabbis have taught on Tannaite authority:*

B.   He who loves his neighbors, he who draws his relatives near, he who marries his sister's daughter, and he who lends a sela to a poor person when he needs it –

C.   concerning such a person Scripture says, "Then you will call, and the Lord will answer" (Is. 58:9).

I.11   A.   *Our rabbis have taught on Tannaite authority:*

B.   "[And if a man take a wife and her mother, it is wickedness; they shall be burned with fire,] both he and they" (Lev. 20:14).

C.   "He and one of them," the words of R. Ishmael.

D.   R. Aqiba says, "He and both of them."

E.   *What is at issue between them?*

F.   *Said Abbayye, "At issue is interpreting the implication of the passage at hand.*

G.   *"R. Ishmael takes the view that t*he meaning of 'he and they' is that they are to burn him and <u>one</u> of them, for in the Greek language, the word for 'one' is <u>hena</u> [in the biblical text at hand, 'THN]. And the penalty against incest with one's mother-in-law's mother derives from exegesis [of Scripture].

H.   *"R. Aqiba maintains that* 'he and they' means 'he and both of them,' in which case the penalty against incest with one's mother-in-law derives from what is explicitly written in the passage at hand directly [and not through exegesis]."

I.   *Raba said, "At issue between them is the case of having sexual relations with his mother-in-law after his wife's death.*

J.   *"R. Ishmael takes the position that* if one has sexual relations with his mother-in-law after his wife's death, he is put to death through burning.

K.   *"R. Aqiba takes the view that* he merely violates a general prohibition [but not penalized]. [Freedman, p. 518, n. 6: R. Ishmael interprets the verse, 'he and one of them' i.e., even if only one of them is alive (viz., his mother-in-law), the penalty for incest is burning, whilst R. Aqiba maintains, 'he and both of them' i.e., only during the lifetime of both is incest with his mother-in-law punished by fire. Otherwise, there is no penalty, though it is forbidden.'"

The fact that the composition was planned at the outset and follows a clear program is shown by the fact that unit I.1 is incomprehensible without the information provided, in an appendix, only at unit I.11. What we want to know is the basis for prohibiting incest with certain female relations: on the one side, the man's mother-in-law after the wife's death, on the other, the man's daughter produced through a rape. The latter of the two categories come under discussion at unit I.2, and the exegesis of the materials of unit I.2 occupies units I.3-4. Unit I.6 then reverts to the proof-texts for the prohibition against incest with a daughter produced by a rape, and units I.7, 8 pursue the same topic. Units I.9, 10 are attached prior to inclusion of the whole in the present composition and do not belong, and then, as I said, unit I.11 presents the <u>locus classicus</u> for the dispute to which unit I has made reference. If then we turn back to the Mishnah-paragraph and ask whether the exegesis of the statements we find there has generated the composition at hand, we look in vain for a reference to the daughter of a man produced by his act of rape. So the issue is essentially a theoretical one, resting on how we can prove, on the basis of Scripture or reason, that such a relationship is incestuous. Then the entire composition is attached to the Mishnah-paragraph at hand, on the pretext supplied by unit I's reading of the exegetical foundations of what turns out to be an oblique and secondary issue – the mother-in-law. In fact, we begin with reference to the mother-in-law, but we mean the daughter produced in a rape. In all, it would be difficult to find a more subtle exercise in the theory of the exegesis of Scripture in relationship to the exegesis of the law.

9:1 D-M

D. **And these are those who are put to death through decapitation:**

E. **the murderer, and the townsfolk of an apostate town.**

F. **A murderer who hit his neighbor with a stone or a piece of iron [Ex. 21:18],**

G. **or who pushed him under water or into fire, and [the other party] cannot get out of there and so perished,**

H. **he is liable.**

I. [If] he pushed him into the water or into the fire, and he can get out of there but [nonetheless] he died, he is exempt.

J. [If] he sicked a dog on him, or sicked a snake on him, he is exempt.

K. [If] he made a snake bite him,

L. R. Judah declares him liable.

M. And sages declare him exempt.

I.1 A. Said Samuel, "Why [at Num. 35:16-18, where we take up murder with iron, stone, or wooden weapons] the word 'hand' is not stated when we speak of an iron weapon [indicating that the weapon must be sufficiently large to be held in the hand only when it is a weapon of stone or wood, but not of iron]?

B. "It is because an iron weapon may inflict death no matter its size."

C. *It has been taught on Tannaite authority to the same effect:*

D. Rabbi says, "It is obvious to Him who spoke and brought the world into being that iron inflicts death no matter what its size.

E. "Therefore the Torah did not assign a minimum measure to it."

F. *That rule pertains, however, only in the case of piercing someone with iron [but if one hit him with iron, it must be of requisite size actually to inflict death].*

II.1 A. **Or pushed him under water [and he cannot get out...he is liable. If he pushed him into water...and he can get out...he is exempt] [M. 9:1G, I]:**

B. *The first of the two statements [M. 9:1G] makes its own point, and the second of the two statements [M. 9:1I] makes its own point, too.*

C. *The former of the two statements makes its own point, namely, even though he is not the one who pushed the other into the water, since the other cannot get up from there and so dies, he is liable.*

D. *The latter of the two statements makes its own point, namely, even though he is the one who pushed the other into the water, since the other can climb up out of the water and nonetheless dies, he is exempt from penalty.*

II.2 A. *How do we know that one keeps the other under [is liable]?*

B. Said Samuel, "It is because Scripture has stated, 'Or if with enmity he smote him with his hand' (Num. 35:21).

C. "This serves to encompass who one holds his neighbor [under the water]."

II.3 A. *A man confined the beast of his fellow in the sun, and it perished.*

B. Rabina declared him liable [to pay the value of the beast].

C. R. Aha, son of Rab, declared him exempt.

D. Rabina declared him liable on the basis of an argument <u>a fortiori</u>:

E. "Now if in the case of murder, in which the law does not treat inadvertent action as equivalent to deliberate action, or action done under constraint as equivalent to action done willfully, the law has imposed liability in the case of one who confines his neighbor [and so causes his death],

F. "[77A] in the case of property damage, in which the law did not distinguish but treated as equivalent an act done inadvertently and one done deliberately, and an act done under constraint as equivalent to an act done willfully, is it not a matter of reason that one should impose liability on one who causes damage by confining [a beast]?"

G. R. Aha, son of Rab, declares such a one exempt [from penalty].

H. *Said R. Mesharshia, "What is the scriptural basis on which the father of my father declares such a one exempt?*

I. *"Scripture has said, 'He who smote him shall surely be put to death, for he is a murderer' (Num. 35:21). It is in the case of a murderer that the law has made such a one liable in the consequence of an act of confinement, but in a case of causing civil damages, the law has not made such a one liable in the consequence of an act of confinement."*

II.4 A. And said Raba, "If one tied up [another person] and the latter dies of starvation, he is exempt."

B. And Raba said, "If one tied up a beast in the heat and it died, or if he did so in the cold and it died, he is liable.

C. "If he did so when the sun was going to come [but had not yet risen], or that the cold had not yet taken effect, he is exempt. [In this case he is merely an indirect cause (Freedman, p. 520, n. 4)]."

D. And Raba said, "If he tied him up before a lion, he is exempt. If he tied him up before mosquitoes, he is liable."

E. *R. Ashi said, "Even if he did so before mosquitoes, he also is exempt, because the ones who are there [when he tied the man up] go along, and others come and take their place."*

II.5 A. *It has been stated on Amoraic authority:*

B. If one turned a vat over upon someone [who died of suffocation] or broke open a ceiling above him [and he caught cold and died],

C. Raba and R. Zira:

D. One said, "He is liable," and the other said, "He is exempt.'"

E. *You may conclude that it is Raba who said that he is exempt, for Raba said, "If he tied him up and he died on account of starvation, he is exempt."*

F. *To the contrary, you may draw the conclusion that R. Zira is the one who has said that he is exempt, for R. Zira said, "He who brought his fellow into a marble chamber and lit a lamp there so that the latter dies [because of the fumes], he is liable."*

G. *What is the reason? It is that he lit a lamp. Lo, had he not lit a lamp, he would not have been liable [even though the other had died because of lack of air]. [So Zira, too, does not impose a penalty for indirectly causing death.]*

H. *One might say that if there had been no lamp, the heat would not have begun [to affect the man]* **[77B]** *at the moment [at which he put him in the room]. But in the present case [that of the overturned vat,] the heat begins to produce its effects immediately.*

II.6 A. Said Raba, "If one pushed someone into a pit, and there was a ladder in the pit, and someone else came along and took it away, or even if he himself removed the ladder, he still is exempt.

B. *"For at the point at which he threw the man into the pit,. [the victim] could climb out of it."*

C.   And Raba said, "If one shot an arrow, and there was a shield in the hand [of the person at whom he shot the arrow], and someone else came long and took the shield away, or even if he came along and took it away, he is exempt.

D.   *"For at the moment at which he shot the arrow at him, the force of the arrow would have been broken [on the shield]."*

E.   And Raba said, "If one shot an arrow at someone, and the latter had ointment in his hand [which would heal the wound of the arrow], and someone else came along and scattered the ointment, or even if he came along and scattered it, he is exempt.

F.   *"For at the moment at which he shot the arrow, the man could have healed himself."*

G.   Said R. Ashi, "Therefore, even in the case of ointment in the market-place [the same rule applies, since someone could have gotten the ointment when it was needed]."

H.   Said R. Aha, son of Raba, to R. Ashi, "If [when the man was hit, he did not have ointment, but] ointment came to hand, what is the law?"

I.   He said to him, "Lo, this one goes forth from court a free man."

J.   And Raba said, "If one threw a stone against the wall and it bounced back and killed someone, he is liable."

K.   *And a Tannaite authority repeats:* "It would be exemplified in a case of people playing with a ball, who deliberately committed murder. They are put to death.

L.   "If this happened inadvertently, they go into exile."

M.   *The point that, if it was inadvertent, they go into exile, is self-evident. It was included only because the framer of the passage wished to make the point concerning those who do so deliberately, stressing that they are put to death. What might you have said? It is a case in which it was an admonition that was subject to doubt. Nor who may say for sure that the ball will bounce back. So we are taught to the contrary.*

II.7   A.   R. Tahalipa of the West repeated on Tannaite authority before R. Abbahu, "In a case of people playing ball, if the one who was killed was within four cubits [of the wall], the player is exempt. If he was outside of four cubits, he is liable."

B.   *Said Rabina to R. Ashi, "What would such a case involve? If it suited [the player that the ball rebound], then even if the man was nearer than four cubits [and the ball rebounded], he should be liable, and if he did not want [the ball to rebound], then even if the man were at a greater distance, he should be exempt from liability."*

C.   *He said to him, "Ordinary ball-players want the ball to rebound more.* [Freedman, p. 522, n. 9: Therefore it may be presumed that he intended it to rebound at least four cubits, hence if less, he is not liable.]"

D.   *May we then conclude that in a case such as this, [the murder is deemed to happen] by the man's direct action? An objection was raised on the basis of the following:* **He who mixes ash and water in a trough and the ash fell on his hand or on the side of the trough and afterward it fell into the trough — the act of mixing is unfit, [since the mixing must be done by human action]** [M. Par. 6:1A-E]. [Here, therefore, in a parallel case, human action does not encompass what happens on a rebound].

F.   *With what sort of a case do we deal? With a case in which [ash] was dripping down [into the trough].* [But had the ash fallen with force, the fall would be regarded as part of the man's action in dropping them onto the utensil (Freedman, p. 523, n. 2)].

G.   *Come and take note:* **A needle which is fixed in an earthenware utensil, and one sprinkled on it – one is in doubt whether he sprinkled on the needle, or whether from the clay utensil water merely dripped on the needle – the sprinkling is unfit [M. Par. 12:2F-H].** [The sprinkling has not been done by human action].

H.   *Said R. Hinena b. R. Judah in the name of Rab, "The word should be read, 'It was <u>found</u>' [so the water was found on the needle, and we do not know how it got there.' That explains the unfitness.]"*

II.8 A.   *Said R. Papa, "If someone tied up his fellow and inundated him with a column of water, it is as if it was done by his arrows and he is liable.*

     B.   *"That is the case if the death was due to the first flow of the water [directly], but if it was through the second flow of the water, he is merely a secondary cause of death.* [Freedman, p. 523, n. 5: If the victim was lying immediately in front of the burst, where the strength of the water's flow is still due to the man's action, the drowning is by his direct agency. But if he was lying at some distance, he is held to be an indirect or secondary cause]."

     C.   And R. Papa said, "If one threw a stone upward and it went to the side and killed someone, he is liable."

     D.   *Said Mar, son of R. Ashi, to R. Pappa, "What is the reason for that ruling? It is because of the man's direct action. But then, if it is because of what the man as done, the stone should continue to go upward. [78A] And if it is not because of his direct action, then it should come straight down. Rather, it is because of his direct action, but it was weakened* [Freedman, p. 524, n.3: Most of the force with which he threw it was already expended but sufficient was left to impel it in the direction in which it fell]."

II.9 A.   *Our rabbis have taught on Tannaite authority:*

     B.   If ten men hit someone with ten sticks and the victim died, whether they did so simultaneously or sequentially, they are exempt.

     C.   R. Judah b. Betera says, "If they did so sequentially, the last one is liable, because he brought the death nearer."

     D.   Said R. Yohanan, "And both authorities [B, C] interpret the same verse: 'And he who kills an entire life of a man shall surely be put to death' (Lev. 24:17).

     E.   *"Rabbis understand by 'an entire life' to mean that one is liable only if the whole of the life of the man is intact [when he inflicts the death blow].*

     F.   *"R. Judah b. Betera takes the position that an aspect of the entire life is at issue* [Freedman, p. 524, n. 8: however little life the man has, even if he is nearly dead, the man who actually kills him is liable]."

G. Said Raba, "Both parties concur in the case of one who kills one afflicted with a fatal disease that he is exempt.

H. "If he killed someone dying because of heavenly action [that is, of natural causes] he is liable.

I. "The dispute concerns only one who is dying on account of the act of man.

J. *"One party compares the case to that of one who is dying because of an incurable diseases [and so exempts the killer]. The other party compares the case to that of one who is dying because of heavenly action [of natural causes, so imposes liability on the murderer].*

K. *"As to the one who compares the case to that of one who is dying because of an incurable disease, what is the reason that he does not compare the case to that of one who is dying because of heavenly action?*

L. *"To one who is dying at the hand of heaven, no concrete injury has been done, while to the other, a concrete injury has been inflicted.*

M. *"As to the one who compares the case to that of one who is dying because of heavenly action, what is the reason that he does not compare the case to that of one who is dying because of an incurable disease? In the case of one who is dying because of an incurable disease,* [Freedman:] the vital organs are affected, while in the case of the other, the vital organs are not affected."

II.10 A. *A Tannaite authority repeated before R. Sheshet:*

B. "'And he that kills all of the life of man' (Lev. 24:17):

C. "This serves to encompass the case of one who hits his fellow, and in his blow there is not sufficient force to inflict death, and then another party comes along and actually delivers the death blow, indicating that the latter is liable."

D. *Since the blow that the former gave him was not sufficient to inflict death, it is self-evident [that the former is not liable].*

E. Rather, it should be that the blow that the former gave <u>was</u> sufficiently strong to inflict death, but another party came and actually inflicted the death blow, and that second party is liable.

F. *The unattributed teaching belongs to R. Judah b. Betera.*

II.11 A. Said Raba, "He who kills someone afflicted with an incurable disease is exempt.

B. "And someone inflicted with an incurable disease who committed murder in the presence of a court is liable.

C. "If it was not in the presence of a court, he is exempt.

D. "If it was in the presence of a court, he is liable, for it is written, 'So shall you put away evil from the midst of you' (Deut. 13:6). [The court acts on what it sees on its own.]

E. If it was not in the presence of the court, he is exempt, for you have in hand an act of testimony that is not subject to the test of conspiratorial perjury [since in this case, the perjurers are beyond penalty. Who so? One has to do to them what they conspired to do to their victim. He is regarded as legally dead.

They therefore cannot have conspired to kill him.] So their testimony is not subject to the usual test and thus is null.

F. And said Raba, "One who commits pederasty with someone afflicted with an incurable disease is liable.

G. "If one inflicted with an incurable disease committed pederasty, if it was before a court, he is liable.

H. "If it was not before a court, he is exempt.

I. "If it was before a court, he is liable, for it is written, 'So shall you put away evil from the midst of you. (Deut. 13:6).

J. "If it was not before the court, he is exempt, for you have in hand an act of testimony that is not subject to the test of conspiratorial perjury."

K. *What need to I have for this further case [having made the same point with reference to the former]? The latter case is identical to the former!*

M. *The matter is at issue because of the clause about having sexual relations with a person dying of an incurable disease.*

N. *So we are informed that, because of the pleasure assumed to have been gained, [a penalty is imposed], and in this case we do invoke the principle that pleasure may be presumed to have been gained through the act [and so penalize the pederast].*

O. And said Raba, "Witnesses who gave testimony against someone dying of an incurable disease and who were then proved to be a conspiracy for perjury are not put to death.

P. "Witnesses who were suffering an incurable disease who were proved to be a conspiracy for perjury are put to death."

Q. R. Ashi said, "Even in the case of witnesses suffering from an incurable disease who were proved to be a conspiracy for perjury are not put to death.,

R. "For the testimony against them [proving that they constituted a conspiracy for perjury] itself is not subject to the same test [since those who testify against them cannot be put to death. Why not? The men were dying anyhow, as Raba originally said]."

S. And said Raba, "An ox, dying of an incurable disease, that killed someone is liable, and an ox belonging to a man suffering from an incurable disease that killed someone is exempt.

T. *"What is the scriptural basis for this rule?*

U. "Scripture has said, 'The ox shall be stoned and its owner shall also be put to death' (Ex. 21:29).

V. *"Wherever we can invoke the rule, 'And also its owner shall be put to death,' we also do not invoke the rule, 'The ox will be stoned.'"*

W. *"And wherever we cannot invoke the rule, 'And also its owner shall be put to death,' we also do not invoke the rule, 'The ox will be stoned.'"*

X. R. Ashi said, "Even an ox that is suffering from an incurable disease that killed a man would be exempt [under the stated circumstance].

Y. *"What is the reason for this ruling? Since, were it the owner, it would have been exempt [dying from an incurable disease, the owner*

would not be liable in this case, as Raba has said], the ox also is
exempt [in a parallel case]."

III.1   A.   **If he sicked a dog on him, etc. [M. 9:1J]:**
         B.   Said R. Aha bar Jacob, "When you look into the matter [A at M.
               9:1K-M], you will find that, in R. Judah's opinion [who holds one
               liable who makes a snake bite a man], the poison of a snake is
               between its teeth. Therefore the one one makes the snake bite a
               man is put to death through decapitation, while the snake itself is
               exempt.
         C.   "In the opinion of sages, the poison of the snake its vomited up out
               of its midst [on its own], and therefore the snake is put to death
               through stoning, and the one who made the snake bite the man is
               exempt. [Freedman, p. 526, n. 8: On Judah's view the fangs
               themselves are poisonous. Consequently the snake does nothing,
               the murder being committed by the person. But the sages maintain
               that even when its fangs are embedded in the flesh, they are not
               poisonous, unless it voluntarily emits poison. Consequently the
               murder is committed by the snake, not the man.]"

Unit I turns immediately to the proof-text on the basis of which the
Mishnah's rule is framed. Unit II.1 then deals with the exegesis of the
Mishnah-paragraph. Unit II.2 provides a proof-text for the same. Unit
II.3 then expands upon the matter. II.4 introduces the first of a long
series of Raba's excellent clarifications of the principle of the law. The
entire composition involving Raba is inserted whole, in the appropriate
position at which a compositor aiming at Mishnah-commentary chose for
it.

9:1 N-T

N.   He who hits his fellow, whether with a stone or with his fist,
O.   and they diagnosed him as likely to die,
P.   but he got better than he was,
Q.   and afterward he got worse and he died
R.   he is liable.
S.   R. Nehemiah says, "He is exempt,
T.   "for there is a basis to the matter [of thinking that he did not die
      from the original injury]."

I.1   A.   *Our rabbis have taught on Tannaite authority:*
       B.   [In T.'s version:] **And this is yet another exegesis which R.
             Nehemiah stated, "[When men quarrel, and one strikes the other
             with a stone or with his fist, and the man does not die but keeps
             his bed], then if the man rises again and walks abroad [78B] with
             his staff, he that struck him shall be clear; only he shall pay for
             the loss of his time, and shall have him thoroughly healed (Ex.
             21:18-19)**
       C.   **"Now would it enter one's mind that this one should walk around
             in the market, while the other should be put to death on his
             account?**

D. **"But the meaning is that, if he should recover somewhat, then get worse, and finally even if he should die [on account of the original blow], the other is exempt," [T. B.Q. 9:7A-C].**

E. *And how do rabbis deal with the proof-text [important to Nehemiah],* "And then shall he who smote him be quit" (Ex. 21:19)?

F. It teaches that the court imprisons the man [until we see whether the victim dies of the original blow].

G. *And how does R. Nehemiah prove that one imprisons the man?*

H. *He derives it from the case of the wood-gatherer (Num. 15:32-36) [who was held in prison until the case was settled on high].*

I. *And why should the rabbis also not derive their principle from the case of the wood-gatherer?*

J. *The wood-gatherer was subject to the death penalty, and what Moses did not know was simply how he was to be put to death. But that would exclude the present case, in which we do not know whether the one who hit the other is subject to the death penalty or not subject to the death penalty.*

K. *And R. Nehemiah points to a parallel in the case from that of the blasphemer, [at Lev. 24:10-14], in which, not knowing whether he was subject to the death penalty or not, the court imprisoned the man [until the decision would come from on high.]*

L. *And rabbis? The case of the blasphemer involved decisions on an ad hoc basis. [Such a decision cannot be taken as precedent for normal procedure.]*

M. *This foregoing report accords with the following teaching on Tannaite authority:*

N. Moses, our rabbi, knew that the wood-gatherer was subject to the death penalty.

O. For it is said, "Those who defile [the Sabbath] shall surely be put to death" (Ex. 31:14).

P. But he did not know by what means he was to be put to death, for it is written, "And they put him in ward, because it was not declared what should be done to him" (Num. 15:34).

Q. But as to the blasphemer, it is stated only, "And they put him in ward, that the mind of the Lord might be showed to them" (Lev. 24:12).

R. This teaches that Moses did not know whether or not he was subject to the death penalty at all.

S. *Now with respect to the view of R. Nehemiah, that is why the Scripture twice makes reference to assessing the man's condition [Ex. 21:18-19: And if men strive together and one smite another with a stone...and he die not but keeps his bed, if he rises again and walk abroad upon his staff, then he that hit him shall be quit."]* [Freedman, p. 528, n. 4: Two phrases are superfluous, that is, "And he die not," and "If he rise again and walk abroad upon his staff," for it is self-evident that the assailant cannot be executed under such circumstances; hence they must refer to two judicial calculations that he would not die, which was, however, subsequently falsified]. One reference to an assessment concerns a case in which the court assessed the victim, holding that he would die, and he turned out to live. The other deals with a case in which the court assessed that he would die, then be recovered somewhat.

T. *But from the perspective of rabbis, what need is there for two assessments of the man's condition?*

V. The one refers to a case in which the court assessed the man's condition and held that he would die and he lived, and the other treats a case in which the court assessed the man's condition and held that he would live, but he died.

W. And in R. Nehemiah's view?

X. The case of the court's assessing the man and holding that he would live, and in which he then dies, does not require a verse of Scripture, since in such a case, the accused has already left the court a free man.

I.2 A. *Our rabbis have taught on Tannaite authority:*

B. "He who hits his fellow, and the court made an assessment that the man would die but he lived – they free the accused.

C. "If they assessed that he would die and he got somewhat better, they make a second assessment as to the monetary compensation that he is to pay.

D. "If after a while the ailment grew worse and the man died, one is guided by the second assessment [and the accused pays for the monetary claim, as originally assessed, but is not liable to death], "the words of R. Nehemiah.

E. And sages say, "There is no assessment after [the original one].

F. *There is a further teaching on Tannaite authority:*

G. **[Tosefta's version:] He who hit his fellow.**

H. **[if] they formed a prognosis that he would die, they again assess that he would live.**

I. **[If they formed a prognosis] that he would live, they do not again assess that he would die.**

J. **[T. adds: If they assessed that he would die, then the defendant is liable to the death penalty but exempt from having to pay monetary compensation. If they made an estimate as to the monetary compensation, the defendant is liable to pay monetary compensation and exempt from the death penalty.]**

K. **If they assessed that he would die, and he got better, they make an estimate of the monetary compensation to be paid a second time.**

L. **[If] they assessed that he would live and he died, [the defendant] pays compensation for injury, pain, medical costs, loss of income, and indignity, to the estate of the deceased.**

M. **From what point does he pay him off?**

N. **From the point at which he hit him [T. B.Q.9:5A-H, 9:6A].**

O. *This unattributed teaching represents the view of R. Nehemiah [that one pays financial compensation and the accused is not put to death].*

Both units of the Talmud take up and analyze the Tosefta's complement to the Mishnah-paragraph at hand.

9:2

A. [If] he intended to kill a beast and killed a man,

B. a gentile and killed an Israelite,

C. an untimely birth and killed an offspring that was viable,

D. he is exempt.

E. [If] he intended to hit him on his loins with a blow that was not sufficient to kill him when it struck his loins, but it went and hit his heart, and there was sufficient force in that blow to kill him when it struck his heart, and he died,

F. he is exempt.

G. [If] he intended to hit him on his heart, [79A] and there was in that blow sufficient force to kill when it struck his heart, and it went and hit him on his loins, and there was not sufficient force in that blow to kill him when it struck his loins, but he died,

H. he is exempt.

I. [If] he intended to hit a large person, and there was not sufficient force in that blow to kill a large person, but it went and hit a small person, and there was sufficient force in that blow to kill a small person, and he died,

J. he is exempt.

K. [If] he intended to hit a small person, and there was in that blow sufficient force to kill a small person, and it went and struck the large person, and there was not sufficient force in that blow to kill the large person, but he died,

L. he is exempt.

M. But: [if] he intended to hit him on his loins, and there was sufficient force in the blow to kill him when it struck his loins, and it went and hit him on his heart and he died,

N. he is liable.

O. [If] he intended to hit a large person, and there was in that blow sufficient force to kill the large person, and it went and hit a small person and he died,

P. he is liable.

Q. R. Simeon says, "Even if he intended to kill this party, and he actually killed some other party, he is exempt."

I.1 A. *To what passage does R. Simeon make reference [at Q]?*

B. *Should we say that it is to the final clause [M-P]? Then what is required is,* "R. Simeon declares exempt," [Freedman, p. 530, n. 2: Why repeat, "Even if he intended..."? Since it bears upon the clause immediately preceding, the circumstances having been stated, it is sufficient just to give Simeon's ruling].

C. *Rather, he refers to the opening clause:* If he intended to kill a beast and killed a man, a gentile and killed an Israelite, an untimely birth and killed an offspring that was viable, he is exempt [M. 9:2A-D].

D. Thus the contrary intent is: "If one intended to kill this party but killed another party, he is liable."

E. [Then the sense of Simeon follows:] R. Simeon says, "Even if he intended to kill this party, and he actually killed some other party, he is exempt" [M. 9:2Q].

F.   *Now the point is self-evident that if Reuben and Simeon were standing [together], and [the killer] said, "I intended Reuben, I did not intend Simeon," here we have the dispute [of R. Simeon and the anonymous authority]. But if he had said, "I had in mind one of them," or if he had said, "I was thinking it was Reuben but it was Simeon," what is the law?*

G.   *Come and take note of the following:* R. Simeon says, "He is liable only if he states, 'I intended to kill So-and-so.'"

I.2   A.   *What is the Scriptural basis for the position of R. Simeon?*

B.   Said Scripture, "[But if any man hates his neighbor] and lies in wait for him" and rises up against him" (Deut. 19:11) meaning that [one is liable only if the killer] has hostile intentions against him in particular.

C.   *And rabbis [view of the language, "for him" and "against him"?]*

D.   *Members of the house of R. Yannai say,* "[The language, 'for him' or 'against him' serves] to exclude one who throws a stone into the midst [of Israelites and gentiles]."

E.   *Now what sort of case is at hand? Should we say that there were nine Samaritans and only one Israelite among them? Then you should conclude that the majority of those [among whom he threw the stone] were Samaritans. Or again, if half were of one group and half of the other group, you have a case of doubt, and in a case of doubt as to capital crimes, one must impose the more lenient ruling.*

F.   *The matter is made pressing by the case in which there were one Samaritan and nine Israelites, in which case the Samaritan is a settled fact [as one of those present], and where there is a settled fact, it counts as one half of the facts at hand [where there is a case of doubt]. [The verse at hand applies to this case and tells us that in such a case, one is not liable; in the other possible cases, it is self-evident that he is not liable, and no proof-text is required].*

I.3   A.   *Now from the viewpoint of rabbis, there is no problem, for they maintain that if one intended to kill one party and killed another, he is liable,* for it is written, "If men strive and hurt a woman with child: (Ex. 21:22). In this connection, said R. Eleazar, "Scripture addresses the case of a fight involving intent to kill, for it is written, 'And if any accident follow, then you shall give life for life' (Ex. 21:23).

B.   *But how does R. Simeon deal with the clause,* "You shall give life for life" (Ex. 21:23) [Freedman, p. 53, n. 8: Since the murder of the woman was unintentional, according to Simeon there is no death penalty]?

C.   *It means that there has to be a payment of monetary compensation for the death, in accord with the view of Rabbi.*

D.   *For it has been taught on Tannaite authority:*

E.   Rabbi says, "'You shall give life for life' (Ex. 21:23).

F.   That means that monetary compensation is paid.

G.   "You maintain that monetary compensation is paid. But perhaps it means that a life must actually be taken?

H.   "The word 'giving' is stated here [at Ex. 21:23] and the same word is stated **[79B]** elsewhere ["If no accident follow, he shall give what the judges determine"].

I.   "Just as in that passage what is at hand is a monetary payment, so here what is expected is a monetary payment."

I.4 A.   *Said Raba, "The following Tannaite authority of the house of Hezekiah differs from both Rabbi and rabbis."*

B.   *For a Tannaite authority of the house of Hezekiah taught, "'And he* who kills a beast [shall pay for it] and he who kills a man [shall be put to death]' (Lev. 24:21). [Freedman, p. 532, n. 4: This verse, by coupling the two, likens them to each other; it also implies that where monetary compensation has to be made for an animal, it is not so for a man, since 'shall pay for it' is only prescribed for the former.]

C.   "Just as in the instance of one who hits a beast, you make no distinction between doing so inadvertently and deliberately, doing so intentionally and unintentionally, doing so with a downward blow or an upward blow, in no instance declaring one exempt from having to make monetary compensation but imposing liability in all cases to monetary compensation,

D.   "so in the case of one who hits [and kills] a man, you should make no distinction between doing so inadvertently and deliberately, doing so intentionally and unintentionally, doing so with a downward blow or an upward blow, in no instance declaring one liable to make monetary compensation but in all cases declaring one exempt from monetary compensation [since the death penalty may be involved]."

E.   *[Reverting to Raba's observation,] "Now what is the sense of 'unintentionally'? Should we say that one is totally unintentional in what he has done? Then we deal with nothing other than a case of inadvertence. Rather, it is self-evident, it is a case that one does not intend to kill this one but rather that one.*

F.   "And it has been taught, '...not imposing a monetary compensation but declaring him free of monetary compensation'? *Now if the person at hand is subject to the death penalty, why is it necessary to indicate that he is exempt from monetary compensation? [Rather, does it not emerge from the passage at hand that such a one is neither subject to the death penalty nor subject to the requirement to pay monetary compensation. [Rabbi, by contrast, imposes the requirement of monetary compensation, and rabbis hold that he is subject to the death penalty]."*

M.9:2 A-C introduce the whole, stating the basic principle which the triplet will proceed to unpack. The matter of intention is at issue. Simeon will reject the entire construction of M.9:2 E-P, because, so far as he is concerned, so long as one's intention has not been carried out, he remains exempt, without regard to the distinctions of the antecedent triplet. Their point is clear in the contrast between E-H+I-L, and M-P. If the death is caused in such a way that the person's original intent in no way leaves him culpable, he is exempt. But if what he did would have caused death to the person to whom he intended to do it, then he is liable on account of the death of the other person, to whom he actually did it.

Units I.1-4 of the Talmud provide a careful exegesis of the meaning of the Mishnah's statements, with special reference to Simeon's position and the scriptural basis for it. Unit I.2 then carries forward discussion of an item introduced by unit I.3, so the whole, at the end, is a unitary composition – and a quite elegant one at that.

9:3

A.   A murderer who was confused with others – all of them are exempt.

B.   R. Judah says, "They put them [all] in prison."

C.   All those who are liable to death who were confused with one another are judged [to be punished] by the more lenient mode of execution.

D.   [If] those to be stoned were confused with those to be burned –

E.   R. Simeon says, "They are to be judged [to be executed] by stoning, for burning is the more severe of the two modes of execution."

F.   And sages say, "They are adjudged [to be executed] by burning, for stoning is the more severe mode of execution of the two."

G.   Said to them R. Simeon, "If burning were not the more severe, it would not have been assigned to the daughter of a priest who committed adultery."

H.   They said to him, "If stoning were not the more severe of the two, it would not have been assigned to the blasphemer and to the one who performs an act of service for idolatry."

I.   Those who are to be decapitated who were confused with those who are to be strangled –

J.   R. Simeon says, "They are killed with the sword."

K.   And sages say, "They are killed by strangling."

I.1   A.   *Who are the others [mentioned at M. 9:3A]? If we should maintain that these others are upright people, then the rule [at M. 9:3A] is self-evident. Furthermore, in such a case would R. Judah say, "They put them into prison"? [Surely not!]*

B.   *Said R. Abbahu said Samuel, "Here we deal with a case in which a* murderer whose trial was not complete got mixed up with other murderers, whose trials had come to an end. *Rabbis maintain that* the court concludes the trial of a person only in that person's presence. Therefore all of them are treated as exempt [and released]. *And R. Judah holds that one cannot free them entirely, since they are, after all, murderers. Therefore,* they put them into prison."

C.   *R. Simeon b. Laqish said, "If it is a case involving human beings all parties concur that they free [all of those who are confused with one another]. But here we deal with a dispute involving the case of an ox, the trial of which had not been completed, and which was confused with other oxen, the trial of which had been completed. Rabbis hold that* the capital trial of the master defines the rules governing the capital trial of the ox, and so the court may conclude the trial of an ox only in that ox's presence. Therefore all of them are treated as exempt [and released]. R. Judah maintains that they put them into prison."

D.   *Said Raba,* **[80A]** *"If so, then we must take up what R. Yosé observed on this passage, namely,* 'Even if my father, Halapta, [a pious man] were among them, [would Judah take the view that he does]?'"

E.   *Rather, said Raba, "The sense [of Yosé's statement] is as follows:* If two people were standing, and an arrow came forth from their midst and killed someone, both of them are exempt [since we do not know who shot the arrow]. And said R. Yosé, 'Even if my father, Halapta, were among them [The rule would be the same, and the thought of Halapta's committing murder is unthinkable. Still, the other party cannot be convicted.] But if an ox that had been tried and convicted was confused with other oxen of a perfectly good [character, not gorers], [the court nonetheless has] them stoned. R. Judah says, 'They are put into prison.'"

F.   *And so it has been taught on Tannaite authority:*

G.   In the case of a cow which killed someone and then gave birth, if before the trial was complete it gave birth, the offspring is permitted.

H.   If after the trial was completed it gave birth, the offspring is forbidden [as part of the mother at the point at which the cow was condemned to stoning. Hence the calf may not be utilized].

I.   If the cow was confused with others, and others with others, they put them all into prison.

J.   R. Eleazar b. R. Simeon says, "They bring them all to court and they stone them."

I.2   A.   A master said: "If before the trial was complete, it gave birth, the offspring is permitted."

B.   *And is that the case, even though, when it gored, it was pregnant?* And has Raba not said, "The offspring of a cow that gored is forbidden [for use in the cult], both the cow and the offspring are deemed to have gored. If the offspring was used for bestiality, both the cow and the offspring are deemed to have been used for bestiality. [If the cow was pregnant, therefore, when it gored, the calf is regarded as identical with its mother (Freedman, p. 534, n. 9)]."

E.   *Then read the passage in this way:* If before the trial was completed, it became pregnant and produced an offspring, the offspring is permitted. If after the trial was complete, the cow became pregnant, and it produced the offspring, the offspring is forbidden.

F.   *That version of matters poses no problem to him who has said,* "[If] both this and that constitute the causes [here: if both an ox and a cow have produced the offspring] [and one of the causes, that is, the cow, is forbidden, then] the offspring is likewise forbidden." **[80B]** *But in the view of him who maintains that in such a case, it is permitted, what is there to be said?*

G.   *Rather, said Rabina, "This is how the rule is to be stated:* If before the trial was completed the cow became pregnant and produced the offspring, the offspring is permitted. And if before the trial was completed, the cow became pregnant, but it was only after the trial was completed that the cow gave birth, the offspring is forbidden. The reason is that the embryo is deemed an integral part of the mother. [Freedman, p. 535, n. 3: In this case, it is forbidden, not because it is the product of its mother, but because before birth it is part of its mother, and the prohibition applicable to the latter applies to the embryo too.]"

II.1   A.   **All those who are liable to death [who were confused with one another are judged to be punished by the more lenient mode of execution] [M. 9:3C]:**

       B.   *That indicates that admonition* [not to commit a crime] *which serves for a more severe infringement of the law applies as an admonition for a less severe infringement of the law.* [The criminals had been admonished with a statement on the mode of execution that applies to the crime they had been about to commit. The admonition referred to a more severe mode of execution. The stated law then indicates that admonition served for a less severe mode of execution.]

       C.   *Said R. Jeremiah, "[Not so,] for with what sort of a case do we deal here? It is with one in which an admonition was given without specification [as to the mode of execution]. And the rule at hand accords with the Tannaite authority who stands behind this following on Tannaite teaching:*

       D.   **"'And as to all others liable to the death penalty imposed by a court, they convict them only on the testimony of witnesses, after warning, and after they inform him that what he is going to do subjects him to liability to the death penalty in court.**

       E.   **"'R. Judah says, "Only if they will inform him specifically as to the sort of death penalty to which he will be subjected"'** [T. San. 11:1A-C].

       F.   *"The former of the two authorities derives the rule from the case of the wood-gatherer, R. Judah takes the view that the wood-gatherer represented an ad hoc case."*

III.1 A.   **If those to be stoned were confused with those to be burned [M. 9:3D]:**

       B.   *R. Ezekiel repeated the passage at hand for Rami, his son, as follows:* 'If those to be burned were confused with those to be stoned, **R. Simeon says, "They are judged to be executed by stoning, for burning is the more severe of the two modes of execution"** [M. 9:3E].'"

       C.   *Said R. Judah to him, "Father, do not repeat it in this way. Why give as the reason, 'Because burning is more stringent'? Rather, derive the fact that the larger number of those who are put to death are put to death through stoning.* [Freedman, p. 536, n. 3: For 'if criminals condemned to burning became mixed up with others condemned to stoning' implies that the latter were in the majority, as the smaller number is lost in the larger]. *Instead, this is how it should be repeated:* **"'If those to be stoned were confused with those to be burned, "R. Simeon says, "They are judged to be executed by stoning, for**

> burning is the more severe of the two modes of execution"' [M. 9:3D-E]."

D. *Then take up the concluding clause:* **But sages say, "They are adjudged to be executed by burning, for stoning is the more severe mode of execution of the two" [M. 9:3F].** *But derive that point from the simple fact that the greater number of those who are put to death are put to death through burning?*

E. *In that case, it is rabbis who frame matters so as to state to R. Simeon, "In accord with your view, for you maintain that burning is more severe, but to the contrary, stoning is the more severe.* [Freedman, p. 536, n. 4: But their ruling could be deduced from the fact that the majority are to be executed through burning]."

F. *Said Samuel to R. Judah, "Sharp one!* **[81A]** *Do not say things in this way to your father! This is what has been taught on Tannaite authority:* Lo, if one's father was violating the teachings of the Torah, he should not say to him, 'Father, you have violated the teachings of the Torah.' Rather, one should say to him, 'Father, this is what is written in the Torah.'"

G. *Still, this is the same as that!*

Q. *Rather, he says to him,* "Father, there is a verse of Scripture that is written in the Torah, and this is what it says. [He does not state the law directly but lets the father draw his own inference (Freedman, p. 536, n. 8)]."

Unit I.1 provides an important clarification for the rule of the Mishnah. Unit I.2 continues unit I. Unit II.1 takes up the implications for an extraneous issue of the rule at M. 9:3C, and unit III.1 clarifies the wording of M. 9:3D.

9:4

A. **He who is declared liable to be put to death through two different modes of execution at the hands of a court is judged [to be executed] by the more severe:**

B. **[if] he committed a transgression which is subject to the death penalty on two separate counts, he is judged on account of the more severe.**

C. **R. Yosé says, "He is judged by the penalty which first applies to what he has done."**

I.1 A. *It is self-evident [that he is subject to the more severe mode of execution]. [For, after all], should he profit [from committing the further crime]?*

B. *Said Raba, "With what sort of case do we deal here? It is one in which* the man committed a lesser transgression and was convicted for the lesser transgression. Then he went and committed a greater transgression. *Now it might have entered your mind to rule that, since he was tried and convicted for the lesser transgression, this man is as if dead [for he is going to be put to death no matter what else he does]. So we are informed [to the contrary, that we do try him for the offense that produces the more severe mode of execution]."*

I.2 A. *The brother of R. Joseph bar Hama asked Rabbah bar Nathan, "What is the source of this view of rabbis:* **He who is declared liable to be put to** death through two different modes of execution at the hands of a court is judged to be executed by the more severe [M. 9:4A]?"

B. [The reply:] "As it is written, 'If [the righteous man] beget a son who is a robber, a shedder of blood...who has eaten upon the mountains and defiled his neighbor's wife' (Ez. 18:10-11).

C. "'If he beget a son who is a robber, a shedder of blood' – such a one is subject to the death penalty of decapitation.

D. "'And defiled his neighbor's wife' – this is adultery, punished through [the more severe penalty] strangulation.

E. "'And has lifted up his eyes to idols' (Ez. 18:12) – this is idolatry, punished through stoning.

F. "And it is written, 'He shall surely die, his blood shall be upon him' (Ex. 18:13) – this refers to stoning. [Freedman, p. 537, n. 6: Thus we see that the severest penalty is imposed, and it must be under the circumstances posited by Raba, for otherwise the verse is unnecessary.]"

G. *To this proof R. Nahman b. Isaac raised an objection, "May I propose that all of the clauses refer to crimes punished by stoning?*

H. "'If he beget a son, a robber, a shedder of blood' – this refers to a wayward and incorrigible son, who is put to death through stoning.

I. "'And defiled his neighbor's wife' – this refers to a betrothed girl, on account of intercourse with whom one is put to death through stoning.

J. "'And has lifted up his eyes to the idols' – this refers to idolatry, penalized by the death-penalty of stoning."

K. *"If that is the case, then what is it that Ezekiel tells us?"*

L. *"Perhaps he was simply reviewing the teachings of the Torah."*

M. *"If so, he should have reviewed it in the way in which Moses, our master, reviewed it."*

I.3 A. *R. Aha, son of R. Hanina, interpreted Scripture, "What is the meaning of the verse, '[But if a man be just and do what is lawful and right...], and has not eaten upon the mountains' (Ez. 18:16)?*

B. "It means that he did not eat only on account of the merit of his ancestors [but on his own merit].

C. "'And did not lift up his eyes to the idols of the house of Israel' – that he did not walk about in a proud way [but in a humble way].

D. "'Nor did he defile his neighbor's wife' – that he did not compete with his fellow in trade.

E. "'And did not have sexual relations with a menstruating woman' – that he did not derive benefit from the charity-fund.

F. "And it is written, '<u>He</u> is just, <u>he</u> shall surely live' (Ez. 18:9)."

G. When Rabban Gamaliel reached this verse of Scripture, he would weep, saying, "If someone did all of these [virtuous deeds], then he will live, but not merely on account of one of them."

H. Said R. Aqiba to him, "But take account of the following: 'Do not defile yourselves in all of these things' (Lev. 18:24). Here too does it mean that one is liable only for doing all of the [vile deeds that are catalogued], but not if he did only one of them?

I.		"Rather, the meaning is in 'only one of these things' [one violates the law], and so here to, if one does only one of all of these things, [he shall live]."
II.1	A.	**If he committed a transgression... [M. 9:4B-C]:**
	B.	*It has been taught on Tannaite authority:*
	C.	**Said R.Yosé, "He is judged by the penalty which first applies to what he has done [M. 9:4C]:**
	D.	**"If he had sexual relations with her when she was his mother-in-law, and then she got married and so was a married woman, he is judged on the count of her being his mother-in-law.**
	E.	**"If she was a married woman and then became his mother-in-law, he is judged on the count of her being a married woman" [T. San. 12:5D-I].**
	F.	Said Ada bar Ahbah to Raba, "If she was his mother-in-law and then became a married woman, should he be judged only on account of having sexual relations with his mother-in-law? *Let him be judged also on account of the prohibition applying to having sexual relations with a married woman!*
	G.	"For lo, R. Abbahu said, 'R. Yosé concurs in the case of a prohibition that adds [to the prohibition already in place].'"
	H.	[81B] *He said to him, "Ada, my son, are you going to kill him twice?"*

The point of concurrence at M. 9:3C is repeated. The important point is not at M. 9:4A, but at M. 9:4B. Once more, we find ourselves engaged in the exposition of the materials of Chapter Seven, now M. 7:4K-R, the sages' view that there may be two counts of culpability on the basis of a single transgression. A's point is that if one has intercourse with a married woman and is liable for strangulation, and afterward he has sexual relations with his mother-in-law and is liable for burning, he is judged on the count of burning. If his mother-in-law had been married, we should have the problem of B. He then would be tried on the count of the mother-in-law, which produces the execution by burning, rather than on the count of the married woman, which produces the penalty of strangulation. Yosé's clarification requires that the woman have passed through several relationships to the lover. First she was a widow, whose daughter he had married, and so she was his mother-in-law. Afterward she was married. He had sexual relations with her. He is tried for having had sexual relations with his mother-in-law, thus for burning, since that was the first aspect in which the woman was prohibited to him. If the story were reversed, he would be tried under the count of strangulation for his sexual relations with a married woman. Unit I.1 of the Talmud clarifies the allegation of M. 9:A, and unit I.2 provides a proof-text for that proposition. Unit I.3 then adds a further exegesis of the same proof-text. Unit II.1 proceeds to the clarification of M. 9:4B-C.

9:5 A-B

A.   He who was flogged [and did the same deed] and was flogged again –

B.   [if he did it yet a third time] the court puts him in prison and feeds him barley until his belly explodes.

I.1   A.   Merely because **he was flogged and flogged again** does **the court put him in prison?**

B.   *Said R. Jeremiah said R. Simeon b. Laqish, "Here we deal with flogging administered in a case in which the real penalty is extirpation [but in which the felon was warned only of the penalty of flogging], so that the felon in point of fact is subject to the death penalty. Now as yet, death has not drawn near this man, and, since he has allowed himself [to violate the law again], we bring him near to death."*

C.   *Said R. Jacob to R. Jeremiah b. Tahalifa, "Come and I shall explain this matter to you. The passage at hand refers to flogging administered on account of a single sort of sin that involves the penalty of extirpation. But in the case of one who commits two or three different sorts of sins that are penalized by extirpation, this man is just trying out [different sorts of sins] and has not abandoned himself to sink to such an extent [that we hasten his death]."*

I.2   A.   **He who was flogged and flogged again [M. 9:5A]:** *He did it twice and not a third time. Then may we say that the Mishnah-passage at hand does not accord with the view of R. Simeon b. Gamaliel?*

C.   *For in the view of Rabban Simeon b. Gamaliel, lo, he has said, "Only in the case of three occurrences [of a given phenomenon] do we recognize a presumption [that such a thing is regularly going to happen]."*

D.   *Said Rabina, "You may maintain even that it is in accord with Rabban Simeon b. Gamaliel.*

E.   *"He takes the view that* in the case of the commission of transgressions, even less than three actions, establish a presumption as to the character of the man."

F.   *An objection was raised [on the basis of the following passage:]*

G.   **Those who are liable for flogging who were flogged [and did the same deed] and were flogged again [M, 9:5A] –**

H.   **and this happened once, twice, and yet a third time –**

I.   **they put him into prison.**

J.   **Abba Saul says, "Also on the third occasion they flog him.**

K.   **"But if he repeats it a fourth time,**

L.   **they put him into prison and feed him barley until his belly explodes" [M. 9:5B]. [T. San. 12:8B-G].**

M.   *May we not say that all parties concur that the fact that one has been flogged establishes a presumption [about his character], and at issue is the dispute between Rabbi and Rabban Simeon b. Gamaliel. [Freedman, p. 540, n. 4:* The first Tannaite authority agrees with Rabbi that twice affords presumption, Abba Saul with R. Simeon b. Gamaliel. But since the first authority is identical with that of our Mishnah, it follows that it cannot agree with R. Simeon b. Gamaliel. This refutes Rabina.]

N.   *No, all parties concur with the view of Rabban Simeon b. Gamaliel. And in the present case, the point at issue is this: One authority takes the view that* the commission of transgressions establishes a presumption [as to one's character] *and the other party takes the view that* inflicting a flogging establishes the presumption [as to one's character].

O. *But has it not been taught on Tannaite authority:*

P. **[If] they warn him and he remains silent,**

Q. **warn him and he nods his head,**

R. **warn him once, twice, and a third time [and he repeated the same transgression],**

S. **they put him into prison [cf. M. 9:5A-B].**

T. **Abba Saul says, "Also on the third occasion they warn him.**

U. **"but if he repeats it a fourth time,**

V. **"they put him into prison and feed him the bread of adversity and the water of affliction (Is. 30:20)" [M. 9:5C] [T. San. 12:7A-G].**

W. *Now in this case there is no issue of flogging!* [Here, therefore, there is no flagellation to afford a basis for presumption (Freedman, p. 540, n. 8)].

X. *So what is at issue?*

Y. *Said Rabina, "What is at issue is whether there is necessity to give an advance admonition concerning the punishment of imprisonment in a cell."*

I.3 A. *And what is a cell?*

B. Said R. Judah, "It was the height of the prisoner."

C. *And where in Scripture do we find an allusion to such a thing?*

D. Said R. Simeon b. Laqish, "'Evil shall slay the wicked' (Ps. 34:2).".

E. *And said R. Simeon b. Laqish, "What is the meaning of that which is written, 'For man also knows not his time, as the fishes that are taken in an evil trap' (Qoh. 9:12)?*

F. *"What is an evil trap?"*

G. Said R. Simeon b. Laqish, "It is a hook."

Unit I clarifies the reasoning behind M. 9:5A. Unit I.2 then investigates its own problem, using the materials of M. 9:5A for that purpose. But the problem is integral to the Mishnah-paragraph, as Tosefta's contribution shows. Unit I.3 then deals with the definition of the prison of M. 9:5B.

9:5C

A. **He who kills a someone not before witnesses they put him in prison and feed him the bread of adversity and the water of affliction (Is. 30:20).**

I.1 A. *How do we know [that this man has killed someone]?*

B. Said Rab, "We deal with a case in which the testimony is disjoined [since the two witnesses saw the act individually, but were not on a line of sight with one another]."

C. And Samuel said, "It was an act committed without prior admonition [as to the consequences]."

D.   *And R. Hisda said Abimi said, "We deal with a case in which the testimony as contradicted in some minor detail as to circumstance but was not disproved as to major details of what had actually been done.*

E.   *"This is as we have learned in the Mishnah:* **There was the case in which Ben Zakkai examined a witness as to the character of the stems of figs under which the incident took place [M. 5:2B]."**

II.1 A.   **And feed him the bread of adversity and the water of affliction [M. 9:5C]:**

B.   *Why does the passage at hand frame matters as,* **And they feed him the bread of adversity and the water of affliction [M. 9:5C],** *while the other passage states,* **The court puts him in prison and feeds him barley until his belly explodes [M. 9:5B]?**

C.   *Said R. Sheshet, "Both, in point of fact, mean that* **they feed him the bread of adversity and the water of affliction.** *This is until his innards shrink.* **Then they give him barley-bread until his belly explodes."**

The Talmud at Unit I.1 asks the obvious question and in unit II.1 explains divergent formulations of the law at hand.

9:6

A.   **He who stole a sacred vessel [of the cult (Num. 4:7)], and he who curses using the name of an idol, and he who has sexual relations with an Aramaean woman –**

B.   **zealots beat him up [on the spot (Num. 25:8, 11)].**

C.   **A priest who performed the rite in a state of uncleanness –**

D.   **his brothers, the priests, do not bring him to court.**

E.   **But the young priests take him outside the courtyard and break his head with clubs.**

F.   **A non-priest who served in the Temple –**

G.   **R. Aqiba says, "[He is put to death] by strangling [Num. 18:7]."**

H.   **And sages say, "[He is put to death] at the hands of Heaven."**

I.1   A.   *What is a sacred vessel [M. 9:6A]?*

B.   *Said R. Judah, "It is a utensil used in the ministry. And so it says, 'And the vessels of libation' (Num. 4:7).*

C.   *"And where in Scripture do we find an allusion to the matter?*

D.   *"'That they come not to see how the holy things are stolen, lest they [who stole them] die' (Num. 4:20)."*

II.1 A.   **He who curses using the name of an idol. [M. 9:6A]:**

B.   *R. Joseph taught on Tannaite authority, "May the idol smite its enchanter."*

C.   *Rabbis, and others say, Rabbah b. Mari, say, "'May the idol slay him, his master, and the one who gives him ownership.'"*

II.2 A.   **...and he who has sexual relations with an Aramaean woman [M. 9:6A]:**

B.   *R. Kahana asked Rab,* **[82A]** *"What is the law if the zealots do not beat him up [M. 9:6B]?"*

C.   *Rab had forgotten his learning on the subject, and in a dream, R. Kahana received the following verse of Scripture, "As Judah has dealt treacherously, and an abomination is committed in Israel and in*

Jerusalem, for Judah has profaned the holiness of the Lord which he loved and has been intimate with the daughter of a strange god" (Mal. 2:11).

D. *He came to Rab and said to him, "This is what I was made to recite in my dream."*

E. *Rab then remembered what he had learned:* "Judah has dealt treacherously – this refers to idolatry, and so it is written, 'Surely as a wife departs treacherously from her husband, so have you dealt treacherously with me, O house of Israel, says the Lord' (Jer. 3:20).

F. "'And an abomination is committed in Israel and in Jerusalem' – this refers to pederasty. And so it is written, 'You shall not lie with mankind as with womankind; it is an abomination' (Lev. 18:22).

G. "'For Judah has profaned the holiness of the Lord' – this refers to prostitution, and so it is written, 'There shall be no consecrated harlot of the daughters of Israel' (Deut. 3:18).

H. "'And has been intimate with the daughter of a strange god' – this refers to one who has sexual relations with a Samaritan woman.

I. "And thereafter it is written, 'The Lord will cut off the men who do this, the master and scholar, out of the tabernacles of Jacob, and him who offers an offering to the Lord of hosts' (Mal. 2:12).

J. "If he is a disciple of a sage, he will have no witness among sages or response among disciples.

K. "If he is a priest, he will have no son to make a meal offering to the Lord of hosts."

II.3 A. Said R. Hiyya bar Abbuyah, "Whoever has sexual relations with a Samaritan woman is as if he marries an idol.

B. "For it is written, 'And has had sexual relations with the daughter of a strange god' (Mal. 2:11).

C. "And does a strange god have a daughter?

D. "Rather, this refers to someone who has sexual relations with a Samaritan woman."

E. And said R. Hiyya bar Abbuyah, "On the skull of Jehoiakim is written 'This and yet another.'"

F. *The grandfather of R. Perida found a skull which was tossed near the gates of Jerusalem, and written on it were the words, "This and yet another."*

G. *He buried it and it came up again. He buried it and it came up again.*

H. *He said, "This must be the skull of Jehoiakim, concerning whom it is written, 'He shall be buried with the burial of an ass, drawn and cast forth beyond the gates of Jerusalem'"* (Jer. 22:19).

I. *He said, "Still, he was a king, and it is not proper to treat him with disrespect."*

J. *He took the skull and wrapped it in silk and put in in a chest.*

K. *His wife came along and saw it. She took it out and showed it to the neighboring women, who said to her, "It must be his [that is, your husband's] first wife, for he cannot forget her." She lit the oven and burned it.*

L. *When he came home he said, "This is in line with what is written on [the skull], 'This and yet another.'"*

II.4 A. When R. Dimi came, he said, "The court of the Hasmoneans made a decree that one who has sexual relations with a Samaritan woman is liable on her account on the counts of having sexual relations with a menstruating woman, a gentile maid servant, a gentile woman, and a married woman."

B.   When Rabin came, he said, "He is liable on the counts of having sexual relations with a menstruating woman, a gentile maidservant, a gentile woman, and a prostitute, *but not on the count of having relations with a married woman, since valid marital relations do not apply to them."*

C.   *And the other [Dimi]?*

D.   *They most assuredly do not allow their women to have sexual relations freely [with any man other than the husband].*

II.5 A.   Said R. Hisda, "[If a zealot] comes to take counsel [as to punishing a law violator, such as is listed at M. 9:6A], they do not give him instructions to do so."

B.   *It has been stated along these same lines on Amoraic authority:*

C.   Said Rabbah bar bar Hannah said R. Yohanan, "[If a zealot] comes to take counsel, they do not give him instructions to do so.

D.   "And not only so, but if Zimri had separated from [his girl-friend] and had Phineas then killed him, Phineas would have been put to death on his account.

E.   "[Under these same conditions] had Zimri turned on Phineas and [in self-defense] had he killed Phineas, he would not have been out to death on his account, for lo, [Phineas then] was in the position of being a pursuer."

The Zealotry of Phineas

II.6 A.   "And Moses said to the judges of Israel, Slay every one his men that were joined to Baal Peor" (Num. 25:5).

B.   The tribe of Simeon went to Zimri b. Salu and said to him, "Lo, the judges are judging capital cases, and you sit silent."

C.   What did he do? He went and called together twenty-four thousand Israelites and went to Kozbi and said to her, "Listen to me [and have sexual relations with me]."

D.   She said to him, "I am a royal princess, and father has told me, 'Listen [I have sexual relations] only with the greatest man among them.'"

E.   He said to her, "Even I am the prince of a tribe, and not only so, but [my tribe] is greater than his [Moses'], for he is second in order of birth, and I am third in order of birth."

F.   He took her by her forelock and brought her to Moses. He said to him, "Ben Amram, is this woman forbidden or permitted? And if you should rule that she is forbidden, as to the daughter of Jethro, who permitted you to marry her?"

G.   Moses forgot the law, and all of them broke out in tears, as it is written, "And they were weeping before the door of the tabernacle of the congregation" (Num. 25:6).

H.	And it is written, "And Phineas, son of Eleazar, son of Aaron the priest, saw" (Num. 25:7).
I.	What did he see?
J.	Said Rab, "He saw the deed and then remembered the law." He said to him, "O brother of the father of my father, have you not taught us as you came down from Mount Sinai, **'He who has sexual relations with an Aramaean woman – zealots beat him up on the spot'** [M. 9:6A-B]?"
K.	*He said to him, "The one who reads the letter should be the one to serve as agent [to carry out its orders] [So, do it.]."*
L.	Samuel said, "He saw that, 'There is no wisdom, understanding, or counsel against the Lord' (Prov. 21:30). In any circumstance in which there is a profanation of the Name [of God], people are not to defer to the master [but are to correct the situation immediately]."
M.	R. Isaac said R. Eleazar said, "He saw that an angel came and destroyed some of the people."
N.	"And he rose up out of the midst of the congregation and took a spear in his hand" (Num. 25:7).
O.	On this basis we learn that people may not enter the school house carrying weapons.
P.	He took off the spear-head and put it in his garment and was **[82B]** leaning on the stock. He went along as if leaning on his staff. When he came to the tribe of Simeon, he said, "Where do we find that the tribe of Levi is greater than the tribe of Simeon? [Let me do it too!]"
Q.	They said, "Let him too do what he needs to do. The people who kept separate now have permitted the matter too."
R.	Said R. Yohanan, "Six miracles were done for Phineas:
S.	"First, that Zimri should have taken out his penis from the woman and he did not do so [leaving Phineas free to act];
T.	"another, that he should have spoken out [for help] but he did not speak out;
U.	"a third, that Phineas got his spear right through the penis of the man and the vagina of the woman'
V.	"fourth, that they did not fall off the spear;
W.	"fifth, that an angel came and raised up the lintel [so he could carry them out on his spear];
X.	"and sixth, that an angel came and destroyed the people [so they paid no attention to what Phineas had done]."
Y.	"Phineas came and cast them down before the Omnipresent, and said, 'Lord of the world, on account of these should twenty-four thousand Israelites die?'
Z.	"For it is said, 'And those that died in the plague were twenty-four thousand' (Num. 25:9).

AA.	"Thus it is written, 'Then Phineas stood up and executed judgment' (Ps. 106:30)."
BB.	Said R. Eleazar, "'And he prayed' is not written, but rather, 'And he argued with ...,' teaching that it was as if he made an argument with his Maker [about punishing them]."
CC.	The ministering angels wanted to push him aside. He said to them, "Let him be. He is a zealot, son of a zealot, he is one who seeks to turn away anger, son of one who seeks to turn away anger."
DD.	The other tribes began to tear him down, "Do you see this son of Puti [Putiel]. For the father of his mother fattened [PTM] calves for idolatry, and he has himself killed the head of a tribe of Israel."
EE.	Scripture came along and spelled out his genealogy: "Phineas, son of Eleazar, son of Aaron the priest" (Num. 25:11).
FF.	Said the Holy One, blessed be he, to Moses, "[When you see him], greet him in peace first, as it is written, 'Wherefore say, Behold, I give to him my covenant of peace' (Num. 25:12).
GG.	"And this act of atonement is worthy that it should continue to make atonement forever."

II.7	A.	*Said R. Nahman said Rab, "What is the meaning of the verse of Scripture, 'A greyhound, a he-goat also, and a king, against whom there is no rising up' (Prov. 30:31)?*
	B.	"Four hundred twenty-four acts of sexual relations did that wicked man have that day.
	C.	"Phineas waited for him until he grew weak, for he did not know that 'a king, against whom there is no rising up' is [God]."
	D.	*In a Tannaite teaching it is taught:*
	E.	He had sexual relations sixty times, until he became like an addled egg, and she became like a furrow filled with water."
	F.	Said R. Kahana, "And her 'seat' was a seah [in size]."
	G.	*R. Joseph taught on Tannaite authority,* "Her womb-opening was a cubit."
II.8	A.	Said R. Sheshet, "Her name was not Cosbi but Shewilani, daughter of Zur.
	B.	"Why was she called Kozbi? Because she violated her father's instructions [in having sexual relations with someone as unimportant as Zimri]."
	C.	Another explanation of Kozbi:
	D.	She said to her father, "Devour (kosbi) this people for me."
	E.	*So it is in line with what people say, "What does Shewilani want among the reeds of the lake, what does Shewilani want among the peeling rushes? Did she embrace her mother?"*

II.9	A.	Said R. Yohana n, "Zimri had five names: Zimri, son of Salu; Saul, son of the Canaanite woman; and Shelumiel, son of Zurishaddai.
	B.	"'Zimri,' because he became like an addled egg.
	C.	"'Son of Salu,' because he outweighed the sins of his family;
	D.	"'Saul,' because he lent himself to sin;
	E.	"'Son of the Canaanite woman,' because he acted like a Canaanite.
	F.	"But what was his real name? It was Shelumiel, son of Zurishaddai."
III.1	A.	**A priest who performed the rite in a state of uncleanness [M. 9:6C]:**
	B.	*R. Aha, son of R. Huna, asked R. Sheshet,* "Is a priest who performed an act of service while in a state of uncleanness liable to the death penalty at the hands of heaven, or is he not liable to the death penalty at the hands of heaven?"
	C.	*He said to him, "You have learned to repeat the following passage of the Mishnah:* **A priest who performed the rite in a state of uncleanness – his brothers, the priests, do not bring him to court. But the young priests take him outside the courtyard and break his head with clubs [M. 9:6C-E].**
	D.	*"Now if you think that he is liable to the death penalty at the hands of heaven, then they should let him be, and let him be put to death at the hands of heaven.*
	E.	*"Then what is the upshot? He is not liable [to death at the hands of heaven]."*
	F.	*But is there any action which the All-Merciful has treated as exempt from penalty, and on account of which we should go and inflict the death penalty?*
	G.	*And is there none? And lo, have we not learned in the Mishnah:*
	H.	**He who was flogged and did the same deed and was flogged again – if he did it yet a third time, the court puts him in prison and feeds him barley until his belly explodes [M. 9:5A-B]?**
	I.	*Here the All-Merciful has treated him as exempt from penalty, but we put him to death.*
	J.	*[That poses no problem], for has not R. Jeremiah said R. Simeon b. Laqish said, "We deal with a case in which the flogging was administered in a case in which the penalty is extirpation, for the man was subject to the death penalty"?*
	K.	*But lo, there is the case of* **one who steals a sacred vessel [M. 9:6A]!**
	L.	*[That too is no problem], for has not R. Judah said, "We deal with utensils used for the cult, and there is an allusion to [the death penalty for stealing them] in that which is written, 'That they come not to see how the holy things are stolen, lest they die' (Num. 4:20)."*
	M.	*And lo, there is the case of* **one who curses using the name of an idol [M. 9:6A]!**
	N.	*Lo, did not R. Joseph repeat on Tannaite authority, "'May the charm slay the enchanter'"? It is because he appears to commit blasphemy.*
	O.	*And lo, there is* **he who has sexual relations with an Aramaean woman [M. 9:6A]?**

P.   *Lo, in that same case R. Kahana in a dream was made to recite a verse of*
      Scripture, and this reminded Rab of the law.

Q.   *An objection was raised:*

R.   **He pours out oil over a meal-offering, he who mixes meal with**
      the oil, he who breaks meal-offering cakes into pieces, he who
      salts meal-offering, he who waves it, he who brings it near
      [opposite the southwest corner of the alter], he who arranges the
      bread on the table, he who trims the lamps, he who takes the
      handful of meal-offering, he who receives the blood [none of
      which actions completes the sacrificial rite] outside of the Temple
      is exempt [from all penalty]. They are not liable on account of
      such actions [83A] either because of being a non-priest or because
      of uncleanness or because of lacking the proper vestments or
      because of having unwashed hands and feet [M. Zeb. 14:3F-I].

S.   *Lo, if such a one had burned incense [and so completed an act of service],*
      he would have been liable. Now is this not <u>liable</u> *to the death penalty?*

T.   *No, it is liable to violating an admonition [not to do so].*

U.   *And is that the case also for a non-priest, that he is merely subject to*
      violating an admonition?

V.   **And is it not written, "And the non-priest who comes near shall be**
      put to death" (Num. 18:7)?

W.   *Each item on the list is subject to its own rule [and for the one who is*
      unclean, on violates a prohibition, but for the one who is a non-priest, the
      death penalty applies].

X.   *Does it then follow that pouring and mingling [oil for the meal-offering]*
      are not violations of a negative commandment?

Y.   *But has it not been taught on Tannaite authority:*

Z.   **Whence in Scripture do we find an admonition [that an unclean**
      priest] nor pour or mingle [oil]?

AA.   **As it is written, "They shall be holy to their God and not profane**
      the name of their God" (Lev. 21:6). [Freedman, p. 550, n. 9: This is
      referred to the performance of one of these acts of service while
      unclean.]

BB.   **It is merely on the authority of rabbis, and the verse provides an**
      additional support.

CC.   *An objection was raised on the basis of the following:*

DD.   **And these are the ones who are subject to the death penalty: an**
      unclean priest who performed an act of service [T. Zeb. 12:17].

EE.   *That indeed refutes the view of R. Sheshet.*

III.2 A.   Reverting to the body of the cited text:

       B.   **And these are the ones who are subject to the death penalty:**

       C.   **He who eats untithed food, and a non-priest, an unclean**
             person, who ate heave-offering, and an unclean priest who
             ate clean heave-offering,

       D.   **and a non-priest, one in the status of Tebul Yom, one lacking**
             priestly vestments, one whose rites of atonement were not yet
             complete, and one with unwashed hands and feet, and those
             with unkempt hair, and those who were drunk, who served
             [at the altar]

       E.   **all of them are subject to the death penalty.**

F.   **But an uncircumcised [priest] and a priest in mourning, and one who was sitting down [while at the altar], lo, these are subject to warning.**

G.   **"A blemished priest [who performed a sacrificial rite] is subject to the death penalty," the words of Rabbi.**

H.   **And sages say, "He is subject to the penalty for transgressing a negative commandment."**

I.   **He who deliberately carried out an act of sacrilege**

J.   **Rabbi says, "He is subject to the death penalty."**

K.   **And sages say, "He is subject to the penalty for transgressing a negative commandment," [T. Zeb. 12:17A-I].**

L.   He who eats untithed food: *Whence in Scripture do we find proof [of the fact that such a one is subject to the death penalty]?*

M.   It is in accord with what Samuel said in the name of R. Eleazar, "How do we know of one who eats untithed food that he is subject to the death penalty?

N.   "It is in accord with the following verse of Scripture: 'And they shall not profane the holy things of the children of Israel, which they shall offer to the Lord' (Lev. 22:15).

O.   "Scripture speaks of what they are going to offer up to the Lord [heave-offering or priestly rations] [and this is in the future, hence, what is going to be designated from the produce, and the produce at this point therefore is liable to tithing and not yet tithed].

P.   "And we establish an analogy between two laws, in the framing of both of which there is reference to 'profanation.' [Reference is to (Lev. 22:9: 'They shall therefore keep my ordinance, lest they bear sin for it and die therefore, if they profane it,' alluding to the eating of priestly rations by a priest who is unclean (Freedman, p. 551, n. 6)].

Q.   "Just as, in that other setting, the penalty is death, so here it is death."

R.   But might we not derive the penalty from the appearance of a reference to "profanation" both here and with regard to what is leftover from sacrificial meat beyond the point at which one is supposed to eat that meat?

S.   [Such a proof would be as follows:] Just as in that case, [as specified at Lev. 19:6-8] the penalty is extirpation, so here too it should be extirpation.

T.   *[We may reject that possibility on the basis of this argument:] It is more reasonable to derive the law from the matter of the penalty for violating the sanctity of the priestly rations,* for the two matters have in common the following points: both are raised up, both are subject to the same rule outside of the Holy Land, both are remitted, both are given in the plural, both are produce of the land, both are subject to the same rule as regards improper priestly intention regarding their disposition, and both are subject to the same rule in regards what is left over [and not to be eaten after a certain point]. [That is, in neither case do the rules apply outside of the Holy Land; the prohibitions in both cases can be annulled, while that concerning what is left over of the offering cannot be annulled; the laws governing priestly intention and the disposition of what is left over do not apply either to what is untithed or to priestly rations].

U. *But to the contrary, [we may argue in a different way]: One should derive the governing analogy from the case of leftover sacrificial meat,* for they share in the traits of being unfit as food and not being subject to remission through the taking of a cultic bath. [In respect to both untithed produce and leftover sacrificial meat, one cannot eat the substance; a priest who is clean, by contrast, may eat priestly rations. The prohibition of untithed produce and leftover sacrificial meat is not affected by a cultic bath.]

V. *The common traits [shared by untithed produce and priestly rations] are more numerous [and therefore the proper analogy for the one is to be drawn from the other].*

W. Rabina said, "The use of the plural with reference to 'profanation' [linking untithed produce and priestly rations] presents a preferable [basis for analogy]."

X. An unclean priest who ate clean heave-offering: *Whence in Scripture do we find proof [of the fact that such a one is subject to the death penalty]?*

Y. *It is in line with what Samuel said,* "How do we know on the basis of Scripture that an unclean priest who ate clean heave-offering is subject to the death penalty at the hands of heaven?

Z. *"Since it is written,* 'Therefore they shall keep my ordinance, lest they bear sin for it and die on that account if they profane it' (Lev. 22:9)."

AA. That statement speaks of what is clean, but not of what is unclean.

BB. For Samuel said R. Eleazar said, "How do we know that an unclean priest who ate unclean priestly rations is not subject to the death penalty?

CC. "As it is said, 'And die on that account, if they profane it' (Lev. 22:9). **[83B].** That excludes [unclean priestly ration], that is already profaned [and cannot be made more profane]."

DD. A non-priest who ate heave-offering:

EE. Rab said, "A non-priest who ate heave-offering is flogged."

FF. *R. Kahana and R. Assi said to Rab, "But should not the master rule that he is subject to the death penalty.*

GG. *"For it is written,* 'There shall no stranger eat of the holy thing [and die on that account]' (Lev. 22:10)?"

HH. "'I the Lord sanctify them' interrupts the matter. [Freedman, p. 552, n. 5: Consequently the penalty of death stated in Lev. 22:9 does not apply to the prohibition at Lev. 22:10.]"

II.	*They raised an objection:* "And these are the ones who are subject to the death penalty...A non-priest who ate heave-offering [T. Zeb. 12:17B]!"

JJ.	*Is teaching on Tannaite authority what you raise in contradiction to Rab?! Rab himself enjoys Tannaite status and differs [from the view expressed by the teaching on the same status, as he has every right to do].*

KK.	A non-priest who served at the altar: As it is written, "And the stranger who comes nigh shall be put to death" (Num. 18:7).

LL.	An unclean person who served at the altar:

MM.	*The answer derives from the inquiry addressed by R. Hiyya bar Abin to R. Joseph,* "How on the basis of Scripture do we know that an unclean priest who served at the altar is subject to the death penalty?

NN.	"Since it is written, 'Speak to Aaron and to his sons, that they separate themselves from the holy things of the children of Israel and that they not profane my holy name' (Lev. 22:2). [Freedman, p. 553, n. 3: The reference is to abstention from sacrificial service during their uncleanness.]

OO.	"We then establish an analogy on the basis of the use of the word 'profanation' both here and with regard to heave-offering.

PP.	"Just as in the case of heave-offering, violation of the law produces the death penalty, so here too violation of the law produces the death penalty."

QQ.	But why not derive the meaning of the word 'profanation' from its use with reference to leftover sacrificial meat [not eaten in the specified span of time]. Then the result would be that, just as in that case, the penalty is extirpation, so too here the penalty is extirpation.

RR.	*It is more reasonable to derive the meaning of the word from its use with reference to heave-offering, for in common in both matters are the considerations of the bodily unfitness [of the person involved], uncleanness, use of the immersion-pool, and use of the plural.*

SS.	*Quite to the contrary, it would be better to derive the sense of the word from its use with respect to leftover sacrificial meat. For to both matters apply the considerations of sanctity, conduct of the rite within the Temple court, the matter of the disqualifying affect of a priest's improper intention, and the issue of the rules governing leftover sacrificial meat themselves.*

TT.	*The use of the plural with reference to "profanation" presents a preferable basis for analogy.*

UU.	One in the status of a Tebul Yom [who had immersed that day but who had to wait for sunset to complete the rite of purification] who served at the altar:

VV.	*How on the basis of Scripture do we know that fact?*

WW.	*It accords with what has been taught on Tannaite authority:*

XX.	R. Simai says, "Whence in Scripture do we find an indication that if a priest awaiting sunset for the completion of his rite of purification performed an act of service, he has profaned [the cult]?
YY.	"Scripture says, 'They shall be holy to their God and not profane the name of their God' (Lev. 21:6).
ZZ.	"If [because we have already proved the matter on another basis] that verse cannot refer to an unclean priest who served at the altar, for we have derived the fact from the reference to 'that they separate themselves' (Lev. 22:2), apply it to he matter of a priest's serving at the altar on the day on which he has immersed but prior to sunset.
AAA.	"And we further derive the sense of 'profane' here from the sense of 'profane' with reference to heave-offering.
BBB.	"Just as in that matter, the death penalty is invoked, so here too the death penalty is invoked."
CCC.	One lacking priestly vestments:
DDD.	*How on the basis of Scripture do we know that fact?*
EEE.	*Said R. Abbahu said R. Yohanan (and some attribute it to the name of R. Eleazar b. R. Simeon), "'And you shall put coats on them and you shall gird them with girdles...[and the priest's office shall be theirs...]' (Ex. 29:9).*
FFF.	"When their garments are upon them, their status as priests applies to them. When their garments are not on them, their status as priests does not apply to them, and they are deemed non-priests, and a master has said, 'A non-priest who served at the altar is subject to the death penalty.'"
GGG.	One whose rites of atonement were not yet complete:
HHH.	*How on the basis of Scripture do we know [that such a one is subject to the death penalty]?*
III.	Said R. Huna, "It is because Scripture has said, 'And the priest shall make an atonement for her and she shall be clean' (Lev. 12:8).
JJJ.	"'And she shall be clean' – indicates that before she had been unclean.
KKK.	"And a master has stated, 'An unclean person who served at the altar is subject to the death penalty.'"
LLL.	And one with unwashed hands and feet:
MMM.	*How on the basis of Scripture do we know that fact?*
NNN.	Scripture states, "And when they go into the tabernacle of the congregation, they shall wash with water, so that they do not die" (Ex. 30:20).
OOO.	And those who were drunk:
PPP.	For it is written, "Do not drink wine or strong drink...lest you die" (Lev. 10:9).
QQQ.	And those with unkempt hair:
RRR.	For it is written, "Neither shall they shave their heads nor suffer their locks to remain unshorn" (Ez. 44:20).
SSS.	And thereafter: "Neither shall they drink wine" (Ez. 44:21).

TTT.	The matter of unkempt hair is thus made comparable to the matter of wine-drinking.
UUU.	Just as ministering while drunk is penalized by death, so ministering with unkempt hair is subject to the death penalty.
VVV.	But an uncircumcised priest, a priest in mourning, and one who was sitting down while at the altar – lo, these are subject to warning [but not to the death penalty]:
WWW.	*How on the basis of Scripture do we know that that is the case for the uncircumcised priest?*
XXX.	Said R. Hisda, "This matter we did not derive from the Torah of Moses, our master, until Ezekiel, son of Buzi, came and taught it to us:
YYY.	"'No stranger, uncircumcised in heart **[84A]** o r uncircumcised in flesh, shall enter my sanctuary' (Ez. 44:20)."
ZZZ.	*How do we know that this is the case for the priest in mourning [who has not yet buried his deceased]?*
AAAA.	As it is written, "Neither shall [the high priest in mourning] go out of the sanctuary, yet shall he not profane the sanctuary of his God" (Lev. 21:12).
BBBB.	Lo, another priest [than the high priest] who did not go forth has profaned the rite [and therefore he is required to deal with his deceased].
CCCC.	Said R. Ada to Raba, "And let us derive the sense of the word 'profane' from the meaning of the word 'profane' as used with reference to heave-offering?
DDDD.	"Just as in that case, the penalty is death, so here too the penalty should be death."
EEEE.	*[He replied,] "But is the prohibition of the priest in mourning stated explicitly in the cited verse of Scripture? It derives, rather, by inference [from the explicit reference to the high priest]. And in respect to any matter which derives only by inference, one does not construct a further argument by analogy."*
FFFF.	*How on the basis of Scripture do we know that one who performs a rite while sitting down [is not subject to the death penalty]?*
GGGG.	Said Raba said R. Nahman, "Scripture has said, 'For the Lord your God has chosen him out of all your tribes, to stand to minister' (Deut. 18:5).
HHHH.	"I have chosen him for standing, and not for sitting."
IIII.	**"A blemished priest who performed a sacrificial rite is subject to the death penalty," the words of Rabbi. And sages say, "He is subject to the penalty for transgressing a negative commandment" [T. Zeb. 12:17G-H].**
JJJJ.	*What is the Scriptural basis for the position of Rabbi?*
KKKK.	Since it is written, "Only he shall not go in to the veil nor come near the altar, because he has a blemish, that he not profane my sanctuaries? (Lev. 21:23).
LLLL.	We then derive the sense of the word "profane" as it is used here from the meaning of the word when used with

reference to heave-offering. Just as, in that context, the penalty is death, so here too, the penalty is death.

MMMM.   But why not derive the sense of the work "profanation" from its use with respect to left-over sacrificial meat?

NNNN.   Just as in that case, the penalty is extirpation, so here too the penalty should be extirpation..

OOOO.   *It is more reasonable to derive the meaning of the work from its use with reference to heave-offering, for in that case, as in the present one, we have the shared trait that what is invalid is the body of the priest himself, and so we derive the rule from a parallel case of bodily invalidity.*

PPPP.   To the contrary, he should derive the rule from the law governing left-over sacrificial meat, for in both cases, we have the considerations of sanctification, conduct of the rite within the Temple court, the priest's capacity to invalidate the rite through an improper intention, and the rule of not eating left-over sacrificial meat.

QQQQ.   Rather, one should derive the analogy [hence the penalty] from the case of an unclean priest who served at the altar, in which case we derive the rule governing the invalidity of the priest's body from another case in which the priest's body is invalid, as well as from the fact that there are the shared considerations, in both matters, of holiness, conduct of the rite inside the Temple, the matter of the priest's invalidating the offering through improper intention, and, finally, the consideration of the rules governing left-over sacrificial meat.

RRRR.   *And rabbis [who ignore these proofs and regard it as merely a negative prohibition]?*

SSSS.   Scripture says, "...and die on that account" (Lev. 22:9) [with respect to an unclean priest who ate heave-offering], meaning for <u>that</u> particular sin, but not for the sin of serving at the altar when one is blemished.

TTTT.   **He who deliberately carried out an act of sacrilege – Rabbi says, "He is subject to the death penalty." And sages says, "He is subject to the penalty for transgressing a negative commandment" [T. Zeb. 12:17I-K]:**

UUUU.   *What is the scriptural basis for the position of Rabbi?*

VVVV.   Said R. Abbahu. "One derives the meaning of the law by analogy based on the use of the word 'sin' both here and in the matter of heave-offering. [Here: 'if a soul commits a trespass and sin through ignorance in the holy things of the Lord' (Lev. 5:15), and, with respect to heave-offering, 'Lest they bear sin for it and die on that account' (Lev. 22:9).]

WWWW.   "Just as in that case, the penalty is death, so here the penalty is death."

XXXX.   And rabbis say, "Scripture has said, '...on that account...' (Lev. 22:9) – and not on account of an act of sacrilege."

IV.1   A.   **A non-priest who served in the Temple:**

        B.   *It has been taught on Tannaite authority:*

C. R. Ishmael says, "Here it is said, 'And the non-priest who comes near shall be put to death' (Num. 18:7), and elsewhere, 'Whosoever comes anything near to the tabernacle of the Lord shall die' (Num. 17:28).

D. "Just as in the latter case [the rebellion of Korah and the subsequent plague], it is death at the hands of heaven, so here it is death at the hands of heaven" [= M. 9:6H].

E. R. Aqiba says, "Here it is said, 'And the non-priest who comes near shall be put to death' (Num. 18:7), and elsewhere, 'And that prophet or that dreamer of dreams shall be put to death' (Deut. 18:6).

F. "Just as there it is by stoning, so here too it is by stoning."

G. R. Yohanan b. Nuri says, "Just as in that case it is by strangling, so here it is by strangling."

H. *What is at issue between R. Ishmael and R. Aqiba?*

I. *R. Aqiba takes the view that* we derive the sense of the work, "shall be put to death" from the meaning of the word "shall be put to death" as it occurs elsewhere, and not from the meaning of the word "shall die."

J. *And R. Ishmael maintains that* we derive the rule governing an ordinary person from the rule governing another ordinary person, and we do not derive the rule governing an ordinary person from the rule governing a prophet.

K. And R. Aqiba?

L. If someone has enticed [a town to commit idolatry], you have no greater evidence that one is an ordinary person than that [for such a one cannot be regarded as a prophet].

M. *What is at issue between R. Aqiba and R. Yohanan b. Nuri?*

N. *At issue is the dispute involving R. Simeon and rabbis.*

O. *For it has been taught on Tannaite authority:*

P. A prophet who enticed [a town to commit idolatry] is subject to the death penalty inflicted by stoning.

Q. R. Simeon says, "It is through strangulation."

R. *But we have learned in the Mishnah:* **R. Aqiba says, "He is put to death by strangling" [M. 9:5G]!**

S. *There are two Tannaite authorities on the view of R. Aqiba. The Mishnah before us is R. Simeon's view of R. Aqiba's rule, and the other Tannaite tradition [holding that a non-priest who served at the altar is put to death through stoning] and deriving that view from the analogy [to the false prophet] represents rabbis' view of R. Aqiba's opinion.*

Our attention is drawn, first of all, to the splendid and satisfying exegesis of the Tosefta-passage at unit III.1. This sort of sustained composition shows the powers of Bavli's authors at their best. The claim that their fundamental approach to their work lay in the exegesis of authoritative materials at hand finds full validation in the elegant unit before us. When we revert to the Mishnah-passage, we have no reason to compare unfavorably the exegetical efforts devoted to the principal document.

10

Bavli Tractate Sanhedrin
Chapter Ten
Folios 84B-90B

10:1A-C

A. These are the ones who are to be strangled:

B. he who hits his father and his mother [Ex. 21:15]; he who steals an Israelite [Ex. 21:16, Deut. 24:7]; an elder who defies the decision of a court, a false prophet, a prophet who prophesies in the name of an idol;

C. He who has sexual relations with a married woman, those who bear false witness against a priest's daughter and against one who has sexual relations with her.

I.1   A. **He who hits his father and his mother:** *How on the basis of Scripture do we [know that such a one is strangled]?*

B. It is in accord with the following verse of Scripture: "And he who hits his father or mother shall surely be put to death" (Ex. 21:15).

C. And any reference without further specification to "death" that is made in Scripture means only strangulation.

D. *But might I say that the one who smites the parents is liable only if he actually kills them.*

E. *Do you imagine that he would have to kill them? If he killed anyone else, he would be decapitated, while if he killed his father, would it be through strangulation [that is not likely. The same penalty would have to apply, and hence at issue here cannot be killing the parent, but only hitting him or her].*

F. *That poses no problem to him who maintains that strangulation is the less severe mode of execution. But in the view of him who has said that strangulation is the more severe mode of execution, what is to be said?*

H. Since it is written, "He who smites a man so that he dies shall surely be put to death" (Ex. 21:12), and it also is written, "Or in enmity smote him with his hand that he

441

die" (Num. 35:21), it bears the implication that, *in any passage in which there is reference to smiting, without further specification, the implication is not that the one has killed the other.* [Hence, here too, the son has not killed the parent but only hit him or her.]

I.2   A.   *It was necessary for Scripture to state, "He who smites a man" (Ex. 21:12), and it also was necessary for Scripture to state, "Who kills any soul" (Num. 35:30).*

B.   *For if the All-Merciful had written, "He who smites a man that he die" (Ex. 21:12), I might have maintained that that rule pertains to smiting by an adult, who is subject to the obligation to carry out the commandments, but it would not apply to smiting by a minor, who is not.*

C.   *Accordingly, the All-Merciful found it necessary to state, "Whoso kills any soul" (Num. 35:30).*

D.   *Had the All-Merciful written only, "Whose kills any soul" (Num. 35:30), I might have concluded that under the law are included even such classifications as abortions or foetuses produced at eight months of conception. [But they are not included.] It was therefore necessary to make both statements.*

I.3   A.   *And might I propose that [one who smites his parents is put to death] even though he does not make a bruise on them?*

B.   *Wherefore do we learn in the Mishnah:* **He who hits his father and his mother is liable only if he will make a lasting bruise on them [M. 10:1D]**?

C.   Scripture has said, "And he who kills a beast [shall restore it] but he who kills a man [shall be put to death]" (Lev. 24:21). [This creates an analogy.]

D.   *Just as he who smites a beast is liable only if he inflicts a bruise, as it is written, "soul" in that connection [at Lev. 24:18], so he who smites a man is liable only if he inflicts a bruise.*

E.   *To this proof R. Jeremiah objected, "How then deal with the following:* If one injured the beast by loading stones on it, [and in this case there is no physical bruise], in such a case also is the person who injured the beast not liable to make it up? [Surely he is liable!]"

F.   Rather, since the reference [to soul] cannot speak of the soul of a beast, for if one injured the ox with heavy stones, he remains liable to make it up, apply the reference to the soul of a man. [Then it would mean, just as claimed, that one is liable only if he makes a wound.]

G.   *If so, what need do I have for the analogy [constructed above, C-D]?*

H.   *It accords with what was taught by the house of Hezekiah [at 79B, with respect to whether we differentiate, in the case of injury to beasts, between doing so deliberately and accidentally].*

I.   *That poses no problems to him who accords with that which was taught on Tannaite authority for the house of Hezekiah.*

J.   *But for the one who does not accord with what was taught on Tannaite authority for the house of Hezekiah, what use is there for the analogy.*

K.   Just as one who hits a beast in order to cure it is exempt [from paying damages], so he who hits a man in order to cure him is exempt from having to pay damages.

I.4   A.   *For the question was raised:*

B.   What is the law on a son's letting blood for his father?

C.   R. Mattena said, "'And you shall love your neighbor as yourself' (Lev. 19:18). [The son surely may do so, since he would do the same for himself.]"

D.   R. Dimi bar Hinena said, "'He who smites a man ... he who smite smites a beast ...': Just as the one who smites a beast for purposes of healing is exempt, so one who smites a man for purposes of healing is exempt."

E.   *Rab would not allow his son to take a thorn out of his flesh.*

F.   *Mar, son of Rabina, would not allow his son to open a boil for him, lest he make a bruise and so be guilty of inadvertently violating a prohibition.*

G.   *If so, then even an outsider also should be prohibited [for a person may not wound someone else].*

H.   *If so, it would be an inadvertent violation of a mere prohibition, while in the case of his son, it is the inadvertent violation of a law penalized by strangulation.*

I.   *And lo, we have learned in the Mishnah:* **[One may handle] a small needle for removing a thorn [M. Shab. 17:2G].**

J.   *And should one not take account of the possibility that the needle will make a bruise, in which case there will be a matter of inadvertent violation of a law for which [a deliberate violation is penalized by] stoning?*

K.   *In the case [of the Sabbath] the person does damage, [which is not penalized on the Sabbath, even when done deliberately].*

L.   *That poses no problem to the one who maintains that one who does damage on the Sabbath is exempt from all penalty.*

M.   *But in the view of him who says that he is liable, what is there to be said?*

N.   *And whom have you heard who takes the view that one who does damage by inflicting a wound is liable [for violating the Sabbath]?*

O.   *It is R. Simeon!*

P.   **[85A]** But R. Simeon also is the one who said, "Any form of labor which is done not for its normal purpose leaves one exempt from having violated the Sabbath." [Freedman, p. 560, n. 5: When a thorn is extracted and wound made, even intentionally, no punishment is involved, because the purpose of the work is extraction, not wounding.]

I.5   A.   *The following question was addressed to R. Sheshet:* "What is the law on appointing a son to be an agent of a court as to his own father, to inflict a flogging on him or to curse him?"

B.   He said to them, "And have they permitted an outsider to do so except for the honor owing to heaven? *It is a superior obligation, and here too, the honor owing to Heaven is a superior obligation. [So a son may act for the court.]*"

C.   *An objection was then raised:* Now if in the case of one whom it is a religious duty to smite [namely, one specified by a court as subject to flogging], it is a religious duty in point of fact not to smite [in that a son may not be agent of a court to flog his own father], one whom it is a religious duty not to smite, is it not a matter of logic that it is a religious duty not to smite such a one [namely, one's father]? *Is the sense, then, not that in both instances we deal with a religious duty, but one refers to one's son, the other to an outsider?* [Thus, as is clear, if one who is subject to flogging may not be flogged by his son as agent of the court, how much the more so may one who is not subject to a flogging, not be flogged by his son.] [Freedman, p. 561, n. 2: Thus by ad majus reasoning, a formal prohibition is deduced against a son's striking his father. For Ex. 21:15 merely prescribes the punishment; but it is a general principle that no punishment can be inflicted unless a prohibition is either stated or deduced from elsewhere. On this interpretation Sheshet's ruling is contradicted.]

D. *No, in both this case and that case there is no difference between one's son and an outsider. But there is no problem, for the one statement speaks of a case in which it is a religious duty, and the other speaks of a case in which it is not a religious duty. And this is the sense of the passage:* Now if in a case in which there is a religious duty to be done, for it is a religious duty to inflict the flogging, it still is a religious duty not to inflict a flogging [in any but the prescribed manner, e.g., with too many lashes], in a case in which no religious duty is involved, in which it is not a religious duty to flog, is it not a matter of reason that it is a religious duty not to inflict a flogging? [So what the teaching at hand tells us is that one may flog only at the order of a court.]

E. *Come and take note:* he who was being taken out to be executed, and his son came along and hit him and cursed him – the son is liable. If another party came along and hit him and cursed him, the other party is exempt. *And we reflected on the matter, asking what the difference is between one's son and a third party. And R. Hisda said, "We deal with a case in which* the court forces the man to go forth and he does not wish to go forth [so the court may not have the son come along and drive the man to his execution, and this contradicts Sheshet's judgment]."

F. *R. Sheshet interprets the passage to speak of a case in which* the court is not forcing the man to go forth.

G. *If so, another party also [should be liable for reviling the condemned man].*

H. *[So far as]* the other party in this case is concerned, the condemned man is already a dead man. *[But the son has to honor the man even after death.]*

I. And did not R. Sheshet say, "If people humiliated a sleeping man and he died [in his sleep], they nonetheless are liable." [Why should mistreating the condemned man be treated any differently?]

J. *With what sort of a case do we deal here?* It is a case in which one hit the condemned man with a blow which is not worth a perutah [so that is why there is no penalty for the third party's action].

K. But did not R. Ammi say R. Yohanan said, "If one smote [another party] with a blow that is not worth a perutah, he is nonetheless flogged"?

L. *What is the sense of "exempt" stated earlier? One is exempt from having to pay a financial reparation.*

M.   *Would it then follow that his son is liable for monetary compensation?!*
    [But what would he pay, since the injury is not worth a perutah!] Rather,
    [he is liable] in accord with the law that applies to him [which is, in the
    case of the son, the death penalty].

N.   *Then [the stranger should be exempt from the law] applying to him, [which*
    is flogging] [so what is the difference between the act of the son and the act
    of a third party]?

O.   *Rather, as to the outsider [who hits the condemned man], the reason that*
    he is exempt is because Scripture has said, "You shall not curse a prince
    among your people" (Ex. 22:27), which applies to one who carries
    on in the manner of your people. [Freedman, p. 562, n. 7: But to
    transgress is not fitting for "your people," and hence the prohibition
    against cursing does not apply to such a case.]

P.   *Now that settles the matter of the curse, but how do we know that*
    that is the case of the actual blow?

Q.   *We draw an analogy between hitting and cursing.*

R.   *If so, then the son also should be subject to the same rule.*

S.   *It accords with what* R. Phineas said, "We deal with a case in
    which he repented." So here too, we deal with a case in which
    the criminal repented.

T.   *If so, then the outsider also [should be prohibited from cursing or*
    hitting the condemned man]. [So, again, what is the difference
    between the son and the outsider?]

U.   *Said R. Mari, "'Among your people' means 'among those who are*
    permanently established among your people [and not a condemned
    criminal, who may be cursed].'"

V.   *If so, his son also [should be allowed to curse or hit him]!*

W.   **[85B]** *The same rule after death applies [that the son may not curse*
    the father].

X.   *What is the upshot of the matter?*

Y.   *Said Rabbah bar R. Huna, and so a Tannaite authority of the house of*
    R. Ishmael taught, "In all cases a son may not serve as an agent
    of a court in flogging or cursing his father, except in the case of
    one who entices a town to apostasy, in which case it is written,
    Neither shall you spare nor conceal him' (Deut. 13:9)."

The entire opening discussion deals only with the matter of hitting
the father or mother. Unit I.1 proves that the penalty is strangulation, as
M. 10:1A states. Unit I.2 carries forward the exegesis begun in Unit I.1.
Unit I.3 then takes up a speculative question, relevant in a general way to
the Mishnah-paragraph, and units I.4, 5 take up further speculative
questions along the same lines.

10:1 D-G

D.   He who hits his father and his mother is liable only if he will
    make a lasting bruise on them.

E.   This rule is more strict in the case of the one who curses than the
    one who hits them.

F.   For the one who curses them after they have died is liable.

G.   But the one who hits them after they have died is exempt.

I.1   A.   *Our rabbis have taught on Tannaite authority:*

        B.   "His father or his mother he has cursed" (Lev. 20:9).

        C.   This applies even after they have died.

        D.   For one might have thought [to the contrary] that since one is liable for hitting them and also liable for cursing them, just as one who hits them is liable only if he does so while they are alive, so the one who curses them is liable only if he does so while they are alive.

        E.   And furthermore there is an argument <u>a fortiori</u>:

        F.   If in the case of one who hits his parents, in which the law treats [a parent] "who is not of your people" as equivalent to one who is "of your people," [so that if the father is a condemned criminal, one still must not hit him], and yet one is not liable after the death of the parents [for hitting them], in the matter of cursing, in which the law has not treated [a parent] who has not conducted himself as if he were "one of your people" as equivalent to one who has conducted himself as if he is "one of you people," is it not a matter of logic that one should not be liable if he curses the parents after death?

        G.   Accordingly, Scripture [is required to] state, "He has cursed his father or his mother" (Lev. 20:9), and this applies to the time after they have died [so one is liable on that account as well].

        H.   *This interpretation poses no problems to the principle of R. Jonathan, who regards as superfluous the verse, "His father or his mother he has cursed."*

        I.   *But in the view of R. Josiah, what is there to be said? [He makes use of the verse at hand for another purpose entirely, as we shall now see.]*

        J.   *For it has been taught on Tannaite authority:*

        K.   "'[For any man that curses his father or his mother shall surely be put to death; his father and his mother she has cursed; his blood shall be upon him' (Lev. 20:9).]" Why does Scripture say 'any man'?

        L.   "It serves to encompass a daughter, one of undefined sexual traits, and one who exhibits the traits of both sexes.

        M.   "'Who curses his father or his mother' – I know only that the law covers his father and his mother. How do I know that it covers his father but not his mother, or his mother but not his father?

        N.   "Scripture says, 'His father and his mother he has cursed; his blood shall be upon him' (Lev. 20:9), that is, 'he has cursed his father,' 'he has cursed his mother,'" the words of R. Josiah.

        O.   R. Jonathan says, "The verse bears the implication that it speaks of the two of them simultaneously, and it bears the implication that it speaks of each by himself or herself, unless the text explicitly treats the two of them together."

        P.   *How then does [Josiah] prove the present matter?*

        Q.   *He derives it from the verse, "And he who curses his father or his mother shall surely be put to death" (Ex. 21:17).*

        R.   *And the other? [How does Jonathan interpret the same verse]?*

        S.   *He requires that verse to encompass within the law a daughter, one of undefined sexual traits, and one who exhibits the sexual traits of both sexes.*

	T.	*And why should he not derive that fact from the usage cited above ["Any man ..."]?*
	U.	The Torah speaks in the language of ordinary people, [and the usage bears no exegetical consequences whatsoever].
	V.	*And should not the framer of the passage teach in addition: "A more strict rule applies to one who hits parents than to one who curses them, for in the case of hitting them the law has treated in the same way a parent who does not conduct himself as "among your people" and the one who conducts himself as "among your people," which is not the case for one who curses parents. [A parent who is a condemned criminal may be cursed by a son, as we saw earlier.]*
	W.	*The framer of the passage takes the view that we do draw an analogy between hitting and cursing, [so the latter also is forbidden, even in the case of a parent who does not conduct himself properly].*
I.2	A.	*May we say that the dispute at hand follows the course of the Tannaite dispute which follows?*
	B.	*For one Tannaite authority teaches:*
	C.	As to a Samaritan, you are commanded against smiting him, but you are not commanded against cursing him. [The two are not treated as comparable.]
	D.	*And another Tannaite authority holds:*
	E.	You are not commanded either against cursing him or against hitting him.
	F.	*Now if we take the view that all parties hold that the Samaritans are true proselytes is not at issue this simple proposition:*
	G.	*one party holds that we draw an analogy between hitting and cursing, and the other party maintains that we do not draw an analogy between hitting and cursing?*
	H.	*No, all parties take the view that we do not draw an analogy between hitting and cursing.*
	I.	*Here then what is at issue?*
	J.	*One party holds that Samaritans are true converts [so they are not to be hit], and the other party maintains that they converted merely because of fear of lions [in the Land of Israel] [so there is no precept against harassing them].*
	K.	*If that is all that is at issue, then what is the sense of the Tannaite teaching on the same passage:*
	L.	And a Samaritan's ox is in the status of ownership of an Israelite's ox.
	M.	*Rather, does that not bear the implication that at issue is whether or not we draw the stated analogy?*
	N.	*It does indeed prove the matter.*

Unit I;1 provides a proof-text for the proposition of the Mishnah, and this proof is subjected to a careful inspection and articulation. Unit I.2 continues the foregoing by introducing what are alleged to be parallel materials.

10:1 H-P

H.   He who steals an Israelite is liable only when he will have brought him into his own domain.

I.   R. Judah says, "Only if he will have brought him into his own domain and will have made use of him,

J.   "as it is said, 'And if he deal with him as a slave or sell him' (Deut. 24:7)."

K.   He who steals his son –

L.   R. Ishmael, son of R. Yohanan b. Beroqah, declares him liable.

M.   And sages declare him exempt.

N.   [If] he stole someone who was half slave and half free –

O.   R. Judah declares him liable.

P.   And sages declare him exempt.

I.1   A.   *Does not the first of the two Tannaite authorities [at M. 10:1H-I] require utilization [of the victim as a prerequisite to liability for kidnapping]?*

B.   *[Of course he does, but,] said R. Aha, son of Raba, "It is utilization of the victim to the extent of work less than a perutah in value that is at issue between the two authorities."*

I.2   A.   R. Jeremiah raised this question, "If one stole and sold a person while he was sleeping, what is the law?

B.   "If one sold a woman for the sake of enslaving the foetus, what is the law?

C.   "Do we maintain that there is an aspect of utilization in such a procedure, or do we not maintain that there is an aspect of utilization in such a procedure?"

D.   *And why not solve the problem by maintaining that there is no aspect of utilization whatsoever [in these actions]?*

E.   *No, it is necessary to raise the issue, so far as the one who was asleep is concerned, to take account of a case in which the kidnapper leaned on the victim,*

F.   *[and,] in the case of a woman, to take account of a case in which the kidnapper used the woman as a screen [against the wind, and if she is pregnant, she makes that much better a screen].*

G.   *Does this constitute a mode of utilization or not?*

H.   *What is the law?*

I.   *The question stands over [there being no clear basis for an answer].*

I.3   A.   *Our rabbis have taught on Tannaite authority:*

B.   "If a man be found stealing any of his brethren of the children of Israel" (Deut. 24:7):

C.   I know only that the law applies to a man who stole someone.

D.   How do I know that the law applies to a woman's doing so?

E.   Scripture says, "And any one who steals a man" (Ex. 21:16).

F.   I know only that the law applies to a man who stole either a woman or a man, and to a woman who stole a man [as specified at Ex. 21:16].

G.   How do I know that a woman who stole a woman [is covered by the law]?

H.   Scripture states, "Then that thief shall die" (Deut. 24:7) – under all circumstances [without regard to the gender of the thief or the victim].

I.4	A.	*It has further been taught on Tannaite authority:*
	B.	"If a a man be found stealing any of his brethren" (Deut. 24:7):
	C.	**All the same are the one who steals a man and the one who steals a woman, a proselyte, a freed slave, and a minor. One is liable [on any of these counts].**
	D.	**If one stole someone but did not sell him, sold him but he is yet within his domain, he is exempt [from liability].**
	E.	**If he sold him to his father or his brothers or to any of his relatives, he is liable.**
	F.	**He who steals slaves is exempt [T. B.Q. 8:1A-I].**
	G.	[86A] *A Tannaite authority repeated this statement before R. Sheshet.*
	H.	He said to him, "I repeat [the matter as follows:] 'R. Simeon says, "['If a man be found stealing a person] from his brethren' [means that one is liable only if] he removes the victim from the domain of his brothers.'"
	I.	"And do you say that he is liable? *Rather, repeat the matter on Tannaite authority as 'exempt.'*"
	J.	*But what is the problem? Perhaps the version at hand is that of R. Simeon as against views of rabbis.*
	K.	*Do not let that possibility come to mind, for R. Yohanan has stated, "An unassigned teaching of the Mishnah represents the view of R. Meir, an unassigned teaching in the Tosefta represents the view of R. Nehemiah, an unassigned teaching in the Sifra represents the view of R. Judah, an unassigned opinion in the Sifré represents the view of R. Simeon, and all of them express their views in line with those of R. Aqiba. [The passage at hand, given anonymously in the Sifré, therefore must stand for the view of Simeon.]"*

II.1	A.	**He who steals his son [M. 10:1K]:**
	B.	*What is the scriptural basis for the view of rabbis?*
	C.	*Said Abbayye, "Scripture has said, 'If a man be found ...' (Deut. 24:7) – excluding a case in which the victim is located [with the kidnapper to begin with]."*
	D.	*Said R. Pappa to Abbayye, "Then how do you deal with the following: 'If a man be found with a woman married to a husband' (Deut. 22:22)? Here too do you maintain: 'If ... be found ...' – so excluding a case in which the woman is commonly found with the lover? For example, [a woman] in the house of Mr. So-and-so, in which women are ordinarily located. In such a case, too, will you regard the man as exempt from all penalty!?"*
	E.	He said to him, "I refer to the passage, '... and he be found in his hand ...' (Ex. 21:16). [Freedman, pp. 567-8, n. 7. This is redundant and therefore shows that the law applies only to a person who is found in his captor's hand as a result of abduction, and not to one who was to be found in his hand before too.]"
	F.	*Said Raba, "Therefore Scripture-teachers and Mishnah-reciters for [young] rabbis fall into the category of those who have [their charges] in their hand and would be exempt [were they to kidnap them]."*

III.1	A.	**If he stole someone who was half slave [M. 10:1N]:**
	B.	*We have learned in the Mishnah:* **R. Judah says, "Slaves do not receive payment for being humiliated" [M. B.Q. 8:3G].**
	C.	*What is the scriptural basis for the position of R. Judah?*

D.   Scripture has said, "When men strive together, a man with his brother" (Deut. 25:11) [yielding compensation for humiliation in the fight].

E.   [Scripture thus assigns compensation for humiliation] to one who is subject to bonds of brotherhood, excluding a slave, who is not subject to bonds of brotherhood.

F.   And rabbis?

G.   He indeed does fall into the category of "brother" so far as keeping the religious duties is concerned.

H.   *In the present case how does R. Judah interpret matters?*

I.   *He takes the view that the reference to stealing "any of his brothers" [at Deut. 24:7] serves to exclude slaves.*

J.   " ... of the children of Israel" *serves to exclude one who is half-slave and half-free.*

K.   "Of the children of Israel" – that likewise serves to exclude one who was half-slave and half-free, so you have one exclusionary clause followed by another exclusionary clause, and in the case of one exclusionary clause followed by another exclusionary clause, the sole outcome is to encompass [what is putatively excluded].

L.   And rabbis?

M.   " ... of his brethren ..." *serving to eliminate slaves is an interpretation that they do not find persuasive. For lo, he indeed is one's brother so far as keeping the religious duties are concerned.*

N.   [Then the sense of] " ... children of Israel ...," " ... of the children of Israel ...," [in their view is such that] *one serves to exclude a slave, and the other serves to exclude one who is half-slave and half-free.*

III.2   A.   *Where in Scripture do we find an admonition against kidnapping [since Deut. 24:7 and Ex. 21:16 state only the penalty for doing so]?*

B.   R. Josiah said, "It is from, 'You shall not steal' (Ex. 20:15)."

C.   R. Yohanan said, "It is from, 'They shall not be sold as a slave is sold' (Lev. 25:42)."

D.   *And there is no dispute between them, for one authority takes into account the admonition against stealing, and the other takes into account the prohibition of selling.*

III.3   A.   *Our rabbis have taught on Tannaite authority:*

B.   "You shall not steal" (Ex. 20:15):

C.   Scripture speaks of kidnapping persons.

D.   You say that it speaks of kidnapping persons. But perhaps it speaks of stealing money.

E.   Do you then say so? Go and derive the matter from the thirteen principles by which the Torah is interpreted, including the one that says that a matter is interpreted in its own context.

F.   [In the present passage], of what subject does the Scripture speak? It deals with crimes against persons.

G.   So here too the commandment takes up capital crimes [such as violating the Sabbath or murder, and so too, kidnapping].

III.4   A.   *A further teaching on Tannaite authority:*

B.   "You shall not steal" (Ex. 20:15):

C.   Scripture speaks of stealing money.

D.   You say that it speaks of stealing money, but perhaps it speaks only of stealing persons?

E. Do you say so? Go and derive the matter from the thirteen principles by which the Torah is interpreted, including the one that says that a matter is interpreted in its own context.

F. [In the present passage], of what subject does the Scripture speak? It speaks of crimes against property [such as envy and false witness].

G. So here too the commandment takes up property crimes.

III.5 A. *It has been stated on Amoraic authority:*

B. If [one set of] witnesses said that there had been a kidnapping and [another set of] witnesses said that there had been a sale of a kidnap-victim, and [both] were proved a conspiracy of perjurers –

C. Hezekiah said, "They are not put to death."

D. R. Yohanan said, "They are put to death."

E. *Hezekiah accords with what R. Aqiba said, for* he said, "'[At the testimony of two witnesses or at the testimony of three witnesses shall] the matter [be established]' (Deut. 19:15) – the whole of the matter, not part of it. [The two witnesses must testify to the entire crime, not only to part of the crime (Freedman, p. 569, n. 11)]." [Hence the witnesses to only part of the matter are not put to death.]

F. *And R. Yohanan rules in accord with the position of rabbis, who maintain, "' ... the matter ...,' – and even part of the matter."*

G. But Hezekiah concedes that the second set of witnesses against a wayward and incorrigible son were proved to be a conspiracy of perjurers, they are put to death, for the first set of witnesses have the power to claim, **[86B]** "It was to see that he was flogged that we came to court *[and on the basis of our testimony, he would have been flogged. Only if he then transgressed a second time, to which the later witnesses testify, would he be put to death.] Accordingly, the second set of witnesses are the ones who inflict on the son the complete penalty [of execution, and the former set of witnesses have no part in the matter]."*

H. *To this allegation R. Pappa objected, "If that is the case, then witnesses to the sale also should be subject to the death penalty, since* the witnesses to the theft have the power to claim, 'It was to see that he was flogged that we came to court, [and not to have him put to death].' *And should you claim that Hezekiah takes the view that, in such a case, the kidnapper is not flogged [for merely stealing the person] lo, it has been stated on Amoraic authority:* As to witnesses to a kidnapping of a person, who were proved to be a conspiracy for perjury, Hezekiah and R. Yohanan: one said, "They are flogged," and the other said, "They are not flogged." *And in that connection we maintained, "One should draw the conclusion that Hezekiah is the one who said that they are flogged, since it is Hezekiah who has ruled that they are not put to death. For so far as R. Yohanan is concerned, since he has maintained that they are put to death,* he has in hand a violation of a negative commandment that is subject to the admonition against committing a crime that, in fact, is punishable by the death penalty inflicted by a court, and in the case of any violation of a negative commandment that is subject to the admonition involving a death penalty at the hands of a court, there is no further penalty of flogging. *If, therefore, the accused would not have been flogged [in accord with the principle just now stated], how can the witnesses against him be flogged? [Clearly, from Yohanan's viewpoint, they cannot be flogged. Thus we have shown that Hezekiah would have the false witnesses flogged. It follows that kidnapping produces the penalty of flogging, and the witnesses would under certain circumstances only be flogged.]"*

I.   *Rather, said R. Pappa, "In the case of witnesses to the sale of the victim, who are proved a conspiracy for perjury], all parties concur that such witnesses are put to death. Where there is a dispute, it concerns witnesses to the abduction.* Hezekiah said, 'They are not put to death, *for the act of kidnapping stands by itself, and the act of sale is treated by itself.'* And R. Yohanan said, 'They are put to death, *because the abduction is the beginning of the act of sale.'* And R. Yohanan concedes in the case of the first set of witnesses against the wayward and incorrigible son who were proved to be a conspiracy for perjury, that they are not put to death, for, since they have the power to claim, 'It was to inflict a flogging on him that we came to court,' [they have not conspired to kill the accused and so they are not made victim to that penalty]."

J.   Said Abbayye, "All concur in one matter concerning the wayward and incorrigible son, all concur in a second matter regarding him, and there is a dispute in yet a third matter. All concur in one matter concerning a wayward and incorrigible son, that the first set of witnesses [proved perjurers] is not put to death, because they have the power to claim, 'It was to inflict a flogging on him that we came to court.' All concur in yet another matter concerning the wayward and incorrigible son, with respect to the second set of witnesses, that they are put to death [should they be proved a conspiracy of perjurers], for the first set of witnesses have the power to claim, 'We came to inflict a flogging on him, *and these others are the ones who committed against the accused the entirety of the act of perjury.* And there is a dispute concerning a third matter having to do with the wayward and incorrigible son: If two witnesses say, 'In our presence, he stole [the food],' and two witnesses say, 'In our presence he ate it,' [each set attests half of the offense]. Freedman, p. 571, n. 4: Hence according to Hezekiah, who agrees with Aqiba's dictum, 'the whole matter but not half the matter,' they are exempt; but in R. Yohanan's view, based on that of the rabbis, 'the matter and even half the matter,' they are liable.]"

III.6   A.   Said R. Assi, "Witnesses against one on account of selling someone, who were proved to form a conspiracy for perjury, are not put to death.

      B.   "For they have the power to claim, '[The one who sold him may say,' "I sold my own slave"' [Freedman, p. 571, n. 5: Hence he was not liable to death on their evidence, and therefore they in turn are also exempt.]"

C.   *Said R. Joseph, "In accord with which authority is this tradition in the name of R. Assi?*

D.   *"It accords with R. Aqiba, who has said, '"A matter ..."* and not part of a matter.'"

E.   *Said Abbayye to him, "But would they, on the view of rabbis, be put to death? Lo, he gives a reason, 'Since ...,' Rather, you may even say that the statement accords with rabbis' view, and it pertains to a case in which no witnesses to the kidnapping came to court."*

F.   *If that is the fact, then what value is there in making such an obvious statement?*

G.   *It was to deal with a case in which, later on, such witnesses [to the actual kidnapping] came, and even so, [the same ruling applies].* [Freedman, p. 572, n. 3: On the combines testimonies the accused was convicted. Yet, if the first witnesses of the sale were falsified, they are not punished, since they can plead, "We did not know that others would testify to the kidnapping."]

H.   *Nonetheless, what need is there to make such an obvious statement?*

I.   *It was indeed necessary, to deal with a case in which the witnesses made surreptitious gestures to one another.*

J.   *What might you have ruled? Such gestures are to be taken into account. So we are informed [by Assi] that a surreptitious gesture has no standing whatsoever.*

As usual, we move from the simplest exegesis of the Mishnah-passage, with special attention to scriptural proofs for its propositions, to rather complex theoretical problems. In the present case, unit I.1 clarifies the intent of one of the authorities at hand, M. 10:1H-I. Unit I.2 raises a theoretical issue continuous with unit I.1. Unit I.3 then introduces the scriptural foundations for the topic as a whole. Work on this same matter continues at unit I.4. Units II.1 and III.1 take up the exposition of sentences of the Mishnah-paragraph, in order. III.2 then turns to the scriptural basis for an admonition, as distinct from a penalty, in the present crime. The remainder forms a secondary, theoretical exercise.

10:2

A.   An elder who defies the decision of a court [M. 10:1B]

B.   as it is said, "If there arise a matter too hard for you in judgment, between blood and blood, between plea and plea" (Deut. 17:8) –

C.   there were three courts there.

D.   One was in session at the door gate of the Temple mount, one was in session at the gate of the courtyard, and one was in session in the hewn-stone chamber.

E.   They come to the one which is at the gate of the Temple mount and say, "Thus I have explained the matter, and thus my colleagues have explained the matter.

F.   "Thus I have ruled in the matter, and thus my colleagues have ruled."

G.   If they had heard a ruling, they told it to them, and if not, they come along to that court which was at the gate of the courtyard.

H.   And he says, "Thus I have explained the matter, and thus my colleagues have explained the matter.

I.   "Thus I have ruled in the matter [lit.: taught], and thus my colleagues have ruled."

J.   If they had heard a ruling, they told it to them, and if not, these and those come along to the high court which was in the hewn-stone chamber,

K.   from which Torah goes forth to all Israel,

L.   as it is said, "From that place which the Lord shall choose" (Deut. 17:12).

M.   [If] he went back to his town and again ruled just as he had ruled before, he is exempt.

N.   But if he instructed [others] to do it in that way, he is liable,

O.   as it is said, "And the man who does presumptuously" (Deut. 17:12).

P.   He is liable only if he will give instructions to people actually to carry out the deed [in accord with the now-rejected view].

Q.   A disciple of a sage who gave instruction to carry out the deed [wrongly] is exempt.

R.   It turns out that the strict ruling concerning him [that he cannot give decisions] also is a lenient ruling concerning him [that he is not punished if he does give decisions].

I.1   A.   *Our rabbis have taught on Tannaite authority:*

B.   "If a thing be outstandingly difficult for you" (Deut. 17:8):

C.   [87A] Scripture speaks of an outstanding figure on a court [and not a disciple].

D.   "You" – this refers to a counsellor, and so it is said, "There is one come out from you, who imagines evil against the Lord, a wicked counsellor" (Nahum 1:11).

E.   "A thing" – refers to a law.

F.   "In judgment" – refers to a ruling based on an influential argument.

G.   "Between blood and blood" – refers to the difference among the types of blood produced by a menstruating woman, a woman in childbirth, and a person suffering flux.

H.   "Between ruling and ruling" – whether capital cases, property cases, or cases involving a flogging.

I.   "Between plague spot and plague spot" – refers to a diseased spot in a human being, a house, and clothing.

J.   "Matters" – refers to decisions on devoted objects and pledges of valuations as well as sanctification of objects to the Temple.

K.   "Contentions" – this speaks of the ordeal of the accused wife, the breaking of the neck of a heifer on the occasion of discovery of a neglected corpse, and decisions on the declaration of purification of a person suffering from saraat [the skin ailment described at Lev. 13-14].

L.   "In your gates" – this refers to gleanings, forgotten sheaves, and the corner of the field.

M.   "Then you shall arise" – from the session of the court.

N. "And go up" – this teaches that the house of the sanctuary is higher than the rest of the Land of Israel, and the Land of Israel is higher than all other lands.

O. "To the place" – this teaches that the place [in which the high court meets] is the decisive factor [in the authority of that court].

P. *Now it is perfectly true that the house of the sanctuary is higher than the Land of Israel, for it is written, "And you shall go up" (Deut. 17:8).*

Q. *But how on the basis of Scripture does one know that the Land of Israel is higher than all other lands?*

R. *As it is written, "Therefore, behold the days are coming, says the Lord, that they shall no more say, 'The Lord lives, which brought up the children of Israel out of the Land of Egypt;' but, 'the Lord lives, who brought up and led the seed of the house of Israel out of the north country and from all other countries whether I have driven them and they shall dwell in their own land' (Jer. 23:7-8)."*

I.2 A. *Our rabbis have taught on Tannaite authority:*

B. "A presumptuous sage is liable only on account of a ruling concerning a matter, the deliberate violation of which is subject to the penalty of extirpation, and the inadvertent violation of which is subject to the penalty of bringing a sin-offering," the words of R. Meir.

C. R. Judah says, "It involves a matter, the principle of which derives from the teachings of the Torah, and the elaboration of which derives from the teachings of scribes."

D. R. Simeon says, "It involves even the most minor detail among the details contributed by scribes."

E. *What is the scriptural basis for the position of R. Meir?*

F. *He derives an analogy based on the meaning of the word "matter" as it occurs in two passages. In one passage it is written, "If there arises a matter too hard for you in judgment" (Deut. 17:8). And in a second passage it is written, "[And if the whole congregation of Israel sin through ignorance,] the matter being hidden from the eyes of the assembly" (Lev. 4:13).*

G. Just as, in this latter passage, "matter" refers to a rule, the deliberate violation of which is punishable by extirpation, and the inadvertent violation of which is punishable through the bringing of a sin-offering, so the word "matter" in the present context refers to a matter, the deliberate violation of which is subject to the penalty of extirpation, and the inadvertent violation of which is subject to the penalty of bringing a sin-offering.

H. And of R. Judah?

I. "According to the Torah which they shall teach you" (Deut. 17:11) – a matter that involves both Torah and what [scribes] shall teach you.

J. And of R. Simeon?

K. "[And you shall do according to the sentence] which they of that place shall show you" (Deut. 17:10) – even the most minor detail.

I.3   A.   *Said R. Huna bar Hinena to Raba, "Explain to me the teaching on Tannaite authority [of unit I] in accord with the view of R. Meir [about what is at issue, that is, distinctions based on types of penalty]."*

       B.   *Said Raba to R. Pappa, "Go out and explain it to him."*

       C.   "'If a thing be outstandingly difficult for you' (Deut. 17:8) – Scripture speaks of an outstanding figure on a court. This refers to a counsellor" – who knows how to intercalate years and designate the appearance of the new moon.

       D.   *As we have learned in the Mishnah:* **They gave testimony that they intercalate the year at any time in Adar.**

       E.   **For they had said, "Only up to Purim."**

       F.   **They gave testimony that they intercalate the year conditionally [M. Ed. 7:7F-H].**

       G.   *[If the presumptuous elder should reject the ruling of the high court], then, if it is to the one side, he will permit the use of leaven on Passover, and, if it is to the other side, he will also permit the use of leaven on Passover.*

I.4   A.   "'A thing' – refers to a law."

       B.   This refers to the law of the eleventh day.
             [Freedman, p. 577, n. 2: According to Biblical Law, a niddah (menstruating woman) can cleanse herself when seven days have passed from the beginning of her menstrual flow, provided it ceased on the seventh day before sunset. During the following eleven days, which are called the eleven days between menses, she cannot become a niddah again, it being axiomatic that a discharge of blood in that period is not a sign of niddah, but may be symptomatic of gonorrhoea. A discharge on one or two days within the eleven days renders her unclean, and she is forbidden cohabitation until the evening of the following day, and must wait for the third to see whether another discharge will follow, rendering her a zabah, or not. Should another discharge follow on the third day, she becomes unclean as a zabah, and cannot become clean until seven days have passed without any issue at all. Should she, however, discharge on the tenth, eleventh, and twelfth days, she is not a zabah, for the twelfth day commences a new period wherein the issue of blood may make her a niddah.]

       C.   *For it has been taught on Amoraic authority:*

       D.   As to the tenth day,

       E.   R. Yohanan said, "The tenth day is in the category of the ninth day."

       F.   R. Simeon b. Laqish said, "The tenth day is in the category of the eleventh day."

       G.   R. Yohanan said, "The tenth day is in the category of the ninth day, *for just as the ninth day requires watchfulness [to see whether there is a discharge of blood on that day], so the tenth day requires watchfulness [for the same reason]."*

       H.   R. Simeon b. Laqish said, "The tenth day falls into the category of the eleventh day, *just as the eleventh day does not require watchfulness [on account of a discharge of blood], so the tenth likewise does not require watchfulness."*

[Freedman, p. 577-8, n. 6: Thus, in R. Yohanan's opinion, there is only one traditional halakhah with respect to the eleventh day, viz., that a blood discharge thereon does not necessitate observation, and this is the only thing in which it differs from the preceding ten days. But if there was a discharge on the tenth, observation is necessary on the eleventh just as on the other days. But according to Resh Laqish it differs in two respects: (i) that a discharge thereon necessitates no further observation, and (ii) that it does not become an observation day on account of the tenth day's discharge. Hence there were two halachoth for that day. This explains the use of the plural in this passage. Now to revert to the main subject, in the opinion of R. Johanan, if a woman had a discharge on the tenth, cohabitation on the eleventh is Biblically forbidden on pain of extinction, whilst according to Resh Laqish it is prohibited only be a Rabbinical ordinance, not by Biblical law; thus this too conforms to R. Meir's requirements.

I. "'In judgment' – refers top a ruling based on an inferential argument."

J. [87B] [This is illustrated by the inferential argument concerning a man's incest with his daughter produced by a woman whom he has raped.

K. *For Raba said, "R. Isaac bar Abodimi said, "'The proof [that incest in such a case is punishable] derives from the common use of the word 'they' in two pertinent passages and also the common use of the word "wickedness" in two related passages.'"*

L. "'Between blood and blood' – refers to the difference among the types of blood produced by a menstruating woman, a woman in childbirth, and a person suffering flux."

M. "Blood produced by a menstruating woman" concerns the dispute of Aqabia b. Mehallel and rabbis.

N. *For we have learned in the Mishnah:*

O. **Blood which is yellow –**

P. **Aqabia b. Mehallel declares it unclean.**

Q. **And sages declare it clean [M. Nid. 2:6E-G].**

R. "A woman in childbirth" *refers to the dispute of Rab and Levi.*

S. *For it has been stated on Amoraic authority:* Rab said, "All blood comes from a single source, and the Torah has declared it unclean [for the first fourteen days after childbirth] and clean for the next sixty-six days."

T. Levi said, "It comes from two different sources. When the source of the clean blood is closed, the source of the unclean blood is opened, and when the source of the clean blood is closed, the source of the clean blood is opened."

U. "The blood of a person suffering flux."

V. *This refers to the dispute of R. Eliezer and R. Joshua, for we have learned in the Mishnah:*

W. **[If] a woman was in hard travail for three days during the eleven days.**

X.   **and [if] she enjoyed a respite for twenty-four hours and [then] gave birth –**

Y.   **"lo, this one is one who has given birth as a Zabah [while in the status of one who has a flux]," the words of R. Eliezer.**

Z.   **R. Joshua says, "A night and a day, like the eve of the Sabbath and its day."**

AA.   **For she has had relief from the pain and not from the blood [M. Nid. 4:4B-F].**

BB.   "'Between ruling and ruling' – whether capital or property cases or cases involving a flogging."

CC.   "Property cases:"

DD.   *This refers to the dispute of Samuel and R. Abbahu.*

EE.   For Samuel said, "If two judges decided a case, their decision is valid, but they are called a presumptuous court."

FF.   And R. Abbahu said, "In the view of all parties their decision is not valid."

            [Freedman, pp. 579-580, n. 3: Extinction may be involved therein in the following way: – If as a result of their decision money was withdrawn from A to B, on Samuel's view, it rightfully belongs to B: on R. Abbahu's, it does not. Now if B married a woman with this money as <u>a token of betrothal</u>, according to Samuel the marriage is valid, and cohabitation with another man is punishable by death or extinction in the absence of witnesses; but according to R. Abbahu, the <u>a token of betrothal</u> is invalid, for if one marries a woman with money or goods not belonging to him, his act is null. Hence, if the Beth din accepted Samuel's view, whilst the rebellious elder accepted R. Abbahu's, he declares a married woman free to others. Now further, if another man C also married the same woman, in Samuel's opinion the second marriage is invalid, and if B subsequently died, she is a free woman. But on R. Abbahu's view this second marriage is valid, since the first was null. Hence, if the Beth din ruled as R. Abbahu, and the rebellious elder as Samuel, he declares her free from C, when in reality she is married to him.]

GG.   "Capital cases:"

HH.   *This refers to the dispute between Rabbi and rabbis.*

II.   *For it has been taught on Tannaite authority:*

JJ.   Rabbi says, "'And you shall give life for life' (Ex. 21:23).

KK.   "This refers to a monetary compensation.

LL.   "You say it refers to monetary compensation, but perhaps it means only that one literally takes a life?

MM.   "Here there is reference to 'giving,' and elsewhere there is a reference to 'giving' [at Ex. 21:22].

NN.   "Just as 'giving' in the latter passage refers to monetary compensation, so 'giving' in the former passage also refers to monetary compensation."

OO. "Or cases involving a flogging" – *this refers to the dispute between R. Ishmael and rabbis.*

PP. *For we have learned in the Mishnah:*

QQ. **Cases involving flogging are judged by a court made up of three judges.**

RR. **In the name of R. Ishmael they have said, "A court made up of twenty three judges" [M. San. 1:2A-B].**

SS. "'Between plague spot and plague spot' – referring to a diseased spot in a human being, a house, and clothing:"

TT. "Plague spots in a human being" *refers to the dispute of R. Joshua and rabbis.*

UU. *For we have learned in the Mishnah:*

VV. **For they have said, If the bright spot preceded the white hair, he is unclean, and if the white hair preceded the bright spot, he is clean.**

WW. **And if there is doubt, he is unclean.**

XX. **And R. Joshua was doubtful [M. Nid. 4:11F-H].**

YY. *What is the meaning of "doubtful"?*

ZZ. Said Raba, "If it is subject to doubt, the man is ruled to be clean."

AAA. "A diseased spot in a house" *refers to the dispute of R. Eleazar b. R. Simeon and rabbis.*

BBB. *For we have learned in the Mishnah:*

CCC. **R. Eleazar b. R. Simeon says, "Until [a spot the size of] two split beans will appear on two stones – on two walls in the corner.**

DDD. **"Its length is two split beans, and its width a split bean" [M. Neg. 12:3G-H].**

EEE. *What is the scriptural basis for the view of R. Eleazar b. R. Simeon?*

FFF. It is written, "wall," and it is further written, "Walls" (at Lev. 14:37, 39). Where do we find one wall as two? It is at the angle.

GGG. "A diseased spot in clothing:"

HHH. *This refers to the dispute between R. Nathan b. Abetolomos and rabbis.*

III. *For it has been taught on Tannaite authority:*

JJJ. R. Nathan b. Abetolomos says, "How do we know **[88A]** that when there is a spreading of disease-signs in clothing, [if it covers the entire garment], it is ruled to be clean?

KKK. "The words 'baldness on the back of the head' and baldness on the front of the head are stated in respect to man, and 'baldness on the back' and 'baldness on the front' are mentioned in connection with clothing.

LLL. "Just as is in the former case, if the baldness spread throughout the whole, the man is clean, so here too, if the baldness spread throughout the whole, the garment is clean."

MMM. "'Matters' refers to decision on devoted objects, pledges of valuations, as well as sanctification of objects to the Temple:"

NNN.   "Pledges of valuations" *refers to the dispute of R. Meir and rabbis,*
as we have learned on Tannaite authority:

OOO.   He who pledges the Valuation of an infant less than a
month old –

PPP.   R. Meir says, "He pays his value [since there is no
Valuation in Scripture]."

QQQ.   And sages say, "He has not made a statement of any
consequence at all [and pays nothing]" [cf. B. Arakhin
5a/1:1HIA-C].

RRR.   " ... decisions on devoted objects:"

SSS.   *This refers to the dispute of R. Judah b. Beterah and rabbis.*

TTT.   *For we have learned in the Mishnah:*

UUU.   R. Judah b. Betera says, "What is declared herem without
further explanation is for the repair of the Temple house,

VVV.   "since it is said, 'Every devoted thing is most holy to the
Lord' (Lev. 27:28)."

WWW.   And sages say, "What is declared herem without further
explanation is for the priests,

XXX.   "since it is said, As a field devoted to the possession
thereof shall be the priest's (Lev. 27:21).

YYY.   "If so, why is it said, And every devoted thing is most
holy to the Lord?

ZZZ.   "That it applies to Most Holy Things and to Lesser Holy
Thing" [M. Ar. 8:6B-G].

AAAA.   " ... as well as sanctification of objects to the Temple:"

BBBB.   *This refers to the dispute of R. Eliezer b. Jacob and rabbis, for it has*
been taught on Tannaite authority:

CCCC.   R. Eliezer b. Jacob says, "The valuation even of a hook that
has been declared sanctified requires the assessment of a
court of ten judges so that it may be redeemed [by the
payment of a monetary equivalent to the value of the
hook]."

DDDD.   "'Contentions' – this speaks of the ordeal of the accused
wife, the breaking of the neck of a heifer on the occasion of
discovery of a neglected corpse, and decisions on the
declaration of purification of a person suffering from
saraat [the skin-ailment described at Lev. 13-14]:"

EEEE.   *"The ordeal of the accused wife" refers to the dispute of R. Eliezer and*
R. Joshua, for we have learned in the Mishnah:

FFFF.   He who expresses jealousy to his wife [concerning her
relations with another man (Num. 5:14) –

GGGG.   R. Eliezer says, "He expresses jealousy before two
witnesses, and he imposes on her the requirement of
drinking the bitter water on the testimony of a single
witness or even on his own evidence [that she has been
alone with the named man]."

HHHH.   R. Joshua says, "He expresses jealousy before two
witnesses, and he requires her to drink the bitter water
before two witnesses" [M. Sot. 1:1A-C].

IIII.   *"The breaking of the neck of a heifer ..." refers to the dispute between*
R. Eliezer and R. Aqiba, for we have learned in the Mishnah:

JJJJ.   **From what point did they measure?**

KKKK.   **R. Eliezer says, "From his belly-button."**

LLLL.   **R. 'Aqiba says, "From his nose."**

MMMM.   **R. Eliezer b. Jacob says, "From the place at which he was turned into a corpse – from his neck" [M. Sot. 9:4A-D].**

NNNN.   *"Decisions on the purification of a person suffering from saraat [the skin-ailment described at Lev. 13-14]" refers to the dispute of R. Simeon and rabbis, for we have learned in the Mishnah:*

OOOO.   **If he did not have a thumb, a big toe, [or] a right ear he can never have purification.**

PPPP.   **R. Eliezer says, "One puts it [the blood] on their place."**

QQQQ.   **R. Simeon says, "If he put it on the left [side instead of the right], he has carried out his obligation" [M. Neg. 14:9E-G].**

RRRR.   *"'In your gates" – this refers to gleanings, forgotten sheaves, and the corner of the field:"*

SSSS.   *As we have learned in the Mishnah:*

TTTT.   **"Two sheaves [of grain which are left side-by-side in a field] are [subject to the restrictions of] the forgotten sheaf.**

UUUU.   **"But three [sheaves left side-by-side in a field] are not [subject to the restrictions of] the forgotten sheaf.**

VVVV.   **"Two piles of olives or carob-[fruit which are left side-by-side in a field] are [subject to the restrictions of] the forgotten sheaf.**

WWWW.   **"But three [such piles left side-by-side in a field] are not [subject to the restrictions of] the forgotten sheaf.**

XXXX.   **But concerning all of them, the House of Shammai say, "Three [measures of produce left side-by-side in a field] belong to the poor, while four [measures] belong to the householder" [M. Pe. 6:5A-D, L (Brooks)].**

YYYY.   *" ... and the corner of the field:"*

ZZZZ.   *This refers to the dispute of R. Ishmael and rabbis.*

AAAAA.   *For it has been taught on Tannaite authority:*

BBBBB.   The religious duty of designating a corner of the field for the poor involves separating standing grain.

CCCCC.   If one did not designate the portion out of standing grain, he should designate it out of grain in sheaves.

DDDDD.   This should be done before he smoothed the stack.

EEEEE.   If he had first smoothed the stack of grain, he should separate tithe and give it to [the poor man].

FFFFF.   In the name of R. Ishmael they said, "One may separate [the share of the poor] even from the dough [of grain that has been processed]."

II.1 A.   **There were three courts there [M. 10:2C]:**

     B.   [With reference to M. 10:2E-F], said R. Kahana, [If] he says, "'[I heard it] from tradition, and they say, '[We heard it] from tradition,' he is not put to death.

     C.   "[If] he says, 'Thus matters appear to me [on this basis of reasoning],' and they say, 'Thus matters appear to us [on the basis of reasoning],' he is not put to death.

D. "And all the more so [if] he says, 'I heard it from tradition,' and they say, 'Thus matters appear to us,' he is not put to death.

E. "[He is put to death] only if he says, 'Thus it appears to me,' while they say, '[We have heard] on the basis of tradition.'

F. "You may know that that is the case, for lo, they did not put Aqabia b. Mehallel to death."

G. But R. Eleazar says, "Even if he says, '[I heard] from tradition,' and they say, 'Thus matters appear to us,' he is put to death, so as to prevent dissension in Israel.

H. "And should you say, On what account did they not put Aqabiah b. Mehallel to death, it was because he did not teach the law as a matter of practical conduct [but only as a theory].

I. "You may know that that is the case, *for lo, we have learned in the Mishnah:* **Thus I have explained the matter and thus my colleagues have explained the matter, thus I have taught and thus my colleagues have taught [M. 10:2H-I].**

J. *"Is this not a case in which he said, '[I heard it] on the basis of tradition,' and they say, 'Thus matters appear to us'?"*

K. No, it is a case in which he says, "Thus it appears to me,'" and they say, "[Thus have we heard] in tradition."

L. *Come and take note:* R. Josiah said, "Three things did Zeira tell me in the name of the men of Jerusalem: 'A husband who retracted his expression of jealousy – his expression of jealousy is null **[88B]**. A disobedient son whom the father and mother wished to forgive is forgiven. A rebellious elder whom a court wished to forgive is forgiven. Now when I came to my colleagues in the south, they concurred with me in two items, but as to the rebellious elder they did not concur with me, so as not to permit the increase of dissension in Israel."

M. *This constitutes a valid refutation [of Kahana's position and support of Eleazar's].*

II.2 A. *It has been taught on Tannaite authority:*

B. Said R. Yosé, "At first there were dissensions in Israel only in the court of seventy in the hewn-stone chamber in Jerusalem.

C. "And there were other courts of twenty-three in the various towns of the land of Israel, and there were other courts of three judges each in Jerusalem, one on the Temple mount, and one on the Rampart.

D. "[If] someone needed to know what the law is, he would go to the court in his town.

E. "[If] there was no court in his town, he would go to the court in the town nearest his.

F. "If they had heard the law, they told him. If not, he and the most distinguished member of that court would come on to the court which was on the Temple mount.

G. "If they had heard the law, they told them. And if not, they and the most distinguished member of that group would come to the court which was on the Rampart.

H. "If they had heard, they told them, and if not, these and those would go to the high court which was in the hewn-stone chamber.

I. "The court which was in the hewn-stone chamber, even though it consists of seventy-one members, may not fall below twenty-three.

J. "[If] one of them had to go out, he looks around to see whether there would be twenty-three left [after he departs]. If there would be twenty-three left he goes out, and if not, he does not go out –

K. "unless there would be twenty-three left.

L. "And there they remained in session from the time of the daily whole-offering of the morning until the time of the daily whole-offering at twilight.

M. "On Sabbaths and on festivals they came only to the study-house which was on the Temple mount.

N. "[If] a question was brought before them, if they had heard the answer, they told them.

O. "if not, they stand for a vote.

P. "[If] those who declare unclean turn out to form the majority, they declared the matter unclean. [If] those who declare the matter clean form the majority, they declared the matter clean.

Q. "From there did the law go forth and circulate in Israel.

R. "From the time that the disciples of Shammai and Hillel who had not served their masters as much as was necessary became numerous, dissensions became many in Israel.

S. "And from there they send for and examine everyone who is wise, prudent, fearful of sin, and of good repute, in whom people found pleasure.

T. "They make him a judge in his town.

U. "Once he has been made a judge in his town, they promote him and seat him on the Rampart's court, and from there they promote him and seat him in he court of the hewn-stone chamber [T. San. 7:1B-U].

II.3 A. They sent from there, "Who is someone who will inherit the world to come?

B. "It is one who is meek and humble, *who bends when he comes and and bends when he goes out, who always is studying the Torah, but does not take pride in himself in on that account.*"

C. *Rabbis gazed at R. Ulla bar Abba.*

III.1 A. If he went back to his town and again ruled [just as he had ruled before he is exempt] [M. 10:2M]:

B. *Our rabbis have taught on Tannaite authority:*

C. He is liable only if he will act in accord with the instruction that he has given, or unless he instructs others to do so and they act in accord with his instruction [T. San. 14:12].

D. *Now there is no problem with the case of his teaching others who act in accord with his instruction. To begin with, he was not subject to the death penalty, but now [after the court has ruled] he is indeed subject to the death penalty. But if he should act in accord with his own instruction, [that is a different matter, for] to begin with, also, he was subject to the death-penalty. There is [to continue the exposition], moreover, no problem if the original ruling had to do with the prohibition of eating forbidden fat or blood, for to begin with he was not subject to the death penalty, while now he is subject to the* *death penalty. But in a case in which he had given instruction concerning matters on account of which the court inflict the death penalty, to begin with he was subject to the death penalty [and it is not only <u>now</u> that the court has made its ruling].*

E.   *[No, that is not a problem, for] to begin with he required admonition [against teaching as he did; barring admonition, he would not be subject to the death penalty], while now, he does not require admonition [and is subject to the death penalty in any event].*

J.   *Then as to the case of one who incites [a whole town to commit idolatry], who does not require an admonition at all, what is to be said?*

K.   *If, [prior to the consultation with the high court], he had given reason for his action, we might have accepted it from him, but now even if he gave a reason, we should not accept it from him.*

The magnificent exposition of unit I.1 at unit I.4 should not distract attention from other impressive traits of systematic exegesis of the fine composition before us. Unit I.1 provides an explanation for the proof-text of Scripture cited by the Mishnah itself. Unit I.2 then defines the matter at issue in the Mishnah-paragraph. Then unit I.3 spells out the materials of unit I, in light of one of the three positions of unit I.2. That the whole is a unity cannot be doubted, a wonderful piece of composition. All of the matters spelled out involve the disjunctive penalty specified by Meir, though this requires explicit exposition only at a few points. From that point forward, the entire passage is laid out as a systematic exposition of the Mishnah.

10:3

A.   A more strict rule applies to the teachings of scribes than to the teachings of Torah.

B.   He who, in order to transgress the teachings of the Torah, rules, "There is no requirement to wear phylacteries," is exempt.

C.   [But if,] in order to add to what the scribes have taught, [he said,] "There are five partitions [in the phylactery, instead of four], he is liable.

I.1   A.   Said R. Eleazar, said R. Oshaia, "The liability applies only to a case in which the principle derives from the teachings of the Torah, the amplification derives from words of scribes, there is a possibility of adding, but if, should there be addition, it constitutes diminution.

      B.   "The only example of such a matter is the case of the phylacteries. [Freedman, p. 587, n. 6: The fundamental law of wearing phylacteries is biblical. By rabbinic interpretation, the phylactery for the head must contain four compartments, with inscriptions in each. Hence it is possible to rule that it should consist of a greater number. But if this is done, the phylactery is unfit, so that the addition amounts to subtraction of its fitness]." *This [A] accords with the principle of R. Judah* [at B. San. 87A, above, who holds that at issue must be both a teaching of the Torah and an amplification based on views of scribes].

C. *But [as against B] there is the matter of the palm-branch [waved on the festival of Tabernacles],* in which the principle of the matter derives from the teaching of the Torah [Lev. 23:40], and the amplification, from the teaching of scribes there is a possibility of adding, but if, should there be addition, it constitutes diminution in the case of the palm-branch.

D. *What is the basic thesis of the present proposal? Is it that it is not necessary to bind together the several components of the palm-branch [that is, the palm with the citron and myrtle]? Then this part is distinct from that* [Freedman, p. 588, n. 5: so that the combination is quite valid]. [Adding further will make no difference.]

E. *If we take the view that the palm-branch does have to be bound together, then the [palm-branch] persists in being invalid [as soon as an additional species, beyond the three required, is bound together with the others].* [Freedman, p. 588, n. 6: But in the case of phylacteries, when four compartments are made, the head-phylactery is valid, while only when a fifth is added, does it become invalid.] *[so this matter of the palm-branch does not constitute a further example to illustrate the conditions set forth at the outset.]*

F. *And lo, there is the case of show-fringes, in which case* the principle derives from a teaching of the Torah, while the amplification of the matter derives from teachings of scribes, and there is a possibility of adding, but if, should there be an addition [of a thread], it constitutes diminution.

G. *But what theory do we espouse in the case of show-fringes? If we take the view that the upper knot [on the show-fringes] does not derive from the requirement of the Torah, then this knot stands apart from that knot.* [Freedman, p. 588, n. 10: The fringes are inserted through a hole and knotted near the edge of the garment. It is disputed whether this is really necessary by biblical law. If not, then even when made, the threads or fringes are regarded as hanging apart and distinct. Consequently, if five instead of four threads were inserted and knotted, four fulfill the precept, while the fifth may be disregarded entirely, without rendering the rest invalid.] *And if we take the view that* **[89A]** *the upper knot does derive from the requirement of the Torah, then to begin with the show-fringes are invalid.*

H. *[This same argument may now apply to the phylacteries, namely,] if so, in the case of phylacteries also, if one made four cubicles and then added a fifth and set it beside the four, [we also may say] that this one is regarded as distinct from the others. And if to begin with one made five cubicles [instead of four], then to begin with the phylactery was invalid [as soon as it was made], for* has not R. Zira said, "In the case of a cubicle that is open to the next [the phylactery is unfit,]" [Freedman, p. 588, n. 12: not having been made according to rule, which requires that each compartment shall be entirely shut off from the next, so it is not a case of phylacteries have been rendered unfit, but of something that was never a phylactery to begin with.]

I. [Freedman supplies from the Munich MS: This must be taught only in the case of one who made a frontlet of four compartments, and then added a fifth thereto and joined it. (By this addition the original is impaired,) even as Raba said, "If the outset compartment does not look upon space, it is invalid..."]

The Talmud provides ample illustration of the Mishnah's principle.

10:4

A. "They put him to death not in the court in his own town or in the court which is in Yabneh, but they bring him up to the high court in Jerusalem.

B. "And they keep him until the festival, and they put him to death on the festival,

C. "as it is said, 'And all the people shall hear and fear and no more do presumptuously' (Deut. 17:13)," the words of R. Aqiba.

D. R. Judah says, "They do not delay the judgment of this one, but they put him to death at once.

E. "And they write messages and send them with messengers to every place:

F. 'Mr. So-and-so, son of Mr. So-and-so, has been declared liable to the death penalty by the court.'"

I.1   A.   *Our rabbis have taught on Tannaite authority:*

B. "They put him to death not in the court in his own town or in the court which is in Yabneh, but they bring him up to the high court in Jerusalem. And they keep him until the festival, and they put him to death on the festival, as it is said, 'And all the people shall hear and fear and no more do presumptuously' (Deut. 17:13)," the words of R. Aqiba [M. 10:4A-C].

C. Said R. Judah to him, "And is it said, 'They shall see and fear'? What is stated is only, 'They shall hear and fear..'

D. "So why delay the judgment of this one? Rather they put him to death at once, and they write messages and send them with messengers to every place:

E. "'Mr. So-and-so has been declared liable to the death penalty by the court'" [M. 10:4D-F].

1.2   A.   *Our rabbis have taught on Tannaite authority:*

B. The condemnation of four classes of criminals requires public announcement:

C. one who entices [a town to apostasy], a wayward and incorrigible son, a rebellious elder, and witnesses who have been proved to form a conspiracy for perjury.

D. And in the case of all of them [except for the fourth], it is written, "And all the people ...," or, "and all Israel ...."

E. But in the case of a conspiracy of perjurers, it is written, "And those that remain shall hear and fear" (Deut. 19:20),

F.   *for not every body is fit to be a witness, [so the admonition is not to all Israel].*

Unit I provides a light gloss to the Mishnah's formulation, giving an answer to the exegetical argument, and unit II likewise amplifies matters.

10:5-6

A.   A false prophet [M.10:1B],

B.   one who prophesies concerning something which he has not actually heard or concerning something which was not actually said to him,

C.   is put to death by man.

D.   But he who holds back his prophesy, he who disregards the words of another prophet, or the prophet who transgresses his word words

E.   is put to death by heaven,

F.   as it is said, "I will require it of him" (Deut. 18;19).

M.10:5

A.   He who prophesies in the name of an idol [M.10:1B5], and says, "Thus did such-and-such an idol say to me,"

B.   even though he got the law right, declaring unclean that which in fact is unclean, and declaring clean that which in fact is clean.

C.   He who has sexual relations with a married woman [M.10:1C1]

D.   as soon as she has entered the domain of the husband in marriage, even though she has not had sexual relations with him

E.   he who has sexual relations with her – lo, this one is put to death by strangling.

F.   And those who bear false witness against a priest's daughter and against one who has sexual relations with her [M. 10:1C2,3] –

G.   for all those who bear false witness first suffer that same mode of execution,

H.   except for those who bear false witness against a priest's daughter and her lover.

M.10:6

I.1   A.   *Our rabbis have taught on Tannaite authority:*

B.   Three [false prophets] are put to death by man, and three are put to death by heaven.

C.   He who prophesies concerning something which he has not actually heard or concerning something which was not actually said to him [M. 10:5B],

D.   and one who prophesies in the name of an idol – such as these are put to death by man.

E.   But he who holds back his prophecy, he who disregards the words of another prophet, or the prophet who transgresses his own words is not to death by heaven [M. 10:5D-F].

I.2   A.   *What is the source of this rule?*

B.   Said R. Judah said Rab, "It is because Scripture has said, 'But the prophet who shall presume to speak a word in may name' (Deut. 18:20) – this refers to a prophet who prophesies concerning something which he has not actually heard.

C.   "'Which I have not commanded him to speak' (Deut. 18:20) – but lo, I have indeed commanded his fellow, [and accordingly], this refers to one who prophesies concerning something which was not actually said to him [but to someone else].

D.   "'Or shall speak in the name of other gods' (Deut. 18:20) – this refers to one who prophesies in the name of an idol.

E.   "And it is written, 'Even that prophet shall die' (Deut. 18:20), and in the case of a death penalty specified in the Torah which is left undefined, it is only through strangulation.

F.   **"But he who holds back his prophecy, he who disregards the words of another prophet, or the prophet who transgresses his own words is put to death by heaven,**

G.   "For it is written, 'And it shall come to pass that whoever will not hearken...' (Deut. 18:19).

H.   *"In regard to such a person applies the statement, 'who will not make heard' and in regard to such a person applies the statement also, 'Who will not listen to my words.'*

I.   "And it is written, 'I shall require it of him' (Deut. 18:19) – meaning, [he is put to death] by heaven."

II.1   A.   **One who prophesies concerning something which he has not actually heard [M. 10:5B].**

B.   **For example, Zedekiah b. Chenaanah [T. San. 14:14A-B],**

C.   for it is written, "And Zedekiah, the son of Chenaanah, had made him horns of iron" (1 Kgs. 22:11).

D.   *What ought he have done? For it was the spirit of Naboth that had confused him!* For it is written, "And the Lord said, Who shall persuade Ahab that he may go up and fall at Ramoth-Gilead? And there came forth a spirit and stood before the Lord and said, I will persuade him...and the Lord said, You shall persuade him and prevail also, go forth and do so" (1 Ks. 22:20ff.)?

E.   Said R. Judah, "What is the meaning of 'go forth'? It is 'go forth' from my vicinity."

F.   *What is the meaning of "spirit"?*

G.   Said R. Yohanan, "It was the spirit of Naboth, the Jezreelite."

H.   [Reverting to the question of what else Zedekiah might have done, we answer:] He might have checked out [the predictions of the other prophets].

I.   *That accords with what R. Isaac said.* For R. Isaac said, "The same message reaches many prophets, but no two prophets prophesy in the same wording. Obadiah said, 'The pride of your heart has deceived you' (Ob. 1:3), while Jeremiah said, 'Your terribleness has deceived you and the pride of your heart' (Jer. 49:16), [and both referred to Edom, but expressed themselves differently.]. [And returning to the argument against Zedekiah:] Since all of these prophets together spoke in the same way, it indicated that they had nothing at all to say [that God had delivered to them as his message]."

J.   *But perhaps [Zedekiah] did not know about this statement of R. Isaac.*

K.   *Jehoshaphat was there, and he spoke to them, for it is written,* "And Jehoshaphat said, Is there not here a prophet of the Lord besides, that we may inquire of him?" (1 Kgs. 22:7).

L.   [Ahab] said to him, "Lo, there are all of these [prophets]. I have received a teaching from the house of my father's father that the same message   reaches many prophets, but no two prophets prophesy in the same wording."

III.1 A. **He who prophesies concerning something which was not actually said to him [M. 10:5B]:**

B. **for example, Hananiah b. Azor [T. San. 14:14D].**

C. *For Jeremiah was standing in the upper market, and saying,* "Thus says the Lord of hosts, Behold I will break the bow of Elam" (Jer. 49:35).

D. Now Hananiah constructed an argument a fortiori on his own, "If concerning Elam, who came only to help Babylonia, the Holy One, blessed be he, has said, 'Behold, I will break the bow of Elam,' the Chaldeans themselves, how much the more so [will the Lord break their bow]!"

E. *He came along to the lower market and said,* "Thus says the Lord of hosts, the God Israel, saying, I have broken the yoke of the kingdom of Babylon: (Jer. 28:2).

F. *Said R. Pappa to Abbayye, "[But this does not constitute violating the rule, for] that message also had not been given to his fellow [Jeremiah]."*

G. *He said to him,* "Since an argument a fortiori has been made available as an exegetical tool,it is as if it had been stated to him."

H. "Accordingly, this falls into the category of saying something that had not been said to him [but had been said to his fellow prophet]."

III.2 A. **He who prophesies in the name of an idol; : He who holds back his prophecy [M. 10:5D]:**

B. **for example Jonah b. Amittai [T. San. 14:15B].**

III.3 A. **He who disregards the words of another prophet [M. 10:5D]:**

B. for example [89B] the friend of Micah,

C. as it is written, "And a certain man of the sons of the prophets said to his fellow in the word of the Lord, Smite me I pray you, and the man refused to smite him" (1 Kgs. 20:35).

D. And it is further written, "And he said to him, Because you have not obeyed [the voice of the Lord, behold as soon as you have departed from me, a lion will kill you]" (1 Kgs. 20:36).

III.4. A. **Or the prophet who transgresses his own words [M. 10:5D]:**

B. **for example, Iddo, the prophet [T. San. 15:15E],**

C. as it is written, "For so it was charged me by the word of the Lord, [saying, Eat not bread not drink water nor turn again by the same way that you come]" (1 Kgs. 13:9).

D. "And [the prophet] said to him, I am a prophet also as you are [and an angel spoke to me by the work of the Lord, saying, Bring him back with you to your house that he may eat bread and drink water" (1 Kgs. 13:18).

E. "So he went back with him," and "When he was gone, a lion met him by the way and slew him" (1 Kgs. 13:24).

III.5 A. *A Tannaite authority repeated before R. Hisda,* "He who holds back his prophecy is flogged."

B. *He said to him,* "He who eats dates out of a sieve is flogged! Who warned [the prophet who withheld his prophecy, since no one could have known about that fact]? [No admonition, no flogging!]"

C. *Said Abbayye,* "His fellow prophets."

D. "How did they know about it?"

E.   *Said Abbayye, "For it is written, 'Surely the Lord will do nothing unless he reveals his secret to his servants, the prophets, (Amos 3:7)."*

F.   *"But perhaps [the heavenly messengers] retracted?"*

G.   *"If it were the case that they had retracted, they would have informed all the other prophets."*

H.   *"And lo, there is the case of Jonah, in which heaven had retracted [its decision], but they had not notified Jonah."*

I.   *"To begin with, Jonah was told that Nineveh would be turned, but he was not informed whether it was for good or for bad."*

III.6 A.   **He who disregards the words of another prophet [M. 10:5D]:**

B.   *How does one know [that the other is a prophet], so that he should be punished?*

C.   *[The other] gives him a sign.*

D.   *And lo, there is the case of Micah, who did not give a sign, and yet [the other prophet] was punished.*

E.   *In a case in which one was already well established as a prophet, the law is different.*

F.   *For if you do not take that view, then in the case of Abraham at Mount Moriah, how could Isaac have listened to Abraham, and in the case of Elijah at Mount Carmel, how could the people have relied on him, so as [in both cases] to make an offering outside of the Temple?*

G.   *It must follow that in a case in which one was already well established, the law is different.*

III.7 A.   "And it came to pass after these words that God tested Abraham" (Gen. 22:1):

B.   What is the meaning of "after"?

C.   Said R. Yohanan in the name of R. Yosé b. Zimra, "It was after the words of Satan.

D.   "For it is written 'And the child grew and was weaned [and Abraham made a great feast the same day that Isaac was weaned' (Gen. 21:8).

E.   "Said Satan to the Holy One, blessed be he, 'Lord of the world, as to this old man, you have shown him grace by giving him the fruit of the womb at one hundred years. Now of the entire meal that he has made, he did not have a single pigeon or a single dove to offer before you.'

F.   "He said to him, 'Has he done anything at all except to honor his son? [But] if I were to say to him, "Sacrifice your son before me," he would sacrifice him immediately.'

G.   "Forthwith: 'And God tested Abraham' (Gen. 22:1)."

H.   "And he said, Take, I pray you, your son" (Gen. 22:2):

I.   Said R. Simeon b. Abba, "The word 'I pray you' bears the meaning only of supplication.

J.   "The matter may be compared to the case of a mortal king, against whom many wars were fought. He had one powerful leader, who won all his battles.

K.   "After a while a very difficult war was waged against him.

L.   "He said to him, 'By your leave, stand up for me in this war too, so that people will not say that, as to the earlier wars, they really did not add up to much.'

M.	"So the Holy One, blessed be he, said to Abraham, 'I tried you in a number of trials and you stood up to all of them. Now stand up for me in this trial as well, so that people will not say that, as to he earlier trials, they really did not add up to much."
N.	"Your son" (Gen. 22:2) – "I have two sons."
O.	"Your only son (Gen. 22:2) – "This one is an only son for his mother, and that one is an only son for his mother."
P.	"Whom you loved" (Gen. 22:2) – *"I love them both."*
Q.	"Isaac" (Gen. 22:2).
R.	Why all this?
S.	So that he should not be confused.
T.	Satan met him on the way and said to him, "If we try to commune with you, will you be grieved? ... Behold you have instructed many, and you have strengthened weak hands. Your words have held up him who was falling, and you have strengthened feeble knees. But now it is come upon you, and you faint" (Job 4:2-5).
U.	He said to him, "I will walk in my integrity." (Ps. 26:2).
V.	He said to him, "But should not your fear by your confidence" (Job 4:6).
W.	He said to him, "Remember, I pray you, whoever perished, being innocent?" (Job 4:6).
X.	*Since [Satan] saw that he would not listen to him, he said to him,* "Now a thing was secretly brought to me" (Job 4:12).
Y.	"This I have heard from the other side of the curtain: 'The lamb is for a burnt-offering (Job 4:7) – and Isaac is not for a burnt-offering."
Z.	This is the penalty paid by a liar, that even when he tells the truth, people do not pay any attention to him.
AA.	[Explaining, "After these words" (Gen. 22:1):] said R. Levi, "After the words between Ishmael and Isaac.
BB.	"Ishmael said to Isaac, 'I am greater than you in the performance of religious duties, for you were circumcised on the eighth day, while I was circumcised in the thirteenth year.'
CC.	"He said to him, 'And on account of one limb are you going to put me down? If the Holy One, blessed be he, were to say to me, 'Sacrifice yourself before me,' I should sacrifice myself immediately.'
DD.	"'And God tried Abraham' (Gen. 22:1)."

III.8	A.	[With reference to M. 10:6A-B], *our rabbis have taught on Tannaite authority:*
	B.	**A prophet who enticed [people to commit idolatry] is put to death through stoning.**
	C.	**R. Simeon says, "It is through strangulation"**
	D.	**Those who entice a whole town to commit idolatry are put to death through stoning.**
	E.	**R. Simeon says, "Through strangulation" [cf. T. San. 11:5D].**
	F.	*What is the scriptural basis for the position of rabbis?*
	G.	They establish an analogy between the matter of the false prophet and the one who enticed a town to commit idolatry on

the basis of the common usage of the word "enticement" in both cases [for the prophet, at Deut. 13:6, and for the one who enticed the town to commit idolatry, at Deut. 13:11].

H.   Just as, in the latter case, the penalty is death through stoning, so in the present case, the penalty is death through stoning.

I.   *And R. Simeon? The penalty is death is ascribed to such a one, and in any case in which in the Torah death is prescribed without further specification, it is is through strangulation.*

J.   **Those who entice a whole town to commit idolatry are put to death through stoning:**

K.   *What is the scriptural basis for the position of rabbis?*

L.   [As before], they establish an analogy between the matter of the one who entices the town to commit idolatry and the prophet who enticed [people to commit idolatry], based on the common use of the word enticement.

M.   And R. Simeon? He derives the penalty applicable to the one who entices the town to commit idolatry from the penalty applicable to the prophet on the basis of the use of the word "enticement" in common to both.

N.   And why not derive the proof from the case of one who entices a community to commit idolatry [at which, at Deut. 13:11, the penalty of stoning is explicitly prescribed]?

O.   We draw an analogy from the case of one who entices the community at large from the case of one who entices the community at large, and we do not derive an analogy concerning the one who entices the community at large from the instance of one who entices an individual.

P.   On the contrary, we should derive an analogy for the penalty applying to a common person from the penalty that applies to another such common person, and we should not establish an analogy concerning a common person from the rule that applies to a prophet!

Q.   And R. Simeon?

R.   Since one has enticed [a community to commit idolatry], you have no more solid grounds than that for regarding one as a common person!

S.   Said R. Hisda, "**[90A]** The dispute concerns the case of one who uprooted the very principle that idolatry is forbidden, or who in part confirmed and in part annulled the principle of idolatry.

T.   "For the All-Merciful has said, '[To entice you]...from the way [which the Lord your God commanded you to walk in]' (Deut. 13:6) – that is, even part of the way.

U.   "But as to one who uprooted the very principle of other religious opinions in the opinion of all parties is put to death through strangulation, and as to one who upholds part and annuls part of any of the other commandments, all parties concur that such a one is exempt."

V.   *R. Hamnuna objected, "'[Because he has spoken ... to entice you from the way which the Lord your God has commanded you] to walk' – this refers to commandments concerning positive deeds.*

W.		"'...in it' – this refers to commandments concerning things not to do.
X.		*"Now if you take that view that at issue is idolatry, where do you find a commandment concerning a duty actually to carry out a deed in connection with idolatry?"*
Y.		R. Hisda explained, "[You do indeed find such a positive commandment: 'And you shall overthrow their altars' (Deut. 12:3)."
Z.		R. Hamnuna said, "The dispute concerns one who uproots the very principle of the law, whether with respect to idolatry or any other religious duties, or the partial fulfillment and the partial nullification of idolatry.
AA.		"For the All-Merciful has said, '...from the way...' (Deut. 13:6) – even part of the way.
BB.		"But if one a one confirms in part and annuls in part the matter of all other commandments, all parties concur that he is exempt."
II.9	A.	*Our rabbis have taught on Tannaite authority:*
	B.	He who prophesies in such a way as to uproot a teaching of the Torah is liable.
	C.	[If he prophesies so as] to confirm part and annul part [of a teaching of the Torah],
	D.	R. Simeon declares him exempt.
	E.	But as for idolatry, even if one says, "Today serve it and tomorrow annul it," all parties concur that he is liable.
	F.	*Abbayye reasons matters in accord with the view of R. Hisda and deals with the matter at hand in accord with the view of R. Hisda, and Raba reasons matters in accord with the view of R. Hamnuna and interprets the matter at hand with the view of R. Hamnuna.*
	G.	*Abbayye reasons matters in accord with the view of R. Hisda and deals with the matter at hand in accord with the view of R. Hisda:*
	H.	As to him who prophesies in such a way as to uproot a teaching of the Torah, all parties concur that he is put to death through strangulation.
	I.	If he so prophesies as to confirm part and annul part, R. Simeon declares him exempt, and that is the view also of rabbis.
	J.	And as to a matter of idolatry, even if he said, "Today serve it and tomorrow annul it," he is liable.
	K.	*Each will condemn him to the death penalty in accord with his established position [so rabbis have him stoned, Simeon has him strangled.].*
	L.	*Raba reasons matters in accord with the view of R. Hamnuna and interprets the matter at hand in accord with the view of R. Hamnuna:*
	M.	He who prophesies as to uproot a teaching of the Torah, whether it concerns idolatry or any of the other religious duties, it is liable.

N.		Each will condemn him to the death penalty in accord with his established position.
O.		If he so prophesies as to confirm part and annul part of another religious duties.
P.		R. Simeon declares him exempt, and that is the view of rabbis. [Freedman, p. 599, n.b. 1: In Hamnuna's view, Simeon is particularly mentioned to show that he is exempt even from strangulation, a more lenient death than stoning, hence certainly from stoning].
Q.		And as idolatry, even if he says, "Today serve it and tomorrow annul it," he is liable.
R.		Each will condemn him to the death penalty in accord with his established position.
III.10	A.	Said R. Abbahu said, R. Yohanan, "In any matter, if a prophet should say to you, 'Violate the teachings of the Torah,' obey him, except for the matter of idolatry.
	B.	"For even if he should make the sun stand still for you in the middle of the firmament, do not listen to him."
	C.	*It has been taught on Tannaite authority:*
	D.	R. Yosé the Galilean says, "The Torah reached the ultimate depth of idolatry, therefore the Torah have [the false prophet] rule over it,
	E.	"so that even if he should make the sun stand still for you in the midst of the firmament, you should not obey him."
	F.	*It has been taught on Tannaite authority:*
	G.	Said R. Aqiba, "Heaven forfend that the Holy One blessed be he should make the sun stand still in behalf of those who violate his will.
	H.	"But it would be like one such as Hananiah, son of Azur, who to begin with had been a true prophet but in the end became a false prophet."
IV.1	A.	**And those who bear false witness against a priest's daughter...[M. 10:F]:**
	B.	*What is the source in Scripture of this rule?*
	C.	*Said R. Aha, son of R. Iqa, "It is in accord with that which has been taught on Tannaite authority:*
	D.	"R. Yosé says, 'What is the meaning of the verse of Scripture, "Then you shall do to him as he had thought to have done to his brother" (Deut. 19:19)?
	E.	"'Since all those in the Torah who are proved to be a conspiracy of perjury, those who prove them to be perjured and lovers are treated as they are [that is, as are the perjured witnesses, so to the death they sought to impose on the women and the lovers to that of the women they had dishonored (Freedman, p. 600, n. 1)],
	F.	"'In the case of the priest's daughter, however, she is executed by burning, but her lover is not executed by burning.
	G.	"'As to perjured witnesses against her, therefore, I do not know whether they are linked to him or to her [and so made to suffer the death they had conspired to bring upon her or upon him].

H.   "'When Scripture says, "to have done to his brother," it teaches, "to his brother and not to his sister" [Freedman, p. 600, n .3: He is executed by her paramour's death, not her own].'"

The Talmud once more follows the Mishnah's topics, systematically and in order. Unit I deals with M. 10:5B-F; units II.1-3 with M. 10:5B, units III.1ff. with M. 10:5D, and IV.1 with M. 10:5F, as indicated. The work is orderly and sensible, and even secondary amplifications are given in a balanced and orderly manner.

11

Bavli Tractate Sanhedrin
Chapter Eleven
Folios 90A-113B

11:1-2

A. All Israelites have a share in the world to come,

B. as it is said, "your people also shall be all righteous, they shall inherit the land forever; the branch of my planting, the work of my hands, that I may be glorified" (Is. 60:21).

C. And these are the ones who have no portion in the world to come:

D. He who says, the resurrection of the dead is a teaching which does not derive from the Torah, and the Torah does not come from Heaven; and an Epicurean.

E. R. Aqiba says, "Also: He who reads in heretical books,

F. "and he who whispers over a wound and says, 'I will put none of the diseases upon you which I have put on the Egyptians, for I am the Lord who heals you' (Ex. 15:26)."

G. Abba Saul says, "Also: He who pronounces the divine Name as it is spelled out."

M. 11:1

A. Three kings and four ordinary folk have no portion in the world to come.

B. Three kings: Jeroboam, Ahab, and Manasseh.

C. R. Judah says, "Manasseh has a portion in the world to come,

D. "since it is said, 'And he prayed to him and he was entreated of him and heard his supplication and brought him again to Jerusalem into his kingdom' (2 Chr. 33:13)."

E. They said to him, "To his kingdom he brought him back, but to the life of the world to come he did not bring him back."

F. Four ordinary folk: Balaam, Doeg, Ahitophel, and Gehazi.

M. 11:2

I.1   A. Why all this [that is, why deny the world to come to those listed]?

477

B. On Tannaite authority [it was stated], "Such a one denied the resurrection of the dead, therefore he will not have a portion in the resurrection of the dead.

C. "For all the measures [meted out by] the Holy One, blessed be he, are in accord with the principle of measure for measure."

D. For R. Samuel bar Nahmani said R. Jonathan said, "How do we know that all the measures [meted out by] the Holy One, blessed be he, accord with the principle of measure for measure?

E. "As it is written, 'Then Elisha said, Hear you the word of the Lord. Thus says the Lord, Tomorrow about this time shall a measure of fine flour be sold for a shekel, and two measures of barley for a shekel in the gates of Samaria' (2 Kgs. 7:1).

F. "And it is written, 'Then a lord on whose hand the king leaned answered the man of God and said, Behold, if the Lord made windows in heaven, might this thing be? And he said, Behold, you shall see it with your eyes, but shall not eat thereof' (2 Kgs. 7:2).

G. [90B] "And it is written, 'And so it fell unto him; for the people trod him in the gate and he died' (2 Kgs. 7:20).

H. *But perhaps it was Elisha's curse that made it happen to him, for R. Judah said Rab said, "The curse of a sage, even for nothing, will come about"?*

I. *If so, Scripture should have said, "They trod upon him and he died." Why say, "They trod upon him in the gate"?*

J. It was that on account of matters pertaining to [the sale of wheat and barley at] the gate [which he had denied, that he died].

I.2 A. How, on the basis of the Torah, do we know about the resurrection of the dead?

B. As it is said, "And you shall give thereof the Lord's heave-offering to Aaron the priest" (Num. 18:28).

C. And will Aaron live forever? And is it not the case that he did not even get to enter the Land of Israel, from the produce of which heave-offering is given? [So there is no point in Aaron's life at which he would receive the priestly rations.]

D. Rather, this teaches that he is destined once more to live, and the Israelites will give him heave-offering.

E. On the basis of this verse, therefore, we see that the resurrection of the dead is a teaching of the Torah.

I.3 A. *A Tannaite authority of the house of R. Ishmael [taught], "' ... to Aaron ..., 'like Aaron. [That is to say,] just as Aaron was in the status of an associate [who ate his produce in a state of cultic cleanness even when not in the Temple], so his sons must be in the status of associates."*

B. Said R. Samuel bar Nahmani said R. Jonathan, "How on the basis of Scripture do we know that people do not give heave-offering to a priest who is in the status of an ordinary person [and not an associate]?

C.	"As it is said, 'Moreover he commanded the people who lived in Jerusalem to give the portion of the Levites, that they might hold fast to the Torah of the Lord' (2 Chr. 31:4).
D.	"Whoever holds fast to the Torah of the Lord has a portion, and whoever does not hold fast to the Torah of the Lord has no portion.:
E.	Said R. Aha bar Ada said R. Judah, "Whoever hands over heave-offering to a priest who is in the status of an ordinary person is as if he throws it in front of a lion.
F.	"Just as, in the case of a lion, it is a matter of doubt whether he will tear at the prey and eat it or not do so,
G.	"so in the case of a priest who is in the status of an ordinary person, it is a matter of doubt whether he will eat it in a condition of cultic cleanness or eat it in a condition of cultic uncleanness."
H.	R. Yohanan said, "[if one gives it to an improper priest], he also causes him to die, for it is said, 'And ... die therefore if they profane it' (Lev. 22:9).
I.	*The Tannaite authority of the house of R. Eliezer B. Jacob [taught],* "One also gets him involved in the sin of guilt [of various kinds], for it is written, 'Or suffer them to bear the iniquity of trespass when they eat their holy things' (Lev. 22:16)."

I.4	A.	*It has been taught on Tannaite authority:*
	B.	R. Simai says, "How on the basis of the Torah do we know about the resurrection of the dead?
	C.	"As it is said, 'And I also have established my covenant with [the patriarchs] to give them the land of Canaan' (Ex. 6:4).
	D.	"'With you' is not stated, but rather, 'with them,' indicating on the basis of the Torah that there is the resurrection of the dead."
I.5	A.	Minim asked Rabban Gamaliel, "How do we know that the Holy One, blessed be he, will resurrect the dead?"
	B.	He said to them, "It is proved from the Torah, from the Prophets, and from the Writings." But they did not accept his proofs.
	C.	"From the Torah: for it is written, 'And the Lord said to Moses, Behold, you shall sleep with your fathers and rise up' (Deut. 31:16)."
	D.	*They said to him, "But perhaps the sense of the passage is, '*And the people will rise up' (Deut. 31:16)?"
	E.	"From the Prophets: as it is written, 'Thy dead men shall live, together with my dead body they shall arise. Awake and sing, you that live in the dust, for your dew is as the dew of herbs, and the earth shall cast out its dead' (Is. 26:19)."
	F.	*"But perhaps that refers to the dead whom Ezekiel raised up."*
	G.	"From the Writings, as it is written, 'And the roof of your mouth, like the best wine of my beloved, that goes down sweetly, causing the lips of those who are asleep to speak' (Song 7:9)."
	H.	*"But perhaps this means that the dead will move their lips?"*
	I.	*That would accord with the view of R. Yohanan.*

J.   For R. Yohanan said in the name of R. Simeon b. Yehosedeq, "Any authority in whose name a law is stated in this world moves his lips in the grave,

K.   "as it is said, 'Causing the lips of those that are asleep to speak.'"

L.   [The minim would not concur in Gamaliel's view] until he cited for them the following verse: "'Which the Lord swore to your fathers to give to them' (Deut. 11:21) – to them and not to you, so proving from the Torah that the dead will live."

M.   And there are those who say that it was the following verse that he cited to them: "'But you who cleaved to the Lord you God are alive, everyone of you this day' (Deut. 4:4). Just as on this day all of you are alive, so in the world to come all of you will live."

I.6 A.   Romans asked R. Joshua b. Hananiah, "How do we know that the Holy One will bring the dead to life and also that he knows what is going to happen in the future?"

B.   *He said to them, "Both propositions derive from the following verse of Scripture:*

C.   "As it is said, 'And the Lord said to Moses, Behold you shall sleep with you fathers and rise up again, and this people shall go awhoring ...' (Deut. 31:16)."

D.   "But perhaps the sense is, '[the people] will rise up and go awhoring'

E.   *He said to them, "Then you have gained half of the matter, that God knows what is going to happen in the future."*

I.7 A.   *It has also been stated on Amoraic authority:*

B.   Said R. Yohanan in the name of R. Simeon b. Yohai, "How do we know that the Holy One, blessed be he, will bring the dead to life and knows what is going to happen in the future?

C.   "As it is said, 'Behold, you shall sleep with you fathers, and ... rise again ... (Deut. 31:16)."

I.8 A.   *It has been taught on Tannaite authority:*

B.   Said R. Eliezer b. R. Yosé, "In this matter I proved false the books of the minim.

C.   "For they would say, 'The principle of the resurrection of the dead does not derive from the Torah.'

D.   "I said to them , 'You have forged your Torah and have gained nothing on that account.

E.   "'For you say, "The principle of the resurrection of the dead does not derive from the Torah."

F.   "'Lo, Scripture says, "[Because he has despised the Lord of the Lord ...] that soul shall be cut off completely, his iniquity shall be upon him" (Num. 15:31).

G.   "'"... shall be utterly cut off ...," in this world, in which case, at what point will "... his iniquity be upon him ..."?

H.   "'Will it not be in the world to come?'"

I.   *Said R. Pappa to Abbayye, "And might one not have replied to them that the words 'utterly ...' '... cut off ...,' signify the two worlds [this and the next]?"*

	J.	*[He said to him,]* "They would have answered, 'The Torah speaks in human language [and the doubling of the verb carries no meaning beyond its normal sense].'"
I.9	A.	*This accords with the following Tannaite dispute:*
	B.	"'That soul shall be utterly cut off' – 'shall be cut off' – in this world, 'utterly' – in the world to come," the words of R. Aqiba.
	C.	Said R. Ishmael to him, "And has it not been said, 'He reproaches the Lord, and that soul shall be cut off' (Num. 15:31). Does this mean that there are three worlds?
	D.	"Rather: '… it will be cut off …,' in this world, '… utterly …,' in the world to come, and 'utterly cut off …,' indicates that the Torah speaks in ordinary human language."
	E.	*Whether from the view of R. Ishmael or of R. Aqiba, what is the meaning of the phrase,* "His iniquity shall be upon him"?
	F.	*It accords with that which has been taught on Tannaite authority:*
	G.	Is it possible that that is the case even if he repented?
	H.	Scripture states, "His iniquity shall be upon him."
	I.	I have made the statement at hand only for a case in which "his iniquity is yet upon him" [but not if he repented].
I.10	A.	*Queen Cleopatra asked R. Meir, saying, "I know that the dead will live, for it is written, 'And [the righteous] shall blossom forth out of your city like the grass of the earth' (Ps. 72:16).*
	B.	"But when they rise, will they rise naked or in their clothing?"
	C.	He said to her, "It is an argument a fortiori based on the grain of wheat.
	D.	"Now if a grain of wheat, which is buried naked, comes forth in many garments, the righteous, who are buried in their garments, all the more so [will rise in many garments]!"
I.11	A.	*Caesar said to Rabban Gamaliel, "You maintain that the dead will live. But they are dust, and can the dust live?"*
	B.	**[91A]** *His daughter said to him, "Allow me to answer him:*
	C.	"There are two potters in our town, one who works with water, the other who works with clay. Which is the more impressive?"
	D.	He said to her, "The one who works with water."
	E.	She said to him, "If he works with water, will he not create even more out of clay?"
I.12	A.	*A Tannaite authority of the house of R. Ishmael [taught],* "[Resurrection] is a matter of an argument a fortiori based on the case of a glass utensil.
	B.	"Now if glassware, which is the work of the breath of a mortal man, when broken, can be repaired,
	C.	"A mortal man, who is made by the breath of the Holy One, blessed be he, how much the more so [that he can be repaired, in the resurrection of the dead]."
I.13	A.	*A min said to R. Ammi, "You say that the dead will live. But they are dust, and will the dust live?"*

B.   He said to him, "I shall draw a parable for you. To what may the matter be compared?

C.   "It may be compared to the case of a mortal king, who said to his staff, 'Go and build a great palace for me, in a place in which there is no water or dirt [for bricks].

D.   "They went and built it, but after a while it collapsed.

E.   "He said to them, 'Go and rebuild it in a place in which there are dirt and water [for bricks].'

F.   "They said to him, 'We cannot do so.'

G.   "He became angry with them and said to them, 'In a place in which there is neither water nor dirt you were able to build, and now in a place in which there are water and dirt, how much the more so [should you be able to build it]!'

H.   "And if you [the min] do not believe it, go to a valley and look at a rat, which today is half-flesh and half-dirt and tomorrow will turn into a creeping thing, made all of flesh. Will you say that it takes much time? Then go up to a mountain and see that today there is only one snail, but tomorrow it will rain and the whole of it will be filled with snails."

I.14   A.   *A min said to Gebiha, son of Pesisa, [a hunchback,] "Woe for you! You are guilty! For you say that the dead will live. Those who are alive die, and will those who are dead live?"*

B.   *He said to him, "Woe for you! You are guilty! For you say that the dead will not live. [Now if we] who were not [alive before birth] now live, will not those who do live all the more so [live again]?"*

C.   *He said to him, "Have you then called me guilty? If I stood up, I could kick you and straighten out your hump."*

D.   *He said to him, "If you could do that, you would be a physician, a specialist who collects enormous fees."*

Topical Appendix on Gebiha, son of Pasisa and Alexander the Great

I.15   A.   *Our rabbis have taught on Tannaite authority:*

B.   *On the twenty-four of Nisan the tax-farmers were dismissed from Judea and Jerusalem.*

C.   When the Africans came to trial with Israel before Alexander of Macedonia, they said to him, "The land of Canaan belongs to us, for it is written, 'The land of Canaan, with the coasts thereof' (Num. 34:2), and Canaan was the father of these men."

D.   Said Gebiha, son of Pasisa, to sages, "Give me permission, and I shall go and defend the case with them before Alexander of Macedonia. If they should win out over me, say, 'You won over a perfectly common person of our group,' and if I should win out over them, say to them, 'It is the Torah of Moses that overcame you.'"

E.   They gave him permission, and he went and engaged in debate with them. He said to them, "From whence do you bring proof?"

F.   They said to him, "From the Torah."

	G.	He said to them, "I too shall bring you proof only from the Torah, for it is said, 'And he said, Cursed be Canaan, a servant of servants shall he be to his brothers' (Gen. 9:25).
	H.	"Now if a slave acquires property, for whom does he acquire it? And to whom is the property assigned?
	I.	"And not only so, but it is quite a number of years since you have served us."
	J.	Said King Alexander to them, "Give him an answer."
	K.	They said to him, "Give us a span of three days time." He gave them time.
	L.	They searched and did not find an answer. They forthwith fled, leaving their fields fully sown and their vineyards laden with fruit, and that year was the Sabbatical Year. [So the Israelites could enjoy the produce in a time in which they most needed it.]
I.16	A.	There was another time, [and] the Egyptians came to lay claim against Israel before Alexander of Macedonia. They said to him, "Lo, Scripture says, 'And the Lord gave the people favor in the sight of the Egyptians, and they lent them gold and precious stones' (Ex. 12:36). Give us back the silver and gold that you took from us."
	B.	Said Gebiha, son of Pasisa, to sages, "Give me permission, and I shall go and defend the case with them before Alexander of Macedonia. If they should win out over me, say, 'You won over a perfectly common person of our group,' and if I should win out over them, say to them, 'It is the Torah of Moses, our master, that overcame you.'"
	C.	They gave him permission, and he went and engaged in debate with them. He said to them, "From whence do you bring proof?"
	D.	They said to him, "From the Torah."
	E.	He said to them , "I too shall bring you proof only from the Torah, for it is said, 'Now the sojourning of the children of Israel, who dwelt in Egypt, was four hundred and thirty years' (Ex. 12:40).
	F.	"Now pay us the salary of six hundred thousand people whom you enslaved in Egypt for four hundred and thirty years."
	G.	Said Alexander of Macedonia to them, "Give him an answer."
	H.	They said to him, "Give us time, a span of three days."
	I.	He gave them time. They searched and found no answer. They forthwith fled, leaving their fields sown and their vineyards laden with fruit, and that year was the Sabbatical Year.
I.17	A.	There was another time, [and] the children of Ishmael and the children of Keturah came to trial with the Israelites before Alexander of Macedonia. They said to him, "The land of Canaan belongs to us as well as to you, for it is written, 'Now these the generations of Ishmael, son of Abraham' (Gen. 25:12), and it is written, 'And these are the

generations of Isaac, Abraham's son' (Gen. 25:19). [Both Ishmael and Isaac have an equal claim on the land, hence so too their descendants]."

B.   Said Gebiha, son of Pasisa, to sages, "Give me permission, and I shall go and defend the case with them before Alexander of Macedonia. If they should win out over me, say, 'You won over a perfectly common person of our group,' and if I should win out over them, say to them, 'It is the Torah of Moses, our master, that overcame you.'"

C.   They gave him permission, and he went and engaged in debate with them. He said to them, "From whence do you bring proof?'

D.   They said to him, "From the Torah."

E.   He said to them, "I too shall bring you proof only from the Torah, for it is said, 'And Abraham gave all that he had to Isaac. But to the sons of the concubines which Abraham had Abraham gave gifts' (Gen. 25:5-6).

F.   "In the case of a father who gave a bequest to his sons while he was yet alive and sent them away from one another, does any one of them have a claim on the other? [Certainly not.]"

G.   *What were the gifts [that he gave]?*

H.   Said R. Jeremiah bar Abba, "This teaches that he gave them [the power of utilizing the divine] Name [for] unclean [purposes]."

Topical Appendix on Antoninus and Rabbi

I.18   A.   Antoninus said to Rabbi, "The body and the soul both can exempt themselves from judgment.

B.   "How so? The body will say, 'The soul is the one that has sinned, for from the day that it left me, lo, I am left like a silent stone in the grave.'

C.   "And the soul will say, 'The body is the one that sinned. For from the day that I left it, lo, I have been flying about in the air like a bird.'"

D.   He said to him, "I shall draw a parable for you. To what may the matter be likened? To the case of a mortal king who had a lovely orchard, and in it were **[91B]** luscious figs. He set in it two watchmen, one crippled and one blind.

E.   "Said the cripple to the blind man, 'There are luscious figs that I see in the orchard. Come and carry me, and let us get some to eat. The cripple rode on the blind man and they got the figs and ate them. After a while the king said to them, 'Where are the luscious figs?'

F.   "Said the cripple, 'Do I have feet to go to them?'

G.   "Said the blind man, 'Do I have eyes to see?'

H.   "What did the king do? He had the cripple climb onto the blind man, and he inflicted judgment on them as one.

I.   "So the Holy One, blessed be he, brings the soul and places it back in the body and judges them as one, as it is said, 'He shall call to the

    heavens from above and to the earth, that he may judge his people'
(Ps. 50:4).

J.   "'He shall to call to the heavens from above' – this is the soul.

K.   "'And to the earth, that he may judge his people' – this is the body."

I.19 A.   Said Antoninus to Rabbi, "Why does the sun rise in the east and set in the west?"

B.   *He said to him, "If thing were opposite, you would still ask me the same thing!"*

C.   *He said to him, "This is what I meant to ask you:* Why does it set in the west?"

D.   He said, "To give a greeting to its maker, as it is written, 'And the host of the heavens make obeisance to you' (Neh. 9:6)..."

E.   *He said to him, "Then let it go half way through the firmament, pay its respects, and then ascend from there [eastward]."*

F.   "It is because of workers and wayfarers [who need to know when the day is over]."

I.20 A.   Said Antoninus to Rabbi, "At what point is the soul placed in man? Is it at the moment that it is decreed [that the person shall be born] or when the embryo is formed?"

B.   He said to him, "From the moment when it is formed."

C.   He said to him, "Is it possible that a piece of flesh should keep for three days of it is not salted and not become rotten?

D.   "Rather, it should be from the time at which it is decreed [that the person should come into being."

E.   Said Rabbi, "This is something that Antoninus taught me, and a verse of Scripture supports his view, for it is said, 'And your decree has preserved my soul' (Job 10:12)."

I.21 A.   And Antoninus said to Rabbi, "At what point does the impulse to do evil take hold of a man? Is it from the moment of creation or from the moment of parturition?"

B.   He said to him, "It is from the moment of creation."

C.   He said to him, "If so, the fetus will kick its mother's womb and escape. Rather, it is from the moment of parturition."

D.   Said Rabbi, "This is something that Antoninus taught me, and a verse of Scripture supports his view, for it is said, 'At the door [of the womb] sin lies in wait' (Gen. 4:7)."

Contrasting Verses of Scripture and the Death of Death

I.22 A.   *R. Simeon b. Laqish contrasted [these two verses]:* "It is written, 'I will gather them ... with the blind and the lame, the woman with child and her that trail travails with child together' (Jer. 31:8), and it is written, 'Then shall the lame man leap as a hart and the tongue of the dumb sing, for in the wilderness shall waters break out and streams in the desert' (Is. 35:6). *How so [will the dead both retain their defects and also be healed]?*

B.   "They will rise [from the grave] bearing their defects and then be healed."

I.23 A.   *Ulla contrasted [these two verses]:* "It is written, 'He will destroy death forever and the Lord God will wipe away tears from all faces' (Is.

25:9), and it is written, 'For the child shall die a hundred years old ... there shall no more thence an infant of days' (Is. 65:20).

B. *"There is no contradiction. The one speaks of Israel, the other of idolators."*

C. *But what do idolators want there* [Freedman, p. 612, n. 9: in the reestablished state after the resurrection]?

D. It is to those concerning whom it is written, "And strangers shall stand and feed your flocks, and the sons of the alien shall be your plowmen and your vinedressers" (Is. 61:5)."

I.24 A. *R. Hisda contrasted [these two verses]: "It is written,* 'Then the moon shall be confounded and the sun ashamed, when the Lord of hosts shall reign' (Is 24:23), *and it is written,* 'Moreover the light of the moon shall be as the light of seven days' (Is 30:26).

B. *"There is no contradiction. The one refers to the days of the Messiah, the other to the world to come."*

C. *And in the view of Samuel, who has said, "There is no difference between the world to come and the days of the messiah, except the end of the subjugation of the exilic communities of Israel"?*

D. *There still is no contradiction. The one speaks of the camp of the righteous, the other the camp of the Presence of God.*

I.25 A. *Raba contrasted [these two verses]: "It is written,* 'I kill and I make alive' (Deut. 32:"39) *and it is written,* 'I wound and I heal' (Deut. 32:39). [Freedman, p. 613, n. 4, 5: The former implies that one is resurrected just as he was at death, thus with blemishes, and the other implies that at the resurrection all wounds are healed].

B. "Said the Holy One, blessed be he, 'What I kill I bring to life,' and then, 'What I have wounded I heal.'"

How on the basis of the Torah
do we know about the resurrection of the dead?

I.26 A. *Our rabbis have taught on Tannaite authority:* "I kill and I make alive" (Deut. 32:39)."

B. Is it possible to suppose that there is death for one person and life for the other, just as the world is accustomed [now]?

C. Scripture says, "I wound and I heal" (Deut. 32:39).

D. Just as wounding and healing happen to one person, so death and then resurrection happen to one person.

E. From this fact we derive an answer to those who say, "There is no evidence of the resurrection of the dead based on the teachings of the Torah."

I.27 A. *It has been taught on Tannaite authority:*

B. R. Meir says, "How on the basis of the Torah do we know about the resurrection of the dead?

C. "As it is said, 'Then shall Moses and the children of Israel sing this song to the Lord' (Ex. 15:1).

D. "What is said is not 'sang' but 'will sing,' on the basis of which there is proof from the Torah of the resurrection of the dead.

E. "Along these same lines: 'Then shall Joshua build an altar to the Lord God of Israel' (Josh. 8:30).

F. "What is said is not 'built' but 'will build,' on the basis of which there is proof from the Torah of the resurrection of the dead.

G. *Then what about this verse:* "Then will Solomon build a high place for Chemosh, abomination of Moab" (1 Kgs.. 11:7)? *Does it mean that he will build it?* Rather, the Scripture treats him as though he had built it [even though he had merely thought about doing so].

I.28 A. Said R. Joshua b. Levi, "How on the basis of Scripture may we prove the resurrection of the dead?

B. "As it is said, 'Blessed are those who dwell in your house, they shall ever praise you, selah' (Ps. 84:5).

C. "What is said is not 'praised you' but 'shall praise you,' on the basis of which there is proof from the Torah of the resurrection of the dead."

D. And R. Joshua b. Levi said, "Whoever recites the song [of praise] in this world will have the merit of saying it in the world to come,

E. "as it is said, 'Happy are those who dwell in you house, they shall ever praise you, selah' (Ps. 84:5)."

F. Said R. Hiyya b. Abba said R. Yohanan, "On what basis do we know about the resurrection of the dead from Scripture."

G. "As it says, 'Your watchman shall lift up the voice, with the voice together they shall sing (Is. 52:8).'"

H. What is said is not 'sang' but 'will sing' on the basis of which there is proof from the Torah of the resurrection of the dead.

I. Said R. Yohanan, "In the future all the prophets will sing in unison, as it is written, 'Your watchman shall lift up the voice, with the voice together they shall sing (Is. 57:8).'"

I.29 A. Said R. Judah said Rab, "Whoever withholds a teaching of law from a disciple is as if he steals the inheritance of his fathers from him,

B. "for it is said, 'Moses commanded us Torah, even the inheritance of the congregation of Jacob' (Deut. 33:4).

C. "It is an inheritance destined for all Israel from the six days of creation."

D. Said R. Hana bar Bizna said R. Simeon the Pious, "Whoever withholds a teaching of law from a disciple is cursed even by the fetuses in their mothers' womb, as it is said, 'He who withholds grain **[92A]** will be cursed by the embryo' (Prov. 11:26), for the word at hand can only mean 'embryo,' as it is written, 'And one embryo shall be stronger than the other people' (Gen. 25:23) [referring to Jacob and Esau in the womb].

E. "And the cited word can only mean 'cursing,' as it is written, 'How shall a curse whom God has not cursed?' (Num. 23:8).

F. "And the word for grain speaks only of 'the Torah,' as it is written, 'Nourish yourselves with grain lest he be angry' (Ps. 2:12)."

G. Ulla bar Ishmael says, "They pierce him like a sieve, for here it is written, 'The people will pierce him,' (Prov. 11:26), and the word means pierce in the verse, 'And he pierced a hole in the lid of it' (2 Kgs. 12:10)."

H. *And Abbayye said, "He will be like a fuller's trough [so perforated as a drainage plank]."*

I. And if he does teach a law, what is his reward?

J.   Said Raba said R. Sheshet, "He will merit blessings like those that came to Joseph, as it is said, 'But blessing shall be upon the head of the one who sells' (Prov. 11:26).

K.   "And the one who sells speaks only of Joseph, as it is said, 'And Joseph was the governor over the land, and he was the one who sells to all the people of the land' (Gen. 47:6)."

I.30   A.   Said R. Sheshet, "Whoever teaches Torah in this world will have the merit of teaching it in the world to come,

B.   "as it is said, 'And he who waters shall water again too' (Prov. 11:25)."

I.31   A.   Said Raba, "How on the basis of the Torah do we find evidence for the resurrection of the dead?

B.   "As it is said, 'Let Reuben live and not die' (Deut. 33:6).

C.   "'Let Reuben live' in this world, and 'not die', in the world to come."

D.   *Rabina said, "Proof derives from here:* 'And many of them that sleep in the dust of the earth shall awake, some to everlasting life, and some to shame and everlasting contempt.' (Den. 12:2)."

E.   *R. Ashi said, "Proof derives from here:* 'But go your way till the end be, for you shall rest and stand in your lot at the end of days' (Dan. 12:13)."

I.32   A.   Said R. Eleazar, "Every authority who leads the community serenely will have the merit of leading them in the world to come, as it is said, 'For he who has mercy on them shall lead them, even by springs of water shall he guide them' (Is. 49:10)."

B.   And said R. Eleazar, "Great is knowledge, for it is set between two names [lit. letters] [of God], as it is written, 'For a God of knowledge is the Lord' (1 Sam. 2:3)."

C.   And said R. Eleazar, "Great is the sanctuary, for it is set between two names [of God], as it is written, 'You have made for yourself, O Lord, a sanctuary, O Lord, your hands have established it' (Ex. 15:17)."

D.   *To this view R. Ada Qarhinaah objected,* "Then how about the following: Great is vengeance, for it is set between two names [of God], as it is written, 'O God of vengeance, O Lord, O God of Vengeance, appear' (Ps. 94:1)."

E.   *He said to him, "In context, that is quite so, in line with what Ulla said."*

F.   For Ulla said, "What purpose is served by these two references to 'appear'? One speaks of the measure of good, the other, the measure of punishment."

G.   And said R. Eleazar, "In the case of any man who has knowledge it is as if the house of the sanctuary had been built in his own time, for this [knowledge] is set between two names of [God], and that [the Temple] likewise is set between two names of [God]."

H.   And said R. Eleazar, "Any man in whom there is knowledge in the end will be rich, for it is said, 'And by knowledge shall the chambers be filled with all precious and pleasant riches' (Prov. 24:4)."

I. And said R. Eleazar, "It is forbidden to have pity on any man in whom there is no knowledge, as it is said, 'For it is a people of no understanding; therefore he that made them will not have mercy upon them, and he that formed them will show them no favor' (Is. 27:11)."

J. And said R. Eleazar, "Whoever gives his bread to someone who does not have knowledge in the end will be afflicted with sufferings, for it is said, 'They who eat your bread have laid a wound under you, there is no understanding in him' (Obad. 1:7), and the word for 'wound' can mean only suffering, as it is written, 'When Ephraim saw his sickness and Judah his suffering' [using the same word] (Hos. 5:13)."

K. And said R. Eleazar, "Any man who has no knowledge in the end will go into exile, as it is said, 'Therefore my people have gone into exile, because they have no knowledge' (Is. 5:13)."

L. And said R. Eleazar, "Any house in which words of Torah are not heard by night will be eaten up by fire, as it is said, 'All darkness is hid in his secret places; a fire not blown shall consume him; he grudges him that is left in his tabernacle' (Job 20:26).

M. "The word for 'grudges' means only a disciple of a sage, as it is written, 'And in those left [using the same root] whom the Lord shall call' (Joel 3:5). [Freedman, p. 616, n. 12: The first part of the verse, 'all darkness is hid ...,' is interpreted as, his secret places are not illumined by the study of the law; the last part, 'he grudges ...,' as, he looks with disfavor upon any student who enters his house for a meal]."

N. And said R. Eleazar, "Whoever does not give a benefit to disciples of sages from his property will see no blessing ever, as it is said, 'There is none who remains to eat it, therefore shall he not hope for prosperity' (Job 20:21).

O. "The word for 'remain' refers only to a disciple of a sage, as it is written, 'And in those left whom the Lord shall call' (Joel 3:5)."

P. And said R. Eleazar, "Anyone who does not leave a piece of bread on his table will never see a sign of blessing, as it is said, 'There be none of his food left, therefore shall he not hope for his prosperity'(Job 20:21)."

Q. But has not R. Eleazar said, "Whoever leaves pieces of bread on his table is as if he worships an idol, as it is said, 'That prepare a table for God and that furnish the drink offering to Meni' (Is. 65:11)"?

R. *There is no contradiction, in the one case [the latter] a complete loaf is left alongside, and in the other case [the former], no complete loaf is left [with the crumbs].*

S. And said R. Eleazar, "Whoever goes back on what he has said is as if he worships an idol.

T. "Here it is written, 'And I seem to him as a deceiver' (Gen. 27:12), and elsewhere it is written, 'They [idols] are vanity and the work of deceivers' (Jer. 10:15)."

U.   And said R. Eleazar, "Whoever stares at a woman's sexual parts will find that his 'bow' is emptied out, as it is said, 'Shame shall empty you bow [of strength]' (Hab. 3:9)."

V.   And said R. Eleazar, "One should always accept [things] and so endure."

W.   *Said R. Zira, "We too also have learned on Tannaite authority:*

X.   **"As to a room without windows, people are not to open windows for it to examine whether or not it is afflicted with a plague-sign [M. Neg. 2:3].** [Thus the possible signs will be missed because of the obscurity of the room. Likewise humility protects one's life.]"

Y.   *That makes the case.*

I.33   A.   *Said R. Tabi said R. Josiah, "What is the meaning of this verse of Scripture: 'The grave and the barren womb and the earth that is not filled by water' (Prov. 30:16).*

B.   "What has the grave to do with the womb?

C.   "It is to say to you, just as the womb takes in and gives forth, so Sheol takes in and gives forth.

D.   "And is it not an argument a fortiori? If in the case of the womb, in which they insert [something] in secret, the womb brings forth in loud cries, Sheol, into which [bodies] are placed with loud cries, is it not reasonable to suppose that from the grave people will be brought forth with great cries?

E.   "On the basis of this argument there is an answer to those who say that the doctrine of the resurrection of the dead does not derive from the Torah."

I.34   A.   *A Tannaite authority of the house of Elisha [taught],* "The righteous whom the Holy One, blessed be he, is going to resurrect will not revert to dust,

B.   "for it is said, 'And it shall come to pass that he that is left in Zion and he that remains in Jerusalem shall be called holy, even everyone that is written among the living in Jerusalem, (Is. 4:3).

C.   "Just as the Holy One lives forever, so they shall live forever.

D.   [92B] "And if you want to ask, as to those years in which the Holy One, blessed be he, will renew his world, as it is said, 'And the Lord alone shall be exalted in that day' (Is. 2:11), during that time what will the righteous do?

E.   "The answer is that the Holy One, blessed be he, will make them wings like eagles, and they will flutter above the water, as it is said, 'Therefore will not fear, when the earth be moved and the mountains be carried in the midst of the sea' (Ps. 44:3).

F.   "And if you should say that they will have pain [in all this], Scripture says, 'But those who wait upon the Lord shall renew their strength, they shall mount up with wings as eagles, they shall run and not be weary, they shall walk and not be faint' (Is. 40:31)."

G.   *And should we derive [the opposite view] from the dead whom Ezekiel resurrected?*

H.   *He accords with the view of him who said that, in truth, it was really a parable.*

I.   *For it has been taught on Tannaite authority:*

J.	R. Eliezer says, "The dead whom Ezekiel resurrected stood on their feet, recited a song, and they died.
K.	"What song did they recite?
L.	"'The Lord kills in righteousness and revives in mercy' (1 Sam. 2:6)."
M.	R. Joshua says, "They recited this song, 'The Lord kills and makes live, he brings down to the grave and brings up' (1 Sam. 2:6)."
N.	R. Judah says, "It was truly a parable."
O.	Said to him R. Nehemiah, "If it was true, then why a parable? And if a parable, why true? But in truth it was a parable."
P.	R. Eliezer, son of R. Yosé the Galilean, says, "The dead whom Ezekiel resurrected went up to the Land of Israel and got married and produced sons and daughters."
Q.	R. Judah b. Betera stood up and said, "I am one of their grandsons, and theses are the phylacteries that father's father left me from them."
R.	*And who were the dead whom Ezekiel resurrected?*
S.	Said Rab, "They were the Ephraimites who reckoned the end of time and erred, as it is said, 'And the sons of Ephraim, Shuthelah and Bared his son and Tahath his son and Eladah his son and Tahath his son. And Zabad his son and Shuthelah his son and Ezzer and Elead, whom the men of Gath that were born in the land slew' (1 Chr. 7:20-21). And it is written, 'And Ephraim their father mourned many days and his brethren came to comfort him' (1 Chr. 7:22)."
T.	And Samuel said, "They were those who denied the resurrection of the dead, as it is said, 'Then he said to me, Son of man, these bones are the whole house of Israel; behold, they say, Our bones are dried and our hope is lost, we are cut off for our parts' (Ez. 37:11)."
U.	Said R. Jeremiah, "These were the men who had not a drop of religious duties to their credit, as it is written, 'O you dry bones, hear the word of the Lord' (Ez. 37:4)."
V.	R. Isaac Nappaha said, "They were the men who had covered the sanctuary entirely with abominations and creeping things, as it is said, 'So I went in and saw, and behold, every form of creeping things and abominable beasts and all the idols of the house of Israel, portrayed upon the wall round about' (Ez. 8:10).
W.	"While [in the case of the dry bones] it is written, 'And caused me to pass by them round about' (Ez. 37:2). [Freedman, p. 620, n. 1: The identification is based on the use of 'round about' in both narratives. In his view even those who in their despair surrender themselves to abominable worship are not excluded from the bliss of resurrection.]"
X.	R. Yohanan said, "They were the dead in the valley of Dura."

Y.   And said R. Yohanan, "From the river Eshel to Rabbath is the valley of Dura. For when Nebuchadnezzar, that wicked man, exiled Israel, there were young men who outshone the sun in their beauty. Chaldean women would see them and reach orgasm [from the mere gaze]. They told their husbands and their husbands told the king. The king ordered them killed. Still, the wives would reach orgasm [merely from laying eyes on the corpses]. The king gave an order and they trampled [the corpses beyond all recognition]."

I.35 A.   *Our rabbis have taught on Tannaite authority:*

B.   When Nebuchadnezzar, the wicked man, cast Hananiah, Mishael, and Azariah, into the fiery furnace, the Holy One, blessed be he, said to Ezekiel, "Go and raise the dead in the valley of Dura."

C.   When he had raised them, the bones came and smacked that wicked man in his face. He said, "What are these things?"

D.   They said to him, "The friend of these is raising the dead in the valley of Dura."

E.   He then said, "'How great are his signs, and how mighty his wonders. His kingdom is an everlasting kingdom, and his dominion is from generation to generation' (Dan. 3:23)."

F.   Said R. Isaac, "May liquid gold pour into the mouth of that wicked man.

G.   "For had not an angel come and slapped his mouth shut, he would have attempted to shame [by the excellence of his composition] all the songs and praises that David had recited in the book of Psalms."

Topical Appendix on Hananiah, Mishael, and Azariah

I.36 A.   *Our rabbis have taught on Tannaite authority:*

B.   Six miracles were done on that day, and these are they:

C.   the furnace floated, the furnace split open, the foundations crumbled, the image was turned over on its face, the four kings were burned up, and Ezekiel raised the dead in the valley of Dura.

D.   *And all of the others were a matter of tradition,* but the [miracle of the] four kings is indicated in a verse of Scripture: "Then Nebuchadnezzar the king sent to gather together the princes, the governors, and the captains, the judges, the treasurers, the counsellors, the sheriffs, and all the rulers of the provinces [to come to the dedication of the image]" (Dan. 3:2),

E.   and it is written, "There are certain Jews ..." (Deut. 3:2),

F.   and also: "And the princes, governors, and captains, and the king's counsellors, being gathered together, saw these men, upon whom the fire had no power" (Dan. 3:27).

I.37   A.   *A Tannaite authority of the house of R. Eliezer b. Jacob [taught],* "Even in time of danger a person should not pretend that he does not hold his high office,

B.   "For it is said, 'Then these men were bound in their coats, their hose, and their other garments' (Dan. 3:21). [Freedman, p. 621, n. 8: These were garments specially worn by men in their exalted position, and they did not doff them though cast into the furnace.]"

I.38   A.   Said R. Yohanan, "**[93A]** The righteous are greater than ministering angels.

B.   "For it is said, 'He answered and said, Lo, I see four men loose, walking in the midst of the fire, and they are not hurt, and the form of the fourth is like the son of God' (Dan. 3:25) [Freedman, p. 621, n. 9: Thus the angel is mentioned last, as being least esteemed]."

I.39   A.   Said R. Tanhum bar Hanilai, "When Hananiah, Mishael, and Azariah went out of the fiery furnace, all the nations of the world came and slapped the enemies of Israel [that is, Israel] on their faces.

B.   "They said to them, 'You have a god such as this, and yet you bow down to an idol!'

C.   "Forthwith they said this verse, 'O Lord, righteousness belongs to you, but to us shamefacedness, as at this day' (Dan. 9:7).:

I.40   A.   *Said R. Samuel bar Nahmani said R. Jonathan,* "What is the meaning of the verse of Scripture, 'I said, I will go up to the palm tree, I will take hold of the boughs thereof' (Song 7:9)?

B.   "'I said I will go up to the palm tree' refers to Israel.

C.   "But now 'I grasped' only one bough, namely, Hananiah, Mishael and Azariah."

I.41   A.   *And said R. Yohanan,* "What is the meaning of the verse of Scripture, 'I saw by night, and behold a man riding upon a red horse, and he stood among the myrtle trees that were in the bottom' (Zech. 1:8).?

B.   What is the meaning of, 'I saw by night'?

C.   "The Holy One blessed be he, sought to turn the entire world into night.

D.   "'And behold, a man riding' – 'man' refers only to the Holy One, blessed be he, as it is said, 'The Lord is a man of war, the Lord is his name' (Ex. 15:3).

E.   "'On a red horse' – the Holy One, blessed be he, sought to turn the entire world to blood.

F.   "When, however, he saw Hananiah, Mishael, and Azariah, he cooled off, as it is said, 'And he stood among the myrtle trees that were in the deep.'

G.   "The word for 'myrtle trees' speaks only of the righteous as it is written, 'And he brought up the myrtle' (Est. 2:7) [another name of Esther].

H.   "And the word for 'deep' speaks only of Babylonia, as it is said, 'That says to the deep, be dry, and I will dry up your rivers' (Is. 44:27) [Freedman, p. 622, n. 11: To Babylon, situated in a hollow].

I.   "Forthwith, those who were filled with [red] anger turned pale, and those who were red turned white [in serenity]."

J.   *Said R. Pappa, "Those proves that a white horse in a dream is a good thing."*

I.42   A.   *The rabbis [Hananiah, Mishael, and Azariah] – where did they go?*

B.   Said Rab, "They died through the working of the evil eye."

C.   And Samuel said, "They drowned in spit."

D.   And R. Yohanan, said, "They went up to the land of Israel, got married, and produced sons and daughters."

E.   *This accords with a Tannaite dispute on the same issue:*

F.   R. Eliezer says, "They died through the working of the evil eye."

G.   R. Joshua says, "They drowned in spit.

H.   And sages say, "They went up to the land of Israel, got married, and produced sons and daughters, as it is said, 'Hear now, Joshua, the high priest, and your fellows who sit before you, for they are men wondered at' (Zech. 3:8).

I.   "Who are men who are wondered at? One must say, This refers to Hananiah, Mishael, and Azariah."

J.   *And where did Daniel go?*

K.   *Said Rab, "To dig a large well at Tiberias."*

L.   *And Samuel said, "To buy fodder."*

M.   *R. Yohanan said, "To buy pigs in Alexandria, Egypt."*

N.   *Can this be true?*

O.   *And have we not learned in the Mishnah:* **Todos the physician said, "A cow or a pig does not leave Alexandria, Egypt, out of which they do not cut its womb, so that it will not breed"** [M. San. 4:4].

P.   *He brought little ones, to which they gave no thought.*

I.43 A.   *Our rabbis have taught on Tannaite authority:*

B.   There were three who were involved in that scheme [to keep Daniel out of the furnace]: the Holy One, blessed be he, Daniel, and Nebuchadnezzar.

C.   *The Holy One, blessed be he, said, "Let Daniel leave here, so that people should not say that they were saved on account of Daniel's merit [and not on their own merit]."*

D.   *Daniel said, "Let me get out of here, so that through me the verse will not be carried out, 'The graven images of their gods you shall burn with fire' (Dan. 7:25). [They may make a god of me.]"*

E.   *Nebuchadnezzar said, "Let Daniel get out of here, lest people say that [the king] has burned up his god [Daniel] in fire."*

F.   *And how do we know that [Nebuchadnezzar] worshipped [Daniel]?*

G.   As it is written, "Then the king Nebuchadnezzar fell upon his face and worshipped Daniel" (Dan. 2:46).

I.44 A.   "Thus says the Lord of hosts, the God of Israel, of Ahab, son of Kolaiah, and of Zedekiah, son of Maaseiah, who prophesy a lie to you in my name" (Jer. 29:21).

B.   And it is written, "And of them shall be taken up a curse by all the captivity of Judah who are in Babylonia, saying, The Lord make you like Zedekiah and like Ahab, whom the king of Babylonia roasted in fire" (Jer. 29:22).

C.   What is said is not "whom he burned in fire" but "whom he roasted in fire."

D.   Said R. Yohanan in the name of R. Simeon b. Yohai, "This teaches that he turned them into pop corn."

I.45 A. "Because they have committed villainy in Israel and have committed adultery with their neighbors' wives" (Jer. 29:23):

B. *What did they do?*

C. *They went to Nebuchadnezzar's daughter.* Ahab said to her, "Thus said the Lord, 'Give yourself to Zedekiah.'"

D. And Zedekiah said, "Thus said the Lord, 'Give yourself to Ahab.'"

E. *She went and told her father. He said to her,* "The god of these men hates lewdness. *When they come to you, send them to me.*"

F. When they came to her, she sent them to her father. *He said to them, "Who said this to you?"*

G. *They said, "The Holy One, blessed be he."*

H. *"But lo, I asked Hananiah, Mishael, and Azariah, and they said to me, 'It is forbidden.'"*

I. *They said to him, "We too are prophets like them. To them the message was not given, to us [God] gave the message."*

J. *He said to him, "I want to test you in the same manner I tested Hananiah, Mishael, and Azariah."*

K. *They said to him, "They were three, and we are two."*

L. *He said to them, "Choose anyone you like to go with you."*

M. *They said to him, "Joshua, the high priest." They were thinking, "Joshua, whose merit is great, will protect us."*

N. *They seized them and tossed them into the fire. They were roasted. As to Joshua, the high priest, his clothing was singed.*

O. For it is said, "And he showed me Joshua, the high priest, standing before the angel of the Lord" (Zech. 3:1), and it is written, "'And the Lord said to Satan, the Lord rebuke you, O Satan" (Zech. 3:2).

P. *[Nebuchadnezzar] said to [Joshua], "I know that you are righteous. But what is the reason that the fire had any power whatsoever over you? Over Hananiah, Mishael, and Azariah the fire had no power at all."*

Q. *He said to him, "They were three, and I am only one."*

R. *He said to him, "Lo, Abraham was only one."*

S. *"But there were no wicked men with him, and the fire was not given power to burn him, while in my case, I was joined with wicked men, so the fire had the power to burn me."*

T.	*This is in line with what people say, "If there are two dry brands and one wet one, the dry ones kindle the wet one."*
U.	*Why was he punished in this way?*
V.	Said R. Pappa, "Because his sons had married wives who were not fit for marriage into the priesthood and he did not object, as it is said, 'Now Joshua was clothed with filthy clothing' (Zech. 3:3).
W.	"Now was it Joshua's way to dress in filthy garments? Rather this teaches that his sons had married women who were not worthy to marry into the priesthood, and he did not object."

I.46

A.	*Said R. Tanhum, "In Sepphoris, Bar Qappara interpreted the following verse:* 'These six [grains] of barley gave he to me' (Ruth 3:17).
B.	*"What are the six of barley? If we should say that* they were actually six of barley, was it the way of Boaz to give out a gift of only six barley grains?
C.	"**[93B]** Rather it must have been six seahs of barley?
D.	"And is it the way of a woman to carry six seahs?
E.	"Rather, this formed an omen to her that six sons are destined to come forth from her, each of whom would receive six blessings, and these are they: David, the Messiah, Daniel, Hananiah, Mishael, and Azariah.
F.	"David, as it is written, 'Then answered one of the servants and said, Behold I have seen the son of Jesse, the Bethlehemite, who is cunning in playing and a mighty, valiant man, and a man of war, and understanding in matters, and a handsome man, and the Lord is with him' (1 Sam. 16:18). [Freedman, p. 626, n. 1: The six epithets, viz., cunning in playing, mighty, valiant, etc., are regarded as blessings applicable to each of the six persons mentioned]."
G.	And said R. Judah said Rab, "The entire verse was stated by Doeg only as vicious gossip.
H.	"'Cunning in playing' – skillful in asking questions;
I.	"'a mighty valiant man' – skillful in answering them;
J.	"'a man of war' – skillful in the battle of Torah-learning;

K.   "'understanding in matters' – understanding in learning one thing from another;

L.   "'and a comely person' – who argues for his position with considerable reasons;

M.   "'and the Lord is with him' – the law everywhere follows his opinion.

N.   "'And in all regards, 'he said to him, 'my son Jonathan is his equal.'

O.   *"When he said, 'The Lord is with him' – something which did not apply to himself – he was humbled and envied him.*

P.   "For of Saul it is written, 'And wherever he turned about, he vexed them' (1 Sam. 14:47), while of David it is written, 'And wherever he turned about he prospered.'"

Q.   *How do we know that this was Doeg?*

R.   It is written here, "then one of the servants answered," meaning, "one who was distinguished from the other young men," and there it is written, "Now a man of the servants of Saul was there that day, detained before the Lord, and his name was Doeg, an Edomite, head herdman that belonged to Saul" (1 Sam. 21:8). [Freedman, p. 626, n. 8: Thus "a man" that is, "one distinguished" is the epithet applied to Doeg.]

S.   [Reverting to Bar Qappara's statement:] "The Messiah, as it is written, 'And the spirit of the Lord shall rest upon him, the spirit of wisdom and understanding, the spirit of counsel and might, the spirit of knowledge of the fear of the Lord, and shall make him of quick understanding in the fear of the Lord' (Is. 11:2-3)."

T.   And R. Alexandri said, "The use of the words 'for quick understanding' indicates that he loaded him down with good deeds and suffering as a mill [which uses the same letters] is loaded down."

U.   [Explaining the same word, now with reference to the formation of the letters of the word to mean "smell,"] said Raba, "[The Messiah] smells and judges, for it is written, 'And he shall judge not after the sight of his eyes nor reprove after the hearing of his ears, yet with righteousness shall he judge the poor' (Ex. 11:3-4)."

V. *Bar Koziba ruled for two and a half years. He said to rabbis, "I am the Messiah."*

W. *They said to him, "In the case of the Messiah it is written that he smells a man and judges. Let us see whether you can smell a man and judge."*

X. *When they saw that he could not smell a man and judge, they killed him.*

Y. [Reverting again to Bar Qappara's statement:] "Daniel, Hananiah, Mishael, and Azariah, as it is written, 'In whom there was no blemish, but well favored, skillful in all wisdom, and cunning in knowledge, understanding science, and such as had ability in them to stand in the king's palace, and whom they might teach the learning and the tongue of the Chaldeans' (Dan. 1:4)."

Z. *What is the meaning of, "In whom there was no blemish" (Dan. 1:4)?*

AA. Said R. Hama bar Hanina, "Even the scar made by bleeding was not on them."

BB. *What is the meaning of, "And such as had ability in them to stand in the king's palace" (Dan. 1:3)?*

CC. Said R. Hama in the name of R. Hanina, "This teaches us that they restrained themselves from laughing and chatting, from sleeping, and they held themselves in when they had to attend to the call of nature, on account of the reverence owing to the king."

I.47 A. "Now among these were of the children of Judah, Daniel, Hananiah, Mishael, and Azariah" (Dan. 1:6):

B. Said R. Eleazar, "All of them came from the children of Judah."

C. And R. Samuel bar Nahmani said, "Daniel came from the children of Judah, but Hananiah, Mishael, and Azariah came from the other tribes."

I.48 A. "And of your sons which shall issue from you, which you shall beget, shall they take away, and they shall be eunuches in the palace of the king of Babylonia" (2 Kgs. 20:18):

B.   *What are these "eunuches"?*

C.   Rab said, "Literally, eunuches."

D.   And R. Hanina said, "The sense is that idolatry was castrated [i.e. made sterile] in their time."

E.   *In the view of him who has said that idolatry was castrated in their time, that is in line with the verse of Scripture, "And there is no hurt in them" (Dan. 3:25).*

F.   *But in the view of him who says that "eunuch" is in its literal sense, what is the meaning of, "And there is no hurt in them" (Dan. 3:25) [Since they had been castrated]?*

G.   *It is that the fire did them no injury.*

H.   But has it not been written, "Nor the smell of fire had passed on them" (Dan. 3:27)?

I.   *There was neither injury nor the smell of fire.*

J.   *In the view of him who has said that idolatry was made a eunuch in their time, that is in line with the following verse: "For thus says the Lord to the eunuches who keep my Sabbaths" (Is. 56:4).*

K.   *But in the view of him who says that eunuch is in its literal sense, would Scripture dwell on what is embarrassing to the righteous?*

L.   Among the group were both sorts [actual eunuches, as well as those in whose day were idols sterilized].

M.   *Now there is no difficulty for the view of him who says that they were literally eunuches in the following verse: "Even to them will I give in my house and within my walls a place and a name better than of sons and of daughters" (Is. 56:5).*

N.   *But in the view of the one who says that the sense is that in their day idolatry was made a eunuch, what is the sense of the statement, "Better than of sons and of daughters"?*

O.   Said R. Nahman bar Isaac, "Better than the sons whom they had already had and who had died."

P.   *What is the meaning of the statement, "I shall give them an everlasting name, that shall not be cut off" (Is. 56:5)?*

Q.   Said R. Tanhum, "Bar Qappara interpreted the matter in Sepphoris:

'This refers to the book of Daniel, which is called by his name."

I.49 A. *Now since whatever concerns Ezra was stated by Nehemiah b. Hachlia, what is the reason that the book was not called by his name?*

B. Said R. Jeremiah bar Abba, "It is because he took pride in himself, as it is written, 'Think up on me for good, my God' (Neh. 5:19)."

C. *David also made such a statement, "Remember me, Lord, with the favor that you bear for your people, visit me with your salvation" (Ps. 106:4).*

D. *It was supplication that David sought.*

E. R. Joseph said, "It was because [Nehemiah] had spoken disparagingly about his predecessors, as it is said, 'But the former governors who had been before me were chargeable unto the people and had taken of them bread and wine, beside forty shekels of silver' (Neh. 5:15).

F. "Furthermore, he spoke in this way even of Daniel, who was greater than he was."

G. And how do we know that Daniel was greater than he was?

H. As it is written, "And I Daniel alone saw the vision, for the men that were with me did not see the vision, but a great quaking fell upon them, so that they fled to hide themselves" (Dan. 10:7).

I. "For the men that were with me did not see the vision" (Dan. 10:7):

J. *Who were they?*

K. R. Jeremiah (some say, R. Hiyya b. Abba) said, "They were Haggai, Zechariah, and Malachi."

L. **[94A]** *They were greater than he, and he was greater than they.*

M. *They were greater than he, for they were prophets, and he was not a prophet.*

N. *And he was greater than they, for he saw a vision and they did not see a vision.*

O. *And since they did not see it, what is the reason that they were frightened?*

P. *Even though they did not see it, their star saw it.*

Q. *Said Rabina, "That yields the conclusion that one who is afraid even though he saw*

	nothing is so because his star saw something.
R.	*"What is his remedy?*
S.	*"Let him jump four cubits from where he is standing.*
T.	*"Or let him recite the Shema.*
U.	*"But if he is standing in an unclean place, let him say, 'The butcher's goat is fatter than I am.'"*

The Messiah. Pharaoh, Sennacherib, Hezekiah, and Other Players in the Messianic Drama

I.50   A.   "Of the increase of his government and peace there shall be no end" (Is. 9:6):

B.   R. Tanhum said, "In Sepphoris, Bar Qappara expounded this verse as follows:

C.   "'On what account is every M in the middle of a word open, but the one in the word "increase" is closed?

D.   "'The Holy One, blessed be he, proposed to make Hezekiah Messiah, and Sennacherib into Gog and Magog.

E.   "'The attribute of justice said before the Holy One, blessed be he, "Lord of the world, Now if David, king of Israel, who recited how many songs and praises before you, you did not make Messiah, Hezekiah, for whom you have done all these miracles, and who did not recite a song before you, surely should not be made Messiah."

F.   "On what account the M was closed.

G.   "'Forthwith, the earth went and said before him, "Lord of the world, I shall say a song before you in the place of this righteous man, so you make him Messiah."

H.   "'The earth went and said a song before him, as it is said, "From the uttermost part of the earth we have heard songs, even glory to the righteous" (Is. 24:16).

I.   "'Said the prince of the world before him, "Lord of the world, [The earth] has carried out your wish in behalf of this righteous man."

J.   "'An echo went forth and said, "It is my secret, it is my secret" (Ps. 24:16).

K.   "'Said the prophet, "Woe is me, woe is me" (Is. 24:16). How long?'

L.   "'How dealt treacherously, yes, the treacherous dealers have dealt very treacherously" (Is. 24:16).'"

M.   *And said Raba, and some say, R. Isaac, "Until spoilers come, and those who spoil spoilers."*

I.51   A.   "The burden of Dumah. He calls to me out of Seir, Watchman, what of the night? Watchman, what of the night?" (Is. 21:11):

B.   Said R. Yohanan, "That angel who is appointed over the souls is named Dumah. All the souls gathered to Dumah, and said to him, "'Watchman, what of the night? Watchman, what of the night?' (Is. 21:11).

C.   "Said the watchman, 'The morning comes and also the night, if you will inquire, inquire, return, come' (Is. 21:11)."

I.52　A.　*A Tannaite authority in the name of R. Pappias [said], "It was a shame for Hezekiah and his associates that they did not recite a song, until the earth opened and said a song, as it is said, 'From the uttermost part of the earth have we hard songs, even glory to the righteous'* (Is. 24:16)."

　　　B.　Along these same lines you may say, "And Jethro said, Blessed be the Lord who has delivered you" (Ex. 18:10).

　　　C.　*A Tannaite authority in the name of R. Pappias said, "It was a shame for Moses and the six hundred thousand, that they did not say, 'Blessed ...,' until Jethro came and said, 'Blessed is the Lord.'"*

I.53　A.　"And Jethro rejoiced" (Ex. 18:9):

　　　B.　Rab and Samuel –

　　　C.　Rab said, "It was that he passed a sharp knife across his flesh [circumcising himself]."

　　　D.　And Samuel said, "All his flesh became goose-pimples [because of the destruction of the Egyptians]."

　　　E.　*Said Rab, "That is in line with what people say, 'As to a proselyte, up to the tenth generation do not insult an Aramaean [since he retains his former loyalty, as Jethro did to the Egyptians]."*

I.54　A.　"Therefore shall the Lord, the Lord of hosts, send among his fat ones leanness" (Is. 10:16):

　　　B.　*What is "among his fat ones leanness"?*

　　　C.　Said the Holy One, blessed be he, "Let Hezekiah come, who has eight names, and exact punishment from Sennacherib, who has eight names."

　　　D.　As to Hezekiah, it is written, "For unto us a child is born, unto us a son is given, and the government shall be upon his shoulder, and his name shall be called wonderful, counsellor, mighty, judge, everlasting, father, prince, and peace" (Is. 9:5).

　　　E.　*And there is yet the name "Hezekiah" too?*

　　　F.　[Hezekiah] means "Whom God has strengthened."

　　　G.　Another matter: it is Hezekiah, for he strengthened Israel for their father in heaven.

　　　H.　As to Sennacherib, it is written, "Tiglath-pileser" (2 Kgs. 15:29), "Pilneser" (1 Chr. 5:26), "Shalmeneser" (2 Kgs. 17:3), "Pul" (2 Kgs. 15:29), "Sargon" (Is. 20:1), "Asnapper" (Ezra 4:10), "Rabba" (Ezra 4:10), and "Yaqqira" (Ezra 4:10).

　　　I.　*And there is yet the name "Sennacherib" too.*

　　　J.　It bears the sense that his conversation is contentious.

　　　K.　Another matter: He talked and babbled against the Most High.

　　　L.　[Referring to Ezra 4:10], said R. Yohanan, "On what account did that wicked man have the merit of being called 'the great and noble Asnapper' (Ezra 4:10)?

　　　M.　"Because he did not speak critically of the land of Israel, as it is said, 'Until I come and take you away to a land like your own land' (2 Kgs. 18:32)."

　　　N.　Rab and Samuel: One said he was a shrewd king, and the other said he was a foolish king.

O.		*In the view of him who said that* he was a shrewd king, *if he had said, "A land that is better than yours," they would have said to him, "You are lying to us."*
P.		*In the view of him who said that* he was a foolish king, *If [the land to which they would be exiled was no better than their own], then what value was there [in their agreeing to go].*
Q.		*Where did he exile them?*
R.		Mar Zutra said, "To Africa."
S.		R. Hanina said, "To the mountains of Salug."
T.		But [for their part], the Israelites spoke critically about the land of Israel. *When they came to Shush, they said, "This is the same as our land."*
U.		*When they got to Elmin, they said, "It is like the house of eternities [Jerusalem]."*
V.		*When they go to Shush Tere, they said, "This is twice as good."*

I.55 A. "And beneath his glory shall he kindle a burning like the burning of a fire" (Is. 10:16):

B. Said R. Yohanan, "Under his glory, but not actually his glory."

C. *That is in line with how R. Yohanan called his clothing* "Those who do me honor."

D. R. Eleazar said, "'Under his glory' literally, just as is the burning of the sons of Aaron.

E. "Just as in that case it was a burning of the soul while the body endured, so here there is a burning of the soul while the body remained intact."

I.56 A. *A Tannaite authority in the name of R. Joshua b. Qorhah taught,* "Since Pharaoh blasphemed personally, the Holy One, blessed be he, exacted punishment from him personally.

B. "Since Sennacherib blasphemed **[94B]** through a messenger, the Holy One, blessed be he, exacted punishment from him through a messenger.

C. "In the case of Pharaoh, it is written, "Who is the Lord, that I should obey his voice' (Ex. 5:2).

D. "The Holy One, blessed be he, exacted punishment from him personally, as it is written, 'And the Lord overthrew the Egyptians in the midst of the sea' (Ex. 14:27), and it also is written, 'You did walk through the sea with your horses' (Hab. 3:15).

E. "In the case of Sennacherib, it is written, 'By your messengers you have reproached the Lord' (2 Kgs. 19:23), so the Holy One, blessed be he, exacted punishment from him through a messenger, as it is written, 'And the angel of the Lord went out and smote in the camp of the Assyrians a hundred fourscore and five thousand' (2 Kgs. 19:23)."

I.57 A. *R. Hanina b. Pappa contrasted two verses:* "It is written, 'I will enter the height of his border' (Is. 37:24), and it is further written, 'I will enter into the lodgings of his borders' (2 Kgs. 19:23).

B. "Said that wicked man, 'First I shall destroy the lower dwelling, and afterward I shall destroy the upper dwelling.'"

I.58   A.   *Said R. Joshua b. Levi, "What is the meaning of the verse of Scripture,* 'Am I now come up without the Lord against this place to destroy it? The Lord said to me, Go up against this land and destroy it' (2 Kgs. 18:25).

       B.   *"What is the sense of the passage?*

       C.   *"He had heard the prophet, who had said,* 'Since this people refuses the waters of Shiloah that go softly and rejoice in Rezina and Ramaliah's son, [now therefore behold the Lord brings up upon them the waters of the river, strong and many, even the king of Assyria and all his glory, and he shall come up over all his channels and go over all his banks]' (Is. 8:6). [Freedman, p. 635, n. 3: This was understood by Sennacherib as an order to possess Jerusalem.]"

       D.   *Said R. Joseph, "Were it not for the following rendering of this verse of Scripture, I should not have understood what it meant: 'Because this people is tired of the rule of the house of David, which rules them mildly, like the waters of Shiloah, which flow gently, and have preferred Razin and the son of Ramaliah.'"*

I.59   A.   *Said R. Yohanan, "What is the meaning of this verse:* 'The curse of the Lord is in the house of the wicked, but he blesses the habitation of the just' (Prov. 3:33)?

       B.   "'The curse of the Lord is in the house of the wicked' refers to Pekah, son of Ramaliah, who would eat forty seahs of pigeons for desert.

       C.   "'But he blesses the habitation of the just' refers to Hezekiah, king of Judea, who would eat a litra of vegetables for a whole meal."

I.60   A.   "Now therefore behold, the Lord brings up upon them the waters of the river, strong and many, even the king of Assyria and all his glory" (Is. 8:7).

       B.   And it is written, "And he shall pass through Judea, he shall overflow and go over, he shall reach even to the neck" (Is. 8:8).

       C.   *Then why was [Sennacherib] punished?*

       D.   *The prophet prophesied about the ten tribes, but [Sennacherib] gave mind to the whole of Jerusalem.*

       E.   The prophet came to him and said to him, "'For the wearied is not for the oppressor' (Is. 8:23)."

       F.   Said R. Eleazar b. R. Berekhiah, "The people that is weary because of its devotion to Torah-study will not be given into the power of the one that oppresses it."

I.61   A.   *What is the meaning of this verse:* "When aforetime the land of Zebulun and the land of Naphtali lightened its burden, but in later times it was made heavy by the way of the sea, beyond Jordan, in Galilee of the nations" (Is. 8:23)?

       B.   It was not like the early generations, who made the yoke of the Torah light for themselves, but the later generations, who made the yoke of the Torah heavy for themselves.

       C.   And these were worthy that a miracle should be done for them, just as was done for those who passed through the sea and trampled over the Jordan.

       D.   If Sennacherib should repent, well and good, but if not, I shall make him into dung among the nations [a play on the latter's GLL, the word for Galilee and dung].

I.62   A.   "After these things, and the truth thereof, Sennacherib, king of Assyria, came and entered Judea and encamped against the fortified cities and thought to win them for himself" (2 Chr. 32:1):

        B.   *Such a recompense [to Hezekiah] for such a gift?* [Freedman, p. 636, n. 9: The previous verse relates that Hezekiah turned earnestly to the service of God. Was then Sennacherib's invasion his just reward?]

        C.   *What is the sense of, "After these things and the truth thereof" (2 Chr. 32:1)?*

        D.   Said Rabina, "After the Holy One, blessed be he, went and took an oath, saying *'If I say to Hezekiah that I am going to bring Sennacherib and hand him over to you, he will say to me, "I don't want him and I don't want his terror either."'*

        E.   "So the Holy One, blessed be he, went ahead and took an oath ahead of time *that he would bring him,* as it is said, 'The Lord of hosts has sworn, saying, Surely as I have thought, so shall it come to pass, and as I have purposed, so shall it stand, that I will break the Assyrian in my land and upon my mountains tread him under foot; then shall his yoke depart from off them, and his burden depart from off their shoulders' (Is. 14:24-25)."

        F.   Said R. Yohanan, "Said the Holy One, blessed be he, 'Let Sennacherib and his company come and serve as a crib for Hezekiah and his company.'"

I.63   A.   "And it shall come to pass in that day that his burden shall be taken away from off your shoulders and his yoke from off your neck, and the yoke shall be destroyed because of the oil" (Is. 10:27):

        B.   Said R. Isaac Nappaha, "The yoke of Sennacherib will be destroyed because of the oil of Hezekiah, which he would kindle in the synagogues and school houses.

        C.   "What did [Hezekiah] do? He affixed a sword at the door of the school house and said, 'Whoever does not take up study of the Torah will be pierced by this sword.'

        D.   "They searched from Dan to Beer Sheba and found no ignoramus, from Gabbath to Antipatris and found no boy or girl, no man or woman, not expert in the laws of uncleanness and cleanness.

        E.   "Concerning that generation Scripture says, 'And it shall come to pass in that day that a man shall nourish a young cow and two sheep' (Is. 7:21), and it says, 'And it shall come to pass on that day that every place shall be, where there were a thousand vines at a thousand silverlings, it shall even be for briers and thorns' (Is. 7:23).

        F.   "Even though 'a thousand vines are worth a thousand pieces of silver,' yet it shall be 'for briers and thorns.'"

I.64   A.   "And your spoil shall be gathered like the gathering of a caterpillar" (Is. 33:4):

        B.   Said the prophet to Israel, "Gather your spoil."

        C.   They said to him, "Is it for individual spoil or for sharing?"

        D.   He said to them, "'Like the gathering of a caterpillar' (Is. 33:4): Just as in the gathering of a caterpillar it is each one for himself, so in your spoil it is each one for himself."

        E.   They said to him, "And is not the money of the ten tribes mixed up with it?"

F. He said to them, "'As the watering of pools does he water it' (Is. 33:4): Just as pools of water serve to raise up a human being from a state of uncleanness to a state of cleanness, so the money that has belonged to Israelites, once it has fallen into the hands of idolators, forthwith imparts cleanness. [Freedman, p. 638, n. 5: When the Israelites have abandoned all hope of the return thereof other Jews may take it.]"

I.65 A. Said R. Huna, "That wicked man [Sennacherib] made ten marches that day,

B. "as it is said, 'He is come to Aiath, he is passed at Migron, at Michmash he has laid up his carriages, they are gone over the passage, they have taken up their lodgings at Geba, Ramah is afraid, Gibeah of Saul is fled, Lift up your voice, O daughter of Gallim, cause it to be heard to Laish, O poor Anathoth, Madmenah is removed, the inhabitants of Gebim gather themselves to flee' (Is. 10:28-31)."

C. *But they are more than [ten]?*

D. [Huna responded,] "Lift up your voice, O daughter of Gallim," *was said by the prophet to the congregation of Israel [as follows]:*

E. "'Lift up your voice, O daughter of Gallim' – daughter of Abraham, Isaac, and Jacob, who carried out religious duties like the waves of the ocean [in number].

F. "'Cause it to be heard to Laish' – *from this one do not fear, but fear the wicked Nebuchadnezzar, who is compared to a lion.*

G. "For it is written, 'The lion is come up from his thicket' (Jer. 4:7)."

H. *What is* **[95A]** *the sense of* "O poor Anathoth" (Is. 10:31)?

I. Jeremiah b. Hilkiah is destined to come up from Anathoth and to prophesy, as it is written, "The words of Jeremiah, son of Hilkiah, of the priests who were in Anathoth in the land of Benjamin" (Jer. 1:1).

J. *But is there any parallel? There [Nebuchadnezzar] is called a lion, but what is written here is laish [another word for lion].*

K. Said R. Yohanan, "A lion is called six things: ari (Jer. 4:7), kefir (Gen. 49:9), labi (Gen. 39:9), laish (Judges 14:5), shahal (Ps. 91:13), and shahaz (Job 28:8)."

L. *If so, they are fewer [than ten]?*

M. *"They are gone over" [and] "the passage" add up to two [more].*

I.66 A. *What is the meaning of the statement,* "As yet shall he halt at Nob that day" (Is. 10:32)?

B. Said R. Huna, "That day alone remained [for the punishment of] the sin committed at Nob [Sam. 22:17-19]. [Freedman, p. 639, n. 9: When the priests of Nob were massacred. God set a term for punishment, of which that day was the last.]

C. *"The Chaldean [soothsayers] said to him, 'If you go now, you will overpower it, and if not, you will not overpower it.'*

D. *"A journey that should require ten days required only one day.*

E. *"When they got to Jerusalem, they piled up mattresses so that, when he climbed up and took up his position on the top one, he could see Jerusalem. When he saw it, it looked tiny in his eyes. He said, 'Is this really the city of Jerusalem, on account of which I moved all my troops and came up and* conquered the entire province? Is it not smaller and weaker than all of the cities of the peoples that by my power I have already conquered?!'

F.   "He went and got up and shook his head and waved his hand backward and forward, with contempt, toward the mountain of the house of the sanctuary in Zion and toward the courts of Jerusalem.'

G.   "They said, 'Let us raise a hand against it right now.'

H.   "He said to them, 'You are tired. Tomorrow each one of your bring me a stone and we shall stone it [Freedman, following Jastrow].'

I.   "Forthwith: 'And it came to pass that night that the angel of the Lord went out and smote in the camp of the Assyrians a hundred fourscore and five thousand, and when they arose early in the morning, behold they were all dead corpses' (2 Kgs. 19:35)."

J.   Said R. Pappa, "That is in line with what people say: 'Justice delayed is justice denied.'"

I.67   A.   "And Ishbi-benob, who was of the sons of the giant, the weight of whose spear weighed three hundred shekels of brass in weight, being girded with a new sword, thought to have slain David" (2 Sam. 21:16):

B.   What is the sense of "Ishbi-be-nob"?

C.   Said R. Judah said Rab, "It was a man [ish] who came on account of the matter of [the sin committed at] Nob.

D.   "Said the Holy One, blessed be he, to David, 'How long will the sin committed [against Nob] be concealed in your hand. On your account, Nob was put to death, the city of priests, on your account, Doeg the Edomite was sent into exile; on your account, Saul and his three sons were killed.

E.   "'Do you want you descendents to be wiped out, or do you want to be handed over into the power of an enemy?'

F.   "He said to him, 'Lord of the world, It is better that I be handed over to an enemy but that my descendents not be wiped out.'"

G.   One day, when he went out to Sekhor Bizzae [Freedman, p. 640, n. 7: literally: "your seed to cease"]. Satan appeared to him in the form of a deer. He shot an arrow at it, and the arrow did not reach [the deer]. It drew him until he came to the land of the Philistines. When Ishbi-benob saw him, he said, 'This is the one who killed Goliath, my brother."

H.   He bound him, doubled him up, and threw him under an olive press. A miracle was done for [David], in that the earth underneath him became soft. This is in line with the following verse of Scripture: "You have enlarged my steps under me, that my feet did not slip" (Ps. 18:37).

I.   That day was the eve of the Sabbath [Friday]. Abishai ben Zeruiah [David's nephew] was washing his head in four casks of water. He saw stains of blood [in the water].

J.   Some say a dove came and slapped its wings before him.

K.   He said, "The congregation of Israel is compared to a dove, for it is said, 'You are as the wings of a dove covered with silver' (Ps. 68:14). This then bears the inference that David, king of Israel, is in trouble."

L.	*He came to his house and did not find him. He said, "We have learned in the Mishnah:* **People are not to ride on his horse or sit on his throne or hand his scepter [M. San. 2:5].**
M.	*"What is the rule about a time of crisis?"*
N.	*He came and asked at the school house. They said to him, "In a time of crisis it is all right."*
O.	*He mounted his mule and rode off and the earth crumbled up [to make the journey quick]. While he was riding along, he saw Orpah, mother of [Ishbi-benob] who was spinning. When she saw him, she broke off the spindle." He threw it at her head and killed her.*
P.	*When Ishbi-benob saw him, he said, "Now there are two against me, and they will kill me."*
Q.	*He threw David up and stuck his spear [into the ground], saying, "Let him fall on it and be killed."*
R.	*[Abishai] shouted the Name [of God], so David was suspended between heaven and earth.*
S.	*But why should David himself not have said it?*
T.	Because one who is bound cannot free himself from his chains.
U.	*He said to him, "What do you want here?"*
V.	*He said to him, "This is what the Holy One, blessed be he, has said to me, and this is what I said to him."*
W.	*He said to him, "Take back your prayer. May your son's son sell wax, but may you not suffer."*
X.	*He said to him, "If so, help me."*
Y.	*That is in accord with what is written, "But Abishai, son of Zeruiah, helped him" (2 Sam. 21:17).*
Z.	Said R. Judah said Rab, "He helped him in prayer."
AA.	*Abishai pronounced the Name and brought [David] down.*
BB.	*He pursued the two of them. When they came to Kubi, they said, "Let us stand against him."*
CC.	*When they came to Bethre, they said, "Will two whelps kill a lion?"*
DD.	*They said to him, "Go find Orpah, your mother, in the grave."*
EE.	*When they mentioned the name of his mother to him, he grew weak, and they killed him.*
FF.	*So it is written, "Then the men of David swore to him, saying, You shall no more go out with us to battle, that you not put out the light of Israel" (2 Sam. 21:17).*

I.68	A.	*Our rabbis have taught on Tannaite authority:*
	B.	For three did the earth fold up [to make their journey quicker]: Eliezer, Abraham's servant, Jacob our father, and Abishai b. Zeruiah.
	C.	As to Abishai, son of Zeruiah, it is as we have just said.
	D.	As to Eliezer, Abraham's servant, it is written, "And I came this day to the well" (Gen. 24:42), meaning that that very day he had set out.
	E.	As to Jacob, our father, **[95B]** as it is written, "And Jacob went out from Beer Sheba and went to Haran" (Gen. 28:10), and it is said, "And he lighted upon a certain place and tarried there all night, because the sun had set" (Gen. 28:11).

F.   When he got to Haran, he said, "Is it possible that I have passed through a place in which my ancestors have prayed, and I did not say a prayer there?"

G.   *He wanted to go back. As soon as the thought of going back had entered his mind, the earth folded up for him. Forthwith:* "He lighted upon a place" (Gen. 28:11).

H.   Another matter: "Lighting upon..." refers only to praying, as it is written, "Therefore do not pray for this people or lift up a cry or prayer for them nor make intercession [using the same root] to me" (Jer. 7:16).

I.   "And he tarried there all night, because the sun had set" (Gen. 28:10):

J.   *After he had prayed, he wanted to go back.* Said the Holy One, blessed be he, "This righteous man has come to the house of my dwelling. Should he go forth without spending the night?"

K.   Forthwith the sun set. That is in line with what is written, "And as he passed over Penuel, the sun rose for him" (Gen. 32:32).

L.   And did it rise only for him? And did not it not rise for the entire world?

M.   "But," said R. Isaac, "Since the sun had set [too soon] on his account, it also rose on his account."

I.69 A.   *And how do we know that the seed of David ceased?*

B.   As it is written, "And when Athaliah, mother of Ahaziah, saw that her son was dead, she rose and destroyed all the royal seed" (2 Kgs. 11:1).

C.   *And lo, Joash remained. Also Abiathar remained, for it is written,* "And one of the sons of Ahimelech, son of Ahitub, named Abiathar, escaped" (1 Sam. 22:20).

D.   Said R. Judah said Rab, "If Abiathar were not left to Ahimelech, son of Ahitub, neither shred nor remnant of the seed of David would have survived."

I.70 A.   Said R. Judah said Rab, "The wicked Sennacherib came against them with forty-five thousand men, sons of kings seated on golden chariots, with their concubines and whores, and with eighty thousand mighty soldiers, garbed in coats of mail, and sixty thousand swordsmen running before him, and the rest cavalry.

B.   And so they came against Abraham, and in the age to come so they will come with Gog and Magog.

C.   *On Tannaite authority it was taught:* The length of his camp was four hundred parasangs, and the breadth of his horses, neck to neck, was forty parasangs, and the total of his army was two million six hundred thousand less one.

D.   *Abbayye asked, "Does this mean less one myriad or one thousand?"*

E.   *The question stands.*

I.71 A.   *A Tannaite statement:*

B.   The first ones crossed by swimming, as it is said, "He shall overflow and go over" (Is. 8:8).

C. The middle ones crossed standing up, as it is said, "He shall reach even to the neck" (Is. 8:8).

D. The last group brought up the dirt [of the river] with their feet and so found no water in the river to drink, so that they had to bring them water from some other place, which they drank, as it is said, "I have digged and drunk water" (Is. 37:25).

E. [How could the army have been so large,] for is it not written, "Then the angel of the Lord went forth and smote in the camp of the Assyrians a hundred and fourscore and five thousand, and when they arose early in the morning, behold, they were all dead corpses" (Is. 37:36)?

F. Said R. Abbahu, "Those were the heads of the troops."

G. *Said R. Ashi, "Read the text closely with the same result, for it is written, '[therefore shall the Lord... send] among his fat ones leanness [i.e. the cream of the crop].*

H. *Said Rabina, "Read the text closely with the same result; for it is written, 'And the Lord sent an angel, which cut off all the men of valor, and the leaders and the princes in the camp of the king of Assyria. So he returned with shamefacedness to his own land, and when he entered into the house of his god, they that came forth of his own bowels slew him there with the sword"* (2 Chr. 32:21).

I. *This proves [that the reference is only to the leaders (Freedman, p. 644, n. 6)].*

I.72 A. How did [the angel] smite [the army]?

B. R. Eliezer says, "He hit them with his hand, as it is said, 'And Israel saw the great hand' (Ex. 14:31), that was destined to exact punishment of Sennacherib."

C. R. Joshua says, "He hit them with a finger, as it is said, 'Then the magicians said to Pharaoh, This is the finger of God' (Ex. 8:14), that finger that was destined to exact punishment of Sennacherib."

D. R. Eleazar, son of R. Yosé the Galilean, says, "Said the Holy One, blessed be he, to Gabriel, 'Is your sickle sharpened?'

E. "He said before him, 'Lord of the world, it has been ready and sharpened since the six days of creation, as it is said, 'For they fled from the swords, from the sharpened sword' (Is. 21:15)."

F. R. Simeon b. Yohai says, "That season was the time for the ripening of the produce. Said the Holy One, blessed be he, to Gabriel, When you go forth to ripen the produce, attack them, as it is said, 'As he passes, he shall take you, for morning by morning shall he pass by, by day and by night, and it shall be a sheer terror to understand the report' (Is. 28:19)."

G. *Said R. Pappa, "This is in line with what people say: 'As you pass by, reveal yourself to your enemy' [and so take revenge whenever you have the chance]."*

H. Others say, "He blew into their noses and they died, as it is said, 'And he shall also blow upon them, and they shall wither' (Is. 40:24)."

I. R. Jeremiah b. Abba said, "He clapped his hands at them and they died, as it is written, 'I will also smite my hands together and I will cause my fury to rest' (Ez. 21:22)."

	J.	R. Isaac Nappaha said, "He opened their ears for them and they heard a song of the living creatures [of the heaven] and they died, as it is written, 'At your exaltation the people were scattered' (Is. 33:3)."
I.73	A.	How many [of Sennacherib's army] remained?
	B.	Rab said, "Ten, as it is said, 'And the rest of the trees of his forest shall be few, that a child may write them' (Is. 10:19).
	C.	"What is the letter representing a number that a child can write? The one that stands for ten."
	D.	Samuel said, "Nine, as it is written, 'Yet gleaning grapes shall be left in it, as the shaking of an olive tree, two and three berries in the top of the uppermost bough, four and five in the utmost fruitful branches thereof' (Is. 17:6). [Freedman, p. 645, n. 12: This is rendered: "just as after the shaking of an olive tree there may remain two olives here and three there, so shall there be left of the arm army four here and five there – nine in all."]
	E.	R. Joshua b. Levi said, "Fourteen, as it is written, 'Two, three..., four, five' (Is. 17:6)."
	F.	R. Yohanan said, "Five: Sennacherib, his two sons, Nebuchadnezzar, and Nebuzaradan.
	G.	"Nebuzaradan['s survival is] a tradition.
	H.	"Nebuchadnezzar, as it is written, 'And the form of the fourth is like an angel of God' (Dan. 3:25).
	I.	*"If he had not seen [an angel], how would he have known?*
	J.	"Sennacherib and his two sons, as it is written, 'And it came to pass, as he was worshipping in the house of Nisroch his god, that Adrammelech and Sharezer, his sons, smote him with the sword' (2 Kgs. 19:37)."
I.74	A.	Said R. Abbahu, "Were it not that a verse of Scripture is explicitly spelled out, it would not have been possible to say it:
	B.	"For it is written, 'In the same day shall the Lord shave with a razor that is hired, namely, by the riverside, by the king of Assyria, the head and the hair of the feet, and it shall consume the beard' (Is. 7:20.
	C.	*"The Holy One, blessed be he, came and appeared before [Sennacherib] as an old man. He said to him, 'When you go against the kings of east and west, whose sons you brought and saw killed, what will you say to them?'*
	D.	*"He said to him, 'This man [I] was also fearful on that account.'*
	E.	*"He said to him, 'What should we do?'*
	F.	*"He said to him, 'Go* **[96A]** *and change your appearance.'*
	G.	*"'How shall I change?'*
	H.	*"He said to him, 'Go and bring me a razor, and I shall shave you.'*
	I.	*"'Where shall I get it?'*
	J.	*"He said to him, 'Go to that house and bring it from there.'*
	K.	*"He went and found it. Ministering angels came and appeared to him in the form of men, grinding palm-nuts.'*
	L.	*"He said to them, 'Give me the razor.'*
	M.	*"They said to him, 'Grind a cask of palm-nuts, and we shall give it to you.'*
	N.	*"He ground a cask of palm-nuts, and they gave the razor to him.*
	O.	*"It got dark before he came back. [God] said to [Sennacherib], 'Go and bring fire.'*

P.   *"He went and brought fire. While he was blowing on it, the fire caught his beard, so [God] shaved his head as well as his beard.* [Freedman, p. 646, n. 8: Thus he was shaved with a razor hired by his own work, a work which is done 'by the riverside,' 'grinding,' the water providing power for the mill.]"

Q.   *They said, "This is in line with what is written:* 'And it shall also consume the beard' (Is. 7:20)."

R.   *Said R. Pappa, "This is in line with what people say: 'If you are singeing an Aramaean's hair and it suits him, light a fire to his beard, so you will not suffer his mockery.'"*

S.   [Reverting to the tale of Abbahu:] *"He went and found a plank from Noah's ark. He said, 'This must be the great god who saved Noah from the flood.'*

T.   *"He said, 'If that man [I] goes and is victorious, he will offer his two sons before you.'*

U.   *"His sons heard and killed him. That is in line with the verse of Scripture,* 'And it came to pass, as he was worshipping in the house of Nisroch his god, that Adrammelech and Sharezer his sons smote him with the sword' (2 Kgs. 19:37)."

I.75   A.   "And he fought against them, he and his servants, by night, and smote them" (Gen. 14:15):

B.   Said R. Yohanan, "That angel who was assigned to Abraham was named 'Night,' as it is said, '[Let the day perish wherein I was born] and the Night which said, There is a man-child conceived' (Job 3:3). [Freedman, p. 647, n. 4: The verse, Gen. 14:15, is translated, and Night fought on their behalf, he and his....']"

C.   R. Isaac Nappaha ["the smith"] said, "It did for him the deeds that are done by night, as it is said, 'They fought from heaven, the stars in their courses fought against Sisera' (Judges 5:20)."

D.   *R. Simeon b. Laqish said, "What the smith [Yohanan] has said is better than what the son of the smith [Isaac] has said."*

E.   "And he pursued them to Dan" (Gen. 14:14):

F.   Said R. Yohanan, "When that righteous man came to Dan, he grew weak. He foresaw that the children of his children were destined to commit acts of idolatry in Dan, as it is said, 'And he set the one in Beth El, and the other he put in Dan' (1 Kgs. 12:29).

G.   "And also that wicked man [Nebuchadnezzar] did not grow strong until he reached Dan, as it is said, 'From Dan the snorting of his horses was heard' (Jer. 8:16)."

I.76   A.   Said R. Zira, "Even though R. Judah b. Beterah sent word from Nisibis, 'Pay heed to an elder who has forgotten his learning through not fault of his own and to cut the jugular veins [in slaughtering a beast], in accord with the view of R. Judah,

B.   "'and take heed of the sons of the ordinary folk, for from them [too] will Torah go forth,'

C.   *"for such a matter as the following we may convey matters to them [and not refrain from teaching this lesson:]*

D.   "'"You are righteous, Lord, when I please with you, yet let met talk to thee of thy judgments, wherefore does the way of the wicked prosper? Wherefore are all they happy who deal very treacherously? You have planted them, yes, they have taken root, they grow, yes, they bring forth fruit" (Jer. 12:1-2).

E.   *"'What did he answer him?* "If you have run with the footmen and they have tired you, then how can you contend with the horses? And if in a land of peace, in which you trust, they have wearied you, how will you do in the prideful swelling of the Jordan" (Jer. 12:5).

F.   "'The matter may be compared to the case of a man who said "I can run in a marsh three parasangs before horses." He happened upon a man on foot and ran before him for only three mils on dry land, and he got tired.

G.   "'He said to him, "Now if matters are this way when you run before a man on foot, all the more so [will you be unable to run] before horses! And if matters are this way for three mils, how much the more so in three parasangs! And if matters are this way in dry land, how much the more so in a marsh!"

H.   "'"So it is with you. If on account of the reward for taking four steps [explained later, J-Y] that I paid that wicked man, which he took in running on account of my honor, you are amazed, when I pay the reward owing to Abraham, Isaac, and Jacob, who ran before me like horses, how much the more so [will you be amazed]!"

I.   "'This is in line with the following verse of Scripture: "My heart within me is broken because of the prophets, all my bones shake, I am like a drunken man, and like a man whose wine has overcome, because of the Lord and because of the words of his holiness" (Jer. 23:9).'"

J.   *As to the reference to the four steps [taken by the wicked man in honor of God], what is its meaning?*

K.   *It is in accord with that which is written:* "At that time Merodach-baladan, son of Baladan, king of Babylonia, sent letters and a present to Hezekiah [for he had heard that he had been sick and recovered]" (Is. 39:1).

L.   And merely because Hezekiah was sick and got better, did he send him letters and a present?!

M.   Yes, so as "to inquire of the wonder that was done in the land" (2 Chr. 32:31).

N.   For R. Yohanan said, "That day on which Ahaz died was only two hours long, *and on the day on which Hezekiah got sick and got better, the Holy One, blessed be he, gave back the other ten hours.*

O.   "For it is written, 'Behold I will bring again the shadow of the degrees which is gone down in the sun dial of Ahaz, ten degrees backward. So the sun returned ten degrees, by which degrees it was gone down' (Is. 38:8). [Freedman, p. 649, ns. 5-6: The sun had set ten hours too soon, to allow no time for funeral eulogies. This was in order to make atonement for his sins, for the disgrace of being deprived of the usual funeral honors expiates one's misdeeds. The return of the ten degrees to which Isaiah refers is assumed to mean a prolongation of the day by ten hours, light having healing powers.]

P.   *"Merodach-baladan] said to [his staff], 'What is going on?'*

Q.	*"They said to him, 'Hezekiah got sick and got better.'*
R.	*"He said, 'Is there such a great man in the world, and should I know want to greet him?'*
S.	*"He wrote him, 'Peace to King Hezekiah, peace to the city of Jerusalem, peace to the Great God!'*
T.	*"Nebuchadnezzar was the scribe of Baladan. At that time he was not there. When he came, he said to him, 'What did you write?'*
U.	*"They said to him, 'This is what we wrote.'*
V.	*"He said to him, 'You called him "the great God" and yet you mentioned him last?'*
W.	*"He said, 'Rather, this is how you should write: "Peace to the great God, peace to the city of Jerusalem, peace to King Hezekiah."'*
X.	*"They said to him, 'Let the one who has read the letter serve as the messenger.'*
Y.	*"He ran after [the messenger] [thus in honor of God]. But when he had run four steps, Gabriel came and froze him in place."*
Z.	Said R. Yohanan, "Had Gabriel not come and kept him standing in place, there would have been no remedy for (the enemies of) Israel." [Freedman, p. 650, n. 3: The learned children of the ordinary folk should thus be informed that the honor paid to them is due to the slight merit of their fathers, as in this case.]

I.77	A.	*What is the meaning of the fact that [Merodach-] Baladan is called "the son of Baladan"?*
	B.	*They say: Baladan was king, and his appearance changed into that of a dog, so his son sat on the throne.*
	C.	*When he would sign a document, he would write his name and the name of his father, "King Baladan."*
	D.	*This is the sense of that which is written: "A son honors his father, and a servant his master" (Mal. 1:6).*
	E.	*"A son honors his father" (Mal. 1:6) refers to what we have just said.*
	F.	*As to "A servant his master" (Mal. 1:6)?*
	G.	*It is in line with that which is written: "Now in the fifth month, on the tenth day of the month, the nineteenth year of Nebuchadnezzar, king of Babylonia, came Nebuzaradan, captain of the guard, and stood before the king of Babylonia in Jerusalem. And he burned the house of the Lord and the house of the king" (Jer. 52:12-13).*
	H.	*[96B] But did Nebuchadnezzar go up to Jerusalem? Has it not been written,* "They carried him up to the King of Babylonia, to Riblah" *(Jer. 52:9)? And, said R. Abbahu, "That town is the same as Antioch."*
	I.	R. Hisda and R. Isaac b. Abudimi: One said, "His picture was engraved on [Nebuzaradan's] chariot."
	J.	"The other said, "He was so much in awe of him that it was as though he were standing before him."

| I.78 | A. | *Said Raba, "It was bearing three hundred mules loaded with iron axes that could break iron that Nebuchadnezzar sent Nebuzaradan. All of them broke on one gate of Jerusalem, as it is said, 'And now they attack its gate together; with axes and hammers they hit it' (Ps. 74:6).* |

B. *"He wanted to go back. He said, 'I am afraid that they might do to me as they did to Sennacherib.*

C. *"A voice came forth: 'Leaper son of a leaper, leap, Nebuzaradan! The time has come for the sanctuary to be destroyed and the palace burned.'*

D. *"Left to him was only a single axe. He went and hit it with its head, ad the gate opened, as it is said, 'A man was famous according as he had lifted up axes upon thick trees' (Ps. 74:5).*

E. *"He continued with the killing until he reached the Temple. He set fire to it. The Temple sought to rise up [to heaven], but from heaven it was pushed down, as it is said, 'The Lord has trodden down the virgin daughter of Judah as in a winepress' (Lam. 1:15).*

F. *"He was elated, but an echo came and said, 'You have killed a dead people, you have burned a burned Temple, you have crushed already ground corn, as it is said, 'Take the millstones and grind meal, uncover your locks, make the leg bare, uncover the thigh, pass over the rivers' (Is. 47:2).*

G. *"What is said is not 'wheat' but 'ground meal.'"*

H. [Nebuzaradan] saw the blood of Zechariah boiling. He said to them, *"What is this?"*

I. They said to him, *"It is the blood of the sacrifices, that has been poured out."*

J. He said to them, *"Come and let us bring [animal blood to make a comparison to see whether they are alike or not alike]."* He slaughtered an animal and the blood was not like [that which was boiling].

K. He said to them, *"Explain it to me, and if not, I shall comb your flesh with iron combs."*

L. They said to him, *"This one was a priest and a prophet, and he prophesied to Israel concerning the destruction of Jerusalem, so they killed him."*

M. He said to them, *"I shall be the one to appease him."* He brought rabbis and killed them over him, but [the blood] did not come to rest. He brought school children and killed them over him, but still the blood did not come to rest. He brought the blossoms of the priesthood and killed them over him, and still the blood did not come to rest, until he had killed over him ninety-four myriads, and still his blood did not rest.

N. He drew near [the blood] and said, "Zechariah, Zechariah, I have destroyed the best of them. *Do you want me to kill them all?"*

O. *Forthwith the blood came to rest.*

P. *He gave thought to repentance, saying,* "Now if they, who killed only a single person, were treated in such a way, that man [I] – what will come of him?"

Q. *He fled, sent his instructions to his household [giving over his property to his family], and then converted [to Judaism].*

I.79 A. *Our rabbis have taught on Tannaite authority:*

B. Naaman was a resident proselyte.

C. Nebuzaradan was a righteous proselyte.

D. Grandsons of Sisera studied Torah in Jerusalem.

E. Grandsons of Sennacherib taught Torah in public.

F. *And who were they? Shemaiah and Abtalion.*

G. Grandsons of Haman studied Torah in Bene Beraq.

H. And so too grandsons of that wicked man [Nebuchadnezzar] did the Holy One, blessed be he, want to bring under the wings of the Presence of God.

I. Said the ministering angels before the Holy One, blessed be he, "Lord of the world, will you bring under the wings of your Presence him who destroyed your house and burned your Temple?"

J. For it is written, "We should have healed Babylonia, but she is not healed" (Jer. 21:9).

K. Said Ulla, "This speaks of Nebuchadnezzar."

L. *Said R. Samuel b. Nahmani, "This refers to the 'canals of Babylonia' (Ps. 137:1), which flow among the palm trees of Babylonia."*

I.80 A. Said Ulla, "Ammon and Moab were bad neighbors of Jerusalem.

B. *"When they heard the prophets prophesying the destruction of Jerusalem, they sent word to Nebuchadnezzar, 'Go out and come here.'*

C. *"He said, 'I am afraid that they will do to me what they did to those who came before me.'*

D. *"They sent to him, '"For the man is not at home" (Prov. 7:19), and "man" can refer only to the Holy One, blessed be he, as it is said, "The Lord is a man of war" (Ex. 15:3).'*

E. *"He replied, 'He is nearby and he will come.'*

F. *"They sent to him, '"He has gone on a far journey" (Prov. 7:19).'*

G. *"He sent to them, 'There are righteous men there, who will pray for mercy and bring him back.'*

H. *"They sent to him, '"He has taken a bag of money with him" (Prov. 7:20), and "money" refers only to the righteous, as it is said, "So I bought her to me for fifteen pieces of silver and for a homer of barley and a half-homer of barley" (Hos. 3:2).'*

I. *"He sent word to them, 'The wicked may repent and pray for mercy and bring him back.'*

J. *"They sent to him, 'He has already set a time for them, as it is said, "And he will come home at the day appointed" (Prov. 7:20), and "day appointed" can refer only to time, as it is said, "In the time appointed on our solemn feast day" (Ps. 81:1,3).'*

K. *"He sent word to them, 'It is winter, and I cannot make the trip because of the snow and rain.'*

L. *"They sent to him, 'Come through the mountains [if need be]. For it is said, "Send you a messenger to the ruler of the earth [that he may come] by way of the rocks to the wilderness to the mountain of the daughter of Zion" (Is. 16:1).'*

M. *"He sent to them, 'If I come, I shall not have a place in which to make camp.'*

N. *"They sent word to him,* 'Their cemeteries are superior to your palaces, as it is written, "At that time, says the Lord, they shall bring out the bones of the king of Judea and the bones of his princes and the bones of the priests and the bones of the prophets and the bones of the inhabitants of Jerusalem, out of their graves. And they shall spread them before the sun and the moon and all the host of heaven, whom they have loved and whom they have served and after whom they have walked" (Jer. 8:1-2).' [Freedman, p. 654, n. 1: The great burial vaults will be cleared out to give shelter to Nebuchadnezzar's army.]"

When Will the Messiah Come?

I.81   A.   *Said R. Nahman to R. Isaac, "Have you heard when the son of 'the fallen one' will come?"*

       B.   *He said to him, "Who is the son of 'the fallen one'?"*

       C.   *He said to him, "It is the Messiah."*

       D.   *"Do you call the Messiah 'the son of the fallen one'?"*

       E.   *He said to him, "Yes, for it is written, 'On that day I will raise up [97A] the tabernacle of David, the fallen one' (Amos 9:11)."*

       F.   *He said to him, "This is what R. Yohanan said, 'The generation to which the son of David will come will be one in which disciples of sages grow fewer,*

       G.   *"'and, as to the others, their eyes will wear out through suffering and sighing,*

       H.   *"'and troubles will be many, and laws harsh, forever renewing themselves so that the new one will hasten onward before the old one has come to an end.'"*

I.82   A.   *Our rabbis have taught on Tannaite authority:*

       B.   The seven year cycle in which the son of David will come:

       C.   As to the first one, the following verse of Scripture will be fulfilled: "And I will cause it to rain upon one city and not upon another" (Amos 4:7).

       D.   As to the second year, the arrows of famine will be sent forth.

       E.   As to the third, there will be a great famine, in which men, women, and children will die, pious men and wonder-workers alike, and the Torah will be forgotten by those that study it.

       F.   As to the fourth year, there will be plenty which is no plenty.

       G.   As to the fifth year, there will be great prosperity, and people will eat, drink, and rejoice, and the Torah will be restored to those that study it.

       H.   As to the sixth year, there will be rumors.

       I.   As to the seventh year, there will be wars.

       J.   As to the end of the seventh year [the eighth year], the son of David will come.

       K.   *Said R. Joseph, "Lo, how many septennates have passed like that one, and yet he has not come."*

       L.   *Said Abbayye, "Were there rumors in the sixth year and wars in the seventh year? And furthermore, did they come in the right order?"*

I.83   A.   *It has been taught on Tannaite authority:*

       B.   R. Judah says, "In the generation in which the son of David will come, **the gathering place will be for prostitution, Galilee will be laid waste, Gablan will be made desolate, and the men of the frontier will go about from town to town, and none will take pity on them; and the wisdom of scribes will putrefy; and those who fear sin will be rejected; and the truth will be herded away [M. Sot. 9:15AA-GG].**

       C.   "For it is said, 'And the truth will be herded away' (Is. 59:15)."

       D.   *What is the meaning of the statement, "The truth will be herded away" (Is. 59:15)?*

       E.   *Said members of the house of Rab, "This teaches that it will be divided into herds and herds, each going its way."*

	F.	*What is the meaning [of the concluding passage of the same verse],* "And he who departs from evil makes himself a prey" (Is. 59:15)?
	G.	*Said members of the house of R. Shila,* "Whoever departs from evil will be treated as a fool [using the same letters as those for prey] by other people."
I.84	A.	[Here is a case of how a righteous man was treated like a fool:] *Said Raba,* "To begin with I had supposed that there is no truth in the world. One of the rabbis, R. Tabut by name (and some say, R. Tabyomi by name), who would not go back on his word even though people gave him all the treasures of the world, said to me that one time he happened to come to a place called Truth.
	B.	"It was a place in which people would not go back on their word, and in which no person died before his day.
	C.	"He took a woman of theirs as wife and had two sons from her.
	D.	"One day his wife was sitting and shampooing her hair. Her neighbor came and knocked on the door. Thinking that it would be improper [to say what his wife was doing], he said to her, 'She is not here.'
	E.	"His two sons died.
	F.	"The people of the place came to him and said to him, 'What is going on?'
	G.	"He said to them, 'This is what happened.'
	H.	"They said to him, 'By your leave, please go away from our place, so as not to incite Satan against these men [us].'"
I.85	A.	*It has been taught on Tannaite authority:*
	B.	R. Nehorai says, "In the generation in which the son of David will come, **children will shame elders, and elders will stand up before children. 'The daughter rises up against the mother, and the daughter-in-law against her mother-in-law' (Mic. 7:6). The face of the generation is the face of a dog, and a son is not ashamed before his father"** [M. Sot. 9:15HH-KK].
I.86	A.	*It has been taught on Tannaite authority:*
	B.	R. Nehemiah says, "In the generation in which the son of David will come, **presumption increases, and dearth increases, and the vine gives its fruit and wine at great cost. The government turns to heresy, and there is no reproof"** [M. Sot. 9:15W-Z].
	C.	*That statement supports the view of R. Isaac.*
	D.	For R. Isaac said, "The son of David will come only when the entire kingdom has turned to heresy."
	E.	*Said Raba,* "What is the text of Scripture that makes that point?
	F.	"'It is all turned white, he is clean' (Lev. 13:13). [Freedman, p. 656, n. 5: When all are heretics, it is a sign that the world is about to be purified by the advent of the Messiah.]"
I.87	A.	*Our rabbis have taught on Tannaite authority:*

B. "For the Lord shall judge his people and repent himself of his servants, when he sees that their power has gone, and there is none shut up or left" (Deut. 32:36).

C. The son of David will come only when traitors are many.

D. Another matter: Only when disciples are few.

E. Another matter: Only when a penny will not be found in anyone's pocket.

F. Another matter: Only when people will have given up hope of redemption, as it is said, "There is none shut up or left" (Deut. 32:36), as it were, when there is none [God being absent] who supports and helps Israel.

G. *That accords with the statement of R. Zira, who, when he would find rabbis involved in [figuring out when the Messiah would come], would say to them, 'By your leave, I ask you not to put it off.*

H. *"For we have learned on Tannaite authority:* Three things come on the spur of the moment, and these are they: the Messiah, a lost object, and a scorpion."

I.88   A. *Said R. Qattina, "The world will exist for six thousand years and be destroyed for one thousand,*

B. "as it is said, 'And the Lord alone shall be exalted in that day' (Is. 2:11)."

C. *Abbayye said, "It will be desolate for two thousand years, as it is said, 'After two days will he revive us, in the third day, he will raise us up and we shall live in his sight' (Hos. 6:2)."*

D. *It has been taught on Tannaite authority in accord with the view of R. Qattina:*

E. Just as at the advent of the Sabbatical Year the world will lie fallow for one out of seven years.

F. so it is with the world. A thousand years will the world lie fallow out of seven thousand years,

G. as it is said, "And the Lord alone shall be exalted in that day" (Is. 2:11), and Scripture says, "A Psalm and song for the Sabbath Day" (Ps. 92:1) – a day that is wholly the Sabbath.

H. And Scripture says, "For a thousand years in your sight are but as yesterday when they are past" (Ps. 90:4). [A day stands for a thousand years.]

I.89   A. *A Tannaite authority of the house of Elijah [said],* "For six thousand years the world will exist.

B. "For two thousand it will be desolate, two thousand years [will be the time of] Torah, and two thousand years will be the days of the Messiah.

C. [97B] but on account of our numerous sins what has been lost [of those years, in which the Messiah should have come but has not come] has been lost.

I.90   A. Said Elijah to R. Sala the Pious, "The world will last for no fewer than eighty-five Jubilees [of fifty years each], and the son of David will come in the last one."

B. He said to him, "Will it be in the first or the last year of the last Jubilee?"

C. He said to him, "I do not know."

D. "Will it come at the end or not come at the end of the fiftieth year?"

E.   He said to him, "I do not know."

F.   *R. Ashi said, "This is what he said to him: 'Up to that time, do not look for his coming, but from that time onward, do look for his coming.'"*

I.91 A.   R. Hanan, son of Tahalipa, sent to R. Joseph, "I came across a man who had in hand a scroll, written in Assyrian [block] letters in the holy language.

B.   "I said to him, 'Where did you get this?'

C.   "He said to me, 'I was employed in the Roman armies, and I found it in the Roman archives.'

D.   "In the scroll it is written that after four thousand two hundred ninety-two years from the creation of the world, the world will be an orphan.

E.   "[As to the years to follow] in some there will be wars of the great dragons, and in some, wars of Gog and Magog, and the rest will be the days of the Messiah.

F.   "And the Holy One, blessed be he, will renew his world only after seven thousand years."

G.   R. Aha, son of Raba, said, "'After five thousand years' *is what is said.*"

I.92 A.   *It has been taught on Tannaite authority:*

B.   R. Nathan says, "This verse of Scripture pierces to the depth:

C.   "'For the vision is yet for an appointed time, but at the end it shall speak and not lie; though he tarry, wait for him; because it will surely come, it will not tarry' (Hab. 2:3)."

D.   This is not in accord with our rabbis, who interpreted, "Until a time and times and the dividing of time" (Dan. 7:25).

E.   Nor does it accord with R. Simlai, who would interpret, "You feed them with the bread of tears and given them tears to drink a third time" (Ps. 80:6).

F.   Nor does it accord with R. Aqiba, who would interpret the verse, "Yet once, it is a little while, and I will shake the heavens and the earth" (Hag. 2:6).

G.   Rather, the first kingdom will last for seventy years, the second kingdom for fifty-two years, and the kingdom of Ben Koziba will be for two and a half years.

I.93 A.   *What is the meaning of the verse,* "But at the end it shall speak and not lie" (Hab. 2:3)?

B.   Said R. Samuel bar Nahmani said R. Jonathan, "[Freedman, p. 659, n. 5: Reading the verse as, 'He will blast him who calculates the end,'] blasted be the bones of those who calculate the end [when the Messiah will come].

C.   "For they might say, 'Since the end has come and he has not come, he will not come.'

D.   "Rather, wait for him, as it is said, 'Though he tarry, wait for him' (Hab. 2:3).

E.   "Should you say that we shall wait, but he may not wait, Scripture responds, 'And therefore will the Lord wait, that he may be gracious to you, and therefore will he be exalted, that he may have mercy upon you' (Is. 30:18).

F.   "Then, since we are waiting and he is waiting, what is holding things up?

G.   "It is the attribute of justice that is holding things up.

H.   "But if the attribute of justice is holding things up, why should we wait?

I.   "It is so as to receive the reward for our patience, as it is written, 'Blessed are all those who wait for him' (Is. 30:9)."

I.94   A.   *Said Abbayye, "There are in the world never fewer than thirty-six righteous men, who look upon the face of the Presence of God every day, for it is said, 'Happy are those who wait for him' (Is. 30:18), and the numerical value of the letters in the word 'for him' is thirty-six."*

       B.   *Is this so? And did not Raba say, "The row of the righteous before the Holy One, blessed be he, is made up of eighteen thousand, as it is said, 'There shall be eighteen thousand round about' (Ez. 48:35)"?*

       C.   *There is no contradiction between the two views. The former number refers to those few who see him through a bright mirror, the latter number refers to those many who see him only through a dirty mirror.*

       D.   *And are they so numerous?*

       E.   And did not Hezekiah said R. Jeremiah said in the name of R. Simeon b. Yohai, "I have myself seen the inhabitants of the upper world, and they are only a few. If they are a thousand, my son and I are among their number. If they are only a hundred, my son and I are among their number. If they are only two, they are only my son and I."

       F.   *There is still no contradiction. The larger number speaks of those who go inside only with permission, the smaller number those who go inside even without permission.*

I.95   A.   Said Rab, "All of the ends have passed, and the matter now depends only on repentance and good deeds."

       B.   And Samuel said, "It is sufficient for a mourner to remain firm in his mourning."

       C.   *This accords with the following dispute among Tannaite authorities:*

       D.   R. Eliezer says, "If the Israelites repent, they will be redeemed, and if not, they will not be redeemed."

       E.   Said R. Joshua to him, "If they do not repent, will they not be redeemed?!

       F.   "Rather, the Holy One, blessed be he, will raise up for them a king whose decrees will be as harsh as those of Haman, and the Israelites will repent, and [God] will restore them to a good path]."

       G.   *A further Tannaite version:*

       H.   R. Eliezer says, "If the Israelites repent, they will be redeemed, as it is said, 'Return, backsliding children, and I will heal your back-slidings' (Jer. 3:22)."

       I.   Said to him R. Joshua, "And is it not written, 'You have sold yourselves for nought, and you shall be redeemed without money' (Is. 52:3)?

       J.   "'You have sold yourselves for nought' – for idolatry.

       K.   "'But you shall be redeemed without money' – with neither repentance nor do good deeds."

	L.	Said to him R. Eliezer, "But is it not written, 'Return to me and I shall return to you' (Mal. 3:7)?"
	M.	Said to him R. Joshua, "But is it not written, 'For I am master over you, and I will take you, one from a city and two from a family and I will bring you to Zion' (Jer. 3:14)?"
	N.	Said to him R. Eliezer, "But it is written, 'In returning and rest you shall be saved' (Is. 30:5)."
	O.	Said R. Joshua to R. Eliezer, "But is it not written, 'Thus says the Lord, the redeemer of Israel, and his holy one, to whom man despises, to him whom the nations abhor, to a servant of rulers, **[98A]** kings shall see and arise, princes also shall worship' (Is. 49:7)?"
	P.	Said to him R. Eliezer, "But is it not written, 'If you will return, O Israel, says the Lord, return to me' (Jer. 4:1)?"
	Q.	Said to him R. Joshua, "But it is written elsewhere, 'And I heard the man clothed in linen, which was upon the waters of the river, when he held up his right hand and his left hand to heaven and swore by him who lives forever that it shall be for a year, two years, and half a year and when he shall have accomplished scattering the power of the holy people, all these things shall be finished' (Dan. 12:7)."
	R.	And R. Eliezer shut up.
I.96	A.	And said R. Abba, "You have no indication of the end more openly stated than the following, as it is said: 'But you, O Mountains of Israel, shall shoot forth your branches and yield your fruit to my people, Israel, for they are at hand to come' (Ez. 36:8)."
	B.	R. Eliezer says, "Also the following, as it is said: 'For before these days there was no hire for man, nor any hire for beast neither was there any peace to him that went out or came in because of the affliction' (Zech. 8:10)."
	C.	*What is the meaning of the phrase,* "Neither was there any peace to him that went out or came in because of the affliction"?
	D.	Rab said, "Even to disciples of sages, concerning whom peace is written in Scripture, as it is written, 'Great peace shall they have who love your Torah' (Ps. 119:165)."
	E.	"Neither was there any peace... because of the affliction" (Zech. 8:10):
	F.	And Samuel said, "Until all prices will be equal."
I.97	A.	Said R. Hanina, "The son of David will come only when a fish will be sought for a sick person and not be found, as it is said, 'Then I will make their waters deep and cause their rivers like oil' (Ez. 32:14), and it is written, 'In that day I will cause the horn of the house of Israel to sprout forth' (Ez. 29:21)."
	B.	Said R. Hama bar Hanina, "The son of David will come only when the rule over Israel by the least of the kingdoms will come to an end, as it is said, 'He shall both cut off the springs with pruning hooks and take away and cut down the branches' (Is. 18:5), and further: 'In that time shall the present be brought to the Lord of hosts of a people that is scattered and peeled' (Is. 18:7)."

C. Said Zeiri said R. Hanina, "The son of David will come only when arrogant people will no longer be [found] in Israel, as it is said, 'For then I will take away out of the midst of you those who rejoice in your pride' (Zeph. 8:11), followed by: 'I will also leave in the midst of you an afflicted and poor people, and they shall take refuge in the name of the Lord' (Zeph. 3:12)."

D. Said R. Simlai in the name of R. Eliezer b. R. Simeon, "The son of David will come only when all judges and rulers come to an end in Israel, as it is said, 'And I will turn my hand upon you and purely purge away your dross and take away all your tin, and I will restore your judges as at the first' (Is. 1:25-26)."

I.98 A. Said Ulla, "Jerusalem will be redeemed only through righteousness, as it is written, 'Zion shall be redeemed with judgment and her converts with righteousness' (Is. 1:27)."

B. *Said R. Pappa, "If the arrogant end [in Israel], the Magi will end [in Iran], if the judges end [in Israel], the rulers of thousands will come to an end [in Iran].*

C. *"If the arrogant end [in Israel], the magi will end [in Iran], as it is written, 'And I will purely purge away your haughty ones and take away all your tin' (Is. 1:25).*

D. *"If judges end [in Israel], the rulers of thousands will come to an end [in Iran], as it is written, 'The Lord has taken away your judgments, he has cast out your enemy' (Zeph. 3:15)."*

I.99 A. Said R. Yohanan, "If you see a generation growing less and less, hope for him, as it is said, 'And the afflicted people will you save' (2 Sam. 22:28)."

B. Said R. Yohanan, "If you see a generation over which many troubles flow like a river, hope for him, as it is written, 'When the enemy shall come in like a flood, the spirit of the Lord shall lift up a standard against him' (Is. 59:19), followed by: 'And the redeemer shall come to Zion' (Is. 59:20)."

C. And said R. Yohanan, "The son of David will come to a generation that is either entirely righteous or entirely wicked.

D. "A generation that is entirely righteous, as it is written, 'Your people also shall be all righteous, they shall inherit the land for ever' (Is. 60:21),

E. "or a generation that is entirely wicked, as it is written, 'And he saw that there was no man and wondered that there was no intercessor' (Is. 59:16), and it is written, 'For my own sake, even for my own sake I will do it' (Is. 60:22)."

I.100 A. *Said R. Alexandri, "R. Joshua b. Levi contrasted verses as follows:*

B. "It is written; 'in its time [will the Messiah come],' and it is also written; 'I [the Lord] will hasten it.'

C. "[What is the meaning of the contrast?]

D. "If [the Israelites] have merit, I will hasten it, if they do not, [the messiah] will come in due course.

E. "'It is written, "And behold, one like the son of man came with the clouds of heaven" (Dan. 7:13, and it is written, "Behold your king comes to you... lowly and riding upon an ass" (Zech. 9:7). [What is the meaning of the contrast?]

F.   "'If [the Israelites] have merit, it will be "with the clouds of heaven" (Dan. 7:13), and if they do not have merit, it will be "lowly and riding upon an ass" (Zech. 9:7).'"

I.101   A.   *Said King Shapur to Samuel, "You say that the Messiah will come on an ass [which is a humble way]. Come and I shall send him a white horse that I have."*

B.   *He said to him, "Do you have one of many colors?"*

I.102   A.   *R. Joshua b. Levi found Elijah standing at the door of the burial vault of R. Simeon b. Yohai. He said to him, "Am I going to come to the world to come?"*

B.   *He said to him, "If this master wants."*

C.   Said R. Joshua b. Levi, "Two did I see, but a third voice did I hear."

D.   *He said to him, "When is the Messiah coming?"*

E.   *He said to him, "Go and ask him."*

F.   *"And where is he sitting?"*

G.   *"At the gate of the city."*

H.   *"And what are the marks that indicate who he is?"*

I.   *"He is sitting among the poor who suffer illness, and all of them untie and tie their bandages all together, but he unties them and ties them one by one. He is thinking, 'Perhaps I may be wanted, and I do not want to be held up.'"*

J.   He went to him, saying to him, "Peace be unto you, my master and teacher."

K.   He said to him, "Peace be unto you, son of Levi."

L.   *He said to him, "When is the master coming?"*

M.   He said to him, "Today."

N.   *He went back to Elijah, who said to him, "What did he tell you?"*

O.   He said to him, "'Peace be unto you, son of Levi.'"

P.   *He said to him, "He [thereby] promised you and your father the world to come."*

Q.   *He said to him, "But he lied to me. For he said to me, 'I am coming today,' but he did not come."*

R.   *He said to him, "This is what he said to you, '"Today, if you will obey his voice" (Ps. 95:7).'"*

I.103   A.   His disciples asked R. Yosé b. Qisma, "When is the son of David coming?"

B.   He said to them, "I am afraid [to answer], lest you ask an omen from me [that my answer is right]."

C.   They said to him, "We shall not ask for an omen from you." He said to them, "When this gate falls and is rebuilt, falls and is rebuilt, and falls a third time. They will not suffice to rebuild it before the son of David will come."

D.   They said to him, "Our master, give us an omen."

E.   He said to them, "But did you not say to me that you would not ask for an omen from me?"

F.   They said to him, "Even so."

G.   He said to them, "Then let the waters of the grotto of Banias turn to blood," and they turned to blood.

H.   When he died, he said to them, "Dig my bier deep into the ground, **[98B]** for there is not a palm tree in Babylonia on which a Persian horse has not been tied, nor is there a bier in the land of Israel from which a Median horse will not eat straw."

I.104   A.   Said Rab, "The son of David will come only when the monarchy [of Rome] will spread over Israel for nine months,

        B.   "as it is said, 'Therefore will he give them up, until the time that she who travails has brought forth; then the remnant of his brethren shall return to the children of Israel' (Mic. 5:2)."

I.105   A.   *Said Ulla, "Let him come, but may I not see him."*

        B.   *Said Rabba, "Let him come, but may I not see him."*

        C.   *R. Joseph said, "May he come, and may I have the merit of sitting in the shade of the dung of his ass."*

        D.   *Said Abbayye to Rabbah, "What is the reason [that some do not wish to see the coming of the messiah]? Is it because of the turmoil of the Messiah?*

        E.   *"And has it not been taught on Tannaite authority:*

        F.   "His disciples asked R. Eliezer, 'What should someone do to save himself from the turmoil of the Messiah?'

        G.   "[He replied to them], 'Let him engage in study of the Torah and acts of loving kindness.'

        H.   "And lo, the master [at hand] practices Torah-study and acts of loving kindness. [So why not want to see him?]"

        I.   He said to him, "Perhaps he fears sin will cause [him to suffer], in line with what R. Jacob bar Idi said."

        J.   *For R. Jacob bar Idi contrasted two verses of Scripture, as follows:* "It is written, 'And behold, I am with you and will keep you wherever you go' (Gen. 28:15), and another verse states, 'Then Jacob was greatly afraid' (Gen. 32:8).

        K.   "[Why the contrast between God's promise and Jacob's fear?] Jacob feared [and thought to himself,] 'Sin which I have done may cause [punishment for me instead].'"

        L.   *That accords with what has been taught on Tannaite authority:*

        M.   "Till your people pass over, O Lord, till your people pass over, that you have acquired" (Ex. 15:16).

        N.   "Till your people pass over" refers to the first entry into the land [in Joshua's time].

        O.   "Till your people pass over, that you have acquired" refers to the second entry into the land [in the time of Ezra and Nehemiah. Thus a miracle was promised not only on the first occasion, but also on the second. But it did not happen the second time around. Why not?]

        P.   On the basis of this statement, sages have said, "The Israelites were worthy of having a miracle performed for them in the time of Ezra also, just as it had been performed for them in the time of Joshua b. Nun, but sin caused the miracle to be withheld."

I.106   A.   *So said R. Yohanan, "Let him come, but let me not see him."*

        B.   *Said R. Simeon b. Laqish to him, "What is the scriptural basis for that view? Shall we say that it is because it is written, 'As if a man fled from a lion and a bear met him, or went into the house and leaned his hand on the wall and a serpent bit him' (Amos 5:19)?*

        C.   "Come and I shall show you an example of such a case in this world.

D.   "When a man goes out to the field and bailiff meets him, it is like one whom a lion meets. He goes into town and a tax-collector meets him, it is like one whom a bear meets.

E.   "He goes into his house and finds his sons and daughters suffering from hunger, it is like one whom a snake bit.

F.   "Rather, it is because it is written, 'Ask you now and see whether a man travails with child? Why do I see every man with his hands on his loins, as women in travail, and all faces are turned into paleness' (Jer. 30:6)."

G.   *What is the sense of, "Why do I see every man..."?*

H.   Said Raba bar Isaac said Rab, "It speaks of him to whom all [manly] power belongs [God]."

I.   *And what is the sense of "all faces are turned into paleness"?*

J.   Said R. Yohanan, "[It speaks of God's] heavenly family and his earthly family, at the moment at which God says, 'These are the creation of my hands, and those are the creation of my hands. How shall I destroy these [gentiles] on account of [what they have done to] those [Israelites]? [Freedman, p. 667, n. 2: to avenge the wrongs suffered by the Jews. Because the suffering would be so great that even the Almighty would lament it, Yohanan desired to be spared the Messiah's coming.]"

K.   *Said R. Pappa, "This is in line with what people say: 'The ox runs and falls, so the horse is put in its stall.' [Freedman, p. 667, n. 3: Then it is hard to get the horse out. So the Israelites, having fallen, were replaced in power by the gentiles, but on their recovery, it will be difficult to remove the gentiles from their position without inflicting much suffering.]"*

I.107 A.   Said R. Giddal said Rab, "The Israelites are going to eat [and not starve] in the years of the Messiah."

B.   *Said R. Joseph, "That is self-evident. If not, then who will eat? Joe and Mo?! [Text: Hiliq and Bileq?]"*

C.   *[The statement at hand] serves to exclude the view of R. Hillel, who has said, "There will be no further Messiah for Israel, for they already consumed him in the time of Hezekiah."*

I.108 A.   Said Rab, "The world was created only for David."

B.   And Samuel said, "For Moses."

C.   And R. Yohanan said, "For the Messiah."

D.   What is his name?

E.   *The house of R. Shila said, "His name is Shiloh, as it is said, 'Until Shiloh come' (Gen. 49:10)."*

F.   *Members of the house of R. Yannai say, "His name is Yinnon, for it is written, 'His name shall endure forever, before the sun was, his name is Yinnon' (Ps. 72:17)."*

G.   *Members of the house of R. Haninah said, "It is Haninah, as it is said, 'Where I will not give you Haninah' (Jer. 16:13)."*

H.   Others say, "His name is Menahem, son of Hezekiah, for it is written, 'Because Menahem that would relieve my soul, is far' (Lam. 1:16)."

I.   *Rabbis said, "His name is 'the leper of the school house,' as it is written,* 'Surely he has borne our griefs and carried our sorrows, yet we did esteem him a leper, smitten of God and afflicted' (Is. 53:4)."

I.109 A.   *Said R. Nahman, "If he is among the living, he is such as I, as it is said,* 'And their nobles shall be of themselves and their governors shall proceed from the midst of them' (Jer. 30:21)."

B.   *Said Rab, "If he is among the living, he is such as our Holy Rabbi [Judah the Patriarch], and if he is among the dead, he is such as Daniel, the most desirable man."*

C.   Said R. Judah said Rab, "The Holy One, blessed be he, is destined to raise up for [Israel] another David, as it is said, 'But they shall serve the Lord their God and David their king, whom I will raise up for them' (Jer. 30:9).

D.   "'Raised up' is not what is said, but rather, 'will raise up.'"

E.   *Said R. Pappa to Abbayye, "But lo, it is written, 'And my servant David shall be their prince forever' (Ez. 37:25) [with the title for prince standing for less than the title for king]."*

F.   [He said to him,] "It is like a king and a viceroy [the second David being king]."

I.110 A.   *R. Simlai interpreted the following verse: "What is the meaning of that which is written, 'Woe to you who desire the day of the Lord! to what end is it for you? the day of the Lord is darkness and not light' (Amos 5:18)?*

B.   "The matter may be compared to the case of the cock and the bat who were waiting for light.

C.   "The cock said to the bat, 'I am waiting for the light, for the light belongs to me, but what do you need light for **[99A]**?'"

D.   *That is in line with what a min said to R. Abbahu, "When is the Messiah coming?"*

E.   *He said to him, "When darkness covers those men."*

F.   *He said to him, "You are cursing me."*

G.   *He said to him, "I am merely citing a verse of Scripture: 'For behold, the darkness shall cover the earth, and great darkness the people, but the Lord shall shine upon you, and his glory shall be seen upon you' (Is. 60:2)."*

I.111 A.   *It has been taught on Tannaite authority:*

B.   R. Eliezer says, "The days of the Messiah will last forty years, as it is said, 'Forty years long shall I take hold of the generation' (Ps. 95:10)."

C.   R. Eliezer b. Azariah says, "Seventy years, as it is said, 'And it shall come to pass in that day that Tyre shall be forgotten seventy years, according to the days of one king' (Is. 23:15).

D.   "Now what would be a one [and singular] king? We must say that it is the Messiah."

E.   Rabbi says, "Three generations, as it is said, 'They shall fear you with the sun and before the moon, a generation and generations' (Ps. 72:5)."

I.112 A.   R. Hillel says, "Israel will have no Messiah, for they consumed him in the time of Hezekiah."

B.   *Said R. Joseph, "May R. Hillel's master forgive him. When did Hezekiah live? It was in the time of the first Temple. But Zechariah prophesied in* the second Temple's time and said, 'Rejoice greatly, O daughter of Zion, shout, O daughter of Jerusalem, behold your king comes to you; he is just and has salvation; lowly and riding upon an ass and upon a colt the foal of an ass' (Zech. 9:9)."

I.113   A.   *A further teaching on Tannaite authority:*

B.   R. Eliezer says, "The days of the Messiah will last for forty years. Here it is written, 'And he afflicted you and made you hunger and fed you with manna' (Deut. 8:3), and elsewhere: 'Make us glad according to the days [forty years in the wilderness] in which you have afflicted us' (Ps. 90:15)."

C.   R. Dosa says, "Four hundred years. Here it is written, 'And they shall serve them and they shall afflict them four hundred years' (Gen. 15:13), and elsewhere: 'Make us glad according to the days wherein you have afflicted us' (Ps. 90:15)."

D.   Rabbi says, "Three hundred and sixty-five years, according to the number of days in the solar year, as it is said, 'For the day of vengeance is in my heart and the year of my redemption has come' (Is. 63:4)."

E.   *What is the meaning of* "the day of vengeance is in my heart" (Is. 63:4)?

F.   Said R. Yohanan, "I have revealed it to my heart, but I have not revealed it to my limbs."

G.   R. Simeon b. Laqish said, "To my heart I have revealed it, to the ministering angels I have not revealed it."

H.   *Abimi, son of R. Abbahu, stated on Tannaite authority,* "The days of the Messiah for Israel will be seven thousand years, as it is said, 'And as the bridegroom rejoices over the bride [a week], so shall your God rejoice over you' (Is. 62:5)."

I.   Said R. Judah said Samuel, "The days of the Messiah are the same as the days that have passed from the day of the creation of the world even to now, as it is said, 'As the days of heaven upon earth' (Deut. 11:21)."

J.   R. Nahman bar Isaac said, "As the days from Noah to now, as it is said, 'For this is as the waters of Noah, which are mine, so I have sworn it' (Is. 54:9)."

I.114   A.   Said R. Hiyya bar Abba said R. Yohanan, "All of the prophets prophesied only concerning the days of the Messiah.

B.   "But as to the world to come [thereafter]: 'Eye has not seen, O Lord, beside you, what he has prepared for him who waits for him' (Is. 64:3)."

C.   *That statement differs from the view of Samuel.*

D.   For said Samuel, "There is no difference between this world and the days of the Messiah except for [Israel's] subjugation to the rule of the empires alone."

E.   And said R. Hiyya bar Abba said R. Yohanan, "All of the prophets prophesied only concerning those who repent, but as to the perfectly righteous people [who have never sinned to begin with]: 'Eye has not seen, O God, beside you, what he has prepared for him who waits for him' (Is. 54:3)."

F.   *That statement differs from the view of R. Abbahu.*

G.   For, said R. Abbahu, "In the place in which those who repent stand, the righteous cannot stand, for it is said, 'Peace, peace to him who is far off and to him that is near' (Is. 57:19).

H.   "'To begin with, he was 'far off,' and then he repented and so became 'near.'

I.   *"What is the sense of 'far off'? Originally far off [a sinner], and what is the sense of 'near'? Originally near and still near.* [Freedman, p. 671, n. 3: Thus he assigns a higher rank to the repentant sinner than to the completely righteous.]"

J.   R. Yohanan said, "'To the one who was distant' because he was far from sin, and 'near' in that he was near sin but distanced himself from it."

K. And said R. Hiyya bar Abba said R. Yohanan, "All of the prophets prophesied only concerning him who marries his daughter off to a disciple of sages, conducts business to the advantage of a disciple of a sage, and benefits a disciple of a sage from his wealth.

L. "But as to disciples of sages themselves: 'Eye has not seen, O God beside you' (Is. 64:3)."

M. *What is the meaning of the phrase, "Eye has not seen"?*

N. Said R. Joshua b. Levi, "This refers to wine that has been kept in the grapes from the six days of creation."

O. R. Simeon b. Laqish said, "This refers to Eden, which no eye has ever seen.

P. "And if you should say, 'Then we where did Adam dwell?' the answer is, in the garden.

Q. "And if you should say, 'But it was the Garden that was Eden,' Scripture says, 'And a river issued from Eden to water the garden' (Gen. 2:10)."

II.1   A.   **And he who says, "The Torah does not come from heaven" [M. 11:1D]:**

B. *Our rabbis have taught on Tannaite authority:*

C. "Because he has despised the word of the Lord and broken his commandment, that soul shall utterly be cut off" (Num. 15:31):

D. This refers to one who says, **"The Torah does not come from heaven."**

E. Another matter:

F. "Because he has despised the word of the Lord": This refers to an Epicurean.

G. Another matter:

H. "Because he has despised the word of the Lord": This refers to one who is without shame in interpreting the Torah.

I. "And broken his commandment": This refers to one who removes the mark fleshly arks of the covenant.

J. "That soul shatter utterly be cut off": "Be cut off" – in this world. "Utterly" in the world to come.

K. On the basis of this exegesis, **said R. Eliezer the Modite, "He who treats Holy Things as secular, he who despises the appointed times, he who humiliates his companion in public, he who removes the signs of the covenant of Abraham, our father, and he**

who exposes aspects of the Torah not in accord with the law, even though he has in hand learning in Torah and good deeds, will have no share in the world to come" [M. Abot 3:11].

L. *A further teaching on Tannaite authority:*

M. "Because he has despised the word of the Lord" (Num. 14:31): This refers to one who says, **"The Torah does not come from heaven."**

N. And even if he had said, "The entire Torah comes from heaven, except for this one verse, which the Holy One, blessed be he, did not say, but which Moses said on his own," such a one falls under the verse, "Because he has despised the word of the Lord" (Num. 15:31).

O. And even if he had said, "The entire Torah comes from heaven, except for one minor point, an argument a fortiori, an argument based on analogy," such a one falls under the verse, "Because he has despised the way of the Lord" (Num. 15:31).

II.2 A. *It has been taught on Tannaite authority:*

B. R. Meir would say, "He who studies the Torah but does not teach it falls under the verse, "Because he has despised the word of the Lord" (Num. 15:31)."

C. R. Nathan says, "Whoever does not pay close attention to the Mishnah."

D. R. Nehorai says, "Whoever has the possibility of taking up the study of the Torah and does not do so."

E. R. Ishmael says, "This refers to one who worships an idol."

F. *What provides the implication that such a one is subject to discussion here?*

G. *It accords with what the Tannaite authority of the house of R. Ishmael [said], "'Because he has despised the word of the Lord' (Num. 15:31) refers to one who despises the statement that was made to Moses at Sinai: 'I am the Lord your God. You shall have no other gods before me' (Ex. 20:2-3)."*

II.3 A. **R. Joshua b. Qorhah says, "Whoever studies the Torah and does not review it is like a man who sows seed but does not harvest it."**

B. **R. Joshua says, "Whoever learns the Torah and forgets it is like a woman who bears and buries."**

C. **R. Aqiba says, "[99B] A song is in me, a song always" [T. Ah. 16:8H-I].**

D. *Said R. Isaac b. Abudimi, "What is the pertinent proof-text? As it is said, 'He who labors labors for himself, for his mouth craves it of him' (Prov. 16:26).*

E. *"He labors in one place, and the Torah labors for him in a different place."*

II.4 A. Said R. Eleazar, "Every man was born to work, as it is said, 'For man is born to work' (Job 5:7).

B. "I do knot know whether it is for work done with the mouth that he is created, or whether it is for labor done through physical work that he was created.

C. "When Scripture says, 'For his mouth craves it of him' (Prov. 16:26), one has to conclude that it is for work done with the mouth that he was created.

D.   "Yet I still do not know whether it was to labor in the Torah or to labor in some sort of other conversation.

E.   "When Scripture says, 'This book of the Torah shall not depart out of your mouth' (Josh. 1:8), one must conclude that it is for labor in the Torah that he is created."

F.   *That is in line with what Raba said, "All bodies serve to bear burdens. Happy are those who have the merit of bearing the burden of the Torah."*

II.5   A.   "Whoever commits adultery with a woman lacks understanding" (Prov. 6:32).:

B.   Said R. Simeon b. Laqish, "This refers to one who studies the Torah at occasional intervals.

C.   "For it is said, 'For it is a pleasant thing if you keep them within you, they shall withal be fitted in your lips' (Prov. 22:18). [Freedman, p. 673, n. 11: One can keep the Torah only if its words are fitted always on his lips, not at rare intervals only.]"

II.6   A.   *Our rabbis have taught on Tannaite authority:*

B.   "But the soul that does anything presumptuously" (Num. 15:30):

C.   This refers to Manasseh, son of Hezekiah, who would go into session and interpret tales seeking flaws in them, saying, "Did Moses have nothing better to do than to write such verses as 'And Lotan's sister was Timna' (Gen. 36:22). 'And Timna was concubine to Eliphaz' (Gen. 36:12). 'And Reuben went in the days of the wheat harvest and found mandrakes in the field' (Gen. 30:14)?"

D.   An echo came forth and said to him, "'You sit and speak against your brother; you slander your own mother's son. These things you have done, and I kept silence, you thought that I was altogether such a one as yourself, but I will reprove you and set them in order before your eyes' (Ps. 50:20-21)."

E.   Concerning him it is spelled out in tradition: "Woe to them who draw iniquity with cords of vanity and sin as it were with a cart rope" (Is. 5:18).

F.   *What is the sense of* "and sin as it were with a cart rope"?

G.   Said R. Assi, "The inclination to do evil to begin with is like a spider's thread and ends up like a cart do rope."

H.   *In any event, what is the meaning of,* "And Lotan's sister was Timna" (Gen. 36:22)?

I.   *She was a princess, as it is written, "Duke Lotan, Duke Timna," and "duke" refers to a kid who has not yet got his crown.*

J.   *She had wanted to convert to Judaism.* She came to Abraham, Isaac, and Jacob, and they did not accept her. She went and became the concubine to Eliphaz, son of Esau, saying, "It is better to he a handmaiden to this nation and not a noble woman to any other nation."

K.   *From her descended Amalak, who distressed Israel.*

L.   *What is the reason? It was because they should not have put her off [but should have accepted her].*

M.   "And Reuben went in the days of the wheat harvest [and found mandrakes in the field]" (Gen. 36:12)"

	N.	Said Raba, son of R. Isaac, said Rab, "On the basis of this verse, we learn that righteous folk do not lay hands on what is stolen."
	O.	"And found mandrakes in the field" (Gen. 36:12):
	P.	*What are these?*
	Q.	Said Rab, "Mandrakes."
	R.	Said Levi, "Violets."
	S.	Said R. Jonathan, "Mandrake flowers."
II.7	A.	Said R. Alexandri, "Whoever is occupied in study of the Torah for the sake of heaven brings peace to the family above and to the family below,
	B.	"as it is said, 'Or let him take hold of my strength that he may make peace with me, and he shall may make peace with me' (Is. 27:5)."
	C.	Rab said, "It is as if he built the palace above and the one below, as it is said, 'And I have put my words in your mouth and I have covered you in the shadow of my hand, that I may plant the heavens and lay the foundations of the earth, and say to Zion, You are my people' (Is. 51:16)."
	D.	R. Yohanan said, "Also he shields the world, as it is said, 'And I have covered you in the shadow of my hand' (Is. 51:16)."
	E.	Levi said, "Also he draws the redemption nearer, as it is said, 'And say to Zion, you are my people' (Is. 51:16)."
II.8	A.	Said R. Simeon b. Laqish, "Whoever teaches Torah to the son of his neighbor is credited by Scripture as if he had made him,
	B.	"as it is said, 'And the souls which they had made in Haran' I (Gen. 12:5)."
	C.	R. Eleazar said, "It is as though he had made the words of Torah, as it is said, 'Therefore keep the words of this covenant and make them' (Deut. 29:9)."
	D.	Raba said, "It is as though he had made himself, as it is said – 'And make them' (Deut. 29:9).
	E.	"Do not read 'them' but 'yourselves.'"
II.9	A.	Said R. Abbahu, "Whoever makes his neighbor carry out a religious duty is credited by Scripture as if he himself had done it, as it is said, 'The Lord said to Moses, Take...your rod, with which you hit the river' (Ex. 17:5).
	B.	"But did Moses hit the river? It was Aaron who hit the river.
	C.	"Rather, this shows, whoever makes his neighbor carry out a religious duty is credited by Scripture as if he himself had done it."
III.1	A.	**...an Epicurean [M. 11:1D]:**
	B.	*Both Rab and R. Hanina say,* "This refers to one who humiliates disciples of sages."
	C.	*Both R. Yohanan and R. Joshua b. Levi say,* "It is one who humiliates his fellow before a disciple of a sage."
	D.	*Now from the viewpoint of him who says* it is one who humiliates his fellow before a sage, it would also encompass a disciple of a sage himself, who **exposes aspects of the Torah not in accord with the law [M. Abot 3:11]** [acts impudently against the Torah (Freedman)].
	E.	*But in the view of him who says that* an Epicurean is one who humiliates a disciple of a sage himself, *then at sort of person would fall*

into the category of one who **exposes aspects of the Torah not in accord with the law [M. Abot 3:11]**?

F.   It would be someone of the sort of Manasseh b. Hezekiah.

G.   *There are those who repeat on Tannaite authority the dispute at hand in conjunction with the latter, rather than the former category, as follows:*

H.   **One who exposes aspects of the Torah [not in accord with the law] [M. Abot 3:11]:**

I.   *Rab and R. Hanina say, "It is one who humiliates a disciple of sages."*

J.   *R. Yohanan and R. Joshua b. Levi say, "It is one who humiliates his fellow before a disciple of a sage."*

K.   *Now from the viewpoint of him who says* it is one who humiliates a disciple of a sage himself, then one who reveals aspects of the Torah, one who humiliates his fellow before a disciple of a sage, would be an Epicurean.

L.   *But from the viewpoint of him who says that it is one who humiliates his fellow before a disciple of a sage, with one who reveals aspects of the Torah [in an improper way] as an Epicurean, then who would fall into that latter category?*

M.   *Said R. Joseph, "It would, for example, be those who say, 'What good are the rabbis for us? It is for their own benefit that they study Scripture. It is for their own benefit that they repeat Mishnah-teachings.'"*

N.   Said Abbayye to him, "That too falls into the category of one who reveals aspects of the Torah in an improper way, for it is written, 'Thus says the Lord, But for my covenant [studied] day and night, I had not appointed the ordinances of heaven and earth' (Jer. 33:25). [Freedman, p. 676, n. 3: The world endures only because the Torah – 'my covenant' – is studied. To deny the utility of scholars therefore is to express disbelief of what is asserted in the Torah.]"

O.   *Said R. Nahman bar Isaac, "The proof derives as well from the following, as it is said, 'Then I will spare all the place for their sakes' (Gen. 18:26)."*

P.   *Rather, it is one who for example was sitting before his master, and the topic of discussion moved to another subject, and he said, "This is what we said on the subject," rather than, "Master, you have said [on that topic]."*

Q.   *Raba said, "It would, for example, be like the members of the house of Benjamin, the physician, who say, 'What good are rabbis to us. They have never* **[100A]** *permitted us to eat a raven or forbidden us to eat a dove [but are limited to what the Torah itself states]."*

R.   *When people of the house of Benjamin brought Raba a problem involving the validity of a beast that had been slaughtered and that may or may not have been able to survive, if he found a reason to permit the matter, he would say to them, "See, I do permit the raven to you."*

S.   *When he found a reason to prohibit it, he would say to them, "See, I do forbid the dove to you."*

	T.	*R. Pappa said, "It would be such as one who said, 'O, these rabbis!'"*
	U.	*R. Pappa forgot himself and said, "O these rabbis!" He sat and fasted.*
III.2	A.	*Levi bar Samuel and R. Huna bar Hiyya were fixing the mantles of the Torah scrolls of the house of R. Judah. When they got to the scroll of Esther, they said, "Lo, this scroll of Esther does not have to have a mantle at all."*
	B.	*He said to them, "This sort of talk also appears to be Epicureanism."*
III.3	A.	R. Nahman said, "It is one who refers to his master by his name."
	B.	For R. Yohanan said, "On what account was Gehazi punished because he called his master by name.
	C.	"as it is said, 'My lord, O King, this is the woman, and this is her son whom Elisha restored to life' (2 Kgs. 8:5)."
III.4	A.	*R. Jeremiah was in session before R. Zira and said, "The Holy One, blessed be he, by which there will be many kinds of delicious produce, as it is said, 'And by the river upon that bank thereof, on this side and on that side, shall grow all trees for meat, whose leaf shall not fade, neither shall the fruit thereof be consumed; it shall bring forth new fruit, according to his months, because their waters they issued out of the sanctuary, and the fruit therefore shall be for meat, and the leaf thereof for medicine' (Ez. 47:12)."*
	B.	*"Said to him a certain old man, 'Well said, and so did R. Yohanan say.'"*
	C.	*Said R. Jeremiah to R. Zira, "Behavior of this sort [condescension to the master] likewise appears to be Epicureanism."*
	D.	*He said to him, "But this represented a mere support for your position.*
	E.	*"But if you have heard any tradition, this is the tradition that you heard:*
	F.	*"R. Yohanan was in session and interpreting Scripture as follows: 'The Holy One, blessed be he, is destined to bring forth precious stones and jewels which are thirty cubits long and thirty cubits high, and engrave on them an engraving ten by twenty cubits, and he will set them up as the gates of Jerusalem, for it is written, "And I will make your windows of agates and your gates of carbuncles" (Is. 54:12).'*
	G.	*"'A disciple ridiculed him, saying "Now if we do not find jewels the size of a dove's egg, are we going to find any that big?"*
	H.	*"'After some time he took a sea voyage, and he saw ministering angels cutting precious stones and jewels. He said to them, "As to these, what are they for?"*
	I.	*"'They said to him, "The Holy One, blessed be he, is destined to set them up as the gates of Jerusalem."*
	J.	*"'When he came back, he found R. Yohanan in session and expounding Scripture. He said to him, "Rabbi, indeed give your exposition, for it is appropriate that you should expound Scripture. Exactly as you said, so I myself saw."*
	K.	*"'He said to him, "Empty head! Had you not seen, would you not have believed me! You are one who ridicules teachings of sages." He set his eye on him and turned him into a hill of bones.'"*
	L.	*An objection was raised [to the teaching of Yohanan]"*
	M.	"And I will make you go upright (Lev. 26:13).

N.   R. Meir says, "It is the height of two hundred cubits, twice the height of Adam."

O.   R. Judah says, "A hundred cubits, the length of the Temple and its walls, as it is written, 'That our sons may be as plants grown up in their youth, that our daughters may be as corner stones, fashioned after the similitude of the Temple' (Ps. 144:12)."

P.   *What R. Yohanan meant was* [Freedman]: *the ventilation – windows.* [These would be ten by twenty, but the gates themselves would be much taller (Freedman, p. 678, n. 7)].

Q.   *What is the meaning of the phrase,* "And the leaf thereof is for medicine" (Ez. 47:12)"

R.   R. Isaac bar. Abodimi and R. Hisda: one said, "It is to open up the upper mouth [and help the dumb to speak]."

S.   One said, "It is to open the lower mouth [and heal the barrenness of a barren woman]."

T.   *It has been taught on Tannaite authority:*

U.   Hezekiah said, "It is to open the mouth of the dumb."

V.   Bar Qappara said, "It is to open the mouth of the barren women."

W.   R. Yohanan said, "It serves as medicine, literally."

X.   *What is the meaning of the statement, "Medicine"?*

Y.   R. Ramual bar Nahmani said, "It is to improve the appearance of masters of mouths [disciples]."

III.5   A.   R. Judah b. R. Simon interpreted, "Whoever blackens his face [in fasting] on account of teachings of Torah in this world will find that the Holy One, blessed be he, polishes his luster in the world to come.

B.   "For it is said, 'His countenance shall be as the Lebanon, excellent as the cedars' (Song 5:15)."

C.   R. Tanhum bar Hanilai said, "Whoever starves himself for words of Torah in his world will the Holy One, blessed be he, feed to satisfaction in the world to come,

D.   "as it is said, 'They shall be abundantly satisfied with the fatness of your house, and you shall make them drink of the river of your pleasures' (Ps. 36:9)."

E.   When R. Dimi came, he said, "The Holy One, blessed be he, is destined to give to every righteous person his full pack-load, as it is said, 'Blessed be the Lord, day by day, who loads us with benefits, even the God of our salvation, Selah' (Ps. 68:20)."

F.   Said Abbayye to him, "And is it possible to say so? Is it not said, 'Who has measured the waters in the hollow of his hand and measured out heaven with the span' (Is. 40:12)?"

G.   *He said to him, "What is the reason that you are not at home in matters of lore. They say in the West in the name of Raba bar Mari,* 'The Holy One, blessed be he, is destined to give each righteous person three hundred and ten worlds, as it is said, "That I may cause those who love me to inherit substance and I will fill their treasures," (Prov. 8:21), and the numerical value of the word for substance is three hundred ten.'"

III.6   A.   *It has been taught on Tannaite authority:*

B. R. Meir says, "By the same measure by which a mate metes out, do they mete out to him [M. Sot. 1:7A],

C. "For it is written, By measure in sending her away thou dost contend with her' (Is. 27:8).

D. Said R. Judah, "And can one say so? If a person gives a handful [to charity] to a poor man in this world, will the Holy One, blessed be he, give him a handful [of his, so much larger hand], in the world to come?

E. "And has it not been written, 'And meted out heaven with a span' (Is. 40:12)?"

F. [Meir replied] "But do you not say so? Which measure is greater? That of goodness or that of punishment?

G. [100B] "One must say, it is the measure of goodness that is greater than the measure of punishment. For with regard to the measure of goodness it is written, 'And he commanded the clouds from above, and opened the doors of heaven and rained down manna upon them to eat' (Ps. 78:23-24).

H. "With regard to the measure of punishment it is written, 'And the windows of heaven were opened' (Gen. 7:11) [Freedman, p. 680, n. 5: 'Doors' implies a greater opening than windows; God metes out reward more fully than punishment.]

I. "In respect to the measure even of punishment it is written, 'And they shall go forth and look upon the carcasses of the men who have transgressed against me, for their worm shall not die, neither shall their fire be quenched, and they shall be a horror to all flesh' (Is. 66:24).

J. "But is it not so that if a person put his finger into a fire in this world, he will be burned right away.

K. "But just as the Holy One, blessed be he, gives the wicked the power to receive their punishment, so the Holy One, blessed be he, gives the righteous the power to receive the goodness that is coming to them."

IV.1 A. R. Aqiba says, "Also: He who reads in heretical books..." [M. 11:1E]:

B. *It was taught on Tannaite authority:* That is the books of the minim.

IV.2 A. R. Joseph said, "It is also forbidden to read in the book of Ben Sira."

B. *Said to him Abbayye, "What is the reason for that view? Should I say that it is because it is written in it, 'Do not skin the fish, even from the ear, so that you will not go and bruise it, but roast it in the fire and eat two loaves with it'? In point of fact in the explicit view of Scripture it is also said,* 'You shall not destroy the trees thereof' (Deut. 20:19). [Freedman, p. 681, ns. 1-2: A fish is fit for consumption even if baked or roasted with its skin and therefore it is wasteful to remove it. Likewise, one must not wantonly destroy what is fit for use]. *And if it is a matter of exegesis [and not the literal sense], then the saying teaches us proper conduct, namely, that one should not have sexual relations in an unnatural way. Rather, might it be because it is written in it, 'A daughter is a worthless treasure for her father. For concern for her, he cannot sleep by night. In her childhood, it is lest she be seduced; in her girlhood, it is lest she play the whore; in her maturity, it is lest she not wed; once she is wed, it is lest she not have sons. In her* old age it is lest she practice witchcraft'? *But rabbis have also made the same statement:* 'The world cannot exist without males and without females. Happy is he whose children are males, and woe is him whose children are females.' *Rather, might it be because it is written in [Ben Sira]:* 'Do not admit despair into your heart, for despair has killed many men'? Lo, Solomon made the same statement; 'Anxiety in the heart of man makes him stoop' (Prov. 12:25)."

C.   R. Ammi and R. Assi: One said, "Let him banish it from his mind."

D.   "The other said, "Let him tell it to others."

E.   *[Reverting to Abbayye's inquiry:]* "*Rather, might it be because it is written in [Ben Sira]:* 'Keep large numbers of people away from your house, and do not let just anyone into your house'? Lo, Rabbi also made that statement. *For it has been taught on Tannaite authority:* Rabbi says, 'A person should never admit a great many friends into his house, as it is said, "A man who has many friends brings evil upon himself" (Prov. 18:24).' *Rather, it is because it is written in it:* 'A man with a thin beard is wise, a man with a thick beard is a fool; one who blows forth his beard is not thirsty. One who says, "What is there to eat with my bread" – take the bread away from him. [He too is not hungry.] He who parts his beard will overpower the world [being very clever.]' [This foolish statement, in point of fact, forms the basis for Joseph's judgment.]"*

J.   *Said R. Joseph, "But the excellent statements in the book [of Ben Sira] we do expound, [such as the following]:*

K.   "A good woman is a good gift, who will be put into the bosom of a God-fearing man. A bad woman is a plague for her husband. *What is his remedy?* Let him drive her from his house and be healed from what is plaguing him.

L.   "A lovely wife – happy is her husband. The number of his days is doubled.

M.   "Keep your eyes from a woman of charm, lest you be taken in her trap. Do not turn to her husband to drink wine with him, or strong drink, for through the looks of a beautiful woman many have been slain, and numerous are those who have been slain by her.

N.   "Many are the blows with which a peddler is smitten [for dealing with women]. Those who make it a habit of committing fornication are like a spark that lights the ember. As a cage is full of birds, so are their houses full of deceit" (Jer. 5:27).

O.   "'Keep large numbers of people away from your house, and do not let just anybody into your house.

P.   "'Let many people ask how you are, but reveal your secret to one out of a thousand. From her who lies in your house keep protected the opening of your mouth.

Q.   "'Do not worry about tomorrow's sorrow,' "For you do not know what a day may bring forth" (Prov. 27:1). Perhaps tomorrow you will no longer exist and it will turn out that you will worry about a world that is not yours.

R.		"'All the days of the poor are evil" (Prov. 15:15). Ben Sira said, "So too his nights. His roof is the lowest in town, his vineyard on the topmost mountain. Rain flows from other roofs onto his and from his vineyard onto other vineyards."
IV.3	A.	*Said R. Zira said Rab, "What is the meaning of the verse of Scripture, 'All the days of the afflicted are evil' (Prov. 15:15)?*
	B.	"This refers to masters of Talmud.
	C.	"'But he that is of a good heart has a continuous banquet' (Prov. 15:15)? This refers to masters of the Mishnah."
	D.	*Raba said, "Matters are just the opposite."*
	E.	*And that is in line with what R. Mesharshayya said in the name of Raba, "What is the meaning of the verse of Scripture: 'Whoever removes stones shall be hurt with them' (Qoh. 10:9)?*
	F.	"This refers to masters of the Mishnah.
	G.	"'But he who cleaves wood shall be warmed by it' (Qoh. 10:9)?
	H.	"This refers to masters of Talmud."
	I.	R. Hanina says, "'All of the days of the afflicted are evil' (Prov. 15:15) refers to a man who has a bad wife.
	J.	"'But he that is of a good heart has a continuous banquet' (Prov. 15:15) refers to a man who has a good wife.
	K.	R. Yannai says, "'All the days of the afflicted are evil' (Prov. 15:15) refers to one who is fastidious.
	L.	"'But he that is of a good heart has a continuous banquet (Prov. 15:15) refers to one who is easy to please."
	M.	R. Yohanan said, "'All the days of the afflicted are evil' (Prov. 15:15) refers to a merciful person.
	N.	"'But he that is of a good heart has a continuous banquet' (Prov. 15:15) refers to someone who is cruel by nature [so nothing bothers him]."
	O.	R. Joshua b. Levi said, "'All the days of the afflicted are evil' (Prov. 15:15) refers to **[101A]** someone who is worrisome.
	P.	"'But he that is of a good heart has a continuous banquet' (Prov. 154:15) refers to one who is serene."
	Q.	R. Joshua b. Levi said, "'All the days of the afflicted are evil' (Prov. 15:1) – *but [not] there are Sabbaths and festival days [on which the afflicted gets some pleasure]?"*
	R.	*The matter accords with what Samuel said. For Samuel said, "The change in diet [for festival meals] is the beginning of stomach ache."*
IV.4	A.	*Our rabbis have taught on Tannaite authority:*
	B.	**He who recites a verse of the Song of Songs and turns it into a kind of love-song, and he who recites a verse in a banquet hall not at the proper time [but in a time of carousal] bring evil into the world [cf. T. San. 12:10A].**
	C.	For the Torah puts on sack cloth and stands before the Holy One, blessed be he, and says before him, "Lord of the world, your children have treated me like a harp which scoffers play.'
	D.	He then says to her, "My daughter, when they eat and drink, what should keep them busy?"
	E.	She will say to him, "Lord of the world, if they are masters of Scripture, let them keep busy with the Torah, prophets, and

writings; if they are masters of the Mishnah, let them keep busy
with the Mishnah, law and lore; and if they are masters of the
Talmud, let them keep busy on Passover with the laws of the
Passover, with the laws of Pentecost on Pentecost, and with the
laws of the Festival [of Tabernacles] on the Festival."

F.   R. Simeon b. Eleazar gave testimony in the name of R. Simeon b.
Hanania, "Whoever recites a verse of Scripture at the proper time
brings good to the world, as it is said, 'And a word spoken in
season, how good is it' (Prov. 15:23)."

V.1   A.   **And he who whispers over a wound [M. 1:1F]:**

B.   Said R. Yohanan, "That is the rule if one spits over the wound, for
people may not make mention of the Name of heaven over spit."

V.2   A.   *It has been stated on Amoraic authority:*

B.   Rab said, "Even 'When the plague of leprosy' (Lev. 1:1) [may not be
recited]."

V.3   A.   *Our rabbis have taught on Tannaite authority:*

B.   People may anoint and massage the intestines on the Sabbath, and
whisper to snakes and scorpions on the Sabbath, and place utensils
on the eyes on the Sabbath.

C.   Said Rabban Simeon b. Gamaliel, "Under what circumstances? In
the case of a utensil that may be carried [on the Sabbath], but in the
case of a utensil that may not be carried, it is forbidden."

D.   And a question may not be addressed on a matter having to do with
demons on the Sabbath.

E.   R. Yosé says, "Even on a weekday it is forbidden to do so.

F.   Said R. Huna, "The decided law accords with the view of R. Yosé.

G.   And R. Yosé made that statement only on account of the danger
involving in doing so.

H.   *This is illustrated by the case of R. Isaac bar Joseph, who got stuck in
a cedar tree,and a miracle was done for him, so that the cedar tree split
open and spit him out* [Freedman, p. 685, n. 5: He consulted a
demon, which turned itself into a tree and swallowed him; it
was only through a miracle that he escaped.]

V.4   A.   *Our rabbis have taught on Tannaite authority:*

B.   People may anoint and massage the intestines on the Sabbath, so
long as one not do so as he does on a weekday.

C.   *How then should one do it?*

D.   R. Hama, son of R. Hanini, said, "One puts on some oil
and then massages."

E.   R. Yohanan said, "One puts on oil and massages
simultaneously."

V.5   A.   *Our rabbis have taught on Tannaite authority:*

B.   As to the spirits of oil or eggs, it is permitted to address questions to
them, except that they prove unreliable.

C.   People whisper over oil that is in a utensil but not over oil that is
held in the hand.

D.   Therefore people apply oil by hand and not out of a utensil.

V.6   A.   *R. Isaac bar Samuel bar Marta happened to stay at a certain inn.
They brought him oil in a utensil, and he anointed himself. He
broke out in blisters all over his face. He went to a market place,*

		and a certain woman saw him and said to him, "The blast of Hamath do I see here."
	B.	*She did something for him, and he was healed.*
V.7	A.	Said R. Abba to Rabba bar Mari, "It is written, 'I will put none of these diseases upon you, which I have brought upon the Egyptians, for I am the Lord who heals you' (Ex. 15:26).
	B.	"But if he does not place those diseases, what need is there for healing anyhow?"
	C.	*He said to him, "This is what R. Yohanan said,* 'This verse of Scripture provides its own interpretation, since it is said, "And he said, If you will diligently obey the voice of the Lord your God" (Ex. 15:16). "If you obey, I shall not place those diseases upon you, and if you will not obey, I will do so."
	D.	"'Yet even so: "I am the Lord who heals you"(Ex. 15:26).'"
V.8	A.	Said Rabbah bar bar Hanah, "When R. Eliezer fell ill, his disciples came in to call on him.
	B.	"He said to them, 'There is great anger in the world [to account for my sickness].'
	C.	"They began to cry, but R. Aqiba began to laugh. They said to him, 'Why are you laughing?'
	D.	"He said to them, 'Why are you crying?'
	E.	"They said to him, 'Is it possible that, when a scroll of the Torah [such as Eliezer] is afflicted with disease, we should not cry?'
	F.	"He said to them, 'For that reason I am laughing. So long as I observed that, as to my master, his wine did not turn to vinegar, his flux was not smitten, his oil did not putrefy, and his honey did not become rancid,
	G.	"I though to myself, "Perhaps, God forbid, my master has received his reward in this world." But now that I see my master in distress, I rejoice [knowing that he will receive his full reward in the world to come.]'
	H.	"[Eliezer] said to him, 'Aqiba, have I left out anything at all from the whole of the Torah?'
	I.	"He said to him, '[Indeed so, for] you have taught us, our master, "For there is not a just man upon earth, who does good and does not sin" (Qoh. 7:20).'"
V.9	A.	*Our rabbis have taught on Tannaite authority:*
	B.	When R. Eliezer fell ill, four elders came to call on him: R. Tarfon, R. Joshua, R. Eleazar b. Azariah, and R. Aqiba.
	C.	R. Tarfon responded first and said, "You are better for Israel than a drop of rain, for a drop of rain is good for this world, but my master is good for this world and the world to come."
	D.	R. Joshua responded and said, "You are better for Israel than the orb of the sun, for the orb of the sun serves for this world, but my master serves for this world and the world to come."
	E.	R. Eleazar b. Azariah responded and said, "You are better for Israel than a father and a mother, for a father and a mother are for this world, but my master is for this world and the world to come."
	F.	R. Aqiba responded and said, "Suffering is precious."

	G.	He said to them, "Prop me up so that I may hear the statement of Aqiba, my disciple, who has said, 'Suffering is precious.'"

G.   He said to them, "Prop me up so that I may hear the statement of Aqiba, my disciple, who has said, 'Suffering is precious.'"

H.   He said to him, "Aqiba, how do you know?"

I.   He said to him, "I interpret a verse of Scripture: "Manasseh was twelve years old when he began to reign, and he reigned fifty five years in Jerusalem...and he did what was evil in the sight of the Lord' (2 Kgs. 21:1-2).

J.   "And it is written **[101B]**, 'These are the proverbs of Solomon, which the men of Hezekiah, king of Judah, copied out' (Prov. 25:1).

K.   "Now is it possible that Hezekiah, king of Judah, taught the Torah to the entire world, but to his son, Manasseh, he did not teach the Torah? [Obviously not!]

L.   "But out of all the trouble that [his father] took with him, and with all the labor that he poured into him, nothing brought him back to the good way except for suffering.

M.   "For it is said, 'And the Lord spoke to Manasseh and to his people, but they would not hearken to him. Therefore the Lord brought upon them the captains of the host of the king of Assyria, who took Manasseh among the thorns and bound him with chains and carried him to Babylonia' (2 Chr. 33:10-11).

N.   "And it is written, 'And when he was in affliction, he sought the Lord his God and humbled himself greatly before the God of his fathers. And he prayed to him and he was entreated of him and heard his supplication and brought him again to Jerusalem to his kingdom, and Manasseh knew that the Lord is God' (2 Chr. 33:12-13).

O.   "So you learn that suffering is precious."

V.10   A.   *Our rabbis have taught on Tannaite authority:*

B.   Three came with a self-serving plea, and these are they: Cain, Esau, and Manasseh.

C.   Cain, as it is written, "Is my sin too great to be forgiven?" (Gen. 4:13).

D.   He said before him, "Lord of the world, Is my sin any greater than that of the six hundred thousand who are destined to sin before you? And yet you will forgive them!"

E.   Esau, as it is written, "Have you but one blessing, my father" (Gen. 27:38).

F.   Manasseh: To begin with he called upon many gods and in the end he called upon the God of his fathers.

VI.1   A.   **Abba Saul says, "Also: he who pronounces the divine Name as it is spelled out" [M. 11:1G].:**

B.   *On Tannaite authority [it was stated]:*

C.   That is the rule in the provinces, and [when it is] in blasphemous language.

VII.1   A.   **Three kings and four ordinary folk [have no portion in the world to come. Three kings: Jeroboam, Ahab, and Manasseh] [M. 11:2A-B]:**

B.   *Our rabbis have taught on Tannaite authority:*

C.   "Jerobam": for he treated the people as his sexual object.

D.   Another matter: "Jeroboam: "for he made strife in the people.

E.   Another matter: "Jeroboam: "for he brought strife between the people of Israel and their father in heaven.

F.   Son of Nebat, a son who saw [a vision] but did not see [its meaning].

VII.2 A.   *On Tannaite [authority it was stated]:*

B.   Nebat is the same as Micah and Sheba son of Bichri.

C.   Nebat: Because he saw a vision but did not see [its meaning].

D.   Micah: because he was [Freedman]: crushed in the building. [Freedman, pp. 688-689, n. 11: According to legend, when the Israelites in Egypt did not complete their tale of bricks, their children were built into the walls instead. On Moses' complaining thereof to God, He answered him that He was thus weeding out the destined wicked. As proof, he was empowered to save Micah, who had already been built it, but only to become an idolator on his reaching manhood. Rashi also gives an alternative rendering: he became impoverished through building – presumably his idolatrous shrine.]

E.   But what was his real name? It was Sheba, son of Bichri.

VII.3 A.   *Our rabbis have taught on Tannaite authority:*

B.   There were three who saw [a vision] but did not see [its meaning], and these are they: Nabat, Ahitophel, and Pharaoh's astrologers.

C.   Nabat saw fire coming forth from his penis. *He thought that [it meant that] he would rule, but that was not the case. It was that Jeroboam would come forth from him [who would rule].*

D.   Ahitophel saw saraat spread over him and over his penis. *He thought that it meant that he would be king, and that was not the case. It was Sheba, his daughter, from whom Solomon would come forth from him.*

E.   The astrologers of Pharaoh: *In line with what R. Hama, son of R. Hanina, said, "What is the meaning of the verse of Scripture, 'These are the waters of rebellion, because they strove' (Num. 20:13)?*

F.   "These are the waters which the astrologers of Pharaoh foresaw, and about which they erred.

G.   "They saw that the savior of Israel would be smitten because of water. So [Pharaoh] decreed, 'Every son that is born you shall cast into the river' (Ex. 1:22).

H.   "But they did not know that it was on account of the water of rebellion that he would be smitten:

VII.4 A.   *And how do we know that [Jeroboam] will not come into the world to come?*

B.   As it is written, "And this thing became sin to the house of Jeroboam, even to cut if off and to destroy it from off the face of the earth" (1 Kgs. 13:34).

C.   "To cut it off" in this world.

D.   "And to destroy it" in the world to come.

VII.5A.   Said R. Yohanan, "On what account did Jeroboam have the merit to rule?

B.   Because he reproved Solomon.

C.   "And on what account was he punished?

D.   "Because he reproved him publicly.

E.   "So it is said, 'And this was the cause that the lifted up his hand against the king: Solomon built Millo and repaired the breaches of the city of David his father' (1 Kgs. 11:27).

F.   "He said to him, 'David your father made breaches in the wall so that the Israelites might come up for the pilgrim-festivals, but you have filled them in so as to collect a tax for the daughter of Pharaoh.'"

G.   *And what is the meaning of the phrase,* "That he lifted up his hand against the king" (1 Kgs. 11:27)?

H.   Said R. Nahman, "Because he took off his phylacteries in his presence."

VII.6 A.   Said R. Nahman, "The arrogance that characterized Jeroboam is what drove him out of the world.

B.   "For it is said, 'Now Jeroboam said in his heart, Now shall the kingdom return to the house of David. If this people go up to sacrifice in the house of the Lord at Jerusalem, then shall the heart of this people turn to their Lord, even to Rehoboam, king of Judah, and they shall kill me and go again to Rehoboam, king of Judah' (1 Kgs. 12:27-26).

C.   *"He said, 'We have a tradition that* no one may sit down in the Temple courtyard except kings of the house of Judah alone. *When the people see that Rehoboam is sitting down and I am standing, they will think that he is king, and I am merely a servant.*

D.   *"'But if I sit down, I shall be in the position of rebelling against the monarchy, and they will kill me and follow.'*

E.   "Forthwith: 'Wherefore the king took counsel and made two calves of gold and said to them, It is too much for you to go up to Jerusalem. Behold your gods O Israel, who brought you up out of the land of Egypt, and he put one in Beth El and the other he put in Dan' (1 Kgs. 12:28)."

F.   *What is the meaning of the phrase,* "The king took counsel"?

G.   Said R. Judah, "That he sat a wicked person next to a righteous person. *He said to them, 'Will you sign everything that I do.'*

H.   *"They said to him, 'Yes.'*

I.   *"He said to them, 'I want to be king.'*

J.   *"They said to him, 'Yes.'*

K.   *"He said to them, 'Will you do whatever I say?'*

L.   *"They said to him, 'Yes.'"'*

M.   *"'Even to worship an idol.'*

N.   "The righteous one said to him, 'God forbid.'

O.   *"The wicked one said to the righteous one, 'Do you think that a person such as Jeroboam would really worship an idol? Rather, what he wants to do is to test us to see whether or not we shall accept his word.'"*

P.   [102A] "Even Ahijah the Shilonite made a mistake and signed, *for Jehu was a very righteous man,* as it is said, And the Lord said to Jehu, Because you have done well in executing what is right in my eyes and have done to the house of Ahab according to all that was in my heart, your

		children of the fourth generation shall sit upon the throne of Israel' (2 Kgs. 10:30).
Q.		"But it is written, 'But Jehu took no heed to walk in the law of the Lord God of Israel with all his heart, for he did not depart from the sins of Jeroboam, which he had made Israel to sin' (2 Kgs. 10:31)."
R.		*What caused it?*
S.		Said Abbayye, "A covenant made orally, as it is said, 'And Jehu gathered all the people together and said to them, Ahab served Baal a little, but Jehu shall serve him much' (2 Kgs. 10:18). [Freedman, p. 691, n. 5: These words, though spoken guilefully, had to be fulfilled.]"
T.		Raba said, "He saw the signature of Ahijah the Shilonite, and he erred on that account."

VII.7 A. It is written, "And the revolters are profound to make slaughter, though I have been a rebuke of all of them" (Hos. 5:2):

B. Said R. Yohanan, "Said the Holy One, blessed be he, 'They have gone deeper than I did. I said, "Whoever does not go up to Jerusalem for the Festival transgresses an affirmative requirement," but they have said, "Whoever does go up to Jerusalem for the festival will be stabbed with a sword."'"

VII.8 A. "And it came to pass at that time, when Jeroboam went out of Jerusalem, that the prophet Ahijah the Shilonite found him in the way, and he had clad himself with a new garment" (1 Kgs. 11:20):

B. *It was taught on Tannaite authority in the name of R. Yosé,* "It was a time designated for punishment. [Freedman, p. 691, n. 9: On that occasion Ahijah prophesied the division of the kingdom as a punishment for Solomon's backsliding.]"

C. "In the time of their visitation they shall perish" (Jer. 51:18):

D. *It was taught on Tannaite authority in the name of R. Yosé,* "A time designated for punishment."

E. "In an acceptable time I have heard you" (Is. 49:8):

F. *It was taught on Tannaite authority in the name of R. Yosé,* "A time designated for good."

G. "Nevertheless in the day when I visit, I will visit their sin upon them: (Ex. 32:34):

H. *It was taught on Tannaite authority in the name of R. Yosé,* "A time designated for punishment."

I. "And it came to pass at that time, that Judah went down from his brethren" (Gen. 38:1):

J. *It was taught on Tannaite authority in the name of R. Yosé,* "A time designated for punishment."

K. "And Rehoboam went to Shechem, for all Israel were come to Shechem to make him king" (1 Kgs. 12:1)"

L. *It was taught on Tannaite authority in the name of R. Yosé,* "A time designated for punishment. In Shechem men raped Dinah, in Shechem his brothers sold Joseph, in Shechem the kingdom of David was divided."

VII.9 A. "Now it came to pass at that time that Jeroboam went out of Jerusalem" (1 Kgs. 11:29)"

	B.	Said R. Hanina bar Pappa, "He went out of the realm of Jerusalem."
VII.10	A.	"And the prophet Ahijah the Shilonite found him in the way, and he clad himself with a new garment, and the two were alone in the field" (1 Kgs. 11:29):
	B.	*What is this "new garment"?*
	C.	said R. Nahman, "It was as with a new garment: just as a new garment has no sort of blemish, so the Torah-learning of Jeroboam had no sort of flaw."
	D.	Another matter: "A new garment:"
	E.	It was that they said things so new that no ear had ever heard them.
	F.	"And the two were alone in the field" (1 Kgs. 11:29): What is the meaning of this statement?
	G.	Said R. Judah said Rab, "It is that all the disciples of sages were as grass of the field before them [and of no account]."
	H.	*And there is he who says,* "It is that the reasons for the rulings of the Torah were revealed to them in the open as in a field."
VII.11	A.	"Therefore shall you give parting gifts to Moresheth-gath, the houses of Achzib shall be a lie to the kings of Israel" (Mic. 1:14):
	B.	Said R. Hanina bar Pappa, "An echo came forth and said to them, 'He who killed the Philistine and gave you possession of Gath – to his sons you will give parting gifts.'"
	C.	"Therefore the houses of Achzib shall be a lie to the kings of Israel" (Mich. 1:14) [Freedman, p. 693, n. 2: "Since you deal treacherously with the house of David, preferring the rule of the kings of Israel, therefore you shall be delivered into the hands of the heathen, whose religion is false."]
VII.12	A.	Said R. Hinnena bar Pappa, "Whoever derives benefit from this world without reciting a blessing is as if he steals from the Holy One, blessed be he, and the community of Israel.
	B.	"For it is said, 'Who robs from his father or his mother and says, It is no transgression, is the companion of a destroyer' (Prov. 28:24).
	C.	"'His father' is only the Holy One, blessed be he, as it is said, 'Is not [God] your father, who has bought you' (Deut. 32:6), and 'his mother' can mean only the congregation of Israel, as it is said, 'My son, hear the instruction of your father and do not forsake the Torah of your mother' (Prov. 1:8)."
	D.	"*What is the sense of* He is the companion of a destroyer (Prov. 28:24)?
	E.	"He is companion of Jeroboam, son of Nebat, who destroyed Israel for their father in heaven."
VII.13	A.	"And Jeroboam drove Israel from following the Lord and made them sin a great sin" (2 Kgs. 17:21)"
	B.	Said R. Hanin, "It was like two sticks that rebound from one another."
VII.14	A.	"[These are the words which Moses spoke to all Israel in the wilderness] and Di Zahab" (Deut. 1:1):
	B.	Said a member of the house of R. Yannai, "Moses said before the Holy One, blessed be he, 'Lord of the world, on account of the silver and gold which you showered on Israel until they said, "Enough," they were caused to make for themselves gods of gold.'

C. "It is comparable to the case of a lion, who does not tear and roar on account of what is in a basket containing straw, but because of what is in a basket of meat."

D. Said R. Oshaia, "Up to the time of Jeroboam, the Israelites would suck from a single calf [sinning on account of only one], but from that time on, it was from two or three calves."

E. Said R. Isaac, "You do not have any sort of punishment that comes upon the world in which is contained at least one twenty-fourth of part of the overweight of a litra of the first calf.

F. "For it is written, 'Nevertheless in the day when I visit, I will visit their sin upon them' (Ex. 32:34)."

G. Said R. Hanina, "After twenty-four generations this verse of Scripture will be exacted: 'He cried also in my ears with a loud voice, saying, Cause the visitations of the city to draw near, even every man with his destroying weapon in his hand' (Ez. 9:1)." [Freedman, p. 694, n. 4: The use of "visitations" suggests that this was the fulfillment of the doom threatened in Ex. 32:34. There were twenty-four generations from that of the wilderness, when the calf was made, to that of Zedekiah, in whose reign the state was overthrown and Judah was deported to Babylonia.]"

VII.15 A. "After this thing Jeroboam did not turn from his evil way" (1 Kgs. 13:33)"

B. What is the sense of "after"?

C. Said R. Abba, "After the Holy One, blessed be he, seized Jeroboam by his garment and said to him, 'Repent, and you and the son of Jesse and I shall walk about in the Garden of Eden.'

D. "He said to him, 'He who will be at the head?'

E. "'The son of Jesse will be at the head.'

F. "If so, I don't want it.'"

VII.16 A. *R. Abbahu would regularly give a public interpretation of the three kings [of M. 11:2A]. He fell ill and undertook not to give such an address [since he thought the illness was punishment for speaking about the king's sins].*

B. *When [102B] he got better, he reversed himself and gave an address. They said to him, "You undertook not to speak about them."*

C. *He said to them, "Did they repent, that I should repent!"*

VII.17 A. *At the house of R. Ashi, [the group] arose [from studying] at the teaching of the three kings. He said, "Tomorrow we shall open discourse with the topic of 'our colleagues' [M. 11:2, that is, the three kings, all of whom were held to be disciples of sages.]"*

B. *Manasseh came and appeared in a dream: "Do you call us 'your colleague' and 'your father's colleague'? [If you are as good as we are, then tell me] from what part of the bread do you take the piece for reciting the blessing, 'Who brings forth bread from the earth'?"*

C. *He said to him, "I don't know."*

D. *He said to him, "If you have not learned from what part of the bread do you take a piece for reciting the blessing, 'Who brings forth bread from the earth,' how can you call us 'your colleague'?"*

E. *He said to him, "Teach me. Tomorrow I shall expound the matter in your name in the class-session."*

F. *He said to him, "One takes the part that is baked into a crust [and not the dough on the inside]."*

G.   *He said to him, "If you are so wise, then what is the reason that you worshipped an idol?"*

H.   *He said to him, "If you had been there, you would have picked up the hem of your garment and run after me."*

I.   *The next day he said to the rabbis, "Let us begin with our teacher."*

VIII.1 A.   **Ahab:** The name 'Ahab' signifies that he was a brother to heaven (ah) but father of idolatry (ab).

B.   "He was brother to heaven, as it is written, 'A brother is born for trouble' (Prov. 17:17).

C.   "He was father to idolatry, as it is written, 'As a father loves his children' (Ps. 103:13)."

VIII.2 A.   "And it came to pass, that it was a light thing for him to walk in the sins of Jeroboam, the son of Nebat" (1 Kgs. 16:31):

B.   Said R. Yohanan, "The lightest [sins] committed by Ahab were as the most severe ones that were committed by Jeroboam.

C.   "And on what account did Scripture blame Jeroboam? It was because he was the beginning of the corruption."

VIII.3 A.   "Yes, their altars are as heaps in the furrows of the fields" (Hos. 12:12):

B.   Said R. Yohanan, "You have no furrow in the whole of the land of Israel in which Ahab did not set up an idol and bow down to it."

VIII.4 A.   *And how do we know that [Ahab] will not enter the world to come?*

B.   As it is written, "And I will cut off from Ahab him who pisses against the wall, him that is shut up and forsaken in Israel" (1 Kgs. 21:21).

C.   "Shut up" in this world.

D.   "Forsaken" in the world to come.

VIII.5 A.   Said R. Yohanan, "On what account did Omri merit the monarchy? Because he added a single town to the land of Israel, as it is written, 'And he bought the hill Samaria of Shemer for two talents of silver and built on the hill and called the name of the city which he built after the name of Shemer, owner of the hill, Samaria' (1 Kgs. 16:24)."

B.   Said R. Yohanan, "On what account did Ahab merit ruling for twenty-two years? Because he honored the Torah, which was given with twenty-two letters [of the Hebrew alphabet], as it is said, 'And he sent messages to Ahab, king of Israel, to the city, and said to him, Thus says Hen-hadad, Your silver and your gold is mine, your wives also and your children, even the goodliest are mine ... Yet will I send my servants to you tomorrow at this time and they shall search your house, and the houses of your servants, and it shall be, that whatsoever is pleasant in your eyes they shall put in their hand and take it away ... Therefore he said to the messengers of Ben-hadad, Tell my lord the king, all that you send for to your servants at the first I will do, but this thing I may not do' (1 Kgs. 20:3, 6, 9).

C.   *"What is the meaning of* 'whatsoever is pleasant in your eyes'? Is it not a scroll of the Torah?"

D.   *But could it not be an idol?*

E.   "Let it not enter your mind, for it is written, 'And all the leader and all the people said to him, Do not listen to him or consent' (1 Kgs. 20:8) [the elders being sages]."

F.   *And perhaps they were elders [who were identified with] the shame [of the idol itself]?*

G.   Is it not written, "And the saying pleased Absalom well and all the elders of Israel" (2 Sam. 17:4)? *On this passage, said R. Joseph, "They were elders [associated with] the shame."*

H.   *"In that passage, it is not written, 'And all the people,' while here it is written, 'And all the people.' It is not possible that among them were no righteous men, for it is written, 'Yet have I left seven thousand in Israel, all the knees which have not bowed to Baal and every mouth which has not kissed him' (1 Kgs. 19:18)."*

VIII.6 A.   Said R. Nahman, "Ahab was right in the middle [between wickedness and righteousness], as it is said, 'And the Lord said, Who shall persuade Ahab, that he may go up and fall at Ramoth-gildean? And one said in this manner, and one said in that manner' (1 Kgs. 22:20). [Freedman, p. 697, n. 1: This shows that it was a difficult matter to lure him to his fate, and that must have been because his righteousness equalled his guilt.]"

B.   *To this proposition R. Joseph objected, "We speak of one concerning whom it is written,* 'But there was none like Ahab, who sold himself to work wickedness in the sight of the Lord, whom Jezebel his wife stirred up' (1 Kgs. 21:25),

C.   *"on which passage it was repeated on Tannaite authority, 'Every day she would weigh out gold shekels for idolatry,' and can you say that he was right in the middle"*

D.   "Rather, Ahab was generous with his money, and because he gave benefit to disciples of sages out of his property, half of his sins were forgiven."

VIII.7 A.   "And there came forth the spirit and stood before the Lord and said, I will persuade him. And the Lord said to him, With what? And he said, I will go forth and I will be a lying spirit in the mouth of his prophets. And he said, You shall persuade him and also prevail. Go forth and do so" (1 Kgs. 22:21-23):

B.   *What spirit was it?*

C.   Said R. Yohanan, "It was the spirit of Naboth the Jezreelite."

D.   *What is meant by "go forth"?*

E.   Said Rabina, "Go forth from my precincts, as it is written, 'He who lies will not tarry in my sight' (Ps. 101:7)."

F.   *Said R. Pappa, "This is in line with what people say, 'He who exacts vengeance destroys his house.'"*

VIII.8 A.   "And Ahab made a grove, and Ahab did more to provoke the Lord God of Israel to anger than all of the kings of Israel that were before him" (1 Kgs. 16:33):

B.   Said R. Yohanan, "It was that he wrote on the gates of Samaria, 'Ahab has denied the God of Israel.' Therefore he has no portion in the God of Israel."

VIII.9 A.   "And he sought Ahaziah, and they caught him for he hid in Samaria" (2 Chr. 22:9):

B.   Said R. Levi, "He was blotting out the mentions of the divine name [in the Torah] and writing in their place the names of idols."

IX.1 A.   **Manasseh** – [Based on the root for the word "forget"] for he forgot the Lord.

	B.	Another explanation: Manasseh – for he made Israel forget their father in heaven.
	C.	*And how do we know that he will not come to the world to come?*
	D.	As it is written, "Manasseh was twelve years old when he began to reign, and he reigned fifty-five years in Jerusalem, ... and he mad a grove as did Ahab, king of Israel" (2 Kgs. 21:2-3).
	E.	Just as Ahab has no share in the world to come, so Manasseh has no share in the world to come.
X.1	A.	**R. Judah says, "Manasseh has a portion in the world to come, since it is said, 'And he prayed to him and he was entreated of him ...' (2 Chr. 33:13)" [M. 11:2C-D]:**
	B.	Said R. Yohanan, "Both authorities [who dispute the fate of Manasseh] interpret the same verse of Scripture, as it is said, 'And I will cause to be removed to all the kingdoms of the earth, because of Manasseh, son of Hezekiah, king of Judah' (Jer. 15:4).
	C.	*"One authority takes the view that it is* 'on account of Manasseh,' who repented, *while they did not repent.*
	D.	*"The other authority takes the view* **[103A]** *that it is* 'because of Manasseh,' *who did not repent."*
X.2	A.	Said R. Yohanan, "Whoever maintains that Manasseh has no share in the world to come weakens the hands of those who repent."
	B.	*For a Tannaite authority repeated before R. Yohanan,* "Manasseh repented for thirty-three years, as it is written, 'Manasseh was twelve years old when he began to reign, and he reigned fifty-five years in Jerusalem and he made a grove as did Ahab, king of Israel' (2 Kgs. 21:2-3).
	C.	*"How long did Ahab rule? Twenty-two years. How long did Manasseh rule? Fifty-five years. Take away twenty-two years, and you are left with thirty-three."*
X.3	A.	*Said R. Yohanan in the name of R. Simeon b. Yohai, "What is the meaning of the verse of Scripture,* 'And he prayed to him and an opening was made for him' (2 Chr. 33:13)?
	B.	*"It should say,* 'and he was entreated of him'!
	C.	"It teaches that the Holy One, blessed be he, made a kind of cave for him in the firmament, so as to receive him in repentance, despite the [contrary will of] the attribute of justice."
	D.	*And said R. Yohanan in the name of R. Simeon b. Yohai,* "What is the meaning of the verse of Scripture, 'In the beginning of the reign of Jehoiakim, son of Josiah, king of Judah' (Jer. 26:1)?
	E.	"And it is written, 'In the beginning of the reign of Zedekiah, king of Judah' (Jer. 28:1).
	F.	*"And is it the case that, up to that time there were no kings?*
	G.	"Rather, the Holy One, blessed be he, planned to return the world to [its beginning condition of] chaos and formlessness on account of Jehoiakim. When, however, he took a close look at his generation, his anger subsided.
	H.	"[Along these same lines], the Holy One, blessed be he, planned to return the world to chaos and formlessness on account of the generation of Zedekiah. But when he took a close look at Zedekiah, his anger subsided."

I. *But with regard to Zedekiah, also, it is written,* "And he did that which was evil in the sight of God" (2 Kgs. 24:19)?

J. He could have stopped others but did not do so.

K. *And said R. Yohanan in the name of R. Simeon b. Yohai, "What is the meaning of the verse of Scripture, 'If a wise man content with a foolish man, whether rage or laughter, there is no satisfaction' (Prov. 29:9)?*

` L. "Said the Holy One, blessed be he, 'I was angry with Ahaz and I handed him over to the kings of Damascus and he sacrificed and offered incense to their gods, as it is said, 'For he sacrificed to the gods of Damascus who smote him, and he said, Because the gods of the kinds of Syria help them, therefore will I sacrifice to them that they may help me. But they were the ruin of him and of all Israel' (2 Chr. 28:23).

M. "'I smiled upon Amaziah and delivered the kings of Edom into his power, so he brought their gods and bowed down to them, a it is said, 'Now it came to pass, after Amaziah was come from the slaughter of the Edomites, that he brought the gods of the children of Seir and set them up to be his gods and bowed down himself before them and burned incense to them' (2 Chr. 25:14)."

N. *Said R. Pappa, "This is in line with what people say: 'Weep for the one who doe not know, laugh for the one who does not know. Woe to him who does not know the difference between good and bad.'"*

O. "And all the princes of the king of Babylonia came in and sat in the middle gate" (Jer. 39:3):

P. Said R. Yohanan in the name of R. Simeon b. Yohai, "It was the place in which laws were mediated."

Q. *Said R. Pappa, "That is in line with what people say: 'In the place in which the master hangs up his sword, the shepherd hangs up his pitcher.' [Freedman, p. 700, n. 3: Where the Jews decided upon their laws, there Nebuchadnezzer issued his decrees.]"*

X.4 A. *Said R. Hisda said R. Jeremiah bar Abba, "What is the meaning of the following verse: 'I went by the field of the slothful and by the vineyard of the man void of understanding. And lo, it was all grown over with thorns and nettles had covered the face thereof, and the stone wall thereof was broken down' (Prov. 24:30-31)?*

B. "'I went by the field of the slothful' – this speaks of Ahaz.

C. "'And by the vineyard of the man void of understanding' – this speaks of Manasseh.

D. "'And lo, it was all grown over with thorns' – this refers to Amon.

E. "'And nettles had covered the face thereof' – this refers to Jehoiakim.

F. "'And the stone wall thereof was broken down' – this refers to Zedekiah, in whose time the Temple was destroyed.

G. And said R. Hisda said R. Jeremiah bar Abba, "There are four categories who will not receive the face of the Presence of God:

H. "The categories of scoffers, flatterers, liars, and slanderers.

I. "The category of scoffers, as it is written, 'He has stretched out his hand against scorners' (Hos. 7:5).

J. "The category of flatterers, as it is written, 'He who speaks lies shall not be established in my sight' (Job. 13:16).

K.   "The category of liars, as it is written, 'He who speaks lies shall not be established in my sight' (Ps. 101:7).

L.   "The category of slanderers, as it is written, 'For you are not a God who has pleasure in wickedness; evil will not dwell with you' (Ps. 5:5). 'You are righteous, O Lord, and evil will not dwell in your house [Ps. 5 addresses slander.]"

M.   *And said R. Hisda said R. Jeremiah bar Abba, "What is the meaning of the verse, 'There shall nor evil befall you, neither shall any plague come near your dwelling'(Ps. 91:10)?*

N.   "There shall not evil befall you' means that the evil impulse will not rule over you.

O.   "'Neither shall any plague come near your dwelling' means that, when you come home from a trip, you will never find that your wife is in doubt as to whether or not she is menstruating."

P.   "Another matter: 'There shall not evil befall you' means that bad dreams and fantasies will never frighten you.

Q.   "'Neither shall any plague come near your dwelling' means that you will not have a son or a disciple who in public burns his food [that is, teaches something heretical].'

R.   "Up to this point is the blessing that his father had given him.

S.   "From this point forward comes the blessing that his mother had given to him: 'For he shall give his angels charge over you, to keep you in all your ways. They shall bear you in their hands ... You shall tread upon the lion and the adder' (Ps. 91:10).

T.   "Up to this point is the blessing that his mother gave him.

U.   "From this point onward comes the blessing that heaven gave him:

V.   "'[103B] Because he has set his love upon me, therefore will I deliver him. I will set him on high, because he has known my name. He shall call upon me, and I will answer him. I will be with him in trouble. I will deliver him and honor him. With long life will I satisfy him and show him my salvation' (Ps. 91:14-16)."

X.5   A.   *Said R. Simeon b. Laqish, "What is the meaning of the following verse of Scripture: 'And from the wicked their light is withheld, and the high arm shall be broken' (Job 38:15)?*

B.   "Why is the letter ayin in the word for wicked suspended [in the text, being written above the level of the line, making it read 'poor,' rather than 'wicked' (Freedman, p. 701, n. 10)]?

C.   "When a person becomes poor below, he is made poor above [Freedman, p. 701, n. 11: Where one earns the disapproval of man, it is proof that he has earned the disapproval of God too.]"

D.   *Then the letter should not be written at all?*

E.   R. Yohanan and R. Eleazar: one said, "It is because of the honor owing to David."

F.   The other said, "It is because the honor owing to Nehemiah B. Hachaliah. [Freedman, p. 702, n. 1: Both had many enemies yet were truly righteous men.]"

X.6   A.   *Our rabbis have taught on Tannaite authority:*

B.   Manasseh would teach the book of Leviticus from fifty-five viewpoints, corresponding to the years of his reign.

C.   Ahab did so in eighty-five ways.

D.   Jeroboam did so in a hundred and three ways.

X.7	A.	*It has been taught on Tannaite authority:*
	B.	R. Meir would say, "Absalom has no share in the world to come,
	C.	"as it is said, 'And they smote Absalom and slew him' (2 Sam. 18:15).
	D.	"'They smote him' in this world.
	E.	"And they slew him' in the world to come."
X.8	A.	*It has been taught on Tannaite authority"*
	B.	R. Simeon b. Eleazar says in the name of R. Meir, "Ahaz, Ahaziah, and all the kings of Israel concerning whom it is written, 'And he did what was evil in the sight of the Lord' will not live or be judged [in the world to come.]"
X.9	A.	"Moreover Manasseh shed much innocent blood, until he had filled Jerusalem from one end to another, beside his sin wherewith he made Judah to sin, in doing that which was evil in the sight of the Lord" (2 Kgs. 21:16):
	B.	*Here [in Babylonia] it is explained that* he killed Isaiah, [and that is the sin at hand].
	C.	*In the West they say that it was that* he made an idol as heavy as a thousand men, and every day it killed them all.
	D.	*In accord with whose position is the following statement made by Raba b. b. Hana:* "The soul of a righteous man is balanced against the whole world"?
	E.	*In accord with whom? With the position of him who has said that* he had killed Isaiah.
X.10	A.	[It is written,] "And he set the graven image" (2 Chr. 33:7), and it is stated, "And the graves and the graven images which he had set up" (2 Chr. 33:19). [was there one image or were there many?]
	B.	Said R. Yohanan, "In the beginning he made one face for it, and in the end he made four faces for it, so that the Presence of God should see it and become angry.
	C.	"Ahaz set it up in the upper chamber, as it is written, 'And the altars that were on top of the upper chamber of Ahaz' (2 Kgs. 23:13).
	D.	"Manasseh set it in the Temple, as it is written, 'And he set up a graven image of the grove that he had made in the house, of which the Lord said to David and to Solomon his son, In this house and in Jerusalem which I have chosen out of all tribes of Israel will I put my name for ever' (2 Kgs. 21:7).
	E.	"Amon put it into the Holy of Holies, as it is said, 'For the bed is shorter than that a man can stretch himself on it, and the covering narrower than that he can wrap himself in it' (Is. 28:20)."
	F.	*What is the sense of,* "For the bed is shorter than that one can stretch himself on it"?
	G.	Said R. Samuel bar Nahmani said R. Jonathan, "This bed is too short for two neighbors to rule over it at one time."
	H.	*What is the sense of* "And the covering is narrower"?
	I.	*Said R. Samuel bar Nahmani, "When R. Jonathan would reach this verse of Scripture, he would cry.* 'He of whom it is written,"He gathers the waters of the sea together as a heap" (Ps. 33:7) — should a molten statue rival him!'"

X.11   A.   Ahaz annulled the sacrificial service and sealed the Torah, for it is said, "Bind up the testimony, seal the Torah among my disciples" (Is. 8:16).

        B.   Manasseh blotted out the mentions of the divine Name and destroyed the altar.

        C.   Amon burned the Torah and let spider webs cover the altar.

        D.   Ahaz permitted consanguineous marriages.

        E.   Manasseh had sexual relations with his sister.

        F.   Amon had sexual relations with his mother, as it is said, "For Amon sinned very much" (2 Chr. 33:23).

        G.   R. Yohanan and R. Eleazar: one said that he burned the torah.

        H.   The other said that he had sexual relations with his mother.

        I.   His mother said to him, "Do you have any pleasure from the place from which you came forth?"

        J.   He said to her, "Am I doing anything except to spite my creator?"

        K.   *When Jehoiakim came, he said, "The ones who came before me really did not know how to anger him.* Do we need him for anything more than his light? We have pure gold, which we use [for light], so let him take away his light."

        L.   They said to him, "But do not silver and gold belong to him, as it is written, 'Mine is the silver, and mine is the gold, saith the Lord of hosts' (Hag. 2:8)."

        M.   "He said to them, "He has already given them to us, as it is said, 'The heavens are the Lord's, and the earth he has given to the children of men' (Ps. 115:16)."

Wicked Monarches Who Nonetheless Merit a Portion in the World to Come, e.g., Jehoiakim, Ahaz, Amon

X.12   A.   Said Raba to Rabbah bar Mari, "On what account did they not count Jehoiakim [among those who do not get the world to come]?

        B.   "For it is written of him, 'And the remaining words of Jehoiakim and the abomination which he wrought and that which was found up upon him' (2 Chr. 36:8)."

        C.   *What is the sense of "that which was found upon him" (2 Chr. 36:8)?*

        D.   R. Yohanan and R. Eleazar: one said that he engraved the name of his idol on his penis.

        E.   The other said that he engraved the name of heaven on his penis.

        F.   [Rabbah b. Mari] said to him, "As to the matter of kings, I have not heard any answer. But a to ordinary people, I have heard an answer.

        G.   "Why did they not count Micah? Because he made his bread available to travellers, for it is said, 'Every traveller turned to the Levites.'"

        H.   "And he shall pad through the sea with affliction and shall smite the waves in the sea" (Zech. 10:11)."

        I.   Said R. Yohanan, "This speaks of the idol of Micah."

        J.   *It has been taught on Tannaite authority:*

K.	R. Nathan says, "From Hareb to Shiloah is three mils, and the smoke of the pile and the smoke of the image of Micah mixed together. The ministering angels wanted to drive [Micah] off. The Holy One, blessed be he, said to them, 'Leave him alone, for his bread is made available to travellers.'"
L.	And for the same matter those involved in the matter of the concubine at Gibeah [Judges 19] were punished.
M.	Said the Holy One, blessed be he, "On account of the honor owing to me you did not protest, and on account of the honor owing to a mortal you protested."

X.13

A.	Said R. Yohanan in the name of R. Yosé b. Qisma, "Great is a mouthful of food, for it set a distance between two families and Israel,
B.	"as it is written, '[An Ammonite or Moabite shall not enter the congregation of the Lord] ... because they did not meet you with bread and water in the way when you came forth from Egypt' (Deut. 33:4-5)."
C.	And R. Yohanan on his own said, "It creates distance among those who are close; it draws near those who are afar; it blinds the eye [of God] from the wicked; it makes the Presence of God rest even on the prophets of Baal, and it makes an unwitting offense appear to be deliberate [if it is performed in connection with care of the wayfarer]."
D.	[Now to spell out the foregoing:] "It creates distance among those who are close:
E.	[Proof derives] from **[104A]** the case of Ammon and Moab.
F.	"It draws near those who are afar:"
G.	[Proof derives] from the case of Jethro.
H.	For said R. Yohanan, "As a reward for saying, 'Call him that he may eat bread' (Ex. 2:20), [Jethro]'s descendants had the merit of going taking seats [as authorities] in the chamber of the hewn stones, it is said, 'And the family of the scribes which dwell at Jabez, the Tirahites, the Shimeathites, and Suchathites. These are the Kenites that came of Hemath, the father of the house of Rechan' (1 Chr. 2:55).
I.	"And elsewhere it is written, 'And the children of the Kenite, Moses' father-in-law, went up out of the city of palm trees with the children of Judah into the wilderness of Judah, which lies in the south of Arab, and they went and dwelt among the people' (Judges 1:16). [Freedman, p. 705, n. 10: This shows that the Kenites were descended from Jethro and they sat in the hall of hewn stones as scribes and sanhedrin.]"
J.	"It blinds the eye [of God] from the wicked:"
K.	[Proof derives] from the case of Micah.
L.	"It makes the Presence of God rest even on the prophets of Baal:"
M.	[Proof derives] from the friend of Iddo, the prophet, for it is written, "And it came to pass, as they sat at the table,

		that the word of the Lord came to the prophet that brought him back" (1 Kgs. 13:20). [Freedman, p. 706, n. 2: He was a prophet of Baal, yet God's word came to him as a reward for his hospitality.]
	N.	"And it makes an unwitting offense appear to be deliberate:"
	O.	[Proof derives] from what R. Judah said Rab, said, "Had Jonathan only brought David two loaves of bread, Nob, the city of priests, would not have been put to death, Doeg the Edomite would not have been troubled, and Saul and his three sons would not have been killed. [Freedman, p. 706, n. 4: For had he provided him with food, he would not have taken any from Ahimelech. Thus all this happened, though Jonathan's initial offense was due to an oversight.]"

X.14   A.   And why did they not list Ahaz [at M. 11:2]?

B.   Said R. Jeremiah bar Abba, "Because he was positioned between two righteous men, between Jotham and Hezekiah."

C.   R. Joseph said, "Because he had the capacity to be ashamed on account of Isaiah, as it is said, 'Then said the Lord to Isaiah, Go forth now to meet Ahaz, you and Shear-jashub your son, at the end of the conduit of the upper pool in the highway of the field of the fuller's trough' (Is. 7:3)."

D.   *What is the source of "fuller's trough"?*

E.   *Some say, "He hid his face [using the same consonants] and fled."*

F.   *Some say, "He dragged a fuller's trough [the meaning of the word in general] on his head and fled."*

X.15   A.   Why did they not list Amon [at M. 11:2]?

B.   On account of the honor owing to Josiah.

C.   In that case, they also should not have listed Manasseh, on account of the honor owing to Hezekiah.

D.   *The son imparts merit to the father, but the father does not give any merit to the son, for it is written,* "Neither is there any one who can deliver out of my hand" (Deut. 32:39).

E.   Abraham cannot save Ishmael. Isaac cannot save Esau.

F.   *If you go that far, then Ahaz also was omitted from the list on account of the honor owing to Hezekiah.*

X.16   A.   And on what account did they not list Jehoiakim?

B.   *It is on account of what R.Hiyya b. R. Abuyyah said.*

C.   *For R. Hiyya b. R. Abuyyah said,* "It was written on the skull of Jehoiakim, 'This and yet another.'"

D.   *The grandfather of R. Perida found a skull tossed at the gates of Jerusalem, on which was written,* "This and yet another."

E.   *He buried it, but it did not stay buried, and he buried it again but it did not stay buried.*

F.   *He said,* "It must be the skull of Jehoiakim, for it is written in that connection, 'He shall be buried with the burial of an ass, drawn and cast forth beyond the gates of Jerusalem' (Jer. 22:19)."

G.   *He said,* "Still, he was a king, and it is not proper to treat him lightly."

H.	*He wrapped the skull in silk and put it in a closet. His wife saw it. She thought, "This is [the bone of] his first wife, whom he has not forgotten."*
I.	*She lit the oven and burned it up, and that is the meaning of what is written,* "This and yet another." [Freedman, p. 707, n. 2: These indignities made sufficient atonement for him that he should share in the future world.]

Hezekiah, the Righteous Monarch on Account of Whom Israel Went into Exile. And the Exegesis of Lamentations

X.17	A.	*It has been taught on Tannaite authority:*
	B.	R. Simeon b. Eleazar said, "On account of [Hezekiah's] statement, 'And I have done that which was good in your sight,' (2 Kgs. 20:3), [he had further to ask,] 'What shall be the sign [that the Lord will heal me]' (2 Kgs. 20:9).
	C.	"On account of the statement, 'What shall be the sign' (2 Kgs. 20:9), gentiles ate at his table.
	D.	"On account of gentiles' eating at his table, [2 Kgs. 20:17-18), he made his children go into exile."
	E.	*That statement supports what Hezekiah said.*
	F.	For Hezekiah said, "Whoever invites an idolator into his house and serves him [as host] causes his children to go into exile, as it is said, 'And of your sons who will issue from you, which you shall beget, shall they take away; and they shall be eunuches in the palace of the king of Babylonia' (2 Kgs. 20:18)."
	G.	"And Hezekiah was happy about them and showed them the treasure house, the silver and gold, spices and precious ointment" (Is. 39:2):
	H.	*Said Rab, "What is the sense of 'his treasure house'?* It means, his wife, who served them drinks."
	I.	Samuel said, "His treasury is what he showed them"
	J.	R. Yohanan said, "His weapons, which had the capacity to consume other weapons, is what he showed them."
X.18	A.	"How does the city sit solitary" (Lam. 1:1):
	B.	Said Rabbah said R. Yohanan, "On what account were the Israelites smitten with the word 'how' [that begins the dirge]? [Since the numerical value of the letters of the word equals thirty-six], it is because they violated the thirty-six rules in the Torah that are penalized by extirpation."
	C.	Said R. Yohanan, "Why were they smitten [with a dirge that is] alphabetical?
	D.	"Because they violated the Torah, which is given through the alphabet. [Freedman, p. 708, n. 6: Its words are formed from the alphabet.]"
X.19	A.	"Sit solitary" (Lam. 1:1)"
	B.	Said Rabbah said R. Yohanan, "Said the Holy One, blessed be he, 'I said, "Israel then shall dwell in safety alone, the foundation of Jacob shall be upon a land of corn and wine, also his heavens shall drop down dew" (Deut. 33:28) [so that sitting

solitary was supposed to be a blessing (Freedman, p. 708, n. 8)], but now, where they dwell will be alone.'"

X.20 A. "The city that was full of people" (Lam. 1:1):

B. Said Rabbah said R. Yohanan, "For they used to marry off a minor girl to an adult male, or an adult woman to a minor boy, so that they should have many children. [But two minors would not marry.]"

X.21 A. "She is become as a widow" (Lam. 1:1):

B. Said R. Judah said Rab, "Like a widow, but not actually a widow, but like a woman whose husband has gone overseas and plans to return to her."

X.22 A. "She was great among the nations and princess among the provinces" (Lam. 1:1):

B. Said R. Rabbah said R. Yohanan, "Everywhere they go they become princes of their masters."

X.23 A. *Our rabbis have taught on Tannaite authority:*

B. There is the case of two men who were captured on Mount Carmel. The kidnapper was walking behind them. **[104B]** One of them said to his fellow, "The camel that is walking before us is blind in one eye, it is carrying two skins, one of wine and one of oil, and of the two men that are leading it, one is an Israelite and the other is a gentile."

C. The kidnapper said to them, "Stiff-necked people, how do you know?"

D. They said to him, "As to the camel, it is eating from the grass before it on the side on which it can see, but on the side on which it cannot see, it is not eating.

E. "And it is carrying two skins, one of wine and one of oil. The one of wine drips and the drippings are absorbed in the ground, while the one of oil drips, and the drippings remain on the surface.

F. "And as the two men who are leading it, one is a gentile and one is an Israelite. The gentile relieves himself right on the road, while the Israelite turns to the side [of the road]."

G. The man ran after them and found that things were just as they had said. He came and kissed them on their head and brought them to his house. He made a great banquet for them and danced before them, saying, "Blessed is he who chose the seed of Abraham and gave part of his wisdom to them, and wherever they go they become princes over their masters."

H. He sent them away and they went home in peace.

X.24 A. "She weeps, yes, she weeps in the night" (Lam. 1:2):

B. Why these two acts of weeping?

C. Said Rabbah said R. Yohanan, "One is for the first Temple and the other is for the second Temple."

D. "At night:"

E. On account of things done in the night, as it is said, "And all the congregation lifted up their voice and cried, and the people wept that night [at the spies' false report]" (Num. 14:1).

	F.	Said Rabbah said R. Yohanan, "That was the ninth of Ab. Said the Holy One, blessed be he, to Israel, 'You have wept tears for nothing. I now shall set up for you weeping for generations to come.'"
	G.	Another interpretation of "At night:"
	H.	Whoever cries at night will find that his voice is heard.
	I.	Another interpretation of "At night:"
	J.	Whoever cries at night finds that the stars and planets will cry with him.
	K.	Another interpretation of "At night:"
	L.	Whoever cries at night finds that whoever hears his voice will cry along with him.
	M.	That was the case of a woman in the neighborhood of Rabban Gamaliel, whose child died. She was weeping by night on account of the child. Rabban Gamaliel heard her voice and cried with her, until his eyelashes fell out. The next day, his disciples recognized what had happened and removed the woman from his neighborhood.
X.25	A.	"And her tears are on her cheeks" (Lam. 1:2):
	B.	Said Rabbah said R. Yohanan, "It is like a woman who weeps for the husband of her youth, as it is said, 'Lamentation like a virgin girded with sackcloth for the husband of her youth' (Joel 1:8)."
X.26	A.	"Her adversaries are the chief" (Lam. 1:5):
	B.	Said Rabbah said R. Yohanan, "Whoever persecutes Israel becomes head,
	C.	"as it is said, 'Nevertheless, there shall be no weariness for her that oppressed her. In the former time he brought into contempt the land of Zebulun and the land of Naphtali, but in the latter time he has made it glorious, by way of the sea, beyond Jordan, the circuit of the nations' (Is. 8:23)."
	D.	Said Rabbah said R. Yohanan, "Whoever oppresses Israel does not get tired."
X.27	A.	"May it not happen to you, all passersby" (Lam. 1:12)."
	B.	Said Rabbah said R. Yohanan, "On this basis we find in the Torah support for saying [when reciting woes], 'May it not happen to you.'"
X.28	A.	"All passersby" (Lam. 1:12):
	B.	Said R. Amram said Rab, "They have turned me into one of those who transgress the law.
	C.	"For in respect to Sodom, it is written, 'And the Lord rained upon Sodom [and upon Gomorrah brimstone and fire' (Gen. 19:24). But in respect to Jerusalem it is written, 'From above he has sent fire against my bones and it prevails against them' (Lam. 1:13). [Freedman, p. 711, n. 4: Thus Jerusalem was treated as Sodom and Gomorrah.]"
	D.	"For the iniquity of the daughter of my people is greater than the sin of Sodom" (Lam. 4:6):
	E.	And is any sort of favoritism shown in such a matter [since Jerusalem was left standing, Sodom was wiped out]?

F. Said Rabbah said R. Yohanan, "[Not at all, in fact] there was a further measure [of punishment] directed against Jerusalem but not against Sodom.

G. "For with respect to Sodom, it is written, 'Behold, this was the iniquity of your sister, Sodom, pride, fullness of bread, and abundance of idleness was in her and in her daughters, neither did she strengthen the hand of the poor and the needy' (Ez. 16:49).

H. "With respect to Jerusalem, by contrast, it is written, 'The hands of merciful women have boiled their own children' (Lam. 4:10). [Freedman, p. 711, n. 8: Jerusalem suffered extreme hunger, which Sodom never did, and this fact counterbalanced her being spared total destruction.]"

X.29 A. "The Lord has trodden under foot all my mighty men in the midst of me" (Lam. 1:15):

B. This is like a man who says to his fellow, "This coin has been invalidated."

C. "All your enemies have opened their mouths against you" (Lam. 2:16):

D. Said Rabbah said R. Yohanan, "On what account does the letter P come before the letter ayin [in the order of verses in the chapter of Lamentation, while in the alphabet, the ayin comes before the P]?

E. "It is on account of the spies, who said with their mouths [and the word for mouth begins with a P] what their eyes had not seen [and the word for eye begins with an ayin.]"

X.30 A. "They eat my people as they eat bread and do not call upon the Lord" (Ps. 14:4):

B. Said Rabbah said R. Yohanan, "Whoever eats the bread of Israelites tastes the flavor of bread, and who does not eat the bread of Israelites does not taste the flavor of bread."

X.31 A. "They do not call upon the Lord" (Ps. 14:4):

B. Rab said, "This refers to judges."

C. And Samuel said, "This refers to those who teach children."

The List of those Who Do Not Enter the World to Come
Kings and Commoners: Summary Judgments

X.32 A. Who counted [the kings and commoners of M. 11:2A]?

B. Said R. Ashi, "The men of the great assembly counted them."

X.33 A. Said R. Judah said Rab, "They wanted to count yet another [namely, Solomon], but an apparition of his father's face came and prostrated himself before them. But they paid no attention to him. A fire came down from heaven and licked around their chairs, but they did not pay attention. An echo come forth and as said to them, 'Do you see a man diligent in his business? He shall stand before kings, he shall not stand before mean men' (Prov. 22:29).

B. "'He who gave precedence to my house over his house, and not only so, but built my house over a span of seven years, while building his own house over a span of thirteen years "he shall stand before kings, he shall not stand before mean men.'"

C.   "But they paid no attention to that either.

D.   "An echo came forth, saying, 'Should it be according to your mind? He will recompense it, whether you refuse or whether you choose, and not I' (Job 34:33)."

X.34   A.   Those who interpret signs [symbolically] would say, "All of them [listed at M. 11:2] will enter the world to come, as it is said, 'Gilead is mine, Manasseh is mine, Ephraim also is the strength of my head, Judah is my lawgiver, Moab is my washpot, over Edom will I cast my shoe, Philistia, you triumph because of me' (Ps. 60:9-10):

     B.   "'Gideon is mine' speaks of Ahab, who fell at Ramoth-gilead.

     C.   "'Manasseh' – literally.

     D.   "'Ephraim also is the strength of my head' speaks of Jeroboam, who comes from Ephraim.

     E.   "'Judah is my lawgiver' refers to Ahitophel, [105A] who comes from Judah.

     F.   "'Moab is my washpot' refers to Gehazi, who was smitten on account of matters having to with washing.

     G.   "'Over Edom will I cast my shoe' refers to Doeg the Edomite.

     H.   "'Philistia, you triumph because of me:' The Ministering angels said before the Holy One, blessed be he, 'Lord of the world, if David should come, who killed the Philistine, and who gave Gath to them as an inheritance, what are you going to do to him?'

     I.   "He said to them, 'It is my task to make them friends of one another.'"

X.35   A.   "Why is this people of Jerusalem slidden back by a perpetual backsliding" (Jer. 8:5):

     B.   Said Rab, "The community of Israel answered the prophet with a lasting reply [a play on the words for backsliding and answer, using the same root].

     C.   "The prophet said to Israel, 'Return in repentance. Your fathers who sinned – where are they now?'

     D.   "They said to him, 'And your prophets, who did not sin, where are they now? For it is said, "Your fathers, where are they? and the prophets, do they live forever" (Zech. 1:5)?'

     E.   "He said to them, 'They repented and confessed as it is said, "But my words and my statutes, which I commanded my servants the prophets, did they not take hold of your fathers? And they returned and said, Like as the Lord of hosts thought to do unto us, according to our ways and according to our doings, so has he dealt with us" (Zech. 1:6).'"

     F.   Samuel said, "Ten men came and sat before him. He said to them, 'Return in repentance.'

     G.   "They said to him, 'If a master has sold his slave, or a husband has divorced his wife, does one party have any further claim upon the other? [Surely not.] Freedman, p. 714, n. 3: Since God has sold us to Nebuchadnezzar, he has no further claim upon us, and we have no cause to repent. This in Samuel's view was the victorious answer.]

H.   "Said the Holy One, blessed be he, to the prophet, 'Go and say to them, 'Thus says the Lord, where is the bill of your mother's divorcement, whom I have put away? Or which of my creditors is it to whom I have sold you? Behold for your iniquities you have sold yourselves, and for you transgressions is your mother put away' (Is. 50:1)."

I.   *And this is in line with what R. Simeon b. Laqish said, "What is the meaning of what is written, 'David my servant [and] Nebuchadnezzar my servant' (Jer. 43:10)?*

J.   "It is perfectly clear before him who spoke and brought the world into being that the Israelites were going to say this, and therefore the Holy One, blessed be he, went ahead and called him 'his servant.' [Why so?] If a slave acquires property, to whom does the slave belong, and to whom does the property belong?' [Freedman, p. 714, n. 7: Even if God had sold them to Nebuchadnezzar, they still belong to God.]'"

X.36   A.   "And that which comes into your mind shall not be at all, that you say, We will be as the heathen, as the families of the countries, to serve wood and stone. As I live, says the Lord God, surely with a mighty hand and with an outstretched arm, and with fury poured out, will I rule over you" (Ez 20:32-33):

B.   *Said R. Nahman, "Even with such anger may the All-Merciful rage against us, so long as he redeems us."*

X.37   A.   "For he chastises him to discretion and his God teaches him" (Is. 28:26):

B.   Said Rabbah bar Hanah, "Said the prophet to Israel, 'Return in repentance.'

C.   "They said to him, 'We cannot do so. The impulse to do evil rules over us.'

D.   "He said to them, 'Reign in your desire.'

E.   "They said to him, 'Let his God teach us.'"

XI.1   A.   **Four ordinary folk: Balaam, Doeg, Ahitophel, and Gehazi [M. 11:2F]:**

B.   [The name] Balaam [means] not with [the rest of] the people [using the same consonants], [who will inherit the world to come].

C.   Another interpretation: Balaam, because he devoured the people.

D.   "Son of Beor" means that he had sexual relations with a cow [a play on the consonants of the word for Beor].

XI.2   A.   *A Tannaite statement:*

B.   Beor, Cushan-rishathaim, and Laban, the Syrian, are one and the same person.

C.   Beor: because he had sexual relations with a cow.

D.   Cushan-rishathaim [two acts of wickedness], for he committed two acts of wickedness against Israel, one in the time of Jacob and one in the time of the Judges.

E.   But what was his real name? It was Laban the Aramaean.

XI.3   A.   It is written, "The son of Beor" (Num. 22:50), but it also is written, "His son was Beor" (Num. 24:3).

B.   Said R. Yohanan, "His father was his son as to prophecy."

XI.4 A. *Balaam is the one who will not come to the world to come. Lo, others will come.*

      B. *In accord with whose view is the Mishnah-passage at hand?*

      C. *It represents the view of R. Joshua.*

      D. *For it has been taught on Tannaite authority:*

      E. [In Tosefta's version:] **R. Eliezer says, "None of the gentiles has a portion in the world to come,**

      F. **"as it is said, 'The wicked shall return to sheol. All the gentiles who forget God' (Ps. (:17).**

      G. **"'The wicked shall return to Sheol' – these are the wicked Israelites.**

      H. **"'And all the gentiles who forget God' – these are the nations."**

      I. **Said to him R. Joshua, "If it had been written, 'The wicked shall return to Sheol – all the gentiles' and then said nothing further, I should have maintained as you do.**

      J. **"Now that it is in fact written, 'All the gentiles who forget God,' it indicates that there also are righteous people among the nations of the world who have a portion in the world to come" [T. San. 13:2E-J].**

      K. And that wicked man [Balaam] also gave a sign concerning his own fate, when he said, "Let me die the death of the righteous" (num. 23:10).

      L. [He said,] "If my soul dies the death of the righteous, may my future be like his, and if not, 'Then behold I go to my people' (Num. 24:14)."

XI.5 A. "And the elders of Moab and the elders of Midian departed" (Num. 22:7):

      B. *A Tannaite statement:*

      C. There was never peace between Midian and Moab. The matter may be compared to two dogs who were in a kennel, barking at one another.

      D. A wolf came and attacked one. The other said, "If I do not help him today, he will kill him, and tomorrow he will come against me."

      E. So the two dogs went and killed the wolf.

      F. *Said R. Pappa, "This is in line with what people say: 'The weasel and the cat can make a banquet on the fat of the unlucky.'"*

XI.6 A. "And the princes of Moab abode with Balaam" (Num. 22:8):

      B. *And as to the princes of Midian, where had they gone?*

      C. *When he said to them, "Lodge here this night and I will bring you word again [as the Lord shall speak to me]," (Num. 22:8), they said, "Does any father hate his son? [No chance!]"*

XI.7 A. *Said R. Nahman, "Hutzbah, even against heaven, serves some good. To begin with, it is written, 'You shall not go with them' (Num. 22:12), and then it is said, 'Rise up and go with them' (Num. 22:20)."*

      B. *Said R. Sheshet, "Hutzbah is dominion without a crown.*

      C. "For it is written, 'And I am this day weak, though anointed king, and these men, the sons of Zeruiah, be too hard for me' (2 Sam. 3:39). [Freedman, p. 717, n. 1: Thus their boldness and impudence outweighed sovereignty.]"

XI.8 A. Said R. Yohanan, "Balaam had one crippled foot, for it is written, 'And he walked haltingly' (Num. 23:3).

B. "Samson had two crippled feet, as it is said, 'An adder in the path that bites the horses' heels' (Gen. 49:17). [Freedman, p. 717, n. 3: This was a prophecy of Samson. "An adder in the path' is taken to mean that he would have to slither along like an adder, being lame in both feet.]

C. "Balaam was blind in one eye, as it is said, 'Whose eye is open' (Num. 24:3).

D. "He practiced enchantment with his penis.

E. "Here it is written, 'Falling but having his eyes open' (Num. 24:3), and elsewhere: 'And Haman was fallen on the bed whereon Esther was' (Est. 7:8).."

F. *It has been stated on Amoraic authority:*

G. Mar Zutra said, "He practiced enchantment with his penis."

H. Mar, son of Rabina, said, "He had sexual relations with his ass."

I. As to the view that he practiced enchantment with his penis it is as we have just now stated.

J. As to the view that he had sexual relations with his ass:

K. Here it is written, "He bowed, he lay down as a lion and as a great lion" (Num. 24:9), and elsewhere it is written, "At her feet [105B] he bowed, he fell" (Jud. 5:27)."

XI.9

A. "He knows the mind of the most high" (Num. 24:16):

B. *Now if he did not know the mind of his own beast, how could he have known the mind of the most high?*

C. *What is the case of the mind of his beast?*

D. *People said to him, "What is the reason that you did not ride on your horse?"*

E. *He said to them, "I put it out to graze in fresh pasture."*

F. [The ass] said to him, "Am I not your ass" (Num. 22:30). [That shows he rode an ass, not a horse.]

G. *"[You are] merely for carrying loads."*

H. "Upon whom you rode" (Num. 22:30).

I. *"It was a happenstance."*

J. "Ever since I was yours, until this day" (Num. 22:30).

K. [The ass continued,] "And not only so, but I serve you for sexual relations by night."

L. *Here it is written, "Did I ever do so to you" (Num. 22:30) and elsewhere it is written, "Let her serve as his companion."* [The same word is used, proving that sexual relations took place as with David and the maiden in his old age.]

M. *Then what is the meaning of the statement, "He knows the mind of the Most High" (Num. 24:16)?*

N. He knew how to tell the exact time at which the Holy One, blessed be he, was angry.

O. *That is in line with what the prophet said to Israel, "O my people, remember now what Balak, king of Moab, consulted, and what Balaam the son of Beor answered him from Shittim to Gilgal, that you may know the righteousness of the Lord" (Mic. 6:5).*

P. *What is the meaning of the statement, "That you may know the righteousness of the Lord" (Mic. 6:5)?*

Q.　　Said the Holy One, blessed be he, to Israel, "Know that I have done many acts of charity with you, that I did not get angry with you in the time of the wicked Balaam.

R.　　"For if I had become angry during all those days, there would not remain out of (the enemies of) Israel a shred or a remnant."

S.　　*That is in line with what Balaam said to Balak,* "How shall I curse one whom God has not cursed? Or shall I rage, when the Lord has not raged?" (Num. 23:8).

T.　　This teaches that for all those days the Lord had not been angry.

U.　　But: "God is angry every day" (Ps. 7:12).

V.　　And how long does his anger last? It is a moment, for it is said, "For his anger endures but a moment, but his favor is life" (Ps. 30:5).

W.　　*If you wish, I shall propose,* "Come, my people, enter into your chambers and shut your doors about you, hide yourself as it were for a brief moment, until the indignation be past" (Is. 26:20).

X.　　*When is he angry? It is in the first three hours [of the day], when the comb of the cock is white.*

Y.　　*But it is white all the time?*

Z.　　*All the other time it has red streaks, but when God is angry, there are no red streaks in it.*

XI.10　A.　　*There was a min living in the neighborhood of R. Joshua b. Levi, who bothered him a great deal. One day he took a chicken and tied it up at the foot of his bed and sat down. He said, "When that moment comes [at which God is angry], I shall curse him."*

　　　　B.　　*When that moment came, he was dozing. He said, "What this teaches is that it is improper [to curse], for it is written, 'Also to punish is not good for the righteous' (Prov. 17:26) – even in the case of a min."*

XI.11　A.　　*A Tannaite authority in the name of R. Meir [said],* "When the sun shines and the kings put their crowns on their heads and bow down to the sun, forthwith he is angry."

XI.12　A.　　"And Balaam rose up in the morning and saddled his ass" (Num. 22:21):

　　　　B.　　*A Tannaite authority taught in the name of R. Simeon b. Eleazar,* "That love annuls the order of proprieties [we learn] from the case of Abraham.

　　　　C.　　"For it is written, 'And Abraham rose up early in the morning and saddled his ass' (Gen. 22:3) [not waiting for the servant to do so].

　　　　D.　　"And that hatred annuls the order of proprieties [we learn] from the case of Balaam.

　　　　E.　　"For it is said, 'And Balaam rose up early in the morning and saddled his ass' (Num. 22.21)."

XI.13　A.　　Said R. Judah said Rab, "Under all circumstances a person should engage in study of Torah and practice of religious duties, even if it is not for their own sake, for out of doing these things not for their own sake one will come to do them for their own sake."

B.   For as a reward for the forty-two offerings that Balak offered, he had the merit that Ruth should come forth from him.

C.   Said R. Yosé bar Huna, "Ruth was the daughter of Eglon, grandson of Balak, king of Moab."

XI.14   A.   *Said Raba to Rabbah bar Mari, "It is written, '[And moreover the king's servants came to bless our lord king David, saying] God make the name of Solomon better than your name, and make his throne greater than your throne' (1 Kgs. 1:47).*

B.   *"Now is this appropriate to speak in such a way to a king?"*

C.   *He said to him, "What they meant is, 'as good as ....'* [Freedman, p. 720, n. 2: 'God make the name of Solomon illustrious even as the nature of your own and make his throne great according to the character of your throne.']

D.   *"For if you do not say this, then [take account of the following:] 'Blessed above women shall be Jael, the wife of Heber the Kenite, be, blessed shall she be above women in the tent' (Jud. 5:24).*

E.   *"Now who are the women in the tent? They are Sarah, Rebecca, Rachel, and Leah.*

F.   *"Is it appropriate to speak in such a way? Rather, what is meant is 'as good as ...,' and here too the sense is, 'as good as ....'"*

G.   *That statement differs from what R. Yosé bar Honi said.*

H.   For R. Yosé bar Honi said , "One may envy anybody except for his son and his disciple.

I.   "One learns the fact about one's son from the case of Solomon.

J.   *"And as to the case of one's disciple, if you wish, I shall propose, 'Let a double quantity of your spirit be upon me.' (2 Kgs. 2:9)*

K.   *"Or if you wish, I shall derive proof from the following: 'And he laid his hands upon him and gave him a charge' (Hum. 27:23)."*

XI.15   A.   "And the Lord put a thing in the mouth of Balaam" (Num. 23:5):

B.   R. Eleazar says, "It was an angel."

C.   R. Jonathan said, "It was a hook."

XI.16   A.   Said R. Yohanan, "From the blessing said by that wicked man, you learn what he had in his heart.

B.   "He wanted to say that they should not have synagogues and school houses: 'How goodly are your tents, O Jacob' (Num. 24:5).

C.   "[He wanted to say that] the Presence of God should not dwell on them: 'And your tabernacles, O Israel' (Num. 24:5).

D.   "[He wanted to say] that their kingdom should not last [thus, to the contrary]: 'As the valleys are they spread forth' (Num. 24:6);

E.   "... that they should have no olives and vineyards: 'As the trees of aloes which the Lord has planted' (Hum. 24:6);

G.   "... that their kings should not be tall: 'And as cedar trees beside the waters' (Num. 24:6).

H.   "... that they should not have a king succeed his father as king: 'He shall pour the water out of his buckets' (Num. 24:6).

I.   "... that their kingdom should not rule over others: 'And his seed shall be in many waters' (Num. 24:6).

J. "... that their kingdom should not be strong: 'And his king shall be higher than Agag' (Num. 24:6).

K. "... that their kingdom not be fearful: 'And his kingdom shall be exalted' (Num. 24:6)."

L. Said R. Abba b. Kahana, "All of them were [ultimately] turned into a curse, except for the one on the synagogues and school houses, as it is said, 'But the Lord your God turned the curse into a blessing for you, because the Lord your God loved you' (Deut. 23:6).

M. "'The curse' – not the [other] curses..."

XI.17 A. *Said R. Samuel bar Nahmani said R. Jonathan, "What is the meaning of the verse of Scripture: 'Faithful are the wounds of a friend, but the kisses of an enemy are deceitful' (Prov. 27:6)?*

B. "Better was the curse with which Ahijah the Shilonite cursed the Israelites than the blessing with which the wicked Balaam blessed them.

C. "Ahijah the Shilonite cursed the Israelites by reference to a reed, as it is said, 'For the Lord shall smite Israel as a reed is shaken in the water' (1 Kgs. 14:15).

D. "Just as a reed stands in a place in which there is water, so its stem [106A] is renewed and its roots abundant, so that, even if all the winds in the world come   and blow against it, they cannot move it from its place, but it goes on swaying with them. When the winds fall silent, the reed stands in its place. [So is Israel].

E. "But the wicked Balaam blessed them by reference to a cedar tree [at 24:6].

F. "Just as a cedar tree does not stand in a place in which there is water, so its roots are few, and its truck is not renewed, so that while, even if all the winds in the world come and blow against it, they will not move it from its place, when the south wind blows against it, it uproots it right away and turns it on its face, [so is Israel].

G. "And not only so, but the reed has the merit that from it a quill is taken for the writing of scrolls of the Torah, prophets, and writings."

XI.18 A. "And he looked on the Kenite and took up his parable" (Num. 24:21):

B. Said Balaam to Jethro the Kenite, "Were you not with us in that conspiracy [of Pharaoh, Ex. 1:22]? [Of course you were.] Then who gave you a seat among the mighty men of the earth [in the sanhedrin]?"

C. *This is in line with what R.Hiyya bar Abba said R. Simai said, "Three participated in that conspiracy [of Ex. 1:22, to destroy the Israelites in the river], Balaam, Job, and Jethro.*

D. "Balaam, who gave the advice, was slain. Job, who kept silent, was judged through suffering. Jethro, who fled, had the merit that some of his sons' sons would go into session [as judges] in the Hewn-Stone Chamber,

E. "as it is said, 'And the families of scribes which dwelt at Jabez, the Tirahites, the Shemathites, the Sucathites. These are the Kenites that came of Hammath, the father of the house of

Rehab' (2 Chr. 2:55). And it is written, 'And the children of the Kenite, Moses' father-in-law ...' (Jud. 1:16)."

XI.19 A. "And he took up his parable and said, Alas, who shall live when God does this" (Num. 24:23):

B. Said R. Yohanan, "Woe to the nation who is at hand when the Holy One, blessed be he, effects the redemption of his children!

C. "Who would want to throw his garment between a lion and a lionness when they are having sexual relations?"

XI.20 A. "And ships shall come from the coast of Chittim" (Num. 24:24):

B. Said Rab, "[Legions will come] from the coast of Chittim" [cf. Freedman, p. 722, n. 12].

C. "And they shall afflict Assyria and they shall afflict Eber" (Num. 24:24):

D. *Up to Assyria they shall kill, from that point they shall enslave.*

XI.21 A. "And now, behold, I go to my people; come and I shall advise you what this people shall do to your people in the end of days" (Num. 24:24):

B. *Rather than saying,* "This people to your people," *it should say,* "Your people to this people." [Freedman, p. 723, n. 4: He advised the Moabites to ensnare Israel through uncharity. Thus he was referring to an action by the former to the latter, while Scripture suggests otherwise.]

C. Said R. Abba, "It is like a man who curses himself but assigns the curse to others. [Scripture alludes to Israel but refers to Moab.]

D. "[Balaam] said to [Balak], 'The God of these people hates fornication, and they lust after linen [clothing, which rich people wear]. Come and I shall give you advice: Make tents and set whores in them, an old one outside and a girl inside. Let them sell linen garments to them.'

E. "He made tents for them from the snowy mountain to Beth Hajeshimoth [north to south] and put whores in them, old women outside, young women inside.

F. "When an Israelite was eating and drinking and carousing and going out for walks in the market, the old lady would say to him, 'Don't you want some linen clothes?'

G. "The old lady would offer them at true value, and the girl would offer them at less.

H. "This would happen two or three times, and then [the young one] would say to him, 'Lo, you are at home here. Sit down and make a choice for yourself.' Gourds of Ammonite wine would be set near her. (At this point the wine of gentiles had not yet been forbidden to Israelites.) She would say to him, 'Do you want to drink a cup of wine?'

I. "When he had drunk a cup of wine, he would become inflamed. He said to her, 'Submit to me.' She would than take her god from her bosom and said to him, 'Worship this.'

J. "He would say to her, 'Am I not a Jew?'

K. "She would say to him, 'What difference does it make to you? Do they ask anything more from you than that you bare yourself?' But he did not know that that was how this idol was served.

	L.	"'And not only so, but I shall not let you do so until you deny the Torah of Moses, your master!'
	M.	"As it is said, 'They went in to Baal-peor and separated themselves unto that shame, and their abominations were according as they loved' (Hos. 9:10)."
XI.22	A.	"And Israel dwelt in Shittim" (Num. 25:1):
	B.	R. Eliezer says, "The name of the place actually was Shittim."
	C.	R. Joshua says, "It was so called because when there they did deeds of idiocy (STWT)."
	D.	"And they called the people to the sacrifices of their gods" (Num. 25:2):
	E.	R. Eliezer says, "They met them naked."
	F.	R. Joshua says, "They all had involuntary seminal emissions."
	G.	*What is the meaning of Rephidim [Ex. 17:8: "Then came Amalek and fought with Israel in Rephidim"]?*
	H.	R. Eliezer says, "It was actually called Rephidim."
	I.	R. Joshua says, "It was a place in which they weakened their [ties to] the teachings of the Torah, as it is written, 'The fathers shall not look back to their children for feebleness of hands' (Jer. 47:3)."
XI.23	A.	R. Yohanan said, "Any passage in which the word, 'And he abode' appears, it means suffering.
	B.	"So: 'And Israel abode in Shittim, and the people began to commit whoredom with the daughters of Moab' (Num. 23:1).
	C.	"'And Jacob dwelt in the land where his father was a stranger, in the land of Canaan' (Gen. 37:1). 'And Joseph brought to his father their evil report' (Gen. 37:3).
	D.	"And Israel dwelt in the land of Egypt, in the country of Goshen' (Gen. 47:27), 'And the time drew near that Israel must die' (Gen. 47:29).
	E.	"'And Judah and Israel dwelt safely, every man under his vine and under his fig tree' (1 Kgs. 5:5). 'And the Lord stirred up an adversary to Solomon, Hadad the Edomite; he was the king's seed in Edom' (1 Kgs. 11:14).."
XI.24	A.	"And they slew the kings of Midian, beside the rest of them that were slain ... Balaam also , the son of Beor, they slew with the sword" (Num. 31:8):
	B.	*What was he doing there anyhow?*
	C.	Said R. Yohanan, "He went to collect a salary on account of the twenty-four thousand Israelites whom he had brought down' [Cf. Num. 25:1-9]."
	D.	*Mar Zutra b. Tobiah said Rab said, "That is in line with what people say: 'When the camel went to ask for horns, the ears that he had they cut off him.'"*
XI.25	A.	"Balaam also, the son of Beor, the soothsayer, [did the children of Israel slay with the sword]" (Josh. 13:22):
	B.	A soothsayer? He was a prophet!
	C.	Said R. Yohanan, "At first he was a prophet, but in the end, a mere soothsayer."
	D.	*Said R. Pappa, "This is in line with what people say: 'She who came from princes and rulers played the whore with a carpenter.'"*

XI.26   A.   [106B] "...did the children of Israel slay with the sword, among those who were slain by them" (Josh. 13:22):

         B.   Said Rab, "They inflicted upon him all four forms of execution: stoning, burning, decapitation, and strangulation."

XI.27   A.   *A min said to R. Hanina, "Have you heard how old Balaam was?"*

         B.   *He said to him, "It is not written out explicitly. But since it is written, 'Bloody and deceitful men shall not live out half their days' (Ps. 55:24), he would have been thirty-three or thirty-four years old."*

         C.   *He said to him,"You have spoken well. I saw the notebook of Balaam, in which it is written, "Balaam, the lame, was thirty-three years old when Phineas, the brigand, killed him.'"*

XI.28   A.   *Said Mar, son of Rabina, to his son, "In regard to all of those [listed as not having a share in the world to come], you should take up the verses relating to them and expound them only in the case of the wicked Balaam. In his case, in whatever way one can expound the relevant passages [to his detriment], you do so."*

XII.1   A.   **Doeg:** It is written, "Doeg" (1 Sam. 21:8) [meaning, "anxious" (Freedman, p. 726, n. 1)] and it is written, "Doeeg" (1 Sam. 22:18) [with letters indicating "woe" being inserted (Freedman, ad loc.)].

         B.   Said R. Yohanan, "To begin with, the Holy One, blessed be he, sits and worries lest such a son one go forth to bad ways. After he has gone forth to bad ways, he says, 'Woe that this one has gone forth!'"

XII.2   A.   *Said R. Isaac, "What is the meaning of the verse of Scripture, 'Why do you boast yourself in mischief, O mighty man? The goodness of God endures forever' (Ps. 52:3)?*

         B.   "Said the Holy One, blessed be he, to Doeg, 'Are you not a hero in Torah-learning! 'Why do you boast in mischief?' Is not the love of God spread over you all day long?'"

         C.   *And said R. Isaac, "What is the meaning of the verse of Scripture, 'But to the wicked God says, What have you to do to declare my statutes?' (Ps. 50:16)?*

         D.   "So the Holy One, blessed be he, said to the wicked Doeg, '"What have you to do to declare my statutes? "When you come to the passages that deal with murderers and slanderers, what have you to say about them!'"

XII.3   A.   "Or that you take my covenant in your mouth?" (Ps. 50:16):

         B.   Said R. Ammi, "The Torah-knowledge of Doeg comes only from the lips and beyond [but not inside his heart]."

XII.4   A.   Said R. Isaac, "What is the meaning of the verse of Scripture, 'The righteous also shall see and fear and shall laugh at him' (Ps. 52:8)?

         B.   "To begin with they shall fear [the wicked], but in the end they shall laugh at him."

         C.   *And said R. Isaac, "What is the meaning of the verse of Scripture: 'He has swallowed down riches and he shall vomit them up again', the God shall cast them out of his belly' (Job 20:15)?*

         D.   "Said David before the Holy One, blessed be he, 'Lord of the world, let Doeg die.'

         E.   "He said to him, '"He has swallowed down riches, and he shall vomit them up again" (Job 20:15).'

         F.   "He said to him, '"Let God cast them out of his belly" (Job 20:15).'"

G.   *And said R. Isaac, "What is the meaning of the verse of Scripture:* 'God shall likewise destroy you forever' *(Ps. 52:7)?*

H.   "Said the Holy One, blessed be he, to David, 'Should I bring Doeg to the world to come?'

I.   "He said to him, '"God shall likewise destroy you forever" (Ps. 52:7).'"

J.   "What is the meaning of the verse: 'He shall take you away and pluck you out of the tent and root you out of the land of the living, selah' (Ps. 52:7)?

K.   "Said the Holy One, blessed be he, *'Let a tradition in the school house be repeated in his name.'*

L.   "He said to him, '"He shall take you away and pluck you out of the tent" (Ps. 52:7).'

M.   *"'Then let his children be rabbis.'*

N.   "'"And your root out of the land of the living, selah!"'"

O.   *And said R. Isaac, "What is the meaning of the verse of Scripture:* 'Where is he who counted, where is he who weighed? Where is he who counted the towers' *(Is. 33:18)?*

P.   "'Where is he who counted all the letters in the Torah? Where is he who weighed all of the arguments a fortiori in the Torah?'

Q.   "'Where is he who counted the towers' – who counted the three hundred decided laws that concern the 'tower that flies in the air' [that is, the laws governing the status of the contents of a closed cabinet not standing on the ground]."

XII.5   A.   *Said R. Ammi, "Four hundred questions did Doeg and Ahitophel raise concerning the 'tower flying in the air,' and they could not answer any one of them."*

      B.   *Said Raba, "Is there any recognition of the achievement of raising questions? In the time of R. Judah, all of their repetition of Mishnah-teachings concerned the civil laws [of Baba Qamma, Baba Mesia, and Baba Batra], while, for our part, we repeat the Mishnah-traditions even dealing with tractate Uqsin [a rather peripheral topic].*

      C.   *"When for his part R. Judah came to the law,* **'A woman who pickles vegetables in a pot' [M. Toh. 2:1],** *or some say,* **'Olives which were pickled with their leaves are insusceptible to uncleanness' (M. Uqs. 2:1],** *he would say, 'I see here all the points of reflection of Rab and Samuel.*

      D.   *"But we repeat the tractate of Uqsin at thirteen sessions [having much more to say about it].*

      E.   *"When R. Judah merely removed his shoes [in preparation for a fast], it would rain.*

      F.   *"When we cry out [in supplication], no one pays any attention to us.*

      G.   *"But the Holy One, blessed be he, demands the heart, as it is written,* 'But the Lord looks on the heart' (1 Sam. 16:7)."

XII.6   A.   *Said R. Mesharshayya, "Doeg and Ahitophel did not know how to reason concerning traditions."*

      B.   *Objected Mar Zutra, "Can it be the case that one concerning whom it is written,* 'Where is he who counted, where is he who weighed, where is he who counted the towers?' (Is. 33:18) *should not be able to reason concerning traditions? But it never turned out that traditions [in their* names] *were stated in accord with the decided law, for it is written,* 'The secret of the Lord is with those who fear him' (Ps. 25:14)."

XII.7 A.   Said R. Ammi, "Doeg did not die before he forgot his learning, as it is said, 'He shall die without instruction, and in the greatness of his folly he shall go astray' (Prov. 5:23)."

B.   Rab said, "He was afflicted with saraat, for it is said, 'You have destroyed all them who go awhoring from you' (Ps. 73:27), and elsewhere it is written, 'And if it not be redeemed within the span of a full year, then the house shall be established finally [to him who bought it]' (Lev. 25:30).

C.   "*[The word indicated as 'finally' and the word for 'destroyed' use the same letters]. And we have learned in the Mishnah:* **The only difference between one who is definitely afflicted with saraat and one who is shut away for observation is in respect to letting the hair grow long and tearing the garment [M. Meg. 1:7]**, [Freedman, p. 729, n. 6: which shows that the term at hand is used to indicate someone is afflicted with saraat. Hence the first of the two verses is to be rendered, 'You have smitten with definite leprosy all those who go awhoring from you.']"

XII.8 A.   Said R. Yohanan, "Three injurious angels were designated for Doeg: one to make him forget his learning, one to burn his soul, and one to scatter his dust among the synagogues and school houses."

B.   And said R. Yohanan, "Doeg and Ahitophel never saw one another. Doeg lived in the time of Saul, and Ahitophel in the time of David.

C.   "And said R. Yohanan, "Doeg and Ahitophel did not live out half their days."

D.   *It has been taught on Tannaite authority along these same lines:*

E.   "Bloody and deceitful men shall not live out half their days" (Ps. 55:24):

F.   Doeg lived only for thirty-four years, Ahitophel for thirty three.

G.   And said R. Yohanan, "At the outset David called Ahitophel his master, at the end he called him his friend, and finally he called him his disciple.

H.   "At the beginning he called him his master: 'But it was you, a man my equal, my guide and my acquaintance' (Ps. 55:14).

I.   "Then his companion: 'We took sweet counsel together and walked into the house of God in company' (Ps. 55:15).

J.   "Finally, his disciple: 'Yea, my own familiar friend, in whom I trusted **[107A]**, who ate my bread, has lifted his heel against me' (Ps. 56:10). [Freedman, p. 729, n. 10: This is understood to refer to Ahitophel, and eating bread is a metaphor for 'who learned of my teaching.']"

King David: His Sin and Atonement

XII.9 A.   Said R. Judah said Rab, "One should never put himself to the test, for lo, David, king of Israel, put himself to the test and he stumbled.

B.   "He said before him, 'Lord of the world, on what account do people say, "God of Abraham, God of Isaac, and God of Jacob, "but they do not say, "God of David"?'

C. *"He said to him, 'They endured a test for me, while you have not endured a test for me.'*

D. "He said before him, 'Lord of the world, here I am. Test me.'

E. "For it is said, 'Examine me, O Lord, and try me' (Ps. 26:1).

F. *"He said to him, 'I shall test you, and I shall do for you something that I did not do for them. I did not inform them [what I was doing], while I shall tell you what I am going to do. I shall try you with a matter having to do with sexual relations.'*

G. "Forthwith: 'And it came to pass in an eventide that David arose from off his bed' (2 Sam. 11:2)."

H. Said R. Judah, "He turned his habit of having sexual relations by night into one of having sexual relations by day.

I. "He lost sight of the following law:

J. "'There is in man a small organ, which makes him feel hungry when he is sated and makes him feel sated when he is hungry.'"

K. "And he walked on the roof of the king's palace, and from the roof he saw a woman washing herself, and the woman was very beautiful to look upon" (2 Sam. 11:2):

L. *Bath Sheba was shampooing her hair behind a screen. Satan came to [David] and appeared to him in the form of a bird. He shot an arrow at [the screen] and broke it down, so that she stood out in the open, and he saw her.*

M. Forthwith: "And David sent and inquired after the woman. And one said, Is not this Bath Sheba, the daughter of Eliam, the wife of Uriah the Hittite? And David sent messengers and took her, and she came to him, and he lay with her; for she was purified from her uncleanness; and she returned to her house; (2 Sam. 11:203).

N. *That is in line with what is written:* "You have tried my heart, you have visited me in the night, you have tried me and shall find nothing; I am purposed that my mouth shall not transgress" (Ps. 17:3).

O. *He said, "Would that a bridle had fallen into my mouth, that I had not said what I said!"*

XII.10 A. *Raba interpreted Scripture, asking,* "What is the meaning of the following verse: 'To the chief musician, a Psalm of David. In the Lord I put my trust, how do you say to my soul, Flee as a bird to your mountain?' (Ps. 11:1)?

B. "Said David before the Holy One, blessed be he, 'Lord of the world, Forgive me for that sin, so that people should not say, "The mountain that is among you [that is, your king] has been driven off by a bird."'"

C. *Raba interpreted Scripture, asking, "What is the meaning of the following verse: 'Against you, you alone, have I sinned, and done this evil in your sight, that you might be justified when you speak and be clear when you judge' (Ps. 11:1)?*

D. *"Said David before the Holy One, blessed be he, 'Lord of the world. It is perfectly clear to you that if I had wanted to overcome my impulse to do evil, I should have done so. But I had in mind that people not say, "The slave has conquered the Master [God, and should then be included as 'God of David'].""*

E.   *Raba interpreted Scripture, asking, "What is the meaning of the following verse: 'For I am ready to halt and my sorrow is continually before me' (Ps. 38:18)?*

F.   "Bath Sheba, daughter of Eliam, was designated for David from the six days of creation, but she came to him through anguish."

G.   *And so did a Tannaite authority of the house of R. Ishmael [teach],* "Bath Sheba, daughter of Eliam, was designated for David, but he 'ate' her while she was yet unripe."

H.   *Raba interpreted Scripture, asking, "What is the meaning of the following verse: 'But in my adversity they rejoiced and gathered themselves together, yes, the abjects gathered themselves together against me and I did not know it, they tore me and did not cease' (Ps. 35:15)?*

I.   "Said David before the Holy One, blessed be he, 'Lord of the world, it is perfectly clear to you that if they had torn my flesh, my blood would not have flowed [because I was so embarrassed].

J.   Not only so, but when they take up the four modes of execution inflicted by a court, they interrupt their Mishnah-study and say to me, "David, he who has sexual relations with a married woman – how is he put to death?"

K.   "'I say to them, "He who has sexual relations with a married woman is put to death through strangulation, but he has a share in the world to come," while he who humiliates his fellow in public has no share in the world to come."'"

XII.11 A.   Said R. Judah said Rab, "Even when David was sick, he carried out the eighteen acts of sexual relations that were owing to his [eighteen] wives, as it is written, 'I am weary with my groaning, all night I make my bed swim, I water my couch with my tears' (Ps. 6:7)."

B.   And said R. Judah said, Rab, "David wanted to worship idols, as it is said, 'And it happened that when David came to the head, where he worshipped God' (2 Sam. 15:32), and 'head' only means idols, as it is written, 'This image's head was of fine gold' (Dan. 2:32).

C.   "'Behold, Hushai, the Archite came to meet him with his coat rent and earth upon his head' (2 Sam. 15:32):

D.   "He said to David, 'Are people to say that a king such as you have worshipped idols?'

E.   "He said to him, 'Will the son of a king such as me kill him? It is better that such a king as me worship an idol and not profane the Name of heaven in public.'

F.   *"He said, 'Why then did you marry a woman captured in battle?* [Freedman, p. 732, n. 7: Absalom's mother, Maachah, the daughter of Talmai, king of Geshur, was a war captive.]"

G.   *"He said to him, 'As to a woman captured in battle, the All-Merciful has permitted marrying her.'*

H.   *"He said to him, 'You did not correctly interpret the meaning of the proximity of two verses. For it is written, 'If a man has stubborn and rebellious son' (Deut. 21:18).*

I.   "'[The proximity teaches that] whoever marries a woman captured in battle will have a stubborn and rebellious son.'"

XII.12 A.   R. Dosetai of Biri interpreted Scripture, "To what may David be likened? To a Samaritan merchant.

B.	"Said David before the Holy One, blessed be he, 'Lord of the world, "Who can understand his errors?" (Ps. 19:13).'
C.	*"He said to him, 'They are remitted for you.'*
D.	"'" Cleanse me of hidden faults" (Ps. 19:13).'
E.	*"'They are remitted to you.'*
F.	"'" Keep back your servant also from presumptuous sins" (Ps. 19:13).'
G.	*"'They are remitted to you.'*
H.	"'" Let them not have dominion over me, then I shall be upright" (Ps. 19:13), *so that the rabbis will not hold me up as an example.'*
I.	*"'They are remitted to you.'*
J.	"'" And I shall be innocent of great transgression" (Ps. 19:13), *so that they will not write down my ruin.'*
K.	"He said to him, 'That is not possible. Now if the Y that I took away from the name of Sarah [changing it from Sarah to Sarah] stood crying for so many years until Joshua came and I added the Y [removed from Sarah's name] to his name, as it is said, "And Moses called Oshea, the son of Nun, Jehoshua" (Num. 13:16), how much the more will a complete passage of Scripture [cry out if I remove that passage from its rightful place]!'"

XII.13	A.	"And I shall be innocent from great transgression: (Ps. 19:13):
	B.	He said before him, "Lord of the world, forgive me for the whole of that sin [as though I had never done it]."
	C.	He said to him, "Solomon, your son, even now is destined to say in his wisdom, 'Can a man take fire in his bosom, and his clothes not be burned? Can one go upon hot coals, and his feet not be burned? So he who goes in to his neighbor's wife, whoever touches her shall not be innocent' (Prov. 6:27-29)."
	D.	*He said to him, "Will I be so deeply troubled?"*
	E.	He said to him, "Accept suffering [as atonement]."
	F.	He accepted the suffering.
XII.14	A.	Said R. Judah said Rab, "For six months David was afflicted with saraat, and the Presence of God left him, and the sanhedrin abandoned him.
	B.	"He was afflicted with saraat, as it is written, 'Purge me with hyssop and I shall be clean, wash me and I shall be whiter than snow/ (Ps. 51:9).
	C.	"The Presence of God left him, as it is written, 'Restore to me the joy of your salvation and uphold me with your free spirit' (Ps. 51:14).
	D.	"The sanhedrin abandoned him, as it is written, 'Let those who fear you turn to me and those who have known your testimonies' (Ps. 119:79).
	E.	"How do we know that this lasted for six months? As it is written, 'And the days that David rules over Israel were forty years: [107B] Seven years he reigned in Hebron, and thirty-three years he reigned in Jerusalem' (1 Kgs. 2:11).
	F.	"Elsewhere it is written, 'In Hebron he reigned over Judah seven years and six months' (2 Sam. 5:5).
	G.	*"So the six months were not taken into account. Accordingly, he was afflicted with saraat [for such a one is regarded as a corpse].*
	H.	"He said before him, 'Lord of the world, forgive me for that sin.'

I.   "'It is forgiven to you.'

J.   "'"Then show me a token for good, that they who hate me may see it and be ashamed, because you, Lord, have helped me and comforted me" (Ps. 86:17).'

K.   "He said to him, 'While you are alive, I shall not reveal [the fact that you are forgiven], but I shall reveal it in the lifetime of your son, Solomon.'

L.   "When Solomon had built the house of the sanctuary, he tried to bring the ark into the house of the Holy of Holies. The gates cleaved to one another. He recited twenty-four prayers [Freedman, p. 734, n. 4: in 2 Chr. 6 words for prayer, supplication and hymn occur twenty-four times], but was not answered.

M.   "He said, 'Lift up your head, O you gates, and be lifted up, you everlasting doors, and the King of glory shall come in. Who is this King of glory? The Lord strong and might, the Lord mighty in battle' (Ps. 24:7ff.).

N.   "And it is further said, 'Lift up your heads, O you gates even lift them up, you everlasting doors/ (Ps. 24:7).

O.   "But he was not answered.

P.   "When he said, 'Lord God, turn not away the face of your anointed, remember the mercies of David, your servant'(2 Chr. 6:42), forthwith he was answered.

Q.   "At that moment the faces of David's enemies turned as black as the bottom of a pot, for all Israel knew that the Holy One, blessed be he, had forgiven him for that sin."

XIII.1   A.   **Gehazi [M. 11:2F]:**

B.   As it is written, "And Elisha came to Damascus" (2 Kgs. 8:7).

C.   *Where was he traveling [when he came to Damascus]?*

D.   Said R. Yohanan, "He went to bring Gehazi back in repentance, but he did not repent.

E.   "He said to him, 'Repent.'

F.   "He said to him, 'This is the tradition that I have received from you: "Whoever has both sinned and caused others to sin will never have sufficient means to do penitence."'"

G.   *What had he done?*

H.   *Some say,* "He hung a lodestone on the sin[ful statue built by] Jeroboam and suspended it between heaven and earth."

I.   *Others say,* "He carved on it the Name of God, so that it would say, 'I [am the Lord your God]...You shall not have [other gods...]' (Ex. 20:1-2)."

J.   *Still others say,* "He drove rabbis away from his presence, as it is said, 'And the sons of the prophets said to Elisha, "See now the place where we swell before you is too small for us"' (2 Kgs. 6:1). *The sense then is that up to that time, it was not too small.*"

XIII.2   A.   *Our rabbis have taught on Tannaite authority:*

B.   Under all circumstances the left hand should push away and the right hand should draw near,

C.   not in the manner of Elisha, who drove away Gehazi with both hands.

D.   What is the case with Gehazi?

E. As it is written, "And Naaman said, 'Be pleased to accept two talents'" (2 Kgs. 5:23).

F. And it is written, "But he said to him, 'Did I not go with you in spirit when the man turned from his chariot to meet you? Was it a time to accept money and garments, olive orchards and vineyards, sheep and oxen, menservants and maidservants'" (2 Kgs. 5:26).

G. *But did he receive all these things? He got only silver and garments.*

H. Said R. Isaac, "At that moment Elisha was occupied with the study of the list of eight dead creeping things (M. Shab. 14:1, Lev. 11:29].

I. Naaman, head of the army of the king of Syria, was afflicted with saraat. *A young girl who had been taken captive from the land of Israel said to him, "If you go to Elisha, he will heal you."*

J. *When he got there, he said to him, "Go, immerse in the Jordan."*

K. *He said to him, "You are making fun of me!"*

L. *Those who were with him said to him, "Go, try it, what difference does it make to you?"*

M. *He went and immersed in the Jordan and was healed.*

N. *He came and brought him everything that he had, but [Elisha] would not take it. Gehazi took leave of Elisha and went and took what he took and hid it.*

O. *When he came back, Elisha saw the marks of saraat, as they blossomed all over his head.*

P. *"He said to Gehazi, 'Wicked one! The time has come to receive the reward for the eight dead creeping things: "Therefore the leprosy of Naaman shall cleave to you and to your descendants forever" (2 Kgs. 8:27).'"*

XIII.3 A. "Now there were four men who were lepers [at the entrance to the gate]" (2 Kgs. 7:3):

B. R. Yohanan said, "This refers to Gehazi and his three sons."

C. *It has been taught on Tannaite authority:* R. Simeon b. Eleazar says, "Also in one's natural impulse, as to a child or a woman, one should push away with the left hand and draw near with the right hand."

[Freedman, p. 736, n. 2: The uncensored edition continues: What of R. Joshua b. Perahjah?--When King Jannai slew our Rabbis, R. Joshua b. Perahjah (and Jesus) fled to Alexandria of Egypt. On the resumption of peace, Simeon b. Shetach sent to him: 'From me, (Jerusalem) the holy city, to thee, Alexandria of Egypt (my sister). My husband dwelleth within thee and I am desolate.' He arose, went, and found himself in a certain inn, where great honour was shown him. 'How beautiful is this Acsania?' (The word denotes both inn and innkeeper. R. Joshua used it in the first sense; the answer assumes the second to be meant.) Thereupon (Jesus) observed, 'Rabbi, her eyes are narrow.' 'Wretch," he rebuked him, 'dost thou thus engage thyself.' He sounded four hundred trumpets and excommunicated him. He (Jesus) came before him many times pleading, 'Receive me!' But he would pay no heed to him. One day he (R. Joshua) was reciting the Shema', when Jesus came before him. He intended to receive him and made a sign to him. He (Jesus) thinking that it was to repel him, went, put up a brick, and worshipped it. 'Repent,' said he (R. Joshua) to him. He replied, 'I have thus learned from thee: He who sins and causes others to sin is not afforded the means of repentance.' And a Master has said, 'Jesus the Nazarene practiced magic and led Israel astray.']

XIII.4 A. *Our rabbis have taught on Tannaite authority:*
        B. Elisha bore three illnesses,
        C. one because he brought the she-bears against the children, one because he pushed Gehazi away with both hands, and one on account of which he died.
        D. For it is said, "Now Elisha had fallen sick of the ailment of which he died" (2 Kgs. 13:14).

XIII.5 A. Until Abraham there was no such thing as [the sign of] old age. Whoever saw Abraham thought, "This is Isaac." Whoever saw Isaac thought, "This is Abraham."
        B. *Abraham prayed for mercy so that he might have [signs of] old age, as it is said,* "And Abraham was old, and well stricken in age" (Gen. 24:1).
        C. *Until the time of Jacob there was no such thing as illness, so he prayed for mercy and illness came about, as it is written,* "And someone told Joseph, behold, your father is sick: (Gen. 48:1).
        D. *"Until the time of Elisha, no one who was sick ever got well. Elisha came along and prayed for mercy and got well, as it is written,* "Now Elisha had fallen sick of the illness of which he died" (2 Kgs. 13:14) [Freedman: This shows that he had been sick on previous occasions too, but recovered.]

The important question at hand is self-evident: how has the compositor of this tractate of monstrous proportions arranged the materials at hand. The answer is given in the outline at Chapter Twelve. There we see that the entire construction devotes itself to the exposition of the Mishnah, with one topical composite after another, but remarkably few secondary insertions and accretions.

11:3A-CC

A. The generation of the flood has no share in the world to come,
B. and they shall not stand in the judgment,
C. since it is written, "My spirit shall not judge with man forever" (Gen. 6:3)
D. neither judgment nor spirit.
E. The generation of the dispersion has no share in the world to come,
F. since it is said, "So the Lord scattered them abroad from there upon the face of the whole earth" (Gen. 11:8).
G. "So the Lord scattered them abroad" – in this world,
H. "and the Lord scattered them from there" – in the world to come.
I. The men of Sodom have no portion in the world to come,
J. since it is said, "Now the men of Sodom were wicked and sinners against the Lord exceedingly" (Gen. 13:13)
K. "Wicked" – in this world,

L. "And sinners" – in the world to come.

M. But they will stand in judgment.

N. R. Nehemiah says, "Both these and those will not stand in judgment,

O. 'for it is said, 'Therefore the wicked shall not stand in judgment [108A], nor sinners in the congregation of the righteous' (Ps. 1:5)

P. 'Therefore the wicked shall not stand in judgment' – this refers to the generation of the flood.

Q. 'Nor sinners in the congregation of the righteous' – this refers to the men of Sodom."

R. They said to him, "They will not stand in the congregation of the righteous, but they will stand in the congregation of the sinners."

S. The spies have no portion in the world to come,

T. as it is said, "Even those men who brought up an evil report of the land died by the plague before the Lord" (Num. 14:37)

U. "Died" – in this world.

V. "By the plague" – in the world to come.

W. "The generation of the wilderness has no portion in the world to come and will not stand in judgment,

X. "for it is written, 'In this wilderness they shall be consumed and there they shall die' (Num. 14:35), "The words of R. Aqiba.

Y. R. Eliezer says, "Concerning them it says, 'Gather my saints together to me, those that have made a covenant with me by sacrifice' (Ps. 50:5)."

Z. "The party of Korah is not destined to rise up,

AA. "for it is written, 'And the earth closed upon them' – in this world.

BB. "'And they perished from among the assembly' – in the world to come," the words of R. Aqiba.

CC. And R. Eliezer says, "Concerning them it says, 'The Lord kills and resurrects, brings down to Sheol and brings up again' (1 Sam. 2:6)."

I.1 A. *Our rabbis have taught on Tannaite authority:*

B. "The generation of the flood has no share in the world to come [M. 11:3A],

C. "nor will they live in the world to come,

D. "as it is said, And he destroyed every living thing that was upon the face of the earth (Gen. 7:23) in this world;

E. "and they perished from the earth in the world to come," the words of R. Aqiba.

F. R. Judah B. Betera says, "They will live nor be judged, as it is said, And the Lord said, My spirit shall not contend with man forever' (Gen. 6:3)

G. "It will not contend, nor will my spirit be in them forever."

H. Another matter: "And the Lord said, My spirit shall not contend: – [Said the Omnipresent,] that their spirit will not return to its sheath.

I. R. Menahem b. R. Joseph says, [In T.'s version:] "It will not contend –

J. "Said the Omnipresent, 'I shall not contend with them when I pay the good reward which is coming to the righteous.'

K. "But the spirit of the evil is harder for them than that of all the others.

L. "as it is written, Their spirit is a fire consuming them (Is. 33:11)'" [T. San. 13:6A-K].

I.2 A. *Our rabbis have taught on Tannaite authority:*

B. The generation of the Flood acted arrogantly before the Omnipresent only on account of the good which he lavished on them, since it is said, "Their houses are safe from fear, neither is the rod of God upon them" (Job 21:9). "Their bull genders and fails not, their cow calves and casts not her calf" (Job 21:10). "They send forth their little ones like a flock, and their children dance" (Job. 21:11). "They spend their days in prosperity and their years in pleasures" (Job 36:11).

C. That is what caused them to say to God, "Depart from us, for we do not desire knowledge of they ways. What is the Almighty, that we should serve Him, and what profit should we have, if we pray to him (Job 21:14).

D. They said, "Do we need Him for anything except a few drops of rain? But look, we have rivers and wells which are more than enough for us in the sunny season and in the rainy season, since it is said, And a mist rose from the earth (Gen. 2:6)."

E. The Omnipresent then said to then, "By the goodness which I lavished on them they take pride before me? By that same good I shall exact punishment from them!"

F. What does it say? "And I, behold, I bring a flood of water upon the earth" (Gen. 6:17).

G. R. Yosé B. Durmasqit says, "The men of the Flood took pride only on account of [the covetousness of] the eyeball, which is like water, as it is said, 'The sons of God saw that the daughter of men were fair, and they took them wives from all which they chose (Gen. 6:2).

H. "Also the Omnipresent exacted punishment from them only through water, which is like the eyeball, as it is written, 'All the fountains of the great deep were broken up, and the windows of heaven were opened' (Gen. 7:11)" [T. Sot. 3:6-9]

I.3 A. Said R. Yohanan, "As to the generation of the flood, they corrupted their way 'greatly,' and they were judged 'greatly.'

B. "They corrupted their way greatly, as it is said, 'And God saw that the wickedness of man was great in the earth' (Gen. 6:5).

C. "They were judged greatly, as it is said, 'All the fountains of the great deep' (Gen. 7:11)."

D. Said R. Yohanan, "Three [of those fountains remained, the gulf of Gaddor, the hot springs of Tiberias, and the great well of Biram.:

I.4 A. "For all flesh had corrupted its way upon the earth" (Gen. 6:12):

B. Said R. Yohanan, "This teaches that [the men of the generation of the flood] made a hybrid match between a domesticated beast and a wild animal, a wild animal and a domesticated beast, and every sort of beast with man and man with every sort of beast."

	C.	Said R. Abba bar Kahana, "And all of them reverted [to the right way] except for the Tartarian lark [Freedman, p. 740, n. 10]."
I.5	A.	"And God said to Noah, the end of all flesh is come before me" (Gen. 6:13).
	B.	Said R. Yohanan, "Come and take note of how great is the power of robbery.
	C.	"For lo, the generation of the flood violated every sort of law, but the decree of punishment against them was sealed only when they went and committed robbery, for it is said, 'For the earth is filled with violence through them, and behold I will destroy them with the earth' (Gen. 6:13).
	D.	"And it is written, 'Violence is risen up into a rod of wickedness, none of them shall remain, nor of their multitude, nor any of theirs, neither shall there be wailing for them' (Ez. 7:11)."
	E.	Said R. Eleazar, "The cited verse teaches that [violence] stood up straight like a staff and stood before the Holy One, blessed be he, and said to him, 'Lord of the world, Neither them, nor of their multitudes, nor of any thing belonging to them, nor will there be wailing for them.'"
I.6	A.	*A Tannaite authority of the house of R. Ishmael [said],* "Also the decree of punishment for Noah was issued, but he pleased the Lord,"
	B.	"as it is said, 'I am sorry that I made them. But Noah found favor in the eyes of the Lord' (Gen. 6:7-8)."
I.7	A.	"And the Lord was comforted that he had made man in the earth" (Gen. 6:6).
	B.	When R. Dimi came, [he said,] "The Holy One, blessed be he, said, 'I did well that I made graves for them in the earth [Freedman, p. 741, n. 6: since the wicked are thereby destroyed].'
	C.	*"How is this indicated? Here it is written,* 'And the Lord was comforted' (Gen. 6:6) *and elsewhere:* 'And he comforted them and spoke kindly to them' (Gen. 50:21)."
	D.	*There are those who say,* "[He said,] 'I did not do well that I made graves for them in the earth.
	E.	*"Here it is written,* 'And the Lord regretted...' (Gen. 6:6) *and elsewhere:* 'And the Lord regretted the evil that he had thought to do to his people' (Ex. 32:14)."
I.8	A.	"These are the generations of Noah: Noah was a righteous man, perfect in his generations" (Gen. 6:9):
	B.	Said R. Yohanan, "By the standards of his generations, but not by the standards of other generations [was he perfect]."
	C.	R. Simeon b. Laqish said, "By the standards of his generations, and all the more so by the standards of other generations."
	D.	Said R. Hanina, "As to the view of R. Yohanan, one may propose a comparison. To what may the matter be compared? To the case of a keg of wine, stored in a wine cellar of vinegar.
	E.	"In its setting, its fragrance is noteworthy, but in any other setting, its fragrance would not be noteworthy."
	F.	Said R. Oshaia, "As to the view of R. Simeon b. Laqish, one may propose a comparison. To what may the matter be compared? To the case of a bottle of perfumed oil lying in a garbage dump.

G.   "If it smells good in such a place, all the more so in a place in which there is spice!"

I.9   A.   "And every living substance was destroyed which was upon the face of the ground, both man and beast" (Gen. 7:23):

B.   While man sinned, what sin had beasts committed?

C.   *It was taught on Tannaite authority in the name of R. Joshua b. Qorha,* "The matter may be compared to the case of a man who made a marriage banquet for his son. He prepared all sorts of food for the banquet. After some days the son died. The man went and threw out [all the food he had prepared for] the banquet.

D.   "He said, 'Did I do anything except for my son? Now that he is died, what need have I for a marriage banquet?'

E.   "So too the Holy One, blessed be he, said, 'Did I create domesticated and wild beasts for any purpose other than for man? Now that man has sinned, what need have I for domesticated beasts or wild beasts?'"

I.10   A.   "All that was on the dry land died" (Gen. 7:22) –

B.   But not the fish in the sea.

I.11A.   R. Yosé of Caesarea expounded as follows: "What is the sense of the verse, 'He is swift as the waters, their portion is cursed in the earth, [he does not behold the way of the vineyards]' (Job 24:18)?

B.   "The verse teaches that Noah, the righteous man, rebuked them, saying to [his generation], 'Carry out an act of repentance, for if not, the Holy One, blessed be he, will bring upon you a flood and your corpses will float on the water like gourds.'

C.   "'So it is written, "He is light upon the waters" (Job 24:18).

D.   "'And not only so, but people will take from your example a curse for all who will pass through the world, as it is said, "Their portion is cursed in the earth" (Job 24:18).'

E.   "They said to him, 'And what is stopping him now?'

F.   "He said to them, '[God] has one dear one to take away from your midst.'

G.   "[They replied], **[108B]** 'If so, we will not turn aside from the way of the vineyards, [that is, we shall continue in our drunkenness].'"

I.12   A.   *Raba expounded as follows: "What is the meaning of the verse, 'He that is ready to slip with his feet is as a stone despised in the thought of him that is at ease' (Job 12:5)?*

B.   "This teaches that the righteous Noah rebuked them, saying to them words as hard as stone, but they despised him, saying, 'Old man, what is this ark for?'

C.   "He said to them, 'The Holy One, blessed be he, is bringing a flood on you.'

D.   "They said to him, 'What sort of flood? If it is a flood of fire, we have something called alitha [Freedman, p. 743, n. 7: a fire-extinguishing demon].

E.   "'And if he brings a flood of water, if it comes from the earth, we have iron plates to cover up the earth [and keep the water down].

F.   "'If it comes from heaven, we have aqob (others say, aqosh) [Freedman, p. 743, n. 8: a legendary fungus, which when donned on the head protects against rain].'

G.   "He said to them, 'He will bring it from between your heels [legs, that is, from your penis], as it is said, "He is ready for the steps of your feet" (Job 12:5).'"

H.   *It has been taught on Tannaite authority:*

I.   The water of the flood was as hard as semen, as it is written, "It is ready for the steps of his feet" (Job 12:5).

I.13   A.   Said R. Hisda, "By hot fluid they corrupted their way in transgression, and by hot fluid they were judged.

B.   "Here it is written, 'And the water cooled' (Gen. 8:1), and elsewhere: 'Then the king's wrath cooled down' (Est. 7:10)."

I.14   A.   "And it came to pass after seven days that the waters of the flood were upon the earth" (Gen. 7:10)"

B.   **Said Rab, "What is the meaning of these seven days?**

C.   **"These are the seven days of mourning for Methuselah, the righteous man. This teaches that lamentation for the righteous held back the retribution from coming upon the world.**

D.   **"Another matter: 'After seven days' teaches that the Holy One, blessed be he, changed the order of the world for them, so that the sun came up in the west and set in the east.**

E.   **"Another matter: It teaches that the Holy One, blessed be he, first set a long a time for them, and then a short time.**

F.   **"Another matter: It teaches that he gave them a taste of the world to come, so that they should know how much good he would withhold from them [T. Sot. 10:3C. 4]."**

I.15   A.   "Of every clean beast you shall take by sevens, man and wife" (Gen. 7:2).:

B.   *Do beasts relate as man and wife?*

C.   Said R. Samuel bar Nahmani said R. Jonathan, "It was to be from among those with whom no transgression had been committed."

D.   *How did he know?*

E.   Said R. Hisda, "He brought them before the ark. Any that the ark received could be known not to have been the object of a transgression, and any that the ark did not receive could be known to be those with whom a transgression had been committed."

F.   R. Abbahu said, "It was from among those who came on their won."

I.16   A.   "Make an ark of gopher wood for yourself" (Gen. 6:14)"

B.   *What is gopher wood?*

C.   *Said R. Adda, "Members of the house of R. Shila say, 'It is a kind of cedar.'*

D.   *"Others say, 'It is a hard wood of cedar.'"*

I.17   A.   "A window (SHR) you shall make in the ark" (Gen. 6:16):

B.   Said R. Yohanan, "The Holy One, blessed be he, said to Noah, 'Put up in its precious stones and pearls, so that they will give light for you as at noon [using the root for window].'"

I.18   A.   "And in a cubit you shall finish the above" (Gen. 6:16)"

B.   *In what way will it stand firm [against the rain].*

C.   "With lower, second, and third stories you shall make it" (Gen. 6:16)"

D.   *It has been taught on Tannaite authority:*

E.   The bottom for dung, the middle for beasts, the upper for man.

I.19   A.   "And he sent forth a raven" (Gen. 8:7):

        B.   Said R. Simeon b. Laqish, "The raven gave Noah a victorious reply, saying to him, 'Your master [God] hates me, and you hate me.

        C.   "'Your master hates me: 'Of the clean, seven, of the unclean, two' [and the raven is unclean].

        D.   "'You hate me, for you exempt the species of which you have seven, and send forth a species of which you have only two.

        E.   "'If I should be injured by the prince of heat or cold, will the world not end up lacking one species?

        F.   "'Or perhaps you need only to make use of my wife?'

        G.   "He said to him, 'Wicked creature! Even sexual relations with one normally permitted to me are presently forbidden [since it was not permitted to have sexual relations in the ark. Is it not an argument a fortiori that I should not desire sexual relations with one who normally is forbidden to me [namely, a bird]?'"

        H.   *And how do we know that sexual relations were forbidden?*

        I.   As it is written, "And you shall enter the ark, you, your sons, your wife, and the wives of your sons with you" (Gen. 6:18).

        J.   And elsewhere: "Go forth from the ark, you, your wife, your sons, and your sons' wives with you" (Gen. 8:16).

        K.   And, said R. Yohanan, "On the basis of this statement they said that sexual relations were forbidden in the ark [ad the instruction to go forth once more permitted sexual relations]."

I.20   A.   *Our rabbis have taught on Tannaite authority:*

        B.   Three species had sexual relations in the ark, and all of them were smitten: the dog, raven, and Ham.

        C.   The dog [was smitten by being condemned to be] tied up.

        D.   The raven was smitten by having to spit [his semen into his mate's mouth].

        E.   Ham was smitten in his skin.

I.21   A.   "Also he sent forth a dove from him to see if the waters had abated" (Gen. 8:8).:

        B.   Said R. Jeremiah, "On the basis of this verse [we learn] that the dwelling of clean fowl was with the righteous."

I.22   A.   "And lo, in her mouth was an olive leaf as food" (Gen. 8:11):

        B.   Said R. Eleazar, "The dove said before the Holy One, blessed be he, 'May my food be as bitter as an olive leaf but placed in our hand, and let it not be as sweet as honey but placed in the hand of mortals.'

        C.   *"What gives evidence that the word at hand means 'as food'?*

        D.   *"From the following:* 'Feed me [using the same root] with food convenient for me' (Prov. 30:8)."

I.23   A.   "After their families they went forth from the ark" (Gen. 8:19).:

        B.   Said R. Yohanan, "'After their families' and not they [Freedman: alone]." [Freedman, p. 746, n. 6: While in the ark, copulation was forbidden. On their exit, it was permitted. That is the significance of "after their families," which denotes that mating was resumed and they ceased to be a group of single entities.]

I.24   A.   Said R. Hana bar Bizna, "Said Eliezer [Abraham's servant] to Shem, the eldest [son], 'It is written, "After their families they went forth from the ark" (Gen. 8:19). *How was it with you? [How did you take* care of all the animals, given their diverse needs, while you were in the ark?]'

B.   "He said to him, 'We had a great deal of trouble in the ark. A beast who usually was to be fed by day we fed by day. One that usually was to be fed by night we fed by night. *As to the chameleon, father did not know what it ate.*

C.   *"'One day he was sitting and cutting up a pomegranate, and a worm fell out of it. [The chameleon] ate it. From that point forth, he would mash bran for it. When it became maggoty, [the chameleon] ate it."*

D.   *As to the lion, it was fed by a fever, for said Rab, "For no fewer than six days and no more than thirteen, fever sustains."*

E.   *[Reverting to Shem's statement,] "'As to the phoenix, father found it lying in the hold of the ark. He said to it, "Don't you want food?"*

F.   *"'It said to him, "I saw that you were occupied and thought not to bother you."*

G.   *"'He said to it, "May it be God's will that you not die, as it is written, 'Then I said I shall die in the nest, but I shall multiply my days as the phoenix' (Job 29:18)."'"*

H.   *Said R. Hanah bar Livai, "Said Shem, the eldest [son] to Eliezer, 'When the kings of the east and the west came against you, what did you do?'*

I.   "He said to him, 'The Holy One, blessed be he, came to Abraham and set him at his right hand, and [God and Abraham] threw dirt, which turned into swords, and [they threw] chaff, which turned into arrows.

J.   "'So it is written, "A Psalm of David. The Lord said to my master, Sit at my right hand until I make your enemies your footstool" (Ps. 110:1). And it is written, "Who raised up the righteous man from the east, called him to his food, gave the nations before him, and made him rule over kings? He made his sword as the dust and his bowl as driven stubble" (Is. 41:2).'"

I.25   A.   *Nahum of Gam Zo ["This too"] was accustomed to say, on the occasion of anything that happened, "This too is for the good." One day, the Israelites wanted to end a gift to Caesar.*

B.   *They said, "With [109A] whom shall we send it? Let us send it with Nahum of Gam Zo, for he is familiar with miracles."*

C.   *When he got to an inn, he wanted to lodge there. They said to him, "What do you have with you?"*

D.   *He said to them, "I'm bringing a gift to Caesar."*

E.   *They got up in the middle of the night and untied his box, took out everything in it, and filled the box with dirt. When he got there [to the capital], it turned out to be dirt. The [courtiers] said to him, "The Jews are ridiculing us."*

F.   *They took him out to kill him. He said, "This too is for the good."*

G.   *Elijah came and appeared to them as one of them. He said to them, "Perhaps this dirt comes from the dirt of Abraham, our father, who threw dirt that turned into swords and chaff that turned into arrows."*

H.   *They looked, and that is what turned out. There was a province that they had not been able to conquer. They threw some of that dirt against it, and they conquered it. They brought [Nahum] to the treasury and said to him, "Take whatever you want."*

	I.	*He filled his box with gold. When he returned, those who were at the inn came and said to him, "What did you bring to the palace?"*
	J.	*He said to them, "What I took from here I brought there."*
	K.	*They took [dirt] ad brought it there, and [the courtiers] put them to death.*
II.1	A.	**The generation of the dispersion has no share in the world to come [M. 10:3E]:**
	B.	*What did they do wrong?*
	C.	*Said members of the house of R. Shila, "[They said], 'Let us build a tower and go up to the firmament and hit it with axes, so that the water will gush forth."*
	D.	*They ridiculed this in the West, "If so, they should have built it on a mountain!"*
	E.	Said R. Jeremiah bar Eleazar, "They divided up into three parties. One said, 'Let us go up and dwell there.'
	F.	"The second said, 'Let us go up and worship an idol.'
	G.	"The third said, 'Let us go up and make war.'
	H.	"The party that said, 'Let us go up and dwell there – the Lord scattered them' (Gen. 11:9).
	I.	"The party that said, 'Let us go up and make war' turned into apes, spirits, devils, and night-demons.
	J.	"The party that said, 'Let us go up and worship an idol' – 'for there the Lord did confound the language of all the earth'(Gen. 11:9)."
II.2	A.	*It has been taught on Tannaite authority:*
	B.	R. Nathan says, "All of them [went up] intending to worship an idol.
	C.	"Here it is written, 'Let us make us a name' (Gen. 11:4), and elsewhere: 'And make no mention of the name of other gods' (Ex. 23:13).
	D.	"Just as in the latter passage [name stands for] idolatry, so here too 'name' stands for idolatry."
II.3	A.	Said R.Yohanan, "As to the tower, a third of it burned, a third of it sank into the earth, and a third is yet standing."
	B.	Said Rab, "The air of the tower makes people forget."
	C.	*Said R. Joseph, "Babylonia and Borsif are a bad sign for Torah-study [because people there forget what they learn (Freedman, p. 748, n. 8)]."*
	D.	*What is the sense of Borsif?*
	E.	*Said R. Asi, "An empty pit [bor: pit: sif/shafi: empty]."*
III.1	A.	**The men of Sodom have no portion in the world to come [M. 10:31]:**
	B.	*Our rabbis have taught on Tannaite authority:*
	C.	**The men of Sodom have no portion in the world to come [M. 11:31],**
	D.	**since it is said, "And the men of Sodom were wicked sinners" (Gen. 13:13) in this world**
	E.	**"against the Lord exceedingly" – in the world to come. [T. San. 13:8A-C].**
III.2	A.	Said R. Judah, "'Wicked' – with their bodies.
	B.	"And 'sinners' – with their money.

C. "'Wicked' – with their bodies, as it is written, 'How then can I do this great wickedness and sin against God?' (Gen. 39:9).

D. "'Sinners' – with their money, as it is written, 'And it be a sin unto you' (Deut. 15:9).

E. "'Before the Lord' – this is blasphemy.

F. "'Very much' – for they intended deliberately to sin."

G. *On Tannaite authority it was taught:*

H. "'Wicked" – with their money.

I. "And sinners" – with their bodies.

J. "Wicked" – with their money, as it is written, "And your eye be wicked against your poor brothers" (Deut. 15:9).

K. "And sinners" – with their bodies, as it is written, "And I will sin against God" (Gen. 39:9).

L. "Before the Lord" – this is blasphemy.

M. "Very much" – this refers to murder, as it is written, "Moreover, Manasseh shed innocent blood exceedingly" (2 Kgs. 21:16).

III.3   A.   *Our rabbis have taught on Tannaite authority:*

B. **The men of Sodom acted arrogantly before the Omnipresent only on account of the good which he lavished on them, since it is said, "As for the land, out of it comes bread...Its stones are the place of sapphires, and it has dust of gold. That path, no bird of prey knows...The proud beasts have not trodden it" (Job 28:5-8).**

C. **Said the men of Sodom, "Since bread comes forth from our land, and silver and gold come forth from our land, and precious stones and pearls come forth from our land, we do not need people to come to us.**

D. **"They come to us only to take things away from us. Let us go and forget how things are usually done among us."**

E. **[Following T.'s version:] The Omnipresent said to them, "Because of the goodness which I have lavished upon you, you deliberately forget how things are usually done among you. I shall make you be forgotten from the world."**

F. **What does it say? "They open shafts in a valley from where men live. They are forgotten by travelers. They hang afar from men, they swing to and fro (Job 28:4). In the thought of one who is at ease there is contempt for misfortune; it is ready for those whose feet slip. The tents of robbers are at peace, and those who provoke God are secure, who bring their god in their hand" (Job 12:5-6).**

G. **And so it says, "As I live, says the Lord God, your sister Sodom and her daughters have not done as you and your daughters have done. Behold, this was the guilt of your sister Sodom: she and her daughters had pride, surfeit of food, and prosperous ease, but did not aid the poor and needy. They were haughty and did abominable things before me. Therefore I removed them when I saw it" (Ez. 16:48-50). [T. Sot. 3:11-2].**

III.4   A.   *Raba expounded [the following verse]: "What is the sense of this verse: 'How long will you imagine mischief against a man? You shall be slain, all of you, you are all as a bowing wall and as a tottering fence' (Ps. 62:4)?*

B.   "This teaches that the [Sodomites] would look enviously at wealthy men, so they would set such a man near a tottering fence and push it over on him and come and take away all his money."

C.   *Raba expounded [the following verse]: "What is the meaning of this verse: 'In the dark they dig through houses, which they had marked for themselves in the daytime; they know not the light' (Job 24:16)?*

D.   "This teaches that the [Sodomites] would look enviously at wealthy men, so they would deposit with such a man valuable balsam. [The wealthy men] would put it into their treasure rooms. In the night [the others] would come and smell it out like a dog [and so know where there treasure was], as it is written, 'They return at evening, they make a noise like a dog, and go around the city' (Ps. 59:7).

E.   "They would then come and dig there and take away the money.

F.   "[As to the victim"] 'They cause him to go naked without clothing' (Job 24:10), 'that they have no covering in the cold' (Job 24:7). 'They lead away the ass of the fatherless, they take the widow's ox for a pledge' (Job 24:3). 'They remove the landmarks, they violently take away flocks and feed them' (Job 24:2). 'And he shall be brought to the grave and remain in the tomb' (Job 21:32)."

G.   *R. Yosé interpreted the passage in this way in Sepphoris. That night three hundred houses in Sepphoris were broken into. They came and blamed him. They said to him, "You have shown the way to thieves."*

H.   *He said to them, "Did I know that thieves would come?"*

I.   *When R. Yosé died, the streets of Sepphoris ran with blood.*

III.5 A.   *[The Sodomites] said, "Whoever has one ox must guard the herd one day, and whoever has no oxen must guard the herd two days."*

B.   *There was an orphan, son of a widow, the whom they gave the herd to pasture. He went and killed the [oxen]. He said to them,* **[109B]** *"He who has one ox may take one hide. He who has no oxen may take two hides."*

C.   *"Why so" they asked him?*

D.   *He said to them "The end of the matter must accord with its beginning. Just as, at the beginning, one who had an ox had to pasture the herd for one day and one who had none had to do it two days, so at the end, one who had an ox takes one hide, and one who has none takes two."*

E.   *One who crosses a river [by a ferry] pays one zuz, and one who does not cross the river by a ferry [but crosses on his own] has to pay two.*

F.   *If one had a row of bricks [drying in the sun], each one of them would take one, saying to him, "I only took one."*

G.   *If one had garlic or onions drying [in the sun], each one of them would take one, saying to him, "I only took one."*

III.6 A.   *There were four judges in Sodom, named Liar, Big Liar, Forger, and Perverter of Justice.*

B.   *If someone beat his neighbor's wife and made her abort, they say to him, "Give her to him, and he will make her pregnant for you."*

C.   *If someone cut off the ear of his neighbor's ass, they say to him, "Give it to him, until it grows a new one."*

D.   *If someone injured his neighbor, they say to [the victim], "Pay him the fee for letting blood from you."*

E.   *One who crosses the river in a ferry pays four zuz, one who crosses through the water pays eight.*

F.   *One day a washerman came by there. They said to him, "Pay four zuz."*

G. *He said to them, "I crossed in the water."*

H. *They said to him, "If so, pay eight, because you crossed through the water."*

I. *He would not pay, so they beat him up. He came before a judge, who said to him, "Pay the fee for his having let blood from you, as well as the eight zuz for crossing through the water."*

J. *Eliezer, Abraham's servant, happened to come there. Someone beat him up. He came before a judge, who said to him, "Pay him a fee for letting blood from you."*

K. *He took a stone and beat the judge. He said to him, "What's this?"*

L. *He said to him, "The fee that you now owe me give to this man, and my money will remain where it is."*

M. *They had beds, on which they would place guests. If someone was too long, they shortened him [by cutting off his legs], and if he was too short, they stretched him [on a rack].*

N. *Eliezer, Abraham's servant, happened by there. They said to him, "Come, lie down on the bed."*

O. *He said to the, "I took a vow from the time that my mother died never to sleep on a bed."*

P. *When a poor man came there, each one of them gave him a denar, on which he wrote his name. But they gave him no bread. When he would die, each one of them came and took back his denar.*

Q. *They made this stipulation among them: Whoever invited someone to a banquet will have to give over his cloak. There was a banquet, and Eliezer happened to come there, but they did not give him any bread. Since he wanted to eat, Eliezer came and sat down at the end of them all. They said to him, "Who invited you here?"*

R. *He said to the one who sat nearby, "You were the one who invited me."*

S. *He said, "Perhaps they will hear that I was the one who invited him and take away the cloak of that man [me]." He took off his cloak and ran away. And so they all did, until all of them were gone, and he ate the entire banquet.*

T. *A certain girl brought out bread hidden in a pitcher to a poor man. The matter became known. They covered her with honey and put her on the parapet of the wall, and a swarm of bees came and ate her up.*

U. *For it is written, "And the Lord said, The cry of Sodom and Gomorrah, because it is great" (Gen. 18:20).*

V. *On this passage, said R. Judah said Rab, "It is on account of the girl [with the consonants for 'girl' and 'great' being the same]."*

IV.1 A. **The spies have no portion in the world to come, as it is said, "Even those men who brought up an evil report of the land died by the plague before the Lord" (Num. 14:37). "Died" in this world. "By the plague" in the world to come.**

B. **"The party of Korah is not destined to rise up, for it is written 'And the earth closed upon them' – in this world. 'And they perished from among the assembly' in the world to come," the words of R. Aqiba. And R. Eliezer says, "Concerning them it says, 'The Lord kills and resurrects, brings down to Sheol and brings up again' (1 Sam. 2:6).**

C. *Our rabbis have taught on Tannaite authority:*

D. "Korah and his company have no portion in the world to come and will not live in the world to come,

E. "since it is said, 'And the earth closed upon them' (Num. 16:33) – in this world.

F. "'And they perished from among the assembly' – in the world to come," the words of R. Aqiba [M. 11:3Z-BB].

G. R. Judah b. Petera says, "Lo, they are like something lost and searched for [T.: They will come to the world to come].

H. "For concerning them it is written, 'I have gone astray like a perishing sheep; seek your servant' (Ps. 119:176)

I. [Following T.:] 'Perishing' is said here, and in the matter of Korah and his company, 'perishing' also is said.

J. "Just as 'perishing' spoken of later on refers to that which is being sought, so 'perishing' spoken of here refers to that which is being sought" [T. San. 13:9C-I].

IV.2   A. "Now Korah took..." (Num. 16:1):

B. He took a bad deal for himself.

C. "Korah" – for he was made a bald-spot ["Korah" and "bald-spot" using the same consonants] in Israel.

D. "Son of Izhar" – a son who turned the heat of the entire world against himself, as the heat of noon ["Izhar" and "noon" use the same consonants].

E. "Son of Kohath" – who set on edge [KHT] the teeth of those who gave birth to him.

F. "Son of Levi" – a son of the company of Gehenna ["Levi" and "company" use the same consonants].

G. Then why not say, "son of Jacob" – a son who followed to Gehenna [with the letters for "Jacob" and "follow" being shared]?

H. Said R. Samuel b. R. Isaac, "'Jacob sought mercy for himself, [that he should not be listed here], as it is said, 'O my soul, come not into their secret, to their assembly my honor be not united' (Gen. 39:6).

I. "'O my soul, come not into their secret' – this refers to the spies.

J. "'Unto their assembly, my honor be not united' refers to the assembly of Korah."

K. "Dathan" (Num. 16:1) [colleague of Korah] – so-called because he transgressed the law [dat] of God.

L. "Abiram" (Num. 16:1) – so-called because he strengthened himself [using the consonants of the name] not to carry out an act of repentance.

M. "On" (Num. 16:1) [whose name means "lamentation"] – so-called because he sat and lamented [what he had done].

N. "Peleth [On's father]" (Num. 16:1) – so-called because wonders [using the same letters as the name] were done for him.

O. "The son of Reuben" (Num. 16:1) – who saw and understood [using the consonants of the name] [not to get involved].

IV.3   A. Said Rab, "As to On, son of Peleth, his wife saved him. *She said to him, 'What do you get out of this matter? If one master is the greater, you are his disciple, and if the other master is the greater, you are still his disciple!'*

B. *"He said to her, 'What should I do? I was in their conspiracy and I took an oath to be with them.'*

C.   *"She said to him, 'I know that they are all a holy congregation, for it is written, "Seeing all the congregation are holy, every one of them"* (Num. 16:3).'

D.   *"She said to him, 'Stay here, and I'll save you.' She got him drunk on wine and laid him down in [the tent]. She sat down at the flap* **[110A]** *and loosened her hair. Whoever came and saw her turned back. [No one would gaze at her.]*

E.   *"Meanwhile Korah's wife joined them, saying to them, 'See what Moses is doing! He is king. His brother made him high priest. His brother's sons he has made assistant priests. If heave-offering is brought, he says, "Give it to the priest." If tithe is brought, which you have every right to take [since it is for the Levites], he says, "Give a tenth of it to the priest."*

F.   *"'Moreover, he has shaved off all your hair [as part of the purification rite, Num. 8:7], and ridicules you as if you were dirt, for he envied your hair.'*

G.   *"He said to her, 'But he did the same thing to himself?'*

H.   *"She said to him, 'It was because all the greatness was coming to him, he said also, "Let my soul die with the Philistines"* (Jud. 16:30). [Freedman, p. 754, n. 5: This was used proverbially to denote readiness to suffer, so that others might suffer too. Moses, retaining all the greatness himself, did not mind shaving his own hair off, seeing that he had caused all the rest to do so, thus depriving them of their beauty.]

I.   *"'And furthermore he has said to you to make [fringes] of blue [on your garments] [Num. 15:38]. But if you think that the blue [fringe] is a religious duty, then produce cloaks of blue and dress your entire academy in them.'*

J.   *"That is in line with what is written, "Every wise woman builds her house'* – referring to the wife of On, son of Peleth.

K.   *"'But the foolish woman tears it down with her own hands'* (Prov. 14:1) – referring to the wife of Korah."

IV.4 A.   "And they rose up before Moses, with certain of the children of Israel, two hundred and fifty" (Num. 16:2):

B.   They were the distinguished members of the community.

C.   "Chosen for the appointed times" (Num. 16:2):

D.   For they knew how to intercalate years and designate the beginnings of the new months.

E.   "Men or renown" (Num. 16:2):

F.   For they were known throughout the world.

IV.5 A.   "And when Moses heard, he fell on his face" (Num. 16:4):

B.   What did he hear?

C.   Said R. Samuel bar Nahmani said R. Jonathan, "That people suspected him of having sexual relations with a married woman, as it is said, 'And they expressed jealousy [as to sexual infidelity] of Moses in the camp' (Ps. 106:16)."

D.   Said R. Samuel bar Isaac, "This teaches that everyone expressed jealousy of his wife [M. Sot. 1:1] with respect to Moses, as it is said, 'And Moses took the tent and pitched it outside the camp.' (Ex. 33:7) [Freedman, p. 755, n. 5: to avoid all ground of suspicion.]"

IV.6 A.   "And Moses rose up and went to Dathan and Abiram" (Num. 16:25):

B.   Said R. Simeon b. Laqish, "On the basis of this verse we learn that one should not hold on to a quarrel [but should be eager to end it, in the model of Moses, who modestly went out to the other side to seek a resolution]."

C.   For Rab said, "Whoever holds on to a quarrel [and does not seek to end it] violates a negative commandment, for it is said, 'And let him not be as Korah and as his company' (Num. 17:5)."

D.   R. Ashi said, "He is worthy of being smitten with *saraat.*

E.   "Here it is written, 'As the Lord said to him by the hand of Moses' (Num. 17:5), and elsewhere it is written, 'And the Lord said to him, Put your hand into your bosom [and when he took it out, behold, his hand was leprous as snow' (Ex. 4:6)."

IV.7   A.   Said R. Yosé, "Whoever contends with the kingdom of the house of David is worthy that a snake bite him.

B.   "Here it is written, 'And Adonijah slew sheep and oxen and fat cattle by the stone of Zoheleth" '(1 Kgs. 1:9), and elsewhere it is written, 'With the poison of serpents [using the same consonants as the word Zoheleth] of the dust' (Deut. 32:24)."

C.   Said R. Hisda, "Whoever is contentious with his master is as if he were contentious with the presence of God, as it is said, 'When they strove against the Lord' (Num. 26:9). [Freedman, p. 755, n. 14: The reference is to Korah's rebellion; though against Moses only, it is stigmatized as being against God.]"

D.   Said R. Hama b. R. Hanina, "Whoever undertakes to quarrel with his master is as if he had quarrelled with the Presence of God, as it is said, 'This is the water of Strife, because the children of Israel strove with the Lord' (Num. 20:13)."

E.   Said R. Hanina bar Pappa, "Whoever complains against his master is as if he complains against the Presence of God, as it is said, 'Your murmurings are not against us but against the Lord' (Ex. 16:8)."

F.   Said R. Abbahu, "Whoever murmurs against his master is as if he murmurs against the Presence of God, as it is said, 'And the people spoke against God and against Moses' (Num. 21:5)."

IV.8   A.   "Riches kept for the owners to their hurt" (Qoh. 5:12):

B.   Said R. Simeon b. Laqish, "This refers to the riches of Korah."

C.   "And all the substance that was at their feet" (Deut. 11:6)"

D.   Said R. Eleazar, "This refers to the wealth of a man, that puts him on his feet."

E.   And said R. Levi, "A load for three hundred white mules were made up by the keys of Korah's treasury, *although all of them were made of leather, both keys and locks [and not metal]."*

F.   Said R. Hama b. R. Hanina, "Joseph hid three treasures in Egypt. One of them was revealed to Korah, one of them was revealed to Antoninus, son of Severus, and one of them is hidden away for the righteous in the world to come."

IV.9   A.   And said R. Yohanan, "Korah was not among those who were swallowed up nor among those who were burned.

B.   "He was not among those who were swallowed up, for it is written, 'And all the men that joined Korah' (Num. 16:32) – but not Korah.

C. "He was not among those who were burned, for it is written, 'When the fire devoured two hundred and fifty men' (Num. 16:10) – but not Korah."

D. *In a Tannaite teaching it was repeated:*

E. Korah was one of those who were burned up, and he was one of those who were swallowed up.

F. He was one of those who were swallowed up, for it is written, "And swallowed them up together with Korah" (Num. 16:10).

G. He was one of those who were burned, since it is written, "And there came up a fire from the Lord and consumed the two hundred fifty men" (Num. 16:35) – *including Korah.*

IV.10 A. *Said Raba, "What is the meaning of that which is written, 'The sun and the moon stood still in their zebul, at the light of your arrows they went' (Hab. 3:1)? [Freedman, p. 757, n. 1: There are seven heavens, of which zebul is one. What were they doing in zebul, seeing that they are set in the firmament, a lower heaven?]*

B. "This teaches that the sun and the moon went up to the firmament called Zebul. They said before the Holy One, blessed be he, 'Lord of the world, if you do justice with the son of Amram, we shall go forth,and if not, we shall not go forth.'

C. "He shot arrows at them and said to them, 'On account of the honor owing to me you never objected, but on account of the honor owing to a mortal man, you make a protest!'

D. *"Nowadays they go forth only when they are driven out."*

IV.11 A. *Raba interpreted a verse of Scripture, "What is the meaning of what is written, 'But if the Lord make a new thing and the earth open her mouth' (Num. 16:30)?*

B. "Said Moses before the Holy One, blessed be he, 'If Gehenna has been created, well and good, and if not, let the Lord now create it.'"

C. *For what purpose? If we say that he was actually to create it then and there, [how can this be so, for] "There is no new thing under the sun" (Qoh. 1:9)?*

D. *Rather, it was to bring its mouth near [to the present place].*

IV.12 A. "But the children of Korah did not die" (Num. 26:11):

B. *A Tannaite authority taught in the name of our Master [Judah the Patriarch]:* "A place was set aside for them in Gehenna, and they sat there and recited a song [for God]."

IV.13 A. *Said Rabbah bar bar Hana, "One time I was going along the way, and a Tai [Arab] said to me, 'Come, and I shall show you where the men of Korah were swallowed up.' I went and saw two crevasses, from which smoke came forth. He took a piece of wool, wet it down, and set it on the tip of his spear and passed it over the spot, and it was singed.*

B. *"I said to him, 'Listen to what you are going to hear.'*

C. *"And I heard him saying, 'Moses and his Torah are true, and they are liars.'*

D. *"[110B] He said to me, 'Every thirty days Gehenna turns them over like meat in a pot, and they say this: 'Moses and his Torah are true, and they are liars.'"*

V.1 A. **The generation of the wilderness has no portion in the world to come [M. 11:3W]:**

B. *Our rabbis have taught on Tannaite authority:*

C.   "The generation of the wilderness has no portion in the world to come [M. 10:3W],

D.   [T. adds:] "and will not live in the world to come,

E.   "for it is said, 'In this wilderness they shall be consumed and there they shall die' (Num. 14:35),

F.   "'In this wilderness they shall be consumed' – in this world,

G.   "and there they will die,' in the world to come.

H.   "And it says, 'Of them I swore in my wrath that they should not enter into my rest' (Ps. 95:11)", the words of R. Aqiba.

I.   R. Eliezer says, "They will come into the world to come,

J.   "for concerning them it is said, 'Gather my saints together to me, those that have made a covenant with me by sacrifice' (Ps. 50:5) [M. 11:3Y] [T. San. 13:10].

K.   "What does Scripture mean, 'I swore in my wrath'?

L.   "'In my wrath I swore, but I retract it.'"

M.   R. Joshua b. Qorha says, "These things were spoken only regarding generations to come,

N.   as it is said, 'Gather my saints together to me' – these are the righteous of every generation [T.: because they did deeds of loving kindness to me];

O.   "'Those that have made a covenant with me' – this refers to Hananiah, Mishael, and Azariah, who gave themselves up to the fiery furnace on my account.

P.   "'By sacrifice' – this refers to R. Aqiba and his colleagues, who gave themselves over to the slaughter on account of the teachings of the Torah."

Q.   R. Simeon b. Menassia says, "They will come [into the world to come],

R.   "and concerning them it is said, 'And the redeemed of the world shall return and come to Zion with gladness' (Is. 35:10) [T. San. 13:11].

S.   *Said Rabbah bar bar Hannah said R. Yohanan, "R. Aqiba abandoned his love [of Israel, when he said that the generation of the wilderness will not enjoy the world to come].*

T.   "For it is written, 'Go and cry in the ears of Jerusalem, saying Thus says the Lord, I remember the loyalty of your youth, the love of your espousals, when you went after me in the wilderness, in an unsown land' (Jer. 2:2). [Freedman, p. 759, n. 1: Thus the merit of this act of faith on the part of the generation of the wilderness stood their descendants in good stead and conferred the privilege on them of a share in the world to come].

U.   "Now if others will come on account of their merit [to the world to come,] how much the more so they themselves!"

The Talmud simply lays forth materials to complement the Mishnah's topics, item by item. The sole point of note is the change in the order of the Mishnah's topics at the final two items. Otherwise the sequence and topical unfolding are just as expected in a commentary to a received text.

11:3DD-FF

DD. "The ten tribes are not destined to return,

EE. "since it is said, 'And he cast them into another land, as on this day' (Deut. 29:28). Just as the day passes and does not return, so they have gone their way and will not return," the words of R. Aqiba.

FF. R. Eliezer says, "Just as this day is dark and then grows light, so the ten tribes for whom it now is dark – thus in the future it is destined to grow light for them."

I.1 A. *Our rabbis have taught on Tannaite authority:*

B. "The ten tribes have no portion in the world to come [T.: and will not live in the world to come],

C. "as it is said, 'And the Lord drove them out of their land with anger and heat and great wrath' (Deut. 29:8) – in this world;

D. "and cast them forth into another land' (Deut. 29:28) – in the world to come," the words of R. Aqiba.

E. R. Simeon b. Judah of Kefar Akkum says in the name of R. Simeon, "Scripture said, 'As at this day' –

F. "if their deeds remains as they are this day, they will [not] reach it, and if not, they will (not) reach it."

G. Rabbi says, "[Both these and those] have a portion in the world to come,

H. "as it is said, 'And it shall come to pass in that day that the trumpet shall be blown [and those who are perishing in the land of Assyria and those who are driven away in to the Land of Egypt shall come and worship the Lord in the holy mountain, in Jerusalem]' (Is. 27:13)." [T. San. 13:12].

I. *Said Rabbah b. b. Hana said R. Yohanan, "R. Aqiba abandoned his love [for Israel in taking the position that he did.]*

J. "For it is written 'Go and proclaim these words toward the north and say, Return, you backsliding Israel, says the Lord, and I will not cause my anger to fall upon you, for I am merciful, says the Lord, and I will not keep my anger forever' (Jer. 3:12)."

K. *What is the reference to [Aqiba's] love?*

L. *As it has been taught on Tannaite authority:*

M. "Minors who are children of the wicked of the Land [of Israel] have no portion in the world to come, as it is said, 'Behold, the day is coming, burning like a furnace, and all the proud, and all who do wickedly, shall be as stubble, and the day coming shall burn them up, said the Lord, that it shall leave them neither root nor branch' (Mal. 3:19).

N. "'Root' – in this world.

O. "'Branch' – in the world to come," the words of Rabban Gamaliel.

P. R. Aqiba says, "They come into the world to come. For it says, 'The Lord preserves the simple' (Ps. 116:6), and in the coastal towns they call a child 'the simple one.' And further, 'Hew down the tree and destroy it, nevertheless, leave the stump of the roots thereof in the earth' (Dan. 4:23)."

Q. Said Rabban Gamaliel said to [Aqiba], "How shall I interpret, 'He shall leave to them neither the root nor the branch'"?

R. [Joshua] said to Gamaliel], "That the Omnipresent will not leave them [the merit of a single] religious duty or the remnant of a religious duty, or for their fathers, forever" [T. San. 13:1 A-D].

S. Another matter:

T. "Root" – this refers to the soul.

U. And "branch" – this refers to the body.

V. And the children of the wicked among the heathen will not live [in the world to come] nor be judged.

W. And Rabban Gamaliel?

X. *He derives the same fact from the verse,* "And you have made all their memory perish" (Is. 26:14).

I.2   A. *It has been stated upon Amoraic authority:*

B. As to an infant, at what point does it enter the world to come?

C. R. Hiyya and R. Simeon b. Rabbi: one said, "From the time that it is born."

D. The other said, "From the time that it cried."

E. *The one who has said,* "From the time that it is born" – as it is said, "They shall come and declare his righteousness to a people that shall be born, that he has done this" (Ps. 22:32).

F. *The one who has said,* "From the time that it spoke" – as it is written, "A seed shall serve him it shall be related of the Lord for a generation" (Ps. 22:31).

G. *It has been stated upon Amoraic authority:*

H. Rabina said, "From the time that of conception as it is written, 'A seed shall serve him' (Ps. 22:31)."

I. R. Nahman b. Isaac said, "From the time of circumcision, as it is written, 'I am afflicted and ready to die from my youth up, while I suffer your terrors I am distracted.' (Ps. 88:16)."

J. *It was taught on Tannaite authority in the name of R. Meir,* "From the time that is said, 'Amen,' as it is said, 'Open you the gates, that the righteous nation which keeps the truth may enter in' (Is. 26:2). Do not read 'which keeps truth' but 'which says, "Amen"'' [rearranging the consonants at hand]."

K. [111A] *What is the meaning of "Amen"?*

L. God, faithful king.

I.3   A. "Therefore hell has enlarged herself and opened her mouth without measure" (Is. 5:15):

B. Said R. Simeon b. Laqish, "For him who leaves over even one law [unobserved]."

C. *Said R. Yohanan, "It is not a pleasing to their Master that you make such a statement to them. Rather:* even if one who has not studied a single statute [it will save a person from Gehenna].'"

D. "And it shall come to pass that in all the land, says the Lord, two parts therein shall be cut off and die, but the third shall be left therein" (Zech. 13:8):

E. Said R. Simeon b. Laqish, "The third of the descendants of Shem."

F. *Said R. Yohanan, "It is not pleasing to their Master that you make such a statement to them [since most of humanity will perish]. Rather:* A third even of the descendants of Noah.'"

G. "For I am married to you and I will take you one of a city and two of a family" (Jer. 3:14):

H. Said R. Simeon b. Laqish, "The matter is to be interpreted just as it is written."

I. *Said R. Yohanan to him, "It is not pleasing to their Master that you should say this to them. Rather:* One in a given city imparts merit to save the entire city, and two of a family impart merit to save the entire family."

J. *R. Kahana was in session before Rab and said [in this same context],* "The matter is to be interpreted just as it is written."

K. *Said Rab to him, "It is not pleasing to their Master that you should say this to them. Rather:* One in a given city imparts merit to save the entire city, and two of a family impart merit to save the entire family."

L. *Rab saw that he straightened out his hair and then went and took up a seat before Rab. He said to him, "'And it shall not be found in the land of the living'* (Job. 28:13)."

M. *He said to him, "You curse me."*

N. *He said to him, "I cite a verse to you:* You shall not find Torah in him who worries about his own needs ahead of it."

I.4 A. *It has been taught on Tannaite authority:*

B. R. Simai says, "It is said, 'I shall take you to me for a people' (Ex. 6:7), and it is said, 'And I will bring you in [to the land]' (Ex. 6:7).

C. "Their exodus from Egypt is compared to their entry into the land. Just as, when they came into the land, they were only two out of the original six hundred thousand [only Caleb and Joshua], so when they lift Egypt, there were only two out of six hundred thousand."

D. Said Raba, "So it will be in the times of the Messiah, as it is said, 'And she shall sing there, as in the days of her youth, and as in the days when she came up out of the land of Egypt' (Hos. 2:17)."

I.5 A. *It has been taught on Tannaite authority:*

B. Said R. Eleazar b. R. Yosé, "One time I went to Alexandria, Egypt. I found an old man there, who said to me, 'Come and I shall show you what my forefathers did to your forefathers.

C. "'Some of [your ancestors] did [my ancestors] drown in the sea, some of them they slew with a sword, some of them they crushed in the buildings.'

D. "And on that account, Moses, our master, was punished, as it is said, 'For since I came to Pharaoh to speak in your name, he has done evil to this people, neither have you delivered your people at all' (Ex. 5:23).

E. "Said to him the Holy One, blessed be he, 'Woe for those who are gone and no longer to be found! How many times did I appear to Abraham, Isaac, and Jacob, as God Almighty, and they did not complain against what I meted out, nor did they ask me, "What is your name?"

F. "'I said to Abraham, "Arise, walk through the land in the length of it and in the breadth of it, for I will give it to you" (Gen. 13:17), [yet] he had to go begging for a place in which to bury Sarah, and he found nothing until he acquired a place for four hundred silver shekels, yet he did not complain against what I meted out.

G. "'I said to Isaac, "Sojourn in this land and I will be with you and will bless you" (Gen. 26:3), and while his servants went begging for water and found none to drink until they had a quarrel, as it is said, "And the herdmen of Gerar did strive with Isaac's herdmen, saying, the water is ours" (Gen. 26:20). Yet he did not complain against what I meted out [to him].

H. "'I said to Jacob, "The land on which you lie will I give to you and to your seed" (Gen. 28:13). Yet he went begging for a place on which to pitch his tent and found none until he bought it for a hundred pieces of money [Gen. 33:19], yet he did not complain against what I meted out.

I. "'And none of them said to me, "What is your name?"

J. "'Yet in the beginning you have said to me, "What is your name?"

K. "'And now you say to me, "Neither have you delivered your people at all" (Ex. 5:23)!

L. "'"Now shall you see what I will do to Pharaoh" (Ex. 6:1). You will see the war against Pharaoh, but you will not see the war against Pharaoh, but you will not see the war against the thirty-one kings' [Josh. 12:24]."

I.6 A. "And Moses made haste and bowed his head toward the earth and worshipped: (Ex. 34:8):

B. What did Moses see?

C. R. Hanina b. Gamula said, "He saw [God's attribute of] being long-suffering [Ex. 34:7]."

D. Rabbis say, "He saw [the attribute of] truth [Ex. 34:7]."

E. *It has been taught on Tannaite authority in accord with him who has said, "He saw God's attribute of being long-suffering."*

F. *For it has been taught on Tannaite authority:*

G. When Moses went up on high, he found the Holy One, blessed be he, sitting and writing, "Long-suffering."

H. He said before him, "Lord of the world, "Long-suffering for the righteous?"

I. He said to him, "Also for the wicked."

J. [Moses] said to him, "Let the wicked perish."

K. He said to him, "Now you will see what you want."

L. When the Israelites sinned, he said to him, "Did I not say to you, 'Long suffering for the righteous'?"

M. [111B] He said to him, "Lord of the world, did I not say to you, 'Also for the wicked'?"

N.   That is in line with what is written, "And now I beseech you, let the power of my Lord be great, according as you have spoken, saying" (Num. 14:17). [Freedman, p. 764, n. 7: What called forth Moses' worship of God when Israel sinned through the Golden Calf was his vision of the Almighty as long-suffering.]

I.7   A.   *R. Hagga was going up the stairs of the house of Rabbah bar Shila. He heard a child saying,* "'Your testimonies are very sure, holiness becomes your house, O Lord, you are for the length of days' (Ps. 93:5).

B.   "And near the same verse: 'A prayer of Moses' (Ps. 90:1)."

C.   He said, "This proves that he saw [the attribute of God's being' long-suffering.]"

I.8   A.   Said R. Eleazar said R. Hanina, "The Holy One, blessed be he, is destined to be a crown on the head of every righteous person, as it is said, 'In that day shall the Lord of Hosts be for a crown of glory and for a diadem of beauty to the remnant of his people' (Is. 28:5)."

B.   *What is the meaning of "a crown of glory and a diadem of beauty"?*

C.   It is for those who do his will and look forward to his salvation. [The word for "glory" uses letters that, in Aramaic, also mean "will" or "desire," and the word for "diadem" contains letters that also mean "look forward" or "hope". The whole reads: In that day shall the Lord of hosts be for a crown of desire and for a diadem of hope (Freedman, pp. 764-5, n. 12)].

D.   Might one suppose that it is for everyone?

E.   Scripture states, "For the remnant of his people" (Is. 28:5). For those who make themselves as a remnant [Freedman, p. 75, n. 1: of no value, hence, to the humble].

F.   "And for a spirit of judgment to him who sits in judgment and for strength to them that turn the battle to the gate" (Is. 28:6)"

G.   "For a spirit of judgment" – this is one who rules over his impulse to do evil.

H.   "To him who sits in judgment" – this refers to one who gives a true and honest judgment.

I.   "And for strength" – to him who is stronger than his impulse to do evil.

J.   "To them that turn the battle" – this refers to one who engages in the give and take of Torah-study.

K.   "To the gate" – this refers to those who get up early in the morning and go to bed late at night to spend time in synagogues and school houses.

L.   The attribute of justice said before the Holy One, blessed be he, "Lord of the world, how do these differ from those? [Why do those who have these qualities differ from those who do not have them them?]?

M.   He said to it, "'But they also have erred through wine and through strong drink are out of the way...they stumble in giving judgment'" (Is. 28:7)."

N.   The word used for "stumble" refers to Gehenna, as it is said, "That this shall be no grief to you" (I 1 Sam. 25:31), and the word for "judgment" refers only to judges, as it is said, "And he shall pay as the judges determine" (Ex. 21:22).

The layout of the whole is explained in Chapter Twelve. I see no major problems, and little secondary material at that.

11:4-6

A. The townsfolk of an apostate town have no portion in the world to come,

B. as it is said, "Certain base fellows [sons of Belial] have gone out from the midst of thee and have drawn away the inhabitants of their city" (Deut. 13:14).

C. And they are not put to death unless those who misled the [town] come from that same town and from that same tribe,

D. and unless the majority is misled,

E. and unless men did the misleading.

F. [If] women or children misled them,

G. of if a minority of the town was misled,

H. or if those who misled the town came from outside of it,

I. lo, they are treated as individuals [and not as a whole town],

J. and they [thus] require [testimony against them] by two witnesses, and a statement of warning, for each and every one of them.

K. This rule is more strict for individuals than for the community:

L. for individuals are out to death by stoning.

M. Therefore their property is saved.

N. But the community is put to death by the sword,

O. Therefore their property is lost.

M.11:4

A. "And you shall surely smite the inhabitants of the city with the edge of the sword" (Deut. 13:15)

B. Ass-drivers, camel-drivers, and people passing from place to place – lo these have the power to save it,

C. as, it is said, "Destroying it utterly and all that is therein and the cattle thereof, with the edge of the sword" (Deut. 13:17).

D. On this basis they said, The property of righteous folk which happens to be located in it is lost. But that which is outside of it is saved.

E. And as to that of evil folk, whether it is in the town or outside of it, lo, it is list.

M.11:5

A. [As it is said,] "And you shall gather all the spoil of it into the midst of the wide place thereof" (Deut. 13:17).

B. If it has no wide place, they make a wide place for it.

C. [If] its wide place is outside of it, they bring it inside.

D. "And you will burn with fire the city and all the spoil thereof, (ever whit, unto the Lord your God)" (Deut. 13:17).

E. "The spoil thereof" – but not the spoil which belongs to heaven.

F. On this basis they have said:

G. Things which have been consecrated which are in it are to be redeemed; heave-offering left therein is allowed to rot; second tithe and sacred scrolls are hidden away.

H. "Ever whit unto the Lord your God"

I. Said R. Simeon, "Said the Holy One, blessed be he: 'If you enter into judgment in the case of an apostate city, I give credit to you as if you had offered a whole burnt-offering before me.'"

J. "And it shall be a heap forever, it shall not be built again"

K. "It should not be made even into vegetable-patches or orchards," the words of R. Yosé the Galilean.

L. R. Aqiba says, "'It shall not be built again' – as it was it may not be rebuilt, but it may be made into vegetable patches and orchards."

M. "And there shall cleave nought of the devoted things to your hand [that the Lord may turn from the fierceness of his anger and show you mercy and have compassion upon you and multiply you]" (Deut. 13:18)

N. for so long as evil people are in the world, fierce anger is in the world.

O. When the evil people have perished from the world, fierce anger departs from the world.

M.11:6

I.1 A. [The townsfolk of an apostate town have no portion in the world to come, as it is said, "Certain base fellows sons fo Belial have gone out from the midst of thee and have drawn away the inhabitants of their city:":] *Our rabbis have taught on Tannaite authority:*

B. "...have gone out..."(Deut. 13:14) – they and not messengers.

C. "...fellows..." – the plural means there must be two.

D. Another matter: "...fellows..." – and not women.

E. "...fellows..." and not children.

F. "...sons of Belial..." – sons who have broken the yoke of heaven from their shoulders.

G. "From your midst" – and not from the border towns.

H. "The inhabitants of their city' – and not the inhabitants of some other city.

I. "Saying" – indicating that there must be proper testimony and admonition for each one [who is involved].

I.2 A. *It has been stated on Amoraic authority:*

B. R. Yohanan said, "They may divide a single town between two tribes [if the boundary between tribes runs through it]."

C. R. Simeon b. Laqish said, "They may not divide a single town between two tribes."

D. *R. Yohanan objected to R. Simeon b. Laqish, "*...unless those misled the town come from that same town and from that same tribe [M. 11:4C] *– does this not bear the implication that even though the ones who led the town astray come from that town only, if they also come from that tribe as well, the law applies, and if not, it does not apply? Then it bears the implication that* a single town may be divided among two tribes."

E.   *[He replied,] "No, it may be a case in which part of the town came to [the one who led it astray] through an inheritance, or it was given to him."*

F.   He objected, "'Nine cities out of these two tribes' (Josh. 21:16) – is that not four and a half from one and four and a half from the other, in which case it follows that they do divide a single town among two tribes?"

G.   *He replied, "No, it means four from one and five from the other."*

H.   *If so, it should be made explicit [which one gave which number].*

I.   *[112A] That is a problem.*

I.3   A.   *The question was raised:*

B.   *If the inhabitants were led astray on their own, what is the law?*

C.   *[Do we say that] the All-Merciful has said, "...have seduced the inhabitants" (Deut. 13:14), and not those who were seduced on their own?*

D.   *Or perhaps, even if the inhabitants were induced on their own, [the law still applies]?*

E.   *Come and take note:* **If women or children misled them...[M. 11:4F]** *– [the people of the town are exempt from punishment]. Now why should this be the case? Let them be in the status of those who were led astray on their own? [It would follow that if a town is led astray on its own, it would be exempt from penalty.]*

F.   *[No, the comparison is apt, for] these followed their own will alone, while the others [in the case specified in the Mishnah-rule] were led astray by women and children.*

II.1   A.   **And unless the majority is misled [M. 11:4D]:**

B.   *[Since each participant is subject to the usual testimony of two witnesses as well as admonition,] how do we handle the matter [of dealing with the majority of a town]?*

C.   Said R. Judah, "The court judges and imprisons, judges and imprisons [again and again, working their way through the population, until a majority has been convicted. Then all are executed.]"

D.   Said Ulla to him, "You turn out to delay the judgment [and execution of those tried earlier, an this is intolerable]."

E.   Rather, said Ulla, "The court judge and executes the death penalty of stoning, judges and executes the death penalty of stoning. [Freedman, p. 769, n. 10: When half of a town have thus been executed and there are still more, the place is declared a condemned city, and the rest are decapitated.]"

F.   *It has been stated on Amoraic authority:*

G.   R. Yohanan said, "The court judges and executes the death penalty through stoning, judges and executes the death penalty through stoning."

H.   R. Simeon b. Laqish said, "They set up many courts [to judge the community more or less simultaneously and the trials are under the aspect of the condemnation of the town as a whole]."

I.   Is this so? And has not R. Hama, son of R. Yosé, said in R. Oshaia's name, "'Then you shall bring forth that man or that woman to your gates' (Deut. 17:5), teaching that a man or a woman do you bring to your gates, but do not bring an entire town to your gates."

J.		Rather, they set up many courts and look into the cases of each of the persons involved [without pronouncing a verdict], then they take the accused out to the high court and complete the trials and put them all to death.
III.1	A.	**And you shall surely smite the inhabitants of the city with the edge of the sword" (Deut. 13:15):**
	B.	*Our rabbis have taught on Tannaite authority:*
	C.	**Ass-drivers, camel-drivers, and people passing from place to place [M. 11:5B] who spent the night in its midst and became apostates with [the others of the town]**
	D.	**if they spent thirty days in the town, they are put to death by the sword, and their property and the town are prohibited.**
	E.	**But if they did not spend thirty days in the town, they are put to death by stoning, but their property is rescued [T. San. 14:2 A-D].**
	F.	*An objection was raised from the following:*
	G.	**How long must a man be in a town to count as one of the men of the town? Twelve months [M. B.B 1:5].**
	H.	*Said Raba, "There is no contradiction [between the two definitions of residency for,] one serves the purpose of designating a person as one of the men of the town [which takes a year], and the other serves the purpose of designating him as one of the permanent residents of the town [which takes thirty days]."*
	I.	*And has it not been taught on Tannaite authority [in support of that view]:*
	J.	**He who is prohibited by vow from deriving benefit from his town or from the people of his town, and someone came from the outside and lived there for thirty days – he who took the vow is permitted to derive benefit from him.**
	K.	**But if he was prohibited by vow from deriving benefit from those who dwell in his town, and someone came from the outside and lived there for thirty days, he is prohibited from deriving benefit from him [T. Ned. 2:10A-D].**
IV.1	A.	**Destroying it utterly and all that is therein and the cattle thereof with the edge of the sword (Deut. 13:17) [M. 11:5C]:**
	B.	*Our rabbis have taught on Tannaite authority:*
	C.	"Destroying it utterly and all that is therein" (Deut. 13:17) –
	D.	excluding **the property of the righteous which is outside of it, [M. 11:5D].**
	E.	"And all that is therein" –
	F.	encompassing **the property of righteous folk which happens to be located in it [M. 11:5D].**
	G.	"The spoil that is in it" (Deut. 13:17) – but not the spoil that belongs to heaven.
	H.	"All the spoil of it" (Deut. 13:17) – encompassing the property of wicked folk that is located outside of it.
IV.2	A.	**Said R. Simeon, "On what account did they rule, The property of the righteous which is in it is lost?**
	B.	**"Because that property caused the righteous to live among evil people.**
	C.	[T. adds: "And is it not a matter of an argument a fortiori? And if property, which does not see, hear, or speak, because it caused

righteous men to live among wicked people, the Scripture has ruled that it must be burned, he who turns his fellow through the way of life to the way of death, all the more so should he be put to death by burning.]" [T. San. 14:4G-K].

IV.3   A.   A master said, "'And all the spoil of it you shall gather' (Deut. 13:17) – encompassing the property of evil folk that is outside of it."

B.   Said R. Hisda, "[But that applies, in particular, to that which can be] gathered together in it."

C.   Said R. Hisda, "Objects left on deposit with men of an apostate city are permitted [to the original owners]."

D.   *To what circumstance does that statement pertain?*

E.   *If one should say that the property belongs to people of a different city but is now within [the apostate city], then it is self-evident that it is permitted, since it does not fall into the category of "its spoil."*

F.   *Rather, they would be objects belonging to the inhabitants of the city located in another town.*

G.   *But if they are capable of being assembled back in the apostate city, then why should they be permitted. And if they are not going to be assembled in he apostate town, he already has made that statement once [and why repeat it in the present form]?*

H.   *In point of fact the property belongs to inhabitants of another town, and has been deposited in the apostate town. And here with what sort of case do we deal? It is with a case in which the resident of the apostate town accepted responsibility to replace the deposited property if lost. What might you have said? Since he has accepted responsibility for the deposited property if it is lost, it falls into the category of his own property.*

I.   *So we are informed that that is not the case.*

J.   Said R. Hisda, "As to a domesticated beast half of which belongs to a resident of an apostate city and half of which belongs to a resident of another town, it is forbidden. But as to dough half of which belongs to a resident of an apostate city and half of which belongs to a resident of another town, it is permitted.

K.   "*What is the difference? The beast is treated as something which has not been divided, while the dough falls into the category of something that already has been divided.*"

L.   *R. Hisda raised the question, "As to a domesticated beast belonging to a resident of an apostate city, what is the law on regarding proper slaughter as an act effective to purify the beast from the uncleanness pertaining to carrion [and so permitting use of the carcass]?*

M.   "*The All-Merciful has said, '[You shall surely smite...the cattle thereof] with the edge of the sword' (Deut. 13:17), and there is no difference whether the beast is properly slaughtered or merely put to death [and not slaughtered as required for ritual use].*

N.	"Or perhaps, once the beast has been properly slaughtered, does the act of slaughter serve [to permit use of the beast]?
O.	"What is the law?"
P.	The question stands over.

IV.4 A. R. Joseph raised the question, "What is the law concerning use of the hair of righteous women [in such a city]?"

B. Said Raba, "Lo, that of wicked women is forbidden [if it is shaved off before they are executed].

C. "Scripture states, 'You shall gather...and you shall burn...' (Deut. 13:17), thus referring to something that lacks only being collected together and burned. Then the present matter is excluded, for it also lacks cutting off, as well as gathering and burning."

D. Rather, said Raba, "We deal with a wig made from the hair of a gentile woman."

E. *If it is a wig made from the hair of a gentile woman, then what is the condition of the wig? If it is attached to her body, it is in the status of her body [and of course is not burned].*

F. *No, it is a question in a case in which the wig is hung on a peg.*

G. *Does it fall into the category of the property of the righteous that are located in the town, in which case it is destroyed?*

H. *Or perhaps, since it is put on and taken off, it falls into the category of the woman's clothing [and is preserved].*

I. *The question stands.*

V.1 A. **"And you shall gather all the spoil of it into the midst of the wide place thereof" (Deut. 13:17):**

B. *Our rabbis have taught on Tannaite authority:*

C. "If it does not have a wide place, it is not declared to be an apostate city," the words of R. Ishmael.

D. R. Aqiba says, **"If it has no wide place, they make a wide place for it" [M. 11:6B].**

E. *What is at issue here?*

F. *One authority takes the view that "its wide place" has the sole meaning of a wide place already present.*

G. *The other authority maintains that "wide place" also bears the meaning of a wide place existing only at present.*

VI.1 A. **[112B] Things which have been consecrated which are in it are to be redeemed; [heave-offering left therein is allowed to rot; second tithe and sacred scrolls are hidden away] [M. 11:6G]:**

B. *Our rabbis have taught on Tannaite authority:*

C. **If there were Holy Things in it, things that have been consecrated for use on the altar are left to die; things which are consecrated for the upkeep of the Temple building are to be redeemed; heave-offering left therein is allowed to rot; second tithe and sacred scrolls are hidden away.**

D. **R. Simeon says, "'Its cattle' – excluding firstlings and tithe of cattle.**

E. **"'And its spoil' – excluding money which has been consecrated, and money which has taken on the status of second tithe" [T. San. 14:5A-D].**

VI.2   A.   A master has said, **"If there were Holy Things in it, things that have been consecrated for use on the altar are left to die:"**

B.   *Now why should they be left to die?* Rather, let them pasture until they are permanently disfigured, at which point let them be sold, and let the proceeds fall for the purchase of a freewill offering [as would be done under ordinary circumstances with such donations].

C.   R. Yohanan said, "'The sacrifice of the wicked is an abomination' (Prov. 21:27)."

D.   R. Simeon b. Laqish said, "It is property belonging to its original owner, for here we deal with Holy Things which the donor is liable to replace if lost."

E.   *At hand, then, is the viewpoint of* R. Simeon, for he has said, "It remains the property of the owners."

F.   *But since the next clause [M. 11:6I] represents the view of R. Simeon, it must follow that the present clause does not stand for his opinion at all.*

G.   *[Rather, we try a different tack:] the passage speaks of Lesser Holy Things and is framed in accord with the position of R. Yosé the Galilean, who has ruled,* "Lesser Holy Things fall into the category of property owned by the original donor."

H.   *Then what would be the rule for Most Holy Things? They should be redeemed [since they belong to the Temple and not to the original donor, that is, the resident of the apostate city].*

I.   *If that is the case, then the framer of the passage should have given the rule concerning things consecrated for the upkeep of the Temple building not separately, but as part of the rule covering Most Holy Things, framing matters in this way:*

J.   "Under what circumstances? In the case of Lesser Holy Things. But as to Most Holy Things, they are to be redeemed." [That would have covered both matters.]

K.   *[The reason he could not frame matters in that way is that is hand also is a sacrifice such as] a beast designated as a sin-offering, the owner of which now is put to death. [Such a beast is killed, but not as a sacrifice.] Accordingly, the framer of the passage could not state matters as a general rule [since the rule would contradict the case of the sin-offering].*

L.   *Now we can understand why R. Yohanan did not rule as did R. Simeon b. Laqish, for it is written,* "The sacrifice of the wicked is an abomination" (Prov. 21:27).

M.   *But why did R. Simeon b. Laqish not reply in the way in which R. Yohanan did [since Yohanan gave a good reply]?*

N.   *He may say to you,* "Where we invoke the rule, 'The sacrifice of the wicked is an abomination,' *it is where the beast is present and at hand, but in the present case, since the status of the beast has changed, [for it is redeemed], the rule likewise may differ [and the cited verse will not apply]."*

VI.3   A.   R. Simeon says, **"'Its cattle' – excluding firstlings and tithe of cattle" [T. San. 14:5C].**

B.   *With what sort of case do we deal?*

C.   *If we say that we deal with those that are unblemished, then this falls into the category of the spoil belonging to heaven.*

D.   *Rather we deal with those that are blemished.*

E.   *In that case, the beasts fall into the category of "the spoil of it" [the city itself, and are to be destroyed].*

F.   Said Rabina, "In point of fact we deal with blemished beasts. What falls into the category of "the cattle thereof" [to be destroyed] are beasts that are eaten as 'its cattle,' excluding the ones at hand, which are not eaten in the category of 'its cattle,' but rather in the category of firstlings and tithes [under a different rule entirely, not as ordinary animals], and so the fall into the category of 'the spoil of heaven.'"

G.   *That then differs from the view of Samuel for Samuel has said, "Everything may be sacrificed and everything may be redeemed."*

H.   *What is the sense of his statement?*

I.   *This is what he means to say:* Whatever may be offered if it is unblemished or redeemed if it is blemished falls into the category of "the spoil of it" [that is to say, all animals designated for offerings of a lesser sanctity, except for firstlings and tithes].

J.   *"But whatever may be offered if unblemished, while not subject to redemption if blemished, for example, the firstling and tithe of cattle, would be excluded by the phrase, "And the cattle thereof."* [This would stand at variance with Rabina's position.]

VII.1 A.   **Heave-offering left therein is allowed to rot [M. 11:6G]:**

B.   Said R. Hisda, "That rule applies only to heave offering in the possession of ordinary Israelites, but as to heave-offering in the possession of a priest, to whom the produce actually belongs, it must be burned."

C.   *To this proposition R. Joseph objected,* "**Second title and sacred scrolls are hidden away [M. 11:6G].** *Now lo, second tithe in the possession of ordinary Israelites is in the same classification as heave-offering in the possession of a priest. And yet, the Mishnah-passage states,* **It is to be hidden away.**"

D.   *Rather, if a statement on Amoraic authority has been made, this is how it has been made:*

E.   Said R. Hisda, "The stated rule [at M. 11:6G] applies only to heave-offering in the possession of priests. But as to heave-offering in the possession of ordinary Israelites, let it be handed over to a priest located in some other town [than the apostate city]."

VII.2 A.   *It has been taught on Tannaite authority:*

B.   "Dough prepared from produce in the status of second tithe [e.g., grain set aside as second tithe that has been milled into flour and made into dough], is exempt from the requirement of the separation of dough-offering," the words of R. Meir.

C.   And sages declare it liable.

D.   Said R. Hisda, "The dispute concerns second tithe that is located in Jerusalem. *For R. Meir takes the view that* produce in the status of second tithe is the property of the Most High [and hence it will not be subject to the requirement of the separation of an additional holy offering, namely, dough-offering.]

E.   *"Sages, by contrast, maintain that* it is in the ownership of the ordinary person [and hence, even in Jerusalem, remains liable to the separation of dough-offering. Since, in Jerusalem, the farmer can eat the produce, it is regarded as his own property, and not property belonging to the Most High].

F.   "But in the provinces, all parties concur that it is exempt to the separation of dough-offering [because the farmer may not make use of the produce as he likes but is subject to the obligation to bring it to Jerusalem. Hence it is subject to God's claim.]"

G.   *To this proposition R. Joseph objected,* "**Second tithe and sacred scrolls are hidden away [M. 11:6G].** *Now with what case do we deal? If we say that it is produce in Jerusalem, can Jerusalem ever fall into the category of an apostate city? And has it not been taught on Tannaite authority:* 'There are ten rules stated with respect to Jerusalem, and this is one of them: it may not be declared an apostate city'?

H.   *"If, furthermore, we deal with another town, the second tithe produce of which they brought up to Jerusalem, then the walls of Jerusalem have enveloped the produce [and imparted to it the status of such produce as it is defined in Jerusalem. It cannot be redeemed for money and removed.] Thus do we not deal with a case of produce in the status of second tithe located in the provinces, and it has been taught in the Mishnah that it* **is hidden away!** [So it is treated as secular property, not as holy property, when it is in Jerusalem, contrary to Hisda's thesis.]"

I.   [In behalf of Hisda, this is the reply:] No, in point of fact it is produce in the status of second tithe that derives from some other town, *which people brought to Jerusalem. There it became unclean.* [Freedman, p. 776, n. 6: In this case it may not be eaten; consequently, it must be hidden away.]

J.   *But then should one not redeem the produce [that has become unclean]? For* said R. Eleazar, "How do we know that even in Jerusalem people are to redeem produce in the status of second tithe that has become unclean? Scripture says, "When you are not able to bear it, then you shall turn it into money" (Deut. 14:25).

K.   "The word for bear has the meaning of 'eat,' as it is said, 'And he took and sent them gifts to them from before him' (Gen. 43:34. [So Freedman, p. 776, n. 10: Thus he translates, If you are not able to eat it – since it is defiled – then you shall turn it into money, that is, redeem it]."

L.   *[No, one need not redeem this produce, for] here with what do we deal? It is with produce that has been purchased* **[113A]** [with the money received in the redemption of the original produce in the status of second tithe. Now the newly purchased produce has become unclean. Freedman, p. 776, n.11: At this stage it is assumed that only the original second tithe can be redeemed if made unclean, but not produce later purchased with the redemption money].

M. *But why not redeem [that produce, too], for it has been taught in the Mishnah:* **If produce that has been purchased with money received for the second tithe has become unclean, it is to be redeemed [M. M.S. 3:10].**

N. *The passage accords with the view of R. Judah, who has said that it should be buried.*

O. *If that is the case, then why do you maintain that at issue is produce in the status of second tithe deriving in particular from an apostate city? Even a city in general [would be subject to the same rule. So we have gained nothing.]*

P. *Rather, we deal with produce in the status of second tithe which is clean, and which has come within the fallen walls of Jerusalem.*

Q. *This accords with the statement of Raba, for Raba has said, "The rule that one must eat produce in the status of second tithe within Jerusalem's walls derives from the Torah.*

R. *"The rule that the walls of Jerusalem envelope the produce [and impart to it the status of second tithe, so that once the produce has entered the walls of the city, it cannot then be redeemed for money and be removed from the city] derives only from the authority of rabbis, "Now when rabbis made that decree, it applied to a time in which the walls were there [to form a barrier], the rule does not apply."* [Freedman, p. 777, n. 2. Hence in this case since it actually belongs to the condemned city, and Jerusalem cannot assimilate it to itself, because its walls had fallen, it must be destroyed, but being sacred, it is hidden instead of burned.]"

VIII.1 A. **Sacred scrolls are hidden away [M. 11:6G]:**

B. *The cited passage of the Mishnah does not accord with the view of R. Eliezer.*

C. *For it has been taught on Tannaite authority:*

D. R. Eliezer says, "Any city in which is to be found even a single mezuzah is not declared to be an apostate city, as it is said, 'And you shall burn the city with fire, and all the spoil thereof, every whit' (Deut. 13:17).

E. *"Now if it contains even a single mezuzah, this would be impossible, as it is written, 'You shall not do so to the Lord your God' (Deut. 12:4)."*

IX.1 A. **R. Simeon says, "The Holy One, blessed be he, said..." [M. 11:6I]:**

B. *[With reference to the dispute of Yosé the Galilean and Aqiba at M. 11:6K-L], may one propose that they dispute about the matter at issue in what R. Abin said R. Ilaa said?*

C. For said R. Abin said R. Ilaa, "In any passage in which you find a generalization concerning an affirmative action, followed by a qualification expressing a negative commandment, people are not to construct on that basis an argument resting on the notion of a general proposition followed by a concrete exemplification only the substance of the concrete exemplification. [Freedman, p. 777-8, n. 8: The rule in such a case is: the general proposition includes only what is enumerated in the particular specification. But when one is thrown into the form of a positive command and the other stated as a negative injunction this does not apply. Now, in the passage under discussion, "And it shall be an heap forever" is a general proposition, implying that it may not be turned even into parks or orchards; whilst "it shall not be built again" is a particular specification, denoting a prohibition against the erection of houses, etc., which require building, but not against parks, etc. Now had they both been expressed in the for of a positive or negative command, the rule of exegesis would be as stated, the particularized expression defining the general proposition. Thus "It shall be an head for ever," and that only in respect of rebuilding, but not i respect of parks, etc. Since, however, they are not both expressed in the same form, this method of exegesis is not followed, but the two clauses are regarded as distinct, a different exegetical rule being followed; viz., 'That which as included in the general proposition and was then separately stated is intended to illumine the former' (for "it shall not be built again," which refers to houses, etc., was really included in the general proposition). Thus: "And it shall be an heap for ever" implies a prohibition of parks and orchards. Now, how is this implication understood? Because Scripture continues, "it shall not be built again," from which we deduce, just as a building is anything erected in a human settlement, so "it shall be an heap for ever" prohibits everything that finds a place in civilization, and therefore includes gardens, etc.]

D. *It would follow [in accord with this theory of what is at issue] that one authority [namely, Yosé] concurs with R. Abin, and the other [Aqiba] does not? [Accordingly, Aqiba prohibits building alone, while Yosé prohibits all sorts of land-use].*

E. *No, all parties concur with the principle of R Abin, and what is at issue here? One authority [Yosé] takes the view that the word "again' bears the meaning, 'entirely, hence, never again," while the other [Aqiba] understands the word to the "again – as it had been" [allowing space for some other usage than the original one].*

X.1 A. **It may not be rebuilt, but it may be made into vegetable patches and orchards [M. 11:6L]:**

B. *Our rabbis have taught on Tannaite authority:*

C. **If the town contained trees that had already been cut down [prior to the trial], they are forbidden. If at the time of the verdict they were yet attached to the ground, they are permitted. But as to the trees of another city, whether they are cut down or attached to the ground, they are forbidden [T. San. 14:5E-G].**

D. *What is this "other city'?*

E. Said R. Hisda, "It is Jericho, as it is written, 'And the city shall be herem to the Lord' (Josh. 6:17)."

"And the city shall be herem to the Lord:" Jericho in Particular

X.2 A. "And Joshua adjured them at that time, saying, Cursed be the man before the Lord who rises up and builds this city, Jericho. He shall lay the foundation thereof in his firstborn, and in his youngest son shall he set up the gates of it." (Josh. 6:17).

	B.	*It has been taught on Tannaite authority:*
	C.	**One may not rebuild it and call it by the name of some other town, and one may not build some other town and call it Jericho." [T. San. 14:6L].**
X.3	A.	It is written, "In his days did Heil the Bethelite build Jericho; he laid the foundations thereof in Abiram his firstborn and set up the gates thereof in his youngest son Segub, according to the word of the Lord which he spoke by Joshua the son of Nun" (1 Kgs. 16:4).
	B.	*It has been taught on Tannaite authority:*
	C.	**"In Abiram his first born" (1 Kgs. 16:34):**
	D.	**That wicked man! To begin with [with Abiram] he had no example from which to learn, but in the case of segub, he had an example from which to learn [T. San. 14:9A-C].**
	E.	*What did Abiram and Segub do [that they, who were not wicked, did not learn the reason for the death]?*
	F.	*This is the sense of the passage:* "From the case of Abiram, his first born, that wicked man should have learned [what would happen to] Segub, his youngest son."
	G.	Since it is said, "In Abiram, his first born" (1 Kgs. 16:34), do I not know that Segub was his youngest son? Why then does Scripture state, "Segub his youngest son"?
	H.	This teaches that he continued burying his sons, from Abiram down to Segub.
	I.	*Ahab had been his groomsman. He and Elijah came to greet him at the house of mourning. [Ahab] went into session and stated, "Perhaps when Joshua made that curse, this was the sense of the curse:*
	J.	"'**One may not rebuild it and call it by the name of some other town, and one may not build some other town and call it Jericho [T. San. 14:6L]'?"**
	K.	*Elijah said to him, "Indeed so."*
	L.	*He said to him, "Now if the curse of Moses has not been carried out –*
	M.	"for it is written, 'And you turn aside and serve other gods and worship them' (Deut. 11:16), followed by, 'And he shut up the heaven that there be no rain' (Deut. 11:17), *while if someone sets up an idol at the end of every furrow, the rain will not allow him to go and bow down to them –*
	N.	*"will the curse of Joshua, his disciple, be carried out? [Surely not!]"*
	O.	Forthwith: "And Elijah, the Tishbite, who was one f the inhabitants of Gilead, said to Ahab, As the Lord God of Israel lives, before whom I stand, there shall not be dew or rain these years, but according to my word" (1 Kgs. 17:1).

	P.	*He sought mercy, and the key of rain was given to him.* *He got up an went his way.*
X.4	A.	"And the word of the Lord came to him, saying, Go away and turn eastward and hide yourself by the brook Cherith, that is before Jordan...And the ravens brought him bread and flesh in the morning" (1 Kgs. 17:2, 6).
	B.	*Where did they get [validly slaughtered meat]?*
	C.	*Said R. Judah said Rab, "They got it from the butchery of Ahab."*
	D.	"And it came to pass, after a while, that the brook dried up, because there had been no rain in the land" (1 Kgs. 17:7):
	E.	*When [God] saw that there was suffering in the world, it is written,* "And the work of the Lord came to him saying, Arise, go to Zarephath" (1 Kgs. 17:8-9).
	F.	And it is written, "And it came to pass after these things that the son of the woman, mistress of the house, fell sick" (1 Kgs. 17:17).
	G.	*[Elijah] prayed for mercy that the keys of the resurrection of the dead might be given to him.*
	H.	*They said to him, "Three keys are not handed over to a messenger: those of birth, rain, and the resurrection of the dead.*
	I.	*"For will people say, 'Two already are in the hand of the disciple [he already had the one for rain] and one in the hand of the master?' Bring the one and take the other."*
	J.	For it is written, "Go, appear to Ahab, and I will send rain upon the earth" (1 Kgs. 18:1).
X.5	A.	*A Galilean gave an exposition before R. Hisda,* "To what may Elijah be compared? To the case of a man who locked his gate and lost the key. [Elijah locked up the rain and could not unlock it]"
	B.	*R. Yosé gave an exposition in Sepphoris,* "Father Elijah **[113B]** *was an impatient man."*
	C.	*[Elijah] had been used earlier to come to visit [Yosé], but he refrained from visiting him for three days and did not come. When he did come, he said to him, "Why did master not come?"*
	D.	*He said to him, "You called me impatient!"*
	E.	*He said to him, "But before us the master has shown himself to be impatient!"*
XI.1	A.	**"And there shall cleave nought of the devoted thing to your hand' (Deut. 13:18), for so long as evil people are in the world, fierce anger – is in the world [M. 11:6M-N]:**
	B.	*Who are these wicked?*
	C.	*Said R. Joseph, "Thieves [who steal property from the apostate city]."*
XI.2	A.	*Our rabbis have taught on Tannaite authority:*

B. When the wicked come into the world, fierce anger comes into the world, for it is written, "When the wicked comes, then comes also contempt, and with ignominy, reproach" (Prov. 18:3).

C. When the wicked departs from the world, goodness comes into the world and retribution leaves the world, as it is written, "And when the wicked perish, there is exultation" (Prov. 11:10).

D. When righteous people leave the world, evil comes into the world, as it is said, "The righteous man perishes, and no one lays it to heart, and merciful men are taken away, none considering that the righteous is taken away from the evil to come" (Is. 57:1).

E. When the righteous come into the world, goodness comes into the world, as it is written, "This one will comfort us in our work and in the toil of our hands" (Gen. 5:29) [T. Sot. 10:1-3].

As the outline in Chapter Twelve shows, the entire composition is organized and worked out in relationship to the Mishnah.

12

The Structure and System of Babylonian Talmud Sanhedrin

Whether or not the Talmud of Babylonia is carefully organized in large-scale, recurrent structures and guided by a program that we may call systematic forms the principal question addressed by an academic commentary. The preceding chapters therefore have pointed toward the presentation set forth here. By "structure" I mean, a clearly-articulated pattern that governs the location of fully-spelled out statements. By "system," I mean, a well-crafted and coherent set of ideas that explain the social order of the community addressed by the writers of a document, a social philosophy, a theory of the way of life, world view, and character of the social entity formed by a given social group. I see a collective, anonymous, and political document, such as the one before us, as a statement to, and about, the way in which people should organize their lives and govern their actions. At issue then in any document such as the remarkable one before us is simple: does this piece of writing present information or a program, facts to whom it may concern, or a philosophically and aesthetically cogent statement about how things should be?

The connection between structure and system is plain to see. From the way in which people consistently frame their thoughts, we move to the world that, in saying things one way rather than in some other, they wish to imagine – the world in which they wish to live, to which they address these thoughts. For if the document exhibits structure and sets forth a system, then it is accessible to questions of rationality. We may ask about the statement that its framers or compilers wished to make by putting the document together as they did. But if we discern no structure and perceive no systematic inquiry or governing points of analysis, then all we find here is inert and miscellaneous information, facts but no propositions, arguments, viewpoints.

Now the Talmud commonly finds itself represented as lacking organization and exhibiting a certain episodic and notional character. That view moreover characterizes the reading and representation of the document by learned and experienced scholars, who have devoted their entire lives to Talmud study and exegesis. It must follow that upon the advocate of the contrary view – the one implicit in the representation of the document for academic analysis – rests the burden of proof. I set forth the allegation that the Talmud exhibits a structure and follows a system and therefore exhibits a commonly-intelligible rationality. The claim to write an academic commentary explicitly states that proposition. For the tractate before us, I have therefore to adduce evidence and argument.

I maintain that through the normal procedures of reasoned analysis we may discern in the tractate a well-crafted structure. I hold that the structure made manifest, we may further identify the purpose and perspective, the governing system of thought and argument, of those who collected and arranged the tractate's composites and put them together in the way in which we now have them. By "structure" I mean, how is a document organized? and by "system," what do the compilers of the document propose to accomplish in producing this complete, organized piece of writing? The answers to both questions derive from a simple outline of the tractate as a whole, underscoring the types of compositions and composites of which it is comprised. Such an outline tells us what is principal and what subordinate, and how each unit – composition formed into composites, composites formed into a complete statement – holds together and also fits with other units, fore and aft. The purpose of the outline then is to identify the character of each component of the whole, and to specify its purpose or statement. The former information permits us to describe the document's structure, the latter, its system.

While the idea of simply outlining a Talmud-tractate beginning to end may seem obvious, I have never made such an outline before, nor has anyone else.[1] Yet, as we shall now see, the character of the outline dictates all further analytical initiatives. Specifically, when we follow the layout of the whole, we readily see the principles of organization that govern. These same guidelines on organizing discourse point also to the character of what is organized: complete units of thought, with a

---

[1] I have provided complete outlines for the Mishnah and for the Tosefta in relationship to the Mishnah, and, not always in outline form, for the Midrash-compilations of late antiquity as well.

beginning, middle, and end, often made up of smaller, equally complete units of thought. The former we know as composites, the latter as compositions.

Identifying and classifying the components of the tractate – the composites, the compositions of which they are made up – we see clearly how the document coheres: the plan and program worked out from beginning to end. When we define that plan and program, we identify the facts of a pattern that permit us to say in a specific and concrete way precisely what the compilers of the tractate intended to accomplish. The structure realizes the system, the program of analysis and thought that takes the form of the presentation we have before us. From what people do, meaning, the way in which they formulate their ideas and organized them into cogent statements, we discern what they proposed to do, meaning, the intellectual goals that they set for themselves.

These goals – the received document they wished to examine, the questions that they brought to that document – realized in the layout and construction of their writing, dictate the points of uniformity and persistence that throughout come to the surface. How people lay out their ideas guides us into what they wished to find out and set forth in their writing, and that constitutes the system that defined the work they set out to accomplish. We move from how people speak to the system that the mode of discourse means to express, in the theory that modes of speech or writing convey modes of thought and inquiry.

We move from the act of thought and its written result backward to the theory of thinking, which is, by definition, an act of social consequence. We therefore turn to the matter of intention that provokes reflection and produces a system of inquiry. That statement does not mean to imply I begin with the premise of order, which sustains the thesis of a prior system that defines the order. To the contrary, the possibility of forming a coherent outline out of the data we have examined defines the first test of whether or not the document exhibits a structure and realizes a system. So everything depends upon the possibility of outlining the writing, from which all else flows. If we can see the order and demonstrate that the allegation of order rests on ample evidence, then we may proceed to describe the structure that gives expression to the order, and the system that the structure sustains.

The present work undertakes the exegesis of exegesis, for the Talmud of Babylonia, like its counterpart in the Land of Israel, is laid out as a commentary to the Mishnah. That obvious fact defined the character of my academic commentary, since we have already faced the reality that our Bavli-tractate is something other than a commentary, though it surely encompasses one. The problems that captured my attention derived from the deeper question of how people make connections and draw conclusions. To ask about how people make connections means that we identify a problem – otherwise we should not have to ask – and what precipitated the problem here has been how a composition or a composite fits into its context, when the context is defined by the tasks of Mishnah-commentary, and the composition or composite clearly does not comment on the Mishnah-passage that is subjected to comment.

The experience of analyzing the document with the question of cogency and coherence in mind therefore yields a simple recognition. Viewed whole, the tractate contains no gibberish but only completed units of thought, sentences formed into intelligible thought and self-contained in that we require no further information to understand those sentences, beginning to end. The tractate organizes these statements as commentary to the Mishnah. But large tracts of the writing do not comment on the Mishnah in the way in which other, still larger tracts do. Then how the former fit together with the latter frames the single most urgent question of structure and system that I can identify.

Since we have already examined enormous composites that find their cogency in an other than exegetical program, alongside composites that hold together by appeal to a common, prior, coherent statement – the Mishnah-sentences at hand – what justifies my insistence that an outline of the document, resting on the premise that we deal with a Mishnah-commentary, govern all further description? To begin with, the very possibility of outlining Babylonian Talmud tractate Sukkah derives from the simple fact that the framers have given to their document the form of a commentary to the Mishnah. It is in the structure of the Mishnah-tractate that they locate everything together that they wished to compile. We know that is the fact because the Mishnah-tractate defines the order of topics and the sequence of problems.

Relationships to the Mishnah are readily discerned; a paragraph stands at the head of a unit of thought; even without the full citation of the paragraph, we should find our way back to the Mishnah because at the head of numerous compositions, laid out in sequence one to the next, clauses of the Mishnah-paragraph are cited in so many words or alluded to in an unmistakable way. So without printing the entire Mishnah-paragraph at the head, we should know that the received code formed the fundamental structure because so many compositions cite and gloss sentences of the Mishnah-paragraph and are set forth in sequence dictated by the order of sentences of said Mishnah-paragraph. Internal evidence alone suffices, then, to demonstrate that the structure of the tractate rests upon the Mishnah-tractate cited and discussed here. Not only so, but the sentences of the Mishnah-paragraphs of our tractate are discussed in no other place in the entire Talmud of Babylonia in the sequence and systematic exegetical framework in which they are set forth here; elsewhere we may find bits or pieces, but only here, the entirety of the tractate.

That statement requires one qualification, and that further leads us to the analytical task of our outline. While the entire Mishnah-tractate of Sukkah is cited in the Talmud, the framers of the Talmud by no means find themselves required to say something about every word, every sentence, every paragraph. On the contrary, they discuss only what they choose to discuss, and glide without comment by large stretches of the tractate. A process of selectivity, which requires description and analysis, has told the compilers of the Talmud's composites and the authors of its compositions[2] what demands attention, and what does not. Our outline has therefore to signal not only what passage of the Mishnah-tractate is discussed, but also what is not discussed, and we require a general theory to explain the principles of selection ("making connections, drawing conclusions" meaning, to begin with, making selections). For that purpose, in the outline, I reproduce the entirety of a Mishnah-paragraph that stands at the head of a Talmudic composite, and I underscore those sentences that are addressed, so highlighting also those that are not.

It follows that the same evidence that justifies identifying the Mishnah-tractate as the structure (therefore also the foundation of the system) of the Talmud-tractate before us also presents puzzles for considerable reflection. The exegesis of Mishnah-exegesis is only one of these. Another concerns the purpose of introducing into the document enormous compositions and composites that clearly hold together

---

[2]This statement requires refinement. I do not know that all available compositions have been reproduced, and that the work of authors of compositions of Mishnah-exegesis intended for a talmud is fully exposed in the document as we have it. That is not only something we cannot demonstrate – we do not have compositions that were not used, only the ones that were – but something that we must regard as unlikely on the face of matters. All we may say is positive: the character of the compositions that address Mishnah-exegesis tells us about the concerns of the writers of those compositions, but we cannot claim to outline all of their concerns, on the one side, or to explain why they chose not to work on other Mishnah-sentences besides the ones treated here. But as to the program of the compositors, that is another matter: from the choices that they made (out of a corpus we cannot begin to imagine or invent for ourselves) we may describe with great accuracy the kinds of materials they wished to include and the shape and structure they set forth out of those materials. We know what they did, and that permits us to investigate why they did what they did. What we cannot know is what they did not do, or why they chose not to do what they did not do. People familiar with the character of speculation and criticism in Talmudic studies will understand why I have to spell out these rather commonplace observations. I lay out an argument based on evidence, not on the silences of evidence, or on the absence of evidence – that alone.

around a shared topic or proposition, e.g., my appendix on one theme or another, my elaborate footnote providing information that is not required but merely useful, and the like. My earlier characterization of composites as appendices and footnotes signalled the fact that the framers of the document chose a not-entirely satisfactory way of setting out the materials they wished to include here, for large components of the tractate do not contribute to Mishnah-exegesis in any way at all. If these intrusions of other-than-exegetical compositions were proportionately modest, or of topical composites negligible in size, we might dismiss them as appendages, not structural components that bear much of the weight of the edifice as a whole. Indeed, the language that I chose for identifying and defining these composites – footnotes, appendices, and the like – bore the implication that what is not Mishnah-commentary also is extrinsic to the Talmud's structure and system.

But that language served only for the occasion. In fact, the outline before us will show that the compositions are large and ambitious, the composites formidable and defining. Any description of the tractate's structure that dismisses as mere accretions or intrusions so large a proportion of the whole misleads. Any notion that "footnotes" and "appendices" impede exposition and disrupt thought, contribute extraneous information or form tacked-on appendages – any such notion begs the question: then why fill up so much space with such purposeless information? The right way is to ask whether the document's topical composites play a role in the re-presentation of the Mishnah-tractate by the compilers of the Talmud. We have therefore to test two hypotheses:

1.   the topical composites ("appendices," "footnotes") do belong and serve the compilers' purpose, or

2.   the topical composites do not participate in the re-presentation of the Mishnah-tractate by the Talmud and do not belong because they add nothing and change nothing.

The two hypotheses may be tested against the evidence framed in response to a single question: is this topical composite necessary? The answer to that question lies in our asking, what happens to the reading of the Mishnah-tractate in light of the topical composites that would not happen were we to read the same tractate without them? The outline that follows systematically raises that question, with results specified in due course. It suffices here to state the simple result of our reading of the tractate, start to finish: the question of structure, therefore also that of system, rests upon the position we identify for that massive component of the tractate that comprises not Mishnah-commentary but free-standing compositions and composites of compositions formed for a purpose other than Mishnah-commentary.

The principal rubrics are given in small caps. The outline takes as its principal rubrics two large-scale organizing principles.

The first is the divisions of the Mishnah-tractate to which the Talmud-tractate serves as a commentary. That simple fact validates the claim that the tractate exhibits a fully-articulated structure. But the outline must also underscore that the Mishnah-tractate provides both more and less than the paramount outline of the Talmud-tractate. It is more because sentences in the Mishnah-tractate are not analyzed at all. These untreated Mishnah-sentences are given in bold face lower case caps, like the rest of the Mishnah, but then are specified by underlining and enclosure in square brackets.

Second, it is less because the structure of the tractate accommodates large composites that address topics not defined by the Mishnah-tractate. That brings us to the second of the two large-scale modes of holding together both sustained analytical exercises and also large sets of compositions formed into cogent composites. These are treated also as major units and are indicated by Roman numerals, alongside the Mishnah-paragraphs themselves; they are also signified in small caps. But the principal rubrics that do not focus on Mishnah-commentary but on free-standing topics or propositions or problems are not given in boldface type. Consequently, for the purposes of a coherent outline we have to identify as autonomous entries in our outline those important composites that treat themes or topics not contributed by the Mishnah-tractate.

I. MISHNAH-TRACTATE SANHEDRIN 1:1

A. PROPERTY CASES ARE DECIDED BY THREE JUDGES; THOSE CONCERNING THEFT AND DAMAGES, BEFORE THREE:

1. I:1: Property cases are decided by three judges; those concerning theft and damages, before three: do not cases concerning theft and damages fall within the classification of property cases that they have to be singled out?

   a. I:2: Clarification of a fact taken for granted in the foregoing: Explaining the matter of three judges in cases involving loans, R. Aha, son of R. Iqa, said, "On the basis of the rules of the Torah itself, a single judge also would be suitable to judge the case. For it is said, 'In justice you singular shall judge your neighbor' (Lev. 19:15). But on account of idle folk who pass their opinion without knowing the law, three are required."

B.   CASES INVOLVING COMPENSATION FOR FULL-DAMAGES, HALF-DAMAGES, TWOFOLD RESTITUTION, FOURFOLD AND FIVEFOLD RESTITUTION, BY THREE:

1.   II:1: Cases involving compensation for full damages fall into the category of cases involving damages. Why then make explicit the fact that these two are tried by three judges?

2.   II:2: How on the basis of Scripture do we know that trials of this classification take place before three judge courts?

3.   II:3: Our rabbis have taught on Tannaite authority: Property cases are brought before three judges. Rabbi says, "Before five, so that the decision may be reached by three" (T. San. 1:1A-B).

  a.   II:4: Amplification of the exegetical principle of the foregoing: Said R. Isaac bar Joseph said R. Yohanan, "Rabbi, R. Judah b. Roes, the House of Shammai, R. Simeon, and R. Aqiba, all take the view that we read Scripture in the way in which the supplied vowels direct it to be read."

4.   II:5: Our rabbis have taught on Tannaite authority: Property cases are to be tried by a court of three judges. But if the judge was recognized by the community as an expert, he may judge even all by himself.

5.   II:6: Said Rab, "One who wants to judge cases with the proviso that, if he makes a judicial error, he is exempt from having to make restitution, had best get authorization from the house of the exilarch." And so said Samuel, "Let such a one gain authorization from the house of the exilarch."

6.   II:7: It is self-evident that authorization granted here for judging cases here, or that granted there for judging cases there in the Land of Israel, or authorization granted here for judging cases there in the Land of Israel is valid. The real question is this: Is authorization granted there valid for judging cases here?

  a.   II:8: Gloss of foregoing: what is authorization?

   I.   II:9: Illustrative case.

   II.   II:10: As above.

   III. II:11: It is self-evident that if authorization is granted only in part for one purpose, not for some other, that is valid as in the case of Rab. What is the rule on authorization granted on the basis of a condition?

C.   JUDGMENT OF CASES BY FEWER THAN THREE JUDGES

  b.   II:12: Gloss of I:2: Reverting to the body of the text cited above at I.2: Said Samuel, "Two who judged a case produce a valid judgment, but they are called 'a presumptuous court.'"

    c.   II:13: Reverting to the text cited above: R. Abbahu said, "If two persons judged a property case, all parties concur that their judgment is invalid."

        I.   II:14: May we propose that the issue between Samuel's and Abbahu's views of whether two persons may judge a case follows lines of a dispute between Tannaite authorities?

D.   COMPOSITE ON ARBITRATION AS ALTERNATIVE TO A LEGAL CONTEST

    1.   II:15: Just as judgment is done before three judges, so an arbitration is reached by three judges. Once the court process has been completed, one has not got the right to arbitrate.

    2.   II:16: R. Eleazar, son of R. Yosé the Galilean, says, "It is forbidden to arbitrate, and whoever arbitrates a case after judgment has been passed – lo, this one sins. And whoever praises the arbitrator – lo, this one curses the Omnipresent."

    3.   II:17: R. Joshua b. Qorha says, "It is a religious duty to arbitrate, as it is said, 'Execute the judgment of truth and peace in your gates' (Zech. 8:16).'

        a.   II:18: Gloss of a detail of the foregoing. What marks the conclusion of the trial?

        b.   II:19: As above. What is the sense of "religious duty" as it was used by R. Joshua b. Qorha?

        c.   II:20: As above. There is a difference of opinion concerning Ps. 10:3, cited above on the part of R. Tanhum bar Hanilai.

        d.   II:21: As above. Now as to the other Tannaite authorities cited above, who favor arbitration even after a case has been heard, how do they interpret the verse, "The beginning of strife is as one that lets out water" (Prov. 17:14)?

           I.   II:22: Further interpretation of a proof-text used in the foregoing.

           A.   II:23: Gloss of foregoing.

E.   ANTHOLOGY IN PRAISE OF JUSTICE AND TRUE JUDGES

    1.   II:24: Said R. Samuel bar Nahmani said R. Jonathan, "Every judge who renders a true and faithful judgment brings the Presence of God to rest on Israel, as it is said, 'God stands in the congregation of God, in the midst of the judges he judges' (Ps. 82:1). And every judge who does not render a

true and faithful judgment drives the Presence of God to abandon Israel, as it is said, 'Because of the oppression of the poor, because of the sighing of the needy, now will I arise, says the Lord' (Ps. 12:6)."

2. II:25: R. Josiah, and some say. R, Nahman bar Isaac, gave an exposition, "What is the meaning of the verse of Scripture, 'O house of David, thus says the Lord, Execute justice in the morning and deliver the spoiled out of the hand of the oppressor' (Jer. 21:12)? Now is it only in the morning that judges work, and do they not work throughout the day? But if a matter is clear to you as the morning light, then state it, and if not, do not state it."

3. II:26: Said R. Joshua b. Levi, "When ten judges go into session to judge a case, an iron chain is hanging on the neck of all of them since responsibility for the decision is shared equally by them."

4. II:27: When R. Dimi came, he said that R. Nahman bar Kohen gave an interpretation, "What is the meaning of that which is written, 'The king by justice established the land, but he who loves gifts overthrows it' (Prov. 29:4)? If the judge is like a king, who needs nothing from anyone else but knows the law on his own, he will establish the land. But if the judge is like a priest who goes begging at the threshing places to collect the priestly gifts, he will destroy it."

5. II:28: The administration of the patriarchate appointed a judge who had not studied the law. They said to Judah bar Nahmani, the spokesman for R. Simeon b. Laqish, "Stand at his side as the spokesman who repeats in a loud voice what the master wishes to say to the assembled throng."

6. II:29: Said R. Simeon b. Laqish, "Whoever appoints a judge who is unworthy is as if he plants an asherah in Israel."

7. II:30: It is written, "You shall not make with me gods of silver or gods of gold" (Ex. 20:23). Gods of silver and gods of gold are what one may not make, but is it permitted to make ones of wood? Said R. Ashi, "The verse refers to a judge who comes on account of silver or a judge who comes on account of gold."

8. II:31: When Rab would come to court, he would say this, "With a bitter soul he goes forth to death. The needs of his house he has not attended to. He goes home empty-handed. Would that his coming home should be as is his going forth."

    a. II:32: Complement to foregoing.

9. II:33: Bar Qappara gave an exposition, "Whence in Scripture do we derive the basis for the rabbis' saying, Be deliberate in judgment M. Abot 1:1?"

10. II:34: "And I shall command your judges at that time" (Deut. 1:16): Said R. Yohanan, "This concerns the rod and strap, to be used cautiously." "Hear the causes between your brothers and judge righteously" (Deut. 1:16): Said R. Hanina, "This is a warning to the court not to listen to the claim of one litigant before the other comes to court, and a warning to the litigants not to plead before the judge before the other party comes to court. The word for 'hear' may also be read 'announce.'"

11. II:35: It has been taught on Tannaite authority: A summons is by the authority of three.

F.   CASES INVOLVING...TWOFOLD RESTITUTION, FOURFOLD AND FIVEFOLD RESTITUTION, BY THREE:

1. III:1: As to cases involving the imposition of penalties fines, how many judges are required?

G.   "CASES INVOLVING HIM WHO RAPES, HIM WHO SEDUCES, AND HIM WHO BRINGS FORTH AN EVIL NAME (DEUT. 22:19), BY THREE," THE WORDS OF R. MEIR. AND SAGES SAY, "HE WHO BRINGS FORTH AN EVIL NAME IS TRIED BEFORE TWENTY-THREE, FOR THERE MAY BE A CAPITAL CASE."

1. IV:1: And should a case involving a case involving a capital crime come forth, what difference would it make?

    a. IV:2: Illustrative problem.

H.   CASES INVOLVING THE PENALTY OF FLOGGING ARE BEFORE THREE.

1. V:1: What is the scriptural source for this rule

I.   IN THE NAME OF R. ISHMAEL THEY SAID, "BEFORE TWENTY-THREE:"

1. VI:1: What is the scriptural basis for the position of R. Ishmael?

J.   THE DECISION TO INTERCALATE THE MONTH IS BEFORE THREE.

1. VII:1: The word choice of the Mishnah-sentence at hand is not "calculation" of the time at which the new month begins, let alone "sanctification" of the new month, when it begins, but rather "intercalation" of the new month. Let the court not sanctify the new month on the thirtieth day, and then, on its own, it will be automatically intercalated.

K.   "THE DECISION TO INTERCALATE THE YEAR IS BEFORE THREE," THE WORDS OF R. MEIR. RABBAN SIMEON B.

GAMALIEL SAYS, "WITH THREE DO THEY BEGIN, WITH FIVE
MORE THEY DEBATE THE MATTER, AND THEY REACH A FINAL
DECISION WITH SEVEN MORE JUDGES. BUT IF THEY REACHED
A DECISION TO INTERCALATE THE YEAR WITH THREE
JUDGES, THE YEAR IS INTERCALATED."

1. VIII:1: It has been taught on Tannaite authority: How is a
    case in which, as Rabban Simeon b. Gamaliel has said, "With
    three do they begin to intercalate the year, with five more
    they debate the matter, and they reach a final decision with
    seven judges?"

2. VIII:2: The year is intercalated only by people who are
    specifically appointed for that task.
    a. VIII:3: Supplementary story about a hero in the
        illustrative story of the foregoing.

3. VIII:4: Our rabbis have taught on Tannaite authority: The
    year is intercalated only if the patriarch approves.

4. VIII:5: Our rabbis have taught on Tannaite authority: They
    intercalate the year only when it needs it, because of the
    condition of the roads, because of the bridges, because of the
    passover ovens, and because of the residents of the Exile,
    who have left home and not been able to reach Jerusalem.

5. VIII:6: Our rabbis have taught on Tannaite authority: They
    do not intercalate the year because the season of the kids,
    lambs, or pigeons has not yet come. But in the case of all of
    them, they regard it as a support for intercalating the year.
    But if they declared the year to be intercalated on the basis of
    their condition, lo, this is deemed intercalated.

6. VIII:7: Our rabbis have taught on Tannaite authority: On
    account of three signs do they intercalate the year, because of
    the premature state of the grain, because of the condition of
    the produce of the trees, and because of the lateness of the
    spring equinox.

7. VIII:8: Our rabbis have taught on Tannaite authority: On
    account of evidence of conditions in three regions viewed as
    distinct districts do they intercalate the year: Judea,
    TransJordan, and Galilee.

8. VIII:9: Our rabbis have taught on Tannaite authority: They
    intercalate the year only in Judah, and if they intercalated in
    Galilee, lo, it is deemed to have been intercalated.

9. VIII:10: Our rabbis have taught on Tannaite authority: The
    court may intercalate the year only by day, and if they have
    conducted the rite at night, it is not deemed to have been
    intercalated.

10. VIII:11: Our rabbis have taught on Tannaite authority: They do not intercalate the year in a time of famine.
11. VIII:12: Our rabbis have taught on Tannaite authority: They do not intercalate the year before the New Year, and if they did intercalate it, it is not deemed intercalated.
12. VIII:13: Our rabbis have taught on Tannaite authority: They do not intercalate a year in advance.
13. VIII:14: Our rabbis have taught on Tannaite authority: They do not intercalate the year either in the case of the Seventh Year or in the case of the year after the Seventh Year.
14. VIII:15: Our rabbis have taught on Tannaite authority: They do not intercalate the year when there is uncleanness.
15. VIII:16: Said R. Judah, said Samuel, "'People intercalate the year only if the summer season is short of completion by the larger part of the month of Tishri so that, in the year that is a candidate for intercalation, if we do not add a month, then the bulk of Tishri will pass before the autumnal equinox has been reached. In simple terms, it means that the larger part of Tishri, must fall prior to September 21.

L. **"THE LAYING OF HANDS ON A COMMUNITY SACRIFICE BY ELDERS...DONE BY THREE JUDGES," THE WORDS OF R. SIMEON. R. JUDAH SAYS, "BY FIVE:"**

1. IX:1: Our rabbis have taught on Tannaite authority: With reference to Lev. 4:15: "And the elders of the congregation shall lay their hands upon the head of the bull before the Lord...": Since it says, "And the elders... shall lay hands," is it possible to suppose that elders from any source whatsoever will suffice? Scripture says, "of the congregation."
2. IX:2: It is taught on Tannaite authority: Laying on of hands and laying on of hands for elders are done with three judges (T. San. 1:1E).
3. IX:3: Since the Mishnah-rule states that the laying on of hands is done by three, we now ask: And can not a single individual lay hands?
4. IX:4: Said R. Joshua b. Levi, "The rite of laying on of hands does not apply outside of the Land."
   a. IX:5: R. Hanina and R. Hoshaia did R. Yohanan aim to subject to the laying on of hands, but the opportunity did not arise. This bothered him very much. They said to him, "Let the master not be troubled about this.
   b. IX:6: Further story.
   c. IX:7: As above.

        d. IX:8: As above.

M.   **AND THE BREAKING OF THE HEIFER'S NECK ...DONE BY THREE JUDGES," THE WORDS OF R. SIMEON. R. JUDAH SAYS, "BY FIVE."**

    1.   X:1: Our rabbis have taught on Tannaite authority: "'Then your elders and your judges shall come forth' (Deut. 21:1-2): 'Your elders' indicate that two are required. 'Your judges' indicates that another two are required. A court cannot be of an even number, so they add on to their number yet another, lo, there are five," the words of R. Judah.

    2.   X:2: The formulation of the Mishnah-paragraph at hand when it specifies that we deal with members of the sanhedrin does not accord with the view of R. Eliezer b. Jacob.

N.   **THE RITE OF REMOVAL OF THE SHOE BREAKING THE LEVIRATE BOND (DEUT. 25:7-9) AND THE EXERCISE OF THE RIGHT OF REFUSAL ARE DONE BEFORE THREE JUDGES.**
    THE EVALUATION OF FRUIT OF FOURTH-YEAR PLANTINGS TO BE REDEEMED (LEV. 19:23-25)

    1.   XI:1: Our rabbis have taught on Tannaite authority: What is the definition of second tithe, the value of which is not known? It is, for example, wine which has formed a film, produce which has begun to rot, or coins which are rusty (M. M.S. 4:26). Produce in the status of second tithe, the value of which is not known is redeemed according to the valuation of three bidders and not according to the valuation of three who are not bidders even if one of the bidders is a non-Israelite, even if one of the bidders is the owner of the produce (T. M.S. 3:5A-D).

O.   **AND OF SECOND TITHE (DEUT. 14:22-26) WHOSE VALUE IS NOT KNOWN IS DONE BEFORE THREE JUDGES.**
    ASSESSMENT OF THE VALUE, FOR PURPOSES OF REDEMPTION, OF THINGS WHICH HAVE BEEN CONSECRATED IS DONE BEFORE THREE JUDGES.

    1.   XII:1: Our version of the Mishnah-law does not accord with the version of the following Tannaite authority.

P.   **PROPERTY PLEDGED AS SECURITY FOR VOWS OF VALUATION, IN THE CASE OF MOVABLES, IS EVALUATED BY THREE JUDGES.**

    1.   XIII:1: What is the meaning of evaluating property pledged as security for vows in the case of movables?

Q.   **R. JUDAH SAYS, "ONE OF THEM MUST BE A PRIEST."**

1. XIV:1: Said R. Pappa to Abbayye, "Now there is no problem to the position of R. Judah in Scripture's referring to a priest in this connection. But as to rabbis who do not require a priest on the board of assessors, why should Scripture have referred to a priest?"

R. AND EVALUATION OF PROPERTY PLEDGED AS SECURITY FOR VOWS FOR VALUATION IN THE CASE OF REAL ESTATE IS DONE BY NINE AND A PRIEST:

1. XV:1: Whence in Scripture do we derive this rule?

S. AND SO FOR THE VALUATION-VOW COVERING MEN.

1. XVI:1: But can a man be declared sanctified for purposes of evaluation for dedication of his value to the Temple?
2. XVI:2: R. Abin raised the question, "As to hair that is ready for shearing, how is it assessed? Is it assessed as if it were already sheared, and therefore by a court of three assessors? Or is it regarded as fully attached as immovable property and therefore assessed by a court of ten?"

T. CASES INVOLVING THE DEATH PENALTY ARE JUDGED BEFORE TWENTY-THREE JUDGES. THE BEAST WHO COMMITS OR IS SUBJECTED TO AN ACT OF SEXUAL RELATIONS WITH A HUMAN BEING IS JUDGED BY TWENTY-THREE, SINCE IT IS SAID, "AND YOU WILL KILL THE WOMAN AND THE BEAST" (LEV. 20:16). AND IT SAYS, "AND THE BEAST YOU WILL SLAY" (LEV. 20:15)

1. XVII:1: The framer of the passage states as a final judgment that there is no distinction between the case of a beast having sexual relations as with a man and one having sexual relations a with a woman.

U. AN OX WHICH IS TO BE STONED IS JUDGED BY TWENTY-THREE, SINCE IT IS SAID, "AND THE OX WILL BE STONED, AND ALSO ITS MASTER WILL BE PUT TO DEATH" (EX. 21:29). JUST AS THE CASE OF THE MASTER, LEADING TO THE DEATH-PENALTY, IS ADJUDGED, SO IS THE CASE OF THE OX, LEADING TO THE DEATH-PENALTY:

1. XVIII:1: Said Abbayye to Raba, "How do we know that the verse, 'And the ox will be stoned and also its master will be put to death' (Ex. 21:29) serves to make the point that just as the case of the master, leading to the death-penalty, is judged, so is the case of the ox, leading to the death-penalty is judged by a court of twenty-three judges?
2. XVIII.2: The question was raised, "An ox that sinned by coming near Mount Sinai cf. (Ex. 19:13) – by what sort of court was it judged?

V.   THE WOLF, LION, BEAR, PANTHER, LEOPARD, AND SNAKE A
      CAPITAL CASE AFFECTING THEM IS JUDGED BY TWENTY-
      THREE. R. ELIEZER SAYS, "WHOEVER KILLS THEM FIRST
      ACQUIRES MERIT."
      1.   XIX:1: Said R. Simeon b. Laqish, "Eliezer's view applies to a
           case in which they have killed someone, but otherwise that is
           not the rule."
W.   R. AQIBA SAYS, "THEIR CAPITAL CASE IS JUDGED BY TWENTY
      THREE."
      1.   XX:1: R. Aqiba says the same thing as the first authority.
X.   THEY JUDGE A TRIBE...ONLY ON THE INSTRUCTIONS OF A
      COURT OF SEVENTY-ONE MEMBERS.
      1.   XXI:1: As to the tribe at hand, what was the sin that it
           committed?
Y.   THEY JUDGE ... A FALSE PROPHET AND A HIGH PRIEST, ONLY
      ON THE INSTRUCTIONS OF A COURT OF SEVENTY-ONE
      MEMBERS.
      1.   XXII:1: What is the scriptural source for this rule?
Y.   THEY JUDGE ...A HIGH PRIEST, ONLY ON THE INSTRUCTIONS
      OF A COURT OF SEVENTY-ONE MEMBERS.
      1.   XXIII:1: What is the scriptural source for this rule?
      2.   XXIII:2: R. Eleazar raised the question, "What sort of court
           would be required to judge the case involving the ox of a
           high priest that had gored and killed a man? Do we place it
           into the classification of the court involving the trial for the
           death-penalty of its master? Or do we place it into the
           category of the court involving the trial for the death penalty
           of any sort of master without reference to the status of the
           high priest?"
Z.   THEY BRING FORTH THE ARMY TO WAGE A WAR FOUGHT BY
      CHOICE ONLY ON THE INSTRUCTIONS OF A COURT OF
      SEVENTY-ONE:
      1.   XXIV:1: What is the scriptural source for this rule?
AA.   THEY MAKE ADDITIONS TO THE CITY OF JERUSALEM AND TO
      THE COURTYARDS OF THE TEMPLE ONLY ON THE
      INSTRUCTIONS OF A COURT OF SEVENTY-ONE:
      1.   XXV:1: What is the scriptural basis for this rule?
BB.   THEY SET UP SANHEDRINS FOR THE TRIBES ONLY ON THE
      INSTRUCTIONS OF A COURT OF SEVENTY-ONE.
      1.   XXVI:1: What is the basis for this rule?
CC.   THEY DECLARE A CITY TO BE "AN APOSTATE CITY" ONLY ON
      THE INSTRUCTIONS OF A COURT OF SEVENTY-ONE:
      1.   XXVII:1: What is the scriptural basis for this rule?

DD. AND THEY DO NOT DECLARE A CITY TO BE "AN APOSTATE CITY" ON THE FRONTIER:

    1. XXVIII:1: What is the scriptural basis for this rule?

EE. NOR DO THEY DECLARE THREE IN ONE LOCALE TO BE APOSTATE CITIES, BUT THEY DO SO IN THE CASE OF ONE OR TWO.

    1. XXIX:1: For it is written, "Concerning one of the cities" (Deut. 13:13 – but they do declare one or two, as it is written, "of your cities" (Deut. 13:13).

FF. THE GREAT SANHEDRIN WAS MADE UP OF SEVENTY-ONE MEMBERS, AND THE SMALL ONE WAS TWENTY-THREE.

    1. XXX:1: What is the reason for the position of rabbis who hold that it was seventy-one, as against Judah, who says that it was only seventy, for they say that Moses was in addition to them M. 1:6E?

    2. XXX:2: Our rabbis have taught on Tannaite authority. "But there remained two men in the camp" (Num. 11:26). But there are those who say, "Their names, Eldad's and Medad's remained in the urn. For when the Holy One, blessed be he, said to Moses, "Gather to me seventy of the elders of Israel" (Num. 11:16), Moses thought to himself, "How shall I do it? If I choose six from each of the twelve tribes, there will be two extra. If I choose five from each tribe, there will be ten too few. If I choose six from one tribe and five from another, I shall cause jealousy among the tribes."

    3. XXX:3: R. Simeon says, "They remained in the camp. When the Holy One blessed be he said to Moses, 'Gather for me seventy men' (Num. 11:16), Eldad and Medad said, 'We are not worthy of that high position.' Said the Holy One, blessed be he, 'Since you diminished yourselves, lo, I shall add greatness to your greatness.'"

GG. AND HOW DO WE KNOW THAT THE GREAT SANHEDRIN WAS TO HAVE SEVENTY-ONE MEMBERS? SINCE IT IS SAID, "GATHER TO ME SEVENTY MEN OF THE ELDERS OF ISRAEL" (NM. 11:16). SINCE MOSES WAS IN ADDITION TO THEM, LO, THERE WERE SEVENTY ONE. R. JUDAH SAYS, "IT IS SEVENTY." AND HOW DO WE KNOW THAT A SMALL ONE IS TWENTY-THREE? SINCE IT IS SAID, "THE CONGREGATION SHALL JUDGE, AND THE CONGREGATION SHALL DELIVER" (NUM. 35: 24, 25) – ONE CONGREGATION JUDGES, AND ONE CONGREGATION SAVES – THUS THERE ARE TWENTY. AND HOW DO WE KNOW THAT A CONGREGATION IS TEN? SINCE IT IS SAID, HOW LONG SHALL I BEAR WITH THIS EVIL

CONGREGATION OF THE TEN SPIES (NUM. 14:27) – EXCLUDING JOSHUA AND CALEB. AND HOW DO WE KNOW THAT WE SHOULD ADD THREE MORE? FROM THE IMPLICATION OF THAT WHICH IS SAID, YOU SHALL NOT FOLLOW AFTER THE MANY TO DO EVIL (EX: 23:20), I DERIVE THE INFERENCE THAT I SHOULD BE WITH THEM TO DO GOOD. IF SO, WHY IS IT SAID, AFTER THE MANY TO DO EVIL? YOUR VERDICT OF ACQUITTAL IS NOT EQUIVALENT TO YOUR VERDICT OF GUILT. YOUR VERDICT OF ACQUITTAL MAY BE ON THE VOTE OF A MAJORITY OF ONE, BUT YOUR VOTE FOR GUILT MUST BE BY A MAJORITY OF TWO. SINCE THERE CANNOT BE A COURT OF AN EVEN NUMBER OF MEMBERS TWENTY-TWO, THEY ADD YET ANOTHER – THUS TWENTY-THREE:

1. XXXI:1: But in the end in a sanhedrin of twenty-three judges you will never come up with a majority of two for a verdict of guilt. If eleven vote for acquittal and twelve for guilt, still it is a majority of one one and that is null, since two are needed for a verdict of guilty. If ten vote for innocence and thirteen for guilt, there is a majority of three for guilt.

2. XXXI:2: Said R. Kahana, "A sanhedrin every member of which reached the conclusion that the accused is guilty must dismiss the accused right away."

3. XXXI:3: Said R. Yohanan, "They seat on a sanhedrin only people of stature, wisdom, good appearance, mature age, who can recognize sorcery, and speak seventy languages, so that there should be no need of a sanhedrin to listen to testimony through an interpreter."

4. XXXI:4: Said R. Judah said Rab, "In any town in which there are not two who can speak and one who can understand seventy languages people may not set up a sanhedrin."

5. XXXI:5: "Those who derive arguments before sages" refers to Levi before Rabbi. "Those who argue before sages" refers to Simeon b. Azzai and Simeon b. Zoma, Hanan the Egyptian and Hananiah b. Hakhinai. R.Nahman bar Isaac repeated the matter in terms of five names: Simeon, Simeon, Simeon, Hanan, and Hananiah.

HH. AND HOW MANY RESIDENTS MUST THERE BE IN A TOWN SO THAT IT MAY BE SUITABLE FOR A SANHEDRIN? ONE HUNDRED TWENTY.

1. XXXII:1: What do these one hundred twenty do?

II.   R. NEHEMIAH SAYS, "TWO HUNDRED AND THIRTY, EQUIVALENT IN NUMBER TO THE CHIEFS OF GROUPS OF TEN:"

1. XXXIII:1: and the law is in accord with his opinion. Rabbi says, "Two hundred and seventy-seven" (T. San. 3:9F-G).

2. XXXIII:2: "And place such over them to be rulers of thousands, rulers of hundreds, rulers of fifties, and rulers of tens" (Ex. 18:21): "The rulers of thousands" were six hundred. "The rulers of hundreds" were six thousand. "The rulers of fifties" were twelve thousand. "The rulers of tens" were sixty-thousand. The total number of judges is Israel was seventy-eight thousand six hundred.

II. MISHNAH-TRACTATE SANHEDRIN 2:1-2

A.   A HIGH PRIEST JUDGES, AND OTHERS JUDGE HIM;

1. I:1: That is self-evident. It was necessary to make that point in the context of the statement that others judge him.

B.   ...GIVES TESTIMONY, AND OTHERS GIVE TESTIMONY ABOUT HIM:

1. II:1: And has it not been taught on Tannaite authority: "And hide yourself from them" (Deut. 22:4) – There are times in which you do hide yourself, and there are times that you do not hide yourself. In the case of a priest, if the man who needs help is in a grave yard where a priest may not go, for fear of contracting corpse uncleanness, or if it is an elder and the work involved is not in accord with the honor owing to him, or if it is a case in which his own work is greater in value than that of his fellow, for such a case it is written, "And you shall hide yourself.

   a. II:2: Gloss of a detail of the foregoing.

C.   ...PERFORMS THE RITE OF REMOVING THE SHOE DEUT. 25:7-9, AND OTHERS PERFORM THE RITE OF REMOVING THE SHOE WITH HIS WIFE. OTHERS ENTER LEVIRATE MARRIAGE WITH HIS WIFE, BUT HE DOES NOT ENTER INTO LEVIRATE MARRIAGE, BECAUSE HE IS PROHIBITED TO MARRY A WIDOW:

1. III:1: Does the Tannaite authority at hand take the view that there is no difference whether the widow was merely betrothed or was partner to a fully consummated marriage?

D.   IF HE SUFFERS A DEATH IN HIS FAMILY, HE DOES NOT FOLLOW THE BIER:

    1.   IV:1: Our rabbis have taught on Tannaite authority: "Neither shall he go out of the sanctuary" (Lev. 21:12): He should not go out with them, but he may go out after them.

E.   "BUT WHEN THE BEARERS OF THE BIER ARE NOT VISIBLE, HE IS VISIBLE; WHEN THEY ARE VISIBLE, HE IS NOT. AND HE GOES WITH THEM TO THE CITY GATE," THE WORDS OF R. MEIR. R. JUDAH SAYS, "HE NEVER LEAVES THE SANCTUARY, SINCE IT SAYS, 'NOR SHALL HE GO OUT OF THE SANCTUARY' (LEV. 21:12):"

    1.   V:1: Has R. Judah given a good argument?

F.   AND WHEN HE GIVES COMFORT TO OTHERS THE ACCEPTED PRACTICE IS FOR ALL THE PEOPLE TO PASS ONE AFTER ANOTHER, AND THE APPOINTED PREFECT OF THE PRIESTS STANDS BETWEEN HIM AND THE PEOPLE:

    1.   VI:1: Our rabbis have taught on Tannaite authority: And when he stands in the line to give comfort to others, the prefect of the priests and the anointed high priests who has now passed out of his position of grandeur are at his right hand, and the head of his father's house, the mourners, and all the people are at his left. When he stands in the line to receive comfort from others as a mourner, the prefect of the priests is at his right hand, and the head of the father's houses the priestly courses and all the people are at his left hand (T. San. 4:1 I, F).

        a.   VI:2: Said R. Pappa, "The present teaching on Tannaite authority yields three points: First, the prefect is the same as the one called in the Mishnah's version 'the one who is appointed.' Second, the mourners stand and the people pass by them. Third, the mourners are to the left of those who come to give comfort."

    2.   VI:3: Our rabbis have taught on Tannaite authority: The original practice was for the mourners to stand still and all the people to pass by them. There were two families in Jerusalem who competed with one another.

G.   AND WHEN HE RECEIVES CONSOLATION FROM OTHERS, ALL THE PEOPLE SAY TO HIM, "LET US BE YOUR ATONEMENT." AND HE SAYS TO THEM, "MAY YOU BE BLESSED BY HEAVEN." AND WHEN THEY PROVIDE HIM WITH THE FUNERAL MEAL, ALL THE PEOPLE SIT ON THE GROUND, WHILE HE SITS ON A STOOL.

    1.   VII:1: The question was raised: When he comforts others, what does he say to them?

H.   THE KING DOES NOT JUDGE, AND OTHERS DO NOT JUDGE HIM; DOES NOT GIVE TESTIMONY, AND OTHERS DO NOT GIVE TESTIMONY ABOUT HIM:

1.   VIII:1: Said R. Joseph, "That law applies only to Israelite kings. But as to the kings of the house of David, such a king judges and others judge them."

I.   HE DOES NOT PERFORM THE RITE OF REMOVING THE SHOE, AND OTHERS DO NOT PERFORM THE RITE OF REMOVING THE SHOE WITH HIS WIFE; DOES NOT ENTER INTO LEVIRATE MARRIAGE, NOR DO HIS BROTHER ENTER LEVIRATE MARRIAGE WITH HIS WIFE. R. JUDAH SAYS, "IF HE WANTED TO PERFORM THE RITE OF REMOVING THE SHOE OR TO ENTER INTO LEVIRATE MARRIAGE, HIS MEMORY IS A BLESSING." THEY SAID TO HIM, "THEY PAY NO ATTENTION TO HIM IF HE EXPRESSED THE WISH TO DO SO."

1.   IX:1: Is what R. Judah says true?

J.   OTHERS DO NOT MARRY HIS WIDOW.

R. JUDAH SAYS, "A KING MAY MARRY THE WIDOW OF A KING. FOR SO WE FIND IN THE CASE OF DAVID, THAT HE MARRIED THE WIDOW OF SAUL, FOR IT IS SAID, 'AND I GAVE YOU YOUR MASTER'S HOUSE AND YOUR MASTER'S WIVES INTO YOUR EMBRACE' (II SAM. 12:8)."

1.   X:1: It has been taught on Tannaite authority: They said to R. Judah, "David married women of the royal family who were permitted to him, Merab and Michal, but these were not his widows."

    a.   X:2: Gloss of foregoing.

    b.   X:3: As above.

III. MISHNAH-TRACTATE SANHEDRIN 2:3

A.   IF THE KING SUFFERS A DEATH IN HIS FAMILY, HE DOES NOT LEAVE THE GATE OF HIS PALACE. R. JUDAH SAYS, "IF HE WANTS TO GO OUT AFTER THE BIER, HE GOES OUT, FOR THUS WE FIND IN THE CASE OF DAVID, THAT HE WENT OUT AFTER THE BIER OF ABNER, SINCE IT IS SAID, 'AND KING DAVID FOLLOWED THE BIER' (2 SAM. 3:31)." THEY SAID TO HIM, "THIS ACTION WAS ONLY TO APPEASE THE PEOPLE:"

1.   I:1: Our rabbis have taught on Tannaite authority: In a place in which women are accustomed to go forth after the bier, they go forth in that way. If they are accustomed to go forth before the bier, they go forth in that manner. R. Judah says, "Women always go forth in front of the bier.

    a.   I:2: Secondary expansion of foregoing.

b. I:3: As above.

B. AND WHEN THEY PROVIDE HIM WITH THE FUNERAL MEAL, ALL THE PEOPLE SIT ON THE GROUND, WHILE HE SITS ON A COUCH.

1. II:1: What is the couch?

IV. MISHNAH-TRACTATE SANHEDRIN 2:4A-D

A. THE KING CALLS OUT THE ARMY TO WAGE A WAR FOUGHT BY CHOICE ON THE INSTRUCTIONS OF A COURT OF SEVENTY-ONE:

1. I:1: But has not the point of M. 2:4A already been made on Tannaite authority: They bring forth the army to wage a war fought by choice only on the instructions of a court of seventy-one?

2. I:2: Said R. Judah said Samuel, "Everything included in the chapter 1 Sam. 8 on the king the king is permitted to do."

   a. I:3: Gloss of a detail of the foregoing: It has been taught on Tannaite authority: R. Yosé says, "Three commandments were imposed upon the Israelites when they came into the land. They were commanded to appoint a king, to cut off the descendents of Amalek, and to build the chosen House" (T. San. 4:5K-L).

      I. I:4: Said R. Simeon b. Laqish, "At first Solomon ruled over the creatures of the upper world, as it is said, 'Then Solomon sat on the throne of the Lord as king' (1 Chr. 29:23). Then he reigned over the creatures of the lower world, as it is written, 'For he had dominion over all the region on this side of the river, From Tifsah even to Gaza' (1 Kgs. 5:4)."

B. HE MAY EXERCISE THE RIGHT TO OPEN A ROAD FOR HIMSELF, AND OTHERS MAY NOT STOP HIM. THE ROYAL ROAD HAS NO REQUIRED MEASURE.
ALL THE PEOPLE PLUNDER AND LAY BEFORE HIM WHAT THEY HAVE GRABBED, AND HE TAKES THE FIRST PORTION.

1. II:1: With reference to M. 2:4D: All the people plunder... and he takes the first portion, our rabbis have taught on Tannaite authority: The royal treasuries of a defeated foe belong to the king, and as to the rest of the spoil that the army takes, half is for the king and the other half is for the people.

V. MISHNAH-TRACTATE SANHEDRIN 2:4E-I

A. "HE SHOULD NOT MULTIPLY WIVES TO HIMSELF" (DEUT. 17:17) – ONLY EIGHTEEN. R JUDAH SAYS, "HE MAY HAVE AS

MANY AS HE WANTS, SO LONG AS THEY DO NOT ENTICE HIM
TO ABANDON THE LORD (DEUT. 7:4)." R. SIMEON SAYS,
"EVEN IF THERE IS ONLY ONE WHO ENTICES HIM TO
ABANDON THE LORD – LO, THIS ONE SHOULD NOT MARRY
HER." IF SO, WHY IS IT SAID, "HE SHOULD NOT MULTIPLY
WIVES TO HIMSELF"? EVEN THOUGH THEY SHOULD BE LIKE
ABIGAIL 1 SAM. 25:3.

1. I:1: Does the dispute at M. 2:4F, G bear the implication that
   R. Judah seeks out the reasoning behind a verse of Scripture,
   and R. Simeon does not seek out the reasoning behind a
   verse of Scripture?
2. I:2: As to the number of eighteen specified at M. 2:4E, what is
   the source for that number?
   a. I:3: Gloss of a detail of the foregoing. Said R. Judah said
      Rab, "David had four hundred sons, all of them born of
      beautiful captive women. All grew long locks plaited
      down the back. All of them seated in golden chariots."

VI. MISHNAH-TRACTATE SANHEDRIN 2:4J-N
A. "HE SHOULD NOT MULTIPLY HORSES TO HIMSELF" (DEUT.
   17:16) – ONLY ENOUGH FOR HIS CHARIOT:
   1. I:1: Our rabbis have taught on Tannaite authority: "He shall
      not multiply horses to himself" (Deut. 17:16). Is it possible to
      suppose that he may not possess even sufficient animals for
      his chariots and horsemen? Scripture says, "To himself,"
      meaning, for his own use he does not multiply them, but he
      does have a multitude for his chariots and horsemen.
B. "NEITHER SHALL HE GREATLY MULTIPLY TO HIMSELF SILVER
   AND GOLD" (DEUT. 17:16) – ONLY ENOUGH TO PAY HIS
   ARMY:
   1. II:1: Our rabbis have taught on Tannaite authority: "Neither
      shall he greatly multiply to himself silver and gold" (Deut.
      17:16): Might one suppose that the prohibition covers even
      enough to pay his army? Scripture says, "To himself" – to
      himself he may not multiply silver and gold, but he may
      multiply silver and gold sufficient to pay his army.
   2. II:2: R. Judah contrasted verses as follows: "It is written,
      'And Solomon had forty thousand stalls of horses for his
      chariots' (1 Kgs. 5:6), and elsewhere, 'And Solomon had four
      thousand stalls for horses and chariots' (2 Chr. 9:25). How
      so? If he had forty thousand stables, each one of them had
      four thousand horse stalls, and if he had four thousand
      stables, each one of them had forty thousand horse stalls."

C.   "AND HE WRITES OUT A SCROLL OF THE TORAH FOR
      HIMSELF" (DEUT. 17:17):
      WHEN HE GOES TO WAR, HE TAKES IT OUT WITH HIM; WHEN
      HE COMES BACK, HE BRINGS IT BACK WITH HIM; WHEN HE IS
      IN SESSION IN COURT, IT IS WITH HIM; WHEN HE IS
      RECLINING, IT IS BEFORE HIM, AS IT IS SAID, "AND IT SHALL
      BE WITH HIM, AND HE SHALL READ IN IT ALL THE DAYS OF
      HIS LIFE" (DEUT. 17:19).
      1.   III:1: It has been taught on Tannaite authority: But that is
           one the condition that he not take credit for one made by his
           ancestors.

D.   COMPOSITE ON THE WRITING AND REVELATION OF THE
      TORAH
      1.   III:2: Said Mar Zutra, and some say Mar Uqba, "In the
           beginning the Torah was given to Israel in Hebrew writing
           and in the Holy Language of Hebrew. Then it was given to
           them in the time of Ezra in Assyrian writing and in the
           Aramaic language. The Israelites chose for themselves
           Assyrian letters and the Holy Language and they left for
           common folk Hebrew letters and the Aramaic language."
      2.   III:3: It has been taught on Tannaite authority: R. Yosé says,
           "Ezra was worthy for the Torah to have been given by him,
           had not Moses come before him."

VII. MISHNAH-TRACTATE SANHEDRIN 2:5
   A.   OTHERS MAY NOT RIDE ON HIS HORSE, SIT ON HIS THRONE,
        HANDLE HIS SCEPTER:
        1.   I:1: Said R. Jacob said R. Yohanan, "Abishag would have
             been permitted to be married to Solomon, but was forbidden
             to be married to Adonijah."
             a.   I:2: And what is the story of Abishag (and Bath Sheba)?
   B.   THE EVILS OF DIVORCE, PARTICULARLY OF AN AGING WIFE
        1.   I:3: Said R. Eliezer, "Whoever divorces his first wife – even
             the altar weeps tears on that account, for it is said, 'And this
             further did you do, you cover the altar of the Lord with tears,
             with weeping and with sighing, in so much that he regards
             not the offering any more, nor receives it with good will at
             your hand' (Mal. 2:13). And it is written, 'Yet you say, Why?
             Because the Lord has been witness between you and the wife
             of your youth, against whom you have dealt treacherously,
             though she is your companion and the wife of your
             covenant' (Mal. 2:14)."

2. I:4: Said R. Yohanan, and some say, R. Eleazar, "A man's wife dies only if people ask for money from him and he does not have it, as it is said, 'If you have not wherewith to pay, why should he take away the bed from under you' (Prov. 22:27)."

   a. I:5: Said Rabbah bar bar Hannah said R. Yohanan, "And it is as difficult to match people up as it is to split the Red Sea, as it is said, 'God sets the solitary in families, he brings prisoners into prosperity' (Ps. 68:7)."

3. I:6: Said R. Samuel bar Nahman, "Everything can be replaced except for the wife of one's youth."

4. I:7: R. Judah repeated on Tannaite authority to his son, R. Isaac, "A man finds true serenity only with his first wife, as it is said, 'Let your fountain be blessed and have joy of the wife of your youth' (Prov. 5:18)."

5. I:8: Said R. Samuel bar Onia in the name of Rab, "A woman is unformed, and she makes a covenant only with him who turns her into a utensil."

C. AND OTHERS MAY NOT WATCH HIM WHILE HE IS GETTING A HAIRCUT, OR WHILE HE IS NUDE, OR IN THE BATH-HOUSE, SINCE IT IS SAID, "YOU SHALL SURELY SET HIM AS KING OVER YOU" (DEUT. 17:15) – THAT REVERENCE FOR HIM WILL BE UPON YOU.

1. II:1: Our rabbis have taught on Tannaite authority: A king gets a haircut every day, a high priest on Fridays, an ordinary priest once in thirty days.

   a. II:2: Said Rabina to R. Ashi, "As to this teaching that priests whose hair is too long should not officiate and are subject to the death-penalty if they do, before Ezekiel came along, who stated it?"

VIII. MISHNAH-TRACTATE SANHEDRIN 3:1

A. PROPERTY-CASES ARE DECIDED BY THREE JUDGES: THIS LITIGANT CHOOSES ONE JUDGE, AND THAT LITIGANT CHOOSES ONE JUDGE, AND THEN THE TWO OF THE LITIGANTS CHOOSE ONE MORE," THE WORDS OF R. MEIR:

1. I:1: What is the meaning of the statement, This litigant chooses one and that litigant chooses one? Surely three judges should be enough? It is assumed each litigant selects a court, and the two courts choose a third court, which tries the case. Why such a clumsy proceeding? Cannot the two litigants jointly select one court which shall try the action?

2.   I:2: May even a debtor hold up matters in the way just described? Or must he go to the court chosen by the creditor?

3.   I:3: But does the stated procedure not apply to court-certified experts? Can these too not be disqualified by the debtor?

4.   I:4: We have learned in the Mishnah: And sages say, The two judges choose a third" – Now if it should enter your mind that matters are as we have proposed, that is, that we speak of each litigant's choosing a court, after the litigants have invalidated a court, will that court go and select yet another court! Surely this is absurd.

B.   AND SAGES SAY, "THE TWO JUDGES CHOOSE ONE MORE:"

1.   II:1: May we say that at issue is the view stated by R. Judah in the name of Rab? For R. Judah said Rab said, "Witnesses are not to sign a bond unless they know who is going to sign with them."

C.   "THIS PARTY HAS THE RIGHT TO INVALIDATE THE JUDGE CHOSEN BY THAT ONE, AND THAT PARTY HAS THE RIGHT TO INVALIDATE THE JUDGE CHOSEN BY THIS ONE," THE WORDS OF R. MEIR. AND SAGES SAY, "UNDER WHAT CIRCUMSTANCES? WHEN HE BRINGS EVIDENCE ABOUT THEM, THAT THEY ARE RELATIVES OR OTHERWISE INVALID. BUT IF THEY ARE VALID JUDGES OR COURT-CERTIFIED EXPERTS, HE HAS NOT GOT THE POWER TO INVALIDATE THEM. THIS PARTY INVALIDATES THE WITNESSES BROUGHT BY THAT ONE, AND THAT PARTY INVALIDATES THE WITNESSES BROUGHT BY THIS ONE," THE WORDS OF R. MEIR. AND SAGES SAY, "UNDER WHAT CIRCUMSTANCES? WHAT HE BRINGS EVIDENCE ABOUT THEM, THAT THEY ARE RELATIVES OR OTHERWISE INVALID. BUT IF THEY ARE VALID TO SERVE AS WITNESSES, HE HAS NOT GOT THE POWER TO INVALIDATE THEM."

1.   III:1: Does a litigant have the power to invalidate a judge?

   a.   III:2: Secondary expansion of the development of the foregoing: May we say that at issue is the same principle debated between Rabbi and Rabban Simeon b. Gamaliel: at issue is whether it is necessary for the defendant to validate his claim.

2.   III:3: When Rabin came, he said R. Yohanan said, "The first clause of the Mishnah speaks of a case in which the witnesses are invalid but the judges are valid. The litigant proposes to reject both the witnesses and the judges, and since he proves his case against the witnesses, we accept his

claim also against the judges. The latter clause of the Mishnah speaks of a case in which the judges are invalid and the witnesses valid. The litigant here proves his case against the judges and not the witnesses, so that, since the judges are invalid, the witnesses also are treated as invalid. That is why, from Meir's position, in both instances we allow one litigant to dismiss the evidence or the judges produced by the other."

a. III:4: Gloss of a detail of the foregoing.
    I. III:5: As above. Illustrating the point of III:4.
    II. III:6: As above.

IX. MISHNAH-TRACTATE SANHEDRIN 3:2

A.   "IF ONE LITIGANT SAID TO THE OTHER, 'I ACCEPT MY FATHER AS RELIABLE,' 'I ACCEPT YOUR FATHER AS RELIABLE,' 'I ACCEPT AS RELIABLE THREE HERDSMEN TO SERVE AS JUDGES,'" R. MEIR SAYS, "HE HAS THE POWER TO RETRACT." AND SAGES SAY, "HE HAS NOT GOT THE POWER TO RETRACT." IF ONE OWED AN OATH TO HIS FELLOW, AND HIS FELLOW SAID, "INSTEAD OF AN OATH, TAKE A VOW TO ME BY THE LIFE OF YOUR HEAD," R. MEIR SAYS, "HE HAS THE POWER TO RETRACT." AND SAGES SAY, "HE HAS NOT GOT THE POWER TO RETRACT:"

1.   I:1: Said R. Dimi, son of R. Nahman, son of R. Joseph, "We deal with a case at M. 3:2A-C in which one of the parties accepted such a person as one of the judges." Said R. Judah said Samuel, "The dispute concerns a case in which the creditor has agreed to say, should the judges favor the debtor, 'The debt is forgiven to you.' But in a case in which the debtor said to the creditor, should the judges favor the creditor, 'I shall pay you,' all parties concur that the debtor has the power to retract his agreement." R. Yohanan said, "The dispute pertains to a case in which the debtor said to the creditor, if the judges rule in favor of the creditor, 'I shall pay.'"

2.   I:2: Said R. Simeon b. Laqish, "There is a dispute about the rule pertaining before the completion of the court decision, but after the completion of the court decision, all agree he cannot retract." And R. Yohanan said, "About retraction after the completion of the court decision there is a dispute."

3.   I:3: R. Nahman bar Rab sent a message to R. Nahman bar Jacob, "May our master teach us: Is the dispute applicable only to the period prior to the completion of the trial, or does

it apply as well to the period after the completion of the trial so that the litigants may retract even then? And in accord with which authority is the decided law?"

X. MISHNAH-TRACTATE SANHEDRIN 3:3

A.   AND THESE ARE THOSE WHO ARE INVALID TO SERVE AS WITNESSES OR JUDGES: HE WHO PLAYS DICE;
1.   I:1: He who plays dice: What does a dice-player do wrong that he should be invalid as a witness or judge?

B.   ...HE WHO LOANS MONEY ON INTEREST;
1.   II:1: Said Raba, "One who borrows money on interest is invalid to serve as a witness."
    a.   II:2: Two witnesses gave testimony against Bar Binithos. One said, "In my presence he lent money on interest." The other party said, "To me he lent money on interest." Raba accepting the evidence of both declared Bar Binithos to be invalid.
    b.   II:3: There was a butcher who was found to be selling terefah-meat under his own authority. R. Nahman declared the man invalid as a butcher and sent him out.

C.   ...THOSE WHO RACE PIGEONS:
1.   III:1: What are pigeon-racers?
2.   III:2: A Tannaite authority stated: They added to the list robbers and those who impose a sale by force even though they pay a fair market value. But a robber is prohibited on the basis of the law of the Torah.
3.   III:3: A Tannaite authority taught: They further added to the list cowboys, tax-collectors, and tax-farmers.
4.   III:4: Said R. Judah, "A shepherd under ordinary circumstances is invalid. A tax-collector under ordinary circumstances is valid."

D.   ...AND THOSE WHO DO BUSINESS IN THE PRODUCE OF THE SEVENTH YEAR.
SAID R. SIMEON, "IN THE BEGINNING THEY CALLED THEM, 'THOSE WHO GATHER SEVENTH YEAR PRODUCE.' WHEN OPPRESSORS BECAME MANY WHO COLLECTED TAXES IN THE SEVENTH YEAR, THEY REVERTED TO CALL THEM, 'THOSE WHO DO BUSINESS IN THE PRODUCE OF THE SEVENTH YEAR.'"
1.   IV:1: What is the sense of this statement?
2.   IV:2: R. Hiyya bar Zaranoqi and R. Simeon b. Yehosedeq were going to intercalate the year in Assya. R. Simeon b. Laqish met them and joined them. He said, "I shall go along

and see how they do it." He saw a man ploughing. He said to them, "He is a priest, and he is ploughing." They said to him, "He can claim, I am an imperial employee in the property."

    a. IV:3: Gloss of a detail of the foregoing: What is a conspiracy of wicked men?

E. SAID R. JUDAH, "UNDER WHAT CIRCUMSTANCES? WHEN THE AFORE-NAMED (B) HAVE ONLY THAT AS THEIR PROFESSION. BUT IF THEY HAVE A PROFESSION OTHER THAN THAT, THEY ARE VALID TO SERVE AS WITNESSES OR JUDGES."

    1. V:1: Said R. Abbahu said R. Eleazar, "The decided law accords with the view of R. Judah."

        a. V:2: There was the case of a deed of gift that bore the signature of two thieves. R. Pappa bar Samuel considered declaring it valid, for lo, no announcement had been made concerning their status as known thieves.

    2. V:3: Said R. Nahman, "Those who 'eat something else' accept charity from gentiles are invalid for testimony. That applies when they do so in public, but if it is in private, the rule does not apply.

        a. V:4: Case.

    3. V:5: As to a witness who is proved to have conspired to commit perjury, Abbayye said, "When between the time he gave his testimony and the time he was proved a perjurer, some days have elapsed, his status as a witness is treated as invalid retrospectively, from the time he began to give his evidence in court, and all the evidence he has given in the intervening period becomes invalidated." And Raba said, "It is only from that point onward that he becomes an invalid witness."

    4. V:6: As to an apostate who eats carrion because he is hungry, all parties concur that he is invalid as a witness.

XI. MISHNAH-TRACTATE SANHEDRIN 3:4-5

A. AND THESE ARE RELATIVES PROHIBITED FROM SERVING AS ONE'S WITNESSES OR JUDGES: (1) ONE'S FATHER: (2) BROTHER, (3) FATHER'S BROTHER, (4) MOTHER'S BROTHER, (5) SISTER'S HUSBAND, (6) FATHER'S SISTER'S HUSBAND, (7) MOTHER'S SISTER'S HUSBAND:

    1. I:1: And these are relatives prohibited from serving as one's witnesses or judges: one's father: What is the scriptural basis for the rule at hand?

2. I:2: We have found proof, therefore, that fathers may not
    testify against children and children against fathers, all the
    more so fathers that is, brothers cannot testify against one
    another. How do we know that sons cannot testify against
    sons that is, cousins, sons of fathers who are brothers? We
    have found proof, therefore, that sons may not testify against
    one another. How do we know that sons brothers may not
    testify together in a case involving a third party?

3. I:3: We now have proven that people related through the
    father may not give evidence together. How do we know
    that people related through the mother may not do so?

B. ...AND THEIR SONS-IN-LAW:

1. II:1: Said Rab, "My father's brother my paternal uncle may
    not give testimony for me, nor may his son or son-in-law,
    and so too, I may not testify for him, nor my son or son-in-
    law. But why should this be the case? Would this not
    involve relationships of the third and first removes? But we
    have learned in the Mishnah at hand that relatives of the
    second remove are forbidden to testify for relatives of the
    second remove e.g., first cousins, and relatives of the second
    remove cannot testify for those of the first remove uncles,
    but not that relatives of the third remove may not testify for
    relatives of the first remove."

2. II:2: Said R. Nahman, "The brother of my mother-in-law may
    not testify for me; the son of the sister of my mother-in-law
    may not testify for me."

3. II:3: Said R. Ashi, "When we were at Ulla's house, the
    question troubled us: As to the brother of one's father-in-
    law, what is his status? As to the son of the brother of one's
    father-in-law, what is his status? As to the son of the sister of
    one's father-in-law, what is his status?"

4. II:4: Rab went to buy parchment. People asked him, "What
    is the law on a man's testifying concerning the wife of his
    step-son?"

C. ...MOTHER'S HUSBAND, (9) FATHER-IN-LAW, AND (10) WIFE'S
    SISTER'S HUSBAND – THEY, THEIR SONS, AND THEIR SONS-
    IN-LAW:

1. III:1: The mother's husband's son is one's brother so this is
    not a new item, and why should the Mishnah repeat itself?

2. III:2: Said R. Hisda, "The father of the groom and the father
    of the bride may give testimony concerning one another."

3. III:3: Said Rabbah bar bar Hannah, "A man may testify concerning his betrothed wife prior to the consummation of the marriage."

D. ...BUT THE STEP-SON ONLY BUT NOT THE STEP-SON'S OFFSPRING:

SAID R. YOSÉ, "THIS IS THE VERSION OF R. AQIBA. BUT THE EARLIER VERSION IS AS FOLLOWS: HIS UNCLE, THE SON OF HIS UNCLE LEV. 25:49 AND ANYONE WHO STANDS TO INHERIT HIM." AND ANYONE WHO IS RELATED TO HIM AT THAT TIME, IF ONE WAS A RELATIVE BUT CEASED TO BE RELATED, LO, THAT PERSON IS VALID."

1. IV:1: Our rabbis have taught on Tannaite authority: The step-son only. R. Yosé says, "A brother-in-law the wife's sister's husband."

2. IV:2: There was a deed of gift which bore as signatories two brothers-in-law. R. Joseph considered validating it, for R. Judah said Samuel said, "The law accords with R. Yosé."

E. R. JUDAH SAYS, "EVEN IF HIS DAUGHTER DIED, IF HE HAS SONS FROM HER, LO, THE SON-IN-LAW IS DEEMED A RELATIVE.

1. V:1: Said R. Tanhum said R. Tabela said R. Barona said Rab, "The decided law accords with the view of R. Judah."

   a. V:2: The sons of the father-in-law of Mar Uqba, who were no longer related to him since their sister, Mar Uqba's wife, had died came to him for a trial. He said to them, "I am not valid to try your case."

F. "ONE KNOWN TO BE A FRIEND AND ONE KNOWN TO BE AN ENEMY – "ONE KNOWN TO BE A FRIEND – THIS IS THE ONE WHO SERVED AS HIS GROOMSMAN:

1. VI:1: For how long does the relationship last?

G. "ONE KNOWN TO BE AN ENEMY – THIS IS ONE WHO HAS NOT SPOKEN WITH HIM FOR THREE DAYS BY REASON O F OUTRAGE."

THEY SAID TO JUDAH, "ISRAELITES ARE NOT SUSPECT FOR SUCH A FACTOR."

1. VII:1: Our rabbis have taught on Tannaite authority: "And he was not an enemy" (Num. 35:23) – then he may give testimony for him. "Neither sought his harm" (Num. 35:23) – then he may judge his case.

XII. MISHNAH-TRACTATE SANHEDRIN 3:6-7

A. HOW DO THEY TEST THE WITNESSES? THEY BRING THEM INTO THE ROOM AND ADMONISH THEM:

1. I:1: How do they speak to the witnesses, when they admonish them?

B. THEN THEY TAKE EVERYONE OUT AND KEEP BACK THE MOST IMPORTANT OF THE GROUP. AND THEY SAY TO HIM, "EXPLAIN: HOW DO YOU KNOW THAT THIS ONE OWES MONEY TO THAT ONE."
IF HE SAID, "HE TOLD ME, 'I OWE HIM,' 'SO-AND-SO TOLD ME THAT HE OWES HIM,'" HE HAS SAID NOTHING WHATSOEVER, UNLESS HE SAYS, "IN OUR PRESENCE HE ADMITTED TO HIM THAT HE OWES HIM TWO HUNDRED ZUZ." AND AFTERWARD THEY BRING IN THE SECOND AND TEST HIM IN THE SAME WAY. IF THEIR TESTIMONY CHECKS OUT, THEY DISCUSS THE MATTER.

1. II:1: This supports the position of R. Judah, for R. Judah said Rab said, "One has to say to the witnesses to a transaction, 'You are my witnesses' at which point the testimony is valid."
   a. II:2: Gloss of a detail of the foregoing: Said R. Samuel bar Nahman said R. Jonathan, "How do we know that a plea is not entered in behalf of an inciter?"
2. II:3: Said Abbayye, "The ruling that one can plead he was joking unless he explicitly recognized the witnesses and validated their testimony of what he was about to do is the case only if the man says, 'I was only joking with you.' But if he had said, 'The incident never happened at all,' he is assumed to be a confirmed liar."
   a. II:4: Someone hid witnesses against his neighbor behind bed-curtains. He said to him, "You have a maneh of mine."
   b. II:5: Someone hid witnesses against his neighbor in a grave. He said to him, "You have a maneh of mine."
3. II:6: Said Rabina, and some say R. Pappa, "From what R. Judah said Rab said, 'One has to say to the witnesses, "You will be my witnesses,"' it follows that there is no difference whether the debtor said it, or the creditor said it and the debtor is silent."
   a. II:7: Someone had the name "A basket of debts." He said, "Who has a claim against me except for Mr. A and Mr. B?"
   b. II:8: There was a man who was called, "A mouse lying on money" that is, a miser. When he lay dying, he said, "Mr. A and Mr. B have a claim of money against me."

> After he died, they came and laid claim against the estate.

4. II:9: If someone admitted the claim before two witnesses, and this was confirmed by an act of acquisition, they may then prepare a bond covering the debt, even though the debtor did not instruct the scribe to do so. But if not, they do not do so.

5. II:10: Said R. Ada bar Ahbah, "Sometimes a deed of acknowledgement of a debt before three witnesses, without an act of acquisition may be written up, sometimes not."

6. II:11: If the debtor conceded a claim for movables and the witnesses effected a formal title given over by the debtor, they write a writ of record, and if not, they do not write one.

7. II:12: Rabina came to Damharia. Said to him R. Dimi, son of R. Huna of Damharia, to Rabina, "What is the law concerning movables that are as his in the domain of the debtor?"

   a. II:13: There was a deed of acknowledgement of debt that lacked the phrase, "He said to us, 'Write and sign and deliver to him...'"

   b. II:14: A deed of acknowledgement had written it, "An aide memoire of the statements of so-and-so," rather than the requisite, "an aide memoire of testimony by witnesses", and was worded wholly as a court document though signed by two, not three men, but omitted the phrase, "We were in session as three judges, and one of them then withdrew."

8. II:15: Our rabbis have taught on Tannaite authority: If someone said to the heirs, "I saw your father hiding money in a box, chest, or cupboard," and he said, "They belong to so-and-so," or "they are in the status of second title to be brought to Jerusalem and there spent on the purchase of food," if the money was in the house, the statement is null. If the money was in the field, his statement is valid.

C. IF TWO JUDGES SAY, "HE IS INNOCENT," AND ONE SAYS, "HE IS GUILTY," HE IS INNOCENT. IF TWO SAY, "HE IS GUILTY," AND ONE SAYS, "HE IS INNOCENT," HE IS GUILTY. IF ONE SAYS, "HE IS INNOCENT," AND ONE SAYS, "HE IS GUILTY," – OR EVEN IF TWO DECLARE HIM INNOCENT AND TWO DECLARE HIM GUILTY – BUT ONE OF THEM SAYS, "I DON'T KNOW," THEY HAVE TO ADD JUDGES.

1. III:1: Where the judges differ, how do they word the court order? R. Yohanan said, "'He is innocent.'" R. Simeon b.

Laqish said, "'Judge X and Judge Y declare him innocent, Judge Z declares him liable.'"

D.   WHEN THEY HAVE COMPLETED THE MATTER, THEY BRING THEM BACK IN. THE CHIEF JUDGE SAYS, "MR. SO-AND-SO, YOU ARE INNOCENT," "MR. SO-AND-SO, YOU ARE GUILTY."

1.   IV:1: Whom do they bring back?

   a.   IV:2: Gloss of foregoing.

   b.   IV:3: Gloss of a cited passage of IV:1: Under no circumstances is their testimony confirmed unless both of them are heard at the same time. R. Nathan says, "They hear out the testimony of this one on one day, and when his fellow comes on the next day, they give a hearing to what he has to say as well" (T. San. 5:5H-I).

   c.   IV:4: R. Simeon b. Eliaqim was watching for an occasion on which to ordain R. Yosé, son of R. Hanina, but nothing came up. One day he was in session before R. Yohanan. He said to them, "Does anybody know whether or not the law follows the view of R. Joshua b. Qorha?"

   d.   IV:5: Said R. Hiyya bar Abin said Rab, "The law is in accord with R. Joshua b. Qorha's view, both in respect to real estate and in respect to movables."

   e.   IV:6: Said R. Joseph, "I say in the name of Ulla, 'The law accords with R. Joshua b. Qorha both as to real estate and as to movables.'"

2.   IV:7: Said R. Judah, "Testimony of two witnesses who contradict one another under examination in respect to peripheral issues, e.g., details of the weather that day is valid in property-cases."

   a.   IV:8: Illustration of foregoing: If one witness says, "It was a jug of wine," and the other witness says, "It was a jug of oil" – there was a case of this kind, which came before R. Ammi. R. Ammi imposed upon the defendant the requirement to pay the value of the jug of wine out of the value of a jug of oil since oil is more expensive, the smaller of the two claims was proved.

   b.   IV:9: Illustration of foregoing: One says, "It was in the upper room," and the other says, "It was in the lower room." Said R. Hanina, "A case of this kind came before Rabbi, who joined the testimony of the two witnesses."

E.   NOW HOW DO WE KNOW THAT WHEN ONE OF THE JUDGES LEAVE THE COURT, HE MAY NOT SAY, "I THINK HE IS INNOCENT, BUT MY COLLEAGUES THINK HE IS GUILTY, SO

WHAT CAN I DO? FOR MY COLLEAGUES HAVE THE VOTES!" CONCERNING SUCH A PERSON, IT IS SAID, "YOU SHALL NOT GO UP AND DOWN AS A TALEBEARER AMONG YOUR PEOPLE" (LEV. 19:16). AND IT IS SAID, "HE WHO GOES ABOUT AS A TALEBEARER AND REVEALS SECRETS, BUT HE THAT IS FAITHFUL CONCEALS THE MATTER" (PROV. 11:13).

1. V:1: Our rabbis have taught on Tannaite authority: How do we know that when one of the judges leaves the court, he may not say, "Lo, I think he is innocent, but my colleagues think he is guilty, so what can I do? For my colleagues have the votes!"?

XIII. MISHNAH-TRACTATE SANHEDRIN 3:8

A. SO LONG AS A LITIGANT BRINGS PROOF, HE MAY REVERSE THE RULING. IF THEY HAD SAID TO HIM, "ALL THE EVIDENCE WHICH YOU HAVE, BRING BETWEEN THIS DATE AND THIRTY DAYS FROM NOW," IF HE FOUND EVIDENCE DURING THE THIRTY-DAY-PERIOD, HE MAY REVERSE THE RULING. IF HE FOUND EVIDENCE AFTER THE THIRTY-DAY-PERIOD, HE MAY NOT REVERSE THE RULING. SAID RABBAN SIMEON B. GAMALIEL, "WHAT SHOULD THIS PARTY DO, WHO COULD NOT FIND THE EVIDENCE DURING THE THIRTY-DAY-PERIOD, BUT FOUND IT AFTER THIRTY DAYS?"

1. I:1: Said Rabbah bar R. Huna, "The decided law accords with the view of Rabban Simeon b. Gamaliel."

B. IF THEY HAD SAID TO HIM, "BRING WITNESSES," AND HE SAID, "I DON'T HAVE WITNESSES," IF THEY HAD SAID, "BRING PROOF," AND HE SAID, "I DON'T HAVE PROOF" AND AFTER A TIME HE BROUGHT PROOF, OR HE FOUND WITNESSES – THIS IS OF NO WEIGHT WHATSOEVER. SAID RABBAN SIMEON B. GAMALIEL, "WHAT SHOULD THIS PARTY DO, WHO DID NOT EVEN KNOW THAT HE HAD WITNESSES ON HIS SIDE BUT FOUND WITNESSES? OR WHO DID NOT EVEN KNOW THAT HE HAD PROOF, BUT WHO FOUND PROOF?" IF THEY HAD SAID TO HIM, "BRING WITNESSES," AND HE SAID, "I HAVE NO WITNESSES," "BRING PROOF," AND HE SAID, "I HAVE NO PROOF," IF HE SAW THAT HE WOULD BE DECLARED LIABLE IN COURT AND SAID, "LET MR. SO-AND-SO AND MR. SUCH-AND-SUCH NOW COME ALONG AND GIVE EVIDENCE IN MY BEHALF," OR IF ON THE SPOT HE BROUGHT PROOF OUT OF HIS POCKET – LO, THIS IS OF NO WEIGHT WHATSOEVER

1. II:1: Said Rabbah bar R. Huna said R. Yohanan, "The decided law accords with the opinion of sages."
   a. II:2: A minor boy was called to court before R. Nahman. He said to him, "Do you have witnesses?"
   b. II:3: There was a woman trustee appointed by creditor and debtor of a bond who produced a bond against a given debtor but said to him, "I know that this bond has been paid off."
2. II:4: When R. Dimi came, he said R. Yohanan said, "One may go on producing proof to contradict the decision, until he runs out of arguments and then says, 'Let Mr. X and Mr. Y come near and testify in my behalf.' This implies that, having stated he has no more evidence, he asks that witnesses be heard."
3. II:5: When R. Dimi came, he said R. Yohanan said, "He who drags his fellow to court – one says, 'Let us have the trial here,' and the other says, 'Let us go to the place of the assembly,' they force him to go to the place of the assembly."
   a. II:6: They sent a message from the court in the Land of Israel to Mar Uqba, "To him whose splendor is like that of the son of Bithia Moses, Peace to you. Uqban, the Babylonian, complained before us, 'Jeremiah, my brother, has placed obstacles in my path.' Speak judge, order to him and get him moving so that he will appear before us in Tiberias."

XIV. MISHNAH-TRACTATE SANHEDRIN 4:1-2

A. THE SAME LAWS APPLY TO PROPERTY CASES AND CAPITAL CASES WITH RESPECT TO EXAMINATION AND INTERROGATION OF WITNESSES, AS IT IS SAID, "YOU WILL HAVE ONE LAW" (LEV. 24:22). WHAT IS THE DIFFERENCE BETWEEN PROPERTY CASES AND CAPITAL CASES?

1. I:1: The same laws apply to property cases and capital cases with respect to examination and interrogation of witnesses: Do property cases require examination and interrogation of witnesses?
2. I:2: Said R. Hanina, "As a matter of Torah-law, the same rules apply to property cases and capital cases with respect to the examination and interrogation of witnesses as it is said, 'You will have one law.' (Lev. 24:22). Then on what account did they rule that property cases do not require examination and interrogation of witnesses? It is so that you

will not shut the door before those who wish to take out loans by making it difficult for the lender to collect."

3. I:3: Raba said, "The rule at hand which requires examination and interrogation of witnesses in property cases deals with cases involving judicial penalties, while the other passages which do not require examination of witnesses deal with cases of admission that a debt exists and cases of transactions in loans. In such cases the procedure would discourage creditors from lending money."

4. I:4: Our rabbis have taught on Tannaite authority: "Justice, justice shall you follow" (Deut. 16:20): This means seek out a well-qualified court."

B. PROPERTY CASES ARE TRIED BY THREE JUDGES, AND CAPITAL CASES BY TWENTY-THREE. IN PROPERTY CASES THEY BEGIN ARGUMENT WITH THE CASE EITHER FOR ACQUITTAL OR FOR CONVICTION, WHILE IN CAPITAL CASES THEY BEGIN ONLY WITH THE CASE FOR ACQUITTAL, AND NOT WITH THE CASE FOR CONVICTION.

1. II:1: What do they say for the defense?

C. IN PROPERTY CASES THEY DECIDE BY A MAJORITY OF ONE, WHETHER FOR ACQUITTAL OR FOR CONVICTION, WHILE IN CAPITAL CASES THEY DECIDE BY A MAJORITY OF ONE FOR ACQUITTAL, BUT ONLY WITH A MAJORITY OF TWO JUDGES FOR CONVICTION.
IN PROPERTY CASES THEY REVERSE THE DECISION WHETHER IN FAVOR OF ACQUITTAL OR IN FAVOR OF CONVICTION, WHILE IN CAPITAL CASES THEY REVERSE THE DECISION SO AS TO FAVOR ACQUITTAL

1. III:1: An objection was raised on the basis of the following: If one judged a case, declaring a liable person to be free of liability, declaring the person free of liability to be liable, declaring what is clean to be unclean, declaring what is unclean to be clean, what he has done is done. But he pays compensation from his own funds (M. Bekh. 4:4D-F). Why not retract the decision, in line with M. 4:1G ?

    a. III:2: Gloss of a detail of the foregoing.

D. IN PROPERTY CASES ALL JUDGES AND EVEN DISCIPLES ARGUE EITHER FOR ACQUITTAL OR CONVICTION. IN CAPITAL CASES ALL ARGUE FOR ACQUITTAL, BUT ALL DO NOT ARGUE FOR CONVICTION.

1. IV:1: How on the basis of Scripture do we know that, if someone goes forth from court having been declared guilty, and one of the judges said, "I have arguments to offer in

behalf of a verdict of innocence," that we bring the convicted man back?

E.   ...BUT THEY DO NOT REVERSE THE DECISION SO AS TO FAVOR CONVICTION:

1.   V:1: Said R. Hiyya bar Abba said R. Yohanan, "And that applies if one has made a mistake about a matter about which the Sadducees do not concur something not in Scripture, but if one has erred in a matter about which the Sadducees concur which is to say, something actually written out in Scripture, then it is something you learn in school and there is no reason to reverse the conviction."

F.   IN CAPITAL CASES ALL ARGUE FOR ACQUITTAL, BUT ALL DO NOT ARGUE FOR CONVICTION:

1.   VI:1: "All" encompasses even the witnesses. May we say that the Mishnah-paragraph represents the view of R. Yosé b. R. Judah and not rabbis?

G.   IN PROPERTY CASES ONE WHO ARGUES FOR CONVICTION MAY ARGUE FOR ACQUITTAL, AND ONE WHO ARGUES FOR ACQUITTAL MAY ALSO ARGUE FOR CONVICTION. IN CAPITAL CASES THE ONE WHO ARGUES FOR CONVICTION MAY ARGUE FOR ACQUITTAL, BUT THE ONE WHO ARGUES FOR ACQUITTAL HAS NOT GOT THE POWER TO RETRACT AND TO ARGUE FOR CONVICTION.

1.   VII:1: Said Rab, "The rule applies only to the time of the give and take of argument in the case. But when the verdict has been reached, one who has argued in favor of innocence may retract and argue in favor of guilt."

a.   VII:2: Amplification of a tangential detail of the foregoing.

H.   IN PROPERTY CASES THEY TRY THE CASE BY DAY AND COMPLETE IT BY NIGHT:

1.   VIII:1: What is the scriptural basis for this rule?

2.   VIII:2: The Mishnah-passage before us does not accord with the view of R. Meir.

a.   VIII:3: There was a blind man in the vicinity of R. Yohanan, who would judge cases, and R. Yohanan did not object in any way.

I.   IN CAPITAL CASES THEY TRY THE CASE BY DAY AND COMPLETE IT THE FOLLOWING DAY.

1.   IX:1: What is the scriptural basis for this rule?

a.   IX:2: Further exegesis of a point tangential in the foregoing proof.

J.   IN PROPERTY CASES THEY COME TO A FINAL DECISION ON
      THE SAME DAY AS THE TRIAL ITSELF, WHETHER IT IS FOR
      ACQUITTAL OR CONVICTION. IN CAPITAL CASES THEY
      COME TO A FINAL DECISION FOR ACQUITTAL ON THE SAME
      DAY, BUT ON THE FOLLOWING DAY FOR CONVICTION:

      1. X:1: What is the scriptural basis for this rule?

K.   THEREFORE THEY DO NOT JUDGE CAPITAL CASES EITHER ON
      THE EVE OF THE SABBATH OR ON THE EVE OF A FESTIVAL:

      1. XI:1: What is the reason? Because it is impossible. How
          could someone do it? If someone were to try a case on
          Friday and complete the verdict on that day, perhaps they
          might find reason to convict the accused, in which case they
          would have to postpone the judgment overnight.

          a. XI:2: Secondary expansion of a tangential detail of the
              foregoing: Said R. Simeon b. Laqish to R. Yohanan, "The
              burial of a neglected corpse should override the
              restrictions of the Sabbath, on the basis of the following
              argument a fortiori: Now if the performance of the
              Temple cult, which overrides the Sabbath is set aside on
              account of the burial of a neglected corpse, the Sabbath,
              restrictions of which are abrogated for the Temple
              service, all the more so should be overridden for the
              burial of a neglected corpse.

L.   IN CASES INVOLVING QUESTIONS OF PROPERTY
      UNCLEANNESS AND CLEANNESS THEY BEGIN VOTING FROM
      THE ELDEST.

      1. XII:1: Said Rab, "I was among those who voted in the house
          of Rabbi, and it was from me that they began to count."

          a. XII:2: Further on the house of Rabbi.

M.   IN CAPITAL CASES THEY BEGIN FROM THE SIDE WITH THE
      YOUNGEST.

      1. XIII:1: What is the scriptural basis for this rule?

      2. XIII:2: Said Rab, "A person may teach his disciple the rule on
          capital offenses and then vote right along side of him in
          capital cases with master and disciple each having a separate
          vote."

      3. XIII:3: Said R. Abbahu speaking of M. 4:1-2), "There are ten
          points of difference in the rules governing trials for property
          cases from those for capital cases. And none of those
          differences pertains to the trial of an ox that is to be stoned,
          except for the requirement of a court of twenty-three judges,
          that alone."

N.   ALL ARE VALID TO ENGAGE IN THE JUDGMENT OF PROPERTY CASES:

    1.   XIV:1: What classification of persons does the specification of "all" serve to include?

O.   BUT ALL ARE NOT VALID TO ENGAGE IN THE JUDGMENT OF CAPITAL CASES, EXCEPT FOR PRIESTS, LEVITES, AND ISRAELITES WHO ARE SUITABLE TO MARRY INTO THE PRIESTHOOD.

    1.   XV:1: What is the reason for this rule?

XV. MISHNAH-TRACTATE SANHEDRIN 4:3-4

A.   THE SANHEDRIN WAS ARRANGED IN THE SHAPE OF A HALF OF A ROUND THRESHING-FLOOR THAT IS, AS AN AMPHITHEATER, SO THAT THE JUDGES SHOULD SEE ONE ANOTHER, AND TWO JUDGES' CLERKS STAND BEFORE THEM, ONE AT THE RIGHT AND ONE AT THE LEFT.

AND THEY WRITE DOWN THE ARGUMENTS OF THOSE WHO VOTE TO ACQUIT AND OF THOSE WHO VOTE TO CONVICT. R. JUDAH SAYS, "THREE: ONE WRITES THE OPINION OF THOSE WHO VOTE TO ACQUIT, ONE WRITES THE OPINION OF THOSE WHO VOTE TO CONVICT, AND THE THIRD WRITES THE OPINIONS BOTH OF THOSE WHO VOTE TO ACQUIT AND OF THOSE WHO VOTE TO CONVICT." AND THREE ROWS OF DISCIPLES OF SAGES SIT BEFORE THEM. EACH AND EVERY ONE KNOWS HIS PLACE. IF THEY FOUND NEED TO ORDAIN A DISCIPLE TO SERVE ON THE COURT, THEY ORDAINED ONE WHO WAS SITTING IN THE FIRST ROW. THEN ONE WHO WAS SITTING IN THE SECOND ROW JOINS THE FIRST ROW, AND ONE WHO WAS SITTING IN THE THIRD ROW MOVES UP TO THE SECOND ROW. AND THEY SELECT FOR THEMSELVES SOMEONE ELSE FROM THE CROWD AND SET HIM IN THE THIRD ROW. THE NEW DISCIPLE DID NOT TAKE A SEAT IN THE PLACE OF THE FIRST PARTY WHO HAD NOW JOINED IN THE COURT BUT IN THE PLACE THAT WAS APPROPRIATE FOR HIM AT THE END OF THE THIRD ROW.

    1.   I:1: What is the scriptural source for the rule at M. 4:3A?

        a.   I:2: Gloss of a detail tangential in the foregoing.

        b.   I:3: As above.

        c.   I:4: As above.

            I.   I:5: Illustrative story.

    2.   I:6: Said Abbayye, "We may infer from this rule that, when they move, all of them move."

XVI. MISHNAH-TRACTATE SANHEDRIN 4:5

A.   HOW DO THEY ADMONISH WITNESSES IN CAPITAL CASES? THEY WOULD BRING THEM IN AND ADMONISH THEM AS FOLLOWS: "PERHAPS IT IS YOUR INTENTION TO GIVE TESTIMONY

1.   I:1: Our rabbis have taught on Tannaite authority: What is the sense of "conjecture'? He says to them, "Perhaps this is what you saw: he was running after his fellow into a ruin with a sword in his hand. The victim ran in front of him into a ruin, and then the other went after him into the ruin. You went in after them and found the victim slain on the floor, with a knife in the hand of the murderer, dripping blood. If this is what you have seen, you have seen nothing you must be admonished that this is not valid evidence."

B.   ON THE BASIS OF SUPPOSITION, HEARSAY, OR OF WHAT ONE WITNESS HAS TOLD ANOTHER:

1.   II:1:It is in capital cases that we do not accept testimony based on supposition or conjecture. Lo, in the case of property cases, we do so.

C.   ...OR YOU MAY BE THINKING, 'WE HEARD IT FROM A RELIABLE PERSON'" OR, YOU MAY NOT KNOW THAT IN THE END WE ARE GOING TO INTERROGATE YOU WITH APPROPRIATE TESTS OF INTERROGATION AND EXAMINATION. YOU SHOULD KNOW THAT THE LAWS GOVERNING A TRIAL FOR PROPERTY CASES ARE DIFFERENT FROM THE LAWS GOVERNING A TRIAL FOR CAPITAL CASES. IN THE CASE OF A TRIAL FOR PROPERTY-CASES, A PERSON PAYS MONEY AND ACHIEVES ATONEMENT FOR HIMSELF. IN CAPITAL CASES THE ACCUSED'S BLOOD AND THE BLOOD OF ALL THOSE WHO WERE DESTINED TO BE BORN FROM HIM WHO WAS WRONGFULLY CONVICTED ARE HELD AGAINST HIM WHO TESTIFIES FALSELY TO THE END OF TIME. "FOR SO WE FIND IN THE CASE OF CAIN WHO SLEW HIS BROTHER, AS IT IS SAID, 'THE BLOODS OF YOUR BROTHER CRY' (GEN. 4:10). IT DOES NOT SAY, 'THE BLOOD OF YOUR BROTHER,' BUT, 'THE BLOODS OF YOUR BROTHER' – HIS BLOOD AND THE BLOOD OF ALL THOSE WHO WERE DESTINED TO BE BORN FROM HIM." ANOTHER MATTER: 'THE BLOODS OF YOUR BROTHER' – FOR HIS BLOOD WAS SPATTERED ON TREES AND STONES:

1.   III:1: Said R. Judah, son of R. Hiyya, "Gen. 4:10, 'The bloods of your brother cry...' teaches that Cain made on Abel, his brother, wound after wound, blow after blow, for he did not

know from which one the soul would go forth, until he came
to his neck."

    a.   III:2: Said R. Judah said Rab, "Exile atones for three
        things."

        I.   III:3: Judah and Hezekiah, sons of R. Hiyya, were
            seated at a meal before Rabbi and they were not
            saying anything. He said to the waiter, "Give more
            strong wine to the young men so that they will say
            something."

    c.   III:4: Said R. Hisda said Mar Uqba, and some say, said R.
        Hisda, Mari bar Mar expounded, "What is the meaning
        of the verse of Scripture, 'And so the Lord has hastened
        the evil and brought it upon us, for the Lord our God is
        righteous' (Dan. 9:14)? Because 'the Lord is righteous'
        'does he hasten the evil and bring it upon us'" "Indeed
        so. The Holy One, blessed be he, acted in a righteous
        way with Israel by bringing the exile of Zedekiah while
        the exile of Jechoniah was still alive.

D.   THEREFORE MAN WAS CREATED ALONE, TO TEACH YOU
       THAT WHOEVER DESTROYS A SINGLE ISRAELITE SOUL IS
       DEEMED BY SCRIPTURE AS IF HE HAD DESTROYED A WHOLE
       WORLD. AND WHOEVER SAVES A SINGLE SOUL IS DEEMED
       BY SCRIPTURE AS IF HE HAD SAVED A WHOLE WORLD.

    1.   IV:1: Our rabbis have taught on Tannaite authority: On what
        account was man created alone? So that the minim should
        not say, "There are many domains in heaven.'

E.   AND IT WAS ALSO FOR THE SAKE OF PEACE AMONG PEOPLE,
       SO THAT SOMEONE SHOULD NOT SAY TO HIS FELLOW, "MY
       FATHER IS GREATER THAN YOUR FATHER." AND IT WAS
       ALSO ON ACCOUNT OF THE MINIM, SO THAT THE MINIM
       SHOULD NOT SAY, "THERE ARE MANY DOMAINS IN
       HEAVEN."

       AND TO PORTRAY THE GRANDEUR OF THE HOLY ONE,
       BLESSED BE HE. FOR A PERSON MINTS MANY COINS WITH A
       SINGLE SEAL, AND THEY ARE ALL ALIKE ONE ANOTHER, BUT
       THE KING OF KINGS OF KINGS, THE HOLY ONE, BLESSED BE
       HE, MINTED ALL HUMAN BEINGS WITH THAT SEAL OF HIS
       WITH WHICH HE MADE THE FIRST PERSON, YET NOT ONE OF
       THEM IS LIKE ANYONE ELSE:

    1.   V:1: Our rabbis have taught on Tannaite authority: Why was
        he created one and alone? To show the grandeur of the king
        of the kings of kings, blessed be he. For if a man mints many
        coins with one mold, all are alike. But the Holy One, blessed

be he, mints every man with the mold of the first man for with a single seal, he created the entire world, and not one of them is like another from a single seal all those many diverse seals have come forth

F.   THE CREATION OF MAN. THE MINIM. DEBATES WITH UNBELIEVERS. THE EMPEROR AND THE PATRIARCH.

1.   V:2: It has been taught on Tannaite authority: R. Meir would say, "The first man was formed out of dust gathered from every part of the world."

2.   V:3: Said R. Yohanan bar Hanina, "The day on which Adam was made was twelve hours. At the first hour the dust for making him was gathered together. At the second hour he was made kneaded into an unformed mass. At the third hour his limbs were shaped. At the fourth hour breath was poured into him. At the fifth hour he stood on his feet. At the sixth hour he named the beasts. At the seventh hour Eve as mated with him. At the eighth hour they went to bed two and came away from bed four. At the ninth hour he was commanded not to eat from the tree. At the tenth hour he went rotten. At the eleventh hour he was judged. At the twelfth hour he was sent off and went his way."

3.   V:4: Said R. Judah said Rab, "When the Holy One, blessed be he, proposed to create man, he created a group of ministering angels. He said to them, 'Shall we make man in our image?' They said to him, 'Lord of the ages, what sort of things will he do?' He said to them, 'These are the sorts of the things he will do.' They said before him, 'Lord of the ages, 'What is man that you are mindful of him, and the son of man that you think of him' (Ps. 8:5)?"

4.   V:5: Said R. Judah said Rab, "The first man stretched from one end of the world to the other, as it is said, 'Since the day that God created man upon the earth, even the one end of heaven to the other' (Deut. 4:32). When he turned rotten, the Holy One, blessed be he, put his hand on him and cut him down to size."

5.   V:6: And said R. Judah said Rab, "The first man spoke Aramaic."

6.   V:7: And R. Judah said Rab said, "The first Man was a min heretic."

7.   V:8: There we have learned in the Mishnah: R. Eliezer says, "Be diligent to study the Torah and know what to say to an unbeliever" M. Abot 2:14. Said R. Yohanan, "That rule

applies to a gentile unbeliever. But as to an Israelite unbeliever, all the more is he beyond the rule."

8. V:9: Said R. Yohanan, "In every passage in which the minim have found evidence for their heresy, in which God is spoken of in the plural, a refutation for their position is provided right at hand."

9. V:10: Said R. Nahman, "If someone knows how to refute the position of the minim as well as does R. Idit, let him undertake to refute them, and if not, he should not reply to them."

10. V:11: A min said to R. Ishmael b. R. Yosé, "It is written, 'Then the Lord caused to rain upon Sodom and Gomorrah brimstone and fire from the Lord' (Gen. 19:24). It should have said, 'From him.'"

11. V:12: Said the emperor to Rabban Gamaliel, "Your God is a thief, for it is written, 'And the Lord God caused a deep sleep to fall upon Adam, and he slept, and he took one of his ribs' (Gen. 2:21)."

12. V:13: The emperor said to Rabban Gamaliel, "I know what your God is doing."

13. V:14: The emperor said to Rabban Gamaliel, "It is written, 'He counts the number of the stars' (Ps. 147:4). What's the big deal? I can count the stars."

14. V:15: The emperor said to Rabban Gamaliel, "He who created the mountains did not create the wind, as it is said, 'For lo, there is one who forms mountains and one who creates wind' (Amos 4:13)."

15. V:16: Said a magus to Amemar, "The part of you from the middle and above belongs to Hormiz, and the part of you from the middle and downward belongs to Ahormiz."

16. V:17: Caesar said to R. Tanhum, "Come, we shall all be one people." He said, "Well and good. But we who are circumcised cannot become like you, so you circumcise and become like us."

17. V:18: An emperor said to Rabban Gamaliel, "You say that wherever there are ten, the Presence of God comes to rest. How many Presences of God are there?"

18. V:19: Said a min to R. Abbahu, "Your God is a joker ridiculing the prophets. For he said to Ezekiel, 'Lie down on your left side' (Ez. 4:4) and it is written, 'Lie on your right side' (Ez. 4:6)."

19. V:20: Said a min to R. Abbahu, "Your God is a priest. For it is written, 'That they take heave-offering for me' (Ex. 25:2)

and that sort of offering is assigned to priests, so God is a priest. Now when he buried Moses, in what did he immerse to remove the corpse-uncleanness he contracted through the burial?"

20. V:21: Said a min to R. Abina, "It is written, 'Who is like your people, Israel, a unique people on earth' (2 Sam. 7:23)? What is so good about you? You are joined in the same category with us, for it is written, 'All the nations are as nothing before him' (Is. 40:17)."

21. V:22: R. Eleazar contrasted verses, "It is written, 'The Lord is good to all' (Ps. 145:9), and it is written, 'The Lord is good to those who wait for him' (Lam. 3:25). The matter may be compared to the case of a man who has an orchard. When he waters it, he waters the whole thing. When he prunes it, he prunes only the good trees."

G. **THEREFORE EVERYONE IS OBLIGATED TO MAINTAIN, "ON MY ACCOUNT THE WORLD WAS CREATED." NOW PERHAPS YOU WITNESSES WOULD LIKE NOW TO SAY, "WHAT BUSINESS HAVE WE GOT WITH THIS TROUBLE?" BUT IT ALREADY HAS BEEN WRITTEN, "HE BEING A WITNESS, WHETHER HE HAS SEEN OR KNOWN, IF HE DOES NOT SPEAK IT, THEN HE SHALL BEAR HIS INIQUITY" (LEV. 5:1). AND PERHAPS YOU MIGHT WANT TO CLAIM, "WHAT BUSINESS IS IT OF OURS TO CONVICT THIS MAN OF A CAPITAL CRIME?" BUT HAS IT NOT ALREADY BEEN SAID, "WHEN THE WICKED PERISH THERE IS REJOICING" (PROV. 11:10).**

H. "AND THERE WENT OUT A SONG THROUGHOUT THE HOST" (1 KGS. 22:36): EXEGESIS OF THE STORY OF AHAB'S DEATH AT RAMOTH IN GILEAD.

1. VI:1: "And there went out a song throughout the host" (1 Kgs. 22:36) at Ahab's death at Ramoth in Gilead. Said R. Aha b. Hanina, "'When the wicked perish, there is song' (Prov. 11:10). When Ahab, b. Omri, perished, there was song."

2. VI:2: "And dogs licked his blood and harlots washed themselves, according to the word of the Lord which he spoke" (1 Kgs. 22:38): Said R. Eleazar, "This was to carry out two visions, one of Micaiah, the other of Elijah."

3. VI:3: It is written, "And Ahab called Obadiah, who was in charge of the household. Now Obadiah fear the Lord very much" (1 Kgs. 18:3): What did he say?

4. VI:4: Said R. Isaac, "On what account did Obadiah have the merit of receiving prophecy? Because he hid a hundred prophets in a cave. For it is said, 'For it was so when Jezebel

cut off the prophets of the Lord that Obadiah took a hundred
prophets and hid them, fifty to a cave' (1 Kgs. 18:4)."

5. VI:5: "The vision of Obadiah. Thus said the Lord God
concerning Edom" (Obad. 1:1): What made Obadiah in
particular the appropriate choice of a prophet to speak
against Edom?

6. VI:6: "Then he took his first-born son, who should have
reigned in his place, and offered him for a burnt offering
upon the wall" (2 Kgs. 3:27): Rab and Samuel: One said, "It
was an offering for the sake of heaven." The other said, "It
was an offering to idolatry."

7. VI:7: "And they departed from him and returned to the
earth" (2 Kgs. 3:27): Said R. Hanina bar Pappa, "At that
moment the wicked ones of Israel descended to the lowest
rung of depravity."

XVII. MISHNAH-TRACTATE SANHEDRIN 5:1-5

A. **THEY INTERROGATED THE WITNESS WITH SEVEN POINTS OF
INTERROGATION: (1) IN WHAT SEPTENNATE? (2) IN WHAT
YEAR? (3) IN WHAT MONTH? (4) ON WHAT DAY OF THE
MONTH? (5) ON WHAT DAY OF THE WEEK? (6) AT WHAT
TIME? (7) IN WHAT PLACE? .**

1. I:1: What is the source of this rule concerning seven points of
interrogation?

2. I:2: Continuation of the foregoing, exegetical argument: Since
trials covering idolatry, punished by stoning, and perjury,
punished by decapitation in the case of perjury in a murder
trial, now have been shown to require cross-examination
through seven questions, we proceed to deal with other
cases, in which the two further modes of inflicting the death
penalty are invoked. We may infer the requirement to cross-
examine witnesses in cases in which the death penalty is
through strangulation, on the basis of an argument a fortiori
from the requirement of the same in cases ending in the
death penalty through stoning or decapitation. The former
are regarded as milder modes of execution than
strangulation. And we infer by an argument a fortiori that
the same mode of careful cross examination is required for
cases involving the death penalty of burning, on the basis of
the fact the same is required in cases ending in stoning.
Here, stoning is regarded as more severe mode of execution
than burning; decapitation is less severe. If we require cross
examination for the one, we surely should do so in the other.

B.   R. YOSÉ SAYS, "(1) ON WHAT DAY? (2) AT WHAT TIME? (3) IN
WHAT PLACE:"

1.   II:1: It has been taught on Tannaite authority: Said R. Yosé to
sages, "In accord with your view, if someone came and said,
'Last night he killed him,' one says to him, 'In what
septennate? In what year? In what month? On what day of
the month?'" They said to him, "But in accord with your
position, if someone came and said, 'He killed him just now,'
one still has to say to him, 'On what day? At what time? In
what place?"

C.   "DO YOU KNOW HIM? (5) DID YOU WARN HIM OF THE
CONSEQUENCES OF HIS DEED? IN CASE OF ONE WHO
WORSHIPS AN IDOL, WHOM DID HE WORSHIP, AND WITH
WHAT DID HE WORSHIP THE IDOL?"

1.   III:1: Our rabbis have taught on Tannaite authority: "Do you
know him? Did he kill a gentile? Did he kill an Israelite?
Did you admonish him? Did he accept the admonishment?
Did he Shachter: admit his liability to the death penalty? Did
he commit murder within the span of the utterance that he
made, admitting his liability?

2.   III:2: Said Ulla, "How on the basis of the Torah do we know
that it is necessary to admonish the felon prior to his act, so
that we may know that what he did was with full knowledge
of the consequences?"

3.   III:3: "Did he admit his liability to the death penalty"? How
do we know that this is a requirement?"

4.   III:4: Said R. Hanan, "Witnesses who have testified against a
betrothed maiden that she has been unfaithful, who then
were proved to have been formed conspiracy for perjury, are
not to put to death. Though had the woman been found
guilty, she would have been put to death, in this case the
perjurers do not suffer retaliation. Why not? Because they
can plead, "Our intent was to prohibit her from
consummating the marriage to her betrothed husband but
not to have her put to death."

5.   III:5: Said R. Hisda, "If one said, 'He killed him with a
sword,' and the other said, 'He killed him with a dagger,'
this is 'not certain' testimony in line with Deut. 13:15, 17:4:
'Behold, if it be truth and the thing certain'. If one says, 'His
clothing was black,' and the other says, 'His clothing was
white,' lo, this is 'certain.' These statements do not refer to
the act, but only to the circumstances."

D.   THE MORE THEY EXPAND THE INTERROGATION, THE MORE
      IS ONE TO BE PRAISED. THE PRECEDENT IS AS FOLLOWS:
      BEN ZAKKAI EXAMINED A WITNESS AS TO THE CHARACTER
      OF THE STALKS OF FIGS UNDER WHICH THE INCIDENT TOOK
      PLACE.

  1.   IV:1: If we should propose that it is R. Yohanan ben Zakkai,
       did he ever sit in a sanhedrin that tried a murder case

E.   THE PRECEDENT IS AS FOLLOWS: BEN ZAKKAI EXAMINED A
      WITNESS AS TO THE CHARACTER OF THE STALKS OF FIGS
      UNDER WHICH THE INCIDENT TOOK PLACE.

  1.   V:1: What is the meaning of, "even if both of them say ..."?
       Surely it is obvious that, if one of them says, "I don't know,"
       the testimony is validated, so if both of them say so, the
       testimony obviously will be valid? For if one is ignorant on a
       certain point, the other's knowledge therefore is valueless.
       Hence whatever evidence is valid when one is ignorant is
       also valid when both are ignorant.

F.   WHAT IS THE DIFFERENCE BETWEEN INTERROGATION
      ABOUT THE DATE, TIME, AND PLACE AND EXAMINATION
      ABOUT   THE   CIRCUMSTANCES?   IN THE CASE OF
      INTERROGATION, IF ONE WITNESS SAYS, "I DON'T KNOW
      THE ANSWER," THE TESTIMONY OF THE WITNESS IS NULL. IN
      THE CASE OF EXAMINATION, IF ONE OF THE WITNESSES SAYS,
      "I DON'T KNOW," OR EVEN IF BOTH OF THEM SAY, "WE
      DON'T KNOW," THEIR TESTIMONY NONETHELESS STANDS.
      ALL THE SAME ARE INTERROGATION AND EXAMINATION:
      WHEN THE WITNESSES CONTRADICT ONE ANOTHER, THEIR
      TESTIMONY IS NULL.

  1.   VI:1: R. Kahana and R. Safra were repeating rules of the
       sanhedrin in the house of Rabbah. Rami bar Hama met
       them. He said to them, "What is it that you people say about
       the laws of the sanhedrin at the house of Rabbah?" They
       said to him, "And what should we say about the rules of
       sanhedrin by themselves without respect to what Rabbah
       has to teach us? What's your problem?" He said to them,
       "On the basis of this passage: What is the difference between
       interrogation about the date, time and place and examination
       about the circumstances, in the case of interrogation, if one
       witness says, 'I don't know the answer,' the testimony of the
       witness is null. In the case of examination, if one of the
       witnesses says, 'I don't know,' or even if both of them say,
       'We don't know,' their testimony nonetheless stands, I have
       the following problem: since the requirement to conduct

both procedures rests on the authority of the Torah, what validates the distinction between interrogation and examination?"

G. IF ONE OF THE WITNESSES SAYS, "IT WAS ON THE SECOND OF THE MONTH," AND ONE OF THE WITNESSES SAYS, "IT WAS ON THE THIRD OF THE MONTH," THEIR TESTIMONY STANDS, FOR ONE OF THEM MAY KNOW ABOUT THE INTERCALATION OF THE MONTH, AND THE OTHER ONE MAY NOT KNOW ABOUT THE INTERCALATION OF THE MONTH. IF ONE OF THEM SAYS, "ON THE THIRD," AND ONE OF THEM SAYS, "ON THE FIFTH," THEIR TESTIMONY IS NULL.

   1. VII:1: Until what day of the month do we assume that people may not know whether it is a full month of thirty days or a defective one of twenty-nine days?

H. TOPICAL APPENDIX ON RECITING THE BLESSING OVER THE NEW MOON

   1. VII:2: And said R. Aha bar Hanina said R. Assi said R. Yohanan, "Up to what point in the month do people say the blessing over the new month?

   2. VII:3: And said R. Aha bar Hanina said R. Assi said R. Yohanan, "Whoever says a blessing for the new moon at the proper time is as if he receives the Presence of God.'

   3. VII:4: Tannaite authority of the house of R. Ishmael stated, "If Israel had had the sole merit of receiving the presence of their father in heaven month by month, it would have been enough for them."

   4. VII:5: Said R. Aha to R. Ashi, "In the West, they say the blessing, 'Blessed ... is he who renews the months.'"

     a. VII:6: "For with wise advice you shall make your war" (Prov. 24:6): Said R. Aha bar Hanina said R. Assi said R. Yohanan, "In whom do you find ability to conduct the 'war of the Torah' of rigorous reasoning? He who possesses 'the wise advice' of Mishnah-learning."

I. IF ONE OF THEM SAYS, "AT TWO," AND ONE OF THEM SAYS, "AT THREE," THEIR TESTIMONY STANDS. IF ONE OF THEM SAYS, "AT THREE," AND ONE OF THEM SAYS, "AT FIVE," THEIR TESTIMONY IS NULL. R. JUDAH SAYS, "IT STANDS."

IF ONE OF THEM SAYS, "AT FIVE," AND ONE OF THEM SAYS, "AT SEVEN," THEIR TESTIMONY IS NULL. FOR AT FIVE THE SUN IS AT THE EAST, AND AT SEVEN THE SUN IS AT THE WEST.

   1. VIII:1: Said R. Shimi bar Ashi, "The rule applies only to differences in hours of the day for there is a margin of error.

But if one of them says, 'It was before dawn,' and the other says, 'It was after dawn,' their testimony is null."

J.   AND AFTERWARD THEY BRING IN THE SECOND WITNESS AND EXAMINE HIM. IF THEIR STATEMENTS CHECK OUT, THEY BEGIN THE ARGUMENT IN FAVOR OF ACQUITTAL. IF ONE OF THE WITNESSES SAID, "I HAVE SOMETHING TO SAY IN FAVOR OF ACQUITTAL," OR IF ONE OF THE DISCIPLES SAID, "I HAVE SOMETHING TO SAY IN FAVOR OF CONVICTION," THEY SHUT HIM UP. IF ONE OF THE DISCIPLES SAID, "I HAVE SOMETHING TO SAY IN FAVOR OF ACQUITTAL," THEY PROMOTE HIM AND SEAT HIM AMONG THE JUDGES, AND HE DID NOT GO DOWN FROM THAT POSITION THAT ENTIRE DAY. IF THERE IS SUBSTANCE IN WHAT HE SAYS, THEY PAY ATTENTION TO HIM. AND EVEN IF THE ACCUSED SAID, "I HAVE SOMETHING TO SAY IN MY OWN BEHALF," THEY PAY ATTENTION TO HIM, SO LONG AS THERE IS SUBSTANCE IN WHAT HE HAS TO SAY.

1.   IX:1: That day and no more?

K.   IF THEY FOUND HIM INNOCENT, THEY SENT HIM AWAY. IF NOT, THEY POSTPONE JUDGING HIM TILL THE NEXT DAY. THEY WOULD GO OFF IN PAIRS AND WOULD NOT EAT VERY MUCH
OR DRINK WINE THAT ENTIRE DAY,
AND THEY WOULD DISCUSS THE MATTER ALL THAT NIGHT. AND THE NEXT DAY THEY WOULD GET UP AND COME TO COURT. THE ONE WHO FAVORS ACQUITTAL SAYS, "I DECLARED HIM INNOCENT YESTERDAY, AND I STAND MY GROUND AND DECLARE HIM INNOCENT TODAY." AND THE ONE WHO DECLARES HIM GUILTY SAYS, "I DECLARED HIM GUILTY YESTERDAY AND I STAND MY GROUND AND DECLARE HIM GUILTY TODAY." THE ONE WHO ARGUES IN FAVOR OF GUILT MAY NOW ARGUE IN FAVOR OF ACQUITTAL, BUT THE ONE WHO ARGUES IN FAVOR OF INNOCENCE MAY NOT NOW GO AND ARGUE IN FAVOR OF GUILT. IF THEY MADE AN ERROR IN SOME MATTER, THE TWO JUDGES' CLERKS REMIND THEM OF WHAT HAD BEEN SAID. IF THEY NOW FOUND HIM INNOCENT, THEY SENT HIM OFF. AND IF NOT, THEY ARISE FOR A VOTE. IF TWELVE VOTE FOR ACQUITTAL AND ELEVEN VOTE FOR CONVICTION, HE IS ACQUITTED. IF TWELVE VOTE FOR CONVICTION AND ELEVEN VOTE FOR ACQUITTAL, AND EVEN IF ELEVEN VOTE FOR ACQUITTAL AND ELEVEN VOTE FOR CONVICTION, BUT ONE SAYS, "I HAVE NO OPINION," AND EVEN IF TWENTY-

TWO VOTE FOR ACQUITTAL OR VOTE FOR CONVICTION, BUT ONE SAYS, "I HAVE NO OPINION, THEY ADD TO THE NUMBER OF THE JUDGES. HOW MANY DO THEY ADD? TWO BY TWO, UNTIL THERE ARE SEVENTY-ONE. IF THIRTY-SIX VOTE FOR ACQUITTAL AND THIRTY-FIVE VOTE FOR CONVICTION, HE IS ACQUITTED:

    1.   X:1: What is the reason for not drinking wine?

L.   IF THIRTY SIX VOTE FOR CONVICTION AND THIRTY-FIVE VOTE FOR ACQUITTAL, THEY DEBATE THE MATTER, UNTIL ONE OF THOSE WHO VOTES FOR CONVICTION ACCEPTS THE ARGUMENTS OF THOSE WHO VOTE FOR ACQUITTAL.

    1.   XI:1: And if they do not accept the arguments?

    2.   XI:2: Our rabbis have taught on Tannaite authority: In property cases the court may rule, "The case is stale." In capital cases the court may not rule, "The case is stale (T. San. 7:7A-B).

XVIII. MISHNAH-TRACTATE SANHEDRIN 6:1A-G

A.   WHEN THE TRIAL IS OVER, AND THE FELON IS CONVICTED, THEY TAKE HIM OUT TO STONE HIM. THE PLACE OF STONING WAS WELL OUTSIDE THE COURT, AS IT IS SAID, "BRING FORTH HIM WHO CURSED TO A PLACE OUTSIDE THE CAMP" (LEV. 24:14).

    1.   I:1: Now was the place of stoning merely outside the court?

    2.   I:2: What is the scriptural basis for the rule that the place of stoning must be outside the three camps?

        a.   I:3: Further proof of the same proposition.

        b.   I:4: As above.

B.   ONE PERSON STANDS AT THE DOOR OF THE COURTHOUSE, WITH FLAGS IN HIS HAND, AND A HORSEMAN IS SOME DISTANCE FROM HIM, SO THAT HE IS ABLE TO SEE HIM:

    1.   II:1: Said R. Huna, "It is obvious to me that the same rule applies to the stone which is used for the stoning, the tree on which the corpse is hung, the sword with which the criminal is put to death, and the scarf with which he is strangled. All of them are paid for by the funds of the community. What is the reason? Because we cannot say to a man to go and supply his own property so that he may be put to death."

C.   IF ONE OF THE JUDGES SAID, "I HAVE SOMETHING TO SAY IN FAVOR OF ACQUITTAL," THE ONE AT THE DOOR WAVES THE FLAGS, AND THE HORSEMAN RACES OFF AND STOPS THE EXECUTION:

1. III:1: R. Aha bar Huna asked R. Sheshet," If one of the disciples said, 'I have an argument to make in behalf of a verdict of innocence,' and then the disciple was struck dumb, what is the law?"

D. AND EVEN IF THE CONVICTED PARTY SAYS, "I HAVE SOMETHING TO SAY IN FAVOR OF MY OWN ACQUITTAL," THEY BRING HIM BACK, EVEN FOUR OR FIVE TIMES, SO LONG AS THERE IS SUBSTANCE IN WHAT HE HAS TO SAY

1. IV:1: Must there be substance in what he has to say even the first and the second time?
2. IV:2: How do the judges know whether or not there is substance?

XIX. MISHNAH-TRACTATE SANHEDRIN 6:1H-J

A. IF THEY THEN FOUND HIM INNOCENT, THEY DISMISS HIM, AND IF NOT, HE GOES OUT TO BE STONED.

1. I:1: Said Abbayye, "And it is necessary to say at M. 6:1J, 'On such and such a day, at such and such an hour, in such and such a place.' Perhaps there are people who have knowledge of the matter and they will come and prove the witnesses against the man to be perjurers."

B. AND A HERALD GOES BEFORE HIM, CRYING OUT, "MR. SO-AND-SO, SON OF MR. SO-AND-SO, IS GOING OUT TO BE STONED BECAUSE HE COMMITTED SUCH-AND-SUCH A TRANSGRESSION, AND MR. SO-AND-SO AND MR. SO-AND-SO ARE THE WITNESSES AGAINST HIM. NOW ANYONE WHO KNOWS GROUNDS FOR ACQUITTAL – LET HIM COME AND SPEAK IN HIS BEHALF!"

1. II:1: Just before the execution, but not prior to that time. This implies, only immediately before the execution, but not previous thereto. In contradiction to this it was taught: On the eve of the Passover Yeshu was hanged. For forty days before the execution took place, a herald went forth and cried, 'He is going forth to be stoned because he has practiced sorcery and enticed Israel to apostasy. Any one who can say anything in his favor, let him come forward and plead on his behalf.' But since nothing was brought forward in his favor he was hanged on the eve of the Passover!

   a. II:2: Exegesis of a verse cited in the foregoing.

XX. MISHNAH-TRACTATE SANHEDRIN 6:2

A. WHEN HE WAS TEN CUBITS FROM THE PLACE OF STONING, THEY SAY TO HIM, "CONFESS," FOR IT IS USUAL FOR THOSE

ABOUT TO BE PUT TO DEATH TO CONFESS. FOR WHOEVER CONFESSES HAS A SHARE IN THE WORLD TO COME. FOR SO WE FIND CONCERNING ACHAN, TO WHOM JOSHUA SAID, "MY SON, I PRAY YOU, GIVE GLORY TO THE LORD, THE GOD OF ISRAEL, AND CONFESS TO HIM, AND TELL ME NOW WHAT YOU HAVE DONE; HIDE IT NOT FROM ME. AND ACHAN ANSWERED JOSHUA AND SAID, TRULY HAVE I SINNED AGAINST THE LORD, THE GOD OF ISRAEL, AND THUS AND THUS I HAVE DONE" (JOSH. 7:19):

1. I:1: The word, "I pray you," at Josh. 7:19 means only supplication. When the Holy One, blessed be he, said to Joshua, "Israel has sinned" (Josh. 7:11), he said to him, "Lord of the world, Who sinned?" He said to him, "Am I a squealer? Go and cast lots."

2. I:2: This matter of sins such as Achan's that have been concealed and then revealed is subject to dispute among Tannaite authorities: "The hidden things belong to the Lord our God, but the things that are revealed belong to us and our children for ever" (Deut. 29:28): Why in the Hebrew version are the words "to us and to our children" as well as the first letter of the word "for ever" dotted on the top? "This teaches that punishment was not inflicted on account of hidden sins until Israel had crossed the Jordan," the words of R. Judah.

3. I:3: "Yes, they have even transgressed my covenant which I have commanded them, yes, they have even taken of the devoted thing and have also stolen it, and dissembled also, and they have even put it among their own property" (Josh. 7:11): Said R. Ilaa in the name of R. Judah bar Misparta, "This teaches that Achan violated all five books of the Torah, for the word 'yes' 'even' is used five times."

4. I:4: "And because he has wrought a wanton deed in Israel" (Josh. 7:19): Said R. Abba bar Zabeda, "This teaches that Achan had sexual relations with a betrothed girl. It is written here, 'Because he has wrought a wanton deed," and it is written elsewhere, 'For she has wrought a wanton deed in Israel' (Deut. 22:21)."

5. I:5: Said the exilarch to R. Huna, "It is written, 'And Joshua took Achan the son of Zerah and the silver and the mantle and the wedge of gold and his sons and his daughters and his oxen and his asses and his sheep and his tent and all that he had' (Josh. 7:24). While he had sinned, how had his sons and daughters sinned?"

6. I:6: And they burned them with fire and stoned them with
    stones" (Josh. 7:25): By two modes of inflicting the death
    penalty?

7. I:7: "And I saw among the spoil a goodly mantle of Shinar
    and two hundred shekels of silver" (Josh. 7:21): Rab said, "It
    was Shachter: a silk mantle." Samuel said, "It was a cloak
    dyed with alum."

8. I:8: "And they laid them down before the Lord" (Josh. 7:23):
    Said R. Nahman, "He came and threw them down before the
    Lord. He said, 'Lord of the world, on account of these will as
    many people as constitute a majority of the great sanhedrin
    thirty-six of seventy-one be put to death?"

9. I:9: Said R. Nahman said Rab, "What is the sense of the verse
    of Scripture, 'The poor uses entreaties, but the rich answers
    insolently' (Prov. 18:23)? 'The poor uses entreaties' refers to
    Moses. 'The rich answers insolently' refers to Joshua."

10. I:10: "And the Lord said to Joshua, Get you up" (Josh. 7:10):
    R. Shila expounded this verse, "Said the Holy one blessed be
    he to him, 'Your sin is more weighty than theirs. For I
    commanded, "And it shall be when you have passed over
    the Jordan you shall set up these stones" (Deut. 27:4), but
    you went a distance of sixty miles to Gerizim and Ebal after
    crossing the Jordan before setting them up.'"

11. I:11: "And it came to pass when Joshua was by Jericho that
    he lifted up his eyes and looked ... And he said, No, but I am
    captain of the host of the Lord, I am now come. And Joshua
    fell on his face to the earth and bowed down" (Josh. 5:13-14):
    How did he do this? And has not R. Yohanan said, "It is
    forbidden for someone to greet his fellow by night, for we
    take account of the possibility that it might be a shade"? So
    how did Joshua greet the man and talk with him?

12. I:12: Said Abbayye to R. Dimi, "How in the West do you
    apply this verse: 'Go not forth hastily to strife, for what will
    you do in the end of it, when your neighbor has put you to
    shame. Debate your cause with your neighbor, but do not
    reveal the secrets of another' (Prov. 25:8-9)?" He said to him,
    "When the Holy One, blessed be he, said to him, 'Go and tell
    Israel, An Amorite was your father, and a Hittite was your
    mother' (Ez. 16:3), the Shachter: intercessory spirit Gabriel
    said before the Holy One, blessed be he, 'Lord of the world,
    if Abraham and Sarah come and stand before them, will you
    speak this way to them and humiliate them? '"Debate your

cause with your neighbor, but do not reveal the secret of another!'"

B.   **AND HOW DO WE KNOW THAT HIS CONFESSION ACHIEVED ATONEMENT FOR HIM? FOR IT IS SAID, "AND JOSHUA SAID, WHY HAVE YOU TROUBLED US? THE LORD WILL TROUBLE YOU THIS DAY" (JOSH. 7:25):**

1.   II:1: And how do we know that his confession achieved atonement for him? For it is said, "And Joshua said, Why have you troubled us? The Lord will trouble you this day" (Josh. 7:25).

C.   **THIS DAY YOU WILL BE TROUBLED, BUT YOU WILL NOT BE TROUBLED IN THE WORLD TO COME:**

1.   III:1: And it is written, "And the sons of Zerah are Zimri, Ethan, Heman, Calcol, Darda, five in all" (1 Chr. 2:6). What is the sense of "five in all"?

D.   **AND IF HE DOES NOT KNOW HOW TO CONFESS, THEY SAY TO HIM, "SAY AS FOLLOWS: 'LET MY DEATH BE ATONEMENT FOR ALL OF MY TRANSGRESSIONS.'" R. JUDAH SAYS, "IF HE KNEW THAT HE HAD BEEN SUBJECTED TO PERJURY, HE SAYS, 'LET MY DEATH BY ATONEMENT FOR ALL MY SINS, EXCEPT FOR THIS PARTICULAR SIN OF WHICH I HAVE BEEN CONVICTED BY FALSE TESTIMONY!'" THEY SAID TO HIM, "IF SO, THEN EVERYONE IS GOING TO SAY THAT, SO AS TO CLEAR HIMSELF."**

1.   IV:1: And why not let them clear themselves?

2.   IV:2: Our rabbis have taught on Tannaite authority: There was the case of a man who went out to be executed. He said, "If I have committed this sin, then let my death not be atonement for all my sins. But if I did not commit this sin, let my death be atonement for all my sins, and the court and all Israel are guiltless, but let the witnesses against me not enjoy forgiveness forever."

XXI.   MISHNAH-TRACTATE SANHEDRIN 6:3

A.   **WHEN HE WAS FOUR CUBITS FROM THE PLACE OF STONING, THEY REMOVE HIS CLOTHES. "IN THE CASE OF A MAN, THEY COVER HIM UP IN FRONT, AND IN THE CASE OF A WOMAN, THEY COVER HER UP IN FRONT AND BEHIND," THE WORDS OF R. JUDAH. AND SAGES SAY, "A MAN IS STONED NAKED, BUT A WOMAN IS NOT STONED NAKED."**

1.   I:1: Our rabbis have taught on Tannaite authority: "When he was four cubits from the place of stoning, they remove his clothes. "In the case of a man, they cover him up in front in

part, and in the case of a woman, in front and in back in part. For a woman is wholly subject to licentious thoughts," the words of R. Judah T. adds: which he said in the name of R. Eliezer. And sages say, "A man is stoned naked, but a woman is not stoned naked" (T. San. 9:6B-D).

2. I:2: Does this then imply that rabbis take account of licentious thoughts, while R. Judah does not?

XXII. MISHNAH-TRACTATE SANHEDRIN 6:4A-G

A. THE PLACE OF STONING WAS TWICE THE HEIGHT OF A MAN:

1. I:1: It has been taught on Tannaite authority: And with his own height, lo, the place of stoning was three heights of a man (T. San. 9:6F).

B. ONE OF THE WITNESSES WOULD PUSH HIM OVER FROM THE HIPS, SO HARD THAT HE TURNED UPWARD IN HIS FALL. HE TURNED HIM OVER ON HIS HIPS AGAIN TO SEE WHETHER HE HAD DIED. IF HE HAD DIED THEREBY, THAT SUFFICED.

1. II:1: Our rabbis have taught: How do we know that the death penalty is executed by throwing someone down? Scripture says, "And he shall be cast down" (Ex. 19:13). And how do we know that the death penalty is executed by stoning? Scripture says, "He shall be stoned" (Ex. 19:13) Cf. Deut. 22:24. And how do we know that it is executed both by stoning and by throwing down? Scripture says, "Stoning, he shall be stoned or thrown down" (Ex. 19:13).

C. IF NOT, THE SECOND WITNESS WOULD TAKE A STONE AND PUT IT ON HIS HEART. IF HE DIED THEREBY, IT SUFFICED.

1. III:1: Takes it? All by himself?! And has it not been taught on Tannaite authority: R. Simeon b. Eleazar says, "There was a stone there, a load so heavy that it was a burden for two to carry. One would take it and put it on his heart. If he died thereby, it sufficed" (T. San. 9:6G-H).

D. AND IF NOT, STONING HIM IS THE DUTY OF ALL ISRAELITES, AS IT IS SAID, "THE HAND OF THE WITNESSES SHALL BE FIRST UPON HIM TO PUT HIM TO DEATH, AND AFTERWARD THE HAND OF ALL THE PEOPLE" (DEUT. 17:7).

1. IV:1: But has it not been taught on Tannaite authority: It was never necessary for someone to do it a second time.

2. IV:2: Said Samuel, "If after they have testified, the hand of the witnesses should be cut off, the condemned is exempt from the penalty of stoning."

XXIII. MISHNAH-TRACTATE SANHEDRIN 6:4H-M

A. "ALL THOSE WHO ARE STONED ARE HUNG ON A TREE AFTERWARD," THE WORDS OF R. ELIEZER. AND SAGES SAY, "ONLY THE BLASPHEMER AND THE ONE WHO WORSHIPS AN IDOL ARE HUNG."

1. I:1: Our rabbis have taught on Tannaite authority: "And if he be put to death, then you shall hang him on a tree" (Deut. 21:22). Might one not think that all those who are put to death are hung? Scripture states, "For he is hanged because of a curse against God" (Deut. 21:23). "Just as the one who blasphemes is executed by stoning, so all who are subject to execution by stoning are hung," the words of R. Eliezer =M.6:4H.

B. "AS TO A MAN, THEY HANG HIM FACING THE PEOPLE, AND AS TO A WOMAN, HER FACE IS TOWARD THE TREE," THE WORDS OF R. ELIEZER. AND SAGES SAY, "THE MAN IS HUNG, BUT THE WOMAN IS NOT HUNG."

1. II:1: What is the scriptural basis for the position of rabbis?

C. SAID TO THEM R. ELIEZER, "AND DID NOT SIMEON B. SHETAH HANG WOMEN IN ASHKELON?" THEY SAID TO HIM, "HE HUNG EIGHTY WOMEN, AND THEY DO NOT JUDGE EVEN TWO ON A SINGLE DAY."

1. III:1: Said R. Hisda, "That teaching applies only when there are two different modes of inflicting the death penalty, but if it is a single mode of inflicting the death penalty, they do judge any number of capital cases in a single day.

2. III:2: It has been taught on Tannaite authority: R. Eliezer b. Jacob says, "I heard that a court may inflict floggings and penalties not in accord with the law of the Torah."

XXIV. MISHNAH-TRACTATE SANHEDRIN 6:4N-S, 6:5

A. HOW DO THEY HANG HIM? THEY DRIVE A POST INTO THE GROUND, AND A BEAM JUTS OUT FROM IT, AND THEY TIE TOGETHER HIS TWO HANDS, AND THUS DO THEY HANG HIM. R. YOSÉ SAYS, "THE POST LEANS AGAINST A WALL, AND THEN ONE SUSPENDS HIM THE WAY BUTCHERS DO IT." AND THEY UNTIE HIM FORTHWITH. AND IF HE IS LEFT OVERNIGHT, ONE TRANSGRESSES A NEGATIVE COMMANDMENT ON HIS ACCOUNT, AS IT IS SAID, "HIS BODY SHALL NOT REMAIN ALL NIGHT ON THE TREE, BUT YOU WILL SURELY BURY HIM ON THE SAME DAY, FOR HE WHO IS HANGED IS A CURSE AGAINST GOD" (DEUT. 21:23):

1. I:1: Our rabbis have taught on Tannaite authority: Had Scripture stated, "If he has sinned, then you shall hang him," I might have maintained that first the felon is hung, and then he is put to death, just as the government does it. Scripture accordingly says, "And he be put to death, then you shall hang him" (Deut. 21:22). The felon is put to death and afterward hung.

2. I:2: Our rabbis have taught on Tannaite authority: "Then you shall hang him on a tree" (Deut. 21:22). May I suppose that that would apply whether the tree is cut down from the ground or whether it is attached to the ground? Scripture says, "You shall surely bury him" (Deut. 21:22). That applies to a tree that now lacks only burial, excluding use of one that lacks both felling and burial. So the tree has to have been cut down before it is used.

B. THAT IS TO SAY, ON WHAT ACCOUNT HAS THIS ONE BEEN HUNG? BECAUSE HE CURSED THE NAME, SO THE NAME OF HEAVEN TURNED OUT TO BE PROFANED.

1. II:1: It has been taught on Tannaite authority: R. Meir says, "Why does Scripture say, 'For one who is hanged is cursed by God' (Deut. 21:23)?

C. SAID R. MEIR, "WHEN A PERSON IS DISTRESSED, WHAT WORDS DOES THE PRESENCE OF GOD SAY? AS IT WERE: 'MY HEAD IS IN PAIN, MY ARM IS IN PAIN'. IF THUS IS THE OMNIPRESENT DISTRESSED ON ACCOUNT OF THE BLOOD OF THE WICKED WHEN IT IS SHED, HOW MUCH THE MORE SO ON ACCOUNT OF THE BLOOD OF THE RIGHTEOUS!"

1. III:1: What is the basis of Meir's interpretation of the word 'a curse of ...' (QLLT)?

D. AND NOT THIS ONLY HAVE SAGES SAID, BUT WHOEVER ALLOWS HIS DECEASED TO STAY UNBURIED OVERNIGHT TRANSGRESSES A NEGATIVE COMMANDMENT BUT IF ONE KEPT A CORPSE OVERNIGHT FOR ITS OWN HONOR, E.G., TO BRING A BIER FOR IT AND SHROUDS, HE DOES NOT TRANSGRESS ON ITS ACCOUNT.

1. IV:1: Said R. Yohanan in the name of R. Simeon b. Yohai, "How on the basis of Scripture do we know that one who keeps his deceased overnight violates a negative commandment? Because Scripture says, 'You shall surely bury him' (Deut. 21:23). On the basis of the cited verse we learn that one who keeps his deceased overnight violates a negative commandment."

E. BURIAL AS THE PREFERRED MODE OF DISPOSITION OF THE DECEASED

1. IV:2: Said King Shapur to R. Hama, "When in the Torah is there proof that one has to bury the deceased?"
2. IV:3: The question was raised: Is burial performed for the purpose of avoiding disgrace or for the sake of atonement?
3. IV:4: The question was raised: Is the eulogy for the sake of the living or for the sake of the dead?

F. AND THEY DID NOT BURY THE FELON IN THE BURIAL GROUNDS OF HIS ANCESTORS. BUT THERE WERE TWO GRAVEYARDS MADE READY FOR THE USE OF THE COURT, ONE FOR THOSE WHO WERE BEHEADED OR STRANGLED, AND ONE FOR THOSE WHO WERE STONED OR BURNED. WHEN THE FLESH HAD ROTTED, THEY THEY DO COLLECT THE BONES AND BURY THEM IN THEIR APPROPRIATE PLACE. AND THE RELATIVES OF THE FELON COME AND INQUIRE AFTER THE WELFARE OF THE JUDGES AND OF THE WITNESS. AS IF TO SAY, "WE HAVE NOTHING AGAINST YOU, FOR YOU JUDGED HONESTLY." AND THEY DID NOT GO INTO MOURNING. BUT THEY OBSERVE A PRIVATE GRIEF, FOR GRIEF IS ONLY IN THE HEART.

1. V:1: Why such arrangements as having two burial grounds, M. 6:5F?
2. V:2: And why not set up four burial grounds to cover the four modes of execution?
3. V:3: Essay on the problem, if a wicked person dies in his wicked state, he gains atonement through his death? If he dies in his wicked state, he does not gain atonement through his death. This long essay both cites our Mishnah-rule as part of its corpus of evidence and also serves as a prologue for the following.
4. V:4: R. Ashi said, "At what point do the rites of mourning commence? It is from when the grave is closed with the grave-stone. When is atonement achieved? When the body has seen a bit of the pain of the grave. Therefore, if the rites have been suspended as in the case of the convicted felon, they are suspended and not required.'
5. V:5: As to the grave of Rab, people would take dirt from it for an attack of fever on the first day.
6. V:6: He who weaves a shroud for a corpse – Abbayye said, "It is forbidden to use for some other purpose." Raba said, "It is permitted."

7. V:7: Our rabbis have taught on Tannaite authority: Those put to death by the court – their property goes to their heirs. But those put to death by the king – their property goes to the king. And R. Judah says, "Those put to death by the king – their property goes to their heirs."

    a. V:8: Secondary development of a theme tangential in the foregoing.

        I. V:9: As above.

XXV. MISHNAH-TRACTATE SANHEDRIN 7:1

A. FOUR MODES OF EXECUTION WERE ASSIGNED TO THE COURT, LISTED IN ORDER OF SEVERITY:

1. I:1: Said Raba said R. Sehora said R. Huna, "Any passage stated by sages in numerical order in fact does not list matters in order of priority or posteriority except for the matter of the seven substances. As we have learned in the Mishnah: Seven substances do they pass over a bloodstain to see whether it is blood or dye: tasteless spit, water from boiled grits, urine, nitre, soap, Cimolian earth, and lion's leaf (M. Nid. 9:6A-B). And it is taught at the end of the same passage: If one rubbed them on out of order, or if one rubbed on all seven substances at once, he has done nothing whatsoever (M. Nid. 9:7K)."

B. (1) STONING, (2) BURNING, (3) DECAPITATION, AND (4) STRANGULATION:

1. II:1: Stoning is a more severe mode of execution than burning as listed in sequence at M. 7:1B, against Simeon's order at M. 7:1C. because it is assigned to the blasphemer and idolator.

C. R. SIMEON SAYS, "(2) BURNING, (1) STONING, (4) STRANGULATION, AND (3) DECAPITATION:"

1. III:1: Burning is a more severe mode of execution than stoning, for it is assigned to a priest's daughter who fornicated.

2. III:2: A betrothed girl, a priest's daughter, who committed adultery is executed by stoning. R. Simeon says, "By burning." If she committed adultery with her father, she is executed by stoning. R. Simeon says, "By burning" (T. San. 12:2).

3. III:3: What evidence is there concerning the view of R. Simeon that the daughter of a priest, whether betrothed or married, is executed for the crime of adultery by burning? It is accord with that which has been taught on Tannaite

authority: R. Simeon says, "Two encompassing principles have been stated with reference to the priest's daughter." One encompassing principle refers to a betrothed girl, the other to a married woman. When the Torah states, "And the man who commits adultery with another man's wife, even he who commits adultery with his neighbor's wife, the adulterer and the adulteress shall surely be put to death" (Lev. 20:10). This is a general law regarding a married woman, in which a priest's daughter should be included. Likewise the law in Deut. 22:23f.: "If a damsel that is a virgin be betrothed to a husband, and a man find her in the city and lie with her, then you shall bring them both out to the gate of the city and stone them." This is a general principle for an adulterous betrothed girl, which should embrace the priest's daughter too.

4. III:4: Our rabbis have taught on Tannaite authority: "And the daughter of any priest, if she profane herself" (Lev. 21:9): Might one think that that is the case even if she had profaned the Sabbath? Scripture states, "by playing the whore" (Lev. 21:9): It is concerning the profanation that involves whoredom that Scripture speaks.

5. III:5: "The daughter of a priest" (Lev. 21:9): I know only that that rule applies if she is married to a priest as will be explained. If she is married to a Levite, an Israelite, an idolator, one of impaired priestly stock, one born of a union of a couple not legally permitted to wed at all, or to a Temple slave, how do we know that the same rule applies?

6. III:6: "And the daughter of a priest, if she profanes herself by playing the harlot, she profanes her father; she shall be burned in fire" (Lev. 21:9). Interpret the latter phrase to mean as follows: She shall be burned but the man who had intercourse with her shall not be burned. She shall be burned, but the witnesses who testify falsely against her shall not be burned.

7. III:7: "'The daughter of a priest' (Lev. 21:9): "I know only that the rule applies if she was married to a priest. If she was married to a Levite, an Israelite, an idolator, one of impaired priestly stock, one who was born of a union of a couple not legally permitted to wed at all, or to a Temple slave, how do we know that the same rule applies? "Scripture says, 'And the daughter of a man who is a priest' (Lev. 21:9) – even though she is herself not of the priestly caste."

8. III:8: The ruling that a priest's daughter married to the offspring of a union of parents who cannot legally married is put to death through burning does not accord with the view of R. Meir who says the penalty is by strangling.

9. III:9: R. Eliezer says, "If she committed adultery with her father, she is put to death through burning, and is if she did so with her father in law, it is through stoning."

10. III:10: What is the source for R. Ishmael's statement?

D. **THIS PROCEDURE IS HOW THE RELIGIOUS REQUIREMENT OF STONING IS CARRIED OUT:**

1. IV:1: What is the sense of the Tannaite authority in saying, This procedure is how the religious requirement of stoning is carried out?

XXVI. MISHNAH-TRACTATE SANHEDRIN 7:2

A. **THE RELIGIOUS REQUIREMENT OF BURNING IS CARRIED OUT AS FOLLOWS: THEY WOULD BURY HIM UP TO HIS ARMPITS IN MANURE, AND PUT A TOWEL OF HARD MATERIAL INSIDE ONE OF SOFT MATERIAL, AND WRAP IT AROUND HIS NECK. THIS WITNESS PULLS IT TO HIM FROM ONE SIDE, AND THAT WITNESS PULLS IT TO HIM AT THE OTHER SIDE, UNTIL HE OPENS UP HIS MOUTH.**
AND ONE KINDLES A WICK
AND THROWS IT INTO HIS MOUTH, AND IT GOES DOWN INTO HIS BOWELS AND BURNS HIS INTESTINES.

1. I:1: What is a wick?

2. I:2: How do we know that death through burning is carried on in this way, rather than in that posited at M. 7:2H?

   a. I:3: Now Moses and Aaron were walking on the way, and Nadab and Abihu were walking behind them, with all Israel after them. Said Nadab to Abihu, "When will these two elders die, so that you and I may become leaders of the generation?" Said the Holy One, blessed be he, to them, "Now let us see who will bury whom."

      I. I:4: Said R. Eleazar, "What is a disciple of a sage like in the view of an ordinary person? At the outset he is like a gold ladle. If he talks with him, he is like a silver ladle. If he accepts some sort of benefit from him, he is like an earthenware ladle.

3. I:5: Imrata, daughter of Teli, was the daughter of a priest who committed an act of adultery. R. Hama bar Tubiah had her surrounded by twigs and burned.

B. R. JUDAH SAYS, "ALSO THIS ONE: IF HE DIED AT THEIR HANDS THROUGH STRANGULATION, THEY WILL NOT HAVE CARRIED OUT THE RELIGIOUS REQUIREMENT OF BURNING IN THE PROPER MANNER. BUT: THEY OPEN HIS MOUTH WITH TONGS, AGAINST HIS WILL, KINDLE A WICK, AND THROW IT INTO HIS MOUTH, AND IT GOES DOWN INTO HIS BOWELS AND BURNS HIS INTESTINES." SAID R. ELEAZAR B. SADOQ, "THERE WAS THE CASE OF A PRIEST WHO COMMITTED ADULTERY. AND THEY PUT BUNDLES OF TWIGS AROUND HER AND BURNED HER." THEY SAID TO HIM, "IT WAS BECAUSE THE COURT OF THAT TIME WAS NOT EXPERT IN THE LAW."

    1. II:1: Said R. Joseph, "It was a court made up of Sadduccees."

XXVII. MISHNAH-TRACTATE SANHEDRIN 7:3A-F

A. THE RELIGIOUS REQUIREMENT OF DECAPITATION IS CARRIED OUT AS FOLLOWS: THEY WOULD CUT OFF HIS HEAD WITH A SWORD, JUST AS THE GOVERNMENT DOES. R. JUDAH SAYS, "THIS IS DISGUSTING. BUT THEY PUT HIS HEAD ON A BLOCK AND CHOP IT OFF WITH AN AX." THEY SAID TO HIM, "THERE IS NO FORM OF DEATH MORE DISGUSTING THAN THIS ONE."

    1. I:1: It has been taught on Tannaite authority: Said R. Judah to sages, "I too recognize that it is a disgusting form of death, but what shall I do? For lo, the Torah has said, 'You will not follow their ordinances' (Lev. 18:3)" (T. San. 9:11C-H).

    2. I:2: And as to what we have learned in the Mishnah: And these are those who are put to death through decapitation: the murderer and the townsfolk of an apostate town (M. San. 9:1D-E), What is the scriptural basis for decapitation in these crimes?

XXVIII. MISHNAH-TRACTATE SANHEDRIN 7:3G-J

A. THE RELIGIOUS REQUIREMENT OF STRANGULATION IS CARRIED OUT AS FOLLOWS: THEY WOULD BURY HIM IN MANURE UP TO HIS ARMPITS, AND PUT A TOWEL OF HARD MATERIAL INSIDE ONE OF SOFT MATERIAL, AND WRAP IT AROUND HIS NECK. THIS WITNESS PULLS IT TO HIM FROM ONE SIDE, AND THAT WITNESS PULLS IT TO HIM AT THE OTHER SIDE, UNTIL HE PERISHES.

    1. I:1: Our rabbis have taught on Tannaite authority: "And the man who commits adultery with another man's wife, even he who commits adultery with his neighbor's wife, the

adulterer and the adulteress shall surely be put to death" (Lev. 20:10). "A man" – excluding a minor. "... who commits adultery with another man's wife" – excluding the wife of a minor.

2. I:2: Said R. Zira to Abbayye, "As to the rest of those who are put to death through stoning, in connection with those cases Scripture does not explicitly specify that stoning is the mode of inflicting the death penalty, so that stoning is the choice mode of execution is a proposition we derive by analogy to the case of the necromancer or wizard put to death through stoning, on the basis of which relevant phrase of those specified at B do we derive that fact?

XXIX. MISHNAH-TRACTATE SANHEDRIN 7:4A-R

A. THESE ARE THE FELONS WHO ARE PUT TO DEATH BY STONING: HE WHO HAS SEXUAL RELATIONS WITH HIS MOTHER,

1. I:1: It has been taught on Tannaite authority: R. Judah says, "If his mother was not fit to be married to his father, he is liable only on the count of her being his mother but not on the count of her being a married woman, (T. San. 10:1A). What is the meaning of his statement if she was not fit to be married to his father?

B. WITH THE WIFE OF HIS FATHER, WITH HIS DAUGHTER-IN-LAW, WITH A MALE, AND WITH A COW; AND THE WOMEN WHO BRINGS AN OX ON TOP OF HERSELF; AND HE WHO BLASPHEMES, HE WHO PERFORMS AN ACT OF WORSHIP FOR AN IDOL, HE WHO GIVES OF HIS SEED TO MOLECH, HE WHO IS A FAMILIAR SPIRIT, AND HE WHO IS A SOOTHSAYER; HE WHO PROFANES THE SABBATH, HE WHO CURSES HIS FATHER OR HIS MOTHER. HE WHO HAS SEXUAL RELATIONS WITH A BETROTHED MAIDEN, HE WHO BEGUILES ENTICES A WHOLE TOWN TO IDOLATRY, A SORCERER, AND A STUBBORN AND INCORRIGIBLE SON. HE WHO HAS SEXUAL RELATIONS WITH HIS MOTHER IS LIABLE ON HER ACCOUNT BECAUSE OF HER BEING HIS MOTHER AND BECAUSE OF HER BEING HIS FATHER'S WIFE LEV. 18:6-7, 20:11.

R. JUDAH SAYS, "HE IS LIABLE ONLY ON ACCOUNT OF HER BEING HIS MOTHER ALONE."

HE WHO HAS SEXUAL RELATIONS WITH HIS FATHER'S WIFE IS LIABLE ON HER ACCOUNT BECAUSE OF HER BEING HIS FATHER'S WIFE AND BECAUSE OF HER BEING A MARRIED WOMAN, WHETHER THIS IS IN THE LIFETIME OF HIS FATHER

OR AFTER THE DEATH OF HIS FATHER, WHETHER SHE IS
ONLY BETROTHED OR ALREADY MARRIED TO THE FATHER:

1. II:1: When R. Isaac came, he repeated the Mishnah passage
   as we have learned it: 'R. Judah says, "He is liable only on
   account of her being his mother" M. 7:4L.' He then said,
   "And what is the scriptural basis for his view that the rule
   applies not only when she is forbidden to the father, but
   under all circumstances?"

C. HE WHO HAS SEXUAL RELATIONS WITH HIS DAUGHTER-IN-
    LAW IS LIABLE ON HER ACCOUNT BECAUSE OF HER BEING
    HIS DAUGHTER-IN-LAW AND BECAUSE OF HER BEING
    ANOTHER MAN'S WIFE, WHETHER THIS IS IN THE LIFETIME
    OF HIS SON OR AFTER THE DEATH OF HIS SON LEV. 20:12,
    WHETHER SHE IS ONLY BETROTHED OR ALREADY MARRIED
    TO THE SON:

1. III:1: While the Mishnah imposes liability on the count of her
   being his daughter-in-law and on the count of her being
   another man's wife, why not in addition impose a penalty on
   the count of her being his son's wife?

XXX. MISHNAH-TRACTATE SANHEDRIN 7:4S-V

A. HE WHO HAS SEXUAL RELATIONS WITH A MALE:

1. I:1: How do we know on the basis of Scripture that the
   penalty of pederasty is stoning?

B. ...OR A COW:

1. II:1: How on the basis of Scripture do we know that the rule
   applies to a beast?

   a. II:2: He who has sexual relations with a male or serves as
      a passive partner of a male – Said R. Abbahu, "In the
      view of R. Ishmael, he is liable on two counts, one on the
      count of, 'You shall not lie with mankind,' and the other
      on the count, 'There shall not be a sodomite of the sons
      of Israel. But on the view of R. Aqiba, he is liable on only
      one count, 'You shall not lie' and 'you shall not be lain
      with' constitute a single statement each one based on
      revocalization of a single passage."

   b. II:3: He who is a passive partner for a male and for a
      beast – Said R. Abbahu, "In the view of R. Aqiba, he is
      liable on two counts, one on the count of, 'You shall not
      lie with mankind' (Lev. 18:2), and the other on the count,
      'You shall not lie with any beast' (Lev. 18:23). But in the
      view of R. Ishmael, he is liable on only one count, both

items deriving from the verse, 'There shall be no sodomite' (Deut. 23:18)."

2. II:4: Our rabbis have taught on Tannaite authority: As to sexual relations with a male, sages have not treated a minor boy as equivalent to an adult, but as to sexual relations with a beast, sages have treated a minor girl as equivalent to an adult.

C. AND THE WOMAN WHO BRINGS AN OX ON TOP OF HERSELF: IF THE HUMAN BEING HAS COMMITTED A SIN, WHAT SIN HAS THE BEAST COMMITTED? BUT BECAUSE A HUMAN BEING HAS OFFENDED THROUGH IT, THEREFORE THE SCRIPTURE HAS SAID, "LET IT BE STONED." ANOTHER MATTER: SO THAT THE BEAST SHOULD NOT AMBLE THROUGH THE MARKET PLACE, WITH PEOPLE SAYING, "THIS IS THE ONE ON ACCOUNT OF WHICH MR. SO-AND-SO GOT HIMSELF STONED."

1. III:I: R. Nahman son of R. Hisda expounded, "In the case of a woman there are two ways in which sexual relations may take place, but in the case of a beast, only one."

2. III:2: It has been taught on Tannaite authority: A male nine years and one day old who has sexual relations with a beast, whether via the vagina or the anus, And a woman who has sexual relations with a beast, whether via the vagina or the anus, is liable

3. III:3: Said Rabina to Raba, "As to him who commits the first stage of sexual relations with a male, what is the law?"

4. III:4: R. Ahadboi bar Ammi asked R. Sheshet, "He who reaches the first stage of sexual activity through masturbation – what is the law?"

5. III:5: The question was asked of R. Sheshet, "As to an idolator who had sexual relations with a beast – what is the law? For the stoning of the beast, we require both a stumbling stock and disgrace, and while the beast indeed is a stumbling block, there is no consideration of disgrace since gentiles do this sort of thing routinely."

XXXI. MISHNAH-TRACTATE SANHEDRIN 7:5

A. HE WHO BLASPHEMES IS LIABLE ONLY WHEN HE HAS FULLY PRONOUNCED THE DIVINE NAME:

1. I:1: A Tannaite authority states, "... When he has cursed the divine Name by Name." What is the source of this rule?

B. THE RELIGIOUS OBLIGATIONS OF THE CHILDREN OF NOAH: IDOLATORS AND SLAVES

1. I:2: Our rabbis have taught on Tannaite authority: "Any man who curses his God shall bear his sin" (Lev. 24:15)": It would have been clear had the text simply said,"A man." Why does it specify, "Any"? It serves to encompass idolators, who are admonished not to curse the Name, just as Israelites are so admonished

2. I:3: Our rabbis have taught on Tannaite authority: Concerning seven religious requirements were the children of Noah commanded: setting up courts of justice, idolatry, blasphemy, cursing the Name of God, fornication, bloodshed, thievery, and cutting a limb from a living beast (T. A.Z. 8:4). R. Hananiah b. Gamaliel says, "Also on account of blood deriving from a living beast." R. Hidqa says, "Also on account of castration." R. Simeon says, "Also on account of witchcraft."

3. I:4: Said R. Joseph, "Disciples of the house of one master said, 'On account of violating three religious duties are children of Noah put to death: on account of adultery, murder, and blasphemy.'"

4. I:5: R. Huna, R. Judah, and all the disciples of Rab say, "On account of seven commandments a son of Noah is put to death. The All-Merciful revealed that fact of one of them, and the same rule applies to all of them."

5. I:6: R. Jacob bar Aha found that it was written in the book of the lore of the house of Rab, "A son of Noah is put to death by a court consisting of a single judge, on the testimony of a single witness, not after appropriate admonition, on the testimony of a man but not on the testimony of a woman, but even if the witness is a relative."

6. I:7: Said R. Abia the elder to R. Pappa, "Might I propose that a daughter of Noah who committed murder should not be put to death? 'At the hand of man who committed murder" – and not the hand of woman' is what is written at Gen. 9:6."

7. I:8: Our rabbis have taught on Tannaite authority: "A man, a man shall not approach any who is near of kin to him, to uncover their nakedness" (Lev. 18:6): As to the word, "A man," why does Scripture say it twice? It serves to encompass Samaritans gentiles, indicating that they are admonished, just like Israelites, against sexual relations with close relatives.

   a. I:9: Gloss of a detail of the foregoing: "In the case of any form of prohibited sexual relationship for which an Israelite court inflicts the death penalty, the children of

Noah are subject to warning. If an Israelite court does not inflict the death penalty in the case at hand, a son of Noah is not subject to warning with respect to it," the words of R. Meir. And sages say, "There are many prohibited relationships with respect to which an Israelite court does not inflict the death-penalty, and the children of Noah are warned with respect to them. If one has had sexual relations with a woman prohibited by Israelite law, he is tried in accord with Israelite law. If he had sexual relations in violation of Noahide law, he is judged in accord with Noahide law. But only the prohibition of sexual relations with a betrothed maiden falls into the category at hand, in which Israelite law prohibits such a relationship and Noahide law does not" (T. A.Z. 8:G-I).

9.   I:10: Said R. Hisda, "A slave is permitted to marry his mother and permitted to marry his daughter, for he has ceased to fall into the category of the Samaritan gentile and has not yet entered the category of Israelite."

10. I:11: When R. Dimi came, he said R. Eliezer said R. Hanina said, "A Noahide who set aside a slave-girl for his slave-boy and then had sexual relations with her is put to death on her account."

11. I:12: Said R. Eleazar said R. Hanina, "A son of Noah who had anal intercourse with his wife is liable, for it is said, 'And he shall cleave' (Gen. 2:24) – by vaginal and not by anal intercourse."

12. I:13: Said R. Hanina, "An idolator who hit an Israelite is liable to the death penalty."

   a.   I:14: Said R. Simeon b. Laqish, "He who raises his hand against his fellow, even though he did not actually hit him, is called a wicked man."

   b.   I:15: And R. Simeon b. Laqish said, "What is the meaning of the verse of Scripture, 'He who serves his land meaning: tills his plot shall be satisfied with bread' (Prov. 12:11)? If a man turns himself into a slave for his property, he shall have enough bread, and if not, he shall not have enough bread."

13. I:16: And R. Simeon b. Laqish said, "An idolator who keeps the Sabbath incurs the death penalty."

14. I:17: And R. Yohanan said, "An idolator who takes up study of the Torah incurs the death penalty."

15. I:18: R. Hanina says, "Also children of Noah must not eat blood drawn from a living beast."

16. I:19: Why was it necessary to state the commandments just cited to the sons of Noah and then to repeat them at Sinai?

17. I:20: Said R. Judah said Rab, "As to the first man, he was not permitted to eat meat."

18. I:21: R. Simeon says, "Also witchcraft is forbidden to the children of Noah" (T. A.Z. 8:6M).

19. I:22: R. Eleazar says, "Also as to mixed seeds" (T. A.Z. 8:8A): What is the scriptural basis for this position?

C.   SAID R. JOSHUA B. QORHA, "ON EVERY DAY OF A TRIAL THEY EXAMINE THE WITNESSES WITH A SUBSTITUTED NAME, SUCH AS, 'MAY YOSÉ SMITE YOSÉ.' ONCE THE TRIAL IS OVER, THEY WOULD NOT PUT HIM TO DEATH ON THE BASIS OF EVIDENCE GIVEN WITH THE SUBSTITUTED EUPHEMISM, BUT THEY CLEAR THE COURT AND ASK THE MOST IMPORTANT OF THE WITNESSES, SAYING TO HIM, 'SAY, WHAT EXACTLY DID YOU HEAR IN DETAIL?' AND HE SAYS WHAT HE HEARD:"

   1. II:1: Said R. Aha bar Jacob, "One is liable only if he curses the name made up of four letters, thus excluding a name made up of two letters, which is not subject to a curse and use of which is not punishable."

D.   ...AND THE JUDGES STAND ON THEIR FEET AND TEAR THEIR CLOTHING:

   1. III:1: How do we know that the judges rise to their feet?

E.   AND NEVER SEW THEM BACK UP.

   1. IV:1: How do we know this?

   2. IV:2: Our rabbis have taught on Tannaite authority: All the same are the one who actually hears the blasphemy and the one who hears it from the one who heard it. Both are liable to tear their garments.

   3. IV:3: Said R. Judah said Samuel, "He who hears the name of God blasphemed by an idolator does not have to tear his clothes, whose blasphemy the king and court tore their clothes, in point of fact, he was an Israelite apostate. And R. Judah said Samuel said, "People tear their clothes only on account of the four-lettered name of God used as a curse."

F.   AND THE SECOND WITNESS SAYS, "ALSO I HEARD WHAT HE HEARD:"

   1. V:1: Said R. Simeon b. Laqish, "It follows from this rule that the language, 'Also I heard what he heard,' is valid in property cases as well as in capital cases."

G.   AND THE THIRD WITNESS SAYS, "ALSO I HEARD WHAT HE HEARD:"

   1.   VI:1: The unattributed statement at hand accords with the principle of R. Aqiba, who treats three witnesses as equivalent to two.

XXXII. MISHNAH-TRACTATE SANHEDRIN 7:6

A.   HE WHO PERFORMS AN ACT OF WORSHIP FOR AN IDOL – ALL THE SAME ARE THE ONE WHO PERFORMS AN ACT OF SERVICE, WHO ACTUALLY SACRIFICES, WHO OFFERS UP INCENSE, WHO POURS OUT A LIBATION OFFERING, WHO BOWS DOWN:

   1.   I:1: What is the meaning of all the same are the one who performs an act of service?

   2.   I:2: What is the biblical source for the fact that these acts of worship impose guilt?

      a.   I:3: Gloss of a detail of the foregoing.

      b.   I:4: Said Raba bar R. Hanan to Abbayye, "Might I say that prostration is subjected to explicit discussion to impose its traits on the general rule at hand the view that prostration was singled out to testify to its own traits, not to impose its traits on the definition of other culpable actions?

   2.   I:5: R. Hamnuna's oxen got lost on him. While searching for them he met Rabbah and laid out for him two passages of the Mishnah which he deemed to contradict one another: "We have learned in the Mishnah: he who performs an act of worship for an idol, meaning that if he actually performed such an act, he is liable but if he merely said, 'I shall do it,' he is not liable. But we have also learned in the Mishnah: He who says, 'I am going to worship,' 'I shall go and worship,' 'Let's go and worship' . This bears the implication that merely saying, not doing, also is penalized."

   3.   I:6: It has been stated on Amoraic authority: He who does an act of worship for an idol, whether from love or from fear, Abbayye said, "He is liable." Raba said, "He is exempt."

   4.   I:7: R. Zakkai repeated on Tannaite authority before R. Yohanan, "If a person sacrificed, burned incense, poured out a libation, and prostrated himself to an idol in one spell of inadvertence not knowing that any form of service to an idol is forbidden, he is liable on only one count."

B.   ...AND THE ONE WHO ACCEPTS IT UPON HIMSELF AS A GOD, SAYING TO IT, "YOU ARE MY GOD:"

    1.   II:1: Said R. Nahman said Rabbah bar Abbuha said Rab, "Once one has said to it, 'You are my god,' he is liable."

C.   BUT THE ONE WHO HUGS, IT, KISSES IT, POLISHES IT, SWEEPS IT, AND WASHES IT, ANOINTS IT, PUTS CLOTHING ON IT, AND PUTS SHOWS ON IT, MERELY TRANSGRESSES A NEGATIVE COMMANDMENT EX. 20:5.

    1.   III:1: When R. Dimi came from Palestine, he said R. Eleazar said, "On account of all of the actions listed at M. 7:6Dff. one is given a flogging, except for the one who takes a vow in its name or who carries out a vow made in its name

D.   HE WHO TAKES A VOW IN ITS NAME, AND HE WHO CARRIES OUT A VOW MADE IN ITS NAME TRANSGRESS A NEGATIVE COMMANDMENT.

    HE WHO UNCOVERS HIMSELF TO BAAL PEOR IS STONED, FOR THIS IS HOW ONE PERFORMS AN ACT OF SERVICE TO IT. HE WHO TOSSES A PEBBLE AT MERKOLIS HERMES IS STONED, FOR THIS IS HOW ONE PERFORMS AN ACT OF SERVICE TO IT.

    1.   IV:1: How do we know that this is the case for him who vows in its name or who carries out a vow made in its name?

    2.   IV:2: When Ulla came, he stayed at the City of Nebo. Said Raba to him, "And where did the master lodge?" He said to him, "In the City of Nebo." He said to him, "Is it not written, 'And do not mention the name of other gods' (Ex. 23:13)?"

    3.   IV:3: Said R. Nahman, "Any form of mockery is forbidden except for mockery of idolatry, which is permitted."

    4.   IV:4: Said R. Isaac, "What is the meaning of the following verse of Scripture: 'And now they sin more and more and have made for themselves molten images of their silver and idols in their image' (Hos. 13:2)? What is the meaning of 'idols in their image'? This teaches that each one of them made an image of his god and put it in his pocket. When he called it to mind, he took it out of his pocket and embraced it and kissed it."

    5.   IV:5: Said R. Judah said Rab, "'And the men of Babylonia made Succoth-benoth' (2 Kgs. 17:30) among idols brought by gentiles who resettled Samaria after the deportation. What was it? It was a chicken."

    6.   IV:6: Said R. Judah said Rab, "The Israelites know that idolatry was of no substance and did not perform acts of idolatry except with the intent of allowing themselves publicly to engage in consanguineous sexual relations."

    7.   IV:7: Said R. Judah said Rab, "There was the case of a gentile woman who was very sick. She said, 'If that woman I

survive this illness, she will go and worship every idol in the world.' She recovered from the illness and went and worshipped every idol in the world...."

8. IV:8: Our rabbis have taught on Tannaite authority: There is the case of Sabta of Eles, who hired his ass to a gentile woman. When she came to Peor, she said to him, "Wait for me while I go in and come out."

    a. IV:9: Illustration of a secondary detail of the foregoing. R. Menassia was going along to Be Torta. They pointed out to him, "There is an idol standing here." He took a stone and threw it at it. They said to him, "It is Mercury."

XXXIII. MISHNAH-TRACTATE SANHEDRIN 7:7A-E

A. HE WHO GIVES OF HIS SEED CHILD TO MOLECH IS LIABLE ONLY WHEN HE WILL BOTH HAVE GIVEN HIM TO MOLECH AND HAVE PASSED HIM THROUGH FIRE. IF HE GAVE HIM TO MOLECH BUT DID NOT PASS HIM THROUGH FIRE, PASSED HIM THROUGH FIRE BUT DID NOT GIVE HIM TO MOLECH, HE IS NOT LIABLE – UNTIL HE WILL BOTH HAVE GIVEN HIM TO MOLECH AND HAVE PASSED HIM THROUGH FIRE.

1. I:1: The Mishnah at M. 7:4 refers to both idolatry in general and giving to Molech in particular treating them as separate. This would imply that giving a child to Molech is not an act of idolatry.

2. I:2: Said R. Yannai, "One is liable only if he hands his son over to the worshippers of an idol."

3. I:3: Said R. Aha, son of Raba, "If one passed all of his children through fire, he is exempt."

4. I:4: R. Ashi raised the question, "If one passed a blind son through fire, what is the law? If he passed through a son who was asleep, what is the law? If he passed through the son of his son or the son of his daughter, what is the law?"

5. I:5: Said R. Judah, "One is liable only when he will have passed him through fire in the usual way (T. San. 10:4B)."

6. I:6: Said R. Yosé bar Hanina, "The three references to extirpation on account of idolatry serve what purpose? These are at Lev. 20:2-5, 'Whoever gives of his seed to Molech will I cut off from among his people,' 'And if the people of the land kill him not, then I will set my face against that man... and will cut him off,' and, at Num. 15:30: 'But the soul that does something presumptuously... shall be cut off from among his people.' One serves to state the penalty for

worship in the normal way, one serves to state the penalty for idol worship not in the normal way, and one states the penalty for worship of Molech."

XXXIV. MISHNAH-TRACTATE SANHEDRIN 7:7F-I

A.   H E   WHO   HAS   A   FAMILIAR SPIRIT   – THIS   IS   A VENTRILOQUIST, WHO SPEAKS FROM HIS ARMPITS; AND HE WHO IS A SOOTHSAYER – THIS IS ONE WHOSE SPIRIT SPEAKS THROUGH HIS MOUTH – LO, THESE ARE PUT TO DEATH BY STONING. AND THE ONE WHO MAKES INQUIRY OF THEM IS SUBJECT TO A WARNING:

1. I:1: What is the reason that, in the present passage, the framer of the passage refers to both one who has a familiar spirit and also a soothsayer at M. 7:7F, G, while at the list of those who are put to their death through extirpation, the one who has a familiar spirit is included in the list, but the one who is a soothsayer is omitted at M. Ker. 1:1? Said R. Yohanan, "It is because both of them are encompassed in a single negative commandment at Lev. 19:31, 'Do not recognize those who have familiar spirits or soothsayers'." R. Simeon b. Laqish said, "The soothsayer is omitted at M. Ker. 1:1, because there is no concrete deed that he does."

2. I:2: He who has a familiar spirit – this is one who has a ventriloquist which speaks from between his joints and from between his elbows. A soothsayer – this one who has the bone of a familiar spirit in his mouth, and it speaks on its own (T. San. 10:6A-B).

3. I:3: Our rabbis have taught on Tannaite authority: He who inquires of the dead (Deut. 18:11) – all the same are the one who raises up the dead by divining and the one who makes inquiry of a skull. What is the difference between one who makes inquiry of a skull and one who raises up the dead by witchcraft? For the one who raises up the dead by witchcraft – the ghost does not come up in his normal way and does not come up on the Sabbath. But the one who makes inquiry of a skull – the spirit comes up in the normal way and comes up on the Sabbath (T. San. 10:7A-D).

   a.   I:4: And so too did Turnus-rufus ask R. Aqiba, "What distinguishes one day the Sabbath from all other days?"

5. I:5: One who asks a question of a familiar spirit – it this not the same as one who seeks after the death?

6. I:6: Our rabbis have taught on Tannaite authority: One who observes the times (Deut. 18:10) – R. Simeon says, "This is

one who rubs the semen of seven sorts of men in his eyes."
And sages say, "This is one who holds peoples' eyes giving
them hallucinations."

XXXV. MISHNAH-TRACTATE SANHEDRIN 7:8A
A.   HE WHO PROFANES THE SABBATH M. 7:4E – IN REGARD TO A
MATTER, ON ACCOUNT OF THE DELIBERATE DOING OF
WHICH THEY ARE LIABLE TO EXTIRPATION, AND ON
ACCOUNT OF THE INADVERTENT DOING OF WHICH THEY
ARE LIABLE TO A SIN-OFFERING.
1.   I:1: This statement bears the implication that there is a form
of profanation of the Sabbath on account of which people are
not liable to a sin-offering should they do it inadvertently, or
to extirpation if they do it deliberately.

XXXVI. MISHNAH-TRACTATE SANHEDRIN 7:8B-E
A.   HE WHO CURSES HIS FATHER AND HIS MOTHER M. 7:4F IS
LIABLE ONLY WHEN HE WILL HAVE CURSED THEM BY THE
DIVINE NAME. IF HE CURSED THEM WITH A EUPHEMISM, R.
MEIR DECLARES HIM LIABLE. AND SAGES DECLARE HIM
EXEMPT.
1.   I:1: Who are the sages of M. 7:8E?
2.   I:2: Our rabbis have taught on Tannaite authority: "For any
man that curses his father of his mother shall surely be put to
death; his father and his mother he has cursed; his blood
shall be upon him" (Lev. 20:9). Why does Scripture say "any
man"? It serves to in encompass a daughter, one of
undefined sexual traits, and one who exhibits the traits of
both sexes.
3.   I:3: "He shall surely be put to death" (Lev. 20:9). That is, by
execution through stoning. You say that it is through
stoning. But perhaps it is by any one of the other modes of
execution that are listed in the Torah.

XXXVII. MISHNAH-TRACTATE SANHEDRIN 7:9
A.   HE WHO HAS SEXUAL RELATIONS WITH A BETROTHED
MAIDEN IS LIABLE ONLY IF SHE IS A VIRGIN MAIDEN,
BETROTHED, WHILE SHE IS YET IN HER FATHER'S HOUSE.
IF TWO DIFFERENT MEN HAD SEXUAL RELATIONS WITH HER,
THE FIRST ONE IS PUT TO DEATH BY STONING, AND THE
SECOND BY STRANGULATION. THE SECOND PARTY, B. HAS
NOT HAD INTERCOURSE WITH A VIRGIN (M. 11:1). THE

MAIDEN IS BETWEEN TWELVE YEARS AND ONE DAY AND TWELVE YEARS SIX MONTHS AND ONE DAY OLD.

1. I:1: Our rabbis have taught on Tannaite authority: "If a girl that is a virgin is betrothed to a husband" (Deut. 22:23): "Girl" and not either a minor, under twelve years, or a mature woman. "A virgin" – and not one who has had sexual relations. "Betrothed" and not one in a fully consummated marriage. "In her father's house" – excluding a case in which the father has given the girl over to the agent of the husband.

2. I:2: R. Jacob bar Ada asked Rab, "If one has had sexual relations with a minor who was betrothed, in R. Meir's view, what is the law? Does he exclude such an act entirely from any sort of punishment or is it from the penalty of stoning that he excludes the action by the exegesis given at unit I.1?"

   a. I:3: The foregoing follows the lines of the following dispute among Tannaite authorities

   b. I:4: Our rabbis have taught on Tannaite authority: "And the daughter of any priest, if she profane herself by playing the whore" (Lev. 21:9). Rabbi says, "The verse refers to the first such action. And so it is written, 'Then the man only who lies with her shall die' (Deut. 22:25)."

XXXVIII. MISHNAH-TRACTATE SANHEDRIN 7:10A-N

A. HE WHO BEGUILES OTHERS TO IDOLATRY M. 7:4H – THIS REFERS TO AN ORDINARY FELLOW:

1. I:1: The one who beguiles others is an ordinary fellow (M. 7:10A) so he is put to death through stoning. But if he were a prophet, he would be put to death through strangulation.

B. ...WHO BEGUILES SOME OTHER ORDINARY FELLOW: IF HE SPOKE IN SUCH A WAY TO TWO, AND THEY SERVE AS WITNESSES AGAINST HIM, THEY BRING HIM TO COURT AND STONE HIM. IF HE SPOKE IN SUCH A WAY TO ONLY ONE PERSON, THE LATTER THEN SAYS TO HIM, "I HAVE SOME FRIENDS WHO WILL WANT THE SAME THING." IF HE WAS CLEVER AND NOT PREPARED TO SPEAK IN THE FRIENDS' PRESENCE, THEY HIDE WITNESSES ON THE OTHER SIDE OF THE PARTITION, AND HE SAYS TO HIM, "TELL ME WHAT YOU WERE SAYING TO ME NOW THAT WE ARE BY OURSELVES." AND THE OTHER PARTY SAYS TO HIM WHAT HE HAD SAID, AND THEN THIS PARTY SAYS, "NOW HOW ARE WE GOING TO ABANDON OUR GOD WHO IS IN HEAVEN AND GO AND WORSHIP STICKS AND STONES?" IF HE REPENTS, WELL AND

GOOD. IF HE SAID, "THIS IS WHAT WE ARE OBLIGATED TO DO, AND THIS IS WHAT IS GOOD FOR US TO DO," THOSE WHO STAND ON THE OTHER SIDE OF THE PARTITION BRING HIM TO COURT AND STONE HIM. HE WHO BEGUILES OTHERS IS ONE WHO SAYS, "I AM GOING TO WORSHIP," "I SHALL MAKE AN OFFERING," "I SHALL OFFER INCENSE," "I SHALL GO AND OFFER INCENSE," "LET'S GO AND OFFER INCENSE," "I SHALL MAKE A LIBATION," "I SHALL GO AND MAKE A LIBATION," "LET'S GO AND MAKE A LIBATION," "I SHALL BOW DOWN," "I SHALL GO AND BOW DOWN," "LET'S GO AND BOW DOWN." IF HE SAID TO HIM, "THERE IS A GOD IN SUCH A PLACE, WHO EATS THUS, DRINKS THUS, DOES GOOD IN ONE WAY, AND HARM IN ANOTHER" – AGAINST ALL THOSE WHO ARE LIABLE TO THE DEATH PENALTY IN THE TORAH THEY DO NOT HIDE WITNESSES FOR THE PURPOSES OF ENTRAPMENT EXCEPT FOR THIS ONE.

1. II:1: But if it had been a community, he would have been put to death through strangulation. In accord with which authority is the Mishnah-paragraph before us? It is R. Simeon.
2. II:2: R. Pappa said, "When the Mishnah says, He who beguiles others refers to an ordinary fellow who beguiles some other ordinary fellow, it is for the purpose of entrapment."

XXXIX. MISHNAH-TRACTATE SANHEDRIN 7:10/O-7:11
A. HE WHO LEADS A WHOLE TOWN ASTRAY M. 10:4H IS ONE WHO SAYS, "LET'S GO AND PERFORM AN ACT OF SERVICE TO AN IDOL."
1. I:1: Said R. Judah said Rab, "Subject to the present statement of the Mishnah are those who entice a whole town to apostasy."
B. THE SORCERER – HE WHO DOES A DEED IS LIABLE, BUT NOT THE ONE WHO MERELY CREATES AN ILLUSION:
1. II:1: Our rabbis have taught on Tannaite authority: "You shall not permit a sorceress to live" (Ex. 22:17). The same rule applies to a sorcerer and to a sorceress. Why then does Scripture speak of a sorceress? It is because it is mainly women who practice sorcery.
2. II:2: How are they put to death? R. Yosé the Galilean says, "Here it is stated, "'You shall not permit a sorceress to live' (Ex. 22:17) and elsewhere it is written, 'You shall not allow anything that breathes to live' (Deut. 20:17 Just as in that

context the Canaanite nations, everything is put to death through decapitation, so here it is through decapitation." R. Aqiba says, "Here it is stated, 'You shall not permit a sorceress to live' (Ex. 22:17), and elsewhere it is stated, 'There shall not a hand touch it, but he shall surely be stoned or shot through, whether it be beast or man it shall not live' (Ex. 19:13). Just as in that passage having to do with the avoidance of Sinai before the giving of the Torah, the penalty is through stoning, so here too the penalty is through stoning."

3. II:3: R. Yohanan said, "Why are they called sorcerers? Because they deny the power of the family above a play on the word for sorcery."

4. II:4: Said Abbayye, "If the sorcerer uses exact methods, it is through a demon. If the sorcery does not work through exact methods, it is through enchantment."

   a. II:5: Case: Said R. Ashi, "I saw the father of Qarna blow his nose hard and ribbons of silk came out of his nostrils."

   b. II:6: Case: "Then the magicians said to Pharaoh, This is the finger of God" (Ex. 8:19). Since the reference is to the creation of lice, which the Egyptian sorcerers could not do, said R. Eleazar, "On the basis of that statement we learn that a demon cannot make a creature smaller than a barley seed."

   c. II:7: Case: Yannai came to an inn. He said to them, "Give me some water to drink." They brought him a flour-and-water drink. He saw that the woman's lips were moving. He poured out a little of the drink, and it turned into scorpions. He said to them, "I drank something of yours, now you take a drink of mine."

   d. II:8: "And the frog came up and covered the land of Egypt" (Ex. 8:6): Said R. Eleazar, "It was one frog, and it multiplied into a swarm and filled the whole land of Egypt."

C.   R. AQIBA SAYS IN THE NAME OF R. JOSHUA, "TWO MAY GATHER CUCUMBERS. ONE GATHERER MAY BE EXEMPT, AND ONE GATHERER MAY BE LIABLE. LIKEWISE: HE WHO DOES A DEED IS LIABLE, BUT HE WHO MERELY CREATES AN ILLUSION IS EXEMPT."

1. III:1: Did R. Aqiba learn his knowledge of magic from R. Joshua? And have we not learned in a Tannaite teaching that he learned his magic from R. Eleazer?

XL. MISHNAH-TRACTATE SANHEDRIN 8:1

A.   A REBELLIOUS AND INCORRIGIBLE SON – AT WHAT POINT DOES A CHILD BECOME LIABLE TO BE DECLARED A REBELLIOUS AND INCORRIGIBLE SON? FROM THE POINT AT WHICH HE WILL PRODUCE TWO PUBIC HAIRS:

    1. I:1: How do we know on the basis of Scripture that a minor is exempt?

B.   ...UNTIL THE 'BEARD' IS FULL – (THAT IS THE LOWER PUBIC, NOT THE UPPER FACIAL, BEARD, BUT THE SAGES USED EUPHEMISMS). AS IT IS SAID, "IF A MAN HAS A SON" (DEUT. 21:18)

    1. II:1: R. Hiyya taught on Tannaite authority, "Until it surrounds the corona."

    2. II:2: Said R. Hisda, "If a minor male produced a child, his son is not subject to the law of a wayward and rebellious son, for it is said, 'If a man has a son' (Deut. 21:18), meaning, when a man has a son, and not 'when a son has a son.'"

    3. II:3: Now as to the Tannaite authority of the house of Ishmael, who taught, 'If a man has a son' (Deut. 21:18) means, a son but not a father so that if the son is himself a father already, the law does not apply, how would such a case be possible? We recall that the Mishnah has defined the period of liability as that interval between the appearance of two pubic hairs and the completion of the pubic corona, a relatively brief span of time.

        a. II:4: Gloss of foregoing.

    4. II:5: Our rabbis have taught on Tannaite authority: A woman who commits lewdness with her minor son, who entered into the first state of cohabitation with her – the House of Shammai invalidate her from marriage into the priesthood. And the House of Hillel declare her valid (T. Sot. 5:7A-C). Said R. Hiyya, son of Rabbah bar Nahmani, said R. Hisda, and some say, said R. Hisda said Zeiri, "All concur in the case of a son nine years and one day old, that his act of sexual relations is entirely valid.'

C.   (1) A SON, NOT A DAUGHTER;
(2) A SON, NOT AN ADULT MAN. AND A MINOR IS EXEMPT, SINCE HE HAS NOT YET ENTERED THE SCOPE OF THE COMMANDMENTS.

    1. III:1: It has been taught on Tannaite authority: Said R. Simeon, "By strict law a daughter also should have been appropriate to fall into the category of the wayward and rebellious child, for everyone comes around to her to commit

a sin and she may turn out to be a whore. But it is the decree of Scripture: 'a son,' not a daughter" (T. San. 11:6C).

XLI. MISHNAH-TRACTATE SANHEDRIN 8:2

A.   AT WHAT POINT IS HE LIABLE? ONCE HE HAS EATEN A TARTEMAR OF MEAT AND DRUNK A HALF-LOG OF ITALIAN WINE. R. YOSÉ SAYS, "A MINA OF MEAT AND A LOG OF WINE:"

1.   I:1: Said R. Zira, "As to this tartemar, I do not know what it is, but since R. Yosé doubles the measure applying to wine, it follows that he doubles the measure in regard to meat. So it turns out that a tartemar is a half mina."

2.   I:2: Said R. Hanan bar Moledah said R. Huna, "He is liable only if he buys meat cheaply and eats it, buys wine cheaply and drinks it, for it is written, 'He is a glutton and a drunkard' (Deut. 21:20) a play on words, since the root for 'glutton' yields 'cheap.'"

3.   I:3: We have learned there: On the eve of the ninth of Ab a person should not eat two prepared dishes, nor should one eat meat or drink wine (M. Ta. 4:7D). In this regard a Tannaite authority taught, "But one may eat salted meat and drink wine fresh from the vat. As to salted meat, how long must it be salted?

B.   THE EVILS OF WINE AND STRONG DRINK

1.   I:4: Said R. Hanan, "Wine has created in this world only for comforting the bereaved and for requiting the wicked."

2.   I:5: Said R. Amram, son of R. Simeon bar Abba, said R. Hanina, "What is the meaning of the verse of Scripture, 'Who has woe? who has sorrow? who has contentions? who has babbling? who has wounds without cause? who has redness of eyes? They who tarry long at wine, they who go to seek mixed wine' (Prov. 23:29-30)?"

3.   I:6: Ubar, the Galilean, expounded as follows: "The word 'and' is stated thirteen times with respect to wine: 'And Noah began to be a husbandman, and he planted a vineyard, and he drank of the wine and was drunken, and he was uncovered within his tent. And Ham the father of Canaan saw the nakedness of his father and told his two brothers outside. And Shem and Japheth took a garment and laid it upon their shoulders and went backward and covered the nakedness of their father, and their faces were backward, and they did not see their father's nakedness. And Noah awoke from his wine and knew what his younger son had

done to him' (Gen. 9:20-24). The conversive waw occurs thirteen times. The combination of waw yod means woe, thus there were thirteen woes; so great are the sorrows caused by drunkenness."

4.   I:7: "And Noah began to be a husbandman and he planted a vineyard" (Gen. 9:25): Said R. Hisda said R. Uqba, and some say, Mar Uqba said R. Zakkai said, "The Holy One, blessed be he, said to Noah, 'Noah, you should have learned from the first man, for whom it was only wine that was the cause of all his troubles.'"

5.   I:8: "The words of King Lemuel, the burden wherewith his mother admonished him" (Prov. 31:1): Said R. Yohanan in the name of R. Simeon b. Yohai, "This verse teaches that his mother had him bound on a post to be flogged. She said to him, 'What, my son? and what, the son of my womb? and what, the son of my vows?' (Prov. 31:1). 'What my son? Everybody knows that your father feared heaven, and now people will say that his mother was the cause of his corruption."

C.   **IF HE ATE IN AN ASSOCIATION FORMED FOR A RELIGIOUS DUTY:**
1.   II:1: Said R. Abbahu, "He is liable only if he eats in an association that is made up entirely of louts."

D.   **IF HE ATE ON THE OCCASION OF THE INTERCALATION OF THE MONTH:**
1.   III:1: Does this bear the implication that on such an occasion they eat meat and wine?

E.   **IF IN JERUSALEM HE ATE FOOD IN THE STATUS OF SECOND TITHE:**
1.   IV:1: Since he eats it in the correct way, he will not be led astray.

F.   **IF HE ATE CARRION AND TEREFAH-MEAT, FORBIDDEN THINGS OR CREEPING THINGS:**
1.   V:1: Said Raba, "If he ate chicken, he is not condemned as a wayward and rebellious son."

G.   **IF HE ATE UNTITHED PRODUCE, FIRST TITHE, THE HEAVE-OFFERING OF WHICH HAD NOT BEEN REMOVED, SECOND TITHE OR CONSECRATED FOOD WHICH HAD NOT BEEN REDEEMED BY MONEY,**
IF HE ATE SOMETHING WHICH FULFILLED A RELIGIOUS DUTY OR WHEREBY HE COMMITTED A TRANSGRESSION,

1. VI:1: Something which fulfilled a religious duty is a meal served to comfort mourners.   Something whereby he committed a transgression is a meal on a public fast.

H. **IF HE ATE ANY SORT OF FOOD EXCEPT MEAT, DRANK ANY SORT OF LIQUID EXCEPT WINE –**

1. VII:1: If he ate any sort of food except meat – "meat" here is meant to include even Keilah-figs. If he drank any sort of liquid except wine – "wine" here is meant to include even honey and milk.

I. **...HE IS NOT DECLARED A REBELLIOUS AND INCORRIGIBLE SON – UNLESS HE EATS MEAT AND DRINKS WINE, SINCE IT IS SAID, "A GLUTTON AND A DRUNKARD" (DEUT. 21:20):**
AND EVEN THOUGH THERE IS NO CLEAR PROOF FOR THE PROPOSITION, THERE IS AT LEAST A HINT FOR IT, FOR IT IS SAID, "DO NOT BE AMONG THE WINE-DRINKERS, AMONG GLUTTONOUS MEAT-EATERS" (PROV. 23:20).

1. VIII:1: Our rabbis have taught on Tannaite authority: If he ate any sort of food but did not eat meat, drank any sort of liquid but did not drink wine, he is not declared a rebellious and incorrigible son, unless he eats meat and drinks wine, since it is said, "A glutton and a drunkard" (Deut. 21:20). Even though there is no clear proof for the proposition, there is at least a hint for it, for it is said, "Do not be among the wine-drinkers, among gluttonous meat-eaters" (Prov. 23:20). And it says, "For the drunkard and glutton shall come to poverty, and drowsiness shall clothe a man with rags" (Prov. 23:21).

XLII. MISHNAH-TRACTATE SANHEDRIN 8:3

A. **IF HE STOLE SOMETHING BELONGING TO HIS FATHER BUT ATE IT IN HIS FATHER'S DOMAIN, OR SOMETHING BELONGING TO OTHERS BUT ATE IT IN THE DOMAIN OF THOSE OTHERS, OR SOMETHING BELONGING TO OTHERS BUT ATE IT IN HIS FATHER'S DOMAIN, HE IS NOT DECLARED A REBELLIOUS AND INCORRIGIBLE SON – UNTIL HE STEALS SOMETHING OF HIS FATHER'S AND EATS IT IN THE DOMAIN OF OTHERS:**

1. I:1: If he stole something belonging to his father but ate it in his father's domain, even though he has ready access to what belongs to his father, he will be afraid and not do this very often. If he stole something belonging to others but ate it in the domain of those others, even though he is not afraid, he does not have ready access and so will not do this very often.

And all the more so if he stole something belonging to others but ate it in his father's domain, in which case he does not have ready access, and, further, is afraid so he will not do this often. Until he steals something of his father's and eats it in the domain of others, in which case he has ready access and will not be afraid and so will make this theft a habitual practice.

B. R. YOSÉ B. JUDAH SAYS, "...UNTIL HE STEALS SOMETHING BELONGING TO HIS FATHER AND HIS MOTHER."

1. II:1: Whence would his mother get domain over property? What a wife buys is as if her husband bought it.

XLIII. MISHNAH-TRACTATE SANHEDRIN 8:4A-E

A. IF HIS FATHER WANTED TO PUT HIM TO JUDGEMENT AS A REBELLIOUS AND INCORRIGIBLE SON BUT HIS MOTHER DID NOT WANT TO DO SO, IF HIS FATHER DID NOT WANT AND HIS MOTHER DID WANT TO PUT HIM TO JUDGMENT, HE IS NOT DECLARED A REBELLIOUS AND INCORRIGIBLE SON – UNTIL BOTH OF THEM WANT TO PUT HIM TO JUDGMENT.
R. JUDAH SAYS, "IF HIS MOTHER WAS UNWORTHY OF HIS FATHER, HE IS NOT DECLARED TO BE A REBELLIOUS AND INCORRIGIBLE SON."

1. I:1: What is the sense of unworthy of his father at M. 8:4E? May I say that it was a marriage that produced liability to extirpation or even to the death penalty at the hands of an earthly court e.g., an incestuous union?

a. I:2: In accord with which authority is the following Tannaite teaching: There has never been, and there never will be, a wayward and rebellious son. So why has the passage been written? To tell you, "Expound and receive a reward" (T. San. 11:6A-B).

XLIV. MISHNAH-TRACTATE SANHEDRIN 8:4F-O

A. IF ONE OF THEM WAS MAIMED IN THE HAND, LAME, DUMB, BLIND, OR DEAF, HE IS NOT DECLARED A REBELLIOUS AND INCORRIGIBLE SON, SINCE IT IS SAID, "THEN HIS FATHER AND HIS MOTHER WILL LAY HOLD OF HIM" (DEUT. 21:20) – SO THEY ARE NOT MAIMED IN THEIR HANDS; "AND BRING THEM OUT" – SO THEY ARE NOT LAME; "AND THEY SHALL SAY" – SO THEY ARE NOT DUMB; "THIS IS OUR SON" – SO THEY ARE NOT BLIND; "HE WILL NOT OBEY OUR VOICE" – SO THEY ARE NOT DEAF.

      1.   I:1: Does this passage prove that the Scripture must be read in a literal way, just as it is written?

B.   THEY WARN HIM BEFORE THREE JUDGES AND FLOG HIM:

      1.   II:1: Why? Should two not suffice?

      2.   II:2: Whence is it stated that a wayward and rebellious son is flogged?

C.   IF HE WENT AND MISBEHAVED AGAIN, HE IS JUDGED BEFORE TWENTY-THREE JUDGES. HE IS STONED ONLY IF THERE WILL BE PRESENT THE FIRST THREE JUDGES, SINCE IT IS SAID, "THIS, OUR SON" – THIS ONE WHO WAS FLOGGED BEFORE YOU:

      1.   III:1: Is the cited verse, "This our son..." not used to make the point at M. 8:4K, "This is our son" – so they are not blind?

XLV. MISHNAH-TRACTATE SANHEDRIN 8:4P-Q

A.   IF HE FLED BEFORE HIS TRIAL WAS OVER, AND AFTERWARD WHILE HE WAS A FUGITIVE, THE LOWER "BEARD" BECAME FULL, HE IS EXEMPT. IF AFTER HIS TRIAL WAS DONE HE FLED, AND AFTERWARD THE LOWER BEARD BECAME FULL, HE IS LIABLE.

      1.   I:1: Said R. Hanina, "A son of Noah who cursed the divine Name and afterward converted to Judaism is exempt from penalty, since the mode of trying him has undergone a change, so too the mode of inflicting the death penalty."

XLVI. MISHNAH-TRACTATE SANHEDRIN 8:5

A.   A REBELLIOUS AND INCORRIGIBLE SON IS TRIED O N ACCOUNT OF WHAT HE MAY END UP TO BE. LET HIM DIE WHILE YET INNOCENT, AND LET HIM NOT DIE WHEN HE IS GUILTY. FOR WHEN THE EVIL FOLK DIE, IT IS A BENEFIT TO THEM AND A BENEFIT TO THE WORLD. BUT WHEN THE RIGHTEOUS FOLK DIE, IT IS BAD FOR THEM AND BAD FOR THE WORLD.

WINE AND SLEEP FOR THE WICKED ARE A BENEFIT FOR THEM AND A BENEFIT FOR THE WORLD. BUT FOR THE RIGHTEOUS, THEY ARE BAD FOR THEM AND BAD FOR THE WORLD. DISPERSION FOR THE EVIL IS A BENEFIT FOR THEM AND A BENEFIT FOR THE WORLD BUT FOR THE RIGHTEOUS, IT IS BAD FOR THEM AND BAD FOR THE WORLD. GATHERING TOGETHER FOR THE EVIL IS BAD FOR THEM AND BAD FOR THE WORLD. BUT FOR THE RIGHTEOUS, IT IS A BENEFIT FOR THEM AND A BENEFIT FOR THE WORLD. TRANQUILITY FOR THE EVIL IS BAD FOR THEM AND BAD FOR THE WORLD. BUT

FOR THE RIGHTEOUS, IT IS A BENEFIT FOR THEM AND A
BENEFIT FOR THE WORLD.

1. I:1: It has been taught on Tannaite authority: R. Yosé the
    Galilean says, "And is it the case that merely because this
    one has eaten a tartemar of meat and drunk a half-log of
    Italian wine, the Torah has said that he should be taken to
    court and tried for the penalty of stoning? Rather, it is
    because the Torah has plumbed the depths of the psychology
    of the wayward and rebellious son. For in the end, he will
    use up his father's wealth and then will want to satisfy his
    gluttony. Not finding the means, he will go out to the
    crossroads and mug people. The Torah has said, Let him die
    while yet innocent, and let him not die when he is guilty.

XLVII. MISHNAH-TRACTATE SANHEDRIN 8:6
   A.   HE WHO BREAKS IN IS JUDGED ON ACCOUNT OF WHAT HE
        MAY END UP TO BE. IF HE BROKE IN AND BROKE A JUG, IF
        BLOOD-GUILT APPLIES TO HIM, HE IS LIABLE. IF BLOOD-
        GUILT DOES NOT APPLY, HE IS EXEMPT.

1. I:1: Said Raba, "What is the reason that the householder may
    kill one who breaks in? It is because we make the
    assumption that no one restrains himself when it comes to
    protecting his property. And this one the thief must have
    taken the view, 'If I go there, the householder will resist me
    and not let me take what I want, so if he resists, I shall kill
    him.' And the Torah has said, 'If he comes to kill you, you
    kill him first' cf. Ex. 22:1."

2. I:2: Our rabbis have taught: "If a thief be found breaking in,
    and he be smitten that he die, there shall no blood be shed
    for him, if the sun be risen upon him" (Ex. 22:1-3). Did the
    sun rise on him alone? But if it is as clear to you as the sun
    that he was not at peace with you, then kill him, but if not,
    do not kill him (T. 11:9F-H).

    a.   I:3: Said Rab, "I would kill anyone who broke in on me,
         except for R. Hanina bar Shila. What is the reason?
         Should I say that it is because he is a righteous man and
         therefore no threat to life but, lo, in the cited possibility,
         he is by definition a housebreaker!..."

3. I:4: Our rabbis have taught on Tannaite authority: "If the sun
    be risen upon him, there shall be blood shed for him" (Ex.
    22:1): That is the case whether on a weekday or on the
    Sabbath. "If the thief be found breaking in, there shall be no

blood shed for him" (Ex. 22:2). That is the case whether on a weekday or on the Sabbath.

4. I:5: Our rabbis have taught on Tannaite authority: "If a thief be found breaking in and be smitten" (Ex. 22:1) – by any one. "And he die" (Ex. 22:1) – by any mode of death by which you can kill him.

5. I:6: Our rabbis have taught on Tannaite authority: "If a thief be found breaking in" (Ex. 22:1): I know that only that the rule applies to a break-in through one's walls. How do I know that the same rule applies to a break-in through one's roof, courtyard, or outer buildings? Scripture says, "If the thief be found" – any where he is found as a thief.

6. I:7: Said R. Huna, "In the case of a minor who is pursuing one, it is permitted to kill him and so to save him at the cost of his own life."

XLVIII. MISHNAH-TRACTATE SANHEDRIN 8:7

A.   AND THESE ARE THOSE WHO ARE TO BE SAVED FROM DOING EVIL EVEN AT THE COST OF THEIR LIVES: HE WHO PURSUES AFTER HIS FELLOW IN ORDER TO KILL HIM – AFTER A MALE, OR AFTER A BETROTHED GIRL:

1. I:1: Our rabbis have taught on Tannaite authority: How do we know that in the case of one who pursues his fellow to kill him, it is permitted to save such a person from sinning at the cost of his life? Scripture says, "You shall not stand by the blood of your neighbor" (Lev. 19:16).

   a. I:2: Gloss of a detail of the foregoing.

2. I:3: Our rabbis have taught on Tannaite authority: All the same are the cases of one who pursues his fellow to kill him, a male, a betrothed girl, other sorts of deeds punishable by death inflicted in the court, and those punishable by death inflicted as extirpation, people save such persons committing these cries at the cost of their own lives. But if it was a widow married to a high priest, or a divorcee or a woman who had performed the rite of removing the shoe married to an ordinary priest, they do not save him at the cost of his life.

   a. I:4: Analysis of the foregoing.

   b. I:5: As above.

   c. I:6: As above.

B.   BUT HE WHO PURSUES A BEAST, HE WHO PROFANES THE SABBATH, HE WHO DOES AN ACT OF SERVICE TO AN IDOL – THEY DO NOT SAVE THEM EVEN AT THE COST OF THEIR LIVES.

1. II:1: It has been taught on Tannaite authority: R. Simeon b. Yohai says, "If one performs an act of service to an idol, it is permitted even at the cost of his own life to save him from sin."

2. II:2: Said R. Yohanan in the name of R. Simeon b. Yehosedeq, "They took a vote and decided in the upper room of the house of Nitzeh in Lod, as follows: 'In the case of all transgressions that are listed in the Torah, if people say to a person, "Commit a transgression and so avoid being executed," one should commit a transgression and avoid execution, except for the matters of idolatry, sexual immorality, and murder.'"

3. II:3: When R. Dimi came, he said R. Yohanan said, "The cited rule about having to give up one's life on account only of the three sins listed applies solely in the time in which there is no royal decree to violate the Torah. But if there is a royal decree, then even on account of the most inconsequential religious duty, one should be put to death and not violate the law."

4. II:4: The question was addressed to R. Ammi, "Is a son of Noah commanded to accept martyrdom in the sanctification of God's name, or is he not commanded to accept martyrdom in the sanctification of God's name?"

5. II:5: Said R. Judah said Rab, "There was the case of a man who gazed upon a woman and whose heart become sick with desire for her. They came and asked physicians, who said, 'He has no remedy unless he has sexual relations with her.' Sages ruled, 'Let him die but not have sexual relations with her. The physicians proposed, 'Let her stand nude before him.' Sages ruled, 'Let him die, but let her not stand nude before him.' 'Let her talk with him behind a wall.' 'Let him die and let her not talk with him behind a wall.'"

XLIX. MISHNAH-TRACTATE SANHEDRIN 9:1A-C

A. AND THESE ARE THOSE WHO ARE PUT TO DEATH THROUGH BURNING: HE WHO HAS SEXUAL RELATIONS WITH BOTH A WOMAN AND HER DAUGHTER, AND A PRIEST'S DAUGHTER WHO COMMITTED ADULTERY: IN THE SAME CATEGORY AS A WOMAN AND HER DAUGHTER ARE THE FOLLOWING: HIS DAUGHTER, HIS DAUGHTER'S DAUGHTER, HIS SON'S DAUGHTER, HIS WIFE'S DAUGHTER, THE DAUGHTER OF HER DAUGHTER, THE DAUGHTER OF HER SON, HIS MOTHER-IN-

LAW, THE MOTHER OF HIS MOTHER-IN-LAW, AND THE MOTHER OF HIS FATHER-IN-LAW.

1. I:1: The framer of the passage does not say, "He who has sexual relations with a woman whose daughter he has married," but rather, He who has sexual relations with both a woman and her daughter (M. 9:1B). What follows is that both of them are prohibited. And who are they? They are his mother-in-law and the mother of his mother-in-law.

2. I:2: What is the source of the rule at hand? It is in accord with what our rabbis have taught on Tannaite authority: "And if a man takes a woman and her mother it is wickedness, they shall be burned with fire, both he and they" (Lev. 20:14). I know only that the law applies to marriage with both a woman and her mother. How do I know that the same law applies to marriage with the daughter of the woman, the daughter of her daughter, or the daughter of her son?

    a. I:3: Gloss of a detail of the foregoing.

    b. I:4: As above.

        I. I:5: Gloss of a detail of I:3.

3. I:6: How do we know that one's own daughter born of a woman one has raped is forbidden?

4. I:7: Further on the question, How do we know that one's own daughter born of a woman one has raped is forbidden?: The father of R. Abin taught on Tannaite authority, "It is because have we have not derived from Scripture that a man's incest with his daughter produced by a rape is punishable that it was necessary for Scripture to state, 'And the daughter of a man and a priest, if she profane herself through her father, she profanes him, she shall be burned with fire' (Lev. 21:9) (cf. T. San. 12:1H).

    a. I:8: Expansion on the foregoing: Whence do we derive the admonition that a man not commit incest with his daughter produced by his act of rape?

B. MARRYING OFF ONE'S CHILDREN IN THE PROPER MANNER

1. I:9: Said R. Kahana in the name of R. Aqiba, "You have none who is poor in Israel except because of one who is clever in acting wickedly and one who delays marrying off his daughter once she has passed puberty."

2. I:10: Our rabbis have taught on Tannaite authority: He who loves his neighbors, he who draws his relatives near, he who marries his sister's daughter, and he who lends a sela to a poor person when he needs it – concerning such a person

Scripture says, "Then you will call, and the Lord will answer" (Is. 58:9).

3. I:11: Our rabbis have taught on Tannaite authority: "And if a man take a wife and her mother, it is wickedness; they shall be burned with fire, both he and they" (Lev. 20:14). "He and one of them," the words of R. Ishmael. R. Aqiba says, "He and both of them."

L. MISHNAH-TRACTATE SANHEDRIN 9:1D-M

A. AND THESE ARE THOSE WHO ARE PUT TO DEATH THROUGH DECAPITATION: THE MURDERER, AND THE TOWNSFOLK OF AN APOSTATE TOWN. A MURDERER WHO HIT HIS NEIGHBOR WITH A STONE OR A PIECE OF IRON:

1. I:1: Said Samuel, "Why at Num. 35:16-18, where we take up murder with iron, stone, or wooden weapons the word 'hand' is not stated when we speak of an iron weapon indicating that the weapon must be sufficiently large to be held in the hand only when it is a weapon of stone or wood, but not of iron? It is because an iron weapon may inflict death no matter its size."

B. ...OR WHO PUSHED HIM UNDER WATER OR INTO FIRE, AND THE OTHER PARTY CANNOT GET OUT OF THERE AND SO PERISHED, HE IS LIABLE. IF HE PUSHED HIM INTO THE WATER OR INTO THE FIRE, AND HE CAN GET OUT OF THERE BUT NONETHELESS HE DIED, HE IS EXEMPT:

1. II:1: The first of the two statements makes its own point, and the second of the two statements makes its own point, too. The former of the two statements makes its own point, namely, even though he is not the one who pushed the other into the water, since the other cannot get up from there and so dies, he is liable. The latter of the two statements makes its own point, namely, even though he is the one who pushed the other into the water, since the other can climb up out of the water and nonetheless dies, he is exempt from penalty.

2. II:2: How do we know that one keeps the other under is liable?

3. II:3: A man confined the beast of his fellow in the sun, and it perished. Rabina declared him liable to pay the value of the beast. R. Aha, son of Rab, declared him exempt.

4. II:4: Said Raba, "If one tied up another person and the latter dies of starvation, he is exempt." And Raba said, "If one tied up a beast in the heat and it died, or if he did so in the cold

and it died, he is liable. If he did so when the sun was going to come but had not yet risen, or that the cold had not yet taken effect, he is exempt. In this case he is merely an indirect cause."

5. II:5: It has been stated on Amoraic authority: If one turned a vat over upon someone who died of suffocation or broke open a ceiling above him and he caught cold and died, Raba and R. Zira: One said, "He is liable," and the other said, "He is exempt.'"

6. II:6: Said Raba, "If one pushed someone into a pit, and there was a ladder in the pit, and someone else came along and took it away, or even if he himself removed the ladder, he still is exempt. For at the point at which he threw the man into the pit,. the victim could climb out of it."

7. II:7: R. Tahalipa of the West repeated on Tannaite authority before R. Abbahu, "In a case of people playing ball, if the one who was killed was within four cubits of the wall, the player is exempt. If he was outside of four cubits, he is liable."

8. II:8: Said R. Papa, "If someone tied up his fellow and inundated him with a column of water, it is as if it was done by his arrows and he is liable. That is the case if the death was due to the first flow of the water directly, but if it was through the second flow of the water, he is merely a secondary cause of death."

9. II:9: Our rabbis have taught on Tannaite authority: If ten men hit someone with ten sticks and the victim died, whether they did so simultaneously or sequentially, they are exempt. R. Judah b. Betera says, "If they did so sequentially, the last one is liable, because he brought the death nearer."

10. II:10: A Tannaite authority repeated before R. Sheshet: "'And he that kills all of the life of man' (Lev. 24:17): This serves to encompass the case of one who hits his fellow, and in his blow there is not sufficient force to inflict death, and then another party comes along and actually delivers the death blow, indicating that the latter is liable."

11. II:11: Said Raba, "He who kills someone afflicted with an incurable disease is exempt. And someone inflicted with an incurable disease who committed murder in the presence of a court is liable. If it was not in the presence of a court, he is exempt."

C.   IF HE SICKED A DOG ON HIM, OR SICKED A SNAKE ON HIM, HE IS EXEMPT. IF HE MADE A SNAKE BITE HIM, R. JUDAH DECLARES HIM LIABLE. AND SAGES DECLARE HIM EXEMPT.

1. III:1: Said R. Aha bar Jacob, "When you look into the matter at M. 9:1K-M, you will find that, in R. Judah's opinion who holds one liable who makes a snake bite a man, the poison of a snake is between its teeth. Therefore the one one makes the snake bite a man is put to death through decapitation, while the snake itself is exempt."

LI. MISHNAH-TRACTATE SANHEDRIN 9:1N-T

A. HE WHO HITS HIS FELLOW, WHETHER WITH A STONE OR WITH HIS FIST, AND THEY DIAGNOSED HIM AS LIKELY TO DIE, BUT HE GOT BETTER THAN HE WAS, AND AFTERWARD HE GOT WORSE AND HE DIED HE IS LIABLE. R. NEHEMIAH SAYS, "HE IS EXEMPT, FOR THERE IS A BASIS TO THE MATTER OF THINKING THAT HE DID NOT DIE FROM THE ORIGINAL INJURY:"

1. I:1: Our rabbis have taught on Tannaite authority: And this is yet another exegesis which R. Nehemiah stated, "When men quarrel, and one strikes the other with a stone or with his fist, and the man does not die but keeps his bed, then if the man rises again and walks abroad 78B with his staff, he that struck him shall be clear; only he shall pay for the loss of his time, and shall have him thoroughly healed (Ex. 21:18-19) Now would it enter one's mind that this one should walk around in the market, while the other should be put to death on his account? But the meaning is that, if he should recover somewhat, then get worse, and finally even if he should die on account of the original blow, the other is exempt," (T. B.Q. 9:7A-C).

2. I:2: Our rabbis have taught on Tannaite authority: "He who hits his fellow, and the court made an assessment that the man would die but he lived – they free the accused. If they assessed that he would die and he got somewhat better, they make a second assessment as to the monetary compensation that he is to pay. If after a while the ailment grew worse and the man died, one is guided by the second assessment and the accused pays for the monetary claim, as originally assessed, but is not liable to death," the words of R. Nehemiah. And sages say, "There is no assessment after the original one."

LII. MISHNAH-TRACTATE SANHEDRIN 9:2

A. IF HE INTENDED TO KILL A BEAST AND KILLED A MAN, A GENTILE AND KILLED AN ISRAELITE, AN UNTIMELY BIRTH

AND KILLED AN OFFSPRING THAT WAS VIABLE, HE IS EXEMPT. IF HE INTENDED TO HIT HIM ON HIS LOINS WITH A BLOW THAT WAS NOT SUFFICIENT TO KILL HIM WHEN IT STRUCK HIS LOINS, BUT IT WENT AND HIT HIS HEART, AND THERE WAS SUFFICIENT FORCE IN THAT BLOW TO KILL HIM WHEN IT STRUCK HIS HEART, AND HE DIED, HE IS EXEMPT. IF HE INTENDED TO HIT HIM ON HIS HEART, AND THERE WAS IN THAT BLOW SUFFICIENT FORCE TO KILL WHEN IT STRUCK HIS HEART, AND IT WENT AND HIT HIM ON HIS LOINS, AND THERE WAS NOT SUFFICIENT FORCE IN THAT BLOW TO KILL HIM WHEN IT STRUCK HIS LOINS, BUT HE DIED, HE IS EXEMPT. IF HE INTENDED TO HIT A LARGE PERSON, AND THERE WAS NOT SUFFICIENT FORCE IN THAT BLOW TO KILL A LARGE PERSON, BUT IT WENT AND HIT A SMALL PERSON, AND THERE WAS SUFFICIENT FORCE IN THAT BLOW TO KILL A SMALL PERSON, AND HE DIED, HE IS EXEMPT. IF HE INTENDED TO HIT A SMALL PERSON, AND THERE WAS IN THAT BLOW SUFFICIENT FORCE TO KILL A SMALL PERSON, AND IT WENT AND STRUCK THE LARGE PERSON, AND THERE WAS NOT SUFFICIENT FORCE IN THAT BLOW TO KILL THE LARGE PERSON, BUT HE DIED, HE IS EXEMPT. BUT: IF HE INTENDED TO HIT HIM ON HIS LOINS, AND THERE WAS SUFFICIENT FORCE IN THE BLOW TO KILL HIM WHEN IT STRUCK HIS LOINS, AND IT WENT AND HIT HIM ON HIS HEART AND HE DIED, HE IS LIABLE. IF HE INTENDED TO HIT A LARGE PERSON, AND THERE WAS IN THAT BLOW SUFFICIENT FORCE TO KILL THE LARGE PERSON, AND IT WENT AND HIT A SMALL PERSON AND HE DIED, HE IS LIABLE.
R. SIMEON SAYS, "EVEN IF HE INTENDED TO KILL THIS PARTY, AND HE ACTUALLY KILLED SOME OTHER PARTY, HE IS EXEMPT."

1. I:1: To what passage does R. Simeon make reference
2. I:2: What is the Scriptural basis for the position of R. Simeon?
3. I:3: Now from the viewpoint of rabbis, there is no problem, for they maintain that if one intended to kill one party and killed another, he is liable, for it is written, "If men strive and hurt a woman with child: (Ex. 21:22). In this connection, said R. Eleazar, "Scripture addresses the case of a fight involving intent to kill, for it is written, 'And if any accident follow, then you shall give life for life' (Ex. 21:23). But how does R. Simeon deal with the clause, "You shall give life for life" (Ex. 21:23) Since the murder of the woman was unintentional, according to Simeon there is no death penalty?

a.   I:4: Amplification of a detail of the foregoing.

LIII. MISHNAH-TRACTATE SANHEDRIN 9:3

A.   A MURDERER WHO WAS CONFUSED WITH OTHERS – ALL OF
     THEM ARE EXEMPT. R. JUDAH SAYS, "THEY PUT THEM ALL IN
     PRISON."

    1.   I:1: Who are the others mentioned at M. 9:3A?

       a.   I:2: Gloss of a detail of the foregoing.

B.   ALL THOSE WHO ARE LIABLE TO DEATH WHO WERE
     CONFUSED WITH ONE ANOTHER ARE JUDGED TO BE
     PUNISHED BY THE MORE LENIENT MODE OF EXECUTION.

    1.   II:1: That indicates that admonition not to commit a crime
     which serves for a more severe infringement of the law
     applies as an admonition for a less severe infringement of
     the law.   The criminals had been admonished with a
     statement on the mode of execution that applies to the crime
     they had been about to commit. The admonition referred to
     a more severe mode of execution. The stated law then
     indicates that admonition served for a less severe mode of
     execution.

C.   IF THOSE TO BE STONED WERE CONFUSED WITH THOSE TO BE
     BURNED – R. SIMEON SAYS, "THEY ARE TO BE JUDGED TO BE
     EXECUTED BY STONING, FOR BURNING IS THE MORE SEVERE
     OF THE TWO MODES OF EXECUTION." AND SAGES SAY,
     "THEY ARE ADJUDGED TO BE EXECUTED BY BURNING, FOR
     STONING IS THE MORE SEVERE MODE OF EXECUTION OF THE
     TWO." SAID TO THEM R. SIMEON, "IF BURNING WERE NOT
     THE MORE SEVERE, IT WOULD NOT HAVE BEEN ASSIGNED TO
     THE DAUGHTER OF A PRIEST WHO COMMITTED ADULTERY."
     THEY SAID TO HIM, "IF STONING WERE NOT THE MORE
     SEVERE OF THE TWO, IT WOULD NOT HAVE BEEN ASSIGNED
     TO THE BLASPHEMER AND TO THE ONE WHO PERFORMS AN
     ACT OF SERVICE FOR IDOLATRY."
     THOSE WHO ARE TO BE DECAPITATED WHO WERE CONFUSED
     WITH THOSE WHO ARE TO BE STRANGLED – R. SIMEON SAYS,
     "THEY ARE KILLED WITH THE SWORD." AND SAGES SAY,
     "THEY ARE KILLED BY STRANGLING."

    1.   III:1: R. Ezekiel repeated the passage at hand for Rami, his
     son, as follows: 'If those to be burned were confused with
     those to be stoned, R. Simeon says, 'They are judged to be
     executed by stoning, for burning is the more severe of the
     two modes of execution.'"

LIV. MISHNAH-TRACTATE SANHEDRIN 9:4

A. HE WHO IS DECLARED LIABLE TO BE PUT TO DEATH THROUGH TWO DIFFERENT MODES OF EXECUTION AT THE HANDS OF A COURT IS JUDGED TO BE EXECUTED BY THE MORE SEVERE.

  1. I:1: It is self-evident that he is subject to the more severe mode of execution. For, after all, should he profit from committing the further crime?

  2. I:2: The brother of R. Joseph bar Hama asked Rabbah bar Nathan, "What is the source of this view of rabbis: He who is declared liable to be put to death through two different modes of execution at the hands of a court is judged to be executed by the more severe ?" The reply: "As it is written, 'If the righteous man beget a son who is a robber, a shedder of blood...who has eaten upon the mountains and defiled his neighbor's wife' (Ez. 18:10-11).

    a. I:3: R. Aha, son of R. Hanina, interpreted Scripture, "What is the meaning of the verse, 'But if a man be just and do what is lawful and right..., and has not eaten upon the mountains' (Ez. 18:16)? It means that he did not eat only on account of the merit of his ancestors but on his own merit.

B. IF HE COMMITTED A TRANSGRESSION WHICH IS SUBJECT TO THE DEATH PENALTY ON TWO SEPARATE COUNTS, HE IS JUDGED ON ACCOUNT OF THE MORE SEVERE. R. YOSÉ SAYS, "HE IS JUDGED BY THE PENALTY WHICH FIRST APPLIES TO WHAT HE HAS DONE."

  1. II:1: It has been taught on Tannaite authority: Said R.Yosé, "He is judged by the penalty which first applies to what he has done: If he had sexual relations with her when she was his mother-in-law, and then she got married and so was a married woman, he is judged on the count of her being his mother-in-law. If she was a married woman and then became his mother-in-law, he is judged on the count of her being a married woman" (T. San. 12:5D-I).

LV. MISHNAH-TRACTATE SANHEDRIN 9:5A-B

A. HE WHO WAS FLOGGED AND DID THE SAME DEED AND WAS FLOGGED AGAIN – IF HE DID IT YET A THIRD TIME THE COURT PUTS HIM IN PRISON AND FEEDS HIM BARLEY UNTIL HIS BELLY EXPLODES.

  1. I:1: Merely because he was flogged and flogged again does the court put him in prison?

2. I:2: He did it twice and not a third time. Then may we say that the Mishnah-passage at hand does not accord with the view of R. Simeon b. Gamaliel? For in the view of Rabban Simeon b. Gamaliel, lo, he has said, "Only in the case of three occurrences of a given phenomenon do we recognize a presumption that such a thing is regularly going to happen."

   a. I:3: And what is a cell?

LVI. MISHNAH-TRACTATE SANHEDRIN 9:5C

A. HE WHO KILLS A SOMEONE NOT BEFORE WITNESSES THEY PUT HIM IN PRISON:

1. I:1: How do we know that this man has killed someone?

B. AND FEED HIM THE BREAD OF ADVERSITY AND THE WATER OF AFFLICTION (IS. 30:20):

1. II:1: Why does the passage at hand frame matters as, And they feed him the bread of adversity and the water of affliction , while the other passage states, The court puts him in prison and feeds him barley until his belly explodes ?

LVII. MISHNAH-TRACTATE SANHEDRIN 9:6

A. HE WHO STOLE A SACRED VESSEL OF THE CULT:

1. I:1: What is a sacred vessel M. 9:6A?

B. AND HE WHO CURSES USING THE NAME OF AN IDOL, AND HE WHO HAS SEXUAL RELATIONS WITH AN ARAMAEAN WOMAN – ZEALOTS BEAT HIM UP ON THE SPOT:

1. II:1: R. Joseph taught on Tannaite authority, "May the idol smite its enchanter."

2. II:2: R. Kahana asked Rab, "What is the law if the zealots do not beat him up?"

3. II:3: Said R. Hiyya bar Abbuyah, "Whoever has sexual relations with a Samaritan woman is as if he marries an idol."

4. II:4: When R. Dimi came, he said, "The court of the Hasmoneans made a decree that one who has sexual relations with a Samaritan woman is liable on her account on the counts of having sexual relations with a menstruating woman, a gentile maid servant, a gentile woman, and a married woman."

5. II:5: Said R. Hisda, "If a zealot comes to take counsel as to punishing a law violator, such as is listed at M. 9:6A, they do not give him instructions to do so."

C. THE ZEALOTRY OF PHINEAS

      a.   II:6: And Moses said to the judges of Israel, Slay every one his men that were joined to Baal Peor" (Num. 25:5). The tribe of Simeon went to Zimri b. Salu and said to him, "Lo, the judges are judging capital cases, and you sit silent." What did he do? He went and called together twenty-four thousand Israelites and went to Kozbi and said to her, "Listen to me and have sexual relations with me."

      b.   II:7: Said R. Nahman said Rab, "What is the meaning of the verse of Scripture, 'A greyhound, a he-goat also, and a king, against whom there is no rising up' (Prov. 30:31)? Four hundred twenty-four acts of sexual relations did that wicked man have that day. Phineas waited for him until he grew weak, for he did not know that 'a king, against whom there is no rising up' is God."

      c.   II:8: Said R. Sheshet, "Her name was not Cosbi but Shewilani, daughter of Zur. Why was she called Kozbi? Because she violated her father's instructions in having sexual relations with someone as unimportant as Zimri."

      d.   II:9: Said R. Yohanan, "Zimri had five names: Zimri, son of Salu; Saul, son of the Canaanite woman; and Shelumiel, son of Zurishaddai.'

D.   A PRIEST WHO PERFORMED THE RITE IN A STATE OF UNCLEANNESS – HIS BROTHERS, THE PRIESTS, DO NOT BRING HIM TO COURT. BUT THE YOUNG PRIESTS TAKE HIM OUTSIDE THE COURTYARD AND BREAK HIS HEAD WITH CLUBS.

   1.   III:1: R. Aha, son of R. Huna, asked R. Sheshet, "Is a priest who performed an act of service while in a state of uncleanness liable to the death penalty at the hands of heaven, or is he not liable to the death penalty at the hands of heaven?"

      a.   III:2: Gloss of a detail of the foregoing.

E.   A NON-PRIEST WHO SERVED IN THE TEMPLE – R. AQIBA SAYS, "HE IS PUT TO DEATH BY STRANGLING NUM. 18:7." AND SAGES SAY, "HE IS PUT TO DEATH AT THE HANDS OF HEAVEN."

   1.   IV:1: It has been taught on Tannaite authority: R. Ishmael says, "Here it is said, 'And the non-priest who comes near shall be put to death' (Num. 18:7), and elsewhere, 'Whosoever comes anything near to the tabernacle of the Lord shall die' (Num. 17:28). Just as in the latter case the rebellion of Korah and the subsequent plague, it is death at

the hands of heaven, so here it is death at the hands of heaven."

LVIII. MISHNAH-TRACTATE SANHEDRIN 10:1A-C

A.   THESE ARE THE ONES WHO ARE TO BE STRANGLED: HE WHO HITS HIS FATHER AND HIS MOTHER; HE WHO STEALS AN ISRAELITE ; AN ELDER WHO DEFIES THE DECISION OF A COURT, A FALSE PROPHET, A PROPHET WHO PROPHESIES IN THE NAME OF AN IDOL;
HE WHO HAS SEXUAL RELATIONS WITH A MARRIED WOMAN, THOSE WHO BEAR FALSE WITNESS AGAINST A PRIEST'S DAUGHTER AND AGAINST ONE WHO HAS SEXUAL RELATIONS WITH HER.

1.   I:1: He who hits his father and his mother: How on the basis of Scripture do we know that such a one is strangled?

   a.   I:2: It was necessary for Scripture to state, "He who smites a man" (Ex. 21:12), and it also was necessary for Scripture to state, "Who kills any soul" (Num. 35:30). For if the All-Merciful had written, "He who smites a man that he die" (Ex. 21:12), I might have maintained that that rule pertains to smiting by an adult, who is subject to the obligation to carry out the commandments, but it would not apply to smiting by a minor, who is not.

2.   I:3: And might I propose that one who smites his parents is put to death even though he does not make a bruise on them?

   a.   I:4: For the question was raised: What is the law on a son's letting blood for his father? R. Mattena said, "'And you shall love your neighbor as yourself' (Lev. 19:18). The son surely may do so, since he would do the same for himself. Just as the one who smites a beast for purposes of healing is exempt, so one who smites a man for purposes of healing is exempt."

3.   I:5: The following question was addressed to R. Sheshet: "What is the law on appointing a son to be an agent of a court as to his own father, to inflict a flogging on him or to curse him?" He said to them, "And have they permitted an outsider to do so except for the honor owing to heaven? It is a superior obligation, and here too, the honor owing to Heaven is a superior obligation. So a son may act for the court."

LIX. MISHNAH-TRACTATE SANHEDRIN 10:1D-G

A.   HE WHO HITS HIS FATHER AND HIS MOTHER IS LIABLE ONLY IF HE WILL MAKE A LASTING BRUISE ON THEM. THIS RULE IS MORE STRICT IN THE CASE OF THE ONE WHO CURSES THAN THE ONE WHO HITS THEM. FOR THE ONE WHO CURSES THEM AFTER THEY HAVE DIED IS LIABLE. BUT THE ONE WHO HITS THEM AFTER THEY HAVE DIED IS EXEMPT.

    1.   I:1: Our rabbis have taught on Tannaite authority: "His father or his mother he has cursed" (Lev. 20:9). This applies even after they have died. For one might have thought to the contrary that since one is liable for hitting them and also liable for cursing them, just as one who hits them is liable only if he does so while they are alive, so the one who curses them is liable only if he does so while they are alive.

        a.   I:2: May we say that the dispute at hand follows the course of the Tannaite dispute which follows?

LX. MISHNAH-TRACTATE SANHEDRIN 10:1H-P

A.   HE WHO STEALS AN ISRAELITE B2 IS LIABLE ONLY WHEN HE WILL HAVE BROUGHT HIM INTO HIS OWN DOMAIN. R. JUDAH SAYS, "ONLY IF HE WILL HAVE BROUGHT HIM INTO HIS OWN DOMAIN AND WILL HAVE MADE USE OF HIM, AS IT IS SAID, 'AND IF HE DEAL WITH HIM AS A SLAVE OR SELL HIM' (DEUT. 24:7)."

    1.   I:1: Does not the first of the two Tannaite authorities at M. 10:1H-I require utilization of the victim as a prerequisite to liability for kidnapping?

    2.   I:2: R. Jeremiah raised this question, "If one stole and sold a person while he was sleeping, what is the law? If one sold a woman for the sake of enslaving the foetus, what is the law?"

    3.   I:3: Our rabbis have taught on Tannaite authority: "If a man be found stealing any of his brethren of the children of Israel" (Deut. 24:7): I know only that the law applies to a man who stole someone. How do I know that the law applies to a woman's doing so?

    4.   I:4: It has further been taught on Tannaite authority: "If a man be found stealing any of his brethren" (Deut. 24:7): All the same are the one who steals a man and the one who steals a woman, a proselyte, a freed slave, and a minor. One is liable on any of these counts. If one stole someone but did not sell him, sold him but he is yet within his domain, he is exempt from liability. If he sold him to his father or his

brothers or to any of his relatives, he is liable. He who steals slaves is exempt (T. B.Q. 8:1A-I).

B.   HE WHO STEALS HIS SON – R. ISHMAEL, SON OF R. YOHANAN B. BEROQAH, DECLARES HIM LIABLE. AND SAGES DECLARE HIM EXEMPT:

1.   II:1: What is the scriptural basis for the view of rabbis?

C.   IF HE STOLE SOMEONE WHO WAS HALF SLAVE AND HALF FREE – R. JUDAH DECLARES HIM LIABLE. AND SAGES DECLARE HIM EXEMPT.

1.   III:1: If he stole someone who was half slave: We have learned in the Mishnah: R. Judah says, "Slaves do not receive payment for being humiliated" M. B.Q. 8:3G. What is the scriptural basis for the position of R. Judah?

2.   III:2: Where in Scripture do we find an admonition against kidnapping since Deut. 24:7 and Ex. 21:16 state only the penalty for doing so?

3.   III:3: Our rabbis have taught on Tannaite authority: "You shall not steal" (Ex. 20:15). Scripture speaks of kidnapping persons.

4.   III:4: Further teaching on Tannaite authority: "You shall not steal" (Ex. 20:15): Scripture speaks of stealing money. You say that it speaks of stealing money, but perhaps it speaks only of stealing persons?

5.   III:5: It has been stated on Amoraic authority: If one set of witnesses said that there had been a kidnapping and another set of witnesses said that there had been a sale of a kidnap-victim, and both were proved a conspiracy of perjurers – Hezekiah said, "They are not put to death." R. Yohanan said, "They are put to death."

6.   III:6: Said R. Assi, "Witnesses against one on account of selling someone, who were proved to form a conspiracy for perjury, are not put to death."

LXI. MISHNAH-TRACTATE SANHEDRIN 10:2

A.   AN ELDER WHO DEFIES THE DECISION OF A COURT, AS IT IS SAID, "IF THERE ARISE A MATTER TOO HARD FOR YOU IN JUDGMENT, BETWEEN BLOOD AND BLOOD, BETWEEN PLEA AND PLEA" (DEUT. 17:8) –

1.   I:1: Our rabbis have taught on Tannaite authority: "If a thing be outstandingly difficult for you" (Deut. 17:8): Scripture speaks of an outstanding figure on a court and not a disciple. "You" – this refers to a counsellor, and so it is said, "There is one come out from you, who imagines evil against the Lord,

a wicked counsellor" (Nahum 1:11). "A thing" – refers to a law. "In judgment" – refers to a ruling based on an influential argument.

2. I:2: Our rabbis have taught on Tannaite authority: "A presumptuous sage is liable only on account of a ruling concerning a matter, the deliberate violation of which is subject to the penalty of extirpation, and the inadvertent violation of which is subject to the penalty of bringing a sin-offering," the words of R. Meir. R. Judah says, "It involves a matter, the principle of which derives from the teachings of the Torah, and the elaboration of which derives from the teachings of scribes." R. Simeon says, "It involves even the most minor detail among the details contributed by scribes."

3. I:3: Said R. Huna bar Hinena to Raba, "Explain to me the teaching on Tannaite authority of unit I in accord with the view of R. Meir about what is at issue, that is, distinctions based on types of penalty."

   a. I:4: Systematic exegesis of the proof of I.1.

B. THERE WERE THREE COURTS THERE. ONE WAS IN SESSION AT THE DOOR GATE OF THE TEMPLE MOUNT, ONE WAS IN SESSION AT THE GATE OF THE COURTYARD, AND ONE WAS IN SESSION IN THE HEWN-STONE CHAMBER.

   THEY COME TO THE ONE WHICH IS AT THE GATE OF THE TEMPLE MOUNT AND SAY, "THUS I HAVE EXPLAINED THE MATTER, AND THUS MY COLLEAGUES HAVE EXPLAINED THE MATTER. THUS I HAVE RULED IN THE MATTER, AND THUS MY COLLEAGUES HAVE RULED." IF THEY HAD HEARD A RULING, THEY TOLD IT TO THEM, AND IF NOT, THEY COME ALONG TO THAT COURT WHICH WAS AT THE GATE OF THE COURTYARD. AND HE SAYS, "THUS I HAVE EXPLAINED THE MATTER, AND THUS MY COLLEAGUES HAVE EXPLAINED THE MATTER. "THUS I HAVE RULED IN THE MATTER AND THUS MY COLLEAGUES HAVE RULED." IF THEY HAD HEARD A RULING, THEY TOLD IT TO THEM, AND IF NOT, THESE AND THOSE COME ALONG TO THE HIGH COURT WHICH WAS IN THE HEWN-STONE CHAMBER, FROM WHICH TORAH GOES FORTH TO ALL ISRAEL, AS IT IS SAID, "FROM THAT PLACE WHICH THE LORD SHALL CHOOSE" (DEUT. 17:12).

1. II:1: With reference to M. 10:2E-F, said R. Kahana, If he says, "'I heard it from tradition, and they say, 'We heard it from tradition,' he is not put to death. If he says, 'Thus matters appear to me on this basis of reasoning,' and they say, 'Thus matters appear to us on the basis of reasoning,' he is not put

to death. And all the more so if he says, 'I heard it from tradition,' and they say, 'Thus matters appear to us,' he is not put to death. He is put to death only if he says, 'Thus it appears to me,' while they say, 'We have heard on the basis of tradition.' You may know that that is the case, for lo, they did not put Aqabia b. Mehallel to death."

2.   II:2: It has been taught on Tannaite authority: Said R. Yosé, "At first there were dissensions in Israel only in the court of seventy in the hewn-stone chamber in Jerusalem. And there were other courts of twenty-three in the various towns of the land of Israel, and there were other courts of three judges each in Jerusalem, one on the Temple mount, and one on the Rampart. If someone needed to know what the law is, he would go to the court in his town...."

    a.   II:3: They sent from there, "Who is someone who will inherit the world to come? It is one who is meek and humble, who bends when he comes and and bends when he goes out, who always is studying the Torah, but does not take pride in himself in on that account."

C.   IF HE WENT BACK TO HIS TOWN AND AGAIN RULED JUST AS HE HAD RULED BEFORE, HE IS EXEMPT. BUT IF HE INSTRUCTED OTHERS TO DO IT IN THAT WAY, HE IS LIABLE, AS IT IS SAID, "AND THE MAN WHO DOES PRESUMPTUOUSLY" (DEUT. 17:12). HE IS LIABLE ONLY IF HE WILL GIVE INSTRUCTIONS TO PEOPLE ACTUALLY TO CARRY OUT THE DEED IN ACCORD WITH THE NOW-REJECTED VIEW. A DISCIPLE OF A SAGE WHO GAVE INSTRUCTION TO CARRY OUT THE DEED WRONGLY IS EXEMPT. IT TURNS OUT THAT THE STRICT RULING CONCERNING HIM THAT HE CANNOT GIVE DECISIONS ALSO IS A LENIENT RULING CONCERNING HIM THAT HE IS NOT PUNISHED IF HE DOES GIVE DECISIONS.

1.   III:1: Our rabbis have taught on Tannaite authority: He is liable only if he will act in accord with the instruction that he has given, or unless he instructs others to do so and they act in accord with his instruction (T. San. 14:12).

LXII. MISHNAH-TRACTATE SANHEDRIN 10:3

A.   A MORE STRICT RULE APPLIES TO THE TEACHINGS OF SCRIBES THAN TO THE TEACHINGS OF TORAH. HE WHO, IN ORDER TO TRANSGRESS THE TEACHINGS OF THE TORAH, RULES, "THERE IS NO REQUIREMENT TO WEAR PHYLACTERIES," IS EXEMPT. BUT IF, IN ORDER TO ADD TO WHAT THE SCRIBES HAVE TAUGHT, HE SAID, "THERE ARE

FIVE PARTITIONS IN THE PHYLACTERY, INSTEAD OF FOUR, HE IS LIABLE.

1. I:1: Said R. Eleazar, said R. Oshaia, "The liability applies only to a case in which the principle derives from the teachings of the Torah, the amplification derives from words of scribes, there is a possibility of adding, but if, should there be addition, it constitutes diminution. The only example of such a matter is the case of the phylacteries. The fundamental law of wearing phylacteries is biblical. By rabbinic interpretation, the phylactery for the head must contain four compartments, with inscriptions in each. Hence it is possible to rule that it should consist of a greater number. But if this is done, the phylactery is unfit, so that the addition amounts to subtraction of its fitness."

LXIII. MISHNAH-TRACTATE SANHEDRIN 10:4

A. "THEY PUT HIM TO DEATH NOT IN THE COURT IN HIS OWN TOWN OR IN THE COURT WHICH IS IN YABNEH, BUT THEY BRING HIM UP TO THE HIGH COURT IN JERUSALEM. AND THEY KEEP HIM UNTIL THE FESTIVAL, AND THEY PUT HIM TO DEATH ON THE FESTIVAL, AS IT IS SAID, 'AND ALL THE PEOPLE SHALL HEAR AND FEAR AND NO MORE DO PRESUMPTUOUSLY' (DEUT. 17:13)," THE WORDS OF R. AQIBA. R. JUDAH SAYS, "THEY DO NOT DELAY THE JUDGMENT OF THIS ONE, BUT THEY PUT HIM TO DEATH AT ONCE. AND THEY WRITE MESSAGES AND SEND THEM WITH MESSENGERS TO EVERY PLACE: 'MR. SO-AND-SO, SON OF MR. SO-AND-SO, HAS BEEN DECLARED LIABLE TO THE DEATH PENALTY BY THE COURT.'"

1. I:1: Our rabbis have taught on Tannaite authority: "They put him to death not in the court in his own town or in the court which is in Yabneh, but they bring him up to the high court in Jerusalem. And they keep him until the festival, and they put him to death on the festival, as it is said, 'And all the people shall hear and fear and no more do presumptuously' (Deut. 17:13)," the words of R. Aqiba M. 10:4A-C.

2. I:2: Our rabbis have taught on Tannaite authority: The condemnation of four classes of criminals requires public announcement: one who entices a town to apostasy, a wayward and incorrigible son, a rebellious elder, and witnesses who have been proved to form a conspiracy for perjury. And in the case of all of them except for the fourth, it is written, "And all the people ...," or, "and all Israel ...."

LXIV. MISHNAH-TRACTATE SANHEDRIN 10:5-6

A. A FALSE PROPHET–ONE WHO PROPHESIES CONCERNING SOMETHING WHICH HE HAS NOT ACTUALLY HEARD OR CONCERNING SOMETHING WHICH WAS NOT ACTUALLY SAID TO HIM, IS PUT TO DEATH BY MAN. BUT HE WHO HOLDS BACK HIS PROPHESY, HE WHO DISREGARDS THE WORDS OF ANOTHER PROPHET, OR THE PROPHET WHO TRANSGRESSES HIS WORD WORDS IS PUT TO DEATH BY HEAVEN, AS IT IS SAID, "I WILL REQUIRE IT OF HIM:"

1. I:1: Our rabbis have taught on Tannaite authority: Three false prophets are put to death by man, and three are put to death by heaven. He who prophesies concerning something which he has not actually heard or concerning something which was not actually said to him and one who prophesies in the name of an idol – such as these are put to death by man.

2. I:2: What is the source of this rule? Said R. Judah said Rab, "It is because Scripture has said, 'But the prophet who shall presume to speak a word in may name' (Deut. 18:20) – this refers to a prophet who prophesies concerning something which he has not actually heard...."

B. ONE WHO PROPHESIES CONCERNING SOMETHING WHICH HE HAS NOT ACTUALLY HEARD:

1. II:1: For example, Zedekiah b. Chenaanah T. San. 14:14A-B, for it is written, "And Zedekiah, the son of Chenaanah, had made him horns of iron" (1 Kgs. 22:11).

C. ...OR CONCERNING SOMETHING WHICH WAS NOT ACTUALLY SAID TO HIM, IS PUT TO DEATH BY MAN

1. III:1: for example, Hananiah b. Azor (T. San. 14:14D). For Jeremiah was standing in the upper market, and saying, "Thus says the Lord of hosts, Behold I will break the bow of Elam" (Jer. 49:35).

2. III:2: He who prophesies in the name of an idol: for example Jonah b. Amittai (T. San. 14:15B).

3. III:3: He who holds back his prophecy: for example for example the friend of Micah, as it is written, "And a certain man of the sons of the prophets said to his fellow in the word of the Lord, Smite me I pray you, and the man refused to smite him" (1 Kgs. 20:35).

4. III:4: He who disregards the words of another prophet (M. 10:5D): for example for example, Iddo, the prophet T. San. 15:15E, as it is written, "For so it was charged me by the word of the Lord, saying, Eat not bread not drink water nor turn again by the same way that you come" (1 Kgs. 13:9).

5. III:5: A Tannaite authority repeated before R. Hisda, "He who holds back his prophecy is flogged." He said to him, "He who eats dates out of a sieve is flogged! Who warned the prophet who withheld his prophecy, since no one could have known about that fact? No admonition, no flogging!"

6. III:6: He who disregards the words of another prophet: How does one know that the other is a prophet, so that he should be punished? The other gives him a sign.

   a. III:7: "And it came to pass after these words that God tested Abraham" (Gen. 22:1): What is the meaning of "after"?

7. III:8: With reference to M. 10:6A-B, our rabbis have taught on Tannaite authority: A prophet who enticed people to commit idolatry is put to death through stoning. R. Simeon says, "It is through strangulation" Those who entice a whole town to commit idolatry are put to death through stoning. R. Simeon says, "Through strangulation" (cf. T. San. 11:5D).

   a. III:9: Our rabbis have taught on Tannaite authority: He who prophesies in such a way as to uproot a teaching of the Torah is liable. If he prophesies so as to confirm part and annul part of a teaching of the Torah, R. Simeon declares him exempt. But as for idolatry, even if one says, "Today serve it and tomorrow annul it," all parties concur that he is liable.

8. III:10: Said R. Abbahu said, R. Yohanan, "In any matter, if a prophet should say to you, 'Violate the teachings of the Torah,' obey him, except for the matter of idolatry. For even if he should make the sun stand still for you in the middle of the firmament, do not listen to him."

D. HE WHO PROPHESIES IN THE NAME OF AN IDOL, AND SAYS, "THUS DID SUCH-AND-SUCH AN IDOL SAY TO ME," EVEN THOUGH HE GOT THE LAW RIGHT, DECLARING UNCLEAN THAT WHICH IN FACT IS UNCLEAN, AND DECLARING CLEAN THAT WHICH IN FACT IS CLEAN.

HE WHO HAS SEXUAL RELATIONS WITH A MARRIED WOMAN AS SOON AS SHE HAS ENTERED THE DOMAIN OF THE HUSBAND IN MARRIAGE, EVEN THOUGH SHE HAS NOT HAD SEXUAL RELATIONS WITH HIM HE WHO HAS SEXUAL RELATIONS WITH HER – LO, THIS ONE IS PUT TO DEATH BY STRANGLING.

AND THOSE WHO BEAR FALSE WITNESS AGAINST A PRIEST'S DAUGHTER AND AGAINST ONE WHO HAS SEXUAL RELATIONS WITH HER. FOR ALL THOSE WHO BEAR FALSE

WITNESS FIRST SUFFER THAT SAME MODE OF EXECUTION,
EXCEPT FOR THOSE WHO BEAR FALSE WITNESS AGAINST A
PRIEST'S DAUGHTER AND HER LOVER.

1.   IV:1: What is the source in Scripture of this rule?

LXV.   MISHNAH-TRACTATE SANHEDRIN 11:1-2

   A.   ALL ISRAELITES HAVE A SHARE IN THE WORLD TO COME, AS
           IT IS SAID, "YOUR PEOPLE ALSO SHALL BE ALL RIGHTEOUS,
           THEY SHALL INHERIT THE LAND FOREVER; THE BRANCH OF
           MY PLANTING, THE WORK OF MY HANDS, THAT I MAY BE
           GLORIFIED" (IS. 60:21).
           AND THESE ARE THE ONES WHO HAVE NO PORTION IN THE
           WORLD TO COME: HE WHO SAYS, THE RESURRECTION OF
           THE DEAD IS A TEACHING WHICH DOES NOT DERIVE FROM
           THE TORAH:

1.   I:1: On Tannaite authority it was stated, "Such a one denied
      the resurrection of the dead, therefore he will not have a
      portion in the resurrection of the dead. For all the measures
      meted out by the Holy One, blessed be he, are in accord with
      the principle of measure for measure."

2.   I:2: How, on the basis of the Torah do we know about the
      resurrection of the dead? As it is said, "And you shall give
      thereof the Lord's heave-offering to Aaron the priest" (Num.
      18:28). And will Aaron live forever? And is it not the case
      that he did not even get to enter the Land of Israel, from the
      produce of which heave-offering is given? Rather, this
      teaches that he is destined once more to live, and the
      Israelites will give him heave-offering. On the basis of this
      verse, therefore, we see that the resurrection of the dead is a
      teaching of the Torah.

   a.   I:3: A Tannaite authority of the house of R. Ishmael
         taught, "' ... to Aaron ...', 'like Aaron. That is to say, just
         as Aaron was in the status of an associate who ate his
         produce in a state of cultic cleanness even when not in
         the Temple, so his sons must be in the status of
         associates."

3.   I:4: It has been taught on Tannaite authority: R. Simai says,
      "How on the basis of the Torah do we know about the
      resurrection of the dead?"

4.   I:5: Minim asked Rabban Gamaliel, "How do we know that
      the Holy One, blessed be he, will resurrect the dead?"

5. I:6: Romans asked R. Joshua b. Hananiah, "How do we know that the Holy One will bring the dead to life and also that he knows what is going to happen in the future?"

6. I:7: It has also been stated on Amoraic authority: Said R. Yohanan in the name of R. Simeon b. Yohai, "How do we know that the Holy One, blessed be he, will bring the dead to life and knows what is going to happen in the future?"

7. I:8: It has been taught on Tannaite authority: Said R. Eliezer b. R. Yosé, "In this matter I proved false the books of the minim. For they would say, 'The principle of the resurrection of the dead does not derive from the Torah.'"

   a. I:9: This accords with the following Tannaite dispute: "'That soul shall be utterly cut off' – 'shall be cut off' – in this world, 'utterly' – in the world to come," the words of R. Aqiba. Said R. Ishmael to him, "And has it not been said, 'He reproaches the Lord, and that soul shall be cut off' (Num. 15:31). Does this mean that there are three worlds? Rather: '... it will be cut off ...,' in this world, '... utterly ...,' in the world to come, and 'utterly cut off ...,' indicates that the Torah speaks in ordinary human language."

8. I:10: Queen Cleopatra asked R. Meir, saying, "I know that the dead will live, for it is written, 'And the righteous shall blossom forth out of your city like the grass of the earth' (Ps. 72:16). But when they rise, will they rise naked or in their clothing?"

9. I:11: Caesar said to Rabban Gamaliel, "You maintain that the dead will live. But they are dust, and can the dust live?"

10. I:12: A Tannaite authority of the house of R. Ishmael taught, "Resurrection is a matter of an argument a fortiori based on the case of a glass utensil. Now if glassware, which is the work of the breath of a mortal man, when broken, can be repaired, A mortal man, who is made by the breath of the Holy One, blessed be he, how much the more so that he can be repaired, in the resurrection of the dead."

11. I:13: A min said to R. Ammi, "You say that the dead will live. But they are dust, and will the dust live?"

12. I:14: A min said to Gebiha, son of Pesisa, a hunchback, "Woe for you! You are guilty! For you say that the dead will live. Those who are alive die, and will those who are dead live?"

B. TOPICAL APPENDIX ON GEBIHA, SON OF PASISA AND ALEXANDER THE GREAT

a.   I:15: Our rabbis have taught on Tannaite authority: When the Africans came to trial with Israel before Alexander of Macedonia, they said to him, "The land of Canaan belongs to us, for it is written, 'The land of Canaan, with the coasts thereof' (Num. 34:2), and Canaan was the father of these men."

b.   I:16: There was another time, and the Egyptians came to lay claim against Israel before Alexander of Macedonia. They said to him, "Lo, Scripture says, 'And the Lord gave the people favor in the sight of the Egyptians, and they lent them gold and precious stones' (Ex. 12:36). Give us back the silver and gold that you took from us."

c.   I:17: There was another time, and the children of Ishmael and the children of Keturah came to trial with the Israelites before Alexander of Macedonia. They said to him, "The land of Canaan belongs to us as well as to you, for it is written, 'Now these are the generations of Ishmael, son of Abraham' (Gen. 25:12), and it is written, 'And these are the generations of Isaac, Abraham's son' (Gen. 25:19). Both Ishmael and Isaac have an equal claim on the land, hence so too their descendants."

C.   TOPICAL APPENDIX ON ANTONINUS AND RABBI

1.   I:18: Antoninus said to Rabbi, "The body and the soul both can exempt themselves from judgment. How so? The body will say, 'The soul is the one that has sinned, for from the day that it left me, lo, I am left like a silent stone in the grave.' And the soul will say, 'The body is the one that sinned. For from the day that I left it, lo, I have been flying about in the air like a bird.'"

2.   I:19: Said Antoninus to Rabbi, "Why does the sun rise in the east and set in the west?"

3.   I:20: Said Antoninus to Rabbi, "At what point is the soul placed in man? Is it at the moment that it is decreed that the person shall be born or when the embryo is formed?"

4.   I:21: And Antoninus said to Rabbi, "At what point does the impulse to do evil take hold of a man? Is it from the moment of creation or from the moment of parturition?"

D.   CONTRASTING VERSES OF SCRIPTURE AND THE DEATH OF DEATH

1.   I:22: R. Simeon b. Laqish contrasted these two verses: "It is written, 'I will gather them ... with the blind and the lame, the woman with child and her that trail travails with child together' (Jer. 31:8), and it is written, 'Then shall the lame

man leap as a hart and the tongue of the dumb sing, for in the wilderness shall waters break out and streams in the desert' (Is. 35:6). How so will the dead both retain their defects and also be healed? They will rise from the grave bearing their defects and then be healed."

2. I:23: Ulla contrasted these two verses: "It is written, 'He will destroy death forever and the Lord God will wipe away tears from all faces' (Is. 25:9), and it is written, 'For the child shall die a hundred years old ... there shall no more thence an infant of days' (Is. 65:20). There is no contradiction. The one speaks of Israel, the other of idolators." But what do idolators want there in the reestablished state after the resurrection? It is to those concerning whom it is written, "And strangers shall stand and feed your flocks, and the sons of the alien shall be your plowmen and your vinedressers" (Is. 61:5)."

3. I:24: R. Hisda contrasted these two verses: "It is written, 'Then the moon shall be confounded and the sun ashamed, when the Lord of hosts shall reign' (Is 24:23), and it is written, 'Moreover the light of the moon shall be as the light of seven days' (Is 30:26). There is no contradiction. The one refers to the days of the Messiah, the other to the world to come."

4. I:25: Raba contrasted these two verses: "It is written, 'I kill and I make alive' (Deut. 32:"39) and it is written, 'I wound and I heal' (Deut. 32:39). The former implies that one is resurrected just as he was at death, thus with blemishes, and the other implies that at the resurrection all wounds are healed. Said the Holy One, blessed be he, 'What I kill I bring to life,' and then, 'What I have wounded I heal.'".

E. HOW ON THE BASIS OF THE TORAH DO WE KNOW ABOUT THE RESURRECTION OF THE DEAD?

1. I:26: Our rabbis have taught on Tannaite authority: "I kill and I make alive" (Deut. 32:39). Is it possible to suppose that there is death for one person and life for the other, just as the world is accustomed now? Scripture says, "I wound and I heal" (Deut. 32:39). Just as wounding and healing happen to one person, so death and then resurrection happen to one person. From this fact we derive an answer to those who say, "There is no evidence of the resurrection of the dead based on the teachings of the Torah."

2. I:27: It has been taught on Tannaite authority: R. Meir says, "How on the basis of the Torah do we know about the resurrection of the dead?"

3. I:28: Said R. Joshua b. Levi, "How on the basis of Scripture may we prove the resurrection of the dead?

4. I:29: Said R. Judah said Rab, "Whoever withholds a teaching of law from a disciple is as if he steals the inheritance of his fathers from him, for it is said, 'Moses commanded us Torah, even the inheritance of the congregation of Jacob' (Deut. 33:4). It is an inheritance destined for all Israel from the six days of creation."

5. I:30: Said R. Sheshet, "Whoever teaches Torah in this world will have the merit of teaching it in the world to come."

6. I:31: Said Raba, "How on the basis of the Torah do we find evidence for the resurrection of the dead?"

7. I:32: Said R. Eleazar, "Every authority who leads the community serenely will have the merit of leading them in the world to come, as it is said, 'For he who has mercy on them shall lead them, even by springs of water shall he guide them' (Is. 49:10)."

8. I:33: Said R. Tabi said R. Josiah, "What is the meaning of this verse of Scripture: 'The grave and the barren womb and the earth that is not filled by water' (Prov. 30:16). What has the grave to do with the womb? It is to say to you, just as the womb takes in and gives forth, so Sheol takes in and gives forth."

9. I:34: A Tannaite authority of the house of Elisha taught, "The righteous whom the Holy One, blessed be he, is going to resurrect will not revert to dust, for it is said, 'And it shall come to pass that he that is left in Zion and he that remains in Jerusalem shall be called holy, even everyone that is written among the living in Jerusalem, (Is. 4:3). Just as the Holy One lives forever, so they shall live forever." The passage concludes with the following, which accounts for the inclusion of I.35's statement on Nebuchadnezzar, thus the entire composite on Hananiah, Mishael, and Azariah: And said R. Yohanan, "From the river Eshel to Rabbath is the valley of Dura. For when Nebuchadnezzar, that wicked man, exiled Israel, there were young men who outshone the sun in their beauty. Chaldean women would see them and reach orgasm from the mere gaze. They told their husbands and their husbands told the king. The king ordered them killed. Still, the wives would reach orgasm merely from

laying eyes on the corpses. The king gave an order and they trampled the corpses beyond all recognition."

    a.   I:35: Our rabbis have taught on Tannaite authority: When Nebuchadnezzar, the wicked man, cast Hananiah, Mishael, and Azariah, into the fiery furnace, the Holy One, blessed be he, said to Ezekiel, "Go and raise the dead in the valley of Dura." When he had raised them, the bones came and smacked that wicked man in his face. He said, "What are these things?" They said to him, "The friend of these is raising the dead in the valley of Dura." He then said, "'How great are his signs, and how mighty his wonders. His kingdom is an everlasting kingdom, and his dominion is from generation to generation' (Dan. 3:23)."

F.   TOPICAL APPENDIX ON HANANIAH, MISHAEL, AND AZARIAH

    I.   I:36: Our rabbis have taught on Tannaite authority: Six miracles were done on that day, and these are they:

    II.   I:37: A Tannaite authority of the house of R. Eliezer b. Jacob taught, "Even in time of danger a person should not pretend that he does not hold his high office, For it is said, 'Then these men were bound in their coats, their hose, and their other garments' (Dan. 3:21). These were garments specially worn by men in their exalted position, and they did not doff them though cast into the furnace."

    III.   I:38: Said R. Yohanan, "The righteous are greater than ministering angels. For it is said, 'He answered and said, Lo, I see four men loose, walking in the midst of the fire, and they are not hurt, and the form of the fourth is like the son of God' (Dan. 3:25). Thus the angel is mentioned last, as being least esteemed."

    IV.   I:39: Said R. Tanhum bar Hanilai, "When Hananiah, Mishael, and Azariah went out of the fiery furnace, all the nations of the world came and slapped the enemies of Israel that is, Israel on their faces."

    V.   I:40: Said R. Samuel bar Nahmani said R. Jonathan, "What is the meaning of the verse of Scripture, 'I said, I will go up to the palm tree, I will take hold of the boughs thereof' (Song 7:9)?'I said I will go up to the palm tree' refers to Israel. But now 'I grasped' only one bough, namely, Hananiah, Mishael and Azariah."

VI. I:41: And said R. Yohanan, "What is the meaning of the verse of Scripture, 'I saw by night, and behold a man riding upon a red horse, and he stood among the myrtle trees that were in the bottom' (Zech. 1:8).? What is the meaning of, 'I saw by night'? The Holy One blessed be he, sought to turn the entire world into night. 'And behold, a man riding' – 'man' refers only to the Holy One, blessed be he, as it is said, 'The Lord is a man of war, the Lord is his name' (Ex. 15:3). 'On a red horse' – the Holy One, blessed be he, sought to turn the entire world to blood. When, however, he saw Hananiah, Mishael, and Azariah, he cooled off, as it is said, 'And he stood among the myrtle trees that were in the deep.'"

VII. I:42: The rabbis Hananiah, Mishael, and Azariah – where did they go?

VIII. I:43: Our rabbis have taught on Tannaite authority: There were three who were involved in that scheme to keep Daniel out of the furnace: the Holy One, blessed be he, Daniel, and Nebuchadnezzar.

IX. I:44: "Thus says the Lord of hosts, the God of Israel, of Ahab, son of Kolaiah, and of Zedekiah, son of Maaseiah, who prophesy a lie to you in my name" (Jer. 29:21) And it is written, "And of them shall be taken up a curse by all the captivity of Judah who are in Babylonia, saying, The Lord make you like Zedekiah and like Ahab, whom the king of Babylonia roasted in fire" (Jer. 29:22). What is said is not "whom he burned in fire" but "whom he roasted in fire."

X. I:45: "Because they have committed villainy in Israel and have committed adultery with their neighbors' wives" (Jer. 29:23): What did they do? They went to Nebuchadnezzar's daughter. Ahab said to her, "Thus said the Lord, 'Give yourself to Zedekiah.'"

XI. I:46: Said R. Tanhum, "In Sepphoris, bar Qappara interpreted the following verse: 'These six grains of barley gave he to me' (Ruth 3:17). What are the six of barley? If we should say that they were actually six of barley, was it the way of Boaz to give out a gift of only six barley grains? Rather it must have been six seahs of barley? And is it the way of a woman to carry six seahs? Rather, this formed an omen to her that six sons are destined to come forth from her, each of whom would receive six blessings, and these are they: David, the Messiah, Daniel, Hananiah, Mishael, and Azariah. David, as it is written, 'Then answered one of the servants and said, Behold I have seen the son of Jesse, the Bethlehemite, who is cunning in playing and a mighty, valiant man, and a man of war, and understanding in matters, and a handsome man, and the Lord is with him' (1 Sam. 16:18). The six epithets, viz., cunning in playing, mighty, valiant, etc., are regarded as blessings applicable to each of the six persons mentioned."

XII. I:47: "Now among these were of the children of Judah, Daniel, Hananiah, Mishael, and Azariah" (Dan. 1:6): Said R. Eleazar, "All of them came from the children of Judah." And R. Samuel bar Nahmani said, "Daniel came from the children of Judah, but Hananiah, Mishael, and Azariah came from the other tribes."

XIII. I:48: "And of your sons which shall issue from you, which you shall beget, shall they take away, and they shall be eunuchs in the palace of the king of Babylonia" (2 Kgs. 20:18): What are these "eunuchs"? Rab said, "Literally, eunuchs." And R. Hanina said, "The sense is that idolatry was castrated i.e. made sterile in their time." In the view of him who has said that idolatry was castrated in their time, that is in line with the verse of Scripture, "And there is no hurt in them" (Dan. 3:25). But in the view of him who says that "eunuch" is in its literal sense, what is the meaning of, "And there is no hurt in them" (Dan. 3:25) Since they had been castrated? It is that the fire did them no injury.

XIV. I:49: Now since whatever concerns Ezra was stated by Nehemiah b. Hachlia, what is the reason that the book was not called by his name? Said R.

Jeremiah bar Abba, "It is because he took pride in himself, as it is written, 'Think up on me for good, my God' (Neh. 5:19)." David also made such a statement, "Remember me, Lord, with the favor that you bear for your people, visit me with your salvation" (Ps. 106:4). It was supplication that David sought. R. Joseph said, "It was because Nehemiah had spoken disparagingly about his predecessors, as it is said, 'But the former governors who had been before me were chargeable unto the people and had taken of them bread and wine, beside forty shekels of silver' (Neh. 5:15). Furthermore, he spoke in this way even of Daniel, who was greater than he was." And how do we know that Daniel was greater than he was?

G.   THE MESSIAH. PHARAOH, SENNACHERIB, HEZEKIAH, AND OTHER PLAYERS IN THE MESSIANIC DRAMA

1.   I:50: Of the increase of his government and peace there shall be no end" (Is. 9:6): R. Tanhum said, "In Sepphoris, Bar Qappara expounded this verse as follows: 'On what account is every M in the middle of a word open, but the one in the word "increase" is closed? 'The Holy One, blessed be he, proposed to make Hezekiah Messiah, and Sennacherib into Gog and Magog. 'The attribute of justice said before the Holy One, blessed be he, "Lord of the world, Now if David, king of Israel, who recited how many songs and praises before you, you did not make Messiah, Hezekiah, for whom you have done all these miracles, and who did not recite a song before you, surely should not be made Messiah."

2.   I:51: "The burden of Dumah. He calls to me out of Seir, Watchman, what of the night? Watchman, what of the night?" (Is. 21:11): Said R. Yohanan, "That angel who is appointed over the souls is named Dumah. All the souls gathered to Dumah, and said to him, "'Watchman, what of the night? Watchman, what of the night?' (Is. 21:11). Said the watchman, 'The morning comes and also the night, if you will inquire, inquire, return, come' (Is. 21:11)."

3.   I:52: A Tannaite authority in the name of R. Pappias said, "It was a shame for Hezekiah and his associates that they did not recite a song, until the earth opened and said a song, as it is said, 'From the uttermost part of the earth have we hard songs, even glory to the righteous' (Is. 24:16)."

a. I:53: "And Jethro rejoiced" (Ex. 18:9) Rab and Samuel – Rab said, "It was that he passed a sharp knife across his flesh circumcising himself." And Samuel said, "All his flesh became goose-pimples because of the destruction of the Egyptians."

4. I:54: "Therefore shall the Lord, the Lord of hosts, send among his fat ones leanness" (Is. 10:16): What is "among his· fat ones leanness"? Said the Holy One, blessed be he, "Let Hezekiah come, who has eight names, and exact punishment from Sennacherib, who has eight names."

5. I:55: "And beneath his glory shall he kindle a burning like the burning of a fire" (Is. 10:16): Said R. Yohanan, "Under his glory, but not actually his glory."

6. I:56: A Tannaite authority in the name of R. Joshua b. Qorhah taught, "Since Pharaoh blasphemed personally, the Holy One, blessed be he, exacted punishment from him personally. Since Sennacherib blasphemed through a messenger, the Holy One, blessed be he, exacted punishment from him through a messenger."

7. I:57: R. Hanina b. Pappa contrasted two verses: "It is written, 'I will enter the height of his border' (Is. 37:24), and it is further written, 'I will enter into the lodgings of his borders' (2 Kgs. 19:23). Said that wicked man, 'First I shall destroy the lower dwelling, and afterward I shall destroy the upper dwelling.'"

8. I:58: Said R. Joshua b. Levi, "What is the meaning of the verse of Scripture, 'Am I now come up without the Lord against this place to destroy it? The Lord said to me, Go up against this land and destroy it' (2 Kgs. 18:25). What is the sense of the passage? He had heard the prophet, who had said, 'Since this people refuses the waters of Shiloah that go softly and rejoice in Rezina and Ramaliah's son, now therefore behold the Lord brings up upon them the waters of the river, strong and many, even the king of Assyria and all his glory, and he shall come up over all his channels and go over all his banks' (Is. 8:6). This was understood by Sennacherib as an order to possess Jerusalem."

9. I:59: Said R. Yohanan, "What is the meaning of this verse: 'The curse of the Lord is in the house of the wicked, but he blesses the habitation of the just' (Prov. 3:33)? 'The curse of the Lord is in the house of the wicked' refers to Pekah, son of Ramaliah, who would eat forty seahs of pigeons for desert. 'But he blesses the habitation of the just' refers to Hezekiah,

king of Judea, who would eat a litra of vegetables for a whole meal."

10. I:60: "Now therefore behold, the Lord brings up upon them the waters of the river, strong and many, even the king of Assyria and all his glory" (Is. 8:7). And it is written, "And he shall pass through Judea, he shall overflow and go over, he shall reach even to the neck" (Is. 8:8). Then why was Sennacherib punished?

11. I:61: What is the meaning of this verse: "When aforetime the land of Zebulun and the land of Naphtali lightened its burden, but in later times it was made heavy by the way of the sea, beyond Jordan, in Galilee of the nations" (Is. 8:23)? It was not like the early generations, who made the yoke of the Torah light for themselves, but the later generations, who made the yoke of the Torah heavy for themselves. And these were worthy that a miracle should be done for them, just as was done for those who passed through the sea and trampled over the Jordan.

12. I:62: "After these things, and the truth thereof, Sennacherib, king of Assyria, came and entered Judea and encamped against the fortified cities and thought to win them for himself" (2 Chr. 32:1): Such a recompense to Hezekiah for such a gift? The previous verse relates that Hezekiah turned earnestly to the service of God. Was then Sennacherib's invasion his just reward?

13. I:63: "And it shall come to pass in that day that his burden shall be taken away from off your shoulders and his yoke from off your neck, and the yoke shall be destroyed because of the oil" (Is. 10:27): Said R. Isaac Nappaha, "The yoke of Sennacherib will be destroyed because of the oil of Hezekiah, which he would kindle in the synagogues and school houses. What did Hezekiah do? He affixed a sword at the door of the school house and said, 'Whoever does not take up study of the Torah will be pierced by this sword.' They searched from Dan to Beer Sheba and found no ignoramus, from Gabbath to Antipatris and found no boy or girl, no man or woman, not expert in the laws of uncleanness and cleanness."

14. I:64: "And your spoil shall be gathered like the gathering of a caterpillar" (Is. 33:4): Said the prophet to Israel, "Gather your spoil." They said to him, "Is it for individual spoil or for sharing?" He said to them, "'Like the gathering of a caterpillar' (Is. 33:4): Just as in the gathering of a caterpillar

it is each one for himself, so in your spoil it is each one for himself."

15. I:65: Said R. Huna, "That wicked man Sennacherib made ten marches that day, as it is said, 'He is come to Aiath, he is passed at Migron, at Michmash he has laid up his carriages, they are gone over the passage, they have taken up their lodgings at Geba, Ramah is afraid, Gibeah of Saul is fled, Lift up your voice, O daughter of Gallim, cause it to be heard to Laish, O poor Anathoth, Madmenah is removed, the inhabitants of Gebim gather themselves to flee' (Is. 10:28-31)."

16. I:66: What is the meaning of the statement, "As yet shall be halt at Nob that day" (Is. 10:32)? Said R. Huna, "That day alone remained for the punishment of the sin committed at Nob Sam. 22:17-19. When the priests of Nob were massacred. God set a term for punishment, of which that day was the last.

17. I:67: "And Ishbi-benob, who was of the sons of the giant, the weight of whose spear weighed three hundred shekels of brass in weight, being girded with a new sword, thought to have slain David" (2 Sam. 21:16): What is the sense of "Ishbi-be-nob"? Said R. Judah said Rab, "It was a man ish who came on account of the matter of the sin committed at Nob. Said the Holy One, blessed be he, to David, 'How long will the sin committed against Nob be concealed in your hand. On your account, Nob was put to death, the city of priests, on your account, Doeg the Edomite was sent into exile; on your account, Saul and his three sons were killed. 'Do you want you descendents to be wiped out, or do you want to be handed over into the power of an enemy?' He said to him, 'Lord of the world, It is better that I be handed over to an enemy but that my descendents not be wiped out.'"

   a. I:68: Our rabbis have taught on Tannaite authority: For three did the earth fold up to make their journey quicker: Eliezer, Abraham's servant, Jacob our father, and Abishai b. Zeruiah. As to Abishai, son of Zeruiah, it is as we have just said. As to Eliezer, Abraham's servant, it is written, "And I came this day to the well" (Gen. 24:42), meaning that that very day he had set out. As to Jacob, our father, as it is written, "And Jacob went out from Beer Sheba and went to Haran" (Gen. 28:10), and it is said, "And he lighted upon a certain place and tarried there all night, because the sun had set" (Gen. 28:11).

18. I:69: And how do we know that the seed of David ceased

19. I:70: Said R. Judah said Rab, "The wicked Sennacherib came against them with forty-five thousand men, sons of kings seated on golden chariots, with their concubines and whores, and with eighty thousand mighty soldiers, garbed in coats of mail, and sixty thousand swordsmen running before him, and the rest cavalry. And so they came against Abraham, and in the age to come so they will come with Gog and Magog."

20. I:71: It was taught on Tannaite authority: The first ones crossed by swimming, as it is said, "He shall overflow and go over" (Is. 8:8). The middle ones crossed standing up, as it is said, "He shall reach even to the neck" (Is. 8:8). The last group brought up the dirt of the river with their feet and so found no water in the river to drink, so that they had to bring them water from some other place, which they drank, as it is said, "I have digged and drunk water" (Is. 37:25).

21. I:72: How did the angel smite the army?

22. I:73: How many of Sennacherib's army remained?

23. I:74: Said R. Abbahu, "Were it not that a verse of Scripture is explicitly spelled out, it would not have been possible to say it: For it is written, 'In the same day shall the Lord shave with a razor that is hired, namely, by the riverside, by the king of Assyria, the head and the hair of the feet, and it shall consume the beard' (Is. 7:20. The Holy One, blessed be he, came and appeared before Sennacherib as an old man. He said to him, 'When you go against the kings of east and west, whose sons you brought and saw killed, what will you say to them?'"

   a. I:75: "And he fought against them, he and his servants, by night, and smote them" (Gen. 14:15): Said R. Yohanan, "That angel who was assigned to Abraham was named 'Night,' as it is said, 'Let the day perish wherein I was born and the Night which said, There is a man-child conceived' (Job 3:3). The verse, Gen. 14:15, is translated, and Night fought on their behalf, he and his....'" Inserted because of the concluding statement: Said R. Yohanan, "When that righteous man came to Dan, he grew weak. He foresaw that the children of his children were destined to commit acts of idolatry in Dan, as it is said, 'And he set the one in Beth El, and the other he put in Dan' (1 Kgs. 12:29). And also that wicked man Nebuchadnezzar did not grow strong until he reached

Dan, as it is said, 'From Dan the snorting of his horses was heard' (Jer. 8:16)."

25. I:76: Said R. Zira, "Even though R. Judah b. Beterah sent word from Nisibis, 'Pay heed to an elder who has forgotten his learning through not fault of his own and to cut the jugular veins in slaughtering a beast, in accord with the view of R. Judah, 'and take heed of the sons of the ordinary folk, for from them too will Torah go forth,' for such a matter as the following we may convey matters to them and not refrain from teaching this lesson: '"You are righteous, Lord, when I please with you, yet let met talk to thee of your judgments, wherefore does the way of the wicked prosper? Wherefore are all they happy who deal very treacherously? You have planted them, yes, they have taken root, they grow, yes, they bring forth fruit" (Jer. 12:1-2).

26. I:77: What is the meaning of the fact that Merodach-Baladan is called "the son of Baladan"? They say: Baladan was king, and his appearance changed into that of a dog, so his son sat on the throne. When he would sign a document, he would write his name and the name of his father, "King Baladan."

27. I:78: Said Raba, "It was bearing three hundred mules loaded with iron axes that could break iron that Nebuchadnezzar sent Nebuzaradan. All of them broke on one gate of Jerusalem, as it is said, 'And now they attack its gate together; with axes and hammers they hit it' (Ps. 74:6). He wanted to go back. He said, 'I am afraid that they might do to me as they did to Sennacherib. A voice came forth: 'Leaper son of a leaper, leap, Nebuzaradan! The time has come for the sanctuary to be destroyed and the palace burned.'"

   a. I:79: Our rabbis have taught on Tannaite authority: Naaman was a resident proselyte. Nebuzaradan was a righteous proselyte. Grandsons of Sisera studied Torah in Jerusalem. Grandsons of Sennacherib taught Torah in public.

28. I:80: Said Ulla, "Ammon and Moab were bad neighbors of Jerusalem. When they heard the prophets prophesying the destruction of Jerusalem, they sent word to Nebuchadnezzar, 'Go out and come here.' He said, 'I am afraid that they will do to me what they did to those who came before me.' They sent to him, '"For the man is not at home" (Prov. 7:19), and "man" can refer only to the Holy One, blessed be he, as it is said, "The Lord is a man of war"

(Ex. 15:3).' He replied, 'He is nearby and he will come.' They sent to him, '"He has gone on a far journey" (Prov. 7:19).' He sent to them, 'There are righteous men there, who will pray for mercy and bring him back.'"

H.   WHEN WILL THE MESSIAH COME?

1.   I:81: Said R. Nahman to R. Isaac, "Have you heard when the son of 'the fallen one' will come?" He said to him, "Who is the son of 'the fallen one'?" He said to him, "It is the Messiah." "Do you call the Messiah 'the son of the fallen one'?" He said to him, "Yes, for it is written, 'On that day I will raise up the tabernacle of David, the fallen one' (Amos 9:11)."

2.   I:82: Our rabbis have taught on Tannaite authority: The seven year cycle in which the son of David will come: As to the first one, the following verse of Scripture will be fulfilled: "And I will cause it to rain upon one city and not upon another" (Amos 4:7). As to the second year, the arrows of famine will be sent forth. As to the third, there will be a great famine, in which men, women, and children will die, pious men and wonder-workers alike, and the Torah will be forgotten by those that study it. As to the fourth year, there will be plenty which is no plenty. As to the fifth year, there will be great prosperity, and people will eat, drink, and rejoice, and the Torah will be restored to those that study it. As to the sixth year, there will be rumors. As to the seventh year, there will be wars.

3.   I:83: It has been taught on Tannaite authority: R. Judah says, "In the generation in which the son of David will come, the gathering place will be for prostitution, Galilee will be laid waste, Gablan will be made desolate, and the men of the frontier will go about from town to town, and none will take pity on them; and the wisdom of scribes will putrefy; and those who fear sin will be rejected; and the truth will be herded away (M. Sot. 9:15AA-GG).

   a.   I:84: Said Raba, "To begin with I had supposed that there is no truth in the world. One of the rabbis, R. Tabut by name (and some say, R. Tabyomi by name), who would not go back on his word even though people gave him all the treasures of the world, said to me that one time he happened to come to a place called Truth."

4.   I:85: It has been taught on Tannaite authority: R. Nehorai says, "In the generation in which the son of David will come, children will shame elders, and elders will stand up before

children. 'The daughter rises up against the mother, and the daughter-in-law against her mother-in-law' (Mic. 7:6). The face of the generation is the face of a dog, and a son is not ashamed before his father" (M. Sot. 9:15HH-KK).

5. I:86: It has been taught on Tannaite authority: R. Nehemiah says, "In the generation in which the son of David will come, presumption increases, and dearth increases, and the vine gives its fruit and wine at great cost. The government turns to heresy, and there is no reproof" (M. Sot. 9:15W-Z).

6. I:87: Our rabbis have taught on Tannaite authority: "For the Lord shall judge his people and repent himself of his servants, when he sees that their power has gone, and there is none shut up or left" (Deut. 32:36). The son of David will come only when traitors are many. Another matter: Only when disciples are few. Another matter: Only when a penny will not be found in anyone's pocket.

7. I:88: Said R. Qattina, "The world will exist for six thousand years and be destroyed for one thousand, as it is said, 'And the Lord alone shall be exalted in that day' (Is. 2:11)." Abbayye said, "It will be desolate for two thousand years, as it is said, 'After two days will he revive us, in the third day, he will raise us up and we shall live in his sight' (Hos. 6:2)."

8. I:89: A Tannaite authority of the house of Elijah said, "For six thousand years the world will exist. For two thousand it will be desolate, two thousand years will be the time of Torah, and two thousand years will be the days of the Messiah."

9. I:90: Said Elijah to R. Sala the Pious, "The world will last for no fewer than eighty-five Jubilees of fifty years each, and the son of David will come in the last one."

10. I:91: R. Hanan, son of Tahalipa, sent to R. Joseph, "I came across a man who had in hand a scroll, written in Assyrian block letters in the holy language. I said to him, 'Where did you get this?' He said to me, 'I was employed in the Roman armies, and I found it in the Roman archives.' In the scroll it is written that after four thousand two hundred ninety-two years from the creation of the world, the world will be an orphan. As to the years to follow in some there will be wars of the great dragons, and in some, wars of Gog and Magog, and the rest will be the days of the Messiah. And the Holy One, blessed be he, will renew his world only after seven thousand years."

11. I:92: It has been taught on Tannaite authority: R. Nathan says, "This verse of Scripture pierces to the depth: 'For the

vision is yet for an appointed time, but at the end it shall speak and not lie; though he tarry, wait for him; because it will surely come, it will not tarry' (Hab. 2:3)."

12. I:93: What is the meaning of the verse, "But at the end it shall speak and not lie" (Hab. 2:3)? Said R. Samuel bar Nahmani said R. Jonathan, " Reading the verse as, 'He will blast him who calculates the end,' blasted be the bones of those who calculate the end when the Messiah will come. For they might say, 'Since the end has come and he has not come, he will not come.' Rather, wait for him, as it is said, 'Though he tarry, wait for him' (Hab. 2:3)."

13. I:94: Said Abbayye, "There are in the world never fewer than thirty-six righteous men, who look upon the face of the Presence of God every day, for it is said, 'Happy are those who wait for him' (Is. 30:18), and the numerical value of the letters in the word 'for him' is thirty-six."

14. I:95: Said Rab, "All of the ends have passed, and the matter now depends only on repentance and good deeds." And Samuel said, "It is sufficient for a mourner to remain firm in his mourning."

15. I:96: And said R. Abba, "You have no indication of the end more openly stated than the following, as it is said: 'But you, O Mountains of Israel, shall shoot forth your branches and yield your fruit to my people, Israel, for they are at hand to come' (Ez. 36:8)."

16. I:97: Said R. Hanina, "The son of David will come only when a fish will be sought for a sick person and not be found, as it is said, 'Then I will make their waters deep and cause their rivers to run like oil' (Ez. 32:14), and it is written, 'In that day I will cause the horn of the house of Israel to sprout forth' (Ez. 29:21)." Said R. Hama bar Hanina, "The son of David will come only when the rule over Israel by the least of the kingdoms will come to an end, as it is said, 'He shall both cut off the springs with pruning hooks and take away and cut down the branches' (Is. 18:5), and further: 'In that time shall the present be brought to the Lord of hosts of a people that is scattered and peeled' (Is. 18:7)."

17. I:98: Said Ulla, "Jerusalem will be redeemed only through righteousness, as it is written, 'Zion shall be redeemed with judgment and her converts with righteousness' (Is. 1:27)." Said R. Pappa, "If the arrogant end in Israel, the Magi will end in Iran, if the judges end in Israel, the rulers of thousands will come to an end in Iran. If the arrogant end in

    Israel, the magi will end in Iran, as it is written, 'And I will purely purge away your haughty ones and take away all your tin' (Is. 1:25). If judges end in Israel, the rulers of thousands will come to an end in Iran, as it is written, 'The Lord has taken away your judgments, he has cast out your enemy' (Zeph. 3:15)."

18. I:99: Said R. Yohanan, "If you see a generation growing less and less, hope for him more and more, as it is said, 'And the afflicted people will you save' (2 Sam. 22:28)." Said R. Yohanan, "If you see a generation over which many troubles flow like a river, hope for him, as it is written, 'When the enemy shall come in like a flood, the spirit of the Lord shall lift up a standard against him' (Is. 59:19), followed by: 'And the redeemer shall come to Zion' (Is. 59:20)."

19. I:100: Said R. Alexandri, "R. Joshua b. Levi contrasted verses as follows: It is written; "in its time will the Messiah come," and it is also written; "I the Lord will hasten it." What is the meaning of the contrast? If the Israelites have merit, I will hasten it, if they do not, the messiah will come in due course."

20. I:101: Said King Shapur to Samuel, "You say that the Messiah will come on an ass which is a humble way. Come and I shall send him a white horse that I have."

21. I:102: . Joshua b. Levi found Elijah standing at the door of the burial vault of R. Simeon b. Yohai. He said to him, "Am I going to come to the world to come?" He said to him, "If this master wants." Said R. Joshua b. Levi, "Two did I see, but a third voice did I hear." He said to him, "When is the Messiah coming?" He said to him, "Go and ask him."

22. I:103: His disciples asked R. Yosé b. Qisma, "When is the son of David coming?"

23. I:104: Said Rab, "The son of David will come only when the monarchy of Rome will spread over Israel for nine months."

24. I:105: Said Ulla, "Let him come, but may I not see him." Said Rabba, "Let him come, but may I not see him." R. Joseph said, "May he come, and may I have the merit of sitting in the shade of the dung of his ass."

25. I:106: So said R. Yohanan, "Let him come, but let me not see him."

26. I:107: Said R. Giddal said Rab, "The Israelites are going to eat and not starve in the years of the Messiah."

27. I:108: Said Rab, "The world was created only for David."
    And Samuel said, "For Moses." And R. Yohanan said, "For
    the Messiah."

28. I:109: Said R. Nahman, "If he is among the living, he is such
    as I, as it is said, 'And their nobles shall be of themselves and
    their governors shall proceed from the midst of them' (Jer.
    30:21)." Said Rab, "If he is among the living, he is such as our
    Holy Rabbi Judah the Patriarch, and if he is among the dead,
    he is such as Daniel, the most desirable man."

29. I:110: R. Simlai interpreted the following verse: "What is the
    meaning of that which is written, 'Woe to you who desire the
    day of the Lord! to what end is it for you? the day of the
    Lord is darkness and not light' (Amos 5:18)? The matter may
    be compared to the case of the cock and the bat who were
    waiting for light. The cock said to the bat, 'I am waiting for
    the light, for the light belongs to me, but what do you need
    light for?' That is in line with what a min said to R. Abbahu,
    "When is the Messiah coming?" He said to him, "When
    darkness covers those men."

30. I:111: It has been taught on Tannaite authority: R. Eliezer
    says, "The days of the Messiah will last forty years, as it is
    said, 'Forty years long shall I take hold of the generation' (Ps.
    95:10)." R. Eliezer b. Azariah says, "Seventy years, as it is
    said, 'And it shall come to pass in that day that Tyre shall be
    forgotten seventy years, according to the days of one king'
    (Is. 23:15)."

31. I:112: R. Hillel says, "Israel will have no Messiah, for they
    consumed him in the time of Hezekiah."

32. I:113: A further teaching on Tannaite authority: R. Eliezer
    says, "The days of the Messiah will last for forty years. Here
    it is written, 'And he afflicted you and made you hunger and
    fed you with manna' (Deut. 8:3), and elsewhere: 'Make us
    glad according to the days forty years in the wilderness in
    which you have afflicted us' (Ps. 90:15)." R. Dosa says, "Four
    hundred years. Here it is written, 'And they shall serve
    them and they shall afflict them four hundred years' (Gen.
    15:13), and elsewhere: 'Make us glad according to the days
    wherein you have afflicted us' (Ps. 90:15)."

33. I:114: Said R. Hiyya bar Abba said R. Yohanan, "All of the
    prophets prophesied only concerning the days of the
    Messiah. But as to the world to come thereafter: 'Eye has
    not seen, O Lord, beside you, what he has prepared for him
    who waits for him' (Is. 64:3)."

I. AND THESE ARE THE ONES WHO HAVE NO PORTION IN THE
    WORLD TO COME: HE WHO SAYS...THE TORAH DOES NOT
    COME FROM HEAVEN:

1. II:1: Our rabbis have taught on Tannaite authority: "Because
    he has despised the word of the Lord and broken his
    commandment, that soul shall utterly be cut off" (Num.
    15:31): This refers to one who says, "The Torah does not
    come from heaven."

2. II:2: It has been taught on Tannaite authority: R. Meir would
    say, "He who studies the Torah but does not teach it falls
    under the verse, "Because he has despised the word of the
    Lord" (Num. 15:31)." R. Nathan says, "Whoever does not
    pay close attention to the Mishnah." R. Nehorai says,
    "Whoever has the possibility of taking up the study of the
    Torah and does not do so." R. Ishmael says, "This refers to
    one who worships an idol."

3. II:3: R. Joshua b. Qorhah says, "Whoever studies the Torah
    and does not review it is like a man who sows seed but does
    not harvest it." R. Joshua says, "Whoever learns the Torah
    and forgets it is like a woman who bears and buries." R.
    Aqiba says, "A song is in me, a song always" (T. Ah. 16:8H-
    I).

4. II:4: Said R. Eleazar, "Every man was born to work, as it is
    said, 'For man is born to work' (Job 5:7). I do not know
    whether it is for work done with the mouth that he is
    created, or whether it is for labor done through physical
    work that he was created. When Scripture says, 'For his
    mouth craves it of him' (Prov. 16:26), one has to conclude
    that it is for work done with the mouth that he was created.
    Yet I still do not know whether it was to labor in the Torah
    or to labor in some sort of other conversation. When
    Scripture says, 'This book of the Torah shall not depart out of
    your mouth' (Josh. 1:8), one must conclude that it is for labor
    in the Torah that he is created."

5. II:5: "Whoever commits adultery with a woman lacks
    understanding" (Prov. 6:32). Said R. Simeon b. Laqish, "This
    refers to one who studies the Torah at occasional intervals."

6. II:6: Our rabbis have taught on Tannaite authority: "But the
    soul that does anything presumptuously" (Num. 15:30):
    This refers to Manasseh, son of Hezekiah, who would go into
    session and interpret tales seeking flaws in them, saying,
    "Did Moses have nothing better to do than to write such
    verses as 'And Lotan's sister was Timna' (Gen. 36:22). 'And

Timna was concubine to Eliphaz' (Gen. 36:12). 'And Reuben went in the days of the wheat harvest and found mandrakes in the field' (Gen. 30:14)?" An echo came forth and said to him, "'You sit and speak against your brother; you slander your own mother's son. These things you have done, and I kept silence, you thought that I was altogether such a one as yourself, but I will reprove you and set them in order before your eyes' (Ps. 50:20-21)."

7. II:7: Said R. Alexandri, "Whoever is occupied in study of the Torah for the sake of heaven brings peace to the family above and to the family below."

8. II:8: Said R. Simeon b. Laqish, "Whoever teaches Torah to the son of his neighbor is credited by Scripture as if he had made him."

9. II:9: Said R. Abbahu, "Whoever makes his neighbor carry out a religious duty is credited by Scripture as if he himself had done it, as it is said, 'The Lord said to Moses, Take...your rod, with which you hit the river' (Ex. 17:5).'"

J. ...AND AN EPICUREAN:

1. III:1: Both Rab and R. Hanina say, "This refers to one who humiliates disciples of sages." Both R. Yohanan and R. Joshua b. Levi say, "It is one who humiliates his fellow before a disciple of a sage."

2. III:2: Levi bar Samuel and R. Huna bar Hiyya were fixing the mantles of the Torah scrolls of the house of R. Judah. When they got to the scroll of Esther, they said, "Lo, this scroll of Esther does not have to have a mantle at all." He said to them, "This sort of talk also appears to be Epicureanism."

3. III:3: R. Nahman said, "It is one who refers to his master by his name."

4. III:4: R. Jeremiah was in session before R. Zira and said, "The Holy One, blessed be he, by which there will be many kinds of delicious produce, as it is said, 'And by the river upon that bank thereof, on this side and on that side, shall grow all trees for meat, whose leaf shall not fade, neither shall the fruit thereof be consumed; it shall bring forth new fruit, according to his months, because their waters they issued out of the sanctuary, and the fruit therefore shall be for meat, and the leaf thereof for medicine' (Ez. 47:12)." "Said to him a certain old man, 'Well said, and so did R. Yohanan say.'" Said R. Jeremiah to R. Zira, "Behavior of this sort condescension to the master likewise appears to be Epicureanism."

5. III:5: R. Judah b. R. Simon interpreted, "Whoever blackens his face in fasting on account of teachings of Torah in this world will find that the Holy One, blessed be he, polishes his luster in the world to come."

6. III:6: It has been taught on Tannaite authority" R. Meir says, "By the same measure by which a mate metes out, do they mete out to him (M. Sot. 1:7A), For it is written, By measure in sending her away thou dost contend with her' (Is. 27:8)." Said R. Judah, "And can one say so? If a person gives a handful to charity to a poor man in this world, will the Holy One, blessed be he, give him a handful of his, so much larger hand, in the world to come? And has it not been written, 'And meted out heaven with a span' (Is. 40:12)?"

K. R. AQIBA SAYS, "ALSO: HE WHO READS IN HERETICAL BOOKS:"

1. IV:1: It was taught on Tannaite authority: That is the books of the minim.

2. IV:2: R. Joseph said, "It is also forbidden to read in the book of Ben Sira."

3. IV:3: Said R. Zira said Rab, "What is the meaning of the verse of Scripture, 'All the days of the afflicted are evil' (Prov. 15:15)? This refers to masters of Talmud. 'But he that is of a good heart has a continuous banquet' (Prov. 15:15)? This refers to masters of the Mishnah."

4. IV:4: Our rabbis have taught on Tannaite authority: He who recites a verse of the Song of Songs and turns it into a kind of love-song, and he who recites a verse in a banquet hall not at the proper time but in a time of carousal bring evil into the world (cf. T. San. 12:10A). For the Torah puts on sack cloth and stands before the Holy One, blessed be he, and says before him, "Lord of the world, your children have treated me like a harp which scoffers play.

L. "...AND HE WHO WHISPERS OVER A WOUND AND SAYS, 'I WILL PUT NONE OF THE DISEASES UPON YOU WHICH I HAVE PUT ON THE EGYPTIANS, FOR I AM THE LORD WHO HEALS YOU:'"

1. V:1: Said R. Yohanan, "That is the rule if one spits over the wound, for people may not make mention of the Name of heaven over spit."

2. V:2: It has been stated on Amoraic authority: Rab said, "Even 'When the plague of leprosy' (Lev. 1:1) may not be recited."

3. V:3: Our rabbis have taught on Tannaite authority: People may anoint and massage the intestines on the Sabbath, and whisper to snakes and scorpions on the Sabbath, and place utensils on the eyes on the Sabbath.

4. V:4: Our rabbis have taught on Tannaite authority: People may anoint and massage the intestines on the Sabbath, so long as one not do so as he does on a weekday.

5. V:5: Our rabbis have taught on Tannaite authority: As to the spirits of oil or eggs, it is permitted to address questions to them, except that they prove unreliable. People whisper over oil that is in a utensil but not over oil that is held in the hand.

   a. V:6: R. Isaac bar Samuel bar Marta happened to stay at a certain inn. They brought him oil in a utensil, and he anointed himself. He broke out in blisters all over his face. He went to a market place, and a certain woman saw him and said to him, "The blast of Hamath do I see here."

6. V:7: Said R. Abba to Rabba bar Mari, "It is written, 'I will put none of these diseases upon you, which I have brought upon the Egyptians, for I am the Lord who heals you' (Ex. 15:26). But if he does not place those diseases, what need is there for healing anyhow?"

7. V:8: Said Rabbah bar bar Hanah, "When R. Eliezer fell ill, his disciples came in to call on him. He said to them, 'There is great anger in the world to account for my sickness.' They began to cry, but R. Aqiba began to laugh. They said to him, 'Why are you laughing?' He said to them, 'Why are you crying?' They said to him, 'Is it possible that, when a scroll of the Torah such as Eliezer is afflicted with disease, we should not cry?' He said to them, 'For that reason I am laughing. So long as I observed that, as to my master, his wine did not turn to vinegar, his flux was not smitten, his oil did not putrefy, and his honey did not become rancid, I though to myself, "Perhaps, God forbid, my master has received his reward in this world." But now that I see my master in distress, I rejoice knowing that he will receive his full reward in the world to come.'

   a. V:9: Our rabbis have taught on Tannaite authority: When R. Eliezer fell ill, four elders came to call on him: R. Tarfon, R. Joshua, R. Eleazar b. Azariah, and R. Aqiba.

    I.   V:10: Our rabbis have taught on Tannaite authority: Three came with a self-serving plea, and these are they: Cain, Esau, and Manasseh.

M. **ABBA SAUL SAYS, "ALSO: HE WHO PRONOUNCES THE DIVINE NAME AS IT IS SPELLED OUT:"**

1. VI:1: On Tannaite authority it was stated: That is the rule in the provinces, and when it is in blasphemous language.

N. **THREE KINGS AND FOUR ORDINARY FOLK HAVE NO PORTION IN THE WORLD TO COME. THREE KINGS: JEROBOAM:**

1. VII:1: Our rabbis have taught on Tannaite authority: "Jerobam": for he treated the people as his sexual object. Another matter: "Jeroboam: "for he made strife in the people. Another matter: "Jeroboam: "for he brought strife between the people of Israel and their father in heaven.

2. VII:2: On Tannaite authority it was stated: Nebat is the same as Micah and Sheba son of Bichri. Nebat: Because he saw a vision but did not see its meaning.

3. VII:3: Our rabbis have taught on Tannaite authority: There were three who saw a vision but did not see its meaning, and these are they: Nabat, Ahitophel, and Pharaoh's astrologers. Nabat saw fire coming forth from his penis. He thought that it meant that he would rule, but that was not the case. It was that Jeroboam would come forth from him who would rule.

4. VII:4: And how do we know that Jeroboam will not come into the world to come?

5. VII:5: Said R. Yohanan, "On what account did Jeroboam have the merit to rule?"

6. VII:6: Said R. Nahman, "The arrogance that characterized Jeroboam is what drove him out of the world."

7. VII:7: It is written, "And the revolters are profound to make slaughter, though I have been a rebuke of all of them" (Hos. 5:2): Said R. Yohanan, "Said the Holy One, blessed be he, 'They have gone deeper than I did. I said, "Whoever does not go up to Jerusalem for the Festival transgresses an affirmative requirement," but they have said, "Whoever does go up to Jerusalem for the festival will be stabbed with a sword."'"

8. VII:8: "And it came to pass at that time, when Jeroboam went out of Jerusalem, that the prophet Ahijah the Shilonite found him in the way, and he had clad himself with a new garment" (1 Kgs. 11:20): It was taught on Tannaite authority in the name of R. Yosé, "It was a time designated for

punishment. On that occasion Ahijah prophesied the division of the kingdom as a punishment for Solomon's backsliding."

9. VII:9: "Now it came to pass at that time that Jeroboam went out of Jerusalem" (1 Kgs. 11:29)" Said R. Hanina bar Pappa, "He went out of the realm of Jerusalem."

10. VII:10: "And the prophet Ahijah the Shilonite found him in the way, and he clad himself with a new garment, and the two were alone in the field" (1 Kgs. 11:29): What is this "new garment"?

11. VII:11: "Therefore shall you give parting gifts to Moresheth-gath, the houses of Achzib shall be a lie to the kings of Israel" (Mic. 1:14): Said R. Hanina bar Pappa, "An echo came forth and said to them, 'He who killed the Philistine and gave you possession of Gath – to his sons you will give parting gifts.'"

12. VII:12: Said R. Hinnena bar Pappa, "Whoever derives benefit from this world without reciting a blessing is as if he steals from the Holy One, blessed be he, and the community of Israel."

13. VII:13: "And Jeroboam drove Israel from following the Lord and made them sin a great sin" (2 Kgs. 17:21)" Said R. Hanin, "It was like two sticks that rebound from one another."

14. VII:14: "These are the words which Moses spoke to all Israel in the wilderness and Di Zahab" (Deut. 1:1): Said a member of the house of R. Yannai, "Moses said before the Holy One, blessed be he, 'Lord of the world, on account of the silver and gold which you showered on Israel until they said, "Enough," they were caused to make for themselves gods of gold.'

15. VII:15: "After this thing Jeroboam did not turn from his evil way" (1 Kgs. 13:33)" What is the sense of "after"?

16. VII:16: R. Abbahu would regularly give a public interpretation of the three kings of M. 11:2A. He fell ill and undertook not to give such an address since he thought the illness was punishment for speaking about the king's sins. When he got better, he reversed himself and gave an address. They said to him, "You undertook not to speak about them." He said to them, "Did they repent, that I should repent!"

17. VII:17: At the house of R. Ashi, the group arose from studying at the teaching of the three kings. He said, "Tomorrow we shall open discourse with the topic of 'our

colleagues' (M. 11:2), that is, the three kings, all of whom were held to be disciples of sages." Manasseh came and appeared in a dream: "Do you call us 'your colleague' and 'your father's colleague'? If you are as good as we are, then tell me from what part of the bread do you take the piece for reciting the blessing, 'Who brings forth bread from the earth'?"

O.   ...AHAB:

1.   VIII:1: The name 'Ahab' signifies that he was a brother to heaven (ah) but father of idolatry (ab).

2.   VIII:2: "And it came to pass, that it was a light thing for him to walk in the sins of Jeroboam, the son of Nebat" (1 Kgs. 16:31) Said R. Yohanan, "The lightest sins committed by Ahab were as the most severe ones that were committed by Jeroboam. And on what account did Scripture blame Jeroboam? It was because he was the beginning of the corruption."

3.   VIII:3: "Yes, their altars are as heaps in the furrows of the fields" (Hos. 12:12): Said R. Yohanan, "You have no furrow in the whole of the land of Israel in which Ahab did not set up an idol and bow down to it."

4.   VIII:4: And how do we know that Ahab will not enter the world to come? As it is written, "And I will cut off from Ahab him who pisses against the wall, him that is shut up and forsaken in Israel" (1 Kgs. 21:21). "Shut up" in this world. "Forsaken" in the world to come.

5.   VIII:5: Said R. Yohanan, "On what account did Omri merit the monarchy? Because he added a single town to the land of Israel, as it is written, 'And he bought the hill Samaria of Shemer for two talents of silver and built on the hill and called the name of the city which he built after the name of Shemer, owner of the hill, Samaria' (1 Kgs. 16:24)."

6.   VIII:6: Said R. Nahman, "Ahab was right in the middle between wickedness and righteousness, as it is said, 'And the Lord said, Who shall persuade Ahab, that he may go up and fall at Ramoth-gildean? And one said in this manner, and one said in that manner' (1 Kgs. 22:20). This shows that it was a difficult matter to lure him to his fate, and that must have been because his righteousness equalled his guilt."

7.   VIII:7: "And there came forth the spirit and stood before the Lord and said, I will persuade him. And the Lord said to him, With what? And he said, I will go forth and I will be a lying spirit in the mouth of his prophets. And he said, You

shall persuade him and also prevail. Go forth and do so" (1 Kgs. 22:21-23): What spirit was it?

8.   VIII:8: "And Ahab made a grove, and Ahab did more to provoke the Lord God of Israel to anger than all of the kings of Israel that were before him" (1 Kgs. 16:33): SaId R. Yohanan, "It was that he wrote on the gates of Samaria, 'Ahab has denied the God of Israel.' Therefore he has no portion in the God of Israel."

9.   VIII:9: "And he sought Ahaziah, and they caught him for he hid in Samaria" (2 Chr. 22:9): Said R. Levi, "He was blotting out the mentions of the divine name in the Torah and writing in their place the names of idols."

P.   ...AND MANASSEH.

1.   IX:1: Manasseh – Based on the root for the word "forget" for he forgot the Lord. And how do we know that he will not come to the world to come?

Q.   R. JUDAH SAYS, "MANASSEH HAS A PORTION IN THE WORLD TO COME, SINCE IT IS SAID, 'AND HE PRAYED TO HIM AND HE WAS ENTREATED OF HIM AND HEARD HIS SUPPLICATION AND BROUGHT HIM AGAIN TO JERUSALEM INTO HIS KINGDOM' (2 CHR. 33:13)." THEY SAID TO HIM, "TO HIS KINGDOM HE BROUGHT HIM BACK, BUT TO THE LIFE OF THE WORLD TO COME HE DID NOT BRING HIM BACK."

1.   X:1: Said R. Yohanan, "Both authorities who dispute the fate of Manasseh interpret the same verse of Scripture, as it is said, 'And I will cause to be removed to all the kingdoms of the earth, because of Manasseh, son of Hezekiah, king of Judah' (Jer. 15:4).

2.   X:2: Said R. Yohanan, "Whoever maintains that Manasseh has no share in the world to come weakens the hands of those who repent."

3.   X:3: Said R. Yohanan in the name of R. Simeon b. Yohai, "What is the meaning of the verse of Scripture, 'And he prayed to him and an opening was made for him' (2 Chr. 33:13)?"

4.   X:4: Said R. Hisda said R. Jeremiah bar Abba, "What is the meaning of the following verse: 'I went by the field of the slothful and by the vineyard of the man void of understanding. And lo, it was all grown over with thorns and nettles had covered the face thereof, and the stone wall thereof was broken down' (Prov. 24:30-31)? 'I went by the field of the slothful' – this speaks of Ahaz. 'And by the vineyard of the man void of understanding' – this speaks of

Manasseh. 'And lo, it was all grown over with thorns' – this refers to Amon. 'And nettles had covered the face thereof' – this refers to Jehoiakim. 'And the stone wall thereof was broken down' – this refers to Zedekiah, in whose time the Temple was destroyed."

5. X:5: Said R. Simeon b. Laqish, "What is the meaning of the following verse of Scripture: 'And from the wicked their light is withheld, and the high arm shall be broken' (Job 38:15)? Why is the letter ayin in the word for wicked suspended in the text, being written above the level of the line, making it read 'poor,' rather than 'wicked' When a person becomes poor below, he is made poor above. Where one earns the disapproval of man, it is proof that he has earned the disapproval of God too."

6. X:6: Our rabbis have taught on Tannaite authority: Manasseh would teach the book of Leviticus from fifty-five viewpoints, corresponding to the years of his reign. Ahab did so in eighty-five ways. Jeroboam did so in a hundred and three ways.

    a. X:7: It has been taught on Tannaite authority: R. Meir would say, "Absalom has no share in the world to come."

    b. X:8: It has been taught on Tannaite authority: R. Simeon b. Eleazar says in the name of R. Meir, "Ahaz, Ahaziah, and all the kings of Israel concerning whom it is written, 'And he did what was evil in the sight of the Lord' will not live or be judged in the world to come."

7. X:9: "Moreover Manasseh shed much innocent blood, until he had filled Jerusalem from one end to another, beside his sin wherewith he made Judah to sin, in doing that which was evil in the sight of the Lord" (2 Kgs. 21:16): Here in Babylonia it is explained that he killed Isaiah, and that is the sin at hand. In the West they say that it was that he made an idol as heavy as a thousand men, and every day it killed them all.

8. X:10: It is written, "And he set the graven image" (2 Chr. 33:7), and it is stated, "And the graves and the graven images which he had set up" (2 Chr. 33:19). was there one image or were there many? Said R. Yohanan, "In the beginning he made one face for it, and in the end he made four faces for it, so that the Presence of God should see it and become angry. Ahaz set it up in the upper chamber, as it is written, 'And the altars that were on top of the upper chamber of Ahaz' (2 Kgs.

23:13). Manasseh set it in the Temple, as it is written, 'And he set up a graven image of the grove that he had made in the house, of which the Lord said to David and to Solomon his son, In this house and in Jerusalem which I have chosen out of all tribes of Israel will I put my name for ever' (2 Kgs. 21:7).

9. X:11: Ahaz annulled the sacrificial service and sealed the Torah, for it is said, "Bind up the testimony, seal the Torah among my disciples" (Is. 8:16). Manasseh blotted out the mentions of the divine Name and destroyed the altar. Amon burned the Torah and let spider webs cover the altar.

R. WICKED MONARCHES WHO NONETHELESS MERIT A PORTION IN THE WORLD TO COME, E.G., JEHOIAKIM, AHAZ, AMON

1. X:12: Said Raba to Rabbah bar Mari, "On what account did they not count Jehoiakim among those who do not get the world to come? For it is written of him, 'And the remaining words of Jehoiakim and the abomination which he wrought and that which was found up upon him' (2 Chr. 36:8)."

   a. X:13: Said R. Yohanan in the name of R. Yosé b. Qisma, "Great is a mouthful of food, for it set a distance between two families and Israel, as it is written, 'An Ammonite or Moabite shall not enter the congregation of the Lord ... because they did not meet you with bread and water in the way when you came forth from Egypt' (Deut. 33:4-5)."

2. X:14: Why did they not list Ahaz at M. 11:2? Said R. Jeremiah bar Abba, "Because he was positioned between two righteous men, between Hotham and Hezekiah."

3. X:15: Why did they not list Amon at M. 11:2? On account of the honor owing to Josiah.

4. X:16: And on what account did they not list Jehoiakim? It is on account of what R.Hiyya b. R. Abuyyah said. For R. Hiyya b. R. Abuyyah said, "It was written on the skull of Jehoiakim, 'This and yet another.'"

S. HEZEKIAH, THE RIGHTEOUS MONARCH ON ACCOUNT OF WHOM ISRAEL WENT INTO EXILE. AND THE EXEGESIS OF LAMENTATIONS

1. X:17: It has been taught on Tannaite authority: R. Simeon b. Eleazar said, "On account of Hezekiah's statement, 'And I have done that which was good in your sight,' (2 Kgs. 20:3), he had further to ask, 'What shall be the sign that the Lord will heal me' (2 Kgs. 20:9)." On account of the statement, 'What shall be the sign' (2 Kgs. 20:9), gentiles ate at his table.

On account of gentiles' eating at his table, 2 Kgs. 20:17-18), he made his children go into exile."

a. X:18: "How does the city sit solitary" (Lam. 1:1): Said Rabbah said R. Yohanan, "On what account were the Israelites smitten with the word 'how' that begins the dirge? Since the numerical value of the letters of the word equals thirty-six, it is because they violated the thirty-six rules in the Torah that are penalized by extirpation."

b. X:19: "Sit solitary" (Lam. 1:1)": Said Rabbah said R. Yohanan, "Said the Holy One, blessed be he, 'I said, "Israel then shall dwell in safety alone, the foundation of Jacob shall be upon a land of corn and wine, also his heavens shall drop down dew" (Deut. 33:28) so that sitting solitary was supposed to be a blessing (Freedman, p. 708, n. 8), but now, where they dwell will be alone.'"

c. X:20: "The city that was full of people" (Lam. 1:1): Said Rabbah said R. Yohanan, "For they used to marry off a minor girl to an adult male, or an adult woman to a minor boy, so that they should have many children. But two minors would not marry."

d. X:21: "She is become as a widow" (Lam. 1:1): Said R. Judah said Rab, "Like a widow, but not actually a widow, but like a woman whose husband has gone overseas and plans to return to her."

e. X:22: "She was great among the nations and princess among the provinces" (Lam. 1:1): Said R. Rabbah said R. Yohanan, "Everywhere they go they become princes of their masters."

    I. X:23: Our rabbis have taught on Tannaite authority: There is the case of two men who were captured on Mount Carmel. The kidnapper was walking behind them. One of them said to his fellow, "The camel that is walking before us is blind in one eye, it is carrying two skins, one of wine and one of oil, and of the two men that are leading it, one is an Israelite and the other is a gentile."

f. X:24: "She weeps, yes, she weeps in the night" (Lam. 1:2): Why these two acts of weeping? Said Rabbah said R. Yohanan, "One is for the first Temple and the other is for the second Temple."

g. X:25: "And her tears are on her cheeks" (Lam. 1:2): Said Rabbah said R. Yohanan, "It is like a woman who weeps for the husband of her youth, as it is said, 'Lamentation like a virgin girded with sackcloth for the husband of her youth' (Joel 1:8)."

h. X:26: "Her adversaries are the chief" (Lam. 1:5): Said Rabbah said R. Yohanan, "Whoever persecutes Israel becomes head, as it is said, 'Nevertheless, there shall be no weariness for her that oppressed her. In the former time he brought into contempt the land of Zebulun and the land of Naphtali, but in the latter time he has made it glorious, by way of the sea, beyond Jordan, the circuit of the nations' (Is. 8:23)."

i. X:27: "May it not happen to you, all passersby" (Lam. 1:12)." Said Rabbah said R. Yohanan, "On this basis we find in the Torah support for saying when reciting woes, 'May it not happen to you.'"

j. X:28: "All passersby" (Lam. 1:12): Said R. Amram said Rab, "They have turned me into one of those who transgress the law. For in respect to Sodom, it is written, 'And the Lord rained upon Sodom and upon Gomorrah brimstone and fire' (Gen. 19:24). But in respect to Jerusalem it is written, 'From above he has sent fire against my bones and it prevails against them' (Lam. 1:13). Thus Jerusalem was treated as Sodom and Gomorrah."

k. X:29: "The Lord has trodden under foot all my mighty men in the midst of me" (Lam. 1:15): This is like a man who says to his fellow, "This coin has been invalidated."

   I. X:30: "They eat my people as they eat bread and do not call upon the Lord" (Ps. 14:4): Said Rabbah said R. Yohanan, "Whoever eats the bread of Israelites tastes the flavor of bread, and who does not eat the bread of Israelites does not taste the flavor of bread."

   II. X:31: "They do not call upon the Lord" (Ps. 14:4): Rab said, "This refers to judges." And Samuel said, "This refers to those who teach children."

T. THE LIST OF THOSE WHO DO NOT ENTER THE WORLD TO COME, KINGS AND COMMONERS: SUMMARY JUDGMENTS

1. X:32: Who counted the kings and commoners of M. 11:2A? Said R. Ashi, "The men of the great assembly counted them."

2. X:33: Said R. Judah said Rab, "They wanted to count yet another namely, Solomon, but an apparition of his father's face came and prostrated himself before them. But they paid no attention to him. A fire came down from heaven and

licked around their chairs, but they did not pay attention. An echo come forth and as said to them, 'Do you see a man diligent in his business? He shall stand before kings, he shall not stand before mean men' (Prov. 22:29). 'He who gave precedence to my house over his house, and not only so, but built my house over a span of seven years, while building his own house over a span of thirteen years "he shall stand before kings, he shall not stand before mean men.'"

3. X:34: Those who interpret signs symbolically would say, "All of them listed at M. 11:2 will enter the world to come, as it is said, 'Gilead is mine, Manasseh is mine, Ephraim also is the strength of my head, Judah is my lawgiver, Moab is my washpot, over Edom will I cast my shoe, Philistia, you triumph because of me' (Ps. 60:9-10): 'Gideon is mine' speaks of Ahab, who fell at Ramoth-gilead. 'Manasseh' – literally. 'Ephraim also is the strength of my head' speaks of Jeroboam, who comes from Ephraim.

4. X:35: "Why is this people of Jerusalem slidden back by a perpetual backsliding" (Jer. 8:5): Said Rab, "The community of Israel answered the prophet with a lasting reply a play on the words for backsliding and answer, using the same root. The prophet said to Israel, 'Return in repentance. Your fathers who sinned – where are they now?' They said to him, 'And your prophets, who did not sin, where are they now? For it is said, "Your fathers, where are they? and the prophets, do they live forever" (Zech. 1:5)?' He said to them, 'They repented and confessed as it is said, "But my words and my statutes, which I commanded my servants the prophets, did they not take hold of your fathers? And they returned and said, Like as the Lord of hosts thought to do unto us, according to our ways and according to our doings, so has he dealt with us" (Zech. 1:6).'"

5. X:36: "And that which comes into your mind shall not be at all, that you say, We will be as the heathen, as the families of the countries, to serve wood and stone. As I live, says the Lord God, surely with a mighty hand and with an outstretched arm, and with fury poured out, will I rule over you" (Ez 20:32-33): Said R. Nahman, "Even with such anger may the All-Merciful rage against us, so long as he redeems us."

6. X:37: "For he chastises him to discretion and his God teaches him" (Is. 28:26): Said Rabbah bar Hanah, "Said the prophet to Israel, 'Return in repentance.' They said to him, 'We

cannot do so. The impulse to do evil rules over us.' He said
to them, 'Reign in your desire.' They said to him, 'Let his
God teach us.'"

U.   FOUR ORDINARY FOLK: BALAAM:

1.   XI:1: The name Balaam means not with the rest of the people
     – using the same consonants – who will inherit the world to
     come.
2.   XI:2: It was taught on Tannaite authority: Beor, Cushan-
     rishathaim, and Laban, the Syrian, are one and the same
     person. Beor: because he had sexual relations with a cow.
3.   XI:3: It is written, "The son of Beor" (Num. 22:50), but it also
     is written, "His son was Beor" (Num. 24:3). Said R. Yohanan,
     "His father was his son as to prophecy."
4.   XI:4: Balaam is the one who will not come to the world to
     come. Lo, others will come.
5.   XI:5: "And the elders of Moab and the elders of Midian
     departed" (Num. 22:7): It was taught on Tannaite authority:
     There was never peace between Midian and Moab. The
     matter may be compared to two dogs who were in a kennel,
     barking at one another.
6.   XI:6: "And the princes of Moab abode with Balaam" (Num.
     22:8): And as to the princess of Midian, where had they
     gone?
7.   XI:7: Said R. Nahman, "Hutzbah, even against heaven,
     serves some good. To begin with, it is written, 'You shall not
     go with them' (Num. 22:12), and then it is said, 'Rise up and
     go with them' (Num. 22:20)." Said R. Sheshet, "Hutzbah is
     dominion without a crown."
8.   XI:8: Said R. Yohanan, "Balaam had one crippled foot, for it
     is written, 'And he walked haltingly' (Num. 23:3)."
9.   XI:9: "He knows the mind of the most high" (Num. 24:16):
     Now if he did not know the mind of his own beast, how
     could he have known the mind of the most high?
     a.   XI:10: There was a min living in the neighborhood of R.
          Joshua b. Levi, who bothered him a great deal. One day
          he took a chicken and tied it up at the foot of his bed and
          sat down. He said, "When that moment comes at which
          God is angry, I shall curse him."
     b.   XI:11: A Tannaite authority in the name of R. Meir said,
          "When the sun shines and the kings put their crowns on
          their heads and bow down to the sun, forthwith he is
          angry."

10. XI:12: "And Balaam rose up in the morning and saddled his ass" (Num. 22:21): A Tannaite authority taught in the name of R. Simeon b. Eleazar, "That love annuls the order of proprieties we learn from the case of Abraham. For it is written, 'And Abraham rose up early in the morning and saddled his ass' (Gen. 22:3) not waiting for the servant to do so. And that hatred annuls the order of proprieties we learn from the case of Balaam. For it is said, 'And Balaam rose up early in the morning and saddled his ass' (Num. 22.21)."

11. XI:13: Said R. Judah said Rab, "Under all circumstances a person should engage in study of Torah and practice of religious duties, even if it is not for their own sake, for out of doing these things not for their own sake one will come to do them for their own sake." For as a reward for the forty-two offerings that Balak offered, he had the merit that Ruth should come forth from him.

12. XI:14: Said Raba to Rabbah bar Mari, "It is written, 'And moreover the king's servants came to bless our lord king David, saying God make the name of Solomon better than your name, and make his throne greater than your throne' (1 Kgs. 1:47). Now is this appropriate to speak in such a way to a king?" He said to him, "What they meant is, 'as good as ....' God make the name of Solomon illustrious even as the nature of your own and make his throne great according to the character of your throne.' For if you do not say this, then take account of the following: 'Blessed above women shall be Jael, the wife of Heber the Kenite, be, blessed shall she be above women in the tent' (Jud. 5:24). Now who are the women in the tent? They are Sarah, Rebecca, Rachel, and Leah. Is it appropriate to speak in such a way? Rather, what is meant is 'as good as ...,' and here too the sense is, 'as good as ....'"

13. XI:15: "And the Lord put a thing in the mouth of Balaam" (Num. 23:5): R. Eleazar says, "It was an angel." R. Jonathan said, "It was a hook."

14. XI:16: Said R. Yohanan, "From the blessing said by that wicked man, you learn what he had in his heart. He wanted to say that they should not have synagogues and school houses: 'How goodly are your tents, O Jacob' (Num. 24:5)."

15. XI:17: Said R. Samuel bar Nahmani said R. Jonathan, "What is the meaning of the verse of Scripture: 'Faithful are the wounds of a friend, but the kisses of an enemy are deceitful' (Prov. 27:6)? Better was the curse with which Ahijah the

Shilonite cursed the Israelites than the blessing with which
the wicked Balaam blessed them."

16. XI:18: "And he looked on the Kenite and took up his
    parable" (Num. 24:21): Said Balaam to Jethro the Kenite,
    "Were you not with us in that conspiracy of Pharaoh, Ex.
    1:22? Of course you were. Then who gave you a seat among
    the mighty men of the earth in the sanhedrin?"
17. XI:19: "And he took up his parable and said, Alas, who shall
    live when God does this" (Num. 24:23): Said R. Yohanan,
    "Woe to the nation who is at hand when the Holy One,
    blessed be he, effects the redemption of his children! Who
    would want to throw his garment between a lion and a
    lioness when they are having sexual relations?"
18. XI:20: "And ships shall come from the coast of Chittim"
    (Num. 24:24): Said Rab, "Legions will come from the coast of
    Chittim"
19. XI:21: "And now, behold, I go to my people; come and I shall
    advise you what this people shall do to your people in the
    end of days" (Num. 24:24): Rather than saying, "This people
    to your people," it should say, "Your people to this people."
    He advised the Moabites to ensnare Israel through uncharity.
    Thus he was referring to an action by the former to the latter,
    while Scripture suggests otherwise.
20. XI:22: "And Israel dwelt in Shittim" (Num. 25:1): R. Eliezer
    says, "The name of the place actually was Shittim." R. Joshua
    says, "It was so called because when there they did deeds of
    idiocy."
21. XI:23: R. Yohanan said, "Any passage in which the word,
    'And he abode' appears, it means suffering. "So: 'And Israel
    abode in Shittim, and the people began to commit
    whoredom with the daughters of Moab' (Num. 23:1).
22. XI:24: "And they slew the kings of Midian, beside the rest of
    them that were slain ... Balaam also , the son of Beor, they
    slew with the sword" (Num. 31:8): What was he doing there
    anyhow?
23. XI:25: "Balaam also, the son of Beor, the soothsayer, did the
    children of Israel slay with the sword" (Josh. 13:22): A
    soothsayer? He was a prophet!
24. XI:26: "...Did the children of Israel slay with the sword,
    among those who were slain by them" (Josh. 13:22): Said
    Rab, "They inflicted upon him all four forms of execution:
    stoning, burning, decapitation, and strangulation."

25. XI:27: A min said to R. Hanina, "Have you heard how old Balaam was?" He said to him, "It is not written out explicitly. But since it is written, 'Bloody and deceitful men shall not live out half their days' (Ps. 55:24), he would have been thirty-three or thirty-four years old."

26. XI:28: Said Mar, son of Rabina, to his son, "In regard to all of those listed as not having a share in the world to come, you should take up the verses relating to them and expound them only in the case of the wicked Balaam. In his case, in whatever way one can expound the relevant passages to his detriment, you do so."

V.   ...DOEG:

1. XII:1: It is written, "Doeg" (1 Sam. 21:8) meaning, "anxious" and it is written, "Doeeg" (1 Sam. 22:18) with letters indicating "woe" being inserted. Said R. Yohanan, "To begin with, the Holy One, blessed be he, sits and worries lest such a son one go forth to bad ways. After he has gone forth to bad ways, he says, 'Woe that this one has gone forth!'"

2. XII:2: Said R. Isaac, "What is the meaning of the verse of Scripture, 'Why do you boast yourself in mischief, O mighty man? The goodness of God endures forever' (Ps. 52:3)? Said the Holy One, blessed be he, to Doeg, 'Are you not a hero in Torah-learning! 'Why do you boast in mischief?' Is not the love of God spread over you all day long?'"

3. XII:3: "Or that you take my covenant in your mouth?" (Ps. 50:16): Said R. Ammi, "The Torah-knowledge of Doeg comes only from the lips and beyond but not inside his heart."

4. XII:4: Said R. Isaac, "What is the meaning of the verse of Scripture, 'The righteous also shall see and fear and shall laugh at him' (Ps. 52:8)? To begin with they shall fear the wicked, but in the end they shall laugh at him." And said R. Isaac, "What is the meaning of the verse of Scripture: 'He has swallowed down riches and he shall vomit them up again, the God shall cast them out of his belly' (Job 20:15)? Said David before the Holy One, blessed be he, 'Lord of the world, let Doeg die.'"

5. XII:5: Said R. Ammi, "Four hundred questions did Doeg and Ahitophel raise concerning the 'tower flying in the air,' and they could not answer any one of them."

6. XII:6: Said R. Mesharshayya, "Doeg and Ahitophel did not know how to reason concerning traditions."

7. XII:7: Said R. Ammi, "Doeg did not die before he forgot his learning, as it is said, 'He shall die without instruction, and in the greatness of his folly he shall go astray' (Prov. 5:23)."

8. XII:8: Said R. Yohanan, "Three injurious angels were designated for Doeg: one to make him forget his learning, one to burn his soul, and one to scatter his dust among the synagogues and school houses."

W. KING DAVID: HIS SIN AND ATONEMENT

1. XII:9: Said R. Judah said Rab, "One should never put himself to the test, for lo, David, king of Israel, put himself to the test and he stumbled. He said before him, 'Lord of the world, on what account do people say, "God of Abraham, God of Isaac, and God of Jacob, "but they do not say, "God of David"?' He said to him, 'They endured a test for me, while you have not endured a test for me.' He said before him, 'Lord of the world, here I am. Test me.' For it is said, 'Examine me, O Lord, and try me' (Ps. 26:1). He said to him, 'I shall test you, and I shall do for you something that I did not do for them. I did not inform them what I was doing, while I shall tell you what I am going to do. I shall try you with a matter having to do with sexual relations.' Forthwith: 'And it came to pass in an eventide that David arose from off his bed' (2 Sam. 11:2)."

2. XII:10: Raba interpreted Scripture, asking, "What is the meaning of the following verse: 'To the chief musician, a Psalm of David. In the Lord I put my trust, how do you say to my soul, Flee as a bird to your mountain?' (Ps. 11:1)? Said David before the Holy One, blessed be he, 'Lord of the world, Forgive me for that sin, so that people should not say, "The mountain that is among you that is, your king has been driven off by a bird."'"

3. XII:11: Said R. Judah said Rab, "Even when David was sick, he carried out the eighteen acts of sexual relations that were owing to his eighteen wives, as it is written, 'I am weary with my groaning, all night I make my bed swim, I water my couch with my tears' (Ps. 6:7)."

4. XII:12: R. Dosetai of Biri interpreted Scripture, "To what may David be likened? To a gentile merchant. Said David before the Holy One, blessed be he, 'Lord of the world, "Who can understand his errors?" (Ps. 19:13).' He said to him, 'They are remitted for you.' '" Cleanse me of hidden faults" (Ps. 19:13).' 'They are remitted to you.' '"Keep back your servant also from presumptuous sins" (Ps. 19:13).' 'They are

remitted to you.' '"Let them not have dominion over me, then I shall be upright" (Ps. 19:13), so that the rabbis will not hold me up as an example.'"

5. XII:13: "And I shall be innocent from great transgression: (Ps. 19:13): He said before him, "Lord of the world, forgive me for the whole of that sin as though I had never done it."

6. XII:14: Said R. Judah said Rab, "For six months David was afflicted with saraat, and the Presence of God left him, and the sanhedrin abandoned him."

X. ...AHITOPHEL AND GEHAZI.

1. XIII:1: As it is written, "And Elisha came to Damascus" (2 Kgs. 8:7). Where was he traveling when he came to Damascus?

2. XIII:2: Our rabbis have taught on Tannaite authority: Under all circumstances the left hand should push away and the right hand should draw near, not in the manner of Elisha, who drove away Gehazi with both hands.

3. XIII:3: "Now there were four men who were lepers at the entrance to the gate" (2 Kgs. 7:3): R. Yohanan said, "This refers to Gehazi and his three sons."

4. XIII:4: Our rabbis have taught on Tannaite authority: Elisha bore three illnesses, one because he brought the she-bears against the children, one because he pushed Gehazi away with both hands, and one on account of which he died.

5. XIII:5: Until Abraham there was no such thing as the sign of old age. Whoever saw Abraham thought, "This is Isaac." Whoever saw Isaac thought, "This is Abraham." Abraham prayed for mercy so that he might have signs of old age, as it is said, "And Abraham was old, and well stricken in age" (Gen. 24:1). Until the time of Jacob there was no such thing as illness, so he prayed for mercy and illness came about, as it is written, "And someone told Joseph, behold, your father is sick: (Gen. 48:1). Until the time of Elisha, no one who was sick ever got well. Elisha came along and prayed for mercy and got well, as it is written, "Now Elisha had fallen sick of the illness of which he died" (2 Kgs. 13:14) Freedman: This shows that he had been sick on previous occasions too, but recovered.

LXVI. MISHNAH-TRACTATE SANHEDRIN 11:3A-CC

A. THE GENERATION OF THE FLOOD HAS NO SHARE IN THE WORLD TO COME, AND THEY SHALL NOT STAND IN THE JUDGMENT, SINCE IT IS WRITTEN, "MY SPIRIT SHALL NOT

JUDGE WITH MAN FOREVER" (GEN. 6:3) NEITHER JUDGMENT NOR SPIRIT:

1. I:1: Our rabbis have taught on Tannaite authority: "The generation of the flood has no share in the world to come, nor will they live in the world to come, as it is said, And he destroyed every living thing that was upon the face of the earth (Gen. 7:23) in this world; and they perished from the earth in the world to come," the words of R. Aqiba. R. Judah B. Betera says, "They will live nor be judged, as it is said, And the Lord said, My spirit shall not contend with man forever' (Gen. 6:3). It will not contend, nor will my spirit be in them forever."

2. I:2: Our rabbis have taught on Tannaite authority: The generation of the Flood acted arrogantly before the Omnipresent only on account of the good which he lavished on them, since it is said, "Their houses are safe from fear, neither is the rod of God upon them" (Job 21:9). "Their bull genders and fails not, their cow calves and casts not her calf" (Job 21:10). "They send forth their little ones like a flock, and their children dance" (Job. 21:11). "They spend their days in prosperity and their years in pleasures" (Job 36:11). That is what caused them to say to God, "Depart from us, for we do not desire knowledge of they ways. What is the Almighty, that we should serve Him, and what profit should we have, if we pray to him (Job 21:14). They said, "Do we need Him for anything except a few drops of rain? But look, we have rivers and wells which are more than enough for us in the sunny season and in the rainy season, since it is said, And a mist rose from the earth (Gen. 2:6)." The Omnipresent then said to then, "By the goodness which I lavished on them they take pride before me? By that same good I shall exact punishment from them!" What does it say? "And I, behold, I bring a flood of water upon the earth" (Gen. 6:17)

3. I:3: Said R. Yohanan, "As to the generation of the flood, they corrupted their way 'greatly,' and they were judged 'greatly.' They corrupted their way greatly, as it is said, 'And God saw that the wickedness of man was great in the earth' (Gen. 6:5). They were judged greatly, as it is said, 'All the fountains of the great deep' (Gen. 7:11)."

4. I:4: "For all flesh had corrupted its way upon the earth" (Gen. 6:12): Said R. Yohanan, "This teaches that the men of the generation of the flood made a hybrid match between a domesticated beast and a wild animal, a wild animal and a

domesticated beast, and every sort of beast with man and man with every sort of beast."

5. I:5: "And God said to Noah, the end of all flesh is come before me" (Gen. 6:13). Said R. Yohanan, "Come and take note of how great is the power of robbery. For lo, the generation of the flood violated every sort of law, but the decree of punishment against them was sealed only when they went and committed robbery, for it is said, 'For the earth is filled with violence through them, and behold I will destroy them with the earth' (Gen. 6:13). And it is written, 'Violence is risen up into a rod of wickedness, none of them shall remain, nor of their multitude, nor any of theirs, neither shall there be wailing for them' (Ez. 7:11)."

6. I:6: A Tannaite authority of the house of R. Ishmael said, "Also the decree of punishment for Noah was issued, but he pleased the Lord,.."

7. I:7: "And the Lord was comforted that he had made man in the earth" (Gen. 6:6). When R. Dimi came, he said, "The Holy One, blessed be he, said, 'I did well that I made graves for them in the earth Freedman, p. 741, n. 6: since the wicked are thereby destroyed.' "How is this indicated? Here it is written, 'And the Lord was comforted' (Gen. 6:6) and elsewhere: 'And he comforted them and spoke kindly to them' (Gen. 50:21)."

8. I:8: "These are the generations of Noah: Noah was a righteous man, perfect in his generations" (Gen. 6:9): Said R. Yohanan, "By the standards of his generations, but not by the standards of other generations was he perfect."

9. I:9: "And every living substance was destroyed which was upon the face of the ground, both man and beast" (Gen. 7:23): While man sinned, what sin had beasts committed?

10. I:10: "All that was on the dry land died" (Gen. 7:22) – But not the fish in the sea.

11. I:11: R. Yosé of Caesarea expounded as follows: "What is the sense of the verse, 'He is swift as the waters, their portion is cursed in the earth, he does not behold the way of the vineyards' (Job 24:18)? The verse teaches that Noah, the righteous man, rebuked them, saying to his generation, 'Carry out an act of repentance, for if not, the Holy One, blessed be he, will bring upon you a flood and your corpses will float on the water like gourds.'

12. I:12: Raba expounded as follows: "What is the meaning of the verse, 'He that is ready to slip with his feet is as a stone

despised in the thought of him that is at ease' (Job 12:5)? This teaches that the righteous Noah rebuked them, saying to them words as hard as stone, but they despised him, saying, 'Old man, what is this ark for?'"

13. I:13: Said R. Hisda, "By hot fluid they corrupted their way in transgression, and by hot fluid they were judged."

14. I:14: "And it came to pass after seven days that the waters of the flood were upon the earth" (Gen. 7:10)" Said Rab, "What is the meaning of these seven days? These are the seven days of mourning for Methuselah, the righteous man. This teaches that lamentation for the righteous held back the retribution from coming upon the world. Another matter: 'After seven days' teaches that the Holy One, blessed be he, changed the order of the world for them, so that the sun came up in the west and set in the east. Another matter: It teaches that the Holy One, blessed be he, first set a long a time for them, and then a short time. Another matter: It teaches that he gave them a taste of the world to come, so that they should know how much good he would withhold from them (T. Sot. 10:3C. 4)."

15. I:15: "Of every clean beast you shall take by sevens, man and wife" (Gen. 7:2).: Do beasts relate as man and wife?

16. I:16: "Make an ark of gopher wood for yourself" (Gen. 6:14) – What is gopher wood?

17. I:17: "A window (SHR) you shall make in the ark" (Gen. 6:16): Said R. Yohanan, "The Holy One, blessed be he, said to Noah, 'Put up in its precious stones and pearls, so that they will give light for you as at noon.'"

18. I:18: "And in a cubit you shall finish the above" (Gen. 6:16)" – In what way will it stand firm against the rain.

19. I:19: "And he set forth a raven" (Gen. 8:7): Said R. Simeon b. Laqish, "The raven gave Noah a victorious reply, saying to him, 'Your master God hates me, and you hate me.

20. I:20: Our rabbis have taught on Tannaite authority: Three species had sexual relations in the ark, and all of them were smitten: the dog, raven, and Ham.

21. I:21: "Also he sent forth a dove from him to see if the waters had abated" (Gen. 8:8) – Said R. Jeremiah, "On the basis of this verse we learn that the dwelling of the clean fowl was with the righteous man."

22. I:22: "And lo, in her mouth was an olive leaf as food" (Gen. 8:11): Said R. Eleazar, "The dove said before the Holy One, blessed be he, 'May my food be as bitter as an olive leaf but

placed in our hand, and let it not be as sweet as honey but placed in the hand of mortals.'

23. I:23: "After their families they went forth from the ark" (Gen. 8:19).: Said R. Yohanan, "'After their families' and not they Freedman: alone." While in the ark, copulation was forbidden. On their exit, it was permitted. That is the significance of "after their families," which denotes that mating was resumed and they ceased to be a group of single entities.

24. I:24: Said R. Hana bar Bizna, "Said Eliezer Abraham's servant to Shem, the eldest son, 'It is written, "After their families they went forth from the ark" (Gen. 8:19). How was it with you? How did you take care of all the animals, given their diverse needs, while you were in the ark?"

    a. I:25: Nahum of Gam Zo "This Too" was accustomed to say, on the occasion of anything that happened, "This too is for the good." One day, the Israelites wanted to end a gift to Caesar.

B. THE GENERATION OF THE DISPERSION HAS NO SHARE IN THE WORLD TO COME, SINCE IT IS SAID, "SO THE LORD SCATTERED THEM ABROAD FROM THERE UPON THE FACE OF THE WHOLE EARTH" (GEN. 11:8). "SO THE LORD SCATTERED THEM ABROAD" – IN THIS WORLD, "AND THE LORD SCATTERED THEM FROM THERE" – IN THE WORLD TO COME.

1. II:1: What did they do wrong?

2. II:2: It has been taught on Tannaite authority: R. Nathan says, "All of them went up intending to worship an idol. Here it is written, 'Let us make us a name' (Gen. 11:4), and elsewhere: 'And make no mention of the name of other gods' (Ex. 23:13). Just as in the latter passage name stands for idolatry, so here too 'name' stands for idolatry."

3. II:3: Said R.Yohanan, "As to the tower, a third of it burned, a third of it sank into the earth, and a third is yet standing."

C. THE MEN OF SODOM HAVE NO PORTION IN THE WORLD TO COME, SINCE IT IS SAID, "NOW THE MEN OF SODOM WERE WICKED AND SINNERS AGAINST THE LORD EXCEEDINGLY" (GEN. 13:13) "WICKED" – IN THIS WORLD, "AND SINNERS" – IN THE WORLD TO COME. BUT THEY WILL STAND IN JUDGMENT.

1. III:1: Our rabbis have taught on Tannaite authority: The men of Sodom have no portion in the world to come M. 11:31, since it is said, "And the men of Sodom were wicked

sinners" (Gen. 13:13) in this world against the Lord exceedingly" – in the world to come. (T. San. 13:8A-C).

2. III:2: Said R. Judah, "'Wicked' – with their bodies. "And 'sinners' – with their money. "'Wicked' – with their bodies, as it is written, 'How then can I do this great wickedness and sin against God?' (Gen. 39:9). 'Sinners' – with their money, as it is written, 'And it be a sin unto you' (Deut. 15:9).

3. III:3: Our rabbis have taught on Tannaite authority: The men of Sodom acted arrogantly before the Omnipresent only on account of the good which he lavished on them, since it is said, "As for the land, out of it comes bread...Its stones are the place of sapphires, and it has dust of gold. That path, no bird of prey knows...The proud beasts have not trodden it" (Job 28:5-8). Said the men of Sodom, "Since bread comes forth from our land, and silver and gold come forth from our land, and precious stones and pearls come forth from our land, we do not need people to come to us. They come to us only to take things away from us. Let us go and forget how things are usually done among us." The Omnipresent said to them, "Because of the goodness which I have lavished upon you, you deliberately forget how things are usually done among you. I shall make you be forgotten from the world."

4. III:4: Raba expounded the following verse: "What is the sense of this verse: 'How long will you imagine mischief against a man? You shall be slain, all of you, you are all as a bowing wall and as a tottering fence' (Ps. 62:4)? This teaches that the Sodomites would look enviously at wealthy men, so they would set such a man near a tottering fence and push it over on him and come and take away all his money."

5. III:5: The Sodomites said, "Whoever has one ox must guard the herd one day, and whoever has no oxen must guard the herd two days. There was an orphan, son of a widow, the whom they gave the herd to pasture. He went and killed the oxen. He said to them, "He who has one ox may take one hide. He who has no oxen may take two hides." "Why so" they asked him?

6. III:6: There were four judges in Sodom, named Liar, Big Liar, Forger, and Perverter of Justice. If someone beat his neighbor's wife and made her abort, they say to him, "Give her to him, and he will make her pregnant for you." If someone cut off the ear of his neighbor's ass, they say to him, "Give it to him, until it grows a new one." If someone

injured his neighbor, they say to the victim, "Pay him the fee for letting blood from you."

D.   R. NEHEMIAH SAYS, "BOTH THESE AND THOSE WILL NOT STAND IN JUDGMENT, FOR IT IS SAID, 'THEREFORE THE WICKED SHALL NOT STAND IN JUDGMENT, NOR SINNERS IN THE CONGREGATION OF THE RIGHTEOUS' (PS. 1:5) THEREFORE THE WICKED SHALL NOT STAND IN JUDGMENT' – THIS REFERS TO THE GENERATION OF THE FLOOD. 'NOR SINNERS IN THE CONGREGATION OF THE RIGHTEOUS' – THIS REFERS TO THE MEN OF SODOM." THEY SAID TO HIM, "THEY WILL NOT STAND IN THE CONGREGATION OF THE RIGHTEOUS, BUT THEY WILL STAND IN THE CONGREGATION OF THE SINNERS."
THE SPIES HAVE NO PORTION IN THE WORLD TO COME, AS IT IS SAID, "EVEN THOSE MEN WHO BROUGHT UP AN EVIL REPORT OF THE LAND DIED BY THE PLAGUE BEFORE THE LORD" (NUM. 14:37) "DIED" – IN THIS WORLD. "BY THE PLAGUE" – IN THE WORLD TO COME.

1.   IV:1: Our rabbis have taught on Tannaite authority: "Korah and his company have no portion in the world to come and will not live in the world to come, since it is said, 'And the earth closed upon them' (Num. 16:33) – in this world. 'And they perished from among the assembly' – in the world to come," the words of R. Aqiba. R. Judah b. Petera says, "Lo, they are like something lost and searched for They will come to the world to come. For concerning them it is written, 'I have gone astray like a perishing sheep; seek your servant' (Ps. 119:176) 'Perishing' is said here, and in the matter of Korah and his company, 'perishing' also is said. Just as 'perishing' spoken of later on refers to that which is being sought, so 'perishing' spoken of here refers to that which is being sought" (T. San. 13:9C-I).

2.   IV:2: "Now Korah took..." (Num. 16:1): He took a bad deal for himself. "Korah" – for he was made a bald-spot "Korah" and "bald-spot" using the same consonants in Israel. "Son of Izhar" – a son who turned the heat of the entire world against himself, as the heat of noon "Izhar" and "noon" use the same consonants.

3.   IV:3: Said Rab, "As to On, son of Peleth, his wife saved him. She said to him, 'What do you get out of this matter? If one master is the greater, you are his disciple, and if the other master is the greater, you are still his disciple!' He said to her, 'What should I do? I was in their conspiracy and I took

an oath to be with them.' She said to him, 'I know that they are all a holy congregation, for it is written, "Seeing all the congregation are holy, every one of them" (Num. 16:3).'"

4.   IV:4: "And they rose up before Moses, with certain of the children of Israel, two hundred and fifty" (Num. 16:2): They were the distinguished members of the community.

5.   IV:5: "And when Moses heard, he fell on his face" (Num. 16:4): What did he hear?

6.   IV:6: "And Moses rose up and went to Dathan and Abiram" (Num. 16:25): Said R. Simeon b. Laqish, "On the basis of this verse we learn that one should not hold on to a quarrel but should be eager to end it, in the model of Moses, who modestly went out to the other side to seek a resolution."

   a.   IV:7: Said R. Yosé, "Whoever contends with the kingdom of the house of David is worthy that a snake bite him. Here it is written, 'And Adonijah slew sheep and oxen and fat cattle by the stone of Zoheleth" '(1 Kgs. 1:9), and elsewhere it is written, 'With the poison of serpents using the same consonants as the word Zoheleth of the dust' (Deut. 32:24)."

7.   IV:8: "Riches kept for the owners to their hurt" (Qoh. 5:12): Said R. Simeon b. Laqish, "This refers to the riches of Korah." "And all the substance that was at their feet" (Deut. 11:6)" Said R. Eleazar, "This refers to the wealth of a man, that puts him on his feet."

8.   IV:9: And said R. Yohanan, "Korah was not among those who were swallowed up nor among those who were burned. "He was not among those who were swallowed up, for it is written, 'And all the men that joined Korah' (Num. 16:32) – but not Korah."

9.   IV:10: Said Raba, "What is the meaning of that which is written, 'The sun and the moon stood still in their zebul, at the light of your arrows they went' (Hab. 3:1)? There are seven heavens, of which zebul is one. What were they doing in zebul, seeing that they are set in the firmament, a lower heaven? This teaches that the sun and the moon went up to the firmament called Zebul. They said before the Holy One, blessed be he, 'Lord of the world, if you do justice with the son of Amram, we shall go forth,and if not, we shall not go forth.'"

10. IV:11: Raba interpreted a verse of Scripture, "What is the meaning of what is written, 'But if the Lord make a new thing and the earth open her mouth' (Num. 16:30)? Said

Moses before the Holy One, blessed be he, 'If Gehenna has been created, well and good, and if not, let the Lord now create it.'"

11. IV:12: "But the children of Korah did not die" (Num. 26:11): A Tannaite authority taught in the name of our Master, Judah the Patriarch: "A place was set aside for them in Gehenna, and they sat there and recited a song for God."

12. IV:13: Said Rabbah bar bar Hana, "One time I was going along the way, and a Tai Arab said to me, 'Come, and I shall show you where the men of Korah were swallowed up.' I went and saw two crevasses, from which smoke came forth. He took a piece of wool, wet it down, and set it on the tip of his spear and passed it over the spot, and it was singed. I said to him, 'Listen to what you are going to hear.'"

E. "THE GENERATION OF THE WILDERNESS HAS NO PORTION IN THE WORLD TO COME AND WILL NOT STAND IN JUDGMENT, FOR IT IS WRITTEN, 'IN THIS WILDERNESS THEY SHALL BE CONSUMED AND THERE THEY SHALL DIE' (NUM. 14:35), "THE WORDS OF R. AQIBA. R. ELIEZER SAYS, "CONCERNING THEM IT SAYS, 'GATHER MY SAINTS TOGETHER TO ME, THOSE THAT HAVE MADE A COVENANT WITH ME BY SACRIFICE' (PS. 50:5)."
"THE PARTY OF KORAH IS NOT DESTINED TO RISE UP, FOR IT IS WRITTEN, 'AND THE EARTH CLOSED UPON THEM' – IN THIS WORLD. 'AND THEY PERISHED FROM AMONG THE ASSEMBLY' – IN THE WORLD TO COME," THE WORDS OF R. AQIBA. AND R. ELIEZER SAYS, "CONCERNING THEM IT SAYS, 'THE LORD KILLS AND RESURRECTS, BRINGS DOWN TO SHEOL AND BRINGS UP AGAIN' (1 SAM. 2:6)."

1. V:1: Our rabbis have taught on Tannaite authority: "The generation of the wilderness has no portion in the world to come, and will not live in the world to come, for it is said, 'In this wilderness they shall be consumed and there they shall die' (Num. 14:35),'In this wilderness they shall be consumed' – in this world, and there they will die, ' in the world to come. And it says, 'Of them I swore in my wrath that they should not enter into my rest' (Ps. 95:11)", the words of R. Aqiba. R. Eliezer says, "They will come into the world to come, for concerning them it is said, 'Gather my saints together to me, those that have made a covenant with me by sacrifice' (Ps. 50:5) (T. San. 13:10).

LXVII. MISHNAH-TRACTATE SANHEDRIN 11:3DD-FF

A.   "THE TEN TRIBES ARE NOT DESTINED TO RETURN, SINCE IT IS SAID, 'AND HE CAST THEM INTO ANOTHER LAND, AS ON THIS DAY' (DEUT. 29:28). JUST AS THE DAY PASSES AND DOES NOT RETURN, SO THEY HAVE GONE THEIR WAY AND WILL NOT RETURN," THE WORDS OF R. AQIBA. R. ELIEZER SAYS, "JUST AS THIS DAY IS DARK AND THEN GROWS LIGHT, SO THE TEN TRIBES FOR WHOM IT NOW IS DARK – THUS IN THE FUTURE IT IS DESTINED TO GROW LIGHT FOR THEM."

1.   I:1: Our rabbis have taught on Tannaite authority: "The ten tribes have no portion in the world to come T.: and will not live in the world to come, as it is said, 'And the Lord drove them out of their land with anger and heat and great wrath' (Deut. 29:8) – in this world; and cast them forth into another land' (Deut. 29:28) – in the world to come," the words of R. Aqiba. R. Simeon b. Judah of Kefar Akkum says in the name of R. Simeon, "Scripture said, 'As at this day' – if their deeds remains as they are this day, they will not reach it, and if not, they will (not) reach it." Rabbi says, "Both these and those have a portion in the world to come, as it is said, 'And it shall come to pass in that day that the trumpet shall be blown and those who are perishing in the land of Assyria and those who are driven away in to the Land of Egypt shall come and worship the Lord in the holy mountain, in Jerusalem' (Is. 27:13)." (T. San. 13:12).

   a.   I:2: It has been stated upon Amoraic authority: As to an infant, at what point does it enter the world to come? R. Hiyya and R. Simeon b. Rabbi: one said, "From the time that it is born." The other said, "From the time that it spoke."

2.   I:3: "Therefore hell has enlarged herself and opened her mouth without measure" (Is. 5:15): Said R. Simeon b. Laqish, "For him who leaves over even one law unobserved." Said R. Yohanan, "It is not a pleasing to their Master that you make such a statement to them. Rather: even if one who has not studied a single statute it will save a person from Gehenna.'"

3.   I:4: It has been taught on Tannaite authority: R. Simai says, "It is said, 'I shall take you to me for a people' (Ex. 6:7), and it is said, 'And I will bring you in to the land' (Ex. 6:7). Their exodus from Egypt is compared to their entry into the land. Just as, when they came into the land, they were only two out of the original six hundred thousand only Caleb and

Joshua, so when they lift Egypt, there were only two out of six hundred thousand."

4. I:5: It has been taught on Tannaite authority: Said R. Eleazar b. R. Yosé, "One time I went to Alexandria, Egypt. I found an old man there, who said to me, 'Come and I shall show you what my forefathers did to your forefathers. Some of your ancestors did my ancestors drown in the sea, some of them they slew with a sword, some of them they crushed in the buildings.' And on that account, Moses, our master, was punished, as it is said, 'For since I came to Pharaoh to speak in your name, he has done evil to this people, neither have you delivered your people at all' (Ex. 5:23)."

5. I:6: "And Moses made haste and bowed his head toward the earth and worshipped: (Ex. 34:8): What did Moses see?

6. I:7: R. Hagga was going up the stairs of the house of Rabbah bar Shila. He heard a child saying, "'Your testimonies are very sure, holiness becomes your house, O Lord, you are for the length of days' (Ps. 93:5). And near the same verse: 'A prayer of Moses' (Ps. 90:1). He said, "This proves that he saw the attribute of God's being' long-suffering."

7. I:8: Said R. Eleazar said R. Hanina, "The Holy One, blessed be he, is destined to be a crown on the head of every righteous person, as it is said, 'In that day shall the Lord of Hosts be for a crown of glory and for a diadem of beauty to the remnant of his people' (Is. 28:5)." What is the meaning of "a crown of glory and a diadem of beauty"?

LXVIII. MISHNAH-TRACTATE SANHEDRIN 11:4-6

A. THE TOWNSFOLK OF AN APOSTATE TOWN HAVE NO PORTION IN THE WORLD TO COME, AS IT IS SAID, "CERTAIN BASE FELLOWS SONS FO BELIAL HAVE GONE OUT FROM THE MIDST OF THEE AND HAVE DRAWN AWAY THE INHABITANTS OF THEIR CITY" (DEUT. 13:14).

1. I:1: Our rabbis have taught on Tannaite authority: "...have gone out..."(Deut. 13:14) – they and not messengers. "...fellows..." – the plural means there must be two. Another matter: "...fellows..." – and not women. "...fellows..." and not children. "...sons of Belial..." – sons who have broken the yoke of heaven from their shoulders. "From your midst" – and not from the border towns.

2. I:2: It has been stated on Amoraic authority: R. Yohanan said, "They may divide a single town between two tribes if the boundary between tribes runs through it." R. Simeon b.

Laqish said, "They may not divide a single town between two tribes."

3. I:3: The question was raised: If the inhabitants were led astray on their own, what is the law? Do we say that the All-Merciful has said, "...have seduced the inhabitants" (Deut. 13:14), and not those who were seduced on their own? Or perhaps, even if the inhabitants were induced on their own, the law still applies?

B. AND THEY ARE NOT PUT TO DEATH UNLESS THOSE WHO MISLED THE TOWN COME FROM THAT SAME TOWN AND FROM THAT SAME TRIBE, AND UNLESS THE MAJORITY IS MISLED, AND UNLESS MEN DID THE MISLEADING.

1. II:1: Since each participant is subject to the usual testimony of two witnesses as well as admonition, how do we handle the matter of dealing with the majority of a town? Said R. Judah, "The court judges and imprisons, judges and imprisons again and again, working their way through the population, until a majority has been convicted. Then all are executed."

C. IF WOMEN OR CHILDREN MISLED THEM, OF IF A MINORITY OF THE TOWN WAS MISLED, OR IF THOSE WHO MISLED THE TOWN CAME FROM OUTSIDE OF IT, LO, THEY ARE TREATED AS INDIVIDUALS AND NOT AS A WHOLE TOWN, AND THEY THUS REQUIRE TESTIMONY AGAINST THEM BY TWO WITNESSES, AND A STATEMENT OF WARNING, FOR EACH AND EVERY ONE OF THEM. THIS RULE IS MORE STRICT FOR INDIVIDUALS THAN FOR THE COMMUNITY: F O R INDIVIDUALS ARE OUT TO DEATH BY STONING. THEREFORE THEIR PROPERTY IS SAVED. BUT THE COMMUNITY IS PUT TO DEATH BY THE SWORD, THEREFORE THEIR PROPERTY IS LOST.

"AND YOU SHALL SURELY SMITE THE INHABITANTS OF THE CITY WITH THE EDGE OF THE SWORD" (DEUT. 13:15). ASS-DRIVERS, CAMEL-DRIVERS, AND PEOPLE PASSING FROM PLACE TO PLACE – LO THESE HAVE THE POWER TO SAVE IT:

1. III:1: Our rabbis have taught on Tannaite authority: Ass-drivers, camel-drivers, and people passing from place to place who spent the night in its midst and became apostates with the others of the town, if they spent thirty days in the town, they are put to death by the sword, and their property and the town are prohibited. But if they did not spend thirty days in the town, they are put to death by stoning, but their property is rescued (T. San. 14:2 A-D).

D.   ...AS IT IS SAID, "DESTROYING IT UTTERLY AND ALL THAT IS THEREIN AND THE CATTLE THEREOF, WITH THE EDGE OF THE SWORD" (DEUT. 13:17). ON THIS BASIS THEY SAID, THE PROPERTY OF RIGHTEOUS FOLK WHICH HAPPENS TO BE LOCATED IN IT IS LOST. BUT THAT WHICH IS OUTSIDE OF IT IS SAVED.

1.   IV.1: Our rabbis have taught on Tannaite authority: "Destroying it utterly and all that is therein" (Deut. 13:17) – excluding the property of the righteous which is outside of it. "And all that is therein" – encompassing the property of righteous folk which happens to be located in it (M. 11:5D). "The spoil that is in it" (Deut. 13:17) – but not the spoil that belongs to heaven. "All the spoil of it" (Deut. 13:17) – encompassing the property of wicked folk that is located outside of it.

2.   IV:2: Said R. Simeon, "On what account did they rule, The property of the righteous which is in it is lost? Because that property caused the righteous to live among evil people. And is it not a matter of an argument a fortiori? And if property, which does not see, hear, or speak, because it caused righteous men to live among wicked people, the Scripture has ruled that it must be burned, he who turns his fellow through the way of life to the way of death, all the more so should he be put to death by burning." (T. San. 14:4G-K).

   a.   IV:3: A master said, "'And all the spoil of it you shall gather' (Deut. 13:17) – encompassing the property of evil folk that is outside of it." Said R. Hisda, "But that applies, in particular, to that which can be gathered together in it."

3.   IV:4: R. Joseph raised the question, "What is the law concerning use of the hair of righteous women in such a city?"

E.   AND AS TO THAT OF EVIL FOLK, WHETHER IT IS IN THE TOWN OR OUTSIDE OF IT, LO, IT IS LEFT TO ROT, AS IT IS SAID, "AND YOU SHALL GATHER ALL THE SPOIL OF IT INTO THE MIDST OF THE WIDE PLACE THEREOF" (DEUT. 13:17). IF IT HAS NO WIDE PLACE, THEY MAKE A WIDE PLACE FOR IT. IF ITS WIDE PLACE IS OUTSIDE OF IT, THEY BRING IT INSIDE.

1.   V:1: Our rabbis have taught on Tannaite authority: "If it does not have a wide place, it is not declared to be an apostate city," the words of R. Ishmael. R. Aqiba says, "If it has no wide place, they make a wide place for it." What is at issue

here? One authority takes the view that "its wide place" has the sole meaning of a wide place already present. The other authority maintains that "wide place" also bears the meaning of a wide place existing only at present.

F.   "AND YOU WILL BURN WITH FIRE THE CITY AND ALL THE SPOIL THEREOF, (EVERY WHIT, UNTO THE LORD YOUR GOD)" (DEUT. 13:17). "THE SPOIL THEREOF" – BUT NOT THE SPOIL WHICH BELONGS TO HEAVEN. ON THIS BASIS THEY HAVE SAID: THINGS WHICH HAVE BEEN CONSECRATED WHICH ARE IN IT ARE TO BE REDEEMED:

1.   VI:1: Our rabbis have taught on Tannaite authority: If there were Holy Things in it, things that have been consecrated for use on the altar are left to die; things which are consecrated for the upkeep of the Temple building are to be redeemed; heave-offering left therein is allowed to rot; second tithe and sacred scrolls are hidden away. R. Simeon says, "'Its cattle' – excluding firstlings and tithe of cattle. 'And its spoil'-- excluding money which has been consecrated, and money which has taken on the status of second tithe" (T. San. 14:5A-D).

   a.   VI:2: A master has said, "If there were Holy Things in it, things that have been consecrated for use on the altar are left to die:" Now why should they be left to die? Rather, let them pasture until they are permanently disfigured, at which point let them be sold, and let the proceeds fall for the purchase of a freewill offering as would be done under ordinary circumstances with such donations.

   b.   VI:3: R. Simeon says, "'Its cattle' – excluding firstlings and tithe of cattle" (T. San. 14:5C). With what sort of case do we deal? If we say that we deal with those that are unblemished, then this falls into the category of the spoil belonging to heaven.

G.   HEAVE-OFFERING LEFT THEREIN IS ALLOWED TO ROT; SECOND TITHE:

1.   VII:1: Said R. Hisda, "That rule applies only to heave offering in the possession of ordinary Israelites, but as to heave-offering in the possession of a priest, to whom the produce actually belongs, it must be burned."

2.   VII:2: It has been taught on Tannaite authority: "Dough prepared from produce in the status of second tithe e.g., grain set aside as second tithe that has been milled into flour and made into dough, is exempt from the requirement of the

separation of dough-offering," the words of R. Meir. And sages declare it liable.

H.   ...AND SACRED SCROLLS ARE HIDDEN AWAY:

    1. VIII:1: The cited passage of the Mishnah does not accord with the view of R. Eliezer.

I.   "EVERY WHIT UNTO THE LORD YOUR GOD" SAID R. SIMEON, "SAID THE HOLY ONE, BLESSED BE HE: 'IF YOU ENTER INTO JUDGMENT IN THE CASE OF AN APOSTATE CITY, I GIVE CREDIT TO YOU AS IF YOU HAD OFFERED A WHOLE BURNT-OFFERING BEFORE ME.' AND IT SHALL BE A HEAP FOREVER, IT SHALL NOT BE BUILT AGAIN" IT SHOULD NOT BE MADE EVEN INTO VEGETABLE-PATCHES OR ORCHARDS," THE WORDS OF R. YOSÉ THE GALILEAN:

    1. IX:1: With reference to the dispute of Yosé the Galilean and Aqiba at M. 11:6K-L, may one propose that they dispute about the matter at issue in what R. Abin said R. Ilaa said? For said R. Abin said R. Ilaa, "In any passage in which you find a generalization concerning an affirmative action, followed by a qualification expressing a negative commandment, people are not to construct on that basis an argument resting on the notion of a general proposition followed by a concrete exemplification only the substance of the concrete exemplification."

J.   R. AQIBA SAYS, "'IT SHALL NOT BE BUILT AGAIN' – AS IT WAS IT MAY NOT BE REBUILT, BUT IT MAY BE MADE INTO VEGETABLE PATCHES AND ORCHARDS."

    1. X:1: Our rabbis have taught on Tannaite authority: If the town contained trees that had already been cut down prior to the trial, they are forbidden. If at the time of the verdict they were yet attached to the ground, they are permitted. But as to the trees of another city, whether they are cut down or attached to the ground, they are forbidden (T. San. 14:5E-G).

K.   "AND THE CITY SHALL BE HEREM TO THE LORD:" JERICHO IN PARTICULAR

    a. X:2: "And Joshua adjured them at that time, saying, Cursed be the man before the Lord who rises up and builds this city, Jericho. He shall lay the foundation thereof in his firstborn, and in his youngest son shall he set up the gates of it." (Josh. 6:17). It has been taught on Tannaite authority: One may not rebuild it and call it by the name of some other town, and one may not build some other town and call it Jericho." (T. San. 14:6L).

b. X:3: It is written, "In his days did Heil the Bethelite build Jericho; he laid the foundations thereof in Abiram his firstborn and set up the gates thereof in his youngest son Segub, according to the word of the Lord which he spoke by Joshua the son of Nun" (1 Kgs. 16:4). It has been taught on Tannaite authority: "In Abiram his first born" (1 Kgs. 16:34): That wicked man! To begin with with Abiram he had no example from which to learn, but in the case of segub, he had an example from which to learn (T. San. 14:9A-C). What did Abiram and Segub do that they, who were not wicked, did not learn the reason for the death?

  I.   X:4: "And the word of the Lord came to him, saying, Go away and turn eastward and hide yourself by the brook Cherith, that is before Jordan...And the ravens brought him bread and flesh in the morning" (1 Kgs. 17:2, 6). Where did they get validly slaughtered meat?

  II. X:5: A Galilean gave an exposition before R. Hisda, "To what may Elijah be compared? To the case of a man who locked his gate and lost the key. Elijah locked up the rain and could not unlock it"

L.   "AND THERE SHALL CLEAVE NOUGHT OF THE DEVOTED THINGS TO YOUR HAND THAT THE LORD MAY TURN FROM THE FIERCENESS OF HIS ANGER AND SHOW YOU MERCY AND HAVE COMPASSION UPON YOU AND MULTIPLY YOU" (DEUT. 13:18) FOR SO LONG AS EVIL PEOPLE ARE IN THE WORLD, FIERCE ANGER IS IN THE WORLD. WHEN THE EVIL PEOPLE HAVE PERISHED FROM THE WORLD, FIERCE ANGER DEPARTS FROM THE WORLD.

1.   XI:1: Who are these wicked?

2.   XI:2: Our rabbis have taught on Tannaite authority: When the wicked come into the world, fierce anger comes into the world, for it is written, "When the wicked comes, then comes also contempt, and with ignominy, reproach" (Prov. 18:3). When the wicked departs from the world, goodness comes into the world and retribution leaves the world, as it is written, "And when the wicked perish, there is exultation" (Prov. 11:10). When righteous people leave the world, evil comes into the world, as it is said, "The righteous man perishes, and no one lays it to heart, and merciful men are taken away, none considering that the righteous is taken away from the evil to come" (Is. 57:1). When the righteous

come into the world, goodness comes into the world, as it is written, "This one will comfort us in our work and in the toil of our hands" (Gen. 5:29) (T. Sot. 10:1-3).

Points of Structure

1. DOES BABYLONIAN TALMUD-TRACTATE SANHEDRIN FOLLOW A COHERENT OUTLINE GOVERNED BY A CONSISTENT RULES?

The Talmud-tractate follows the program of the Mishnah-tractate of the same name and rarely diverges from it. Where we have a large composite that does not expound a topic or proposition set forth by the Mishnah-tractate, it complements one that does. This tractate more slavishly adheres to the program of the Mishnah than any other, and that is the fact despite the appearance of prolixity.

2. WHAT ARE THE SALIENT TRAITS OF ITS STRUCTURE?

For the first ten chapters, the Mishnah sets forth topics or propositions inviting analysis. For the eleventh chapter, the Mishnah defines a topical program, which the Talmud richly augments with collections of information.

3. WHAT IS THE RATIONALITY OF THE STRUCTURE?

The Mishnah defines what is orderly and what is not. There is no other organizing principle that governs throughout. What I have marked as secondary or derivative or complementary nearly everywhere carries forward what has begun as Mishnah-commentary. I see only very, very few entries – compositions, never composites – that are parachuted down on their own. All composites and nearly all compositions can be shown to stand in logical or at least topical relationship to the Mishnah's program: propositional or topical.

4. WHERE ARE THE POINTS OF IRRATIONALITY IN THE STRUCTURE?

I have identified a variety of composites that serve a purpose other than that of Mishnah-commentary. These are to be divided into three groups, only one of which requires further comment. The first group is made up of composites that do not directly comment upon a proposition of the Mishnah or deal with a topic introduced by the Mishnah. These I list below, in my discussion of topical composites that the Talmud contributes but that the Mishnah does not require on its own. The second group comprises composites that form appendices to the treatment of a Mishnah-topic or proposition, e.g., clarifying a subsidiary point or otherwise standing in subordinate relationship to the Mishnah. These I list below, indenting the items and so differentiating them from the ones that change the character of the Talmud's re-presentation of the Mishnah. The third set are items that have no clear relationship whatever to the work of Mishnah-commentary, e.g., formal composites, in which an extrinsic trait, not one intrinsic to what is said, accounts for the agglutination of compositions. These I indicate by underlining. Readers are referred to the treatment of topical composites in what follows.

Points of System

1. DOES THE BABYLONIAN TALMUD-TRACTATE SANHEDRIN SERVE ONLY AS A RE-PRESENTATION OF THE MISHNAH-TRACTATE OF THE SAME NAME?

Enough of the Mishnah is covered by the Talmud to require an affirmative response to this question. Certainly the net effect is to treat the Mishnah as principal and as privileged, and all composites are set into the Talmud in relationship to the Mishnah's requirements. I cannot find a single exception to that rule, and that is now an established fact. That the Talmud must be described as a commentary to the Mishnah and as nothing other than a commentary to the Mishnah is the outcome of this work to date.

2. HOW DO THE TOPICAL COMPOSITES FIT INTO THE TALMUD-TRACTATE SANHEDRIN AND WHAT DO THEY CONTRIBUTE THAT THE MISHNAH-TRACTATE OF THE SAME NAME WOULD LACK WITHOUT THEM?

> I.C: The judgment of cases by fewer than three judges is simply a question invited by the law of the Mishnah.
>
> I.D: Arbitration as an alternative to a legal contest falls into the same category as the foregoing.

I.E: In praise of justice and true judges: This entry is invited by the general theme and premise of the Mishnah-rule and does not vastly change our impression of the Mishnah's topic, which is, the judgment of cases and the fair conduct of trials.

> > VI.D   Composite on the Writing and Revelation of the Torah: This is a thematic composite, inserted because of the discussion, by the Mishnah, of the King's writing out a scroll of the Torah and carrying it about with him. I do not see how this composite vastly changes our perception of the Mishnah's rule or its context.
> >
> > VII.B   The evils of divorce, particularly of an aging wife: This composite is inserted without any

clear relationship to the Mishnah;'s rule. Including the set has probably been provoked by the story of Abishad and Bath Sheba.

XVI.F: The creation of man, the minim, debates with unbelievers, the emperor and the patriarch. This is a vast and important composite on a variety of topics. It is added as a complement to the Mishnah's statement that God put his mint-mark on everyone, yet not one is like another. While this passage moves in a variety of directions, it seems to me wholly complementary to the Mishnah's interests and statements and in no way does the composite (or, really, set of composites) reshape the setting or context in which we are to read the Mishnah's statements. To the contrary, what we have is a rich and dense extension of what the Mishnah clearly wishes to emphasize.

XVI.H: The exegesis of the story of Ahab's death illustrates the statement of the Mishnah immediately preceding, which is, "When the wicked perish there is rejoicing." This item then illustrates that point. But of course, the composite moves in its own direction, guided by the requirements of the theme that it pursues.

XVII.H: Topical appendix on reciting the blessing over the New Moon. The Mishnah's statement introduces this theme, which is then a compendium of useful information, nothing more.

XXIV.E: Burial as the preferred mode of disposition. This is a clear appendix to the statement that one may not leave the deceased to stay unburied overnight. The composite simply reenforces the Mishnah's premise.

XXXI.B: The religious obligations of the children of Noah: idolators and slaves. This composite begins with the statement that idolators as much as Israelites are admonished not to curse God, which is precisely the topic that the Mishnah has introduced. The composite goes off in its own direction, but blasphemy remains a principal consideration throughout, even though the governing topic is now not blasphemy but the obligations of non-Israelites.

XLI.B: The evils of wine: This is a topical composite added after a reference to the rebellious son's drinking a half-log of Italian wine. The Mishnah's general interests thus are advanced, and the premise of Scripture and the Mishnah, that drunkenness is evil, is reenforced.

XLIX.B: Marrying off one's children in the proper manner: This item forms a positive side to the Mishnah's negative, that is, those put to death for incest and similar sexual crimes. Now we are given the opposite: how matters should be carried on.

LVII.C: The zealotry of Phineas: This is a first-rate illustration of the Mishnah's interest in how zealots may enforce the law outside the normal framework of court procedures.

LXV.B: Topical Appendix on Gebiha and Alexander: This is added because of the reference in the foregoing to Gebiha's proof for the resurrection of the dead.

LXV.C: Topical Appendix on Antoninus and Rabbi: My best guess is that this composite was joined to the foregoing as part of a set on sages and emperors; I see no point of topical, let alone propositional, intersection with our Mishnah.

LXV.D: The death of Death: Here we really do have a point of extension, beyond the limits of the Mishnah, so as to recast the Mishnah's topic and set forth a proposition that the exegesis of the Mishnah does not require and that greatly changes our sense of the Mishnah's meaning. The Mishnah's interest in the resurrection of the dead is now shown to be part of a larger proposition, which is, in time to come, death itself will die.

LXV.E: How on the basis of the Torah do we know about the resurrection of the dead. This large composite carries forward the exegesis of the Mishnah, proving in various ways on the strength of Scripture the facticity of the Mishnah's claim.

LXV.F: Topical appendix on Hananiah, Mishael, and Azariah: Here is an example of how death is overcome.

LXV.G: The Messiah. Pharaoh, Sennacherib, Hezekiah, and other Players in the Messianic drama. Here is the point in our tractate at which the Mishnah's program really comes under considerable revision. The Talmud treats as self-evident the link between the Messiah and the resurrection of the dead, but the Mishnah has not done so, indeed, has no introduced the Messiah-theme at all. The Talmud then wants to know how the Messiah's coming relates to the resurrection of the dead. Various salvific occasions are then introduced, Pharaoh and Moses; Sennacherib and Hezekiah. These form secondary expositions of the general theme of the Messiah.

LXV.H: When will the Messiah come? Here is yet another major revision in the presentation of the Mishnah, a systematic recasting of matters to link the resurrection to that other, and quite separate, issue. The upshot is that Israel's historical fate and its salvation at the end of time form a component in the exposition of the theme of the resurrection of the dead. Since this passage of the Mishnah does not introduce the Messiah-theme, the radical re-presentation of matters emerges with great force.

LXV.R: Wicked monarchs who nonetheless merit a portion in the world to come: This is a clear extension of the Mishnah, since the point of interest is to form a catalogue of kings who, despite their evil, will inherit the world to come.

LXV.S: The special case of Hezekiah. The Exegesis of Lamentations. Since Hezekiah is designated as a player in the Messianic drama, and since the exegesis of Lamentations is introduced as if out of nowhere, it seems to me we should regard this composite, mostly devoted to Lamentations, as a further treatment of the Messiah-theme. Here is why Israel requires the Messiah: the city sits solitary.

LXV.T: Summary judgments. What we have here is yet another secondary amplification of the Mishnah's topic. The composite is situated where it belongs for the purpose of Mishnah-commentary, precisely at the end of the account of the kings who do not merit the world to come, and at the outset of the account of the commoners who likewise lose out.

LXV.W: After Doeg we deal with David, who is matched against Doeg. I am somewhat puzzled by the introduction of this composite, but it does seem to me continuous in its general proposition with the preceding one.

LXVIII.K: Jericho in Particular. Here we have a fine illustration of the one case in which a town really was treated in accord with the law of the Torah governing the apostate city.

3. CAN WE STATE WHAT THE COMPILERS OF THIS DOCUMENT PROPOSE TO ACCOMPLISH IN PRODUCING THIS COMPLETE, ORGANIZED PIECE OF WRITING?

The first ten chapters of the tractate conform to the general rules of sustained, analytical investigation that govern in the Talmud in general. Chapter Eleven contains much information, many well-crafted compositions and purposive composites, but it exhibits singular deficiencies in the analytical process to which we become accustomed. But the rules of large-scale conglomeration remain firm. When we take a second look at Chapter Eleven, we find a sustained effort at recasting the Mishnah's topic by introducing themes that the Mishnah either omits altogether or treats in a casual way. These emerge in unit LXV: the death of death; the coming of the Messiah – past time; the coming of the Messiah – future time; the special case of Hezekiah and the pertinence of the book of Lamentations. Here in a single set of composites we find introduced a set of propositions concerning the Messiah and Israel's history that the Mishnah has neglected. The Mishnah, after all, has focused upon private persons – specific kings and commoners who have lost the world to come. The Talmud, by contrast, introduces the dimension of the Israelite community seen whole. The Mishnah tells us how individuals lose out, e.g., by denying that the Torah itself teaches that the dead will be raised. The Talmud turns to the more profound question of the death of death, which itself then comes as the prologue to the advent of the Messiah. As though to underscore the main point – the issue is Israel the holy people, not merely individual players in Israelite life – the exegesis of Lamentations is inserted, whole and in no clear connection to what has preceded. The result of this analysis leaves no doubt that the framers of the Talmud have both commented upon the Mishnah in a rich and remarkably profound way but also recast the context in which the Mishnah is to be received and understood. The Talmud truly forms the re-presentation of the Mishnah. And what the Talmud's framers find self-evident in the exposition of the Mishnah's statements that the Mishnah's authors treated casually or not at all speaks for itself.